PV	Present value
Q	Unit sales
ρ	Correlation coefficient (lowercase rho)
r	Discount rate, rate of return, cost of capital, or required return
r^*	Real interest rate
$\hat{r}$	Expected rate of return
$\bar{r}$	Historical, or realized, rate of return
r_{Nom}	Nominal rate of return
r_c	Composite, or overall, cost of capital
r_d	Before-tax cost of debt
r_e	Cost of newly issued common stock
r_i	Required return on asset i
r_M	Required rate of return on "the market"
r_{ps}	Cost of preferred stock
r_{RF}	Rate of return on a riskless asset
r_s	Cost of common stock
ROA	Return on assets
ROE	Return on equity
ROIC	Return on invested capital
RP	Risk premium
	RP_M Market risk premium
S	(1) Dollar sales
	(2) Total market value of equity
SML	Security Market Line
Σ	Summation sign (capital sigma)
σ	Standard deviation (lowercase sigma)
T	Tax rate
t	Time
TIE	Times-interest-earned ratio
V	(1) Value
	(2) Variable cost per unit
V_L	Total market value of a levered firm
V_U	Total market value of an unlevered firm
w	Proportion or weight
	w_d Weight of debt
	w_{ps} Weight of preferred stock
	w_{ce} Weight of common equity
WACC	Weighted average cost of capital
YTC	Yield to call
YTM	Yield to maturity

2ND EDITION

CORPORATE FINANCE

A Focused Approach

MICHAEL C. EHRHARDT
University of Tennessee

EUGENE F. BRIGHAM
University of Florida

THOMSON
™
SOUTH-WESTERN

Australia · Canada · Mexico · Singapore · Spain · United Kingdom · United States

THOMSON
SOUTH-WESTERN

Corporate Finance, **Second Edition**
Michael C. Ehrhardt and Eugene F. Brigham

VP/Editorial Director:
Jack W. Calhoun

VP/Editor-in-Chief:
Dave Shaut

Executive Editor:
Michael R. Reynolds

Senior Developmental Editor:
Elizabeth R. Thomson

Marketing Manager:
Heather MacMaster

Senior Production Editor:
Kara ZumBahlen

Manager of Technology, Editorial:
Vicky True

Technology Project Editor:
John Barans

Web Coordinator:
Karen Schaffer

Senior Manufacturing Coordinator:
Sandee Milewski

Production House:
Elm Street Publishing Services, Inc.

Printer:
R. R. Donnelley, Willard, OH

Composition:
Lachina Publishing Services

Art Director:
Anne Marie Rekow

Internal Designer:
Anne Marie Rekow

Cover Designer:
Fuson Design Group

Cover Images:
© Getty Images

For permission to use material from this text or product, submit a request online at http://www.thomsonrights.com.

Library of Congress Control Number: 2004110765

For more information about our products, contact us at:

Thomson Learning Academic Resource Center

1-800-423-0563

Asia (including India)
Thomson Learning
5 Shenton Way
#01-01 UIC Building
Singapore 068808

Australia/New Zealand
Thomson Learning Australia
102 Dodds Street
Southbank, Victoria 3006
Australia

Canada
Thomson Nelson
1120 Birchmount Road
Toronto, Ontario
M1K 5G4
Canada

Latin America
Thomson Learning
Seneca, 53
Colonia Polanco
11560 Mexico
D.F.Mexico

UK/Europe/Middle East/Africa
Thomson Learning
High Holborn House
50/51 Bedford Row
London WC1R 4LR
United Kingdom

Spain (including Portugal)
Thomson Paraninfo
Calle Magallanes, 25
28015 Madrid, Spain

PREFACE

When we wrote the first edition of this book, we had four goals in mind: (1) to create a book that would help people make better financial decisions, (2) to motivate students by demonstrating that finance is both interesting and relevant, (3) to make the book clear enough for students to go through the material without wasting time trying to figure out what we were trying to say, and (4) to provide a book that covers the core material necessary for a one-semester introductory MBA course but without all the other interesting-but-not-essential material that is contained in most MBA texts. This last goal is the main factor that differentiates *Corporate Finance: A Focused Approach* from the other MBA texts.

Finance theory and applications have dramatically expanded during the last decade, and so have finance textbooks, including some that we have written. As a result, professors teaching the introductory MBA course must choose between breadth and depth. They can assign most of the chapters in one of the other textbooks and teach finance as a survey course, going for breadth at the expense of depth. Alternatively, they can cover fewer chapters (and parts of chapters), explore them in depth, and ignore the remaining chapters. We learned from a review of course syllabi that the vast majority of professors, including us, choose the second alternative. Finance majors will probably cover much of the omitted material in later courses, but nonmajors end up having to buy a larger, more expensive book than they need. Also, instructors must make difficult choices, including having to decide what parts of selected chapters are most important. Drawing on our own classroom experience, we wrote *Corporate Finance* for those professors who want to cover the critical finance topics in depth but not require their students to purchase chapters that will not be covered.

This book combines theory with practical applications. An understanding of finance theory is essential if people are to develop and implement effective financial strategies; students also need a good working knowledge of the financial environment. Therefore, the book begins with basic background information and essential concepts, including the economic and financial environment, the time value of money, cash flows versus accounting profits, the relationship between risk and return, and stock and bond valuation. With this background, students can understand the specific techniques, decision rules, and financial policies that are used to help maximize the value of the firm. This structure has three important advantages:

1. Financial management is designed to help maximize the value of a firm. Value is determined, in the long run, by cash flows as revealed in financial statements. Therefore, financial managers make decisions based on how

e-resource

For more information about the text, visit the Web site at **http://ehrhardt .swlearning.com**.

those decisions will affect future financial statements. Our early coverage of financial statements thus helps students see what financial management is all about and how the effects of particular financial decisions are transmitted throughout the firm. Also, most financial decisions today are analyzed using spreadsheets, and, if an instructor plans to emphasize spreadsheets in the course, financial statements provide an excellent starting point to illustrate this tool.

2. *Giving students an early exposure to risk analysis, discounted cash flow techniques, valuation procedures, and EVA/MVA permits us to use and reinforce these key concepts throughout the book.*

3. *Students, even those who do not plan to major in finance, generally enjoy working with stock and bond valuation, rates of return, and the like. Since a student's ability to learn a subject is a function of his or her interest and motivation, and since* Corporate Finance *covers security markets and prices early on, the book's organization is sound from a pedagogic standpoint.*

INTENDED MARKET AND USE

Corporate Finance is designed for use in a one-term introductory MBA course. The book can also be used in executive programs and as an undergraduate introductory text with exceptionally good students.

MAJOR CHANGES IN THE SECOND EDITION

As in any revision, we updated and clarified sections throughout the text. In addition, we always make a few major changes, including the six discussed in this section.

1. **The big picture: a corporate valuation framework.** We have always emphasized cash flows and valuation, and we extended that emphasis in this edition through the addition of a corporate valuation box early in each chapter. These boxes explicitly show how the chapter's material is related to corporate valuation, which helps students keep the big picture in mind as they focus on a chapter's specific topics.

2. **Corporate governance: failures, fraud, and ethics.** The accounting and ethical fiascos of 2001 and 2002 have left a mark on finance and financial markets. Although the repercussions of these events are still unfolding, it is important for students to understand how corporate ethics interacts with operating performance to affect firms' values. The recent abuses are discussed in Chapter 1 and elsewhere throughout the book. In addition, Chapter 13 specifically addresses corporate governance and the actions both firms and governmental units can take to minimize such events.

3. **Thomson ONE—Business School Edition.** Students receive access to Thomson ONE—Business School Edition, provided by Thomson Financial, a global leader in financial information. Thomson ONE provides financial information downloadable into *Excel* for 500 well-known companies, along with I/B/E/S earnings estimates, ratio comparisons with peer companies, Datastream stock prices, Thomson Financial market data, Worldscope market data, and current company news. Students can develop "real-world" skills through end-of-chapter problems that require them to access and use these data sources.

4. **Financial options and their use in corporate finance.** Chapter 8 now focuses only on financial options, including an introduction to the binomial pricing approach. This chapter also explains how financial options are used in corporate finance, including risk management, real options, compensation, and capital structure applications.

5. **Updated *PowerPoint* presentations and flexible designs.** We have updated the first edition's *PowerPoint* slides and put them into a standard design template that comes with *PowerPoint*. This allows instructors to easily change the design format to any other Microsoft *PowerPoint* design template that they prefer. To do this, an instructor should follow these steps: (a) Open one of the textbook's *PowerPoint* files; (b) select Format, then Slide Design; and (c) pick the preferred design. It may be necessary to reapply a particular slide's format (such as for some slides with tables); a ***Read Me*** file explaining this process in detail is included with the *PowerPoint* files.

6. **Instructor control over access to Mini Case solutions and *PowerPoint* shows.** Each chapter has a Mini Case as part of its end-of-chapter materials. Many instructors, including us, use the Mini Cases as a way to structure class lectures. In the first edition, we provided *PowerPoint* and *Excel* solutions for these Mini Cases directly to students (on the Student section of the Web site) so that they could follow along in class. However, some instructors want to assign the Mini Cases as homework. Therefore, we no longer provide the Mini Case solutions on the Student Web site. For those instructors who wish to provide the solutions to students for use as course notes, there are several options: (a) Instructors can post the files to their own password-protected Web sites (this is what we do). (b) Instructors can e-mail the files to their students. (c) Instructors can print the solutions and make them available to students. (d) Instructors can contact the Publisher and order a custom publication containing the solutions, which can be packaged with the textbook.

OTHER CHANGES IN THE SECOND EDITION

The entire book has been reviewed for completeness, ease of exposition, and currency. Hundreds of small changes have been made to keep the text up-to-date. Particular emphasis was placed on updating the real-world examples and including the latest changes in the financial environment and in financial theory. Some examples of changes include the following:

e-resource

The Corporate Finance *Web site is http://ehrhardt .swlearning.com.*

1. **Improved e-resources.** *Corporate Finance's* Web site is both a learning and teaching tool, with separate areas for students and instructors. For a complete list of e-resources, see the Instructional Package section later in this Preface.

2. **Duration and zero coupon bonds.** The Web Extension to Chapter 6 explains how duration is used to measure a bond's risk. In addition, the Extension describes zero coupon bonds, including the calculation of imputed interest for tax purposes.

3. **Separate coverage of financial options and real options.** Chapter 8 is now devoted solely to financial options, with increased coverage of binomial pricing and the uses of options in corporate finance. An introduction to real options is delayed until we get to capital budgeting in Chapter 11. Separating the financial options and real options is easier for students and provides more flexibility to instructors.

4. **Empirical studies of capital structure.** We have added a section to Chapter 14 that explains and synthesizes the results of the most recent empirical studies on capital structure.

5. **International topics.** Chapter 17 provides an updated explanation of international monetary systems. We also added a detailed explanation and illustration of capital budgeting for international projects.

THE INSTRUCTIONAL PACKAGE: AN INTEGRATED APPROACH TO LEARNING

Corporate Finance includes a broad range of ancillary materials designed both to enhance students' learning and to make it easier for instructors to prepare for and conduct classes. All the ancillaries are available on the textbook's Web site. In addition, the Instructor's Resource CD-ROM and Instructor's section of the Web site provide material specifically for instructors. The ancillaries are described here:

1. *Instructor's Manual.* This comprehensive manual contains solutions to all end-of-chapter materials. It is available in print form and electronic form at the book's Instructor's Web site.

2. *Excel* **Tool Kits.** Proficiency with spreadsheets is an absolute necessity for all MBA students. With this in mind, we created *Excel* spreadsheets, called "Tool Kits," for each chapter to show how the analysis in the chapter is done with *Excel*. The Tool Kit models include explanations and screen shots that show students how to use many of the features and functions of *Excel*, enabling the Tool Kits to serve as self-taught tutorials on *Excel*. In addition, a file containing an index to the tutorial is also available with the *Excel* files so that a reader can find the Tool Kit tutorial that explains a particular *Excel* feature.

3. *PowerPoint* **slides.** There is a Mini Case located at the end of each chapter. These cases cover all the essential issues presented in the chapter, and they provide the structure for our class lectures. For each Mini Case, we developed a set of *Power-Point* slides that present graphs, tables, lists, and calculations for use in lectures. Although they are based on the Mini Cases, the slides are self-contained in the sense that they can be used for lectures regardless of whether students are required to read the Mini Cases. Instructors can easily customize the slides because they can be converted quickly into any *PowerPoint* design template.[1] In addition, several chapters have "bonus slides" for those professors who wish to cover selected investments topics in slightly more detail. Copies of these files are on the book's Instructor's Web site and the Instructor's CD-ROM. Note: Some instructors assign the Mini Cases as homework problems, so we do not include the *PowerPoint* slides on the Student Resources Web site. Other instructors, including us, want to provide students with a set of class notes. In this case, the instructor must make these *PowerPoint* slides available to the students.

4. **Mini Case spreadsheets.** In addition to the *PowerPoint* slides, we also provide *Excel* spreadsheets that do the calculations required in the Mini Cases. These spreadsheets are similar to the Tool Kits except (a) the numbers in Mini Case models correspond to the Mini Cases rather than the chapter examples, and (b) we added some features that make it possible to do what-if analysis on a real-time basis in class. For example, we usually begin our lectures with the *PowerPoint* presentation, but, after we have explained a basic concept, we "toggle" to the Mini Case *Excel* file and show how the analysis is done in *Excel*.[2] For example, when teaching bond pricing, we begin with the *PowerPoint* show and cover the basic concepts and calculations. Then we toggle to the *Excel* sheet and use a graph to show how bond prices change as interest rates and time to maturity vary. More and more students are bringing their laptops to class, and they can follow along, doing the what-if analysis for themselves. Note: Some instructors assign the Mini

---

[1] To convert in *PowerPoint*, select Format, Apply Design Template, and then pick any template. Always double-check the conversion, because some templates use differently sized fonts, which can cause some slide titles to run over their allotted space.

[2] Note: To toggle between two open programs, such as *Excel* and *PowerPoint*, hold the Alt key down and hit the Tab key until you have selected the program you want to show.

Cases as homework problems, so we do not include the *Excel* files on the Student Resources Web site. Other instructors, including us, want to provide students with a set of class notes. In this case, the instructor must make these files available to the students.

5. **Web Safaris.** The book's Web site provides a series of links, called Web Safaris, which facilitate Internet searches for useful financial data. Each Web Safari has a specific goal, such as finding the current spreads between Treasury bonds and risky bonds with different ratings. The Web Safari provides a hyperlink to the appropriate Web site and shows how to navigate to the desired information. As noted earlier, we usually begin our lecture with the *PowerPoint* presentation, but when we teach in an Internet-accessible classroom, we occasionally "toggle" to a Web Safari and pull up data in real time.

6. **End-of-chapter spreadsheet problems.** Each chapter has a "Build a Model" problem, where students start with a spreadsheet that contains financial data plus instructions for solving a particular problem. The model is partially completed, with headings but no formulas, so the student must literally build the model. This structure guides the student through the problem, and it also makes it easy to grade the work, since all students' answers are in the same locations on the spreadsheet. The partial spreadsheets for the "Build a Model" problems are available to students on the book's Student Resources Web site, while the completed models are in files on the Instructor's Resource CD-ROM and on Instructor's portion of the Web site.

7. **Thomson ONE—Business School Edition Problem sets.** The book's Web site has a set of problems that require accessing Thomson ONE—Business School Edition Web data. Using this real-world data, students are able to develop real-world skills.

8. **Cyberproblems.** The Web site also contains "Cyberproblems," which require students to go to specific Web sites and answer a series of questions. Answers are available on the Instructors' portion of the Web site.

9. *Test Bank.* The *Test Bank* contains more than 1,200 class-tested questions and problems. Information regarding the topic and degree of difficulty, along with the complete solution for all numerical problems, is provided with each question. The *Test Bank* is available in three forms: (a) in a printed book; (b) in Microsoft *Word* files; and (c) in a computerized test bank, *ExamView,* which has many features that make test preparation, scoring, and grade recording easy. An especially useful feature is *ExamView's* ability to export the Test Bank so that it can be used with *Blackboard,* a widely available classroom management system. We use this feature to create homework "quizzes" that students take over the Web and that are then automatically graded and recorded in a gradesheet that is exportable to *Excel.* We usually specify a pool of 20 questions and have *Blackboard* randomly choose 10 for each student's homework quiz.

10. **Student Resources Web site.** Students who purchase a new textbook have access to a variety of restricted supplementary materials available on the Student Resources Web site at **http://ehrhardt-student.swlearning.com**. These resources include the *Excel* Tool Kits, Web Safaris, partially completed Build a Model spreadsheets, Cyberproblems, Web Extensions, and Interactive Quizzing. Used book buyers may purchase access to this site online. Students can also link to the Student Resources Web site from **http://ehrhardt.swlearning.com**.

11. **Instructor's Resource CD-ROM.** This CD contains all of the student supplements plus *PowerPoint, Word* files for the *Instructor's Manual* and the *Test Bank,* along with completed *Excel* models for the Build a Model problems. This material is also available on the Instructor's portion of the Web site.

12. **Internet applications.** The book's Web site at **http://ehrhardt.swlearning.com** has clickable hyperlinks corresponding to all Web addresses mentioned in each chapter.

13. *Finance Online Case Library.* More than 175 cases, written by Eugene F. Brigham and Linda Klein, are now available via the Web, and new cases are added every year. These cases are in a customized case database that allows instructors to select cases and create their own customized casebooks. Most of the cases have accompanying spreadsheet models that, while not essential for working the case, do reduce number crunching and thus leave more time for students to consider conceptual issues. The models also show students how computers can be used to make better financial decisions. Cases that we have found particularly useful for the different chapters are listed in the end-of-chapter references.

14. *NewsWire: Finance in the News.* A problem inherent in printed textbooks is keeping them up-to-date in a constantly changing world. When an Enron goes bankrupt, or the Nasdaq stock market crashes, it would be useful to relate these events to the textbook. This can be done by use of *NewsWire: Finance in the News,* the book's Web site that provides summaries of recent articles in *The Wall Street Journal, BusinessWeek,* and other business publications, along with discussion questions and references to the text. This helps instructors incorporate late-breaking news into classroom discussions. Instructors can also use the accompanying questions for quizzes and/or exams.

15. *Technology Supplement.* This print ancillary contains tutorials for five commonly used financial calculators and for Microsoft *Excel* and *PowerPoint.* The calculator tutorials cover everything a student needs to know about calculators to work the problems in the text. In our classes, we provide the tutorials for selected calculators as a part of our course pack. The rather large manuals that accompany most calculators intimidate some students, and they find our 12-page, course-specific tutorials far easier to use. The spreadsheet tutorials teach students the basics plus some advanced spreadsheet features, and they prepare students to work with the specific finance models provided in the Tool Kits and Mini Case models. Finally, the *PowerPoint* tutorial is useful to students who must make presentations or to instructors who want to make slides for use in their lectures.

16. *Study Guide.* This supplement outlines the key sections of each chapter, and it provides students with a set of questions and problems similar to those in the text and in the *Test Bank,* along with worked-out solutions. Instructors seldom use the *Study Guide* themselves, but students often find it useful, so we recommend that instructors ask their bookstores to have copies available. Our bookstore generally has to reorder it, which attests to its popularity with students.

Thomson South-Western College Publishing will provide complimentary supplements or supplement packages to those adopters qualified under South-Western's adoption policy. Please contact your sales representative to learn how you may qualify. If, as an adopter or potential user, you receive supplements you do not need, please return them to your sales representative.

ACKNOWLEDGMENTS

This book reflects the efforts of a great many people over a number of years. First, we would like to thank the following people who helped with the second edition: Kurt Jesswein, Murray State University; Lynn Phillips Kugele, Christian Brothers University; Stuart E. Michelson, Stetson University; and Mark D. Walker, North Carolina State University.

Second, professors and professionals who are experts on specific topics reviewed earlier versions of individual chapters or groups of chapters. We are grateful for the insights provided by Edward I. Altman, New York University; Mary Schary Amram, Analysis Group Economics; Nasser Arshadi, University of Missouri; Abdul Aziz, Humboldt State University; William Beranek, University of Georgia; Gordon R. Bonner, University of Delaware;

Ben S. Branch, Bank of New England and University of Massachusetts; David T. Brown, University of Florida; Mark Flannery, University of Florida; E. Bruce Frederickson, Syracuse University; Myron Gordon, University of Toronto; Hal Heaton, Brigham Young University; John Helmuth, Rochester Institute of Technology; Hugh Hunter, Eastern Washington University; James E. Jackson, Oklahoma State University; Vahan Janjigian, Northeastern University; Keith H. Johnson, University of Kentucky; Robert Kieschnick, George Mason University; Richard LeCompte, Wichita State University; Ilene Levin, University of Minnesota–Duluth; James T. Lindley, University of South Mississippi; R. Daniel Pace, Valparaiso University; Ralph A. Pope, California State University–Sacramento; Jay Ritter, University of Florida; Allen Rappaport, University of Northern Iowa; Michael Ryngaert, University of Florida; Fiona Robertson, Seattle University; James Schallheim, University of Utah; G. Bennett Stewart, Stern Stewart & Co.; Robert Strong, University of Maine at Orono; Eugene Swinnerton, University of Detroit–Mercy; Robert Taggart, Boston College; Jonathan Tiemann, Wells Fargo Nikko Investment Advisors; Sheridan Titman, University of Texas at Austin; Alan L. Tucker, Pace University; David Vang, University of St. Thomas; Gary R. Wells, Idaho State University; and David Ziebart, University of Illinois at Urbana.

In addition, we would like to thank the following people, whose reviews and comments on companion books have contributed to this edition: Mike Adler, Syed Ahmad, Sadhana M. Alangar, Ed Altman, Bruce Anderson, Ron Anderson, Bob Angell, Vince Apilado, Henry Arnold, Bob Aubey, Gil Babcock, Peter Bacon, Kent Baker, Tom Bankston, Les Barenbaum, Charles Barngrover, Michael Barry, Bill Beedles, Moshe Ben-Horim, Bill Beranek, Tom Berry, Bill Bertin, Roger Bey, Dalton Bigbee, John Bildersee, Russ Boisjoly, Keith Boles, Geof Booth, Kenneth Boudreaux, Helen Bowers, Oswald Bowlin, Don Boyd, G. Michael Boyd, Pat Boyer, Joe Brandt, Elizabeth Brannigan, Greg Brauer, Mary Broske, Dave Brown, Kate Brown, Bill Brueggeman, Kirt Butler, Robert Button, Bill Campsey, Bob Carleson, Severin Carlson, David Cary, K. Michael Casey, Steve Celec, Karen Chambliss, Don Chance, Antony Chang, Susan Chaplinsky, Arjun Chatrath, Jay Choi, S. K. Choudhury, Lal Chugh, Maclyn Clouse, Margaret Considine, Phil Cooley, Joe Copeland, David Cordell, John Cotner, Charles Cox, David Crary, John Crockett, Roy Crum, Brent Dalrymple, Bill Damon, Joel Dauten, Steve Dawson, Sankar De, Miles Delano, Fred Dellva, Anand Desai, Bernard Dill, Greg Dimkoff, Les Dlabay, Mark Dorfman, Gene Drycimski, Dean Dudley, David Durst, Ed Dyl, Dick Edelman, Charles Edwards, John Ellis, Dave Ewert, John Ezzell, Richard Fendler, Michael Ferri, Jim Filkins, John Finnerty, Susan Fischer, Steven Flint, Russ Fogler, Dan French, Tina Galloway, Phil Gardial, Michael Garlington, Jim Garvin, Adam Gehr, Jim Gentry, Philip Glasgo, Rudyard Goode, Walt Goulet, Bernie Grablowsky, Theoharry Grammatikos, Ed Grossnickle, John Groth, Alan Grunewald, Manak Gupta, Sam Hadaway, Don Hakala, Janet Hamilton, Sally Hamilton, Gerald Hamsmith, William Hardin, Joel Harper, John Harris, Paul Hastings, Bob Haugen, Steve Hawke, Del Hawley, Robert Hehre, George Hettenhouse, Hans Heymann, Kendall Hill, Roger Hill, Tom Hindelang, Linda Hittle, Ralph Hocking, J. Ronald Hoffmeister, Jim Horrigan, John Houston, John Howe, Keith Howe, Steve Isberg, Jim Jackson, Kose John, Arnell D. Johnson, Craig Johnson, Keith Johnson, Ramon Johnson, Ray Jones, Manuel Jose, Gus Kalogeras, Mike Keenan, Bill Kennedy, Joe Kiernan, Rick Kish, Linda Klein, Don Knight, Dorothy Koehl, Theodor Kohers, Jaroslaw Komarynsky, Duncan Kretovich, Harold Krogh, Charles Kroncke, Joan Lamm, P. Lange, Howard Lanser, Martin Laurence, Ed Lawrence, Wayne Lee, Jim LePage, Jules Levine, John Lewis, Chuck Linke, Bill Lloyd, Susan Long, Judy Maese, Bob Magee, Ileen Malitz, Phil Malone, Terry Maness, Chris Manning, Terry Martell, D. J. Masson, John Mathys, John McAlhany, Andy McCollough, Bill McDaniel, Robin McLaughlin, Tom McCue, Jamshid Mehran, Ilhan Meric, Joseph H. Meredith, Larry Merville, Rick Meyer, Stuart Michelson, Vassil Mihov, Jim Millar, Ed Miller, John Mitchell, Carol Moerdyk, Bob Moore, Barry Morris, Gene Morris, Fred Morrissey, Chris Muscarella, Stu Myers, David Nachman, Tim Nantell, Don Nast, Bill Nelson, Bob Nelson, James Nelson, Bob Niendorf, Tom O'Brien, Dennis O'Connor, John O'Donnell, Jim Olsen,

Robert Olsen, Frank O'Meara, David Overbye, Coleen Pantalone, Jim Pappas, Stephen Parrish, Pam Peterson, Glenn Petry, Jim Pettijohn, Rich Pettit, Dick Pettway, Hugo Phillips, John Pinkerton, Gerald Pogue, R. Potter, Franklin Potts, R. Powell, Chris Prestopino, Jerry Prock, Howard Puckett, Herbert Quigley, George Racette, Bob Radcliffe, Bill Rentz, Ken Riener, Charles Rini, John Ritchie, Pietra Rivoli, Menahem Rosenberg, Antonio Rodriguez, E. M. Roussakis, Dexter Rowell, Mike Ryngaert, Jim Sachlis, Abdul Sadik, Thomas Scampini, Kevin Scanlon, Frederick Schadler, Mary Jane Scheuer, Carl Schweser, John Settle, Alan Severn, Sol Shalit, Elizabeth Shields, Frederic Shipley, Dilip Shome, Ron Shrieves, Neil Sicherman, J. B. Silvers, Clay Singleton, Joe Sinkey, Stacy Sirmans, Jaye Smith, Steve Smith, Don Sorenson, David Speairs, Ken Stanly, Ed Stendardi, Alan Stephens, Don Stevens, Jerry Stevens, Mark Stohs, Glen Strasburg, Philip Swensen, Ernie Swift, Paul Swink, Gary Tallman, Dennis Tanner, Craig Tapley, Russ Taussig, Richard W. Taylor, Richard Teweles, Ted Teweles, Andrew Thompson, George Trivoli, George Tsetsekos, Charles Tu, Mel Tysseland, C. Joe Ueng, David Upton, Howard Van Auken, Pretorious Van den Dool, Pieter Vanderburg, Paul Vanderheiden, Jim Verbrugge, Patrick Vincent, Steve Vinson, Susan Visscher, John Wachowicz, Mike Walker, Sam Weaver, Kuo Chiang Wei, Bill Welch, Fred Weston, Norm Williams, Tony Wingler, Ed Wolfe, Larry Wolken, Don Woods, Thomas Wright, Michael Yonan, Zhong-guo Zhou, Dennis Zocco, and Kent Zumwalt.

Special thanks are due to Fred Weston, Myron Gordon, Merton Miller, and Franco Modigliani, who have done much to help develop the field of financial management and who provided us with instruction and inspiration; to Roy Crum, who co-authored the multinational finance chapter; to Larry Wolken, who offered his hard work and advice for the development of the *PowerPoint* shows; to Dana Aberwald Clark, Susan Ball, and Chris Buzzard, who helped us develop the spreadsheet models; to Amelia Bell and Stephanie Hodge, who provided editorial support; and to Joel Houston and Phillip Daves, whose work with us on other books is reflected in this text. We owe special thanks to Lou Gapenski for his many past contributions.

Our colleagues and our students at the Universities of Florida and Tennessee gave us many useful suggestions, and the South-Western and Elm Street Publishing Services staffs—especially Elizabeth Thomson, Kara ZumBahlen, Vicky True, John Barans, Sue Nodine, Cate Rzasa, Heather MacMaster, and Mike Reynolds—helped greatly with all phases of text development, production, and marketing.

ERRORS IN THE TEXT

At this point, authors generally say something like this: "We appreciate all the help we received from the people listed above, but any remaining errors are, of course, our own responsibility." And in many books, there are plenty of remaining errors. Having experienced difficulties with errors ourselves, both as students and as instructors, we resolved to avoid this problem in *Corporate Finance*. As a result of our error detection procedures, we are convinced that the book is relatively free of mistakes.

Partly because of our confidence that few such errors remain, but primarily because we want to detect any errors in the textbook that may have slipped by so we can correct them in subsequent printings, we decided to offer a reward of $10 per error to the first person who reports a textbook error to us. For purposes of this reward, errors in the textbook are defined as misspelled words, nonrounding numerical errors, incorrect statements, and any other error that inhibits comprehension. Typesetting problems such as irregular spacing and differences in opinion regarding grammatical or punctuation conventions do not qualify for this reward. Also, given the ever-changing nature of the World Wide Web, changes in Web addresses do not qualify as errors, although we would appreciate reports of changed Web addresses. Finally, any qualifying error that has follow-through effects is counted as two errors only. **Please report any errors to Michael C. Ehrhardt at the e-mail address given below.**

CONCLUSION

Finance is, in a real sense, the cornerstone of the free enterprise system. Good financial management is therefore vitally important to the economic health of business firms, hence to the nation and the world. Because of its importance, corporate finance should be thoroughly understood. However, this is easier said than done—the field is relatively complex, and it is undergoing constant change in response to shifts in economic conditions. All of this makes corporate finance not only stimulating and exciting, but also challenging and sometimes perplexing. We sincerely hope that *Corporate Finance: A Focused Approach* will help readers understand and solve the financial problems faced by businesses today.

Michael C. Ehrhardt
University of Tennessee
ehrhardt@utk.edu

Eugene F. Brigham
University of Florida
gene.brigham@cba.ufl.edu

January 2005

Brief Contents

CONTENTS

PART 3 PROJECTS AND THEIR VALUATION 275

APPENDIXES

Fundamental Concepts of Corporate Finance

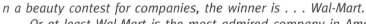

CHAPTER 1

An Overview of Corporate Finance and the Financial Environment

I n a beauty contest for companies, the winner is . . . Wal-Mart.

Or at least Wal-Mart is the most admired company in America, according to Fortune *magazine's annual survey. The other top-ten finalists are Berkshire Hathaway, Southwest Airlines, General Electric, Dell, Microsoft, Johnson & Johnson, Starbucks, FedEx, and IBM. What do these companies have that separates them from the rest of the pack?*

According to more than 10,000 executives, directors, and security analysts, these companies have the highest average scores across eight attributes: (1) innovativeness, (2) quality of management, (3) employee talent, (4) quality of products and services, (5) long-term investment value, (6) financial soundness, (7) social responsibility, and (8) use of corporate assets. These companies also have an incredible focus on using technology to reduce costs, to reduce inventory, and to speed up product delivery. For example, Wal-Mart's success is driven by the three S's: scale, scope, and speed. Wal-Mart's scale is truly astounding, with more than $240 billion in sales, giving it the largest U.S. market share in many products. Wal-Mart's wide scope of products and state-of-the-art information systems allow it to tailor its product mix to fit demand, so its shelves are always full of the products that people currently want. But products don't stay on its shelves very long. Wal-Mart moves merchandise so fast that it sells 70 percent of its goods before it has paid the suppliers.

Many companies have a difficult time attracting employees. Not so for the most admired companies, which average 26 applicants for each job opening. These companies are on the leading edge when it comes to training employees and providing a workplace in which people can thrive.

In a nutshell, these companies reduce costs by having innovative production processes, they create value for customers by providing high-quality products and services, and they create value for employees through training and fostering an environment that allows employees to utilize all of their skills and talents.

Do investors benefit from this focus on processes, customers, and employees? During the most recent five-year period, these ten companies posted an average annual stock return of 7.0 percent, which is quite impressive when compared with the 3.2 percent annual decline in the S&P 500. These superior returns are due to superior cash flow generation. But, as you will see throughout this book, a company can generate cash flow only if it also creates value for its customers, employees, and suppliers.

Visit **http://www.fortune .com** *for updates on the U.S. ranking.* Fortune *also ranks the Global Most Admired.*

This chapter should give you an idea of what corporate finance is all about, including an overview of the financial markets in which corporations operate. Before getting into details, let's look at the big picture. You're probably back in school because you want an interesting, challenging, and rewarding career. To see where finance fits in, here's a five-minute MBA.

THE FIVE-MINUTE MBA

e-resource

Visit http://ehrhardt .swlearning.com to see the Web site accompanying this text. This ever-evolving site, for students and instructors, is a tool for teaching, learning, financial research, and job searches.

Okay, we realize you can't get an MBA in five minutes. But just as an artist quickly sketches the outline of a picture before filling in the details, we can sketch the key elements of an MBA education. In a nutshell, the objective of an MBA is to provide managers with the knowledge and skills they need to run successful companies, so we start our sketch with some common characteristics of successful companies. In particular, all successful companies are able to accomplish two goals.

1. They identify, create, and deliver products or services that are highly valued by customers—so highly valued that customers choose to purchase them from the company rather than from its competitors.
2. All successful companies sell their products/services at prices that are high enough to cover costs and to compensate owners and creditors for their exposure to risk.

It's easy to talk about satisfying customers and investors, but it's not so easy to accomplish these goals. If it were, then all companies would be successful, and you wouldn't need an MBA!

The Key Attributes Required for Success

First, *successful companies have skilled people* at all levels inside the company, including leaders, managers, and a capable workforce.

Second, *successful companies have strong relationships* with groups outside the company. For example, successful companies develop win–win relationships with suppliers and excel in customer relationship management.

Third, *successful companies have enough funding* to execute their plans and support their operations. For example, most companies need cash to purchase land, buildings, equipment, and materials. Companies can reinvest a portion of their earnings, but most must also raise additional funds externally, by some combination of selling stock and/or borrowing in the financial markets.

Just as a stool needs all three legs to stand, a successful company must have all three attributes: skilled people, strong external relationships, and sufficient capital.

The MBA, Finance, and Your Career

Consult http://www .careers-in-finance .com for an excellent site containing information on a variety of business career areas, listings of current jobs, and other reference materials.

To be successful, a company must meet its first goal—identifying, creating, and delivering highly valued products and services to its customers. This requires that it possess all three of the key attributes. Therefore, it's not surprising that most of your MBA courses are directly related to these attributes. For example, courses in economics, communication, strategy, organizational behavior, and human resources should prepare you for a leadership role and enable you to effectively manage your company's work force. Other courses, such as marketing, operations management, and information technology, increase your knowledge of specific disciplines, enabling you to develop the efficient business processes and strong external relationships your company needs. Portions of this finance course will address raising the capital your company needs to implement its plans. In short, your MBA courses will give you the skills you need to help a company achieve its first goal—producing goods and services that customers want.

Recall, though, that it's not enough just to have highly valued products and satisfied customers. Successful companies must also meet their second goal, which is generating enough cash to compensate the investors who provided the necessary capital. To help accomplish this second goal, you must be able to evaluate any proposal, whether it relates to marketing, production, strategy, or any other area, and implement only the projects that add value for your investors. For this, you must have expertise in finance, no matter your major. Thus, finance is a critical part of an MBA education, and it will help you throughout your career.

SELF-TEST QUESTIONS
What are the goals of successful companies?
What are the three key attributes common to all successful companies?
How does expertise in finance help a company become successful?

THE CORPORATE LIFE CYCLE

Many major corporations had humble origins, perhaps even in a garage, including Apple Computer and Hewlett-Packard. How is it possible for such companies to grow into the giants we see today? No two companies develop in exactly the same way, but the following sections describe some typical stages in the corporate life cycle.

Starting Up as a Proprietorship

Many companies begin as a **proprietorship,** which is an unincorporated business owned by one individual. Starting a business as a proprietor is easy—one merely begins business operations, after obtaining any required city or state business licenses. The proprietorship has three important advantages: (1) It is easily and inexpensively formed, (2) it is subject to few government regulations, and (3) its income is not subject to corporate taxation but is taxed only as a part of the proprietor's personal income.

However, the proprietorship has three important limitations: (1) It is difficult for a proprietorship to obtain the capital needed for growth; (2) the proprietor has unlimited personal liability for the business's debts, which can result in losses that exceed the money he or she invested in the company (creditors may even be able to seize a proprietor's house or other personal property!); and (3) the life of a proprietorship is limited to the life of its founder. For these three reasons, sole proprietorships are used primarily for small businesses. In fact, proprietorships account for only about 13 percent of all sales, based on dollar values, even though about 80 percent of all companies are proprietorships.

More Than One Owner: A Partnership

Some companies start with more than one owner, and some proprietors decide to add a partner as the business grows. A **partnership** exists whenever two or more persons associate to conduct a noncorporate business for profit. Partnerships may operate under different degrees of formality, ranging from informal, oral understandings to formal agreements filed with the secretary of the state in which the partnership was formed. Partnership agreements define the ways any profits and losses are shared between partners. A partnership's advantages and disadvantages are similar to those of a proprietorship.

Regarding liability, the partners can potentially lose all of their personal assets, even assets not invested in the business, because under partnership law, each partner is liable for the business's debts. Therefore, if any partner is unable to meet his or her pro rata liability in the event the partnership goes bankrupt, the remaining partners must make good on the unsatisfied claims, drawing on their personal assets to the extent necessary. To avoid this, it is possible to limit the liabilities of some of the partners by establishing a **limited partnership,** wherein certain partners are designated **general partners** and others **limited partners.** In a limited partnership, the limited partners are liable only for the amount of their investment in the partnership, while the general partners have unlimited liability. However, the limited partners typically have no control, which rests solely with the general partners, and their returns are likewise limited. Limited partnerships are common in real estate, oil, equipment leasing ventures, and venture capital. However, they are not widely used in general business situations because no one partner is usually willing to be the general partner and thus accept the majority of the business's risk, and none of the others are willing to be limited partners and give up all control.

In both regular and limited partnerships, at least one partner is liable for the debts of the partnership. However, in a **limited liability partnership (LLP)**, sometimes called a **limited liability company (LLC)**, all partners enjoy limited liability with regard to the business's liabilities, with their potential losses limited to their investment in the LLP. Of course, this increases the risk faced by an LLP's lenders, customers, and suppliers.

Many Owners: A Corporation

Most partnerships have difficulty attracting substantial amounts of capital. This is generally not a problem for a slow-growing business, but if a business's products or services really catch on, and if it needs to raise large sums of money to capitalize on its opportunities, the difficulty in attracting capital becomes a real drawback. Thus, many growth companies, such as Hewlett-Packard and Microsoft, began life as a proprietorship or partnership, but at some point their founders found it necessary to convert to a corporation. Some companies, in anticipation of growth, actually begin as corporations. A **corporation** is a legal entity created by a state, and it is separate and distinct from its owners and managers. This separation gives the corporation three major advantages: (1) *unlimited* life—a corporation can continue after its original owners and managers are deceased; (2) *easy transferability of ownership interest*—ownership interests can be divided into shares of stock, which can be transferred far more easily than can proprietorship or partnership interests; and (3) *limited liability*—losses are limited to the actual funds invested.

To illustrate limited liability, suppose you invested $10,000 in a partnership that then went bankrupt owing $1 million. Because the owners are liable for the debts of a partnership, you could be assessed for a share of the company's debt, and you could be held liable for the entire $1 million if your partners could not pay their shares. On the other hand, if you invested $10,000 in the stock of a corporation that then went bankrupt, your potential loss on the investment would be limited to your $10,000 investment.[1] Unlimited life, easy transferability of ownership interest, and limited liability—make it much easier for corporations than for proprietorships or partnerships to raise money in the financial markets and grow into large companies.

The corporate form offers significant advantages over proprietorships and partnerships, but it also has two disadvantages: (1) Corporate earnings may be subject to double taxation—the earnings of the corporation are taxed at the corporate level, and then earnings paid out as dividends are taxed again as income to the stockholders.[2] (2) Setting up a corporation involves preparing a charter, writing a set of bylaws, and filing the many required state and federal reports, which is more complex and time-consuming than creating a proprietorship or a partnership.

The **charter** includes the following information: (1) name of the proposed corporation, (2) types of activities it will pursue, (3) amount of capital stock, (4) number of directors, and (5) names and addresses of directors. The charter is filed with the secretary of the state in which the firm will be incorporated, and when it is approved, the corporation is officially in existence.[3] After the corporation begins operating, quarterly and annual employment, financial, and tax reports must be filed with state and federal authorities.

---

[1] In the case of very small corporations, the limited liability may be fiction because lenders frequently require personal guarantees from the stockholders.

[2] The 2003 tax act reduced, but did not eliminate, the taxation of dividends received by investors.

[3] More than 60 percent of major U.S. corporations are chartered in Delaware, which has, over the years, provided a favorable legal environment for corporations. It is not necessary for a firm to be headquartered, or even to conduct operations, in its state of incorporation, or even in its country of incorporation.

The **bylaws** are a set of rules drawn up by the founders of the corporation. Included are such points as (1) how directors are to be elected (all elected each year, or perhaps one-third each year for three-year terms); (2) whether the existing stockholders will have the first right to buy any new shares the firm issues; and (3) procedures for changing the bylaws themselves, should conditions require it.

There are actually several different types of corporations. Professionals such as doctors, lawyers, and accountants often form a **professional corporation (PC)** or a **professional association (PA)**. These provide most of incorporation's benefits but do not relieve the participants of professional (malpractice) liability. Indeed, the primary motivation behind the professional corporation was to provide a way for groups of professionals to incorporate and thus avoid certain types of unlimited liability, yet still be held responsible for professional liability.

Finally, if certain requirements are met, particularly with regard to size and number of stockholders, owners can establish a corporation but elect to be taxed as if the business were a proprietorship or partnership. Such firms, which differ not in organizational form but only in how their owners are taxed, are called **S corporations.**

Once a corporation has been established, how does it evolve?

Growing and Managing a Corporation

When entrepreneurs start a company, they usually provide all the financing from their personal resources, which may include savings, second mortgages, or even credit cards. As the corporation grows, it needs factories, equipment, inventory, and other resources to support its growth. In time, the entrepreneurs usually deplete their own resources and must turn to external financing. Many young companies are too risky for banks, so the founders must sell stock to outsiders, such as friends, family, private investors (often called angels), or venture capitalists. If the corporation continues to grow, it may become successful enough to attract lending from banks, or it may even raise additional funds through an **initial public offering (IPO)** by selling stock to the public at large. After an IPO, corporations support their growth by borrowing from banks, issuing debt, or selling additional shares of stock. In short, a corporation's ability to grow depends on its interactions with the financial markets, which we describe in much more detail later in this chapter.

For proprietorships, partnerships, and small corporations, the firm's owners are also its managers. This is usually not true for a large corporation, which means that large firms' stockholders, who are its owners, face a very serious problem. What is to prevent managers from acting in their own best interests, rather than in the best interests of the owners? This is called an **agency problem** because managers are hired as agents to act on behalf of the owners. We will have much more to say about agency problems throughout the book, especially in Chapters 13 and 14.

SELF-TEST QUESTIONS

What are the key differences between proprietorships, partnerships, and corporations?

Describe some special types of partnerships and corporations, and explain the differences among them.

THE PRIMARY OBJECTIVE OF THE CORPORATION: VALUE MAXIMIZATION

Shareholders are the owners of a corporation, and they purchase stocks because they want to earn a good return on their investment without undue risk exposure. In most cases, shareholders elect directors, who then hire managers to run the corporation on a day-to-day basis. Because managers are supposed to be working on behalf of shareholders, they should pursue policies that enhance shareholder value. Consequently, throughout this book we operate on the assumption that management's primary objective should be **stockholder wealth maximization.**

The **market price** is the stock price that we observe in the financial markets. We later explain in detail how stock prices are determined, but for now it is enough to say that a company's market price incorporates the information available to investors. If the market price reflects all *relevant* information, then the observed price is also the **fundamental,** or **intrinsic price.** However, investors rarely have all relevant information. For example, companies report most major decisions, but sometimes withhold critical information to prevent competitors from gaining strategic advantages.

Unfortunately, some managers deliberately mislead investors by taking actions to make their companies appear more valuable than they truly are. Sometimes these actions are illegal, such as those taken by the senior managers at Enron. Sometimes the actions are legal, but they are taken to push the current market price above its fundamental price in the short term. For example, suppose a utility's stock price is equal to its fundamental price of $50 per share. What would happen if the utility substantially reduced its tree-trimming program, but didn't tell investors? This would lower current costs and thus boost current earnings and current cash flow, but it would also lead to major expenditures in the future when breaking limbs damage the lines. If investors are told about the major repair costs facing the company, the market price would immediately drop to a new fundamental value of $45. But if investors are kept in the dark, they might misinterpret the higher-than-expected current earnings, and the market price might go up to $52. Investors would eventually understand the situation when the company later incurs large costs to repair the damaged lines; when that happens, the price would fall to its fundamental value of $45.

Consider the sequence of events. The company's managers deceived investors, and the price rose to $52 when it would have fallen to $45 if not for the deception. Of course, this benefited those who owned the stock at the time of the deception, including managers with stock options. But when the deception came to light, those stockholders who still owned the stock would suffer a significant loss, ending up with stock worth less than its original fundamental value. If the managers cashed in their stock options prior to this, then only the stockholders were hurt by the deception. Because the managers were hired to act in the interests of stockholders, their deception was a breach of their fiduciary responsibility. In addition, the managers' deception damaged the company's credibility, making it harder to raise capital in the future.

Therefore, when we say management's objective should be to maximize stockholder wealth, we really mean it is to *maximize the fundamental price of the firm's common stock*—and not just the current market price. Firms do, of course, have other objectives—in particular, the managers who make the actual decisions are interested in their own personal satisfaction, in their employees' welfare, and in the good of the community and of society at large. Still, for the reasons set forth in the following sections, *maximizing the fundamental stock price is the most important objective for most corporations.*

Stock Price Maximization and Social Welfare

If a firm attempts to maximize its fundamental stock price, is this good or bad for society? In general, it is good. Aside from such illegal actions as fraudulent accounting, exploiting monopoly power, violating safety codes, and failing to meet environmental standards, *the same actions that maximize fundamental stock prices also benefit society.* Here are some of the reasons:

1. **To a large extent, the owners of stock *are* society.** Seventy-five years ago this was not true, because most stock ownership was concentrated in the hands of a relatively small segment of society, comprised of the wealthiest individuals. Since then, there has been explosive growth in pension funds, life insurance companies, and mutual

funds. These institutions now own more than 61 percent of all stock, which means that most individuals have an indirect stake in the stock market. In addition, more than 48 percent of all U.S. households now own stock directly, as compared with only 32.5 percent in 1989. Thus, most members of society now have an important stake in the stock market, either directly or indirectly. Therefore, when a manager takes actions to maximize the stock price, this improves the quality of life for millions of ordinary citizens.

2. **Consumers benefit.** Stock price maximization requires efficient, low-cost businesses that produce high-quality goods and services at the lowest possible cost. This means that companies must develop products and services that consumers want and need, which leads to new technology and new products. Also, companies that maximize their stock price must generate growth in sales by creating value for customers in the form of efficient and courteous service, adequate stocks of merchandise, and well-located business establishments.

   People sometimes argue that firms, in their efforts to raise profits and stock prices, increase product prices and gouge the public. In a reasonably competitive economy, which we have, prices are constrained by competition and consumer resistance. If a firm raises its prices beyond reasonable levels, it will simply lose its market share. Even giant firms such as General Motors lose business to Japanese and German firms, as well as to Ford and Chrysler, if they set prices above the level necessary to cover production costs plus a "normal" profit. Of course, firms *want* to earn more, and they constantly try to cut costs, develop new products, and so on, and thereby earn above-normal profits. Note, though, that if they are indeed successful and do earn above-normal profits, those very profits will attract competition, which will eventually drive prices down, so again, the main long-term beneficiary is the consumer.

3. **Employees benefit.** There are cases in which a stock increases when a company announces a plan to lay off employees, but viewed over time this is the exception rather than the rule. In general, companies that successfully increase stock prices also grow and add more employees, thus benefiting society. Note too that many governments across the world, including U.S. federal and state governments, are privatizing some of their state-owned activities by selling these operations to investors. Perhaps not surprisingly, the sales and cash flows of recently privatized companies generally improve. Moreover, studies show that these newly privatized companies tend to grow and thus require more employees when they are managed with the goal of stock price maximization.

   One of *Fortune* magazine's key criteria in determining their list of most admired companies is a company's ability to attract, develop, and retain talented people. Their results consistently show high correlations among a company's being admired, its ability to satisfy employees, and its creation of value for shareholders. Employees find that it is both fun and financially rewarding to work for successful companies. Thus, successful companies get the cream of the employee crop, and skilled, motivated employees are one of the keys to corporate success.

Managerial Actions to Maximize Shareholder Wealth

What types of actions can managers take to maximize shareholder wealth? To answer this question, we first need to ask, "What determines a firm's value?" In a nutshell, it is *a company's ability to generate cash flows now and in the future.*

We address different aspects of this in detail throughout the book, but we can lay out three basic facts now: (1) Any financial asset, including a company's stock, is valuable only to the extent that it generates cash flows; (2) the timing of cash flows matters—cash received sooner is better; and (3) investors are averse to risk, so all else equal, they will pay more for a stock whose cash flows are relatively certain than for one whose cash flows are more risky. Because of these three facts, managers can enhance their firms' value

The Security Industry Association's Web site, http://www.sia .com, is a great source of information. To find data on stock ownership, go to their Web page, click on Research/ Statistical/Surveys, click on Securities Industry Fact Book, and look at the section on Investor Participation. You can purchase the most recent data, or look at the prior year for free.

by increasing the size of the expected cash flows, by speeding up their receipt, and by reducing their risk.

The cash flows that matter are called **free cash flows (FCFs)**, not because they are free, but because they are available (or free) for distribution to all of the company's investors, including creditors and stockholders. As shown in Figure 1-1, the three primary determinants of free cash flows are (1) sales revenues, (2) operating costs and taxes, and (3) required investments in operations.

Sales revenues depend on the *current level of unit sales, the price per unit,* and *expected future growth rates.* Managers can increase unit sales, hence cash flows, by truly understanding their customers and then providing the goods and services that customers want. Some companies may luck into a situation that creates rapid sales growth, but the unfortunate reality is that market saturation and competition will, in the long term, cause the unit sales growth rate to decline to a level that is limited by population growth. Companies may try to increase prices, but in a competitive economy such as ours, higher prices can be charged only for products that meet the needs of customers better than competitors' products. Therefore, managers must constantly strive to create new products, services, and brand identities that cannot be easily replicated by competitors, and thus to extend the period of high growth and high prices for as long as possible.

The second determinant of cash flows is the combined impact of operating costs and taxes, which determines the amount of after-tax profit that is available to investors after the company pays its employees and suppliers. One way to increase operating profit is to reduce direct expenses such as labor and materials. However, and paradoxically, sometimes companies can create even higher profit by spending *more* on labor and materials. For example, choosing the lowest-cost supplier might result in using poor materials that lead to costly production problems. Therefore, managers should understand *supply chain management,* which often means developing long-term relationships with suppliers. Similarly, increased employee training adds to costs, but it often pays off through increased productivity and lower turnover. Therefore, the *human resources staff* can have a huge effect on operating profits.

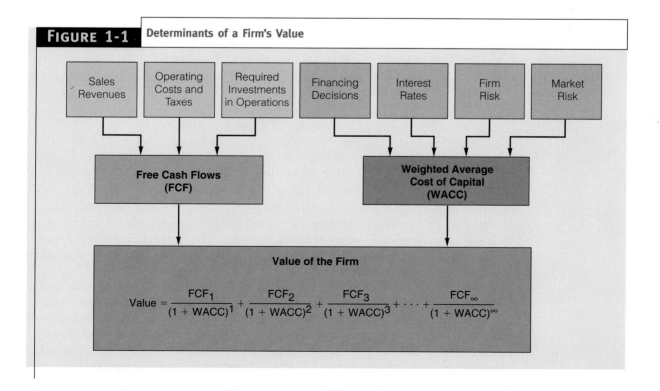

FIGURE 1-1   Determinants of a Firm's Value

CORPORATE SCANDALS AND MAXIMIZING STOCK PRICE

The list of corporate scandals seems to go on for- ever: Sunbeam, Enron, ImClone, WorldCom, Tyco, Adelphia . . . At first glance, it's tempting to say, "Look what happens when managers care only about maximizing stock price." But a closer look reveals a much different story. In fact, if these man- agers were trying to maximize stock price, they failed dismally, given the resulting values of these companies.

Although details vary from company to com- pany, a few common themes emerge. First, mana- gerial compensation was linked to the short-term performance of the stock price via poorly designed stock option and stock grant programs. This pro- vided managers with a powerful incentive to drive up the stock price at the option vesting date with- out worrying about the future. Second, it is virtu- ally impossible to take *legal* actions that drive up the stock price in the short term but harm it in the long term because the value of a company is based on all of its future free cash flows and not just cash flows in the immediate future. Because legal actions to quickly drive up the stock price didn't

exist (other than the old-fashioned ones, such as increasing sales, cutting costs, or reducing capital requirements), these managers began bending a few rules. Third, as they initially got away with bending rules, their egos and hubris grew to such an extent that they felt they were above all rules, and so they began breaking even more rules.

Stock prices did go up, at least temporarily. But as Abraham Lincoln said, "You can't fool all of the people all of the time." As the scandals became public, the stocks' prices plummeted, and in some cases the companies were ruined.

There are several important lessons to be learned from these examples. First, people respond to incen- tives, and poorly designed incentives can cause dis- astrous results. Second, ethical violations usually begin with small steps; if stockholders want man- agers to avoid large ethical violations, then don't let them make the small ones. Third, there is no short- cut to creating lasting value. It takes hard work to increase sales, cut costs, and reduce capital require- ments, but this is the formula for success.

The third factor affecting cash flows is the amount of money a company must invest in its operations (including assets such as factories, equipment, computer systems, and inventory). In short, it takes cash to create cash. But each dollar tied up in operations is a dollar that is unavailable for distribution to investors. Therefore, reducing asset require- ments increases cash flows, which increases the stock price. For example, companies that successfully implement *just-in-time inventory systems* generally increase their cash flows because they have less cash tied up in inventory.

As these examples indicate, there are many ways to improve free cash flows. All of them require the active participation of many departments—including marketing, engi- neering, and logistics. One of the financial manager's roles is to show others how their actions will affect the company's ability to generate cash flow.

Financial managers also must make financing decisions relating to *how to finance the firm*. In particular, what mix of debt and equity should be used, and what specific types of debt and equity securities should be issued? Also, what percentage of current earnings should be retained and reinvested rather than paid out as dividends? Along with these financing decisions, the general level of interest rates in the economy, the risk of the firm's operations, and stock market investors' overall attitude toward risk determine the rate of return that is required to satisfy a firm's investors. This is a return from investors' per- spectives, but it is a cost from the company's point of view. Therefore, it is called the **weighted average cost of capital (WACC)**.

Figure 1-1 summarizes these points. A firm generates sales, pays its costs and taxes, and makes the necessary investments in assets to support its growth. The result is free cash flow, which is available for distribution to all investors. The firm's capital structure and the risk of its operations determine the total risk of the free cash flows to the investors. This risk is combined with the level of interest rates in the economy and investors' overall attitude toward risk, resulting in the rate of return that investors require, which is the weighted average cost of capital to the company. Finally, the stream of annual expected future free cash flows, combined with the cost of capital, determine the value of the company.

Growing firms need access to financial markets, and, as indicated in Figure 1-1, financial markets have a significant impact on a firm's cost of capital. The rest of this chapter focuses upon financial markets and interest rates.

What is management's primary objective?
How does stock price maximization benefit society?
What three basic factors determine the price of a stock?
What three factors determine cash flows?

THE FINANCIAL MARKETS

Businesses often need capital to implement growth plans; governments require funds to finance building projects; and individuals frequently want loans to purchase cars, homes, and education. Where can they get this money? Fortunately, there are other individuals and firms with incomes greater than their expenditures. **Financial markets** bring together people and organizations needing money with those having surplus funds.

There are many different financial markets in a developed economy such as ours. Each market deals with a somewhat different type of instrument, customer, or geographic location. Here are some of the major types of markets:

1. **Physical asset markets** (also called "tangible" or "real" asset markets) are those for such products as wheat, autos, real estate, computers, and machinery. **Financial asset markets,** on the other hand, deal with stocks, bonds, notes, mortgages, and other **financial instruments.** All of these instruments are simply pieces of paper with contractual provisions that entitle their owners to specific rights and claims on real assets. For example, a corporate bond issued by IBM entitles its owner to a specific claim on the cash flows produced by IBM's physical assets, while a share of IBM stock entitles its owner to a different set of claims on IBM's cash flows. Unlike these conventional financial instruments, the contractual provisions of **derivatives** are not direct claims on either real assets or their cash flows. Instead, derivatives are claims whose values depend on, or are *derived* from, the value of some other asset. Futures and options are two important types of derivatives, and their values depend on the prices of other assets, say, IBM stock, Japanese yen, or pork bellies.
2. **Spot markets** and **futures markets** are markets where assets are being bought or sold for "on-the-spot" delivery (literally, within a few days) or for delivery at some future date, such as six months or a year into the future.
3. **Money markets** are the markets for short-term, highly liquid debt securities. **Capital markets** are the markets for intermediate- or long-term debt and corporate stocks. The New York Stock Exchange is an example of a capital market. When describing debt markets, "short term" generally means less than one year, "intermediate term" means one to five years, and "long term" means more than five years.
4. **Mortgage markets** deal with loans on residential, agricultural, commercial, and industrial real estate, while **consumer credit markets** involve loans for autos, appliances, education, vacations, and so on.
5. **World, national, regional, and local markets** also exist. Thus, depending on an organization's size and scope of operations, it may be able to borrow all around the world, or it may be confined to a strictly local, even neighborhood, market.
6. **Primary markets** are the markets in which corporations raise new capital. If Microsoft were to sell a new issue of common stock to raise capital, this would be a

primary market transaction. The corporation selling the newly created stock receives the proceeds from the sale in a primary market transaction.

7. The **initial public offering (IPO) market** is a subset of the primary market. Here firms "go public" by offering shares to the public for the first time. Microsoft had its IPO in 1986. Previously, Bill Gates and other insiders owned all the shares. In many IPOs, the insiders sell some of their shares plus the company sells newly created shares to raise additional capital.

8. **Secondary markets** are markets in which existing, already outstanding, securities are traded among investors. Thus, if you decided to buy 1,000 shares of AT&T stock, the purchase would occur in the secondary market. The New York Stock Exchange is a secondary market, since it deals in outstanding, as opposed to newly issued, stocks. Secondary markets also exist for bonds, mortgages, and other financial assets. The corporation whose securities are being traded is not involved in a secondary market transaction and, thus, does not receive any funds from such a sale.

9. **Private markets,** where transactions are worked out directly between two parties, are differentiated from **public markets,** where standardized contracts are traded on organized exchanges. Bank loans and private placements of debt with insurance companies are examples of private market transactions. Since these transactions are private, they may be structured in any manner that appeals to the two parties. By contrast, securities that are issued in public markets (for example, common stock and corporate bonds) are ultimately held by a large number of individuals. Public securities must have fairly standardized contractual features, both to appeal to a broad range of investors and also because public investors cannot afford the time to study unique, nonstandardized contracts. Private market securities are, therefore, more tailor-made but less liquid, whereas public market securities are more liquid but subject to greater standardization.

You can access current and historical interest rates and economic data as well as regional economic data for the states of Arkansas, Illinois, Indiana, Kentucky, Mississippi, Missouri, and Tennessee from the Federal Reserve Economic Data (FRED) site at http://www .stls.frb.org/fred/.

Other classifications could be made, but this breakdown is sufficient to show that there are many types of financial markets. Also, note that the distinctions among markets are often blurred and unimportant, except as a general point of reference. For example, it makes little difference if a firm borrows for 11, 12, or 13 months, hence, whether we have a "money" or "capital" market transaction. You should recognize the big differences among types of markets, but don't get hung up trying to distinguish them at the boundaries.

Table 1-1 gives a listing of the most important instruments traded in the various financial markets. The instruments are arranged from top to bottom in ascending order of typical length of maturity and risk. Notice that as maturity and risk increase, interest rates usually increase. As we go through the book, we will look in much more detail at many of the instruments listed in Table 1-1 and their effect on corporate valuation.

SELF-TEST QUESTIONS Distinguish between (1) physical asset markets and financial asset markets, (2) spot and futures markets, (3) money and capital markets, (4) primary and secondary markets, and (5) private and public markets.

What are derivatives?

FINANCIAL INSTITUTIONS

Transfers of capital between savers and those who need capital take place in the three different ways diagrammed in Figure 1-2. *Direct transfers* of money and securities, as shown in the top section, occur when a business sells its stocks or bonds directly to savers, without going through any type of financial institution. The business delivers its securities to savers, who in turn give the firm the money it needs.

TABLE 1-1 | Summary of Major Financial Instruments

Instrument	Major Participants	Risk	Original Maturity	Interest Rates on 3/25/04[a]
U.S. Treasury bills	Sold by U.S. Treasury	Default-free	91 days to 1 year	0.94%
Banker's acceptances	A firm's promise to pay, guaranteed by a bank	Low if strong bank guarantees	Up to 180 days	1.04
Commercial paper	Issued by financially secure firms to large investors	Low default risk	Up to 270 days	1.00
Negotiable certificates of deposit (CDs)	Issued by major banks to large investors	Depends on strength of issuer	Up to 1 year	1.04
Money market mutual funds	Invest in short-term debt; held by individuals and businesses	Low degree of risk	No specific maturity (instant liquidity)	0.50
Eurodollar market time deposits	Issued by banks outside U.S.	Depends on strength of issuer	Up to 1 year	1.04
Consumer credit loans	Loans by banks/credit unions/finance companies	Risk is variable	Variable	Variable
Commercial loans	Loans by banks to corporations	Depends on borrower	Up to 7 years	Tied to prime rate (4.00%) or LIBOR (1.11%)[b]
U.S. Treasury notes and bonds	Issued by U.S. government	No default risk, but price falls if interest rates rise	2 to 30 years	4.73
Mortgages	Loans secured by property	Risk is variable	Up to 30 years	5.08
Municipal bonds	Issued by state and local governments to individuals and institutions	Riskier than U.S. government bonds, but exempt from most taxes	Up to 30 years	4.41
Corporate bonds	Issued by corporations to individuals and institutions	Riskier than U.S. government debt; depends on strength of issuer	Up to 40 years[c]	5.28
Leases	Similar to debt; firms lease assets rather than borrow and then buy them	Risk similar to corporate bonds	Generally 3 to 20 years	Similar to bond yields
Preferred stocks	Issued by corporations to individuals and institutions	Riskier than corporate bonds	Unlimited	6 to 9%
Common stocks[d]	Issued by corporations to individuals and institutions	Riskier than preferred stocks	Unlimited	9 to 15%

[a]Data are from *The Wall Street Journal* (**http://online.wsj.com**) or the *Federal Reserve Statistical Release* (**http://www.federalreserve.gov/releases/H15/update**). Money market rates assume a 3-month maturity. The corporate bond rate is for AAA-rated bonds.

[b]The prime rate is the rate U.S. banks charge to good customers. LIBOR (London Interbank Offered Rate) is the rate that U.K. banks charge one another.

[c]A few corporations have issued 100-year bonds; however, the majority have issued bonds with maturities less than 40 years.

[d]Common stocks are expected to provide a "return" in the form of dividends and capital gains rather than interest. Of course, if you buy a stock, your *actual* return may be considerably higher or lower than your *expected* return.

As shown in the middle section, transfers may also go through an **investment banking house** such as Merrill Lynch, which *underwrites* the issue. An underwriter serves as a middleman and facilitates the issuance of securities. The company sells its stocks or bonds to the investment bank, which in turn sells these same securities to savers. Because new securities are involved and the corporation receives the proceeds of the sale, this is a primary market transaction.

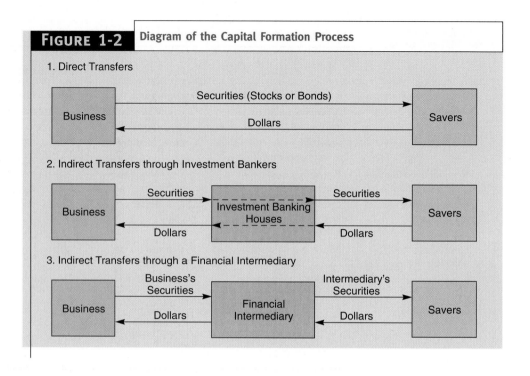

FIGURE 1-2 Diagram of the Capital Formation Process

1. Direct Transfers

Business → Securities (Stocks or Bonds) → Savers
Business ← Dollars ← Savers

2. Indirect Transfers through Investment Bankers

Business → Securities → Investment Banking Houses → Securities → Savers
Business ← Dollars ← Investment Banking Houses ← Dollars ← Savers

3. Indirect Transfers through a Financial Intermediary

Business → Business's Securities → Financial Intermediary → Intermediary's Securities → Savers
Business ← Dollars ← Financial Intermediary ← Dollars ← Savers

Transfers can also be made through a **financial intermediary** such as a bank or mutual fund. Here the intermediary obtains funds from savers in exchange for its own securities. The intermediary then uses this money to purchase and then hold businesses' securities. For example, a saver might give dollars to a bank, receiving from it a certificate of deposit, and then the bank might lend the money to a small business in the form of a mortgage loan. Thus, intermediaries literally create new forms of capital.

In the United States and other developed nations, a set of specialized, highly efficient financial intermediaries has evolved. The situation is changing rapidly, however, with different types of institutions performing services that were formerly reserved for others, causing institutional distinctions to blur. Still, there is a degree of institutional identity, and here are the major classes of intermediaries:

1. **Commercial banks,** the traditional "department stores of finance," serve a wide variety of savers and borrowers. Historically, commercial banks were the major institutions that lent money, handled checking accounts, and provided a channel through which the Federal Reserve System expanded or contracted the money supply. Today, however, several other institutions also provide checking services and significantly influence the money supply. Conversely, commercial banks are providing an ever-widening range of services, including stock brokerage services and insurance.

   Prior to 1933, commercial banks offered investment banking services, but the Glass-Steagall Act, which was passed in 1933, prohibited commercial banks from engaging in investment banking. Thus, the Morgan Bank was broken up into two separate organizations, one of which became the Morgan Guaranty Trust Company, a commercial bank, while the other became Morgan Stanley, a major investment banking house. Note also that Japanese and European banks can offer both commercial and investment banking services. This hindered U.S. banks in global competition, so in 1999 Congress basically repealed the Glass-Steagall Act. Then, U.S. commercial and investment banks began merging with one another, creating such giants as Citigroup and J. P. Morgan Chase.

2. **Savings and loan associations (S&Ls),** which have traditionally served individual savers and residential and commercial mortgage borrowers, take the funds of many small savers and then lend this money to home buyers and other types of borrowers. Because the savers obtain a degree of liquidity that would be absent if they made the mortgage loans directly, perhaps the most significant economic function of the S&Ls is to "create liquidity" that would otherwise be lacking. Also, the S&Ls have more expertise in analyzing credit, setting up loans, and making collections than individual savers, so S&Ls can reduce the costs of processing loans, thereby increasing the availability of real estate loans. Finally, the S&Ls hold large, diversified portfolios of loans and other assets and thus spread risks in a manner that would be impossible if small savers were making mortgage loans directly. Because of these factors, savers benefit by being able to invest in more liquid, better managed, and less risky assets, whereas borrowers benefit by being able to obtain more capital, and at a lower cost, than would otherwise be possible.

3. **Mutual savings banks** are similar to S&Ls, but they operate primarily in the northeastern states.

4. **Credit unions** are cooperative associations whose members are supposed to have a common bond, such as being employees of the same firm. Members' savings are loaned only to other members, generally for auto purchases, home improvement loans, and home mortgages. Credit unions are often the cheapest source of funds available to individual borrowers.

5. **Life insurance companies** take savings in the form of premiums; invest these funds in stocks, bonds, real estate, and mortgages; and make payments to beneficiaries. Life insurance companies also offer a variety of tax-deferred savings plans designed to provide retirement benefits.

6. **Mutual funds** are corporations that accept money from savers and then use these funds to buy financial instruments. These organizations pool funds and thus reduce risks by diversification. They also achieve economies of scale in analyzing securities, managing portfolios, and buying and selling securities. Different funds are designed to meet the objectives of different types of savers. Hence, there are bond funds for those who desire safety, stock funds for savers who are willing to accept significant risks in the hope of higher returns, and still other funds that are used as interest-bearing checking accounts (the **money market funds**). There are literally thousands of different mutual funds with dozens of different goals and purposes.

7. **Pension funds** are retirement plans funded by corporations or government agencies for their workers and administered generally by the trust departments of commercial banks or by life insurance companies. Pension funds invest primarily in bonds, stocks, mortgages, and real estate.

Financial institutions have historically been heavily regulated, with the primary purpose of this regulation being to ensure the safety of the institutions and thus to protect investors. However, these regulations—which have taken the form of prohibitions on nationwide branch banking, restrictions on the types of assets the institutions can buy, ceilings on the interest rates they can pay, and limitations on the types of services they can provide—tended to impede the free flow of capital and thus hurt the efficiency of our capital markets. Recognizing this, Congress has removed many of these restrictions.

The result has been a blurring of the distinctions between the different types of institutions. Indeed, the trend in the United States today is toward huge **financial service corporations,** which own banks, S&Ls, investment banking houses, insurance companies, pension plan operations, and mutual funds, and which have branches across the country and around the world. Examples of financial service corporations, most of which started in one area but have now diversified to cover most of the financial spectrum, include Merrill Lynch, American Express, Citigroup, Fidelity, and Prudential.

SELF-TEST QUESTIONS Identify three ways capital is transferred between savers and borrowers.

What is the difference between a commercial bank and an investment bank?

Distinguish between investment banking houses and financial intermediaries.

List the major types of intermediaries and briefly describe the primary function of each.

SECONDARY MARKETS

Financial institutions play a key role in matching primary market players who need money with those who have extra funds, but the vast majority of trading actually occurs in the **secondary markets.** Although there are many secondary markets for a wide variety of securities, we can classify their trading procedures along two dimensions. First, the secondary market can be either a **physical location exchange** or a **computer/telephone network.** For example, the New York Stock Exchange, the American Stock Exchange (AMEX), the Chicago Board of Trade (the CBOT trades futures and options), and the Tokyo Stock Exchange are all physical location exchanges. In other words, the traders actually meet and trade in a specific part of a specific building. In contrast, Nasdaq, which trades U.S. stocks, is a network of linked computers. Other examples are the markets for U.S. Treasury bonds and foreign exchange, which are conducted via telephone and/or computer networks. In these electronic markets, the traders never see one another.

The second dimension is the way orders from sellers and buyers are matched. This can occur through an open outcry **auction** system, through dealers, or by automated order matching. An example of an outcry auction is the CBOT, where traders actually meet in a pit and sellers and buyers communicate with one another through shouts and hand signals.

In a **dealer market,** there are "market makers" who keep an inventory of the stock (or other financial instrument) in much the same way that any merchant keeps an inventory. These dealers list bid and ask quotes, which are the prices at which they are willing to buy or sell. Computerized quotation systems keep track of all bid and ask prices, but they don't actually match buyers and sellers. Instead, traders must contact a specific dealer to complete the transaction. Nasdaq (U.S. stocks) is one such market, as are the London SEAQ (U.K. stocks) and the Neuer Market (stocks of small German companies).

The third method of matching orders is through an **electronic communications network (ECN).** Participants in an ECN post their orders to buy and sell, and the ECN automatically matches orders. For example, someone might place an order to buy 1,000 shares of IBM stock (this is called a "market order" since it is to buy the stock at the current market price). Suppose another participant had placed an order to sell 1,000 shares of IBM at a price of $91 per share, and this was the lowest price of any "sell" order. The ECN would automatically match these two orders, execute the trade, and notify both participants that the trade has occurred. Participants can also post "limit orders," which might state that the participant is willing to buy 1,000 shares of IBM at $90 per share if the price falls that low during the next two hours. In other words, there are limits on the price and/or the duration of the order. The ECN will execute the limit order if the conditions are met, that is, if someone offers to sell IBM at a price of $90 or less during the next two hours. The two largest ECNs for trading U.S. stocks are Instinet (owned by Reuters) and Island. Other large ECNs include Eurex, a Swiss-German ECN that trades futures contracts, and SETS, a U.K. ECN that trades stocks.

SELF-TEST QUESTIONS What are the major differences between physical location exchanges and computer/telephone networks?

What are the differences among open outcry auctions, dealer markets, and ECNs?

THE STOCK MARKET

Because the primary objective of financial management is to maximize the firm's stock price, a knowledge of the stock market is important to anyone involved in managing a business. The two leading stock markets today are the New York Stock Exchange and the Nasdaq stock market.

The New York Stock Exchange

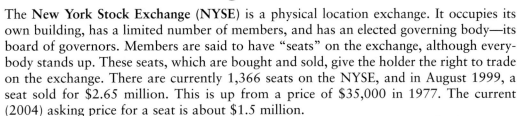

You can access the home pages of the major U.S. stock markets by typing http://www.nyse .com or http://www .nasdaq.com. These sites provide back-ground information as well as the opportunity to obtain individual stock quotes.

The **New York Stock Exchange (NYSE)** is a physical location exchange. It occupies its own building, has a limited number of members, and has an elected governing body—its board of governors. Members are said to have "seats" on the exchange, although everybody stands up. These seats, which are bought and sold, give the holder the right to trade on the exchange. There are currently 1,366 seats on the NYSE, and in August 1999, a seat sold for $2.65 million. This is up from a price of $35,000 in 1977. The current (2004) asking price for a seat is about $1.5 million.

Most of the larger investment banking houses operate *brokerage departments,* and they own seats on the NYSE and designate one or more of their officers as members. The NYSE is open on all normal working days, with the members meeting in a large room equipped with electronic equipment that enables each member to communicate with his or her firm's offices throughout the country. For example, Merrill Lynch (the largest brokerage firm) might receive an order in its Atlanta office from a customer who wants to buy shares of AT&T stock. Simultaneously, Morgan Stanley's Denver office might receive an order from a customer wishing to sell shares of AT&T. Each broker communicates electronically with the firm's representative on the NYSE. Other brokers throughout the country are also communicating with their own exchange members. The exchange members with *sell orders* offer the shares for sale, and they are bid for by the members with *buy orders.* Thus, the NYSE operates as an *auction market.*[4]

The Nasdaq Stock Market

The **National Association of Securities Dealers (NASD)** is a self-regulatory body that licenses brokers and oversees trading practices. The computerized network used by the NASD is known as the NASD Automated Quotation System, or Nasdaq. Nasdaq started as just a quotation system, but it has grown to become an organized securities market with its own listing requirements. Nasdaq lists about 5,000 stocks, although not all trade through the same Nasdaq system. For example, the Nasdaq National Market lists the larger Nasdaq stocks, such as Microsoft and Intel, while the Nasdaq SmallCap Market lists smaller companies with the potential for high growth. Nasdaq also operates the Nasdaq OTC Bulletin Board, which lists quotes for stock that is registered with the Securities

---

[4] The NYSE is actually a modified auction market, wherein people (through their brokers) bid for stocks. Originally—about 200 years ago—brokers would literally shout, "I have 100 shares of Erie for sale; how much am I offered?" and then sell to the highest bidder. If a broker had a buy order, he or she would shout, "I want to buy 100 shares of Erie; who'll sell at the best price?" The same general situation still exists, although the exchanges now have members known as *specialists* who facilitate the trading process by keeping an inventory of shares of the stocks in which they specialize. If a buy order comes in at a time when no sell order arrives, the specialist will sell off some inventory. Similarly, if a sell order comes in, the specialist will buy and add to inventory. The specialist sets a *bid price* (the price the specialist will pay for the stock) and an *asked price* (the price at which shares will be sold out of inventory). The bid and asked prices are set at levels designed to keep the inventory in balance. If many buy orders start coming in because of favorable developments or sell orders come in because of unfavorable events, the specialist will raise or lower prices to keep supply and demand in balance. Bid prices are somewhat lower than asked prices, with the difference, or *spread,* representing the specialist's profit margin.

Special facilities are available to help institutional investors such as mutual funds or pension funds sell large blocks of stock without depressing their prices. In essence, brokerage houses that cater to institutional clients will purchase blocks (defined as 10,000 or more shares) and then resell the stock to other institutions or individuals. Also, when a firm has a major announcement that is likely to cause its stock price to change sharply, it will ask the exchanges to halt trading in its stock until the announcement has been made and digested by investors.

MEASURING THE MARKET

A *stock index* is designed to show the performance of the stock market. The problem is that there are many stock indexes, and it is difficult to determine which index best reflects market actions. Some are designed to represent the whole equity market, some to track the returns of certain industry sectors, and others to track the returns of small-cap, mid-cap, or large-cap stocks. "Cap" is short for capitalization, which means the total market value of a firm's stock. We discuss below three of the leading indexes.

Dow Jones Industrial Average

Unveiled in 1896 by Charles H. Dow, the Dow Jones Industrial Average (DJIA) provided a benchmark for comparing individual stocks with the overall market and for comparing the market with other economic indicators. The industrial average began with just 10 stocks, was expanded in 1916 to 20 stocks, and then to 30 in 1928. Also, in 1928 *The Wall Street Journal* editors began adjusting it for stock splits, and making substitutions. Today, the DJIA still includes 30 companies. They represent almost a fifth of the market value of all U.S. stocks, and all are both leading companies in their industries and widely held by individual and institutional investors.

S&P 500 Index

Created in 1926, the S&P 500 Index is widely regarded as the standard for measuring large-cap U.S. stock market performance. The stocks in the S&P 500 are selected by the Standard & Poor's Index Committee for being the leading companies in the leading industries, and for accurately reflecting the U.S. stock market. It is value weighted, so the largest companies (in terms of value) have the greatest influence. The S&P 500 Index is used as a comparison benchmark by 97 percent of all U.S. money managers and pension plan sponsors, and approximately $700 billion is managed so as to obtain the same performance as this index (that is, in indexed funds).

Nasdaq Composite Index

The Nasdaq Composite Index measures the performance of all common stocks listed on the Nasdaq stock market. Currently, it includes more than 5,000 companies, and because many of the technology-sector companies are traded on the computer-based Nasdaq exchange, this index is generally regarded as an economic indicator of the high-tech industry. Microsoft, Intel, and Cisco Systems are the three largest Nasdaq companies, and they comprise a high percentage of the index's value-weighted market capitalization. For this reason, substantial movements in the same direction by these three companies can move the entire index.

Trading the Market

Through the use of exchange traded funds (ETFs), it is now possible to buy and sell the market in much the same way as an individual stock. For example, the Standard & Poor's depository receipt (SPDR) is a share of a fund comprised of the stocks in the S&P 500. SPDRs trade during regular market hours, making it possible to buy or sell the S&P 500 any time during the day. There are hundreds of other ETFs, including ones for the Nasdaq and Dow Jones Industrial Average.

Recent Performance

Go to the Web site **http://finance.yahoo.com/**. Enter the symbol for any of the indices (^DJI for the Dow Jones, ^SPC for the S&P 500, and ^IXIC for the Nasdaq) and click GO. This will bring up the current value of the index, shown in a table. Click Basic Chart in the panel on the left, and it will bring up a chart showing the historical performance of the index. Immediately above the chart is a series of buttons that allows you to choose the number of years and to plot the relative performance of several indices on the same chart. You can even download the historical data in spreadsheet form by clicking Historical Prices in the left panel.

Exchange Commission (SEC) but that is not listed on any exchange, usually because the company is too small or too unprofitable.[5] Finally, Nasdaq operates the Pink Sheets, which provide quotes on companies that are not registered with the SEC.

---

[5] OTC stands for over-the-counter. Before Nasdaq, the quickest way to trade a stock that was not listed at a physical location exchange was to find a brokerage firm that kept shares of that stock in inventory. The stock certificates were actually kept in a safe and were literally passed over the counter when bought or sold. Nowadays the certificates for almost all listed stocks and bonds in the United States are stored in a vault beneath Manhattan, operated by the Depository Trust and Clearing Corporation (DTCC). Most brokerage firms have an account with the DTCC, and most investors leave their stocks with their brokers. Thus, when stocks are sold, the DTCC simply adjusts the accounts of the brokerage firms that are involved, and no stock certificates are actually moved.

"Liquidity" is the ability to trade quickly at a net price (that is, after any commissions) that is very close to the security's recent market value. In a dealer market, such as Nasdaq, a stock's liquidity depends on the number and quality of the dealers who make a market in the stock. Nasdaq has more than 400 dealers, most making markets in a large number of stocks. The typical stock has about 10 market makers, but some stocks have more than 50 market makers. Obviously, there are more market makers, and liquidity, for the Nasdaq National Market than for the SmallCap Market. There is very little liquidity for stocks on the OTC Bulletin Board or the Pink Sheets.

Over the past decade the competition between the NYSE and Nasdaq has been fierce. In an effort to become more competitive with the NYSE and with international markets, the NASD and the AMEX merged in 1998 to form what might best be referred to as an *organized investment network*. This investment network is often referred to as Nasdaq, but stocks continue to be traded and reported separately on the two markets. Increased competition among global stock markets assuredly will result in similar alliances among other exchanges and markets in the future.

Since most of the largest companies trade on the NYSE, the market capitalization of NYSE-traded stocks is much higher than for stocks traded on Nasdaq (about $11.6 trillion compared with $2.9 trillion in early 2004). However, reported volume (number of shares traded) is often larger on Nasdaq, and more companies are listed on Nasdaq.[6] For comparison, the market capitalizations for global exchanges are $3.0 trillion in Tokyo, $2.5 trillion in London, and $1.1 trillion in Germany.

Interestingly, many high-tech companies such as Microsoft and Intel have remained on Nasdaq even though they easily meet the listing requirements of the NYSE. At the same time, however, other high-tech companies such as Gateway 2000, America Online, and Iomega have left Nasdaq for the NYSE. Despite these defections, Nasdaq's growth over the past decade has been impressive. In the years ahead, the competition will no doubt remain fierce.

| SELF-TEST QUESTION | What are some major differences between the NYSE and the Nasdaq stock market? |

THE COST OF MONEY AND INTEREST RATE LEVELS

In a free economy, capital from providers with available funds is allocated through the price system to users that have a demand for funds. The interaction of the providers' supply and the users' demand determines the cost (or price) of money, which is the rate users pay to providers. For debt, we call this price the **interest rate.** For equity, we call this price the **cost of equity,** and it consists of the dividends and capital gains stockholders expect.

Factors That Affect the Cost of Money

The four most fundamental factors affecting the cost of money are (1) **production opportunities,** (2) **time preferences for consumption,** (3) **risk,** and (4) **inflation.** By production opportunities, we mean the ability to turn capital into benefits. If a business raises capital, the benefits are determined by the expected rates of return on its production opportunities. If a student borrows to finance education, the benefits are higher expected future salaries (and, of course, the sheer joy of learning!). If a homeowner borrows, the benefits are the pleasure from living in his or her own home, plus any expected appreciation in the value of the home. Notice that the expected rates of return on these "production opportunities" put an upper limit on how much users can pay to providers.

---

[6] One transaction on Nasdaq generally shows up as two separate trades (the buy and the sell). This "double counting" makes it difficult to compare the volume between stock markets.

Providers can use their current funds for consumption or saving. By saving, they give up consumption now in the expectation of having more consumption in the future. If providers have a strong preference for consumption now, then it takes high interest rates to induce them to trade current consumption for future consumption. Therefore, the time preference for consumption has a major impact on the cost of money. Notice that the time preference for consumption varies for different individuals, for different age groups, and for different cultures. For example, people in Japan have a lower time preference for consumption than those in the United States, which partially explains why Japanese families tend to save more than U.S. families, even though interest rates are lower in Japan.

If the expected rate of return on an investment is risky, then providers require a higher expected return to induce them to take the extra risk, which drives up the cost of money. Inflation also leads to higher interest rates. For example, suppose you earned 10 percent one year on your investment, but inflation caused prices to increase by 20 percent. This means you can't consume as much at the end of the year as when you originally invested your money. Obviously, if you had expected 20 percent inflation, you would have required a higher rate of return than 10 percent.

Interest Rate Levels

Figure 1-3 shows how long- and short-term interest rates to business borrowers have varied during the past 32 years. Notice that short-term interest rates tend to rise during booms and then fall during recessions. (The shaded areas of the chart indicate recessions.) When the economy is expanding, firms need capital, and this demand for capital pushes

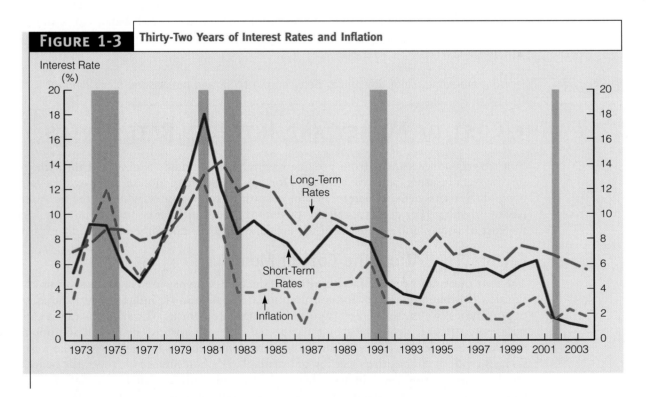

FIGURE 1-3 Thirty-Two Years of Interest Rates and Inflation

Notes:

[a]The shaded areas designate business recession as defined by the National Bureau of Economic Research; see **http://www.nber.org/cycles**. Tick marks represent January 2 of the year.

[b]Short-term rates are for three-month nonfinancial commercial paper (the borrowing rate for very large, strong corporations), long-term rates are for AAA corporate bonds; see **http://www.federalreserve.gov/releases**.

[c]Inflation is measured by the annual rate of change for the Consumer Price Index (CPI); see **http://research.stlouisfed.org/fred/**.

rates up. Conditions are reversed during recessions such as the one beginning in 2001. Slack business reduces the demand for credit, and the result is a drop in interest rates. Furthermore, the Federal Reserve deliberately lowers rates during recessions to help stimulate the economy, and it tightens during booms.

Interest rates reflect investors' expectations for *future* inflation, while the actual inflation rate measures *past* inflation. Therefore, interest rates usually fall before reported inflation falls and rise before reported inflation rises, although there occasionally are exceptions. For example, inflation began to fall in 1980, but interest rates continued to rise because investors feared the decline in inflation would be temporary.

In the years ahead, we can be sure that the level of interest rates will vary with (1) economic activity, (2) changes in the current rate of inflation, and (3) changes in expectations about future inflation.

SELF-TEST QUESTIONS

What four fundamental factors affect the cost of money?

Why does the price of capital change during booms and recessions?

How does inflation affect interest rates?

THE DETERMINANTS OF MARKET INTEREST RATES

In general, the quoted (or nominal) interest rate on a debt security, r, is composed of a real risk-free rate of interest, r*, plus several premiums that reflect inflation, the riskiness of the security, and the security's marketability (or liquidity).[7] This relationship can be expressed as follows:

$$\text{Quoted interest rate} = r = r^* + IP + DRP + LP + MRP. \qquad \text{(1-1)}$$

Here

e-resource

*The textbook's Web site contains an Excel file that will guide you through the chapter's calculations. The file for this chapter is **CF2 Ch 01 Tool Kit.xls,** and we encourage you to open the file and follow along as you read the chapter.*

r = the quoted, or nominal, rate of interest on a given security.[8] There are many different securities, hence many different quoted interest rates.

r^* = the real risk-free rate of interest. r^* is pronounced "r-star," and it is the rate that would exist on a riskless security if zero inflation were expected.

IP = inflation premium. IP is equal to the average expected inflation rate over the life of the security. The expected future inflation rate is not necessarily equal to the current inflation rate, so IP is not necessarily equal to current inflation as reported in Figure 1-3.

r_{RF} = $r^* + IP$, and it is the quoted risk-free rate of interest on a security such as a U.S. Treasury bill, which is very liquid and also free of most risks. Note that r_{RF} includes the premium for expected inflation, because $r_{RF} = r^* + IP$.

DRP = default risk premium. This premium reflects the possibility that the issuer will not pay interest or principal at the stated time and in the stated amount. DRP is zero for U.S. Treasury securities, but it rises as the riskiness of issuers increases.

[7] Sometimes "i" or "I" is used to denote interest rates because financial calculators, covered in Chapter 2, use these terms. Also, "k" has been used in the past, but "r" is the most commonly used term today.

[8] The term *nominal* as it is used here means the *stated* rate as opposed to the *real* rate, which is adjusted to remove inflation effects. Suppose you bought a 10-year Treasury bond with a quoted, or nominal, rate of about 4.6 percent. If inflation averages 2.5 percent over the next 10 years, the real rate would be about 4.6% − 2.5% = 2.1%. To be technically correct, we should find the real rate by solving for r* in the following equation: $(1 + r^*)(1 + 0.025) = (1 + 0.046)$. If we solved the equation, we would find r* = 2.05%. Since this is very close to the 2.1 percent calculated above, we will continue to approximate the real rate by subtracting inflation from the nominal rate.

> LP = liquidity, or marketability, premium. This is a premium charged by lenders to reflect the fact that some securities cannot be converted to cash on short notice at a "reasonable" price. LP is very low for Treasury securities and for securities issued by large, strong firms, but it is relatively high on securities issued by very small firms.
>
> MRP = maturity risk premium. As we will explain later, longer-term bonds, even Treasury bonds, are exposed to a significant risk of price declines, and a maturity risk premium is charged by lenders to reflect this risk.

As noted above, since $r_{RF} = r^* + IP$, we can rewrite Equation 1-1 as follows:

$$\text{Nominal, or quoted, rate} = r = r_{RF} + DRP + LP + MRP.$$

We discuss the components whose sum makes up the quoted, or nominal, rate on a given security in the following sections.

The Real Risk-Free Rate of Interest, r*

See *http://www .bloomberg.com* and select *MARKETS* and then *U.S. Treasuries* for a partial listing of indexed Treasury bonds and their interest rates. See *http://www .publicdebt.treas .gov* for a complete listing of all indexed treasuries.

The **real risk-free rate of interest, r***, is defined as the interest rate that would exist on a risk-less security if no inflation were expected, and it may be thought of as the rate of interest on *short-term* U.S. Treasury securities in an inflation-free world. The real risk-free rate is not static—it changes over time depending on economic conditions, especially (1) on the rate of return corporations and other borrowers expect to earn on productive assets and (2) on people's time preferences for current versus future consumption.[9]

In addition to its regular bond offerings, in 1997 the U.S. Treasury began issuing **indexed bonds,** with payments linked to inflation. To date, the Treasury has issued ten of these indexed bonds, with maturities ranging (at time of issue) from 5 to 31 years. In March 2004, the indexed bond with a five-year maturity had a 0.45 percent yield. This is a pretty good estimate of the real risk-free rate, r^*, although ideally we would prefer an even shorter-term indexed bond.

Inflation Premium (IP)

Inflation has a major effect on interest rates because it erodes the purchasing power of the dollar and lowers the real rate of return on investments. To illustrate, suppose you saved $1,000 and invested it in a Treasury bill that matures in one year and pays a 5 percent interest rate. At the end of the year, you will receive $1,050—your original $1,000 plus $50 of interest. Now suppose the inflation rate during the year is 10 percent, and it affects all items equally. If gas had cost $1 per gallon at the beginning of the year, it would cost $1.10 at the end of the year. Therefore, your $1,000 would have bought $1,000/$1 = 1,000 gallons at the beginning of the year, but only $1,050/$1.10 = 955 gallons at the end. In *real terms*, you would be worse off—you would receive $50 of interest, but it would not be sufficient to offset inflation. You would thus be better off buying 1,000 gallons of gas (or some other storable asset such as land, timber, apartment buildings, wheat, or gold) than buying the Treasury bill.

Investors are well aware of all this, so when they lend money, they build in an **inflation premium (IP)** equal to the average expected inflation rate over the life of the security.

---

[9] The real rate of interest as discussed here is different from the *current* real rate as often discussed in the press. The current real rate is the current interest rate minus the current (or latest past) inflation rate, while the real rate, as used here (and in the fields of finance and economics generally) without the word "current," is the current interest rate minus the *expected future* inflation rate over the life of the security. For example, suppose the current quoted rate for a one-year Treasury bill is 5 percent, inflation during the latest year was 2 percent, and inflation expected for the coming year is 4 percent. Then the *current* real rate would be 5% − 2% = 3%, but the *expected* real rate would be 5% − 4% = 1%.

For a short-term, default-free U.S. Treasury bill, the actual interest rate charged, $r_{\text{T-bill}}$, would be the real risk-free rate, r^*, plus the inflation premium (IP):

$$r_{\text{T-bill}} = r_{RF} = r^* + IP.$$

Therefore, if the real short-term risk-free rate of interest were $r^* = 0.6\%$, and if inflation were expected to be 1.0 percent (and hence $IP = 1.0\%$) during the next year, then the quoted rate of interest on one-year T-bills would be $0.6\% + 1.0\% = 1.6\%$.

It is important to note that the inflation rate built into interest rates is *the inflation rate expected in the future*, not the rate experienced in the past. Thus, the latest reported figures might show an annual inflation rate of 2 percent, but that is for the *past* year. If people on average expect a 6 percent inflation rate in the future, then 6 percent would be built into the current interest rate. Note also that the inflation rate reflected in the quoted interest rate on any security is the *average rate of inflation expected over the security's life*. Thus, the inflation rate built into a one-year bond is the expected inflation rate for the next year, but the inflation rate built into a 30-year bond is the average rate of inflation expected over the next 30 years. For example, in March 2004, the rate on a five-year nonindexed T-bond was 2.79 percent and the rate on a five-year indexed T-bond was 0.45. Thus, the five-year inflation premium was $2.79\% - 0.45\% = 2.34\%$, implying that investors expected inflation to average 2.34 percent over the next five years.[10] Similarly, the rate on a 27-year nonindexed T-bond was 4.77 percent and the rate on a 28-year indexed T-bond was 1.87. Thus, the long-term inflation premium was approximately $4.77\% - 1.87\% = 2.90\%$, implying that investors expected inflation to average 2.9 percent over the next three decades.[11]

Expectations for future inflation are closely, but not perfectly, correlated with rates experienced in the recent past. Therefore, if the inflation rate reported for last month increased, people would tend to raise their expectations for future inflation, and this change in expectations would cause an increase in interest rates.

Note that Germany, Japan, and Switzerland have, over the past several years, had lower inflation rates than the United States, hence their interest rates have generally been lower than ours. South Africa and most South American countries have experienced high inflation, and that is reflected in their interest rates.

The Nominal, or Quoted, Risk-Free Rate of Interest, r_{RF}

The **nominal**, or **quoted, risk-free rate**, r_{RF}, is the real risk-free rate plus a premium for expected inflation: $r_{RF} = r^* + IP$. To be strictly correct, the risk-free rate should mean the interest rate on a totally risk-free security—one that has no risk of default, no maturity risk, no liquidity risk, no risk of loss if inflation increases, and no risk of any other type. There is no such security, hence there is no observable truly risk-free rate. If the term "risk-free rate" is used without either the modifier "real" or the modifier "nominal," people generally mean the quoted (nominal) rate, and we will follow that convention in this book. Therefore, when we use the term "risk-free rate, r_{RF}," we mean the nominal risk-free rate, which includes an inflation premium equal to the average expected inflation rate over the life of the security. In general, we use the T-bill rate to approximate the short-term

---

[10] To be theoretically precise, we should use a *geometric average* by solving the following equation: $(1 + IP)(1.0045) = 1.0279$. Solving for IP gives $IP = 2.33\%$, which is very close to our approximation.

[11] There are several sources for the estimated inflation premium. The Congressional Budget Office regularly updates the estimates of inflation that it uses in its forecasted budgets; see **http://www.cbo.gov/**, select Current Economic Projections. A second source is the University of Michigan's Institute for Social Research, which regularly polls consumers regarding their expectations for price increases during the next year; see **http://www.isr.umich.edu/src/projects.html**, select the Surveys of Consumers, and then select the table for Expected Change in Prices. We prefer using inflation premiums derived from indexed and nonindexed Treasury securities, as described in the text, since these are based on how investors actually spend their money, not on theoretical models or opinions.

risk-free rate, and the T-bond rate to approximate the long-term risk-free rate (even though it also includes a maturity premium). So, whenever you see the term "risk-free rate," assume that we are referring either to the quoted U.S. T-bill rate or to the quoted T-bond rate.

Default Risk Premium (DRP)

The risk that a borrower will *default* on a loan, which means not pay the interest or the principal, also affects the market interest rate on the security: the greater the default risk, the higher the interest rate. Treasury securities have no default risk, hence they carry the lowest interest rates on taxable securities in the United States. For corporate bonds, the higher the bond's rating, the lower its default risk, and, consequently, the lower its interest rate.[12] Here are some representative interest rates on long-term bonds during March 2004:

To see current estimates of DRP, go to http://www .bondsonline.com; under the section on Corporate Bonds, select Industrial Spreads.

Long-Term Bonds	Rate		DRP	
	2001	2004	2001	2004
U.S. Treasury	5.5%	4.8%	—	—
AAA	6.5	5.3	1.0	0.5
AA	6.8	5.5	1.3	0.7
A	7.3	5.7	1.8	0.9
BBB	7.9	6.5	2.4	1.7
BB+	10.5	7.8	5.0	3.0

The difference between the quoted interest rate on a T-bond and that on a corporate bond with similar maturity, liquidity, and other features is the **default risk premium (DRP)**, sometimes called the **bond spread.** Therefore, if the bonds listed above were otherwise similar, the default risk premium in 2004 would be DRP = 5.3% − 4.8% = 0.5 percentage point for AAA corporate bonds, 5.5% − 4.8% = 0.7 percentage point for AA, and so forth. Default risk premiums vary somewhat over time, but the figures above are representative of levels in recent years.

Liquidity Premium (LP)

A "liquid" asset can be converted to cash quickly and at a "fair market value." Financial assets are generally more liquid than real assets. Because liquidity is important, investors include **liquidity premiums (LPs)** when market rates of securities are established. Although it is difficult to accurately measure liquidity premiums, a differential of at least two and probably four or five percentage points exists between the least liquid and the most liquid financial assets of similar default risk and maturity.

Maturity Risk Premium (MRP)

U.S. Treasury securities are free of default risk in the sense that one can be virtually certain that the federal government will meet the scheduled interest and principal payments on its bonds. Therefore, the default risk premium on Treasury securities is essentially zero. Further, active markets exist for Treasury securities, so their liquidity premiums are also close to zero. Thus, as a first approximation, the rate of interest on a Treasury bond should be the risk-free rate, r_{RF}, which is equal to the real risk-free rate, r^*, plus an inflation premium, IP. However, an adjustment is needed for long-term Treasury bonds. The prices of long-term bonds decline sharply whenever interest rates rise, and since interest rates can and do occasionally rise, all long-term bonds, even Treasury bonds, have an ele-

---

[12] Bond ratings, and bonds' riskiness in general, are discussed in detail in Chapter 6. For now, merely note that bonds rated AAA are judged to have less default risk than bonds rated AA, while AA bonds are less risky than A bonds, and so on. Ratings are designated AAA or Aaa, AA or Aa, and so forth, depending on the rating agency. In this book, the designations are used interchangeably.

ment of risk called **interest rate risk.** As a general rule, the bonds of any organization have more interest rate risk the longer the maturity of the bond.[13] Therefore, a **maturity risk premium (MRP),** which is higher the longer the years to maturity, must be included in the required interest rate.

The effect of maturity risk premiums is to raise interest rates on long-term bonds relative to those on short-term bonds. This premium, like the others, is difficult to measure, but (1) it varies somewhat over time, rising when interest rates are more volatile and uncertain, then falling when interest rates are more stable, and (2) in recent years, the maturity risk premium on 30-year T-bonds appears to have generally been in the range of one to three percentage points.

We should mention that although long-term bonds are heavily exposed to interest rate risk, short-term bills are heavily exposed to **reinvestment rate risk.** When short-term bills mature and the funds are reinvested, or "rolled over," a decline in interest rates would necessitate reinvestment at a lower rate, and this would result in a decline in interest income. To illustrate, suppose you had $100,000 invested in one-year T-bills, and you lived on the income. In 1981, short-term rates were about 15 percent, so your income would have been about $15,000. However, your income would have declined to about $9,000 by 1983, and to just $5,700 by 2001. Had you invested your money in long-term T-bonds, your income (but not the value of the principal) would have been stable.[14] Thus, although "investing short" preserves one's principal, the interest income provided by short-term T-bills is less stable than the interest income on long-term bonds.

Write out an equation for the nominal interest rate on any debt security.

Distinguish between the *real* risk-free rate of interest, r*, and the *nominal,* or *quoted,* risk-free rate of interest, r_{RF}.

How is inflation incorporated into interest rates?

Does the interest rate on a T-bond include a default risk premium? Explain.

Identify some assets that are liquid and some that are illiquid.

Briefly explain the following statement: "Long-term bonds are heavily exposed to interest rate risk."

THE TERM STRUCTURE OF INTEREST RATES

You can find current U.S. Treasury yield curve graphs and other global and domestic interest rate information at Bloomberg markets' site at http://www .bloomberg.com/ markets/rates/index .html.

The **term structure of interest rates** describes the relationship between long- and short-term rates. The term structure is important to corporate treasurers who must decide whether to borrow by issuing long- or short-term debt and to investors who must decide whether to buy long- or short-term bonds. Thus, it is important to understand (1) how long- and short-term rates relate to each other and (2) what causes shifts in their relative positions.

Interest rates for bonds with different maturities can be found in a variety of publications, including *The Wall Street Journal* and the *Federal Reserve Bulletin,* and on a number of Web sites, including Bloomberg, Yahoo, and CNN Financial. From interest rate

---

[13] For example, if someone had bought a 30-year Treasury bond for $1,000 in 1998, when the long-term interest rate was 5.25 percent, and held it until 2000, when long-term T-bond rates were about 6.6 percent, the value of the bond would have declined to about $830. That would represent a loss of 17 percent, and it demonstrates that long-term bonds, even U.S. Treasury bonds, are not riskless. Even indexed Treasuries aren't riskless. An increase in real interest rates between October 1998 and January 2000 caused the price of indexed bonds to fall from $980 to $890, a decline of almost 10 percent.

[14] Long-term bonds also have some reinvestment rate risk. If one is saving and investing for some future purpose, say, to buy a house or for retirement, then to actually earn the quoted rate on a long-term bond, the interest payments must be reinvested at the quoted rate. However, if interest rates fall, the interest payments must be reinvested at a lower rate; thus, the realized return would be less than the quoted rate. Note, though, that reinvestment rate risk is lower on a long-term bond than on a short-term bond because only the interest payments (rather than interest plus principal) on the long-term bond are exposed to reinvestment rate risk. Zero coupon bonds, which are discussed in Chapter 6, are completely free of reinvestment rate risk during their life.

data obtained from these sources, we can construct the term structure at a given point in time. For example, the tabular section below Figure 1-4 presents interest rates for different maturities on three different dates. The set of data for a given date, when plotted on a graph such as that in Figure 1-4, is called the **yield curve** for that date.

The yield curve changes both in position and in slope over time. In March 1980, all rates were relatively high, and since short-term rates were higher than long-term rates, the yield curve was *downward sloping*. In March 2004, all rates had fallen, and because short-term rates were lower than long-term rates, the yield curve was *upward sloping*. In February 2000, the yield curve was *humped*—medium-term rates were higher than both short- and long-term rates.

Figure 1-4 shows yield curves for U.S. Treasury securities, but we could have constructed curves for corporate bonds issued by ExxonMobil, IBM, Delta Air Lines, or any

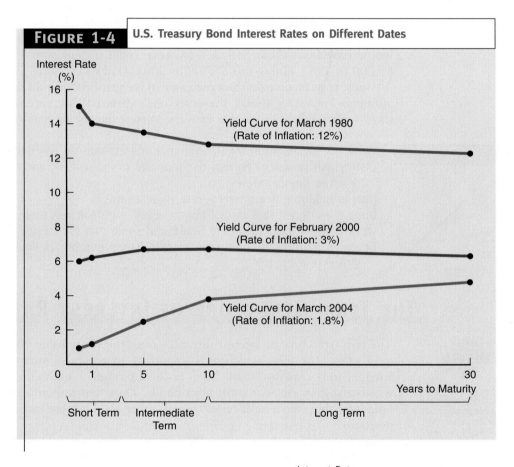

FIGURE 1-4 **U.S. Treasury Bond Interest Rates on Different Dates**

Term to Maturity	Interest Rate		
	March 1980	February 2000	March 2004
6 months	15.0%	6.0%	1.0%
1 year	14.0	6.2	1.2
5 years	13.5	6.7	2.7
10 years	12.8	6.7	3.8
30 years[a]	12.3	6.3	4.8

Notes:

[a]The Treasury last issued a 30-year bond in 2001, so the March 2004 observation actually has 27 years until it matures.

other company that borrows money over a range of maturities. Had we constructed corporate curves and plotted them on Figure 1-4, they would have been above those for Treasury securities because corporate yields include default risk premiums. However, the corporate yield curves would have had the same general shape as the Treasury curves. Also, the riskier the corporation, the higher its yield curve, so Delta Air Lines, which has a lower bond rating than either ExxonMobil or IBM, would have a higher yield curve than those of ExxonMobil and IBM.

Historically, in most years long-term rates have been above short-term rates, so the yield curve usually slopes upward. For this reason, people often call an upward-sloping yield curve a **"normal" yield curve** and a yield curve that slopes downward an **inverted,** or **"abnormal," curve.** Thus, in Figure 1-4 the yield curve for March 1980 was inverted and the one for March 2004 was normal. However, the February 2000 curve is **humped,** which means that interest rates on medium-term maturities are higher than rates on both short- and long-term maturities. We explain in detail in the next section why an upward slope is the normal situation, but briefly, the reason is that short-term securities have less interest rate risk than longer-term securities, hence smaller MRPs. Therefore, short-term rates are normally lower than long-term rates.

SELF-TEST QUESTIONS	What is a yield curve, and what information would you need to draw this curve? Explain the shapes of a "normal" yield curve, an "abnormal" curve, and a "humped" curve.

WHAT DETERMINES THE SHAPE OF THE YIELD CURVE?

Since maturity risk premiums are positive, then if other things were held constant, long-term bonds would have higher interest rates than short-term bonds. However, market interest rates also depend on expected inflation, default risk, and liquidity, and each of these factors can vary with maturity.

Expected inflation has an especially important effect on the yield curve's shape. To see why, consider U.S. Treasury securities. Because Treasuries have essentially no default or liquidity risk, the yield on a Treasury bond that matures in t years can be found using the following equation:

$$r_t = r^* + IP_t + MRP_t.$$

While the real risk-free rate, r^*, may vary somewhat over time because of changes in the economy and demographics, these changes are random rather than predictable, so it is reasonable to assume that r^* will remain constant. However, the inflation premium, IP, does vary significantly over time, and in a somewhat predictable manner. Recall that the inflation premium is simply the average level of expected inflation over the life of the bond. For example, during a recession inflation is usually abnormally low. Investors will expect higher future inflation, leading to higher inflation premiums for long-term bonds. On the other hand, if the market expects inflation to decline in the future, long-term bonds will have a smaller inflation premium than short-term bonds. Finally, if investors consider long-term bonds to be riskier than short-term bonds, the maturity risk premium will increase with maturity.

Panel a of Figure 1-5 shows the yield curve when inflation is expected to increase. Here long-term bonds have higher yields for two reasons: (1) Inflation is expected to be higher in the future, and (2) there is a positive maturity risk premium. Panel b of Figure 1-5 shows the yield curve when inflation is expected to decline, causing the yield curve to be downward sloping. Downward sloping yield curves often foreshadow economic downturns, because weaker economic conditions tend to be correlated with declining inflation, which in turn leads to lower long-term rates.

Now let's consider the yield curve for corporate bonds. Recall that corporate bonds include a default-risk premium (DRP) and a liquidity premium (LP). Therefore, the yield on a corporate bond that matures in t years can be expressed as follows:

$$r_{Ct} = r^* + IP_t + MRP_t + DRP_t + LP_t.$$

A corporate bond's default and liquidity risks are affected by its maturity. For example, the default risk on Coca-Cola's short-term debt is very small, since there is almost no chance that Coca-Cola will go bankrupt over the next few years. However, Coke has some 100-year bonds, and while the odds of Coke defaulting on these bonds still might not be high, the default risk on these bonds is considerably higher than that on its short-term debt.

Longer-term corporate bonds are also less liquid than shorter-term debt, hence the liquidity premium rises as maturity lengthens. The primary reason for this is that, for the reasons discussed earlier, short-term debt has less default and interest rate risk, so a buyer can buy short-term debt without having to do as much credit checking as would be nec-

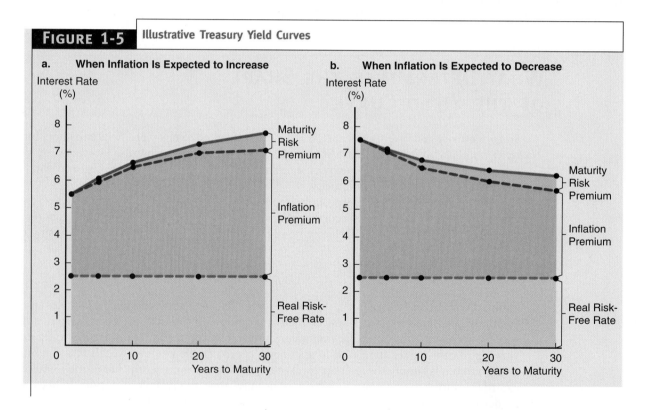

FIGURE 1-5 Illustrative Treasury Yield Curves

	With Increasing Expected Inflation					With Decreasing Expected Inflation			
Maturity	r*	IP	MRP	Yield	Maturity	r*	IP	MRP	Yield
1 year	2.50%	3.00%	0.00%	5.50%	1 year	2.50%	5.00%	0.00%	7.50%
5 years	2.50	3.40	0.18	6.08	5 years	2.50	4.60	0.18	7.28
10 years	2.50	4.00	0.28	6.78	10 years	2.50	4.00	0.28	6.78
20 years	2.50	4.50	0.42	7.42	20 years	2.50	3.50	0.42	6.42
30 years	2.50	4.67	0.53	7.70	30 years	2.50	3.33	0.53	6.36

essary for long-term debt. Thus, people can move into and out of short-term corporate debt much more rapidly than long-term debt. The end result is that short-term corporate debt is more liquid, hence has a smaller liquidity premium than the same company's long-term debt.

Figure 1-6 shows yield curves for an AA-rated corporate bond with minimal default risk and a BBB-rated bond with more default risk, along with the yield curve for Treasury securities as taken from Panel a of Figure 1-5. Here we assume that inflation is expected to increase, so the Treasury yield curve is upward sloping. Because of their additional default and liquidity risk, corporate bonds always trade at a higher yield than Treasury bonds with the same maturity, and BBB-rated bonds trade at higher yields than AA-rated bonds. Finally, note that the yield spread between corporate bonds and Treasury bonds is larger the longer the maturity. This occurs because longer-term corporate bonds have more default and liquidity risk than shorter-term bonds, and both of these premiums are absent in Treasury bonds.

A few academics and practitioners contend that large bond traders who buy and sell securities of different maturities each day dominate the market. According to this view, a bond trader is just as willing to buy a 30-year bond to pick up a short-term profit as to buy a three-month security. Strict proponents of this view argue that the shape of the yield

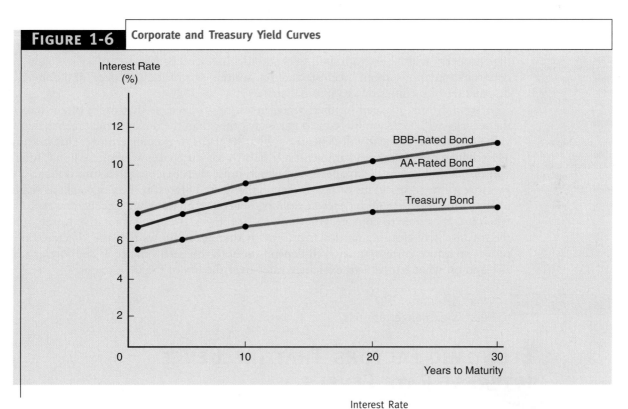

FIGURE 1-6 Corporate and Treasury Yield Curves

Term to Maturity	Interest Rate					
	Treasury Bond	AA-Rated Bond	AA Spread over T-Bond	BBB-Rated Bond	BBB Spread over T-Bond	BBB Spread over AA
1 year	5.5%	6.7%	1.2%	7.4%	1.9%	0.7%
5 years	6.1	7.4	1.3	8.1	2.0	0.7
10 years	6.8	8.2	1.4	9.1	2.3	0.9
20 years	7.4	9.2	1.8	10.2	2.8	1.0
30 years	7.7	9.8	2.1	11.1	3.4	1.3

CF

e-resource

See the Chapter 1 Web Extension.

curve is therefore determined only by market expectations about future interest rates, a position that is called the **pure expectations theory,** or sometimes just the **expectations theory.** If this were true, then the maturity risk premium (MRP) would be zero, and long-term interest rates would simply be a weighted average of current and expected future short-term interest rates. See the Web Extension to this chapter for a more detailed discussion of the expectations theory.

How do maturity risk premiums affect the yield curve?

If the rate of inflation is expected to increase, would this increase or decrease the slope of the yield curve?

Explain why corporate bonds' default and liquidity premiums are likely to increase with maturity.

INTERNATIONAL RISK FACTORS

Euromoney magazine publishes rankings, based on country risk. Students can access the home page of Euromoney magazine by typing ***http://www.euromoney .com.*** *Although the site requires users to register, the site is free to use (although some data sets and articles are available only to subscribers). Yahoo also provides country risk evaluations at* ***http://biz .yahoo.com/ifc/.***

Investors should consider additional risk factors before investing overseas. First there is **country risk,** which refers to the risk that arises from investing or doing business in a particular country. This risk depends on the country's economic, political, and social environment. Countries with stable economic, social, political, and regulatory systems provide a safer climate for investment, and therefore have less country risk than less stable nations. Examples of country risk include the risk associated with changes in tax rates, regulations, currency conversion, and exchange rates. Country risk also includes the risk that property will be expropriated without adequate compensation, as well as new host country stipulations about local production, sourcing or hiring practices, and damage or destruction of facilities due to internal strife.

A second thing to keep in mind when investing overseas is that more often than not the security will be denominated in a currency other than the dollar, which means that the value of your investment will depend on what happens to exchange rates. This is known as **exchange rate risk.** For example, if a U.S. investor purchases a Japanese bond, interest will probably be paid in Japanese yen, which must then be converted into dollars if the investor wants to spend his or her money in the United States. If the yen weakens relative to the dollar, then it will buy fewer dollars, hence the investor will receive fewer dollars when it comes time to convert. Alternatively, if the yen strengthens relative to the dollar, the investor will earn higher dollar returns. It therefore follows that the effective rate of return on a foreign investment will depend on both the performance of the foreign security and on what happens to exchange rates over the life of the investment.

What is country risk?

What is exchange rate risk?

ECONOMIC FACTORS THAT INFLUENCE INTEREST RATE LEVELS

Economic factors also influence both the general level of interest rates and the shape of the yield curve. The four most important factors are (1) Federal Reserve policy; (2) the federal budget deficit or surplus; (3) international factors, including the foreign trade balance and interest rates in other countries; and (4) the level of business activity.

Federal Reserve Policy

As you probably learned in your economics courses, (1) the money supply has a major effect on both the level of economic activity and the inflation rate, and (2) in the United

The home page for the Board of Governors of the Federal Reserve System can be found at http:// www.federalreserve .gov. You can access general information about the Federal Reserve, including press releases, speeches, and monetary policy.

States, the Federal Reserve Board controls the money supply. If the Fed wants to stimulate the economy, it increases growth in the money supply. The initial effect would be to cause interest rates to decline. However, a larger money supply may also lead to an increase in expected inflation, which would push interest rates up. The reverse holds if the Fed tightens the money supply. During periods when the Fed is actively intervening in the markets, the yield curve may be temporarily distorted. Short-term rates will be temporarily "too low" if the Fed is easing credit, and "too high" if it is tightening credit. Long-term rates are not affected as much by Fed intervention.

Budget Deficits or Surpluses

If the federal government spends more than it takes in from tax revenues, it runs a deficit, and that deficit must be covered either by borrowing or by printing money (increasing the money supply). If the government borrows, this added demand for funds pushes up interest rates. If it prints money, this increases expectations for future inflation, which also drives up interest rates. Thus, the larger the federal deficit, other things held constant, the higher the level of interest rates. Whether long- or short-term rates are more affected depends on how the deficit is financed, so we cannot state, in general, how deficits will affect the slope of the yield curve.

International Trade Deficits or Surpluses

Businesses and individuals in the United States buy from and sell to people and firms in other countries. If we buy more than we sell (that is, if we import more than we export), we are said to be running a *foreign trade deficit*. When trade deficits occur, they must be financed, and the main source of financing is debt. In other words, if we import $200 billion of goods but export only $100 billion, we run a trade deficit of $100 billion, and we would probably borrow the $100 billion.[15] Therefore, the larger our trade deficit, the more we must borrow, and as we increase our borrowing, this drives up interest rates. Also, foreigners are willing to hold U.S. debt if and only if the rate paid on this debt is competitive with interest rates in other countries. Therefore, if the Federal Reserve attempts to lower interest rates in the United States, causing our rates to fall below rates abroad, then foreigners will sell U.S. bonds, those sales will depress bond prices, and that in turn will result in higher U.S. rates. Thus, if the trade deficit is large relative to the size of the overall economy, it will hinder the Fed's ability to combat a recession by lowering interest rates.

The United States has been running annual trade deficits since the mid-1970s, and the cumulative effect of these deficits is that the United States has become the largest debtor nation of all time. As a result, our interest rates are very much influenced by interest rates in other countries around the world—higher rates abroad lead to higher U.S. rates, and vice versa. Because of all this, U.S. corporate treasurers—and anyone else who is affected by interest rates—must keep up with developments in the world economy.

Business Activity

Figure 1-3, presented earlier, shows how business conditions influence interest rates. The shaded areas in the graph represent recessions. Consumer demand slows during a recession, keeping companies from increasing prices, which reduces price inflation. Companies also cut back on hiring, which reduces wage inflation. Less disposable income causes consumers to reduce their purchases of homes and automobiles, reducing consumer demand for loans. Companies reduce investments in new operations, which reduces their demand

---

[15] The deficit could also be financed by selling assets, including gold, corporate stocks, entire companies, and real estate. The United States has financed its massive trade deficits by all of these means in recent years, but the primary method has been by borrowing from foreigners.

for funds. The cumulative effect is downward pressure on inflation and interest rates. The Federal Reserve is also active during recessions, trying to stimulate the economy. One way it does this is by purchasing Treasury bonds that are held by banks. This has two effects. Because they sell some of their bonds, the banks have more cash, which increases their supply of loanable funds, which in turn makes them willing to lend at lower interest rates. Also, the Fed's bond purchases drive up bond prices, which drive down bond interest rates. The combined effect of the Fed's activities is to reduce interest rates.

There are two reasons that short-term rates tend to decline more sharply than long-term rates during recessions. First, the Fed operates mainly in the short-term sector, so its intervention has the strongest effect there. Second, long-term rates reflect the average expected inflation rate over the next 20 to 30 years, and this expectation generally does not change drastically, even when the current inflation rate is low because of a recession or high because of a boom. So, short-term rates are more volatile than long-term rates.

SELF-TEST QUESTIONS

Name some economic factors that influence interest rates, and explain their effects. How does the Fed stimulate the economy? How does the Fed affect interest rates?

A PREVIEW OF WHAT IS AHEAD

A manager's primary job is to increase the value of his or her company. Figure 1-1 shows the determinants of a firm's value, and it also provides a good preview for the rest of the book. Chapter 2 shows how to determine the value today of a future cash flow, a topic called the time value of money. Chapter 3 explains financial statements and how to calculate free cash flows, along with taxation and its role in valuation. Chapter 4 shows how to use financial statements to identify a firm's strengths and risks. Chapter 5 discusses risk and return, which are critical for understanding and estimating the cost of capital. In Part Two, Chapters 6 and 7 focus on bonds and stock valuation, which are the cost of capital's two most important components. Chapter 8 discusses financial options, which often play an important role in managerial compensation, agency costs, and valuation. Part Three applies the valuation concepts in Figure 1-1 to individual projects, beginning with estimating the cost of capital in Chapter 9 and continuing with project evaluation in Chapters 10 and 11.

Part Four explicitly addresses corporate valuation. Chapter 12 develops techniques for forecasting future financial statements and free cash flows. Chapter 13 directly uses the concepts in Figure 1-1 to determine a corporation's value, including the value of its stock. Chapter 13 also discusses corporate governance, which has a direct effect on how much value companies create for their shareholders.

Part Five discusses basic corporate financing decisions. Chapter 14 examines capital structure theory, or the issue of how much debt versus equity the firm should use. Chapter 15 considers the firm's distribution policy, that is, how much of its free cash flow should be paid out, either as dividends or as share repurchases. In Part Six, we address special topics that draw upon the earlier chapters, including working capital management and multinational financial management.

E-RESOURCES

The Web site at **http://ehrhardt.swlearning.com** contains several types of files:

1. It contains *Excel* files, called Tool Kits, that provide well-documented models for almost all of the text's calculations. Not only will these Tool Kits help you with this finance course, but they will serve as tool kits for you in other courses and in your career.

2. There are problems at the end of the chapters that require spreadsheets, and the Web site contains the models you will need to begin work on these problems.

e-resource

When we think it might be helpful for you to look at one of the Web site's files, we'll show an icon in the margin like the one that is shown here.

Other resources are also on the Web page, including *Web Safaris,* which are links to useful Web data and descriptions for navigating the sites to access the data.

SUMMARY

In this chapter, we provided an overview of financial management and of the financial environment. We discussed the fundamental determinants of a firm's value, the nature of financial markets, the types of institutions that operate in these markets, and how interest rates are determined. The key concepts covered are listed below:

- The three main forms of business organization are the **proprietorship,** the **partnership,** and the **corporation.**
- Although each form of organization offers advantages and disadvantages, **corporations conduct most business in the United States.**
- The primary objective of management should be to **maximize stockholders' wealth,** and this means **maximizing the stock price.** Legal actions that maximize stock prices usually increase social welfare.
- Firms increase cash flows by creating value for **customers, suppliers,** and **employees.**
- **Free cash flows (FCFs)** are the cash flows available for distribution to all of a firm's investors (shareholders and creditors) after the firm has paid all expenses (including taxes) and made the required investments in operations to support growth.
- Three factors determine free cash flows: (1) **sales revenues,** (2) **operating costs and taxes,** and (3) **required investments in operations.**
- The **value of a firm** depends on the **size of the firm's free cash flows,** the **timing of those flows,** and **their risk.**
- The **weighted average cost of capital (WACC)** is the average return required by all of the firm's investors. It is determined by the firm's **capital structure** (the firm's relative amounts of debt and equity), **interest rates,** the firm's **risk,** and the **market's attitude toward risk.**
- A **firm's value** is defined by

$$\text{Value} = \frac{\text{FCF}_1}{(1 + \text{WACC})} + \frac{\text{FCF}_2}{(1 + \text{WACC})^2} + \cdots + \frac{\text{FCF}_\infty}{(1 + \text{WACC})^\infty}.$$

- There are many different types of **financial markets.** Each market serves a different region or deals with a different type of security.
- **Physical asset markets,** also called tangible or real asset markets, are those for such products as wheat, autos, and real estate.
- **Financial asset markets** deal with stocks, bonds, notes, mortgages, and other claims on real assets.
- **Spot markets** and **futures markets** are terms that refer to whether the assets are bought or sold for "on-the-spot" delivery or for delivery at some future date.
- **Money markets** are the markets for debt securities with maturities of less than one year.
- **Capital markets** are the markets for long-term debt and corporate stocks.
- **Primary markets** are the markets in which corporations raise new capital.

- **Secondary markets** are markets in which existing, already outstanding, securities are traded among investors.
- A **derivative** is a security whose value is derived from the price of some other "underlying" asset.
- Transfers of capital between borrowers and savers take place (1) by **direct transfers** of money and securities; (2) by transfers through **investment banking houses**, which act as middlemen; and (3) by transfers through **financial intermediaries**, which create new securities.
- The major intermediaries include **commercial banks, savings and loan associations, mutual savings banks, credit unions, pension funds, life insurance companies,** and **mutual funds.**
- One result of ongoing regulatory changes has been a blurring of the distinctions between the different financial institutions. The trend in the United States has been toward **financial service corporations** that offer a wide range of financial services, including investment banking, brokerage operations, insurance, and commercial banking.
- The **stock market** is an especially important market because this is where stock prices (which are used to "grade" managers' performances) are established.
- There are two basic types of stock markets—**the physical location exchanges** (such as the NYSE) and **computer/telephone networks** (such as Nasdaq).
- Orders from buyers and sellers can be matched in one of three ways: (1) in an open outcry **auction,** (2) through **dealers,** and (3) automatically through an **electronic communications network (ECN).**
- Capital is allocated through the price system—a price must be paid to "rent" money. Lenders charge **interest** on funds they lend, while equity investors receive **dividends and capital gains** in return for letting firms use their money.
- Four fundamental factors affect the cost of money: (1) **production opportunities,** (2) **time preferences for consumption,** (3) **risk,** and (4) **inflation.**
- The **risk-free rate of interest,** r_{RF}, is defined as the real risk-free rate, r^*, plus an inflation premium, IP, hence $r_{RF} = r^* + IP$.
- The **nominal** (or **quoted**) **interest rate** on a debt security, **r,** is composed of the real risk-free rate, r^*, plus premiums that reflect inflation (IP), default risk (DRP), liquidity (LP), and maturity risk (MRP):

$$r = r^* + IP + DRP + LP + MRP.$$

- The relationship between the yields on securities and the securities' maturities is known as the **term structure of interest rates,** and the **yield curve** is a graph of this relationship.
- The shape of the yield curve depends on two key factors: (1) **expectations about future inflation** and (2) **perceptions about the relative riskiness of securities with different maturities.**
- The yield curve is normally **upward sloping**—this is called a **normal yield curve.** However, the curve can slope downward (an **inverted yield curve**) if the inflation rate is expected to decline. The yield curve can be **humped,** which means that interest rates on medium-term maturities are higher than rates on both short- and long-term maturities.

QUESTIONS

(1-1) Define each of the following terms:
a. Proprietorship; partnership; corporation
b. Limited partnership; limited liability partnership; professional corporation
c. Stockholder wealth maximization
d. Money market; capital market; primary market; secondary market
e. Private markets; public markets; derivatives
f. Investment banker; financial service corporation; financial intermediary

g. Mutual fund; money market fund
h. Physical location exchanges; computer/telephone network
i. Open outcry auction; dealer market; electronic communications network (ECN)
j. Production opportunities; time preferences for consumption
k. Real risk-free rate of interest, r*; nominal risk-free rate of interest, r_{RF}
l. Inflation premium (IP); default risk premium (DRP); liquidity; liquidity premium (LP)
m. Interest rate risk; maturity risk premium (MRP); reinvestment rate risk
n. Term structure of interest rates; yield curve
o. "Normal" yield curve; inverted ("abnormal") yield curve
p. Expectations theory
q. Foreign trade deficit

(1-2) What are the three principal forms of business organization? What are the advantages and disadvantages of each?

(1-3) What are the three primary determinants of a firm's cash flow?

(1-4) What are financial intermediaries, and what economic functions do they perform?

(1-5) Which fluctuate more, long-term or short-term interest rates? Why?

(1-6) Suppose the population of Area Y is relatively young while that of Area O is relatively old, but everything else about the two areas is equal.
   a. Would interest rates likely be the same or different in the two areas? Explain.
   b. Would a trend toward nationwide branching by banks and savings and loans, and the development of nationwide diversified financial corporations, affect your answer to part a?

(1-7) Suppose a new and much more liberal Congress and administration were elected, and their first order of business was to take away the independence of the Federal Reserve System, and to force the Fed to greatly expand the money supply. What effect would this have
   a. On the level and slope of the yield curve immediately after the announcement?
   b. On the level and slope of the yield curve that would exist 2 or 3 years in the future?

SELF-TEST PROBLEM Solution Appears in Appendix A

(ST-1)
Inflation Rates
Assume that it is now January 1. The rate of inflation is expected to be 4 percent throughout the year. However, increased government deficits and renewed vigor in the economy are then expected to push inflation rates higher. Investors expect the inflation rate to be 5 percent in Year 2, 6 percent in Year 3, and 7 percent in Year 4. The real risk-free rate, r*, is expected to remain at 2 percent over the next 5 years. Assume that no maturity risk premiums are required on bonds with 5 years or less to maturity. The current interest rate on 5-year T-bonds is 8 percent.
   a. What is the average expected inflation rate over the next 4 years?
   b. What should be the prevailing interest rate on 4-year T-bonds?
   c. What is the implied expected inflation rate in Year 5, given that Treasury bonds which mature at the end of that year yield 8 percent?

PROBLEMS

(1-1)
Expected Rate of Interest
The real risk-free rate of interest is 3 percent. Inflation is expected to be 2 percent this year and 4 percent during the next 2 years. Assume that the maturity risk premium is zero. What is the yield on 2-year Treasury securities? What is the yield on 3-year Treasury securities?

(1-2)
Default Risk
Premium

A Treasury bond that matures in 10 years has a yield of 6 percent. A 10-year corporate bond has a yield of 8 percent. Assume that the liquidity premium on the corporate bond is 0.5 percent. What is the default risk premium on the corporate bond?

(1-3)
Maturity Risk
Premium

The real risk-free rate is 3 percent, and inflation is expected to be 3 percent for the next 2 years. A 2-year Treasury security yields 6.2 percent. What is the maturity risk premium for the 2-year security?

(1-4)
Expected Rate
of Interest

The real risk-free rate is 3 percent. Inflation is expected to be 3 percent this year, 4 percent next year, and then 3.5 percent thereafter. The maturity risk premium is estimated to be $0.0005 \times (t - 1)$, where t = number of years to maturity. What is the nominal interest rate on a 7-year Treasury security?

(1-5)
Maturity Risk
Premium

Assume that the real risk-free rate, r^*, is 3 percent and that inflation is expected to be 8 percent in Year 1, 5 percent in Year 2, and 4 percent thereafter. Assume also that all Treasury securities are highly liquid and free of default risk. If 2-year and 5-year Treasury notes both yield 10 percent, what is the difference in the maturity risk premiums (MRPs) on the two notes; that is, what is MRP_5 minus MRP_2?

(1-6)
Inflation Rates

Due to a recession, the inflation rate expected for the coming year is only 3 percent. However, the inflation rate in Year 2 and thereafter is expected to be constant at some level above 3 percent. Assume that the real risk-free rate is $r^* = 2\%$ for all maturities and that there are no maturity premiums. If 3-year Treasury notes yield 2 percentage points more than 1-year notes, what inflation rate is expected after Year 1?

(1-7)
Yield Curves

Suppose you and most other investors expect the inflation rate to be 7 percent next year, to fall to 5 percent during the following year, and then to remain at a rate of 3 percent thereafter. Assume that the real risk-free rate, r^*, will remain at 2 percent and that maturity risk premiums on Treasury securities rise from zero on very short-term securities (those that mature in a few days) to a level of 0.2 percentage point for 1-year securities. Furthermore, maturity risk premiums increase 0.2 percentage point for each year to maturity, up to a limit of 1.0 percentage point on 5-year or longer-term T-notes and T-bonds.

a. Calculate the interest rate on 1-, 2-, 3-, 4-, 5-, 10-, and 20-year Treasury securities, and plot the yield curve.
b. Now suppose ExxonMobil, an AAA-rated company, had bonds with the same maturities as the Treasury bonds. As an approximation, plot an ExxonMobil yield curve on the same graph with the Treasury bond yield curve. (Hint: Think about the default risk premium on ExxonMobil's long-term versus its short-term bonds.)
c. Now plot the approximate yield curve of Long Island Lighting Company, a risky nuclear utility.

SPREADSHEET PROBLEM

(1-8)
Build a Model:
Analyzing Interest
Rates

a. Start with the partial model in the file *CF2 Ch 01 P08 Build a Model.xls* from the textbook's Web site. Suppose you are considering two possible investment opportunities: a 12-year Treasury bond and a 7-year, A-rated corporate bond. The current real risk-free rate is 4 percent, and inflation is expected to be 2 percent for the next 2 years, 3 percent for the following 4 years, and 4 percent thereafter. The maturity risk premium is estimated by this formula: MRP = 0.1% (t − 1). The liquidity premium for the corporate bond is estimated to be 0.7 percent. Finally, you may determine the default risk premium, given the company's bond rating, from the default risk premium table in the text. What yield would you predict for each of these two investments?
b. Given the following Treasury bond yield information from the March 26, 2004, *Federal Reserve Statistical Release*, construct a graph of the yield curve as of that date.

Maturity	Yield
3 months	0.94%
6 months	0.99
1 year	1.15
2 years	1.51
3 years	1.91
5 years	2.70
7 years	3.23
10 years	3.75
20 years	4.65

c. Based on the information about the corporate bond that was given in part a, calculate yields and then construct a new yield curve graph that shows both the Treasury and the corporate bonds.

CYBERPROBLEM

Please go to our Web site, **http://ehrhardt.swlearning.com**, to access any Cyberproblems.

THOMSON ONE
Business School Edition

Please go to **http://ehrhardt.swlearning.com** to access any Thomson ONE—Business School Edition problems.

MINI CASE

Assume that you recently graduated with a degree in finance and have just reported to work as an investment advisor at the brokerage firm of Balik and Kiefer Inc. One of the firm's clients is Michelle DellaTorre, a professional tennis player who has just come to the United States from Chile. DellaTorre is a highly ranked tennis player who would like to start a company to produce and market apparel that she designs. She also expects to invest substantial amounts of money through Balik and Kiefer. DellaTorre is very bright, and, therefore, she would like to understand in general terms what will happen to her money. Your boss has developed the following set of questions that you must ask and answer to explain the U.S. financial system to DellaTorre.

a. Why is corporate finance important to all managers?

b. Describe the organizational forms a company might have as it evolves from a startup to a major corporation. List the advantages and disadvantages of each form.

c. How do corporations "go public" and continue to grow? What are "agency" problems?

d. What should be the primary objective of managers?

    (1)   Do firms have any responsibilities to society at large?

    (2)   Is stock price maximization good or bad for society?

    (3)   Should firms behave ethically?

e. What three aspects of cash flows affect the value of any investment?

f. What are free cash flows? What are the three determinants of free cash flows?

g. What is the weighted average cost of capital? What affects it?

h. How do free cash flows and the weighted average cost of capital interact to determine a firm's value?

i. What are financial assets? Describe some financial instruments.

j. Who are the providers (savers) and users (borrowers) of capital? How is capital transferred between savers and borrowers?

k. List some financial intermediaries.

l. What are some different types of markets?

m. How are secondary markets organized?

   (1) List some physical location markets and some computer/telephone networks.

   (2) Explain the differences between open outcry auctions, dealer markets, and electronic communications networks (ECNs).

n. What do we call the price that a borrower must pay for debt capital? What is the price of equity capital? What are the four most fundamental factors that affect the cost of money, or the general level of interest rates, in the economy?

o. What is the real risk-free rate of interest (r^*) and the nominal risk-free rate (r_{RF})? How are these two rates measured?

p. Define the terms inflation premium (IP), default risk premium (DRP), liquidity premium (LP), and maturity risk premium (MRP). Which of these premiums is included when determining the interest rate on (1) short-term U.S. Treasury securities, (2) long-term U.S. Treasury securities, (3) short-term corporate securities, and (4) long-term corporate securities? Explain how the premiums would vary over time and among the different securities listed above.

q. What is the term structure of interest rates? What is a yield curve?

r. Suppose most investors expect the inflation rate to be 5 percent next year, 6 percent the following year, and 8 percent thereafter. The real risk-free rate is 3 percent. The maturity risk premium is zero for securities that mature in 1 year or less, 0.1 percent for 2-year securities, and then the MRP increases by 0.1 percent per year thereafter for 20 years, after which it is stable. What is the interest rate on 1-year, 10-year, and 20-year Treasury securities? Draw a yield curve with these data. What factors can explain why this constructed yield curve is upward sloping?

s. At any given time, how would the yield curve facing an AAA-rated company compare with the yield curve for U.S. Treasury securities? At any given time, how would the yield curve facing a BB-rated company compare with the yield curve for U.S. Treasury securities? Draw a graph to illustrate your answer.

t. What is the pure expectations theory? What does the pure expectations theory imply about the term structure of interest rates?

u. Finally, DellaTorre is also interested in investing in countries other than the United States. Describe the various types of risks that arise when investing overseas.

SELECTED ADDITIONAL REFERENCES

For *views on firms' objectives, see*

Jensen, Michael C., "Value Maximization, Stakeholder Theory, and the Corporate Objective Function," *Journal of Applied Corporate Finance,* Fall 2001, 8–21.

Textbooks that focus on interest rates and financial markets include

Fabozzi, Frank J., *Bond Markets, Analysis and Strategies* (Upper Saddle River, NJ: Prentice-Hall, 2000).

Johnson, Hazel J., *Financial Institutions and Markets: A Global Perspective* (New York: McGraw-Hill, 1993).

Kidwell, David S., Richard Peterson, and David Blackwell, *Financial Institutions,* *Markets, and Money* (Hoboken, NJ: J. Wiley & Sons, 2003).

Kohn, Mier, *Money, Banking, and Financial Markets* (Fort Worth, TX: The Dryden Press, 1993).

Livingston, Miles, *Money and Capital Markets* (Cambridge, MA: Blackwell, 1996).

For additional information on financial institutions, see

Greenbaum, Stuart I., and Anjan V. Thakor, *Contemporary Financial Intermediation* (Fort Worth, TX: The Dryden Press, 1995).

Kaufman, George G., *The U.S. Financial System* (Englewood Cliffs, NJ: Prentice-Hall, 1995).

CHAPTER 2

Time Value of Money[1]

Will you be able to retire? Your reaction to this question is probably, "First things first! I'm worried about getting a job, not retiring!" However, an awareness of the retirement situation could help you land a job because (1) this is an important issue today, (2) employers prefer to hire people who know the issues, and (3) professors often test students on time value of money with problems related to saving for some future purpose, including retirement. So read on.

Here are some interesting facts: (1) The U.S. savings rate is the lowest of any industrial nation. (2) The ratio of U.S. workers to retirees, which was 17 to 1 in 1950, is down to 3.2 to 1, and it will decline to less than 2 to 1 after 2020. (3) With so few people paying into the Social Security System and so many drawing funds out, Social Security may soon be in serious trouble. In fact, many of today's college students may have to support their parents.

If Ms. Jones, who earns $85,000, retires in 2005, expects to live for another 20 years after retirement, and needs 80 percent of her pre-retirement income, she would require $68,000 during 2005. However, if inflation amounts to 5 percent per year, her income requirement would increase to $110,765 in 10 years and to $180,424 in 20 years. If inflation were 7 percent, her Year 20 requirement would jump to $263,139! How much wealth would Ms. Jones need at retirement to maintain her standard of living, and how much would she have had to save during each working year to accumulate that wealth?

The answer depends on a number of factors, including the rate she could earn on savings, the inflation rate, and when her savings program began. Also, the answer would depend on how much she will get from Social Security and from her corporate retirement plan, if she has one. (She might not get much from Social Security unless she is really down and out.) Note, too, that her plans could be upset if the inflation rate increased, if the return on her savings changed, or if she lived beyond 20 years.

Many organizations have done studies relating to the retirement issue, using the tools and techniques described in this chapter. The general conclusion is that most Americans have been putting their heads in the sand—many of us have been ignoring what is almost certainly going to be a huge personal and social problem. But if you study this chapter carefully, you can avoid the trap that seems to be catching so many people.

*Excellent retirement calculators are available at **http://www.ssa.gov** and **http://www.asec.org**. These allow you to input hypothetical retirement savings information, and the program shows graphically if current retirement savings will be sufficient to meet retirement needs.*

---

[1] This chapter was written on the assumption that most students will have a financial calculator or personal computer. Calculators are relatively inexpensive, and students who cannot use them run the risk of being deemed obsolete and uncompetitive before they even graduate. Therefore, the chapter has been written to include a discussion of financial calculator solutions along with computer solutions using *Excel*.

Note also that tutorials on how to use both *Excel* and several Hewlett-Packard, Texas Instruments, and Sharp calculators are provided in the *Technology Supplement* to this book, which is available to adopting instructors.

In Chapter 1, we saw that the primary objective of financial management is to maximize the value of the firm's stock. We also saw that stock values depend in part on the timing of the cash flows investors expect to receive from an investment—a dollar expected soon is worth more than a dollar expected in the distant future. Therefore, it is essential for financial managers to have a clear understanding of the time value of money and its impact on stock prices. These concepts are discussed in this chapter, where we show how the timing of cash flows affects asset values and rates of return.

The principles of time value analysis have many applications, ranging from setting up schedules for paying off loans to decisions about whether to acquire new equipment. *In fact, of all the concepts used in finance, none is more important than the* **time value of money,** *which is also called* **discounted cash flow (DCF) analysis.** Since this concept is used throughout the remainder of the book, it is vital that you understand the material in this chapter before you move on to other topics.

TIME LINES

e-resource

The textbook's Web site contains an Excel file that will guide you through the chapter's calculations. The file for this chapter is CF2 Ch 02 Tool Kit.xls, and we encourage you to open the file and follow along as you read the chapter.

One of the most important tools in time value analysis is the **time line,** which is used by analysts to help visualize what is happening in a particular problem and then to help set up the problem for solution. To illustrate the time line concept, consider the following diagram:

Time: 0   1   2   3   4   5

Time 0 is today; Time 1 is one period from today, or the end of Period 1; Time 2 is two periods from today, or the end of Period 2; and so on. Thus, the numbers above the tick marks represent end-of-period values. Often the periods are years, but other time intervals such as semiannual periods, quarters, months, or even days can be used. If each period on the time line represents a year, the interval from the tick mark corresponding to 0 to the tick mark corresponding to 1 would be Year 1, the interval from 1 to 2 would be Year 2, and so on. Note that each tick mark corresponds to the end of one period as well as the beginning of the next period. In other words, the tick mark at Time 1 represents the *end* of Year 1, and it also represents the *beginning* of Year 2 because Year 1 has just passed.

Cash flows are placed directly below the tick marks, and interest rates are shown directly above the time line. Unknown cash flows, which you are trying to find in the analysis, are indicated by question marks. Now consider the following time line:

Time: 0   5%   1   2   3
Cash flows: −100   ?

Here the interest rate for each of the three periods is 5 percent; a single amount (or lump sum) cash *outflow* is made at Time 0; and the Time 3 value is an unknown *inflow.* Since the initial $100 is an outflow (an investment), it has a minus sign. Since the Period 3 amount is an inflow, it does not have a minus sign, which implies a plus sign. Note that no cash flows occur at Times 1 and 2. Note also that we generally do not show dollar signs on time lines to reduce clutter.

Now consider a different situation, where a $100 cash outflow is made today, and we will receive an unknown amount at the end of Time 2:

0   5%   1   10%   2
−100   ?

CORPORATE VALUATION AND THE TIME VALUE OF MONEY

In Chapter 1, we told you that managers should strive to make their firms more valuable, and that the value of a firm is determined by the size, timing, and risk of its free cash flows (FCF). Recall that free cash flows are the cash flows available for distribution to all of a firm's investors (stockholders and creditors) and that the weighted average cost of capital is the average rate of return required by all of the firm's investors. We showed you a formula, highlighted below, for calculating value. That formula takes future cash flows and adjusts them to show how much those future risky cash flows are worth today. That formula relies on time value of money concepts, which we explain in this chapter.

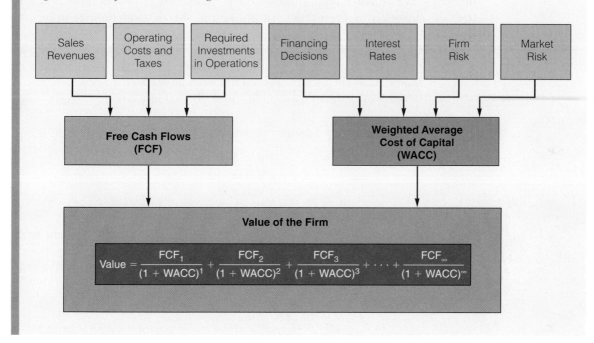

Here the interest rate is 5 percent during the first period, but it rises to 10 percent during the second period. If the interest rate is constant in all periods, we show it only in the first period, but if it changes, we show all the relevant rates on the time line.

Time lines are essential when you are first learning time value concepts, but even experts use time lines to analyze complex problems. We use time lines throughout the book, and you should get into the habit of using them when you work problems.

SELF-TEST QUESTION   Draw a three-year time line to illustrate the following situation: (1) An outflow of $10,000 occurs at Time 0. (2) Inflows of $5,000 then occur at the end of Years 1, 2, and 3. (3) The interest rate during all three years is 10 percent.

FUTURE VALUE

A dollar in hand today is worth more than a dollar to be received in the future because, if you had it now, you could invest it, earn interest, and end up with more than one dollar in the future. The process of going from today's values, or present values (PVs), to future values (FVs) is called **compounding**. To illustrate, suppose you deposit $100 in a bank that pays 5 percent interest each year. How much would you have at the end of one year? To begin, we define the following terms:

> PV = present value, or beginning amount, in your account. Here $PV = \$100$.
>
> i = interest rate the bank pays on the account per year. The interest earned is based on the balance at the beginning of each year, and we assume that it is paid at the end of the year. Here $i = 5\%$, or, expressed as a decimal, $i = 0.05$. Throughout this chapter, we designate the interest rate as i (or I) because that symbol is used on most financial calculators. Note, though, that in later chapters we use the symbol r to denote interest rates because r is used more often in the financial literature.
>
> INT = dollars of interest you earn during the year = Beginning amount $\times\ i$. Here $INT = \$100(0.05) = \$5$.
>
> FV_n = future value, or ending amount, of your account at the end of n years. Whereas PV is the value now, or the *present value*, FV_n is the value n years into the *future*, after the interest earned has been added to the account.
>
> n = number of periods involved in the analysis. Here $n = 1$.

In our example, $n = 1$, so FV_n can be calculated as follows:

$$\begin{aligned} FV_n = FV_1 &= PV + INT \\ &= PV + PV(i) \\ &= PV(1 + i) \\ &= \$100(1 + 0.05) = \$100(1.05) = \$105. \end{aligned}$$

Thus, the **future value (FV)** at the end of one year, FV_1, equals the present value multiplied by 1 plus the interest rate, so you will have $105 after one year.

What would you end up with if you left your $100 in the account for five years? Here is a time line set up to show the amount at the end of each year:

	0 5%	1	2	3	4	5
Initial deposit:	−100	$FV_1 = ?$	$FV_2 = ?$	$FV_3 = ?$	$FV_4 = ?$	$FV_5 = ?$
Interest earned:		5.00	5.25	5.51	5.79	6.08
Amount at the end of each period = FV_n:		105.00	110.25	115.76	121.55	**127.63**

Note the following points: (1) You start by depositing $100 in the account—this is shown as an outflow at $t = 0$. (2) You earn $100(0.05) = \$5$ of interest during the first year, so the amount at the end of Year 1 (or $t = 1$) is $100 + \$5 = \$105$. (3) You start the second year with $105, earn $5.25 on the now larger amount, and end the second year with $110.25. Your interest during Year 2, $5.25, is higher than the first year's interest, $5, because you earned $5(0.05) = \$0.25$ interest on the first year's interest. (4) This process continues, and because the beginning balance is higher in each succeeding year, the annual interest earned increases. (5) The total interest earned, $27.63, is reflected in the final balance at $t = 5$, $127.63.

Note that the value at the end of Year 2, $110.25, is equal to

$$\begin{aligned} FV_2 &= FV_1(1 + i) \\ &= PV(1 + i)(1 + i) \\ &= PV(1 + i)^2 \\ &= 100(1.05)^2 = \$110.25. \end{aligned}$$

Continuing, the balance at the end of Year 3 is

$$
\begin{aligned}
FV_3 &= FV_2(1 + i) \\
&= PV(1 + i)^2(1 + i) \\
&= PV(1 + i)^3 \\
&= \$100(1.05)^3 = \$115.76,
\end{aligned}
$$

and

$$FV_5 = \$100(1.05)^5 = \$127.63.$$

In general, the future value of an initial lump sum at the end of n years can be found by applying Equation 2-1:

$$FV_n = PV(1 + i)^n = PV(FVIF_{i,n}). \qquad \textbf{(2-1)}$$

The last term in Equation 2-1 defines the **Future Value Interest Factor for i and n, $FVIF_{i,n}$,** as $(1 + i)^n$. This provides a shorthand way to refer to the actual formula in Equation 2-1.

Equation 2-1 and most other time value of money equations can be solved in three ways: numerically with a regular calculator, with a financial calculator, or with a computer spreadsheet program.[2] Most work in financial management will be done with a financial calculator or on a computer, but when learning basic concepts it is best to also work the problem numerically with a regular calculator.

NUMERICAL SOLUTION

We can use a regular calculator and either multiply $(1 + i)$ by itself $n − 1$ times or else use the exponential function to raise $(1 + i)$ to the *n*th power. With most calculators, you would enter $1 + i = 1.05$ and multiply it by itself four times, or else enter 1.05, then press the y^x (exponential) function key, and then enter 5. In either case, your answer would be 1.2763 (if you set your calculator to display four decimal places), which you would multiply by \$100 to get the final answer, \$127.6282, which would be rounded to \$127.63.

In certain problems, it is extremely difficult to arrive at a solution using a regular calculator. We will tell you this when we have such a problem, and in these cases we will not show a numerical solution. Also, at times we show the numerical solution just below the time line, as a part of the diagram, rather than in a separate section.

FINANCIAL CALCULATOR SOLUTION

A version of Equation 2-1, along with a number of other equations, has been programmed directly into financial calculators, and these calculators can be used to find future values. Note that calculators have five keys that correspond to the five most commonly used time value of money variables:

N   I   PV   PMT   FV

Here

N = the number of periods. Some calculators use n rather than N.
I = interest rate per period. Some calculators use i or I/YR rather than I.
PV = present value.

e-resource

---

[2] Prior to the widespread use of financial calculators, a fourth method was used. It is called the "tabular approach," and it is described in the Chapter 2 Web Extension, available on the textbook's Web site.

> PMT = payment. This key is used only if the cash flows involve a series of equal, or constant, payments (an annuity). If there are no periodic payments in a particular problem, then PMT = 0.
>
> FV = future value.

On some financial calculators, these keys are actually buttons on the face of the calculator, while on others they are shown on a screen after going into the time value of money (TVM) menu. To find the future value of $100 after five years at 5 percent, most financial calculators solve a version of Equation 2-2:

$$PV(1 + i)^n + FV_n = 0. \tag{2-2}$$

The equation has four variables, FV_n, PV, i, and n. If we know any three, we can solve for the fourth. In our example, we enter N = 5, I = 5, PV = −100, and PMT = 0. Then, when we press the FV key, we get the answer, FV = 127.63 (rounded to two decimal places).[3]

Notice that either PV or FV_n in Equation 2-2 must be negative to make the equation true, assuming nonnegative interest rates. Thus, most financial calculators require that all cash flows be designated as either inflows or outflows, with outflows being entered as negative numbers. In our illustration, you deposit, or put in, the initial amount (which is an outflow to you) and you take out, or receive, the ending amount (which is an inflow to you). Therefore, you enter the PV as −100. Enter the −100 by keying in 100 and then pressing the "change sign" or +/− key. (If you entered 100, then the FV would appear as −127.63.) Also, on some calculators you are required to press a "Compute" key before pressing the FV key.

Sometimes the convention of changing signs can be confusing. For example, if you have $100 in the bank now and want to find out how much you will have after five years if your account pays 5 percent interest, the calculator will give you a negative answer, in this case −127.63, because the calculator assumes you are going to withdraw the funds. This sign convention should cause you no problem if you think about what you are doing.

We should also note that financial calculators permit you to specify the number of decimal places that are displayed. Twelve significant digits are actually used in the calculations, but we generally use two places for answers when working with dollars or percentages and four places when working with decimals. The nature of the problem dictates how many decimal places should be displayed.

SPREADSHEET SOLUTION

e-resource

See CF2 Ch 02 Tool Kit.xls.

Spreadsheet programs are ideally suited for solving many financial problems, including time value of money problems.[4] With very little effort, the spreadsheet itself becomes a time line. Here is how the problem would look in a spreadsheet:

---

[3] Here we assume that compounding occurs once each year. Most calculators have a setting that can be used to designate the number of compounding periods per year. For example, the HP-10B comes preset with payments at 12 per year. You would need to change it to 1 per year to get FV = 127.63. With the HP-10B, you would do this by typing 1, pressing the gold key, and then pressing the P/YR key.

[4] In this section, and in other sections and chapters, we discuss spreadsheet solutions to various financial problems. If a reader is not familiar with spreadsheets and has no interest in them, then these sections can be omitted. For those who are interested, **CF2 Ch 02 Tool Kit.xls** is the file on the Web site for this chapter that does the various calculations using *Excel*. If you have the time, we *highly recommend* that you go through the models. This will give you practice with *Excel*, which will help tremendously in later courses, in the job market, and in the workplace. Also, going through the models will enhance your understanding of financial concepts.

	A	B	C	D	E	F	G
1	Interest rate	0.05					
2	Time	0	1	2	3	4	5
3	Cash flow	−100					
4	Future value		105.00	110.25	115.76	121.55	**127.63**

Cell B1 shows the interest rate, entered as a decimal number, 0.05. Row 2 shows the periods for the time line. With *Microsoft Excel,* you could enter 0 in Cell B2, then the formula =B2 + 1 in Cell C2, and then copy this formula into Cells D2 through G2 to produce the time periods shown on Row 2. Note that if your time line had many years, say, 50, you would simply copy the formula across more columns.

Row 3 shows the cash flows. In this case, there is only one cash flow, shown in Cell B3. Row 4 shows the future value of this cash flow at the end of each year. Cell C4 contains the formula for Equation 2-1. The formula could be written as =−B3*(1+.05)^C2, but we wrote it as =−B3*(1+B1)^C2, which gives us the flexibility to change the interest rate in Cell B1 to see how the future value changes with changes in interest rates. Note that the formula has a minus sign for the PV (which is in Cell B3) to account for the minus sign of the cash flow. This formula was then copied into Cells D4 through G4. As Cell G4 shows, the value of $100 compounded for five years at 5 percent per year is $127.63.

You could also find the FV by putting the cursor on Cell G4, then clicking the function wizard, then Financial, then scrolling down to FV, and then clicking OK to bring up the FV dialog box. Then enter B1 or .05 for Rate, G2 or 5 for Nper, 0 or leave blank for Pmt because there are no periodic payments, B3 or −100 for Pv, and 0 or leave blank for Type to indicate that payments occur at the end of the period. Then, when you click OK, you get the future value, $127.63.

Note that the dialog box prompts you to fill in the arguments in an equation. The equation itself, in *Excel* format, is FV(Rate,Nper,Pmt,Pv,Type) = FV(.05,5,0,−100,0). Rather than insert numbers, you could input cell references for Rate, Nper, Pmt, and Pv. Either way, when *Excel* sees the equation, it knows to use our Equation 2-2 to fill in the specified arguments, and to deposit the result in the cell where the cursor was located when you began the process. If someone really knows what they are doing and has memorized the formula, they can skip both the time line and the function wizard and just insert data into the formula to get the answer. But until you become an expert, we recommend that you use time lines to visualize the problem and the function wizard to complete the formula.

Comparing the Three Procedures

The first step in solving any time value problem is to understand the verbal description of the problem well enough to diagram it on a time line. Woody Allen said that 90 percent of success is just showing up. With time value problems, 90 percent of success is correctly setting up the time line.

After you diagram the problem on a time line, your next step is to pick an approach to solve the problem. Which of the three approaches should you use—numerical, financial calculator, or spreadsheet? In general, you should use the easiest approach. But which is easiest? The answer depends on the particular situation.

All business students should know Equation 2-1 by heart and should also know how to use a financial calculator. So, for simple problems such as finding the future value of a single payment, it is probably easiest and quickest to use either the numerical approach or a financial calculator.

THE POWER OF COMPOUND INTEREST

Suppose you are 26 years old and just received your MBA. After reading the introduction to this chapter, you decide to start investing in the stock market for your retirement. Your goal is to have $1 million when you retire at age 65. Assuming you earn a 10 percent annual rate on your stock investments, how much must you invest at the end of each year in order to reach your goal?

The answer is $2,490.98, but this amount depends critically on the return earned on your investments. If returns drop to 8 percent, your required annual contributions would rise to $4,185.13, while if returns rise to 12 percent, you would need to put away only $1,461.97 per year.

What if you are like most of us and wait until later to worry about retirement? If you wait until age 40, you will need to save $10,168 per year to reach your $1 million goal, assuming you earn 10 percent, and $13,679 per year if you earn only 8 percent. If you wait until age 50 and then earn 8 percent, the required amount will be $36,830 per year.

While $1 million may seem like a lot of money, it won't be when you get ready to retire. If inflation averages 5 percent a year over the next 39 years, your $1 million nest egg will be worth only $116,861 in today's dollars. At an 8 percent rate of return, and assuming you live for 20 years after retirement, your annual retirement income in today's dollars would be only $11,903 before taxes. So, after celebrating graduation and your new job, start saving!

For problems with more than a couple of cash flows, the numerical approach is usually too time consuming, so here either the calculator or spreadsheet approaches would generally be used. Calculators are portable and quick to set up, but if many calculations of the same type must be done, or if you want to see how changes in an input such as the interest rate affect the future value, the spreadsheet approach is generally more efficient. If the problem has many irregular cash flows, or if you want to analyze many scenarios with different cash flows, then the spreadsheet approach is definitely the most efficient. The important thing is that you understand the various approaches well enough to make a rational choice, given the nature of the problem and the equipment you have available. In any event, you must understand the concepts behind the calculations and know how to set up time lines in order to work complex problems. This is true for stock and bond valuation, capital budgeting, lease analysis, and many other important financial problems.

Graphic View of the Compounding Process: Growth

e-resource

Figure 2-1 shows how $1 (or any other lump sum) grows over time at various interest rates. We generated the data and then made the graph with a spreadsheet model in the file *CF2 Ch 02 Tool Kit.xls*. The higher the rate of interest, the faster the rate of growth. The interest rate is, in fact, a growth rate: If a sum is deposited and earns 5 percent interest, then the funds on deposit will grow at a rate of 5 percent per period. Note also that time value concepts can be applied to anything that is growing—sales, population, earnings per share, or your future salary.

SELF-TEST QUESTIONS Explain what is meant by the following statement: "A dollar in hand today is worth more than a dollar to be received next year."

What is compounding? Explain why earning "interest on interest" is called "compound interest."

Explain the following equation: $FV_1 = PV + INT$.

You deposit $100 in an account that pays 5 percent interest annually. Write an equation that shows how much money you will have at the end of three years.

What are the five TVM (time value of money) input keys on a financial calculator?

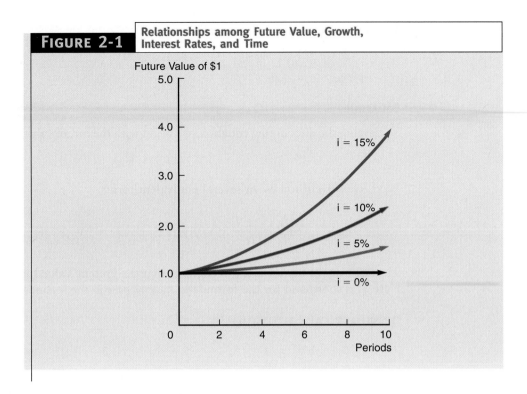

FIGURE 2-1 | Relationships among Future Value, Growth, Interest Rates, and Time

PRESENT VALUE

Suppose you have some extra cash, and you have a chance to buy a low-risk security that will pay $127.63 at the end of five years. Your local bank is currently offering 5 percent interest on five-year certificates of deposit (CDs), and you regard the security as being exactly as safe as a CD. The 5 percent rate is defined as your **opportunity cost rate,** or the rate of return you could earn on an alternative investment of similar risk. How much should you be willing to pay for the security?

From the future value example presented in the previous section, we saw that an initial amount of $100 invested at 5 percent per year would be worth $127.63 at the end of five years. As we will see in a moment, you should be indifferent between $100 today and $127.63 at the end of five years. The $100 is defined as the **present value,** or **PV,** of $127.63 due in five years when the opportunity cost rate is 5 percent. If the price of the security were less than $100, you should buy it, because its price would then be less than the $100 you would have to spend on a similar-risk alternative to end up with $127.63 after five years. Conversely, if the security cost more than $100, you should not buy it, because you would have to invest only $100 in a similar-risk alternative to end up with $127.63 after five years. If the price were exactly $100, then you should be indifferent—you could either buy the security or turn it down. Therefore, $100 is defined as the security's **fair,** or **equilibrium, value.**

In general, *the present value of a cash flow due n years in the future is the amount which, if it were on hand today, would grow to equal the future amount.* Since $100 would grow to $127.63 in five years at a 5 percent interest rate, $100 is the present value of $127.63 due in five years when the opportunity cost rate is 5 percent.

Finding present values is called **discounting,** and it is the reverse of compounding—if you know the PV, you can compound to find the FV, while if you know the FV, you can discount to find the PV. When discounting, you would follow these steps:

TIME LINE:

EQUATION:

To develop the discounting equation, we begin with the future value equation, Equation 2-1:

$$FV_n = PV(1 + i)^n \qquad \textbf{(2-1)}$$

Next, we solve it for PV in several equivalent forms:

$$PV = \frac{FV_n}{(1 + i)^n} = FV_n \left(\frac{1}{1 + i} \right)^n = FV_n(PVIF_{i,n}). \qquad \textbf{(2-3)}$$

The last form of Equation 2-3 recognizes that the **Present Value Interest Factor for i and n, PVIF$_{i,n}$,** is shorthand for the formula in parentheses in the second version of the equation.

1. NUMERICAL SOLUTION

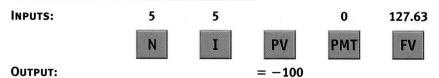

Divide $127.63 by 1.05 five times, or by $(1.05)^5$, to find PV = $100.

2. FINANCIAL CALCULATOR SOLUTION

INPUTS:

	5	5		0	127.63
	N	I	PV	PMT	FV

OUTPUT: = −100

Enter N = 5, I = 5, PMT = 0, and FV = 127.63, and then press PV to get PV = −100.

3. SPREADSHEET SOLUTION

	A	B	C	D	E	F	G
1	Interest rate	0.05					
2	Time	0	1	2	3	4	5
3	Cash flow		0	0	0	0	127.63
4	Present value	100					

CF

e-resource

See CF2 Ch 02 Tool Kit.xls.

You could enter the spreadsheet version of Equation 2-3 in Cell B4, **=127.63/(1+0.05) ^5,** but you could also use the built-in spreadsheet PV function. In *Excel,* you would put the cursor on Cell B4, then click the function wizard, indicate that you want a Financial function, scroll down, and double click PV. Then, in the dialog box, enter B1 or 0.05 for Rate, G2 or 5 for Nper, 0 for Pmt (because there are no annual payments), G3 or 127.63 for Fv, and 0 (or leave blank) for Type because the cash flow occurs at the end of the year. Then, press OK to get the answer, PV = −$100.00. Note that the PV function returns a negative value, the same as the financial calculator.

Graphic View of the Discounting Process

Figure 2-2 shows how the present value of $1 (or any other sum) to be received in the future diminishes as the years to receipt and the interest rate increase. The graph shows (1) that the present value of a sum to be received at some future date decreases and approaches zero as the payment date is extended further into the future, and (2) that the rate of decrease is greater the higher the interest (discount) rate. At relatively high interest rates, funds due in the future are worth very little today, and even at a relatively low discount rate, the present value of a sum due in the very distant future is quite small. For example, at a 20 percent discount rate, $1 million due in 100 years is worth approximately 1 cent today. (However, 1 cent would grow to almost $1 million in 100 years at 20 percent.)

SELF-TEST QUESTIONS What is meant by the term "opportunity cost rate"?

What is discounting? How is it related to compounding?

How does the present value of an amount to be received in the future change as the time is extended and the interest rate increased?

SOLVING FOR INTEREST RATE AND TIME

At this point, you should realize that compounding and discounting are related, and that we have been dealing with one equation that can be solved for either the FV or the PV:

$$FV_n = PV(1 + i)^n. \tag{2-1}$$

There are four variables in the equation—PV, FV, i, and n—and if you know the values of any three, you can find the value of the fourth. Thus far, we have always given you the interest rate (i) and the number of years (n), plus either the PV or the FV. In many situations, though, you will need to solve for either i or n, as we discuss below.

Solving for i

Suppose you can buy a security at a price of $78.35, and it will pay you $100 after five years. Here you know PV, FV, and n, and you want to find i, the interest rate you would earn if you bought the security. Such problems are solved as follows:

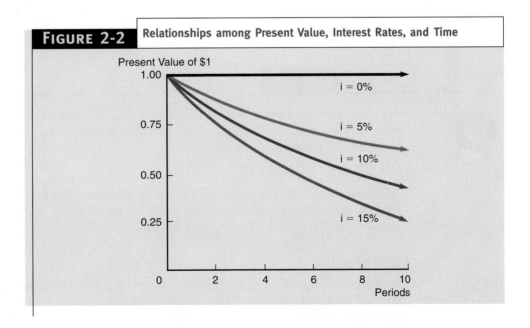

FIGURE 2-2   **Relationships among Present Value, Interest Rates, and Time**

Present Value of $1

1.00 — i = 0%

0.75 — i = 5%

i = 10%

0.50

0.25 — i = 15%

0   2   4   6   8   10

Periods

TIME LINE:

```
    0    i = ?    1           2           3           4           5
    ├──────────┼───────────┼───────────┼───────────┼───────────┤
  −78.35                                                      100
```

EQUATION:

$$FV_n = PV(1 + i)^n$$
$$\$100 = \$78.35(1 + i)^5. \text{ Solve for i.}$$

(2-1)

1. NUMERICAL SOLUTION

Use Equation 2-1 to solve for i:

$$\$100 = \$78.35(1 + i)^5$$
$$\frac{\$100}{\$78.35} = (1 + i)^5$$
$$(1 + i)^5 = 1.276$$
$$1 + i = (1.276)^{(1/5)}$$
$$1 + i = 1.050$$
$$i = 0.05 = 5\%.$$

Therefore, the interest rate is 5 percent.

2. FINANCIAL CALCULATOR SOLUTION

INPUTS: 5   −78.35   0   100

| N | I | PV | PMT | FV |

OUTPUT: = 5.0

Enter N = 5, PV = −78.35, PMT = 0, and FV = 100, and then press I to get I = 5%. This procedure is easy, and it can be used for any interest rate or for any value of n, including fractional values.

3. SPREADSHEET SOLUTION

	A	B	C	D	E	F	G
1	Time	0	1	2	3	4	5
2	Cash flow	−78.35	0	0	0	0	100
3	Interest rate	5%					

CF

e-resource

See CF2 Ch 02 Tool Kit.xls.

Most spreadsheets have a built-in function to find the interest rate. In *Excel,* you would put the cursor on Cell B3, then click the function wizard, indicate that you want a Financial function, scroll down to RATE, and click OK. Then, in the dialog box, enter G1 or 5 for Nper, 0 for Pmt because there are no periodic payments, B2 or −78.35 for Pv, G2 or 100 for Fv, 0 for type, and leave "Guess" blank to let *Excel* decide where to start its iterations. Then, when you click OK, *Excel* solves for the interest rate, 5.00 percent. *Excel* also has other procedures that could be used to find the 5 percent, but for this problem the RATE function is easiest to apply.

Solving for n

Suppose you invest $78.35 at an interest rate of 5 percent per year. How long will it take your investment to grow to $100? You know PV, FV, and i, but you do not know n, the number of periods. Here is the situation:

TIME LINE:

```
0      5%     1              2                        n−1         n=?
|-------------|--------------|----- · · · -----|-----------|
−78.35                                                      100
```

EQUATION:

$$FV_n = PV(1 + i)^n$$
$$\$100 = \$78.35(1.05)^n. \text{ Solve for n.}$$

(2-1)

1. NUMERICAL SOLUTION

Use Equation 2-1 to solve for n:

$$\$100 = \$78.35 (1 + 0.05)^n.$$

Transform to

$$\$100/\$78.35 = 1.276 = (1 + 0.05)^n.$$

Take the natural log of both sides, and then solve for n:

$$n \, LN(1.05) = LN(1.276)$$
$$n = LN(1.276)/LN(1.05)$$

Find the logs with a calculator, and complete the solution:

$$n = 0.2437/0.0488$$
$$= 4.9955 \approx 5.0.$$

Therefore, 5 is the number of years it takes for $78.35 to grow to $100 if the interest rate is 5 percent.

2. FINANCIAL CALCULATOR SOLUTION

INPUTS: 5   −78.35   0   100

N	I	PV	PMT	FV

OUTPUT: = 5.0

Enter I = 5, PV = −78.35, PMT = 0, and FV = 100, and then press N to get N = 5.

3. SPREADSHEET SOLUTION

	A	B	C	D	E	F	G
1	Time	0	1	2	3	...	?
2	Cash flow	−78.35	0	0	0	...	100
3	Interest rate	5%					
4	Payment	0					
5	N	5.00					

e-resource

Most spreadsheets have a built-in function to find the number of periods. In *Excel*, you would put the cursor on Cell B5, then click the function wizard, indicate that you want a Financial function, scroll down to NPER, and click OK. Then, in the dialog box, enter

B3 or 5% for Rate, 0 for Pmt because there are no periodic payments, B2 or -78.35 for Pv, G2 or 100 for Fv, and 0 for Type. When you click OK, *Excel* solves for the number of periods, 5.

SELF-TEST QUESTIONS   Assuming that you are given PV, FV, and the time period, n, write out an equation that can be used to determine the interest rate, i.

Assuming that you are given PV, FV, and the interest rate, i, write out an equation that can be used to determine the time period, n.

FUTURE VALUE OF AN ANNUITY

An **annuity** is a series of equal payments made at fixed intervals for a specified number of periods. For example, $100 at the end of each of the next three years is a three-year annuity. The payments are given the symbol PMT, and they can occur at either the beginning or the *end* of each period. If the payments occur at the *end* of each period, as they typically do, the annuity is called an **ordinary,** or **deferred, annuity.** Payments on mortgages, car loans, and student loans are typically set up as ordinary annuities. If payments are made at the *beginning* of each period, the annuity is an **annuity due.** Rental payments for an apartment, life insurance premiums, and lottery payoffs are typically set up as annuities due. Since ordinary annuities are more common in finance, when the term "annuity" is used in this book, you should assume that the payments occur at the end of each period unless otherwise noted.

Ordinary Annuities

An ordinary, or deferred, annuity consists of a series of equal payments made at the *end* of each period. If you deposit $100 at the end of each year for three years in a savings account that pays 5 percent interest per year, how much will you have at the end of three years? To answer this question, we must find the future value of the annuity, **FVA$_n$**. Each payment is compounded out to the end of Period n, and the sum of the compounded payments is the future value of the annuity, FVA$_n$.

TIME LINE:

Here we show the regular time line as the top portion of the diagram, but we also show how each cash flow is compounded to produce the value FVA$_n$ in the lower portion of the diagram.

EQUATION:

$$
\begin{aligned}
FVA_n &= PMT(1+i)^{n-1} + PMT(1+i)^{n-2} + PMT(1+i)^{n-3} + \cdots + PMT(1+i)^0 \\
&= PMT \sum_{t=1}^{n} (1+i)^{n-t} \\
&= PMT \left(\frac{(1+i)^n - 1}{i} \right) \\
&= PMT(FVIFA_{i,n}).
\end{aligned}
$$

(2-4)

The first line of Equation 2-4 represents the application of Equation 2-1 to each individual payment of the annuity. In other words, each term is the compounded amount of a single payment, with the superscript in each term indicating the number of periods during which the payment earns interest. For example, because the first annuity payment was made at the end of Period 1, interest would be earned in Periods 2 through n only, so compounding would be for n − 1 periods rather than n periods. Compounding for the second payment would be for Period 3 through Period n, or n − 2 periods, and so on. The last payment is made at the end of the annuity's life, so there is no time for interest to be earned.

The second line of Equation 2-4 is just a shorthand version of the first form. The Greek letter Σ means to replace t in the formula with 1, then replace t with 2, then with 3, until you finally replace t with n, and then add all those terms together. The third line is found by applying the algebra of geometric progressions. This form of Equation 2-4 is especially useful when no financial calculator is available. Finally, the fourth line shows the payment multiplied by the **Future Value Interest Factor for an Annuity** (**FVIFA**$_{i,n}$), which is the shorthand version of the formula.

1. NUMERICAL SOLUTION

The lower section of the time line shows the numerical solution, which involves using the first line of Equation 2-4. The future value of each cash flow is found, and those FVs are summed to find the FV of the annuity, $315.25. If a long annuity were being evaluated, this process would be quite tedious, and in that case you probably would use the form of Equation 2-4 found on the third line:

$$FVA_n = PMT\left(\frac{(1 + i)^n - 1}{i}\right)$$

$$= \$100\left(\frac{(1 + 0.05)^3 - 1}{0.05}\right) = \$100(3.1525) = \$315.25.$$

(2-4)

2. FINANCIAL CALCULATOR SOLUTION

INPUTS:

	3	5	0	−100	
	N	I	PV	PMT	FV

OUTPUT: = 315.25

Note that in annuity problems, the PMT key is used in conjunction with the N and I keys, plus either the PV or the FV key, depending on whether you are trying to find the PV or the FV of the annuity. In our example, you want the FV, so press the FV key to get the answer, $315.25. Since there is no initial payment, we input PV = 0.

3. SPREADSHEET SOLUTION

	A	B	C	D	E
1	Interest rate	0.05			
2	Time	0	1	2	3
3	Cash flow		100	100	100
4	Future value				315.25

Most spreadsheets have a built-in function for finding the future value of an annuity. In *Excel,* we could put the cursor on Cell E4, then click the function wizard, Financial, FV,

e-resource

See *CF2 Ch 02 Tool Kit.xls*.

and OK to get the FV dialog box. Then, we would enter .05 or B1 for Rate, 3 or E2 for Nper, and −100 for Pmt. (Like the financial calculator approach, the payment is entered as a negative number to show that it is a cash outflow.) We would leave Pv blank because there is no initial payment, and we would leave Type blank to signify that payments come at the end of the periods. Then, when we clicked OK, we would get the FV of the annuity, $315.25. Note that it isn't necessary to show the time line, since the FV function doesn't require you to input a range of cash flows. Still, the time line is useful to help visualize the problem.

Annuities Due

Had the three $100 payments in the previous example been made at the *beginning* of each year, the annuity would have been an *annuity due*. On the time line, each payment would be shifted to the left one year, so each payment would be compounded for one extra year.

TIME LINE:

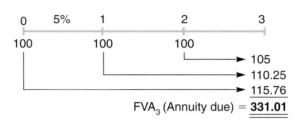

Again, the time line is shown at the top of the diagram, and the values as calculated with a regular calculator are shown under Year 3. The future value of each cash flow is found, and those FVs are summed to find the FV of the annuity due. The payments occur earlier, so more interest is earned. Therefore, the future value of the annuity due is larger— $331.01 versus $315.25 for the ordinary annuity.

EQUATION:

$$
\begin{aligned}
FVA_n(Due) &= PMT(1+i)^n + PMT(1+i)^{n-1} + PMT(1+i)^{n-2} + \cdots + PMT(1+i) \\
&= PMT \sum_{t=1}^{n} (1+i)^{n+1-t} \\
&= PMT\left(\frac{(1+i)^n - 1}{i}\right)(1+i) \\
&= PMT(FVIFA_{i,n})(1+i).
\end{aligned}
$$

(2-4a)

The only difference between Equation 2-4a for annuities due and Equation 2-4 for ordinary annuities is that every term in Equation 2-4a is compounded for one extra period, reflecting the fact that each payment for an annuity due occurs one period earlier than for a corresponding ordinary annuity.

1. NUMERICAL SOLUTION

The lower section of the time line shows the numerical solution using the first line of Equation 2-4a. The future value of each cash flow is found, and those FVs are summed to find the FV of the annuity, $331.01. Because this process is quite tedious for long annuities, you probably would use the third line of Equation 2-4a:

$$
FVA_n(Due) = PMT\left(\frac{(1+i)^n - 1}{i}\right)(1+i)
$$

(2-4a)

$$
= \$100\left(\frac{(1+0.05)^3 - 1}{0.05}\right)(1+0.05) = \$100(3.1525)(1.05) = \$331.01.
$$

2. FINANCIAL CALCULATOR SOLUTION

Most financial calculators have a switch, or key, marked "DUE" or "BEG" that permits you to switch from end-of-period payments (ordinary annuity) to beginning-of-period payments (annuity due). When the beginning mode is activated, the display will normally show the word "BEGIN." Thus, to deal with annuities due, switch your calculator to "BEGIN" and proceed as before:

BEGIN

INPUTS:	3	5	0	−100	
	N	I	PV	PMT	FV

OUTPUT: = **331.01**

Enter N = 3, I = 5, PV = 0, PMT = −100, and then press FV to get the answer, $331.01. *Since most problems specify end-of-period cash flows, you should always switch your calculator back to "END" mode after you work an annuity due problem.*

3. SPREADSHEET SOLUTION

For the annuity due, use the FV function just as for the ordinary annuity except enter 1 for Type to indicate that we now have an annuity due. Then, when you click OK, the answer $331.01 will appear.

SELF-TEST QUESTIONS

What is the difference between an ordinary annuity and an annuity due?

How do you modify the equation for determining the value of an ordinary annuity to find the value of an annuity due?

Other things held constant, which annuity has the greater *future* value: an ordinary annuity or an annuity due? Why?

PRESENT VALUE OF AN ANNUITY

Suppose you were offered the following alternatives: (1) a three-year annuity with payments of $100 or (2) a lump sum payment today. You have no need for the money during the next three years, so if you accept the annuity, you would deposit the payments in a bank account that pays 5 percent interest per year. Similarly, the lump sum payment would be deposited into a bank account. How large must the lump sum payment today be to make it equivalent to the annuity?

Ordinary Annuities

If the payments come at the end of each year, then the annuity is an ordinary annuity, and it would be set up as follows:

TIME LINE:

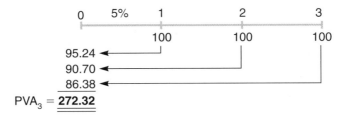

The regular time line is shown at the top of the diagram, and the numerical solution values are shown in the left column. The PV of the annuity, PVA_n, is $272.32.

EQUATION:

The general equation used to find the PV of an ordinary annuity is shown below:

$$PVA_n = PMT\left(\frac{1}{1+i}\right)^1 + PMT\left(\frac{1}{1+i}\right)^2 + \cdots + PMT\left(\frac{1}{1+i}\right)^n$$

$$= PMT \sum_{t=1}^{n}\left(\frac{1}{1+i}\right)^t$$

$$= PMT\left(\frac{1 - \dfrac{1}{(1+i)^n}}{i}\right)$$

$$= PMT(PVIFA_{i,n}).$$

(2-5)

The **Present Value Interest Factor of an Annuity for i and n, PVIFA$_{i,n}$,** is a shorthand notation for the formula.

1. NUMERICAL SOLUTION

The lower section of the time line shows the numerical solution, $272.32, calculated by using the first line of Equation 2-5, where the present value of each cash flow is found and then summed to find the PV of the annuity. If the annuity has many payments, it is easier to use the third line of Equation 2-5:

$$PVA_n = PMT\left(\frac{1 - \dfrac{1}{(1+i)^n}}{i}\right)$$

$$= \$100\left(\frac{1 - \dfrac{1}{(1+0.05)^3}}{0.05}\right) = \$100(2.7232) = \$272.32.$$

2. FINANCIAL CALCULATOR SOLUTION

INPUTS:	3	5		−100	0
	N	I	PV	PMT	FV
OUTPUT:			= 272.32		

Enter N = 3, I = 5, PMT = −100, and FV = 0, and then press the PV key to find the PV, $272.32.

3. SPREADSHEET SOLUTION

	A	B	C	D	E
1	Interest rate	0.05			
2	Time	0	1	2	3
3	Cash flow		100	100	100
4	Present value	272.32			

In *Excel*, put the cursor on Cell B4 and then click the function wizard, Financial, PV, and OK. Then enter B1 or 0.05 for Rate, E2 or 3 for Nper, −100 for Pmt, 0 or leave blank for Fv, and 0 or leave blank for Type. Then, when you click OK, you get the answer, $272.32.

One especially important application of the annuity concept relates to loans with constant payments, such as mortgages and auto loans. With such loans, called *amortized loans,* the amount borrowed is the present value of an ordinary annuity, and the payments constitute the annuity stream. We will examine constant payment loans in more depth in a later section of this chapter.

Annuities Due

Had the three $100 payments in the preceding example been made at the beginning of each year, the annuity would have been an *annuity due.* Each payment would be shifted to the left one year, so each payment would be discounted for one less year. Here is the time line:

TIME LINE:

	0	5%	1	2	3
	100		100	100	
	95.24	←			
	90.70	←			

PVA_3 (Annuity due) = **285.94**

Again, we find the PV of each cash flow and then sum these PVs to find the PV of the annuity due. This procedure is illustrated in the lower section of the time line diagram. Since the cash flows occur sooner, the PV of the annuity due exceeds that of the ordinary annuity, $285.94 versus $272.32.

EQUATION:

$$PVA_n(\text{Due}) = PMT\left(\frac{1}{1+i}\right)^0 + PMT\left(\frac{1}{1+i}\right)^1 + \cdots + PMT\left(\frac{1}{1+i}\right)^{n-1}$$

$$= PMT \sum_{t=1}^{n}\left(\frac{1}{1+i}\right)^{t-1}$$

$$= PMT\left(\frac{1 - \dfrac{1}{(1+i)^n}}{i}\right)(1+i)$$

$$= PMT(PVIFA_{i,n})(1+i).$$

(2-5a)

1. NUMERICAL SOLUTION

The lower section of the time line shows the numerical solution, $285.94, calculated by using the first line of Equation 2-5a, where the present value of each cash flow is found and then summed to find the PV of the annuity due. If the annuity has many payments, it is easier to use the third line of Equation 2-5a:

$$PVA_n(\text{Due}) = PMT\left(\frac{1 - \dfrac{1}{(1+i)^n}}{i}\right)(1+i)$$

(2-5a)

$$= \$100\left(\frac{1 - \dfrac{1}{(1+0.05)^3}}{0.05}\right)(1+0.05).$$

$$= \$100(2.7232)(1+0.05) = \$285.94.$$

2. FINANCIAL CALCULATOR SOLUTION

BEGIN

INPUTS:	3	5		−100	0
	N	I	PV	PMT	FV

OUTPUT: = 285.94

Switch to the beginning-of-period mode, and then enter N = 3, I = 5, PMT = −100, and FV = 0, and then press PV to get the answer, $285.94. *Again, since most problems deal with end-of-period cash flows, don't forget to switch your calculator back to the "END" mode.*

3. SPREADSHEET SOLUTION

For an annuity due, use the PV function just as for a regular annuity except enter 1 rather than 0 for Type to indicate that we now have an annuity due.

SELF-TEST QUESTIONS

Which annuity has the greater present value: an ordinary annuity or an annuity due? Why?

Explain how financial calculators can be used to find the present value of annuities.

ANNUITIES: SOLVING FOR INTEREST RATE, NUMBER OF PERIODS, OR PAYMENT

Sometimes it is useful to calculate the interest rate, payment, or number of periods for a given annuity. For example, suppose you can lease a computer from its manufacturer for $78 per month. The lease runs for 36 months, with payments due at the end of the month. As an alternative, you can buy it for $1,988.13. In either case, at the end of the 36 months the computer will be worth zero. You would like to know the "interest rate" the manufacturer has built into the lease; if that rate is too high, you should buy the computer rather than lease it.

Or suppose you are thinking ahead to retirement. If you save $4,000 per year at an interest rate of 8 percent, how long will it take for you to accumulate $1 million? Or, viewing the problem another way, if you earn an interest rate of 8 percent, how much must you save for each of the next 20 years to accumulate the $1 million?

To solve problems such as these, we can use an equation that is built into financial calculators and spreadsheets:[5]

$$PV(1 + i)^n + PMT\left(\frac{(1 + i)^n - 1}{i}\right) + FV = 0. \qquad (2\text{-}6)$$

Note that some value must be negative. There are five variables: n, i, PV, PMT, and FV. In each of the three problems above, you know four of the variables. For example, in the computer leasing problem, you know that n = 36, PV = 1,988.13 (this is positive, since you get to keep this amount if you choose to lease rather than purchase), PMT = −78 (this is negative since it is what you must pay each month), and FV = 0. Therefore, the equation is

$$(1,988.13)(1 + i)^{36} + (-78)\left(\frac{(1 + i)^{36} - 1}{i}\right) + 0 = 0. \qquad (2\text{-}6a)$$

---

[5] This is the equation for an ordinary annuity. Calculators and spreadsheets have a slightly different equation for an annuity due.

Unless you use a financial calculator or a spreadsheet, the only way to solve for i is by trial-and-error. However, with a financial calculator, you simply enter the values for the four known variables (N = 36, PV = 1988.13, PMT = −78, and FV = 0), and then hit the key for the unknown fifth variable, in this case, I = 2. Since this is an interest rate of 2 percent per month or 12(2%) = 24% per year, you would probably want to buy the computer rather than lease it.

It is worth pointing out that the left side of the equation cannot equal zero if you put both the PV and PMT as positive numbers (assuming positive interest rates). If you do this by mistake, most financial calculators will make a rude beeping noise, while spreadsheets will display an error message.

In an *Excel* spreadsheet, you would use the same RATE function that we discussed earlier. In this example, enter 36 for Nper, −78 for Pmt, 1988.13 for Pv, 0 for Fv, and 0 for Type: **=RATE(36,−78,1988.13,0,0)**. The result is again 0.02, or 2 percent.

Regarding how long you must save until you accumulate $1 million, you know i = 8%, PV = 0 (since you don't have any savings when you start), PMT = −4,000 (it is negative since the payment comes out of your pocket), and FV = 1,000,000 (it is positive since you will get the $1 million). Substituting into Equation 2-6 gives:

$$(0)(1 + 0.08)^n + (-4,000)\left(\frac{(1 + 0.08)^n - 1}{0.08}\right) + 1,000,000 = 0. \qquad \textbf{(2-6a)}$$

Using algebra, you could solve for n, but it is easier to find n with a financial calculator. Input I = 8, PV = 0, PMT = −4000, FV = 1000000, and solve for N, which is equal to 39.56. Thus, it will take almost 40 years to accumulate $1 million if you earn 8 percent interest and save only $4,000 per year. On a spreadsheet, you could use the same NPER function that we discussed earlier. In this case, enter 8% for Rate, −4000 for Pmt, 0 for Pv, 1000000 for Fv, and 0 for Type: **=NPER(8%,−4000,0,1000000,0)**. The result is again 39.56.

If you plan to save for only 20 years, how much must you save each year to accumulate $1 million? In this case, we know that n = 20, i = 8%, PV = 0, and FV = 1000000. The equation is

$$(0)(1 + 0.08)^{20} + PMT\left(\frac{(1 + 0.08)^{20} - 1}{0.08}\right) + 1,000,000 = 0. \qquad \textbf{(2-6a)}$$

You could use algebra to solve for PMT, or you could use a financial calculator and input N = 20, I = 8, PV = 0, and FV = 1000000. The result is PMT = −21,852.21. On a spreadsheet, you would use the PMT function, inputting 8% for Rate, 20 for Nper, 0 for Pv, 1000000 for Fv, and 0 for Type: **=PMT(8%,20,0,1000000,0)**. The result is again −21,852.21.

SELF-TEST QUESTIONS

Write out the equation that is built into a financial calculator.
Explain why a financial calculator cannot find a solution if PV, PMT, and FV all are positive.

PERPETUITIES

Most annuities call for payments to be made over some finite period of time—for example, $100 per year for three years. However, some annuities go on indefinitely, or perpetually, and these are called **perpetuities**. The present value of a perpetuity is found by applying Equation 2-7.

$$PV(\text{Perpetuity}) = \frac{\text{Payment}}{\text{Interest rate}} = \frac{PMT}{i}. \qquad \textbf{(2-7)}$$

Perpetuities can be illustrated by some British securities issued after the Napoleonic Wars. In 1815, the British government sold a huge bond issue and used the proceeds to pay off many smaller issues that had been floated in prior years to pay for the wars. Since the purpose of the bonds was to consolidate past debts, the bonds were called **consols.** Suppose each consol promised to pay $100 per year in perpetuity. (Actually, interest was stated in pounds.) What would each bond be worth if the opportunity cost rate, or discount rate, was 5 percent? The answer is $2,000:

$$\text{PV(Perpetuity)} = \frac{\$100}{0.05} = \$2,000 \text{ if i} = 5\%.$$

Suppose the interest rate rose to 10 percent; what would happen to the consol's value? The value would drop to $1,000:

$$\text{PV(Perpetuity)} = \frac{\$100}{0.10} = \$1,000 \text{ at i} = 10\%.$$

Thus, we see that the value of a perpetuity changes dramatically when interest rates change.

SELF-TEST QUESTIONS What happens to the value of a perpetuity when interest rates increase? What happens when interest rates decrease?

UNEVEN CASH FLOW STREAMS

The definition of an annuity includes the words *constant payment*—in other words, annuities involve payments that are the same in every period. Although many financial decisions do involve constant payments, other important decisions involve uneven, or nonconstant, cash flows. For example, common stocks typically pay an increasing stream of dividends over time, and fixed asset investments such as new equipment normally do not generate constant cash flows. Consequently, it is necessary to extend our time value discussion to include **uneven cash flow streams.**

Throughout the book, we will follow convention and reserve the term **payment (PMT)** for annuity situations where the cash flows are equal amounts, and we will use the term **cash flow (CF)** to denote uneven cash flows. Financial calculators are set up to follow this convention, so if you are dealing with uneven cash flows, you will need to use the "cash flow register."

Present Value of an Uneven Cash Flow Stream

The PV of an uneven cash flow stream is found as the sum of the PVs of the individual cash flows of the stream. For example, suppose we must find the PV of the following cash flow stream, discounted at 6 percent:

0	6%	1	2	3	4	5	6	7
PV = ?		100	200	200	200	200	0	1,000

The PV will be found by applying this general present value equation:

$$PV = CF_1\left(\frac{1}{1+i}\right)^1 + CF_2\left(\frac{1}{1+i}\right)^2 + \cdots + CF_n\left(\frac{1}{1+i}\right)^n$$

$$= \sum_{t=1}^{n} CF_t\left(\frac{1}{1+i}\right)^t = \sum_{t=1}^{n} CF_t(PVIF_{i,t}).$$

(2-8)

We could find the PV of each individual cash flow using the numerical, financial calculator, or spreadsheet methods, and then sum these values to find the present value of the stream. Here is what the process would look like:

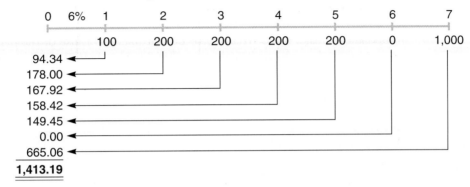

All we did was to apply Equation 2-8, show the individual PVs in the left column of the diagram, and then sum these individual PVs to find the PV of the entire stream.

The present value of a cash flow stream can always be found by summing the present values of the individual cash flows as shown above. However, cash flow regularities within the stream may allow the use of shortcuts. For example, notice that the cash flows in periods 2 through 5 represent an annuity. We can use that fact to solve the problem in a slightly different manner:

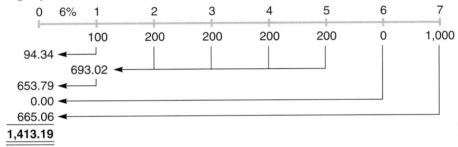

Cash flows during Years 2 to 5 represent an ordinary annuity, and we find its PV at Year 1 (one period before the first payment). This PV ($693.02) must then be discounted back one more period to get its Year 0 value, $653.79.

Problems involving uneven cash flows can be solved in one step with most financial calculators. First, you input the individual cash flows, in chronological order, into the cash flow register. Cash flows are usually designated CF_0, CF_1, CF_2, CF_3, and so on. Next, you enter the interest rate, I. At this point, you have substituted in all the known values of Equation 2-8, so you only need to press the NPV key to find the present value of the stream. The calculator has been programmed to find the PV of each cash flow and then to sum these values to find the PV of the entire stream. To input the cash flows for this problem, enter 0 (because $CF_0 = 0$), 100, 200, 200, 200, 200, 0, 1000 in that order into the cash flow register, enter I = 6, and then press NPV to obtain the answer, $1,413.19.

Two points should be noted. First, when dealing with the cash flow register, the calculator uses the term "NPV" rather than "PV." The N stands for "net," so NPV is the abbreviation for "Net Present Value," which is simply the net present value of a series of positive and negative cash flows, including the cash flow at time zero.

The second point to note is that annuities can be entered into the cash flow register more efficiently by using the N_j key.[6] In this illustration, you would enter $CF_0 = 0$, CF_1

---

[6] On some calculators, you are prompted to enter the number of times the cash flow occurs, and on still other calculators, the procedures for inputting data, as we discuss next, may be different. You should consult your calculator manual or our *Technology Supplement* to determine the appropriate steps for your specific calculator.

= 100, CF_2 = 200, N_j = 4 (which tells the calculator that the 200 occurs 4 times), CF_6 = 0, and CF_7 = 1000.[7] Then enter I = 6 and press the NPV key, and 1,413.19 will appear in the display. Also, note that amounts entered into the cash flow register remain in the register until they are cleared. Thus, if you had previously worked a problem with eight cash flows, and then moved to a problem with only four cash flows, the calculator would simply add the cash flows from the second problem to those of the first problem. Therefore, you must be sure to clear the cash flow register before starting a new problem.

Spreadsheets are especially useful for solving problems with uneven cash flows. Just as with a financial calculator, you must enter the cash flows in the spreadsheet:

	A	B	C	D	E	F	G	H	I
1	Interest rate	0.06							
2	Time	0	1	2	3	4	5	6	7
3	Cash flow		100	200	200	200	200	0	1,000
4	Present value	1,413.19							

e-resource

See CF2 Ch 02 Tool Kit.xls.

To find the PV of these cash flows with *Excel,* put the cursor on Cell B4, click the function wizard, click Financial, scroll down to NPV, and click OK to get the dialog box. Then enter B1 or 0.06 for Rate and the range of cells containing the cash flows, C3:I3, for Value 1. Be very careful when entering the range of cash flows. With a financial calculator, you begin by entering the time zero cash flow. With *Excel,* you do not include the time zero cash flow; instead, you begin with the Year 1 cash flow. Now, when you click OK, you get the PV of the stream, $1,413.19. Note that you use the PV function if the cash flows (or payments) are constant, but the NPV function if they are not constant. Note too that one of the advantages of spreadsheets over financial calculators is that you can see the cash flows, which makes it easy to spot any typing errors.

Notice that the corporate valuation equation shown in the box at the beginning of the chapter is simply a formula to find the present value of an uneven stream of cash flows where the cash flows are free cash flows (FCF) and the interest rate is the weighted average cost of capital (WACC):

$$V = \frac{FCF_1}{(1 + WACC)} + \frac{FCF_2}{(1 + WACC)^2} + \cdots + \frac{FCF_\infty}{(1 + WACC)^\infty}$$

$$= \sum_{t=1}^{\infty} \frac{FCF_t}{(1 + WACC)^t}.$$

(2-9)

In Chapter 6 we will show you how to solve such an equation, even if it has an infinite number of cash flows.

Future Value of an Uneven Cash Flow Stream

The future value of an uneven cash flow stream (sometimes called the **terminal value**) is found by compounding each payment to the end of the stream and then summing the future values:

---

[7] On some calculators, instead of entering CF_6 = 0 and CF_7 = 1000, you enter CF_3 = 0 and CF_4 = 1000, since these are the third and fourth *different* cash flows.

$$FV_n = CF_1(1 + i)^{n-1} + CF_2 (1 + i)^{n-2} + \cdots + CF_{n-1}(1 + i) + CF_n$$

$$= \sum_{t=1}^{n} CF_t(1 + i)^{n-t} = \sum_{t=1}^{n} CF_t(FVIF_{i,n-t}).$$

(2-10)

The future value of our illustrative uneven cash flow stream is $2,124.92:

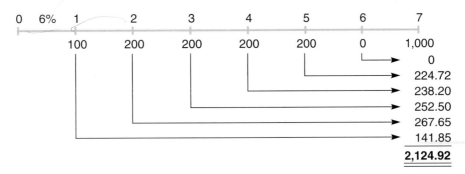

Some financial calculators have a net future value (NFV) key which, after the cash flows and interest rate have been entered, can be used to obtain the future value of an uneven cash flow stream. Even if your calculator doesn't have the NFV feature, you can use the cash flow stream's net present value to find its net future value: $NFV = NPV (1 + i)^n$. Thus, in our example, you could find the PV of the stream, then find the FV of that PV, compounded for n periods at i percent. In the illustrative problem, find PV = 1,413.19 using the cash flow register and I = 6. Then enter N = 7, I = 6, PV = −1413.19, and PMT = 0, and then press FV to find FV = 2,124.92, which equals the NFV shown on the time line above.

Solving for i with Uneven Cash Flow Streams

It is relatively easy to solve for i numerically when the cash flows are lump sums or annuities. However, it is *extremely difficult* to solve for i if the cash flows are uneven, because then you would have to go through many tedious trial-and-error calculations. With a spreadsheet program or a financial calculator, though, it is easy to find the value of i. Simply input the CF values into the cash flow register and then press the IRR key. IRR stands for "internal rate of return," which is the percentage return on an investment. We will defer further discussion of this calculation for now, but we will take it up later, in our discussion of capital budgeting methods in Chapter 10.[8]

SELF-TEST QUESTIONS

Give two examples of financial decisions that would typically involve uneven cash flows. (Hint: Think about a bond or a stock that you plan to hold for five years.)

What is meant by the term "terminal value"?

GROWING ANNUITIES

Normally, an annuity is defined as a series of *constant* payments to be received over a specified number of periods. However, the term **growing annuity** is used to describe a

---

[8] To obtain an IRR solution, at least one of the cash flows must have a negative sign, indicating that it is an investment. Since none of the CFs in our example were negative, the cash flow stream has no IRR. However, had we input a cost for CF_0, say, −$1,000, we could have obtained an IRR, which would be the rate of return earned on the $1,000 investment. Here IRR would be 13.96 percent.

series of payments that is growing at a constant rate for a specified number of periods. The most common application of growing annuities is in the area of financial planning, where someone wants to maintain a constant *real,* or *inflation-adjusted,* income over some specified number of years. For example, suppose a 65-year-old person is contemplating retirement, expects to live for another 20 years, has $1 million of investment funds, expects to earn 10 percent on the investments, expects inflation to average 5 percent per year, and wants to withdraw a constant *real* amount per year. What is the maximum amount that he or she can withdraw at the end of each year?

e-resource

We explain in the spreadsheet model for this chapter, *CF2 Ch 02 Tool Kit.xls,* that the problem can be solved in three ways. (1) Use the real rate of return for I in a financial calculator. (2) Use a relatively complicated formula.[9] Or (3) use a spreadsheet model, with *Excel*'s Goal Seek feature used to find the maximum withdrawal that will leave a zero balance in the account at the end of 20 years. The financial calculator approach is the easiest to use, but the spreadsheet model provides the clearest picture of what is happening. Also, the spreadsheet approach can be adapted to find other parameters of the general model, such as the maximum number of years a given constant income can be provided by the initial portfolio.

To implement the calculator approach, first calculate the expected real rate of return as follows, where r_r is the real rate and r_{nom} is the nominal rate of return:

$$\text{Real rate} = r_r = [(1 + r_{nom})/(1 + \text{Inflation})] - 1.0$$

$$= [1.10/1.05] - 1.0 = 4.761905\%.$$

e-resource

Now, with a financial calculator, input N = 20, I = 4.761905, PV = −1000000, and FV = 0, and then press PMT to get the answer, $78,630.64. Thus, a portfolio worth $1 million will provide 20 annual payments with a current dollar value of $78,630.64 under the stated assumptions. The actual payments will be growing at 5 percent per year to offset inflation. The (nominal) value of the portfolio will be growing at first and then declining, and it will hit zero at the end of the 20th year. The *CF2 Ch 02 Tool Kit.xls* shows all this in both tabular and graphic form.

SELF-TEST QUESTIONS

Differentiate between a "regular" and a growing annuity.

What three methods can be used to deal with growing annuities?

SEMIANNUAL AND OTHER COMPOUNDING PERIODS

In almost all of our examples thus far, we have assumed that interest is compounded once a year, or annually. This is called **annual compounding.** Suppose, however, that you put $100 into a bank which states that it pays a 6 percent annual interest rate but that interest is credited each six months. This is called **semiannual compounding.** How much would you have accumulated at the end of one year, two years, or some other period under semiannual compounding? Note that virtually all bonds pay interest semiannually, most stocks pay dividends quarterly, and most mortgages, student loans, and auto loans require monthly payments. Therefore, it is essential that you understand how to deal with nonannual compounding.

---

[9] The formula used to find the payment is shown below. Other formulas can be developed to solve for n and other terms, but they are even more complex.

$$\text{PVIF of a growing annuity} = \text{PVIFGA} = [1 - [(1 + g)/(1 + i)]^n]/[(i - g)/(1 + g)]$$
$$= 12.72.$$
$$\text{Payment} = \text{PMT} = \text{PV}/\text{PVIFGA} = \$1,000,000/12.72$$
$$= \$78,630.64.$$

Types of Interest Rates

Compounding involves three types of interest rates: nominal rates, i_{Nom}; periodic rates, i_{PER}; and effective annual rates, EAR or EFF%.

1. **Nominal, or quoted, rate, i_{Nom}.**[10] This is the rate that is quoted by banks, brokers, and other financial institutions. So, if you talk with a banker, broker, mortgage lender, auto finance company, or student loan officer about rates, the nominal rate is the one he or she will normally quote you. However, to be meaningful, the quoted nominal rate must also include the number of compounding periods per year. For example, a bank might offer 6 percent, compounded quarterly, on CDs, or a mutual fund might offer 5 percent, compounded monthly, on its money market account.

    The nominal rate on loans to consumers is also called the **Annual Percentage Rate (APR)**. For example, if a credit card issuer quotes an annual rate of 18 percent, this is the APR.

    Note that the nominal rate is never shown on a time line, and it is never used as an input in a financial calculator, unless compounding occurs only once a year. If more frequent compounding occurs, you should use the periodic rate as discussed below.

2. **Periodic rate, i_{PER}.** This is the rate charged by a lender or paid by a borrower each period. It can be a rate per year, per six-month period, per quarter, per month, per day, or per any other time interval. For example, a bank might charge 1.5 percent per month on its credit card loans, or a finance company might charge 3 percent per quarter on installment loans. We find the periodic rate as follows:

$$\text{Periodic rate, } i_{PER} = i_{Nom}/m, \qquad \text{(2-11)}$$

which implies that

$$\text{Nominal annual rate} = i_{Nom} = (\text{Periodic rate})(m). \qquad \text{(2-12)}$$

Here i_{Nom} is the nominal annual rate and m is the number of compounding periods per year. To illustrate, consider a finance company loan at 3 percent per quarter:

$$\text{Nominal annual rate} = i_{Nom} = (\text{Periodic rate})(m) = (3\%)(4) = 12\%,$$

or

$$\text{Periodic rate} = i_{Nom}/m = 12\%/4 = 3\% \text{ per quarter.}$$

If there is only one payment per year, or if interest is added only once a year, then m = 1, and the periodic rate is equal to the nominal rate.

The periodic rate is the rate that is generally shown on time lines and used in calculations.[11] To illustrate use of the periodic rate, suppose you invest $100 in an

---

[10] The term *nominal rate* as it is used here has a different meaning than the way it was used in Chapter 1. There, nominal interest rates referred to stated market rates as opposed to real (zero inflation) rates. In this chapter, the term *nominal rate* means the stated, or quoted, annual rate as opposed to the effective annual rate, which we explain later. In both cases, though, *nominal* means *stated,* or *quoted,* as opposed to some adjusted rate.

[11] The only exception is in situations where (1) annuities are involved and (2) the payment periods do not correspond to the compounding periods. If an annuity is involved and if its payment periods do not correspond to the compounding periods—for example, if you are making quarterly payments into a bank account to build up a specified future sum, but the bank pays interest on a daily basis—then the calculations are more complicated. For such problems, one can proceed in two alternative ways. (1) Determine the periodic (daily) interest rate by dividing the nominal rate by 360 (or 365 if the bank uses a 365-day year), then compound each payment over the exact number of days from the payment date to the terminal point, and then sum the compounded payments to find the future value of the annuity. This is what would generally be done in the real world, because with a computer, it would be a simple process. (2) Calculate the EAR, as defined on the next page, based on daily compounding, then find the corresponding nominal rate based on quarterly compounding (because the annuity payments are made quarterly), then find the quarterly periodic rate, and then use that rate with standard annuity procedures. The second procedure is faster with a calculator, but hard to explain and generally not used in practice given the ready availability of computers.

account that pays a nominal rate of 12 percent, compounded quarterly. How much would you have after two years?

For compounding more frequently than annually, we use the following modification of Equation 2-1:

$$FV_n = PV(1 + i_{PER})^{\text{Number of periods}} = PV\left(1 + \frac{i_{Nom}}{m}\right)^{mn}. \qquad \text{(2-13)}$$

TIME LINE AND EQUATION:

$$FV_n = PV(1 + i_{PER})^{\text{Number of periods}}.$$

1. NUMERICAL SOLUTION

Using Equation 2-13,

$$FV = \$100 (1 + 0.03)^8$$
$$= \$126.68.$$

2. FINANCIAL CALCULATOR SOLUTION

INPUTS:	8	3	−100	0	
	N	I	PV	PMT	FV
OUTPUT:					= 126.68

Input N = 2 × 4 = 8, I = 12/4 = 3, PV = −100, and PMT = 0, and then press the FV key to get FV = \$126.68.

Most financial calculators have a feature that allows you to set the number of payments per year and then use the nominal annual interest rate. However, in our experience, students make fewer errors when using the periodic rate with their calculators set for one payment per year, so this is what we recommend.

3. SPREADSHEET SOLUTION

A spreadsheet could be developed as we did earlier in the chapter in our discussion of the future value of a lump sum. Rows would be set up to show the interest rate, time, cash flow, and future value of the lump sum. The interest rate used in the spreadsheet would be the periodic interest rate (i_{Nom}/m) and the number of time periods shown would be (m)(n).

3. **Effective (or equivalent) annual rate (EAR).** This is the annual rate that produces the same result as if we had compounded at a given periodic rate m times per year. The EAR, also called EFF% (for effective percentage), is found as follows:

$$EAR \text{ (or EFF\%)} = \left(1 + \frac{i_{Nom}}{m}\right)^m - 1.0. \qquad \text{(2-14)}$$

You could also use the interest conversion feature of a financial calculator.[12]

---

[12] Most financial calculators are programmed to find the EAR or, given the EAR, to find the nominal rate. This is called "interest rate conversion," and you simply enter the nominal rate and the number of compounding periods per year and then press the EFF% key to find the effective annual rate.

In the EAR equation, i_{Nom}/m is the periodic rate, and m is the number of periods per year. For example, suppose you could borrow using either a credit card that charges 1 percent per month or a bank loan with a 12 percent quoted nominal interest rate that is compounded quarterly. Which should you choose? To answer this question, the cost rate of each alternative must be expressed as an EAR:

$$\text{Credit card loan: EAR} = (1 + 0.01)^{12} - 1.0 = (1.01)^{12} - 1.0$$
$$= 1.126825 - 1.0 = 0.126825 = 12.6825\%.$$
$$\text{Bank loan: EAR} = (1 + 0.03)^{4} - 1.0 = (1.03)^{4} - 1.0$$
$$= 1.125509 - 1.0 = 0.125509 = 12.5509\%.$$

Thus, the credit card loan is slightly more costly than the bank loan. This result should have been intuitive to you—both loans have the same 12 percent nominal rate, yet you would have to make monthly payments on the credit card versus quarterly payments under the bank loan.

The EAR rate is not used in calculations. However, it should be used to compare the effective cost or rate of return on loans or investments when payment periods differ, as in the credit card versus bank loan example.

The Result of Frequent Compounding

Suppose you plan to invest $100 for five years at a nominal annual rate of 10 percent. What will happen to the future value of your investment if interest is compounded more frequently than once a year? Because interest will be earned on interest more often, you might expect the future value to increase as the frequency of compounding increases. Similarly, you might also expect the effective annual rate to increase with more frequent compounding. As Table 2-1 shows, you would be correct—the future value and EAR do in fact increase as the frequency of compounding increases. Notice that the biggest increases in FV and EAR occur when compounding goes from annual to semiannual, and that moving from monthly to daily compounding has a relatively small impact. Although Table 2-1 shows daily compounding as the smallest interval, it is possible to compound even more frequently. At the limit, one can have **continuous compounding**. This is explained in the Chapter 2 Web Extension, available on the textbook's Web site.

CF

e-resource

Define the nominal (or quoted) rate, the periodic rate, and the effective annual rate. Which rate should be shown on time lines and used in calculations?

What changes must you make in your calculations to determine the future value of an amount that is being compounded at 8 percent semiannually versus one being compounded annually at 8 percent?

Why is semiannual compounding better than annual compounding from a saver's standpoint? What about a borrower's standpoint?

TABLE 2-1 | The Impact of Frequent Compounding

Frequency of Compounding	Nominal Annual Rate	Effective Annual Rate (EAR)[a]	Future Value of $100 Invested for 5 Years[b]
Annual	10%	10.000%	$161.05
Semiannual	10	10.250	162.89
Quarterly	10	10.381	163.86
Monthly	10	10.471	164.53
Daily[c]	10	10.516	164.86

[a]The EAR is calculated using Equation 2-14.
[b]The future value is calculated using Equation 2-13.
[c]The daily calculations assume 365 days per year.

FRACTIONAL TIME PERIODS

In all the examples used thus far in the chapter, we have assumed that payments occur at either the beginning or the end of periods, but not at some date *within* a period. However, we often encounter situations that require compounding or discounting over fractional periods. For example, suppose you deposited $100 in a bank that adds interest to your account daily, that is, uses daily compounding, and pays a nominal rate of 10 percent with a 360-day year. How much will be in your account after nine months? The answer is $107.79:[13]

$$\text{Periodic rate} = i_{PER} = 0.10/360 = 0.00027778 \text{ per day.}$$
$$\text{Number of days} = 0.75(360) = 270.$$
$$\text{Ending amount} = \$100(1.00027778)^{270} = \$107.79.$$

Now suppose you borrow $100 from a bank that charges 10 percent per year "simple interest," which means annual rather than daily compounding, but you borrow the $100 for only 270 days. How much interest would you have to pay for the use of $100 for 270 days? Here we would calculate a daily interest rate, i_{PER}, as above, but multiply by 270 rather than use it as an exponent:

$$\text{Interest owed} = \$100(0.00027778)(270) = \$7.50 \text{ interest charged.}$$

You would owe the bank a total of $107.50 after 270 days. This is the procedure most banks actually use to calculate interest on loans, except that they generally require you to pay the interest on a monthly basis rather than after 270 days.

Finally, let's consider a somewhat different situation. Say an Internet access firm had

---

[13] Here we assumed a 360-day year, and we also assumed that the nine months all have 30 days. This convention is often used. However, some contracts specify that actual days be used. Computers (and many financial calculators) have a built-in calendar, and if you input the beginning and ending dates, the computer or calculator would tell you the exact number of days, taking account of 30-day months, 31-day months, and 28- or 29-day months.

100 customers, and its customer base is expected to grow steadily at the rate of 10 percent per year. What is the estimated customer base nine months later? This problem would be set up exactly like the bank account with daily compounding, and the estimate would be 107.79 customers, rounded to 108.

The most important thing in problems like these, as in all time value problems, is to be careful! Think about what is involved in a logical, systematic manner, draw a time line if it would help you visualize the situation, and then apply the appropriate equations.

SELF-TEST QUESTION   How do you solve a time value problem with a fractional time period?

AMORTIZED LOANS

One of the most important applications of compound interest involves loans that are paid off in installments over time. Included are automobile loans, home mortgage loans, student loans, and most business loans other than very short-term loans and long-term bonds. If a loan is to be repaid in equal periodic amounts (monthly, quarterly, or annually), it is said to be an **amortized loan.**[14]

Table 2-2 illustrates the amortization process. A firm borrows $1,000, and the loan is to be repaid in three equal payments at the end of each of the next three years. (In this case, there is only one payment per year, so years = periods and the stated rate = periodic rate.) The lender charges a 6 percent interest rate on the loan balance that is outstanding at the beginning of each year. The first task is to determine the amount the firm must repay each year, or the constant annual payment. To find this amount, recognize that the $1,000 represents the present value of an annuity of PMT dollars per year for three years, discounted at 6 percent:

TIME LINE:

TABLE 2-2 | Loan Amortization Schedule, 6 Percent Interest Rate

Year	Beginning Amount (1)	Payment (2)	Interest[a] (3)	Repayment of Principal[b] (2) − (3) = (4)	Remaining Balance (1) − (4) = (5)
1	$1,000.00	$ 374.11	$ 60.00	$ 314.11	$685.89
2	685.89	374.11	41.15	332.96	352.93
3	352.93	374.11	21.18	352.93	0.00
		$1,122.33	$122.33	$1,000.00	

[a]Interest is calculated by multiplying the loan balance at the beginning of the year by the interest rate. Therefore, interest in Year 1 is $1,000(0.06) = $60; in Year 2 it is $685.89(0.06) = $41.15; and in Year 3 it is $352.93(0.06) = $21.18.
[b]Repayment of principal is equal to the payment of $374.11 minus the interest charge for each year.

---

[14] The word *amortized* comes from the Latin *mors,* meaning "death," so an amortized loan is one that is "killed off" over time.

EQUATION:

The same general equation used to find the PV of an ordinary annuity is shown below:

$$PVA_n = PMT\left(\frac{1}{1+i}\right)^1 + PMT\left(\frac{1}{1+i}\right)^2 + \cdots + PMT\left(\frac{1}{1+i}\right)^n$$

$$= PMT\sum_{t=1}^{n}\left(\frac{1}{1+i}\right)^t \qquad\qquad (2\text{-}5)$$

$$= PMT\left(\frac{1 - \dfrac{1}{(1+i)^n}}{i}\right)$$

$$= PMT(PVIFA_{i,n})$$

1. NUMERICAL SOLUTION

We know the present value, the interest rate, and the number of periods. The only unknown variable is the payment. Using Equation 2-5, we can solve the equation for the payment:

$$\$1,000 = PMT\left(\frac{1 - \dfrac{1}{(1+0.06)^3}}{0.06}\right) = PMT(2.6730)$$

$$PMT = \$1,000/2.6730 = \$374.11.$$

2. FINANCIAL CALCULATOR SOLUTION

INPUTS:	3	6	1000		0
	N	I	PV	PMT	FV
OUTPUT:				= −374.11	

Enter N = 3, I = 6, PV = 1000, and FV = 0, and then press the PMT key to find PMT = −$374.11.

3. SPREADSHEET SOLUTION

e-resource

See *CF2 Ch 02 Tool Kit.xls* for details.

The spreadsheet is ideal for developing amortization tables. The setup is similar to Table 2–2, but you would want to include "input" cells for the interest rate, principal value, and the length of the loan. This would make the spreadsheet flexible in the sense that the loan terms could be changed and a new amortization table would be recalculated instantly. Then use the function wizard to find the payment. If you had I = 6% in B1, N = 3 in B2, and PV = 1000 in B3, then the function = **PMT(B1, B2, B3)** would return a result of −$374.11.

Therefore, the firm must pay the lender $374.11 at the end of each of the next three years, and the percentage cost to the borrower, which is also the rate of return to the lender, will be 6 percent. Each payment consists partly of interest and partly of repayment of principal. This breakdown is given in the **amortization schedule** shown in Table 2-2. The interest component is largest in the first year, and it declines as the outstanding balance of the loan decreases. For tax purposes, a business borrower or homeowner reports the interest component shown in Column 3 as a deductible cost each year, while the lender reports this same amount as taxable income.

Financial calculators are programmed to calculate amortization tables—you simply enter the input data, and then press one key to get each entry in Table 2-2. If you have a financial calculator, it is worthwhile to read the appropriate section of the calculator manual and learn how to use its amortization feature. As we show in the model for this chapter, with a spreadsheet such as *Excel* it is easy to set up and print out a full amortization schedule.

SELF-TEST QUESTIONS

To construct an amortization schedule, how do you determine the amount of the periodic payments?

How do you determine the amount of each payment that goes to interest and to principal?

SUMMARY

Most financial decisions involve situations in which someone pays money at one point in time and receives money at some later time. Dollars paid or received at two different points in time are different, and this difference is recognized and accounted for by *time value of money (TVM) analysis*.

- **Compounding** is the process of determining the **future value (FV)** of a cash flow or a series of cash flows. The compounded amount, or future value, is equal to the beginning amount plus the interest earned.
- Future value of a single payment: $FV_n = PV(1 + i)^n$.
- **Discounting** is the process of finding the **present value (PV)** of a future cash flow or a series of cash flows; discounting is the reciprocal, or reverse, of compounding.

- Present value of a single payment: $PV = \dfrac{FV_n}{(1 + i)^i}$.

- An **annuity** is defined as a series of equal periodic payments (PMT) for a specified number of periods.
- Future value of an annuity:

$$FVA_n = PMT \sum_{t=1}^{n} (1 + i)^{n-t} = PMT\left(\frac{(1 + i)^n - 1}{i}\right).$$

- Present value of an annuity: $PVA_n = PMT\left(\dfrac{1 - \dfrac{1}{(1 + i)^n}}{i}\right).$

- An annuity whose payments occur at the *end* of each period is called an **ordinary annuity.** The formulas above are for ordinary annuities.
- If each payment occurs at the beginning of the period rather than at the end, then we have an **annuity due.** The PV of each payment would be larger, because each payment would be discounted back one year less, so the PV of the annuity would also be larger. Similarly, the FV of the annuity due would also be larger because each payment would be compounded for an extra year. The following formulas can be used to convert the PV and FV of an ordinary annuity to an annuity due:

$$PVA \text{ (annuity due)} = PVA \text{ of an ordinary annuity} \times (1 + i).$$
$$FVA \text{ (annuity due)} = FVA \text{ of an ordinary annuity} \times (1 + i).$$

- A **perpetuity** is an annuity with an infinite number of payments.

$$\text{Value of perpetuity} = \frac{PMT}{i}.$$

- To find the PV or FV of an uneven series, find the PV or FV of each individual cash flow and then sum them.
- If you know the cash flows and the PV (or FV) of a cash flow stream, you can **determine the interest rate.**
- When compounding occurs more frequently than once a year, the nominal rate must be converted to a periodic rate, and the number of years must be converted to periods:

$$i_{PER} = \text{Stated rate/Periods per year.}$$
$$\text{Periods} = \text{Years} \times \text{Periods per year.}$$

The periodic rate and number of periods would be used for calculations and shown on time lines.

- If comparing the costs of loans that require payments more than once a year, or the rates of return on investments that pay interest more frequently, then the comparisons should be based on **equivalent** (or **effective**) rates of return using this formula:

$$\text{Effective annual rate} = \text{EAR (or EFF\%)} = \left(1 + \frac{i_{Nom}}{m}\right)^m - 1.0.$$

- The general equation for finding the future value for any number of compounding periods per year is

$$FV_n = PV\left(1 + \frac{i_{Nom}}{m}\right)^{mn},$$

where

$$i_{Nom} = \text{quoted interest rate.}$$
$$m = \text{number of compounding periods per year.}$$
$$n = \text{number of years.}$$

- An **amortized loan** is one that is paid off in equal payments over a specified period. An **amortization schedule** shows how much of each payment constitutes interest, how much is used to reduce the principal, and the unpaid balance at each point in time.

QUESTIONS

(2-1) Define each of the following terms:
  a. PV; i; INT; FV_n; PVA_n; FVA_n; PMT; m; i_{Nom}
  b. $FVIF_{i,n}$; $PVIF_{i,n}$; $FVIFA_{i,n}$; $PVIFA_{i,n}$
  c. Opportunity cost rate
  d. Annuity; lump sum payment; cash flow; uneven cash flow stream
  e. Ordinary (deferred) annuity; annuity due
  f. Perpetuity; consol
  g. Outflow; inflow; time line; terminal value
  h. Compounding; discounting
  i. Annual, semiannual, quarterly, monthly, and daily compounding
  j. Effective annual rate (EAR); nominal (quoted) interest rate; APR; periodic rate
  k. Amortization schedule; principal versus interest component of a payment; amortized loan

(2-2) What is an *opportunity cost rate?* How is this rate used in discounted cash flow analysis, and where is it shown on a time line? Is the opportunity rate a single number that is used in all situations?

(2-3) An *annuity* is defined as a series of payments of a fixed amount for a specific number of periods. Thus, $100 a year for 10 years is an annuity, but $100 in Year 1, $200 in Year 2, and $400 in Years 3 through 10 does *not* constitute an annuity. However, the second series *contains* an annuity. Is this statement true or false?

(2-4) If a firm's earnings per share grew from $1 to $2 over a 10-year period, the *total growth* would be 100 percent, but the *annual growth rate* would be *less than* 10 percent. True or false? Explain.

(2-5) Would you rather have a savings account that pays 5 percent interest compounded semiannually or one that pays 5 percent interest compounded daily? Explain.

SELF-TEST PROBLEMS   Solutions Appear in Appendix A

(ST-1)
Future Value

Assume that one year from now, you will deposit $1,000 into a savings account that pays 8 percent.
a. If the bank compounds interest annually, how much will you have in your account 4 years from now?
b. What would your balance 4 years from now be if the bank used quarterly compounding rather than annual compounding?
c. Suppose you deposited the $1,000 in 4 payments of $250 each at Year 1, Year 2, Year 3, and Year 4. How much would you have in your account at Year 4, based on 8 percent annual compounding?
d. Suppose you deposited 4 equal payments in your account at Year 1, Year 2, Year 3, and Year 4. Assuming an 8 percent interest rate, how large would each of your payments have to be for you to obtain the same ending balance as you calculated in part a?

(ST-2)
Time Value of Money

Assume that 4 years from now you will need $1,000. Your bank compounds interest at an 8 percent annual rate.
a. How much must you deposit 1 year from now to have a balance of $1,000 4 years from now?
b. If you want to make equal payments at Years 1 through 4, to accumulate the $1,000, how large must each of the 4 payments be?
c. If your father were to offer either to make the payments calculated in part b ($221.92) or to give you a lump sum of $750 one year from now, which would you choose?
d. If you have only $750 one year from now, what interest rate, compounded annually, would you have to earn to have the necessary $1,000 four years from now?
e. Suppose you can deposit only $186.29 each at Years 1 through 4, but you still need $1,000 at Year 4. What interest rate, with annual compounding, must you seek out to achieve your goal?
f. To help you reach your $1,000 goal, your father offers to give you $400 one year from now. You will get a part-time job and make 6 additional payments of equal amounts each 6 months thereafter. If all of this money is deposited in a bank which pays 8 percent, compounded semiannually, how large must each of the 6 payments be?
g. What is the effective annual rate being paid by the bank in part f?

(ST-3)
Effective Annual Rates

Bank A pays 8 percent interest, compounded quarterly, on its money market account. The managers of Bank B want its money market account to equal Bank A's effective annual rate, but interest is to be compounded on a monthly basis. What nominal, or quoted, rate must Bank B set?

PROBLEMS

(2-1)
Present and Future Values for Different Periods

Find the following values, *using the equations*, and then work the problems using a financial calculator to check your answers. Disregard rounding differences. (Hint: If you are using a financial calculator, you can enter the known values and then press the appropriate key to find the unknown variable. Then, without clearing the TVM register, you can "override" the variable which changes by simply entering a new value for it and then pressing the key for the unknown variable to obtain the second answer. This procedure can be used in parts b and d, and in many other situations, to see how changes in input variables affect the output variable.)

a. An initial $500 compounded for 1 year at 6 percent.
b. An initial $500 compounded for 2 years at 6 percent.
c. The present value of $500 due in 1 year at a discount rate of 6 percent.
d. The present value of $500 due in 2 years at a discount rate of 6 percent.

(2-2)
Present and Future
Values for Different
Interest Rates

Use equations and a financial calculator to find the following values. See the hint for Problem 2-1.

a. An initial $500 compounded for 10 years at 6 percent.
b. An initial $500 compounded for 10 years at 12 percent.
c. The present value of $500 due in 10 years at a 6 percent discount rate.
d. The present value of $1,552.90 due in 10 years at a 12 percent discount rate and at a 6 percent rate. Give a verbal definition of the term *present value,* and illustrate it using a time line with data from this problem. As a part of your answer, explain why present values are dependent upon interest rates.

(2-3)
Time for a Lump
Sum to Double

To the closest year, how long will it take $200 to double if it is deposited and earns the following rates? [Notes: (1) See the hint for Problem 2-1. (2) This problem cannot be solved exactly with some financial calculators. For example, if you enter PV = −200, PMT = 0, FV = 400, and I = 7 in an HP-12C, and then press the N key, you will get 11 years for part a. The correct answer is 10.2448 years, which rounds to 10, but the calculator rounds up. However, the HP-10B gives the correct answer.]

a. 7 percent.
b. 10 percent.
c. 18 percent.
d. 100 percent.

(2-4)
Future Value of
an Annuity

Find the *future value* of the following annuities. The first payment in these annuities is made at the *end* of Year 1; that is, they are *ordinary annuities*. (Note: See the hint to Problem 2-1. Also, note that you can leave values in the TVM register, switch to "BEG," press FV, and find the FV of the annuity due.)

a. $400 per year for 10 years at 10 percent.
b. $200 per year for 5 years at 5 percent.
c. $400 per year for 5 years at 0 percent.
d. Now rework parts a, b, and c assuming that payments are made at the *beginning* of each year; that is, they are *annuities due.*

(2-5)
Present Value of
an Annuity

Find the *present value* of the following *ordinary annuities* (see note to Problem 2-4):

a. $400 per year for 10 years at 10 percent.
b. $200 per year for 5 years at 5 percent.
c. $400 per year for 5 years at 0 percent.
d. Now rework parts a, b, and c assuming that payments are made at the *beginning* of each year; that is, they are *annuities due.*

(2-6)
Uneven Cash
Flow Stream

a. Find the present values of the following cash flow streams. The appropriate interest rate is 8 percent. (Hint: It is fairly easy to work this problem dealing with the individual cash flows. However, if you have a financial calculator, read the section of the manual that describes how to enter cash flows such as the ones in this problem. This will take a little time, but the investment will pay huge dividends throughout the course. Note, if you do work with the cash flow register, then you must enter $CF_0 = 0$.)

Year	Cash Stream A	Cash Stream B
1	$100	$300
2	400	400
3	400	400
4	400	400
5	300	100

b. What is the value of each cash flow stream at a 0 percent interest rate?

(2-7)
Effective Rate of Interest

Find the interest rates, or rates of return, on each of the following:
a. You *borrow* $700 and promise to pay back $749 at the end of 1 year.
b. You *lend* $700 and receive a promise to be paid $749 at the end of 1 year.
c. You borrow $85,000 and promise to pay back $201,229 at the end of 10 years.
d. You borrow $9,000 and promise to make payments of $2,684.80 per year for 5 years.

(2-8)
Future Value for Various Compounding Periods

Find the amount to which $500 will grow under each of the following conditions:
a. 12 percent compounded annually for 5 years.
b. 12 percent compounded semiannually for 5 years.
c. 12 percent compounded quarterly for 5 years.
d. 12 percent compounded monthly for 5 years.

(2-9)
Present Value for Various Compounding Periods

Find the present value of $500 due in the future under each of the following conditions:
a. 12 percent nominal rate, semiannual compounding, discounted back 5 years.
b. 12 percent nominal rate, quarterly compounding, discounted back 5 years.
c. 12 percent nominal rate, monthly compounding, discounted back 1 year.

(2-10)
Future Value of an Annuity for Various Compounding Periods

Find the future values of the following ordinary annuities:
a. FV of $400 each 6 months for 5 years at a nominal rate of 12 percent, compounded semiannually.
b. FV of $200 each 3 months for 5 years at a nominal rate of 12 percent, compounded quarterly.
c. The annuities described in parts a and b have the same amount of money paid into them during the 5-year period and both earn interest at the same nominal rate, yet the annuity in part b earns $101.75 more than the one in part a over the 5 years. Why does this occur?

(2-11)
Effective versus Nominal Interest Rates

Universal Bank pays 7 percent interest, compounded annually, on time deposits. Regional Bank pays 6 percent interest, compounded quarterly.
a. Based on effective interest rates, in which bank would you prefer to deposit your money?
b. Could your choice of banks be influenced by the fact that you might want to withdraw your funds during the year as opposed to at the end of the year? In answering this question, assume that funds must be left on deposit during the entire compounding period in order for you to receive any interest.

(2-12)
Amortization Schedule

a. Set up an amortization schedule for a $25,000 loan to be repaid in equal installments at the end of each of the next 5 years. The interest rate is 10 percent.
b. How large must each annual payment be if the loan is for $50,000? Assume that the interest rate remains at 10 percent and that the loan is paid off over 5 years.
c. How large must each payment be if the loan is for $50,000, the interest rate is 10 percent, and the loan is paid off in equal installments at the end of each of the next 10 years? This loan is for the same amount as the loan in part b, but the payments are spread out over twice as many periods. Why are these payments not half as large as the payments on the loan in part b?

(2-13)
Growth Rates

Hanebury Corporation's current sales were $12 million. Sales were $6 million 5 years earlier.
a. To the nearest percentage point, at what rate have sales been growing?
b. Suppose someone calculated the sales growth for Hanebury Corporation in part a as follows: "Sales doubled in 5 years. This represents a growth of 100 percent in 5 years, so, dividing 100 percent by 5, we find the growth rate to be 20 percent per year." Explain what is wrong with this calculation.

(2-14)
Expected Rate of Return

Washington-Pacific invests $4 million to clear a tract of land and to set out some young pine trees. The trees will mature in 10 years, at which time Washington-Pacific plans to sell the forest at an expected price of $8 million. What is Washington-Pacific's expected rate of return?

(2-15)
Effective Rate
of Interest
A mortgage company offers to lend you $85,000; the loan calls for payments of $8,273.59 per year for 30 years. What interest rate is the mortgage company charging you?

(2-16)
Required Lump
Sum Payment
To complete your last year in business school and then go through law school, you will need $10,000 per year for 4 years, starting next year (that is, you will need to withdraw the first $10,000 one year from today). Your rich uncle offers to put you through school, and he will deposit in a bank paying 7 percent interest a sum of money that is sufficient to provide the 4 payments of $10,000 each. His deposit will be made today.
a. How large must the deposit be?
b. How much will be in the account immediately after you make the first withdrawal? After the last withdrawal?

(2-17)
Repaying a Loan
While Mary Corens was a student at the University of Tennessee, she borrowed $12,000 in student loans at an annual interest rate of 9 percent. If Mary repays $1,500 per year, how long, to the nearest year, will it take her to repay the loan?

(2-18)
Reaching a Financial Goal
You need to accumulate $10,000. To do so, you plan to make deposits of $1,250 per year, with the first payment being made a year from today, in a bank account that pays 12 percent annual interest. Your last deposit will be less than $1,250 if less is needed to round out to $10,000. How many years will it take you to reach your $10,000 goal, and how large will the last deposit be?

(2-19)
Present Value of
a Perpetuity
What is the present value of a perpetuity of $100 per year if the appropriate discount rate is 7 percent? If interest rates in general were to double and the appropriate discount rate rose to 14 percent, what would happen to the present value of the perpetuity?

(2-20)
PV and Effective
Annual Rate
Assume that you inherited some money. A friend of yours is working as an unpaid intern at a local brokerage firm, and her boss is selling some securities that call for four payments, $50 at the end of each of the next 3 years, plus a payment of $1,050 at the end of Year 4. Your friend says she can get you some of these securities at a cost of $900 each. Your money is now invested in a bank that pays an 8 percent nominal (quoted) interest rate but with quarterly compounding. You regard the securities as being just as safe, and as liquid, as your bank deposit, so your required effective annual rate of return on the securities is the same as that on your bank deposit. You must calculate the value of the securities to decide whether they are a good investment. What is their present value to you?

(2-21)
Loan Amortization
Assume that your aunt sold her house on December 31 and that she took a mortgage in the amount of $10,000 as part of the payment. The mortgage has a quoted (or nominal) interest rate of 10 percent, but it calls for payments every 6 months, beginning on June 30, and the mortgage is to be amortized over 10 years. Now, 1 year later, your aunt must inform the IRS and the person who bought the house of the interest that was included in the two payments made during the year. (This interest will be income to your aunt and a deduction to the buyer of the house.) To the closest dollar, what is the total amount of interest that was paid during the first year?

(2-22)
Loan Amortization
Your company is planning to borrow $1,000,000 on a 5-year, 15%, annual payment, fully amortized term loan. What fraction of the payment made at the end of the second year will represent repayment of principal?

(2-23)
Nonannual
Compounding
a. It is now January 1. You plan to make 5 deposits of $100 each, one every 6 months, with the first payment being made *today*. If the bank pays a nominal interest rate of 12 percent but uses semiannual compounding, how much will be in your account after 10 years?
b. You must make a payment of $1,432.02 ten years from today. To prepare for this payment, you will make 5 equal deposits, beginning today and for the next 4 quarters, in a bank that pays a nominal interest rate of 12 percent, quarterly compounding. How large must each of the 5 payments be?

(2-24)
Nominal Rate of Return
Anne Lockwood, manager of Oaks Mall Jewelry, wants to sell on credit, giving customers 3 months in which to pay. However, Anne will have to borrow from her bank

to carry the accounts payable. The bank will charge a nominal 15 percent, but with monthly compounding. Anne wants to quote a nominal rate to her customers (all of whom are expected to pay on time) that will exactly cover her financing costs. What nominal annual rate should she quote to her credit customers?

(2-25)
Required Annuity
Payments

Assume that your father is now 50 years old, that he plans to retire in 10 years, and that he expects to live for 25 years after he retires, that is, until he is 85. He wants a fixed retirement income that has the same purchasing power at the time he retires as $40,000 has today (he realizes that the real value of his retirement income will decline year by year after he retires). His retirement income will begin the day he retires, 10 years from today, and he will then get 24 additional annual payments. Inflation is expected to be 5 percent per year from today forward; he currently has $100,000 saved up; and he expects to earn a return on his savings of 8 percent per year, annual compounding. To the nearest dollar, how much must he save during each of the next 10 years (with deposits being made at the end of each year) to meet his retirement goal?

SPREADSHEET PROBLEM

(2-26)
Build a Model: The
Time Value of Money

e-resource

Start with the partial model in the file *CF2 Ch 02 P26 Build a Model.xls* from the textbook's Web site. Answer the following questions, using a spreadsheet model to do the calculations.

a. Find the FV of $1,000 invested to earn 10 percent after 5 years. Answer this question by using a math formula and also by using the *Excel* function wizard.

b. Now create a table that shows the FV at 0 percent, 5 percent, and 20 percent for 0, 1, 2, 3, 4, and 5 years. Then create a graph with years on the horizontal axis and FV on the vertical axis to display your results.

c. Find the PV of $1,000 due in 5 years if the discount rate is 10 percent. Again, work the problem with a formula and also by using the function wizard.

d. A security has a cost of $1,000 and will return $2,000 after 5 years. What rate of return does the security provide?

e. Suppose California's population is 30 million people, and its population is expected to grow by 2 percent per year. How long would it take for the population to double?

f. Find the PV of an annuity that pays $1,000 at the end of each of the next 5 years if the interest rate is 15 percent. Then find the FV of that same annuity.

g. How would the PV and FV of the annuity change if it were an annuity due rather than an ordinary annuity?

h. What would the FV and the PV for parts a and c be if the interest rate were 10 percent with semiannual compounding rather than 10 percent with annual compounding?

i. Find the PV and the FV of an investment that makes the following end-of-year payments. The interest rate is 8 percent.

Year	Payment
1	$100
2	200
3	400

j. Suppose you bought a house and took out a mortgage for $50,000. The interest rate is 8 percent, and you must amortize the loan over 10 years with equal end-of-year payments. Set up an amortization schedule that shows the annual payments and the amount of each payment that goes to pay off the principal and the amount that constitutes interest expense to the borrower and interest income to the lender.

(1) Create a graph that shows how the payments are divided between interest and principal repayment over time.

(2) Suppose the loan called for 10 years of monthly payments, with the same original amount and the same nominal interest rate. What would the amortization schedule show now?

CYBERPROBLEM

Please go to our Web site, **http://ehrhardt.swlearning.com**, to access any Cyberproblems.

THOMSON ONE
Business School Edition

Please go to **http://ehrhardt.swlearning.com** to access any Thomson ONE—Business School Edition problems.

MINI CASE

Assume that you are nearing graduation and that you have applied for a job with a local bank. As part of the bank's evaluation process, you have been asked to take an examination that covers several financial analysis techniques. The first section of the test addresses discounted cash flow analysis. See how you would do by answering the following questions.

a. Draw time lines for (a) a $100 lump sum cash flow at the end of Year 2, (b) an ordinary annuity of $100 per year for 3 years, and (c) an uneven cash flow stream of −$50, $100, $75, and $50 at the end of Years 0 through 3.

b. (1) What is the future value of an initial $100 after 3 years if it is invested in an account paying 10 percent annual interest?

(2) What is the present value of $100 to be received in 3 years if the appropriate interest rate is 10 percent?

c. We sometimes need to find how long it will take a sum of money (or anything else) to grow to some specified amount. For example, if a company's sales are growing at a rate of 20 percent per year, how long will it take sales to double?

d. If you want an investment to double in 3 years, what interest rate must it earn?

e. What is the difference between an ordinary annuity and an annuity due? What type of annuity is shown below? How would you change it to the other type of annuity?

f. (1) What is the future value of a 3-year ordinary annuity of $100 if the appropriate interest rate is 10 percent?

(2) What is the present value of the annuity?

(3) What would the future and present values be if the annuity were an annuity due?

g. What is the present value of the following uneven cash flow stream? The appropriate interest rate is 10 percent, compounded annually.

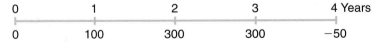

h. (1) Define (a) the stated, or quoted, or nominal rate (i_{Nom}) and (b) the periodic rate (i_{PER}).

(2) Will the future value be larger or smaller if we compound an initial amount more often than annually, for example, every 6 months, or *semiannually,* holding the stated interest rate constant? Why?

(3) What is the future value of $100 after 5 years under 12 percent annual compounding? Semiannual compounding? Quarterly compounding? Monthly compounding? Daily compounding?

(4) What is the effective annual rate (EAR)? What is the EAR for a nominal rate of 12 percent, compounded semiannually? Compounded quarterly? Compounded monthly? Compounded daily?

i. Will the effective annual rate ever be equal to the nominal (quoted) rate?

j. (1) Construct an amortization schedule for a $1,000, 10 percent annual rate loan with 3 equal installments.

(2) What is the annual interest expense for the borrower, and the annual interest income for the lender, during Year 2?

k. Suppose on January 1 you deposit $100 in an account that pays a nominal, or quoted, interest rate of 11.33463 percent, with interest added (compounded) daily. How much will you have in your account on October 1, or after 9 months?

l. (1) What is the value at the end of Year 3 of the following cash flow stream if the quoted interest rate is 10 percent, compounded semiannually?

(2) What is the PV of the same stream?

(3) Is the stream an annuity?

(4) An important rule is that you should never show a nominal rate on a time line or use it in calculations unless what condition holds? (Hint: Think of annual compounding, when i_{Nom} = EAR = i_{Per}.) What would be wrong with your answer to Questions l (1) and l (2) if you used the nominal rate (10%) rather than the periodic rate ($i_{Nom}/2$ = 10%/2 = 5%)?

m. Suppose someone offered to sell you a note calling for the payment of $1,000 fifteen months from today. They offer to sell it to you for $850. You have $850 in a bank time deposit that pays a 6.76649 percent nominal rate with daily compounding, which is a 7 percent effective annual interest rate, and you plan to leave the money in the bank unless you buy the note. The note is not risky—you are sure it will be paid on schedule. Should you buy the note? Check the decision in three ways: (1) by comparing your future value if you buy the note versus leaving your money in the bank, (2) by comparing the PV of the note with your current bank account, and (3) by comparing the EAR on the note versus that of the bank account.

SELECTED ADDITIONAL REFERENCES

For a more complete discussion of the mathematics of finance, see

Atkins, Allen B., and Edward A. Dyl, "The Lotto Jackpot: The Lump Sum versus the Annuity," *Financial Practice and Education,* Fall/Winter 1995, 107–111.

Lindley, James T., "Compounding Issues Revisited," *Financial Practice and Education,* Fall 1993, 127–129.

Shao, Lawrence P., and Stephen P. Shao, *Mathematics for Management and Finance* (Mason, OH: South-Western, 8th ed. 1998).

To learn more about using financial calculators, see the manual that came with your calculator or see

White, Mark A., *Financial Analysis with an Electronic Calculator,* 4th ed. (Burr Ridge, IL: McGraw-Hill/Irwin, 2004).

_____, "Financial Problem Solving with an Electronic Calculator: Texas Instruments' BA II Plus," *Financial Practice and Education,* Fall 1993, 123–126.

CHAPTER 3

Financial Statements, Cash Flow, and Taxes

When evaluating a company, who can you trust? The analysts at top brokerage firms rate companies, using terms such as buy, hold, or sell. Maybe you think you can trust their ratings, since these analysts are highly trained and have access to great data sources. Think again. When the market was recently in the middle of a long, steady decline, these analysts made 7,033 buy recommendations, but only 57 sells. What could possibly cause such optimism? How about their own personal compensation and their own firms' profits, rather than their clients' best interests? Most brokerage firms are members of a corporate family that includes an investment bank. If analysts assign a negative rating, the company will take its investment banking business to a firm that gives it a better rating. To prevent this defection, analysts are pressured to not make any offensive ratings. Analysts who don't fall in line are often fired, such as Mike Mayo, formerly of Credit Suisse First Boston, who gave some honest (and subsequently shown to be accurate) negative ratings. In fact, at CSFB, the analysts actually reported to investment bankers, and internal e-mails revealed that analysts were often switched around to keep investment banking clients happy.

At Merrill Lynch, e-mail revealed an even more disturbing situation. Analysts consistently gave positive ratings to firms, but then blasted the firms in internal e-mails. For example, analysts gave one company a strong buy rating but wrote that the company was "a piece of junk" in their internal e-mails. That's actually better than the e-mail for another positively rated company, which was called a "piece of s – – t." Another company was rated "Neutral in the short term/Minimum 40% appreciation long term," but e-mails stated that there was nothing interesting about the company, "except banking fees."

New York attorney general Eliot Spitzer brought action against Wall Street, which eventually settled for $1.4 billion (this doesn't stop the many suits now being brought against them by individual investors). Some are making additional efforts, such as CSFB's reassignment of analysts so that they report to its general counsel instead of its securities division. At Morgan Stanley, analysts have actually increased the number of unfavorable ratings from 2 percent to over 22 percent.

Who can you trust? Your best bet is to learn how to analyze a company, starting with this chapter, and then trust yourself.

Sources: Jeremy Kahn, "Frank Quattrone's Heavy Hand," *Fortune*, December 30, 2002, 78; Jeremy Kahn and Nelson D. Schwartz, "A New Investor Era? Ha!" *Fortune*, November 25, 2002, 35–38; David Rynecki, "The Price of Being Right," *Fortune*, February 4, 2001, 126–141; Nelson D. Schwartz and Jeremy Kahn, "Can This Bull Run Again," *Fortune*, December 30, 2002, 68–82; and Alynda Wheat, "Hall of Shame: Merrill Lynch-to-English Dictionary," *Fortune*, April 29, 2002, 28.

e-resource

The textbook's Web site contains an Excel file that will guide you through the chapter's calculations. The file for this chapter is **CF2 Ch 03 Tool Kit.xls,** *and we encourage you to open the file and follow along as you read the chapter.*

A manager's primary goal is to maximize the value of his or her firm's stock. Value is based on the stream of cash flows the firm will generate in the future. But how does an investor go about estimating future cash flows, and how does a manager decide which actions are most likely to increase cash flows? The answers to both questions lie in a study of the financial statements that publicly traded firms must provide to investors. Here "investors" include both institutions (banks, insurance companies, pension funds, and the like) and individuals. Thus, this chapter begins with a discussion of what the basic financial statements are, how they are used, and what kinds of financial information users need.

The value of any business asset—whether it is a *financial asset* such as a stock or a bond, or a *real (physical) asset* such as land, buildings, and equipment—depends on the usable, after-tax cash flows the asset is expected to produce. Therefore, the chapter also explains the difference between accounting income and cash flow. Finally, since it is *after-tax* cash flow that is important, the chapter provides an overview of the federal income tax system.

FINANCIAL STATEMENTS AND REPORTS

A source for links to the annual reports of many companies is **http://www .annualreportservice .com.**

Of the various reports corporations issue to their stockholders, the **annual report** is probably the most important. Two types of information are provided. First, there is a verbal section, often presented as a letter from the chairman, that describes the firm's operating results during the past year and then discusses new developments that will affect future operations. Second, the annual report presents four basic financial statements—the *balance sheet,* the *income statement,* the *statement of retained earnings,* and the *statement of cash flows.* Taken together, these statements give an accounting picture of the firm's operations and financial position. Detailed data are provided for the two or three most recent years, along with historical summaries of key operating statistics for the past five or ten years.[1]

The quantitative and verbal materials are equally important. The financial statements report *what has actually happened* to assets, earnings, and dividends over the past few years, whereas the verbal statements attempt to explain why things turned out the way they did.

For illustrative purposes, we use data on MicroDrive Inc., a producer of disk drives for microcomputers. Formed in 1982, MicroDrive has grown steadily and has earned a reputation for being one of the best firms in the microcomputer components industry. Micro-Drive's earnings dropped a bit in the most recent year. Management blamed a three-month strike that kept the firm from fully utilizing a new plant that had been financed mostly with debt. However, management went on to paint a more optimistic picture for the future, stating that full operations had been resumed, that several new products had been introduced, and that profits were expected to rise sharply. Of course, the profit increase may not occur, and analysts should compare management's past statements with subsequent results when judging the credibility of the projected improvement. In any event, *the information contained in an annual report is used by investors to help form expectations about future earnings and dividends.*

SELF-TEST QUESTIONS

What is the annual report, and what two types of information are given in it?
Why is the annual report of great interest to investors?
What four types of financial statements are typically included in the annual report?

---

[1] Firms also provide less comprehensive quarterly reports. Larger firms file even more detailed statements, giving breakdowns for each major division or subsidiary, with the Securities and Exchange Commission (SEC). These reports, called *10-K reports,* are available on the SEC's Web site at **http://www.sec.gov** under the heading "EDGAR."

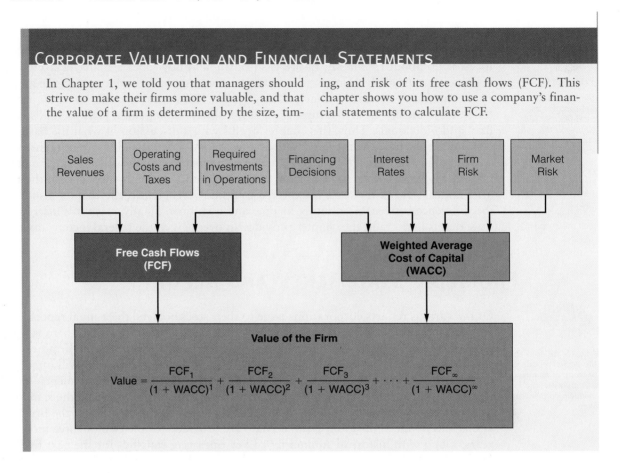

CORPORATE VALUATION AND FINANCIAL STATEMENTS

In Chapter 1, we told you that managers should strive to make their firms more valuable, and that the value of a firm is determined by the size, tim-ing, and risk of its free cash flows (FCF). This chapter shows you how to use a company's finan-cial statements to calculate FCF.

THE BALANCE SHEET

Table 3-1 shows MicroDrive's most recent **balance sheets**, which represent "snapshots" of its financial position on the last day of each year. Although most companies report their balance sheets only on the last day of a given period, the "snapshot" actually changes daily as inventories are bought and sold, as fixed assets are added or retired, or as bank loan balances are increased or paid down. Moreover, a retailer will have much larger invento-ries before Christmas than later in the spring, so balance sheets for the same company can look quite different at different times during the year.

The left side of a balance sheet lists assets, which are the "things" the company owns. They are listed in order of "liquidity," or length of time it typically takes to convert them to cash at fair market values. The right side lists the claims that various groups have against the company's value, listed in the order in which they must be paid. For example, suppli-ers may have a claim called accounts payable that is due within 30 days, banks may have claims called notes payable that are due within 90 days, and bondholders may have claims that are not due for 20 years or more. Stockholders come last, for two reasons. First, their claim represents ownership (or equity) and need never be "paid off." Second, they have a residual claim in the sense that they may receive payments only if the other claimants have already been paid. The nonstockholder claims are liabilities from the stockholders' per-spective. The amounts shown on the balance sheets are called **book values** since they are based on the amounts recorded by bookkeepers when assets are purchased or liabilities are

e-resource

*See CF2
Ch 03 Tool
Kit.xls for
details.*

TABLE 3-1 | MicroDrive Inc.: December 31 Balance Sheets (Millions of Dollars)

Assets	2005	2004	Liabilities and Equity	2005	2004
Cash and equivalents	$ 10	$ 15	Accounts payable	$ 60	$ 30
Short-term investments	0	65	Notes payable	110	60
Accounts receivable	375	315	Accruals	140	130
Inventories	615	415	Total current liabilities	$ 310	$ 220
Total current assets	$1,000	$ 810	Long-term bonds	754	580
Net plant and equipment	1,000	870	Total liabilities	$1,064	$ 800
			Preferred stock (400,000 shares)	40	40
			Common stock (50,000,000 shares)	130	130
			Retained earnings	766	710
			Total common equity	$ 896	$ 840
Total assets	$2,000	$1,680	Total liabilities and equity	$2,000	$1,680

issued. As you will see throughout this textbook, book values may be very different from **market values,** which are the current values as determined in the marketplace.

The following sections provide more information about specific asset, liability, and equity accounts.

Assets

Cash, short-term investments, accounts receivable, and inventories are listed as current assets, because MicroDrive is expected to convert them into cash within a year. All assets are stated in dollars, but only cash represents actual money that can be spent. Some marketable securities mature very soon, and can be converted quickly into cash at prices close to their book values. These securities are called "cash equivalents," and they are included with cash. Therefore, MicroDrive could write checks for a total of $10 million. Other types of marketable securities have a longer time until maturity, and their market values are less predictable. These securities are classified as "short-term investments."

When MicroDrive sells its products to a customer but doesn't demand immediate payment, the customer then has an obligation called an account receivable. The $375 million shown in accounts receivable is the amount of sales for which MicroDrive has not yet been paid.

Inventories show the dollars MicroDrive has invested in raw materials, work-in-process, and finished goods available for sale. MicroDrive uses the **FIFO (first-in, first-out)** method to determine the inventory value shown on its balance sheet ($615 million). It could have used the **LIFO (last-in, first-out)** method. During a period of rising prices, by taking out old, low-cost inventory and leaving in new, high-cost items, FIFO will produce a higher balance sheet inventory value but a lower cost of goods sold on the income statement. (This is strictly accounting; companies actually use older items first.) Because MicroDrive uses FIFO, and because inflation has been occurring, (1) its balance sheet inventories are higher than they would have been had it used LIFO, (2) its cost of goods sold is lower than it would have been under LIFO, and (3) its reported profits are therefore higher. In MicroDrive's case, if the company had elected to switch to LIFO, its balance sheet would have inventories of $585 million rather than $615 million, and its earnings (discussed in the next section) would have been reduced by $18 million. Thus, the inventory valuation method can have a significant effect on financial statements, which is important to know when comparing different companies.

Rather than treat the entire purchase price of a long-term asset (such as a factory, plant, or equipment) as an expense in the purchase year, accountants "spread" the purchase cost over the asset's useful life.[2] The amount they charge each year is called the **depreciation** expense. Some companies report an amount called "gross plant and equipment," which is the total cost of the long-term assets they have in place, and another amount called "accumulated depreciation," which is the total amount of depreciation that has been charged on those assets. Some companies, such as MicroDrive, only report net plant and equipment, which is gross plant and equipment less accumulated depreciation. Chapter 11 provides a more detailed explanation of depreciation methods.

Liabilities

Accounts payable, notes payable, and accruals are listed as current liabilities, because MicroDrive is expected to pay them within a year. When MicroDrive purchases supplies but doesn't immediately pay for them, it takes on an obligation called an account payable. Similarly, when MicroDrive takes out a loan that must be repaid within a year, it signs an IOU called a note payable. MicroDrive doesn't pay its taxes or its employees' wages daily, and the amount it owes on these items at any point in time is called an accrual, or an accrued expense. Long-term bonds are also liabilities because they, too, reflect a claim held by someone other than a stockholder.

Preferred stock is a hybrid, or a cross between common stock and debt. In the event of bankruptcy, preferred stock ranks below debt but above common stock. Also, the preferred dividend is fixed, so preferred stockholders do not benefit if the company's earnings grow. Most firms do not use much, or even any, preferred stock, so "equity" usually means "common equity" unless the words "total" or "preferred" are included.

When a company sells shares of stock, the proceeds are recorded in the common stock account.[3] Retained earnings are the cumulative amount of earnings that have not been paid out as dividends. The sum of common stock and retained earnings is called common equity, or sometimes just equity. If a company's assets could actually be sold at their book value, and if the liabilities and preferred stock were actually worth their book values, then a company could sell its assets, pay off its liabilities and preferred stock, and the remaining cash would belong to common stockholders. Therefore, common equity is sometimes called **net worth**—it's the assets net of the liabilities.

SELF-TEST QUESTIONS What is the balance sheet, and what information does it provide?
How is the order of the information shown on the balance sheet determined?
Why might a company's December 31 balance sheet differ from its June 30 balance sheet?

THE INCOME STATEMENT

Table 3-2 gives the **income statements** for MicroDrive, which show its financial performance over each of the last two years. Income statements can cover any period of time, but they are usually prepared monthly, quarterly, and annually. Unlike the balance sheet, which is a snapshot of a firm at a point in time, the income statement reflects performance during the period.

Subtracting operating costs from net sales, but excluding depreciation and amortization, results in **EBITDA**, which stands for earnings before interest, taxes, depreciation,

---

[2] This is called *accrual accounting,* which attempts to match revenues to the periods in which they are earned and expenses to the periods in which the effort to generate income occurred. Students sometimes call this "a cruel rule" because it can be confusing.

[3] Companies sometimes break the total proceeds into two parts, one called "par" and the other called "paid-in-capital" or "capital surplus." For example, if a company sells shares of stock for $10, it might record $1 of par and $9 of paid-in-capital. For most purposes, the distinction between par and paid-in-capital is not important, and most companies use no-par stock.

TABLE 3-2	MicroDrive Inc.: Income Statements for Years Ending December 31 (Millions of Dollars, Except for Per-Share Data)		
		2005	2004
Net sales		$3,000.0	$2,850.0
Operating costs excluding depreciation and amortization		2,616.2	2,497.0
Earnings before interest, taxes, depreciation, and amortization (EBITDA)		$ 383.8	$ 353.0
Depreciation		100.0	90.0
Amortization		0.0	0.0
Depreciation and amortization		$ 100.0	$ 90.0
Earnings before interest and taxes (EBIT, or operating income)		$ 283.8	$ 263.0
Less interest		88.0	60.0
Earnings before taxes (EBT)		$ 195.8	$ 203.0
Taxes (40%)		78.3	81.2
Net income before preferred dividends		$ 117.5	$ 121.8
Preferred dividends		4.0	4.0
Net income		$ 113.5	$ 117.8
Common dividends		$ 57.5	$ 53.0
Addition to retained earnings		$ 56.0	$ 64.8
Per-Share Data			
Common stock price		$23.00	$26.00
Earnings per share (EPS)[a]		$ 2.27	$ 2.36
Dividends per share (DPS)[a]		$ 1.15	$ 1.06
Book value per share (BVPS)[a]		$17.92	$16.80
Cash flow per share (CFPS)[a]		$ 4.27	$ 4.16

[a] There are 50,000,000 shares of common stock outstanding. Note that EPS is based on earnings after preferred dividends—that is, on net income available to common stockholders. Calculations of the most recent EPS, DPS, BVPS, and CFPS are shown below.

$$\text{Earnings per share} = \text{EPS} = \frac{\text{Net income}}{\text{Common shares outstanding}} = \frac{\$113,500,000}{50,000,000} = \$2.27.$$

$$\text{Dividends per share} = \text{DPS} = \frac{\text{Dividends paid to common stockholders}}{\text{Common shares outstanding}} = \frac{\$57,500,000}{50,000,000} = \$1.15.$$

$$\text{Book value per share} = \text{BVPS} = \frac{\text{Total common equity}}{\text{Common shares outstanding}} = \frac{\$896,000,000}{50,000,000} = \$17.92.$$

$$\text{Cash flow per share} = \text{CFPS} = \frac{\text{Net income} + \text{Depreciation} + \text{Amortization}}{\text{Common shares outstanding}} = \frac{\$213,500,000}{50,000,000} = \$4.27.$$

and amortization. Depreciation and amortization are annual charges that reflect the estimated costs of the assets used up each year. Depreciation applies to tangible assets, such as plant and equipment, whereas amortization applies to intangible assets such as patents, copyrights, trademarks, and goodwill.[4] Because neither depreciation nor amortization is paid in cash, some analysts claim that EBITDA is a better measure of financial strength than is net income. However, as we show later in the chapter, EBITDA is not as important as free cash flow. In fact, some financial wags have stated that EBITDA really stands for "earnings before anything bad happens."

---

[4] The accounting treatment of goodwill resulting from mergers has changed in recent years. Rather than an annual charge, companies are required to periodically evaluate the value of goodwill and reduce net income only if the goodwill's value has decreased materially (become impaired, in the language of accountants). For example, in 2002 AOL Time Warner wrote off almost $100 billion associated with the AOL merger. It doesn't take too many $100 billion expenses to really hurt net income!

The net income available to common shareholders, which is revenues less expenses, taxes, and preferred dividends (but before paying common dividends), is generally referred to as **net income,** although it is also called **profit** or **earnings,** particularly in the news or financial press. Dividing net income by the number of shares outstanding gives earnings per share (EPS), which is often called "the bottom line." Throughout this book, unless otherwise indicated, net income means net income available to common stockholders.[5]

What is an income statement, and what information does it provide?

Why is earnings per share called "the bottom line"?

What is EBITDA?

Regarding the time period reported, how does the income statement differ from the balance sheet?

STATEMENT OF RETAINED EARNINGS

Table 3-3, the **statement of retained earnings,** shows that MicroDrive began 2005 with $710 million of retained earnings, that during the year it earned $113.5 million and paid out $57.5 in dividends, and that it plowed the difference, $56 million, back into the business. These "corporate savings" caused retained earnings to increase from $710 million at the end of 2004 to $766 million at the end of 2005.

Note that "retained earnings" represents a *claim against assets,* not an asset per se. In 2005 MicroDrive's stockholders allowed it to reinvest $56 million instead of distributing the money as dividends, and management spent this money on new assets. Thus, retained earnings as reported on the balance sheet does not represent cash and is not "available" for the payment of dividends or anything else.[6]

What is the statement of retained earnings, and what information does it provide?

Why do changes in retained earnings occur?

Explain why the following statement is true: "Retained earnings as reported on the balance sheet do not represent cash and are not 'available' for the payment of dividends or anything else."

NET CASH FLOW

Many financial analysts focus on **net cash flow.** A business's *net cash flow* generally differs from its **accounting** profit because some of the revenues and expenses listed on the income statement were not received or paid in cash during the year. The relationship between net cash flow and net income can be expressed as follows:

---

[5] Companies report "comprehensive income" as well as net income. Comprehensive income is equal to net income plus several comprehensive income items. One example of comprehensive income is the unrealized gain or loss that occurs when a marketable security, classified as available for sale, is marked-to-market. For our purposes, we assume that there are no comprehensive income items, so we present only basic income statements throughout the text. Although not required, some companies also report "pro forma income." For example, if a company incurs an expense that it doesn't expect to recur, such as closing a plant, it might calculate pro forma income as though it had not incurred the one-time expense. There are no hard and fast rules for calculating pro forma income, and companies report it on a voluntary basis. As a result, it is often subject to abuse, with many companies finding ingenious ways to make pro forma income higher than traditional income. The SEC and the Public Company Accounting Oversight Board (PCAOB) are taking steps to reduce deceptive uses of pro forma reporting.

[6] The amount reported in the retained earnings account is *not* an indication of the amount of cash the firm has. Cash (as of the balance sheet date) is found in the cash account, an asset account. A positive number in the retained earnings account indicates only that in the past the firm earned some income, but its dividends paid were less than its earnings. Even though a company reports record earnings and shows an increase in its retained earnings account, it still may be short of cash.

The same situation holds for individuals. You might own a new BMW (no loan), lots of clothes, and an expensive stereo, hence have a high net worth, but if you have only 23 cents in your pocket plus $5 in your checking account, you would still be short of cash.

e-resource

See *CF2 Ch 03
Tool Kit.xls* for
details.

TABLE 3-3	MicroDrive Inc.: Statement of Retained Earnings for Year Ending December 31, 2005 (Millions of Dollars)
Balance of retained earnings, December 31, 2004	$710.0
Add: Net income, 2005	113.5
Less: Dividends to common stockholders	(57.5)[a]
Balance of retained earnings, December 31, 2005	$766.0

[a]Here, and throughout the book, parentheses are used to denote negative numbers.

$$\text{Net cash flow} = \text{Net income} - \text{Noncash revenues} + \text{Noncash charges.} \quad (3\text{-}1)$$

The primary examples of noncash charges are depreciation and amortization. These items reduce net income but are not paid out in cash, so we add them back to net income when calculating net cash flow. Another example of a noncash charge is deferred taxes. In some instances, companies are allowed to defer tax payments to a later date even though the tax payment is reported as an expense on the income statement. Therefore, deferred tax payments would be added to net income when calculating net cash flow.[7] At the same time, some revenues may not be collected in cash during the year, and these items must be subtracted from net income when calculating net cash flow.

Typically, depreciation and amortization are by far the largest noncash items, and in many cases the other noncash items roughly net out to zero. For this reason, many analysts assume that net cash flow equals net income plus depreciation and amortization:

$$\text{Net cash flow} = \text{Net income} + \text{Depreciation and amortization.} \quad (3\text{-}2)$$

To keep things simple, we will generally assume that Equation 3-2 holds. However, you should remember that Equation 3-2 will not accurately reflect net cash flow in those instances where there are significant noncash items beyond depreciation and amortization.

We can illustrate Equation 3-2 with 2005 data for MicroDrive taken from Table 3-2:

$$\text{Net cash flow} = \$113.5 + \$100.0 = \$213.5 \text{ million.}$$

To illustrate depreciation's effect, suppose a machine with a life of five years and a zero expected salvage value was purchased in 2004 for $100,000 and placed into service in 2005. This $100,000 cost is not expensed in the purchase year; rather, it is charged against production over the machine's five-year depreciable life. If the depreciation expense were not taken, profits would be overstated, and taxes would be too high. So, the annual depreciation charge is deducted from sales revenues, along with such other costs as labor and raw materials, to determine income. However, because the $100,000 was actually expended back in 2004, the depreciation charged against income in 2005 and subsequent years is not a cash outlay, as are labor or raw materials charges. *Depreciation is a noncash charge, so it must be added back to net income to obtain the net cash flow*. If we assume that all other noncash items (including amortization) sum to zero, then net cash flow is simply equal to net income plus depreciation.

SELF-TEST QUESTIONS

Differentiate between net cash flow and accounting profit.

In accounting, the emphasis is on net income. What is emphasized in finance, and why is that item emphasized?

Assuming that depreciation is its only noncash expense, how can someone calculate a business's net cash flow?

[7]Deferred taxes may arise, for example, if a company uses accelerated depreciation for tax purposes but straight-line depreciation for reporting its financial statements to investors.

FINANCIAL ANALYSIS ON THE INTERNET

A wide range of valuable financial information is available on the Internet. With just a couple of clicks, an investor can easily find the key financial statements for most publicly traded companies. Here's a partial (but by no means a complete) list of places you can go to get started:

- One of the very best sources of financial information is Thomson Financial. Go to the textbook's Web site, **http://ehrhardt.swlearning.com** and follow the directions to access Thomson ONE—Business School Edition. An especially useful feature is the ability to download up to ten years of financial statements in spreadsheet form. First, enter the ticker for a company and then click Go. From the top tab (in dark blue), select Financials. This will show a second row of items (in light blue). Selecting More from this row will reveal a drop-down menu. Select SEC Database Reports & Charts. This will bring up another drop-down menu which includes the ten-year balance sheets, income statements, and statement of cash flows. To download the financial statements into a spreadsheet, first select one of the statements, such as the 10YR Balance Sheet. The balance sheets will then be displayed on your browser page. To download, click on the *Excel* icon toward the right of the light blue row at the top of the Thomson ONE panel. This will bring up a dialog box that lets you download the *Excel* file to your computer.

- Try Yahoo's finance Web site, **http://finance .yahoo.com**. Here you will find updated market information along with links to a variety of interesting research sites. Enter a stock's ticker symbol, click GO, and you will see the stock's current price, along with recent news about the company. The panel on the left has links to key statistics, the company's income statement, balance sheet, statement of cash flows, and more. The Yahoo site also has a list of insider transactions, so you can tell if a company's CEO

and other key insiders are buying or selling their company's stock. In addition, there is a message board where investors share opinions about the company, and there is a link to the company's filings with the Securities and Exchange Commission (SEC). Note that, in most cases, a more complete list of the SEC filings can be found at **http://www.sec.gov**.

- Other sources for up-to-date market information are **http://money.cnn.com**, **http:// www.bloomberg.com**, and **http://www.cbs .marketwatch.com**. Each also has an area where you can obtain stock quotes along with company financials, links to Wall Street research, and links to SEC filings.

- Another good source is **http://www.quicken .com**. Enter the ticker symbol in the area labeled quotes and research. The site will take you to an area where you can find a link to the company's financial statements, along with analysts' earnings estimates and SEC filings.

- If you are looking for charts of key accounting variables (for example, sales, inventory, depreciation and amortization, and reported earnings), along with the financial statements, take a look at **http://www.smartmoney.com**.

- Another good place to look is **http://www .investor.reuters.com**. Here you find links to analysts' research reports along with the key financial statements.

- Two other places to consider: **http://www .hoovers.com** and **http://www.zacks.com**. Each has free research available along with more detailed information provided to subscribers.

Once you have accumulated all of this information, you may be looking for sites that provide opinions regarding the direction of the overall market and views regarding individual stocks. Two popular sites in this category are The Motley Fool's Web site, **http://www.fool.com**, and the Web site for The Street.com, **http://www.thestreet.com**.

STATEMENT OF CASH FLOWS

Even if a company reports a large net income during a year, the *amount of cash* reported on its year-end balance sheet may be the same or even lower than its beginning cash. The reason is that its net income can be used in a variety of ways, not just kept as cash in the bank. For example, the firm may use its net income to pay dividends, to increase inventories, to finance accounts receivable, to invest in fixed assets, to reduce debt, or to buy back common stock. Indeed, the company's *cash position* as reported on its balance sheet is affected by a great many factors, including the following:

1. **Net income before preferred dividends.** Other things held constant, a positive net income will lead to more cash in the bank. However, as we discuss below, other things generally are not held constant.
2. **Noncash adjustments to net income.** To calculate cash flow, it is necessary to adjust net income to reflect noncash revenues and expenses, such as depreciation and deferred taxes, as shown above in the calculation of net cash flow.
3. **Changes in working capital.** Increases in current assets other than cash, such as inventories and accounts receivable, decrease cash, whereas decreases in these accounts increase cash. For example, if inventories are to increase, the firm must use some of its cash to acquire the additional inventory. Conversely, if inventories decrease, this generally means the firm is selling inventories and not replacing all of them, hence generating cash. On the other hand, if payables increase, the firm has received additional credit from its suppliers, which saves cash, but if payables decrease, this means it has used cash to pay off its suppliers. Therefore, increases in current liabilities such as accounts payable increase cash, whereas decreases in current liabilities decrease cash.
4. **Fixed assets.** If a company invests in fixed assets, this will reduce its cash position. On the other hand, if it sells some fixed assets this will increase cash.
5. **Security transactions and dividend payments.** If a company issues stock or bonds during the year, the funds raised will increase its cash position. On the other hand, if the company uses cash to buy back outstanding stock or to pay off debt, or if it pays dividends to its shareholders, this will reduce cash.

Each of the above factors is reflected in the **statement of cash flows,** which summarizes the changes in a company's cash position. The statement separates activities into three categories, plus a summary section:

1. **Operating activities,** which includes net income, depreciation, changes in current assets and liabilities other than cash, short-term investments, and short-term debt.
2. **Investing activities,** which includes investments in or sales of fixed assets.
3. **Financing activities,** which includes raising cash by selling short-term investments or by issuing short-term debt, long-term debt, or stock. Also, because both dividends paid and cash used to buy back outstanding stock or bonds reduce the company's cash, such transactions are included here.

Accounting texts explain how to prepare the statement of cash flows, but the statement is used to help answer questions such as these: Is the firm generating enough cash to purchase the additional assets required for growth? Is the firm generating any extra cash that can be used to repay debt or to invest in new products? Such information is useful both for managers and investors, so the statement of cash flows is an important part of the annual report.

Table 3-4 shows MicroDrive's statement of cash flows as it would appear in the company's annual report. The top section shows cash generated by and used in operations—for MicroDrive, operations provided net cash flows of *minus* $2.5 million. This subtotal, the minus $2.5 million net cash flow provided by operating activities, is in many respects the most important figure in any of the financial statements. Profits as reported on the income statement can be "doctored" by such tactics as depreciating assets too slowly, not recognizing bad debts promptly, and the like. However, it is far more difficult to simultaneously doctor profits and the working capital accounts. Therefore, it is not uncommon for a company to report positive net income right up to the day it declares bankruptcy. In such cases, however, the net cash flow from operations almost always began to deteriorate much earlier, and analysts who kept an eye on cash flow could have predicted trouble. Therefore, if you are ever analyzing a company and are pressed for time, look first at the trend in net cash flow provided by operating activities, because it will tell you more than any other number.

e-resource

See **CF2 Ch 03 Tool Kit.xls** *for details.*

TABLE 3-4 | MicroDrive Inc.: Statement of Cash Flows for 2005 (Millions of Dollars)

	Cash Provided or Used
Operating Activities	
Net income before preferred dividends	$117.5
Adjustments:	
Noncash adjustments:	
Depreciation[a]	100.0
Due to changes in working capital:[b]	
Increase in accounts receivable	(60.0)
Increase in inventories	(200.0)
Increase in accounts payable	30.0
Increase in accruals	10.0
Net cash provided by operating activities	($ 2.5)
Long-Term Investing Activities	
Cash used to acquire fixed assets[c]	($230.0)
Financing Activities	
Sale of short-term investments	$ 65.0
Increase in notes payable	50.0
Increase in bonds outstanding	174.0
Payment of preferred and common dividends	(61.5)
Net cash provided by financing activities	$227.5
Summary	
Net change in cash	($ 5.0)
Cash at beginning of year	15.0
Cash at end of year	$ 10.0

[a]Depreciation is a noncash expense that was deducted when calculating net income. It must be added back to show the correct cash flow from operations.
[b]An increase in a current asset *decreases* cash. An increase in a current liability *increases* cash. For example, inventories increased by $200 million, so that reduced cash by a like amount.
[c]The net increase in fixed assets is $130 million; however, this net amount is after a deduction for the year's depreciation expense. Depreciation expense would have to be added back to find the increase in gross fixed assets. From the company's income statement, we see that the 2005 depreciation expense is $100 million; thus, expenditures on fixed assets were actually $230 million.

The second section shows long-term fixed-asset investing activities. MicroDrive purchased fixed assets totaling $230 million; this was the only long-term investment it made during 2005.

The third section, financing activities, includes borrowing from banks (notes payable), selling new bonds, and paying dividends on common and preferred stock. MicroDrive raised $289 million by borrowing and by selling off its short-term investments, but it paid $61.5 million in preferred and common dividends. Therefore, its net inflow of funds from financing activities was $227.5 million.

In the summary, where all of these sources and uses of cash are totaled, we see that MicroDrive's cash outflows exceeded its cash inflows by $5 million during 2005; that is, its net change in cash was a *negative* $5 million.

MicroDrive's statement of cash flows should be worrisome to its managers and to outside analysts. The company had a $2.5 million cash shortfall from operations, it spent an additional $230 million on new fixed assets, and it paid out another $61.5 million in dividends. It covered these cash outlays by borrowing heavily and by liquidating $65 million of short-term investments. Obviously, this situation cannot continue year after year, so something will have to be done. Later in the chapter we consider some of the actions MicroDrive's financial staff might recommend to ease the cash flow problem.

SELF-TEST QUESTIONS   What types of questions does the statement of cash flows answer?

Identify and briefly explain the three different categories of activities shown in the statement of cash flows.

MODIFYING ACCOUNTING DATA FOR MANAGERIAL DECISIONS

Thus far in the chapter we have focused on financial statements as they are presented in the annual report. However, these statements are designed more for use by creditors and tax collectors than for managers and stock analysts. Therefore, certain modifications are needed for use in corporate decision making. In the following sections we discuss how financial analysts combine stock prices and accounting data to make the statements more useful.

Operating Assets and Total Net Operating Capital

Different firms have different financial structures, different tax situations, and different amounts of nonoperating assets. These differences affect traditional accounting measures such as the rate of return on equity. They can cause two firms, or two divisions within a single firm, that actually have similar operations to appear to be operated with different efficiency. This is important, because if managerial compensation systems are to function properly, operating managers must be judged and compensated for those things that are under their control, not on the basis of things outside their control. Therefore, to judge managerial performance, we need to compare managers' ability to generate *operating income (EBIT)* with the *operating assets* under their control.

The first step in modifying the traditional accounting framework is to divide total assets into two categories, **operating assets,** which consist of the assets necessary to operate the business, and **nonoperating assets,** which would include cash and short-term investments above the level required for normal operations, investments in subsidiaries, land held for future use, and the like. Moreover, operating assets are further divided into **operating current assets,** such as inventory, and **long-term operating assets,** such as plant and equipment. Obviously, if a manager can generate a given amount of profit and cash flow with a relatively small investment in operating assets, then the amount of capital investors must put up is reduced and the rate of return on that capital increases.

Most capital used in a business is supplied by investors—stockholders, bondholders, and lenders such as banks. Investors must be paid for the use of their money, with payment coming as interest in the case of debt and as dividends plus capital gains in the case of stock. So, if a company buys more assets than it actually needs, and thus raises too much capital, then its capital costs will be unnecessarily high.

Must all of the capital used to acquire assets be obtained from investors? The answer is no, because some of the funds are provided as a normal consequence of operations. For example, some funds will come from suppliers and be reported as *accounts payable,* while other funds will come as *accrued wages and accrued taxes,* which amount to short-term loans from workers and tax authorities. Such funds are called **operating current liabilities.** Therefore, if a firm needs $100 million of assets, but it has $10 million of accounts payable and another $10 million of accrued wages and taxes, then its *investor-supplied capital* would be only $80 million.

Those current assets used in operations are called **operating working capital,** and operating working capital less operating current liabilities is called **net operating working capital.** Therefore, net operating working capital is the working capital acquired with investor-supplied funds. Here is the definition in equation form:

$$\text{Net operating} \atop \text{working capital} = {\text{Operating current} \atop \text{assets}} - {\text{Operating current} \atop \text{liabilities}}. \qquad \text{(3-3)}$$

Now think about how these concepts can be used in practice. First, all companies must carry some cash to "grease the wheels" of their operations. Companies continuously receive checks from customers and write checks to suppliers, employees, and so on. Because inflows and outflows do not coincide perfectly, a company must keep some cash in its bank account. In other words, some cash is required to conduct operations. The same is true for most other current assets, such as inventory and accounts receivable, which are required for normal operations. However, any short-term securities the firm holds generally result from investment decisions made by the treasurer, and they are not used in the core operations. Therefore, short-term investments are normally excluded when calculating net operating working capital.[8]

Some current liabilities—especially accounts payable and accruals—arise in the normal course of operations. Moreover, each dollar of such current liabilities is a dollar that the company does not have to raise from investors to acquire current assets. Therefore, to calculate net operating working capital, we deduct these operating current liabilities from the operating current assets. Other current liabilities that charge interest, such as notes payable to banks, are treated as investor-supplied capital and thus are not deducted when calculating net working capital.

If you are ever uncertain about an item, ask yourself whether it is a natural consequence of operations or if it is a discretionary choice, such as a particular method of financing, or an investment in a financial asset. If it is discretionary, it is not an operating asset or liability.

We can apply these definitions to MicroDrive, using the balance sheet data given in Table 3-1. Here is the net operating working capital for 2005:

$$
\begin{aligned}
\text{Net operating working capital} &= (\text{Cash} + \text{Accounts receivable} + \text{Inventories}) \\
&\quad - (\text{Accounts payable} + \text{Accruals}) \\
&= (\$10 + \$375 + \$615) - (\$60 + \$140) \\
&= \$800 \text{ million.}
\end{aligned}
$$

MicroDrive's total net operating capital at year-end 2005 was the sum of its net operating working capital and its operating long-term assets (which consist only of net plant and equipment):

$$
\begin{aligned}
\text{Total net operating capital} &= (\text{Net operating working capital}) \\
&\quad + (\text{Operating long-term assets}) \qquad \text{(3-4)} \\
&= \$800 + \$1{,}000 \\
&= \$1{,}800 \text{ million.}
\end{aligned}
$$

---

[8] If the marketable securities are held as a substitute for cash, and therefore reduce the cash requirements, then they may be classified as part of operating working capital. Generally, though, large holdings of marketable securities are held as a reserve for some contingency or else as a temporary "parking place" for funds prior to an acquisition, a major capital investment program, or the like.

For the previous year, net operating working capital was

$$\text{Net operating working capital} = (\$15 + \$315 + \$415) - (\$30 + \$130)$$
$$= \$585 \text{ million.}$$

Adding the $870 million of fixed assets, its total operating capital at year-end 2004 was

$$\text{Total net operating capital} = \$585 + \$870$$
$$= \$1,455 \text{ million.}$$

Notice that we have defined total net operating capital as the sum of net operating working capital and operating long-term assets. In other words, our definition is in terms of operating assets and liabilities. However, we can also calculate total net operating capital by adding up the funds provided by investors, such as notes payable, long-term bonds, preferred stock, and common stock. For MicroDrive, the total capital provided by investors at year-end 2004 was $60 + $580 + $40 + $840 = $1,520 million. Of this amount, $65 million was tied up in short-term investments, which are not directly related to MicroDrive's operations. Therefore, only $1,520 − $65 = $1,455 million of investor-supplied capital was used in operations. Notice that this is exactly the same value as calculated above. This shows that we can calculate total net operating capital either from net operating working capital and operating long-term assets or from the investor-supplied funds. We usually base our calculations upon the first definition since it is possible to perform this calculation for a division, whereas it is not possible to do so using the definition based on investor-supplied capital.

We use the terms total net operating capital, operating capital, net operating assets, and capital to mean the same thing. Unless we specifically say "investor-supplied capital," we are referring to total net operating capital.

MicroDrive increased its operating capital to $1,800 from $1,455 million, or by $345 million, during 2005. Furthermore, most of this increase went into working capital, which rose from $585 to $800 million, or by $215 million. This 37 percent increase in net operating working capital versus a sales increase of only 5 percent (from $2,850 to $3,000 million) should set off warning bells in your head: Why did MicroDrive tie up so much additional cash in working capital? Is the company gearing up for a big increase in sales, or are inventories not moving and receivables not being collected? We will address these questions in detail in Chapter 4, when we cover ratio analysis.

Net Operating Profit after Taxes (NOPAT)

If two companies have different amounts of debt, hence different amounts of interest charges, they could have identical operating performances but different net incomes—the one with more debt would have a lower net income. Net income is certainly important, but it does not always reflect the true performance of a company's operations or the effectiveness of its operating managers. A better measurement for comparing managers' performance is **net operating profit after taxes,** or **NOPAT,** which is the amount of profit a company would generate if it had no debt and held no financial assets. NOPAT is defined as follows:[9]

$$\text{NOPAT} = \text{EBIT}(1 - \text{Tax rate}). \qquad (3\text{-}5)$$

---

[9] For firms with a more complicated tax situation, it is better to define NOPAT as follows: NOPAT = (Net income before preferred dividends) + (Net interest expense)(1 − Tax rate). Also, if firms are able to defer paying some of their taxes, perhaps by the use of accelerated depreciation, then NOPAT should be adjusted to reflect the taxes that the company actually paid on its operating income. See P. Daves, M. Ehrhardt, and R. Shrieves, *Corporate Valuation: A Guide for Managers and Investors* (Mason, OH: Thomson South-Western, 2004) for a detailed explanation of these and other adjustments.

FINANCIAL BAMBOOZLING: HOW TO SPOT IT

Recent accounting frauds by Enron, WorldCom, Xerox, Merck, Arthur Andersen, Tyco, and many others have shown that analysts can no longer blindly assume that a firm's published financial statements are the best representation of its financial position. Clearly, many companies were "pushing the envelope" if not outright lying in an effort to make their companies look better.

A recent *Fortune* article points out that there are only three basic ways to manipulate financial statements: moving earnings from the future to the present, avoiding taxes, or hiding debt. For example, suppose one telecom firm (think World-Com or Global Crossing) sold the right to use parts of its fiber-optic network for ten years to another telecom for $100 million. The seller would immediately record revenues of $100 million. The buyer, however, could spread the expense over ten years and report an expense of only $10 million this year. The buyer would simultaneously sell similar rights to the original seller for $100 million. This way, no cash changes hands, both companies report an extra $100 million in revenue, but each reports a cost of only $10 million. Thus, both companies "created" an extra $90 million in pre-tax profits, without doing anything. Of course, both companies will have to report an extra $10 million expense each year for the remaining nine years, but they have each boosted short-term profits and thus this year's executive bonuses. To boost earnings next year, all they have to do is play the same game, but on a bigger scale.

For hiding debt, it's hard to beat Enron's special purpose entities (SPEs). These SPEs owed hundreds of millions of dollars, and it turned out that Enron was responsible for this debt, even though it never showed up on Enron's financial statements.

How can you spot bamboozling? Here are some tips. When companies have lots of write-offs or charges for restructuring, it could be that they are planning on managing earnings in the future. In other words, they sandbag this year to pad next year's earnings. Beware of serial acquirers, especially if they use their own stock to buy other companies. This can increase reported earnings, but it often erodes value since the acquirer usually pays a large premium for the target. Watch out for companies that depreciate their assets much slower than others in the industry (this is shown in the financial statement's footnotes). This causes current earnings to look larger than their competitors, even though they aren't actually performing any better. Perhaps the best evidence of bamboozling is if earnings are consistently growing faster than cash flows, which almost always indicates a financial scam.

In response to these and other abuses, Congress passed the Sarbanes-Oxley Act of 2002. One of its provisions requires both the CEO and the CFO to sign a statement certifying that the "financial statements and disclosures fairly represent, in all material respects, the operations and financial condition" of the company. This will make it easier to haul off in handcuffs a CEO or CFO who has been misleading investors. Whether this will prevent future bamboozling remains to be seen.

Sources: Geoffrey Colvin, "Bamboozling: A Field Guide," *Fortune,* July 8, 2002, 51; and Shawn Tully, "Don't Get Burned," *Fortune,* February 18, 2002, 87–90.

Using data from the income statements of Table 3-2, MicroDrive's 2005 NOPAT is found to be

$$\text{NOPAT} = \$283.8(1 - 0.4) = \$283.8(0.6) = \$170.3 \text{ million.}$$

This means MicroDrive generated an after-tax operating profit of $170.3 million, a little better than its previous NOPAT of $263(0.6) = $157.8 million. However, the income statements in Table 3-2 show that MicroDrive's earnings per share actually declined. This decrease in EPS was caused by an increase in interest expense, and not by a decrease in operating profit. Moreover, the balance sheets in Table 3-1 show an increase in debt. But why did MicroDrive increase its debt? As we just saw, its investment in operating capital increased dramatically during 2005, and that increase was financed primarily with debt.

Free Cash Flow

Earlier in this chapter, we defined net cash flow as net income plus noncash adjustments, which typically means net income plus depreciation. Note, though, that cash flows cannot be maintained over time unless depreciated fixed assets are replaced, so management is not completely free to use net cash flows however it chooses. Therefore, we now define another term, **free cash flow (FCF)**, which is the cash flow actually available for distribution to investors *after the company has made all the investments in fixed assets and working capital necessary to sustain ongoing operations.*

When you studied income statements in accounting, the emphasis was probably on the firm's net income, which is its **accounting profit.** However, the value of a company's operations is determined by the stream of cash flows that the operations will generate now and in the future. To be more specific, the value of operations depends on all the future expected free cash flows (FCF), defined as after-tax operating profit minus the amount of new investment in working capital and fixed assets necessary to sustain the business. Thus, free cash flow represents the cash that is actually available for distribution to investors. *Therefore, the way for managers to make their companies more valuable is to increase free cash flow.*

Calculating Free Cash Flow

As shown earlier in the chapter, MicroDrive had $1,455 million of total net operating capital at the end of 2004, but $1,800 million at the end of 2005. Therefore, during 2005, it made a **net investment in operating capital** of

Net investment in operating capital = $1,800 − $1,455 = $345 million.

MicroDrive's free cash flow in 2005 was

$$\text{FCF} = \text{NOPAT} - \text{Net investment in operating capital} \qquad \text{(3-6)}$$

$$= \$170.3 - \$345$$
$$= -\$174.7 \text{ million.}$$

Net fixed assets rose from $870 to $1,000 million, or by $130 million. However, Micro-Drive reported $100 million of depreciation, so its gross investment in fixed assets was $130 + $100 = $230 million for the year. With this background, we find the **gross investment in operating capital** as follows:

$$\text{Gross investment} = \text{Net investment} + \text{Depreciation} \qquad \text{(3-7)}$$

$$= \$345 + \$100 = \$445 \text{ million.}$$

An algebraically equivalent expression for free cash flow is

$$\text{FCF} = (\text{NOPAT} + \text{Depreciation}) - \frac{\text{Gross investment}}{\text{in operating capital}} \qquad \text{(3-6a)}$$

$$= (\$170.3 + \$100) - \$445$$
$$= -\$174.7 \text{ million.}$$

The two equations are equivalent because depreciation is added to both NOPAT and net investment in Equation 3-6 to arrive at Equation 3-6a. We usually use Equation 3-6, because it saves us this step.

The Uses of FCF

Recall that free cash flow (FCF) is the amount of cash that is available for distribution to all investors, including both shareholders and debtholders. There are five good uses for FCF:

1. Pay interest to debtholders, keeping in mind that the net cost to the company is the after-tax interest expense.
2. Repay debtholders, that is, pay off some of the debt.
3. Pay dividends to shareholders.
4. Repurchase stock from shareholders.
5. Buy marketable securities or other nonoperating assets.

Recall that the company does not have to use FCF to acquire operating assets since, by definition, FCF already takes into account the purchase of all operating assets needed to support growth. Unfortunately, there is evidence to suggest that some companies with high FCF tend to make unnecessary investments that don't add value, such as paying too much to acquire some other company. Thus, high FCF can cause waste if managers fail to act in the best interest of shareholders. As discussed in Chapter 1, this is called an agency cost, since managers are hired as agents to act on behalf of stockholders. We discuss agency costs and ways to control them in Chapter 13, where we discuss value-based management and corporate governance, and in Chapter 14, where we discuss the choice of capital structure.

In practice, most companies combine these five uses in such a way that the net total is equal to FCF. For example, a company might pay interest and dividends, issue new debt, and also sell some of its marketable securities. Some of these activities are cash outflows (for example, paying interest and dividends) and some are cash inflows (for example, issuing debt and selling marketable securities), but the net cash flow from these five activities is equal to FCF.

FCF and Corporate Value

FCF is the amount of cash available for distribution to investors, and, as a result, the value of a company depends on the present value of its expected future FCFs, discounted at the company's weighted average cost of capital (WACC). Subsequent chapters will develop the tools needed to forecast FCFs and evaluate their risk. Chapter 13 ties all this together with a model that is used to calculate the value of a company. Even though you do not yet have all the tools to apply the model, it's important that you understand this basic concept: *FCF is the cash available for distribution to investors. Therefore, the value of a firm primarily depends on its expected future FCFs.*

Evaluating FCF, NOPAT, and Operating Capital

Even though MicroDrive had a positive NOPAT, its very high investment in operating assets resulted in a negative free cash flow. Because free cash flow is what is available for distribution to investors, not only was there nothing for investors, but investors actually had to provide *additional* money to keep the business going. Investors provided most of this new money as debt.

Is a negative free cash flow always bad? The answer is, "Not necessarily. It depends on why the free cash flow was negative." If FCF was negative because NOPAT was negative, that is a bad sign, because then the company is probably experiencing operating problems. However, many high-growth companies have positive NOPAT but negative free cash flow because they are making large investments in operating assets to support growth. There is nothing wrong with profitable growth, even if it causes negative cash flows.

One way to determine whether growth is profitable is by examining the **return on invested capital (ROIC)**, which is the ratio of NOPAT to total operating capital. If the ROIC exceeds the rate of return required by investors, then a negative free cash flow caused by high growth is nothing to worry about. Chapter 13 discusses this in detail.

To calculate the ROIC, we first calculate NOPAT and operating capital. The return on invested capital (ROIC) is a performance measure that indicates how much NOPAT is generated by each dollar of operating capital:

$$\text{ROIC} = \frac{\text{NOPAT}}{\text{Operating capital}}. \qquad \text{(3-8)}$$

If ROIC is greater than the rate of return investors require, which is the weighted average cost of capital (WACC), then the firm is adding value.

As noted earlier, a negative current FCF is not necessarily bad, provided it is due to high growth. For example, Home Depot had negative FCF due to its rapid growth, but it also had a very high ROIC, and this high ROIC resulted in a high market value for the stock.

MicroDrive had an ROIC in 2005 of 9.46 percent ($170.3/$1,800 = 0.0946). Is this enough to cover its cost of capital? We'll answer that question in the next section.

SELF-TEST QUESTIONS

What is net operating working capital? Why does it exclude most short-term investments and also notes payable?

What is total net operating capital? Why is it important for managers to calculate a company's capital requirements?

Why is NOPAT a better performance measure than net income?

What is free cash flow? Why is it important?

MVA AND EVA

Neither traditional accounting data nor the modified data discussed in the preceding section incorporates stock prices, even though the primary goal of management is to maximize the firm's stock price. Financial analysts have therefore developed two additional performance measures, MVA, or Market Value Added, and EVA, or Economic Value Added. These concepts are discussed in this section.[10]

Market Value Added (MVA)

The primary goal of most firms is to maximize shareholders' wealth. This goal obviously benefits shareholders, but it also helps to ensure that scarce resources are allocated efficiently, which benefits the economy. Shareholder wealth is maximized by maximizing the *difference* between the market value of the firm's stock and the amount of equity capital that was supplied by shareholders. This difference is called the **Market Value Added (MVA):**

For an updated estimate of Coca-Cola's MVA, go to http:// finance.yahoo.com, enter KO, and click GO. This shows the market value of equity, called Mkt Cap. To get the book value of equity, select Balance Sheet from the left panel.

$$\begin{aligned} \text{MVA} &= \text{Market value of stock} - \text{Equity capital supplied by shareholders} \\ &= (\text{Shares outstanding})(\text{Stock price}) - \text{Total common equity.} \end{aligned} \qquad \text{(3-9)}$$

To illustrate, consider Coca-Cola. In March 2004, its total market equity value was $123.0 billion, while its balance sheet showed that stockholders had put up only $14.1 billion. Thus, Coca-Cola's MVA was $123.0 − $14.1 = $108.9 billion. This $108.9 billion represents the difference between the money that Coca-Cola's stockholders have invested

---

[10] The concepts of EVA and MVA were developed by Joel Stern and Bennett Stewart, co-founders of the consulting firm Stern Stewart & Company. Stern Stewart copyrighted the terms "EVA" and "MVA," so other consulting firms have given other names to these values. Still, EVA and MVA are the terms most commonly used in practice.

in the corporation since its founding—including retained earnings—versus the cash they could get if they sold the business. The higher its MVA, the better the job management is doing for the firm's shareholders.

Sometimes MVA is defined as the total market value of the company minus the total amount of investor-supplied capital:

$$
\begin{aligned}
\text{MVA} &= \text{Total market value} - \text{Total capital} \\
&= (\text{Market value of stock} + \text{Market value of debt}) \\
&\quad - \text{Total capital.}
\end{aligned}
\tag{3-9a}
$$

For most companies, the total amount of investor-supplied capital is the sum of equity, debt, and preferred stock. We can calculate the total amount of investor-supplied capital directly from their reported values in the financial statements. The total market value of a company is the sum of the market values of common equity, debt, and preferred stock. It is easy to find the market value of equity, since stock prices are readily available, but it is not always easy to find the market value of debt. Hence, many analysts use the value of debt that is reported in the financial statements, or the debt's book value, as an estimate of its market value.

For Coca-Cola, the total amount of reported debt was about $5.4 billion, and Coca-Cola had no preferred stock. Using this as an estimate of the market value of debt, Coke's total market value was $123.0 + $5.4 = $128.4 billion. The total amount of investor-supplied funds was $14.1 + $5.4 = $19.5 billion. Using these total values, the MVA was $128.4 − $19.5 = $108.9 billion. Note that this is the same answer that we got using the previous definition of MVA. Both methods will give the same results if the market value of debt is approximately equal to its book value.

Economic Value Added (EVA)

Whereas MVA measures the effects of managerial actions since the very inception of a company, **Economic Value Added (EVA)** focuses on managerial effectiveness in a given year. The basic EVA formula is as follows:

$$
\begin{aligned}
\text{EVA} &= \text{Net operating profit after taxes (NOPAT)} \\
&\quad - \text{After-tax dollar cost of capital used to support operations} \\
&= \text{EBIT}(1 - \text{Tax rate}) - (\text{Total net operating capital})(\text{WACC}).
\end{aligned}
\tag{3-10}
$$

We can also calculate EVA in terms of ROIC:

$$
\text{EVA} = (\text{Operating capital})(\text{ROIC} - \text{WACC}).
\tag{3-10a}
$$

As this equation shows, a firm adds value—that is, has a positive EVA—if its ROIC is greater than its WACC. If WACC exceeds ROIC, then new investments in operating capital will reduce the firm's value.

EVA is an estimate of a business's true economic profit for the year, and it differs sharply from accounting profit.[11] EVA represents the residual income that remains after the cost of *all* capital, including equity capital, has been deducted, whereas accounting profit is determined without imposing a charge for equity capital. As we discuss in Chap-

---

[11] The most important reason EVA differs from accounting profit is that the cost of equity capital is deducted when EVA is calculated. Other factors that could lead to differences include adjustments that might be made to depreciation, to research and development costs, to inventory valuations, and so on. These other adjustments also can affect the calculation of investor supplied capital, which affects both EVA and MVA. See Stewart, *The Quest for Value*, listed in the Selected Additional References at the end of the chapter.

ter 9, equity capital has a cost, because funds provided by shareholders could have been invested elsewhere, where they would have earned a return. Shareholders give up the opportunity to invest elsewhere when they provide capital to the firm. The return they could earn elsewhere in investments of equal risk represents the cost of equity capital. This cost is an *opportunity cost* rather than an *accounting cost,* but it is quite real nevertheless.

Note that when calculating EVA we do not add back depreciation. Although it is not a cash expense, depreciation is a cost since worn-out assets must be replaced, and it is therefore deducted when determining both net income and EVA. Our calculation of EVA assumes that the true economic depreciation of the company's fixed assets exactly equals the depreciation used for accounting and tax purposes. If this were not the case, adjustments would have to be made to obtain a more accurate measure of EVA.

EVA measures the extent to which the firm has increased shareholder value. Therefore, if managers focus on EVA, this will help to ensure that they operate in a manner that is consistent with maximizing shareholder wealth. Note too that EVA can be determined for divisions as well as for the company as a whole, so it provides a useful basis for determining managerial performance at all levels. Consequently, EVA is being used by an increasing number of firms as the primary basis for determining managerial compensation.

Table 3-5 shows how MicroDrive's MVA and EVA are calculated. The stock price was $23 per share at year-end 2005, down from $26 per share the previous year. Its WACC, which is the percentage after-tax cost of capital, was 10.8 percent in 2004 and 11.0 percent in 2005, and its tax rate was 40 percent. Other data in Table 3-5 were given in the basic financial statements provided earlier in the chapter.

Note first that the lower stock price and the higher book value of equity (due to retaining earnings during 2005) combined to reduce the MVA. The 2005 MVA is still positive, but $460 − $254 = $206 million of stockholders' value was lost during the year.

e-resource

See CF2 Ch 03 Tool Kit.xls for details.

TABLE 3-5 | MVA and EVA for MicroDrive (Millions of Dollars)

	2005	2004
MVA Calculation		
Price per share	$ 23.0	$ 26.0
Number of shares (millions)	50.0	50.0
Market value of equity = Share price (number of shares)	$1,150.0	$1,300.0
Book value of equity	$ 896.0	$ 840.0
MVA = Market value − Book value	$ 254.0	$ 460.0
EVA Calculation		
EBIT	$ 283.8	$ 263.0
Tax rate	40%	40%
NOPAT = EBIT(1 − T)	$ 170.3	$ 157.8
Total investor-supplied operating capital[a]	$1,800.0	$1,455.0
Weighted average cost of capital, WACC (%)	11.0%	10.8%
Dollar cost of capital = Operating capital (WACC)	$ 198.0	$ 157.1
EVA = NOPAT − Capital cost	($ 27.7)	$ 0.7
ROIC = NOPAT/Operating capital	9.46%	10.85%
ROIC − Cost of capital = ROIC − WACC	(1.54%)	0.05%
EVA = (Operating capital)(ROIC − WACC)	($ 27.7)	$ 0.7

[a]Investor-supplied operating capital equals the sum of notes payable, long-term debt, preferred stock, and common equity, less short-term investments. It could also be calculated as total liabilities and equity minus accounts payable, accruals, and short-term investments. It is also equal to total net operating capital.

EVA for 2004 was just barely positive, and in 2005 it was negative. Operating income (NOPAT) rose, but EVA still declined, primarily because the amount of capital rose more sharply than NOPAT—by about 26 percent versus 8 percent—and the cost of this additional capital pulled EVA down.

Recall also that net income fell, but not nearly so dramatically as the decline in EVA. Net income does not reflect the amount of equity capital employed, but EVA does. Because of this omission, net income is not as useful as EVA for setting corporate goals and measuring managerial performance.

We will have more to say about both MVA and EVA later in the book, but we can close this section with two observations. First, there is a relationship between MVA and EVA, but it is not a direct one. If a company has a history of negative EVAs, then its MVA will probably be negative, and vice versa if it has a history of positive EVAs. However, the stock price, which is the key ingredient in the MVA calculation, depends more on expected future performance than on historical performance. Therefore, a company with a history of negative EVAs could have a positive MVA, provided investors expect a turnaround in the future.

The second observation is that when EVAs or MVAs are used to evaluate managerial performance as part of an incentive compensation program, EVA is the measure that is typically used. The reasons are (1) EVA shows the value added during a given year, whereas MVA reflects performance over the company's entire life, perhaps even including times before the current managers were born, and (2) EVA can be applied to individual divisions or other units of a large corporation, whereas MVA must be applied to the entire corporation.

SELF-TEST QUESTIONS	Define "Market Value Added (MVA)" and "Economic Value Added (EVA)." How does EVA differ from accounting profit?

THE FEDERAL INCOME TAX SYSTEM

H&R Block provides information for the current and next year at http://www.hrblock.com/taxes/tools/rate_tables.html. A Web site explaining federal tax law is http://www.taxsites.com. From this home page one can visit other sites that provide summaries of recent tax legislation or current information on corporate and individual tax rates. The official government site is http://www.irs.gov.

e-resource

See CF2 Ch 03 Tool Kit.xls for details.

The value of any financial asset (including stocks, bonds, and mortgages), as well as most real assets such as plants or even entire firms, depends on the stream of cash flows produced by the asset. Cash flows from an asset consist of *usable* income plus depreciation, and usable income means income *after taxes*. The following sections describe the key features of corporate and individual taxation.

Corporate Income Taxes

The corporate tax structure, shown in Table 3-6, is relatively simple. The **marginal tax rate** is the rate paid on the last dollar of income, while the **average tax rate** is the average

TABLE 3-6 | Corporate Tax Rates as of January 2004

If a Corporation's Taxable Income Is	It Pays This Amount on the Base of the Bracket	Plus This Percentage on the Excess over the Base	Average Tax Rate at Top of Bracket
Up to $50,000	$ 0	15%	15.0%
$50,000–$75,000	7,500	25	18.3
$75,000–$100,000	13,750	34	22.3
$100,000–$335,000	22,250	39	34.0
$335,000–$10,000,000	113,900	34	34.0
$10,000,000–$15,000,000	3,400,000	35	34.3
$15,000,000–$18,333,333	5,150,000	38	35.0
Over $18,333,333	$6,416,667	35	35.0

rate paid on all income. To illustrate, if a firm had $65,000 of taxable income, its tax bill would be

$$Taxes = \$7,500 + 0.25(\$65,000 - \$50,000)$$
$$= \$7,500 + \$3,750 = \$11,250.$$

Its marginal rate would be 25 percent, and its average tax rate would be $11,250/$65,000 = 17.3%. Note that corporate income above $18,333,333 has an average and marginal tax rate of 35 percent.[12]

INTEREST AND DIVIDEND INCOME RECEIVED BY A CORPORATION

Interest income received by a corporation is taxed as ordinary income at regular corporate tax rates. *However, 70 percent of the dividends received by one corporation from another is excluded from taxable income, while the remaining 30 percent is taxed at the ordinary tax rate.*[13] Thus, a corporation earning more than $18,333,333 and paying a 35 percent marginal tax rate would pay only $(0.30)(0.35) = 0.105 = 10.5\%$ of its dividend income as taxes, so its effective tax rate on dividends received would be 10.5 percent. If this firm had $10,000 in pre-tax dividend income, its after-tax dividend income would be $8,950:

$$\begin{aligned}\text{After-tax income} &= \text{Before-tax income} - \text{Taxes}\\ &= \text{Before-tax income} - (\text{Before-tax income})(\text{Effective tax rate})\\ &= \text{Before-tax income}(1 - \text{Effective tax rate})\\ &= \$10,000[1 - (0.30)(0.35)]\\ &= \$10,000(1 - 0.105) = \$10,000(0.895) = \$8,950.\end{aligned}$$

If the corporation pays its own after-tax income out to its stockholders as dividends, the income is ultimately subjected to *triple taxation:* (1) the original corporation is first taxed, (2) the second corporation is then taxed on the dividends it received, and (3) the individuals who receive the final dividends are taxed again. This is the reason for the 70 percent exclusion on intercorporate dividends.

If a corporation has surplus funds that can be invested in marketable securities, the tax factor favors investment in stocks, which pay dividends, rather than in bonds, which pay interest. For example, suppose GE had $100,000 to invest, and it could buy either bonds that paid interest of $8,000 per year or preferred stock that paid dividends of $7,000. GE is in the 35 percent tax bracket; therefore, its tax on the interest, if it bought bonds, would be $0.35(\$8,000) = \$2,800$, and its after-tax income would be $5,200. If it bought preferred (or common) stock, its tax would be $0.35[(0.30)(\$7,000)] = \$735$, and its after-tax

---

[12] Prior to 1987, many large, profitable corporations such as General Electric and Boeing paid no income taxes. The reasons for this were as follows: (1) expenses, especially depreciation, were defined differently for calculating taxable income than for reporting earnings to stockholders, so some companies reported positive profits to stockholders but losses—hence no taxes—to the Internal Revenue Service; and (2) some companies that did have tax liabilities used various tax credits to offset taxes that would otherwise have been payable. This situation was effectively eliminated in 1987.

The principal method used to eliminate this situation is the Alternative Minimum Tax (AMT). Under the AMT, both corporate and individual taxpayers must figure their taxes in two ways, the "regular" way and the AMT way, and then pay the higher of the two. The AMT is calculated as follows: (1) Figure your regular taxes. (2) Take your taxable income under the regular method and then add back certain items, especially income on certain municipal bonds, depreciation in excess of straight line depreciation, certain research and drilling costs, itemized or standard deductions (for individuals), and a number of other items. (3) The income determined in (2) is defined as AMT income, and it must then be multiplied by the AMT tax rate to determine the tax due under the AMT system. An individual or corporation must then pay the higher of the regular tax or the AMT tax. In 2004, there were two AMT tax rates for individuals (26 percent and 28 percent, depending on the level of AMT income and filing status). Most corporations have an AMT of 20 percent. However, there is no AMT for very small companies, defined as those that have had average sales of less than $7.5 million for the last three years.

[13] The size of the dividend exclusion actually depends on the degree of ownership. Corporations that own less than 20 percent of the stock of the dividend-paying company can exclude 70 percent of the dividends received; firms that own more than 20 percent but less than 80 percent can exclude 80 percent of the dividends; and firms that own more than 80 percent can exclude the entire dividend payment. We will, in general, assume a 70 percent dividend exclusion.

income would be $6,265. Other factors might lead GE to invest in bonds, but the tax factor certainly favors stock investments when the investor is a corporation.[14]

INTEREST AND DIVIDENDS PAID BY A CORPORATION A firm's operations can be financed with either debt or equity capital. If it uses debt, it must pay interest on this debt, whereas if it uses equity, it is expected to pay dividends to the equity investors (stockholders). The interest *paid* by a corporation is deducted from its operating income to obtain its taxable income, but dividends paid are not deductible. Therefore, a firm needs $1 of pre-tax income to pay $1 of interest, but if it is in the 40 percent federal-plus-state tax bracket, it must earn $1.67 of pre-tax income to pay $1 of dividends:

$$\frac{\text{Pre-tax income needed}}{\text{to pay \$1 of dividends}} = \frac{\$1}{1 - \text{Tax rate}} = \frac{\$1}{0.60} = \$1.67.$$

Working backward, if a company has $1.67 in pre-tax income, it must pay $0.67 in taxes [(0.4)($1.67) = $0.67]. This leaves it with after-tax income of $1.00.

Of course, it is generally not possible to finance exclusively with debt capital, and the risk of doing so would offset the benefits of the higher expected income. *Still, the fact that interest is a deductible expense has a profound effect on the way businesses are financed—our corporate tax system favors debt financing over equity financing.* This point is discussed in more detail in Chapters 9 and 14.

CORPORATE CAPITAL GAINS Before 1987, corporate long-term capital gains were taxed at lower rates than corporate ordinary income, so the situation was similar for corporations and individuals. Under current law, however, corporations' capital gains are taxed at the same rates as their operating income.

CORPORATE LOSS CARRY-BACK AND CARRY-FORWARD Ordinary corporate operating losses can be carried back (**carry-back**) to each of the preceding 2 years and forward (**carry-forward**) for the next 20 years and used to offset taxable income in those years. For example, an operating loss in 2005 could be carried back and used to reduce taxable income in 2003 and 2004, and forward, if necessary, and used in 2006, 2007, and so on, to the year 2025. After carrying back two years, any remaining loss is typically carried forward first to the next year, then to the one after that, and so on, until losses have been used up or the 20-year carry-forward limit has been reached.[15]

To illustrate, suppose Apex Corporation had $2 million of *pre-tax* profits (taxable income) in 2003 and 2004, and then, in 2005, Apex lost $12 million. Also, assume that Apex's federal-plus-state tax rate is 40 percent. As shown in Table 3-7, the company would use the carry-back feature to recompute its taxes for 2003, using $2 million of the 2005 operating losses to reduce the 2003 pre-tax profit to zero. This would permit it to recover the taxes paid in 2003. Therefore, in 2005 Apex would receive a refund of its 2003 taxes because of the loss experienced in 2005. Because $10 million of the unrecovered losses would still be available, Apex would repeat this procedure for 2004. Thus, in 2005 the company would pay zero taxes for 2005 and also would receive a refund for taxes paid in 2003 and 2004. Apex would still have $8 million of unrecovered losses to

---

[14] This illustration demonstrates why corporations favor investing in lower-yielding preferred stocks over higher-yielding bonds. When tax consequences are considered, the yield on the preferred stock, [1 − 0.35(0.30)] (7.0%) = 6.265%, is higher than the yield on the bond, (1 − 0.35)(8.0%) = 5.2%. Also, note that corporations are restricted in their use of borrowed funds to purchase other firms' preferred or common stocks. Without such restrictions, firms could engage in *tax arbitrage*, whereby the interest on borrowed funds reduces taxable income on a dollar-for-dollar basis, but taxable income is increased by only $0.30 per dollar of dividend income. Thus, current tax laws reduce the 70 percent dividend exclusion in proportion to the amount of borrowed funds used to purchase the stock.

[15] In the wake of the terrorist attacks on the World Trade Center and Pentagon on September 11, 2001, Congress temporarily changed the carry-back provision in the Tax Code. The new provision allows operating losses incurred in tax years ending in 2001 or 2002 to be carried back five years rather than the normal two years. This provision is set to expire before this edition goes to print, so we will use a two-year carry-back provision in all of the examples.

e-resource

See CF2 Ch 03 Tool Kit.xls for details.

TABLE 3-7	Apex Corporation: Calculation of $12 Million Loss Carry-Back and Amount Available for Carry-Forward		
	Past Year 2003	Past Year 2004	Current Year 2005
Original taxable income	$2,000,000	$2,000,000	−$12,000,000
Carry-back credit	2,000,000	2,000,000	
Adjusted profit	$ 0	$ 0	
Taxes previously paid (40%)	800,000	800,000	
Difference = Tax refund due	$ 800,000	$ 800,000	
Total tax refund received			$ 1,600,000
Amount of loss carry-forward available Current loss			−$12,000,000
Carry-back losses used			4,000,000
Carry-forward losses still available			−$ 8,000,000

carry forward, subject to the 20-year limit. This $8 million could be used to offset future taxable income. The purpose of this loss treatment is to avoid penalizing corporations whose incomes fluctuate substantially from year to year.

IMPROPER ACCUMULATION TO AVOID PAYMENT OF DIVIDENDS Corporations could refrain from paying dividends and thus permit their stockholders to avoid personal income taxes on dividends. To prevent this, the Tax Code contains an **improper accumulation** provision that states that earnings accumulated by a corporation are subject to penalty rates *if the purpose of the accumulation is to enable stockholders to avoid personal income taxes*. A cumulative total of $250,000 (the balance sheet item "retained earnings") is by law exempted from the improper accumulation tax for most corporations. This is a benefit primarily to small corporations.

The improper accumulation penalty applies only if the retained earnings in excess of $250,000 are *shown by the IRS to be unnecessary to meet the reasonable needs of the business*. A great many companies do indeed have legitimate reasons for retaining more than $250,000 of earnings. For example, earnings may be retained and used to pay off debt, to finance growth, or to provide the corporation with a cushion against possible cash drains caused by losses. How much a firm should be allowed to accumulate for uncertain contingencies is a matter of judgment. We shall consider this matter again in Chapter 15, which deals with corporate dividend policy.

CONSOLIDATED CORPORATE TAX RETURNS If a corporation owns 80 percent or more of another corporation's stock, it can aggregate income and file one consolidated tax return; thus, the losses of one company can be used to offset the profits of another. (Similarly, one division's losses can be used to offset another division's profits.) No business ever wants to incur losses (you can go broke losing $1 to save 35¢ in taxes), but tax offsets do help make it more feasible for large, multidivisional corporations to undertake risky new ventures or ventures that will suffer losses during a developmental period.

TAXES ON OVERSEAS INCOME Many U.S. corporations have overseas subsidiaries, and those subsidiaries must pay taxes in the countries where they operate. Often, foreign tax rates are lower than U.S. rates. As long as foreign earnings are reinvested overseas, no U.S. tax is due on those earnings. However, when foreign earnings are repatriated to the U.S. parent, they are taxed at the applicable U.S. rate, less a credit for taxes paid to the foreign country. As a result, U.S. corporations such as IBM, Coca-Cola, and Microsoft have been able to defer billions of dollars of taxes. This procedure has stimulated overseas investments by U.S. multinational firms—they can continue the deferral indefinitely, but only if they reinvest the earnings in their overseas operations.[16]

Taxation of Small Businesses: S Corporations

The Tax Code provides that small businesses that meet certain restrictions as spelled out in the code may be set up as corporations and thus receive the benefits of the corporate form of organization—especially limited liability—yet still be taxed as proprietorships or partnerships rather than as corporations. These corporations are called **S corporations.** ("Regular" corporations are called C corporations.) If a corporation elects S corporation status for tax purposes, all of the business's income is reported as personal income by its stockholders, on a pro rata basis, and thus is taxed at the rates that apply to individuals. This is an important benefit to the owners of small corporations in which all or most of the income earned each year will be distributed as dividends, because then the income is taxed only once, at the individual level.

Personal Taxes

e-resource

See the Chapter 3 Web Extension for details.

The Web Extension to this chapter provides a more detailed treatment of individual taxation, but the key elements are presented here. **Ordinary income** consists primarily of wages or profits from a proprietorship or partnership, plus investment income. For the 2004 tax year, individuals with less than $7,150 of taxable income are subject to a federal income tax rate of 10 percent. For those with higher income, tax rates increase and go up to 35 percent, depending on the level of income. This is called a **progressive tax,** because the higher one's income, the larger the percentage paid in taxes.

As noted above, individuals are taxed on investment income as well as earned income, but with a few exceptions and modifications. For example, interest received from most state and local government bonds, called **municipals** or **"munis,"** is not subject to federal taxation. However, interest earned on most other bonds or lending is taxed as ordinary income. This means that a lower-yielding muni can provide the same after-tax return as a higher-yielding corporate bond. For a taxpayer in the 35 percent marginal tax bracket, a muni yielding 5.5 percent provides the same after-tax return as a corporate bond with a pre-tax yield of 8.46 percent: $8.46\%(1 - 0.35) = 5.5\%$.

Assets such as stocks, bonds, and real estate are defined as capital assets. If you own a capital asset and its price goes up, then your wealth increases, but you are not liable for any taxes on your increased wealth until you sell the asset. If you sell the asset for more than you originally paid, the profit is called a **capital gain;** if you sell it for less, then you suffer a **capital loss.** The length of time you owned the asset determines the tax treatment. If held for less than one year, then your gain or loss is simply added to your other ordinary income. If held for more than a year, then gains are called *long-term capital gains* and are taxed at a lower rate. See the Chapter 3 Web Extension for details, but the long-term capital gains rate is 15 percent for most situations.

Under the 2003 tax law changes, dividends are now taxed as though they were capital gains. As stated earlier, corporations may deduct interest payments, but not dividends when computing their corporate tax liability, which means that dividends are taxed twice, once at the corporate level and again at the personal level. This differential treatment motivates corporations to use debt relatively heavily, and to pay small (or even no) dividends. The 2003 tax law did not eliminate the differential treatment of dividends and interest payments from the corporate perspective, but it did make the tax treatment of dividends more similar to that of capital gains from investors' perspectives. To see this,

---

[16] This is a contentious political issue. U.S. corporations argue that our tax system is similar to systems in the rest of the world, and if they were taxed immediately on all overseas earnings they would be at a competitive disadvantage vis-á-vis their global competitors. Others argue that taxation encourages overseas investments at the expense of domestic investments, contributing to the jobs outsourcing problem and also to the federal budget deficit.

consider a company that doesn't pay a dividend but instead reinvests the cash it could have paid. The company's stock price should increase, leading to a capital gain, which would be taxed at the same rate as the dividend. Of course, the stock price appreciation isn't actually taxed until the stock is sold, whereas the dividend is taxed in the year it is paid, so dividends will still be more costly than capital gains for many investors.

Finally, note that the income of both S corporations and noncorporate businesses is reported as income by the firms' owners. Since there are far more S corporations, partnerships, and proprietorships than C corporations (which are subject to the corporate tax), individual tax considerations play an important role in business finance.

SELF-TEST QUESTIONS	Explain what is meant by this statement: "Our tax rates are progressive."
	Explain the difference between marginal tax rates and average tax rates.
	What is a "municipal bond," and how are these bonds taxed?
	What are capital gains and losses, and how are they taxed?
	How does the federal income tax system treat dividends received by a corporation versus those received by an individual?
	What is the difference in the tax treatment of interest and dividends paid by a corporation? Does this factor favor debt or equity financing?
	Briefly explain how tax loss carry-back and carry-forward procedures work.

SUMMARY

The primary purposes of this chapter were (1) to describe the basic financial statements, (2) to present some background information on cash flows, and (3) to provide an overview of the federal income tax system. The key concepts covered are listed below.

- The four basic statements contained in the **annual report** are the balance sheet, the income statement, the statement of retained earnings, and the statement of cash flows. Investors use the information provided in these statements to form expectations about the future levels of earnings and dividends, and about the firm's riskiness.
- The **balance sheet** shows assets on the left-hand side and liabilities and equity, or claims against assets, on the right-hand side. (Sometimes assets are shown at the top and claims at the bottom of the balance sheet.) The balance sheet may be thought of as a snapshot of the firm's financial position at a particular point in time.
- The **income statement** reports the results of operations over a period of time, and it shows earnings per share as its "bottom line."
- The **statement of retained earnings** shows the change in retained earnings between balance sheet dates. Retained earnings represent a claim against assets, not assets per se.
- The **statement of cash flows** reports the effect of operating, investing, and financing activities on cash flows over an accounting period.
- **Net cash flow** differs from **accounting profit** because some of the revenues and expenses reflected in accounting profits may not have been received or paid out in cash during the year. Depreciation is typically the largest noncash item, so net cash flow is often expressed as net income plus depreciation. Investors are at least as interested in a firm's projected net cash flow as in reported earnings because it is cash, not paper profit, that is paid out as dividends and plowed back into the business to produce growth.
- **Operating current assets** are the current assets that are used to support operations, such as cash, inventory, and accounts receivable. They do not include short-term investments.
- **Operating current liabilities** are the current liabilities that occur as a natural consequence of operations, such as accounts payable and accruals. They do not include notes payable or any other short-term debts that charge interest.

- **Net operating working capital** is the difference between operating current assets and operating current liabilities. Thus, it is the working capital acquired with investor-supplied funds.
- **Operating long-term assets** are the long-term assets used to support operations, such as net plant and equipment. They do not include any long-term investments that pay interest or dividends.
- **Total net operating capital** (which means the same as **operating capital** and **net operating assets**) is the sum of net operating working capital and operating long-term assets. It is the total amount of capital needed to run the business.
- **NOPAT** is net operating profit after taxes. It is the after-tax profit a company would have if it had no debt and no investments in nonoperating assets. Because it excludes the effects of financial decisions, it is a better measure of operating performance than is net income.
- **Free cash flow (FCF)** is the amount of cash flow remaining after a company makes the asset investments necessary to support operations. In other words, FCF is the amount of cash flow available for distribution to investors, *so the value of a company is directly related to its ability to generate free cash flow*. It is defined as NOPAT minus the net investment in operating capital.
- **Market Value Added (MVA)** represents the difference between the total market value of a firm and the total amount of investor-supplied capital. If the market values of debt and preferred stock equal their values as reported on the financial statements, then MVA is the difference between the market value of a firm's stock and the amount of equity its shareholders have supplied.
- **Economic Value Added (EVA)** is the difference between after-tax operating profit and the total dollar cost of capital, including the cost of equity capital. EVA is an estimate of the value created by management during the year, and it differs substantially from accounting profit because no charge for the use of equity capital is reflected in accounting profit.
- The value of any asset depends on the stream of **after-tax cash flows** it produces. Tax rates and other aspects of our tax system are changed by Congress every year or so.
- Interest income received by a corporation is taxed as **ordinary income;** however, 70 percent of the dividends received by one corporation from another are excluded from **taxable income.**
- Because interest paid by a corporation is a **deductible** expense while dividends are not, our tax system favors debt over equity financing.
- Ordinary corporate operating losses can be **carried back** to each of the preceding 2 years and **forward** for the next 20 years and used to offset taxable income in those years.
- **S corporations** are small businesses that have the limited-liability benefits of the corporate form of organization yet are taxed as a partnership or a proprietorship.
- In the United States, tax rates are **progressive**—the higher one's income, the larger the percentage paid in taxes.
- Assets such as stocks, bonds, and real estate are defined as **capital assets**. If a capital asset is sold for more than its cost, the profit is called a **capital gain**. If the asset is sold for a loss, it is called a **capital loss**. Assets held for more than a year provide **long-term** gains or losses.
- Dividends are taxed as though they were capital gains.

QUESTIONS

(3-1) Define each of the following terms:
   a. Annual report; balance sheet; income statement
   b. Common stockholders' equity, or net worth; retained earnings

c. Statement of retained earnings; statement of cash flows
d. Depreciation; amortization; EBITDA
e. Operating current assets; operating current liabilities; net operating working capital; total net operating capital
f. Accounting profit; net cash flow; NOPAT; free cash flow
g. Market Value Added; Economic Value Added
h. Progressive tax; taxable income; marginal and average tax rates
i. Capital gain or loss; tax loss carry-back and carry-forward
j. Improper accumulation; S corporation

(3-2) What four statements are contained in most annual reports?

(3-3) If a "typical" firm reports $20 million of retained earnings on its balance sheet, could its directors declare a $20 million cash dividend without any qualms whatsoever?

(3-4) Explain the following statement: "While the balance sheet can be thought of as a snapshot of the firm's financial position *at a point in time*, the income statement reports on operations *over a period of time*."

(3-5) What is operating capital, and why is it important?

(3-6) Explain the difference between NOPAT and net income. Which is a better measure of the performance of a company's operations?

(3-7) What is free cash flow? Why is it the most important measure of cash flow?

(3-8) If you were starting a business, what tax considerations might cause you to prefer to set it up as a proprietorship or a partnership rather than as a corporation?

SELF-TEST PROBLEM   Solution Appears in Appendix A

(ST-1)
Net Income, Cash Flow, and EVA
Last year Rattner Robotics had $5,000,000 in operating income (EBIT). The company had a net depreciation expense of $1,000,000 and an interest expense of $1,000,000; its corporate tax rate was 40 percent. The company has $14,000,000 in operating current assets and $4,000,000 in operating current liabilities; it has $15,000,000 in net plant and equipment. It estimates that it has an after-tax cost of capital of 10 percent. Assume that Rattner's only noncash item was depreciation.
a. What was the company's net income for the year?
b. What was the company's net cash flow?
c. What was the company's net operating profit after taxes (NOPAT)?
d. If capital in the previous year was $24,000,000, what was the company's free cash flow (FCF) for the year?
e. What was the company's Economic Value Added (EVA)?

PROBLEMS

Note: By the time this book is published, Congress might have changed rates and/or other provisions of current tax law—as noted in the chapter, such changes occur fairly often. Work all problems on the assumption that the information in the chapter is applicable.

(3-1)
Personal After-Tax Yield
An investor recently purchased a corporate bond which yields 9 percent. The investor is in the 36 percent combined federal and state tax bracket. What is the bond's after-tax yield?

(3-2)
Personal After-Tax Yield
Corporate bonds issued by Johnson Corporation currently yield 8 percent. Municipal bonds of equal risk currently yield 6 percent. At what tax rate would an investor be indifferent between these two bonds?

(3-3)
Corporate Tax Liability
The Talley Corporation had a taxable income of $365,000 from operations after all operating costs but before (1) interest charges of $50,000, (2) dividends received of $15,000, (3) dividends paid of $25,000, and (4) income taxes. What is the firm's income tax liability and its after-tax income? What are the company's marginal and average tax rates on taxable income?

(3-4)
Corporate Tax Liability
The Wendt Corporation had $10.5 million of taxable income.
a. What is the company's federal income tax bill for the year?
b. Assume the firm receives an additional $1 million of interest income from some bonds it owns. What is the tax on this interest income?
c. Now assume that Wendt does not receive the interest income but does receive an additional $1 million as dividends on some stock it owns. What is the tax on this dividend income?

(3-5)
Corporate After-Tax Yield
The Shrieves Corporation has $10,000 that it plans to invest in marketable securities. It is choosing among AT&T bonds, which yield 7.5 percent, state of Florida muni bonds, which yield 5 percent, and AT&T preferred stock, with a dividend yield of 6 percent. Shrieves's corporate tax rate is 35 percent, and 70 percent of the dividends received are tax exempt. Assuming that the investments are equally risky and that Shrieves chooses strictly on the basis of after-tax returns, which security should be selected? What is the after-tax rate of return on the highest-yielding security?

(3-6)
Cash Flow
The Klaven Corporation has operating income (EBIT) of $750,000. The company's depreciation expense is $200,000. Klaven is 100 percent equity financed, and it faces a 40 percent tax rate. What is the company's net income? What is its net cash flow?

(3-7)
Income and Cash Flow Analysis
The Menendez Corporation expects to have sales of $12 million. Costs other than depreciation are expected to be 75 percent of sales, and depreciation is expected to be $1.5 million. All sales revenues will be collected in cash, and costs other than depreciation must be paid for during the year. Menendez's federal-plus-state tax rate is 40 percent.
a. Set up an income statement. What is Menendez's expected net cash flow?
b. Suppose Congress changed the tax laws so that Menendez's depreciation expenses doubled. No changes in operations occurred. What would happen to reported profit and to net cash flow?
c. Now suppose that Congress, instead of doubling Menendez's depreciation, reduced it by 50 percent. How would profit and net cash flow be affected?
d. If this were your company, would you prefer Congress to cause your depreciation expense to be doubled or halved? Why?

(3-8)
Free Cash Flow
You have just obtained financial information for the past 2 years for Powell Panther Corporation. Answer the following questions.
a. What is the net operating profit after taxes (NOPAT) for 2005?
b. What are the amounts of net operating working capital for both years?
c. What are the amounts of total net operating capital for both years?
d. What is the free cash flow for 2005?
e. How can you explain the large increase in dividends in 2005?

Powell Panther Corporation: Income Statements for Year Ending December 31 (Millions of Dollars)

	2005	2004
Sales	$1,200.0	$1,000.0
Operating costs excluding depreciation	1,020.0	850.0
Depreciation	30.0	25.0
Earnings before interest and taxes	$ 150.0	$ 125.0
Less interest	21.7	20.2
Earnings before taxes	$ 128.3	$ 104.8
Taxes (40%)	51.3	41.9
Net income available to common stockholders	$ 77.0	$ 62.9
Common dividends	60.5	4.4

Powell Panther Corporation: Balance Sheets as of December 31 (Millions of Dollars)

	2005	2004
Assets		
Cash and equivalents	$ 12.0	$ 10.0
Short-term investments	0.0	0.0
Accounts receivable	180.0	150.0
Inventories	180.0	200.0
Total current assets	$372.0	$360.0
Net plant and equipment	300.0	250.0
Total assets	$672.0	$610.0
Liabilities and Equity		
Accounts payable	$108.0	$ 90.0
Notes payable	67.0	51.5
Accruals	72.0	60.0
Total current liabilities	$247.0	$201.5
Long-term bonds	150.0	150.0
Total liabilities	$397.0	$351.5
Common stock (50 million shares)	50.0	50.0
Retained earnings	225.0	208.5
Common equity	$275.0	$258.5
Total liabilities and equity	$672.0	$610.0

(3-9)
Loss Carry-Back,
Carry-Forward
The Herrmann Company has made $150,000 before taxes during each of the last 15 years, and it expects to make $150,000 a year before taxes in the future. However, in 2005 the firm incurred a loss of $650,000. The firm will claim a tax credit at the time it files its 2005 income tax return, and it will receive a check from the U.S. Treasury. Show how it calculates this credit, and then indicate the firm's tax liability for each of the next 5 years. Assume a 40 percent tax rate on *all* income to ease the calculations.

SPREADSHEET PROBLEM

(3-10)
Build a Model: Financial
Statements, EVA, and MVA
Start with the partial model in the file *CF2 Ch 03 P10 Build a Model.xls* from the textbook's Web site. Cumberland Industries' most recent balance sheets (in thousands of dollars) are shown below and in the partial model in the file:

e-resource

	2005	2004
Cash	$ 91,450	$ 74,625
Short-term investments	11,400	15,100
Accounts receivable	103,365	85,527
Inventories	38,444	34,982
Total current assets	$244,659	$210,234
Net fixed assets	67,165	42,436
Total assets	$311,824	$252,670
Accounts payable	$ 30,761	$ 23,109
Accruals	30,477	22,656
Notes payable	16,717	14,217
Total current liabilities	$ 77,955	$ 59,982
Long-term debt	76,264	63,914
Total liabilities	$154,219	$123,896

	2005	2004
Common stock	100,000	90,000
Retained earnings	57,605	38,774
Total common equity	$157,605	$128,774
Total liabilities and equity	$311,824	$252,670

a. The company's sales for 2005 were $455,150,000, and EBITDA was 15 percent of sales. Furthermore, depreciation amounted to 11 percent of net fixed assets, interest charges were $8,575,000, the state-plus-federal corporate tax rate was 40 percent, and Cumberland pays 40 percent of its net income out in dividends. Given this information, construct Cumberland's 2005 income statement. (Hint: Start with the partial model in the file.)

b. Next, construct the firm's statement of retained earnings for the year ending December 31, 2005, and then its 2005 statement of cash flows.

c. Calculate net operating working capital, total net operating capital, net operating profit after taxes, and free cash flow for 2005.

d. Calculate the firm's EVA and MVA for 2005. Assume that Cumberland had 10 million shares outstanding, that the year-end closing stock price was $17.25 per share, and its after-tax cost of capital (WACC) was 12 percent.

CYBERPROBLEM

Please go to our Web site, **http://ehrhardt.swlearning.com**, to access any Cyberproblems.

THOMSON ONE
Business School Edition

Please go to **http://ehrhardt.swlearning.com** to access any Thomson ONE—Business School Edition problems.

MINI CASE

Donna Jamison, a graduate of the University of Tennessee with four years of banking experience, was recently brought in as assistant to the chairman of the board of Computron Industries, a manufacturer of electronic calculators.

The company doubled its plant capacity, opened new sales offices outside its home territory, and launched an expensive advertising campaign. Computron's results were not satisfactory, to put it mildly. Its board of directors, which consisted of its president and vice-president plus its major stockholders (who were all local businesspeople), was most upset when directors learned how the expansion was going. Suppliers were being paid late and were unhappy, and the bank was complaining about the deteriorating situation and threatening to cut off credit. As a result, Al Watkins, Computron's president, was informed that changes would have to be made, and quickly, or he would be fired. Also, at the board's insistence Donna Jamison was brought in and given the job of assistant to Fred Campo, a retired banker who was Computron's chairman and largest stockholder. Campo agreed to give up a few of his golfing days and to help nurse the company back to health, with Jamison's help.

Jamison began by gathering financial statements and other data.

	2004	2005
BALANCE SHEETS		
Assets		
Cash	$ 9,000	$ 7,282
Short-term investments	48,600	20,000
Accounts receivable	351,200	632,160

	2004	2005
Inventories	715,200	1,287,360
Total current assets	$1,124,000	$1,946,802
Gross fixed assets	491,000	1,202,950
Less: Accumulated depreciation	146,200	263,160
Net fixed assets	$ 344,800	$ 939,790
Total assets	$1,468,800	$2,886,592

Liabilities and Equity		
Accounts payable	$ 145,600	$ 324,000
Notes payable	200,000	720,000
Accruals	136,000	284,960
Total current liabilities	$ 481,600	$1,328,960
Long-term debt	323,432	1,000,000
Common stock (100,000 shares)	460,000	460,000
Retained earnings	203,768	97,632
Total equity	$ 663,768	$ 557,632
Total liabilities and equity	$1,468,800	$2,886,592

INCOME STATEMENTS

Sales	$3,432,000	$5,834,400
Cost of goods sold	2,864,000	4,980,000
Other expenses	340,000	720,000
Depreciation	18,900	116,960
Total operating costs	$3,222,900	$5,816,960
EBIT	$ 209,100	$ 17,440
Interest expense	62,500	176,000
EBT	$ 146,600	$ (158,560)
Taxes (40%)	58,640	(63,424)
Net income	$ 87,960	$ (95,136)

OTHER DATA

Stock price	$ 8.50	$ 6.00
Shares outstanding	100,000	100,000
EPS	$ 0.880	$ (0.951)
DPS	$ 0.220	$ 0.110
Tax rate	40%	40%

STATEMENT OF RETAINED EARNINGS, 2005

Balance of retained earnings, 12/31/2004	$ 203,768
Add: Net income, 2005	(95,136)
Less: Dividends paid, 2005	(11,000)
Balance of retained earnings, 12/31/2005	$ 97,632

STATEMENT OF CASH FLOWS, 2005

Operating Activities

Net income	($ 95,136)
Adjustments:	
Noncash adjustments:	
Depreciation	116,960
Changes in working capital:	
Change in accounts receivable	(280,960)
Change in inventories	(572,160)

	2004	2005
Change in accounts payable		178,400
Change in accruals		148,960
Net cash provided by operating activities		($ 503,936)
Long-Term Investing Activities		
Cash used to acquire fixed assets		($ 711,950)
Financing Activities		
Change in short-term investments		$ 28,600
Change in notes payable		520,000
Change in long-term debt		676,568
Change in common stock		—
Payment of cash dividends		(11,000)
Net cash provided by financing activities		$1,214,168
Summary		
Net change in cash		($ 1,718)
Cash at beginning of year		9,000
Cash at end of year		$ 7,282

Assume that you are Jamison's assistant, and you must help her answer the following questions for Campo.

a. What effect did the expansion have on sales and net income? What effect did the expansion have on the asset side of the balance sheet? What effect did it have on liabilities and equity?

b. What do you conclude from the statement of cash flows?

c. What is free cash flow? Why is it important? What are the five uses of FCF?

d. What are operating current assets? What are operating current liabilities? How much net operating working capital and total net operating capital does Computron have?

e. What are Computron's net operating profit after taxes (NOPAT) and free cash flow (FCF)?

f. Calculate Computron's return on invested capital. Computron has a 10 percent cost of capital (WACC). Do you think Computron's growth added value?

g. Jamison also has asked you to estimate Computron's EVA. She estimates that the after-tax cost of capital was 10 percent in both years.

h. What happened to Computron's market value added (MVA)?

i. Assume that a corporation has $100,000 of taxable income from operations plus $5,000 of interest income and $10,000 of dividend income. What is the company's federal tax liability?

j. Assume that you are in the 25 percent marginal tax bracket and that you have $5,000 to invest. You have narrowed your investment choices down to California bonds with a yield of 7 percent or equally risky ExxonMobil bonds with a yield of 10 percent. Which one should you choose and why? At what marginal tax rate would you be indifferent to the choice between California and ExxonMobil bonds?

SELECTED ADDITIONAL REFERENCES

The effects of alternative accounting policies on financial statements are discussed in the investment textbooks referenced in Chapter 5 and also in the many excellent texts on financial statement analysis. For example, see

Fraser, Lyn M., and Aileen Ormiston, *Understanding Financial Statements* (Upper Saddle River, NJ: Prentice-Hall, 2004).

For treatments of the relationship between free cash flows and the value of a company, see

Copeland, Tom, Tim Koller, and Jack Murrin, *Valuation: Measuring and Managing the Value of Companies* (New York: John Wiley & Sons, Inc., 2001).

Daves, P., M. Ehrhardt, and R. Shrieves, *Corporate Valuation: A Guide for Managers and Investors* (Mason, OH: Thomson South-Western, 2004).

Stewart, G. Bennett, *The Quest for Value* (New York: Harper Collins, 1991).

CHAPTER 4

Analysis of Financial Statements

On May 19, 1999, Dell Computer Corp. announced that its first-quarter earnings were 42 percent higher than those reported one year earlier. This dramatic increase in earnings was roughly in line with Wall Street projections. Nevertheless, Dell's stock fell nearly $4 a share immediately after the announcement.

At first glance, the market's response appeared puzzling. However, analysts zeroed in on the fact that Dell's profit margin in the first quarter had fallen considerably. The computer business had become a lot more competitive, and the increased competition had pushed down computer prices, lowering profit margins for Dell.

Wall Street's response to Dell's announced earnings brings home several important points. First, investors and others outside the company use reported earnings and other financial statement data as inputs when determining a company's value. Second, analysts are primarily concerned about future performance—past performance is useful only to the extent that it provides information about the company's future. Finally, analysts go beyond reported profits—they dig into the financial statements.

So, while many people regard financial statements as "just accounting," they are really much more. As we see in this chapter, the statements provide a wealth of information that is used by managers, investors, lenders, customers, suppliers, and regulators. An analysis of its statements can highlight a company's strengths and shortcomings, and this information can be used by management to help improve performance and by others to predict future results. Financial analysis can be used to predict how such strategic decisions as the sale of a division, a major marketing program, or expanding a plant are likely to affect future financial performance.

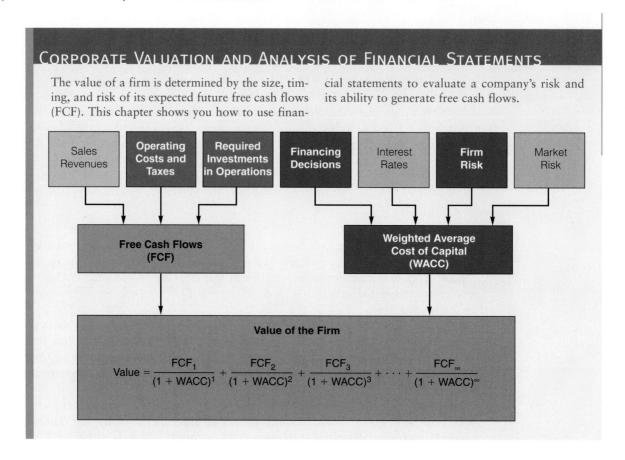

CORPORATE VALUATION AND ANALYSIS OF FINANCIAL STATEMENTS

The value of a firm is determined by the size, timing, and risk of its expected future free cash flows (FCF). This chapter shows you how to use financial statements to evaluate a company's risk and its ability to generate free cash flows.

Financial statement analysis involves (1) comparing the firm's performance with that of other firms in the same industry and (2) evaluating trends in the firm's financial position over time. This analysis helps managers identify deficiencies and then take actions to improve performance. The real value of financial statements lies in the fact that they can be used to help predict future earnings, dividends, and free cash flow. From an investor's standpoint, *predicting the future is what financial statement analysis is all about,* while from management's standpoint, *financial statement analysis is useful both to help anticipate future conditions and, more important, as a starting point for planning actions that will improve the firm's future performance.*[1]

RATIO ANALYSIS

Financial ratios are designed to help evaluate financial statements. For example, Firm A might have debt of $5,248,760 and interest charges of $419,900, while Firm B might have debt of $52,647,980 and interest charges of $3,948,600. Which company is stronger? The burden of these debts, and the companies' ability to repay them, can best be evaluated by comparing (1) each firm's debt to its assets and (2) the interest it must pay to the income it has available for payment of interest. Such comparisons are made by *ratio analysis.*

We will calculate the Year 2005 financial ratios for MicroDrive Inc., using data from the balance sheets and income statements given in Table 4-1. We will also evaluate the ratios in relation to the industry averages. Note that dollar amounts are in millions.

---

[1] As we said in Chapter 1 and again in Chapter 3, widespread accounting fraud has cast doubt on whether all firms' published financial statements can be trusted. New regulations by the SEC and the exchanges, and new laws enacted by Congress, have both improved oversight of the accounting industry and increased the criminal penalties on management for fraudulent reporting.

LIQUIDITY RATIOS

A **liquid asset** is one that trades in an active market and hence can be quickly converted to cash at the going market price, and a firm's "liquidity ratios" deal with this question: Will the firm be able to pay off its debts as they come due over the next year or so? As shown in Table 4-1, MicroDrive has current liabilities of $310 million that must be paid off within the coming year. Will it have trouble satisfying those obligations? A full liquidity analysis requires the use of cash budgets, but by relating the amount of cash and other current assets to current obligations, ratio analysis provides a quick, easy-to-use measure of liquidity. Two commonly used **liquidity ratios** are discussed in this section.

e-resource

See CF2 Ch 04 Tool Kit.xls for details.

TABLE 4-1 | **MicroDrive Inc.: Balance Sheets and Income Statements for Years Ending December 31 (Millions of Dollars, Except for Per Share Data)**

Assets	2005	2004	Liabilities and Equity	2005	2004
Cash and equivalents	$ 10	$ 15	Accounts payable	$ 60	$ 30
Short-term investments	0	65	Notes payable	110	60
Accounts receivable	375	315	Accruals	140	130
Inventories	615	415	Total current liabilities	$ 310	$ 220
Total current assets	$1,000	$ 810	Long-term bonds[a]	754	580
Net plant and equipment	1,000	870	Total liabilities	$1,064	$ 800
			Preferred stock		
			(400,000 shares)	40	40
			Common stock		
			(50,000,000 shares)	130	130
			Retained earnings	766	710
			Total common equity	$ 896	$ 840
Total assets	$2,000	$1,680	Total liabilities and equity	$2,000	$1,680

	2005	2004
Net sales	$3,000.0	$2,850.0
Operating costs excluding depreciation and amortization[b]	2,616.2	2,497.0
Earnings before interest, taxes, depreciation, and amortization (EBITDA)	$ 383.8	$ 353.0
Depreciation	100.0	90.0
Amortization	0.0	0.0
Depreciation and amortization	$ 100.0	$ 90.0
Earnings before interests and taxes (EBIT, or operating income)	$ 283.8	$ 263.0
Less interest	88.0	60.0
Earnings before taxes (EBT)	$ 195.8	$ 203.0
Taxes (40%)	78.3	81.2
Net income before preferred dividends	$ 117.5	$ 121.8
Preferred dividends	4.0	4.0
Net income	$ 113.5	$ 117.8
Common dividends	$ 57.5	$ 53.0
Addition to retained earnings	$ 56.0	$ 64.8
Per-Share Data		
Common stock price	$ 23.00	$ 26.00
Earnings per share (EPS)	$ 2.27	$ 2.36
Book value per share (BVPS)	$ 17.92	$ 16.80
Cash flow per share (CFPS)	$ 4.27	$ 4.16

[a]The bonds have a sinking fund requirement of $20 million a year.
[b]The costs include lease payments of $28 million a year.

Ability to Meet Short-Term Obligations: The Current Ratio

The **current ratio** is calculated by dividing current assets by current liabilities:

$$\text{Current ratio} = \frac{\text{Current assets}}{\text{Current liabilities}}$$

$$= \frac{\$1,000}{\$310} = 3.2 \text{ times.}$$

Industry average = 4.2 times.

Current assets normally include cash, marketable securities, accounts receivable, and inventories. Current liabilities consist of accounts payable, short-term notes payable, current maturities of long-term debt, accrued taxes, and other accrued expenses (principally wages).

MicroDrive has a lower current ratio than the average for its industry. Is this good or bad? Sometimes the answer depends on who is asking the question. For example, suppose a supplier is trying to decide whether to extend credit to MicroDrive. In general, creditors like to see a high current ratio. If a company is getting into financial difficulty, it will begin paying its bills (accounts payable) more slowly, borrowing from its bank, and so on, so its current liabilities will be increasing. If current liabilities are rising faster than current assets, the current ratio will fall, and this could spell trouble. Because the current ratio provides the best single indicator of the extent to which the claims of short-term creditors are covered by assets that are expected to be converted to cash fairly quickly, it is the most commonly used measure of short-term solvency.

Now consider the current ratio from the perspective of a shareholder. A high current ratio could mean that the company has a lot of money tied up in nonproductive assets, such as excess cash or marketable securities. Or perhaps the high current ratio is due to large inventory holdings, which might well become obsolete before they can be sold. Thus, shareholders might not want a high current ratio.

An industry average is not a magic number that all firms should strive to maintain—in fact, some very well-managed firms will be above the average while other good firms will be below it. However, if a firm's ratios are far removed from the averages for its industry, this is a red flag, and analysts should be concerned about why the variance occurs. For example, suppose a low current ratio is traced to low inventories. Is this a competitive advantage resulting from the firm's mastery of just-in-time inventory management, or an Achilles heel that is causing the firm to miss shipments and lose sales? Ratio analysis doesn't answer such questions, but it does point to areas of potential concern.

Quick, or Acid Test, Ratio

The **quick,** or **acid test, ratio** is calculated by deducting inventories from current assets and then dividing the remainder by current liabilities:

$$\text{Quick, or acid test, ratio} = \frac{\text{Current assets} - \text{Inventories}}{\text{Current liabilities}}$$

$$= \frac{\$385}{\$310} = 1.2 \text{ times.}$$

Industry average = 2.1 times.

Inventories are typically the least liquid of a firm's current assets, hence they are the current assets on which losses are most likely to occur in a bankruptcy. Therefore, a measure of the firm's ability to pay off short-term obligations without relying on the sale of inventories is important.

The industry average quick ratio is 2.1, so MicroDrive's 1.2 ratio is low in comparison with other firms in its industry. Still, if the accounts receivable can be collected, the company can pay off its current liabilities without having to liquidate its inventory.

Identify two ratios that are used to analyze a firm's liquidity position, and write out their equations.

What are the characteristics of a liquid asset? Give some examples.

Which current asset is typically the least liquid?

ASSET MANAGEMENT RATIOS

The second group of ratios, the **asset management ratios,** measure how effectively the firm is managing its assets. These ratios are designed to answer this question: Does the total amount of each type of asset as reported on the balance sheet seem reasonable, too high, or too low in view of current and projected sales levels? If a company has excessive investments in assets, then its operating assets and capital will be unduly high, which will reduce its free cash flow and its stock price. On the other hand, if a company does not have enough assets, it will lose sales, which will hurt profitability, free cash flow, and the stock price. Therefore, it is important to have the *right* amount invested in assets. Ratios that analyze the different types of assets are described in this section.

Evaluating Inventories: The Inventory Turnover Ratio

The **inventory turnover ratio** is defined as sales divided by inventories:

$$\text{Inventory turnover ratio} = \frac{\text{Sales}}{\text{Inventories}}$$

$$= \frac{\$3,000}{\$615} = 4.9 \text{ times.}$$

Industry average = 9.0 times.

As a rough approximation, each item of MicroDrive's inventory is sold out and restocked, or "turned over," 4.9 times per year. "Turnover" is a term that originated many years ago with the old Yankee peddler, who would load up his wagon with goods and then go off to peddle his wares. The merchandise was called "working capital" because it was what he actually sold, or "turned over," to produce his profits, whereas his "turnover" was the number of trips he took each year. Annual sales divided by inventory equaled turnover, or trips per year. If he made 10 trips per year, stocked 100 pans, and made a gross profit of $5 per pan, his annual gross profit would be $(100)(\$5)(10) = \$5,000$. If he went faster and made 20 trips per year, his gross profit would double, other things held constant. So, his turnover directly affected his profits.

MicroDrive's turnover of 4.9 times is much lower than the industry average of 9 times. This suggests that MicroDrive is holding too much inventory. Excess inventory is, of course, unproductive, and it represents an investment with a low or zero rate of return. MicroDrive's low inventory turnover ratio also makes us question the current ratio. With such a low turnover, we must wonder whether the firm is actually holding obsolete goods not worth their stated value.[2]

---

[2] A problem arises calculating and analyzing the inventory turnover ratio. Sales are stated at market prices, so if inventories are carried at cost, as they generally are, the calculated turnover overstates the true turnover ratio. Therefore, it would be more appropriate to use cost of goods sold in place of sales in the formula's numerator. However, established compilers of financial ratio statistics such as Dun & Bradstreet use the ratio of sales to inventories carried at cost. To develop a figure that can be compared with those published by Dun & Bradstreet and similar organizations, it is necessary to measure inventory turnover with sales in the numerator, as we do here.

Note that sales occur over the entire year, whereas the inventory figure is for one point in time. For this reason, it is better to use an average inventory measure.[3] If the firm's business is highly seasonal, or if there has been a strong upward or downward sales trend during the year, it is especially useful to make some such adjustment. To maintain comparability with industry averages, however, we did not use the average inventory figure.

Evaluating Receivables: The Days Sales Outstanding

Days sales outstanding (DSO), also called the "average collection period" (ACP), is used to appraise accounts receivable, and it is calculated by dividing accounts receivable by average daily sales to find the number of days' sales that are tied up in receivables.[4] Thus, the DSO represents the average length of time that the firm must wait after making a sale before receiving cash, which is the average collection period. MicroDrive has 46 days sales outstanding, well above the 36-day industry average:

$$\text{DSO} = \frac{\text{Days sales outstanding}}{} = \frac{\text{Receivables}}{\text{Average sales per day}} = \frac{\text{Receivables}}{\text{Annual sales/365}}$$

$$= \frac{\$375}{\$3,000/365} = \frac{\$375}{\$8.219} = 45.6 \text{ days} \approx 46 \text{ days.}$$

$$\text{Industry average} = 36 \text{ days.}$$

The DSO can also be evaluated by comparison with the terms on which the firm sells its goods. For example, MicroDrive's sales terms call for payment within 30 days, so the fact that 45 days' sales, not 30 days', are outstanding indicates that customers, on the average, are not paying their bills on time. This deprives MicroDrive of funds that it could use to invest in productive assets. Moreover, in some instances the fact that a customer is paying late may signal that the customer is in financial trouble, in which case MicroDrive may have a hard time ever collecting the receivable. Therefore, if the trend in DSO over the past few years has been rising, but the credit policy has not been changed, this would be strong evidence that steps should be taken to expedite the collection of accounts receivable.

Evaluating Fixed Assets: The Fixed Assets Turnover Ratio

The **fixed assets turnover ratio** measures how effectively the firm uses its plant and equipment. It is the ratio of sales to net fixed assets:

$$\text{Fixed assets turnover ratio} = \frac{\text{Sales}}{\text{Net fixed assets}}$$

$$= \frac{\$3,000}{\$1,000} = 3.0 \text{ times.}$$

$$\text{Industry average} = 3.0 \text{ times.}$$

MicroDrive's ratio of 3.0 times is equal to the industry average, indicating that the firm is using its fixed assets about as intensively as are other firms in its industry. Therefore, MicroDrive seems to have about the right amount of fixed assets in relation to other firms.

A potential problem can exist when interpreting the fixed assets turnover ratio. Recall from accounting that fixed assets reflect the historical costs of the assets. Inflation has

---

[3] Preferably, the average inventory value should be calculated by summing the monthly figures during the year and dividing by 12. If monthly data are not available, one can add the beginning and ending annual figures and divide by 2. However, most industry ratios are calculated as above, using end-of-year values.

[4] It would be better to use *average* receivables, but we used year-end values for comparability with the industry average.

caused the value of many assets that were purchased in the past to be seriously understated. Therefore, if we were comparing an old firm that had acquired many of its fixed assets years ago at low prices with a new company that had acquired its fixed assets only recently, we would probably find that the old firm had the higher fixed assets turnover ratio. However, this would be more reflective of the difficulty accountants have in dealing with inflation than of any inefficiency on the part of the new firm. Financial analysts must recognize that this problem exists and deal with it judgmentally.

Evaluating Total Assets: The Total Assets Turnover Ratio

The final asset management ratio, the **total assets turnover ratio,** measures the turnover of all the firm's assets; it is calculated by dividing sales by total assets:

$$\text{Total assets turnover ratio} = \frac{\text{Sales}}{\text{Total assets}}$$

$$= \frac{\$3,000}{\$2,000} = 1.5 \text{ times.}$$

Industry average $= 1.8$ times.

MicroDrive's ratio is somewhat below the industry average, indicating that the company is not generating a sufficient volume of business given its total asset investment. Sales should be increased, some assets should be sold, or a combination of these steps should be taken.

SELF-TEST QUESTIONS

Identify four ratios that are used to measure how effectively a firm is managing its assets, and write out their equations.

How might rapid growth distort the inventory turnover ratio?

What potential problem might arise when comparing different firms' fixed assets turnover ratios?

DEBT MANAGEMENT RATIOS

The extent to which a firm uses debt financing, or **financial leverage,** has three important implications: (1) By raising funds through debt, stockholders can maintain control of a firm without increasing their investment. (2) If the firm earns more on investments financed with borrowed funds than it pays in interest, then its shareholders' returns are magnified, or "leveraged," but their risks are also magnified. (3) Creditors look to the equity, or owner-supplied funds, to provide a margin of safety, so the higher the proportion of funding supplied by stockholders, the less risk creditors face. Chapter 14 explains the first two points in detail, while the following ratios examine leverage from a creditor's point of view.

How the Firm Is Financed: Total Liabilities to Total Assets

The ratio of total liabilities to total assets is called the **debt ratio,** or sometimes the **total debt ratio.** It measures the percentage of funds provided by sources other than equity:

$$\text{Debt ratio} = \frac{\text{Total liabilities}}{\text{Total assets}}$$

$$= \frac{\$310 + \$754}{\$2,000} = \frac{\$1,064}{\$2,000} = 53.2\%.$$

Industry average $= 40.0\%$.

Creditors prefer low debt ratios because the lower the ratio, the greater the cushion against creditors' losses in the event of liquidation. Stockholders, on the other hand, may want more leverage because it magnifies expected earnings.

MicroDrive's debt ratio is 53.2 percent, which means that its creditors have supplied more than half the total financing. As we will discuss in Chapter 14, a variety of factors determine a company's optimal debt ratio. Nevertheless, the fact that MicroDrive's debt ratio exceeds the industry average raises a red flag and may make it costly for MicroDrive to borrow additional funds without first raising more equity capital. Creditors may be reluctant to lend the firm more money, and management would probably be subjecting the firm to the risk of bankruptcy if it increased the debt ratio by borrowing additional funds.

If you use a debt ratio that you did not calculate yourself, be sure to find out how the ratio was defined. Some sources provide the ratio of long-term debt to total assets, and some provide the ratio of debt to equity, so be sure to check the source's definition.[5]

Ability to Pay Interest: Times-Interest-Earned

The **times-interest-earned (TIE) ratio** is determined by dividing earnings before interest and taxes (EBIT in Table 14-1) by the interest charges:

$$\text{Times-interest-earned (TIE) ratio} = \frac{\text{EBIT}}{\text{Interest charges}}$$

$$= \frac{\$283.8}{\$88} = 3.2 \text{ times.}$$

Industry average $= 6.0$ times.

The TIE ratio measures the extent to which operating income can decline before the firm is unable to meet its annual interest costs. Failure to meet this obligation can bring legal action by the firm's creditors, possibly resulting in bankruptcy. Note that earnings before interest and taxes, rather than net income, is used in the numerator. Because interest is paid with pre-tax dollars, the firm's ability to pay current interest is not affected by taxes.

MicroDrive's interest is covered 3.2 times. Since the industry average is 6 times, MicroDrive is covering its interest charges by a relatively low margin of safety. Thus, the TIE ratio reinforces the conclusion from our analysis of the debt ratio that MicroDrive would face difficulties if it attempted to borrow additional funds.

Ability to Service Debt: EBITDA Coverage Ratio

The TIE ratio is useful for assessing a company's ability to meet interest charges on its debt, but this ratio has two shortcomings: (1) Interest is not the only fixed financial charge—companies must also reduce debt on schedule, and many firms lease assets and thus must make lease payments. If they fail to repay debt or meet lease payments, they can be forced into bankruptcy. (2) EBIT does not represent all the cash flow available to service debt, especially if a firm has high depreciation and/or amortization charges. To account for these deficiencies, bankers and others have developed the **EBITDA coverage ratio,** defined as follows:[6]

---

[5] The debt-to-assets (D/A) and debt-to-equity (D/E) ratios are simply transformations of each other:

$$D/E = \frac{D/A}{1 - D/A}, \text{ and } D/A = \frac{D/E}{1 + D/E}.$$

[6] Different analysts define the EBITDA coverage ratio in different ways. For example, some would omit the lease payment information, and others would "gross up" principal payments by dividing them by $(1 - T)$ because these payments are not tax deductions, hence must be made with after-tax cash flows. We included lease payments because, for many firms, they are quite important, and failing to make them can lead to bankruptcy just as surely as can failure to make payments on "regular" debt. We did not gross up principal payments because, if a company is in financial difficulty, its tax rate will probably be zero, hence the gross up is not necessary whenever the ratio is really important.

$$\text{EBITDA coverage ratio} = \frac{\text{EBITDA} + \text{Lease payments}}{\text{Interest} + \text{Principal payments} + \text{Lease payments}}$$

$$= \frac{\$383.8 + \$28}{\$88 + \$20 + \$28} = \frac{\$411.8}{\$136} = 3.0 \text{ times.}$$

Industry average = 4.3 times.

MicroDrive had $383.8 million of earnings before interest, taxes, depreciation, and amortization (EBITDA). Also, lease payments of $28 million were deducted while calculating EBITDA. That $28 million was available to meet financial charges, hence it must be added back, bringing the total available to cover fixed financial charges to $411.8 million. Fixed financial charges consisted of $88 million of interest, $20 million of sinking fund payments, and $28 million for lease payments, for a total of $136 million.[7] Therefore, MicroDrive covered its fixed financial charges by 3.0 times. However, if EBITDA declines, the coverage will fall, and EBITDA certainly can decline. Moreover, MicroDrive's ratio is well below the industry average, so again, the company seems to have a relatively high level of debt.

The EBITDA coverage ratio is most useful for relatively short-term lenders such as banks, which rarely make loans (except real estate-backed loans) for longer than about five years. Over a relatively short period, depreciation-generated funds can be used to service debt. Over a longer time, those funds must be reinvested to maintain the plant and equipment or else the company cannot remain in business. Therefore, banks and other relatively short-term lenders focus on the EBITDA coverage ratio, whereas long-term bondholders focus on the TIE ratio.

SELF-TEST QUESTIONS

How does the use of financial leverage affect current stockholders' control position?

In what way do taxes influence a firm's willingness to finance with debt?

In what way does the use of debt involve a risk-versus-return trade-off?

Explain the following statement: "Analysts look at both balance sheet and income statement ratios when appraising a firm's financial condition."

Name three ratios that are used to measure the extent to which a firm uses financial leverage, and write out their equations.

PROFITABILITY RATIOS

Profitability is the net result of a number of policies and decisions. The ratios examined thus far provide useful clues as to the effectiveness of a firm's operations, but the **profitability ratios** go on to show the combined effects of liquidity, asset management, and debt on operating results.

Profit Margin on Sales

The **profit margin on sales,** calculated by dividing net income by sales, gives the profit per dollar of sales:

$$\frac{\text{Profit margin}}{\text{on sales}} = \frac{\text{Net income available to common stockholders}}{\text{Sales}}$$

$$= \frac{\$113.5}{\$3,000} = 3.8\%.$$

Industry average = 5.0%.

---

[7] A sinking fund is a required annual payment designed to reduce the balance of a bond or preferred stock issue.

INTERNATIONAL ACCOUNTING DIFFERENCES CREATE HEADACHES FOR INVESTORS

You must be a good financial detective to analyze financial statements, especially if the company operates overseas. Despite attempts to standardize accounting practices, there are many differences in the way financial information is reported in different countries, and these differences create headaches for investors trying to make cross-border company comparisons.

A study by two Rider College accounting professors demonstrated that huge differences can exist. The professors developed a computer model to evaluate the net income of a hypothetical but typical company operating in different countries. Applying the standard accounting practices of each country, the hypothetical company would have reported net income of $34,600 in the United States, $260,600 in the United Kingdom, and $240,600 in Australia.

Such variances occur for a number of reasons. In most countries, including the United States, an asset's balance sheet value is reported at original cost less any accumulated depreciation. However, in some countries, asset values are adjusted to reflect current market prices. Also, inventory valuation methods vary from country to country, as does the treatment of goodwill. Other differences arise from the treatment of leases, research and development costs, and pension plans.

These differences arise from a variety of legal, historical, cultural, and economic factors. For exam-

ple, in Germany and Japan large banks are the key source of both debt and equity capital, whereas in the United States public capital markets are most important. As a result, U.S. corporations disclose a great deal of information to the public, while German and Japanese corporations use very conservative accounting practices that appeal to the banks.

There are two basic trends regarding international accounting standards. The first is a movement toward a single set of accounting standards. For example, the European Union recently passed regulations requiring all EU-listed companies to comply by 2005 with standards defined by the International Accounting Standards Board (IASB). There are also ongoing discussions between the IASB and the U.S. Financial Accounting Standards Board (FASB) to develop a single set of financial standards for all companies worldwide. Second, IASB standards rely on general principles, while FASB standards are rules based. As the recent accounting scandals demonstrate, many U.S. companies have been able to comply with U.S. rules while violating the principle, or intent, underlying the rules. This is fueling a debate over the relative effectiveness of principles-based versus rules-based standards.

Sources: See the Web sites of the IASB and the FASB: **http://www .iasc.org.uk** and **http://www.fasb.org**. Also, see Lee Burton, "All Accountants Soon May Speak the Same Language," *The Wall Street Journal,* August 29, 1995, A15.

MicroDrive's profit margin is below the industry average of 5 percent. This sub-par result occurs because costs are too high. High costs, in turn, generally occur because of inefficient operations. However, MicroDrive's low profit margin is also a result of its heavy use of debt. Recall that net income is income *after interest*. Therefore, if two firms have identical operations in the sense that their sales, operating costs, and EBIT are the same, but if one firm uses more debt than the other, it will have higher interest charges. Those interest charges will pull net income down, and since sales are constant, the result will be a relatively low profit margin. In such a case, the low profit margin would not indicate an operating problem—rather, it would indicate a difference in financing strategies. Thus, the firm with the low profit margin might end up with a higher rate of return on its stockholders' investment due to its use of financial leverage. We will see exactly how profit margins and the use of debt interact to affect the return on stockholders' equity later in the chapter, when we examine the Du Pont model.

Basic Earning Power (BEP)

The **basic earning power (BEP) ratio** is calculated by dividing earnings before interest and taxes (EBIT) by total assets:

$$\text{Basic earning power ratio (BEP)} = \frac{\text{EBIT}}{\text{Total assets}}$$

$$= \frac{\$283.8}{\$2,000} = 14.2\%.$$

Industry average = 17.2%.

This ratio shows the raw earning power of the firm's assets, before the influence of taxes and leverage, and it is useful for comparing firms with different tax situations and different degrees of financial leverage. Because of its low turnover ratios and low profit margin on sales, MicroDrive is not getting as high a return on its assets as is the average company in its industry.[8]

Return on Total Assets

The ratio of net income to total assets measures the **return on total assets (ROA)** after interest and taxes:

$$\text{Return on total assets} = \text{ROA} = \frac{\text{Net income available to common stockholders}}{\text{Total assets}}$$

$$= \frac{\$113.5}{\$2,000} = 5.7\%.$$

Industry average = 9.0%.

MicroDrive's 5.7 percent return is well below the 9 percent average for the industry. This low return results from (1) the company's low basic earning power plus (2) high interest costs resulting from its above-average use of debt, both of which cause its net income to be relatively low.

Return on Common Equity

Ultimately, the most important, or "bottom line," accounting ratio is the ratio of net income to common equity, which measures the **return on common equity (ROE)**:

$$\text{Return on common equity} = \text{ROE} = \frac{\text{Net income available to common stockholders}}{\text{Common equity}}$$

$$= \frac{\$113.5}{\$896} = 12.7\%.$$

Industry average = 15.0%.

Stockholders invest to get a return on their money, and this ratio tells how well they are doing in an accounting sense. MicroDrive's 12.7 percent return is below the 15 percent industry average, but not as far below as the return on total assets. This somewhat better result is due to the company's greater use of debt, a point that is analyzed in detail later in the chapter.

SELF-TEST QUESTIONS

Identify and write out the equations for four ratios that show the combined effects of liquidity, asset management, and debt management on profitability.

Why is the basic earning power ratio useful?

Why does the use of debt lower the ROA?

What does ROE measure? Since interest expense lowers profits, does using debt lower ROE?

---

[8] Notice that EBIT is earned throughout the year, whereas the total assets figure is an end-of-the-year number. Therefore, it would be conceptually better to calculate this ratio as EBIT/Average assets = EBIT/[(Beginning assets + Ending assets)/2]. We have not made this adjustment because the published ratios used for comparative purposes do not include it. However, when we construct our own comparative ratios, we do make the adjustment. Incidentally, the same adjustment would also be appropriate for the next two ratios, ROA and ROE.

MARKET VALUE RATIOS

A final group of ratios, the **market value ratios,** relates the firm's stock price to its earnings, cash flow, and book value per share. These ratios give management an indication of what investors think of the company's past performance and future prospects. If the liquidity, asset management, debt management, and profitability ratios all look good, then the market value ratios will be high, and the stock price will probably be as high as can be expected.

Price/Earnings Ratio

The **price/earnings (P/E) ratio** shows how much investors are willing to pay per dollar of reported profits. MicroDrive's stock sells for $23, so with an EPS of $2.27 its P/E ratio is 10.1:

$$\text{Price/earnings (P/E) ratio} = \frac{\text{Price per share}}{\text{Earnings per share}}$$

$$= \frac{\$23.00}{\$2.27} = 10.1 \text{ times.}$$

Industry average = 12.5 times.

P/E ratios are higher for firms with strong growth prospects, other things held constant, but they are lower for riskier firms. Because MicroDrive's P/E ratio is below the average, this suggests that the company is regarded as being somewhat riskier than most, as having poorer growth prospects, or both.

Price/Cash Flow Ratio

In some industries, stock price is tied more closely to cash flow rather than net income. Consequently, investors often look at the **price/cash flow ratio,** where cash flow is defined as net income plus depreciation and amortization:

$$\text{Price/cash flow} = \frac{\text{Price per share}}{\text{Cash flow per share}}$$

$$= \frac{\$23.00}{\$4.27} = 5.4 \text{ times.}$$

Industry average = 6.8 times.

MicroDrive's price/cash flow ratio is also below the industry average, once again suggesting that its growth prospects are below average, its risk is above average, or both.

Note that some analysts look at multiples beyond just the price/earnings and the price/cash flow ratios. For example, depending on the industry, some may look at measures such as price/sales, price/customers, or price/EBITDA per share. Ultimately, though, value depends on free cash flows, so if these "exotic" ratios do not forecast future free cash flow, they may turn out to be misleading. This was true in the case of the dot-com retailers before they crashed and burned in 2000, costing investors many billions.

Market/Book Ratio

The ratio of a stock's market price to its book value gives another indication of how investors regard the company. Companies with relatively high rates of return on equity generally sell at higher multiples of book value than those with low returns. First, we find MicroDrive's book value per share:

$$\text{Book value per share} = \frac{\text{Common equity}}{\text{Shares outstanding}}$$

$$= \frac{\$896}{50} = \$17.92.$$

Now we divide the market price by the book value to get a **market/book (M/B) ratio** of 1.3 times:

$$\text{Market/book ratio} = \text{M/B} = \frac{\text{Market price per share}}{\text{Book value per share}}$$

$$= \frac{\$23.00}{\$17.92} = 1.3 \text{ times.}$$

$$\text{Industry average} = 1.7 \text{ times.}$$

Investors are willing to pay relatively little for a dollar of MicroDrive's book value.

The average company in the S&P 500 had a market/book ratio of about 4.52 in the spring of 2004. Since M/B ratios typically exceed 1.0, this means that investors are willing to pay more for stocks than their accounting book values. The book value is a record of the past, showing the cumulative amount that stockholders have invested, either directly by purchasing newly issued shares or indirectly through retaining earnings. In contrast, the market price is forward-looking, incorporating investors' expectations of future cash flows. For example, in spring 2004 Alaska Air had a market/book ratio of only 1.01, reflecting the crisis in the airlines industry caused by the terrorist attacks, whereas Dell Computer's market/book ratio was 14.11, indicating that investors expect Dell's past successes to continue.

Table 4-2 summarizes MicroDrive's financial ratios. As the table indicates, the company has many problems.

CF

e-resource

See CF2 Ch 04 Tool Kit.xls for details.

SELF-TEST QUESTIONS

Describe three ratios that relate a firm's stock price to its earnings, cash flow, and book value per share, and write out their equations.

How do market value ratios reflect what investors think about a stock's risk and expected rate of return?

What does the price/earnings (P/E) ratio show? If one firm's P/E ratio is lower than that of another, what are some factors that might explain the difference?

How is book value per share calculated? Explain why book values often deviate from market values.

TREND ANALYSIS, COMMON SIZE ANALYSIS, AND PERCENT CHANGE ANALYSIS

It is important to analyze trends in ratios as well as their absolute levels, for trends give clues as to whether a firm's financial condition is likely to improve or to deteriorate. To do a **trend analysis,** one simply plots a ratio over time, as shown in Figure 4-1. This graph shows that MicroDrive's rate of return on common equity has been declining since 2002, even though the industry average has been relatively stable. All the other ratios could be analyzed similarly.

TABLE 4-2 | **MicroDrive Inc.: Summary of Financial Ratios (Millions of Dollars)**

Ratio	Formula for Calculation	Calculation	Ratio	Industry Average	Comment
Liquidity					
Current	$\dfrac{\text{Current assets}}{\text{Current liabilities}}$	$\dfrac{\$1{,}000}{\$310}$	= 3.2×	4.2×	Poor
Quick, or acid test	$\dfrac{\text{Current assets} - \text{Inventories}}{\text{Current liabilities}}$	$\dfrac{\$385}{\$310}$	= 1.2×	2.1×	Poor
Asset Management					
Inventory turnover	$\dfrac{\text{Sales}}{\text{Inventories}}$	$\dfrac{\$3{,}000}{\$615}$	= 4.9×	9.0×	Poor
Days sales outstanding (DSO)	$\dfrac{\text{Receivables}}{\text{Annual sales}/365}$	$\dfrac{\$375}{\$8.219}$	= 46 days	36 days	Poor
Fixed assets turnover	$\dfrac{\text{Sales}}{\text{Net fixed assets}}$	$\dfrac{\$3{,}000}{\$1{,}000}$	= 3.0×	3.0×	OK
Total assets turnover	$\dfrac{\text{Sales}}{\text{Total assets}}$	$\dfrac{\$3{,}000}{\$2{,}000}$	= 1.5×	1.8×	Somewhat low
Debt Management					
Debt ratio	$\dfrac{\text{Total liabilities}}{\text{Total assets}}$	$\dfrac{\$1{,}064}{\$2{,}000}$	= 53.2%	40.0%	High (risky)
Times-interest-earned (TIE)	$\dfrac{\text{Earnings before interest and taxes (EBIT)}}{\text{Interest charges}}$	$\dfrac{\$283.8}{\$88}$	= 3.2×	6.0×	Low (risky)
EBITDA coverage	$\dfrac{\text{EBITDA} + \text{Lease payments}}{\text{Interest} + \text{Principal payments} + \text{Lease payments}}$	$\dfrac{\$411.8}{\$136}$	= 3.0×	4.3×	Low (risky)
Profitability					
Profit margin on sales	$\dfrac{\text{Net income available to common stockholders}}{\text{Sales}}$	$\dfrac{\$113.5}{\$3{,}000}$	= 3.8%	5.0%	Poor
Basic earning power (BEP)	$\dfrac{\text{Earnings before interest and taxes (EBIT)}}{\text{Total assets}}$	$\dfrac{\$283.8}{\$2{,}000}$	= 14.2%	17.2%	Poor
Return on total assets (ROA)	$\dfrac{\text{Net income available to common stockholders}}{\text{Total assets}}$	$\dfrac{\$113.5}{\$2{,}000}$	= 5.7%	9.0%	Poor
Return on common equity (ROE)	$\dfrac{\text{Net income available to common stockholders}}{\text{Common equity}}$	$\dfrac{\$113.5}{\$896}$	= 12.7%	15.0%	Poor
Market Value					
Price/earnings (P/E)	$\dfrac{\text{Price per share}}{\text{Earnings per share}}$	$\dfrac{\$23.00}{\$2.27}$	= 10.1×	12.5×	Low
Price/cash flow	$\dfrac{\text{Price per share}}{\text{Cash flow per share}}$	$\dfrac{\$23.00}{\$4.27}$	= 5.4×	6.8×	Low
Market/book (M/B)	$\dfrac{\text{Market price per share}}{\text{Book value per share}}$	$\dfrac{\$23.00}{\$17.92}$	= 1.3×	1.7×	Low

Common size analysis and **percent change analysis** are two other techniques that can be used to identify trends in financial statements. Common size analysis is also useful in comparative analysis, and some sources of industry data, such as Robert Morris Associates, are presented exclusively in common size form.

In a common size analysis, all income statement items are divided by sales, and all balance sheet items are divided by total assets. Thus, a common size income statement shows each item as a percentage of sales, and a common size balance sheet shows each item as

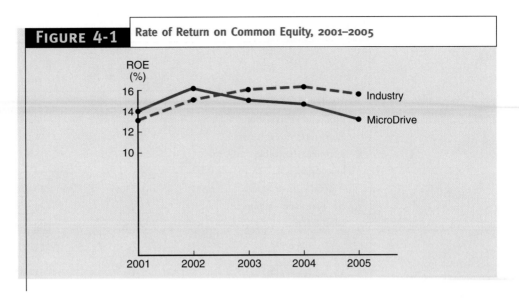

FIGURE 4-1 | Rate of Return on Common Equity, 2001–2005

a percentage of total assets. The advantage of common size analysis is that it facilitates comparisons of balance sheets and income statements over time and across companies.

Table 4-3 contains MicroDrive's 2004 and 2005 common size income statements, along with the composite statement for the industry. (Note: Rounding may cause addition/subtraction differences in Tables 4-3 and 4-4.) MicroDrive's operating costs are slightly above average, as are its interest expenses, but its taxes are relatively low because of its low EBIT. The net effect of all these forces is a relatively low profit margin.

Table 4-4 shows MicroDrive's common size balance sheets, along with the industry average. Its accounts receivable are significantly higher than the industry average, its inventories are significantly higher, and it uses far more fixed charge capital (debt and preferred) than the average firm.

A final technique used to help analyze a firm's financial statements is percentage change analysis. In this type of analysis, growth rates are calculated for all income statement items and balance sheet accounts. To illustrate, Table 4-5 contains MicroDrive's income statement

e-resource

See CF2 Ch 04 Tool Kit.xls for details.

TABLE 4-3 | MicroDrive Inc.: Common Size Income Statements

	2004	2005	2005 Industry Composite
Net sales	100.0%	100.0%	100.0%
Costs excluding depreciation	87.6	87.2	87.6
Depreciation	3.2	3.3	2.8
Total operating costs	90.8%	90.5%	90.4%
Earnings before interest and taxes (EBIT)	9.2%	9.5%	9.6%
Less interest	2.1	2.9	1.3
Earnings before taxes (EBT)	7.1%	6.5%	8.3%
Taxes (40%)	2.8	2.6	3.3
Net income before preferred dividends	4.3%	3.9%	5.0%
Preferred dividends	0.1	0.1	0.0
Net income available to common stockholders (profit margin)	4.1%	3.8%	5.0%

Note: Percentages may not total exactly due to rounding.

TABLE 4-4 | MicroDrive Inc.: Common Size Balance Sheets

	2004	2005	2005 Industry Composite
Assets			
Cash and equivalents	0.9%	0.5%	3.2%
Short-term investments	3.9	0.0	0.0
Accounts receivable	18.8	18.8	17.8
Inventories	24.7	30.8	19.8
Total current assets	48.2%	50.0%	40.8%
Net plant and equipment	51.8	50.0	59.2
Total assets	100.0%	100.0%	100.0%
Liabilities and Equity			
Accounts payable	1.8%	3.0%	1.8%
Notes payable	3.6	5.5	4.4
Accruals	7.7	7.0	3.6
Total current liabilities	13.1%	15.5%	9.8%
Long-term bonds	34.5	37.7	30.2
Total liabilities	47.6%	53.2%	40.0%
Preferred equity	2.4	2.0	0.0
Common equity	50.0	44.8	60.0
Total liabilities and equity	100.0%	100.0%	100.0%

percentage change analysis for 2005. Sales increased at a 5.3 percent rate during 2005, while total operating costs increased at a slower 5.0 percent rate, leading to 7.9 percent growth in EBIT. The fact that sales increased faster than operating costs is positive, but this "good news" was offset by a 46.7 percent increase in interest expense. The significant growth in interest expense caused growth in both earnings before taxes and net income to be negative. Thus, the percentage change analysis points out that the decrease in reported

e-resource

See *CF2 Ch 04 Tool Kit.xls* for details.

TABLE 4-5 | MicroDrive Inc.: Income Statement Percentage Change Analysis (Millions of Dollars)

	2004	2005	Percent Change
Net sales	$2,850	$3,000.0	5.3%
Costs excluding depreciation	$2,497	$2,616.2	4.8%
Depreciation	90	100.0	11.1
Total operating costs	$2,587	$2,716.2	5.0%
Earnings before interest and taxes (EBIT)	$ 263	$ 283.8	7.9%
Less interest	60	88.0	46.7
Earnings before taxes (EBT)	$ 203	$ 195.8	(3.5%)
Taxes (40%)	81	78.3	(3.3)
Net income before preferred dividends	$ 122	$ 117.5	(3.7%)
Preferred dividends	4	4.0	0
Net income available to common stockholders	$ 118	$ 113.5	(3.8%)

income in 2005 resulted almost exclusively from an increase in interest expense. This conclusion could be reached by analyzing dollar amounts, but percentage change analysis simplifies the task. The same type of analysis applied to the balance sheets would show that assets grew at a 19.0 percent rate, largely because inventories grew at a whopping 48.2 percent rate. With only a 5.3 percent growth in sales, the extreme growth in inventories should be of great concern to MicroDrive's managers.

The conclusions reached in common size and percentage change analyses generally parallel those derived from ratio analysis. However, occasionally a serious deficiency is highlighted by only one of the three analytical techniques. Also, it is often useful to have all three and to drive home to management, in slightly different ways, the need to take corrective actions. Thus, a thorough financial statement analysis will include ratio, percentage change, and common size analyses, as well as a Du Pont analysis as described next.

SELF-TEST QUESTIONS

How does one do a trend analysis?

What important information does a trend analysis provide?

What is common size analysis?

What is percent change analysis?

TYING THE RATIOS TOGETHER: THE DU PONT EQUATION

The profit margin times the total assets turnover is called the **Du Pont equation,** and it gives the rate of return on assets (ROA):

$$\text{ROA} = \text{Profit margin} \times \text{Total assets turnover}$$
$$= \frac{\text{Net income}}{\text{Sales}} \times \frac{\text{Sales}}{\text{Total assets}} \tag{4-1}$$

$$= 3.8\% \times 1.5 = 5.7\%.$$

MicroDrive made 3.8 percent, or 3.8 cents, on each dollar of sales, and its assets were "turned over" 1.5 times during the year. Therefore, the company earned a return of 5.7 percent on its assets.

If the company were financed only with common equity, the rate of return on assets (ROA) and the return on equity (ROE) would be the same because the total assets would equal the common equity:

$$\text{ROA} = \frac{\text{Net income}}{\text{Total assets}} = \frac{\text{Net income}}{\text{Common equity}} = \text{ROE}.$$

This equality holds if and only if Total assets = Common equity, that is, if the company uses no debt. MicroDrive does use debt, so its common equity is less than total assets. Therefore, the return to the common stockholders (ROE) must be greater than the ROA of 5.7 percent. To find the ROE, multiply the rate of return on assets (ROA) by the *equity multiplier,* which is the ratio of assets to common equity:

$$\text{Equity multiplier} = \frac{\text{Total assets}}{\text{Common equity}}.$$

Firms that use a large amount of debt financing (a lot of leverage) will necessarily have a high equity multiplier—the more the debt, the less the equity, hence the higher the equity multiplier. For example, if a firm has $1,000 of assets and is financed with $800 (or 80 percent) debt, then its equity will be $200, and its equity multiplier will be $1,000/$200 = 5. Had it used only $200 of debt, then its equity would have been $800, and its equity multiplier would have been only $1,000/$800 = 1.25.[9]

MicroDrive's return on equity (ROE) depends on its ROA and its use of leverage.

$$\text{ROE} = \text{ROA} \times \text{Equity multiplier}$$
$$= \frac{\text{Net income}}{\text{Total assets}} \times \frac{\text{Total assets}}{\text{Common equity}} \tag{4-2}$$

$$= 5.7\% \times \$2,000/\$896$$
$$= 5.7\% \times 2.23$$
$$= 12.7\%.$$

Now we can combine Equations 4-1 and 4-2 to form the *extended Du Pont equation*, which shows how the profit margin, the assets turnover ratio, and the equity multiplier combine to determine the ROE:

$$\text{ROE} = (\text{Profit margin})(\text{Total assets turnover})(\text{Equity multiplier})$$
$$= \frac{\text{Net income}}{\text{Sales}} \times \frac{\text{Sales}}{\text{Total assets}} \times \frac{\text{Total assets}}{\text{Common equity}}. \tag{4-3}$$

For MicroDrive, we have

$$\text{ROE} = (3.8\%)(1.5)(2.23)$$
$$= 12.7\%.$$

The 12.7 percent rate of return could, of course, be calculated directly: both Sales and Total assets cancel, leaving Net income/Common equity = $113.5/$896 = 12.7%. However, the Du Pont equation shows how the profit margin, the total assets turnover, and the use of debt interact to determine the return on equity.

The insights provided by the Du Pont model are valuable, and it can be used for "quick and dirty" estimates of the impact that operating changes have on returns. For example, holding all else equal, if MicroDrive can drive up its ratio of sales/total assets to 1.8, then its ROE will improve to (3.8%)(1.8)(2.23) = 15.25%. For a more complete "what if" analysis, most companies use a forecasting model such as the one described in Chapter 12.

SELF-TEST QUESTIONS

Explain how the extended, or modified, Du Pont equation can be used to reveal the basic determinants of ROE.

What is the equity multiplier?

COMPARATIVE RATIOS AND "BENCHMARKING"

Ratio analysis involves comparisons—a company's ratios are compared with those of other firms in the same industry, that is, with industry average figures. However, like most firms, MicroDrive's managers go one step further—they also compare their ratios with those of a smaller set of the leading computer companies. This technique is called **benchmarking**, and the companies used for the comparison are called **benchmark companies**.

---

[9] Expressed algebraically,

$$\text{Debt ratio} = \frac{\text{D}}{\text{A}} = \frac{\text{A} - \text{E}}{\text{A}} = \frac{\text{A}}{\text{A}} - \frac{\text{E}}{\text{A}} = 1 - \frac{1}{\text{Equity multiplier}}.$$

Here D is debt, E is equity, A is total assets, and A/E is the equity multiplier. This equation ignores preferred stock.

For example, MicroDrive benchmarks against five other firms that its management considers to be the best-managed companies with operations similar to its own.

Many companies also benchmark various parts of their overall operation against top companies, whether they are in the same industry or not. For example, MicroDrive has a division that sells hard drives directly to consumers through catalogs and the Internet. This division's shipping department benchmarks against L.L. Bean, even though they are in different industries, because L.L. Bean's shipping department is one of the best. MicroDrive wants its own shippers to strive to match L.L. Bean's record for on-time shipments.

Comparative ratios are available from a number of sources, including *Value Line*, Dun and Bradstreet (D&B), and the *Annual Statement Studies* published by Robert Morris Associates, which is the national association of bank loan officers. Table 4-6 reports selected ratios from Reuters available through Yahoo!.

Each data-supplying organization uses a somewhat different set of ratios designed for its own purposes. For example, D&B deals mainly with small firms, many of which are proprietorships, and it sells its services primarily to banks and other lenders. Therefore, D&B is concerned largely with the creditor's viewpoint, and its ratios emphasize current assets and liabilities, not market value ratios. So, when you select a comparative data source, you should be sure that your emphasis is similar to that of the agency whose ratios you plan to use. Additionally, there are often definitional differences in the ratios presented by different sources, so before using a source, be sure to verify the exact definitions of the ratios to ensure consistency with your own work.

SELF-TEST QUESTIONS

Differentiate between trend analysis and comparative ratio analysis.
Why is it useful to do a comparative ratio analysis?
What is benchmarking?

TABLE 4-6 | Comparative Ratios for Dell Computer Corporation, the Computer Hardware Industry, the Technology Sector, and the S&P 500

Ratio	Dell	Computer Hardware Industry[a]	Technology Sector[b]	S&P 500
P/E ratio	34.32	28.13	35.97	24.84
Market to book	14.11	7.86	5.19	4.52
Price to tangible book	14.11	9.11	7.06	8.02
Price to cash flow	31.23	20.64	25.87	18.07
Net profit margin	6.38	5.76	9.81	13.06
Quick ratio	0.81	1.03	2.55	1.28
Current ratio	0.98	1.26	3.03	1.78
Long-term debt to equity	0.08	0.38	0.24	0.68
Total debt to equity	0.08	0.52	0.29	0.85
Interest coverage (TIE)[c]	—	11.24	9.95	11.81
Return on assets	15.53	8.18	5.98	6.42
Return on equity	47.89	29.43	11.91	18.73
Inventory turnover	105.06	20.94	9.61	10.52
Asset turnover	2.43	1.45	0.76	0.92

[a]The computer hardware industry is comprised of 50 firms, including IBM, Dell, Sun Microsystems, Hewlett-Packard, and Hitachi.
[b]The technology sector contains 11 industries, including communications equipment, computer hardware, computer networks, semiconductors, and software and programming.
[c]Dell had more interest income than interest expense.

Source: http://www.reuters.com, accessed through Yahoo!, on April 7, 2004.

USES AND LIMITATIONS OF RATIO ANALYSIS

To find quick information about a company, go to **http://www.investor.reuters.com**. Here you can find company profiles, stock price and share information, and several key ratios.

Ratio analysis is used by three main groups: (1) *managers*, who employ ratios to help analyze, control, and thus improve their firms' operations; (2) *credit analysts*, including bank loan officers and bond rating analysts, who analyze ratios to help ascertain a company's ability to pay its debts; and (3) *stock analysts*, who are interested in a company's efficiency, risk, and growth prospects. In later chapters we will look more closely at the basic factors that underlie each ratio, which will give you a better idea about how to interpret and use ratios. Note, though, that while ratio analysis can provide useful information concerning a company's operations and financial condition, it does have limitations that necessitate care and judgment. Some potential problems are listed below:

1. Many large firms operate different divisions in different industries, and for such companies it is difficult to develop a meaningful set of industry averages. Therefore, ratio analysis is more useful for small, narrowly focused firms than for large, multidivisional ones.

2. Most firms want to be better than average, so merely attaining average performance is not necessarily good. As a target for high-level performance, it is best to focus on the industry leaders' ratios. Benchmarking helps in this regard.

3. Inflation may have badly distorted firms' balance sheets—recorded values are often substantially different from "true" values. Further, because inflation affects both depreciation charges and inventory costs, profits are also affected. Thus, a ratio analysis for one firm over time, or a comparative analysis of firms of different ages, must be interpreted with judgment.

4. Seasonal factors can also distort a ratio analysis. For example, the inventory turnover ratio for a food processor will be radically different if the balance sheet figure used for inventory is the one just before versus just after the close of the canning season. This problem can be minimized by using monthly averages for inventory (and receivables) when calculating turnover ratios.

5. Firms can employ **"window dressing" techniques** to make their financial statements look stronger. To illustrate, a Chicago builder borrowed on a two-year basis in late December. Because the loan was for more than one year, it was not included in current liabilities. The builder held the proceeds of the loan as cash. This improved his current and quick ratios, and made his year-end balance sheet look

stronger. However, the improvement was strictly window dressing; a week later the builder paid off the loan and the balance sheet was back at the old level.

6. Different accounting practices can distort comparisons. As noted earlier, inventory valuation and depreciation methods can affect financial statements and thus distort comparisons among firms. Also, if one firm leases a substantial amount of its productive equipment, then its assets may appear low relative to sales because leased assets often do not appear on the balance sheet. At the same time, the liability associated with the lease obligation may not be shown as a debt. Therefore, leasing can artificially improve both the turnover and the debt ratios.

7. It is difficult to generalize about whether a particular ratio is "good" or "bad." For example, a high current ratio may indicate a strong liquidity position, which is good, or excessive cash, which is bad (because excess cash in the bank is a non-earning asset). Similarly, a high fixed assets turnover ratio may denote either that a firm uses its assets efficiently or that it is undercapitalized and cannot afford to buy enough assets.

8. A firm may have some ratios that look "good" and others that look "bad," making it difficult to tell whether the company is, on balance, strong or weak. However, statistical procedures can be used to analyze the *net effects* of a set of ratios. Many banks and other lending organizations use discriminant analysis, a statistical technique, to analyze firms' financial ratios, and then classify the firms according to their probability of getting into financial trouble.

9. Effective use of financial ratios requires that the financial statements upon which they are based be accurate. Revelations in 2001 and 2002 of accounting fraud by such industry giants as WorldCom and Enron showed that financial statements are not always accurate, hence information based on reported data can be misleading.

Ratio analysis is useful, but analysts should be aware of these problems and make adjustments as necessary. Ratio analysis conducted in a mechanical, unthinking manner is dangerous, but used intelligently and with good judgment, it can provide useful insights into a firm's operations. Your judgment in interpreting a set of ratios is bound to be weak at this point, but it will improve as you go through the remainder of the book.

SELF-TEST QUESTIONS

List three types of users of ratio analysis. Would the different users emphasize the same or different types of ratios?

List several potential problems with ratio analysis.

LOOKING BEYOND THE NUMBERS

AAII's educational Web site at http:// www.aaii.com provides information on investing basics, financial planning, portfolio management, and the like, so individuals can manage their own assets more effectively.

Hopefully, working through this chapter has helped your understanding of financial statements and improved your ability to interpret accounting numbers. These important and basic skills are necessary when making business decisions, evaluating performance, and forecasting likely future developments.

Sound financial analysis involves more than just calculating numbers—good analysis requires that certain qualitative factors be considered when evaluating a company. These factors, as summarized by the American Association of Individual Investors (AAII), include the following:

1. **Are the company's revenues tied to one key customer?** If so, the company's performance may decline dramatically if the customer goes elsewhere.

2. **To what extent are the company's revenues tied to one key product?** Companies that rely on a single product may be more efficient and focused, but a lack of diversification increases risk.

3. **To what extent does the company rely on a single supplier?** Depending on a single supplier may lead to unanticipated shortages and thus to lower profits.

4. **What percentage of the company's business is generated overseas?** Companies with a large percentage of overseas business are often able to realize higher growth and larger profit margins. However, firms with large overseas operations also find that the value of their operations depends in large part on the value of the local currency. Thus, fluctuations in currency markets create additional risks for firms with large overseas operations. In addition, the political stability of the region is important.

5. **Competition.** It is important to consider both the likely actions of the current competition and the likelihood of new competitors in the future.

6. **Future prospects.** Does the company invest heavily in research and development? If so, its future prospects may depend critically on the success of products currently in the pipeline.

7. **Legal and regulatory environment.** It is crucial to factor in the effects of proposed regulations and pending or likely lawsuits.

SELF-TEST QUESTION

What are some qualitative factors analysts should consider when evaluating a company's likely future financial performance?

SUMMARY

The primary purpose of this chapter was to discuss techniques used by investors and managers to analyze financial statements. The key concepts covered are listed below.

- **Financial statement analysis** generally begins with a set of **financial ratios** designed to reveal a company's strengths and weaknesses as compared with other companies in the same industry, and to show whether its financial position has been improving or deteriorating over time.
- **Liquidity ratios** show the relationship of a firm's current assets to its current liabilities, and thus its ability to meet maturing debts. Two commonly used liquidity ratios are the **current ratio** and the **quick,** or **acid test, ratio.**
- **Asset management ratios** measure how effectively a firm is managing its assets. These ratios include **inventory turnover, days sales outstanding, fixed assets turnover,** and **total assets turnover.**
- **Debt management ratios** reveal (1) the extent to which the firm is financed with debt and (2) its likelihood of defaulting on its debt obligations. They include the **debt ratio, times-interest-earned ratio,** and **EBITDA coverage ratio.**
- **Profitability ratios** show the combined effects of liquidity, asset management, and debt management policies on operating results. They include the **profit margin on sales,** the **basic earning power ratio,** the **return on total assets,** and the **return on common equity.**
- **Market value ratios** relate the firm's stock price to its earnings, cash flow, and book value per share, thus giving management an indication of what investors think of the company's past performance and future prospects. These include the **price/earnings ratio, price/cash flow ratio,** and the **market/book ratio.**
- **Trend analysis,** where one plots a ratio over time, is important, because it reveals whether the firm's condition has been improving or deteriorating over time.
- The **Du Pont system** is designed to show how the profit margin on sales, the assets turnover ratio, and the use of debt interact to determine the rate of return on equity. The firm's management can use the Du Pont system to analyze ways of improving performance.
- **Benchmarking** is the process of comparing a particular company with a group of "benchmark" companies.
- **ROE** is important, but it does not take account of either the amount of investment or risk.

Ratio analysis has limitations, but used with care and judgment, it can be very helpful.

QUESTIONS

(4-1) Define each of the following terms:
a. Liquidity ratios: current ratio; quick, or acid test, ratio
b. Asset management ratios: inventory turnover ratio; days sales outstanding (DSO); fixed assets turnover ratio; total assets turnover ratio
c. Financial leverage: debt ratio; times-interest-earned (TIE) ratio; coverage ratio
d. Profitability ratios: profit margin on sales; basic earning power (BEP) ratio; return on total assets (ROA); return on common equity (ROE)
e. Market value ratios: price/earnings (P/E) ratio; price/cash flow ratio; market/book (M/B) ratio; book value per share
f. Trend analysis; comparative ratio analysis; benchmarking
g. Du Pont equation; "window dressing"; seasonal effects on ratios

(4-2) Financial ratio analysis is conducted by managers, equity investors, long-term creditors, and short-term creditors. What is the primary emphasis of each of these groups in evaluating ratios?

(4-3) Over the past year, M. D. Ryngaert & Co. has realized an increase in its current ratio and a drop in its total assets turnover ratio. However, the company's sales, quick ratio, and fixed assets turnover ratio have remained constant. What explains these changes?

(4-4) Profit margins and turnover ratios vary from one industry to another. What differences would you expect to find between a grocery chain such as Safeway and a steel company? Think particularly about the turnover ratios, the profit margin, and the Du Pont equation.

(4-5) How might (a) seasonal factors and (b) different growth rates distort a comparative ratio analysis? Give some examples. How might these problems be alleviated?

(4-6) Why is it sometimes misleading to compare a company's financial ratios with other firms that operate in the same industry?

SELF-TEST PROBLEMS   Solutions Appear in Appendix A

(ST-1)
Debt Ratio
K. Billingsworth & Co. had earnings per share of $4 last year, and it paid a $2 dividend. Total retained earnings increased by $12 million during the year, while book value per share at year-end was $40. Billingsworth has no preferred stock, and no new common stock was issued during the year. If Billingsworth's year-end debt (which equals its total liabilities) was $120 million, what was the company's year-end debt/assets ratio?

(ST-2)
Ratio Analysis
The following data apply to A. L. Kaiser & Company (millions of dollars):

Cash and marketable securities	$100.00
Fixed assets	$283.50
Sales	$1,000.00
Net income	$50.00
Quick ratio	2.0×
Current ratio	3.0×
DSO	40.55 days
ROE	12%

Kaiser has no preferred stock—only common equity, current liabilities, and long-term debt.

    a. Find Kaiser's (1) accounts receivable (A/R), (2) current liabilities, (3) current assets, (4) total assets, (5) ROA, (6) common equity, and (7) long-term debt.

    b. In part a, you should have found Kaiser's accounts receivable (A/R) = $111.1 million. If Kaiser could reduce its DSO from 40.55 days to 30.4 days while holding other things constant, how much cash would it generate? If this cash were used to buy back common stock (at book value), thus reducing the amount of common equity, how would this affect (1) the ROE, (2) the ROA, and (3) the total debt/total assets ratio?

PROBLEMS

(4-1)
Liquidity Ratios

Ace Industries has current assets equal to $3 million. The company's current ratio is 1.5, and its quick ratio is 1.0. What is the firm's level of current liabilities? What is the firm's level of inventories?

(4-2)
Days Sales Outstanding

Baker Brothers has a DSO of 40 days. The company's average daily sales are $20,000. What is the level of its accounts receivable? Assume there are 365 days in a year.

(4-3)
Debt Ratio

Bartley Barstools has an equity multiplier of 2.4. The company's assets are financed with some combination of long-term debt and common equity. What is the company's debt ratio?

(4-4)
Du Pont Analysis

Doublewide Dealers has an ROA of 10 percent, a 2 percent profit margin, and a return on equity equal to 15 percent. What is the company's total assets turnover? What is the firm's equity multiplier?

(4-5)
Ratio Calculations

Assume you are given the following relationships for the Brauer Corporation:

Sales/Total assets	1.5×
Return on assets (ROA)	3%
Return on equity (ROE)	5%

Calculate Brauer's profit margin and debt ratio.

(4-6)
Liquidity Ratios

The Petry Company has $1,312,500 in current assets and $525,000 in current liabilities. Its initial inventory level is $375,000, and it will raise funds as additional notes payable and use them to increase inventory. How much can Petry's short-term debt (notes payable) increase without pushing its current ratio below 2.0? What will be the firm's quick ratio after Petry has raised the maximum amount of short-term funds?

(4-7)
Ratio Calculations

The Kretovich Company had a quick ratio of 1.4, a current ratio of 3.0, an inventory turnover of 6 times, total current assets of $810,000, and cash and marketable securities of $120,000. What were Kretovich's annual sales and its DSO? Assume a 365-day year.

(4-8)
Times-Interest-Earned Ratio

The H. R. Pickett Corporation has $500,000 of debt outstanding, and it pays an interest rate of 10 percent annually: Pickett's annual sales are $2 million, its average tax rate is 30 percent, and its net profit margin on sales is 5 percent. If the company does not maintain a TIE ratio of at least 5 times, its bank will refuse to renew the loan, and bankruptcy will result. What is Pickett's TIE ratio?

(4-9)
Ratio Analysis

Data for Barry Computer Company and its industry averages follow.

    a. Calculate the indicated ratios for Barry.

    b. Construct the extended Du Pont equation for both Barry and the industry.

    c. Outline Barry's strengths and weaknesses as revealed by your analysis.

    d. Suppose Barry had doubled its sales as well as its inventories, accounts receivable, and common equity during 2005. How would that information affect the validity of your ratio analysis? (Hint: Think about averages and the effects of rapid growth on ratios if averages are not used. No calculations are needed.)

Barry Computer Company: Balance Sheet as of December 31, 2005 (In Thousands)

Cash	$ 77,500	Accounts payable	$129,000
Receivables	336,000	Notes payable	84,000
Inventories	241,500	Other current liabilities	117,000
Total current assets	$655,000	Total current liabilities	$330,000
Net fixed assets	292,500	Long-term debt	256,500
		Common equity	361,000
Total assets	$947,500	Total liabilities and equity	$947,500

Barry Computer Company: Income Statement for Year Ended December 31, 2005 (In Thousands)

Sales	$1,607,500
Cost of goods sold	1,392,500
Selling, general, and administrative expenses	145,000
Earnings before interest and taxes (EBIT)	$ 70,000
Interest expense	24,500
Earnings before taxes (EBT)	$ 45,500
Federal and state income taxes (40%)	18,200
Net income	$ 27,300

Ratio	Barry	Industry Average
Current assets/current liabilities	_____	2.0×
Days sales outstanding[a]	_____	35 days
Sales/inventory	_____	6.7×
Sales/fixed assets	_____	12.1×
Sales/total assets	_____	3.0×
Net income/sales	_____	1.2%
Net income/total assets	_____	3.6%
Net income/common equity	_____	9.0%
Total debt/total assets	_____	60.0%

[a]Calculation is based on a 365-day year.

(4-10)
Balance Sheet Analysis
Complete the balance sheet and sales information in the table that follows for Hoffmeister Industries using the following financial data:

Debt ratio: 50%
Quick ratio: 0.80×
Total assets turnover: 1.5×
Days sales outstanding: 36.5 days[a]
Gross profit margin on sales: (Sales − Cost of goods sold)/Sales = 25%
Inventory turnover ratio: 5×

[a]Calculation is based on a 365-day year.

BALANCE SHEET

Cash	_____	Accounts payable	_____
Accounts receivable	_____	Long-term debt	60,000
Inventories	_____	Common stock	_____
Fixed assets	_____	Retained earnings	97,500
Total assets	$300,000	Total liabilities and equity	_____
Sales	_____	Cost of goods sold	_____

(4-11)
Ratio Analysis
The Corrigan Corporation's forecasted 2006 financial statements follow, along with some industry average ratios.

a. Calculate Corrigan's 2006 forecasted ratios, compare them with the industry average data, and comment briefly on Corrigan's projected strengths and weaknesses.

b. What do you think would happen to Corrigan's ratios if the company initiated cost-cutting measures that allowed it to hold lower levels of inventory and substantially decreased the cost of goods sold? No calculations are necessary. Think about which ratios would be affected by changes in these two accounts.

Corrigan Corporation: Forecasted Balance Sheet as of December 31, 2006

Cash	$ 72,000
Accounts receivable	439,000
Inventories	894,000
Total current assets	$1,405,000
Fixed assets	431,000
Total assets	$1,836,000
Accounts and notes payable	$ 432,000
Accruals	170,000
Total current liabilities	$ 602,000
Long-term debt	404,290
Common stock	575,000
Retained earnings	254,710
Total liabilities and equity	$1,836,000

Corrigan Corporation: Forecasted Income Statement for 2006

Sales	$4,290,000
Cost of goods sold	3,580,000
Selling, general, and administrative expenses	370,320
Depreciation	159,000
Earnings before taxes (EBT)	$ 180,680
Taxes (40%)	72,272
Net income	$ 108,408

Per-Share Data	
EPS	$4.71
Cash dividends per share	$0.95
P/E ratio	5×
Market price (average)	$23.57
Number of shares outstanding	23,000
Industry Financial Ratios (2005)[a]	
Quick ratio	1.0×
Current ratio	2.7×
Inventory turnover[b]	7.0×
Days sales outstanding[c]	32 days
Fixed assets turnover[b]	13.0×
Total assets turnover[b]	2.6×
Return on assets	9.1%
Return on equity	18.2%
Debt ratio	50.0%
Profit margin on sales	3.5%
P/E ratio	6.0×
P/cash flow ratio	3.5×

[a]Industry average ratios have been constant for the past 4 years.
[b]Based on year-end balance sheet figures.
[c]Calculation is based on a 365-day year.

SPREADSHEET PROBLEM

(4-12)
Build a Model:
Ratio Analysis

CF

e-resource

Start with the partial model in the file *CF2 Ch 04 P12 Build a Model.xls* from the textbook's Web site. This problem requires you to further analyze the financial data given for Cumberland Industries in the Build a Model problem for Chapter 3.

Cumberland Industries' common stock has increased in price from $14.75 to $17.25 from the end of 2004 to the end of 2005, and its shares outstanding increased from 9 to 10 million shares during that same period. Cumberland has annual lease payments of $75,000 (which is included in operating costs on the income statement), but no sinking fund payments are required. Now answer the following questions.

Using Cumberland's financial statements as given in the Chapter 3 Build a Model problem, perform a ratio analysis for 2004 and 2005. Consider its liquidity, asset management, debt management, profitability, and market value ratios.

a. Has Cumberland's liquidity position improved or worsened? Explain.
b. Has Cumberland's ability to manage its assets improved or worsened? Explain.
c. How has Cumberland's profitability changed during the last year?
d. Perform an extended Du Pont analysis for Cumberland for 2004 and 2005.
e. Perform a common size analysis. What has happened to the composition (that is, percentage in each category) of assets and liabilities?
f. Perform a percent change analysis. What does this tell you about the change in profitability and asset utilization?

CYBERPROBLEM

Please go to our Web site, **http://ehrhardt.swlearning.com**, to access any Cyberproblems.

THOMSON ONE
Business School Edition

Please go to **http://ehrhardt.swlearning.com** to access any Thomson ONE—Business School Edition problems.

MINI CASE

The first part of the case, presented in Chapter 3, discussed the situation that Computron Industries was in after an expansion program. Thus far, sales have not been up to the forecasted level, costs have been higher than were projected, and a large loss occurred in 2005, rather than the expected profit. As a result, its managers, directors, and investors are concerned about the firm's survival.

Donna Jamison was brought in as assistant to Fred Campo, Computron's chairman, who had the task of getting the company back into a sound financial position. Computron's 2004 and 2005 balance sheets and income statements, together with projections for 2006, are shown in the following tables. Also, the tables show the 2004 and 2005 financial ratios, along with industry average data. The 2006 projected financial statement data represent Jamison's and Campo's best guess for 2006 results, assuming that some new financing is arranged to get the company "over the hump."

BALANCE SHEETS

	2004	2005	2006E
Assets			
Cash	$ 9,000	$ 7,282	$ 14,000
Short-term investments	48,600	20,000	71,632
Accounts receivable	351,200	632,160	878,000
Inventories	715,200	1,287,360	1,716,480
Total current assets	$1,124,000	$1,946,802	$2,680,112
Gross fixed assets	491,000	1,202,950	1,220,000
Less: Accumulated depreciation	146,200	263,160	383,160
Net fixed assets	$ 344,800 ·	$ 939,790	$ 836,840
Total assets	$1,468,800	$2,886,592	$3,516,952
Liabilities and Equity			
Accounts payable	$ 145,600	$ 324,000	$ 359,800
Notes payable	200,000	720,000	300,000
Accruals	136,000	284,960	380,000
Total current liabilities	$ 481,600	$1,328,960	$1,039,800
Long-term debt	323,432	1,000,000	500,000
Common stock (100,000 shares)	460,000	460,000	1,680,936
Retained earnings	203,768	97,632	296,216
Total equity	$ 663,768	$ 557,632	$1,977,152
Total liabilities and equity	$1,468,800	$2,886,592	$3,516,952

Note: "E" indicates estimated. The 2006 data are forecasts.

INCOME STATEMENTS

	2004	2005	2006E
Sales	$3,432,000	$5,834,400	$7,035,600
Cost of goods sold	2,864,000	4,980,000	5,800,000
Other expenses	340,000	720,000	612,960
Depreciation	18,900	116,960	120,000
Total operating costs	$3,222,900	$5,816,960	$6,532,960
EBIT	$ 209,100	$ 17,440	$ 502,640
Interest expense	62,500	176,000	80,000
EBT	$ 146,600	$ 158,560	$ 422,640
Taxes (40%)	58,640	(63,424	169,056
Net income	$ 87,960	$ 95,136	$ 253,548
Other Data			
Stock price	$8.50	$6.00	$12.17
Shares outstanding	100,000	100,000	250,000
EPS	$0.880	($0.951)	$1.014
DPS	$0.220	0.110	0.220
Tax rate	40%	40%	40%
Book value per share	$6.638	$5.576	$7.909
Lease payments	$40,000	$40,000	$40,000

Note: "E" indicates estimated. The 2006 data are forecasts.

RATIO ANALYSIS

	2004	2005	2006E	Industry Average
Current	2.3×	1.5×	—	2.7×
Quick	0.8×	0.5×	—	1.0×
Inventory turnover	4.8×	4.5×	—	6.1×
Days sales outstanding	37.3	39.6	—	32.0
Fixed assets turnover	10.0×	6.2×	—	7.0×
Total assets turnover	2.3×	2.0×	—	2.5×
Debt ratio	54.8%	80.7%	—	50.0%
TIE	3.3×	0.1×	—	6.2×
EBITDA coverage	2.6×	0.8×	—	8.0×
Profit margin	2.6%	−1.6%	—	3.6%
Basic earning power	14.2%	0.6%	—	17.8%
ROA	6.0%	−3.3%	—	9.0%
ROE	13.3%	−17.1%	—	17.9%
Price/earnings (P/E)	9.7×	−6.3×	—	16.2×
Price/cash flow	8.0×	27.5×	—	7.6×
Market/book	1.3×	1.1×	—	2.9×

Note: "E" indicates estimated. The 2006 data are forecasts.

Jamison examined monthly data for 2005 (not given in the case), and she detected an improving pattern during the year. Monthly sales were rising, costs were falling, and large losses in the early months had turned to a small profit by December. Thus, the annual data looked somewhat worse than final monthly data. Also, it appears to be taking longer for the advertising program to get the message across, for the new sales offices to generate sales, and for the new manufacturing facilities to operate efficiently. In other words, the lags between spending money and deriving benefits were longer than Computron's managers had anticipated. For these reasons, Jamison and Campo see hope for the company—provided it can survive in the short run.

Jamison must prepare an analysis of where the company is now, what it must do to regain its financial health, and what actions should be taken. Your assignment is to help her answer the following questions. Provide clear explanations, not yes or no answers.

a. Why are ratios useful? What are the five major categories of ratios?

b. Calculate the 2006 current and quick ratios based on the projected balance sheet and income statement data. What can you say about the company's liquidity position in 2004, 2005, and as projected for 2006? We often think of ratios as being useful (1) to managers to help run the business, (2) to bankers for credit analysis, and (3) to stockholders for stock valuation. Would these different types of analysts have an equal interest in the liquidity ratios?

c. Calculate the 2006 inventory turnover, days sales outstanding (DSO), fixed assets turnover, and total assets turnover. How does Computron's utilization of assets stack up against other firms in its industry?

d. Calculate the 2006 debt, times-interest-earned, and EBITDA coverage ratios. How does Computron compare with the industry with respect to financial leverage? What can you conclude from these ratios?

e. Calculate the 2006 profit margin, basic earning power (BEP), return on assets (ROA), and return on equity (ROE). What can you say about these ratios?

f. Calculate the 2006 price/earnings ratio, price/cash flow ratio, and market/book ratio. Do these ratios indicate that investors are expected to have a high or low opinion of the company?

g. Perform a common size analysis and percent change analysis. What do these analyses tell you about Computron?

h. Use the extended Du Pont equation to provide a summary and overview of Computron's financial condition as projected for 2006. What are the firm's major strengths and weaknesses?

i. What are some potential problems and limitations of financial ratio analysis?

j. What are some qualitative factors analysts should consider when evaluating a company's likely future financial performance?

SELECTED ADDITIONAL REFERENCES AND CASES

The effects of alternative accounting policies on both financial statements and ratios based on these statements are discussed in the books referenced in Chapter 3.

The following cases from the Finance Online Case Library *cover many of the concepts discussed in this chapter and are available at* ***http://www.textchoice.com:***

Case 35, "Mark X Company (A)," which illustrates the use of ratio analysis in the evaluation of a firm's existing and potential financial positions.

Case 36, "Garden State Container Corporation," which is similar in content to Case 35.

Case 36A, "Safe Packaging Corporation," which updates Case 36.

CHAPTER 5

Risk and Return

S kill or luck? That's the question The Wall Street Journal's *Investment Dartboard Contest sought to answer by pitting the stock-picking ability of professional analysts against amateurs and dart throwers. Here's how the contest worked. First,* The Wall Street Journal (WSJ) *picked four professional analysts, and each of those pros formed a portfolio by picking four stocks. The stocks had to trade on the NYSE, AMEX, or Nasdaq; have a market capitalization of at least $50 million and a stock price of at least $2; and have average daily trades of at least $100,000. Second, amateurs could enter the contest by e-mailing their pick of a single stock to the WSJ, which then picked four amateurs at random and combined their choices to make a four-stock portfolio. Third, a group of WSJ editors formed a portfolio by throwing four darts at the stock tables. At the beginning of each contest, the WSJ announced the six resulting portfolios, and at the end of six months, the paper announced the results. The top two pros were invited back for the next contest.*

Since 1990 there have been 142 completed contests. The pros beat the darts 87 times and lost 55 times. The pros also beat the Dow Jones Industrial Average in 54 percent of the contests. The pros had an average six-month portfolio return of 10.2 percent; much higher than either the DJIA six-month average of 5.6 percent or the darts' return of only 3.5 percent. The readers, meantime, lost an average of 4 percent versus a same-period (30 contests) gain of 7.2 percent for the pros.

Do these results mean that skill is more important than luck when it comes to investing in stocks? Not necessarily, according to Burton Malkiel, an economics professor at Princeton and the author of the widely read book, A Random Walk Down Wall Street. *Since the dart-selected portfolios consist of randomly chosen stocks, they should have average risk. However, the pros have consistently picked high-risk stocks. Because there was a bull market during most of the contest, one would expect high-risk stocks to outperform the average stock. According to Malkiel, the pros' performance could be due to a rising market rather than superior analytical skills. The WSJ stopped that contest in 2002, so we won't know for sure whether Malkiel was right or wrong.*

The WSJ *now runs a new contest, pitting six amateurs against six darts. In the recently completed Contest No. 13, the readers trounced the darts by gaining 139 percent versus the darts' gain of 86 percent. If you would like to enter the contest, e-mail your stock pick to* **sundaydartboard@wsj.com.**

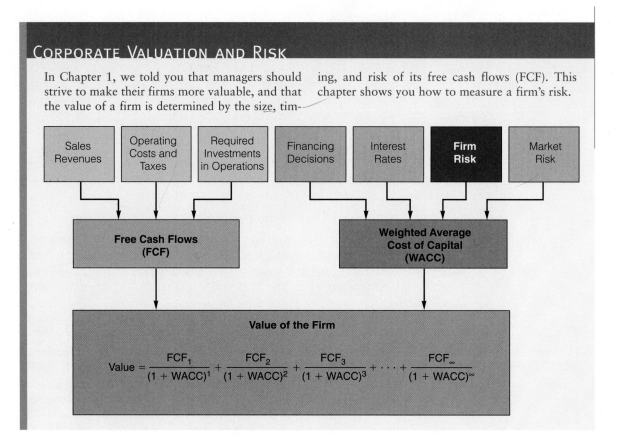

CORPORATE VALUATION AND RISK

In Chapter 1, we told you that managers should strive to make their firms more valuable, and that the value of a firm is determined by the size, tim-

ing, and risk of its free cash flows (FCF). This chapter shows you how to measure a firm's risk.

e-resource

The textbook's Web site contains an Excel *file that will guide you through the chapter's calculations. The file for this chapter is* **CF2 Ch 05 Tool Kit .xls,** *and we encourage you to open the file and follow along as you read the chapter.*

In this chapter, we start from the basic premise that investors like returns and dislike risk. Therefore, people will invest in riskier assets only if they expect to receive higher returns. We define precisely what the term *risk* means as it relates to investments. We examine procedures managers use to measure risk, and we discuss the relationship between risk and return. In later chapters we extend these relationships to show how risk and return interact to determine security prices. Managers must understand and apply these concepts as they plan the actions that will shape their firms' futures.

INVESTMENT RETURNS

With most investments, an individual or business spends money today with the expectation of earning even more money in the future. The concept of *return* provides investors with a convenient way to express the financial performance of an investment. To illustrate, suppose you buy 10 shares of a stock for $1,000. The stock pays no dividends, but at the end of one year, you sell the stock for $1,100. What is the return on your $1,000 investment?

One way to express an investment return is in *dollar terms*. The dollar return is simply the total dollars received from the investment less the amount invested:

$$\text{Dollar return} = \text{Amount received} - \text{Amount invested}$$
$$= \$1,100 - \$1,000$$
$$= \$100.$$

If, at the end of the year, you sell the stock for only $900, your dollar return would be −$100.

Although expressing returns in dollars is easy, two problems arise: (1) To make a meaningful judgment about the return, you need to know the scale (size) of the investment; a $100 return on a $100 investment is a good return (assuming the investment is held for one year), but a $100 return on a $10,000 investment would be a poor return. (2) You also need to know the timing of the return; a $100 return on a $100 investment is a very good return if it occurs after one year, but the same dollar return after 20 years would not be very good.

The solution to the scale and timing problems is to express investment results as *rates of return,* or *percentage returns.* For example, the rate of return on the 1-year stock investment, when $1,100 is received after one year, is 10 percent:

$$\text{Rate of return} = \frac{\text{Amount received} - \text{Amount invested}}{\text{Amount invested}}$$

$$= \frac{\text{Dollar return}}{\text{Amount invested}} = \frac{\$100}{\$1,000}$$

$$= 0.10 = 10\%.$$

The rate of return calculation "standardizes" the return by considering the annual return per unit of investment. Although this example has only one outflow and one inflow, the annualized rate of return can easily be calculated in situations where multiple cash flows occur over time by using time value of money concepts.

SELF-TEST QUESTIONS

Differentiate between dollar returns and rates of return.

Why are rates of return superior to dollar returns in terms of accounting for the size of investment and the timing of cash flows?

STAND-ALONE RISK

Risk is defined in *Webster's* as "a hazard; a peril; exposure to loss or injury." Thus, risk refers to the chance that some unfavorable event will occur. If you engage in skydiving, you are taking a chance with your life—skydiving is risky. If you bet on the horses, you are risking your money. If you invest in speculative stocks (or, really, *any* stock), you are taking a risk in the hope of making an appreciable return.

An asset's risk can be analyzed in two ways: (1) on a stand-alone basis, where the asset is considered in isolation, and (2) on a portfolio basis, where the asset is held as one of a number of assets in a portfolio. Thus, an asset's **stand-alone risk** is the risk an investor would face if he or she held only this one asset. Obviously, most assets are held in portfolios, but it is necessary to understand stand-alone risk in order to understand risk in a portfolio context.

To illustrate the risk of financial assets, suppose an investor buys $100,000 of short-term Treasury bills with an expected return of 5 percent. In this case, the rate of return on the investment, 5 percent, can be estimated quite precisely, and the investment is defined as being essentially *risk free.* However, if the $100,000 were invested in the stock of a company just being organized to prospect for oil in the mid-Atlantic, then the investment's return could not be estimated precisely. One might analyze the situation and conclude that the *expected* rate of return, in a statistical sense, is 20 percent, but the investor should recognize that the *actual* rate of return could range from, say, +1,000 percent to −100 percent. Because there is a significant danger of actually earning much less than the expected return, the stock would be relatively risky.

No investment should be undertaken unless the expected rate of return is high enough to compensate the investor for the perceived risk of the investment. In our example, it is clear that few if any investors would be willing to buy the oil company's stock if its expected return were the same as that of the T-bill.

Risky assets rarely actually produce their expected rates of return—generally, risky assets earn either more or less than was originally expected. Indeed, if assets always produced their expected returns, they would not be risky. Investment risk, then, is related to the probability of actually earning a low or negative return—the greater the chance of a low or negative return, the riskier the investment. However, risk can be defined more precisely, and we do so in the next section.

Probability Distributions

An event's *probability* is defined as the chance that the event will occur. For example, a weather forecaster might state, "There is a 40 percent chance of rain today and a 60 percent chance that it will not rain." If all possible events, or outcomes, are listed, and if a probability is assigned to each event, the listing is called a **probability distribution.** Keep in mind that the probabilities must sum to 1.0, or 100 percent.

With this in mind, consider the possible rates of return due to dividends and stock price changes that you might earn next year on a $10,000 investment in the stock of either Sale.com or Basic Foods Inc. Sale.com is an Internet company offering deep discounts on factory seconds and overstocked merchandise. Because it faces intense competition, its new services may or may not be competitive in the marketplace, so its future earnings cannot be predicted very well. Indeed, some new company could develop better services and literally bankrupt Sale.com. Basic Foods, on the other hand, distributes essential food staples to grocery stores, and its sales and profits are relatively stable and predictable.

The rate-of-return probability distributions for the two companies are shown in Table 5-1. There is a 30 percent chance of strong demand, in which case both companies will have high earnings, pay high dividends, and enjoy capital gains. There is a 40 percent probability of normal demand and moderate returns, and there is a 30 percent probability of weak demand, which will mean low earnings and dividends as well as capital losses. Notice, however, that Sale.com's rate of return could vary far more widely than that of Basic Foods. There is a fairly high probability that the value of Sale.com's stock will drop substantially, resulting in a 70 percent loss, while there is a much smaller possible loss for Basic Foods.

Expected Rate of Return

If we multiply each possible outcome by its probability of occurrence and then sum these products, as in Table 5-2, we have a *weighted average* of outcomes. The weights are the

TABLE 5-1 | Probability Distributions for Sale.com and Basic Foods

Demand for the Company's Products	Probability of This Demand Occurring	RATE OF RETURN ON STOCK IF THIS DEMAND OCCURS	
		Sale.com	Basic Foods
Strong	0.3	100%	40%
Normal	0.4	15	15
Weak	0.3	(70)	(10)
	1.0		

TABLE 5-2	Calculation of Expected Rates of Return: Payoff Matrix				
		SALE.COM		BASIC FOODS	
Demand for the Company's Products (1)	Probability of This Demand Occurring (2)	Rate of Return if This Demand Occurs (3)	Product: $(2) \times (3)$ $= (4)$	Rate of Return if This Demand Occurs (5)	Product: $(2) \times (5)$ $= (6)$
Strong	0.3	100%	30%	40%	12%
Normal	0.4	15	6	15	6
Weak	0.3	(70)	(21)	(10)	(3)
	1.0		$\hat{r} = 15\%$		$\hat{r} = 15\%$

probabilities, and the weighted average is the **expected rate of return, $\hat{r}$,** called "r-hat."[1] The expected rates of return for both Sale.com and Basic Foods are shown in Table 5-2 to be 15 percent. This type of table is known as a *payoff matrix*.

The expected rate of return calculation can also be expressed as an equation that does the same thing as the payoff matrix table:

$$\text{Expected rate of return} = \hat{r} = P_1 r_1 + P_2 r_2 + \cdots + P_n r_n$$
$$= \sum_{i=1}^{n} P_i r_i. \tag{5-1}$$

Here r_i is the *i*th possible outcome, P_i is the probability of the *i*th outcome, and n is the number of possible outcomes. Thus, $\hat{r}$ is a weighted average of the possible outcomes (the r_i values), with each outcome's weight being its probability of occurrence. Using the data for Sale.com, we obtain its expected rate of return as follows:

$$\hat{r} = P_1(r_1) + P_2(r_2) + P_3(r_3)$$
$$= 0.3(100\%) + 0.4(15\%) + 0.3(-70\%)$$
$$= 15\%.$$

Basic Foods' expected rate of return is also 15 percent:

$$\hat{r} = 0.3(40\%) + 0.4(15\%) + 0.3(-10\%)$$
$$= 15\%.$$

We can graph the rates of return to obtain a picture of the variability of possible outcomes; this is shown in the Figure 5-1 bar charts. The height of each bar signifies the probability that a given outcome will occur. The range of probable returns for Sale.com is from -70 to $+100$ percent, with an expected return of 15 percent. The expected return for Basic Foods is also 15 percent, but its range is much narrower.

Thus far, we have assumed that only three situations can exist: strong, normal, and weak demand. Actually, of course, demand could range from a deep depression to a fantastic boom, and there are an unlimited number of possibilities in between. Suppose we had the time and patience to assign a probability to each possible level of demand (with

---

[1] In later chapters, we will use $\hat{r}_d$ and $\hat{r}_s$ to signify the returns on bonds and stocks, respectively. However, this distinction is unnecessary in this chapter, so we just use the general term, $\hat{r}$, to signify the expected return on an investment.

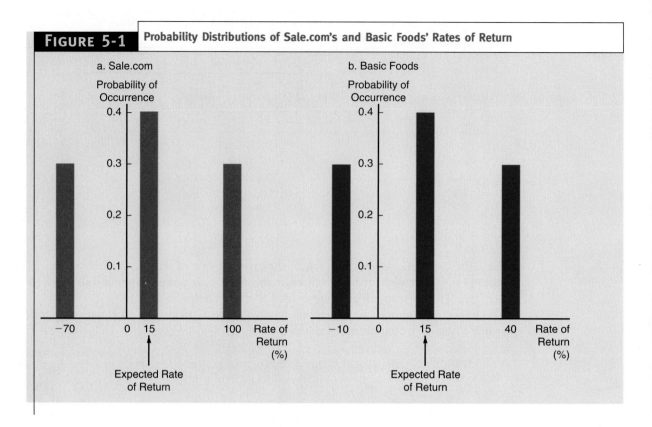

FIGURE 5-1   Probability Distributions of Sale.com's and Basic Foods' Rates of Return

the sum of the probabilities still equaling 1.0) and to assign a rate of return to each stock for each level of demand. We would have a table similar to Table 5-1, except that it would have many more entries in each column. This table could be used to calculate expected rates of return as shown previously, and the probabilities and outcomes could be approximated by continuous curves such as those presented in Figure 5-2. Here we have changed the assumptions so that there is essentially a zero probability that Sale.com's return will be less than −70 percent or more than 100 percent, or that Basic Foods' return will be less than −10 percent or more than 40 percent, but virtually any return within these limits is possible.

The tighter, or more peaked, the probability distribution, the more likely it is that the actual outcome will be close to the expected value, and, consequently, the less likely it is that the actual return will end up far below the expected return. Thus, the tighter the probability distribution, the lower the risk assigned to a stock. Since Basic Foods has a relatively tight probability distribution, its *actual return* is likely to be closer to its 15 percent *expected return* than is that of Sale.com.

Measuring Stand-Alone Risk: The Standard Deviation

Risk is a difficult concept to grasp, and a great deal of controversy has surrounded attempts to define and measure it. However, a common definition, and one that is satisfactory for many purposes, is stated in terms of probability distributions such as those presented in Figure 5-2: *The tighter the probability distribution of expected future returns, the smaller the risk of a given investment.* According to this definition, Basic Foods is less risky than Sale.com because there is a smaller chance that its actual return will end up far below its expected return.

To be most useful, any measure of risk should have a definite value—we need a measure of the tightness of the probability distribution. One such measure is the **standard deviation,** the symbol for which is **σ,** pronounced "sigma." The smaller the standard deviation,

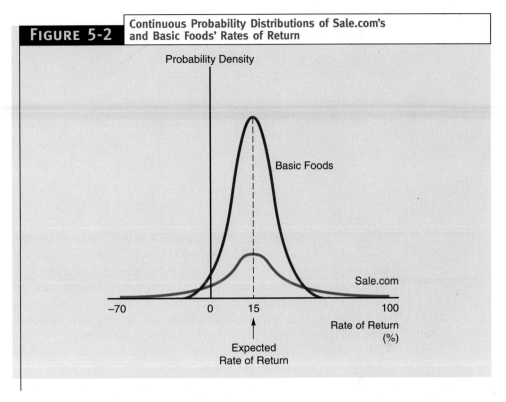

FIGURE 5-2	Continuous Probability Distributions of Sale.com's and Basic Foods' Rates of Return

Note: The assumptions regarding the probabilities of various outcomes have been changed from those in Figure 5-1. There the probability of obtaining exactly 15 percent was 40 percent; here it is much smaller because there are many possible outcomes instead of just three. With continuous distributions, it is more appropriate to ask what the probability is of obtaining at least some specified rate of return than to ask what the probability is of obtaining exactly that rate. This topic is covered in detail in statistics courses.

the tighter the probability distribution, and, accordingly, the less risky the stock. To calculate the standard deviation, we proceed as shown in Table 5-3, taking the following steps:

1. Calculate the expected rate of return:

$$\text{Expected rate of return} = \hat{r} = \sum_{i=1}^{n} P_i r_i.$$

   For Sale.com, we previously found $\hat{r} = 15\%$.

2. Subtract the expected rate of return ($\hat{r}$) from each possible outcome (r_i) to obtain a set of deviations about $\hat{r}$ as shown in Column 1 of Table 5-3:

$$\text{Deviation}_i = r_i - \hat{r}.$$

3. Square each deviation, then multiply the result by the probability of occurrence for its related outcome, and then sum these products to obtain the **variance** of the probability distribution as shown in Columns 2 and 3 of the table:

$$\text{Variance} = \sigma^2 = \sum_{i=1}^{n} (r_i - \hat{r})^2 P_i. \qquad \text{(5-2)}$$

4. Finally, find the square root of the variance to obtain the standard deviation:

$$\text{Standard deviation} = \sigma = \sqrt{\sum_{i=1}^{n} (r_i - \hat{r})^2 P_i}. \qquad \text{(5-3)}$$

TABLE 5-3 | Calculating Sale.com's Standard Deviation

$r_i - \hat{r}$ (1)		$(r_i - \hat{r})^2$ (2)	$(r_i - \hat{r})^2 P_i$ (3)
$100 - 15 =$	85	$7,225$	$(7,225)(0.3) = 2,167.5$
$15 - 15 =$	0	0	$(0)(0.4) = 0.0$
$-70 - 15 =$	-85	$7,225$	$(7,225)(0.3) = \underline{2,167.5}$
			Variance $= \sigma^2 = \underline{\underline{4,335.0}}$
			Standard deviation $= \sigma = \sqrt{\sigma^2} = \sqrt{4,335} = 65.84\%.$

Thus, the standard deviation is essentially a weighted average of the deviations from the expected value, and it provides an idea of how far above or below the expected value the actual value is likely to be. Sale.com's standard deviation is seen in Table 5-3 to be $\sigma = 65.84\%$. Using these same procedures, we find Basic Foods' standard deviation to be 19.36 percent. Sale.com has the larger standard deviation, which indicates a greater variation of returns and thus a greater chance that the actual return may be substantially lower than the expected return. Therefore, Sale.com is a riskier investment than Basic Foods when held alone.

If a probability distribution is normal, the *actual* return will be within ±1 standard deviation of the *expected* return 68.26 percent of the time. Figure 5-3 illustrates this point, and it also shows the situation for ±2σ and ±3σ. For Sale.com, $\hat{r} = 15\%$ and $\sigma = 65.84\%$, whereas $\hat{r} = 15\%$ and $\sigma = 19.36\%$ for Basic Foods. Thus, if the two distributions were normal, there would be a 68.26 percent probability that Sale.com's actual return would be in the range of 15 ± 65.84 percent, or from -50.84 to 80.84 percent. For Basic Foods, the

e-resource

For more discussion of probability distributions, see the Chapter 5 Web Extension on the textbook's Web site at http://ehrhardt .swlearning.com.

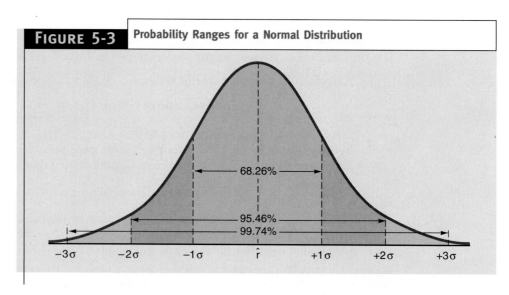

FIGURE 5-3 | **Probability Ranges for a Normal Distribution**

Notes:

a. The area under the normal curve always equals 1.0, or 100 percent. *Thus, the areas under any pair of normal curves drawn on the same scale, whether they are peaked or flat, must be equal.*

b. Half of the area under a normal curve is to the left of the mean, indicating that there is a 50 percent probability that the actual outcome will be less than the mean, and half is to the right of $\hat{r}$, indicating a 50 percent probability that it will be greater than the mean.

c. Of the area under the curve, 68.26 percent is within ±1σ of the mean, indicating that the probability is 68.26 percent that the actual outcome will be within the range $\hat{r} - 1\sigma$ to $\hat{r} + 1\sigma$.

68.26 percent range is 15 ± 19.36 percent, or from -4.36 to 34.36 percent. For the average firm listed on the New York Stock Exchange, σ has generally been in the range of 35 to 40 percent in recent years.

Using Historical Data to Measure Risk

In the previous example, we described the procedure for finding the mean and standard deviation when the data are in the form of a known probability distribution. Suppose only sample returns data over some past period are available. The past **realized rate of return** in period t is denoted by $\bar{r}_t$ ("r bar t") and the average annual return over the last n years is $\bar{r}_{Avg}$. The standard deviation of returns can be estimated using this formula:

$$\text{Estimated } \sigma = S = \sqrt{\frac{\sum_{t=1}^{n} (\bar{r}_t - \bar{r}_{Avg})^2}{n - 1}}. \tag{5-3a}$$

When estimated from past data, the standard deviation is often denoted by S. Here is an example:[2]

Year	$\bar{r}_t$
2003	15%
2004	-5
2005	20

$$\bar{r}_{Avg} = \frac{(15 - 5 + 20)}{3} = 10.0\%.$$

$$\text{Estimated } \sigma \text{ (or S)} = \sqrt{\frac{(15 - 10)^2 + (-5 - 10)^2 + (20 - 10)^2}{3 - 1}}$$

$$= \sqrt{\frac{350}{2}} = 13.2\%.$$

The historical σ is often used as an estimate of the future σ. Because past variability is likely to be repeated, S may be a good estimate of future risk. However, it is usually incorrect to used $\bar{r}_{Avg}$ for some past period as an estimate of $\hat{r}$, the expected future return. For example, just because a stock had a 75 percent return in the past year, there is no reason to expect a 75 percent return this year.

Measuring Stand-Alone Risk: The Coefficient of Variation

If a choice has to be made between two investments that have the same expected returns but different standard deviations, most people would choose the one with the lower standard deviation and, therefore, the lower risk. Similarly, given a choice between two investments with the same risk (standard deviation) but different expected returns, investors would generally prefer the investment with the higher expected return. To most people, this is common sense—return is "good," risk is "bad," and consequently investors want as much return and as little risk as possible. But how do we choose between two investments if one has a higher expected return but the other a lower standard deviation? To help

---

[2] Equation 5-3a is built into all financial calculators, and it is very easy to use. We simply enter the rates of return and press the key marked S (or S_x) to get the standard deviation. Note, though, that calculators have no built-in formula for finding S where unequal probabilities are involved; there you must go through the process outlined in Table 5-3 and Equation 5-3. The same situation holds for computer spreadsheet programs.

answer this question, we often use another measure of risk, the **coefficient of variation (CV)**, which is the standard deviation divided by the expected return:

$$\text{Coefficient of variation} = CV = \frac{\sigma}{\hat{r}}. \qquad (5\text{-}4)$$

The coefficient of variation shows the risk per unit of return, and it provides a more meaningful basis for comparison when the expected returns on two alternatives are not the same. Since Basic Foods and Sale.com have the same expected return, the coefficient of variation is not necessary in this case. The firm with the larger standard deviation, Sale.com, must have the larger coefficient of variation when the means are equal. In fact, the coefficient of variation for Sale.com is 65.84/15 = 4.39 and that for Basic Foods is 19.36/15 = 1.29. Thus, Sale.com is more than three times as risky as Basic Foods on the basis of this criterion. Because the coefficient of variation captures the effects of both risk and return, it is a better measure than just standard deviation for evaluating stand-alone risk in situations where two or more investments have substantially different expected returns.

Risk Aversion and Required Returns

Suppose you have worked hard and saved $1 million, which you now plan to invest. You can buy a 5 percent U.S. Treasury security, and at the end of one year you will have a sure $1.05 million, which is your original investment plus $50,000 in interest. Alternatively, you can buy stock in Genetic Advances. If Genetic Advances' research programs are successful, your stock will increase in value to $2.1 million. However, if the research is a failure, the value of your stock will go to zero, and you will be penniless. You regard Genetic Advances' chances of success or failure as being 50–50, so the expected value of the stock investment is 0.5($0) + 0.5($2,100,000) = $1,050,000. Subtracting the $1 million cost of the stock leaves an expected profit of $50,000, or an expected (but risky) 5 percent rate of return: $50,000/$1,000,000 = 0.05 = 5%.

Thus, you have a choice between a sure $50,000 profit (representing a 5 percent rate of return) on the Treasury security and a risky expected $50,000 profit (also representing a 5 percent expected rate of return) on the Genetic Advances stock. Which one would you choose? *If you choose the less risky investment, you are risk averse. Most investors are indeed risk averse, and certainly the average investor is risk averse with regard to his or her "serious money." Because this is a well-documented fact, we shall assume* **risk aversion** *throughout the remainder of the book.*

What are the implications of risk aversion for security prices and rates of return? The answer is that, other things held constant, the higher a security's risk, the lower its price and the higher its required return. To see how risk aversion affects security prices, consider again Basic Foods and Sale.com. Suppose each stock is expected to pay an annual dividend of $15 forever. The price of each stock is just the present value of a perpetuity, as calculated in Chapter 2. If each stock had an expected return of 15 percent, then each stock's price would be P = $15/0.15 = $100. Investors are averse to risk, so under these conditions there would be a general preference for Basic Foods—it has the same expected return as Sale.com but less risk. People with money to invest would bid for Basic Foods rather than Sale.com stock, and Sale.com stockholders would start selling their stock and using the money to buy Basic Foods. Buying pressure would drive up Basic Foods' stock, and selling pressure would simultaneously cause Sale.com's price to decline.

These price changes, in turn, would cause changes in the expected rates of return on the two securities.[3] Suppose, for example, that Basic Foods' stock price was bid up from $100 to $150, whereas Sale.com's stock price declined from $100 to $75. This would

---

[3] Recall from Chapter 2 that the present value of a perpetuity is P = CF/r, where CF is the constant annual cash flow of the perpetuity. Solving for r, the expected return for Basic Foods is $15/$150 = 0.10 = 10%. The expected return for Sale.com is $15/$75 = 0.20 = 20%.

THE TRADE-OFF BETWEEN RISK AND RETURN

The table accompanying this box summarizes the historical trade-off between risk and return for different classes of investments from 1926 through 2003. As the table shows, those assets that produced the highest average returns also had the highest standard deviations and the widest ranges of returns. For example, small-company stocks had the highest average annual return, but their standard deviation of returns was also the highest. By contrast, U.S. Treasury bills had the lowest standard deviation, but they also had the lowest average return.

Note that a T-bill is riskless *if you hold it until maturity,* but if you invest in a rolling portfolio of T-bills and hold the portfolio for a number of years, your investment income will vary depending on what happens to the level of interest rates in each year. While you can be sure of the return you will earn on a T-bill in a given year, you cannot be sure of the return you will earn on a portfolio of T-bills over a number of years.

Distribution of Realized Returns, 1926–2003

	Small-Company Stocks	Large-Company Stocks	Long-Term Corporate Bonds	Long-Term Government Bonds	U.S. Treasury Bills	Inflation
Average return	17.5%	12.4%	6.2%	5.8%	3.8%	3.1%
Standard deviation	33.3	20.4	8.6	9.4	3.1	4.3
Excess return over T-bonds[a]	11.7	6.6	0.4			

[a]The excess return over T-bonds is called the "historical risk premium." If and only if investors expect returns in the future to be similar to returns earned in the past, the excess return will also be the current risk premium that is reflected in security prices.

Source: Based on *Stocks, Bonds, Bills, and Inflation: Valuation Edition 2004 Yearbook* (Chicago: Ibbotson Associates, 2004).

cause Basic Foods' expected return to fall to 10 percent, while Sale.com's expected return would rise to 20 percent. The difference in returns, 20% − 10% = 10%, is a **risk premium, RP,** which represents the additional compensation investors require for assuming the additional risk of Sale.com stock.

This example demonstrates a very important principle: *In a market dominated by risk-averse investors, riskier securities must have higher expected returns, as estimated by the marginal investor, than less risky securities. If this situation does not exist, buying and selling in the market will force it to occur.* We will consider the question of how much higher the returns on risky securities must be later in the chapter, after we see how diversification affects the way risk should be measured. Then, in later chapters, we will see how risk-adjusted rates of return affect the prices investors are willing to pay for bonds and stocks.

SELF-TEST QUESTIONS

What does "investment risk" mean?
Set up an illustrative probability distribution for an investment.
What is a payoff matrix?
Which of the two stocks graphed in Figure 5-2 is less risky? Why?
How does one calculate the standard deviation?
Which is a better measure of risk if assets have different expected returns: (1) the standard deviation or (2) the coefficient of variation? Why?
Explain the following statement: "Most investors are risk averse."
How does risk aversion affect rates of return?

RISK IN A PORTFOLIO CONTEXT

In the preceding section, we considered the risk of assets held in isolation. Now we analyze the risk of assets held in portfolios. As we shall see, an asset held as part of a portfolio is less risky than the same asset held in isolation. Accordingly, most financial assets are actually held as parts of portfolios. Banks, pension funds, insurance companies, mutual funds, and other financial institutions are required by law to hold diversified portfolios. Even individual investors—at least those whose security holdings constitute a significant part of their total wealth—generally hold portfolios, not the stock of only one firm. This being the case, from an investor's standpoint the fact that a particular stock goes up or down is not very important; *what is important is the return on his or her portfolio, and the portfolio's risk. Logically, then, the risk and return of an individual security should be analyzed in terms of how that security affects the risk and return of the portfolio in which it is held.*

To illustrate, Pay Up Inc. is a collection agency that operates nationwide through 37 offices. The company is not well known, its stock is not very liquid, its earnings have fluctuated quite a bit in the past, and it doesn't pay a dividend. All this suggests that Pay Up is risky and that the required rate of return on its stock, r, should be relatively high. However, Pay Up's required rate of return in 2005, and all other years, was quite low in relation to those of most other companies. This indicates that investors regard Pay Up as being a low-risk company in spite of its uncertain profits. The reason for this counterintuitive fact has to do with diversification and its effect on risk. Pay Up's earnings rise during recessions, whereas most other companies' earnings tend to decline when the economy slumps. It's like fire insurance—it pays off when other things go badly. Therefore, adding Pay Up to a portfolio of "normal" stocks tends to stabilize returns on the entire portfolio, thus making the portfolio less risky.

Portfolio Returns

The **expected return on a portfolio**, $\hat{r}_p$, is simply the weighted average of the expected returns on the individual assets in the portfolio, with the weights being the fraction of the total portfolio invested in each asset:

$$\hat{r}_p = w_1\hat{r}_1 + w_2\hat{r}_2 + \cdots + w_n\hat{r}_n \qquad (5\text{-}5)$$

$$= \sum_{i=1}^{n} w_i\,\hat{r}_i.$$

Here the $\hat{r}_i$'s are the expected returns on the individual stocks, the w_i's are the weights, and there are n stocks in the portfolio. Note that (1) w_i is the fraction of the portfolio's dollar value invested in Stock i (that is, the value of the investment in Stock i divided by the total value of the portfolio) and (2) the w_i's must sum to 1.0.

Assume that in August 2005, a security analyst estimated that the following returns could be expected on the stocks of four large companies:

	Expected Return, $\hat{r}$
Microsoft	12.0%
General Electric	11.5
Pfizer	10.0
Coca-Cola	9.5

If we formed a $100,000 portfolio, investing $25,000 in each stock, the expected portfolio return would be 10.75 percent:

$$\hat{r}_p = w_1\hat{r}_1 + w_2\hat{r}_2 + w_3\hat{r}_3 + w_4\hat{r}_4$$

$$= 0.25(12\%) + 0.25(11.5\%) + 0.25(10\%) + 0.25(9.5\%)$$

$$= 10.75\%.$$

Of course, the actual realized rates of return will almost certainly be different from their expected values, so the realized portfolio return, $\bar{r}_p$, will be different from the expected return. For example, Coca-Cola might double and provide a return of +100%, whereas Microsoft might have a terrible year, fall sharply, and have a return of −75%. Note, though, that those two events would be somewhat offsetting, so the portfolio's return might still be close to its expected return, even though the individual stocks' actual returns were far from their expected returns.

Portfolio Risk

As we just saw, the expected return on a portfolio is simply the weighted average of the expected returns on the individual assets in the portfolio. However, unlike returns, the risk of a portfolio, σ_p, is generally *not* the weighted average of the standard deviations of the individual assets in the portfolio; the portfolio's risk will almost always be *smaller* than the weighted average of the assets' σ's. In fact, it is theoretically possible to combine stocks that are individually quite risky as measured by their standard deviations to form a portfolio that is completely riskless, with $\sigma_p = 0$.

To illustrate the effect of combining assets, consider the situation in Figure 5-4. The bottom section gives data on rates of return for Stocks W and M individually, and also for a portfolio invested 50 percent in each stock. The three graphs plot the data in a time series format. The two stocks would be quite risky if they were held in isolation, but when they are combined to form Portfolio WM, they not risky at all. (Note: These stocks are called W and M because the graphs of their returns in Figure 5-5 resemble a W and an M.)

The reason Stocks W and M can be combined to form a riskless portfolio is that their returns move countercyclically to each other—when W's returns fall, those of M rise, and

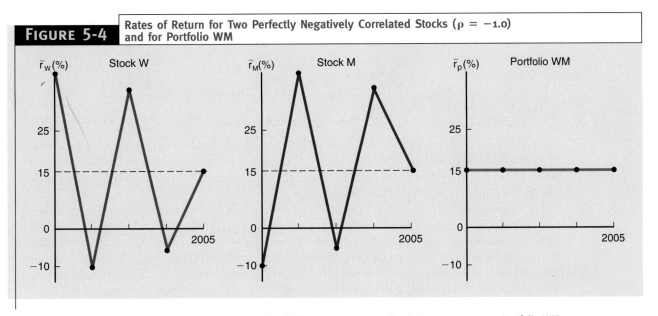

| **FIGURE 5-4** | Rates of Return for Two Perfectly Negatively Correlated Stocks ($\rho = -1.0$) and for Portfolio WM |

Year	Stock W $(\bar{r}_W)$	Stock M $(\bar{r}_M)$	Portfolio WM $(\bar{r}_p)$
2001	40.0%	(10.0%)	15.0%
2002	(10.0)	40.0	15.0
2003	35.0	(5.0)	15.0
2004	(5.0)	35.0	15.0
2005	15.0	15.0	15.0
Average return	15.0%	15.0%	15.0%
Standard deviation	22.6%	22.6%	0.0%

FIGURE 5-5	Rates of Return for Two Perfectly Positively Correlated Stocks ($\rho = +1.0$) and for Portfolio MM′

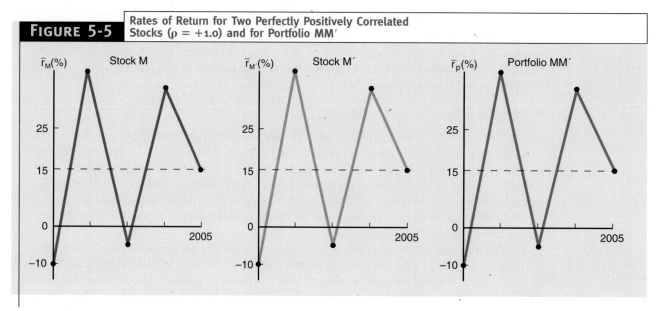

Year	Stock M $(\bar{r}_M)$	Stock M′ $(\bar{r}_{M'})$	Portfolio MM′ $(\bar{r}_p)$
2001	(10.0%)	(10.0%)	(10.0%)
2002	40.0	40.0	40.0
2003	(5.0)	(5.0)	(5.0)
2004	35.0	35.0	35.0
2005	15.0	15.0	15.0
Average return	15.0%	15.0%	15.0%
Standard deviation	22.6%	22.6%	22.6%

vice versa. The tendency of two variables to move together is called **correlation,** and the **correlation coefficient** measures this tendency.[4] The symbol for the correlation coefficient is the Greek letter rho, ρ (pronounced roe). In statistical terms, we say that the returns on Stocks W and M are *perfectly negatively correlated,* with $\rho = -1.0$.

The opposite of perfect negative correlation, with $\rho = -1.0$, is *perfect positive correlation,* with $\rho = +1.0$. Returns on two perfectly positively correlated stocks (M and M′) would move up and down together, and a portfolio consisting of two such stocks would be exactly as risky as each individual stock. This point is illustrated in Figure 5-5, where we see that the portfolio's standard deviation is equal to that of the individual stocks. *Thus, diversification does nothing to reduce risk if the portfolio consists of perfectly positively correlated stocks.*

---

[4] The *correlation coefficient,* ρ, can range from $+1.0$, denoting that the two variables move up and down in perfect synchronization, to -1.0, denoting that the variables always move in exactly opposite directions. A correlation coefficient of zero indicates that the two variables are not related to each other—that is, changes in one variable are *independent* of changes in the other.

The correlation is called R when it is estimated using historical data. Here is the formula to estimate the correlation between stocks i and j ($\bar{r}_{i,t}$ is the actual return for stock i in period t and $\bar{r}_{i,\text{Avg}_i}$ is the average return during the period; similar notation is used for stock j):

$$R = \frac{\sum_{t=1}^{n} (\bar{r}_{i,t} - \bar{r}_{i,\text{Avg}_i})(\bar{r}_{j,t} - \bar{r}_{j,\text{Avg}_j})}{\sqrt{\sum_{t=1}^{n} (\bar{r}_{i,t} - \bar{r}_{i,\text{Avg}_i})^2 \sum_{t=1}^{n} (\bar{r}_{j,t} - \bar{r}_{j,\text{Avg}_j})^2}}.$$

Fortunately, it is easy to calculate correlation coefficients with a financial calculator. Simply enter the returns on the two stocks and then press a key labeled "r." In *Excel,* use the **CORREL** function.

Figures 5-4 and 5-5 demonstrate that when stocks are perfectly negatively correlated ($\rho = -1.0$), all risk can be diversified away, but when stocks are perfectly positively correlated ($\rho = +1.0$), diversification does no good whatsoever. In reality, most stocks are positively correlated, but not perfectly so. On average, the correlation coefficient for the returns on two randomly selected stocks would be about $+0.6$, and for most pairs of stocks, ρ would lie in the range of $+0.5$ to $+0.7$. *Under such conditions, combining stocks into portfolios reduces risk but does not eliminate it completely.* Figure 5-6 illustrates this point with two stocks whose correlation coefficient is $\rho = +0.67$. The portfolio's average return is 15 percent, which is exactly the same as the average return for each of the two stocks, but its standard deviation is 20.6 percent, which is less than the standard deviation of either stock. Thus, the portfolio's risk is *not* an average of the risks of its individual stocks—diversification has reduced, but not eliminated, risk.

From these two-stock portfolio examples, we have seen that in one extreme case ($\rho = -1.0$), risk can be completely eliminated, while in the other extreme case ($\rho = +1.0$), diversification does nothing to limit risk. The real world lies between these extremes, so in general combining two stocks into a portfolio reduces, but does not eliminate, the risk inherent in the individual stocks.

What would happen if we included more than two stocks in the portfolio? *As a rule, the risk of a portfolio will decline as the number of stocks in the portfolio increases.* If we added enough partially correlated stocks, could we completely eliminate risk? In general,

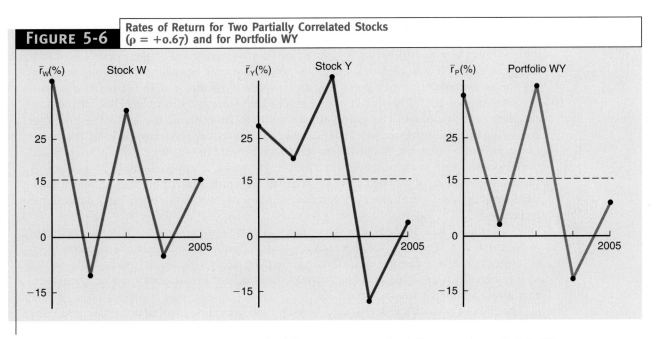

| FIGURE 5-6 | Rates of Return for Two Partially Correlated Stocks ($\rho = +0.67$) and for Portfolio WY |

Year	Stock W ($\bar{r}_W$)	Stock Y ($\bar{r}_Y$)	Portfolio WY ($\bar{r}_p$)
2001	40.0%	28.0%	34.0%
2002	(10.0)	20.0	5.0
2003	35.0	41.0	38.0
2004	(5.0)	(17.0)	(11.0)
2005	15.0	3.0	9.0
Average return	15.0%	15.0%	15.0%
Standard deviation	22.6%	22.6%	20.6%

the answer is no, but the extent to which adding stocks to a portfolio reduces its risk depends on the *degree of correlation* among the stocks: The smaller the positive correlation coefficients, the lower the risk in a large portfolio. If some stocks had correlations of −1.0, all risk could be eliminated. *In the real world, where the correlations among the individual stocks are generally positive but less than +1.0, some, but not all, risk can be eliminated.*

To test your understanding, would you expect to find higher correlations between the returns on two companies in the same or in different industries? For example, would the correlation of returns on Ford's and General Motors' stocks be higher, or would the correlation coefficient be higher between either Ford or GM and AT&T, and how would those correlations affect the risk of portfolios containing them?

Answer: Ford's and GM's returns have a correlation coefficient of about 0.9 with one another because both are affected by auto sales, but their correlation is only about 0.6 with AT&T.

Implications: A two-stock portfolio consisting of Ford and GM would be less well diversified than a two-stock portfolio consisting of Ford or GM, plus AT&T. Thus, to minimize risk, portfolios should be diversified across industries.

Diversifiable Risk versus Market Risk

As noted above, it is difficult if not impossible to find stocks whose expected returns are negatively correlated—most stocks tend to do well when the national economy is strong and badly when it is weak. Thus, even very large portfolios end up with a substantial amount of risk, but not as much risk as if all the money were invested in only one stock.

To see more precisely how portfolio size affects portfolio risk, consider Figure 5-7, which shows how portfolio risk is affected by forming larger and larger portfolios of randomly selected New York Stock Exchange (NYSE) stocks. Standard deviations are plotted for an average one-stock portfolio, a two-stock portfolio, and so on, up to a portfolio consisting of all 2,000-plus common stocks that were listed on the NYSE at the time the data were graphed. The graph illustrates that, in general, the risk of a portfolio consisting of large-company stocks tends to decline and to approach some limit as the size of the portfolio increases. According to data accumulated in recent years, σ_1, the standard deviation of a one-stock portfolio (or an average stock), is approximately 35 percent. A portfolio consisting of all stocks, which is called the **market portfolio,** would have a standard deviation, σ_M, of about 20.1 percent, which is shown as the horizontal dashed line in Figure 5-7.

Thus, almost half of the risk inherent in an average individual stock can be eliminated if the stock is held in a reasonably well-diversified portfolio, which is one containing 40 or more stocks in a number of different industries. Some risk always remains, however, so it is virtually impossible to diversify away the effects of broad stock market movements that affect almost all stocks.

The part of a stock's risk that *can* be eliminated is called *diversifiable risk,* while the part that *cannot* be eliminated is called *market risk*.[5] The fact that a large part of the risk of any individual stock can be eliminated is vitally important, because rational investors *will* eliminate it and thus render it irrelevant.

Diversifiable risk is caused by such random events as lawsuits, strikes, successful and unsuccessful marketing programs, winning or losing a major contract, and other events that are unique to a particular firm. Because these events are random, their effects on a portfolio can be eliminated by diversification—bad events in one firm will be offset by good events in another. **Market risk,** on the other hand, stems from factors that systematically

---

[5] Diversifiable risk is also known as *company-specific,* or *unsystematic,* risk. Market risk is also known as *nondiversifiable,* or *systematic,* or *beta,* risk; it is the risk that remains after diversification.

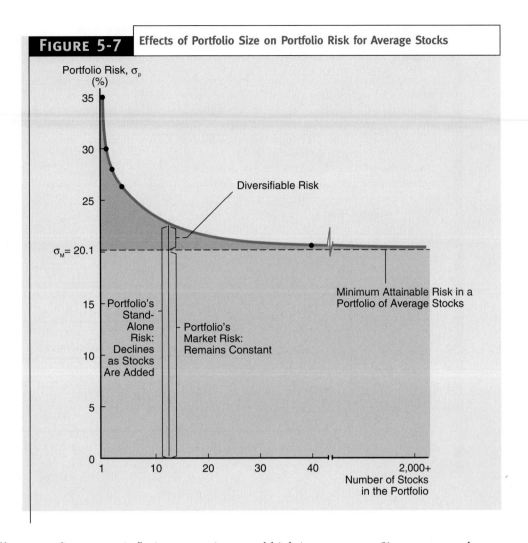

FIGURE 5-7 Effects of Portfolio Size on Portfolio Risk for Average Stocks

Portfolio Risk, σ_p (%)

Diversifiable Risk

$\sigma_M = 20.1$

Minimum Attainable Risk in a Portfolio of Average Stocks

Portfolio's Stand-Alone Risk: Declines as Stocks Are Added

Portfolio's Market Risk: Remains Constant

Number of Stocks in the Portfolio

affect most firms: war, inflation, recessions, and high interest rates. Since most stocks are negatively affected by these factors, market risk cannot be eliminated by diversification.

We know that investors demand a premium for bearing risk; that is, the higher the risk of a security, the higher its expected return must be to induce investors to buy (or to hold) it. However, if investors are primarily concerned with the risk of their *portfolios* rather than the risk of the individual securities in the portfolio, how should the risk of an individual stock be measured? One answer is provided by the **Capital Asset Pricing Model (CAPM),** an important tool used to analyze the relationship between risk and rates of return.[6] The primary conclusion of the CAPM is this: *The relevant risk of an individual stock is its contribution to the risk of a well-diversified portfolio.* A stock might be quite risky if held by itself, but if half of its risk can be eliminated by diversification, then its **relevant risk,** which is its *contribution to the portfolio's risk,* is much smaller than its stand-alone risk.

A simple example will help make this point clear. Suppose you are offered the chance to flip a coin once. If a head comes up, you win $20,000, but if a tail comes up, you lose $16,000. This is a good bet—the expected return is 0.5($20,000) + 0.5(−$16,000) = $2,000. However, it is a highly risky proposition, because you have a 50 percent chance

---

[6] Indeed, the 1990 Nobel Prize was awarded to the developers of the CAPM, Professors Harry Markowitz and William F. Sharpe. The CAPM is a relatively complex theory, and only its basic elements are presented in this chapter.

THE BENEFITS OF DIVERSIFYING OVERSEAS

Figure 5-7, presented earlier, demonstrated that an investor can significantly reduce the risk of his or her portfolio by holding a large number of stocks. The figure accompanying this box suggests that investors may be able to reduce risk even further by holding a large portfolio of stocks from all around the world, because the returns of domestic and international stocks are not perfectly correlated.

Although U.S. investors have traditionally been relatively reluctant to hold international assets, it is a safe bet that in the years ahead U.S. investors will shift more and more of their assets to overseas investments.

Source: Kenneth Kasa, "Measuring the Gains from International Portfolio Diversification," *Federal Reserve Bank of San Francisco Weekly Letter,* Number 95-14, April 8, 1994.

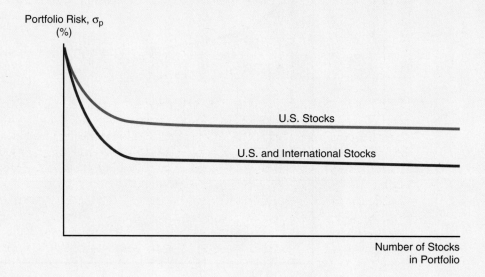

of losing $16,000. Thus, you might well refuse to make the bet. Alternatively, suppose you were offered the chance to flip a coin 100 times, and you would win $200 for each head but lose $160 for each tail. It is theoretically possible that you would flip all heads and win $20,000, and it is also theoretically possible that you would flip all tails and lose $16,000, but the chances are very high that you would actually flip about 50 heads and about 50 tails, winning a net of about $2,000. Although each individual flip is a risky bet, collectively you have a low-risk proposition because most of the risk has been diversified away. This is the idea behind holding portfolios of stocks rather than just one stock, except that with stocks all of the risk cannot be eliminated by diversification—those risks related to broad, systematic changes in the stock market will remain.

Are all stocks equally risky in the sense that adding them to a well-diversified portfolio would have the same effect on the portfolio's riskiness? The answer is no. Different stocks will affect the portfolio differently, so different securities have different degrees of relevant risk. How can the relevant risk of an individual stock be measured? As we have seen, all risk except that related to broad market movements can, and presumably will, be diversified away. After all, why accept risk that can be easily eliminated? *The risk that remains after diversifying is market risk, or the risk that is inherent in the market, and it can be measured by the degree to which a given stock tends to move up or down with the market.* In the next section, we develop a measure of a stock's market risk, and then, in a later section, we introduce an equation for determining the required rate of return on a stock, given its market risk.

The Concept of Beta

As we noted above, the primary conclusion of the CAPM is that the relevant risk of an individual stock is the amount of risk the stock contributes to a well-diversified portfolio. The benchmark for a well-diversified stock portfolio is the market portfolio, which is a portfolio containing all stocks. Therefore, the relevant risk of an individual stock, which is called its **beta coefficient,** is defined under the CAPM as the amount of risk that the stock contributes to the market portfolio. In CAPM terminology, ρ_{iM} is the correlation between the ith stock's return and the return on the market, σ_i is the standard deviation of the ith stock's return, and σ_M is the standard deviation of the market's return. In the literature on the CAPM, it is proved that the beta coefficient of the ith stock, denoted by b_i, can be found as follows:

$$b_i = \left(\frac{\sigma_i}{\sigma_M} \right) \rho_{iM}. \tag{5-6}$$

This tells us that a stock with a high standard deviation, σ_i, will tend to have a high beta. This makes sense, because if all other things are equal, a stock with high stand-alone risk will contribute a lot of risk to the portfolio. Note too that a stock with a high correlation with the market, ρ_{iM}, will also have a large beta, hence be risky. This also makes sense, because a high correlation means that diversification is not helping much, hence the stock contributes a lot of risk to the portfolio.

Calculators and spreadsheets can use Equation 5-6 to calculate beta, but there is another way. Suppose you plotted the stock's returns on the y-axis of a graph and the market portfolio's returns on the x-axis, as shown in Figure 5-8. The tendency of a stock to move up and down with the market is reflected in its beta coefficient. An *average-risk stock* is defined as one with a beta equal to 1.0. Such a stock's returns tend to move up and down, on average, by about the same amount as the general market, which is measured by some index such as the Dow Jones Industrials, the S&P 500, or the New York Stock Exchange Index. A portfolio of such b = 1.0 stocks will move up and down with the broad market indexes, and it will be just as risky as the indexes. A portfolio of b = 0.5 stocks will be half as risky as the market. On the other hand, a portfolio of b = 2.0 stocks will be twice as risky as the market. The value of such a portfolio could double—or halve—in a short time, and if you held such a portfolio, you could quickly go from millionaire to pauper.

Figure 5-8 graphs the relative volatility of three stocks. The data below the graph assume that in 2003 the "market," defined as a portfolio consisting of all stocks, had a total return (dividend yield plus capital gains yield) of $\bar{r}_M = 10\%$, and Stocks H, A, and L (for High, Average, and Low risk) also all had returns of 10 percent. In 2004, the market went up sharply, and the return on the market portfolio was $\bar{r}_M = 20\%$. Returns on the three stocks also went up: H soared to 30 percent; A went up to 20 percent, the same as the market; and L only went up to 15 percent. Now suppose the market dropped in 2005, and the market return was $\bar{r}_M = -10\%$. The three stocks' returns also fell, H plunging to −30 percent, A falling to −10 percent, and L going down to $\bar{r}_L = 0\%$. Thus, the three stocks all moved in the same direction as the market, but H was by far the most volatile; A was just as volatile as the market; and L was less volatile.

Beta measures a stock's volatility relative to the market, which by definition has b = 1.0. As we noted above, a stock's beta can be calculated by plotting a line like those in Figure 5-8. The slopes of the lines show how each stock moves in response to a movement in the general market—indeed, *the slope coefficient of such a "regression line" is defined as a beta coefficient.* (Procedures for actually calculating betas are described later in this chapter.) Most stocks have betas in the range of 0.50 to 1.50, and the average beta for all stocks is 1.0 by definition.

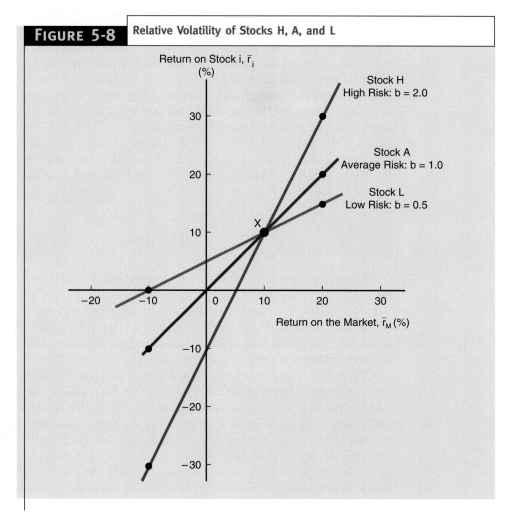

| **Figure 5-8** | **Relative Volatility of Stocks H, A, and L** |

Year	$\bar{r}_H$	$\bar{r}_A$	$\bar{r}_L$	$\bar{r}_M$
2003	10%	10%	10%	10%
2004	30	20	15	20
2005	(30)	(10)	0	(10)

Note: These three stocks plot exactly on their regression lines. This indicates that they are exposed only to market risk. Mutual funds that concentrate on stocks with betas of 2.0, 1.0, and 0.5 would have patterns similar to those shown in the graph.

Theoretically, it is possible for a stock to have a negative beta. In this case, the stock's returns would tend to rise whenever the returns on other stocks fall. In practice, very few stocks have a negative beta. Keep in mind that a stock in a given period may move counter to the overall market, even though the stock's beta is positive. If a stock has a positive beta, we would *expect* its return to increase whenever the overall stock market rises. However, company-specific factors may cause the stock's realized return to decline, even though the market's return is positive.

The beta of a portfolio is a weighted average of its individual securities' betas:

$$b_p = w_1 b_1 + w_2 b_2 + \cdots + w_n b_n$$
$$= \sum_{i=1}^{n} w_i b_i. \tag{5-7}$$

Here b_p is the beta of the portfolio, and it shows how volatile the portfolio is in relation to the market; w_i is the fraction of the portfolio invested in the ith stock; and b_i is the beta coefficient of the ith stock. For example, if an investor holds a \$100,000 portfolio consisting of \$33,333.33 invested in each of three stocks, and if each of the stocks has a beta of 0.7, then the portfolio's beta will be $b_p = 0.7$:

$$b_p = 0.3333(0.7) + 0.3333(0.7) + 0.3333(0.7) = 0.7.$$

Such a portfolio will be less risky than the market, so it should experience relatively narrow price swings and have relatively small rate-of-return fluctuations. In terms of Figure 5-8, the slope of its regression line would be 0.7, which is less than that for a portfolio of average stocks.

Now suppose one of the existing stocks is sold and replaced by a stock with $b_i = 2.0$. This action will increase the beta of the portfolio from $b_{p1} = 0.7$ to $b_{p2} = 1.13$:

$$b_{p2} = 0.3333(0.7) + 0.3333(0.7) + 0.3333(2.0)$$
$$= 1.13.$$

Had a stock with $b_i = 0.2$ been added, the portfolio beta would have declined from 0.7 to 0.53. Adding a low-beta stock, therefore, would reduce the risk of the portfolio. Consequently, adding new stocks to a portfolio can change the riskiness of that portfolio. *Thus, since a stock's beta measures its contribution to the risk of a portfolio, beta is the theoretically correct measure of the stock's risk.*

The preceding analysis of risk in a portfolio context is part of the Capital Asset Pricing Model (CAPM), and we can summarize our discussion to this point as follows:

1. A stock's risk consists of two components, market risk and diversifiable risk.
2. Diversifiable risk can be eliminated by diversification, and most investors do indeed diversify, either by holding large portfolios or by purchasing shares in a mutual fund. We are left, then, with market risk, which is caused by general movements in the stock market and which reflects the fact that most stocks are systematically affected by events like war, recessions, and inflation. Market risk is the only relevant risk to a rational, diversified investor because such an investor would eliminate diversifiable risk.
3. Investors must be compensated for bearing risk—the greater the risk of a stock, the higher its required return. However, compensation is required only for risk that cannot be eliminated by diversification. If risk premiums existed on stocks due to diversifiable risk, well-diversified investors would start buying those securities (which would not be especially risky to such investors) and bidding up their prices, and the stocks' final (equilibrium) expected returns would reflect only non-diversifiable market risk.
4. The market risk of a stock is measured by its beta coefficient, which is an index of the stock's relative volatility. If b equals 1.0, then the stock is about as risky as the market, if held in a diversified portfolio. If b is less than 1.0, the stock is less risky than the market. If beta is greater than 1.0, the stock is more risky.
5. The beta of a portfolio is a weighted average of the individual securities' betas.
6. *Since a stock's beta coefficient determines how the stock affects the risk of a diversified portfolio, beta is the most relevant measure of any stock's risk.*

SELF-TEST QUESTIONS

Explain the following statement: "An asset held as part of a portfolio is generally less risky than the same asset held in isolation."

What is meant by *perfect positive correlation, perfect negative correlation,* and *zero correlation?*

In general, can the risk of a portfolio be reduced to zero by increasing the number of stocks in the portfolio? Explain.

What is the beta of a stock that is as risky as the market?

Why is beta the theoretically correct measure of a stock's risk?

If you plotted the returns on a particular stock versus those on the Dow Jones Index over the past five years, what would the slope of the regression line you obtained indicate about the stock's market risk?

CALCULATING BETA COEFFICIENTS

e-resource

The CAPM is an *ex ante* model, which means that all of the variables represent before-the-fact, *expected* values. In particular, the beta coefficient used by investors should reflect the expected volatility of a given stock's return versus the return on the market during some *future* period. However, people generally calculate betas using data from some *past* period, and then assume that the stock's relative volatility will be the same in the future as it was in the past.

Table 5-4 shows the betas for some well-known companies, as provided by two different financial organizations, Thomson ONE—Business School Edition and Yahoo!Finance. Notice that their estimates of beta usually differ, because they calculate beta in slightly different ways. Given these differences, many analysts choose to calculate their own betas.

Recall from Figure 5-8 how betas are calculated. The actual historical returns for a company are plotted on the y-axis and the market portfolio's returns are plotted on the x-axis. A regression line is then fitted through the points, and the slope of the regression line provides an estimate of the stock's beta. Although it is possible to calculate beta coefficients with a calculator, they are usually calculated with a computer, either with a statistical software program or a spreadsheet program. The file *CF2 Ch 05 Tool Kit.xls* on your textbook's Web site shows how GE's beta coefficient is calculated using *Excel's* regression function.[7]

The first step in a regression analysis is compiling the data. Most analysts use four to five years of monthly data, although some use 52 weeks of weekly data. We decided to use four years of monthly data, so we began by downloading 49 months of stock prices for GE from the Yahoo!Finance Web site. We used the S&P 500 Index as the market port-

To see updated estimates, go to **Thomson ONE—Business School Edition,** log in using the card that comes with your book, enter a ticker symbol, and click GO. After the quote appears, select Company Earnings, then GO. Or go to *http://finance .yahoo.com* and enter the ticker symbol. When the page with results comes up, select Key Statistics from the left panel to find beta.

TABLE 5-4 | Beta Coefficients for Some Actual Companies

Stock (Ticker Symbol)	Beta: Thomson ONE	Beta: Yahoo!Finance
Cisco Systems (CSCO)	1.74	2.18
Merrill Lynch (MER)	1.49	1.53
Amazon.com (AMZN)	1.41	2.23
Dell Computer (DELL)	1.33	1.64
General Electric (GE)	1.32	1.10
Microsoft Corp. (MSFT)	1.20	1.62
Coca-Cola (KO)	0.46	0.28
Empire District Electric (EDE)	0.44	0.00
Procter & Gamble (PG)	0.44	−0.16
Energen Corp. (EGN)	0.39	0.10
Heinz (HNZ)	0.34	0.28

Sources: **Thomson ONE—Business School Edition** and http://finance.yahoo.com.

[7] For an explanation of calculating beta with a financial calculator, see the Chapter 5 Web Extension on the textbook's Web site, **http://ehrhardt.swlearning.com**.

e-resource

folio because most analysts use this index. Table 5-5 shows a portion of this data; the full data set is in the file **CF2 Ch 05 Tool Kit.xls** on your textbook's Web site.

The second step is to convert the stock prices into rates of return. For example, to find the April 2004 return for GE, we find the percentage change from the previous month: ($30.48 − $30.52)/$30.52 = −0.001 = −0.1%.[8] We also find the percent change of the S&P Index level, and use this as the market return.

As Table 5-5 shows, GE had an average annual return of −26.3 percent during this four-year period, while the market had an average annual return of −4.6 percent. As we noted before, it is usually unreasonable to think that the future expected return for a stock will equal its average historical return over a relatively short period, such as four years. However, we might well expect past volatility to be a reasonable estimate of future volatility, at least during the next couple of years. Note that the standard deviation for GE's return during this period was 41.5 percent versus 16.9 percent for the market. Thus, the market's volatility is less than that of GE. This is what we would expect, since the market is a well-diversified portfolio and thus much of its risk has been diversified away. The correlation between GE's stock returns and the market returns is about 42 percent, which is a little lower than the correlation for a typical stock.

Figure 5-9 shows a plot of GE's returns against the market returns. As you will notice if you look in the file **CF2 Ch 05 Tool Kit.xls**, we used the *Excel* Chart feature to add a trend line and to display the equation and R^2 value on the chart itself. Alternatively, we could have used the *Excel* regression analysis feature, which would have provided more detailed data.

e-resource

Check out *http://finance.yahoo.com* for General Electric using its ticker symbol of GE. You can also download data for the S&P 500 index using its symbol of ^SPX.

TABLE 5-5 | Stock Return Data for General Electric

Date	Market Level (S&P 500 Index)	Market Return	GE Adjusted Stock Price	GE Return
April 2004	1,128.17	0.2%	30.48	−0.1%
March 2004	1,126.21	−1.6	30.52	−6.2
February 2004	1,144.94	1.2	32.52	−2.7
January 2004	1,131.13	1.7	33.43	8.6
.	.	.	.	.
.	.	.	.	.
.	.	.	.	.
July 2000	1,430.83	−1.6	47.71	−2.2
June 2000	1,454.60	2.4	48.79	0.7
May 2000	1,420.60	−2.2	48.45	0.4
April 2000	1,452.43	NA	48.26	NA
Average return (annual)		−4.6%		−26.3%
Standard deviation (annual)		16.9%		41.5%
Correlation between GE and the market		42.2%		

---

[8] The prices reported in Yahoo!Finance are adjusted for dividends and stock splits so we can calculate the return as the percentage change in the adjusted price. If you use a source that reports actual market prices, then you have to make the adjustment yourself when calculating returns. For example, suppose the stock price is $100 in July, the company has a 2-for-1 split, and the actual price is then $60 in August. The reported adjusted price for August would be $60, but the reported price for July would be lowered to $50 to reflect the stock split. This gives an accurate stock return of 20 percent: ($60 − $50)/$50 = 20%, the same as if there had not been a split, in which case the return would have been ($120 − $100)/$100 = 20%.

Or suppose the actual price in September were $50, the company paid a $10 dividend, and the actual price in October was $60. Shareholders have earned a return of ($60 + $10 − $50)/$50 = 40%. Yahoo reports an adjusted price of $60 for October, and an adjusted price of $42.857 for September, which gives a return of ($60 − $42.857)/$42.857 = 40%. Again, the percentage change in the adjusted price accurately reflects the actual return.

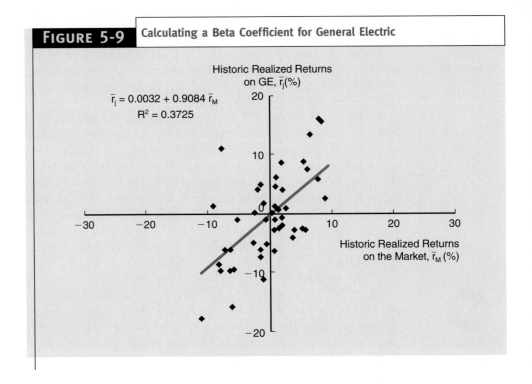

FIGURE 5-9 Calculating a Beta Coefficient for General Electric

$$\bar{r}_j = 0.0032 + 0.9084\,\bar{r}_M$$
$$R^2 = 0.3725$$

Figure 5-9 shows that GE's beta is about 0.91, as shown by the slope coefficient in the regression equation displayed on the chart. This means that GE's beta is a little less than the 1.0 average beta. Thus, GE moves up and down slightly less than the market. Note, however, that the points are not clustered very tightly around the regression line. Sometimes GE does much better than the market, while at other times it does much worse. The R^2 value shown in the chart measures the degree of dispersion about the regression line. Statistically speaking, it measures the percentage of the variance that is explained by the regression equation. An R^2 of 1.0 indicates that all points lie exactly on the line, hence that all of the variance of the y-variable is explained by the x-variable. GE's R^2 is about 0.37, which is higher than for most individual stocks. This indicates that about 37 percent of the variance in GE's returns is explained by the market returns. If we had done a similar analysis for a portfolio of 40 randomly selected stocks, then the points would probably have been clustered tightly around the regression line, and the R^2 would have probably been over 0.9.

Finally, note that the intercept shown in the regression equation on the chart is about -0.0032. Since the regression equation is based on monthly data, this means that over this period GE's stock earned 0.32 percent less per month than an average stock as a result of factors other than a general increase in stock prices.

SELF-TEST QUESTIONS

What types of data are needed to calculate a beta coefficient for an actual company? What does the R^2 measure? What is the R^2 for a typical company?

THE RELATIONSHIP BETWEEN RISK AND RATES OF RETURN

In the preceding section, we saw that under the CAPM theory, beta is the appropriate measure of a stock's relevant risk. Now we must specify the relationship between risk and return: For a given level of risk as measured by beta, what rate of return should investors require to compensate them for bearing that risk? To begin, let us define the following terms:

$\hat{r}_i$ = *expected* rate of return on the ith stock.

r_i = *required* rate of return on the ith stock. This is the minimum expected return that is required to induce an average investor to purchase the stock.

$\bar{r}$ = realized, after-the-fact return.

r_{RF} = risk-free rate of return. In this context, r_{RF} is generally measured by the expected return on long-term U.S. Treasury bonds.

b_i = beta coefficient of the ith stock.

r_M = required rate of return on a portfolio consisting of all stocks, which is called the *market portfolio*.

RP_M = risk premium on "the market". $RP_M = (r_M - r_{RF})$ is the additional return over the risk-free rate required to induce an average investor to invest in the market portfolio.

RP_i = risk premium on the ith stock: $RP_i = (RP_M)b_i$.

The **market risk premium, RP_M,** shows the premium investors require for bearing the risk of an average stock, and it depends on the degree of risk aversion that investors on average have. Let us assume that at the current time, Treasury bonds yield r_{RF} = 6%, and the market has a required return of r_M = 11%. The market risk premium is 5 percent:

$$RP_M = r_M - r_{RF} = 11\% - 6\% = 5\%.$$

We can measure a stock's relative riskiness by its beta coefficient. The risk premium for the ith stock is

Risk premium for Stock i = $RP_i = (RP_M)b_i$.　　(5-8)

If we know the market risk premium, RP_M, and the stock's risk as measured by its beta coefficient, b_i, we can find the stock's risk premium as the product $(RP_M)b_i$. For example, if b_i = 0.5 and RP_M = 5%, then RP_i is 2.5 percent:

$$\begin{aligned} RP_i &= (5\%)(0.5) \\ &= 2.5\%. \end{aligned}$$

It follows that if one stock were twice as risky as another, its risk premium would be twice as high, while if its risk were only half as much, its risk premium would be half as large.

The required return for any investment can be expressed in general terms as

Required return = Risk-free return + Premium for risk.

Here the risk-free return includes a premium for expected inflation, and we assume that the assets under consideration have similar maturities and liquidity. Under these conditions, the relationship between the required return and risk is called the **Security Market Line (SML):**

SML Equation:　$\begin{array}{c} \text{Required return} \\ \text{on Stock i} \end{array} = \begin{array}{c} \text{Risk-free} \\ \text{rate} \end{array} + \left(\begin{array}{c} \text{Market risk} \\ \text{premium} \end{array}\right)\left(\begin{array}{c} \text{Stock i's} \\ \text{beta} \end{array}\right)$

$$\begin{aligned} r_i &= r_{RF} + (r_M - r_{RF})b_i \\ &= r_{RF} + (RP_M)b_i. \end{aligned}$$

(5-9)

The required return for Stock i can be written as follows:

$$r_i = 6\% + 5\%(0.5)$$
$$= 8.5\%.$$

If some other Stock j were riskier than Stock i and had $b_j = 2.0$, then its required rate of return would be 16 percent:

$$r_j = 6\% + (5\%)2.0 = 16\%.$$

An average stock, with $b = 1.0$, would have a required return of 11 percent, the same as the market return:

$$r_A = 6\% + (5\%)1.0 = 11\% = r_M.$$

As noted above, Equation 5-9 is called the Security Market Line (SML) equation, and it is often expressed in graph form, as in Figure 5-10, which shows the SML when $r_{RF} = 6\%$ and $RP_M = 5\%$. Note the following points:

1. Required rates of return are shown on the vertical axis, while risk as measured by beta is shown on the horizontal axis. This graph is quite different from the one shown in Figure 5-8, where the returns on individual stocks were plotted on the vertical axis and returns on the market index were shown on the horizontal axis. The slopes of the three lines in Figure 5-8 were used to calculate the three stocks' betas, and those betas were then plotted as points on the horizontal axis of Figure 5-10.

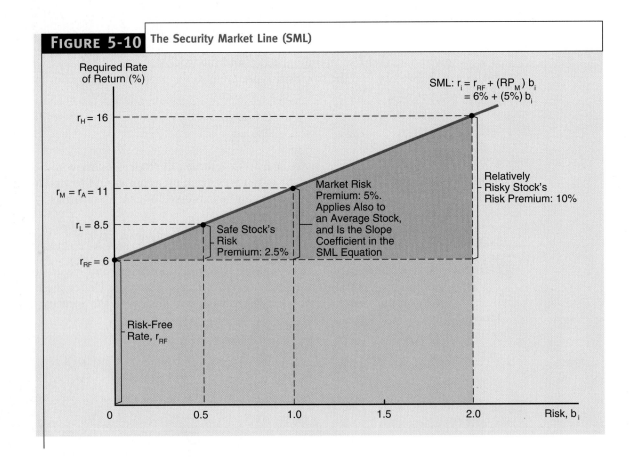

FIGURE 5-10   The Security Market Line (SML)

2. Riskless securities have $b_i = 0$; therefore, r_{RF} appears as the vertical axis intercept in Figure 5-10. If we could construct a portfolio that had a beta of zero, it would have a required return equal to the risk-free rate.
3. The slope of the SML (5% in Figure 5-10) reflects the degree of risk aversion in the economy—the greater the average investor's aversion to risk, then (a) the steeper the slope of the line, (b) the greater the risk premium for all stocks, and (c) the higher the required rate of return on all stocks.[9] These points are discussed further in a later section.
4. The values we worked out for stocks with $b_i = 0.5$, $b_i = 1.0$, and $b_i = 2.0$ agree with the values shown on the graph for r_L, r_A, and r_H.

Both the Security Market Line and a company's position on it change over time due to changes in interest rates, investors' aversion to risk, and individual companies' betas. Such changes are discussed in the following sections.

The Impact of Inflation

Interest amounts to "rent" on borrowed money, or the price of money. Thus, r_{RF} is the price of money to a riskless borrower. The risk-free rate as measured by the rate on U.S. Treasury securities is called the *nominal*, or *quoted, rate,* and it consists of two elements: (1) a *real inflation-free rate of return, r**, and (2) an *inflation premium, IP,* equal to the anticipated rate of inflation.[10] Thus, $r_{RF} = r^* + IP$. The real rate on long-term Treasury bonds has historically ranged from 2 to 4 percent, with a mean of about 3 percent. Therefore, if no inflation were expected, long-term Treasury bonds would yield about 3 percent. However, as the expected rate of inflation increases, a premium must be added to the real risk-free rate of return to compensate investors for the loss of purchasing power that results from inflation. Therefore, the 6 percent r_{RF} shown in Figure 5-10 might be thought of as consisting of a 3 percent real risk-free rate of return plus a 3 percent inflation premium: $r_{RF} = r^* + IP = 3\% + 3\% = 6\%$.

If the expected inflation rate rose by 2 percent, to $3\% + 2\% = 5\%$, this would cause r_{RF} to rise to 8 percent. Such a change is shown in Figure 5-11. Notice that under the CAPM, the increase in r_{RF} leads to an *equal* increase in the rate of return on all risky assets, because the same inflation premium is built into the required rate of return of both riskless and risky assets. For example, the rate of return on an average stock, r_M, increases from 11 to 13 percent. Other risky securities' returns also rise by two percentage points.

The discussion above also applies to any change in the nominal risk-free interest rate, whether it is caused by a change in expected inflation or in the real interest rate. The key point to remember is that a change in r_{RF} will not necessarily cause a change in the market risk premium, which is the required return on the market, r_M, minus the risk-free rate, r_{RF}. In other words, as r_{RF} changes, so may the required return on the market, keeping the market risk premium stable. Think of a sailboat floating in a harbor. The distance from the ocean floor to the ocean surface is like the risk-free rate, and it moves up and down with the tides. The distance from the top of the ship's mast to the ocean floor is like the required market return: it, too, moves up and down with the tides. But the distance from the masttop to the ocean surface is like the market risk premium—it generally stays the same, even

---

[9] Students sometimes confuse beta with the slope of the SML. This is a mistake. The slope of any straight line is equal to the "rise" divided by the "run," or $(Y_1 - Y_0)/(X_1 - X_0)$. Consider Figure 5-10. If we let $Y = r$ and $X = \text{beta}$, and we go from the origin to $b = 1.0$, we see that the slope is $(r_M - r_{RF})/(b_M - b_{RF}) = (11\% - 6\%)/(1 - 0) = 5\%$. Thus, the slope of the SML is equal to $(r_M - r_{RF})$, the market risk premium. In Figure 5-10, $r_i = 6\% + 5\%b_i$, so an increase of beta from 1.0 to 2.0 would produce a 5 percentage point increase in r_i.

[10] Long-term Treasury bonds also contain a maturity risk premium, MRP. Here we include the MRP in r^* to simplify the discussion.

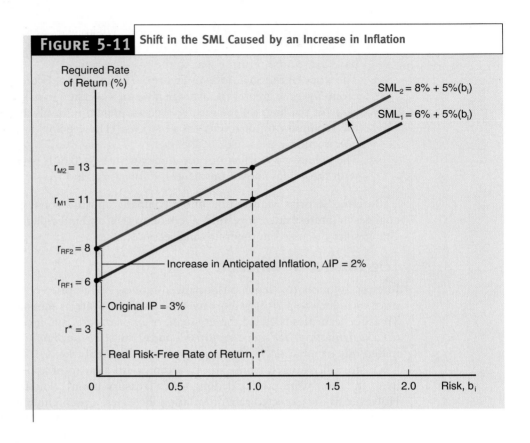

FIGURE 5-11   Shift in the SML Caused by an Increase in Inflation

though tides move the ship up and down. In other words, a change in the risk-free rate also causes a change in the required market return, r_M, resulting in a relatively stable market risk premium, $r_M - r_{RF}$.

Changes in Risk Aversion

The slope of the Security Market Line reflects the extent to which investors are averse to risk—the steeper the slope of the line, the greater the average investor's risk aversion. Suppose investors were indifferent to risk; that is, they were not risk averse. If r_{RF} were 6 percent, then risky assets would also provide an expected return of 6 percent, because if there were no risk aversion, there would be no risk premium, and the SML would be plotted as a horizontal line. As risk aversion increases, so does the risk premium, and this causes the slope of the SML to become steeper.

Figure 5-12 illustrates an increase in risk aversion. The market risk premium rises from 5 to 7.5 percent, causing r_M to rise from $r_{M1} = 11\%$ to $r_{M2} = 13.5\%$. The returns on other risky assets also rise, and the effect of this shift in risk aversion is more pronounced on riskier securities. For example, the required return on a stock with $b_i = 0.5$ increases by only 1.25 percentage points, from 8.5 to 9.75 percent, whereas that on a stock with $b_i = 1.5$ increases by 3.75 percentage points, from 13.5 to 17.25 percent.

Changes in a Stock's Beta Coefficient

As we shall see later in the book, a firm can influence its market risk, hence its beta, through changes in the composition of its assets and also through its use of debt. A company's beta can also change as a result of external factors such as increased competition in its industry, the expiration of basic patents, and the like. When such changes occur, the required rate of return also changes.

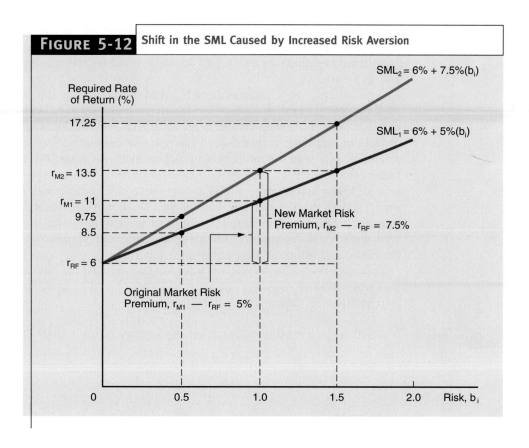

FIGURE 5-12 Shift in the SML Caused by Increased Risk Aversion

Differentiate among the expected rate of return ($\hat{r}$), the required rate of return (r), and the realized, after-the-fact return ($\bar{r}$) on a stock. Which would have to be larger to get you to buy the stock, $\hat{r}$ or r? Would $\hat{r}$, r, and $\bar{r}$ typically be the same or different for a given company?

What are the differences between the relative volatility graph (Figure 5-8), where "betas are made," and the SML graph (Figure 5-10), where "betas are used"? Discuss both how the graphs are constructed and the information they convey.

What happens to the SML graph in Figure 5-10 when inflation increases or decreases?

What happens to the SML graph when risk aversion increases or decreases? What would the SML look like if investors were indifferent to risk, that is, had zero risk aversion?

How can a firm influence its market risk as reflected in its beta?

SOME CONCERNS ABOUT BETA AND THE CAPM

The Capital Asset Pricing Model (CAPM) is more than just an abstract theory described in textbooks—it is also widely used by analysts, investors, and corporations. However, despite the CAPM's intuitive appeal, a number of studies have raised concerns about its validity. In particular, a study by Eugene Fama of the University of Chicago and Kenneth French of Yale cast doubt on the CAPM.[11] Fama and French found two variables that are consistently related to stock returns: (1) the firm's size and (2) its market/book ratio. After

---

[11] See Eugene F. Fama and Kenneth R. French, "The Cross-Section of Expected Stock Returns," *Journal of Finance*, Vol. 47, 1992, 427–465; and Eugene F. Fama and Kenneth R. French, "Common Risk Factors in the Returns on Stocks and Bonds," *Journal of Financial Economics*, Vol. 33, 1993, 3–56.

adjusting for other factors, they found that smaller firms have provided relatively high returns, and that returns are relatively high on stocks with low market/book ratios. At the same time, and contrary to the CAPM, they found no relationship between a stock's beta and its return.

As an alternative to the traditional CAPM, researchers and practitioners have begun to look to more general multi-beta models that expand on the CAPM and address its shortcomings. The multi-beta model is an attractive generalization of the traditional CAPM model's insight that market risk, or the risk that cannot be diversified away, underlies the pricing of assets. In the multi-beta model, market risk is measured relative to a set of risk factors that determine the behavior of asset returns, whereas the CAPM gauges risk only relative to the market return. It is important to note that the risk factors in the multi-beta model are all nondiversifiable sources of risk. Empirical research investigating the relationship between economic risk factors and security returns is ongoing, but it has discovered several risk factors, including the bond default premium, the bond term structure premium, and inflation, that affect most securities.

Practitioners and academicians have long recognized the limitations of the CAPM, and they are constantly looking for ways to improve it. The multi-beta model is a potential step in that direction.

| SELF-TEST QUESTION | Are there any reasons to question the validity of the CAPM? Explain. |

SUMMARY

In this chapter, we described the trade-off between risk and return. We began by discussing how to calculate risk and return for both individual assets and portfolios. In particular, we differentiated between stand-alone risk and risk in a portfolio context, and we explained the benefits of diversification. Finally, we developed the CAPM, which explains how risk affects rates of return. In the chapters that follow, we will give you the tools to estimate the required rates of return for bonds, preferred stock, and common stock, and we will explain how firms use these returns to develop their costs of capital. As you will see, the cost of capital is an important element in the firm's capital budgeting process. The key concepts covered in this chapter are listed below.

- **Risk** can be defined as the chance that some unfavorable event will occur.
- The risk of an asset's cash flows can be considered on a **stand-alone basis** (each asset by itself) or in a **portfolio context,** where the investment is combined with other assets and its risk is reduced through **diversification.**
- Most rational investors hold **portfolios of assets,** and they are more concerned with the riskiness of their portfolios than with the risk of individual assets.
- The **expected return** on an investment is the mean value of its probability distribution of returns.
- The **greater the probability** that the actual return will be far below the expected return, the **greater the stand-alone risk** associated with an asset.
- The average investor is **risk averse,** which means that he or she must be compensated for holding risky assets. Therefore, riskier assets have higher required returns than less risky assets.
- An asset's risk consists of (1) **diversifiable risk,** which can be eliminated by diversification, plus (2) **market risk,** which cannot be eliminated by diversification.
- The **relevant risk** of an individual asset is its contribution to the riskiness of a well-diversified **portfolio,** which is the asset's **market risk.** Since market risk cannot be eliminated by diversification, investors must be compensated for bearing it.

CU = σ/E(R)

- A stock's **beta coefficient, b,** is a measure of its market risk. Beta measures the extent to which the stock's returns move relative to the market.
- A **high-beta stock** is more volatile than an average stock, while a **low-beta stock** is less volatile than an average stock. An average stock has b = 1.0.
- The **beta of a portfolio** is a **weighted average** of the betas of the individual securities in the portfolio.
- The **Security Market Line (SML)** equation shows the relationship between a security's market risk and its required rate of return. The return required for any security i is equal to the **risk-free rate** plus the **market risk premium** times the security's beta: $r_i = r_{RF} + (RP_M)b_i$.
- Even though the expected rate of return on a stock is generally equal to its required return, a number of things can happen to cause the required rate of return to change: (1) **the risk-free rate can change** because of changes in either real rates or anticipated inflation, (2) **a stock's beta can change,** and (3) **investors' aversion to risk can change.**
- Because returns on assets in different countries are not perfectly correlated, **global diversification** may result in lower risk for multinational companies and globally diversified portfolios.

QUESTIONS

(5-1) Define the following terms, using graphs or equations to illustrate your answers wherever feasible:
   a. Stand-alone risk; risk; probability distribution
   b. Expected rate of return, $\hat{r}$
   c. Continuous probability distribution
   d. Standard deviation, σ; variance, σ^2; coefficient of variation, CV
   e. Risk aversion; realized rate of return, $\bar{r}$
   f. Risk premium for Stock i, RP_i; market risk premium, RP_M
   g. Capital Asset Pricing Model (CAPM)
   h. Expected return on a portfolio, $\hat{r}_p$; market portfolio
   i. Correlation coefficient, ρ; correlation
   j. Market risk; diversifiable risk; relevant risk
   k. Beta coefficient, b; average stock's beta, b_A
   l. Security Market Line (SML); SML equation
   m. Slope of SML as a measure of risk aversion

(5-2) The probability distribution of a less risky return is more peaked than that of a riskier return. What shape would the probability distribution have for (a) completely certain returns and (b) completely uncertain returns?

(5-3) Security A has an expected return of 7 percent, a standard deviation of returns of 35 percent, a correlation coefficient with the market of −0.3, and a beta coefficient of −1.5. Security B has an expected return of 12 percent, a standard deviation of returns of 10 percent, a correlation with the market of 0.7, and a beta coefficient of 1.0. Which security is riskier? Why?

(5-4) Suppose you owned a portfolio consisting of $250,000 worth of long-term U.S. government bonds.
   a. Would your portfolio be riskless?
   b. Now suppose you hold a portfolio consisting of $250,000 worth of 30-day Treasury bills. Every 30 days your bills mature, and you reinvest the principal ($250,000) in a new batch of bills. Assume that you live on the investment income from your portfolio and that you want to maintain a constant standard of living. Is your portfolio truly riskless?
   c. Can you think of any asset that would be completely riskless? Could someone develop such an asset? Explain.

(5-5) If investors' aversion to risk increased, would the risk premium on a high-beta stock increase more or less than that on a low-beta stock? Explain.

(5-6) If a company's beta were to double, would its expected return double?

(5-7) Is it possible to construct a portfolio of stocks which has an expected return equal to the risk-free rate?

SELF-TEST PROBLEMS   Solutions Appear in Appendix A

(ST-1) Stocks A and B have the following historical returns:

Realized Rates of Return

Year	Stock A's Returns, r_A	Stock B's Returns, r_B
2001	(18%)	(24%)
2002	44	24
2003	(22)	(4)
2004	22	8
2005	34	56

a. Calculate the average rate of return for each stock during the 5-year period. Assume that someone held a portfolio consisting of 50 percent of Stock A and 50 percent of Stock B. What would have been the realized rate of return on the portfolio in each year? What would have been the average return on the portfolio during this period?

b. Now calculate the standard deviation of returns for each stock and for the portfolio. Use Equation 5-3a.

c. Looking at the annual returns data on the two stocks, would you guess that the correlation coefficient between returns on the two stocks is closer to 0.8 or to -0.8?

d. If you added more stocks at random to the portfolio, which of the following is the most accurate statement of what would happen to σ_p?
   (1) σ_p would remain constant.
   (2) σ_p would decline to somewhere in the vicinity of 20 percent.
   (3) σ_p would decline to zero if enough stocks were included.

(ST-2) ECRI Corporation is a holding company with four main subsidiaries. The percentage of its business coming from each of the subsidiaries, and their respective betas, are as follows:

Beta and Required Rate of Return

Subsidiary	Percentage of Business	Beta
Electric utility	60%	0.70
Cable company	25	0.90
Real estate	10	1.30
International/special projects	5	1.50

a. What is the holding company's beta?

b. Assume that the risk-free rate is 6 percent and the market risk premium is 5 percent. What is the holding company's required rate of return?

c. ECRI is considering a change in its strategic focus: it will reduce its reliance on the electric utility subsidiary, so the percentage of its business from this subsidiary will be 50 percent. At the same time, ECRI will increase its reliance on the international/special projects division, so the percentage of its business from that subsidiary will rise to 15 percent. What will be the shareholders' required rate of return if they adopt these changes?

PROBLEMS

(5-1)   A stock's return has the following distribution:

Expected Return

Demand for the Company's Products	Probability of This Demand Occurring	Rate of Return if This Demand Occurs
Weak	0.1	(50%)
Below average	0.2	(5)
Average	0.4	16
Above average	0.2	25
Strong	0.1	60
	1.0	

Calculate the stock's expected return, standard deviation, and coefficient of variation.

(5-2)   An individual has $35,000 invested in a stock which has a beta of 0.8 and $40,000
Portfolio Beta   invested in a stock with a beta of 1.4. If these are the only two investments in her
portfolio, what is her portfolio's beta?

(5-3)   Assume that the risk-free rate is 5 percent and the market risk premium is 6 percent.
Expected and Required   What is the expected return for the overall stock market? What is the required rate
Rates of Return   of return on a stock that has a beta of 1.2?

(5-4)   Assume that the risk-free rate is 6 percent and the expected return on the market
Required Rate   is 13 percent. What is the required rate of return on a stock that has a beta
of Return   of 0.7?

(5-5)   The market and Stock J have the following probability distributions:

Expected Returns

Probability	r_M	r_J
0.3	15%	20%
0.4	9	5
0.3	18	12

a.   Calculate the expected rates of return for the market and Stock J.
b.   Calculate the standard deviations for the market and Stock J.
c.   Calculate the coefficients of variation for the market and Stock J.

(5-6)   Suppose $r_{RF} = 5\%$, $r_M = 10\%$, and $r_A = 12\%$.
Required Rate   a.   Calculate Stock A's beta.
of Return   b.   If Stock A's beta were 2.0, what would be A's new required rate of return?

(5-7)   Suppose $r_{RF} = 9\%$, $r_M = 14\%$, and $b_i = 1.3$.
Required Rate   a.   What is r_i, the required rate of return on Stock i?
of Return   b.   Now suppose r_{RF} (1) increases to 10 percent or (2) decreases to 8 percent.
The slope of the SML remains constant. How would this affect r_M and r_i?
c.   Now assume r_{RF} remains at 9 percent but r_M (1) increases to 16 percent or
(2) falls to 13 percent. The slope of the SML does not remain constant.
How would these changes affect r_i?

(5-8)   Suppose you hold a diversified portfolio consisting of a $7,500 investment in each
Portfolio Beta   of 20 different common stocks. The portfolio beta is equal to 1.12. Now, suppose
you have decided to sell one of the stocks in your portfolio with a beta equal to 1.0
for $7,500 and to use these proceeds to buy another stock for your portfolio.
Assume the new stock's beta is equal to 1.75. Calculate your portfolio's new beta.

(5-9)
Portfolio Required
Return
Suppose you are the money manager of a $4 million investment fund. The fund consists of 4 stocks with the following investments and betas:

Stock	Investment	Beta
A	$ 400,000	1.50
B	600,000	(0.50)
C	1,000,000	1.25
D	2,000,000	0.75

If the market required rate of return is 14 percent and the risk-free rate is 6 percent, what is the fund's required rate of return?

(5-10)
Portfolio Beta
You have a $2 million portfolio consisting of a $100,000 investment in each of 20 different stocks. The portfolio has a beta equal to 1.1. You are considering selling $100,000 worth of one stock which has a beta equal to 0.9 and using the proceeds to purchase another stock which has a beta equal to 1.4. What will be the new beta of your portfolio following this transaction?

(5-11)
Required Rate
of Return
Stock R has a beta of 1.5, Stock S has a beta of 0.75, the expected rate of return on an average stock is 13 percent, and the risk-free rate of return is 7 percent. By how much does the required return on the riskier stock exceed the required return on the less risky stock?

(5-12)
Realized Rates
of Return
Stocks A and B have the following historical returns:

Year	Stock A's Returns, r_A	Stock B's Returns, r_B
2001	(18.00%)	(14.50%)
2002	33.00	21.80
2003	15.00	30.50
2004	(0.50)	(7.60)
2005	27.00	26.30

a. Calculate the average rate of return for each stock during the 5-year period.
b. Assume that someone held a portfolio consisting of 50 percent of Stock A and 50 percent of Stock B. What would have been the realized rate of return on the portfolio in each year? What would have been the average return on the portfolio during this period?
c. Calculate the standard deviation of returns for each stock and for the portfolio.
d. Calculate the coefficient of variation for each stock and for the portfolio.
e. If you are a risk-averse investor, would you prefer to hold Stock A, Stock B, or the portfolio? Why?

(5-13)
Expected and
Required Rates of
Return; Financial
Calculator Needed
You have observed the following returns over time:

Year	Stock X	Stock Y	Market
2001	14%	13%	12%
2002	19	7	10
2003	−16	−5	−12
2004	3	1	1
2005	20	11	15

Assume that the risk-free rate is 6 percent and the market risk premium is 5 percent.
a. What are the betas of Stocks X and Y?
b. What are the required rates of return for Stocks X and Y?
c. What is the required rate of return for a portfolio consisting of 80 percent of Stock X and 20 percent of Stock Y?
d. If Stock X's expected return is 22 percent, is Stock X under- or overvalued?

SPREADSHEET PROBLEM

(5-14)

Build a Model:
Evaluating Risk
and Return

e-resource

Start with the partial model in the file *CF2 Ch 05 P14 Build a Model.xls* from the textbook's Web site. Bartman Industries' and Reynolds Incorporated's stock prices and dividends, along with the Market Index, are shown below. Stock prices are reported for December 31 of each year, and dividends reflect those paid during the year. The Market data are adjusted to include dividends.

	BARTMAN INDUSTRIES		REYNOLDS INCORPORATED		MARKET INDEX
Year	Stock Price	Dividend	Stock Price	Dividend	Includes Divs.
2005	$17.250	$1.15	$48.750	$3.00	11,663.98
2004	14.750	1.06	52.300	2.90	8,785.70
2003	16.500	1.00	48.750	2.75	8,679.98
2002	10.750	0.95	57.250	2.50	6,434.03
2001	11.375	0.90	60.000	2.25	5,602.28
2000	7.625	0.85	55.750	2.00	4,705.97

a. Use the data given to calculate annual returns for Bartman, Reynolds, and the Market Index, and then calculate average returns over the 5-year period. (Hint: Remember, returns are calculated by subtracting the beginning price from the ending price to get the capital gain or loss, adding the dividend to the capital gain or loss, and dividing the result by the beginning price. Assume that dividends are already included in the index. Also, you cannot calculate the rate of return for 2000 because you do not have 1999 data.)

b. Calculate the standard deviations of the returns for Bartman, Reynolds, and the Market Index. (Hint: Use the sample standard deviation formula given in the chapter, which corresponds to the STDEV function in *Excel*.)

c. Now calculate the coefficients of variation for Bartman, Reynolds, and the Market Index.

d. Construct a scatter diagram graph that shows Bartman's and Reynolds's returns on the vertical axis and the Market Index's returns on the horizontal axis.

e. Estimate Bartman's and Reynolds's betas by running regressions of their returns against the Index's returns. Are these betas consistent with your graph?

f. The risk-free rate on long-term Treasury bonds is 6.04 percent. Assume that the market risk premium is 5 percent. What is the expected return on the market? Now use the SML equation to calculate the two companies' required returns.

g. If you formed a portfolio that consisted of 50 percent of Bartman stock and 50 percent of Reynolds stock, what would be its beta and its required return?

h. Suppose an investor wants to include Bartman Industries' stock in his or her portfolio. Stocks A, B, and C are currently in the portfolio, and their betas are 0.769, 0.985, and 1.423, respectively. Calculate the new portfolio's required return if it consists of 25 percent of Bartman, 15 percent of Stock A, 40 percent of Stock B, and 20 percent of Stock C.

CYBERPROBLEM

Please go to our Web site, **http://ehrhardt.swlearning.com**, to access any Cyberproblems.

THOMSON ONE
Business School Edition

Please go to **http://ehrhardt.swlearning.com** to access any Thomson ONE—Business School Edition problems.

MINI CASE

Assume that you recently graduated with a major in finance, and you just landed a job as a financial planner with Barney Smith Inc., a large financial services corporation. Your first assignment is to invest $100,000 for a client. Because the funds are to be invested in a business at the end of 1 year, you have been instructed to plan for a 1-year holding period. Further, your boss has restricted you to the following investment alternatives, shown with their probabilities and associated outcomes. (Disregard for now the items at the bottom of the data; you will fill in the blanks later.)

Barney Smith's economic forecasting staff has developed probability estimates for the state of the economy, and its security analysts have developed a sophisticated computer program which was used to estimate the rate of return on each alternative under each state of the economy. Alta Industries is an electronics firm; Repo Men Inc. collects past-due debts; and American Foam manufactures mattresses and various other foam products. Barney Smith also maintains an "index fund" which owns a market-weighted fraction of all publicly traded stocks; you can invest in that fund, and thus obtain average stock market results. Given the situation as described, answer the following questions.

a. What are investment returns? What is the return on an investment that costs $1,000 and is sold after 1 year for $1,100?

b. (1) Why is the T-bill's return independent of the state of the economy? Do T-bills promise a completely risk-free return? (2) Why are Alta Industries' returns expected to move with the economy whereas Repo Men's are expected to move counter to the economy?

c. Calculate the expected rate of return on each alternative and fill in the blanks on the row for r̂ in the table below.

d. You should recognize that basing a decision solely on expected returns is appropriate only for risk-neutral individuals. Because your client, like virtually everyone, is risk averse, the riskiness of each alternative is an important aspect of the decision. One possible measure of risk is the standard deviation of returns. (1) Calculate this value for each alternative, and fill in the blank on the row for σ in the table below. (2) What type of risk is measured by the standard deviation? (3) Draw a graph that shows *roughly* the shape of the probability distributions for Alta Industries, American Foam, and T-bills.

e. Suppose you suddenly remembered that the coefficient of variation (CV) is generally regarded as being a better measure of stand-alone risk than the standard deviation when the alternatives being considered have widely differing expected returns. Calculate the missing CVs, and fill in the blanks on the row for CV in the table below. Does the CV produce the same risk rankings as the standard deviation?

RETURNS ON ALTERNATIVE INVESTMENTS

ESTIMATED RATE OF RETURN

State of the Economy	Probability	T-Bills	Alta Industries	Repo Men	American Foam	Market Portfolio	2-Stock Portfolio
Recession	0.1	8.0%	(22.0%)	28.0%	10.0%[a]	(13.0%)	3.0%
Below average	0.2	8.0	(2.0)	14.7	(10.0)	1.0	
Average	0.4	8.0	20.0	0.0	7.0	15.0	10.0
Above average	0.2	8.0	35.0	(10.0)	45.0	29.0	
Boom	0.1	8.0	50.0	(20.0)	30.0	43.0	15.0
r̂				1.7%	13.8%	15.0%	
σ		0.0		13.4	18.8	15.3	
CV				7.9	1.4	1.0	
b				−0.86	0.68		

[a]Note that the estimated returns of American Foam do not always move in the same direction as the overall economy. For example, when the economy is below average, consumers purchase fewer mattresses than they would if the economy were stronger. However, if the economy is in a flat-out recession, a large number of consumers who were planning to purchase a more expensive inner spring mattress may purchase, instead, a cheaper foam mattress. Under these circumstances, we would expect American Foam's stock price to be higher if there is a recession than if the economy was just below average.

f. Suppose you created a 2-stock portfolio by investing $50,000 in Alta Industries and $50,000 in Repo Men. (1) Calculate the expected return ($\hat{r}_p$), the standard deviation (σ_p), and the coefficient of variation (CV_p) for this portfolio and fill in the appropriate blanks in the table. (2) How does the risk of this 2-stock portfolio compare with the risk of the individual stocks if they were held in isolation?

g. Suppose an investor starts with a portfolio consisting of one randomly selected stock. What would happen (1) to the risk and (2) to the expected return of the portfolio as more and more randomly selected stocks were added to the portfolio? What is the implication for investors? Draw a graph of the two portfolios to illustrate your answer.

h. (1) Should portfolio effects impact the way investors think about the risk of individual stocks? (2) If you decided to hold a 1-stock portfolio, and consequently were exposed to more risk than diversified investors, could you expect to be compensated for all of your risk; that is, could you earn a risk premium on that part of your risk that you could have eliminated by diversifying?

i. How is market risk measured for individual securities? How are beta coefficients calculated?

j. Suppose you have the following historical returns for the stock market and for another company, P. Q. Unlimited. Explain how to calculate beta, and use the historical stock returns to calculate the beta for PQU. Interpret your results.

Year	Market	PQU
1	25.7%	40.0%
2	8.0	−15.0
3	−11.0	−15.0
4	15.0	35.0
5	32.5	10.0
6	13.7	30.0
7	40.0	42.0
8	10.0	−10.0
9	−10.8	−25.0
10	−13.1	25.0

k. The expected rates of return and the beta coefficients of the alternatives as supplied by Barney Smith's computer program are as follows:

Security	Return ($\hat{r}$)	Risk (Beta)
Alta Industries	17.4%	1.29
Market	15.0	1.00
American Foam	13.8	0.68
T-bills	8.0	0.00
Repo Men	1.7	(0.86)

(1) Do the expected returns appear to be related to each alternative's market risk? (2) Is it possible to choose among the alternatives on the basis of the information developed thus far?

l. (1) Write out the Security Market Line (SML) equation, use it to calculate the required rate of return on each alternative, and then graph the relationship between the expected and required rates of return. (2) How do the expected rates of return compare with the required rates of return? (3) Does the fact that Repo Men has an expected return that is less than the T-bill rate make any sense? (4) What would be the market risk and the required return of a 50-50 portfolio of Alta Industries and Repo Men? Of Alta Industries and American Foam?

m. (1) Suppose investors raised their inflation expectations by 3 percentage points over current estimates as reflected in the 8 percent T-bill rate. What effect would higher inflation have on the SML and on the returns required on high- and low-risk securities? (2) Suppose instead that investors' risk aversion increased enough to cause the market risk premium to increase by 3 percentage points. (Inflation remains constant.) What effect would this have on the SML and on returns of high- and low-risk securities?

SELECTED ADDITIONAL REFERENCES AND CASES

Probably the best sources of additional information on probability distributions and single-asset risk measures are statistics textbooks. For example, see

Kohler, Heinz, *Statistics for Business and Economics* (New York: HarperCollins, 1994).

Mendenhall, William, Richard L. Schaeffer, and Dennis D. Wackerly, *Mathematical Statistics with Applications* (Pacific Grove, CA: Duxbury, 2002).

Probably the best place to find an extension of portfolio theory concepts is one of the investments textbooks. These are some good ones:

Francis, Jack C., *Investments: Analysis and Management* (New York: McGraw-Hill, 1991).

Radcliffe, Robert C., *Investment: Concepts, Analysis, and Strategy* (Reading, MA: Addison-Wesley, 1997).

Reilly, Frank K., and Keith C. Brown, *Investment Analysis and Portfolio Management* (Fort Worth, TX: South-Western Publishing, 2000).

The following case from the Finance Online Case Library *covers many of the concepts discussed in this chapter and is available at* **http://www.textchoice.com:**

Case 2, "Peachtree Securities, Inc. (A)."

Securities and Their Valuation

CHAPTER 6

Bonds and Their Valuation

A lot of U.S. bonds have been issued, and we mean a LOT! According to the Federal Reserve, there are about $4.0 trillion of outstanding U.S. Treasury securities, more than $1.8 trillion of municipal securities, $2.8 trillion of corporate bonds, and more than $384 billion of bonds issued by foreign governments and companies in the United States. Not only is the dollar amount mind-boggling, so is the variety. Bonds come in many shapes and flavors, with new varieties introduced each year. Two of the most interesting bonds don't pay any interest, and one actually has a negative interest rate.

How can a bond not pay interest? An investor might buy such a bond today for $558, and then receive $1,000 in 10 years. An investor doesn't receive any cash interest payments, but the 10-year increase from the original purchase price to the $1,000 repayment equals a 6 percent annual return on the investment. Although there isn't any annual cash interest payment, the government allows corporate issuers to deduct an annual interest expense from their taxable income based on the investor's annual value appreciation. Thus, the company gets a tax deduction each year, even though it isn't making actual interest payments! Of course, the downside is that the company will have to come up with the full $1,000 per bond in 10 years to pay off the bondholders.

Berkshire Hathaway (chaired by Warren Buffett) issued bonds with a negative interest rate in 2002. Technically, Berkshire issued bonds with a 3 percent interest payment, but they also had an attached warrant that allows an investor to purchase shares of Berkshire Hathaway stock at a fixed price in the future. If the stock price rises above the stated price, then investors can profit by exercising the warrants. However, Berkshire Hathaway didn't just give away the warrants—it required investors to make an annual installment payment equal to 3.75 percent of the bond's face value. Thus, investors receive a 3 percent interest payment, but they must then pay a 3.75 percent warrant fee, for a net interest rate of negative 0.75 percent. Berkshire Hathaway can deduct the 3 percent interest payment for tax purposes, but the 3.75 percent warrant fee is not taxable, further increasing Berkshire Hathaway's annual after-tax cash flow.

Think about these and other bonds as you read this chapter.

Source: **http://www.federalreserve.gov/releases/Z1/current/,** "Flow of Funds Accounts of the United States, Section L.2, Credit Market Debt Owed by Nonfinancial Sectors."

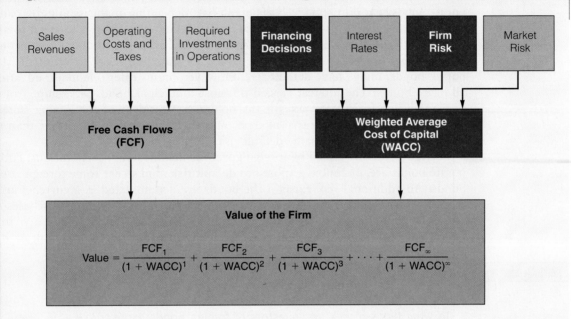

CORPORATE VALUATION AND RISK

In Chapter 1, we told you that managers should strive to make their firms more valuable, and that the value of a firm is determined by the size, timing, and risk of its free cash flows (FCF). This chapter shows you how to measure a bond's risk and the return demanded by a firm's bond holders, which affects the firm's weighted average cost of capital.

CF

e-resource

The textbook's Web site contains an Excel file that will guide you through the chapter's calculations. The file for this chapter is **CF2 Ch 06 Tool Kit.xls,** *and we encourage you to open the file and follow along as you read the chapter.*

Growing companies must acquire land, buildings, equipment, inventory, and other operating assets. The debt markets are a major source of funding for such purchases. Therefore, every manager should have a working knowledge of the types of bonds companies and government agencies issue, the terms that are contained in bond contracts, the types of risks to which both bond investors and issuers are exposed, and procedures for determining the values of and rates of return on bonds.

WHO ISSUES BONDS?

A **bond** is a long-term contract under which a borrower agrees to make payments of interest and principal, on specific dates, to the holders of the bond. For example, on January 5, 2006, MicroDrive Inc. borrowed $50 million by issuing $50 million of bonds. For convenience, we assume that MicroDrive sold 50,000 individual bonds for $1,000 each. Actually, it could have sold one $50 million bond, 10 bonds with a $5 million face value, or any other combination that totals to $50 million. In any event, MicroDrive received the $50 million, and in exchange it promised to make annual interest payments and to repay the $50 million on a specified maturity date.

Investors have many choices when investing in bonds, but bonds are classified into four main types: Treasury, corporate, municipal, and foreign. Each type differs with respect to expected return and degree of risk.

Treasury bonds, sometimes referred to as government bonds, are issued by the U.S. federal government.[1] It is reasonable to assume that the federal government will make good on its promised payments, so these bonds have no default risk. However, Treasury bond prices decline when interest rates rise, so they are not free of all risks.

Corporate bonds, as the name implies, are issued by corporations. Unlike Treasury bonds, corporate bonds are exposed to default risk—if the issuing company gets into trouble, it may be unable to make the promised interest and principal payments. Different corporate bonds have different levels of default risk, depending on the issuing company's characteristics and the terms of the specific bond. Default risk often is referred to as "credit risk," and the larger the default or credit risk, the higher the interest rate the issuer must pay.

Municipal bonds, or "munis," are issued by state and local governments. Like corporate bonds, munis have default risk. However, munis offer one major advantage over all other bonds: The interest earned on most municipal bonds is exempt from federal taxes and also from state taxes if the holder is a resident of the issuing state. Consequently, municipal bonds carry interest rates that are considerably lower than those on corporate bonds with the same default risk.

Foreign bonds are issued by foreign governments or foreign corporations. Foreign corporate bonds are, of course, exposed to default risk, and so are some foreign government bonds. An additional risk exists if the bonds are denominated in a currency other than that of the investor's home currency. For example, if a U.S. investor purchases a corporate bond denominated in Japanese yen and the yen subsequently falls relative to the dollar, then the investor will lose money, even if the company does not default on its bonds.

SELF-TEST QUESTIONS

What is a bond?

What are the four main types of bonds?

Why are U.S. Treasury bonds not riskless?

To what types of risk are investors of foreign bonds exposed?

KEY CHARACTERISTICS OF BONDS

Although all bonds have some common characteristics, they do not always have identical contractual features, as described below.

Par Value

The **par value** is the stated face value of the bond; for illustrative purposes we generally assume a par value of $1,000, although any multiple of $1,000 (for example, $5,000) can be used. The par value generally represents the amount of money the firm borrows and promises to repay on the maturity date.

Coupon Interest Rate

MicroDrive's bonds require the company to pay a fixed number of dollars of interest each year (or, more typically, each six months). When this **coupon payment,** as it is called, is divided by the par value, the result is the **coupon interest rate.** For example, MicroDrive's bonds have a $1,000 par value, and they pay $100 in interest each year. The bond's coupon interest is $100, so its coupon interest rate is $100/$1,000 = 10%. The coupon payment, which is fixed at the time the bond is issued, remains in force during the life of

---

[1] The U.S. Treasury actually issues three types of securities: "bills," "notes," and "bonds." A bond makes an equal payment every six months until it matures, at which time it makes an additional lump sum payment. If the maturity at the time of issue is less than 10 years, it is called a note rather than a bond. A T-bill has a maturity of 52 weeks or less at the time of issue, and it makes no payments at all until it matures. Thus, bills are sold initially at a discount to their face, or maturity, value.

e-resource

See the Chapter 6 Web Extension for more on zero coupon bonds.

the bond.[2] Typically, at the time a bond is issued its coupon payment is set at a level that will enable the bond to be issued at or near its par value.

In some cases, a bond's coupon payment will vary over time. For these **floating-rate bonds,** the coupon rate is set for, say, the initial six-month period, after which it is adjusted every six months based on some market rate. Some corporate issues are tied to the Treasury bond rate, while other issues are tied to other rates, such as LIBOR. Many additional provisions can be included in floating-rate issues. For example, some are convertible to fixed-rate debt, whereas others have upper and lower limits ("caps" and "floors") on how high or low the rate can go.

Floating-rate debt is popular with investors who are worried about the risk of rising interest rates, since the interest paid on such bonds increases whenever market rates rise. This causes the market value of the debt to be stabilized, and it also provides institutional buyers, such as banks, with income that is better geared to their own obligations. Banks' deposit costs rise with interest rates, so the income on floating-rate loans that they have made rises at the same time their deposit costs are rising. The savings and loan industry was almost destroyed as a result of their former practice of making fixed-rate mortgage loans but borrowing on floating-rate terms. If you are earning 6 percent fixed but paying 10 percent floating—which they were—you soon go bankrupt—which they did. Moreover, floating-rate debt appeals to corporations that want to issue long-term debt without committing themselves to paying a historically high interest rate for the entire life of the loan.

Some bonds pay no coupons at all, but are offered at a substantial discount below their par values and hence provide capital appreciation rather than interest income. These securities are called **zero coupon bonds** ("*zeros*"). Other bonds pay some coupon interest, but not enough to be issued at par. In general, any bond originally offered at a price significantly below its par value is called an **original issue discount (OID) bond.** Corporations first used zeros in a major way in 1981. In recent years IBM, Alcoa, JCPenney, ITT, Cities Service, GMAC, and Lockheed Martin have used zeros to raise billions of dollars.

Some bonds don't pay cash coupons but pay coupons consisting of additional bonds (or a percentage of an additional bond). These are called **payment in kind bonds,** or just **PIK bonds.** PIK bonds are usually issued by companies with cash flow problems, which makes them risky.

Some bonds have a step-up provision: If the company's bond rating is downgraded, then it must increase the bond's coupon rate. Step-ups are more popular in Europe than in the United States, but that is beginning to change. Note that a step-up is quite dangerous from the company's standpoint. The downgrade means that it is having trouble servicing its debt, and the step-up will exacerbate the problem. This has led to a number of bankruptcies.

Maturity Date

Bonds generally have a specified **maturity date** on which the par value must be repaid. MicroDrive's bonds, which were issued on January 5, 2006, will mature on January 5, 2021; thus, they had a 15-year maturity at the time they were issued. Most bonds have **original maturities** (the maturity at the time the bond is issued) ranging from 10 to 40 years, but any maturity is legally permissible.[3] Of course, the effective maturity of a bond declines each year after it has been issued. Thus, MicroDrive's bonds had a 15-year original maturity, but in 2007, a year later, they will have a 14-year maturity, and so on.

---

[2] At one time, bonds literally had a number of small (1/2- by 2-inch), dated coupons attached to them, and on each interest payment date the owner would clip off the coupon for that date and either cash it at his or her bank or mail it to the company's paying agent, who would then mail back a check for the interest. For example, a 30-year, semiannual bond would start with 60 coupons. Today, most new bonds are *registered*—no physical coupons are involved, and interest checks are mailed automatically to the registered owners.

[3] In July 1993, Walt Disney Co., attempting to lock in a low interest rate, issued the first 100-year bonds to be sold by any borrower in modern times. Soon after, Coca-Cola became the second company to stretch the meaning of "long-term bond" by selling $150 million of 100-year bonds.

Provisions to Call or Redeem Bonds

Most corporate bonds contain a **call provision,** which gives the issuing corporation the right to call the bonds for redemption.[4] The call provision generally states that the company must pay the bondholders an amount greater than the par value if they are called. The additional sum, which is termed a **call premium,** is often set equal to one year's interest if the bonds are called during the first year, and the premium declines at a constant rate of INT/N each year thereafter, where INT = annual interest and N = original maturity in years. For example, the call premium on a $1,000 par value, 10-year, 10 percent bond would generally be $100 if it were called during the first year, $90 during the second year (calculated by reducing the $100, or 10 percent, premium by one-tenth), and so on. However, bonds are often not callable until several years (generally 5 to 10) after they were issued. This is known as a **deferred call,** and the bonds are said to have **call protection.**

Suppose a company sold bonds when interest rates were relatively high. Provided the issue is callable, the company could sell a new issue of low-yielding securities if and when interest rates drop. It could then use the proceeds of the new issue to retire the high-rate issue and thus reduce its interest expense. This process is called a **refunding operation.**

A call provision is valuable to the firm but potentially detrimental to investors. If interest rates go up, the company will not call the bond, and the investor will be stuck with the original coupon rate on the bond, even though interest rates in the economy have risen sharply. However, if interest rates fall, the company *will* call the bond and pay off investors, who then must reinvest the proceeds at the current market interest rate, which is lower than the rate they were getting on the original bond. In other words, the investor loses when interest rates go up, but doesn't reap the gains when rates fall. To induce an investor to take this type of risk, a new issue of callable bonds must provide a higher interest rate than an otherwise similar issue of noncallable bonds. For example, Pacific Timber Company issued bonds yielding 9.5 percent; these bonds were callable immediately. On the same day, Northwest Milling Company sold an issue with similar risk and maturity that yielded 9.2 percent, but these bonds were noncallable for 10 years. Investors were willing to accept a 0.3 percent lower interest rate on Northwest's bonds for the assurance that the 9.2 percent interest rate would be earned for at least 10 years. Pacific, on the other hand, had to incur a 0.3 percent higher annual interest rate to obtain the option of calling the bonds in the event of a subsequent decline in rates.

Bonds that are **redeemable at par** at the holder's option protect investors against a rise in interest rates. If rates rise, the price of a fixed-rate bond declines. However, if holders have the option of turning their bonds in and having them redeemed at par, they are protected against rising rates. Examples of such debt include Transamerica's $50 million issue of 25-year, 8½ percent bonds. The bonds are not callable by the company, but holders can turn them in for redemption at par five years after the date of issue. If interest rates have risen, holders will turn in the bonds and reinvest the proceeds at a higher rate. This feature enabled Transamerica to sell the bonds with an 8½ percent coupon at a time when other similarly rated bonds had yields of 9 percent.

In late 1988, the corporate bond markets were sent into turmoil by the leveraged buyout of RJR Nabisco. RJR's bonds dropped in value by 20 percent within days of the LBO announcement, and the prices of many other corporate bonds also plunged, because investors feared that a boom in LBOs would load up many companies with excessive debt, leading to lower bond ratings and declining bond prices. All this led to a resurgence of concern about **event risk,** which is the risk that some sudden event, such as an LBO, will occur and increase the credit risk of the company, hence lowering the firm's bond rating and the value of its outstanding bonds. Investors' concern over event risk meant that

---

[4] A majority of municipal bonds also contain call provisions. Although the U.S. Treasury no longer issues callable bonds, some past Treasury issues were callable.

those firms deemed most likely to face events that could harm bondholders had to pay dearly to raise new debt capital, if they could raise it at all. In an attempt to control debt costs, a new type of protective covenant was devised to minimize event risk. This covenant, called a **super poison put,** enables a bondholder to turn in, or "put" a bond back to the issuer at par in the event of a takeover, merger, or major recapitalization.

Poison puts had actually been around since 1986, when the leveraged buyout trend took off. However, the earlier puts proved to be almost worthless because they allowed investors to "put" their bonds back to the issuer at par value only in the event of an unfriendly takeover. But because almost all takeovers are eventually approved by the target firm's board, mergers that started as hostile generally ended as friendly. Also, the earlier poison puts failed to protect investors from voluntary recapitalizations, in which a company sells a big issue of bonds to pay a big, one-time dividend to stockholders or to buy back its own stock. The "super" poison puts that were used following the RJR buyout announcement protected against both of these actions. This is a good illustration of how quickly the financial community reacts to changes in the marketplace.

Finally, some bonds have a **make-whole call provision.** This allows a company to call the bond, but it must pay a call price that is essentially equal to the market value of a similar noncallable bond. This provides companies with an easy way to repurchase bonds as part of a financial restructuring, such as a merger.

Sinking Funds

Some bonds also include a **sinking fund provision** that facilitates the orderly retirement of the bond issue. On rare occasions the firm may be required to deposit money with a trustee, which invests the funds and then uses the accumulated sum to retire the bonds when they mature. Usually, though, the sinking fund is used to buy back a certain percentage of the issue each year. A failure to meet the sinking fund requirement causes the bond to be thrown into default, which may force the company into bankruptcy. Obviously, a sinking fund can constitute a significant cash drain on the firm.

In most cases, the firm is given the right to handle the sinking fund in either of two ways:

1. The company can call in for redemption (at par value) a certain percentage of the bonds each year; for example, it might be able to call 5 percent of the total original amount of the issue at a price of $1,000 per bond. The bonds are numbered serially, and those called for redemption are determined by a lottery administered by the trustee.
2. The company may buy the required number of bonds on the open market.

The firm will choose the least-cost method. If interest rates have risen, causing bond prices to fall, it will buy bonds in the open market at a discount; if interest rates have fallen, it will call the bonds. Note that a call for sinking fund purposes is quite different from a refunding call as discussed above. A sinking fund call typically requires no call premium, but only a small percentage of the issue is normally callable in any one year.[5]

Although sinking funds are designed to protect bondholders by ensuring that an issue is retired in an orderly fashion, you should recognize that sinking funds can work to the detriment of bondholders. For example, suppose the bond carries a 10 percent interest rate, but yields on similar bonds have fallen to 7.5 percent. A sinking fund call at par would require an investor to give up a bond that pays $100 of interest and then to reinvest in a bond that pays only $75 per year. This obviously harms those bondholders whose bonds are called. On balance, however, bonds that have a sinking fund are regarded as being safer than those without such a provision, so at the time they are issued sinking fund bonds have lower coupon rates than otherwise similar bonds without sinking funds.

---

[5] Some sinking funds require the issuer to pay a call premium.

Other Features

Several other types of bonds are used sufficiently often to warrant mention. First, **convertible bonds** are bonds that are convertible into shares of common stock, at a fixed price, at the option of the bondholder. Convertibles have a lower coupon rate than nonconvertible debt, but they offer investors a chance for capital gains in exchange for the lower coupon rate. Bonds issued with **warrants** are similar to convertibles. Warrants are options that permit the holder to buy stock for a stated price, thereby providing a capital gain if the price of the stock rises. Bonds that are issued with warrants, like convertibles, carry lower coupon rates than straight bonds.

Another type of bond is an **income bond,** which pays interest only if the interest is earned. These securities cannot bankrupt a company, but from an investor's standpoint they are riskier than "regular" bonds. Yet another bond is the **indexed,** or **purchasing power, bond,** which first became popular in Brazil, Israel, and a few other countries plagued by high inflation rates. The interest rate paid on these bonds is based on an inflation index such as the consumer price index, so the interest paid rises automatically when the inflation rate rises, thus protecting the bondholders against inflation. In January 1997, the U.S. Treasury began issuing indexed bonds, and they currently pay a rate that is roughly 1 to 4 percent plus the rate of inflation during the past year.

SELF-TEST QUESTIONS

Define floating-rate bonds and zero coupon bonds.

Why is a call provision advantageous to a bond issuer?

What are the two ways a sinking fund can be handled? Which method will be chosen by the firm if interest rates have risen? If interest rates have fallen?

Are securities that provide for a sinking fund regarded as being riskier than those without this type of provision? Explain.

What are income bonds and indexed bonds?

Why do bonds with warrants and convertible bonds have lower coupons than similarly rated bonds that do not have these features?

BOND VALUATION

The value of any financial asset—a stock, a bond, a lease, or even a physical asset such as an apartment building or a piece of machinery—is simply the present value of the cash flows the asset is expected to produce.

The cash flows from a specific bond depend on its contractual features as described above. For a standard coupon-bearing bond such as the one issued by MicroDrive, the cash flows consist of interest payments during the 15-year life of the bond, plus the amount borrowed (generally the $1,000 par value) when the bond matures. In the case of a floating-rate bond, the interest payments vary over time. In the case of a zero coupon bond, there are no interest payments, only the face amount when the bond matures. For a "regular" bond with a fixed coupon rate, here is the situation:

0	$r_d\%$	1	2	3	N
Bond's Value		INT	INT	INT	INT
					M

Here

r_d = the bond's market rate of interest = 10%. This is the discount rate that is used to calculate the present value of the bond's cash flows. It is also called the "yield" or "going rate of interest." Note that r_d is *not* the coupon interest rate. It is equal to the coupon rate only if (as in this case) the bond is selling at par. Generally, most coupon bonds are issued at par, which implies that the coupon rate is set at r_d. Thereafter, interest rates, as measured by r_d, will fluctuate, but the coupon rate is fixed, so r_d will equal the coupon rate only by chance. We used the term "i" or "I" to designate the interest rate for many calculations because those terms are used on financial calculators, but "r," with the subscript "d" to designate the rate on a debt security, is normally used in finance.[6]

N = the number of years before the bond matures = 15. Note that N declines each year after the bond was issued, so a bond that had a maturity of 15 years when it was issued (original maturity = 15) will have N = 14 after one year, N = 13 after two years, and so on. Note also that at this point we assume that the bond pays interest once a year, or annually, so N is measured in years. Later on, we will deal with semiannual payment bonds, which pay interest each six months.

INT = dollars of interest paid each year = Coupon rate × Par value = 0.10($1,000) = $100. In calculator terminology, INT = PMT = 100. If the bond had been a semiannual payment bond, the payment would have been $50 every six months. The payment would be zero if MicroDrive had issued zero coupon bonds, and it would vary if the bond was a "floater."

M = the par, or maturity, value of the bond = $1,000. This amount must be paid off at maturity.

The following general equation, written in several forms, can be used to find the value of any bond, V_B:

$$
\begin{aligned}
V_B &= \frac{INT}{(1 + r_d)^1} + \frac{INT}{(1 + r_d)^2} + \cdots + \frac{INT}{(1 + r_d)^N} + \frac{M}{(1 + r_d)^N} \\
&= \sum_{t=1}^{N} \frac{INT}{(1 + r_d)^t} + \frac{M}{(1 + r_d)^N} \\
&= INT\left(\frac{1 - \dfrac{1}{(1 + r_d)^N}}{r_d} \right) + \frac{M}{(1 + r_d)^N}.
\end{aligned}
\tag{6-1}
$$

Note that the cash flows consist of an annuity of N years plus a lump sum payment at the end of Year N, and this fact is reflected in Equation 6-1. Further, Equation 6-1 can be solved by one of three procedures: (1) numerically, (2) with a financial calculator, and (3) with a spreadsheet.

NUMERICAL SOLUTION

Inserting values for MicroDrive's bond, we have

$$
\begin{aligned}
V_B &= \sum_{t=1}^{15} \frac{\$100}{(1.10)^t} + \frac{\$1,000}{(1.10)^{15}} \\
&= \$100\left(\frac{1 - \dfrac{1}{(1.1)^{15}}}{0.1} \right) + \frac{\$1,000}{(1.1)^{15}} = \$1,000.
\end{aligned}
\tag{6-1a}
$$

---

[6] The appropriate interest rate on a bond depends on its risk, liquidity, and years to maturity, as well as supply and demand conditions in the capital markets.

Or one could simply discount each cash flow back to the present and sum these PVs to find the bond's value; see Figure 6-1. This procedure is not very efficient, especially if the bond has many years to maturity. Alternatively, you could use the formula in the second row of Equation 6-1a with a simple or scientific calculator, although this would still be somewhat cumbersome.

FINANCIAL CALCULATOR SOLUTION

All five financial calculator keys are used with bonds. Here is the setup:

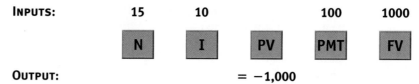

INPUTS: 15   10   100   1000

| N | I | PV | PMT | FV |

OUTPUT: = −1,000

Simply input N = 15, I = r_d = 10, INT = PMT = 100, M = FV = 1000, and then press the PV key to find the value of the bond, $1,000. Since the PV is an outflow to the investor, it is shown with a negative sign. The calculator is programmed to solve Equation 6-1: It finds the PV of an annuity of $100 per year for 15 years, discounted at 10 percent, then it finds the PV of the $1,000 maturity payment, and then it adds these two PVs to find the value of the bond. Notice that even though the time line in Figure 6-1 shows a total of $1,100 at Year 15, you should not enter FV = 1100! When you entered N = 15 and PMT = 100, you told the calculator that there is a $100 payment at Year 15. Thus, the FV = 1000 accounts for any *extra* payment at Year 15, above and beyond the $100 payment.

SPREADSHEET SOLUTION

e-resource

See CF2 Ch 06 Tool Kit.xls.

Here we want to find the PV of the cash flows, so we would use the PV function. Put the cursor on Cell B10, click the function wizard, then Financial, PV, and OK. Then fill in the dialog box with Rate = 0.1 or F3, Nper = 15 or Q5, Pmt = 100 or C6, Fv = 1000 or Q7, and Type = 0 or leave it blank. Then, when you click OK, you will get the value of

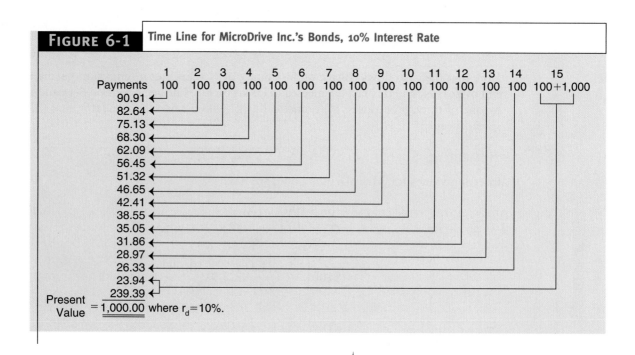

FIGURE 6-1   Time Line for MicroDrive Inc.'s Bonds, 10% Interest Rate

	1	2	3	4	5	6	7	8	9	10	11	12	13	14	15
Payments	100	100	100	100	100	100	100	100	100	100	100	100	100	100	100+1,000

90.91
82.64
75.13
68.30
62.09
56.45
51.32
46.65
42.41
38.55
35.05
31.86
28.97
26.33
23.94
239.39

Present Value = 1,000.00 where r_d = 10%.

the bond, −$1,000. Like the financial calculator solution, this is negative because the Pmt and Fv are positive.

An alternative, and in this case somewhat easier, procedure given that the time line has been created, is to use the NPV function. Click the function wizard, then Financial, NPV, and OK. Then input Rate = 0.1 or F3 and Value 1 = C8:Q8. Then click OK to get the answer, $1,000.

Note that by changing the interest rate in F3, we can instantly find the value of the bond at any other discount rate. Note also that *Excel* provides specialized functions for bond prices. For example, in *Excel* you could use the function wizard to enter this formula:

$$= PRICE(Date(2006,1,5),Date (2021,1,5),10\%,10\%,100,1,0).$$

The first two arguments in the function give the current and maturity dates. The next argument is the bond's coupon rate, followed by the current market interest rate, or yield. The fifth argument, 100, is the redemption value of the bond at maturity, expressed as a percent of the face value. The sixth argument is the number of payments per year, and the last argument, 0, tells the program to use the U.S. convention for counting days, which is to assume 30 days per month and 360 days per year. This function produces the value 100, which is the current price expressed as a percent of the bond's par value, which is $1,000. Therefore, you can multiply $1,000 by 100 percent to get the current price, which is $1,000. This function is essential if a bond is being evaluated between coupon payment dates.

	A	B	C	D	E	F	G	H	I	J	K	L	M	N	O	P	Q
1	Spreadsheet for bond value calculation																
2				Going rate, or yield													
3	Coupon rate	10%				10%											
4																	
5	Time	0	1	2	3	4	5	6	7	8	9	10	11	12	13	14	15
6	Interest Pmt		100	100	100	100	100	100	100	100	100	100	100	100	100	100	100
7	Maturity Pmt																1000
8	Total CF		100	100	100	100	100	100	100	100	100	100	100	100	100	100	1100
9																	
10	PV of CF	1000															

Changes in Bond Values over Time

At the time a coupon bond is issued, the coupon is generally set at a level that will cause the market price of the bond to equal its par value. If a lower coupon were set, investors would not be willing to pay $1,000 for the bond, while if a higher coupon were set, investors would clamor for the bond and bid its price up over $1,000. Investment bankers can judge quite precisely the coupon rate that will cause a bond to sell at its $1,000 par value.

A bond that has just been issued is known as a **new issue**. (Investment bankers classify a bond as a new issue for about one month after it has first been issued. New issues are usually actively traded, and are called "on-the-run" bonds.) Once the bond has been on the market for a while, it is classified as an **outstanding bond**, also called a **seasoned issue**. Newly issued bonds generally sell very close to par, but the prices of seasoned bonds vary widely from par. Except for floating-rate bonds, coupon payments are constant, so when economic conditions change, a bond with a $100 coupon that sold at par when it was issued will sell for more or less than $1,000 thereafter.

MicroDrive's bonds with a 10 percent coupon rate were originally issued at par. If r_d remained constant at 10 percent, what would the value of the bond be one year after it was issued? Now the term to maturity is only 14 years—that is, N = 14. With a financial calculator, just override N = 15 with N = 14, press the PV key, and you find a value of $1,000. If we continued, setting N = 13, N = 12, and so forth, we would see that the value of the bond will remain at $1,000 as long as the going interest rate remains constant at the coupon rate, 10 percent.[7]

Now suppose interest rates in the economy fell after the MicroDrive bonds were issued, and, as a result, r_d *fell below the coupon rate*, decreasing from 10 to 5 percent. Both the coupon interest payments and the maturity value remain constant, but now 5 percent values for PVIF and PVIFA would have to be used in Equation 6-1. The value of the bond at the end of the first year would be $1,494.93:

$$V_B = \$100\left(\frac{1 - \dfrac{1}{(1.05)^{14}}}{0.05}\right) + \frac{\$1,000}{(1.05)^{14}}$$

$$= \$1,494.93.$$

With a financial calculator, just change r_d = I from 10 to 5, and then press the PV key to get the answer, $1,494.93. Thus, if r_d fell *below* the coupon rate, the bond would sell above par, or at a **premium**.

The arithmetic of the bond value increase should be clear, but what is the logic behind it? The fact that r_d has fallen to 5 percent means that if you had $1,000 to invest, you could buy new bonds like MicroDrive's (every day some 10 to 12 companies sell new bonds), except that these new bonds would pay $50 of interest each year rather than $100. Naturally, you would prefer $100 to $50, so you would be willing to pay more than $1,000 for a MicroDrive bond to obtain its higher coupons. All investors would react similarly, and as a result, the MicroDrive bonds would be bid up in price to $1,494.93, at which point they would provide the same rate of return to a potential investor as the new bonds, 5 percent.

Assuming that interest rates remain constant at 5 percent for the next 14 years, what would happen to the value of a MicroDrive bond? It would fall gradually from $1,494.93 at present to $1,000 at maturity, when MicroDrive will redeem each bond for $1,000. This point can be illustrated by calculating the value of the bond 1 year later, when it has 13 years remaining to maturity. With a financial calculator, merely input the values for N, I, PMT, and FV, now using N = 13, and press the PV key to find the value of the bond, $1,469.68. Thus, the value of the bond will have fallen from $1,494.93 to $1,469.68, or by $25.25. If you were to calculate the value of the bond at other future dates, the price would continue to fall as the maturity date approached.

---

[7] The bond prices quoted by brokers are calculated as described. However, if you bought a bond between interest payment dates, you would have to pay the basic price plus accrued interest. Thus, if you purchased a MicroDrive bond six months after it was issued, your broker would send you an invoice stating that you must pay $1,000 as the basic price of the bond plus $50 interest, representing one-half the annual interest of $100. The seller of the bond would receive $1,050. If you bought the bond the day before its interest payment date, you would pay $1,000 + (364/365)($100) = $1,099.73. Of course, you would receive an interest payment of $100 at the end of the next day.

Throughout the chapter, we assume that bonds are being evaluated immediately after an interest payment date. The more expensive financial calculators have a built-in calendar that permits the calculation of exact values between interest payment dates, as do spreadsheet programs. For example, see *Excel*'s PRICE function, which is illustrated in the *CF2 Ch 06 Tool Kit.xls* file.

e-resource

Note that if you purchased the bond at a price of $1,494.93 and then sold it one year later with r_d still at 5 percent, you would have a capital loss of $25.25, or a total return of $100.00 − $25.25 = $74.75. Your percentage rate of return would consist of an **interest yield** (also called a **current yield**) plus a **capital gains yield,** calculated as follows:

$$\begin{aligned}
\text{Interest, or current, yield} &= \$100/1,494.93 &&= 0.0669 &&= 6.69\% \\
\text{Capital gains yield} &= -\$25.25/\$1,494.93 &&= -0.0169 &&= -1.69\% \\
\text{Total rate of return, or yield} &= \$74.75/\$1,494.93 &&= 0.0500 &&= \underline{5.00\%}
\end{aligned}$$

Had interest rates risen from 10 to 15 percent during the first year after issue rather than fallen from 10 to 5 percent, then you would enter N = 14, I = 15, PMT = 100, and FV = 1000, and then press the PV key to find the value of the bond, $713.78. In this case, the bond would sell below its par value, or at a **discount.** The total expected future return on the bond would again consist of a current yield and a capital gains yield, but now the capital gains yield would be *positive.* The total return would be 15 percent. To see this, calculate the price of the bond with 13 years left to maturity, assuming that interest rates remain at 15 percent. With a calculator, enter N = 13, I = 15, PMT = 100, and FV = 1000, and then press PV to obtain the bond's value, $720.84.

Note that the capital gain for the year is the difference between the bond's value at Year 2 (with 13 years remaining) and the bond's value at Year 1 (with 14 years remaining), or $720.84 − $713.78 = $7.06. The interest yield, capital gains yield, and total yield are calculated as follows:

$$\begin{aligned}
\text{Interest, or current, yield} &= \$100/\$713.78 &&= 0.1401 = 14.01\% \\
\text{Capital gains yield} &= \$7.06/\$713.78 &&= 0.0099 = \underline{\ 0.99\%} \\
\text{Total rate of return, or yield} &= \$107.06/\$713.78 &&= 0.1500 = \underline{15.00\%}
\end{aligned}$$

Figure 6-2 graphs the value of the bond over time, assuming that interest rates in the economy (1) remain constant at 10 percent, (2) fall to 5 percent and then remain constant at

e-resource

See CF2 Ch 06 Tool Kit.xls for details.

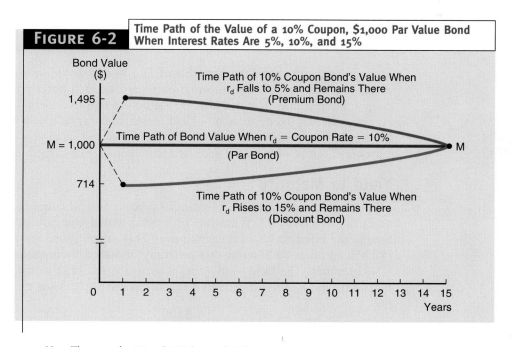

FIGURE 6-2 Time Path of the Value of a 10% Coupon, $1,000 Par Value Bond When Interest Rates Are 5%, 10%, and 15%

Note: The curves for 5% and 15% have a slight bow.

that level, or (3) rise to 15 percent and remain constant at that level. Of course, if interest rates do *not* remain constant, then the price of the bond will fluctuate. However, regardless of what future interest rates do, the bond's price will approach $1,000 as it nears the maturity date (barring bankruptcy, in which case the bond's value might fall dramatically).

Figure 6-2 illustrates the following key points:

1. Whenever the going rate of interest, r_d, is equal to the coupon rate, a *fixed-rate* bond will sell at its par value. Normally, the coupon rate is set equal to the going rate when a bond is issued, causing it to sell at par initially.
2. Interest rates do change over time, but the coupon rate remains fixed after the bond has been issued. Whenever the going rate of interest *rises above* the coupon rate, a fixed-rate bond's price will *fall below* its par value. Such a bond is called a **discount bond.**
3. Whenever the going rate of interest *falls below* the coupon rate, a fixed-rate bond's price will *rise above* its par value. Such a bond is called a **premium bond.**
4. Thus, an *increase* in interest rates will cause the prices of outstanding bonds to *fall*, whereas a *decrease* in rates will cause bond prices to *rise*.
5. The market value of a bond will always approach its par value as its maturity date approaches, provided the firm does not go bankrupt.

These points are very important, for they show that bondholders may suffer capital losses or make capital gains, depending on whether interest rates rise or fall after the bond was purchased.

SELF-TEST QUESTIONS

Explain how to calculate a bond's price.

What is meant by the terms "new issue" and "seasoned issue"?

Explain what happens to the price of a fixed-rate bond if (1) interest rates rise above the bond's coupon rate or (2) interest rates fall below the bond's coupon rate.

Why do the prices of fixed-rate bonds fall if expectations for inflation rise?

What is a "discount bond"? A "premium bond"?

BOND YIELDS

If you examine the bond market table of *The Wall Street Journal* or a bond dealer's price sheet, you will typically see information regarding each bond's maturity date, price, and coupon interest rate. You will also see the bond's reported yield. Unlike the coupon interest rate, which is fixed, the bond's yield varies from day to day depending on current market conditions. Moreover, the yield can be calculated in three different ways, and three "answers" can be obtained. These different yields are described in the following sections.

Yield to Maturity

Suppose you were offered a 14-year, 10 percent annual coupon, $1,000 par value bond at a price of $1,494.93. What rate of interest would you earn on your investment if you bought the bond and held it to maturity? This rate is called the bond's **yield to maturity (YTM)**, and it is the interest rate generally discussed by investors when they talk about rates of return. The yield to maturity is generally the same as the market rate of interest, r_d, and to find it, all you need to do is solve Equation 6-1 for r_d:

$$V_B = \$1{,}494.93 = \frac{\$100}{(1 + r_d)^1} + \cdots + \frac{\$100}{(1 + r_d)^{14}} + \frac{\$1{,}000}{(1 + r_d)^{14}}.$$

You could substitute values for r_d until you find a value that "works" and forces the sum of the PVs on the right side of the equal sign to equal \$1,494.93. Alternatively, you could substitute values of r_d into the third form of Equation 6-1 until you find a value that works.

Finding r_d = YTM by trial-and-error would be a tedious, time-consuming process, but as you might guess, it is easy with a financial calculator.[8] Here is the setup:

INPUTS:	14		−1494.93	100	1000
	N	I	PV	PMT	FV
OUTPUT:		= 5			

Simply enter N = 14, PV = −1494.93, PMT = 100, and FV = 1000, and then press the I key. The answer, 5 percent, will then appear.

The yield to maturity is identical to the total rate of return discussed in the preceding section. The yield to maturity can also be viewed as the bond's *promised rate of return,* which is the return that investors will receive if all the promised payments are made. However, the yield to maturity equals the *expected rate of return* only if (1) the probability of default is zero and (2) the bond cannot be called. If there is some default risk, or if the bond may be called, then there is some probability that the promised payments to maturity will not be received, in which case the calculated yield to maturity will differ from the expected return.

The YTM for a bond that sells at par consists entirely of an interest yield, but if the bond sells at a price other than its par value, the YTM will consist of the interest yield plus a positive or negative capital gains yield. Note also that a bond's yield to maturity changes whenever interest rates in the economy change, and this is almost daily. One who purchases a bond and holds it until it matures will receive the YTM that existed on the purchase date, but the bond's calculated YTM will change frequently between the purchase date and the maturity date.

Yield to Call

If you purchased a bond that was callable and the company called it, you would not have the option of holding the bond until it matured. Therefore, the yield to maturity would not be earned. For example, if MicroDrive's 10 percent coupon bonds were callable, and if interest rates fell from 10 percent to 5 percent, then the company could call in the 10 percent bonds, replace them with 5 percent bonds, and save \$100 − \$50 = \$50 interest per bond per year. This would be beneficial to the company, but not to its bondholders.

If current interest rates are well below an outstanding bond's coupon rate, then a callable bond is likely to be called, and investors will estimate its expected rate of return as the **yield to call (YTC)** rather than as the yield to maturity. To calculate the YTC, solve this equation for r_d:

$$\text{Price of bond} = \sum_{t=1}^{N} \frac{\text{INT}}{(1 + r_d)^t} + \frac{\text{Call price}}{(1 + r_d)^N}. \tag{6-2}$$

e-resource

---

[8] You could also find the YTM with a spreadsheet. In *Excel,* you would use the RATE function for this bond, inputting Nper = 14, Pmt = 100, Pv = −1494.93, Fv = 1000, 0 for Type, and leave Guess blank. In *Excel,* the YIELD function allows the user to input specific purchase and maturity dates. See the **CF2 Ch 06 Tool Kit.xls** file for details.

Here N is the number of years until the company can call the bond; call price is the price the company must pay in order to call the bond (it is often set equal to the par value plus one year's interest); and r_d is the YTC.

To illustrate, suppose MicroDrive's bonds had a provision that permitted the company, if it desired, to call the bonds 10 years after the issue date at a price of $1,100. Suppose further that interest rates had fallen, and one year after issuance the going interest rate had declined, causing the price of the bonds to rise to $1,494.93. Here is the time line and the setup for finding the bond's YTC with a financial calculator:

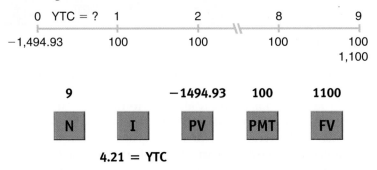

The YTC is 4.21 percent—this is the return you would earn if you bought the bond at a price of $1,494.93 and it was called nine years from today. (The bond could not be called until 10 years after issuance, and one year has gone by, so there are nine years left until the first call date.)

Do you think MicroDrive *will* call the bonds when they become callable? MicroDrive's action would depend on what the going interest rate is when the bonds become callable. If the going rate remains at $r_d = 5\%$, then MicroDrive could save $10\% - 5\% = 5\%$, or $50 per bond per year, by calling them and replacing the 10 percent bonds with a new 5 percent issue. There would be costs to the company to refund the issue, but the interest savings would probably be worth the cost, so MicroDrive would probably refund the bonds. Therefore, you would probably earn YTC = 4.21% rather than YTM = 5% if you bought the bonds under the indicated conditions.

In the balance of this chapter, we assume that bonds are not callable unless otherwise noted, but some of the end-of-chapter problems deal with yield to call.

Current Yield

If you examine brokerage house reports on bonds, you will often see reference to a bond's **current yield.** The current yield is the annual interest payment divided by the bond's current price. For example, if MicroDrive's bonds with a 10 percent coupon were currently selling at $985, the bond's current yield would be 10.15 percent ($100/$985).

Unlike the yield to maturity, the current yield does not represent the rate of return that investors should expect on the bond. The current yield provides information regarding the amount of cash income that a bond will generate in a given year, but since it does not take account of capital gains or losses that will be realized if the bond is held until maturity (or call), it does not provide an accurate measure of the bond's total expected return.

The fact that the current yield does not provide an accurate measure of a bond's total return can be illustrated with a zero coupon bond. Since zeros pay no annual income, they always have a current yield of zero. This indicates that the bond will not provide any cash interest income, but since the bond will appreciate in value over time, its total rate of return clearly exceeds zero.

Explain the difference between the yield to maturity and the yield to call.
How does a bond's current yield differ from its total return?
Could the current yield exceed the total return?

BONDS WITH SEMIANNUAL COUPONS

Although some bonds pay interest annually, the vast majority actually pay interest semiannually. To evaluate semiannual payment bonds, we must modify the valuation model as follows:

1. Divide the annual coupon interest payment by 2 to determine the dollars of interest paid each six months.
2. Multiply the years to maturity, N, by 2 to determine the number of semiannual periods.
3. Divide the nominal (quoted) interest rate, r_d, by 2 to determine the periodic (semiannual) interest rate.

By making these changes, we obtain the following equation for finding the value of a bond that pays interest semiannually:

$$V_B = \sum_{t=1}^{2N} \frac{INT/2}{(1 + r_d/2)^t} + \frac{M}{(1 + r_d/2)^{2N}}. \tag{6-3}$$

To illustrate, assume now that MicroDrive's bonds pay $50 interest each six months rather than $100 at the end of each year. Thus, each interest payment is only half as large, but there are twice as many of them. The coupon rate is thus "10 percent, semiannual payments." This is the nominal, or quoted, rate.[9]

When the going (nominal) rate of interest is 5 percent with semiannual compounding, the value of this 15-year bond is found as follows:

INPUTS:	30	2.5		50	1000
	N	I	PV	PMT	FV
OUTPUT:			= −1,523.26		

---

[9] In this situation, the nominal coupon rate of "10 percent, semiannually," is the rate that bond dealers, corporate treasurers, and investors generally would discuss. Of course, the *effective annual rate* would be higher than 10 percent at the time the bond was issued:

$$EAR = EFF\% = \left(1 + \frac{r_{Nom}}{m}\right)^m - 1 = \left(1 + \frac{0.10}{2}\right)^2 - 1 = (1.05)^2 - 1 = 10.25\%.$$

Note also that 10 percent with annual payments is different than 10 percent with semiannual payments. Thus, we have assumed a change in effective rates in this section from the situation in the preceding section, where we assumed 10 percent with annual payments.

Enter N = 30, r_d = I = 2.5, PMT = 50, FV = 1000, and then press the PV key to obtain the bond's value, $1,523.26. The value with semiannual interest payments is slightly larger than $1,518.98, the value when interest is paid annually. This higher value occurs because interest payments are received somewhat faster under semiannual compounding.

SELF-TEST QUESTION Describe how the annual bond valuation formula is changed to evaluate semiannual coupon bonds. Then, write out the revised formula.

ASSESSING THE RISK OF A BOND

Interest Rate Risk

Interest rates go up and down over time, and an increase in interest rates leads to a decline in the value of outstanding bonds. This risk of a decline in bond values due to rising interest rates is called **interest rate risk.** To illustrate, suppose you bought some 10 percent MicroDrive bonds at a price of $1,000, and interest rates in the following year rose to 15 percent. As we saw earlier, the price of the bonds would fall to $713.78, so you would have a loss of $286.22 per bond.[10] Interest rates can and do rise, and rising rates cause a loss of value for bondholders. Thus, people or firms who invest in bonds are exposed to risk from changing interest rates.

One's exposure to interest rate risk is higher on bonds with long maturities than on those maturing in the near future.[11] This point can be demonstrated by showing how the value of a 1-year bond with a 10 percent annual coupon fluctuates with changes in r_d, and then comparing these changes with those on a 14-year bond as calculated previously. The 1-year bond's value for r_d = 5% is shown below:

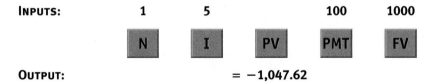

INPUTS: 1   5   100   1000

| N | I | PV | PMT | FV |

OUTPUT: = −1,047.62

You would obtain the first value with a financial calculator by entering N = 1, I = 5, PMT = 100, and FV = 1000, and then pressing PV to get $1,047.62. With everything still in your calculator, enter I = 10 to override the old I = 5, and press PV to find the bond's value at r_d = I = 10; it is $1,000. Then enter I = 15 and press the PV key to find the last value, $956.52.

The values of the 1-year and 14-year bonds at several current market interest rates are summarized and plotted in Figure 6-3. Note how much more sensitive the price of the 14-year bond is to changes in interest rates. At a 10 percent interest rate, both the 14-year and the 1-year bonds are valued at $1,000. When rates rise to 15 percent, the 14-year bond falls to $713.78, but the 1-year bond falls only to $956.52.

---

[10] You would have an *accounting* (and tax) loss only if you sold the bond; if you held it to maturity, you would not have such a loss. However, even if you did not sell, you would still have suffered a *real economic loss in an opportunity cost sense* because you would have lost the opportunity to invest at 15 percent and would be stuck with a 10 percent bond in a 15 percent market. In an economic sense, "paper losses" are just as bad as realized accounting losses.

[11] Actually, a bond's maturity and coupon rate both affect interest rate risk. Low coupons mean that most of the bond's return will come from repayment of principal, whereas on a high coupon bond with the same maturity, more of the cash flows will come in during the early years due to the relatively large coupon payments. A measurement called "duration," which finds the average number of years the bond's PV of cash flows remain outstanding, has been developed to combine maturity and coupons. A zero coupon bond, which has no interest payments and whose payments all come at maturity, has a duration equal to the bond's maturity. Coupon bonds all have durations that are shorter than maturity, and the higher the coupon rate, the shorter the duration. Bonds with longer duration are exposed to more interest rate risk. *Excel*'s DURATION function provides an easy way to calculate a bond's duration. See the Web Extension to this chapter for more on duration.

CF

e-resource

See the Chapter 6 Web Extension.

e-resource

See CF2 Ch 06 Tool Kit.xls for details.

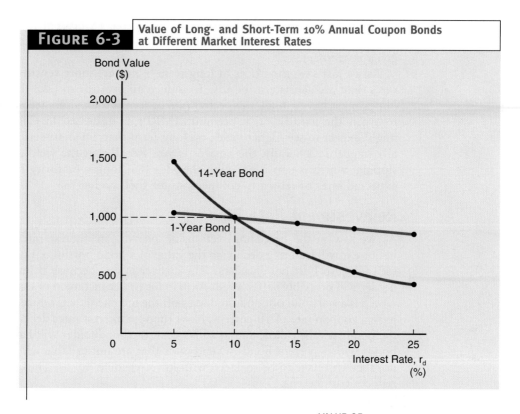

	VALUE OF	
Current Market Interest Rate, r_d	1-Year Bond	14-Year Bond
5%	$1,047.62	$1,494.93
10	1,000.00	1,000.00
15	956.52	713.78
20	916.67	538.94
25	880.00	426.39

Note: Bond values were calculated using a financial calculator assuming annual, or once-a-year, compounding.

For bonds with similar coupons, this differential sensitivity to changes in interest rates always holds true—the longer the maturity of the bond, the more its price changes in response to a given change in interest rates. Thus, even if the risk of default on two bonds is exactly the same, the one with the longer maturity is exposed to more risk from a rise in interest rates.[12]

The logical explanation for this difference in interest rate risk is simple. Suppose you bought a 14-year bond that yielded 10 percent, or $100 a year. Now suppose interest rates on comparable-risk bonds rose to 15 percent. You would be stuck with only $100 of interest for the next 14 years. On the other hand, had you bought a 1-year bond, you would have a low return for only 1 year. At the end of the year, you would get your $1,000

---

[12] If a 10-year bond were plotted in Figure 6-3, its curve would lie between those of the 14-year bond and the 1-year bond. The curve of a 1-month bond would be almost horizontal, indicating that its price would change very little in response to an interest rate change, but a 100-year bond (or a perpetuity) would have a very steep slope. Also, zero coupon bond prices are quite sensitive to interest rate changes, and the longer the maturity of the zero, the greater its price sensitivity. Therefore, 30-year zero coupon bonds have a huge amount of interest rate risk.

back, and you could then reinvest it and receive 15 percent, or $150 per year, for the next 13 years. Thus, interest rate risk reflects the length of time one is committed to a given investment.

As we just saw, the prices of long-term bonds are more sensitive to changes in interest rates than are short-term bonds. To induce an investor to take this extra risk, long-term bonds must have a higher expected rate of return than short-term bonds. This additional return is the maturity risk premium (MRP) as discussed in Chapter 1. Therefore, one might expect to see higher yields on long-term than on short-term bonds. Does this actually happen? Generally, the answer is yes. Recall that the yield curve usually is upward sloping, which is consistent with the idea that longer maturity bonds must have higher expected rates of return to compensate for their higher risk.

Reinvestment Rate Risk

As we saw in the preceding section, an *increase* in interest rates will hurt bondholders because it will lead to a decline in the value of a bond portfolio. But can a *decrease* in interest rates also hurt bondholders? The answer is yes, because if interest rates fall, a bondholder will probably suffer a reduction in his or her income. For example, consider a retiree who has a portfolio of bonds and lives off the income they produce. The bonds, on average, have a coupon rate of 10 percent. Now suppose interest rates decline to 5 percent. Many of the bonds will be called, and as calls occur, the bondholder will have to replace 10 percent bonds with 5 percent bonds. Even bonds that are not callable will mature, and when they do, they will have to be replaced with lower-yielding bonds. Thus, our retiree will suffer a reduction of income.

The risk of an income decline due to a drop in interest rates is called **reinvestment rate risk.** Reinvestment rate risk is obviously high on callable bonds. It is also high on short maturity bonds, because the shorter the maturity of a bond, the fewer the years when the relatively high old interest rate will be earned, and the sooner the funds will have to be reinvested at the new low rate. Thus, retirees whose primary holdings are short-term securities, such as bank CDs and short-term bonds, are hurt badly by a decline in rates, but holders of long-term bonds continue to enjoy their old high rates.

Comparing Interest Rate and Reinvestment Rate Risk

Note that interest rate risk relates to the *value* of the bonds in a portfolio, while reinvestment rate risk relates to the *income* the portfolio produces. If you hold long-term bonds, you will face a lot of interest rate risk because the value of your bonds will decline if interest rates rise, but you will not face much reinvestment rate risk, so your income will be stable. On the other hand, if you hold short-term bonds, you will not be exposed to much interest rate risk because the value of your portfolio will be stable, but you will be exposed to considerable reinvestment rate risk because your income will fluctuate with changes in interest rates.

We see, then, that no fixed-rate bond can be considered totally riskless—even most Treasury bonds are exposed to both interest rate and reinvestment rate risk.[13] One can minimize interest rate risk by holding short-term bonds, or one can minimize reinvestment rate risk by holding long-term bonds, but the actions that lower one type of risk increase the other. Bond portfolio managers try to balance these two risks, but some risk generally remains.

SELF-TEST QUESTIONS	Differentiate between interest rate risk and reinvestment rate risk.

To which type of risk are holders of long-term bonds more exposed? Short-term bondholders?

---

[13] Note, though, that indexed Treasury bonds are almost riskless, but they pay a relatively low real rate. Also, risks have not disappeared—they are simply transferred from bondholders to taxpayers.

DEFAULT RISK

Another important risk associated with bonds is default risk. If the issuer defaults, investors receive less than the promised return on the bond. Therefore, investors need to assess a bond's default risk before making a purchase. Recall from Chapter 1 that the quoted interest rate includes a default risk premium—the greater the default risk, the higher the bond's yield to maturity. The default risk on Treasury securities is zero, but default risk can be substantial for corporate and municipal bonds.

Suppose two bonds have the same promised cash flows, coupon rate, maturity, liquidity, and inflation exposure, but one bond has more default risk than the other. Investors will naturally pay less for the bond with the greater chance of default. As a result, bonds with higher default risk will have higher interest rates: $r_d = r^* + IP + DRP + LP + MRP$.

If its default risk changes, this will affect the price of a bond. For example, if the default risk of the MicroDrive bonds increases, the bonds' price will fall and the yield to maturity (YTM = r_d) will increase.

In this section we consider some issues related to default risk. First, we show that corporations can influence the default risk of their bonds by changing the type of bonds they issue. Second, we discuss bond ratings, which are used to measure default risk. Third, we describe the "junk bond market," which is the market for bonds with a relatively high probability of default. Finally, we consider bankruptcy and reorganization, which affect how much an investor will recover if a default occurs.

Bond Contract Provisions That Influence Default Risk

Default risk is affected by both the financial strength of the issuer and the terms of the bond contract, especially whether collateral has been pledged to secure the bond. Several types of contract provisions are discussed below.

BOND INDENTURES   An **indenture** is a legal document that spells out the rights of both bondholders and the issuing corporation, and a **trustee** is an official (usually a bank) who represents the bondholders and makes sure the terms of the indenture are carried out. The indenture may be several hundred pages in length, and it will include **restrictive covenants** that cover such points as the conditions under which the issuer can pay off the bonds prior to maturity, the levels at which certain of the issuer's ratios must be maintained if the company is to issue additional debt, and restrictions against the payment of dividends unless earnings meet certain specifications.

The trustee is responsible for monitoring the covenants and for taking appropriate action if a violation does occur. What constitutes "appropriate action" varies with the circumstances. It might be that to insist on immediate compliance would result in bankruptcy and possibly large losses on the bonds. In such a case, the trustee might decide that the bondholders would be better served by giving the company a chance to work out its problems and thus avoid forcing it into bankruptcy.

The Securities and Exchange Commission (1) approves indentures and (2) makes sure that all indenture provisions are met before allowing a company to sell new securities to the public. Also, it should be noted that the indentures of many larger corporations were actually written in the 1930s or 1940s, and that many issues of new bonds sold since then were covered by the same indenture. The interest rates on the bonds, and perhaps also the maturities, vary depending on market conditions at the time of each issue, but bondholders' protection as spelled out in the indenture is the same for all bonds of the same type. A firm will have different indentures for each of the major types of bonds it issues. For example, one indenture will cover its first mortgage bonds, another its debentures, and a third its convertible bonds.

MORTGAGE BONDS   Under a **mortgage bond,** the corporation pledges certain assets as security for the bond. To illustrate, in 2005 Billingham Corporation needed $10 million to build a major regional distribution center. Bonds in the amount of $4 million, secured by a *first mortgage* on the property, were issued. (The remaining $6 million was financed with equity capital.) If Billingham defaults on the bonds, the bondholders can foreclose on the property and sell it to satisfy their claims.

If Billingham chose, it could issue *second mortgage bonds* secured by the same $10 million of assets. In the event of liquidation, the holders of these second mortgage bonds would have a claim against the property, but only after the first mortgage bondholders had been paid off in full. Thus, second mortgages are sometimes called *junior mortgages,* because they are junior in priority to the claims of *senior mortgages,* or *first mortgage bonds.*

All mortgage bonds are subject to an indenture. The indentures of many major corporations were written 20, 30, 40, or more years ago. These indentures are generally "open ended," meaning that new bonds can be issued from time to time under the same indenture. However, the amount of new bonds that can be issued is virtually always limited to a specified percentage of the firm's total "bondable property," which generally includes all land, plant, and equipment.

DEBENTURES   A **debenture** is an unsecured bond, and as such it provides no lien against specific property as security for the obligation. Debenture holders are, therefore, general creditors whose claims are protected by property not otherwise pledged. In practice, the use of debentures depends both on the nature of the firm's assets and on its general credit strength. Extremely strong companies often use debentures; they simply do not need to put up property as security for their debt. Debentures are also issued by weak companies that have already pledged most of their assets as collateral for mortgage loans. In this latter case, the debentures are quite risky, and they will bear a high interest rate.

SUBORDINATED DEBENTURES   The term *subordinate* means "below," or "inferior to," and, in the event of bankruptcy, subordinated debt has claims on assets only after senior debt has been paid off. **Subordinated debentures** may be subordinated either to designated notes payable (usually bank loans) or to all other debt. In the event of liquidation or reorganization, holders of subordinated debentures cannot be paid until all senior debt, as named in the debentures' indenture, has been paid.

DEVELOPMENT BONDS   Some companies may be in a position to benefit from the sale of either **development bonds** or **pollution control bonds.** State and local governments may set up both *industrial development agencies* and *pollution control agencies.* These agencies are allowed, under certain circumstances, to sell **tax-exempt bonds,** then to make the proceeds available to corporations for specific uses deemed (by Congress) to be in the public interest. Thus, an industrial development agency in Florida might sell bonds to provide funds for a paper company to build a plant in the Florida Panhandle, where unemployment is high. Similarly, a Detroit pollution control agency might sell bonds to provide Ford with funds to be used to purchase pollution control equipment. In both cases, the income from the bonds would be tax exempt to the holders, so the bonds would sell at relatively low interest rates. Note, however, that these bonds are guaranteed by the corporation that will use the funds, not by a governmental unit, so their rating reflects the credit strength of the corporation using the funds.

MUNICIPAL BOND INSURANCE   Municipalities can have their bonds insured, which means that an insurance company guarantees to pay the coupon and principal payments should the issuer default. This reduces risk to investors, who will thus accept a lower coupon rate for an insured bond vis-à-vis an uninsured one. Even though the municipality must pay a fee to get its bonds insured, its savings due to the lower coupon rate often make insurance cost effective. Keep in mind that the insurers are private companies, and the value added by the insurance depends on the creditworthiness of the insurer. However, the larger ones are strong companies, and their own ratings are AAA. Therefore, the bonds they insure are also rated AAA, regardless of the credit strength of the municipal issuer. Bond ratings are discussed in the next section.

Bond Ratings

Since the early 1900s, bonds have been assigned quality ratings that reflect their probability of going into default. The three major rating agencies are Moody's Investors Service (Moody's), Standard & Poor's Corporation (S&P), and Fitch Investors Service. Moody's and S&P's rating designations are shown in Table 6-1.[14] The triple- and double-A bonds are extremely safe. Single-A and triple-B bonds are also strong enough to be called **investment grade bonds,** and they are the lowest-rated bonds that many banks and other institutional investors are permitted by law to hold. Double-B and lower bonds are speculative, or **junk bonds.** These bonds have a significant probability of going into default. A later section discusses junk bonds in more detail.

BOND RATING CRITERIA   Bond ratings are based on both qualitative and quantitative factors, some of which are listed below:

1. *Various ratios,* including the debt ratio, the times-interest-earned ratio, and the EBITDA coverage ratio. The better the ratios, the higher the rating.[15]
2. *Mortgage provisions:* Is the bond secured by a mortgage? If it is, and if the property has a high value in relation to the amount of bonded debt, the bond's rating is enhanced.
3. *Subordination provisions:* Is the bond subordinated to other debt? If so, it will be rated at least one notch below the rating it would have if it were not subordinated. Conversely, a bond with other debt subordinated to it will have a somewhat higher rating.
4. *Guarantee provisions:* Some bonds are guaranteed by other firms. If a weak company's debt is guaranteed by a strong company (usually the weak company's parent), the bond will be given the strong company's rating.
5. *Sinking fund:* Does the bond have a sinking fund to ensure systematic repayment? This feature is a plus factor to the rating agencies.
6. *Maturity:* Other things the same, a bond with a shorter maturity will be judged less risky than a longer-term bond, and this will be reflected in the ratings.
7. *Stability:* Are the issuer's sales and earnings stable?

TABLE 6-1 | Moody's and S&P Bond Ratings

	INVESTMENT GRADE				JUNK BONDS			
Moody's	Aaa	Aa	A	Baa	Ba	B	Caa	C
S&P	AAA	AA	A	BBB	BB	B	CCC	D

Note: Both Moody's and S&P use "modifiers" for bonds rated below triple-A. S&P uses a plus and minus system; thus, A+ designates the strongest A-rated bonds and A− the weakest. Moody's uses a 1, 2, or 3 designation, with 1 denoting the strongest and 3 the weakest; thus, within the double-A category, Aa1 is the best, Aa2 is average, and Aa3 is the weakest.

---

[14] In the discussion to follow, reference to the S&P code is intended to imply the Moody's and Fitch's codes as well. Thus, triple-B bonds mean both BBB and Baa bonds; double-B bonds mean both BB and Ba bonds; and so on.

[15] See Chapter 4 for an explanation of these and other ratios.

8. *Regulation:* Is the issuer regulated, and could an adverse regulatory climate cause the company's economic position to decline? Regulation is especially important for utilities and telephone companies.
9. *Antitrust:* Are any antitrust actions pending against the firm that could erode its position?
10. *Overseas operations:* What percentage of the firm's sales, assets, and profits are from overseas operations, and what is the political climate in the host countries?
11. *Environmental factors:* Is the firm likely to face heavy expenditures for pollution control equipment?
12. *Product liability:* Are the firm's products safe? The tobacco companies today are under pressure, and so are their bond ratings.
13. *Pension liabilities:* Does the firm have unfunded pension liabilities that could pose a future problem?
14. *Labor unrest:* Are there potential labor problems on the horizon that could weaken the firm's position? As this is written, a number of airlines face this problem, and it has caused their ratings to be lowered.
15. *Accounting policies:* If a firm uses relatively conservative accounting policies, its reported earnings will be of "higher quality" than if it uses less conservative procedures. Thus, conservative accounting policies are a plus factor in bond ratings.

Representatives of the rating agencies have consistently stated that no precise formula is used to set a firm's rating; all the factors listed, plus others, are taken into account, but not in a mathematically precise manner. Nevertheless, as we see in Table 6-2, there is a strong correlation between bond ratings and many of the ratios described in Chapter 4. Not surprisingly, companies with lower debt ratios, higher cash flow to debt, higher returns on capital, higher EBITDA interest coverage ratios, and EBIT interest coverage ratios typically have higher bond ratings.

IMPORTANCE OF BOND RATINGS Bond ratings are important both to firms and to investors. First, because a bond's rating is an indicator of its default risk, the rating has a direct, measurable influence on the bond's interest rate and the firm's cost of debt. Second, most bonds are purchased by institutional investors rather than individuals, and many institutions are restricted to investment-grade securities. Thus, if a firm's bonds fall below BBB, it will have a difficult time selling new bonds because many potential purchasers will

TABLE 6-2 | **Bond Rating Criteria: Median Financial Ratios for Different Bond Rating Classifications**

Ratios	AAA	AA	A	BBB	BB	B	CCC
EBIT interest coverage (EBIT/Interest)	23.4×	13.3×	6.3×	3.9×	2.2×	1.0×	0.1×
EBITDA interest coverage (EBITDA/Interest)	25.3	16.9	8.5	5.4	3.2	1.7	0.7
Funds from operations/Total debt	214.2%	65.7%	42.2%	30.6%	19.7%	10.4%	3.2%
Free operating cash flow/ Total debt	156.6	33.6	22.3	12.8	7.3	1.5	−2.8
Return on capital	35.0	26.6	18.1	13.1	11.5	8.0	1.2
Operating income/Sales	23.4	24.0	18.1	15.5	15.4	14.7	8.8
Long-term debt/Long-term capital	−1.1	21.1	33.8	40.3	53.6	72.6	78.3
Total debt/Total capital	5.0	35.9	42.6	47.0	57.7	75.1	91.7

Source: Standard & Poor's 2003 Corporate Ratings Criteria, September 8, 2003. For ratio definitions and updates, go to **http://www.standardandpoors.com**; select Fixed Income, then Industrials (under Browse by Sector), then Ratings Criteria.

not be allowed to buy them. In addition, the covenants may stipulate that the interest rate is automatically increased if the rating falls below a specified level.

As a result of their higher risk and more restricted market, lower-grade bonds have higher required rates of return, r_d, than high-grade bonds. Figure 6-4 illustrates this point. In each of the years shown on the graph, U.S. government bonds have had the lowest yields, AAAs have been next, and BBB bonds have had the highest yields. The figure also shows that the gaps between yields on the three types of bonds vary over time, indicating that the cost differentials, or risk premiums, fluctuate from year to year.[16]

Table 6-3 reports yields and risk premiums for selected years. As Column (4) shows, the average risk premium for a AAA bond relative to a Treasury bond during this period was 1.0 percent, but it varied quite a bit, ranging from 0.2 percent in 1979 to 2.1 percent in 2001. For BBB bonds, Column (5) shows that the risk premium relative to a T-bond

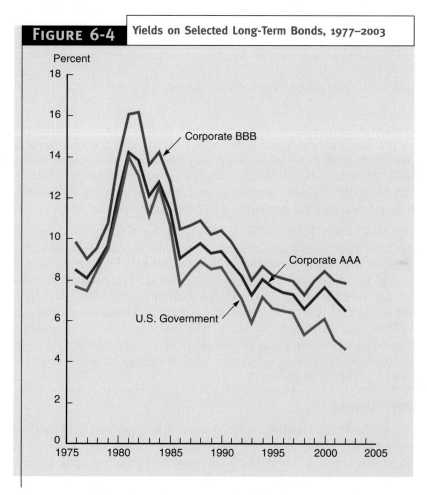

| **FIGURE 6-4** | Yields on Selected Long-Term Bonds, 1977–2003 |

Source: Federal Reserve Board, http://www.federalreserve.gov.

---

[16] The term *risk premium* ought to reflect only the difference in expected (and required) returns between two securities that results from differences in their risk. However, the differences between *yields to maturity* on different types of bonds consist of (1) a true risk premium; (2) a liquidity premium, which reflects the fact that U.S. Treasury bonds are more readily marketable than most corporate bonds; (3) a call premium, because most Treasury bonds are not callable whereas corporate bonds are; and (4) an expected loss differential, which reflects the probability of loss on the corporate bonds. As an example of the last point, suppose the yield to maturity on a BBB bond was 8.0 percent versus 5.5 percent on government bonds, but there was a 5 percent probability of total default loss on the corporate bond. In this case, the expected return on the BBB bond would be 0.95(8.0%) + 0.05(0%) = 7.6%, and the risk premium would be 2.1 percent, not the full 2.5 percentage points difference in "promised" yields to maturity. Because of all these points, the risk premiums given in Table 6-3 overstate somewhat the true (but unmeasurable) theoretical risk premiums.

TABLE 6-3 | Selected Yields and Risk Premiums (1977–2003)

	Yields			Risk Premiums		
	Treasury Bonds (1)	AAA Corporate Bonds (2)	BBB Corporate Bonds (3)	AAA (4) = (2) − (1)	BBB (5) = (3) − (1)	BBB − AAA (6) = (3) − (2)
1978	8.4%	8.7%	9.5%	0.3%	1.1%	0.8%
1979	9.4	9.6	10.7	0.2	1.3	1.1
1982	13.0	13.8	16.1	0.8	3.1	2.3
1997	6.4	7.3	7.9	0.9	1.5	0.6
2001	5.0	7.1	8.0	2.1	3.0	0.9
2002	4.6	6.5	7.8	1.9	3.2	1.3
2003	4.0	5.7	6.8	1.7	2.8	1.1
			27-year average:	1.0	2.1	1.1
			Maximum:	2.1	3.2	2.3
			Minimum:	0.2	1.1	0.6

Source: Federal Reserve Board, **http://www.federalreserve.gov.**

averaged 2.1 percent, but it ranged from 1.1 percent in 1978 to 3.2 percent in 2002. The risk premiums for AAA and BBB bonds tend to move together (their correlation is about 0.66), with BBB bond yields averaging about 1.1 percentage points more than AAA bonds. However, there are times when the risk premium of a BBB bond relative to an AAA bond differs significantly from its average. For example, Column (6) shows that the premium was only 0.6 percent in 1997 but 2.3 percent in 1982.

CHANGES IN RATINGS   Changes in a firm's bond rating affect both its ability to borrow long-term capital and the cost of that capital. Rating agencies review outstanding bonds on a periodic basis, occasionally upgrading or downgrading a bond as a result of its issuer's changed circumstances. For example, in May 2003, Standard & Poor's reported that it had increased the rating on Bio-Rad Laboratories from BB− to BB+ due to its "success with integrating the 1999 acquisition of Pasteur Sanofi Diagnostics, more than doubling EBITDA, and extending its well-established positions in competitive niche markets." However, S&P also lowered the rating of Interface Inc., an Atlanta-based carpet manufacturer, from B+ to B−, following "weaker than expected revenue and margin pressures across all business segments."

See the Standard & Poor's Web site, **http://www .standardandpoors .com,** *for this and other changes in ratings.*

Junk Bonds

Prior to the 1980s, fixed-income investors such as pension funds and insurance companies were generally unwilling to buy risky bonds, so it was almost impossible for risky companies to raise capital in the public bond markets. Then, in the late 1970s, Michael Milken of the investment banking firm Drexel Burnham Lambert, relying on historical studies that showed that risky bonds yielded more than enough to compensate for their risk, began to convince institutional investors of the merits of purchasing risky debt. Thus was born the "junk bond," a high-risk, high-yield bond issued to finance a leveraged buyout, a merger, or a troubled company.[17] For example, Public Service of New Hampshire financed construction of its troubled Seabrook nuclear plant with junk bonds, and junk bonds were used by Ted Turner to finance the development of CNN and Turner Broadcasting. In junk bond

---

[17] Another type of junk bond is one that was highly rated when it was issued but whose rating has fallen because the issuing corporation has fallen on hard times. Such bonds are called "fallen angels."

deals, the debt ratio is generally extremely high, so the bondholders must bear as much risk as stockholders normally would. The bonds' yields reflect this fact—a promised return of 25 percent per annum was required to sell some Public Service of New Hampshire bonds.

The emergence of junk bonds as an important type of debt is another example of how the investment banking industry adjusts to and facilitates new developments in capital markets. In the 1980s, mergers and takeovers increased dramatically. People like T. Boone Pickens and Henry Kravis thought that certain old-line, established companies were run inefficiently and were financed too conservatively, and they wanted to take these companies over and restructure them. Michael Milken and his staff at Drexel Burnham Lambert began an active campaign to persuade certain institutions (often S&Ls) to purchase high-yield bonds. Milken developed expertise in putting together deals that were attractive to the institutions yet feasible in the sense that projected cash flows were sufficient to meet the required interest payments. The fact that interest on the bonds was tax deductible, combined with the much higher debt ratios of the restructured firms, also increased after-tax cash flows and helped make the deals feasible.

The development of junk bond financing has done much to reshape the U.S. financial scene. The existence of these securities contributed to the loss of independence of Gulf Oil and hundreds of other companies, and it led to major shake-ups in such companies as CBS, Union Carbide, and USX (formerly U.S. Steel). It also caused Drexel Burnham Lambert to leap from essentially nowhere in the 1970s to become the most profitable investment banking firm during the 1980s.

The phenomenal growth of the junk bond market was impressive, but controversial. In 1989, Drexel Burnham Lambert was forced into bankruptcy, and "junk bond king" Michael Milken, who had earned $500 million two years earlier, was sent to jail. Those events led to the collapse of the junk bond market in the early 1990s. Since then, however, the junk bond market has rebounded, and junk bonds are here to stay as an important form of corporate financing.

Bankruptcy and Reorganization

During recessions, bankruptcies normally rise, and recent recessions are no exception. The 2001 recession claimed Worldcom, Enron, Conseco, Global Crossing, United Airlines, Adelphia Communications, Pacific Gas and Electric, Kmart, and the FINOVA Group. The total assets of these companies, prior to filing for bankruptcy, were about $355 billion dollars! A brief discussion of bankruptcy follows.

When a business becomes *insolvent,* it does not have enough cash to meet its interest and principal payments. A decision must then be made whether to dissolve the firm through *liquidation* or to permit it to *reorganize* and thus stay alive. These issues are addressed in Chapters 7 and 11 of the federal bankruptcy statutes, and the final decision is made by a federal bankruptcy court judge.

The decision to force a firm to liquidate versus permit it to reorganize depends on whether the value of the reorganized firm is likely to be greater than the value of the firm's assets if they are sold off piecemeal. In a reorganization, the firm's creditors negotiate with management on the terms of a potential reorganization. The reorganization plan may call for a *restructuring* of the firm's debt, in which case the interest rate may be reduced, the term to maturity lengthened, or some of the debt may be exchanged for equity. The point of the restructuring is to reduce the financial charges to a level that the firm's cash flows can support. Of course, the common stockholders also have to give up something—they often see their position diluted as a result of additional shares being given to debtholders in exchange for accepting a reduced amount of debt principal and interest. In fact, the original common stockholders often end up with nothing. A trustee may be appointed by the court to oversee the reorganization, but generally the existing management is allowed to retain control.

Liquidation occurs if the company is deemed to be too far gone to be saved—if it is worth more dead than alive. If the bankruptcy court orders a liquidation, assets are sold off and the cash obtained is distributed as specified in Chapter 7 of the Bankruptcy Act. Here is the priority of claims:

1. Secured creditors are entitled to the proceeds from the sale of the specific property that was used to support their loans.
2. The trustee's costs of administering and operating the bankrupt firm are next in line.
3. Expenses incurred after bankruptcy was filed come next.
4. Wages due workers, up to a limit of $2,000 per worker, follow.
5. Claims for unpaid contributions to employee benefit plans are next. This amount, together with wages, cannot exceed $2,000 per worker.
6. Unsecured claims for customer deposits up to $900 per customer are sixth in line.
7. Federal, state, and local taxes due come next.
8. Unfunded pension plan liabilities are next although some limitations exist.
9. General unsecured creditors are ninth on the list.
10. Preferred stockholders come next, up to the par value of their stock.
11. Common stockholders are finally paid, if anything is left, which is rare.

The key points for you to know are (1) the federal bankruptcy statutes govern both reorganization and liquidation, (2) bankruptcies occur frequently, and (3) a priority of the specified claims must be followed when distributing the assets of a liquidated firm.

SELF-TEST QUESTIONS	Differentiate between mortgage bonds and debentures.
	Name the major rating agencies, and list some factors that affect bond ratings.
	Differentiate between a Chapter 7 liquidation and a Chapter 11 reorganization.
	List the priority of claims for the distribution of a liquidated firm's assets.

BOND MARKETS

Corporate bonds are traded primarily in the over-the-counter market rather than in organized exchanges. Most bonds are owned by and traded among the large financial institutions (for example, life insurance companies, mutual funds, and pension funds, all of which deal in very large blocks of securities), and it is relatively easy for the over-the-counter bond dealers to arrange the transfer of large blocks of bonds among the relatively few holders of the bonds.

Information on bond trades in the over-the-counter market is not widely published, but a representative group of bonds is listed and traded on the bond division of the NYSE and is reported on the bond market page of *The Wall Street Journal*. Bond data are also available on the Internet, at sites such as **http://www.bondsonline.com**. Figure 6-5 reports data for selected bonds of BellSouth Corporation. Note that BellSouth actually had more issues outstanding, but Figure 6-5 reports data for only six bonds.

The bonds of BellSouth and other companies can have various denominations, but for convenience we generally think of each bond as having a par value of $1,000—this is how much per bond the company borrowed and how much it must someday repay. However, since other denominations are possible, for trading and reporting purposes bonds are quoted as percentages of par. Looking at the fourth bond listed in the data in Figure 6-5, we see that the bond is of the series that pays a 7 percent coupon, or 0.07($1,000) = $70.00 of interest per year. The BellSouth bonds, and most others, pay interest semiannually, so

FIGURE 6-5 — Selected Bond Market Data

S&P Bond Rating	Issue Name	Coupon Rate	Maturity Date[a]	Yield to Maturity	Yield to Call[b]	Price[c]
A+	BellSouth	6.500	6/15/2005	1.410	NC	105.715
A+	BellSouth	5.000	10/15/2006	2.796	NC	105.223
A+	BellSouth	6.000	10/15/2011	4.749	NC	107.790
A+	**BellSouth**	**7.000**	**10/1/2025**	**6.251**	**NC**	**108.778**
A+	BellSouth	6.875	10/15/2031	6.216	NC	108.626
A+	BellSouth	7.625	5/15/2035C	6.799	0.927	110.625

Notes:
[a]C denotes a callable bond.
[b]NC indicates that the bond is not callable.
[c]The price is reported as a percentage of par.

Source: April 21, 2004: **http://www.bondsonline.com**. At the left of the Web page, select Corporate Bonds beneath Bond Search/Quote Center. When the bond-search dialog box appears, type in BellSouth for issue and click the Find Bonds button.

all rates are nominal, not EAR rates. This bond matures and must be repaid on October 1, 2025; it is not shown in the figure, but this bond was issued in 1995, so it had a 30-year original maturity. The price shown in the last column is expressed as a percentage of par, 108.778 percent, which translates to $1,087.78. This bond has a yield to maturity of 6.251 percent. This bond is not callable, but the last bond in Figure 6-5 has a yield to call of only 0.927 percent compared with its yield to maturity of 6.799 percent. This bond can be called in 2005. At that time BellSouth can call it, get rid of bonds with a coupon of 7.625 percent, and replace them with new bonds that carry a coupon of about 6.8 percent (assuming interest rates remain at their 2004 level). Therefore, investors expect the bond to be called, and someone buying it would think of it as a one-year bond with a yield of about 0.9 percent.

Coupon rates are generally set at levels that reflect the "going rate of interest" on the day a bond is issued. If the rates were set lower, investors simply would not buy the bonds at the $1,000 par value, so the company could not borrow the money it needed. Thus, bonds generally sell at their par values on the day they are issued, but their prices fluctuate thereafter as interest rates change.

As shown in Figure 6-6, the BellSouth bonds initially sold at par, but then fell below par in 1996 when interest rates rose. The price rose above par in 1997 and 1998 when interest rates fell, but the price fell again in 1999 and 2000 after increases in interest rates. It rose again in 2001 through 2003, when interest rates fell. It fell in 2004 due to expectations of rising rates. The dashed line in Figure 6-6 shows the projected price of the bonds, in the unlikely event that interest rates remain constant from 2004 to 2025. Looking at the actual and projected price history of these bonds, we see (1) the inverse relationship between interest rates and bond values and (2) the fact that bond values approach their par values as their maturity date approaches.

SELF-TEST QUESTIONS Why do most bond trades occur in the over-the-counter market?
If a bond issue is to be sold at par, how will its coupon rate be determined?

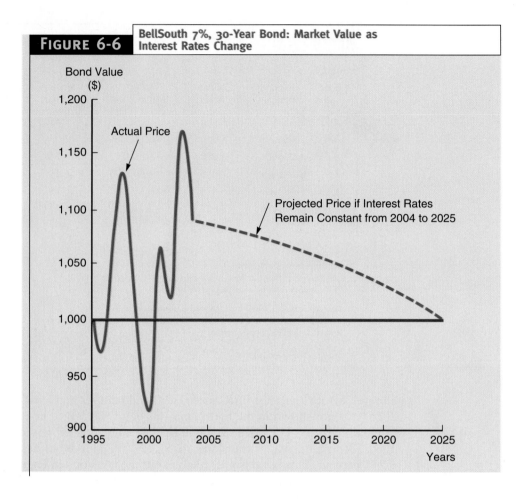

FIGURE 6-6 BellSouth 7%, 30-Year Bond: Market Value as Interest Rates Change

SUMMARY

This chapter described the different types of bonds governments and corporations issue, explained how bond prices are established, and discussed how investors estimate the rates of return they can expect to earn. We also discussed the various types of risks that investors face when they buy bonds. The key concepts covered are summarized below.

- A **bond** is a long-term promissory note issued by a business or governmental unit. The issuer receives money in exchange for promising to make interest payments and to repay the principal on a specified future date.
- Some recent innovations in long-term financing include **zero coupon bonds,** which pay no annual interest, but are issued at a discount; **floating-rate debt,** whose interest payments fluctuate with changes in the general level of interest rates; and **junk bonds,** which are high-risk, high-yield instruments issued by firms that use a great deal of financial leverage.
- A **call provision** gives the issuing corporation the right to redeem the bonds prior to maturity under specified terms, usually at a price greater than the maturity value (the difference is a **call premium**). A firm will typically call a bond if interest rates fall substantially below the coupon rate.
- A **redeemable bond** gives the investor the right to sell the bond back to the issuing company at a previously specified price. This is a useful feature (for investors) if interest rates rise or if the company engages in unanticipated risky activities.

- A **sinking fund** is a provision that requires the corporation to retire a portion of the bond issue each year. The purpose of the sinking fund is to provide for the orderly retirement of the issue. A sinking fund typically requires no call premium.
- The **value of a bond** is found as the present value of an **annuity** (the interest payments) plus the present value of a lump sum (the **principal**). The bond is evaluated at the appropriate periodic interest rate over the number of periods for which interest payments are made.
- The equation used to find the value of an annual coupon bond is

$$V_B = \sum_{t=1}^{N} \frac{INT}{(1 + r_d)^t} + \frac{M}{(1 + r_d)^N}.$$

- An adjustment to the formula must be made if the bond pays interest **semi-annually**: divide INT and r_d by 2, and multiply N by 2.
- The return earned on a bond held to maturity is defined as the bond's **yield to maturity (YTM)**. If the bond can be redeemed before maturity, it is **callable,** and the return investors receive if it is called is defined as the **yield to call (YTC).** The YTC is found as the present value of the interest payments received while the bond is outstanding plus the present value of the call price (the par value plus a call premium).
- The longer the maturity of a bond, the more its price will change in response to a given change in interest rates; this is called **interest rate risk.** However, bonds with short maturities expose investors to high **reinvestment rate risk,** which is the risk that income from a bond portfolio will decline because cash flows received from bonds will be rolled over at lower interest rates.
- Corporate and municipal bonds have **default risk.** If an issuer defaults, investors receive less than the promised return on the bond. Therefore, investors should evaluate a bond's default risk before making a purchase.
- There are many different types of bonds with different sets of features. These include **convertible bonds, bonds with warrants, income bonds, purchasing power (indexed) bonds, mortgage bonds, debentures, subordinated debentures, junk bonds, development bonds,** and **insured municipal bonds.** The return required on each type of bond is determined by the bond's riskiness.
- Bonds are assigned **ratings** that reflect the probability of their going into default. The highest rating is AAA, and they go down to D. The higher a bond's rating, the lower its risk and therefore its interest rate.

QUESTIONS

(6-1) Define each of the following terms:
   a. Bond; Treasury bond; corporate bond; municipal bond; foreign bond
   b. Par value; maturity date; coupon payment; coupon interest rate
   c. Floating-rate bond; zero coupon bond; original issue discount bond (OID)
   d. Call provision; redeemable bond; sinking fund
   e. Convertible bond; warrant; income bond; indexed, or purchasing power, bond
   f. Premium bond; discount bond
   g. Current yield (on a bond); yield to maturity (YTM); yield to call (YTC)
   h. Reinvestment risk; interest rate risk; default risk
   i. Indentures; mortgage bond; debenture; subordinated debenture
   j. Development bond; municipal bond insurance; junk bond; investment-grade bond

(6-2) "The values of outstanding bonds change whenever the going rate of interest changes. In general, short-term interest rates are more volatile than long-term interest rates. Therefore, short-term bond prices are more sensitive to interest rate changes than are long-term bond prices." Is this statement true or false? Explain.

(6-3) The rate of return you would get if you bought a bond and held it to its maturity date is called the bond's yield to maturity. If interest rates in the economy rise after a bond has been issued, what will happen to the bond's price and to its YTM? Does the length of time to maturity affect the extent to which a given change in interest rates will affect the bond's price?

(6-4) If you buy a *callable* bond and interest rates decline, will the value of your bond rise by as much as it would have risen if the bond had not been callable? Explain.

(6-5) A sinking fund can be set up in one of two ways:
(1) The corporation makes annual payments to the trustee, who invests the proceeds in securities (frequently government bonds) and uses the accumulated total to retire the bond issue at maturity.
(2) The trustee uses the annual payments to retire a portion of the issue each year, either calling a given percentage of the issue by a lottery and paying a specified price per bond or buying bonds on the open market, whichever is cheaper.
Discuss the advantages and disadvantages of each procedure from the viewpoint of both the firm and its bondholders.

SELF-TEST PROBLEM   Solution Appears in Appendix A

(ST-1)
Bond Valuation

The Pennington Corporation issued a new series of bonds on January 1, 1982. The bonds were sold at par ($1,000), have a 12 percent coupon, and mature in 30 years, on December 31, 2011. Coupon payments are made semiannually (on June 30 and December 31).
a. What was the YTM of Pennington's bonds on January 1, 1982?
b. What was the price of the bond on January 1, 1987, five years later, assuming that the level of interest rates had fallen to 10 percent?
c. Find the current yield and capital gains yield on the bond on January 1, 1987, given the price as determined in part b.
d. On July 1, 2005, Pennington's bonds sold for $916.42. What was the YTM at that date?
e. What were the current yield and capital gains yield on July 1, 2005?
f. Now, assume that you purchased an outstanding Pennington bond on March 1, 2005, when the going rate of interest was 15.5 percent. How large a check must you have written to complete the transaction? This is a hard question!

PROBLEMS

(6-1)
Bond Valuation

Callaghan Motors' bonds have 10 years remaining to maturity. Interest is paid annually, the bonds have a $1,000 par value, and the coupon interest rate is 8 percent. The bonds have a yield to maturity of 9 percent. What is the current market price of these bonds?

(6-2)
Yield to Maturity;
Financial Calculator Needed

Wilson Wonders' bonds have 12 years remaining to maturity. Interest is paid annually, the bonds have a $1,000 par value, and the coupon interest rate is 10 percent. The bonds sell at a price of $850. What is their yield to maturity?

(6-3)
Yield to Maturity and Call;
Financial Calculator Needed

Thatcher Corporation's bonds will mature in 10 years. The bonds have a face value of $1,000 and an 8 percent coupon rate, paid semiannually. The price of the bonds is $1,100. The bonds are callable in 5 years at a call price of $1,050. What is the yield to maturity? What is the yield to call?

(6-4)
Current Yield

Heath Foods' bonds have 7 years remaining to maturity. The bonds have a face value of $1,000 and a yield to maturity of 8 percent. They pay interest annually and have a 9 percent coupon rate. What is their current yield?

(6-5)
Bond Valuation
Nungesser Corporation has issued bonds that have a 9 percent coupon rate, payable semiannually. The bonds mature in 8 years, have a face value of $1,000, and a yield to maturity of 8.5 percent. What is the price of the bonds?

(6-6)
Bond Valuation
The Garraty Company has two bond issues outstanding. Both bonds pay $100 annual interest plus $1,000 at maturity. Bond L has a maturity of 15 years, and Bond S a maturity of 1 year.
a. What will be the value of each of these bonds when the going rate of interest is (1) 5 percent, (2) 8 percent, and (3) 12 percent? Assume that there is only one more interest payment to be made on Bond S.
b. Why does the longer-term (15-year) bond fluctuate more when interest rates change than does the shorter-term bond (1 year)?

(6-7)
Yield to Maturity
The Heymann Company's bonds have 4 years remaining to maturity. Interest is paid annually; the bonds have a $1,000 par value; and the coupon interest rate is 9 percent.
a. What is the yield to maturity at a current market price of (1) $829 or (2) $1,104?
b. Would you pay $829 for one of these bonds if you thought that the appropriate rate of interest was 12 percent—that is, if $r_d = 12\%$? Explain your answer.

(6-8)
Yield to Call
Six years ago, The Singleton Company sold a 20-year bond issue with a 14 percent annual coupon rate and a 9 percent call premium. Today, Singleton called the bonds. The bonds originally were sold at their face value of $1,000. Compute the realized rate of return for investors who purchased the bonds when they were issued and who surrender them today in exchange for the call price.

(6-9)
Bond Yields; Financial Calculator Needed
A 10-year, 12 percent semiannual coupon bond, with a par value of $1,000, may be called in 4 years at a call price of $1,060. The bond sells for $1,100. (Assume that the bond has just been issued.)
a. What is the bond's yield to maturity?
b. What is the bond's current yield?
c. What is the bond's capital gain or loss yield?
d. What is the bond's yield to call?

(6-10)
Yield to Maturity; Financial Calculator Needed
You just purchased a bond which matures in 5 years. The bond has a face value of $1,000, and has an 8 percent annual coupon. The bond has a current yield of 8.21 percent. What is the bond's yield to maturity?

(6-11)
Current Yield; Financial Calculator Needed
A bond that matures in 7 years sells for $1,020. The bond has a face value of $1,000 and a yield to maturity of 10.5883 percent. The bond pays coupons semiannually. What is the bond's current yield?

(6-12)
Nominal Interest Rate
Lloyd Corporation's 14 percent coupon rate, semiannual payment, $1,000 par value bonds, that mature in 30 years, are callable 5 years from now at a price of $1,050. The bonds sell at a price of $1,353.54, and the yield curve is flat. Assuming that interest rates in the economy are expected to remain at their current level, what is the best estimate of Lloyd's nominal interest rate on new bonds?

(6-13)
Bond Valuation
Suppose Ford Motor Company sold an issue of bonds with a 10-year maturity, a $1,000 par value, a 10 percent coupon rate, and semiannual interest payments.
a. Two years after the bonds were issued, the going rate of interest on bonds such as these fell to 6 percent. At what price would the bonds sell?
b. Suppose that, 2 years after the initial offering, the going interest rate had risen to 12 percent. At what price would the bonds sell?
c. Suppose that the conditions in part a existed—that is, interest rates fell to 6 percent 2 years after the issue date. Suppose further that the interest rate remained at 6 percent for the next 8 years. What would happen to the price of the Ford Motor Company bonds over time?

(6-14)
Interest Rate Sensitivity; Financial Calculator Needed
A bond trader purchased each of the following bonds at a yield to maturity of 8 percent. Immediately after she purchased the bonds, interest rates fell to 7 percent. What is the percentage change in the price of each bond after the decline in interest rates?

Fill in the following table:

	Price @ 8%	Price @ 7%	Percentage Change
10-year, 10% annual coupon	_____	_____	_____
10-year zero	_____	_____	_____
5-year zero	_____	_____	_____
30-year zero	_____	_____	_____
$100 perpetuity	_____	_____	_____

(6-15)
Bond Valuation;
Financial Calculator
Needed

An investor has two bonds in his portfolio. Each bond matures in 4 years, has a face value of $1,000, and has a yield to maturity equal to 9.6 percent. One bond, Bond C, pays an annual coupon of 10 percent; the other bond, Bond Z, is a zero coupon bond.

a. Assuming that the yield to maturity of each bond remains at 9.6 percent over the next 4 years, what will be the price of each of the bonds at the following time periods? Fill in the following table:

t	Price of Bond C	Price of Bond Z
0	_____	_____
1	_____	_____
2	_____	_____
3	_____	_____
4	_____	_____

b. Plot the time path of the prices for each of the two bonds.

SPREADSHEET PROBLEM

(6-16)
Build a Model;
Bond Valuation

Start with the partial model in the file *CF2 Ch 06 P16 Build a Model.xls* from the textbook's Web site. Rework Problem 6-9. After completing parts a through d, answer the following related questions.

e. How would the price of the bond be affected by changing interest rates? (Hint: Conduct a sensitivity analysis of price to changes in the yield to maturity, which is also the going market interest rate for the bond. Assume that the bond will be called if and only if the going rate of interest *falls below* the coupon rate. That is an oversimplification, but assume it anyway for purposes of this problem.)

f. Now assume that the date is October 25, 2005. Assume further that our 12 percent, 10-year bond was issued on July 1, 2005, is callable on July 1, 2009, at $1,060, will mature on June 30, 2015, pays interest semiannually (January 1 and July 1), and sells for $1,100. Use your spreadsheet to find (1) the bond's yield to maturity and (2) its yield to call.

CF
e-resource

CYBERPROBLEM

Please go to our Web site, **http://ehrhardt.swlearning.com**, to access any Cyberproblems.

THOMSON ONE
Business School Edition

Please go to **http://ehrhardt.swlearning.com** to access any Thomson ONE—Business School Edition problems.

MINI CASE

Sam Strother and Shawna Tibbs are vice-presidents of Mutual of Seattle Insurance Company and codirectors of the company's pension fund management division. An important new client, the North-Western Municipal Alliance, has requested that Mutual of Seattle present an investment seminar to the mayors of the represented cities, and Strother and Tibbs, who will make the actual presentation, have asked you to help them by answering the following questions. Because the Boeing Company operates in one of the league's cities, you are to work Boeing into the presentation.

a. What are the key features of a bond?

b. What are call provisions and sinking fund provisions? Do these provisions make bonds more or less risky?

c. How is the value of any asset whose value is based on expected future cash flows determined?

d. How is the value of a bond determined? What is the value of a 10-year, $1,000 par value bond with a 10 percent annual coupon if its required rate of return is 10 percent?

e. (1) What would be the value of the bond described in part d if, just after it had been issued, the expected inflation rate rose by 3 percentage points, causing investors to require a 13 percent return? Would we now have a discount or a premium bond?

   (2) What would happen to the bond's value if inflation fell, and r_d declined to 7 percent? Would we now have a premium or a discount bond?

   (3) What would happen to the value of the 10-year bond over time if the required rate of return remained at 13 percent, or if it remained at 7 percent? [Hint: With a financial calculator, enter PMT, I, FV, and N, and then change (override) N to see what happens to the PV as the bond approaches maturity.]

f. (1) What is the yield to maturity on a 10-year, 9 percent, annual coupon, $1,000 par value bond that sells for $887.00? That sells for $1,134.20? What does the fact that a bond sells at a discount or at a premium tell you about the relationship between r_d and the bond's coupon rate?

   (2) What are the total return, the current yield, and the capital gains yield for the discount bond? (Assume the bond is held to maturity and the company does not default on the bond.)

g. What is *interest rate (or price) risk?* Which bond has more interest rate risk, an annual payment 1-year bond or a 10-year bond? Why?

h. What is *reinvestment rate risk?* Which has more reinvestment rate risk, a 1-year bond or a 10-year bond?

i. How does the equation for valuing a bond change if semiannual payments are made? Find the value of a 10-year, semiannual payment, 10 percent coupon bond if nominal $r_d = 13\%$.

j. Suppose you could buy, for $1,000, either a 10 percent, 10-year, annual payment bond or a 10 percent, 10-year, semiannual payment bond. They are equally risky. Which would you prefer? If $1,000 is the proper price for the semiannual bond, what is the equilibrium price for the annual payment bond?

k. Suppose a 10-year, 10 percent, semiannual coupon bond with a par value of $1,000 is currently selling for $1,135.90, producing a nominal yield to maturity of 8 percent. However, the bond can be called after 5 years for a price of $1,050.

   (1) What is the bond's *nominal yield to call (YTC)?*

   (2) If you bought this bond, do you think you would be more likely to earn the YTM or the YTC? Why?

l. Boeing's bonds were issued with a yield to maturity of 7.5 percent. Does the yield to maturity represent the promised or expected return on the bond?

m. Boeing's bonds were rated AA− by S&P. Would you consider these bonds investment grade or junk bonds?

n. What factors determine a company's bond rating?

o. If this firm were to default on the bonds, would the company be immediately liquidated? Would the bondholders be assured of receiving all of their promised payments?

SELECTED ADDITIONAL REFERENCES AND CASES

Many investment textbooks cover bond valuation models in depth and detail. Some of the better ones are listed in the Chapter 5 references.

For some works on valuation, see

Bey, Roger P., and J. Markham Collins, "The Relationship between Before- and After-Tax Yields on Financial Assets," *The Financial Review,* August 1988, 313–343.

Taylor, Richard W., "The Valuation of Semiannual Bonds Between Interest Payment Dates," *The Financial Review,* August 1988, 365–368.

Tse, K. S. Maurice, and Mark A. White, "The Valuation of Semiannual Bonds between Interest Payment Dates: A Correction," *Financial Review,* November 1990, 659–662.

The following cases in the Finance Online Case Library *cover many of the concepts discussed in this chapter and are available at* ***http://www.textchoice.com:***

Case 3, "Peachtree Securities, Inc. (B)"; Case 43, "Swan Davis"; Case 49, "Beatrice Peabody"; and Case 56, "Laura Henderson."

CHAPTER 7

Stocks and Their Valuation

F rom slightly less than 4,000 in early 1995, the Dow surged to 11,723 in early 2000. To put this remarkable 7,723-point rise in perspective, consider that the Dow first reached 1,000 in 1965, then took another 22 years to hit 2,000, then four more years to reach 3,000, and another four to get to 4,000 (in 1995). Then, in just over five years, it reached 11,723. Thus, in those five years investors made almost twice as much in the stock market as they made in the previous 70 years!

That bull market made it possible for many people to take early retirement, buy expensive homes, and afford large expenditures such as college tuition. Encouraged by this performance, more and more investors flocked to the market, and today more than 79 million Americans own stock. Moreover, a rising stock market made it easier and cheaper for corporations to raise equity capital, which facilitated economic growth.

However, some observers were concerned that many investors did not realize just how risky the stock market is. Indeed, the Dow fell all the way to 8,236 in the days following the terrorist attacks of September 11, 2001. It surged back up to 10,635 in early 2002, but fell to 7,286 by late 2002. In mid 2004, the market stood at about 10,500.

Note too that while all boats may rise with the tide, the same does not hold for stock markets—regardless of the trend, some individual stocks always make huge gains while others suffer substantial losses. Even though the market itself was up more than 28 percent in 2003, many individual stocks performed much better while others performed worse. For example, Best Buy rose more than 116 percent, but Eastman Kodak was down 26.7 percent. In terms of market value, Cisco added more than $77 billion of wealth to its stockholders. On the other hand, Verizon's shareholders saw more than $10 billion in wealth evaporate.

While it is difficult to predict prices, we are not completely in the dark when it comes to valuing stocks. After studying this chapter, you should have a reasonably good understanding of the factors that influence stock prices. With that knowledge—and a little luck—you may be able to find the next Best Buy and avoid future Eastman Kodaks.

In Chapter 6 we examined bonds. We now turn to common and preferred stock, beginning with some important background material that helps establish a framework for valuing these securities.

While it is generally easy to predict the cash flows received from bonds, forecasting the cash flows on common stocks is much more difficult. However, two fairly straightforward models can be used to help estimate the "true," or intrinsic, value of a common stock: (1) the dividend growth model, which we describe in this chapter, and (2) the total corporate value model, which we explain in Chapter 13.

The concepts and models developed here will also be used when we estimate the cost of capital in Chapter 9. In subsequent chapters, we demonstrate how the cost of capital is used to help make many important decisions, especially the decision to invest or not invest in new assets. Consequently, it is critically important that you understand the basics of stock valuation.

LEGAL RIGHTS AND PRIVILEGES OF COMMON STOCKHOLDERS

e-resource

The textbook's Web site contains an Excel file that will guide you through the chapter's calculations. The file for this chapter is CF2 Ch 07 Tool Kit.xls, and we encourage you to open the file and follow along as you read the chapter.

The common stockholders are the *owners* of a corporation, and as such they have certain rights and privileges as discussed in this section.

Control of the Firm

Its common stockholders have the right to elect a firm's directors, who, in turn, elect the officers who manage the business. In a small firm, the largest stockholder typically assumes the positions of president and chairperson of the board of directors. In a large, publicly owned firm, the managers typically have some stock, but their personal holdings are generally insufficient to give them voting control. Thus, the managements of most publicly owned firms can be removed by the stockholders if the management team is not effective.

State and federal laws stipulate how stockholder control is to be exercised. First, corporations must hold an election of directors periodically, usually once a year, with the vote taken at the annual meeting. Frequently, one-third of the directors are elected each year for a three-year term. Each share of stock has one vote; thus, the owner of 1,000 shares has 1,000 votes for each director.[1] Stockholders can appear at the annual meeting and vote in person, but typically they transfer their right to vote to a second party by means of a **proxy**. Management always solicits stockholders' proxies and usually gets them. However, if earnings are poor and stockholders are dissatisfied, an outside group may solicit the proxies in an effort to overthrow management and take control of the business. This is known as a **proxy fight**. Proxy fights are discussed in detail in Chapter 13.

The Preemptive Right

Common stockholders often have the right, called the **preemptive right**, to purchase any additional shares sold by the firm. In some states, the preemptive right is automatically included in every corporate charter; in others, it is necessary to insert it specifically into the charter.

The preemptive right enables current stockholders to maintain control and prevents a transfer of wealth from current stockholders to new stockholders. If it were not for this

---

[1] In the situation described, a 1,000-share stockholder could cast 1,000 votes for each of three directors if there were three contested seats on the board. An alternative procedure that may be prescribed in the corporate charter calls for *cumulative voting*. Here the 1,000-share stockholder would get 3,000 votes if there were three vacancies, and he or she could cast all of them for one director. Cumulative voting helps small groups get representation on the board.

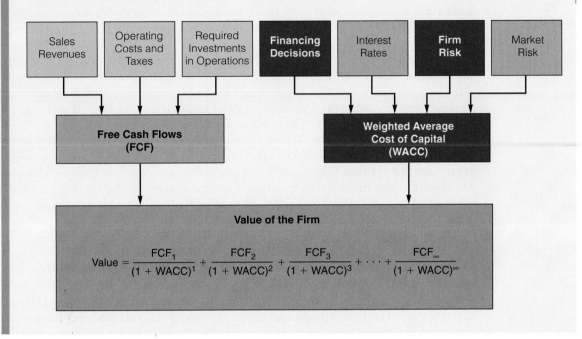

CORPORATE VALUATION AND STOCK RISK

In Chapter 1, we told you that managers should strive to make their firms more valuable and that the value of a firm is determined by the size, timing, and risk of its free cash flows (FCF). This chapter provides additional insights in how to measure the risk and return demanded by a firm's stockholders, which affects the firm's weighted average cost of capital. It also shows you how to estimate the stock's value, which is a key part of the firm's total value.

| Sales Revenues | Operating Costs and Taxes | Required Investments in Operations | Financing Decisions | Interest Rates | Firm Risk | Market Risk |

Free Cash Flows (FCF)

Weighted Average Cost of Capital (WACC)

Value of the Firm

$$\text{Value} = \frac{\text{FCF}_1}{(1 + \text{WACC})^1} + \frac{\text{FCF}_2}{(1 + \text{WACC})^2} + \frac{\text{FCF}_3}{(1 + \text{WACC})^3} + \cdots + \frac{\text{FCF}_\infty}{(1 + \text{WACC})^\infty}$$

safeguard, the management of a corporation could issue a large number of additional shares at a low price and purchase these shares itself. Management could thereby seize control of the corporation and steal value from the current stockholders. For example, suppose 1,000 shares of common stock, each with a price of $100, were outstanding, making the total market value of the firm $100,000. If an additional 1,000 shares were sold at $50 a share, or for $50,000, this would raise the total market value to $150,000. When total market value is divided by new total shares outstanding, a value of $75 a share is obtained. The old stockholders thus lose $25 per share, and the new stockholders have an instant profit of $25 per share. Thus, selling common stock at a price below the market value would dilute its price and transfer wealth from the present stockholders to those who were allowed to purchase the new shares. The preemptive right prevents such occurrences.

SELF-TEST QUESTIONS

What is a proxy fight?

What are the two primary reasons for the existence of the preemptive right?

TYPES OF COMMON STOCK

Although most firms have only one type of common stock, in some instances **classified stock** is used to meet the special needs of the company. Generally, when special classifications are used, one type is designated *Class A*, another *Class B*, and so on. Small, new companies seeking funds from outside sources frequently use different types of common stock. For example, when Genetic Concepts went public, its Class A stock was sold to the public and paid a dividend, but this stock had no voting rights for five years. Its Class B stock, which was retained by the organizers of the company, had full voting rights for five years, but the legal terms stated that dividends could not be paid on the Class B stock until the company had established its earning power by building up retained earnings to a designated level. The use of classified stock thus enabled the public to take a position in a conservatively financed growth company without sacrificing income, while the founders retained absolute control during the crucial early stages of the firm's development. At the same time, outside investors were protected against excessive withdrawals of funds by the original owners. As is often the case in such situations, the Class B stock was called **founders' shares.**

Note that "Class A," "Class B," and so on, have no standard meanings. Most firms have no classified shares, but a firm that does could designate its Class B shares as founders' shares and its Class A shares as those sold to the public, while another could reverse these designations. Still other firms could use stock classifications for entirely different purposes. For example, when General Motors acquired Hughes Aircraft for $5 billion, it paid in part with a new Class H common, GMH, which had limited voting rights and whose dividends were tied to Hughes's performance as a GM subsidiary. The reasons for the new stock were reported to be (1) that GM wanted to limit voting privileges on the new classified stock because of management's concern about a possible takeover and (2) that Hughes employees wanted to be rewarded more directly on Hughes's own performance than would have been possible through regular GM stock.

GM's deal posed a problem for the NYSE, which had a rule against listing a company's common stock if the company had any nonvoting common stock outstanding. GM made it clear that it was willing to delist if the NYSE did not change its rules. The NYSE concluded that such arrangements as GM had made were logical and were likely to be made by other companies in the future, so it changed its rules to accommodate GM. In reality, though, the NYSE had little choice. In recent years, the Nasdaq market has proven that it can provide a deep, liquid market for common stocks, and the defection of GM would have hurt the NYSE much more than GM.

As these examples illustrate, the right to vote is often a distinguishing characteristic between different classes of stock. Suppose two classes of stock differ in but one respect: One class has voting rights but the other does not. As you would expect, the stock with voting rights would be more valuable. In the United States, which has a legal system with fairly strong protection for minority stockholders (that is, noncontrolling stockholders), voting stock typically sells at a price 4 to 6 percent above that of otherwise similar nonvoting stock. Thus, if a stock with no voting rights sold for $50, then one with voting rights would probably sell for $52 to $53. In countries with legal systems that provide less protection for minority stockholders, the right to vote is far more valuable. For example, voting stock on average sells for 45 percent more than nonvoting stock in Israel, and for 82 percent more in Italy.

As we noted above, General Motors created its Class H common stock as a part of its acquisition of Hughes Aircraft. This type of stock, with dividends tied to a particular part of a company, is called **tracking stock.** It also is called **target stock.** Although GM used its tracking stock in an acquisition, other companies are attempting to use such stock to increase shareholder value. For example, in 1995 US West had several business areas with very different growth prospects, ranging from slow-growth local telephone services to high-growth cellular, cable television, and directory services. US West felt that investors were unable to correctly value its high-growth lines of business, since cash flows from slow-growth and high-growth businesses were mingled. To separate the cash flows and to allow separate valuations, the company issued tracking stocks. Similarly, Georgia-Pacific Corp. issued tracking stock for its timber business, and USX Corp. used tracking stocks for its oil, natural gas, and steel divisions. Despite this trend, many analysts are skeptical as to whether tracking stock increases a company's total market value. Companies still report consolidated financial statements for the entire company, and they have considerable leeway in allocating costs and reporting the financial results for the various divisions, even those with tracking stock. Thus, a tracking stock is not the same as the stock of an independent, stand-alone company.

SELF-TEST QUESTION   What are some reasons a company might use classified stock?

THE MARKET FOR COMMON STOCK

Note that http:// finance.yahoo.com provides an easy way to find stocks meeting specified criteria. Under the section on Stock Research, select Stock Screener. To find the largest companies in terms of market value, for example, choose More Preset Screens, then select Largest Market Cap. You can also create custom screens to find stocks meeting other criteria.

Some companies are so small that their common stocks are not actively traded; they are owned by only a few people, usually the companies' managers. The stock in such firms is said to be **closely held.** In contrast, the stocks of most larger companies are owned by a large number of investors, most of whom are not active in management. Such stock is called **publicly held stock.**

A recent study found that institutional investors owned more than 60 percent of all publicly held common stocks. Included are pension plans, mutual funds, foreign investors, insurance companies, and brokerage firms. These institutions buy and sell relatively actively, so they account for about 75 percent of all transactions. Thus, institutional investors have a heavy influence on the prices of individual stocks.

Types of Stock Market Transactions

We can classify stock market transactions into three distinct types:

1. *Trading in the outstanding shares of established, publicly owned companies: the secondary market.* For example, if the owner of 100 shares of publicly held stock sells his or her stock, the trade is said to have occurred in the **secondary market.** Thus, the market for outstanding shares, or *used shares,* is the secondary market. The company receives no new money when sales occur in this market.
2. *Additional shares sold by established, publicly owned companies: the primary market.* If a company decides to sell (or issue) additional shares to raise new equity capital, this transaction is said to occur in the **primary market.**
3. *Initial public offerings by privately held firms: the IPO market.* Whenever stock in a closely held corporation is offered to the public for the first time, the company is said to be **going public.** The market for stock that is just being offered to the public is called the **initial public offering (IPO) market.**

For updates, see IPO Monitor's Year End Review at http:// www.ipomonitor.com. The Wall Street Journal also provides IPO data in its Year End Review of Markets & Finance, at http:// wsj.online.com.

There were 81 IPOs in 2003, bringing in a total of $13.5 billion. The average first-day return was 11.87 percent, although some firms had spectacular first-day price run-ups. For example, Kintera was up 54 percent on its first day of trading, and it gained more than 77 percent for the year. However, not all companies fared so well—Nitromed was down 15.5 percent its first day, and it lost a total of 34.7 percent for the year. Moreover, even if you are able to identify a "hot" issue, it is often difficult to purchase shares in the initial offering. These deals are generally *oversubscribed,* which means that the demand for shares at the offering price exceeds the number of shares issued. In such instances, investment bankers favor large institutional investors (who are their best customers), and small investors find it hard, if not impossible, to get in on the ground floor. They can buy the stock in the aftermarket, but evidence suggests that if you do not get in on the ground floor, the average IPO underperforms the overall market over the longer run.[2]

---

[2] See Jay R. Ritter, "The Long-Run Performance of Initial Public Offerings," *Journal of Finance,* March 1991, Vol. 46, No. 1, 3–27.

AUSTRALIAN BORDELLO'S IPO: FIRST DAY PERFORMANCE IS UP

The Daily Planet Ltd. made history on May 1, 2003, by becoming the world's first publicly traded brothel. Technically, the Daily Planet only owns property, including a hotel with 18 rooms, each with a different theme, but all having multiperson showers and very large beds. The Daily Planet charges guests a room fee of A$115 per hour; clients also pay a fee of A$115 directly to individual members of the staff.

The IPO was for 7.5 million shares of stock, initially priced at A$0.50. However, the price ended the first day of trading at A$1.09, for a first-day return of 118 percent. The price closed the second day at A$1.56, for a two-day return of 212 percent, one of the largest returns since the days of the dot-com boom. Institutional investors normally buy about 60 to 70 percent of IPO stock, but they didn't participate in this offering. The Daily Planet plans to use some of the proceeds to pay down debt and the rest for expansion, possibly through franchising.

The company is named after the fictitious newspaper where comic strip character Clark Kent was a reporter. All receptionists have "Lois Lane" nametags, and there is a telephone box in the lobby. What would Superman think!

Before you conclude that it isn't fair to let only the best customers have the stock in an initial offering, think about what it takes to become a best customer. Best customers are usually investors who have done lots of business in the past with the investment banking firm's brokerage department. In other words, they have paid large sums as commissions in the past, and they are expected to continue doing so in the future. As is so often true, there is no free lunch—most of the investors who get in on the ground floor of an IPO have in fact paid for this privilege.

<table>
<tr><td>SELF-TEST QUESTIONS</td><td>Differentiate between closely held stock and publicly owned stock.
Differentiate between primary and secondary markets.
What is an IPO?</td></tr>
</table>

COMMON STOCK VALUATION

Common stocks provide an expected future cash flow stream, and a stock's value is found in the same manner as the values of other financial assets—namely, as the present value of the expected future cash flow stream. The expected cash flows consist of two elements: (1) the dividends expected in each year and (2) the price investors expect to receive when they sell the stock. The expected final stock price includes the return of the original investment plus an expected capital gain.

Definitions of Terms Used in Stock Valuation Models

We saw in Chapter 1 that managers seek to maximize the values of their firms' stocks. A manager's actions affect both the stream of income to investors and the riskiness of that stream. Therefore, managers need to know how alternative actions are likely to affect stock prices. At this point we develop some models to help show how the value of a share of stock is determined. We begin by defining the following terms:

> D_t = dividend the stockholder *expects* to receive at the end of Year t. D_0 is the most recent dividend, which has already been paid; D_1 is the first dividend expected, and it will be paid at the end of this year; D_2 is the dividend expected at the end of two years; and so forth. D_1 represents the first cash flow a new purchaser of the stock will receive. Note that D_0, the dividend

that has just been paid, is known with certainty. However, all future dividends are expected values, so the estimate of D_t may differ among investors.[3]

P_0 = actual **market price** of the stock today.

$\hat{P}_t$ = expected price of the stock at the end of each Year t (pronounced "P hat t"). $\hat{P}_0$ is the **intrinsic, or fundamental, value** of the stock today as seen by the particular investor doing the analysis; $\hat{P}_1$ is the price expected at the end of one year; and so on. Note that $\hat{P}_0$ is the intrinsic value of the stock today based on a particular investor's estimate of the stock's expected dividend stream and the riskiness of that stream. Hence, whereas the market price P_0 is fixed and is identical for all investors, $\hat{P}_0$ could differ among investors depending on how optimistic they are regarding the company. The caret, or "hat," is used to indicate that $\hat{P}_t$ is an estimated value. $\hat{P}_0$, the individual investor's estimate of the intrinsic value today, could be above or below P_0, the current stock price, but an investor would buy the stock only if his or her estimate of $\hat{P}_0$ were equal to or greater than P_0.

Since there are many investors in the market, there can be many values for $\hat{P}_0$. However, we can think of a group of "average," or "marginal," investors whose actions actually determine the market price. For these marginal investors, P_0 must equal $\hat{P}_0$; otherwise, a disequilibrium would exist, and buying and selling in the market would change P_0 until $P_0 = \hat{P}_0$ for the marginal investor.

D_1/P_0 = expected **dividend yield** during the coming year. If the stock is expected to pay a dividend of $D_1 = \$1$ during the next 12 months, and if its current price is $P_0 = \$10$, then the expected dividend yield is $\$1/\$10 = 0.10 = 10\%$.

$\dfrac{\hat{P}_1 - P_0}{P_0}$ = expected **capital gains yield** during the coming year. If the stock sells for $10 today, and if it is expected to rise to $10.50 at the end of one year, then the expected capital gain is $\hat{P}_1 - P_0 = \$10.50 - \$10.00 = \$0.50$, and the expected capital gains yield is $\$0.50/\$10 = 0.05 = 5\%$.

g = expected **growth rate** in dividends as predicted by a marginal investor. If dividends are expected to grow at a constant rate, g is also equal to the expected rate of growth in earnings and in the stock's price. Different investors may use different g's to evaluate a firm's stock, but the market price, P_0, is set on the basis of the g estimated by marginal investors.

r_s = minimum acceptable, or **required, rate of return** on the stock, considering both its riskiness and the returns available on other investments. Again, this term generally relates to marginal investors. The primary determinants of r_s include the real rate of return, expected inflation, and risk.

$\hat{r}_s$ = **expected rate of return** that an investor who buys the stock expects to receive in the future. $\hat{r}_s$ (pronounced "r hat s") could be above or below r_s, but one would buy the stock only if $\hat{r}_s$ were equal to or greater than r_s. $\hat{r}_s$ is equal to the expected dividend yield (D_1/P_0) plus expected capital gains yield $[(\hat{P}_1 - P_0)/P_0]$. In our example, $\hat{r}_s = 10\% + 5\% = 15\%$.

$\bar{r}_s$ = **actual, or realized**, *after-the-fact* **rate of return**, pronounced "r bar s." You may *expect* to obtain a return of $\hat{r}_s = 15$ percent if you buy ExxonMobil today, but if the market goes down, you may end up next year with an actual realized return that is much lower, perhaps even negative.

---

[3] Stocks generally pay dividends quarterly, so theoretically we should evaluate them on a quarterly basis. However, in stock valuation, most analysts work on an annual basis because the data generally are not precise enough to warrant refinement to a quarterly model. For additional information on the quarterly model, see Charles M. Linke and J. Kenton Zumwalt, "Estimation Biases in Discounted Cash Flow Analysis of Equity Capital Cost in Rate Regulation," *Financial Management*, Autumn 1984, 15–21.

Expected Dividends as the Basis for Stock Values

Like all financial assets, equilibrium stock prices are the present value of a stream of cash flows. What are the cash flows that corporations provide to their stockholders? First, think of yourself as an investor who buys a stock with the intention of holding it (in your family) forever. In this case, all that you (and your heirs) will receive is a stream of dividends, and the value of the stock today is calculated as the present value of an infinite stream of dividends:

$$
\begin{aligned}
\text{Value of stock} = \hat{P}_0 &= \text{PV of expected future dividends} \\
&= \frac{D_1}{(1 + r_s)^1} + \frac{D_2}{(1 + r_s)^2} + \cdots + \frac{D_\infty}{(1 + r_s)^\infty} \\
&= \sum_{t=1}^{\infty} \frac{D_t}{(1 + r_s)^t}.
\end{aligned}
\tag{7-1}
$$

What about the more typical case, where you expect to hold the stock for a finite period and then sell it—what is the value of $\hat{P}_0$ in this case? Unless the company is likely to be liquidated or sold and thus to disappear, *the value of the stock is again determined by Equation 7-1*. To see this, recognize that for any individual investor, the expected cash flows consist of expected dividends plus the expected sale price of the stock. However, the sale price the current investor receives will depend on the dividends some future investor expects. Therefore, for all present and future investors in total, expected cash flows must be based on expected future dividends. Put another way, unless a firm is liquidated or sold to another concern, the cash flows it provides to its stockholders will consist only of a stream of dividends; therefore, the value of a share of its stock must be the present value of that expected dividend stream.

The general validity of Equation 7-1 can also be confirmed by asking the following question: Suppose I buy a stock and expect to hold it for one year. I will receive dividends during the year plus the value $\hat{P}_1$ when I sell out at the end of the year. But what will determine the value of $\hat{P}_1$? The answer is that it will be determined as the present value of the dividends expected during Year 2 plus the stock price at the end of that year, which, in turn, will be determined as the present value of another set of future dividends and an even more distant stock price. This process can be continued ad infinitum, and the ultimate result is Equation 7-1.[4]

SELF-TEST QUESTIONS What are the two parts of most stocks' expected total return?

How does one calculate the capital gains yield and the dividend yield of a stock?

CONSTANT GROWTH STOCKS

Equation 7-1 is a generalized stock valuation model in the sense that the time pattern of D_t can be anything: D_t can be rising, falling, fluctuating randomly, or it can even be zero for several years, and Equation 7-1 will still hold. With a computer spreadsheet we can easily use this equation to find a stock's intrinsic value for any pattern of dividends.[5] In prac-

---

[4] We should note that investors periodically lose sight of the long-run nature of stocks as investments and forget that in order to sell a stock at a profit, one must find a buyer who will pay the higher price. If you analyze a stock's value in accordance with Equation 7-1, conclude that the stock's market price exceeds a reasonable value, and then buy the stock anyway, then you would be following the "bigger fool" theory of investment—you think that you may be a fool to buy the stock at its excessive price, but you also think that when you get ready to sell it, you can find someone who is an even bigger fool. The bigger fool theory was widely followed in the spring of 2000, just before the Nasdaq market lost more than one-third of its value.

[5] Actually, we can find an approximate price. If we project dividends for 100 years or more, the present value of that finite dividend stream is approximately equal to the present value of the infinite dividend stream.

tice, the hard part is getting an accurate forecast of the future dividends. However, in many cases, the stream of dividends is expected to grow at a constant rate. If this is the case, Equation 7-1 may be rewritten as follows:[6]

$$\hat{P}_0 = \frac{D_0(1+g)^1}{(1+r_s)^1} + \frac{D_0(1+g)^2}{(1+r_s)^2} + \cdots + \frac{D_0(1+g)^\infty}{(1+r_s)^\infty}$$

$$= D_0 \sum_{t=1}^{\infty} \frac{(1+g)^t}{(1+r_s)^t} \qquad (7\text{-}2)$$

$$= \frac{D_0(1+g)}{r_s - g} = \frac{D_1}{r_s - g}.$$

The last term of Equation 7-2 is called the **constant growth model**, or the **Gordon model** after Myron J. Gordon, who did much to develop and popularize it.

A necessary condition for the validity of Equation 7-2 is that r_s be greater than g. Look back at the second form of Equation 7-2. If g is larger than r_s, then $(1+g)^t/(1+r_s)^t$ must always be greater than one. In this case, the second line of Equation 7-2 is the sum of an infinite number of terms, with each term being a number larger than one. Therefore, if the constant g were greater than r_s, the resulting stock price would be infinite! Since no company is worth an infinite price, it is impossible to have a constant growth rate that is greater than r_s. Occasionally, a student will plug a value for g greater than r_s into the last form of Equation 7-2 and report a negative stock price. This is nonsensical. The last form of Equation 7-2 is valid only when g is less than r_s. *If g is greater than r_s the constant growth model cannot be used and the answer you would get from using Equation 7-2 would be wrong and misleading.*

Illustration of a Constant Growth Stock

Assume that MicroDrive just paid a dividend of $1.15 (that is, $D_0 = \$1.15$). Its stock has a required rate of return, r_s, of 13.4 percent, and investors expect the dividend to grow at a constant 8 percent rate in the future. The estimated dividend one year hence would be $D_1 = \$1.15(1.08) = \$1.24$; D_2 would be $1.34; and the estimated dividend five years hence would be $1.69:

$$D_t = D_0(1+g)^t = \$1.15(1.08)^5 = \$1.69.$$

We could use this procedure to estimate each future dividend, and then use Equation 7-1 to determine the current stock value, $\hat{P}_0$. In other words, we could find each expected future dividend, calculate its present value, and then sum all the present values to find the intrinsic value of the stock.

Such a process would be time consuming, but we can take a short cut—just insert the illustrative data into Equation 7-2 to find the stock's intrinsic value, $23:

$$\hat{P}_0 = \frac{\$1.15(1.08)}{0.134 - 0.08} = \frac{\$1.242}{0.054} = \$23.00.$$

The concept underlying the valuation process for a constant growth stock is graphed in Figure 7-1. Dividends are growing at the rate g = 8%, but because $r_s > g$, the present value of each future dividend is declining. For example, the dividend in Year 1 is $D_1 = D_0(1+g)^1 = \$1.15(1.08) = \$1.242$. However, the present value of this dividend, discounted at 13.4 percent, is $PV(D_1) = \$1.242/(1.134)^1 = \$1.095$. The dividend expected

CF
e-resource

---

[6] The last term in Equation 7-2 is derived in the Web Extension to this chapter.

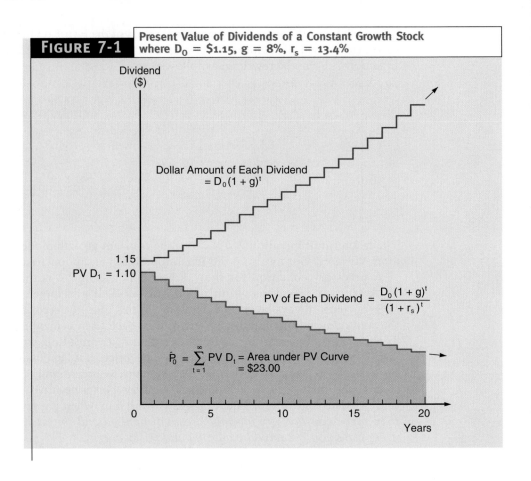

FIGURE 7-1 Present Value of Dividends of a Constant Growth Stock where $D_0 = \$1.15$, $g = 8\%$, $r_s = 13.4\%$

in Year 2 grows to $\$1.242(1.08) = \$1.341$, but the present value of this dividend falls to $\$1.043$. Continuing, $D_3 = \$1.449$ and $PV(D_3) = \$0.993$, and so on. Thus, the expected dividends are growing, but the present value of each successive dividend is declining, because the dividend growth rate (8%) is less than the rate used for discounting the dividends to the present (13.4%).

If we summed the present values of each future dividend, this summation would be the value of the stock, $\hat{P}_0$. When g is a constant, this summation is equal to $D_1/(r_s - g)$, as shown in Equation 7-2. Therefore, if we extended the lower step function curve in Figure 7-1 on out to infinity and added up the present values of each future dividend, the summation would be identical to the value given by Equation 7-2, $\$23.00$.

Although Equation 7-2 assumes that dividends grow to infinity, most of the value is based on dividends during a relatively short time period. In our example, 70 percent of the value is attributed to the first 25 years, 91 percent to the first 50 years, and 99.4 percent to the first 100 years. So, companies don't have to live forever for the Gordon growth model to be used.

Dividend and Earnings Growth

Growth in dividends occurs primarily as a result of growth in *earnings per share (EPS)*. Earnings growth, in turn, results from a number of factors, including (1) inflation, (2) the amount of earnings the company retains and reinvests, and (3) the rate of return the company earns on its equity (ROE). Regarding inflation, if output (in units) is stable, but both sales prices and input costs rise at the inflation rate, then EPS will also grow at the inflation rate. Even without inflation, EPS will also grow as a result of the reinvestment, or plowback, of earnings. If the firm's earnings are not all paid out as dividends (that is, if some fraction of earnings is retained), the dollars of investment behind each share will rise over time, which should lead to growth in earnings and dividends.

Even though a stock's value is derived from expected dividends, this does not necessarily mean that corporations can increase their stock prices by simply raising the current dividend. Shareholders care about *all* dividends, both current and those expected in the future. Moreover, there is a trade-off between current dividends and future dividends. Companies that pay high current dividends necessarily retain and reinvest less of their earnings in the business, and that reduces future earnings and dividends. So, the issue is this: Do shareholders prefer higher current dividends at the cost of lower future dividends, the reverse, or are stockholders indifferent? There is no simple answer to this question. Shareholders prefer to have the company retain earnings, hence pay less current dividends, if it has highly profitable investment opportunities, but they want the company to pay earnings out if investment opportunities are poor. Taxes also play a role—since dividends and capital gains are taxed differently, dividend policy affects investors' taxes. We will consider dividend policy in detail in Chapter 15.

Do Stock Prices Reflect Long-Term or Short-Term Events?

Managers often complain that the stock market is shortsighted, and that it cares only about next quarter's performance. Let's use the constant growth model to test this assertion. MicroDrive's most recent dividend was $1.15, and it is expected to grow at a rate of 8 percent per year. Since we know the growth rate, we can forecast the dividends for each of the next five years and then find their present values:

$$
\begin{aligned}
PV &= \frac{D_0(1+g)^1}{(1+r_s)^1} + \frac{D_0(1+g)^2}{(1+r_s)^2} + \frac{D_0(1+g)^3}{(1+r_s)^3} + \frac{D_0(1+g)^4}{(1+r_s)^4} + \frac{D_0(1+g)^5}{(1+r_s)^5} \\
&= \frac{\$1.15(1.08)^1}{(1.134)^1} + \frac{\$1.15(1.08)^2}{(1.134)^2} + \frac{\$1.15(1.08)^3}{(1.134)^3} + \frac{\$1.15(1.08)^4}{(1.134)^4} + \frac{\$1.15(1.08)^5}{(1.134)^5} \\
&= \frac{\$1.242}{(1.134)^1} + \frac{\$1.341}{(1.134)^2} + \frac{\$1.449}{(1.134)^3} + \frac{\$1.565}{(1.134)^4} + \frac{\$1.690}{(1.134)^5} \\
&= 1.095 + 1.043 + 0.993 + 0.946 + 0.901 \\
&\approx \$5.00.
\end{aligned}
$$

Recall that MicroDrive's stock price is $23.00. Therefore, only $5.00, or 22 percent, of the $23.00 stock price is attributable to short-term cash flows. This means that Micro-Drive's managers will have a bigger effect on the stock price if they work to increase long-term cash flows rather than focus on short-term flows. This situation holds for most companies. Indeed, a number of professors and consulting firms have used actual company data to show that more than 80 percent of a typical company's stock price is due to cash flows expected more than five years in the future.

This brings up an interesting question. If most of a stock's value is due to long-term cash flows, why do managers and analysts pay so much attention to quarterly earnings? Part of the answer lies in the information conveyed by short-term earnings. For example, if actual quarterly earnings are lower than expected, not because of fundamental problems but only because a company has increased its research and development (R&D) expenditures, studies have shown that the stock price probably won't decline and may actually increase. This makes sense, because R&D should increase future cash flows. On the other hand, if quarterly earnings are lower than expected because customers don't like the company's new products, then this new information will have negative implications for future values of g, the long-term growth rate. As we show later in this chapter, even small changes in g can lead to large changes in stock prices. Therefore, quarterly earnings themselves might not be very important, but the information they convey about future prospects can be terribly important.

Another reason many managers focus on short-term earnings is that some firms pay managerial bonuses on the basis of current earnings rather than stock prices (which reflect future earnings). For these managers, the concern with quarterly earnings is not due to their effect on stock prices—it's due to their effect on bonuses.[7]

When Can the Constant Growth Model Be Used?

The constant growth model is often appropriate for mature companies with a stable history of growth. Expected growth rates vary somewhat among companies, but dividend growth for most mature firms is generally expected to continue in the future at about the same rate as nominal gross domestic product (real GDP plus inflation). On this basis, one might expect the dividends of an average, or "normal," company to grow at a rate of 5 to 8 percent a year.

Note too that Equation 7-2 is sufficiently general to handle the case of a **zero growth stock**, where the dividend is expected to remain constant over time. If g = 0, Equation 7-2 reduces to Equation 7-3:

$$\hat{P}_0 = \frac{D}{r_s}. \tag{7-3}$$

This is essentially the equation for a perpetuity, and it is simply the dividend divided by the discount rate.

SELF-TEST QUESTIONS

Write out and explain the valuation formula for a constant growth stock.
Are stock prices affected more by long-term or short-term events?

EXPECTED RATE OF RETURN ON A CONSTANT GROWTH STOCK

We can solve Equation 7-2 for r_s, again using the hat to indicate that we are dealing with an expected rate of return:[8]

$$\begin{array}{ccccc}
\text{Expected rate} & & \text{Expected} & & \text{Expected growth} \\
\text{of return} & = & \text{dividend} & + & \text{rate, or capital} \\
& & \text{yield} & & \text{gains yield} \\
\hat{r}_s & = & \dfrac{D_1}{P_0} & + & g.
\end{array} \tag{7-4}$$

Thus, if you buy a stock for a price P_0 = \$23, and if you expect the stock to pay a dividend D_1 = \$1.242 one year from now and to grow at a constant rate g = 8% in the future, then your expected rate of return will be 13.4 percent:

$$\hat{r}_s = \frac{\$1.242}{\$23} + 8\% = 5.4\% + 8\% = 13.4\%.$$

---

[7] Many apparent puzzles in finance can be explained either by managerial compensation systems or by peculiar features of the Tax Code. So, if you can't explain a firm's behavior in terms of economic logic, look to bonuses or taxes as possible explanations.

[8] The r_s value in Equation 7-2 is a *required* rate of return, but when we solve for r_s to obtain Equation 7-4, we are finding an *expected* rate of return. Obviously, the solution requires that $r_s = \hat{r}_s$. This equality holds if the stock market is in equilibrium, a condition that will be discussed later in the chapter.

In this form, we see that $\hat{r}_s$ is the *expected total return* and that it consists of an *expected dividend yield*, $D_1/P_0 = 5.4\%$, plus an *expected growth rate or capital gains yield*, $g = 8\%$.

Suppose this analysis had just been conducted, with the current price, P_0, equal to $23 and the Year 1 expected dividend, D_1, equal to $1.242. What is the expected price at the end of the first year, immediately after D_1 has been paid? We would again apply Equation 7-2, but this time we would use the Year 2 dividend, $D_2 = D_1 (1 + g) = \$1.242(1.08) = \$1.3414$:

$$\hat{P}_1 = \frac{D_2}{r_s - g} = \frac{\$1.3414}{0.134 - 0.08} = \$24.84.$$

Now, note that $24.84 is 8 percent larger than P_0, the $23 price found one year earlier:

$$\$23(1.08) = \$24.84.$$

Thus, we would expect to make a capital gain of $24.84 − $23.00 = $1.84 during the year, which would provide a capital gains yield of 8 percent:

$$\text{Capital gains yield} = \frac{\text{Capital gain}}{\text{Beginning price}} = \frac{\$1.84}{\$23.00} = 0.08 = 8\%.$$

We could extend the analysis, and in each future year the expected capital gains yield would always equal g, the expected dividend growth rate.

The dividend yield during the year could be estimated as follows:

$$\text{Dividend yield} = \frac{D_2}{\hat{P}_1} = \frac{\$1.3414}{\$24.84} = 0.054 = 5.4\%.$$

The dividend yield for the next year could also be calculated, and again it would be 5.4 percent. Thus, *for a constant growth stock,* the following conditions must hold:

1. The dividend is expected to grow forever at a constant rate, g.
2. The stock price is expected to grow at this same rate.
3. The expected dividend yield is constant.
4. The expected capital gains yield is also constant, and it is equal to g.
5. The expected total rate of return, $\hat{r}_s$, is equal to the expected dividend yield plus the expected growth rate: $\hat{r}_s$ = dividend yield + g.

The popular Motley Fool Web site http:// www.fool.com/ school/introduction tovaluation.htm provides a good description of some of the benefits and drawbacks of a few of the more commonly used valuation procedures.

The term *expected* should be clarified—it means expected in a probabilistic sense, as the "statistically expected" outcome. Thus, if we say the growth rate is expected to remain constant at 8 percent, we mean that the best prediction for the growth rate in any future year is 8 percent, not that we literally expect the growth rate to be exactly 8 percent in each future year. In this sense, the constant growth assumption is a reasonable one for many large, mature companies.

SELF-TEST QUESTIONS

What conditions must hold if a stock is to be evaluated using the constant growth model?

What does the term "expected" mean when we say expected growth rate?

VALUING STOCKS THAT HAVE A NONCONSTANT GROWTH RATE

For many companies, it is inappropriate to assume that dividends will grow at a constant rate. Firms typically go through *life cycles*. During the early part of their lives, their growth is much faster than that of the economy as a whole; then they match the economy's growth; and finally their growth is slower than that of the economy.[9] Automobile manu-facturers in the 1920s, computer software firms such as Microsoft in the 1990s, and tech-nology firms such as Cisco in the 2000s are examples of firms in the early part of the cycle; these firms are called **supernormal, or nonconstant, growth** firms. Figure 7-2 illus-trates nonconstant growth and also compares it with normal growth, zero growth, and negative growth.[10]

In the figure, the dividends of the supernormal growth firm are expected to grow at a 30 percent rate for three years, after which the growth rate is expected to fall to 8 per-cent, the assumed average for the economy. The value of this firm, like any other, is the present value of its expected future dividends as determined by Equation 7-1. When D_t is growing at a constant rate, we simplified Equation 7-1 to $\hat{P}_0 = D_1/(r_s - g)$. In the super-normal case, however, the expected growth rate is not a constant—it declines at the end of the period of supernormal growth.

Because Equation 7-2 requires a constant growth rate, we obviously cannot use it to value stocks that have nonconstant growth. However, assuming that a company currently enjoying supernormal growth will eventually slow down and become a constant growth stock, we can combine Equations 7-1 and 7-2 to form a new formula, Equation 7-5, for valuing it. First, we assume that the dividend will grow at a nonconstant rate (generally

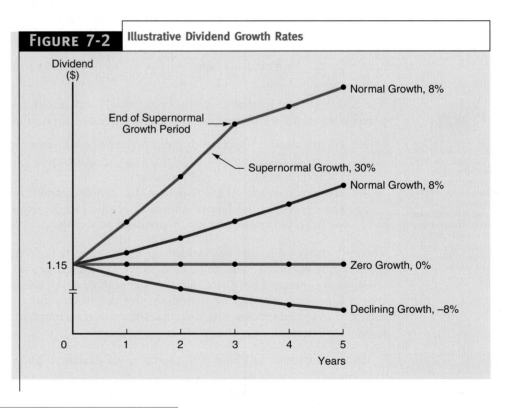

FIGURE 7-2 Illustrative Dividend Growth Rates

a relatively high rate) for N periods, after which it will grow at a constant rate, g. N is often called the **terminal date**, or **horizon date**.

We can use the constant growth formula, Equation 7-2, to determine what the stock's **horizon**, or **terminal, value** will be N periods from today:

$$\text{Horizon value} = \hat{P}_N = \frac{D_{N+1}}{r_s - g} = \frac{D_N(1 + g)}{r_s - g}. \tag{7-2a}$$

The stock's intrinsic value today, $\hat{P}_0$, is the present value of the dividends during the non-constant growth period plus the present value of the horizon value:

$$\hat{P}_0 = \underbrace{\frac{D_1}{(1 + r_s)^1} + \frac{D_2}{(1 + r_s)^2} + \cdots + \frac{D_N}{(1 + r_s)^N}}_{\substack{\text{PV of dividends during the} \\ \text{nonconstant growth period} \\ t = 1, \cdots N.}} + \underbrace{\frac{D_{N+1}}{(1 + r_s)^{N+1}} + \cdots + \frac{D_\infty}{(1 + r_s)^\infty}}_{\substack{\text{PV of dividends during the} \\ \text{constant growth period} \\ t = N + 1, \cdots \infty.}}$$

$$\hat{P}_0 = \underbrace{\frac{D_1}{(1 + r_s)^1} + \frac{D_2}{(1 + r_s)^2} + \cdots + \frac{D_N}{(1 + r_s)^N}}_{\substack{\text{PV of dividends during the} \\ \text{nonconstant growth period} \\ t = 1, \cdots N.}} + \underbrace{\frac{\hat{P}_N}{(1 + r_s)^N}}_{\substack{\text{PV of horizon} \\ \text{value}, \hat{P}_N: \\ \frac{[(D_{N+1})/(r_s - g)]}{(1 + r_s)^N}.}} \tag{7-5}$$

To implement Equation 7-5, we go through the following three steps:

1. Estimate the expected dividends for each year during the period of nonconstant growth.
2. Find the expected price of the stock at the end of the nonconstant growth period, at which point it has become a constant growth stock.
3. Find the present values of the expected dividends during the nonconstant growth period and the present value of the expected stock price at the end of the nonconstant growth period. Their sum is the intrinsic value of the stock, $\hat{P}_0$.

Figure 7-3 can be used to illustrate the process for valuing nonconstant growth stocks. Here we assume the following five facts exist:

r_s = stockholders' required rate of return = 13.4%. This rate is used to discount the cash flows.

N = years of supernormal growth = 3.

g_s = rate of growth in both earnings and dividends during the supernormal growth period = 30%. This rate is shown directly on the time line. (Note: The growth rate during the supernormal growth period could vary from year to year. Also, there could be several different supernormal growth periods, e.g., 30 percent for three years, then 20 percent for three years, and then a constant 8 percent.)

g_n = rate of normal, constant growth after the supernormal period = 8 percent. This rate is also shown on the time line, between Periods 3 and 4.

D_0 = last dividend the company paid = $1.15.

FIGURE 7-3   Process for Finding the Value of a Supernormal Growth Stock

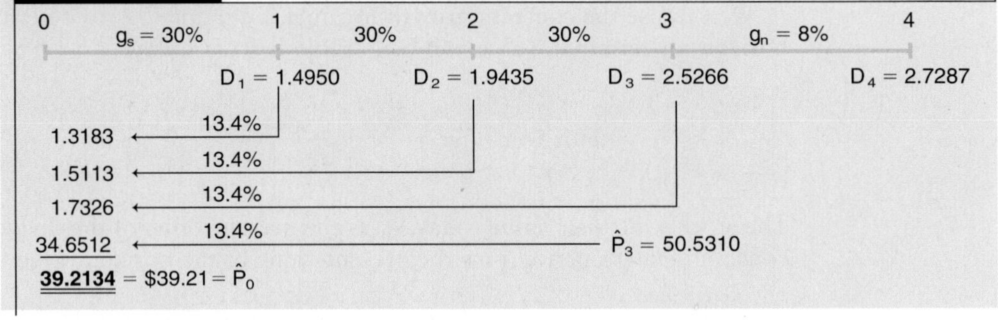

Notes to Figure 7-3:

STEP 1. Calculate the dividends expected at the end of each year during the nonconstant growth period. Calculate the first dividend, $D_1 = D_0(1 + g_s) = \$1.15(1.30) = \$1.4950$. Here g_s is the growth rate during the three-year supernormal growth period, 30 percent. Show the \$1.4950 on the time line as the cash flow at Time 1. Then, calculate $D_2 = D_1(1 + g_s) = \$1.4950(1.30) = \$1.9435$, and then $D_3 = D_2(1 + g_s) = \$1.9435(1.30) = \$2.5266$. Show these values on the time line as the cash flows at Time 2 and Time 3. Note that D_0 is used only to calculate D_1.

STEP 2. At Time 3, the stock becomes a constant growth stock. Therefore, we can use the constant growth formula to find $\hat{P}_3$, which is the PV of the dividends from Time 4 to infinity as evaluated at Time 3. First, we determine $D_4 = \$2.5266(1.08) = \$2.7287$ for use in the formula, and then we calculate $\hat{P}_3$ as follows:

$$\hat{P}_3 = \frac{D_4}{r_s - g_n} = \frac{\$2.7287}{0.134 - 0.08} = \$50.5310.$$

We show this \$50.5310 on the time line as a second cash flow at Time 3. The \$50.5310 is a Time 3 cash flow in the sense that the owner of the stock could sell it for \$50.5310 at Time 3 and also in the sense that \$50.5310 is the present value of the dividend cash flows from Time 4 to infinity.

STEP 3. Now that the cash flows have been placed on the time line, we can discount each cash flow at the required rate of return, $r_s = 13.4\%$. This produces the PVs shown to the left below the time line, and the sum of the PVs is the value of the supernormal growth stock, \$39.21.

With a financial calculator, you can find the PV of the cash flows as shown on the time line with the cash flow (CFLO) register of your calculator. Enter 0 for CF_0 because you get no cash flow at Time 0, $CF_1 = 1.495$, $CF_2 = 1.9435$, and $CF_3 = 2.5266 + 50.531 = 53.0576$. Then enter I = 13.4, and press the NPV key to find the value of the stock, \$39.21.

The valuation process as diagrammed in Figure 7-3 is explained in the steps set forth below the time line. The estimated value of the supernormal growth stock is \$39.21.

SELF-TEST QUESTIONS   Explain how one would find the value of a supernormal growth stock.

Explain what is meant by "horizon (terminal) date" and "horizon (terminal) value."

STOCK VALUATION BY THE FREE CASH FLOW APPROACH

The box at the beginning of the chapter showed that the value of a firm is the present value of its future expected free cash flows (FCFs), discounted at the weighted average cost of capital (WACC). Following is a simple example illustrating this approach to stock valuation.

Suppose a firm had a free cash flow of \$200 million at the end of the most recent year. Chapter 12 shows how to forecast financial statements and free cash flows, but for now let's assume that the firm's FCFs are expected to grow at a constant rate of 5 percent per year forever. Chapter 9 explains how to estimate the weighted average cost of capital, but for now let's assume that the firm's WACC is 9 percent. The present value of the expected future free cash flows is the PV of a growing annuity, so we can use a variation of Equation 7-2, the value of a constantly growing stream of dividends:

$$V = \frac{FCF(1 + g)}{WACC - g} = \frac{\$200(1.05)}{0.09 - 0.05} = \$5,250 \text{ million.} \qquad (7\text{-}6)$$

FCFs are the cash flow available for distribution to *all* of the firm's investors, not just the shareholders. The WACC is the average rate of return required by *all* of the firm's investors, not just shareholders. Therefore, V is the value of the entire firm's operations, not just the value of its equity. If the firm had any nonoperating assets, such as short-term investments in marketable securities, we would add them to V to find the total value. The firm in this example has no nonoperating assets, so its total value is $5,250 million. To find the value of equity, subtract the value of claims held by all groups other than common shareholders, such as debtholders and preferred stock holders. If the value of debt and preferred stock equal $2,000 million, then the firm's equity has a value of $5,250 − $2,000 = $3,250 million. If 325 million shares of stock are outstanding, then the intrinsic stock value $3,250/325 = $10 per share. This example should give you the general idea behind the free cash flow approach to stock valuation, but see Chapter 13 for a more comprehensive example, including the situation where free cash flows are growing initially at a nonconstant rate.

SELF-TEST QUESTION   Explain how to find the stock price using the free cash flow approach.

MARKET MULTIPLE ANALYSIS

Another method of stock valuation is **market multiple analysis,** which applies a market-determined multiple to net income, earnings per share, sales, book value, or, for businesses such as cable TV or cellular telephone systems, the number of subscribers. While the discounted dividend method applies valuation concepts in a precise manner, focusing on expected cash flows, market multiple analysis is more judgmental. To illustrate the concept, suppose that a company's forecasted earnings per share is $7.70. The average price per share to earnings per share (P/E) ratio for similar publicly traded companies is 12.

To estimate the company's stock value using the market P/E multiple approach, simply multiply its $7.70 earnings per share by the market multiple of 12 to obtain the value of $7.70(12) = $92.40. This is its estimated stock price per share.

Note that measures other than net income can be used in the market multiple approach. For example, another commonly used measure is *earnings before interest, taxes, depreciation, and amortization (EBITDA)*. The EBITDA multiple is the total value of a company (the market value of equity plus debt) divided by EBITDA. This multiple is based on total value, since EBITDA measures the entire firm's performance. Therefore, it is called an **entity multiple**. The EBITDA market multiple is the average EBITDA multiple for similar publicly traded companies. Multiplying a company's EBITDA by the market multiple gives an estimate of the company's total value. To find the company's estimated stock price per share, subtract debt from total value, and then divide by the number of shares of stock.

As noted above, in some businesses such as cable TV and cellular telephone, an important element in the valuation process is the number of customers a company has. For example, telephone companies have been paying about $2,000 per customer when acquiring cellular operators. Managed care companies such as HMOs have applied similar logic in acquisitions, basing their valuations on the number of people insured. Some Internet companies have been valued by the number of "eyeballs," which is the number of hits on the site.

SELF-TEST QUESTIONS   What is market multiple analysis?
What is an entity multiple?

Stock Market Equilibrium

Recall that r_i, the required return on Stock i, can be found using the Security Market Line (SML) equation as it was developed in our discussion of the Capital Asset Pricing Model (CAPM) back in Chapter 5:

$$r_i = r_{RF} + (RP_M)b_i.$$

If the risk-free rate of return is 8 percent, the market risk premium, RP_M, is 4 percent, and Stock i has a beta of 2, then the marginal investor will require a return of 16 percent on Stock i:

$$r_i = 8\% + (4\%)\,2.0$$
$$= 16\%.$$

The **marginal investor** will want to buy Stock i if its expected rate of return is more than 16 percent, will want to sell it if the expected rate of return is less than 16 percent, and will be indifferent, hence will hold but not buy or sell, if the expected rate of return is exactly 16 percent. Now suppose the investor's portfolio contains Stock i, and he or she analyzes the stock's prospects and concludes that its earnings, dividends, and price can be expected to grow at a constant rate of 5 percent per year. The last dividend was $D_0 = \$2.8571$, so the next expected dividend is

$$D_1 = \$2.8571(1.05) = \$3.$$

Our marginal investor observes that the present price of the stock, P_0, is $30. Should he or she purchase more of Stock i, sell the stock, or maintain the present position?

The investor can calculate Stock i's *expected rate of return* as follows:

$$\hat{r}_i = \frac{D_1}{P_0} + g = \frac{\$3}{\$30} + 5\% = 15\%.$$

Because the expected rate of return is less than the required return of 16 percent, this marginal investor would want to sell the stock, as would most other holders. However, few people would want to buy at the $30 price, so the present owners would be unable to find buyers unless they cut the price of the stock. Thus, the price would decline, and this decline would continue until the price reached $27.27, at which point the stock would be in **equilibrium,** defined as the price at which the expected rate of return, 16 percent, is equal to the required rate of return:

$$\hat{r}_i = \frac{\$3}{\$27.27} + 5\% = 11\% + 5\% = 16\% = r_i.$$

Had the stock initially sold for less than $27.27, say, at $25, events would have been reversed. Investors would have wanted to buy the stock because its expected rate of return would have exceeded its required rate of return, and buy orders would have driven the stock's price up to $27.27.

To summarize, in equilibrium two related conditions must hold:

1. A stock's expected rate of return as seen by the marginal investor must equal its required rate of return: $\hat{r}_i = r_i$.
2. The actual market price of the stock must equal its intrinsic value as estimated by the marginal investor: $P_0 = \hat{P}_0$.

Of course, some individual investors may believe that $\hat{r}_i > r_i$ and $\hat{P}_0 > P_0$, hence they would invest in the stock, while other investors may have an opposite view and would sell all of their shares. However, it is the marginal investor who establishes the actual market price, and for this investor, we must have $\hat{r}_i = r_i$ and $P_0 = \hat{P}_0$. If these conditions do not hold, trading will occur until they do.

Changes in Equilibrium Stock Prices

Stock prices are not constant—they undergo violent changes at times. For example, on September 17, 2001, the first day of trading after the terrorist attacks of September 11, the Dow Jones average dropped 685 points. This was the largest decline ever in the Dow, but not the largest percentage loss, which was -24.4 percent on December 12, 1914. More recently, the Dow fell by 22.6 percent on October 19, 1987. The Dow has also had some spectacular increases. In fact, its eighth-largest increase was 368 points on September 24, 2001, shortly after its largest-ever decline. The Dow's largest increase ever was 499 points on April 16, 2000, and its largest percentage gain of 15.4 percent occurred on March 15, 1933. At the risk of understatement, the stock market is volatile!

To see how such changes can occur, assume that Stock i is in equilibrium, selling at a price of $27.27. If all expectations were exactly met, during the next year the price would gradually rise to $28.63, or by 5 percent. However, many different events could occur to cause a change in the equilibrium price. To illustrate, consider again the set of inputs used to develop Stock i's price of $27.27, along with a new set of assumed input variables:

	VARIABLE VALUE	
	Original	New
Risk-free rate, r_{RF}	8%	7%
Market risk premium, $r_M - r_{RF}$	4%	3%
Stock i's beta coefficient, b_i	2.0	1.0
Stock i's expected growth rate, g_i	5%	6%
D_0	$2.8571	$2.8571
Price of Stock i	$27.27	?

Now give yourself a test: How would the indicated change in each variable, by itself, affect the price, and what is your guess as to the new stock price?

Every change, taken alone, would lead to an *increase* in the price. Taken together, the first three changes lower r_i, which declines from 16 to 10 percent:

$$\text{Original } r_i = 8\% + 4\%(2.0) = 16\%.$$
$$\text{New } r_i = 7\% + 3\%(1.0) = 10\%.$$

Using these values, together with the new g value, we find that $\hat{P}_0$ rises from $27.27 to $75.71:[11]

$$\text{Original } \hat{P}_0 = \frac{\$2.8571(1.05)}{0.16 - 0.05} = \frac{\$3}{0.11} = \$27.27.$$

$$\text{New } \hat{P}_0 = \frac{\$2.8571(1.06)}{0.10 - 0.06} = \frac{\$3.0285}{0.04} = \$75.71.$$

At the new price, the expected and required rates of return are equal:[12]

$$\hat{r}_i = \frac{\$3.0285}{\$75.71} + 6\% = 10\% = r_i.$$

[11] A price change of this magnitude is by no means rare for an individual stock. The prices of *many* stocks double or halve during a year. For example, Ciena, a phone equipment maker, fell by 76.1 percent in 1998, increased by 183 percent in 2000, declined by 84 percent in 2001, and declined by another 64 percent in 2002.

[12] It should be obvious by now that *actual realized* rates of return are not necessarily equal to expected and required returns. Thus, an investor might have *expected* to receive a return of 15 percent if he or she had bought Ciena stock, but after the fact, the realized return was far above 15 percent in 2000 and was far below in 1998, 2001, and 2002.

As this example illustrates, even small changes in the size or riskiness of expected future dividends can cause large changes in stock prices. What might cause investors to change their expectations about future dividends? It could be new information about the company, such as preliminary results for an R&D program, initial sales of a new product, or the discovery of harmful side effects from the use of an existing product. Or, new information that will affect many companies could arrive, such as a tightening of interest rates by the Federal Reserve. Given the existence of computers and telecommunications networks, new information hits the market on an almost continuous basis, and it causes frequent and sometimes large changes in stock prices. In other words, *ready availability of information causes stock prices to be volatile!*

If a stock's price is stable, that probably means that little new information is arriving. But if you think it's risky to invest in a volatile stock, imagine how risky it would be to invest in a company that rarely released new information about its sales or operations. It may be bad to see your stock's price jump around, but it would be a lot worse to see a stable quoted price most of the time but then to see huge moves on the rare days when new information was released. Fortunately, in our economy timely information is readily available, and evidence suggests that stocks, especially those of large companies, adjust rapidly to new information. Consequently, equilibrium ordinarily exists for any given stock, and required and expected returns are generally equal. Stock prices certainly change, sometimes violently and rapidly, but this simply reflects changing conditions and expectations. There are, of course, times when a stock appears to react for several months to favorable or unfavorable developments. However, this does not signify a long adjustment period; rather, it simply indicates that as more new pieces of information about the situation become available, the market adjusts to them. The ability of the market to adjust to new information is discussed in the next section.

The Efficient Markets Hypothesis

A body of theory called the **Efficient Markets Hypothesis (EMH)** holds (1) that stocks are always in equilibrium and (2) that it is impossible for an investor to consistently "beat the market." Essentially, those who believe in the EMH note that there are 100,000 or so full-time, highly trained, professional analysts and traders operating in the market, while there are fewer than 3,000 major stocks. Therefore, if each analyst followed 30 stocks (which is about right, as analysts tend to specialize in the stocks in a specific industry), there would on average be 1,000 analysts following each stock. Further, these analysts work for organizations such as Citigroup, Merrill Lynch, Prudential Insurance, and the like, which have billions of dollars available with which to take advantage of bargains. In addition, as a result of SEC disclosure requirements and electronic information networks, as new information about a stock becomes available, these 1,000 analysts generally receive and evaluate it at about the same time. Therefore, the price of a stock will adjust almost immediately to any new development.

Levels of Market Efficiency

If markets are efficient, stock prices will rapidly reflect all available information. This raises an important question: What types of information are available and, therefore, incorporated into stock prices? Financial theorists have discussed three forms, or levels, of market efficiency.

WEAK-FORM EFFICIENCY   The **weak form** of the EMH states that all information contained in past price movements is fully reflected in current market prices. If this were true, then information about recent trends in stock prices would be of no use in selecting stocks—the fact that a stock has risen for the past three days, for example, would give us no useful clues as to what it will do today or tomorrow. People who believe that weak-form efficiency exists also believe that "tape watchers" and "chartists" are wasting their time.[13]

For example, after studying the past history of the stock market, a chartist might "discover" the following pattern: If a stock falls three consecutive days, its price typically rises 10 percent the following day. The technician would then conclude that investors could make money by purchasing a stock whose price has fallen three consecutive days.

But if this pattern truly existed, wouldn't other investors also discover it, and if so, why would anyone be willing to sell a stock after it had fallen three consecutive days if he or she knows its price is expected to increase by 10 percent the next day? In other words, if a stock is selling at $40 per share after falling three consecutive days, why would investors sell the stock if they expected it to rise to $44 per share one day later? Those who believe in weak-form efficiency argue that if the stock was really likely to rise to $44 tomorrow, its price *today* would actually rise to somewhere near $44 immediately, thereby eliminating the trading opportunity. Consequently, weak-form efficiency implies that any information that comes from past stock prices is rapidly incorporated into the current stock price.

SEMISTRONG-FORM EFFICIENCY   The **semistrong form** of the EMH states that current market prices reflect all *publicly available* information. Therefore, if semistrong-form efficiency exists, it would do no good to pore over annual reports or other published data because market prices would have adjusted to any good or bad news contained in such reports back when the news came out. With semistrong-form efficiency, investors should expect to earn the returns predicted by the SML, but they should not expect to do any better unless they have either good luck or access to information that is not publicly available. However, insiders (for example, the presidents of companies) who have information that is not publicly available can earn consistently abnormal returns (returns higher than those predicted by the SML) even under semistrong-form efficiency.

Another implication of semistrong-form efficiency is that whenever information is released to the public, stock prices will respond only if the information is different from what had been expected. If, for example, a company announces a 30 percent increase in earnings, and if that increase is about what analysts had been expecting, the announcement should have little or no effect on the company's stock price. On the other hand, the stock price would probably fall if analysts had expected earnings to increase by more than 30 percent, but it probably would rise if they had expected a smaller increase.

STRONG-FORM EFFICIENCY   The **strong form** of the EMH states that current market prices reflect all pertinent information, whether publicly available or privately held. If this form holds, even insiders would find it impossible to earn consistently abnormal returns in the stock market.

Implications of Market Efficiency

What bearing does the EMH have on financial decisions? If stock prices already reflect all publicly available information, and hence are fairly priced, one can "beat the market" consistently only by luck, and it is difficult, if not impossible, for anyone to consistently outperform the market averages. For the most part, empirical tests support the EMH in

---

[13] Tape watchers focus on the trade-by-trade behavior of stock prices, which used to be reported on a paper tape. Chartists plot past patterns of stock price movements. Both are called "technical analysts," and both believe that they can tell if something is happening to the stock that will cause its price to move up or down in the near future.

its weak and semistrong forms.[14] However, people such as corporate officers, who have inside information, can do better than the averages.[15]

Some investors may be able to analyze and react more quickly than others to releases of new information, and these investors may have a temporary advantage over others. However, the buy-sell actions of those investors quickly bring market prices into equilibrium. For most stocks, most of the time it is generally safe to assume that $\hat{r}_i = r_i$, that $\hat{P}_0 = P_0$, and that the stocks plot on the SML.

Market efficiency also has important implications for managerial decisions, especially stock issues, stock repurchases, and tender offers. If the market prices stocks fairly, then managerial decisions based on the premise that a stock is undervalued or overvalued might not make sense. Managers may have better information about their own companies than outsiders, but they cannot use this information for their own advantage, nor can they deliberately defraud any investors.

SELF-TEST QUESTIONS For a stock to be in equilibrium, what two conditions must hold?

What is the Efficient Markets Hypothesis (EMH)?

What are the differences among the three forms of the EMH?

What are the implications of the EMH for financial decisions?

ACTUAL STOCK PRICES AND RETURNS

Our discussion thus far has focused on *expected* stock prices and *expected* rates of return. Anyone who has ever invested in the stock market knows that there can be, and there generally are, large differences between *expected* and *realized* prices and returns. Figure 7-4 shows how the stock market has moved in recent years. We know from theory that expected returns, as estimated by a marginal investor, are always positive, but in some years, as Figure 7-4 shows, stock prices fall. Of course, even in bad years some individual companies do well, so "the name of the game" in security analysis is to pick the winners. In subsequent chapters, we will examine the actions that managers can take to increase the odds of their firms doing relatively well even in a falling market.

Investing in International Stocks

The U.S. stock market amounts to only about 40 percent of the world stock market, and this is prompting many U.S. investors to also hold foreign stocks. Analysts have long touted the benefits of investing overseas, arguing that foreign stocks improve diversification and provide good growth opportunities. Table 7-1 shows how stocks in different countries performed in 2003. The number on the right indicates how stocks in each country performed in terms of its local currency, while the left numbers show how the country's stocks performed in terms of the U.S. dollar. For example, in 2003 Swiss stocks rose by 19.38 percent, but the Swiss Franc rose by about 13.76 percent versus the U.S. dollar. Therefore, if U.S. investors had bought Swiss stocks, they would have made 19.38 percent in Swiss Franc terms, but those Swiss Francs would have bought 13.76 percent more U.S.

---

[14] Virtually no academic studies have shown that excess returns (that is, above those predicted by the CAPM) can be earned by using past stock prices to predict future stock prices. One possible exception is in the area of long-term reversals, where portfolios of stocks with poor past long-term performance tend to do slightly better than average in the long term, and vice versa. With respect to other publicly available information, there have been periods when small stocks and "value" stocks (those with a high book-to-market ratio) had excess returns, but those patterns may not still persist. When a way to "beat" the market becomes known, the actions of investors tend to eliminate it.

[15] Several cases of illegal insider trading have made the headlines, and the Enron, WorldCom, and other scandals were reported in 2001 and 2002. These cases involved employees of several corporations and major investment banking houses, and even an employee of the SEC. In one famous case during the 1980s, Ivan Boesky admitted to making $50 million by purchasing the stock of firms he knew were about to merge. He went to jail, and he had to pay a large fine, but he helped disprove the strong-form EMH.

FIGURE 7-4 S&P 500 Index, 1968–2003

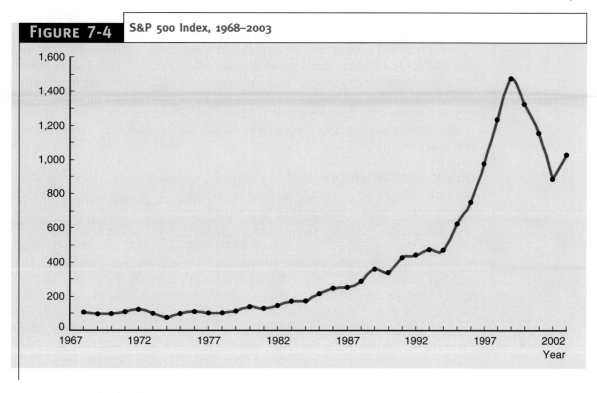

Source: Data taken from **http://finance.yahoo.com**.

TABLE 7-1 2003 Performance of the Dow Jones Global Stock Indexes (Rates of Return)

Country	U.S. Dollars	Local Currency	Country	U.S. Dollars	Local Currency
Thailand	+138.70%	+119.29%	Belgium	+40.78%	+17.26%
Brazil	+131.40	+89.01	Norway	+40.62	+35.32
Venezuela	+119.88	+152.70	France	+39.11	+15.87
Chile	+83.53	+51.13	Hong Kong	+38.69	+38.07
Indonesia	+65.95	+56.17	Portugal	+38.53	+15.39
Greece	+65.08	+37.50	Italy	+38.35	+15.24
Germany	+61.33	+34.37	Japan	+37.61	+24.40
Sweden	+60.06	+32.63	Taiwan	+36.63	+33.91
Austria	+58.26	+31.82	Singapore	+36.27	+33.43
Spain	+55.59	+29.59	Switzerland	+33.14	+19.38
Canada	+51.54	+25.15	Mexico	+31.46	+42.50
New Zealand	+50.85	+20.84	South Korea	+31.45	+32.14
Philippines	+49.62	+55.66	Great Britain	+28.54	+15.82
Denmark	+49.35	+25.03	U.S.	+28.44	+28.44
Australia	+45.95	+9.07	Malaysia	+26.19	+26.18
Ireland	+44.26	+20.16	Netherlands	+25.27	+4.34
South Africa	+41.78	+10.69	Finland	+17.33	−2.27

Source: "The Year of the Bull," *The Wall Street Journal,* January 2, 2004, R6.

dollars, so the effective return would have been 33.14 percent. So, the results of foreign investments depend in part on what happens to the exchange rate. Indeed, when you invest overseas, you are making two bets: (1) that foreign stocks will increase in their local markets and (2) that the currencies in which you will be paid will rise relative to the dollar.

Even though foreign stocks have exchange rate risk, this by no means suggests that investors should avoid foreign stocks. Foreign investments still improve diversification, and it is inevitable that there will be years when foreign stocks outperform domestic stocks. When this occurs, U.S. investors will be glad they put some of their money in overseas markets.

Stock Market Reporting

Up until a couple of years ago, the best source of stock quotations was the business section of a daily newspaper, such as *The Wall Street Journal*. One problem with newspapers, however, is that they are printed only once a day. Now it is possible to get quotes all during the day from a wide variety of Internet sources.[16] One of the best is provided by Bloomberg at **http://www.bloomberg.com**. Figure 7-5 shows a quote for Abbott Labs, which is traded on the NYSE under the symbol ABT. As Figure 7-5 shows, Abbott Labs' stock ended the day at $43.90, for a loss of $0.35, which is a 0.791 percent decrease from the previous day. The data also show that Abbott opened the current day at $44.00, reached a high during the day of $44.32, and fell as low as $43.77. During the past year, the price has been as high as $47.25 and as low as $37.65. More than 3.7 million shares traded during the day. If this quote had been during trading hours, it would also have provided information about the quotes at which the stock could be bought (the Ask quote) or sold (the Bid quote). In addition to this information, the Web page has links to research and much more detailed data for Abbott Labs.

SELF-TEST QUESTIONS

Explain how financial markets adjust to bring stocks into equilibrium.

Explain why expected, required, and realized returns are often different.

What are the key benefits and risks of adding foreign stocks to a portfolio?

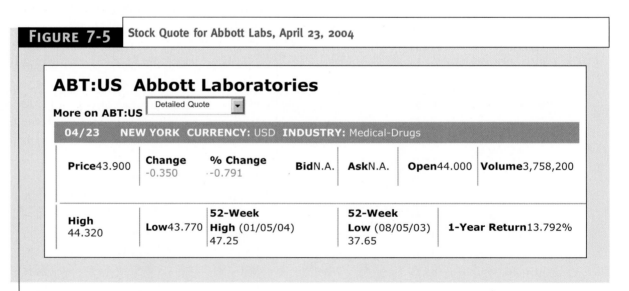

FIGURE 7-5   Stock Quote for Abbott Labs, April 23, 2004

ABT:US Abbott Laboratories

More on ABT:US   Detailed Quote

04/23   NEW YORK CURRENCY: USD INDUSTRY: Medical-Drugs

| Price 43.900 | Change -0.350 | % Change -0.791 | Bid N.A. | Ask N.A. | Open 44.000 | Volume 3,758,200 |

| High 44.320 | Low 43.770 | 52-Week High (01/05/04) 47.25 | | 52-Week Low (08/05/03) 37.65 | 1-Year Return 13.792% |

Source: http://www.bloomberg.com.

[16] Most free sources actually provide quotes that are delayed by 20 minutes.

A NATION OF TRADERS

A story in *Fortune* profiled the dramatic revolution in the way investors trade stocks. Just a few years ago, the vast majority of investors bought and sold stocks by calling a full-service broker. The typical broker would execute orders, maintain records, assist with stock selection, and provide guidance regarding long-run asset allocations. Those services came at a price—when investors bought stocks, the commissions were often well in excess of $100 a trade.

While the full-service broker is far from dead, many are on the ropes. Now large and small investors have online access to the same type of company and market information that brokers provide, and they can trade stocks online for less than $10 a trade. Online trading is by no means relegated to just a few investors—it now represents a significant percentage of all trades that occur. In 1989 only 28 percent of households owned stock, while 10 years later this percentage had risen to 48 percent.

Changing technology is encouraging more and more investors to take control of their own finances. While this trend has lowered traditional brokers' incomes, it has reduced transaction costs, increased information, and empowered investors. Of course, concerns have been raised about whether individual investors fully understand the risks involved, and whether they have sound strategies in place for long-run investing. The tech stock crash of 2000 and the subsequent bear market showed how vulnerable individual investors are to market movements.

Source: Andy Serwer, Christine Y. Chen, and Angel Key, "A Nation of Traders," *Fortune* (1999), 116–120. Copyright © 1999 Time Inc. All rights reserved. Reprinted by permission.

PREFERRED STOCK

Preferred stock is a *hybrid*—it is similar to bonds in some respects and to common stock in others. Like bonds, preferred stock has a par value and a fixed amount of dividends that must be paid before dividends can be paid on the common stock. However, if the preferred dividend is not earned, the directors can omit (or "pass") it without throwing the company into bankruptcy. So, although preferred stock has a fixed payment like bonds, a failure to make this payment will not lead to bankruptcy.

As noted above, a preferred stock entitles its owners to regular, fixed dividend payments. If the payments last forever, the issue is a perpetuity whose value, V_{ps}, is found as follows:

$$V_{ps} = \frac{D_{ps}}{r_{ps}}. \tag{7-7}$$

V_{ps} is the value of the preferred stock, D_{ps} is the preferred dividend, and r_{ps} is the required rate of return. MicroDrive has preferred stock outstanding that pays a dividend of $10 per year. If the required rate of return on this preferred stock is 10 percent, then its value is $100, found by solving Equation 7-7 as follows:

$$V_{ps} = \frac{\$10.00}{0.10} = \$100.00.$$

If we know the current price of a preferred stock and its dividend, we can solve for the rate of return as follows:

$$r_{ps} = \frac{D_{ps}}{V_{ps}}. \tag{7-7a}$$

Some preferred stocks have a stated maturity date, say, 50 years. If MicroDrive's preferred matured in 50 years, paid a $10 annual dividend, and had a required return of 8 percent, then we could find its price as follows: Enter N = 50, I = 8, PMT = 10, and FV = 100.

Then press PV to find the price, $V_{ps} = \$124.47$. If $r_{ps} = I = 10\%$, change $I = 8$ to $I = 10$, and find $P = V_{ps} = PV = \$100$. If you know the price of a share of preferred stock, you can solve for I to find the expected rate of return, $\hat{r}_{ps}$.

Most preferred stocks pay dividends quarterly. This is true for MicroDrive, so we could find the effective rate of return on its preferred stock (perpetual or maturing) as follows:

$$\text{EFF\%} = \text{EAR}_p = \left(1 + \frac{r_{Nom}}{m}\right)^m - 1 = \left(1 + \frac{0.10}{4}\right)^4 - 1 = 10.38\%.$$

If an investor wanted to compare the returns on MicroDrive's bonds and its preferred stock, it would be best to convert the nominal rates on each security to effective rates and then compare these "equivalent annual rates."

SELF-TEST QUESTIONS

Explain the following statement: "Preferred stock is a hybrid security."

Is the equation used to value preferred stock more like the one used to evaluate a perpetual bond or the one used for common stock?

SUMMARY

Corporate decisions should be analyzed in terms of how alternative courses of action are likely to affect a firm's value. However, it is necessary to know how stock prices are established before attempting to measure how a given decision will affect a specific firm's value. This chapter showed how stock values are determined, and also how investors go about estimating the rates of return they expect to earn. The key concepts covered are listed below.

- A **proxy** is a document that gives one person the power to act for another, typically the power to vote shares of common stock. A **proxy fight** occurs when an outside group solicits stockholders' proxies in an effort to vote a new management team into office.
- A **takeover** occurs when a person or group succeeds in ousting a firm's management and takes control of the company.
- Stockholders often have the right to purchase any additional shares sold by the firm. This right, called the **preemptive right**, protects the control of the present stockholders and prevents dilution of their value.
- Although most firms have only one type of common stock, in some instances **classified stock** is used to meet the special needs of the company. One type is **founders' shares**. This is stock owned by the firm's founders that carries sole voting rights but restricted dividends for a specified number of years.
- **Closely held stock** is owned by a few individuals who are typically associated with the firm's management.
- **Publicly owned stock** is owned by a relatively large number of individuals who are not actively involved in the firm's management.
- Whenever stock in a closely held corporation is offered to the public for the first time, the company is said to be **going public**. The market for stock that is just being offered to the public is called the **initial public offering (IPO) market**.
- The intrinsic **value of a share of stock** is calculated as the **present value of the stream of dividends** the stock is expected to provide in the future.
- The equation used to find the **value of a constant growth stock** is:

$$\hat{P}_0 = \frac{D_1}{r_s - g}.$$

- The **expected total rate of return** from a stock consists of an **expected dividend yield** plus an **expected capital gains yield**. For a constant growth firm, both the expected dividend yield and the expected capital gains yield are constant.

- The equation for $\hat{r}_s$, the **expected rate of return on a constant growth stock,** can be expressed as follows:

$$\hat{r}_s = \frac{D_1}{P_0} + g.$$

- A **zero growth stock** is one whose future dividends are not expected to grow at all, while a **supernormal growth stock** is one whose earnings and dividends are expected to grow much faster than the economy as a whole over some specified time period and then to grow at the "normal" rate.
- To find the **present value of a supernormal growth stock,** (1) find the dividends expected during the supernormal growth period, (2) find the price of the stock at the end of the supernormal growth period, (3) discount the dividends and the projected price back to the present, and (4) sum these PVs to find the current value of the stock, $\hat{P}_0$.
- The **horizon (terminal) date** is the date when individual dividend forecasts are no longer made because the dividend growth rate is assumed to be constant.
- The **horizon (terminal) value** is the value at the horizon date of all future dividends after that date.
- The **marginal investor** is a representative investor whose actions reflect the beliefs of those people who are currently trading a stock. It is the marginal investor who determines a stock's price.
- **Equilibrium** is the condition under which the expected return on a security as seen by the marginal investor is just equal to its required return, $\hat{r} = r$. Also, the stock's intrinsic value must be equal to its market price, $\hat{P}_0 = P_0$.
- The **Efficient Markets Hypothesis (EMH)** holds (1) that stocks are always in equilibrium and (2) that it is impossible for an investor who does not have inside information to consistently "beat the market." Therefore, according to the EMH, stocks are always fairly valued ($\hat{P}_0 = P_0$), the required return on a stock is equal to its expected return ($r = \hat{r}$), and all stocks' expected returns plot on the SML.
- Differences can and do exist between expected and realized returns in the stock and bond markets—only for short-term, risk-free assets are expected and actual (or realized) returns equal.
- When U.S. investors purchase foreign stocks, they hope (1) that stock prices will increase in the local market and (2) that the foreign currencies will rise relative to the U.S. dollar.
- **Preferred stock** is a hybrid security having some characteristics of debt and some of equity.
- Most preferred stocks are **perpetuities,** and the value of a share of perpetual preferred stock is found as the dividend divided by the required rate of return:

$$V_{ps} = \frac{D_{ps}}{r_{ps}}.$$

- **Maturing preferred stock** is evaluated with a formula that is identical in form to the bond value formula.

QUESTIONS

(7-1) Define each of the following terms:
   a. Proxy; proxy fight; takeover; preemptive right; classified stock; founders' shares
   b. Closely held stock; publicly owned stock
   c. Secondary market; primary market; going public; initial public offering (IPO)
   d. Intrinsic value ($\hat{P}_0$); market price (P_0)
   e. Required rate of return, r_s; expected rate of return, $\hat{r}_s$; actual, or realized, rate of return, $\bar{r}_s$
   f. Capital gains yield; dividend yield; expected total return
   g. Normal, or constant, growth; supernormal, or nonconstant, growth; zero growth stock

h. Equilibrium; Efficient Markets Hypothesis (EMH); three forms of EMH
i. Preferred stock

(7-2) Two investors are evaluating AT&T's stock for possible purchase. They agree on the expected value of D_1 and also on the expected future dividend growth rate. Further, they agree on the riskiness of the stock. However, one investor normally holds stocks for 2 years, while the other normally holds stocks for 10 years. On the basis of the type of analysis done in this chapter, they should both be willing to pay the same price for AT&T's stock. True or false? Explain.

(7-3) A bond that pays interest forever and has no maturity date is a perpetual bond. In what respect is a perpetual bond similar to a no-growth common stock, and to a share of preferred stock?

SELF-TEST PROBLEMS   Solutions Appear in Appendix A

(ST-1)
Constant Growth
Stock Valuation
Ewald Company's current stock price is $36, and its last dividend was $2.40. In view of Ewald's strong financial position and its consequent low risk, its required rate of return is only 12 percent. If dividends are expected to grow at a constant rate, g, in the future, and if r_s is expected to remain at 12 percent, what is Ewald's expected stock price 5 years from now?

(ST-2)
Supernormal Growth
Stock Valuation
Snyder Computer Chips Inc. is experiencing a period of rapid growth. Earnings and dividends are expected to grow at a rate of 15 percent during the next 2 years, at 13 percent in the third year, and at a constant rate of 6 percent thereafter. Snyder's last dividend was $1.15, and the required rate of return on the stock is 12 percent.
a. Calculate the value of the stock today.
b. Calculate $\hat{P}_1$ and $\hat{P}_2$.
c. Calculate the dividend yield and capital gains yield for Years 1, 2, and 3.

PROBLEMS

(7-1)
DPS Calculation
Warr Corporation just paid a dividend of $1.50 a share (i.e., $D_0 = \$1.50$). The dividend is expected to grow 5 percent a year for the next 3 years, and then 10 percent a year thereafter. What is the expected dividend per share for each of the next 5 years?

(7-2)
Constant Growth
Valuation
Thomas Brothers is expected to pay a $0.50 per share dividend at the end of the year (i.e., $D_1 = \$0.50$). The dividend is expected to grow at a constant rate of 7 percent a year. The required rate of return on the stock, r_s, is 15 percent. What is the value per share of the company's stock?

(7-3)
Constant Growth
Valuation
Harrison Clothiers' stock currently sells for $20 a share. The stock just paid a dividend of $1.00 a share (i.e., $D_0 = \$1.00$). The dividend is expected to grow at a constant rate of 10 percent a year. What stock price is expected 1 year from now? What is the required rate of return on the company's stock?

(7-4)
Preferred Stock
Valuation
Fee Founders has preferred stock outstanding which pays a dividend of $5 at the end of each year. The preferred stock sells for $60 a share. What is the preferred stock's required rate of return?

(7-5)
Supernormal Growth
Valuation
A company currently pays a dividend of $2 per share, $D_0 = 2$. It is estimated that the company's dividend will grow at a rate of 20 percent per year for the next 2 years, then the dividend will grow at a constant rate of 7 percent thereafter. The company's stock has a beta equal to 1.2, the risk-free rate is 7.5 percent, and the market risk premium is 4 percent. What would you estimate is the stock's current price?

(7-6)
Constant Growth
Rate, g
A stock is trading at $80 per share. The stock is expected to have a year-end dividend of $4 per share ($D_1 = 4$), which is expected to grow at some constant rate g throughout time. The stock's required rate of return is 14 percent. If you are an analyst who believes in efficient markets, what is your forecast of g?

(7-7)
Constant Growth
Valuation
You are considering an investment in the common stock of Keller Corp. The stock is expected to pay a dividend of $2 a share at the end of the year ($D_1 = \$2.00$). The stock has a beta equal to 0.9. The risk-free rate is 5.6 percent, and the market risk premium is 6 percent. The stock's dividend is expected to grow at some constant rate g. The stock currently sells for $25 a share. Assuming the market is in equilibrium, what does the market believe will be the stock price at the end of 3 years? (That is, what is $\hat{P}_3$?)

(7-8)
Preferred Stock
Rate of Return
What will be the nominal rate of return on a preferred stock with a $100 par value, a stated dividend of 8 percent of par, and a current market price of (a) $60, (b) $80, (c) $100, and (d) $140?

(7-9)
Declining Growth
Stock Valuation
Martell Mining Company's ore reserves are being depleted, so its sales are falling. Also, its pit is getting deeper each year, so its costs are rising. As a result, the company's earnings and dividends are declining at the constant rate of 5 percent per year. If $D_0 = \$5$ and $r_s = 15\%$, what is the value of Martell Mining's stock?

(7-10)
Rates of Return
and Equilibrium
The beta coefficient for Stock C is $b_C = 0.4$, whereas that for Stock D is $b_D = -0.5$. (Stock D's beta is negative, indicating that its rate of return rises whenever returns on most other stocks fall. There are very few negative beta stocks, although collection agency stocks are sometimes cited as an example.)
a. If the risk-free rate is 9 percent and the expected rate of return on an average stock is 13 percent, what are the required rates of return on Stocks C and D?
b. For Stock C, suppose the current price, P_0, is $25; the next expected dividend, D_1, is $1.50; and the stock's expected constant growth rate is 4 percent. Is the stock in equilibrium? Explain, and describe what will happen if the stock is not in equilibrium.

(7-11)
Supernormal Growth
Stock Valuation
Assume that the average firm in your company's industry is expected to grow at a constant rate of 6 percent and its dividend yield is 7 percent. Your company is about as risky as the average firm in the industry, but it has just successfully completed some R&D work that leads you to expect that its earnings and dividends will grow at a rate of 50 percent $[D_1 = D_0(1 + g) = D_0(1.50)]$ this year and 25 percent the following year, after which growth should match the 6 percent industry average rate. The last dividend paid (D_0) was $1. What is the value per share of your firm's stock?

(7-12)
Supernormal Growth
Stock Valuation
Microtech Corporation is expanding rapidly, and it currently needs to retain all of its earnings, hence it does not pay any dividends. However, investors expect Microtech to begin paying dividends, with the first dividend of $1.00 coming 3 years from today. The dividend should grow rapidly—at a rate of 50 percent per year—during Years 4 and 5. After Year 5, the company should grow at a constant rate of 8 percent per year. If the required return on the stock is 15 percent, what is the value of the stock today?

(7-13)
Preferred Stock
Valuation
Ezzell Corporation issued preferred stock with a stated dividend of 10 percent of par. Preferred stock of this type currently yields 8 percent, and the par value is $100. Assume dividends are paid annually.
a. What is the value of Ezzell's preferred stock?
b. Suppose interest rate levels rise to the point where the preferred stock now yields 12 percent. What would be the value of Ezzell's preferred stock?

(7-14)
Constant Growth
Stock Valuation
Your broker offers to sell you some shares of Bahnsen & Co. common stock that paid a dividend of $2 *yesterday*. You expect the dividend to grow at the rate of 5 percent per year for the next 3 years, and, if you buy the stock, you plan to hold it for 3 years and then sell it.
a. Find the expected dividend for each of the next 3 years; that is, calculate D_1, D_2, and D_3. Note that $D_0 = \$2$.
b. Given that the appropriate discount rate is 12 percent and that the first of these dividend payments will occur 1 year from now, find the present value of the dividend stream; that is, calculate the PV of D_1, D_2, and D_3, and then sum these PVs.
c. You expect the price of the stock 3 years from now to be $34.73; that is, you expect $\hat{P}_3$ to equal $34.73. Discounted at a 12 percent rate, what is the present value of this expected future stock price? In other words, calculate the PV of $34.73.

    d. If you plan to buy the stock, hold it for 3 years, and then sell it for $34.73, what is the most you should pay for it?

    e. Use Equation 7-2 to calculate the present value of this stock. Assume that g = 5%, and it is constant.

    f. Is the value of this stock dependent upon how long you plan to hold it? In other words, if your planned holding period were 2 years or 5 years rather than 3 years, would this affect the value of the stock today, $\hat{P}_0$?

(7-15)
Return on
Common Stock

You buy a share of The Ludwig Corporation stock for $21.40. You expect it to pay dividends of $1.07, $1.1449, and $1.2250 in Years 1, 2, and 3, respectively, and you expect to sell it at a price of $26.22 at the end of 3 years.

    a. Calculate the growth rate in dividends.

    b. Calculate the expected dividend yield.

    c. Assuming that the calculated growth rate is expected to continue, you can add the dividend yield to the expected growth rate to get the expected total rate of return. What is this stock's expected total rate of return?

(7-16)
Constant Growth
Stock Valuation

Investors require a 15 percent rate of return on Levine Company's stock ($r_s = 15\%$).

    a. What will be Levine's stock value if the previous dividend was $D_0 = \$2$ and if investors expect dividends to grow at a constant compound annual rate of (1) −5 percent, (2) 0 percent, (3) 5 percent, and (4) 10 percent?

    b. Using data from part a, what is the Gordon (constant growth) model value for Levine's stock if the required rate of return is 15 percent and the expected growth rate is (1) 15 percent or (2) 20 percent? Are these reasonable results? Explain.

    c. Is it reasonable to expect that a constant growth stock would have $g > r_s$?

(7-17)
Supernormal Growth
Stock Valuation

Wayne-Martin Electric Inc. (WME) has just developed a solar panel capable of generating 200 percent more electricity than any solar panel currently on the market. As a result, WME is expected to experience a 15 percent annual growth rate for the next 5 years. By the end of 5 years, other firms will have developed comparable technology, and WME's growth rate will slow to 5 percent per year indefinitely. Stockholders require a return of 12 percent on WME's stock. The most recent annual dividend (D_0), which was paid yesterday, was $1.75 per share.

    a. Calculate WME's expected dividends for t = 1, t = 2, t = 3, t = 4, and t = 5.

    b. Calculate the value of the stock today, $\hat{P}_0$. Proceed by finding the present value of the dividends expected at t = 1, t = 2, t = 3, t = 4, and t = 5 plus the present value of the stock price which should exist at t = 5, $\hat{P}_5$. The $\hat{P}_5$ stock price can be found by using the constant growth equation. Notice that to find $\hat{P}_5$, you use the dividend expected at t = 6, which is 5 percent greater than the t = 5 dividend.

    c. Calculate the expected dividend yield, D_1/P_0, the capital gains yield expected during the first year, and the expected total return (dividend yield plus capital gains yield) during the first year. (Assume that $\hat{P}_0 = P_0$, and recognize that the capital gains yield is equal to the total return minus the dividend yield.) Also calculate these same three yields for t = 5 (e.g., D_6/P_5).

(7-18)
Supernormal Growth
Stock Valuation

Taussig Technologies Corporation (TTC) has been growing at a rate of 20 percent per year in recent years. This same growth rate is expected to last for another 2 years.

    a. If $D_0 = \$1.60$, $r_s = 10\%$, and $g_n = 6\%$, what is TTC's stock worth today? What are its expected dividend yield and capital gains yield at this time?

    b. Now assume that TTC's period of supernormal growth is to last another 5 years rather than 2 years. How would this affect its price, dividend yield, and capital gains yield? Answer in words only.

    c. What will be TTC's dividend yield and capital gains yield once its period of supernormal growth ends? (Hint: These values will be the same regardless of whether you examine the case of 2 or 5 years of supernormal growth; the calculations are very easy.)

    d. Of what interest to investors is the changing relationship between dividend yield and capital gains yield over time?

(7-19)

Equilibrium Stock Price

The risk-free rate of return, r_{RF}, is 11 percent; the required rate of return on the market, r_M, 14 percent; and Upton Company's stock has a beta coefficient of 1.5.

   a. If the dividend expected during the coming year, D_1, is $2.25, and if g = a constant 5%, at what price should Upton's stock sell?

   b. Now, suppose the Federal Reserve Board increases the money supply, causing the risk-free rate to drop to 9 percent and r_M to fall to 12 percent. What would this do to the price of the stock?

   c. In addition to the change in part b, suppose investors' risk aversion declines; this fact, combined with the decline in r_{RF}, causes r_M to fall to 11 percent. At what price would Upton's stock sell?

   d. Now, suppose Upton has a change in management. The new group institutes policies that increase the expected constant growth rate to 6 percent. Also, the new management stabilizes sales and profits, and thus causes the beta coefficient to decline from 1.5 to 1.3. Assume that r_{RF} and r_M are equal to the values in part c. After all these changes, what is Upton's new equilibrium price? (Note: D_1 goes to $2.27.)

e-resource

SPREADSHEET PROBLEM

(7-20)

Build a Model:
Supernormal Growth and
Corporate Valuation

Start with the partial model in the file *CF2 Ch 07 P20 Build a Model.xls* from the textbook's Web site. Rework Problem 7-18, parts a, b, and c, using a spreadsheet model. For part b, calculate the price, dividend yield, and capital gains yield as called for in the problem.

CYBERPROBLEM

Please go to our Web site, **http://ehrhardt.swlearning.com**, to access any Cyberproblems.

THOMSON ONE
Business School Edition

Please go to **http://ehrhardt.swlearning.com** to access any Thomson ONE—Business School Edition problems.

MINI CASE

Sam Strother and Shawna Tibbs are senior vice-presidents of Mutual of Seattle. They are co-directors of the company's pension fund management division, with Strother having responsibility for fixed income securities (primarily bonds) and Tibbs being responsible for equity investments. A major new client, the Northwestern Municipal Alliance, has requested that Mutual of Seattle present an investment seminar to the mayors of the represented cities, and Strother and Tibbs, who will make the actual presentation, have asked you to help them.

To illustrate the common stock valuation process, Strother and Tibbs have asked you to analyze the Temp Force Company, an employment agency that supplies word processor operators and computer programmers to businesses with temporarily heavy workloads. You are to answer the following questions.

a. Describe briefly the legal rights and privileges of common stockholders.

b. (1) Write out a formula that can be used to value any stock, regardless of its dividend pattern.

   (2) What is a constant growth stock? How are constant growth stocks valued?

   (3) What happens if a company has a constant g which exceeds its r_s? Will many stocks have expected g > r_s in the short run (i.e., for the next few years)? In the long run (i.e., forever)?

c. Assume that Temp Force has a beta coefficient of 1.2, that the risk-free rate (the yield on T-bonds) is 7.0 percent, and that the market risk premium is 5 percent. What is the required rate of return on the firm's stock?

d. Assume that Temp Force is a constant growth company whose last dividend (D_0, which was paid yesterday) was $2.00 and whose dividend is expected to grow indefinitely at a 6 percent rate.

   (1) What is the firm's expected dividend stream over the next 3 years?

   (2) What is the firm's current stock price?

   (3) What is the stock's expected value 1 year from now?

   (4) What are the expected dividend yield, the capital gains yield, and the total return during the first year?

e. Now assume that the stock is currently selling at $30.29. What is the expected rate of return on the stock?

f. What would the stock price be if its dividends were expected to have zero growth?

g. Now assume that Temp Force is expected to experience supernormal growth of 30 percent for the next 3 years, then to return to its long-run constant growth rate of 6 percent. What is the stock's value under these conditions? What is its expected dividend yield and capital gains yield in Year 1? In Year 4?

h. Is the stock price based more on long-term or short-term expectations? Answer this by finding the percentage of Temp Force's current stock price based on dividends expected more than 3 years in the future.

i. Suppose Temp Force is expected to experience zero growth during the first 3 years and then to resume its steady-state growth of 6 percent in the fourth year. What is the stock's value now? What is its expected dividend yield and its capital gains yield in Year 1? In Year 4?

j. Finally, assume that Temp Force's earnings and dividends are expected to decline by a constant 6 percent per year, that is, $g = -6\%$. Why would anyone be willing to buy such a stock, and at what price should it sell? What would be the dividend yield and capital gains yield in each year?

k. What is market multiple analysis?

l. Why do stock prices change? Suppose the expected D_1 is $2, the growth rate is 5 percent, and r_s is 10 percent. Using the constant growth model, what is the price? What is the impact on stock price if g is 4 percent or 6 percent? If r_s is 9 percent or 11 percent?

m. What does market equilibrium mean?

n. If equilibrium does not exist, how will it be established?

o. What is the Efficient Markets Hypothesis, what are its three forms, and what are its implications?

p. Temp Force recently issued preferred stock. It pays an annual dividend of $5, and the issue price was $50 per share. What is the expected return to an investor on this preferred stock?

SELECTED ADDITIONAL REFERENCES AND CASES

Many investment textbooks cover stock valuation models in depth, and some are listed in the Chapter 5 references.

For some works on valuation, see

Bey, Roger P., and J. Markham Collins, "The Relationship between Before- and After-Tax Yields on Financial Assets," *The Financial Review,* August 1988, 313–343.

Brooks, Robert, and Billy Helms, "An N-Stage, Fractional Period, Quarterly Dividend Discount Model," *Financial Review,* November 1990, 651–657.

The following cases from the Finance Online Case Library *cover many of the concepts discussed in this chapter and are available at http://www.textchoice.com:*

Case 3, "Peachtree Securities, Inc. (B)"; Case 43, "Swan-Davis"; Case 49, "Beatrice Peabody"; and Case 101, "TECO Energy."

CHAPTER 8

Financial Options, Their Valuation, and Applications in Corporate Finance

Microsoft has granted more than 800 million options to its employees, or about 16,000 options per person. Of course, many employees have fewer options and some have more, but any way you cut it, that's a lot of options. Microsoft is not the only company making mega-grants: Bank of America, Citigroup, IBM, JP Morgan Chase, and Ford are among the many companies that have granted more than 100 million options to their employees. Whether your next job is with a high-tech firm like Microsoft, a financial services company like Citigroup, or a manufacturer like Ford, you will probably receive stock options, so it's important for you to understand them.

In a typical grant, you receive stock options allowing you to purchase shares of stock at a fixed "exercise" price on or before an expiration date. Most plans have a vesting period, during which you can't exercise the options. For example, suppose you are granted 1,000 options with an exercise price of $50, an expiration date of 10 years, and a vesting period of three years. Even if the stock price rises above $50 during the first three years, you can't exercise the options, due to the vesting requirement. After three years, if you have remained with the company, you have the right to exercise the options. For example, if the stock goes up to $110, you could pay the company $50(1,000) = $50,000 and receive stock worth $110,000. However, if you don't exercise the options within ten years, they expire worthless.

Even though the vesting requirement prevents you from exercising the options at the moment they are granted to you, the options clearly have some value. Therefore, when evaluating different job offers, you will need a way to determine the value of those options. This chapter will describe two valuation approaches, so read on.

Every manager should understand the basic principles of option pricing. First, many projects allow managerial intervention as market conditions change. These "embedded options" often mean the difference between a successful project and a failure. Understanding basic financial options helps to manage the value inherent in these real options. Second, many companies use derivatives to manage risk, and understanding financial options is necessary before tackling derivatives. Third, option pricing theory provides insights into the optimal debt/equity choice, especially when convertible securities are involved. Finally, understanding financial options will help you with any employee stock options that you receive.

FINANCIAL OPTIONS

e-resource

The textbook's Web site contains an Excel file that will guide you through the chapter's calculations. The file for this chapter is **CF2 Ch 08 Tool Kit.xls,** *and we encourage you to open the file and follow along as you read the chapter.*

An **option** is a contract that gives its holder the right to buy (or sell) an asset at some predetermined price within a specified period of time. The following sections explain the different features that affect an option's value.

Option Types and Markets

There are many types of options and option markets.[1] To illustrate how options work, suppose you owned 100 shares of General Computer Corporation (GCC), which on Friday, January 9, 2005, sold for $53.50 per share. You could sell to someone the right to buy your 100 shares at any time until May 14, 2005, at a price of, say, $55 per share. This is called an **American option,** because it can be exercised any time before it expires. By contrast, a **European option** can only be exercised on its expiration date. The $55 is called the **strike,** or **exercise, price.** The last day that the option can be exercised is called the **expiration date.** Such options exist, and they are traded on a number of exchanges, with the Chicago Board Options Exchange (CBOE) being the oldest and the largest. This type of option is defined as a **call option,** because the buyer has a "call" on 100 shares of stock. The seller of an option is called the option *writer.* An investor who "writes" call options against stock held in his or her portfolio is said to be selling **covered options.** Options sold without the stock to back them up are called **naked options.** When the exercise price exceeds the current stock price, a call option is said to be **out-of-the-money.** When the exercise price is less than the current price of the stock, the option is **in-the-money.**

You can also buy an option that gives you the right to *sell* a stock at a specified price within some future period—this is called a **put option.** For example, suppose you think GCC's stock price is likely to decline from its current level of $53.50 sometime during the next four months. A put option will give you the right to sell at a fixed price even after the market price declines. You could then buy at the new lower market price, sell at the higher fixed price, and earn a profit. Table 8-1 provides data on GCC's options. You could buy the four-month May put option for $218.75 ($2\frac{3}{16} \times 100$). That would give you the right to sell 100 shares (that you would not necessarily own) at a price of $50 per share ($50 is the strike price). Suppose you bought this 100-share contract for $218.75 and then GCC's stock fell to $45. You could buy the stock on the open market at $45 and exercise your put option by selling the stock at $50. Your profit from exercising the option would be ($50 –$45)(100) = $500. After subtracting the $218.75 you paid for the option, your profit (before taxes and commissions) would be $281.25.

Table 8-1 contains an extract from the Listed Options Quotations Table as it would appear the next day in a daily newspaper. Sport World's February $55 call option sold for $0.50. Thus, for $0.50(100) = $50 you could buy options that would give you the right

---

[1] For an in-depth treatment of options, see Don M. Chance, *An Introduction to Derivatives and Risk Management* (Mason, OH: South-Western Publishing, 2001).

TABLE 8-1 | January 7, 2005, Listed Options Quotations

Closing Price	Strike Price	CALLS—LAST QUOTE			PUTS—LAST QUOTE		
		February	March	May	February	March	May
General Computer Corporation (GCC)							
53½	50	4¼	4¾	5½	⅝	1⅜	2³⁄₁₆
53½	55	1⁵⁄₁₆	2¹⁄₁₆	3⅛	2⅝	r	4½
53½	60	⁵⁄₁₆	¹¹⁄₁₆	1½	6⅝	r	8
U.S. Medical							
56⅝	55	4¼	5⅛	7	2¼	3¾	r
Sport World							
53⅛	55	½	1⅛	r	2⅛	r	r

Note: r means not traded on January 7.

The Chicago Board Options Exchange provides 20-minute delayed quotes for equity, index, and LEAPS options at http://www.cboe.com.

to buy 100 shares of Sport World stock at a price of $55 per share from January until February, or during the next month.[2] If the stock price stayed below $55 during that period, you would lose your $50, but if it rose to $65, your $50 investment would increase in value to ($65 − $55)(100) = $1,000 in less than 30 days. That translates into a very healthy annualized rate of return. Incidentally, if the stock price did go up, you would not actually exercise your options and buy the stock—rather, you would sell the options, which would then have a value of at least $1,000 versus the $50 you paid, to another option buyer or to the original seller.

In addition to options on individual stocks, options are also available on several stock indexes such as the NYSE Index and the S&P 100 Index. Index options permit one to hedge (or bet) on a rise or fall in the general market as well as on individual stocks.

Option trading is one of the hottest financial activities in the United States. The leverage involved makes it possible for speculators with just a few dollars to make a fortune almost overnight. Also, investors with sizable portfolios can sell options against their stocks and earn the value of the option (less brokerage commissions), even if the stock's price remains constant. Most importantly, though, options can be used to create *hedges* that protect the value of an individual stock or portfolio.[3]

Conventional options are generally written for six months or less, but a type of option called a **Long-term Equity AnticiPation Security (LEAPS)** is different. Like conventional options, LEAPS are listed on exchanges and are available on both individual stocks and stock indexes. The major difference is that LEAPS are long-term options, having maturities of up to 2½ years. One-year LEAPS cost about twice as much as the matching three-month option, but because of their much longer time to expiration, LEAPS provide buyers with more potential for gains and offer better long-term protection for a portfolio.

Corporations on whose stocks options are written have nothing to do with the option market. Corporations do not raise money in the option market, nor do they have any direct transactions in it. Moreover, option holders do not vote for corporate directors or receive dividends. There have been studies by the SEC and others as to whether option

---

[2] Actually, the expiration date is the Friday before the third Saturday of the exercise month. Also, note that option contracts are generally written in 100-share multiples.

[3] Insiders who trade illegally generally buy options rather than stock because the leverage inherent in options increases the profit potential. Note, though, that it is illegal to use insider information for personal gain, and an insider using such information would be taking advantage of the option seller. Insider trading, in addition to being unfair and essentially equivalent to stealing, hurts the economy: Investors lose confidence in the capital markets and raise their required returns because of an increased element of risk, and this raises the cost of capital and thus reduces the level of real investment.

trading stabilizes or destabilizes the stock market, and whether this activity helps or hinders corporations seeking to raise new capital. The studies have not been conclusive, but option trading is here to stay, and many regard it as the most exciting game in town.

Factors That Affect the Value of a Call Option

Table 8-1 can provide some insights into call option valuation. First, we see that at least three factors affect a call option's value:

1. *Market price versus strike price.* The higher the stock's market price in relation to the strike price, the higher will be the call option price. Thus, Sport World's $55 February call option sells for $0.50, whereas U.S. Medical's $55 February option sells for $4.25. This difference arises because U.S. Medical's current stock price is $56⅝ versus only $53⅛ for Sport World.

2. *Level of strike price.* The higher the strike price, the lower the call option price. Thus, all of GCC's call options, regardless of exercise month, decline as the strike price increases.

3. *Length of option.* The longer the option period, the higher the option price. This occurs because the longer the time before expiration, the greater the chance that the stock price will climb substantially above the exercise price. Thus, option prices increase as the expiration date is lengthened.

Other factors that affect option values, especially the volatility of the underlying stock, are discussed in later sections.

Exercise Value versus Option Price

How is the actual price of a call option determined in the market? In a later section, we present a widely used model (the Black-Scholes model) for pricing call options, but first it is useful to establish some basic concepts. To begin, we define a call option's **exercise value** as follows:[4]

$$\text{Exercise value} = \text{MAX [Current price of the stock} - \text{Strike price, 0]}.$$

The exercise value is what the option would be worth if it expired immediately. For example, if a stock sells for $50 and its option has a strike price of $20, then you could buy the stock for $20 by exercising the option. You would own a stock worth $50, but you would have to pay only $20. Therefore, the option would be worth $30 if you had to exercise it immediately. The minimum exercise value is zero, because no one would exercise an out-of-the-money option.

Figure 8-1 presents some data on Space Technology Inc. (STI), a company that recently went public and whose stock price has fluctuated widely during its short history. The third column in the tabular data shows the exercise values for STI's call option when the stock was selling at different prices; the fourth column gives the actual market prices for the option; and the fifth column shows the premium of the actual option price over its exercise value.

First, notice that the market value of the option is zero when the stock price is zero. This is because a stock price falls to zero only when there is no possibility that the company would ever generate any future cash flows; in other words, the company must be out of business. In such a situation, an option would be worthless.

Second, notice that the market price of the option is always greater than or equal to the exercise value. If the option price ever fell below the exercise value, then you could

---

[4] MAX means choose the maximum. For example, MAX[15,0] = 15, and MAX[−10,0] = 0.

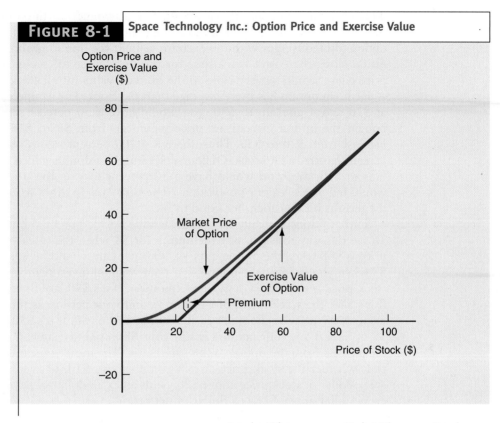

FIGURE 8-1   Space Technology Inc.: Option Price and Exercise Value

Price of Stock (1)	Strike Price (2)	Exercise Value of Option MAX[(1) − (2), o] = (3)	Market Price of Option (4)	Premium (4) − (3) = (5)
$10.00	$20.00	$ 0.00	$ 2.00	$2.00
20.00	20.00	0.00	8.00	8.00
21.00	20.00	1.00	8.75	7.75
22.00	20.00	2.00	9.50	7.50
30.00	20.00	10.00	16.00	6.00
40.00	20.00	20.00	24.50	4.50
50.00	20.00	30.00	33.50	3.50
73.00	20.00	53.00	54.50	1.50
98.00	20.00	78.00	79.00	1.00

buy the option and immediately exercise it, reaping a riskless profit. Because everyone would try to do this, the price of the option would be driven up until it was at least as high as the exercise value.

Third, notice that the market value of the option is greater than zero even when the option is out-of-the-money. For example, the option price is $2 when the stock price is only $10. Depending on the remaining time until expiration and the stock's volatility, there is a chance that the stock price will rise above $20, so the option has value even if it is out-of-the-money.

Fourth, Figure 8-1 shows the value of the option steadily increasing as the stock price increases. This shouldn't be surprising, since the option's expected payoff increases along with the stock price. But notice that as the stock price rises, the option price and exercise value begin to converge, causing the premium to get smaller and smaller. This happens because there is virtually no chance that the stock will be out-of-the-money at expiration if the stock price is presently very high. Thus, owning the option is like owning the stock, less the exercise price. Although we don't show it in Figure 8-1, the market price of the option also converges with the exercise value if the option is about to expire. With expiration close, there isn't much time for the stock price to change, so the option's market price curve would be very close to the exercise value for all stock prices.

Fifth, an option has more leverage than the stock. For example, if you buy STI's stock at $20 and it goes up to $30, you would have a 50 percent rate of return. But if you bought the option instead, its price would go from $8 to $16 versus the stock price increase from $20 to $30. Thus, there is a 100 percent return on the option versus a 50 percent return on the stock. Of course, leverage is a double-edged sword: If the stock price falls to $10, then you would have a 50 percent loss on the stock, but the option price would fall to $2, leaving you with a 75 percent loss. In other words, the option magnifies the returns on the stock, for good or ill.

Sixth, options typically have considerable upside potential but limited downside risk. To see this, suppose you buy the option for $8 when the stock price is $20. If the stock price is $28 when the option expires, your net gain would be $0: you gain $28 − $20 = $8 when you exercise the option, but your original investment was $8. Now suppose the stock price is either $30 or $20 at expiration. If it's $30, your net gain is $10 − $8 = $2. If it's $20, the stock is out-of-the-money, and your net loss is the $8 cost of your investment. Now suppose the stock price is either $50 or $5. If it's $50, your net gain is $30 − $8 = $22; if $5, your net loss is still your $8 initial investment. As this example shows, the payoffs from the option aren't symmetric. The most you can lose is $8, and this happens whether the stock price at expiration is $20, $10, or even $1. On the other hand, every dollar of stock price above $20 yields an extra dollar of payoff from the option, and every dollar above $28 is a dollar of net profit.

In addition to the stock price and the exercise price, the price of an option depends on three other factors: (1) the option's term to maturity, (2) the variability of the stock price, and (3) the risk-free rate. We will explain precisely how these factors affect call option prices later, but for now, note these points:

1. The longer a call option has to run, the greater its value and the larger its premium. If an option expires at 4 P.M. today, there is not much chance that the stock price will go up very much, so the option will sell at close to its exercise value and its premium will be small. On the other hand, if the expiration date is a year away, the stock price could rise sharply, pulling the option's value up with it.

2. An option on an extremely volatile stock is worth more than one on a very stable stock. If the stock price rarely moves, then there is little chance of a large gain on the stock, hence the option will not be worth much. However, if the stock is highly volatile, the option could easily become very valuable. At the same time, losses on options are limited—you can make an unlimited amount, but you can lose only what you paid for the option. Therefore, a large decline in a stock's price does not have a corresponding bad effect on option holders. As a result of the unlimited upside but limited downside potential, the more volatile a stock, the higher the value of its options.

3. Options will be exercised in the future, and part of a call option's value depends on the present value of the cost to exercise it. If interest rates are high, then the present value of the cost to exercise is low, which increases the option's value.

Because of Points 1 and 2, a graph such as Figure 8-1 would show that the longer an option's life, the higher its market price line would be above the exercise value line. Similarly, the more volatile the price of the underlying stock, the higher would be the market price line. We will see precisely how these factors, and also the risk-free rate, affect option values when we discuss the Black-Scholes model.

FINANCIAL STATEMENTS AND EMPLOYEE STOCK OPTIONS

When granted to executives and other employees, options are a "hybrid" form of compensation. At some companies, especially small ones, option grants may be a substitute for cash wages—employees are willing to take lower cash salaries if they also have options. Options also provide an incentive for employees to work harder. Whether issued to motivate employees or to conserve cash, options clearly have value at the time they are granted, and they transfer wealth from existing shareholders to employees to the extent that they do not reduce cash expenditures or increase employee productivity sufficiently to offset their value at the time of issue.

Companies like the fact that an option grant requires no immediate cash expenditure, although it might dilute shareholder wealth if it is later exercised. Employees, and especially CEOs, like the potential wealth that they receive when they are granted options. When option grants were relatively small, they didn't show up on investors' radar screens. However, as the high-tech sector began making mega-grants in the 1990s, and as other industries followed suit in the heavy use of

options, stockholders began to realize that large grants were making some CEOs filthy rich at the stockholders' expense.

Before 2005, option grants were not very visible in companies' financial reports. Even though such grants are clearly a wealth transfer to employees, companies were only required to footnote the grants and could ignore them when reporting their income statements and balance sheets before 2005. As we write this in late 2004, the Financial Accounting Standard Board has proposed that companies must show option grants as an expense on the income statement. To do this, the value of the grant is estimated at the time of the grant and then expensed during the vesting period. For example, if the initial value is $100 million and the vesting period is two years, the company would report a $50 million expense for each of the next two years. This approach isn't perfect because it isn't a cash expense, and it does not take into account changes in the option's value after it is initially granted. However, it does make the option grant more visible to investors, which is a good thing.

What is an option? A call option? A put option?

Define a call option's exercise value. Why is the actual market price of a call option usually above its exercise value?

What are some factors that affect a call option's value?

INTRODUCTION TO OPTION PRICING MODELS: THE BINOMIAL APPROACH

All option pricing models are based on the concept of a **riskless hedge.** The purpose of such a hedge isn't to create a riskless security—you can buy Treasury securities for that—but, instead, to determine how much an option is worth. To see how this works, suppose a hypothetical investor, we'll call her the *hedger*, buys some shares of stock and simultaneously writes a call option on the stock. As a result of writing the call option, our hedger (1) receives a payment from the call option's purchaser and (2) assumes an obligation to satisfy the purchaser if he or she chooses to exercise the option. Let's focus only on the hedger's portfolio, which contains stock and the obligation to satisfy the option's purchaser (we'll solve for the amount the hedger receives for selling the option in just a bit). If the stock price goes up, the hedger will earn a profit on the stock. However, the option holder will then exercise the option, our hedger will have to sell a share of stock to the option holder at the exercise price (which is below the market price) and that will reduce our hedger's profit on the stock's gain. Conversely, if the stock goes down, our hedger will lose on her stock investment, but she won't lose as much in satisfying the option: If the stock goes down a lot, the option holder won't exercise the option, and the hedger will owe nothing; if the stock goes down a little, then the hedger might still have to sell a share at a below-market price to satisfy the option holder, but the market price will be closer to the exercise price, so the hedger will lose less. As we will soon show, it is possible to create the portfolio such that the hedger will end up with a riskless position—the value of the portfolio will be the same regardless of what the stock does.

If the portfolio is riskless, then its return must be equal to the riskless rate in order to keep the market in equilibrium. If the portfolio offered a higher rate of return than the riskless rate, arbitrageurs would buy the portfolio and in the process push the price up and the rate of return down, and vice versa if it offered less than the riskless rate. Given the price of the stock, its volatility, the option's exercise price, the life of the option, and the risk-free rate, there is a single option price that satisfies the equilibrium condition, namely, that the portfolio will earn the riskless rate.

The following example applies the **binomial approach**, so named because we assume the stock price can take on only one of two possible values at the end of each period. The stock of Western Cellular, a manufacturer of cell phones, sells for $40 per share. Options exist that permit the holder to buy one share of Western at an exercise price of $35. These options will expire at the end of one year. The steps to the binomial approach are shown below.

STEP 1. **Define the possible ending prices of the stock.** Let's assume that Western's stock will be selling at one of two prices at the end of the year, either $50 or $32. If there is a 70 percent chance of the $50 price, then Western's expected price is 0.7($50) + 0.3($32) = $44.6.[5] Because the current stock price is $40, Western has an 11.5 percent expected return: ($44.6 − $40)/$40 = 0.115 = 11.5%. If Western were a riskier stock, then we would have assumed different ending prices that had a wider range and possibly a higher expected return. See the Web Extension to this chapter for a more detailed explanation of the relationship between the stock's risk and the possible ending stock prices. Figure 8-2 illustrates the stock's possible price paths, and contains additional information that is explained below.

STEP 2. **Find the range of values at expiration.** When the option expires at the end of the year, Western's stock will sell for either $50 or $32, a range of $50 − $32 = $18. As shown in Figure 8-2, the option will pay $15 if the stock is $50, because this is above the exercise price of $35: $50 − $35 = $15. The option will pay nothing if the stock price is $32, because this is below the exercise price. The range of option payoffs is $15 − $0 = $15. The hedger's portfolio consists of the stock and the obligation to satisfy the option holder, so the value of the portfolio in one year is the stock price minus the option payoff.

STEP 3. **Buy exactly enough stock to equalize the range of payoffs for the stock and the option.** Figure 8-2 shows that the ranges of payoffs for the stock and the option are $18 and $15. To construct the riskless portfolio, we need to equalize these ranges so that the profits from the stock exactly offset the losses in satisfying the option holder. We do so by buying $15/$18 = 0.8333 share and selling one option (or 8,333 shares and 10,000 options).[6] In this case, the current value of the stock in the portfolio is $40(0.8333) = $33.33. The value of the portfolio's stock at the end of the year will be either $50(0.8333) = $41.67 or $32(0.8333) = $26.67. As shown in Figure 8-3, the range of the stock's ending value is now $41.67 − $26.67 = $15.

---

[5] As we'll soon show, we don't have to specify the probability of the ending prices to calculate the option price.

[6] Here is why equalizing ranges gives the correct number of shares of stock. Let P_u be the stock price if it goes up, P_d the stock price if it goes down, C_u the call option payoff if the stock goes up, C_d the call option payoff if the stock goes down, and N the number of shares of stock. We want the portfolio value to be the same whether the stock is high or low. The portfolio value for a high stock price is $N(P_u) - C_u$, and the value for a low stock price is $N(P_d) - C_d$. Setting these equal and solving for N yields $N = \dfrac{C_u - C_d}{P_u - P_d}$, which is the same as equalizing the ranges.

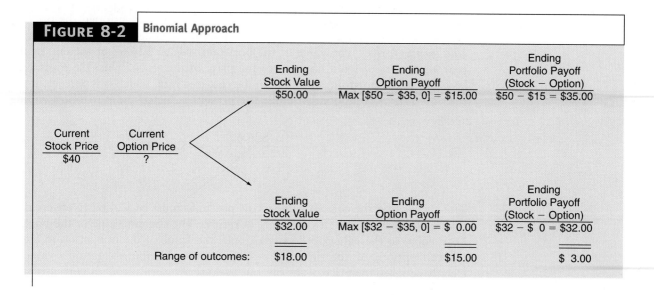

FIGURE 8-2   **Binomial Approach**

STEP 4. **Create a riskless hedged investment.** We created a riskless portfolio by buying 0.8333 share of the stock and selling one call option, as shown in Figure 8-3. The stock in the portfolio will have a value of either $41.67 or $26.67, depending on the ending price of Western's stock. The call option that was sold will have no effect on the value of the portfolio if Western's price falls to $32 because it will not be exercised—it will expire worthless. However, if the stock price ends at $50, the holder of the option will exercise it, paying the $35 exercise price for stock that would cost $50 on the open market. The option holder's profit is the option writer's loss, so the option will cost the hedger $15. Now note that the value of the portfolio is $26.67 regardless of whether Western's stock goes up or down, so the portfolio is riskless. A hedge has been created that protects against both increases and decreases in the price of the stock.

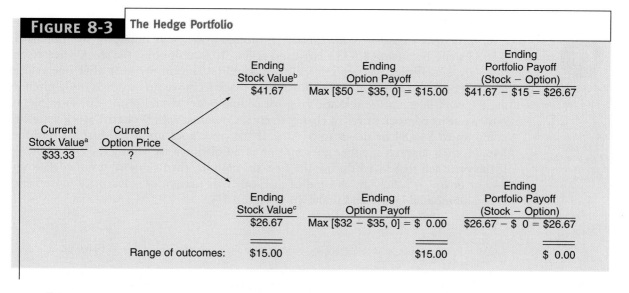

FIGURE 8-3   **The Hedge Portfolio**

Notes:

[a]The portfolio contains 0.8333 share of stock, with a stock price of $40, so its value is 0.8333($40) = $33.33.
[b]The ending stock price is $50, so the value is 0.8333($50) = $41.67.
[c]The ending stock price is $32, so the value is 0.8333($32) = $26.67.

STEP 5. **Find the call option's price.** To this point, we have not mentioned the price of the call option that was sold to create the riskless hedge. What is the *fair*, or *equilibrium*, price? The value of the portfolio will be $26.67 at the end of the year, regardless of what happens to the price of the stock. This $26.67 is riskless, and so the portfolio should earn the risk-free rate, which is 8 percent. If the risk-free rate is compounded daily, the present value of the portfolio's ending value is[7]

$$PV = \frac{\$26.67}{\left(1 + \dfrac{0.08}{365}\right)^{365}} = \$24.62.$$

This means that the current value of the portfolio must be $24.62 to ensure that the portfolio earns the risk-free rate of return. The current value of the portfolio is equal to the value of the stock minus the value of the obligation to cover the call option. At the time the call option is sold, the obligation's value is exactly equal to the price of the option. Because Western's stock is currently selling for $40, and because the portfolio contains 0.8333 share, the value of the stock in the portfolio is 0.8333($40) = $33.33. What remains is the price of the option:

PV of portfolio = Current value of stock in portfolio − Current option price

Current option price = Current value of stock in portfolio − PV of portfolio

= $33.33 − $24.62 = $8.71.

If this option sold at a price higher than $8.71, other investors could create riskless portfolios as described above and earn more than the riskless rate. Investors (especially the large investment banking firms) would create such portfolios and sell options until their price fell to $8.71, at which point the market would be in equilibrium. Conversely, if the options sold for less than $8.71, investors would create an "opposite" portfolio by buying a call option and selling short the stock.[8] The resulting supply shortage would drive the price up to $8.71. Thus, investors (or arbitrageurs) would buy and sell in the market until the options were priced at their equilibrium level.

e-resource

See the Web Extension for this chapter for more details of the binomial approach. CF2 Ch 08 Tool Kit.xls also illustrates the binomial approach.

Clearly, this example is unrealistic. Although you could duplicate the purchase of 0.8333 share by buying 8,333 shares and selling 10,000 options, the stock price assumptions are unrealistic; Western's stock price could be almost anything after one year, not just $50 or $32. However, if we allowed the stock to move up or down more often during the year, then a more realistic range of ending prices would result. For example, suppose we allowed stock prices to change every six months, with Western's stock price either going up to $46.84 or down to $34.16. If the price goes up in the first six months to $46.84, then suppose it either goes up to $54.84 or down to $40 by the end of the year. If the price fell to $34.16 during the first six months, then suppose it either goes up to $40 or down to $29.17 by the end of the year. This pattern of stock price movements is called a **binomial lattice** and is shown in Figure 8-4.

---

[7] To be technically correct, we should discount the ending value using a continuously compounded interest rate, as discussed in the Chapter 2 Web Extension.

[8] Suppose an investor (or speculator) does not own any IBM stock. If the investor anticipates a rise in the stock price and consequently buys IBM stock, he or she is said to have *gone long* in IBM. On the other hand, if the investor thinks IBM's stock is likely to fall, he or she could *go short*, or *sell IBM short*. Because the short seller has no IBM stock, he or she would have to borrow the shares from a broker and sell the borrowed shares. If the stock price falls, the short seller could, later on, buy shares on the open market and pay back the ones borrowed from the broker. The short seller's profit, before commissions and taxes, would be the difference between the price received from the short sale and the price paid later to purchase the replacement stock.

e-resource

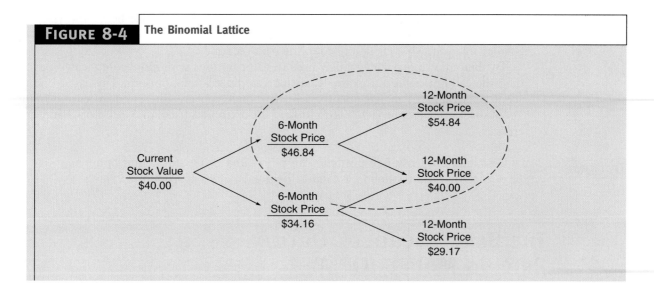

FIGURE 8-4   **The Binomial Lattice**

e-resource

See the Chapter 8 Web Extension for a more complete discussion. See CF2 Ch 08 Tool Kit.xls for all calculations.

There are many free binomial option-pricing programs on the Web, including one at http://www .kellogg.nwu.edu/ faculty/benzoni/ftp/ D6o/Files/options/ options.xls.

If we focus only on the upper right portion of the lattice shown inside the oval, it is very similar to the problem we just solved in Figures 8-2 and 8-3. We can apply the same solution procedure to find the value of the option at the end of six months, given a six-month stock price of $46.84. As explained in the Web Extension to this chapter, the value of the option at the end of six months is $13.21, given that the stock price goes up to $46.84; see **CF2 Ch 08 Tool Kit.xls** for all calculations. Applying the same approach to the lower-right portion of the lattice, the Web Extension and Tool Kit show that the option value at the end of six months is $2.83, given a six-month stock price of $34.16. These values are shown in Figure 8-5. Using the values in Figure 8-5 and the same approach as before, we can calculate the current price, which is $8.60. Notice that by solving three binomial problems, we are able to find the current option price.

If we break the year into smaller periods and allow the stock price to move up or down more often, the lattice would have a more realistic range of possible outcomes. Of course, estimating the current option price would require solving lots of binomial problems within the lattice, but each problem is very simple, and computers can solve them very rapidly. With more outcomes, the resulting estimated option price is more accurate. For example, if we divide the year into 10 periods, the estimated price is $8.38. With 100 periods, the price is $8.41. With 1,000, it is still $8.41, which shows that the solution converges to its

FIGURE 8-5   **Six-Month Stock Prices and Option Values for the First Section of the Binomial Lattice**

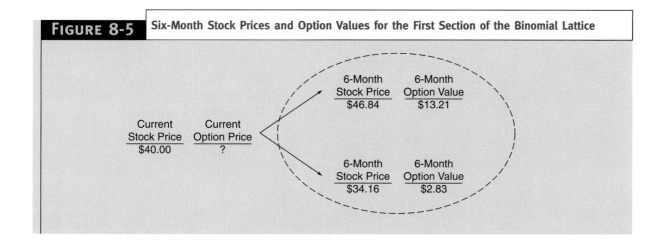

final value with a relatively small number of steps. In fact, as we break the year into smaller and smaller periods, the solution for the binomial approach converges to the Black-Scholes solution, which is described in the next section.

The binomial approach is widely used to value options with more complicated payoffs than the call option in our example, such as employee stock options. This is beyond the scope of a financial management textbook, but if you are interested in learning more about the binomial approach, take a look at the textbooks listed in the end-of-chapter references.

SELF-TEST QUESTIONS   Describe how a risk-free portfolio can be created using stocks and options. How can such a portfolio be used to help estimate a call option's value?

THE BLACK-SCHOLES OPTION PRICING MODEL (OPM)

The **Black-Scholes Option Pricing Model (OPM)**, developed in 1973, helped give rise to the rapid growth in options trading. This model, which has even been programmed into some hand-held and Web-based calculators, is widely used by option traders.

OPM Assumptions and Equations

For a Web-based option calculator, see http://www.cfo .com, select Tools, and then Stock Options Calculator.

In deriving their option pricing model, Fischer Black and Myron Scholes made the following assumptions:

1. The stock underlying the call option provides no dividends or other distributions during the life of the option.
2. There are no transaction costs for buying or selling either the stock or the option.
3. The short-term, risk-free interest rate is known and is constant during the life of the option.
4. Any purchaser of a security may borrow any fraction of the purchase price at the short-term, risk-free interest rate.
5. Short selling is permitted, and the short seller will receive immediately the full cash proceeds of today's price for a security sold short.
6. The call option can be exercised only on its expiration date.
7. Trading in all securities takes place continuously, and the stock price moves randomly.

The derivation of the Black-Scholes model rests on the concept of a riskless hedge such as the one we set up in the last section. By buying shares of a stock and simultaneously selling call options on that stock, an investor can create a risk-free investment position, where gains on the stock will exactly offset losses on the option. This riskless hedged position must earn a rate of return equal to the risk-free rate. Otherwise, an arbitrage opportunity would exist, and people trying to take advantage of this opportunity would drive the price of the option to the equilibrium level as specified by the Black-Scholes model.

The Black-Scholes model consists of the following three equations:

$$V = P[N(d_1)] - Xe^{-r_{RF}t}[N(d_2)].$$ (8-1)

$$d_1 = \frac{\ln(P/X) + [r_{RF} + (\sigma^2/2)]t}{\sigma\sqrt{t}}.$$ (8-2)

$$d_2 = d_1 - \sigma\sqrt{t}.$$ (8-3)

Here

$$
\begin{aligned}
V &= \text{current value of the call option.}\\
P &= \text{current price of the underlying stock.}\\
N(d_i) &= \text{probability that a deviation less than } d_i \text{ will occur in a standard normal}\\
&\quad\text{distribution. Thus, } N(d_1) \text{ and } N(d_2) \text{ represent areas under a standard nor-}\\
&\quad\text{mal distribution function.}\\
X &= \text{exercise, or strike, price of the option.}\\
e &\approx 2.7183.\\
r_{RF} &= \text{risk-free interest rate.}^9\\
t &= \text{time until the option expires (the option period).}\\
\ln(P/X) &= \text{natural logarithm of } P/X.\\
\sigma^2 &= \text{variance of the rate of return on the stock.}
\end{aligned}
$$

Note that the value of the option is a function of the variables we discussed earlier: (1) P, the stock's price; (2) t, the option's time to expiration; (3) X, the strike price; (4) σ^2, the variance of the underlying stock; and (5) r_{RF}, the risk-free rate. We do not derive the Black-Scholes model—the derivation involves some extremely complicated mathematics that go far beyond the scope of this text. However, it is not difficult to use the model. Under the assumptions set forth previously, if the option price is different from the one found by Equation 8-1, this would provide the opportunity for arbitrage profits, which would force the option price back to the value indicated by the model.[10] As we noted earlier, the Black-Scholes model is widely used by traders, so actual option prices conform reasonably well to values derived from the model.

Loosely speaking, the first term of Equation 8-1, $P[N(d_1)]$, can be thought of as the expected present value of the terminal stock price, given that $P > X$ and the option will be exercised. The second term, $Xe^{-r_{RF}t}[N(d_2)]$, can be thought of as the present value of the exercise price, given that the option will be exercised. However, rather than try to figure out exactly what the equations mean, it is more productive to plug in some numbers to see how changes in the inputs affect the value of an option. The following example is also in the file *CF2 Ch 08 Tool Kit.xls,* on the textbook's Web site.

OPM Illustration

The current stock price, P, the exercise price, X, and the time to maturity, t, can all be obtained from a newspaper such as *The Wall Street Journal*. The risk-free rate, r_{RF}, is the yield on a Treasury bill with a maturity equal to the option expiration date. The annualized variance of stock returns, σ^2, can be estimated by multiplying the variance of the percentage change in daily stock prices for the past year [that is, the variance of $(P_t - P_{t-1})/P_{t-1}$] by 365 days.

Assume that the following information has been obtained:

$$
\begin{aligned}
P &= \$20.\\
X &= \$20.\\
t &= 3 \text{ months or } 0.25 \text{ year.}\\
r_{RF} &= 6.4\% = 0.064.\\
\sigma^2 &= 0.16. \text{ Note that if } \sigma^2 = 0.16, \text{ then } \sigma = \sqrt{0.16} = 0.4.
\end{aligned}
$$

---

[9] The risk-free rate should be expressed as a continuously compounded rate. If r is a continuously compounded rate, then the effective annual yield is $e^r - 1.0$. An 8 percent continuously compounded rate of return yields $e^{0.08} - 1 = 8.33\%$. In all of the Black-Scholes option pricing model examples, we will assume that the rate is expressed as a continuously compounded rate.

[10] *Programmed trading*, in which stocks are bought and options are sold, or vice versa, is an example of arbitrage between stocks and options.

Given this information, we can now use the OPM by solving Equations 8-1, 8-2, and 8-3. Since d_1 and d_2 are required inputs for Equation 8-1, we solve Equations 8-2 and 8-3 first:

$$d_1 = \frac{\ln(\$20/\$20) + [0.064 + (0.16/2)](0.25)}{0.40(0.50)}$$

$$= \frac{0 + 0.036}{0.20} = 0.180.$$

$$d_2 = d_1 - 0.4\sqrt{0.25} = 0.180 - 0.20 = -0.020.$$

Note that $N(d_1) = N(0.180)$ and $N(d_2) = N(-0.020)$ represent areas under a standard normal distribution function. From the table in Appendix D, or from the *Excel* function NORMSDIST, we see that the value $d_1 = 0.180$ implies a probability of $0.0714 + 0.5000 = 0.5714$, so $N(d_1) = 0.5714$. Since d_2 is negative, $N(d_2) = 0.500 - 0.0080 = 0.4920$. We can use those values to solve Equation 8-1:

$$V = \$20[N(d_1)] - \$20e^{-(0.064)(0.25)}[N(d_2)]$$

$$= \$20[N(0.180)] - \$20(0.9841)[N(-0.020)]$$

$$= \$20(0.5714) - \$19.68(0.4920)$$

$$= \$11.43 - \$9.69 = \$1.74.$$

Thus the value of the option, under the assumed conditions, is $1.74. Suppose the actual option price was $2.25. Arbitrageurs could simultaneously sell the option, buy the underlying stock, and earn a riskless profit. Such trading would occur until the price of the option was driven down to $1.74. The reverse would occur if the option sold for less than $1.74. Thus, investors would be unwilling to pay more than $1.74 for the option, and they could not buy it for less, so $1.74 is the *equilibrium value* of the option.

To see how the five OPM factors affect the value of the option, consider Table 8-2. Here the top row shows the base-case input values that were used above to illustrate the OPM and the resulting option value, V = $1.74. In each of the subsequent rows, the boldfaced factor is increased, while the other four are held constant at their base-case levels. The resulting value of the call option is given in the last column. Now let's consider the effects of the changes:

1. *Current stock price.* If the current stock price, P, increases from $20 to $25, the option value increases from $1.74 to $5.57. Thus, the value of the option increases as the stock price increases, but by less than the stock price increase, $3.83 versus $5.00. Note, though, that the percentage increase in the option value, ($5.57 − $1.74)/$1.74 = 220%, far exceeds the percentage increase in the stock price, ($25 − $20)/$20 = 25%.

TABLE 8-2 | Effects of OPM Factors on the Value of a Call Option

	INPUT FACTORS					OUTPUT
Case	P	X	t	r_{RF}	σ^2	V
Base case	$20	$20	0.25	6.4%	0.16	$1.74
Increase P by $5	**25**	20	0.25	6.4	0.16	5.57
Increase X by $5	20	**25**	0.25	6.4	0.16	0.34
Increase t to 6 months	20	20	**0.50**	6.4	0.16	2.54
Increase r_{RF} to 9%	20	20	0.25	**9.0**	0.16	1.81
Increase σ^2 to 0.25	20	20	0.25	6.4	**0.25**	2.13

2. *Exercise price.* If the exercise price, X, increases from $20 to $25, the value of the option declines. Again, the decrease in the option value is less than the exercise price increase, but the percentage change in the option value, ($0.34 − $1.74)/$1.74 = −78%, exceeds the percentage change in the exercise price, ($25 − $20)/$20 = 25%.

3. *Option period.* As the time to expiration increases from t = 3 months (or 0.25 year) to t = 6 months (or 0.50 year), the value of the option increases from $1.74 to $2.54. This occurs because the value of the option depends on the chances for an increase in the price of the underlying stock, and the longer the option has to go, the higher the stock price may climb. Thus, a six-month option is worth more than a three-month option.

4. *Risk-free rate.* As the risk-free rate increases from 6.4 to 9 percent, the value of the option increases slightly, from $1.74 to $1.81. Equations 8-1, 8-2, and 8-3 suggest that the principal effect of an increase in r_{RF} is to reduce the present value of the exercise price, $Xe^{-r_{RF}t}$, hence to increase the current value of the option.[11] The risk-free rate also plays a role in determining the values of the normal distribution functions $N(d_1)$ and $N(d_2)$, but this effect is of secondary importance. Indeed, option prices in general are not very sensitive to interest rate changes, at least not to changes within the ranges normally encountered.

5. *Variance.* As the variance increases from the base case 0.16 to 0.25, the value of the option increases from $1.74 to $2.13. Therefore, the riskier the underlying security, the more valuable the option. This result is logical. First, if you bought an option to buy a stock that sells at its exercise price, and if $\sigma^2 = 0$, then there would be a zero probability of the stock going up, hence a zero probability of making money on the option. On the other hand, if you bought an option on a high-variance stock, there would be a higher probability that the stock would go way up, hence that you would make a large profit on the option. Of course, a high-variance stock could go way down, but as an option holder, your losses would be limited to the price paid for the option—only the right-hand side of the stock's probability distribution counts. Put another way, an increase in the price of the stock helps option holders more than a decrease hurts them, so the greater the variance, the greater is the value of the option. This makes options on risky stocks more valuable than those on safer, low-variance stocks.

Myron Scholes and Robert Merton were awarded the 1997 Nobel Prize in Economics, and Fischer Black would have been a co-recipient had he still been living. Their work provided analytical tools and methodologies that are widely used to solve many types of financial problems, not just option pricing. Indeed, the entire field of modern risk management is based primarily on their contributions. Although the Black-Scholes model was derived for a European option that can be exercised only on its maturity date, it also applies to American options that don't pay any dividends prior to expiration. The textbooks listed in the end-of-chapter references show adjusted models for dividend-paying stocks.

SELF-TEST QUESTIONS

What is the purpose of the Black-Scholes Option Pricing Model?
Explain what a "riskless hedge" is and how the riskless hedge concept is used in the Black-Scholes OPM.

---

[11] At this point, you may be wondering why the first term in Equation 8-1, $P[N(d_1)]$, is not discounted. In fact, it has been, because the current stock price, P, already represents the present value of the expected stock price at expiration. In other words, P is a discounted value, and the discount rate used in the market to determine today's stock price includes the risk-free rate. Thus, Equation 8-1 can be thought of as the present value of the end-of-option-period spread between the stock price and the strike price, adjusted for the probability that the stock price will be higher than the strike price.

TAXES AND STOCK OPTIONS

If an employee stock option grant meets certain conditions, it is called a "tax-qualifying grant," or sometimes an "Incentive Stock Option"; otherwise, it is a "nonqualifying grant." For example, suppose you receive a grant of 1,000 options with an exercise price of $50. If the stock price goes to $110 and you exercise the options, you must pay $50(1,000) = $50,000 for stock that is worth $110,000, which is a sweet deal. But what is your tax liability? If you receive a nonqualifying grant, you are liable for ordinary income taxes on 1,000($110 − $50) = $60,000 when you exercise the option. If it were a tax-qualified grant, you owe no regular taxes when exercised. If you then wait at least a year and sell the stock, say, for $150, you would have a long-term capital gain of 1,000($150 − $50) = $100,000, which would be taxed at the lower capital gains rate.

Before you gloat over your newfound wealth, you had better consult your accountant. Your "profit" when you exercise the tax-qualified options isn't taxable under the regular tax code, but it is under the Alternative Minimum Tax (AMT) code. With an AMT tax rate of up to 28 percent, you might owe as much as 0.28($110 − $50)(1,000) = $16,800. Here's where people get into trouble. The AMT tax isn't due until the following April, so you might think about waiting until then to sell some stock to pay your AMT tax (so that the sale will qualify as a long-term capital gain).

But what happens if the stock price falls to $5 by next April? You can sell your stock, which raises only $5(1,000) = $5,000 in cash. Without getting into the details, you have a long-term capital loss of 1,000($50 − $5) = $45,000, but IRS regulations limit your net capital loss in a single year to $3,000. In other words, the cash from the sale and the tax benefit from the capital loss aren't nearly enough to cover the AMT tax. You may be able to reduce your taxes in future years because of the AMT tax you pay this year and the carry-forward of the remaining long-term capital loss, but that doesn't help right now. You lost $45,000 of your original $50,000 investment, you now have very little cash, and, adding insult to injury, the IRS will insist that you also pay the $16,800 AMT tax.

This is exactly what happened to many people who made paper fortunes in the dot-com boom only to see them evaporate in the ensuing bust. They were left with worthless stock but multi-million-dollar AMT tax obligations. In fact, many still have IRS liens garnishing their wages until they eventually pay their AMT tax. So if you receive stock options, we congratulate you. But unless you want to be the next poster child for poor financial planning, we advise you to settle your AMT tax when you incur it.

Describe the effect of a change in each of the following factors on the value of a call option:
(1) Stock price.
(2) Exercise price.
(3) Option life.
(4) Risk-free rate.
(5) Stock price variance, that is, riskiness of stock.

THE VALUATION OF PUT OPTIONS

A put option gives its owner the right to sell a share of stock. If the stock pays no dividends and the option can only be exercised upon its maturity date, what is its value? Rather than reinventing the wheel, consider the payoffs for two portfolios, as shown in Table 8-3. The first portfolio consists of a put option and a share of stock; the second has a call option (with the same exercise price and expiration date as the call option) and some cash. The amount of cash is equal to the present value of the exercise cost, discounted at the continuously compounded risk-free rate, which is $Xe^{-r_{RF}t}$. At expiration, the value of this cash will equal the exercise cost, X.

TABLE 8-3 | Portfolio Payoffs

	STOCK PRICE AT EXPIRATION IF:	
	P < X	P ≥ X
Put	X − P	0
Stock	P	P
Portfolio 1:	X	P
Call	0	P − X
Cash	X	X
Portfolio 2:	X	P

If the stock price, P, is less than the exercise price, X, when the option expires, then the value of the put option is X − P. Therefore, the value of Portfolio 1, which contains the put and the stock, is equal to X − P plus P, or just X. For Portfolio 2, the value of the call is zero (because the call option is out-of-the-money), and the value of the cash is X, for a total value of X. Notice that both portfolios have the same payoffs if the stock price is less than the exercise price.

What if the stock price is greater than the exercise price? In this case, the put is worth nothing, so the value of Portfolio 1 is equal to the stock price, P. The call option is worth P − X, and the cash is worth X, so the value of Portfolio 2 is P. Therefore, the values of the two portfolios are equal, whether the stock price is below or above the exercise price.

If the two portfolios have identical payoffs, they must have identical values. This is known as the **put-call parity relationship**:

Put option + Stock = Call option + PV of exercise price.

If V is the Black-Scholes value of the call option, then the value of a put is[12]

$$\text{Put option} = V - P + Xe^{-r_{RF}t} \qquad (8\text{-}4)$$

where V is the value of the call option.

For example, consider a put option written on the stock discussed in the previous section. If the put option has the same exercise price and expiration date as the call, its price is

$$\text{Put option} = \$1.74 - \$20 + \$20\,e^{-0.064(0.25)}$$
$$= \$1.74 - \$20 + \$19.68 = \$1.42.$$

SELF-TEST QUESTION In words, what is put-call parity?

APPLICATIONS OF OPTION PRICING IN CORPORATE FINANCE

Option pricing is used in four major areas in corporate finance: (1) real options analysis for project evaluations and strategic decisions, (2) risk management, (3) capital structure decisions, and (4) compensation plans.

---

[12] This model cannot be applied to an American put option on a stock that pays a dividend prior to expiration. The textbooks listed in the end-of-chapter references show valuation approaches for this situation.

Real Options

Suppose a company has a one-year proprietary license to develop a software application for use in a new generation of wireless cellular telephones. Hiring programmers and marketing consultants to complete the project will cost $30 million. The good news is that if consumers love the new cell phones, there will be a tremendous demand for the new software. The bad news is that if sales of the new cell phones are low, the software project will be a disaster. Should the company spend the $30 million and develop the software?

Because the company has a license, it has the option of waiting for a year, at which time it might have a much better insight into market demand for the new cell phones. If demand is high in a year, then the company can spend the $30 million and develop the software. If demand is low, it can avoid losing the $30 million development cost by simply letting the license expire. Notice that the license is analogous to a call option: It gives the company the right to buy something (in this case, software for the new cell phones) at a fixed price ($30 million) at any time during the next year. The license gives the company a **real option,** because the underlying asset (the software) is a real asset and not a financial asset.

There are many other types of real options, including the option to increase capacity at a plant, to expand into new geographical regions, to introduce new products, to switch inputs (such as gas versus oil), to switch outputs (such as producing sedans versus SUVs), and to abandon a project. Many companies now evaluate real options with techniques similar to those described earlier in the chapter for pricing financial options.

Risk Management

Suppose a company plans to issue $400 million of bonds in six months to pay for a new plant now under construction. The plant will be profitable if interest rates remain at current levels, but if rates rise, it will be unprofitable. To hedge against rising rates, the company could purchase a put option on Treasury bonds. If interest rates go up, the company would "lose" because its bonds would carry a high interest rate, but it would have an offsetting gain on its put options. Conversely, if rates fall, the company would "win" when it issues its own low-rate bonds, but it would lose on the put options. By purchasing puts, the company has hedged the risk it would otherwise face due to possible interest rate changes.

Another example of risk management is a firm that bids on a foreign contract. For example, suppose a winning bid means the firm will receive a payment of 12 million euros in nine months. At a current exchange rate of $1.04 per euro, the project would be profitable. But if the exchange rate falls to $0.80 per euro, the project would be a loser. To avoid exchange rate risk, the firm could take a short position in a forward contract, which would allow it to convert 12 million euros into dollars at a fixed rate of $1.00 per euro in nine months, which would still ensure a profitable project. This eliminates exchange rate risk if the firm wins the contract, but what if the firm loses the contract? It would still be obligated to sell 12 million euros at a price of $1.00 per euro, which could be a disaster. For example, if the exchange rate rises to $1.25 per euro, the firm would have to spend $15 million to purchase 12 million euros at a price of $1.25/€, and then sell the euros for $12 million = ($1.00/€)(€12 million), a loss of $3 million.

To eliminate this risk, the firm could also purchase a currency call option that allows it to buy 12 million euros at a fixed price of $1.00 per euro. If the company wins the bid, it will let the option expire, but it will use the forward contract to convert the euros at the forward contract's rate of $1.00 per euro. If the firm loses the bid, then it will exercise the call option and purchase 12 million euros for $1.00 per euro. It will then use those proceeds to close out the forward contract. Thus, the company is able to lock in the future exchange rate if it wins the bid and avoid any net payments at all if it loses the bid. The total cost in either scenario is equal to the initial cost of the option. In other words, the cost of the option is like insurance that guarantees the exchange rate if the company wins the bid and guarantees no net obligations if it loses the bid.

Many other applications of risk management involve futures contracts and other complex derivatives rather than calls and puts. However, the principles used in pricing derivatives are similar to those used earlier in this chapter for pricing options. Thus, financial options and their valuation techniques play key roles in risk management.

Capital Structure Decisions

Decisions regarding the mix of debt and equity used to finance operations are quite important. One interesting aspect of the capital structure decision is based on option pricing. For example, consider a firm with debt requiring a final principal payment of $60 million in one year. If the company's value one year from now is $61 million, then it can pay off the debt and have $1 million left for stockholders. If the firm's value is less than $60 million, then it might well file for bankruptcy and turn over its assets to the creditors, resulting in stockholders' equity of zero. In other words, the value of the stockholders' equity is analogous to a call option: The equity holders have the right to buy the assets for $60 million (which is the face value of the debt) in one year (when the debt matures).

Suppose the firm's owner-managers are considering two projects. One has very little risk, and it will result in an asset value of either $59 million or $61 million. The other has high risk, and it will result in an asset value of either $20 million or $100 million. Notice that the equity will be worth zero if the assets are worth less than $60 million, so the stockholders will be hurt no more if the assets end up at $20 million than $59 million. On the other hand, the stockholders would benefit much more if the assets were worth $100 million rather than $61 million. Thus, the owner-managers have an incentive to choose risky projects, which is consistent with an option's value rising with the risk of the underlying asset. Potential lenders recognize this situation, so they build covenants into loan agreements that restrict managers from making excessively risky investments.

Not only does option pricing theory help explain why managers might want to choose risky projects (for example, think about Enron) and why debtholders might want very restrictive covenants, but options also play a direct role in capital structure choices. For example, a firm might choose to issue convertible debt, which gives bondholders the option to convert their debt into stock if the value of the company turns out to be higher than expected. In exchange for this option, bondholders charge a lower interest rate than for nonconvertible debt. Because owner-managers must share the wealth with convertible bond holders, they have a smaller incentive to gamble with high-risk projects.

Compensation Plans

Many companies use stock options as a part of their compensation plans. It is important for boards of directors to understand the value of these options before they grant them to employees. This is likely to become an even more important issue if FASB's 2004 proposal to expense stock options is implemented.

SELF-TEST QUESTION Describe four ways that option pricing is used in corporate finance.

SUMMARY

In this chapter we discussed option pricing topics, including the following:
- **Financial options** are instruments that (1) are created by exchanges rather than firms, (2) are bought and sold primarily by investors, and (3) are of importance to both investors and financial managers.
- The two primary types of financial options are (1) **call options,** which give the holder the right to purchase a specified asset at a given price (the **exercise,** or **strike, price**) for a given period of time, and (2) **put options,** which give the holder the right to sell an asset at a given price for a given period of time.

- A call option's **exercise value** is defined as the maximum of zero or the current price of the stock less the strike price.
- The **Black-Scholes Option Pricing Model (OPM)** can be used to estimate the value of a call option.
- The five inputs to the Black-Scholes model are (1) P, the current stock price; (2) X, the exercise price; (3) r_{RF}, the risk-free interest rate; (4) t, the remaining time until expiration; and (5) σ^2, the variance of the stock's rate of return.
- A call option's value increases if: P increases, X decreases, r_{RF} increases, t increases, or σ^2 increases.
- The **put-call parity relationship** states that: Put option + Stock = Call option + PV of exercise price.

QUESTIONS

(8-1) Define each of the following terms:
a. Option; call option; put option
b. Exercise value; strike price
c. Black-Scholes Option Pricing Model

(8-2) Why do options sell at prices higher than their exercise values?

(8-3) Describe the effect on a call option's price caused by an increase in each of the following factors: (1) stock price, (2) exercise price, (3) time to expiration, (4) risk-free rate, and (5) variance of stock return.

SELF-TEST PROBLEMS   Solutions Appear in Appendix A

(ST-1) A call option on the stock of Bedrock Boulders has a market price of $7. The stock
Options sells for $30 a share, and the option has an exercise price of $25 a share.
a. What is the exercise value of the call option?
b. What is the premium on the option?

(ST-2) Which of the following events are likely to increase the market value of a call option
Options on a common stock? Explain.
a. An increase in the stock's price.
b. An increase in the volatility of the stock price.
c. An increase in the risk-free rate.
d. A decrease in the time until the option expires.

PROBLEMS

(8-1) Assume you have been given the following information on Purcell Industries:
Black-Scholes Model

Current stock price = $15	Exercise price of option = $15
Time to maturity of option = 6 months	Risk-free rate = 6%
Variance of stock return = 0.12	d_1 = 0.24495
d_2 = 0.00000	$N(d_1)$ = 0.59675
$N(d_2)$ = 0.50000	

Using the Black-Scholes Option Pricing Model, what would be the value of the option?

(8-2) The exercise price on one of Flanagan Company's options is $15, its exercise value is
Options $22, and its premium is $5. What are the option's market value and the price of the stock?

(8-3)
Black-Scholes Model
Use the Black-Scholes model to find the price for a call option with the following inputs: (1) current stock price is $30, (2) exercise price is $35, (3) time to expiration is 4 months, (4) annualized risk-free rate is 5%, and (5) variance of stock return is 0.25.

(8-4)
Binomial Model
The current price of a stock is $20. In 1 year, the price will be either $26 or $16. The annual risk-free rate is 5 percent. Find the price of a call option on the stock that has an exercise price of $21 and that expires in 1 year. (Hint: Use daily compounding.)

(8-5)
Binomial Model
The current price of a stock is $15. In 6 months, the price will be either $18 or $13. The annual risk-free rate is 6 percent. Find the price of a call option on the stock that has an exercise price of $14 and that expires in 6 months. (Hint: Use daily compounding.)

(8-6)
Put-Call Parity
The current price of a stock is $33, and the annual risk-free rate is 6 percent. A call option with an exercise price of $32 and 1 year until expiration has a current value of $6.56. What is the value of a put option written on the stock with the same exercise price and expiration date as the call option?

SPREADSHEET PROBLEM

(8-7)
Build a Model:
Black-Scholes Model

CF
e-resource

Start with the partial model in the file *CF2 Ch 08 P07 Build a Model.xls* from the textbook's Web site. Rework Problem 8-1. Then work the next two parts of this problem given below.
a. Construct data tables for the exercise value and Black-Scholes option value for this option, and graph this relationship. Include possible stock price values ranging up to $30.00.
b. Suppose this call option is purchased today. Draw the profit diagram of this option position at expiration.

CYBERPROBLEM

Please go to our Web site, **http://ehrhardt.swlearning.com**, to access any Cyberproblems.

THOMSON ONE
Business School Edition

Please go to **http://ehrhardt.swlearning.com** to access any Thomson ONE—Business School Edition problems.

MINI CASE

Assume that you have just been hired as a financial analyst by Triple Trice Inc., a mid-sized California company that specializes in creating exotic clothing. Because no one at Triple Trice is familiar with the basics of financial options, you have been asked to prepare a brief report that the firm's executives could use to gain at least a cursory understanding of the topic.

To begin, you gathered some outside materials on the subject and used these materials to draft a list of pertinent questions that need to be answered. In fact, one possible approach to the paper is to use a question-and-answer format. Now that the questions have been drafted, you have to develop the answers.

a. What is a financial option? What is the single most important characteristic of an option?

b. Options have a unique set of terminology. Define the following terms:
(1) Call option
(2) Put option

(3) Exercise price
(4) Striking, or strike, price
(5) Option price
(6) Expiration date
(7) Exercise value
(8) Covered option
(9) Naked option
(10) In-the-money call
(11) Out-of-the-money call
(12) LEAPS

c. Consider Triple Trice's call option with a $25 strike price. The following table contains historical values for this option at different stock prices:

Stock Price	Call Option Price
$25	$ 3.00
30	7.50
35	12.00
40	16.50
45	21.00
50	25.50

(1) Create a table that shows (a) stock price, (b) strike price, (c) exercise value, (d) option price, and (e) the premium of option price over exercise value.
(2) What happens to the premium of option price over exercise value as the stock price rises? Why?

d. In 1973, Fischer Black and Myron Scholes developed the Black-Scholes Option Pricing Model (OPM).
(1) What assumptions underlie the OPM?
(2) Write out the three equations that constitute the model.
(3) What is the value of the following call option according to the OPM?

Stock price = $27.00

Exercise price = $25.00

Time to expiration = 6 months

Risk-free rate = 6.0%

Stock return variance = 0.11

e. What impact does each of the following call option parameters have on the value of a call option?
(1) Current stock price
(2) Exercise price
(3) Option's term to maturity
(4) Risk-free rate
(5) Variability of the stock price

f. What is put-call parity?

SELECTED ADDITIONAL REFERENCES

For more information on the derivatives markets, see

Chance, Don M., *An Introduction to Derivatives and Risk Management* (Mason, OH: South-Western Publishing, 2004).

Hull, John C., *Options, Futures, and Other Derivatives* (Upper Saddle River, NJ: Prentice Hall, 2003).

Projects and Their Valuation

CHAPTER 9

The Cost of Capital

General Electric has long been recognized as one of the world's best-managed companies, and it has rewarded its shareholders with outstanding returns. During its corporate life, GE has raised a cumulative $79 billion in capital from its stockholders, but it has turned that $79 billion into a market capitalization worth more than $299 billion. Its Market Value Added (MVA), the difference between its market capitalization and the capital shareholders put up, is a whopping $220 billion! Not surprisingly, GE is always at or near the top of all companies in MVA.

When investors provide a corporation with funding, they expect the company to generate an appropriate return on those funds. From the company's perspective, the investors' expected return is a cost of using the funds, and it is called the cost of capital. A variety of factors influence a firm's cost of capital. Some, such as the level of interest rates, state and federal tax policies, and the regulatory environment, are outside the firm's control. However, the degree of risk in the projects it undertakes and the types of funds it raises are under the company's control, and both have a profound effect on its cost of capital.

We estimated GE's overall cost of capital to be about 8.2 percent. Therefore, to satisfy its investors, GE must generate a return on an average project of at least 8.2 percent. Some of GE's projects are "home grown" in the sense that the company has developed a new product or entered a new geographic market. For example, GE's appliance division introduced the Advantium speedcooking oven and the ultra-quiet Triton dishwasher. GE began Lexan® polycarbonate production at a new plastics plant in Cartagena, Spain. Sometimes GE creates completely new lines of business, such as its entry into e-commerce. When GE evaluates potential projects such as these, it must determine whether the return on the capital invested in the project will exceed the cost of that capital.

GE also invests by acquiring other companies. In recent years, GE has spent billions annually to acquire hundreds of companies, such as its acquisition of SI Pressure Instruments. GE must estimate its expected return on capital, and the cost of that capital, for each of these acquisitions, and then make the investment only if the expected return is greater than the cost.

How has GE done with its investments? It has produced a 15.6 percent return on capital, well above its 8.2 percent estimated cost of capital. With such a large differential, it's no wonder GE has created a great deal of value for its investors.

Sources: Various issues of *Fortune* and the General Electric Web site, **http://www.ge.com**.

e-resource

The textbook's Web site contains an Excel file that will guide you through the chapter's calculations. The file for this chapter is **CF2 Ch 09 Tool Kit.xls,** *and we encourage you to open the file and follow along as you read the chapter.*

Most important business decisions require capital. For example, when Daimler-Benz decided to develop the Mercedes ML 320 sport utility vehicle and to build a plant in Alabama to produce it, Daimler had to estimate the total investment that would be required and the cost of the required capital. The expected rate of return exceeded the cost of the capital, so Daimler went ahead with the project. Microsoft had to make a similar decision with Windows XP, Pfizer with Viagra, and South-Western when it decided to publish this textbook.

Mergers and acquisitions often require enormous amounts of capital. For example, Vodafone Group, a large telecommunications company in the United Kingdom, spent $60 billion to acquire AirTouch Communications, a U.S. telecommunications company, in 1999. The resulting company, Vodafone AirTouch, later made a $124 billion offer for Mannesmann, a German company. In both cases, Vodafone estimated the incremental cash flows that would result from the acquisition, and then discounted those cash flows at the estimated cost of capital. The resulting values were greater than the targets' market prices, so Vodafone made the offers.

Recent survey evidence indicates that almost half of all large companies have elements in their compensation plans that use the concept of Economic Value Added (EVA). As described in Chapter 3, EVA is the difference between net operating profit after taxes and a charge for capital, where the capital charge is calculated by multiplying the amount of capital by the cost of capital. Thus, the cost of capital is an increasingly important component of compensation plans.

The cost of capital is also a key factor in choosing the mixture of debt and equity used to finance the firm. As these examples illustrate, the cost of capital is a critical element in business decisions.[1]

THE WEIGHTED AVERAGE COST OF CAPITAL

What precisely do the terms "cost of capital" and "weighted average cost of capital" mean? To begin, note that it is possible to finance a firm entirely with common equity. However, most firms employ several types of capital, called **capital components,** with common and preferred stock, along with debt, being the three most frequently used types. All capital components have one feature in common: The investors who provided the funds expect to receive a return on their investment.

If a firm's only investors were common stockholders, then the cost of capital would be the required rate of return on equity. However, most firms employ different types of capital, and, due to differences in risk, these different securities have different required rates of return. The required rate of return on each capital component is called its **component cost,** and the cost of capital used to analyze capital budgeting decisions should be a *weighted average* of the various components' costs. We call this weighted average just that, the **weighted average cost of capital,** or **WACC.**

Most firms set target percentages for the different financing sources. For example, National Computer Corporation (NCC) plans to raise 30 percent of its required capital as debt, 10 percent as preferred stock, and 60 percent as common equity. This is its **target capital structure.** We discuss how targets are established in Chapter 14, but for now simply accept NCC's 30/10/60 debt, preferred, and common percentages as given.

---

[1] The cost of capital is an important factor in the regulation of electric, gas, and telephone companies. These utilities are natural monopolies in the sense that one firm can supply service at a lower cost than could two or more firms. Because it has a monopoly, your electric or telephone company could, if it were unregulated, exploit you. Therefore, regulators (1) determine the cost of the capital investors have provided the utility and (2) then set rates designed to permit the company to earn its cost of capital, no more and no less.

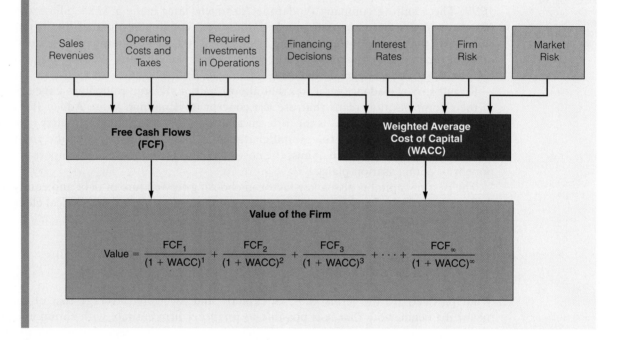

CORPORATE VALUATION AND THE COST OF CAPITAL

In Chapter 1, we told you that managers should strive to make their firms more valuable and that the value of a firm is determined by the size, timing, and risk of its free cash flows (FCF). In particular, a firm's value is the present value of its FCFs, discounted at the weighted average cost of capital (WACC). In the previous chapters, we examined the major sources of financing (stocks, bonds, and preferred stock) on an individual basis. In this chapter, we put those pieces together and estimate the WACC.

The following sections discuss each of the component costs in more detail, and then we show how to combine them to calculate the weighted average cost of capital.

SELF-TEST QUESTIONS

What are the three major capital components?

What is a component cost?

What is a target capital structure?

COST OF DEBT, $r_d(1 - T)$

The first step in estimating the cost of debt is to determine the rate of return debtholders require, or r_d. Although estimating r_d is conceptually straightforward, some problems arise in practice. Companies use both fixed- and floating-rate debt, straight and convertible debt, and debt with and without sinking funds, and each form has a somewhat different cost.

It is unlikely that the financial manager will know at the start of a planning period the exact types and amounts of debt that will be used during the period. The type or types used will depend on the specific assets to be financed and on capital market conditions as they develop over time. Even so, the financial manager does know what types of debt are typical for his or her firm. For example, NCC typically issues commercial paper to raise short-term money to finance working capital, and it issues 30-year bonds to raise long-term debt used to finance its capital budgeting projects. Since the WACC is used primarily in capital budgeting, NCC's treasurer uses the cost of 30-year bonds in her WACC estimate.

Assume that it is January 2006, and NCC's treasurer is estimating the WACC for the coming year. How should she calculate the component cost of debt? Most financial managers would begin by discussing current and prospective interest rates with their investment bankers. Assume that NCC's bankers state that a new 30-year, non-callable, straight bond issue would require an 11 percent coupon rate with semiannual payments, and that it would be offered to the public at its $1,000 par value. Therefore, r_d is equal to 11 percent.[2]

Note that the 11 percent is the cost of **new, or marginal, debt,** and it will probably not be the same as the average rate on NCC's previously issued debt, which is called the **historical, or embedded, rate.** The embedded cost is important for some decisions but not for others. For example, the average cost of all the capital raised in the past and still outstanding is used by regulators when they determine the rate of return a public utility should be allowed to earn. However, in financial management the WACC is used primarily to make investment decisions, and these decisions hinge on projects' expected future returns versus the cost of new, or marginal, capital. *Thus, for our purposes, the relevant cost is the marginal cost of new debt to be raised during the planning period.*

Suppose NCC had issued debt in the past, and its bonds are publicly traded. The financial staff could use the market price of the bonds to find their yield to maturity (or yield to call if the bonds sell at a premium and are likely to be called). The yield is the rate of return the existing bondholders expect to receive, and it is also a good estimate of r_d, the rate of return that new bondholders would require.

If NCC had no publicly traded debt, its staff could look at yields on publicly traded debt of similar firms. This too should provide a reasonable estimate of r_d.

The required return to debtholders, r_d, is not equal to the company's cost of debt because, since interest payments are deductible, the government in effect pays part of the total cost. As a result, the cost of debt to the firm is less than the rate of return required by debtholders.

The **after-tax cost of debt, $r_d(1-T)$,** is used to calculate the weighted average cost of capital, and it is the interest rate on debt, r_d, less the tax savings that result because interest is deductible. This is the same as r_d multiplied by $(1-T)$, where T is the firm's marginal tax rate.[3]

$$\text{After-tax component cost of debt} = \text{Interest rate} - \text{Tax savings}$$
$$= r_d - r_d T \qquad (9\text{-}1)$$
$$= r_d(1-T).$$

Therefore, if NCC can borrow at an interest rate of 11 percent, and if it has a marginal federal-plus-state tax rate of 40 percent, then its after-tax cost of debt is 6.6 percent:

$$r_d(1-T) = 11\%(1.0 - 0.4)$$
$$= 11\%(0.6)$$
$$= 6.6\%.$$

---

[2] The effective annual rate is $(1 + 0.11/2)^2 - 1 = 11.3\%$, but NCC and most other companies use nominal rates for all component costs.

[3] The federal tax rate for most corporations is 35 percent. However, most corporations are also subject to state income taxes, so the marginal tax rate on most corporate income is about 40 percent. For illustrative purposes, we assume that the effective federal-plus-state tax rate on marginal income is 40 percent. The effective tax rate is *zero* for a firm with such large current or past losses that it does not pay taxes. In this situation the after-tax cost of debt is equal to the pre-tax interest rate.

Flotation costs are usually fairly small for most debt issues, and so most analysts ignore them when estimating the cost of debt. Later in the chapter we show how to incorporate flotation costs for those cases in which they are significant.

SELF-TEST QUESTIONS Why is the after-tax cost of debt rather than the before-tax cost used to calculate the weighted average cost of capital?

Is the relevant cost of debt the interest rate on already *outstanding* debt or that on *new* debt? Why?

COST OF PREFERRED STOCK, r_{ps}

A number of firms, including NCC, use preferred stock as part of their permanent financing mix. Preferred dividends are not tax deductible. Therefore, the company bears their full cost, and *no tax adjustment is used when calculating the cost of preferred stock*. Note too that while some preferreds are issued without a stated maturity date, today most have a sinking fund that effectively limits their life. Finally, although it is not mandatory that preferred dividends be paid, firms generally have every intention of doing so, because otherwise (1) they cannot pay dividends on their common stock, (2) they will find it difficult to raise additional funds in the capital markets, and (3) in some cases preferred stockholders can take control of the firm.

The **component cost of preferred stock** used to calculate the weighted average cost of capital, r_{ps}, is the preferred dividend, D_{ps}, divided by the net issuing price, P_n, which is the price the firm receives after deducting flotation costs:

$$\text{Component cost of preferred stock} = r_{ps} = \frac{D_{ps}}{P_n}. \qquad \text{(9-2)}$$

Flotation costs are higher for preferred stock than for debt, hence they are incorporated into the formula for preferred stocks' costs.

To illustrate the calculation, assume that NCC has preferred stock that pays a $10 dividend per share and sells for $100 per share. If NCC issued new shares of preferred, it would incur an underwriting (or flotation) cost of 2.5 percent, or $2.50 per share, so it would net $97.50 per share. Therefore, NCC's cost of preferred stock is 10.3 percent:

$$r_{ps} = \$10/\$97.50 = 10.3\%.$$

SELF-TEST QUESTIONS Does the component cost of preferred stock include or exclude flotation costs? Explain.

Why is no tax adjustment made to the cost of preferred stock?

COST OF COMMON STOCK, r_s

Companies can raise common equity in two ways: (1) directly, by issuing new shares, and (2) indirectly, by retaining earnings. If new shares are issued, what rate of return must the company earn to satisfy the new stockholders? In Chapter 5, we saw that investors require a return of r_s. However, a company must earn more than r_s on new external equity to provide this rate of return to investors because there are commissions and fees, called flotation costs, when a firm issues new equity.

Few mature firms issue new shares of common stock.[4] In fact, less than 2 percent of all new corporate funds come from the external equity market. There are three reasons for this:

1. Flotation costs can be quite high, as we show later in this chapter.
2. Investors perceive issuing equity as a negative signal with respect to the true value of the company's stock. Investors believe that managers have superior knowledge about companies' future prospects, and that managers are most likely to issue new stock when they think the current stock price is higher than the true value. Therefore, if a mature company announces plans to issue additional shares, this typically causes its stock price to decline.
3. An increase in the supply of stock will put pressure on the stock's price, forcing the company to sell the new stock at a lower price than existed before the new issue was announced.

Therefore, we assume that the companies in the following examples do not plan to issue new shares.[5]

Does new equity capital raised indirectly by retaining earnings have a cost? The answer is a resounding yes. If some of its earnings are retained, then stockholders will incur an **opportunity cost**—the earnings could have been paid out as dividends (or used to repurchase stock), in which case stockholders could then have reinvested the money in other investments. *Thus, the firm should earn on its reinvested earnings at least as much as its stockholders themselves could earn on alternative investments of equivalent risk.*

What rate of return can stockholders expect to earn on equivalent-risk investments? The answer is r$_s$, because they expect to earn that return by simply buying the stock of the firm in question or that of a similar firm. *Therefore, r$_s$ is the cost of common equity raised internally by reinvesting earnings.* If a company cannot earn at least r$_s$ on reinvested earnings, then it should pass those earnings on to its stockholders and let them invest the money themselves in assets that do provide r$_s$.

Whereas debt and preferred stock are contractual obligations that have easily determined costs, it is more difficult to estimate r$_s$. However, we can employ the principles described in Chapters 5 and 7 to produce reasonably good cost of equity estimates. Three methods typically are used: (1) the Capital Asset Pricing Model (CAPM), (2) the discounted cash flow (DCF) method, and (3) the bond-yield-plus-risk-premium approach. These methods are not mutually exclusive—no method dominates the others, and all are subject to error when used in practice. Therefore, when faced with the task of estimating a company's cost of equity, we generally use all three methods and then choose among them on the basis of our confidence in the data used for each in the specific case at hand.

SELF-TEST QUESTIONS	What are the two sources of equity capital?

Why do most established firms not issue additional shares of common equity?

Explain why there is a cost to using retained earnings; that is, why aren't retained earnings a free source of capital?

---

[4] A few companies issue new shares through new-stock dividend reinvestment plans, which we discuss in Chapter 15. Also, quite a few companies sell stock to their employees, and companies occasionally issue stock to finance huge projects or mergers.

[5] There are times when companies should issue stock in spite of these problems, hence we discuss stock issues later in the chapter.

THE CAPM APPROACH

To estimate the cost of common stock using the Capital Asset Pricing Model (CAPM) as discussed in Chapter 5, we proceed as follows:

STEP 1. Estimate the risk-free rate, r_{RF}.

STEP 2. Estimate the current expected market risk premium, RP_M, which is the expected market return minus the risk-free rate.

STEP 3. Estimate the stock's beta coefficient, b_i, and use it as an index of the stock's risk. The i signifies the *i*th company's beta.

STEP 4. Substitute the preceding values into the CAPM equation to estimate the required rate of return on the stock in question:

$$r_s = r_{RF} + (RP_M)b_i. \qquad (9\text{-}3)$$

Equation 9-3 shows that the CAPM estimate of r_s begins with the risk-free rate, r_{RF}, to which is added a risk premium set equal to the risk premium on the market, RP_M, scaled up or down to reflect the particular stock's risk as measured by its beta coefficient. The following sections explain how to implement the four-step process.

Estimating the Risk-Free Rate

The starting point for the CAPM cost of equity estimate is r_{RF}, the risk-free rate. There is really no such thing as a truly riskless asset in the U.S. economy. Treasury securities are essentially free of default risk, but nonindexed long-term T-bonds will suffer capital losses if interest rates rise, and a portfolio of short-term T-bills will provide a volatile earnings stream because the rate earned on T-bills varies over time.

Since we cannot in practice find a truly riskless rate upon which to base the CAPM, what rate should we use? A recent survey of highly regarded companies shows that about two-thirds of the companies use the rate on long-term Treasury bonds.[6] We agree with their choice, and here are our reasons:

To find the rate on a T-bond, go to **http:// www.federalreserve .gov.** Select "Economic Research and Data," and then select "Statistics: Releases and Historical Data." Click on the "Daily Update" for H.15, "Selected Interest Rates."

1. Common stocks are long-term securities, and although a particular stockholder may not have a long investment horizon, most stockholders do invest on a long-term basis. Therefore, it is reasonable to think that stock returns embody long-term inflation expectations similar to those reflected in bonds rather than the short-term expectations in bills.

2. Treasury bill rates are more volatile than are Treasury bond rates and, most experts agree, more volatile than r_s.[7]

3. In theory, the CAPM is supposed to measure the expected return over a particular holding period. When it is used to estimate the cost of equity for a project, the theoretically correct holding period is the life of the project. Since many projects have long lives, the holding period for the CAPM also should be long. Therefore, the rate on a long-term T-bond is a logical choice for the risk-free rate.

In light of the preceding discussion, we believe that the cost of common equity is more closely related to Treasury bond rates than to T-bill rates. This leads us to favor T-bonds

---

[6] See Robert E. Bruner, Kenneth M. Eades, Robert S. Harris, and Robert C. Higgins, "Best Practices in Estimating the Cost of Capital: Survey and Synthesis," *Financial Practice and Education*, Spring/Summer 1998, 13–28.

[7] Economic events usually have a larger impact on short-term rates than on long-term rates. For example, see the analysis of 1995–1996 federal debt limit disagreement between the White House and Congress provided in Srinivas Nippani, Pu Liu, and Craig T. Schulman, "Are Treasury Securities Free of Default?" *Journal of Financial and Quantitative Analysis*, June 2001, 251–266.

as the base rate, or r_{RF}, in a CAPM cost of equity analysis. T-bond rates can be found in *The Wall Street Journal* or the *Federal Reserve Bulletin*. Generally, we use the yield on a 10-year T-bond as the proxy for the risk-free rate.

Estimating the Market Risk Premium

The market risk premium, RP_M, is the expected market return minus the risk-free rate. This is also called the **equity risk premium**, or just the **equity premium**. It is caused by investor risk aversion: Since most investors are averse to risk, they require a higher expected return (a risk premium) to induce them to invest in risky equities versus relatively low-risk debt. The premium can be estimated on the basis of (1) historical data or (2) forward-looking data.

HISTORICAL RISK PREMIUM   Historical risk premium data for U.S. securities, updated annually, are available from Ibbotson Associates.[8] Their study includes historical data on stocks, T-bills, T-bonds, and corporate bonds from 1926 through the latest year (2003 currently). Ibbotson calculates the actual realized rates of return on each set of securities and defines the historical market risk premium on common stocks as the difference between the historical realized returns on stocks and T-bonds. Ibbotson's latest study reports a 6.6 percent arithmetic average historical risk premium and a 5.0 percent geometric average historical risk premium. If investor risk aversion had actually been constant during their sample period, then the arithmetic average would be the best estimate for next year's risk premium, while the geometric average would be the best estimate for the longer-term risk premium, say, for the next 20 years.

For many years, academic researchers and corporate analysts used the Ibbotson historical risk premium to estimate the current equity risk premium, under the assumption that the risk premium doesn't change over time. However, this approach has come under fire in recent years. For example, in 2000, 2001, and 2002, bonds had higher returns than stocks. This caused negative realized risk premiums during those years, which reduced the historical average risk premium. However, most knowledgeable observers believe that the true equity risk premium actually increased during the 2000–2002 period and that the increasing premium contributed to the declining stock market during those years: An increasing risk premium caused higher costs of equity, lower stock prices, and, thus, lower stock returns. As this shows, an increase in the current risk premium causes a decrease in the historical premium, and vice versa. Thus, greater risk aversion by investors will cause a lower historical risk premium as reported by Ibbotson, the exact opposite of its true effect. If risk aversion does vary over time, as many experts believe, it throws a lot of cold water on those who use the historical risk premium to estimate the current premium.

FORWARD-LOOKING RISK PREMIUMS   An alternative to the historical risk premium is to estimate a forward-looking, or ex ante, risk premium. The most common approach is to use the discounted cash flow (DCF) model to estimate the expected market rate of return, $\hat{r}_M = r_M$, and then calculate RP_M as $r_M - r_{RF}$. This procedure recognizes that if markets are in equilibrium, the expected rate of return on the market is also its required rate of return, so when we estimate $\hat{r}_M$, we are also estimating r_M:

$$\begin{array}{c} \text{Expected} \\ \text{rate of return} \end{array} = \hat{r}_M = \frac{D_1}{P_0} + g = r_{RF} + RP_M = r_M = \begin{array}{c} \text{Required} \\ \text{rate of return} \end{array}.$$

In words, the required return on the market is the sum of the expected dividend yield plus the expected growth rate. Note that the expected dividend yield, D_1/P_0, can be found using the current dividend yield and the expected growth rate: $D_1/P_0 = D_0(1 + g)/P_0$. Therefore, to

---

[8] See *Stocks, Bonds, Bills and Inflation: 2004 Yearbook* (Chicago: Ibbotson Associates, 2004).

estimate the required return on the market, all you need are estimates of the current dividend yield and the expected growth rate in dividends. Several data sources report the current dividend yield on the market, as measured by the S&P 500. For example, Yahoo! reports a current dividend yield of 1.98 percent for the S&P 500.

It is much more difficult to obtain an estimate of the expected dividend growth rate. What we really need is the long-run dividend growth rate that a marginal investor expects to obtain if he or she bought a broad portfolio of stocks. Since we cannot identify the marginal investors, let alone get inside their heads, it is impossible to obtain a direct estimate of the relevant growth rate. Faced with these data limitations, analysts usually estimate the expected dividend growth rate in one of two ways: (1) the historical dividend growth rate or (2) analysts' forecasts for earnings growth rates as an approximation for expected dividend growth.

For example, Yahoo! reports a 7.09 percent annual growth rate of dividends for the S&P 500 during the past five years. Using the current dividend yield of 1.98 percent, the estimated market return is

$$r_M = \left[\frac{D_0}{P_0} (1 + g) \right] + g$$
$$= [0.0198 \, (1 + 0.0709)] + 0.0709$$
$$= 0.0921 = 9.21\%.$$

Given a current long-term T-bond rate of around 4.4 percent, the estimated forward-looking risk premium from this approach is about $9.21 - 4.4 = 4.81\%$. However, the problems here are similar to those encountered with historical risk premiums—there is no compelling reason to believe that investors expect future growth to be exactly like past growth, and past growth rates are extremely sensitive to the period over which growth is measured. In addition, many companies have small dividend payments but repurchase stock as a way to return free cash flow to investors. We discuss this more in Chapter 15, but the implication here is that historical dividend growth rates don't truly reflect the cash distributions to investors.

The second approach for estimating the expected dividend growth rate is to obtain published forecasts from security analysts. Unfortunately, there are problems with this approach, too: (1) Analysts generally forecast earnings growth rates, not dividend growth rates, and the longest forecast period is typically five years.[9] (2) The accuracy (and truthfulness) of analysts who work for investment banking firms has been questioned in recent years. This suggests that it might be better to use the forecasts of independent analysts, such as those who work for publications like *Value Line,* rather than those who work for the large investment banking firms. (3) Different analysts have different opinions, leading to very different growth rate estimates.

Yahoo! reports a 10.76 percent forecasted earnings five-year growth rate for the S&P 500. Using the current dividend yield of 1.98 percent, the estimated market risk premium is

$$r_M = \left[\frac{D_0}{P_0} (1 + g) \right] + g$$
$$= [0.0198 \, (1 + 0.1076)] + 0.1076$$
$$= 0.1295 = 12.95\%.$$

Given a current long-term T-bond rate of 4.4 percent, the estimated forward-looking risk premium from this approach is $12.95 - 4.4 = 8.55\%$. Notice that this is quite a bit higher than our previous estimate based on the historical dividend growth rate.

To find an estimate of earnings growth, go to *http://finance .yahoo.com,* get a quote for any stock, and then select Analyst Estimates from the column on the left.

---

[9] In theory, the constant growth rate for sales, earnings, and dividends ought to be equal. However, this has not been true for past growth rates. For example, the S&P 500 has had past five-year annual average growth rates of 9.52 percent for sales, 12.35 percent for earnings per share, and 7.09 percent for dividends.

To muddy the water a bit further, some academics have recently argued for a much lower market risk premium. Eugene Fama and Kenneth French examined earnings and dividend growth rates during the period from 1951 to 2000 and found the forward-looking market risk premium to be 2.55 percent. Jay Ritter argues that the forward-looking market risk premium should be based on inflation-adjusted expected returns and should be even lower—closer to 1 percent.[10]

OUR VIEW ON THE MARKET RISK PREMIUM   After reading the previous sections, you might well be confused about the correct market risk premium, since the different approaches give different results. Here is our opinion. The risk premium is driven primarily by investors' attitudes toward risk, and there are good reasons to believe that investors are less risk averse today than 50 years ago. The advent of pension plans, Social Security, health insurance, and disability insurance means that people today can take more chances with their investments, which should make them less risk averse. Also, many households have dual incomes, which also allows investors to take more chances. Finally, the historical average return on the market as Ibbotson measures it is probably too high due to a survivorship bias. Putting it all together, we conclude that the true risk premium in 2005 is lower than the long-term historical average.

But how much lower is the current premium? In our consulting, we typically use a risk premium of about 5 percent, but we would have a hard time arguing with someone who used a risk premium in the range of 3.5 to 6.5 percent. We believe that investor risk aversion is relatively stable but not absolutely constant from year to year. When market prices are relatively high, then investors are feeling less risk averse, so we use a risk premium at the low end of our range. Conversely, we use a risk premium at the high end of our range when market prices are relatively low. The bottom line is that there is no way to prove that a particular risk premium is either right or wrong, although we would be suspicious of an estimated market premium that is less than 3.5 percent or greater than 6.5 percent.

Estimating Beta

To find an estimate of beta, go to *http:// www.finance.yahoo .com,* and enter the ticker symbol for a stock quote. Then select Key Statistics. Or go to Thomson ONE—Business School Edition. Beta is shown in the section of Key Fundamentals.

Recall from Chapter 5 that beta is usually estimated as the slope coefficient in a regression, with the company's stock returns on the y-axis and market returns on the x-axis. The resulting beta is called the *historical beta,* since it is based on historical data. Although this approach is conceptually straightforward, complications quickly arise in practice.

First, there is no theoretical guidance as to the correct holding period over which to measure returns. The returns for a company can be calculated using daily, weekly, or monthly time periods, and the resulting estimates of beta will differ. Beta is also sensitive to the number of observations used in the regression. With too few observations, the regression loses statistical power, but with too many, the "true" beta may have changed during the sample period. In practice, it is common to use either four to five years of monthly returns or one to two years of weekly returns.

Second, the market return should, theoretically, reflect every asset, even the human capital being built by students. In practice, however, it is common to use only an index of common stocks such as the S&P 500, the NYSE Composite, or the Wilshire 5000. Even though these indexes are highly correlated with one another, using different indexes in the regression will often result in different estimates of beta.

Third, some organizations modify the calculated historical beta in order to produce what they deem to be a more accurate estimate of the "true" beta, where the true beta is the one that reflects the risk perceptions of the marginal investor. One modification, called an *adjusted beta,* attempts to correct a possible statistical bias by adjusting the historical beta to make it closer to the average beta of 1.0. Another modification, called a *fundamental*

[10] See Eugene F. Fama and Kenneth R. French, "The Equity Premium," *Journal of Finance,* Vol. 27, no. 2, April 2002, 637–659; and Jay Ritter, "The Biggest Mistakes We Teach," *Journal of Financial Research,* Summer 2002, 159–168.

beta, incorporates information about the company, such as changes in its product lines and capital structure.

Fourth, even the best estimates of beta for an individual company are statistically imprecise. The average company has an estimated beta of 1.0, but the 95 percent confidence interval ranges from about 0.6 to 1.4. For example, if your regression produces an estimated beta of 1.0, then you can be 95 percent sure that the true beta is in the range of 0.6 to 1.4.

The preceding discussion refers to conditions in the United States and other countries with well-developed financial markets, where relatively good data are available. Still, as we have seen, beta can only be estimated within a fairly wide range. When we move on to countries with less-developed financial markets, we are even less certain about the true size of a company's beta.

Moreover, further complications arise when we are dealing with multinational companies, especially those that raise equity capital in different parts of the world. We might, for example, be relatively confident in the beta calculated for the parent company in its home country but less confident of the betas for subsidiaries located in other countries. When such complications arise, we are often forced to make "educated guesses" as to the appropriate beta. It would, of course, be nice to have exact, precise numbers for everything and thus be able to make decisions with a great deal of confidence. However, that's just not the way the world is—we are often forced to use judgment, and our discussion should help improve your judgment regarding the choice of beta for use in cost of capital studies.

An Illustration of the CAPM Approach

To illustrate the CAPM approach for NCC, assume that $r_{RF} = 8\%$, $RP_M = 6\%$, and $b_i = 1.1$, indicating that NCC is somewhat riskier than average. Therefore, NCC's cost of equity is 14.6 percent:

$$
\begin{aligned}
r_s &= 8\% + (6\%)(1.1) \\
&= 8\% + 6.6\% \\
&= 14.6\%.
\end{aligned}
$$

It should be noted that although the CAPM approach appears to yield an accurate, precise estimate of r_s, it is hard to know the correct estimates of the inputs required to make it operational because (1) it is hard to estimate precisely the beta that investors expect the company to have in the future, and (2) it is difficult to estimate the market risk premium. Despite these difficulties, surveys indicate that CAPM is the preferred choice for the vast majority of companies.

SELF-TEST QUESTIONS What is generally considered to be the most appropriate estimate of the risk-free rate, the yield on a short-term T-bill or the yield on a long-term T-bond?

Explain the two methods for estimating the market risk premium, that is, the historical data approach and the forward-looking approach.

What are some of the problems encountered when estimating beta?

DIVIDEND-YIELD-PLUS-GROWTH-RATE, OR DISCOUNTED CASH FLOW (DCF), APPROACH

In Chapter 7, we saw that if dividends are expected to grow at a constant rate, then the price of a stock is

$$
P_0 = \frac{D_1}{r_s - g}. \tag{9-4}
$$

Here P_0 is the current price of the stock; D_1 is the dividend expected to be paid at the end of Year 1, and r_s is the required rate of return. We can solve for r_s to obtain the required rate of return on common equity, which for the marginal investor is also equal to the expected rate of return:

$$r_s = \hat{r}_s = \frac{D_1}{P_0} + \text{Expected g.} \qquad \text{(9-5)}$$

Thus, investors expect to receive a dividend yield, D_1/P_0, plus a capital gain, g, for a total expected return of $\hat{r}_s$. In equilibrium this expected return is also equal to the required return, r_s. This method of estimating the cost of equity is called the **discounted cash flow, or DCF, method.** Henceforth, we will assume that markets are at equilibrium, hence $r_s = \hat{r}_s$, so we can use the terms r_s and $\hat{r}_s$ interchangeably.

Estimating Inputs for the DCF Approach

Three inputs are required to use the DCF approach: the current stock price, the current dividend, and the expected growth in dividends. Of these inputs, the growth rate is by far the most difficult to estimate. The following sections describe the most commonly used approaches for estimating the growth rate: (1) historical growth rates, (2) the retention growth model, and (3) analysts' forecasts.

HISTORICAL GROWTH RATES   First, if earnings and dividend growth rates have been relatively stable in the past, and if investors expect these trends to continue, then the past realized growth rate may be used as an estimate of the expected future growth rate.

CF
e-resource

We explain several different methods for estimating historical growth rates in the Web Extension to this chapter, found on the textbook's Web site; the spreadsheet in the file *CF2 Ch 09 Tool Kit.xls* shows the calculations. For NCC, these different methods produce estimates of historical growth ranging from 4.6 percent to 11.0 percent, with most estimates fairly close to 7 percent.

As the *CF2 Ch 09 Tool Kit.xls* shows, one can take a given set of historical data and, depending on the years and the calculation method used, obtain a large number of quite different growth rates. Now recall our purpose in making these calculations: We are seeking the future dividend growth rate that investors expect, and we reasoned that, if past growth rates have been stable, then investors might base future expectations on past trends. This is a reasonable proposition, but, unfortunately, we rarely find much historical stability. Therefore, the use of historical growth rates in a DCF analysis must be applied with judgment, and also be used (if at all) in conjunction with other growth estimation methods as discussed next.

RETENTION GROWTH MODEL   Most firms pay out some of their net income as dividends and reinvest, or retain, the rest. The payout ratio is the percent of net income that the firm pays out as a dividend, defined as total dividends divided by net income; see Chapter 4 for more details on ratios. The retention ratio is the complement of the payout ratio: Retention ratio = (1 − Payout ratio). ROE is the return on equity, defined as net income available for common stockholders divided by common equity. Although we don't prove it here, you should find it reasonable that the growth rate of a firm will depend on the amount of net income that it retains and the rate it earns on the retentions. Using this logic, we can write the **retention growth model:**

$$g = \text{ROE (Retention ratio).} \qquad \text{(9-6)}$$

Equation 9-6 produces a constant growth rate, but when we use it we are, by implication, making four important assumptions: (1) We expect the payout rate, and thus the retention rate, to remain constant; (2) we expect the return on equity on new investment to remain constant; (3) the firm is not expected to issue new common stock, or, if it does, we expect this new stock to be sold at a price equal to its book value; and (4) future projects are expected to have the same degree of risk as the firm's existing assets.

NCC has had an average return on equity of about 14.5 percent over the past 15 years. The ROE has been relatively steady, but even so it has ranged from a low of 11.0 percent to a high of 17.6 percent. In addition, NCC's dividend payout rate has averaged 0.52 over the past 15 years, so its retention rate has averaged $1.0 - 0.52 = 0.48$. Using Equation 9-6, we estimate g to be 7 percent:

$$g = 14.5\%(0.48) = 7\%.$$

ANALYSTS' FORECASTS   A third technique calls for using security analysts' forecasts. Analysts publish earnings' growth rate estimates for most of the larger publicly owned companies. For example, *Value Line* provides such forecasts on 1,700 companies, and all of the larger brokerage houses provide similar forecasts. Further, several companies compile analysts' forecasts on a regular basis and provide summary information such as the median and range of forecasts on widely followed companies. These growth rate summaries, such as those compiled by Zack's or by Thomson ONE, can be found on the Internet. These earnings' growth rates are often used as estimates of dividend growth rates.

However, these forecasts often involve nonconstant growth. For example, some analysts were forecasting that NCC would have a 10.4 percent annual growth rate in earnings and dividends over the next five years, but a growth rate beyond that of 6.5 percent.

This nonconstant growth forecast can be used to develop a proxy constant growth rate. Computer simulations indicate that dividends beyond Year 50 contribute very little to the value of any stock—the present value of dividends beyond Year 50 is virtually zero, so for practical purposes, we can ignore anything beyond 50 years. If we consider only a 50-year horizon, we can develop a weighted average growth rate and use it as a constant growth rate for cost of capital purposes. In the NCC case, we assumed a growth rate of 10.4 percent for 5 years followed by a growth rate of 6.5 percent for 45 years. We weight the short-term growth by $5/50 = 10\%$ and the long-term growth by $45/50 = 90\%$. This produces an average growth rate of $0.10(10.4\%) + 0.90(6.5\%) = 6.9\%$.

Rather than convert nonconstant growth estimates into an approximate average growth rate, it is possible to use the nonconstant growth estimates to directly estimate the required return on common stock. See the Web Extension to this chapter for an explanation of this approach; all calculations are in the file *CF2 Ch 09 Tool Kit.xls*.

For example, see http://www.zacks .com Also, see Thomson ONE— Business School Edition. After selecting a company, choose the tab for Estimates.

e-resource

Illustration of the Discounted Cash Flow Approach

To illustrate the DCF approach, suppose NCC's stock sells for $32; its next expected dividend is $2.40; and its expected growth rate is 7 percent. NCC's expected and required rate of return, hence its cost of common stock, would then be 14.5 percent:

$$\hat{r}_s = r_s = \frac{\$2.40}{\$32.00} + 7.0\%$$
$$= 7.5\% + 7.0\%$$
$$= 14.5\%.$$

Evaluating the Methods for Estimating Growth

Note that the DCF approach expresses the cost of common equity as the dividend yield (the expected dividend divided by the current price) plus the growth rate. The dividend yield can be estimated with a high degree of certainty, but uncertainty in the growth estimate induces uncertainty in the DCF cost estimate. We discussed three methods for estimating future growth: (1) historical growth rates, (2) retention growth model, and (3) analysts' forecasts. Of these three methods, studies have shown that analysts' forecasts usually represent the best source of growth rate data for DCF cost of capital estimates.[11]

SELF-TEST QUESTIONS

What inputs are required for the DCF method?
What are the ways to estimate the dividend growth rate?
Which of these methods provides the best estimate?

BOND-YIELD-PLUS-RISK-PREMIUM APPROACH

Some analysts use a subjective, ad hoc procedure to estimate a firm's cost of common equity: They simply add a judgmental risk premium of 3 to 5 percentage points to the interest rate on the firm's own long-term debt. It is logical to think that firms with risky, low-rated, and consequently high-interest-rate debt will also have risky, high-cost equity, and the procedure of basing the cost of equity on a readily observable debt cost utilizes this logic. In this approach,

$$r_s = \text{Bond yield} + \text{Bond risk premium}.$$

The bonds of NCC have a yield of 11.0 percent. If its bond risk premium is 3.7 percent, its estimated cost of equity is 14.7 percent:

$$r_s = 11.0\% + 3.7\% = 14.7\%.$$

Because the 3.7 percent risk premium is a judgmental estimate, the estimated value of r_s is also judgmental. Empirical work suggests that the risk premium over a firm's own bond yield has generally ranged from 3 to 5 percentage points, with recent values close to 3 percent. With such a large range, this method is not likely to produce a precise cost of equity. However, it can get us "into the right ballpark."

SELF-TEST QUESTION   What is the reasoning behind the bond-yield-plus-risk-premium approach?

COMPARISON OF THE CAPM, DCF, AND BOND-YIELD-PLUS-RISK-PREMIUM METHODS

We have discussed three methods for estimating the required return on common stock. For NCC, the CAPM estimate is 14.6 percent, the DCF constant growth estimate is 14.5 percent, and the bond-yield-plus-risk-premium is 14.7 percent. The overall average of these three methods is (14.6% + 14.5% + 14.7%)/3 = 14.6%. These results are unusually consistent, so it would make little difference which one we used. However, if the methods produced widely varied estimates, then a financial analyst would have to use his or her judgment as to the relative merits of each estimate and then choose the estimate that seemed most reasonable under the circumstances.

Recent surveys found that the CAPM approach is by far the most widely used method. Although most firms use more than one method, almost 74 percent of respondents in one survey, and 85 percent in the other, used the CAPM.[12] This is in sharp contrast to a 1982

---

[11] See Robert Harris, "Using Analysts' Growth Rate Forecasts to Estimate Shareholder Required Rates of Return," *Financial Management,* Spring 1986, 58–67. Analysts' forecasts are the best predictors of actual future growth, and also the growth rate investors say they use in valuing stocks.

[12] See John R. Graham and Campbell Harvey, "The Theory and Practice of Corporate Finance: Evidence from the Field," *Journal of Financial Economics,* Vol. 60, nos. 2–3, 2001, 187–243, and the paper cited in Footnote 6. Interestingly, a growing number of firms (about 34 percent) also are using CAPM-type models with more than one factor. Of these firms, over 40 percent include factors for interest-rate risk, foreign exchange risk, and business cycle risk (proxied by gross domestic product). More than 20 percent of these firms include a factor for inflation, size, and exposure to particular commodity prices. Less than 20 percent of these firms make adjustments due to distress factors, book-to-market ratios, or momentum factors.

survey, which found that only 30 percent of respondents used the CAPM.[13] Approximately 16 percent now use the DCF approach, down from 31 percent in 1982. The bond-yield-plus-risk-premium is used primarily by companies that are not publicly traded.

People experienced in estimating the cost of equity recognize that both careful analysis and sound judgment are required. It would be nice to pretend that judgment is unnecessary and to specify an easy, precise way of determining the exact cost of equity capital. Unfortunately, this is not possible—finance is in large part a matter of judgment, and we simply must face that fact.

SELF-TEST QUESTION | Which approach is used most often by businesses today?

COMPOSITE, OR WEIGHTED AVERAGE, COST OF CAPITAL, WACC

As we see in Chapter 14, each firm has an optimal capital structure, defined as that mix of debt, preferred, and common equity that causes its stock price to be maximized. Therefore, a value-maximizing firm will establish a *target (optimal) capital structure* and then raise new capital in a manner that will keep the actual capital structure on target over time. In this chapter, we assume that the firm has identified its optimal capital structure, that it uses this optimum as the target, and that it finances so as to remain constantly on target. How the target is established is examined in Chapter 14.

The target proportions of debt, preferred stock, and common equity, along with the component costs of capital, are used to calculate the firm's WACC. To illustrate, suppose NCC has a target capital structure calling for 30 percent debt, 10 percent preferred stock, and 60 percent common equity. Its before-tax cost of debt, r_d, is 11 percent; its after-tax cost of debt is $r_d(1 - T) = 11\%(0.6) = 6.6\%$; its cost of preferred stock, r_{ps}, is 10.3 percent; its cost of common equity, r_s, is 14.6 percent; its marginal tax rate is 40 percent; and all of its new equity will come from retained earnings. We can calculate NCC's weighted average cost of capital, WACC, as follows:

$$WACC = w_d r_d(1 - T) + w_{ps} r_{ps} + w_{ce} r_s \qquad (9\text{-}7)$$
$$= 0.3(11.0\%)(0.6) + 0.1(10.3\%) + 0.6(14.6\%)$$
$$= 11.76\% \approx 11.8\%.$$

Here w_d, w_{ps}, and w_{ce} are the weights used for debt, preferred, and common equity, respectively.

Every dollar of new capital that NCC obtains will on average consist of 30 cents of debt with an after-tax cost of 6.6 percent, 10 cents of preferred stock with a cost of 10.3 percent, and 60 cents of common equity with a cost of 14.6 percent. The average cost of each whole dollar, the WACC, is 11.8 percent.

Two points should be noted. First, the WACC is the current weighted average cost the company would face for a new, or *marginal,* dollar of capital—it is not the average cost of dollars raised in the past. Second, the percentages of each capital component, called weights, should be based on management's target capital structure, which is presumably an estimate of the firm's optimal capital structure. Here are the rationales for those points.

The required rates of return for a company's investors, whether they are new or old, are always marginal rates. For example, a stockholder might have invested in a company last year when the risk-free interest rate was 6 percent and might have had a required

---

[13] See Lawrence J. Gitman and Vincent Mecurio, "Cost of Capital Techniques Used by Major U.S. Firms: Survey Analysis of *Fortune's* 1000," *Financial Management,* Vol. 14, 1982, 21–29.

return on equity of 12 percent. If the risk-free rate subsequently falls and is now 4 percent, then the investor's required return on equity is now 10 percent (holding all else constant). This is the same required rate of return that a new equity holder would have, whether the new investor bought stock in the secondary market or through a new equity offering. In other words, whether the shareholders are already equity holders or are brand new equity holders, all have the same required rate of return, which is the current required rate of return on equity. The same reasoning applies for the firm's bondholders. All bondholders, whether old or new, have a required rate of return equal to the yield on the firm's debt, which is based on current market conditions.

Because all investors have required rates of return based on current market conditions rather than the past market conditions at the investment's purchase date, the cost of capital depends on current conditions, not on historic or past market conditions. It is in this sense that the cost of capital is a marginal cost, since it depends upon current market rates, which are the rates the company would pay on any new capital (ignoring flotation costs, which we discuss later in the chapter).

We have heard managers (and students!) say, "We are only raising debt this year, and it has a 5 percent after-tax cost, so we should use this, and not our 10 percent WACC, to evaluate this year's projects." Here is the flaw in that line of reasoning. Although some investors, such as debtholders, have higher-priority claims relative to other investors, *all* investors have claims on *all* future cash flows. For example, if a company raises debt and also invests in a new project that same year, the new debtholders don't have a specific claim on that specific project's cash flows (assuming it is not nonrecourse project financing). In fact, new debtholders receive a claim on the cash flows being generated by existing as well as new projects, while old debtholders (and equity holders) have claims on both new and existing projects. Thus, the decision to take on a new project should depend on the project's ability to satisfy all of the company's investors, not just the new debtholders, even if only debt is being raised that year.

An investor expects to receive a rate of return on the full amount that is at stake, which is the current market value of the investment. Therefore, the weights used in estimating the WACC should be based on market values, not book values. Recall from Chapter 6 that a firm's risk, as measured by its bond rating, affects its cost of debt. Recall also that the bond rating depends in part on the percentage of the firm that is financed with debt. As we show in Chapter 14, this also affects the cost of equity. In other words, the costs of debt and equity depend on the capital structure weights. However, these costs depend more on the future weights that investors expect than the current weights, which fluctuate due to market conditions and the most recent form of external financing (debt or equity). Thus, the weights used in calculating the WACC should also be based on the expected future weights, which are the firm's target weights.

SELF-TEST QUESTIONS How is the weighted average cost of capital calculated? Write out the equation.
On what should the weights be based?

FACTORS THAT AFFECT THE WEIGHTED AVERAGE COST OF CAPITAL

The cost of capital is affected by a number of factors. Some are beyond the firm's control, but others are influenced by its financing and investment policies.

Factors the Firm Cannot Control

The three most important factors that are beyond a firm's direct control are (1) the level of interest rates, (2) the market risk premium, and (3) tax rates.

For U.S. firms to be competitive with foreign companies, they must have a cost of capital no greater than that faced by their international competitors. In the past, many experts argued that U.S. firms were at a disadvantage. In particular, Japanese firms enjoyed a very low cost of capital, which lowered their total costs and thus made it hard for U.S. firms to compete. Recent events, however, have considerably narrowed cost of capital differences between U.S. and Japanese firms. In particular, the U.S. stock market has outperformed the Japanese market in the last decade, which has made it easier and cheaper for U.S. firms to raise equity capital.

As capital markets become increasingly integrated, cross-country differences in the cost of capital are disappearing. Today, most large corporations raise capital throughout the world, hence we are moving toward one global capital market rather than distinct capital markets in each country. Although government policies and market conditions can affect the cost of capital within a given country, this primarily affects smaller firms that do not have access to global capital markets, and even these differences are becoming less important as time goes by. What matters most is the risk of the individual firm, not the market in which it raises capital.

THE LEVEL OF INTEREST RATES   If interest rates in the economy rise, the cost of debt increases because firms will have to pay bondholders a higher interest rate to obtain debt capital. Also, recall from our discussion of the CAPM that higher interest rates increase the costs of common and preferred equity. During the 1990s, interest rates in the United States declined significantly. This reduced the cost of both debt and equity capital for all firms, which encouraged additional investment. Lower interest rates also enabled U.S. firms to compete more effectively with German and Japanese firms, which in the past had enjoyed relatively low costs of capital.

MARKET RISK PREMIUM   The perceived risk inherent in stocks and investors' aversion to risk determine the market risk premium. Individual firms have no control over this factor, but it affects the cost of equity and, through a substitution effect, the cost of debt, and thus the WACC.

TAX RATES   Tax rates, which are largely beyond the control of an individual firm (although firms do lobby for more favorable tax treatment), have an important effect on the cost of capital. Tax rates are used in the calculation of the cost of debt as used in the WACC, and there are other less obvious ways in which tax policy affects the cost of capital. For example, lowering the capital gains tax rate relative to the rate on ordinary income would make stocks more attractive, which would reduce the cost of equity relative to that of debt. That would, as we see in Chapter 14, lead to a change in a firm's optimal capital structure toward less debt and more equity.

Factors the Firm Can Control

A firm can affect its cost of capital through (1) its capital structure policy, (2) its dividend policy, and (3) its investment (capital budgeting) policy.

CAPITAL STRUCTURE POLICY   In this chapter, we assume that a firm has a given target capital structure, and we use weights based on that target structure to calculate the WACC. It is clear, though, that a firm can change its capital structure, and such a change can affect its cost of capital. First, beta is a function of financial leverage, so capital structure affects the cost of equity. Second, the after-tax cost of debt is lower than the cost of equity. Therefore, if the firm decides to use more debt and less common equity, this change in the weights in the WACC equation will tend to lower the WACC. However, an increase in the use of debt will increase the riskiness of both the debt and the equity, and increases in component costs will tend to offset the effects of the change in the weights.

In Chapter 14 we discuss this in more depth, and we will demonstrate that a firm's optimal capital structure is the one that minimizes its cost of capital.

DIVIDEND POLICY   As we see in Chapter 15, the percentage of earnings paid out in dividends may affect a stock's required rate of return, r_s. Also, if a firm's payout ratio is so high that it must issue new stock to fund its capital budget, this will force it to incur flotation costs, and this too will affect its cost of capital. This second point is discussed in detail later in this chapter and also in Chapter 15.

INVESTMENT POLICY   When we estimate the cost of capital, we use as the starting point the required rates of return on the firm's outstanding stock and bonds. Those rates reflect the risk of the firm's existing assets. Therefore, we have implicitly been assuming that new capital will be invested in assets with the same degree of risk as existing assets. This assumption is generally correct, as most firms do invest in assets similar to those they currently use. However, it would be incorrect if a firm dramatically changed its investment policy. For example, if a firm invests in an entirely new line of business, its marginal cost of capital should reflect the riskiness of that new business. To illustrate, Time Warner's merger with AOL undoubtedly increased its risk and cost of capital.

SELF-TEST QUESTIONS   What three factors that affect the cost of capital are generally beyond the firm's control? What three policies under the firm's control are likely to affect its cost of capital? Explain how a change in interest rates in the economy would affect each component of the weighted average cost of capital.

ADJUSTING THE COST OF CAPITAL FOR RISK

As we have calculated it, the cost of capital reflects the average risk and overall capital structure of the entire firm. But what if a firm has divisions in several business lines that differ in risk? Or what if a company is considering a project that is much riskier than its typical project? It doesn't make sense for a company to use its overall cost of capital to discount divisional or project-specific cash flows that don't have the same risk as the company's average cash flows. The following sections explain how to adjust the cost of capital for divisions and for specific projects.

The Divisional Cost of Capital

Consider Starlight Sandwich Shops, a company with two divisions—a bakery operation and a chain of cafes. The bakery division is low risk and has a 10 percent cost of capital. The cafe division is riskier and has a 14 percent cost of capital. Each division is approximately the same size, so Starlight's overall cost of capital is 12 percent. The bakery manager has a project with an 11 percent expected rate of return, and the cafe division manager has a project with a 13 percent expected return. Should these projects be accepted or rejected? Starlight can create value if it accepts the bakery's project, since its rate of return is greater than its cost of capital (11% > 10%), but the cafe project's rate of return is less than its cost of capital (13% < 14%), so it should be rejected. However, if one simply compared the two projects' returns with Starlight's 12 percent overall cost of capital, then the bakery's value-adding project would be rejected while the cafe's value-destroying project would be accepted.

Many firms use the CAPM to estimate the cost of capital for specific divisions. To begin, recall that the Security Market Line equation expresses the risk/return relationship as follows:

$$r_s = r_{RF} + (RP_M)b_i.$$

As an example, consider the case of Huron Steel Company, an integrated steel producer operating in the Great Lakes region. For simplicity, assume that Huron has only one division and uses only equity capital, so its cost of equity is also its corporate cost of capital, or WACC. Huron's beta = b = 1.1; r_{RF} = 7%; and RP_M = 6%. Thus, Huron's cost of equity is 13.6 percent:

$$r_s = 7\% + (6\%)1.1 = 13.6\%.$$

This suggests that investors should be willing to give Huron money to invest in average-risk projects if the company expects to earn 13.6 percent or more on this money. By average risk we mean projects having risk similar to the firm's existing division.

Now suppose Huron creates a new transportation division consisting of a fleet of barges to haul iron ore, and barge operations have betas of 1.5 rather than 1.1. The barge division, with b = 1.5, has a 16.0 percent cost of capital:

$$r_{Barge} = 7\% + (6\%)1.5 = 16.0\%.$$

On the other hand, if Huron adds a low-risk division, such as a new distribution center with a beta of only 0.5, its divisional cost of capital would be 10 percent:

$$r_{Center} = 7\% + (6\%)0.5 = 10.0\%.$$

A firm itself may be regarded as a "portfolio of assets," and since the beta of a portfolio is a weighted average of the betas of its individual assets, adding the barge and distribution center divisions will change Huron's overall beta. The exact value of the new beta would depend on the relative size of the investment in the new divisions versus Huron's original steel operations. If 70 percent of Huron's total value ends up in the steel division, 20 percent in the barge division, and 10 percent in the distribution center, then its new corporate beta would be

$$\text{New beta} = 0.7(1.1) + 0.2(1.5) + 0.1(0.5) = 1.12.$$

Thus, investors in Huron's stock would have a required return of:

$$r_{Huron} = 7\% + (6\%)1.12 = 13.72\%.$$

Even though the investors require an overall return of 13.72 percent, they would expect a return of at least 13.6 percent from the steel division, 16.0 percent from the barge division, and 10.0 percent from the distribution center.

Figure 9-1 gives a graphic summary of these concepts as applied to Huron Steel. Note the following points:

1. If the expected rate of return on a given capital project lies *above* the SML, the expected rate of return on the project is more than enough to compensate for its risk, and the project should be accepted. Conversely, if the project's rate of return lies *below* the SML, it should be rejected. Thus, Project M in Figure 9-1 is acceptable, whereas Project N should be rejected. N has a higher expected return than M, but the differential is not enough to offset its much higher risk.

2. For simplicity, the Huron Steel illustration is based on the assumption that the company used no debt financing, which allows us to use the SML to plot the company's cost of capital. The basic concepts presented in the Huron illustration also hold for companies that use debt financing. When debt financing is used, the division's cost of equity must be combined with the division's cost of debt and target capital structure to obtain the division's overall cost of capital.

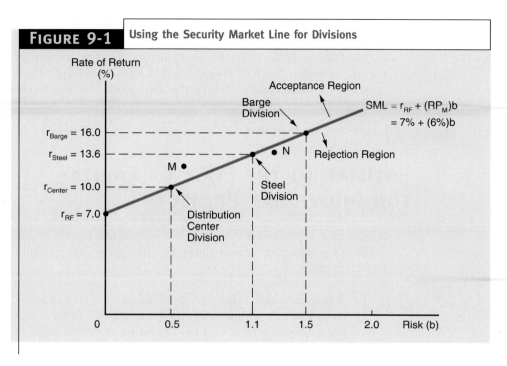

FIGURE 9-1 | Using the Security Market Line for Divisions

Rate of Return (%)

Acceptance Region

Barge Division

$SML = r_{RF} + (RP_M)b$
$= 7\% + (6\%)b$

$r_{Barge} = 16.0$

$r_{Steel} = 13.6$

N

Rejection Region

M

$r_{Center} = 10.0$

Steel Division

$r_{RF} = 7.0$

Distribution Center Division

0   0.5   1.1   1.5   2.0   Risk (b)

SELF-TEST QUESTIONS Based on the CAPM, how would one find the cost of capital for a low-risk division, and for a high-risk division?

Explain why you should accept a given capital project if its expected rate of return lies above the SML and reject it if its expected return is below the SML.

TECHNIQUES FOR MEASURING DIVISIONAL BETAS

In Chapter 5 we discussed the estimation of betas for stocks and indicated the difficulties in estimating beta. The estimation of divisional betas is much more difficult, and more fraught with uncertainty. However, two approaches have been used to estimate individual assets' betas—the pure play method and the accounting beta method.

The Pure Play Method

In the **pure play method,** the company tries to find several single-product companies in the same line of business as the division being evaluated, and it then averages those companies' betas to determine the cost of capital for its own division. For example, suppose Huron could find three existing single-product firms that operate barges, and suppose also that Huron's management believes its barge division would be subject to the same risks as those firms. Huron could then determine the betas of those firms, average them, and use this average beta as a proxy for the barge division's beta.[14]

The Accounting Beta Method

As noted above, it may be impossible to find single-product, publicly traded firms suitable for the pure play approach. If that is the case, we may be able to use the **accounting**

---

[14] If the pure play firms employ different capital structures than that of Huron, this fact must be dealt with by adjusting the beta coefficients. See Chapter 14 for a discussion of this aspect of the pure play method. For a technique that can be used when pure play firms are not available, see Yatin Bhagwat and Michael Ehrhardt, "A Full Information Approach for Estimating Divisional Betas," *Financial Management*, Summer 1991, 60–69.

beta method. Betas normally are found by regressing the returns of a particular company's *stock* against returns on a *stock market index*. However, we could run a regression of the division's *accounting return on assets* against the *average return on assets* for a large sample of companies, such as those included in the S&P 500. Betas determined in this way (that is, by using accounting data rather than stock market data) are called **accounting betas.**

SELF-TEST QUESTION   Describe the pure play and the accounting beta methods for estimating divisional betas.

ESTIMATING THE COST OF CAPITAL FOR INDIVIDUAL PROJECTS

Although it is intuitively clear that riskier projects have a higher cost of capital, it is difficult to estimate project risk. First, note that three separate and distinct types of risk can be identified:

1. **Stand-alone risk** is the variability of the project's expected returns.
2. **Corporate, or within-firm, risk** is the variability the project contributes to the corporation's returns, giving consideration to the fact that the project represents only one asset of the firm's portfolio of assets, hence that some of its risk effects will be diversified away.
3. **Market, or beta, risk** is the riskiness of the project as seen by a well-diversified stockholder. Market risk is measured by the project's effect on the firm's beta coefficient.

Taking on a project with a high degree of either stand-alone or corporate risk will not necessarily affect the firm's beta. However, if the project has highly uncertain returns, and if those returns are highly correlated with returns on the firm's other assets and with most other assets in the economy, then the project will have a high degree of all types of risk. For example, suppose General Motors decides to undertake a major expansion to build electric autos. GM is not sure how its technology will work on a mass production basis, so there is much risk in the venture—its stand-alone risk is high. Management also estimates that the project will do best if the economy is strong, for then people will have more money to spend on the new autos. This means that the project will tend to do well if GM's other divisions are doing well and will tend to do badly if other divisions are doing badly. This being the case, the project will also have high corporate risk. Finally, since GM's profits are highly correlated with those of most other firms, the project's beta will also be high. Thus, this project will be risky under all three definitions of risk.

Of the three measures, market risk is theoretically the most relevant because of its direct effect on stock prices. Unfortunately, the market risk for a project is also the most difficult to estimate. In practice, most decision makers consider all three risk measures in a judgmental manner.

The first step is to determine the divisional cost of capital, and then to group divisional projects into subjective risk categories. Then, using the divisional WACC as a starting point, **risk-adjusted costs of capital** are developed for each category. For example, a firm might establish three risk classes—high, average, and low—then assign average-risk projects the divisional cost of capital, higher-risk projects an above-average cost, and lower-risk projects a below-average cost. Thus, if a division's WACC were 10 percent, its managers might use 10 percent to evaluate average-risk projects in the division, 12 percent for high-risk projects, and 8 percent for low-risk projects. While this approach is better than not risk adjusting at all, these risk adjustments are necessarily subjective and somewhat arbitrary. Unfortunately, given the data, there is no completely satisfactory way to specify exactly how much higher or lower we should go in setting risk-adjusted costs of capital.

What are the three types of project risk?

Which type of risk is theoretically the most relevant? Why?

Describe a procedure firms can use to develop costs of capital for projects with differing degrees of risk.

ADJUSTING THE COST OF CAPITAL FOR FLOTATION COSTS

Most debt is privately placed, and most equity is raised internally as retained earnings. In these cases, there are no flotation costs, hence the component costs of debt and equity should be estimated as discussed earlier. However, if companies issue debt or new stock to the public, then flotation costs can become important. In the following sections, we explain how to estimate the component costs of publicly issued debt and stock, and we show how these new component costs affect the marginal cost of capital.

Axis Goods Inc., a retailer of trendy sportswear, has a target capital structure of 45 percent debt, 2 percent preferred stock, and 53 percent common stock. Its common stock sells for $23, the next expected dividend is $1.24, and the expected constant growth rate is 8 percent. Based on the constant growth DCF model, Axis' cost of common equity is $r_s = 13.4\%$ when the equity is raised as retained earnings. Axis' cost of preferred stock is 10.3 percent, based on the method discussed in the chapter, which incorporates flotation costs. In the following sections, we examine the effects of flotation costs on the component costs of debt and common stock, and on the marginal cost of capital.

Flotation Costs and the Component Cost of Debt

Axis can issue a 30-year, $1,000 par value bond with an interest rate of 10 percent, paid annually. Here $T = 40\%$, so the after-tax component cost of debt is $r_d(1 - T) = 10\%(1.0 - 0.4) = 6.0\%$. However, if Axis must incur flotation costs, F, of 1 percent of the value of the issue, then this formula must be used to find the after-tax cost of debt:

$$M(1 - F) = \sum_{t=1}^{N} \frac{INT(1 - T)}{[1 + r_d(1 - T)]^t} + \frac{M}{[1 + r_d(1 - T)]^N}. \tag{9-8}$$

Here M is the bond's par value, F is the flotation percentage, N is the bond's maturity, T is the firm's tax rate, INT is the dollars of interest per period, and $r_d(1 - T)$ is the after-tax cost of debt adjusted for flotation costs. With a financial calculator, enter $N = 30$, $PV = -990$, $PMT = 60$, and $FV = 1000$. Solving for I, we find $I = r_d(1 - T) = 6.07\%$, which is the after-tax component cost of debt. Note that the 6.07 percent theoretically correct after-tax cost of debt is quite close to the original 6.00 percent after-tax cost, so in this instance adjusting for flotation costs doesn't make much difference.

However, the flotation adjustment would be higher if F were larger or if the bond's life were shorter. For example, if F were 10 percent rather than 1 percent, then the flotation-adjusted $r_d(1 - T)$ would have been 6.79 percent. With N at 1 year rather than 30 years, and F still equal to 1 percent, then $r_d(1 - T) = 7.07\%$. Finally, if $F = 10\%$ and $N = 1$, then $r_d(1 - T) = 17.78\%$. In all of these cases the differential would be too high to ignore.[15]

---

[15] Strictly speaking, the after-tax cost of debt should reflect the *expected* cost of debt. While Axis' bonds have a promised return of 10 percent, there is some chance of default, so its bondholders' expected return (and consequently Axis' cost) is a bit less than 10 percent. However, for a relatively strong company such as Axis, this difference is quite small. Also, the after-tax cash flows in Equation 9-8 are for a bond issued at or close to par. If the bond is issued at a price substantially below par, then the discount will have an impact on the after-tax cash flows.

Cost of Newly Issued Common Stock, or External Equity, r_e

The **cost of new common equity, r_e**, or external equity, is higher than the cost of equity raised internally by reinvesting earnings, r_s, because of flotation costs involved in issuing new common stock. What rate of return must be earned on funds raised by selling new stock to make issuing stock worthwhile? To put it another way, what is the cost of new common stock?

The answer for a constant growth stock is found by applying this formula:

$$r_e = \frac{D_1}{P_0\,(1 - F)} + g. \qquad \text{(9-9)}$$

In Equation 9-9, F is the **percentage flotation cost** incurred in selling the new stock, so $P_0(1 - F)$ is the net price per share received by the company.

Assuming that Axis has a flotation cost of 10 percent, its cost of new outside equity is computed as follows:

$$r_e = \frac{\$1.24}{\$23(1 - 0.10)} + 8.0\%$$

$$= \frac{\$1.24}{\$20.70} + 8.0\%$$

$$= 6.0\% + 8.0\% = 14.0\%.$$

Investors require a return of $r_s = 13.4\%$ on the stock.[16] However, because of flotation costs the company must earn *more* than 13.4 percent on the net funds obtained by selling stock if investors are to receive a 13.4 percent return on the money they put up. Specifically, if the firm earns 14 percent on funds obtained by issuing new stock, then earnings per share will remain at the previously expected level, the firm's expected dividend can be maintained, and, as a result, the price per share will not decline. If the firm earns less than 14 percent, then earnings, dividends, and growth will fall below expectations, causing the stock price to decline. If the firm earns more than 14 percent, the stock price will rise.

As we noted earlier, most analysts use the CAPM to estimate the cost of equity. Suppose the CAPM cost of equity for Axis is 13.8 percent. How could the analyst incorporate flotation costs? In the example above, application of the DCF methodology gives a cost of equity of 13.4 percent if flotation costs are ignored and a cost of equity of 14.0 percent if flotation costs are included. Therefore, flotation costs add 0.6 percentage point to the cost of equity $(14.0 - 13.4 = 0.6)$. To incorporate flotation costs into the CAPM estimate, you would add the 0.6 percentage point to the 13.8 percent CAPM estimate, resulting in a 14.4 percent estimated cost of external equity. As an alternative, you could find the average of the CAPM, DCF, and bond-yield-plus-risk-premium costs of equity ignoring flotation costs, and then add to it the 0.6 percentage point due to flotation costs.

How Much Does It Cost to Raise External Capital?

Table 9-1 shows the average flotation cost for debt and equity issued by U.S. corporations in the 1990s. The common stock flotation costs are for non-IPOs. Costs associated with IPOs are even higher—about 17 percent of gross proceeds for common equity if the amount raised is less than $10 million and about 6 percent if more than $500 million is raised. The data include both utility and nonutility companies. If utilities were excluded, flotation costs would be even higher.

---

[16]If there were no flotation costs, $r_s = \dfrac{\$1.24}{\$23} + 8.0\% = 13.4\%$.

TABLE 9-1 | Average Flotation Costs for Debt and Equity

Amount of Capital Raised (Millions of Dollars)	Average Flotation Cost for Common Stock (% of Total Capital Raised)	Average Flotation Cost for New Debt (% of Total Capital Raised)
2–9.99	13.28	4.39
10–19.99	8.72	2.76
20–39.99	6.93	2.42
40–59.99	5.87	2.32
60–79.99	5.18	2.34
80–99.99	4.73	2.16
100–199.99	4.22	2.31
200–499.99	3.47	2.19
500 and up	3.15	1.64

Source: Inmoo Lee, Scott Lochhead, Jay Ritter, and Quanshui Zhao, "The Costs of Raising Capital," *The Journal of Financial Research,* Vol XIX, no. 1, Spring 1996, 59–74. Reprinted with permission.

SELF-TEST QUESTIONS

What are flotation costs?

Are flotation costs higher for debt or equity?

SOME PROBLEM AREAS IN COST OF CAPITAL

A number of difficult issues relating to the cost of capital either have not been mentioned or were glossed over in this chapter. These topics are beyond the scope of this text, but they deserve some mention both to alert you to potential dangers and to provide you with a preview of some of the matters dealt with in specialty courses.

1. *Privately owned firms.* Our discussion of the cost of equity was related primarily to publicly owned corporations, and we concentrated on the rate of return required by public stockholders. However, there is a serious question about how one should measure the cost of equity for a firm whose stock is not traded. Tax issues are also especially important in these cases. As a general rule, the same principles of cost of capital estimation apply to both privately held and publicly owned firms, but the problems of obtaining input data are somewhat different for each.
2. *Small businesses.* Small businesses are generally privately owned, making it difficult to estimate their cost of equity.
3. *Measurement problems.* We cannot overemphasize the practical difficulties encountered when estimating the cost of equity. It is very difficult to obtain good input data for the CAPM, for g in the formula $r_s = D_1/P_0 + g$, and for the bond risk premium in the formula $r_s = $ Bond yield + Bond risk premium. As a result, we can never be sure just how accurate our estimated cost of capital is.
4. *Costs of capital for projects of differing riskiness.* As we see in Chapter 11, it is difficult to measure projects' risks, hence to assign risk-adjusted discount rates to capital budgeting projects of differing degrees of riskiness.
5. *Capital structure weights.* In this chapter, we simply took as given the target capital structure and used this target to obtain the weights used to calculate WACC. As we see in Chapter 14, establishing the target capital structure is a major task in itself.

Although this list of problems may appear formidable, the state of the art in cost of capital estimation is really not in bad shape. The procedures outlined in this chapter can be used to obtain cost of capital estimates that are sufficiently accurate for practical purposes, and the problems listed here merely indicate the desirability of refinements. The refinements are not unimportant, but the problems we have identified do not invalidate the usefulness of the procedures outlined in the chapter.

SELF-TEST QUESTION

Identify some problem areas in cost of capital analysis. Do these problems invalidate the cost of capital procedures discussed in the chapter?

FOUR MISTAKES TO AVOID

We often see managers and students make the following mistakes when estimating the cost of capital. Although we have discussed these errors previously at separate places in the chapter, they are worth repeating here:

1. *Never use the coupon rate on a firm's existing debt as the pre-tax cost of debt.* The relevant pre-tax cost of debt is the interest rate the firm would pay if it issued debt today.

2. *When estimating the market risk premium for the CAPM method, never use the historical average return on stocks in conjunction with the current risk-free rate.* The historical average return on common stocks has been about 12.4 percent, the historical return on long-term Treasury bonds about 5.8 percent, and the difference between them, which is the **historical risk premium**, is 6.6 percent. The **current risk premium** is found as the difference between an estimate of the current expected rate of return on common stocks and the current expected yield on T-bonds. To illustrate, suppose an estimate of the future return on common stock is 10 percent, and the current rate on long-term T-bonds is 4 percent. This implies that you expect to earn 10 percent if you buy stock today and 4 percent if you buy bonds. Therefore, this implies a current market risk premium of 10% − 4% = 6%. A case could be made for using either the historical or the current risk premium, but it would be wrong to take the *historical* rate of return on the market, 12.4 percent, subtract from it the *current* 4 percent rate on T-bonds, and then use 12.4% − 4% = 8.4% as the risk premium.

3. *Never use the book value of equity when estimating the capital structure weights for the WACC.* Your first choice should be to use the target capital structure to determine the weights. If you are an outside analyst and do not know the target weights, it is better to estimate weights based on the current market values of the capital components than on their book values. This is especially true for equity. For example, the stock of an average S&P 500 firm in 2004 had a market value that was about 4.19 times its book value, and in general, stocks' market values are rarely close to their book values. If the company's debt is not publicly traded, then it is reasonable to use the book value of debt to estimate the weights, since book and market values of debt, especially short-term debt, are usually close to one another. To summarize, if you don't know the target weights, then use market values of equity rather than book values to obtain the weights used to calculate WACC.

To find the current S&P 500 market to book ratio, go to *http://yahoo .investor.reuters.com,* get the stock quote for any company, and select Ratios, then look for the Price to Book ratio.

4. *Always remember that capital components are funds that come from investors.* If it's not from an investor, then it's not a capital component. Sometimes the argument is made that accounts payable and accruals are sources of funding and should be included in the calculation of the WACC. However, these accounts are due to operating relationships with suppliers and employees, and they are deducted when determining the investment requirement for a project. Therefore, they should not be included in the WACC. Of course, they are not ignored in either corporate valuation or capital budgeting. As we saw in Chapter 3, current liabilities do affect

cash flow, hence have an effect on corporate valuation. Moreover, in Chapter 11 we show that the same is true for capital budgeting, namely, that current liabilities affect the cash flows of a project, but not its WACC.[17]

| SELF-TEST QUESTION | What are four common mistakes people make when estimating the WACC? |

---

[17] The same reasoning could be applied to other items on the balance sheet, such as deferred taxes. The existence of deferred taxes means that the government has collected less in taxes than a company would owe if the same depreciation and amortization rates were used for taxes as for stockholder reporting. In this sense, the government is "making a loan to the company." However, the deferred tax account is not a source of funds from investors, hence it is not considered to be a capital component. Moreover, the cash flows that are used in capital budgeting and in corporate valuation reflect the actual taxes that the company must pay, not the "normalized" taxes it might report on its income statement. In other words, the correct adjustment for the deferred tax account is made in the cash flows, not in the WACC.

SUMMARY

This chapter showed how the cost of capital is developed for use in capital budgeting. The key concepts covered are listed below.
- The cost of capital used in capital budgeting is a **weighted average** of the types of capital the firm uses, typically debt, preferred stock, and common equity.
- The **component cost of debt** is the **after-tax cost of new debt.** It is found by multiplying the cost of new debt by $(1 - T)$, where T is the firm's marginal tax rate: $r_d(1 - T)$.
- The **component cost of preferred stock** is calculated as the preferred dividend divided by the net issuing price, where the net issuing price is the price the firm receives after deducting flotation costs: $r_{ps} = D_{ps}/P_n$.
- The **cost of common equity, r_s,** is also called the **cost of common stock.** It is the rate of return required by the firm's stockholders, and it can be estimated by three methods: (1) the **CAPM approach,** (2) the **dividend-yield-plus-growth-rate,** or **DCF, approach,** and (3) the **bond-yield-plus-risk-premium approach.**
- To use the **CAPM approach,** (1) estimate the firm's beta, (2) multiply this beta by the market risk premium to determine the firm's risk premium, and (3) add the firm's risk premium to the risk-free rate to obtain the cost of common stock: $r_s = r_{RF} + (RP_M)b_i$.
- The best proxy for the **risk-free rate** is the yield on long-term T-bonds.
- To use the **dividend-yield-plus-growth-rate approach,** which is also called the **discounted cash flow (DCF) approach,** add the firm's expected growth rate to its expected dividend yield: $r_s = D_1/P_0 + g$.
- The growth rate can be estimated from **historical earnings and dividends** or by use of the **retention growth model, g = (1 − Payout)(Return on equity),** or it can be based on **analysts' forecasts.**
- The **bond-yield-plus-risk-premium approach** calls for adding a risk premium of from 3 to 5 percentage points to the firm's interest rate on long-term debt: $r_s =$ Bond yield + Bond RP.
- Each firm has a **target capital structure,** defined as that mix of debt, preferred stock, and common equity that minimizes its **weighted average cost of capital (WACC):**

$$WACC = w_d r_d (1 - T) + w_{ps} r_{ps} + w_{ce} r_s.$$

- **Various factors affect a firm's cost of capital.** Some of these factors are determined by the financial environment, but the firm influences others through its financing, investment, and dividend policies.
- Ideally, the **cost of capital** for each project should reflect the risk of the project itself, not the risks associated with the firm's average project as reflected in its composite WACC.

- **Failing to adjust for differences in project risk** would lead a firm to accept too many value-destroying risky projects and reject too many value-adding safe ones. Over time, the firm would become more risky, its WACC would increase, and its shareholder value would decline.
- A project's **stand-alone risk** is the risk the project would have if it were the firm's only asset and if stockholders held only that one stock. Stand-alone risk is measured by the variability of the asset's expected returns.
- **Corporate, or within-firm, risk** reflects the effects of a project on the firm's risk, and it is measured by the project's effect on the firm's earnings variability.
- **Market, or beta, risk** reflects the effects of a project on the riskiness of stockholders, assuming they hold diversified portfolios. Market risk is measured by the project's effect on the firm's beta coefficient.
- Most decision makers consider all three risk measures in a judgmental manner and then classify projects into subjective risk categories. Using the composite WACC as a starting point, risk-adjusted costs of capital are developed for each category. The **risk-adjusted cost of capital** is the cost of capital appropriate for a given project, given the riskiness of that project. The greater the risk, the higher the cost of capital.
- Firms may be able to use the **CAPM** to estimate the cost of capital for specific projects or divisions. However, estimating betas for projects is difficult.
- The **pure play** and **accounting beta methods** can sometimes be used to estimate betas for large projects or for divisions.
- Companies generally hire an investment banker to assist them when they issue common stock, preferred stock, or bonds. In return for a fee, the investment banker helps the company with the terms, price, and sale of the issue. The banker's fees are often referred to as **flotation costs.** The total cost of capital should include not only the required return paid to investors but also the flotation fees paid to the investment banker for marketing the issue.
- When calculating the **cost of new common stock,** the DCF approach can be adapted to account for flotation costs. For a constant growth stock, this cost can be expressed as: $r_e = D_1/[P_0(1 - F)] + g$. Note that flotation costs cause r_e to be greater than r_s.
- **Flotation cost adjustments** can also be made for debt. The bond's issue price is reduced for flotation expenses and then used to solve for the after-tax yield to maturity.
- The three equity cost estimating techniques discussed in this chapter have **serious limitations** when applied to small firms, thus increasing the need for the small-business manager to use judgment.

The cost of capital as developed in this chapter is used in the following chapters to determine the value of a corporation and to evaluate capital budgeting projects. In addition, we extend the concepts developed here in Chapter 14, where we consider the effect of the capital structure on the cost of capital.

QUESTIONS

(9-1) Define each of the following terms:
 a. Weighted average cost of capital, WACC; after-tax cost of debt, $r_d(1 - T)$
 b. Cost of preferred stock, r_{ps}; cost of common equity or cost of common stock, r_s
 c. Target capital structure
 d. Flotation cost, F; cost of new external common equity, r_e

(9-2) In what sense is the WACC an average cost? A marginal cost?

(9-3) How would each of the following affect a firm's cost of debt, $r_d(1 - T)$; its cost of equity, r_s; and its weighted average cost of capital, WACC? Indicate by a plus (+), a minus (−), or a zero (0) if the factor would raise, lower, or have an indeterminate effect on the item in question. Assume other things are held constant. Be prepared to justify your answer, but recognize that several of the parts probably have no single correct answer; these questions are designed to stimulate thought and discussion.

	EFFECT ON		
	$r_d(1-T)$	r_s	WACC
a. The corporate tax rate is lowered.	____	____	____
b. The Federal Reserve tightens credit.	____	____	____
c. The firm uses more debt.	____	____	____
d. The firm doubles the amount of capital it raises during the year.	____	____	____
e. The firm expands into a risky new area.	____	____	____
f. Investors become more risk averse.	____	____	____

(9-4) Distinguish between beta (or market) risk, within-firm (or corporate) risk, and stand-alone risk for a potential project. Of the three measures, which is theoretically the most relevant, and why?

(9-5) Suppose a firm estimates its cost of capital for the coming year to be 10 percent. What might be reasonable costs of capital for average-risk, high-risk, and low-risk projects?

SELF-TEST PROBLEM   Solution Appears in Appendix A

(ST-1)
WACC
Longstreet Communications Inc. (LCI) has the following capital structure, which it considers to be optimal: debt = 25%, preferred stock = 15%, and common stock = 60%.

LCI's tax rate is 40 percent and investors expect earnings and dividends to grow at a constant rate of 6 percent in the future. LCI paid a dividend of $3.70 per share last year (D_0), and its stock currently sells at a price of $60 per share. Treasury bonds yield 6 percent, the market risk premium is 5 percent, and LCI's beta is 1.3. These terms would apply to new security offerings:

Preferred: New preferred could be sold to the public at a price of $100 per share, with a dividend of $9. Flotation costs of $5 per share would be incurred.
Debt: Debt could be sold at an interest rate of 9 percent.

a. Find the component costs of debt, preferred stock, and common stock. Assume LCI does not have to issue any additional shares of common stock.
b. What is the WACC?

PROBLEMS

(9-1)
Cost of Equity
David Ortiz Motors has a target capital structure of 40 percent debt and 60 percent equity. The yield to maturity on the company's outstanding bonds is 9 percent, and the company's tax rate is 40 percent. Ortiz's CFO has calculated the company's WACC as 9.96 percent. What is the company's cost of equity capital?

(9-2)
Cost of Preferred Stock
Tunney Industries can issue perpetual preferred stock at a price of $50 a share. The issue is expected to pay a constant annual dividend of $3.80 a share. The flotation cost on the issue is estimated to be 5 percent. What is the company's cost of preferred stock, r_{ps}?

(9-3)
Cost of Equity
Javits & Sons' common stock is currently trading at $30 a share. The stock is expected to pay a dividend of $3.00 a share at the end of the year (D_1 = $3.00), and the dividend is expected to grow at a constant rate of 5 percent a year. What is the cost of common equity?

(9-4)
After-Tax Cost of Debt
Calculate the after-tax cost of debt under each of the following conditions:
a. Interest rate, 13 percent; tax rate, 0 percent.
b. Interest rate, 13 percent; tax rate, 20 percent.
c. Interest rate, 13 percent; tax rate, 35 percent.

(9-5)
After-Tax Cost of Debt
The Heuser Company's currently outstanding 10 percent coupon bonds have a yield to maturity of 12 percent. Heuser believes it could issue at par new bonds that would provide a similar yield to maturity. If its marginal tax rate is 35 percent, what is Heuser's after-tax cost of debt?

(9-6)
Cost of Preferred Stock
Trivoli Industries plans to issue some $100 par preferred stock with an 11 percent dividend. The stock is selling on the market for $97.00, and Trivoli must pay flotation costs of 5 percent of the market price. What is the cost of the preferred stock for Trivoli?

(9-7)
After-Tax Cost of Debt
A company's 6 percent coupon rate, semiannual payment, $1,000 par value bond which matures in 30 years sells at a price of $515.16. The company's federal-plus-state tax rate is 40 percent. What is the firm's component cost of debt for purposes of calculating the WACC? (Hint: Base your answer on the *nominal* rate.)

(9-8)
Cost of Equity
The earnings, dividends, and stock price of Carpetto Technologies Inc. are expected to grow at 7 percent per year in the future. Carpetto's common stock sells for $23 per share, its last dividend was $2.00, and the company will pay a dividend of $2.14 at the end of the current year.
a. Using the discounted cash flow approach, what is its cost of equity?
b. If the firm's beta is 1.6, the risk-free rate is 9 percent, and the expected return on the market is 13 percent, what will be the firm's cost of equity using the CAPM approach?
c. If the firm's bonds earn a return of 12 percent, what will r_s be using the bond-yield-plus-risk-premium approach? (Hint: Use the midpoint of the risk premium range.)
d. On the basis of the results of parts a through c, what would you estimate Carpetto's cost of equity to be?

(9-9)
Cost of Equity
The Bouchard Company's current EPS is $6.50. It was $4.42 5 years ago. The company pays out 40 percent of its earnings as dividends, and the stock sells for $36.
a. Calculate the past growth rate in earnings. (Hint: This is a 5-year growth period.)
b. Calculate the *next* expected dividend per share, D_1. ($D_0 = 0.4(\$6.50) = \$2.60$.) Assume that the past growth rate will continue.
c. What is the cost of equity, r_s, for the Bouchard Company?

(9-10)
Calculation of g and EPS
Sidman Products' stock is currently selling for $60 a share. The firm is expected to earn $5.40 per share this year and to pay a year-end dividend of $3.60.
a. If investors require a 9 percent return, what rate of growth must be expected for Sidman?
b. If Sidman reinvests earnings in projects with average returns equal to the stock's expected rate of return, what will be next year's EPS? [Hint: g = ROE(Retention ratio).]

(9-11)
WACC Estimation
On January 1, the total market value of the Tysseland Company was $60 million. During the year, the company plans to raise and invest $30 million in new projects. The firm's present market value capital structure, shown below, is considered to be optimal. Assume that there is no short-term debt.

Debt	$30,000,000
Common equity	30,000,000
Total capital	$60,000,000

New bonds will have an 8 percent coupon rate, and they will be sold at par. Common stock is currently selling at $30 a share. Stockholders' required rate of return is estimated to be 12 percent, consisting of a dividend yield of 4 percent and an expected constant growth rate of 8 percent. (The next expected dividend is $1.20, so $1.20/$30 = 4%.) The marginal corporate tax rate is 40 percent.
a. To maintain the present capital structure, how much of the new investment must be financed by common equity?
b. Assume that there is sufficient cash flow such that Tysseland can maintain its target capital structure without issuing additional shares of equity. What is the WACC?

c. Suppose now that there is not enough internal cash flow and the firm must issue new shares of stock. Qualitatively speaking, what will happen to the WACC?

(9-12) Suppose the Schoof Company has this *book value* balance sheet:

Market Value
Capital Structure

Current assets	$30,000,000	Current liabilities	$10,000,000
Fixed assets	50,000,000	Long-term debt	30,000,000
		Common equity	
		Common stock (1 million shares)	1,000,000
		Retained earnings	39,000,000
Total assets	$80,000,000	Total claims	$80,000,000

The current liabilities consist entirely of notes payable to banks, and the interest rate on this debt is 10 percent, the same as the rate on new bank loans. The long-term debt consists of 30,000 bonds, each of which has a par value of $1,000, carries an annual coupon interest rate of 6 percent, and matures in 20 years. The going rate of interest on new long-term debt, r_d, is 10 percent, and this is the present yield to maturity on the bonds. The common stock sells at a price of $60 per share. Calculate the firm's market value capital structure.

(9-13) A summary of the balance sheet of Travellers Inn Inc. (TII), a company which was
WACC Estimation formed by merging a number of regional motel chains and which hopes to rival Holiday Inn on the national scene, is shown in the table:

Travellers Inn: December 31, 2005 (Millions of Dollars)

Cash	$ 10	Accounts payable	$ 10
Accounts receivable	20	Accruals	10
Inventories	20	Short-term debt	5
Current assets	$ 50	Current liabilities	$ 25
Net fixed assets	50	Long-term debt	30
		Preferred stock	5
		Common equity	
		Common stock	$ 10
		Retained earnings	30
		Total common equity	$ 40
Total assets	$100	Total liabilities and equity	$100

These facts are also given for TII:
(1) Short-term debt consists of bank loans that currently cost 10 percent, with interest payable quarterly. These loans are used to finance receivables and inventories on a seasonal basis, so in the off-season, bank loans are zero.
(2) The long-term debt consists of 20-year, semiannual payment mortgage bonds with a coupon rate of 8 percent. Currently, these bonds provide a yield to investors of $r_d = 12\%$. If new bonds were sold, they would yield investors 12 percent.
(3) TII's perpetual preferred stock has a $100 par value, pays a quarterly dividend of $2, and has a yield to investors of 11 percent. New perpetual preferred would have to provide the same yield to investors, and the company would incur a 5 percent flotation cost to sell it.
(4) The company has 4 million shares of common stock outstanding. $P_0 = \$20$, but the stock has recently traded in a range of $17 to $23. $D_0 = \$1$ and $EPS_0 = \$2$. ROE based on average equity was 24 percent in 2005, but management expects to increase this return on equity to 30 percent; however, security analysts are not aware of management's optimism in this regard.

(5) Betas, as reported by security analysts, range from 1.3 to 1.7; the T-bond rate is 10 percent; and RP_M is estimated by various brokerage houses to be in the range of 4.5 to 5.5 percent. Brokerage house reports forecast growth rates in the range of 10 to 15 percent over the foreseeable future. However, some analysts do not explicitly forecast growth rates, but they indicate to their clients that they expect TII's historical trends as shown in the table below to continue.

(6) At a recent conference, TII's financial vice president polled some pension fund investment managers on the minimum rate of return they would have to expect on TII's common to make them willing to buy the common rather than TII bonds, when the bonds yielded 12 percent. The responses suggested a risk premium over TII bonds of 4 to 6 percentage points.

(7) TII is in the 40 percent federal-plus-state tax bracket.

(8) TII's principal investment banker, Henry, Kaufman & Company, predicts a decline in interest rates, with r_d falling to 10 percent and the T-bond rate to 8 percent, although Henry, Kaufman & Company acknowledges that an increase in the expected inflation rate could lead to an increase rather than a decrease in rates.

(9) Here is the historical record of EPS and DPS:

Year	EPS	DPS	Year	EPS	DPS
1991	$0.09	$0.00	1999	0.78	0.00
1992	−0.20	0.00	2000	0.80	0.00
1993	$0.40	$0.00	2001	$1.20	$0.20
1994	0.52	0.00	2002	0.95	0.40
1995	$0.10	$0.00	2003	1.30	0.60
1996	0.57	0.00	2004	1.60	0.80
1997	0.61	0.00	2005	2.00	1.00
1998	0.70	0.00			

Assume that you are a recently hired financial analyst, and your boss, the treasurer, has asked you to estimate the company's WACC; assume no new equity will be issued. Your cost of capital should be appropriate for use in evaluating projects which are in the same risk class as the firm's average assets now on books.

(9-14) Rework Problem 9-3, assuming that new stock will be issued. The stock will be issued
Flotation Costs and for $30 and the flotation cost is 10 percent of the issue proceeds. The expected divi-
the Cost of Equity dend and growth remain at $3.00 per share and 5 percent, respectively.

(9-15) Suppose a company will issue new 20-year debt with a par value of $1,000 and a
Flotation Costs and coupon rate of 9 percent, paid annually. The tax rate is 40 percent. If the flotation
the Cost of Debt cost is 2 percent of the issue proceeds, what is the after-tax cost of debt?

SPREADSHEET PROBLEM

(9-16) Start with the partial model in the file *CF2 Ch 09 P16 Build a Model.xls* from the
Build a Model: WACC textbook's Web site. The stock of Gao Computing sells for $50, and last year's dividend was $2.10. A flotation cost of 10 percent would be required to issue new common stock. Gao's preferred stock pays a dividend of $3.30 per share, and new preferred could be sold at a price to net the company $30 per share. Security analysts are projecting that the common dividend will grow at a rate of 7 percent a year. The firm can also issue additional long-term debt at an interest rate (or before-tax cost) of 10 percent, and its marginal tax rate is 35 percent. The market risk premium is 6 percent, the risk-free rate is 6.5 percent, and Gao's beta is 0.83. In its cost of capital calculations, Gao uses a target capital structure with 45 percent debt, 5 percent preferred stock, and 50 percent common equity.

e-resource

a. Calculate the cost of each capital component (that is, the after-tax cost of debt), the cost of preferred stock (including flotation costs), and the cost of equity (ignoring flotation costs) with the DCF method and the CAPM method.

b. Calculate the cost of new stock using the DCF model.

c. What is the cost of new common stock, based on the CAPM? (Hint: Find the difference between r_e and r_s as determined by the DCF method and add that differential to the CAPM value for r_s.)

d. Assuming that Gao will not issue new equity and will continue to use the same target capital structure, what is the company's WACC?

e. Suppose Gao is evaluating three projects with the following characteristics:

   (1) Each project has a cost of $1 million. They will all be financed using the target mix of long-term debt, preferred stock, and common equity. The cost of the common equity for each project should be based on the beta estimated for the project. All equity will come from retained earnings.

   (2) Equity invested in Project A would have a beta of 0.5 and an expected return of 9.0 percent.

   (3) Equity invested in Project B would have a beta of 1.0 and an expected return of 10.0 percent.

   (4) Equity invested in Project C would have a beta of 2.0 and an expected return of 11.0 percent.

f. Analyze the company's situation and explain why each project should be accepted or rejected.

CYBERPROBLEM

Please go to our Web site, **http://ehrhardt.swlearning.com**, to access any Cyberproblems.

THOMSON ONE
Business School Edition

Please go to **http://ehrhardt.swlearning.com** to access any Thomson ONE—Business School Edition problems.

MINI CASE

During the last few years, Harry Davis Industries has been too constrained by the high cost of capital to make many capital investments. Recently, though, capital costs have been declining, and the company has decided to look seriously at a major expansion program that had been proposed by the marketing department. Assume that you are an assistant to Leigh Jones, the financial vice president. Your first task is to estimate Harry Davis's cost of capital. Jones has provided you with the following data, which she believes may be relevant to your task:

(1) The firm's tax rate is 40 percent.

(2) The current price of Harry Davis's 12 percent coupon, semiannual payment, noncallable bonds with 15 years remaining to maturity is $1,153.72. Harry Davis does not use short-term interest-bearing debt on a permanent basis. New bonds would be privately placed with no flotation cost.

(3) The current price of the firm's 10 percent, $100 par value, quarterly dividend, perpetual preferred stock is $113.10. Harry Davis would incur flotation costs of $2.00 per share on a new issue.

(4) Harry Davis's common stock is currently selling at $50 per share. Its last dividend (D_0) was $4.19, and dividends are expected to grow at a constant rate of 5 percent in the foreseeable future. Harry Davis's beta is 1.2, the yield on T-bonds is 7 percent, and the market risk premium is estimated to

be 6 percent. For the bond-yield-plus-risk-premium approach, the firm uses a 4 percentage point risk premium.

(5) Harry Davis's target capital structure is 30 percent long-term debt, 10 percent preferred stock, and 60 percent common equity.

To structure the task somewhat, Jones has asked you to answer the following questions.

a. (1) What sources of capital should be included when you estimate Harry Davis's weighted average cost of capital (WACC)?

   (2) Should the component costs be figured on a before-tax or an after-tax basis?

   (3) Should the costs be historical (embedded) costs or new (marginal) costs?

b. What is the market interest rate on Harry Davis's debt and its component cost of debt?

c. (1) What is the firm's cost of preferred stock?

   (2) Harry Davis's preferred stock is riskier to investors than its debt, yet the preferred's yield to investors is lower than the yield to maturity on the debt. Does this suggest that you have made a mistake? (Hint: Think about taxes.)

d. (1) What are the two primary ways companies raise common equity?

   (2) Why is there a cost associated with reinvested earnings?

   (3) Harry Davis doesn't plan to issue new shares of common stock. Using the CAPM approach, what is Harry Davis's estimated cost of equity?

e. (1) What is the estimated cost of equity using the discounted cash flow (DCF) approach?

   (2) Suppose the firm has historically earned 15 percent on equity (ROE) and retained 35 percent of earnings, and investors expect this situation to continue in the future. How could you use this information to estimate the future dividend growth rate, and what growth rate would you get? Is this consistent with the 5 percent growth rate given earlier?

   (3) Could the DCF method be applied if the growth rate was not constant? How?

f. What is the cost of equity based on the bond-yield-plus-risk-premium method?

g. What is your final estimate for the cost of equity, r_s?

h. What is Harry Davis's weighted average cost of capital (WACC)?

i. What factors influence a company's WACC?

j. Should the company use the composite WACC as the hurdle rate for each of its divisions?

k. What procedures are used to determine the risk-adjusted cost of capital for a particular division? What approaches are used to measure a division's beta?

l. Harry Davis is interested in establishing a new division, which will focus primarily on developing new Internet-based projects. In trying to determine the cost of capital for this new division, you discover that stand-alone firms involved in similar projects have on average the following characteristics:

   • Their capital structure is 10 percent debt and 90 percent common equity.

   • Their cost of debt is typically 12 percent.

   • The beta is 1.7.

   Given this information, what would your estimate be for the division's cost of capital?

m. What are three types of project risk? How is each type of risk used?

n. Explain in words why new common stock that is raised externally has a higher percentage cost than equity that is raised internally by reinvesting earnings.

o. (1) Harry Davis estimates that if it issues new common stock, the flotation cost will be 15 percent. Harry Davis incorporates the flotation costs into the DCF approach. What is the estimated cost of newly issued common stock, taking into account the flotation cost?

   (2) Suppose Harry Davis issues 30-year debt with a par value of $1,000 and a coupon rate of 10 percent, paid annually. If flotation costs are 2 percent, what is the after-tax cost of debt for the new bond issue?

p. What four common mistakes in estimating the WACC should Harry Davis avoid?

SELECTED ADDITIONAL REFERENCES AND CASES

For a comprehensive treatment of the cost of capital, see

Ehrhardt, Michael C., *The Search for Value: Measuring the Company's Cost of Capital* (Boston: Harvard Business School Press, 1994).

The following articles provide some valuable insights into the CAPM approach to estimating the cost of equity:

Amihud, Yakov, and Haim Mendelson, "Liquidity and Cost of Capital: Implications for Corporate Management," *Journal of Applied Corporate Finance,* Fall 1989, 65–73.

Brigham, Eugene F., Dilip K. Shome, and Steve R. Vinson, "The Risk Premium Approach to Measuring a Utility's Cost of Equity," *Financial Management,* Spring 1985, 33–45.

Chen, Carl R., "Time-Series Analysis of Beta Stationarity and Its Determinants: A Case of Public Utilities," *Financial Management,* Autumn 1982, 64–70.

Harris, Robert S., and Felecia C. Marston, "Estimating Shareholder Risk Premia Using Analysts' Growth Forecasts," *Financial Management,* Summer 1992, 63–70.

Taggart, Robert A., Jr., "Consistent Valuation and Cost of Capital Expressions with Corporate and Personal Taxes," *Financial Management,* Autumn 1991, 8–20.

Timme, Stephen G., and Peter C. Eisemann, "On the Use of Consensus Forecasts of Growth in the Constant Growth Model: The Case of Electric Utilities," *Financial Management,* Winter 1989, 23–35.

The following cases from the Finance Online Case Library *cover many of the concepts discussed in this chapter and are available at* *http://www.textchoice.com:*

Case 4A, "West Coast Semiconductor"; Case 4B, "Ace Repair"; Case 4C, "Premier Paint & Body"; Case 6, "Randolph Corporation"; and Case 57, "Auto Hut."

CHAPTER 10

The Basics of Capital Budgeting:
Evaluating Cash Flows

In 1970, the Adolph Coors Company was a small brewer serving a regional market. But because of its quality products and aggressive marketing, by 1990 Coors had risen to the number three brand in the U.S. beer market. During this high-growth phase, the corporate emphasis was on marketing, technology, engineering, and capacity additions. When investing in new equipment or factories, Coors always went "the Cadillac route," with little scrutiny of proposed projects. In effect, their motto was "If you build it, they will come." Indeed, for two decades consumers did switch to Coors.

However, the brewing industry began to experience major problems in the 1990s. Many consumers were drawn to wine, causing growth in beer sales to fall below 1 percent per year. In addition, large numbers of microbreweries opened, providing beer drinkers with an alternative to the national brands. These events proved particularly painful to Coors, whose lack of financial discipline had led to a frivolous use of capital and thus to a high-cost infrastructure.

Coors hired a new CFO, Timothy Wolf, who soon learned that Coors had a low return on invested capital, negative free cash flow, and an unreliable planning/forecasting process. Wolf quickly created an in-house education program to teach managers and engineers how to conduct a rational project analysis. Even more important, he began to shift the corporate culture from a focus on undisciplined growth and high-technology engineering to creating shareholder value. This new focus was put to the test when Coors reexamined its plans for a major new bottle-washing facility in Virginia. Using the capital budgeting processes established by Wolf, the project team was able to reduce the cost of the investment by 25 percent. They also implemented design changes that led to lower operating costs.

Under Wolf's guidance, Coors steadily improved both its return on invested capital and its free cash flow. Financial analysts were impressed with Wolf's efforts. Skip Carpenter of Donaldson, Lufkin & Jenrette said, "From a financial perspective, there's absolutely no question Coors is better positioned to deal with the difficulties of the beer industry."[1] Investors seem to agree; Coors' stock price has climbed from about $14 per share when Wolf joined in 1995 to over $65 per share in May 2004, an annualized average gain of more than 18 percent.

---

[1] See Stephen Barr, "Coors's New Brew," *CFO*, March 1998, 91–93.

CORPORATE VALUATION AND CAPITAL BUDGETING

You can calculate the free cash flows (FCFs) for a project in much the same way as for a firm. When the project's free cash flows are discounted at the appropriate risk-adjusted rate, the result is the project's value. One difference between valuing a firm and valuing a project is the rate that is used to discount cash flows. For a firm, it is the overall weighted cost of capital; for a project, it is r, the project's risk adjusted cost of capital.

Subtracting the initial cost of the project gives the net present value (NPV). If a project has a positive NPV, then it adds value to the firm. In fact, the firm's market value added (MVA) is the sum of all its projects' NPVs. Therefore, the process for evaluating projects, called **capital budgeting,** is critical for a firm's success.

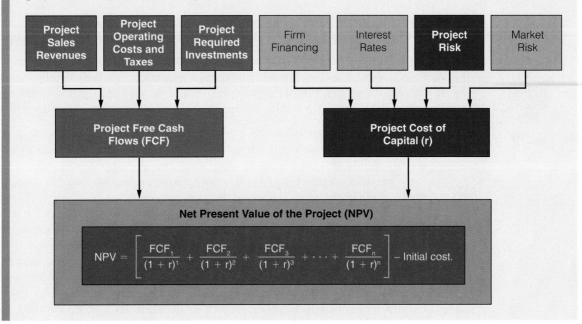

$$NPV = \left[\frac{FCF_1}{(1+r)^1} + \frac{FCF_2}{(1+r)^2} + \frac{FCF_3}{(1+r)^3} + \cdots + \frac{FCF_n}{(1+r)^n} \right] - \text{Initial cost.}$$

Capital budgeting is the process of evaluating a company's potential investments and deciding which ones to accept. This chapter provides an overview of the capital budgeting process and explains the basic techniques used to evaluate potential projects, given that their expected cash flows have already been estimated. Chapter 11 then explains how to estimate a project's cash flows and analyze its risk.

OVERVIEW OF CAPITAL BUDGETING

Capital budgeting is the decision process that managers use to identify those projects that add to the firm's value, and as such it is perhaps the most important task faced by financial managers and their staffs. First, a firm's capital budgeting decisions define its strategic direction, because moves into new products, services, or markets must be preceded by capital expenditures. Second, the results of capital budgeting decisions continue for many years, reducing flexibility. Third, poor capital budgeting can have serious financial consequences. If the firm invests too much, it will waste investors' capital on excess capacity. On the other hand, if it does not invest enough, its equipment and computer software may not be sufficiently modern to enable it to produce competitively. Also, if it has inadequate capacity, it may lose market share to rival firms, and regaining lost customers requires heavy selling expenses, price reductions, or product improvements, all of which are costly.

A firm's growth, and even its ability to remain competitive and to survive, depends on a constant flow of ideas for new products, for ways to make existing products better, and for ways to operate at a lower cost. Accordingly, a well-managed firm will go to great lengths to encourage good capital budgeting proposals from its employees. If a firm has capable and imaginative executives and employees, and if its incentive system is working properly, many ideas for capital investment will be advanced. Some ideas will be good ones, but others will not. Therefore, companies must screen projects for those that add value, the primary topic of this chapter.

SELF-TEST QUESTIONS Why are capital budgeting decisions so important?
What are some ways firms get ideas for capital projects?

PROJECT CLASSIFICATIONS

Analyzing capital expenditure proposals is not a costless operation—benefits can be gained, but analysis does have a cost. For certain types of projects, a relatively detailed analysis may be warranted; for others, simpler procedures should be used. Accordingly, firms generally categorize projects and then analyze those in each category somewhat differently:

1. *Replacement: maintenance of business.* Replacement of worn-out or damaged equipment is necessary if the firm is to continue in business. The only issues here are (a) should this operation be continued and (b) should we continue to use the same production processes? If the answers are yes, maintenance decisions are normally made without an elaborate decision process.

2. *Replacement: cost reduction.* These projects lower the costs of labor, materials, and other inputs such as electricity by replacing serviceable but less efficient equipment. These decisions are discretionary, and require a detailed analysis.

3. *Expansion of existing products or markets.* Expenditures to increase output of existing products, or to expand retail outlets or distribution facilities in markets now being served, are included here. These decisions are more complex because they require an explicit forecast of growth in demand, so a more detailed analysis is required. Also, the final decision is generally made at a higher level within the firm.

4. *Expansion into new products or markets.* These projects involve strategic decisions that could change the fundamental nature of the business, and they normally require the expenditure of large sums with delayed paybacks. Invariably, a detailed analysis is required, and the final decision is generally made at the very top—by the board of directors as a part of the firm's strategic plan.

5. *Safety and/or environmental projects.* Expenditures necessary to comply with government orders, labor agreements, or insurance policy terms are called *mandatory investments,* and they often involve *non-revenue-producing projects.* How they are handled depends on their size, with small ones being treated much like the Category 1 projects described above.

6. *Research and development.* The expected cash flows from R&D are often too uncertain to warrant a standard discounted cash flow (DCF) analysis. Instead, decision tree analysis and the real options approach are often used.

7. *Long-term contracts.* Companies often make long-term contractual arrangements to provide products or services to specific customers. For example, IBM has signed agreements to handle computer services for other companies for periods of 5 to 10 years. There may or may not be much up-front investment, but costs and revenues will accrue over multiple years, and a DCF analysis should be performed before the contract is signed.

Within each category, projects are classified by their dollar costs: Larger investments require increasingly detailed analysis and approval at a higher level within the firm. Thus, a plant manager may be authorized to approve maintenance expenditures up to $10,000 on the basis of a relatively unsophisticated analysis, but the full board of directors may have to approve decisions that involve either amounts over $1 million or expansions into new products or markets.

Identify the major project classification categories, and explain how they are used.

CAPITAL BUDGETING DECISION RULES

Six key methods are used to rank projects and to decide whether or not they should be accepted for inclusion in the capital budget: (1) payback, (2) discounted payback, (3) net present value (NPV), (4) internal rate of return (IRR), (5) modified internal rate of return (MIRR), and (6) profitability index (PI). We explain how each ranking criterion is calculated, and then we evaluate how well each performs in terms of identifying those projects that will maximize the firm's stock price.

The first, and most difficult, step in project analysis is estimating the relevant cash flows, a step that Chapter 11 explains in detail. Our present focus is on the different decision rules, so we provide the cash flows used in this chapter, starting with the expected cash flows of Project S and L in Figure 10-1. These projects are equally risky, and the cash flows for each year, CF_t, reflect purchase cost, investments in working capital, taxes, depreciation, and salvage values. Finally, we assume that all cash flows occur at the end of the designated year. Incidentally, the S stands for *short* and the L for *long*: Project S is a short-term project in the sense that its cash inflows come in sooner than L's.

CF

e-resource

The Web Extension explains a seventh method, the accounting rate of return (ARR) approach. The ARR approach has major flaws, and the Web Extension explains why it should not be used.

Payback Period

The **payback period,** defined as the expected number of years required to recover the original investment, was the first formal method used to evaluate capital budgeting projects. The payback calculation is diagrammed in Figure 10-2, and it is explained below for Project S.

The cumulative net cash flow at t = 0 is just the initial cost of −$1,000. At Year 1 the cumulative net cash flow is the previous cumulative of −$1,000 plus the Year 1 cash flow of $500: −$1,000 + $500 = −$500. Similarly, the cumulative for Year 2 is the previous cumulative of −$500 plus the Year 2 inflow of $400, resulting in −$100. We see that by the end of Year 3 the cumulative inflows have more than recovered the initial outflow. Thus, the payback occurred during the third year. If the $300 of inflows comes in evenly during Year 3, then the exact payback period can be found as follows:

$$\text{Payback}_S = \text{Year before full recovery} + \frac{\text{Unrecovered cost at start of year}}{\text{Cash flow during year}}$$

$$= 2 + \frac{\$100}{\$300} = 2.33 \text{ years.}$$

Applying the same procedure to Project L, we find $\text{Payback}_L = 3.33$ years.

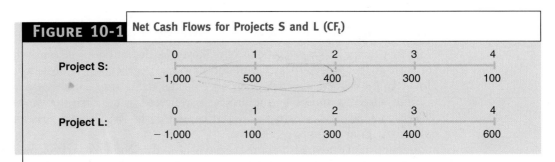

FIGURE 10-1	Net Cash Flows for Projects S and L (CF$_t$)

	0	1	2	3	4
Project S:	− 1,000	500	400	300	100

	0	1	2	3	4
Project L:	− 1,000	100	300	400	600

Note: CF$_0$ represents the cash flow experienced at the project's inception.

| FIGURE 10-2 | Payback Period for Projects S and L |

Project S:		0	1	2	3	4
Net cash flow		– 1,000	500	400	300	100
Cumulative NCF		– 1,000	– 500	– 100	200	300
Payback$_S$ = 2.33 years.						

Project L:		0	1	2	3	4
Net cash flow		– 1,000	100	300	400	600
Cumulative NCF		– 1,000	– 900	– 600	– 200	400
Payback$_L$ = 3.33 years.						

The shorter the payback period, the better. Therefore, if the firm required a payback of three years or less, Project S would be accepted but Project L would be rejected. If the projects were **mutually exclusive,** S would be ranked over L because S has the shorter payback. *Mutually exclusive* means that if one project is taken on, the other must be rejected. For example, the installation of a conveyor-belt system in a warehouse and the purchase of a fleet of forklifts for the same warehouse would be mutually exclusive projects—accepting one implies rejection of the other. **Independent projects** are projects whose cash flows don't affect one another.

Discounted Payback Period

Some firms use a variant of the regular payback, the **discounted payback period,** which is similar to the regular payback period except that the expected cash flows are discounted by the project's cost of capital. Thus, the discounted payback period is defined as the number of years required to recover the investment from *discounted* net cash flows. Figure 10-3 contains the discounted net cash flows for Projects S and L, assuming both projects have a cost of capital of 10 percent. To construct Figure 10-3, each cash inflow is divided by $(1 + r)^t = (1.10)^t$, where t is the year in which the cash flow occurs and r is the project's cost of capital. After three years, Project S will have generated $1,011 in discounted cash inflows. Because the cost is $1,000, the discounted payback is just under three years, or, to be precise, 2 + ($214/$225) = 2.95 years. Project L's discounted payback is 3.88 years:

$$\text{Discounted payback}_S = 2.0 + \$214/\$225 = 2.95 \text{ years.}$$
$$\text{Discounted payback}_L = 3.0 + \$360/\$410 = 3.88 \text{ years.}$$

For Projects S and L, the rankings are the same regardless of which payback method is used; that is, Project S is preferred to Project L, and Project S would still be selected if the firm were to require a discounted payback of three years or less. Often, however, the regular and the discounted paybacks produce conflicting rankings.

Evaluating Payback and Discounted Payback

Note that the payback is a type of "breakeven" calculation in the sense that if cash flows come in at the expected rate until the payback year, then the project will break even. However, the regular payback does not consider the cost of capital—no cost for the debt or equity used to undertake the project is reflected in the cash flows or the calculation. The discounted payback does consider capital costs—it shows the breakeven year after covering debt and equity costs.

An important drawback of both the payback and discounted payback methods is that they ignore cash flows that are paid or received after the payback period. For example, suppose

FIGURE 10-3 Projects S and L: Discounted Payback Period

Project S:	0	1	2	3	4
Net cash flow	− 1,000	500	400	300	100
Discounted NCF (at 10%)	− 1,000	455	331	225	68
Cumulative discounted NCF	− 1,000	− 545	− 214	11	79

Payback_S = 2.95 years.

Project L:	0	1	2	3	4
Net cash flow	− 1,000	100	300	400	600
Discounted NCF (at 10%)	− 1,000	91	248	301	410
Cumulative discounted NCF	− 1,000	− 909	− 661	− 360	50

Payback_L = 3.88 years.

Project L had an additional cash flow of $5,000 at Year 5. Common sense suggests that Project L would be more valuable than Project S, yet its payback and discounted payback make it look worse than Project S. Consequently, both payback methods have serious deficiencies.

Although the payback methods have serious faults as ranking criteria, they do provide information on how long funds will be tied up in a project. Thus, the shorter the payback period, other things held constant, the greater the project's *liquidity*. Also, since cash flows expected in the distant future are generally riskier than near-term cash flows, the payback is often used as an indicator of a project's *riskiness*.

Net Present Value (NPV)

As the flaws in the payback were recognized, people began to search for ways to improve the effectiveness of project evaluations. One such method is the **net present value (NPV) method**, which relies on **discounted cash flow (DCF) techniques.** To implement this approach, we proceed as follows:

1. Find the present value of each cash flow, including all inflows and outflows, discounted at the project's cost of capital.
2. Sum these discounted cash flows; this sum is defined as the project's NPV.
3. If the NPV is positive, the project should be accepted, while if the NPV is negative, it should be rejected. If two projects with positive NPVs are mutually exclusive, the one with the higher NPV should be chosen.

The equation for the NPV is as follows:

$$\text{NPV} = \text{CF}_0 + \frac{\text{CF}_1}{(1 + r)^1} + \frac{\text{CF}_2}{(1 + r)^2} + \cdots + \frac{\text{CF}_n}{(1 + r)^n}$$

$$= \sum_{t=0}^{n} \frac{\text{CF}_t}{(1 + r)^t}.$$

(10-1)

Here CF_t is the expected net cash flow at Period t, r is the project's cost of capital, and n is its life. Cash outflows (expenditures such as the cost of buying equipment or building factories) are treated as *negative* cash flows. In evaluating Projects S and L, only CF_0 is negative, but for many large projects such as the Alaska Pipeline, an electric generating plant, or a new Boeing jet aircraft, outflows occur for several years before operations begin and cash flows turn positive.

At a 10 percent cost of capital, Project S's NPV is $78.82:

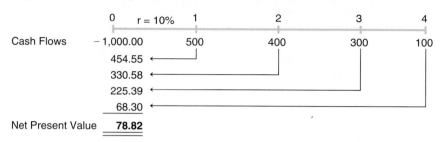

By a similar process, we find NPV_L = $49.18. On this basis, both projects should be accepted if they are independent, but S should be chosen over L if they are mutually exclusive.

It is not hard to calculate the NPV as was done in the time line by using Equation 10-1 and a regular calculator. However, it is more efficient to use a financial calculator. Different calculators are set up somewhat differently, but they all have a section of memory called the "cash flow register" that is used for uneven cash flows such as those in Projects S and L (as opposed to equal annuity cash flows). A solution process for Equation 10-1 is literally programmed into financial calculators, and all you have to do is enter the cash flows (being sure to observe the signs), along with the value of r = I. At that point, you have (in your calculator) this equation:

$$NPV_S = -1,000 + \frac{500}{(1.10)^1} + \frac{400}{(1.10)^2} + \frac{300}{(1.10)^3} + \frac{100}{(1.10)^4}.$$

Note that the equation has one unknown, NPV. Now all you need to do is to ask the calculator to solve the equation for you, which you do by pressing the NPV button (and, on some calculators, the "compute" button). The answer, 78.82, will appear on the screen.[2]

Most projects last for more than four years, and, as we see in Chapter 11, we must go through a number of steps to develop the estimated cash flows. Therefore, financial analysts generally use spreadsheets when dealing with capital budgeting projects. For Project S, this spreadsheet could be used (disregard for now the IRR on Row 6; we discuss it in the next section):

	A	B	C	D	E	F
1	Project S					
2	r =	10%				
3	Time	0	1	2	3	4
4	Cash flow =	−1000	500	400	300	100
5	NPV =	$78.82				
6	IRR =	14.5%				

In *Excel*, the formula in Cell B5 is =B4+NPV(B2,C4:F4), and it results in a value of $78.82.[3] For a simple problem such as this, setting up a spreadsheet may not seem worth

---

[2] The *Technology Supplement* for this text explains commonly used calculator applications for a variety of calculators.

[3] You could click the function wizard, f_x, then Financial, then NPV, and then OK. Then insert B2 as the rate and C4:F4 as "Value 1," which is the cash flow range. Then click OK, and edit the equation by adding B4. Note that you cannot enter the −$1,000 cost as part of the NPV range because the *Excel* NPV function assumes that the first cash flow in the range occurs at t = 1.

the trouble. However, in real-world problems there will be a number of rows above our cash flow line, starting with expected sales, then deducting various costs and taxes, and ending up with the cash flows shown on Row 4. Moreover, once a spreadsheet has been set up, it is easy to change input values to see what would happen under different conditions. For example, we could see what would happen if lower sales caused all cash flows to decline by $15, or if the cost of capital rose to 10.5 percent. Using *Excel*, it is easy to make such changes and then see the effects on NPV.

Rationale for the NPV Method

The rationale for the NPV method is straightforward. An NPV of zero signifies that the project's cash flows are exactly sufficient to repay the invested capital and to provide the required rate of return on that capital. If a project has a positive NPV, then it is generating more cash than is needed to service the debt and to provide the required return to shareholders, and this excess cash accrues solely to the firm's stockholders. Therefore, if a firm takes on a project with a positive NPV, the wealth of the stockholders increases. In our example, shareholders' wealth would increase by $78.82 if the firm takes on Project S, but by only $49.18 if it takes on Project L. Viewed in this manner, it is easy to see why S is preferred to L, and it is also easy to see the logic of the NPV approach.[4]

There is also a direct relationship between NPV and EVA (economic value added, as discussed in Chapter 3)—NPV is equal to the present value of the project's future EVAs. Therefore, accepting positive NPV projects should result in a positive EVA and a positive MVA (market value added, or the excess of the firm's market value over its book value). So, a reward system that compensates managers for producing positive EVA will lead to the use of NPV for making capital budgeting decisions.

Internal Rate of Return (IRR)

In Chapter 6 we presented procedures for finding the yield to maturity, or rate of return, on a bond—if you invest in a bond, hold it to maturity, and receive all of the promised cash flows, you will earn the YTM on the money you invested. Exactly the same concepts are employed in capital budgeting when the **internal rate of return (IRR) method** is used. The IRR is defined as the discount rate that forces the NPV to equal zero:

$$CF_0 + \frac{CF_1}{(1 + IRR)^1} + \frac{CF_2}{(1 + IRR)^2} + \cdots + \frac{CF_n}{(1 + IRR)^n} = 0$$

$$NPV = \sum_{t=0}^{n} \frac{CF_t}{(1 + IRR)^t} = 0.$$

(10-2)

For our Project S, here is the time line setup:

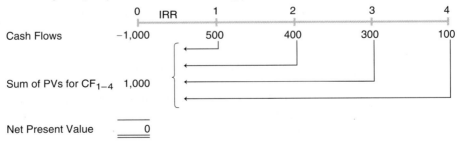

4 This description of the process is somewhat oversimplified. Both analysts and investors anticipate that firms will identify and accept positive NPV projects, and current stock prices reflect these expectations. Thus, stock prices react to announcements of new capital projects only to the extent that such projects were not already expected.

$$-1,000 + \frac{500}{(1 + \text{IRR})^1} + \frac{400}{(1 + \text{IRR})^2} + \frac{300}{(1 + \text{IRR})^3} + \frac{100}{(1 + \text{IRR})^4} = 0.$$

Thus, we have an equation with one unknown, IRR, and we need to solve for IRR.

Although it is easy to find the NPV without a financial calculator, this is *not* true of the IRR. If the cash flows are constant from year to year, then we have an annuity, and we can use annuity formulas to find the IRR. However, if the cash flows are not constant, as is generally the case in capital budgeting, then it is difficult to find the IRR without a financial calculator. Without a calculator, you must solve Equation 10-2 by trial-and-error—try some discount rate and see if the equation solves to zero, and if it does not, try a different discount rate, and continue until you find the rate that forces the equation to equal zero. The discount rate that causes the equation (and the NPV) to equal zero is defined as the IRR. For a realistic project with a fairly long life, the trial-and-error approach is a tedious, time-consuming task.

Fortunately, it is easy to find IRRs with a financial calculator. You follow procedures almost identical to those used to find the NPV. First, you enter the cash flows as shown on the preceding time line into the calculator's cash flow register. In effect, you have entered the cash flows into the equation shown below the time line. Note that we have one unknown, IRR, which is the discount rate that forces the equation to equal zero. The calculator has been programmed to solve for the IRR, and you activate this program by pressing the button labeled "IRR." Then the calculator solves for IRR and displays it on the screen. Here are the IRRs for Projects S and L as found with a financial calculator:

$$\text{IRR}_S = 14.5\%.$$

$$\text{IRR}_L = 11.8\%.$$

It is also easy to find the IRR using the same spreadsheet we used for the NPV. With *Excel*, we simply enter this formula in Cell B6: **=IRR(B4:F4)**. For Project S, the result is 14.5 percent.[5]

If both projects have a cost of capital, or **hurdle rate**, of 10 percent, then the internal rate of return rule indicates that if the projects are independent, both should be accepted—they are both expected to earn more than the cost of the capital needed to finance them. If they are mutually exclusive, S ranks higher and should be accepted, so L should be rejected. If the cost of capital is above 14.5 percent, both projects should be rejected.

Notice that the internal rate of return formula, Equation 10-2, is simply the NPV formula, Equation 10-1, solved for the particular discount rate that forces the NPV to equal zero. Thus, the same basic equation is used for both methods, but in the NPV method the discount rate, r, is specified and the NPV is found, whereas in the IRR method the NPV is specified to equal zero, and the interest rate that forces this equality (the IRR) is calculated.

Mathematically, the NPV and IRR methods will always lead to the same accept/reject decisions for independent projects. This occurs because if NPV is positive, IRR must exceed r. However, NPV and IRR can give conflicting rankings for mutually exclusive projects. This point will be discussed in more detail in a later section.

Rationale for the IRR Method

Why is the particular discount rate that equates a project's cost with the present value of its receipts (the IRR) so special? The reason is based on this logic: (1) The IRR on a project is its expected rate of return. (2) If the internal rate of return exceeds the cost of the

---

[5] Note that the full range is specified, because *Excel*'s IRR function assumes that the first cash flow (the negative $1,000) occurs at t = 0. You can use the function wizard if you don't have the formula memorized.

funds used to finance the project, a surplus will remain after paying for the capital, and this surplus will accrue to the firm's stockholders. (3) Therefore, taking on a project whose IRR exceeds its cost of capital increases shareholders' wealth. On the other hand, if the internal rate of return is less than the cost of capital, then taking on the project will impose a cost on current stockholders. It is this "break-even" characteristic that makes the IRR useful in evaluating capital projects.

SELF-TEST QUESTIONS
What four capital budgeting ranking methods were discussed in this section? Describe each method, and give the rationale for its use.

What two methods always lead to the same accept/reject decision for independent projects?

What two pieces of information does the payback period convey that are not conveyed by the other methods?

COMPARISON OF THE NPV AND IRR METHODS

In many respects the NPV method is better than IRR, so it is tempting to explain NPV only, to state that it should be used to select projects, and to go on to the next topic. However, the IRR is familiar to many corporate executives, it is widely entrenched in industry, and it does have some virtues. Therefore, it is important for you to understand the IRR method but also to be able to explain why, at times, a project with a lower IRR may be preferable to a mutually exclusive alternative with a higher IRR.

NPV Profiles

CF

e-resource

See CF2 Ch 10 Tool Kit.xls for all calculations.

A graph that plots a project's NPV against the cost of capital rates is defined as the project's **net present value profile;** profiles for Projects L and S are shown in Figure 10-4. To construct NPV profiles, first note that at a zero cost of capital, the NPV is simply the total of the projects' undiscounted cash flows. Thus, at a zero cost of capital $NPV_S = \$300$, and $NPV_L = \$400$. These values are plotted as the vertical axis intercepts in Figure 10-4. Next, we calculate the projects' NPVs at three costs of capital, 5, 10, and 15 percent, and plot these values. The four points plotted on our graph for each project are shown at the bottom of the figure.

Recall that the IRR is defined as the discount rate at which a project's NPV equals zero. Therefore, *the point where its net present value profile crosses the horizontal axis indicates a project's internal rate of return.* Since we calculated IRR_S and IRR_L in an earlier section, we can confirm the validity of the graph.

When we plot a curve through the data points, we have the net present value profiles. NPV profiles can be very useful in project analysis, and we will use them often in the remainder of the chapter.

NPV Rankings Depend on the Cost of Capital

Figure 10-4 shows that the NPV profiles of both Project L and Project S decline as the cost of capital increases. But notice in the figure that Project L has the higher NPV when the cost of capital is low, while Project S has the higher NPV if the cost of capital is greater than the 7.2 percent crossover rate. Notice also that Project L's NPV is "more sensitive" to changes in the cost of capital than is NPV_S; that is, Project L's net present value profile has the steeper slope, indicating that a given change in r has a greater effect on NPV_L than on NPV_S.

Recall that a long-term bond has greater sensitivity to interest rates than a short-term bond. Similarly, if a project has most of its cash flows coming in the early years, its NPV will not decline very much if the cost of capital increases, but a project whose cash flows

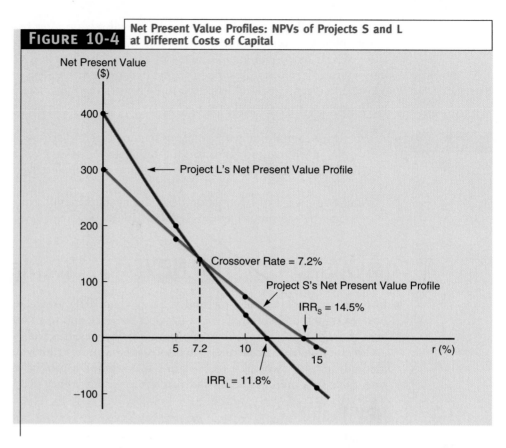

FIGURE 10-4 Net Present Value Profiles: NPVs of Projects S and L at Different Costs of Capital

r	NPV$_S$	NPV$_L$
0%	$300.00	$400.00
5	180.42	206.50
10	78.82	49.18
15	(8.33)	(80.14)

come later will be severely penalized by high capital costs. Accordingly, Project L, which has its largest cash flows in the later years, is hurt badly if the cost of capital is high, while Project S, which has relatively rapid cash flows, is affected less by high capital costs. Therefore, Project L's NPV profile has the steeper slope.

Evaluating Independent Projects

If *independent* projects are being evaluated, then the NPV and IRR criteria always lead to the same accept/reject decision: if NPV says accept, IRR also says accept. To see why this is so, assume that Projects L and S are independent, look at Figure 10-4, and notice (1) that the IRR criterion for acceptance for either project is that the project's cost of capital is less than (or to the left of) the IRR and (2) that whenever a project's cost of capital is less than its IRR, its NPV is positive. Thus, at any cost of capital less than 11.8 percent, Project L will be acceptable by both the NPV and the IRR criteria, while both methods reject Project L if the cost of capital is greater than 11.8 percent. Project S—and all other independent projects under consideration—could be analyzed similarly, and it will always turn out that if the IRR method says accept, then so will the NPV method.

Evaluating Mutually Exclusive Projects

Now assume that Projects S and L are *mutually exclusive* rather than independent. That is, we can choose either Project S or Project L, or we can reject both, but we cannot accept both projects. Notice in Figure 10-4 that as long as the cost of capital is *greater than* the crossover rate of 7.2 percent, then (1) NPV_S is larger than NPV_L and (2) IRR_S exceeds IRR_L. Therefore, if r is *greater than* the crossover rate of 7.2 percent, the two methods both lead to the selection of Project S. However, if the cost of capital is *less than* the crossover rate, the NPV method ranks Project L higher, but the IRR method indicates that Project S is better. *Thus, a conflict exists if the cost of capital is less than the crossover rate.*[6] NPV says choose mutually exclusive L, while IRR says take S. Which is correct? Logic suggests that the NPV method is better, because it selects the project that adds the most to shareholder wealth. But what causes the conflicting recommendations?

Two basic conditions can cause NPV profiles to cross, and thus conflicts to arise between NPV and IRR: (1) when *project size (or scale) differences* exist, meaning that the cost of one project is larger than that of the other, or (2) when *timing differences* exist, meaning that the timing of cash flows from the two projects differs such that most of the cash flows from one project come in the early years while most of the cash flows from the other project come in the later years, as occurred with our Projects L and S.

When either size or timing differences are present, the firm will have different amounts of funds to invest in the various years, depending on which of the two mutually exclusive projects it chooses. For example, if one project costs more than the other, then the firm will have more money at t = 0 to invest elsewhere if it selects the smaller project. Similarly, for projects of equal size, the one with the larger early cash inflows—in our example, Project S—provides more funds for reinvestment in the early years. Given this situation, the rate of return at which differential cash flows can be invested is a critical issue.

The key to resolving conflicts between mutually exclusive projects is this: How useful is it to generate cash flows sooner rather than later? The value of early cash flows depends on the return we can earn on those cash flows, that is, the rate at which we can reinvest them. *The NPV method implicitly assumes that the rate at which cash flows can be reinvested is the cost of capital, whereas the IRR method assumes that the firm can reinvest at the IRR.* These assumptions are inherent in the mathematics of the discounting process. The cash flows may actually be withdrawn as dividends by the stockholders and spent on beer and pizza, but the NPV method still assumes that cash flows can be reinvested at the cost of capital, while the IRR method assumes reinvestment at the project's IRR.

Which is the better assumption—that cash flows can be reinvested at the cost of capital, or that they can be reinvested at the project's IRR? The best assumption is that projects' cash flows can be reinvested at the cost of capital, which means that the NPV method is more reliable.

We should reiterate that, when projects are independent, the NPV and IRR methods both lead to exactly the same accept/reject decision. However, *when evaluating mutually exclusive projects, especially those that differ in scale and/or timing, the NPV method should be used.*

Multiple IRRs

There is another reason the IRR approach may not be reliable—when projects have non-normal cash flows. A project has **normal cash flows** if it has one or more cash outflows (costs) followed by a series of cash inflows. Notice that normal cash flows have only one change in sign—they begin as negative cash flows, change to positive cash flows, and then

---

[6] The crossover rate is easy to calculate. Simply go back to Figure 10-1, where we set forth the two projects' cash flows, and calculate the difference in those flows in each year. The differences are $CF_S - CF_L = \$0, +\$400, +\$100, -\$100,$ and $-\$500$, respectively. Enter these values in the cash flow register of a financial calculator, press the IRR button, and the crossover rate, $7.17\% \approx 7.2\%$, appears. Be sure to enter $CF_0 = 0$ or else you will not get the correct answer.

remain positive.[7] **Nonnormal cash flows** occur when there is more than one change in sign. For example, a project may begin with negative cash flows, switch to positive cash flows, and then switch back to negative cash flows. This cash flow stream has two sign changes—negative to positive and then positive to negative—so it is a nonnormal cash flow. Projects with nonnormal cash flows can actually have two or more IRRs, or **multiple IRRs!**

To see this, consider the equation that one solves to find a project's IRR:

$$\sum_{t=0}^{n} \frac{CF_t}{(1 + IRR)^t} = 0. \tag{10-2}$$

Notice that Equation 10-2 is a polynomial of degree n, so it may have as many as n different roots, or solutions. All except one of the roots are imaginary numbers when investments have normal cash flows (one or more cash outflows followed by cash inflows), so in the normal case, only one value of IRR appears. However, the possibility of multiple real roots, hence multiple IRRs, arises when the project has nonnormal cash flows (negative net cash flows occur during some year after the project has been placed in operation).

To illustrate, suppose a firm is considering the expenditure of $1.6 million to develop a strip mine (Project M). The mine will produce a cash flow of $10 million at the end of Year 1. Then, at the end of Year 2, $10 million must be expended to restore the land to its original condition. Therefore, the project's expected net cash flows are as follows (in millions of dollars):

EXPECTED NET CASH FLOWS		
Year 0	End of Year 1	End of Year 2
−$1.6	+$10	−$10

These values can be substituted into Equation 10-2 to derive the IRR for the investment:

$$NPV = \frac{-\$1.6 \text{ million}}{(1 + IRR)^0} + \frac{\$10 \text{ million}}{(1 + IRR)^1} + \frac{-\$10 \text{ million}}{(1 + IRR)^2} = 0.$$

When solved, we find that NPV = 0 when IRR = 25% and also when IRR = 400%.[8] Therefore, the IRR of the investment is both 25 and 400 percent. This relationship is depicted graphically in Figure 10-5. Note that no dilemma would arise if the NPV method were used; we would simply use Equation 10-1, find the NPV, and use this to evaluate the project. If Project M's cost of capital were 10 percent, then its NPV would be −$0.77 million, and the project should be rejected. If r were between 25 and 400 percent, the NPV would be positive.

The example illustrates how multiple IRRs can arise when a project has nonnormal cash flows. In contrast, the NPV criterion can easily be applied, and this method leads to conceptually correct capital budgeting decisions.

---

[7] Normal cash flows can also begin with positive cash flows, switch to negative cash flows, and then remain negative. The key is that there is only one change in sign.

[8] If you attempted to find the IRR of Project M with many financial calculators, you would get an error message. This same message would be given for all projects with multiple IRRs. However, you can still find Project M's IRR by first calculating NPVs using several different values for r and then plotting the NPV profile. The intersection with the X-axis gives a rough idea of the IRR value. Finally, you can use trial-and-error to find the exact value of r that forces NPV = 0.

The IRR function in spreadsheets begins its trial-and-error search for a solution with an initial guess. If you omit the initial guess, the *Excel* default starting point is 10 percent. Now suppose the values −1.6, +10, and −10 were in Cells A1:C1. You could use this *Excel* formula, **=IRR(A1:C1,10%)**, where 10 percent is the initial guess, and it would produce a result of 25 percent. If you used a guess of 150 percent, you would have this formula, **=IRR(A1:C1,150%)**, and it would produce a result of 400 percent.

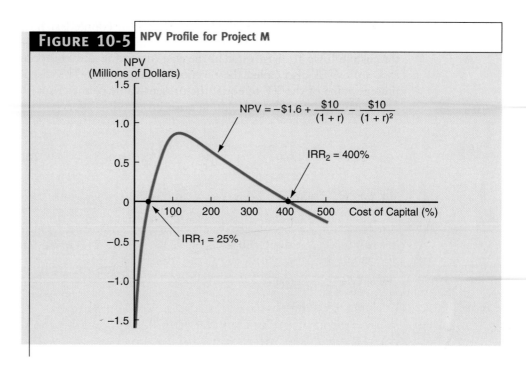

FIGURE 10-5 NPV Profile for Project M

NPV
(Millions of Dollars)

$$NPV = -\$1.6 + \frac{\$10}{(1 + r)} - \frac{\$10}{(1 + r)^2}$$

$IRR_2 = 400\%$

$IRR_1 = 25\%$

Cost of Capital (%)

Describe how NPV profiles are constructed, and define the crossover rate.

How does the "reinvestment rate" assumption differ between the NPV and IRR methods?

If a conflict exists, should the capital budgeting decision be made on the basis of the NPV or the IRR ranking? Why?

Explain the difference between normal and nonnormal cash flows, and their relationship to the "multiple IRR problem."

MODIFIED INTERNAL RATE OF RETURN (MIRR)

In spite of a strong academic preference for NPV, surveys indicate that many executives prefer IRR over NPV. Apparently, managers find it intuitively more appealing to evaluate investments in terms of percentage rates of return than dollars of NPV. Given this fact, can we devise a percentage evaluator that is better than the regular IRR? The answer is yes—we can modify the IRR and make it a better indicator of relative profitability, hence better for use in capital budgeting. The new measure is called the **modified IRR**, or **MIRR**, and it is defined as follows:

$$\sum_{t=0}^{n} \frac{COF_t}{(1 + r)^t} = \frac{\sum_{t=0}^{n} CIF_t(1 + r)^{n-t}}{(1 + MIRR)^n}$$

$$\text{PV of costs} = \frac{\text{Terminal value}}{(1 + MIRR)^n}$$

$$= \text{PV of terminal value.}$$

(10-2a)

Here COF refers to cash outflows (negative numbers), or the cost of the project, CIF refers to cash inflows (positive numbers), and r is the cost of capital. The left term is simply the present value of the investment outlays when discounted at the cost of capital, and the numerator of the right term is the compounded future value of the inflows, assuming that the cash inflows are reinvested at the cost of capital. The compounded future value of the cash inflows is also called the *terminal value,* or *TV.* The discount rate that forces the present value of the TV to equal the present value of the costs is defined as the MIRR.[9]

We can illustrate the calculation with Project S:

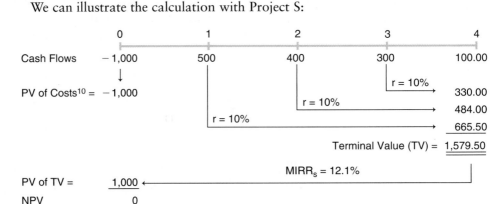

Using the cash flows as set out on the time line, first find the terminal value by compounding each cash inflow at the 10 percent cost of capital. Then enter $N = 4$, $PV = -1000$, $PMT = 0$, $FV = 1579.5$, and then press the I button to find $MIRR_S = 12.1\%$. Similarly, we find $MIRR_L = 11.3\%$.[11]

The modified IRR has a significant advantage over the regular IRR. MIRR assumes that cash flows from all projects are reinvested at the cost of capital, while the regular IRR assumes that the cash flows from each project are reinvested at the project's own IRR. Because reinvestment at the cost of capital is generally more correct, the modified IRR is a better indicator of a project's true profitability. The MIRR also eliminates the multiple IRR problem. To illustrate, with $r = 10\%$, Project M (the strip mine project) has MIRR $= 5.6\%$ versus its 10 percent cost of capital, so it should be rejected. This is consistent with the decision based on the NPV method, because at $r = 10\%$, NPV $= -\$0.77$ million.

Is MIRR as good as NPV for choosing between mutually exclusive projects? If two projects are of equal size and have the same life, then NPV and MIRR will always lead to the same decision. Thus, for any set of projects like our Projects S and L, if $NPV_S > NPV_L$, then $MIRR_S > MIRR_L$, and the kinds of conflicts we encountered between NPV and the regular IRR will not occur. Also, if the projects are of equal size, but differ in lives, the MIRR will always lead to the same decision as the NPV if the MIRRs are both calculated using as the terminal year the life of the longer project. (Just fill in zeros for the shorter project's missing cash flows.) However, if the projects differ in size, then conflicts can still occur. For example, if we were choosing between a large project and a small mutually exclusive one, then we might find $NPV_L > NPV_S$, but $MIRR_S > MIRR_L$.

---

[9] There are several alternative definitions for the MIRR. The differences primarily relate to whether negative cash flows that occur after positive cash flows begin should be compounded and treated as part of the TV or discounted and treated as a cost. A related issue is whether negative and positive flows in a given year should be netted or treated separately. For a complete discussion, see William R. McDaniel, Daniel E. McCarty, and Kenneth A. Jessell, "Discounted Cash Flow with Explicit Reinvestment Rates: Tutorial and Extension," *The Financial Review,* August 1988, 369–385; and David M. Shull, "Interpreting Rates of Return: A Modified Rate of Return Approach," *Financial Practice and Education,* Fall 1993, 67–71.

[10] In this example, the only negative cash flow occurs at $t = 0$, so the PV of costs is equal to CF_0.

[11] Most spreadsheets have a function for finding the MIRR. Refer back to our spreadsheet for Project S, with cash flows of $-1,000$, 500, 400, 300, and 100 in Cells B4:F4. You could use the *Excel* function wizard to set up the following formula: **=MIRR(B4:F4,10%,10%)**. Here the first 10 percent is the cost of capital used for discounting, and the second one is the rate used for compounding, or the reinvestment rate. In our definition of the MIRR, we assume that reinvestment is at the cost of capital, so we enter 10 percent twice. The result is an MIRR of 12.1 percent.

Our conclusion is that the MIRR is superior to the regular IRR as an indicator of a project's "true" rate of return, or "expected long-term rate of return," but the NPV method is still the best way to choose among competing projects because it provides the best indication of how much each project will add to the value of the firm.

Describe how the modified IRR (MIRR) is calculated.

What are the primary differences between the MIRR and the regular IRR?

What condition can cause the MIRR and NPV methods to produce conflicting rankings?

PROFITABILITY INDEX

Another method used to evaluate projects is the **profitability index (PI)**:

$$PI = \frac{\text{PV of future cash flows}}{\text{Initial cost}} = \frac{\sum_{t=1}^{n} \frac{CF_t}{(1 + r)^t}}{CF_0}. \tag{10-3}$$

Here CF_t represents the expected future cash flows, and CF_0 represents the initial cost. The PI shows the *relative* profitability of any project, or the present value per dollar of initial cost. The PI for Project S, based on a 10 percent cost of capital, is 1.079:

$$PI_S = \frac{\$1,078.82}{\$1,000} = 1.079.$$

Thus, on a present value basis, Project S is expected to produce $1.079 for each $1 of investment. Project L, with a PI of 1.049, should produce $1.049 for each dollar invested.

A project is acceptable if its PI is greater than 1.0, and the higher the PI, the higher the project's ranking. Therefore, both S and L would be accepted by the PI criterion if they were independent, and S would be ranked ahead of L if they were mutually exclusive.

Mathematically, the NPV, IRR, MIRR, and PI methods will always lead to the same accept/reject decisions for *independent* projects: If a project's NPV is positive, its IRR and MIRR will always exceed r, and its PI will always be greater than 1.0. However, these methods can give conflicting rankings for *mutually exclusive* projects. This point is discussed in more detail in the next section.

Explain how the PI is calculated. What does it measure?

CONCLUSIONS ON CAPITAL BUDGETING METHODS

We have discussed six capital budgeting decision methods, compared the methods with one another, and highlighted their relative strengths and weaknesses. In the process, we probably created the impression that "sophisticated" firms should use only one method in the decision process, NPV. However, virtually all capital budgeting decisions are analyzed by computer, so it is easy to calculate and list all the decision measures: payback and discounted payback, NPV, IRR, modified IRR (MIRR), and profitability index (PI). In making the accept/reject decision, most large, sophisticated firms calculate and consider all of the measures, because each one provides decision makers with a somewhat different piece of relevant information.

Payback and discounted payback provide an indication of both the *risk* and the *liquidity* of a project—a long payback means (1) that the investment dollars will be locked up for many years, hence the project is relatively illiquid, and (2) that the project's cash flows must be forecasted far out into the future, hence the project is probably quite risky. A good analogy for this is the bond valuation process. An investor should never compare the yields to maturity on two bonds without also considering their terms to maturity, because a bond's riskiness is affected by its maturity.

NPV is important because it gives a direct measure of the dollar benefit of the project to shareholders. Therefore, we regard NPV as the best single measure of *profitability*. IRR also measures profitability, but here it is expressed as a percentage rate of return, which many decision makers prefer. Further, IRR contains information concerning a project's "safety margin." To illustrate, consider the following two projects: Project S (for small) costs $10,000 and is expected to return $16,500 at the end of one year, while Project L (for large) costs $100,000 and has an expected payoff of $115,500 after one year. At a 10 percent cost of capital, both projects have an NPV of $5,000, so by the NPV rule we should be indifferent between them. However, Project S has a much larger margin for error. Even if its realized cash inflow were 39 percent below the $16,500 forecast, the firm would still recover its $10,000 investment. On the other hand, if Project L's inflows fell by only 13 percent from the forecasted $115,500, the firm would not recover its investment. Further, if no inflows were generated at all, the firm would lose only $10,000 with Project S, but $100,000 if it took on Project L.

The NPV provides no information about either of these factors—the "safety margin" inherent in the cash flow forecasts or the amount of capital at risk. However, the IRR does provide "safety margin" information—Project S's IRR is a whopping 65 percent, while Project L's IRR is only 15.5 percent. As a result, the realized return could fall substantially for Project S, and it would still make money. The modified IRR has all the virtues of the IRR, but (1) it incorporates a better reinvestment rate assumption, and (2) it avoids the multiple rate of return problem.

The PI measures profitability relative to the cost of a project—it shows the "bang per buck." Like the IRR, it gives an indication of the project's risk, because a high PI means that cash flows could fall quite a bit and the project would still be profitable.

The different measures provide different types of information to decision makers. Since it is easy to calculate all of them, all should be considered in the decision process. For any specific decision, more weight might be given to one measure than another, but it would be foolish to ignore the information provided by any of the methods.

Just as it would be foolish to ignore these capital budgeting methods, it would also be foolish to make decisions based *solely* on them. One cannot know at Time 0 the exact cost of future capital, or the exact future cash flows. These inputs are simply estimates, and if they turn out to be incorrect, then so will be the calculated NPVs and IRRs. *Thus, quantitative methods provide valuable information, but they should not be used as the sole criteria for accept/reject decisions* in the capital budgeting process. Rather, managers should use quantitative methods in the decision-making process but also consider the likelihood that actual results will differ from the forecasts. Qualitative factors, such as the chances of a tax increase, or a war, or a major product liability suit, should also be considered. *In summary, quantitative methods such as NPV and IRR should be considered as an aid to informed decisions but not as a substitute for sound managerial judgment.*

In this same vein, managers should ask sharp questions about any project that has a large NPV, a high IRR, or a high PI. In a perfectly competitive economy, there would be no positive NPV projects—all companies would have the same opportunities, and competition would quickly eliminate any positive NPV. Therefore, positive NPV projects must be predicated on some imperfection in the marketplace, and the longer the life of the project, the longer that imperfection must last. Therefore, managers should be able to identify the imperfection and explain why it will persist before accepting that a project will really have a positive NPV. Valid explanations might include patents or proprietary technology, which is how pharmaceutical and software firms create positive NPV projects. Aventis's Allegra® allergy medicine and Microsoft's Windows XP® operating system are examples. Companies can also create positive NPV by being the first entrant into a new market or by creating new products that meet some previously unidentified consumer needs. The Post-it® notes invented by 3M are an example. Similarly, Dell developed procedures for direct sales of microcomputers, and in the process created projects with enormous NPV. Also, companies such as Southwest Airlines have managed to train and motivate their workers better than their competitors, and this has led to positive NPV projects. In all of these cases, the companies developed some source of competitive advantage, and that advantage resulted in positive NPV projects.

This discussion suggests three things: (1) If you can't identify the reason a project has a positive projected NPV, then its actual NPV will probably not be positive. (2) Positive NPV projects don't just happen—they result from hard work to develop some competitive advantage. At the risk of oversimplification, the primary job of a manager is to find and develop areas of competitive advantage. (3) Some competitive advantages last longer than others, with their durability depending on competitors' ability to replicate them. Patents, the control of scarce resources, or large size in an industry where strong economies of scale exist can keep competitors at bay. However, it is relatively easy to replicate nonpatentable features on products. The bottom line is that managers should strive to develop nonreplicatible sources of competitive advantage, and if such an advantage cannot be demonstrated, then you should question projects with high NPV, especially if they have long lives.

SELF-TEST QUESTIONS

Describe the advantages and disadvantages of the six capital budgeting methods discussed in this chapter.

Should capital budgeting decisions be made solely on the basis of a project's NPV?

What are some possible reasons that a project might have a large NPV?

BUSINESS PRACTICES

The findings of a 1993 survey of the capital budgeting methods used by the *Fortune* 500 industrial companies are shown below:[12]

1. Every responding firm used some type of DCF method. In 1955, a similar study reported that only 4 percent of large companies used a DCF method. Thus, large firms' usage of DCF methodology increased dramatically in the last half of the 20th century.
2. The payback period was used by 84 percent of Bierman's surveyed companies. However, no company used it as the primary method, and most companies gave the greatest weight to a DCF method. In 1955, surveys similar to Bierman's found that payback was the most important method.
3. In 1993, 99 percent of the *Fortune* 500 companies used IRR, while 85 percent used NPV. Thus, most firms actually used both methods.
4. Ninety-three percent of Bierman's companies calculated a weighted average cost of capital as part of their capital budgeting process. A few companies apparently used the same WACC for all projects, but 73 percent adjusted the corporate WACC to account for project risk, and 23 percent made adjustments to reflect divisional risk.
5. An examination of surveys done by other authors led Bierman to conclude that there has been a strong trend toward the acceptance of academic recommendations, at least by large companies.

---

[12] Harold Bierman, "Capital Budgeting in 1993: A Survey," *Financial Management*, Autumn 1993, 24.

A second 1993 study, conducted by Joe Walker, Richard Burns, and Chad Denson (WBD), focused on small companies.[13] WBD began by noting the same trend toward the use of DCF that Bierman cited, but they reported that only 21 percent of small companies used DCF versus 100 percent for Bierman's large companies. WBD also noted that within their sample, the smaller the firm, the smaller the likelihood that DCF would be used. The focal point of the WBD study was *why* small companies use DCF so much less frequently than large firms. The three most frequently cited reasons, according to the survey, were (1) small firms' preoccupation with liquidity, which is best indicated by payback, (2) a lack of familiarity with DCF methods, and (3) a belief that small project sizes make DCF not worth the effort.

The general conclusion one can reach from these studies is that large firms should and do use the procedures we recommend, and that managers of small firms, especially managers with aspirations for future growth, should at least understand DCF procedures well enough to make rational decisions about using or not using them. Moreover, as computer technology makes it easier and less expensive for small firms to use DCF methods, and as more and more of their competitors begin using these methods, survival will necessitate increased DCF usage.

SELF-TEST QUESTION   What general considerations can be reached from these studies?

THE POST-AUDIT

An important aspect of the capital budgeting process is the **post-audit,** which involves (1) comparing actual results with those predicted by the project's sponsors and (2) explaining why any differences occurred. For example, many firms require that the operating divisions send a monthly report for the first six months after a project goes into operation, and a quarterly report thereafter, until the project's results are up to expectations. From then on, reports on the operation are reviewed on a regular basis like those of other operations.

The post-audit has three main purposes:

1. *Improve forecasts.* When decision makers are forced to compare their projections to actual outcomes, there is a tendency for estimates to improve. Conscious or unconscious biases are observed and eliminated; new forecasting methods are sought as the need for them becomes apparent; and people simply tend to do everything better, including forecasting, if they know that their actions are being monitored.
2. *Improve operations.* Businesses are run by people, and people can perform at higher or lower levels of efficiency. When a divisional team has made a forecast about an investment, its members are, in a sense, putting their reputations on the line and will strive to improve operations if they are evaluated with post-audits. In a discussion related to this point, one executive made this statement: "You academicians worry only about making good decisions. In business, we also worry about making decisions good."
3. *Identify termination opportunities.* Although the decision to undertake a project may be the correct one based on information at hand, things don't always turn out as expected. The post-audit can help identify projects that should be terminated because they have lost their economic viability.

---

[13] Joe Walker, Richard Burns, and Chad Denson, "Why Small Manufacturing Firms Shun DCF," *Journal of Small Business Finance,* 1993, 233–249.

How Does Industry Evaluate Projects?

Has industry adopted the capital budgeting techniques that business schools are teaching? Professors John Graham and Campbell Harvey of Duke University recently asked this very question of 392 chief financial officers (CFOs). Of those firms, 26 percent had sales less than $100 million, 32 percent had sales between $100 million and $1 billion, and 42 percent exceeded $1 billion.

Graham and Harvey found that when estimating the cost of equity, 73.5 percent of the firms used the Capital Asset Pricing Model (CAPM), 34.3 percent used a multi-beta version of the CAPM, and 15.7 percent used the dividend discount model. In addition, although the CFOs used a variety of risk adjustment techniques, most still used a single hurdle rate to evaluate all corporate projects.

When it came to choosing a method for evaluating projects, most of the companies used NPV (74.9 percent) and IRR (75.7 percent), but many (56.7 percent) also used the payback approach. It seems obvious, then, that most firms use more than one approach to evaluate projects.

The survey also found that small firms (less than $1 billion in sales) and large firms (more than $1 billion in sales) employ different capital budgeting practices. Consistent with the earlier studies by Bierman and by Walker, Burns, and Denson (WBD) described in the text, Graham and Harvey found that smaller firms are more likely to rely on the payback approach, while larger firms are more likely to rely on NPV and/or IRR.

Source: John R. Graham and Campbell R. Harvey, "The Theory and Practice of Corporate Finance: Evidence from the Field," *Journal of Financial Economics,* Vol. 60, no. 2–3, 2001, 187–243.

The results of post-audits often conclude that (1) the actual NPVs of most cost reduction projects exceed their expected NPVs by a slight amount, (2) expansion projects generally fall short of their expected NPVs by a slight amount, and (3) new product and new market projects often fall short by relatively large amounts. Thus, biases seem to exist, and companies that understand them can build in corrections and thus design better capital budgeting programs. Our observations of businesses and governmental units suggest that the best-run and most successful organizations put great emphasis on post-audits. Accordingly, we regard the post-audit as being one of the most important elements in a good capital budgeting system.

SELF-TEST QUESTIONS   What is done in the post-audit?

Identify several purposes of the post-audit.

SPECIAL APPLICATIONS OF CASH FLOW EVALUATION

Misapplication of the NPV method can lead to errors when two mutually exclusive projects have unequal lives. There are also situations in which an asset should not be operated for its full life. The following sections explain how to evaluate cash flows in these situations.

Comparing Projects with Unequal Lives

Note that a replacement decision involves comparing two mutually exclusive projects: retaining the old asset versus buying a new one. When choosing between two mutually exclusive alternatives with significantly different lives, an adjustment is necessary. For example, suppose a company is planning to modernize its production facilities, and it is considering either a conveyor system (Project C) or some forklift trucks (Project F) for moving materials. Figure 10-6 shows both the expected net cash flows and the NPVs for these two mutually exclusive alternatives. We see that Project C, when discounted at the firm's 11.5 percent cost of capital, has the higher NPV and thus appears to be the better project.

Although the NPV shown in Figure 10-6 suggests that Project C should be selected, this analysis is incomplete, and the decision to choose Project C is actually incorrect. If we choose Project F, we will have an opportunity to make a similar investment in three years, and if cost and revenue conditions continue at the Figure 10-6 levels, this second investment will also be profitable. However, if we choose Project C, we cannot make this second investment. Two different approaches can be used to correctly compare Projects C and F. The first is the **equivalent annual annuity (EAA) approach,** and the second is the **replacement chain (common life) approach.** Both methods are theoretically correct, but the replacement chain approach is the most widely used method in practice because it is very easy to apply using spreadsheets and because it enables analysts to incorporate a variety of assumptions regarding future inflation and efficiency gains. For those reasons, we focus here upon the replacement chain approach. However, we provide a full description of the EAA approach in the Web Extension to this chapter, and the *CF2 Ch 10 Tool Kit.xls* illustrates the application of both methods.

e-resource

The key to the replacement chain approach is to analyze both projects using a common life. In this example, we will find the NPV of Project F over a six-year period, and then compare this extended NPV with Project C's NPV over the same six years. The NPV for Project C as calculated in Figure 10-6 is already over the six-year common life. For Project F, however, we must add in a second project to extend the overall life of the combined projects to six years. Here we assume (1) that Project F's cost and annual cash inflows will not change if the project is repeated in three years and (2) that the cost of capital will remain at 11.5 percent:

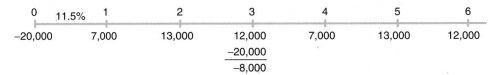

NPV at 11.5% = $9,281; IRR = 25.2%.

The NPV of this extended Project F is $9,281, and its IRR is 25.2 percent. (The IRR of two Project Fs is the same as the IRR for one Project F.) Since the $9,281 extended NPV

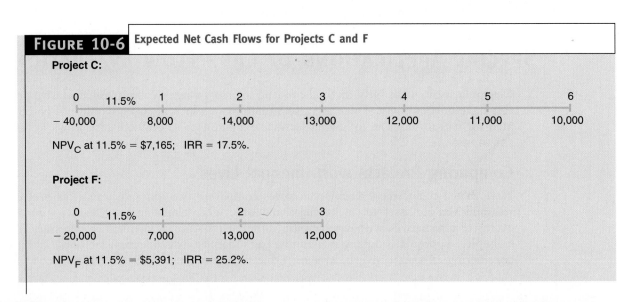

FIGURE 10-6   **Expected Net Cash Flows for Projects C and F**

Project C:

NPV$_C$ at 11.5% = $7,165; IRR = 17.5%.

Project F:

NPV$_F$ at 11.5% = $5,391; IRR = 25.2%.

of Project F over the six-year common life is greater than the $7,165 NPV of Project C, Project F should be selected.[14]

When should we worry about unequal life analysis? The unequal life issue (1) does not arise for independent projects, but (2) it can arise if mutually exclusive projects with significantly different lives are being compared. However, even for mutually exclusive projects, it is not always appropriate to extend the analysis to a common life. This should be done only if there is a high probability that the projects will actually be repeated at the end of their initial lives.

We should note several potentially serious weaknesses inherent in this type of analysis: (1) If inflation is expected, then replacement equipment will have a higher price. Moreover, both sales prices and operating costs will probably change. Thus, the static conditions built into the analysis would be invalid. (2) Replacements that occur down the road would probably employ new technology, which in turn might change the cash flows. (3) It is difficult enough to estimate the lives of most projects, and even more so to estimate the lives of a series of projects.

In view of these problems, no experienced financial analyst would be too concerned about comparing mutually exclusive projects with lives of, say, eight years and ten years. Given all the uncertainties in the estimation process, such projects would, for all practical purposes, be assumed to have the same life. Still, it is important to recognize that a problem exists if mutually exclusive projects have substantially different lives. When we encounter such problems in practice, we use a computer spreadsheet and build expected inflation and/or possible efficiency gains directly into the cash flow estimates, and then use the replacement chain approach. The cash flow estimation is a bit more complicated, but the concepts involved are exactly the same as in our example.

Economic Life versus Physical Life

Projects are normally analyzed under the assumption that the firm will operate the asset over its full physical life. However, this may not be the best course of action—it may be best to terminate a project before the end of its potential life, and this possibility can materially affect the project's estimated profitability. The situation in Table 10-1 can be used to illustrate this concept and its effects on capital budgeting. The salvage values listed in the third column are after taxes, and they have been estimated for each year of Project A's life.

TABLE 10-1 | Project A: Investment, Operating, and Salvage Cash Flows

Year (t)	Initial (Year 0) Investment and After-tax Operating Cash Flows	Net Salvage Value at End of Year t
0	($4,800)	$4,800
1	2,000	3,000
2	2,000	1,650
3	1,750	0

---

[14] Alternatively, we could recognize that the value of the cash flow stream of two consecutive Project Fs can be summarized by two NPVs: one at Year 0 representing the value of the initial project, and one at Year 3 representing the value of the replication project:

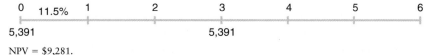

NPV = $9,281.

Ignoring rounding differences, the present value of these two cash flows, when discounted at 11.5 percent, is again $9,281.

Using a 10 percent cost of capital, the expected NPV based on three years of operating cash flows and the zero abandonment (salvage) value is $-\$14.12$:

0	10%	1	2	3
($4,800)		$2,000	$2,000	$1,750
				0

$$NPV = -\$4,800 + \$2,000/(1.10)^1 + \$2,000/(1.10)^2 + \$1,750/(1.10)^3$$
$$= -\$14.12.$$

Thus, Project A would not be accepted if we assume that it will be operated over its full three-year life. However, what would its NPV be if the project were terminated after two years? In this case, we would receive operating cash flows in Years 1 and 2, plus the salvage value at the end of Year 2, and the project's NPV would be $34.71:

0	10%	1	2
($4,800)		$2,000	$2,000
			1,650

$$NPV = -\$4,800 + \$2,000/(1.10)^1 + \$2,000/(1.10)^2 + \$1,650/(1.10)^2$$
$$= \$34.71.$$

Thus, Project A would be profitable if we operate it for two years and then dispose of it. To complete the analysis, note that if the project were terminated after one year, its NPV would be $-\$254.55$. Thus, the optimal life for this project is two years.

This type of analysis can be used to determine a project's **economic life**, which is the life that maximizes the NPV and thus maximizes shareholder wealth. For Project A, the economic life is two years versus the three-year **physical**, or **engineering, life.** Note that this analysis was based on the expected cash flows and the expected salvage values, and it should always be conducted as a part of the capital budgeting evaluation if salvage values are relatively high.

SELF-TEST QUESTIONS   Briefly describe the replacement chain (common life) approach.
Define the economic life of a project (as opposed to its physical life).

THE OPTIMAL CAPITAL BUDGET

The **optimal capital budget** is the set of projects that maximizes the value of the firm. Finance theory states that all projects with positive NPVs should be accepted, and the optimal capital budget consists of these positive NPV projects. However, two complications arise in practice: (1) an increasing marginal cost of capital and (2) capital rationing.

An Increasing Marginal Cost of Capital

The cost of capital may depend on the size of the capital budget. As we discussed in Chapter 9, the flotation costs associated with issuing new equity or public debt can be quite high. This means that the cost of capital jumps upward after a company invests all of its internally generated cash and must sell new common stock. In addition, investors often perceive extremely large capital investments to be riskier, which may also drive up the cost of capital as the size of the capital budget increases. As a result, a project might have a positive NPV if it is part of a "normal size" capital budget, but the same project might have a negative NPV if it is part of an unusually large capital budget. Fortunately, this problem occurs very rarely for most firms, and it is unusual for an established firm to require new outside equity. Still, the Web Extension for this chapter contains a more detailed discussion of this problem and shows how to deal with the existence of an increasing marginal cost of capital.

e-resource

See the Web Extension for a more detailed discussion.

Capital Rationing

Armbrister Pyrotechnics, a manufacturer of fireworks and lasers for light shows, has identified 40 potential independent projects, with 15 having a positive NPV based on the firm's 12 percent cost of capital. The total cost of implementing these 15 projects is $75 million. Based on finance theory, the optimal capital budget is $75 million, and Armbrister should accept the 15 projects with positive NPVs. However, Armbrister's management has imposed a limit of $50 million for capital expenditures during the upcoming year. Due to this restriction, the company must forego a number of value-adding projects. This is an example of **capital rationing,** defined as a situation in which a firm limits its capital expenditures to less than the amount required to fund the optimal capital budget. Despite being at odds with finance theory, this practice is quite common.

Why would any company forego value-adding projects? Here are some potential explanations, along with some suggestions for better ways to handle these situations:

1. *Reluctance to issue new stock.* Many firms are extremely reluctant to issue new stock, so all of their capital expenditures must be funded out of debt and internally generated cash. Also, most firms try to stay near their target capital structure, and, combined with the limit on equity, this limits the amount of debt that can be added during any one year. The result can be a serious constraint on the amount of funds available for investment in new projects.

    This reluctance to issue new stock could be based on some sound reasons: (a) flotation costs can be very expensive; (b) investors might perceive new stock offerings as a signal that the company's equity is overvalued; and (c) the company might have to reveal sensitive strategic information to investors, thereby reducing some of its competitive advantages. To avoid these costs, many companies simply limit their capital expenditures.

    However, rather than placing a somewhat artificial limit on capital expenditures, a company might be better off explicitly incorporating the costs of raising external capital into its cost of capital. If there still are positive NPV projects even using this higher cost of capital, then the company should go ahead and raise external equity and accept the projects. See the Web Extension for this chapter on the textbook's Web site for more details concerning an increasing marginal cost of capital.

2. *Constraints on nonmonetary resources.* Sometimes a firm simply does not have the necessary managerial, marketing, or engineering talent to immediately accept all positive NPV projects. In other words, the potential projects are not really independent, because the firm cannot accept them all. To avoid potential problems due to spreading existing talent too thinly, many firms simply limit the capital budget to a size that can be accommodated by their current personnel.

    A better solution might be to employ a technique called **linear programming.** Each potential project has an expected NPV, and each potential project requires a certain level of support by different types of employees. A linear program can identify the set of projects that maximizes NPV, subject to the constraint that the total amount of support required for these projects does not exceed the available resources.[15]

3. *Controlling estimation bias.* Many managers become overly optimistic when estimating the cash flows for a project. Some firms try to control this estimation bias by requiring managers to use an unrealistically high cost of capital. Others try to control the bias by limiting the size of the capital budget. Neither solution is generally effective since managers quickly learn the rules of the game and then increase

CF
e-resource

---

[15] See Stephen P. Bradley and Sherwood C. Frey, Jr., "Equivalent Mathematical Programming Models of Pure Capital Rationing," *Journal of Financial and Quantitative Analysis,* June 1978, 345–361.

their own estimates of project cash flows, which might have been biased upward to begin with.

A better solution is to implement a post-audit program and to link the accuracy of forecasts to the compensation of the managers who initiated the projects.

SELF-TEST QUESTIONS

What factors can lead to an increasing marginal cost of capital? How might this affect capital budgeting?

What is capital rationing?

What are three explanations for capital rationing? How might firms handle these situations?

SUMMARY

This chapter has described six techniques (payback, discounted payback, NPV, IRR, MIRR, and PI) that are used in capital budgeting analysis. Each approach provides a different piece of information, so in this age of computers, managers often look at all of them when evaluating projects. However, NPV is the best single measure, and almost all firms now use NPV. The key concepts covered in this chapter are listed below:

- Capital budgeting is the process of analyzing potential projects. Capital budgeting decisions are probably the most important ones managers must make.
- The **payback period** is defined as the number of years required to recover a project's cost. The regular payback method ignores cash flows beyond the payback period, and it does not consider the time value of money. The payback does, however, provide an indication of a project's risk and liquidity, because it shows how long the invested capital will be "at risk."
- The **discounted payback method** is similar to the regular payback method except that it discounts cash flows at the project's cost of capital. It considers the time value of money, but it ignores cash flows beyond the payback period.
- The **net present value (NPV) method** discounts all cash flows at the project's cost of capital and then sums those cash flows. The project should be accepted if the NPV is positive.
- The **internal rate of return (IRR)** is defined as the discount rate that forces a project's NPV to equal zero. The project should be accepted if the IRR is greater than the cost of capital.
- The NPV and IRR methods make the same accept/reject decisions for **independent projects,** but if projects are **mutually exclusive,** then ranking conflicts can arise. If conflicts arise, the NPV method should be used. The NPV and IRR methods are both superior to the payback, but NPV is superior to IRR.
- The NPV method assumes that cash flows will be reinvested at the firm's cost of capital, while the IRR method assumes reinvestment at the project's IRR. **Reinvestment at the cost of capital is generally a better assumption** because it is closer to reality.
- The **modified IRR (MIRR) method** corrects some of the problems with the regular IRR. MIRR involves finding the **terminal value (TV)** of the cash inflows, compounded at the firm's cost of capital, and then determining the discount rate that forces the present value of the TV to equal the present value of the outflows.
- The **profitability index (PI)** shows the dollars of present value divided by the initial cost, so it measures relative profitability.
- Sophisticated managers consider all of the project evaluation measures because each measure provides a useful piece of information.

- The **post-audit** is a key element of capital budgeting. By comparing actual results with predicted results and then determining why differences occurred, decision makers can improve both their operations and their forecasts of projects' outcomes.
- Small firms tend to use the payback method rather than a discounted cash flow method. This may be rational, because (1) the cost of conducting a DCF analysis **may outweigh the benefits** for the project being considered, (2) **the firm's cost of capital cannot be estimated accurately,** or (3) the small-business owner may be considering **nonmonetary goals.**
- If mutually exclusive projects have **unequal lives,** it may be necessary to adjust the analysis to put the projects on an equal life basis. This can be done using the **replacement chain (common life) approach.**
- A project's true value may be greater than the NPV based on its **physical life** if it can be **terminated** at the end of its **economic life.**
- Flotation costs and increased riskiness associated with unusually large expansion programs can cause the **marginal cost of capital** to rise as the size of the capital budget increases.
- **Capital rationing** occurs when management places a constraint on the size of the firm's capital budget during a particular period.

QUESTIONS

(10-1) Define each of the following terms:
    a. Capital budgeting; regular payback period; discounted payback period
    b. Independent projects; mutually exclusive projects
    c. DCF techniques; net present value (NPV) method; internal rate of return (IRR) method
    d. Modified internal rate of return (MIRR) method; profitability index
    e. NPV profile; crossover rate
    f. Nonnormal cash flow projects; normal cash flow projects; multiple IRRs
    g. Hurdle rate; reinvestment rate assumption; post-audit
    h. Replacement chain; economic life; capital rationing

(10-2) How is a project classification scheme (for example, replacement, expansion into new markets, and so forth) used in the capital budgeting process?

(10-3) Explain why the NPV of a relatively long-term project, defined as one for which a high percentage of its cash flows are expected in the distant future, is more sensitive to changes in the cost of capital than is the NPV of a short-term project.

(10-4) Explain why, if two mutually exclusive projects are being compared, the short-term project might have the higher ranking under the NPV criterion if the cost of capital is high, but the long-term project might be deemed better if the cost of capital is low. Would changes in the cost of capital ever cause a change in the IRR ranking of two such projects?

(10-5) In what sense is a reinvestment rate assumption embodied in the NPV, IRR, and MIRR methods? What is the assumed reinvestment rate of each method?

(10-6) Suppose a firm is considering two mutually exclusive projects. One has a life of 6 years and the other a life of 10 years. Would the failure to employ some type of replacement chain analysis bias an NPV analysis against one of the projects? Explain.

SELF-TEST PROBLEM   Solution Appears in Appendix A

(ST-1)
Project Analysis

You are a financial analyst for the Hittle Company. The director of capital budgeting has asked you to analyze two proposed capital investments, Projects X and Y. Each project has a cost of $10,000, and the cost of capital for each project is 12 percent. The projects' expected net cash flows are as follows:

	EXPECTED NET CASH FLOWS	
Year	Project X	Project Y
0	($10,000)	($10,000)
1	6,500	3,500
2	3,000	3,500
3	3,000	3,500
4	1,000	3,500

a. Calculate each project's payback period, net present value (NPV), internal rate of return (IRR), and modified internal rate of return (MIRR).
b. Which project or projects should be accepted if they are independent?
c. Which project should be accepted if they are mutually exclusive?
d. How might a change in the cost of capital produce a conflict between the NPV and IRR rankings of these two projects? Would this conflict exist if r were 5%? (Hint: Plot the NPV profiles.)
e. Why does the conflict exist?

PROBLEMS

(10-1)
Decision Methods
Project K has a cost of $52,125, its expected net cash inflows are $12,000 per year for 8 years, and its cost of capital is 12 percent. (Hint: Begin by constructing a time line.)
a. What is the project's payback period (to the closest year)?
b. What is the project's discounted payback period?
c. What is the project's NPV?
d. What is the project's IRR?
e. What is the project's MIRR?

(10-2)
NPV
Your division is considering two investment projects, each of which requires an up-front expenditure of $15 million. You estimate that the investments will produce the following net cash flows:

Year	Project A	Project B
1	$ 5,000,000	$20,000,000
2	10,000,000	10,000,000
3	20,000,000	6,000,000

What are the two projects' net present values, assuming the cost of capital is 10 percent? 5 percent? 15 percent?

(10-3)
NPVs, IRRs, and
MIRRs for
Independent Projects
Edelman Engineering is considering including two pieces of equipment, a truck and an overhead pulley system, in this year's capital budget. The projects are independent. The cash outlay for the truck is $17,100, and that for the pulley system is $22,430. The firm's cost of capital is 14 percent. After-tax cash flows, including depreciation, are as follows:

Year	Truck	Pulley
1	$5,100	$7,500
2	5,100	7,500
3	5,100	7,500
4	5,100	7,500
5	5,100	7,500

Calculate the IRR, the NPV, and the MIRR for each project, and indicate the correct accept/reject decision for each.

(10-4)
NPVs and IRRs for
Mutually Exclusive
Projects

Davis Industries must choose between a gas-powered and an electric-powered forklift truck for moving materials in its factory. Since both forklifts perform the same function, the firm will choose only one. (They are mutually exclusive investments.) The electric-powered truck will cost more, but it will be less expensive to operate; it will cost $22,000, whereas the gas-powered truck will cost $17,500. The cost of capital that applies to both investments is 12 percent. The life for both types of truck is estimated to be 6 years, during which time the net cash flows for the electric-powered truck will be $6,290 per year and those for the gas-powered truck will be $5,000 per year. Annual net cash flows include depreciation expenses. Calculate the NPV and IRR for each type of truck, and decide which to recommend.

(10-5)
Capital Budgeting
Methods

Project S has a cost of $10,000 and is expected to produce benefits (cash flows) of $3,000 per year for 5 years. Project L costs $25,000 and is expected to produce cash flows of $7,400 per year for 5 years. Calculate the two projects' NPVs, IRRs, MIRRs, and PIs, assuming a cost of capital of 12 percent. Which project would be selected, assuming they are mutually exclusive, using each ranking method? Which should actually be selected?

(10-6)
MIRR and NPV

Your company is considering two mutually exclusive projects, X and Y, whose costs and cash flows are shown below:

Year	X	Y
0	($1,000)	($1,000)
1	100	1,000
2	300	100
3	400	50
4	700	50

The projects are equally risky, and their cost of capital is 12 percent. You must make a recommendation, and you must base it on the modified IRR (MIRR). What is the MIRR of the better project?

(10-7)
NPV and IRR Analysis

After discovering a new gold vein in the Colorado mountains, CTC Mining Corporation must decide whether to mine the deposit. The most cost-effective method of mining gold is sulfuric acid extraction, a process that results in environmental damage. To go ahead with the extraction, CTC must spend $900,000 for new mining equipment and pay $165,000 for its installation. The gold mined will net the firm an estimated $350,000 each year over the 5-year life of the vein. CTC's cost of capital is 14 percent. For the purposes of this problem, assume that the cash inflows occur at the end of the year.
a. What are the NPV and IRR of this project?
b. Should this project be undertaken, ignoring environmental concerns?
c. How should environmental effects be considered when evaluating this, or any other, project? How might these effects change your decision in part b?

(10-8)
NPV and IRR Analysis

Cummings Products Company is considering two mutually exclusive investments. The projects' expected net cash flows are as follows:

	EXPECTED NET CASH FLOWS	
Year	Project A	Project B
0	($300)	($405)
1	(387)	134
2	(193)	134
3	(100)	134
4	600	134
5	600	134
6	850	134
7	(180)	0

    a. Construct NPV profiles for Projects A and B.

    b. What is each project's IRR?

    c. If you were told that each project's cost of capital was 10 percent, which project should be selected? If the cost of capital was 17 percent, what would be the proper choice?

    d. What is each project's MIRR at a cost of capital of 10 percent? At 17%? (Hint: Consider Period 7 as the end of Project B's life.)

    e. What is the crossover rate, and what is its significance?

(10-9)
Timing Differences

The Ewert Exploration Company is considering two mutually exclusive plans for extracting oil on property for which it has mineral rights. Both plans call for the expenditure of $10,000,000 to drill development wells. Under Plan A, all the oil will be extracted in 1 year, producing a cash flow at t = 1 of $12,000,000, while under Plan B, cash flows will be $1,750,000 per year for 20 years.

    a. What are the annual incremental cash flows that will be available to Ewert Exploration if it undertakes Plan B rather than Plan A? (Hint: Subtract Plan A's flows from B's.)

    b. If the firm accepts Plan A, then invests the extra cash generated at the end of Year 1, what rate of return (reinvestment rate) would cause the cash flows from reinvestment to equal the cash flows from Plan B?

    c. Suppose a company has a cost of capital of 10 percent. Is it logical to assume that it would take on all available independent projects (of average risk) with returns greater than 10 percent? Further, if all available projects with returns greater than 10 percent have been taken, would this mean that cash flows from past investments would have an opportunity cost of only 10 percent, because all the firm could do with these cash flows would be to replace money that has a cost of 10 percent? Finally, does this imply that the cost of capital is the correct rate to assume for the reinvestment of a project's cash flows?

    d. Construct NPV profiles for Plans A and B, identify each project's IRR, and indicate the crossover rate of return.

(10-10)
Scale Differences

The Pinkerton Publishing Company is considering two mutually exclusive expansion plans. Plan A calls for the expenditure of $50 million on a large-scale, integrated plant which will provide an expected cash flow stream of $8 million per year for 20 years. Plan B calls for the expenditure of $15 million to build a somewhat less efficient, more labor-intensive plant which has an expected cash flow stream of $3.4 million per year for 20 years. The firm's cost of capital is 10 percent.

    a. Calculate each project's NPV and IRR.

    b. Set up a Project Δ by showing the cash flows that will exist if the firm goes with the large plant rather than the smaller plant. What are the NPV and the IRR for this Project Δ?

    c. Graph the NPV profiles for Plan A, Plan B, and Project Δ.

    d. Give a logical explanation, based on reinvestment rates and opportunity costs, as to why the NPV method is better than the IRR method when the firm's cost of capital is constant at some value such as 10 percent.

(10-11)
Multiple Rates of Return

The Ulmer Uranium Company is deciding whether or not it should open a strip mine, the net cost of which is $4.4 million. Net cash inflows are expected to be $27.7 million, all coming at the end of Year 1. The land must be returned to its natural state at a cost of $25 million, payable at the end of Year 2.

    a. Plot the project's NPV profile.

    b. Should the project be accepted if r = 8%? If r = 14%? Explain your reasoning.

    c. Can you think of some other capital budgeting situations where negative cash flows during or at the end of the project's life might lead to multiple IRRs?

    d. What is the project's MIRR at r = 8%? At r = 14%? Does the MIRR method lead to the same accept/reject decision as the NPV method?

(10-12)
Present Value of Costs

The Aubey Coffee Company is evaluating the within-plant distribution system for its new roasting, grinding, and packing plant. The two alternatives are (1) a conveyor system with a high initial cost, but low annual operating costs, and (2) several forklift trucks, which cost less, but have considerably higher operating costs. The decision to construct the plant has already been made, and the choice here will have no effect on the overall revenues of the project. The cost of capital for the plant is 8 percent, and the projects' expected net costs are listed in the table:

	EXPECTED NET COST	
Year	Conveyor	Forklift
0	($500,000)	($200,000)
1	(120,000)	(160,000)
2	(120,000)	(160,000)
3	(120,000)	(160,000)
4	(120,000)	(160,000)
5	(20,000)	(160,000)

  a. What is the IRR of each alternative?
  b. What is the present value of costs of each alternative? Which method should be chosen?

(10-13)
Payback, NPV, and MIRR
Your division is considering two investment projects, each of which requires an up-front expenditure of $25 million. You estimate that the cost of capital is 10 percent and that the investments will produce the following after-tax cash flows (in millions of dollars):

Year	Project A	Project B
1	5	20
2	10	10
3	15	8
4	20	6

  a. What is the regular payback period for each of the projects?
  b. What is the discounted payback period for each of the projects?
  c. If the two projects are independent and the cost of capital is 10 percent, which project or projects should the firm undertake?
  d. If the two projects are mutually exclusive and the cost of capital is 5 percent, which project should the firm undertake?
  e. If the two projects are mutually exclusive and the cost of capital is 15 percent, which project should the firm undertake?
  f. What is the crossover rate?
  g. If the cost of capital is 10 percent, what is the modified IRR (MIRR) of each project?

(10-14)
Unequal Lives
Shao Airlines is considering two alternative planes. Plane A has an expected life of 5 years, will cost $100 million, and will produce net cash flows of $30 million per year. Plane B has a life of 10 years, will cost $132 million, and will produce net cash flows of $25 million per year. Shao plans to serve the route for 10 years. Inflation in operating costs, airplane costs, and fares is expected to be zero, and the company's cost of capital is 12 percent. By how much would the value of the company increase if it accepted the better project (plane)?

(10-15)
Unequal Lives
The Perez Company has the opportunity to invest in one of two mutually exclusive machines that will produce a product it will need for the foreseeable future. Machine A costs $10 million but realizes after-tax inflows of $4 million per year for 4 years. After 4 years, the machine must be replaced. Machine B costs $15 million and realizes after-tax inflows of $3.5 million per year for 8 years, after which it must be replaced. Assume that machine prices are not expected to rise because inflation will be offset by cheaper components used in the machines. If the cost of capital is 10 percent, which machine should the company use?

(10-16)
Unequal Lives
Filkins Fabric Company is considering the replacement of its old, fully depreciated knitting machine. Two new models are available: Machine 190-3, which has a cost

of $190,000, a 3-year expected life, and after-tax cash flows (labor savings and depreciation) of $87,000 per year; and Machine 360-6, which has a cost of $360,000, a 6-year life, and after-tax cash flows of $98,300 per year. Knitting machine prices are not expected to rise, because inflation will be offset by cheaper components (microprocessors) used in the machines. Assume that Filkins' cost of capital is 14 percent. Should the firm replace its old knitting machine, and, if so, which new machine should it use?

(10-17)
Economic Life

The Scampini Supplies Company recently purchased a new delivery truck. The new truck cost $22,500, and it is expected to generate net after-tax operating cash flows, including depreciation, of $6,250 per year. The truck has a 5-year expected life. The expected salvage values after tax adjustments for the truck are given below. The company's cost of capital is 10 percent.

Year	Annual Operating Cash Flow	Salvage Value
0	($22,500)	$22,500
1	6,250	17,500
2	6,250	14,000
3	6,250	11,000
4	6,250	5,000
5	6,250	0

a. Should the firm operate the truck until the end of its 5-year physical life, or, if not, what is its optimal economic life?
b. Would the introduction of salvage values, in addition to operating cash flows, ever *reduce* the expected NPV and/or IRR of a project?

SPREADSHEET PROBLEM

(10-18)
Build a Model:
Capital Budgeting Tools

e-resource

Start with the partial model in the file *CF2 Ch 10 P18 Build a Model.xls* from the textbook's Web site. Gardial Fisheries is considering two mutually exclusive investments. The projects' expected net cash flows are as follows:

	EXPECTED NET CASH FLOWS	
Year	Project A	Project B
0	($375)	($575)
1	(300)	190
2	(200)	190
3	(100)	190
4	600	190
5	600	190
6	926	190
7	(200)	0

a. If you were told that each project's cost of capital was 12 percent, which project should be selected? If the cost of capital was 18 percent, what would be the proper choice?
b. Construct NPV profiles for Projects A and B.
c. What is each project's IRR?
d. What is the crossover rate, and what is its significance?
e. What is each project's MIRR at a cost of capital of 12 percent? At r = 18%? (Hint: Consider Period 7 as the end of Project B's life.)
f. What is the regular payback period for these two projects?
g. At a cost of capital of 12 percent, what is the discounted payback period for these two projects?

CYBERPROBLEM

Please go to our Web site, **http://ehrhardt.swlearning.com**, to access any Cyberproblems.

THOMSON ONE
Business School Edition

Please go to **http://ehrhardt.swlearning.com** to access any Thomson ONE—Business School Edition problems.

MINI CASE

You have just graduated from the MBA program of a large university, and one of your favorite courses was "Today's Entrepreneurs." In fact, you enjoyed it so much you have decided you want to "be your own boss." While you were in the master's program, your grandfather died and left you $1 million to do with as you please. You are not an inventor, and you do not have a trade skill that you can market; however, you have decided that you would like to purchase at least one established franchise in the fast-foods area, maybe two (if profitable). The problem is that you have never been one to stay with any project for too long, so you figure that your time frame is 3 years. After 3 years you will go on to something else.

You have narrowed your selection down to two choices: (1) Franchise L, Lisa's Soups, Salads, & Stuff, and (2) Franchise S, Sam's Wonderful Fried Chicken. The net cash flows shown below include the price you would receive for selling the franchise in Year 3 and the forecast of how each franchise will do over the 3-year period. Franchise L's cash flows will start off slowly but will increase rather quickly as people become more health conscious, while Franchise S's cash flows will start off high but will trail off as other chicken competitors enter the marketplace and as people become more health conscious and avoid fried foods. Franchise L serves breakfast and lunch, while Franchise S serves only dinner, so it is possible for you to invest in both franchises. You see these franchises as perfect complements to one another: You could attract both the lunch and dinner crowds and the health conscious and not so health conscious crowds without the franchises directly competing against one another.

Here are the net cash flows (in thousands of dollars):

	EXPECTED NET CASH FLOW	
Year	Franchise L	Franchise S
0	($100)	($100)
1	10	70
2	60	50
3	80	20

Depreciation, salvage values, net working capital requirements, and tax effects are all included in these cash flows.

You also have made subjective risk assessments of each franchise, and concluded that both franchises have risk characteristics that require a return of 10 percent. You must now determine whether one or both of the franchises should be accepted.

a. What is capital budgeting?

b. What is the difference between independent and mutually exclusive projects?

c. (1) What is the payback period? Find the paybacks for Franchises L and S.

    (2) What is the rationale for the payback method? According to the payback criterion, which franchise or franchises should be accepted if the firm's maximum acceptable payback is 2 years, and if Franchises L and S are independent? If they are mutually exclusive?

    (3) What is the difference between the regular and discounted payback periods?

    (4) What is the main disadvantage of discounted payback? Is the payback method of any real usefulness in capital budgeting decisions?

d. (1) Define the term *net present value (NPV)*. What is each franchise's NPV?

    (2) What is the rationale behind the NPV method? According to NPV, which franchise or franchises should be accepted if they are independent? Mutually exclusive?

    (3)   Would the NPVs change if the cost of capital changed?

e. (1)   Define the term *internal rate of return (IRR)*. What is each franchise's IRR?

    (2)   How is the IRR on a project related to the YTM on a bond?

    (3)   What is the logic behind the IRR method? According to IRR, which franchises should be accepted if they are independent? Mutually exclusive?

    (4)   Would the franchises' IRRs change if the cost of capital changed?

f. (1)   Draw NPV profiles for Franchises L and S. At what discount rate do the profiles cross?

    (2)   Look at your NPV profile graph without referring to the actual NPVs and IRRs. Which franchise or franchises should be accepted if they are independent? Mutually exclusive? Explain. Are your answers correct at any cost of capital less than 23.6 percent?

g. (1)   What is the underlying cause of ranking conflicts between NPV and IRR?

    (2)   What is the "reinvestment rate assumption," and how does it affect the NPV versus IRR conflict?

    (3)   Which method is the best? Why?

h. (1)   Define the term *modified IRR (MIRR)*. Find the MIRRs for Franchises L and S.

    (2)   What are the MIRR's advantages and disadvantages vis-à-vis the regular IRR? What are the MIRR's advantages and disadvantages vis-à-vis the NPV?

i. As a separate project (Project P), you are considering sponsoring a pavilion at the upcoming World's Fair. The pavilion would cost $800,000, and it is expected to result in $5 million of incremental cash inflows during its 1 year of operation. However, it would then take another year, and $5 million of costs, to demolish the site and return it to its original condition. Thus, Project P's expected net cash flows look like this (in millions of dollars):

Year	Net Cash Flows
0	($0.8)
1	5.0
2	(5.0)

The project is estimated to be of average risk, so its cost of capital is 10 percent.

    (1)   What are normal and nonnormal cash flows?

    (2)   What is Project P's NPV? What is its IRR? Its MIRR?

    (3)   Draw Project P's NPV profile. Does Project P have normal or nonnormal cash flows? Should this project be accepted?

j. What does the profitability index (PI) measure? What are the PI's of Franchises S and L?

k. In an unrelated analysis, you have the opportunity to choose between the following two mutually exclusive projects:

Year	EXPECTED NET CASH FLOW	
	Project S	Project L
0	($100,000)	($100,000)
1	60,000	33,500
2	60,000	33,500
3	—	33,500
4	—	33,500

The projects provide a necessary service, so whichever one is selected is expected to be repeated into the foreseeable future. Both projects have a 10 percent cost of capital.

    (1)   What is each project's initial NPV without replication?

    (2)   Now apply the replacement chain approach to determine the projects' extended NPVs. Which project should be chosen?

(3) Now assume that the cost to replicate Project S in 2 years will increase to $105,000 because of inflationary pressures. How should the analysis be handled now, and which project should be chosen?

l. You are also considering another project which has a physical life of 3 years; that is, the machinery will be totally worn out after 3 years. However, if the project were terminated prior to the end of 3 years, the machinery would have a positive salvage value. Here are the project's estimated cash flows:

Year	Initial Investment and Operating Cash Flows	End-of-Year Net Salvage Value
0	($5,000)	$5,000
1	2,100	3,100
2	2,000	2,000
3	1,750	0

Using the 10 percent cost of capital, what is the project's NPV if it is operated for the full 3 years? Would the NPV change if the company planned to terminate the project at the end of Year 2? At the end of Year 1? What is the project's optimal (economic) life?

m. After examining all the potential projects, you discover that there are many more projects this year with positive NPVs than in a normal year. What two problems might this extra large capital budget cause?

SELECTED ADDITIONAL REFERENCES AND CASES

For an in-depth treatment of capital budgeting techniques, see

Bierman, Harold, Jr., *The Capital Budgeting Decision* (Boston: Kluwer Academic Publishers, 2003.)

Levy, Haim, and Marshall Sarnat, *Capital Investment and Financial Decisions* (Englewood Cliffs, NJ: Prentice-Hall, 1994).

Seitz, Neil E., and Mitch Ellison, *Capital Budgeting and Long-Term Financing Decisions* (Mason, OH: South-Western Publishing, 2004).

These articles are related directly to the topics in this chapter:

Chaney, Paul K., "Moral Hazard and Capital Budgeting," *Journal of Financial Research,* Summer 1989, 113–128.

Miller, Edward M., "Safety Margins and Capital Budgeting Criteria," *Managerial Finance,* Number 2/3, 1988, 1–8.

Woods, John C., and Maury R. Randall, "The Net Present Value of Future Investment Opportunities: Its Impact on Shareholder Wealth and Implications for Capital Budgeting Theory," *Financial Management,* Summer 1989, 85–92.

For some articles that discuss the capital budgeting methods actually used in practice, see

Kim, Suk H., Trevor Crick, and Seung H. Kim, "Do Executives Practice What Academics Preach?" *Management Accounting,* November 1986, 49–52.

Mukherjee, Tarun K., "Capital Budgeting Surveys: The Past and the Future," *Review of Business and Economic Research,* Spring 1987, 37–56.

———, "The Capital Budgeting Process of Large U.S. Firms: An Analysis of Capital Budgeting Manuals," *Managerial Finance,* Number 2/3, 1988, 28–35.

Ross, Marc, "Capital Budgeting Practices of Twelve Large Manufacturers," *Financial Management,* Winter 1986, 15–22.

Runyan, L. R., "Capital Expenditure Decision Making in Small Firms," *Journal of Business Research,* September 1983, 389–397.

Weaver, Samuel C., Donald Peters, Roger Cason, and Joe Daleiden, "Capital Budgeting," *Financial Management,* Spring 1989, 10–17.

Additional capital budgeting references are provided in Chapter 11.

The following case from the Finance Online *Case Library covers many of the concepts discussed in this chapter and is available at* http://www.textchoice.com:

Case 11, "Chicago Valve Company."

CHAPTER 11

Cash Flow Estimation and Risk Analysis

H ome Depot Inc. grew phenomenally during the 1990s, and it is still growing rapidly. At the beginning of 1990, it had 118 stores and annual sales of $2.8 billion. It now has more than 1,700 stores, and sales of more than $64 billion. The stock has also performed quite well—a $10,000 investment in 1990 would now be worth about $350,000, for an annual return of more than 25 percent!

It costs Home Depot, on average, $16 million to purchase land, construct a new store, and stock it with inventory. (The inventory costs about $5 million, but about $2 million of this is financed through accounts payable.) Each new store thus represents a major capital expenditure, so the company must use capital budgeting techniques to determine if a potential store's expected cash flows are sufficient to cover its costs. Home Depot uses information from its existing stores to forecast new stores' expected cash flows. Thus far, its forecasts have been outstanding, but there are always risks that must be considered. First, sales might be less than projected if the economy weakens. Second, some of Home Depot's customers might in the future bypass it altogether and buy directly from manufacturers through the Internet or from competitors such as Lowe's. Third, new stores could "cannibalize," that is, take sales away from, existing stores. This last point was made in the July 16, 1999, issue of Value Line:

> The retailer has picked the "low-hanging fruit"; it has already entered the most attractive markets. To avoid "cannibalization"—which occurs when duplicative stores are located too closely together—the company is developing complementary formats. For example, Home Depot is beginning to roll out its Expo Design Center chain, which offers one-stop sales and service for kitchen and bath and other remodeling and renovation work . . .

The decision to expand requires a detailed assessment of the forecasted cash flows, including the risk that the forecasted level of sales might not be realized. In this chapter, we describe techniques for estimating a project's cash flows and their associated risk. As you read this chapter, think about Home Depot and how it might use these techniques to evaluate its capital budgeting decisions.

CORPORATE VALUATION, CASH FLOWS, AND RISK ANALYSIS

You can calculate the free cash flows (FCFs) for a project in much the same way as for a firm. When the project's expected free cash flows are discounted at the appropriate risk-adjusted rate, the result is the project's value. This chapter focuses on how to estimate the size and risk of a project's cash flows.

Project Sales Revenues	Project Operating Costs and Taxes	Project Required Investments	Firm Financing	Interest Rates	Project Risk	Market Risk

Project Free Cash Flows (FCF)

Project Cost of Capital (r)

Net Present Value of the Project (NPV)

$$NPV = \left[\frac{FCF_1}{(1+r)^1} + \frac{FCF_2}{(1+r)^2} + \frac{FCF_3}{(1+r)^3} + \cdots + \frac{FCF_n}{(1+r)^n} \right] - \text{Initial cost.}$$

The basic principles of capital budgeting were covered in Chapter 10. Given a project's expected cash flows, it is easy to calculate its payback, discounted payback, NPV, IRR, MIRR, and PI. Unfortunately, cash flows are rarely just given—rather, managers must estimate them based on information collected from sources both inside and outside the company. Moreover, uncertainty surrounds the cash flow estimates, and some projects are riskier than others. In the first part of the chapter, we develop procedures for estimating the cash flows associated with capital budgeting projects. Then, in the second part, we discuss techniques used to measure and take account of project risk.

ESTIMATING CASH FLOWS

CF
e-resource

The textbook's Web site contains an Excel file that will guide you through the chapter's calculations. The file for this chapter is CF2 Ch 11 Tool Kit.xls, and we encourage you to open the file and follow along as you read the chapter.

The most important, but also the most difficult, step in capital budgeting is estimating projects' cash flows—the investment outlays and the annual net cash flows after a project goes into operation. Many variables are involved, and many individuals and departments participate in the process. For example, the forecasts of unit sales and sales prices are normally made by the marketing group, based on their knowledge of price elasticity, advertising effects, the state of the economy, competitors' reactions, and trends in consumers' tastes. Similarly, the capital outlays associated with a new product are generally obtained from the engineering and product development staffs, while operating costs are estimated by cost accountants, production experts, personnel specialists, purchasing agents, and so forth.

A proper analysis includes (1) obtaining information from various departments such as engineering and marketing, (2) ensuring that everyone involved with the forecast uses a consistent set of realistic economic assumptions, and (3) making sure that no biases are inherent in the forecasts. This last point is extremely important, because some managers become emotionally involved with pet projects, and others seek to build empires. Both problems cause cash flow forecast biases which make bad projects look good—on paper.

SELF-TEST QUESTIONS What is the most important step in a capital budgeting analysis?
What departments are involved in estimating a project's cash flows?

IDENTIFYING THE RELEVANT CASH FLOWS

The first step in capital budgeting is to identify the **relevant cash flows,** defined as the specific set of cash flows that should be considered in the decision at hand. Analysts often make errors in estimating cash flows, but two cardinal rules can help you minimize mistakes: (1) Capital budgeting decisions must be based on *cash flows,* not accounting income. (2) Only *incremental cash flows* are relevant.

Free cash flow is the cash flow available for distribution to investors. In a nutshell, the relevant cash flow for a project is the *additional* free cash flow that the company can expect if it implements the project. It is the cash flow above and beyond what the company could expect if it doesn't implement the project. The following sections discuss the relevant cash flows in more detail.

Project Cash Flow versus Accounting Income

Free cash flow is calculated as follows:[1]

$$
\begin{aligned}
\text{Free cash flow} &= \begin{array}{c}\text{Net operating} \\ \text{profit after taxes} \\ \text{(NOPAT)}\end{array} + \text{Depreciation} - \begin{array}{c}\text{Gross fixed asset} \\ \text{expenditures}\end{array} - \begin{array}{c}\text{Change in net} \\ \text{operating} \\ \text{working capital}\end{array} \\
&= \text{EBIT}(1 - T) + \text{Depreciation} - \begin{array}{c}\text{Gross fixed asset} \\ \text{expenditures}\end{array} - \left[\begin{array}{c}\Delta\ \text{Operating current assets} - \\ \Delta\ \text{Operating current liabilities}\end{array}\right].
\end{aligned}
$$

Just as a firm's value depends on its free cash flows, so does the value of a project. We illustrate the estimation of project cash flow later in the chapter with a comprehensive example, but it is important for you to understand that project cash flow differs from accounting income.

COSTS OF FIXED ASSETS   Most projects require assets, and asset purchases represent *negative* cash flows. Even though the acquisition of assets results in a cash outflow, accountants do not show the purchase of fixed assets as a deduction from accounting income. Instead, they deduct a depreciation expense each year throughout the life of the asset.

Note that the full cost of fixed assets includes any shipping and installation costs. When a firm acquires fixed assets, it often must incur substantial costs for shipping and installing the equipment. These charges are added to the price of the equipment when the project's cost is being determined. Then, the full cost of the equipment, including shipping and installation costs, is used as the **depreciable basis** when depreciation charges are being calculated. For example, if a company bought a computer with an invoice price of $100,000 and paid another $10,000 for shipping and installation, then the full cost of the computer (and its depreciable basis) would be $110,000. Note too

---

[1] Chapter 3 explains the calculation of free cash flow. Note that EBIT stands for earnings before interest and taxes, and it is also called pre-tax operating profit.

that fixed assets can often be sold at the end of a project's life. If this is the case, then the after-tax cash proceeds represent a positive cash flow. We will illustrate both depreciation and cash flow from asset sales later in the chapter.

NONCASH CHARGES   In calculating net income, accountants usually subtract depreciation from revenues. So, while accountants do not subtract the purchase price of fixed assets when calculating accounting income, they do subtract a charge each year for depreciation. Depreciation shelters income from taxation, and this has an impact on cash flow, but depreciation itself is not a cash flow. Therefore, depreciation must be added to NOPAT when estimating a project's cash flow.

CHANGES IN NET OPERATING WORKING CAPITAL   Normally, additional inventories are required to support a new operation, and expanded sales tie up additional funds in accounts receivable. However, payables and accruals increase as a result of the expansion, and this reduces the cash needed to finance inventories and receivables. The difference between the required increase in operating current assets and the increase in operating current liabilities is the **change in net operating working capital.** If this change is positive, as it generally is for expansion projects, then additional financing, over and above the cost of the fixed assets, will be needed.

Toward the end of a project's life, inventories will be used but not replaced, and receivables will be collected without corresponding replacements. As these changes occur, the firm will receive cash inflows, and as a result, the investment in net operating working capital will be returned by the end of the project's life.

INTEREST EXPENSES ARE NOT INCLUDED IN PROJECT CASH FLOWS   Recall from Chapter 10 that we discount a project's cash flows by its cost of capital, and that the cost of capital is a weighted average (WACC) of the costs of debt, preferred stock, and common equity, adjusted for the project's risk. This WACC is the rate of return necessary to satisfy all of the firm's investors, both stockholders and debtholders. A common mistake made by many students and financial managers is to subtract interest payments when estimating a project's cash flows. This is a mistake because the cost of debt is already embedded in the WACC, so subtracting interest payments from the project's cash flows would amount to double counting interest costs.

If someone subtracted interest (or interest plus principal payments) from the project's cash flows, then they would be calculating the cash flows available to the equity holders, and these cash flows should be discounted at the cost of equity. This technique can give the correct answer, but in order for it to work you must be very careful to adjust the amount of debt outstanding each year in order to keep the riskiness of the equity cash flows constant. This process is very complicated, and we do not recommend it. Here is one final caution: If someone subtracts interest, then it is definitely wrong to discount the resulting cash flows by the WACC, and no amount of care can correct that error.

Note that this differs from the procedures used to calculate accounting income. Accountants measure the profit available for stockholders, so interest expenses are subtracted. However, project cash flow is the cash flow available for all investors, bondholders as well as stockholders, so interest expenses are not subtracted. This is completely analogous to the procedures used in the corporate valuation model of Chapter 13, where the company's free cash flows are discounted at the WACC. *Therefore, you should not subtract interest expenses when finding a project's cash flows.*

Incremental Cash Flows

In evaluating a project, we focus on those cash flows that occur if and only if we accept the project. These cash flows, called **incremental cash flows,** represent the change in the firm's total cash flow that occurs as a direct result of accepting the project. Three special problems in determining incremental cash flows are discussed next.

SUNK COSTS   A **sunk cost** is an outlay that has already occurred, hence is not affected by the decision under consideration. Since sunk costs are not incremental costs, they should not be included in the analysis. To illustrate, in 2005, Northeast BankCorp was considering whether to establish a branch office in a newly developed section of Boston. To help with its evaluation, Northeast had, back in 2004, hired a consulting firm to perform a site analysis; the cost was $100,000, and this amount was expensed for tax purposes in 2004. Is this 2004 expenditure a relevant cost with respect to the 2005 capital budgeting decision? The answer is no—the $100,000 is a *sunk cost,* and it will not affect Northeast's future cash flows regardless of whether or not the new branch is built. It often turns out that a particular project has a negative NPV if all the associated costs, including sunk costs, are considered. However, on an incremental basis, the project may be a good one because the *future incremental cash flows* are large enough to produce a positive NPV on the *incremental investment.*

OPPORTUNITY COSTS   A second potential problem relates to **opportunity costs,** which are cash flows that could be generated from an asset the firm already owns if it is not used for the project in question. To illustrate, Northeast BankCorp already owns a piece of land that is suitable for the branch location. When evaluating the prospective branch, should the cost of the land be disregarded because no additional cash outlay would be required? The answer is no, because there is an *opportunity cost* inherent in the use of the property. In this case, the land could be sold to yield $150,000 after taxes. Use of the site for the branch would require forgoing this inflow, so the $150,000 must be charged as an opportunity cost against the project. Note that the proper land cost in this example is the $150,000 market-determined value, irrespective of whether Northeast originally paid $50,000 or $500,000 for the property. (What Northeast paid would, of course, have an effect on taxes, hence on the after-tax opportunity cost.)

EFFECTS ON OTHER PARTS OF THE FIRM: EXTERNALITIES   The third potential problem involves the effects of a project on other parts of the firm, which economists call **externalities.** For example, some of Northeast's customers who would use the new branch are already banking with Northeast's downtown office. The loans and deposits, hence profits, generated by these customers would not be new to the bank; rather, they would represent a transfer from the main office to the branch. Thus, the net income produced by these customers should not be treated as incremental income in the capital budgeting decision. On the other hand, having a suburban branch would help the bank attract new business to its downtown office, because some people like to be able to bank both close to home and close to work. In this case, the additional income that would actually flow to the downtown office should be attributed to the branch. Although they are often difficult to quantify, *externalities* (which can be either positive or negative) should be considered.

When a new project takes sales from an existing product, this is often called **cannibalization.** Naturally, firms do not like to cannibalize their existing products, but it often turns out that if they do not, someone else will. To illustrate, IBM for years refused to provide full support for its PC division because it did not want to steal sales from its highly profitable mainframe business. That turned out to be a huge strategic error, because it allowed Intel, Microsoft, Dell, and others to become dominant forces in the computer industry. Therefore, when considering externalities, the full implications of the proposed new project should be taken into account.

A few young firms, including Dell Computer, have been successful selling their products only over the Internet. Many firms, however, had established retail channels long before the Internet became a reality. For these firms, the decision to begin selling directly to consumers over the Internet is not a simple one. For example, Nautica Enterprises Inc. is an international company that designs, sources, markets, and distributes sportswear.

Nautica sells its products to traditional retailers such as Saks Fifth Avenue and Parisian, who then sell to consumers. If Nautica opens its own online Internet store, it could potentially increase its profit margin by avoiding the substantial markup added by dealers. However, Internet sales would probably cannibalize sales through its retailer network. Even worse, retailers might react adversely to Nautica's Internet sales by redirecting the marketing effort and display space they now provide Nautica to other brands that do not compete over the Internet. Nautica, and many other producers, must determine whether the new profits from Internet sales will compensate for lost profits from existing channels. Thus far, Nautica has decided to stay with its traditional retailers.

Rather than focusing narrowly on the project at hand, analysts must anticipate the project's impact on the rest of the firm, which requires imagination and creative thinking. As the IBM and Nautica examples illustrate, it is critical to identify and account for all externalities when evaluating a proposed project.

e-resource

See CF2 Ch 11 Tool Kit.xls for all calculations.

REPLACEMENT PROJECTS   If a project involves replacing existing assets with new ones, then we must estimate cash flows on an incremental basis. For example, suppose a more efficient machine would cost $100,000, but it would lead to increased output, higher sales, and lower costs. Moreover, the firm would receive $40,000 after taxes for the old machine, reducing the incremental investment to $60,000. The new machine would result in sales of $40,000 per year versus old sales of $25,000, so the incremental revenue would be $15,000, and the new costs would be $10,000 versus old costs of $15,000. Thus, the incremental costs would be −$5,000, which means a saving. Finally, the old machine was being depreciated at the rate of $8,000 per year, but the new machine would have $20,000 of annual depreciation, so the incremental depreciation would be +$12,000. Based on these figures, and assuming the new and old machines both have a life of five years, the incremental cash flows are given in Table 11-1.

If we looked only at the cash flows for the replacement machine without considering the old machine, then the NPV would be negative and the IRR less than the WACC. However, if we properly considered the incremental cash flows, then we would see that the NPV *on the incremental investment* is positive, so the old machine should be replaced. The example demonstrates the fundamentals of a replacement analysis and the importance of focusing on incremental cash flows.

TABLE 11-1 | Incremental Cash Flows and Project Analysis

	New		Old		Incremental
Initial investment	$100,000	−	$40,000	=	$60,000
Annual Revenues and Costs					
Sales revenues	$ 40,000	−	$25,000	=	$15,000
Operating costs	−10,000	−	−15,000	=	− 5,000
Depreciation	−20,000	−	−8,000	=	−12,000
Taxable income	$ 10,000	−	$ 2,000	=	$ 8,000
Taxes (40%)	$ 4,000	−	$ 800	=	$ 3,200
Net income	$ 6,000	−	$ 1,200	=	$ 4,800
Add back depreciation	$ 20,000	−	$ 8,000	=	$12,000
Net cash flow	$ 26,000	−	$ 9,200	=	$16,800
WACC = 10%					
Life = 5 years					
NPV:	−$ 1,440				$ 3,685
IRR:	9.4%				12.4%

Timing of Cash Flows

We must account properly for the timing of cash flows. Accounting income statements are for periods such as years or months, so they do not reflect exactly when during the period cash revenues or expenses occur. Because of the time value of money, capital budgeting cash flows should in theory be analyzed exactly as they occur. Of course, there must be a compromise between accuracy and feasibility. A time line with daily cash flows would in theory be most accurate, but daily cash flow estimates would be costly to construct, unwieldy to use, and probably no more accurate than annual cash flow estimates because we simply cannot forecast well enough to warrant this degree of detail. Therefore, in most cases, we simply assume that all cash flows occur at the end of every year. However, for some projects, it may be useful to assume that cash flows occur at mid-year, or even quarterly or monthly.

SELF-TEST QUESTIONS Why should companies use project cash flow rather than accounting income when finding the NPV of a project?

How do shipping and installation costs affect the depreciable basis?

What is the most common noncash charge that must be added back when finding project cash flows?

What is net operating working capital, and how does it affect a project's cash flows in capital budgeting?

Explain the following terms: incremental cash flow, sunk cost, opportunity cost, externality, and cannibalization.

TAX EFFECTS

Taxes have a major effect on cash flows, and in many cases tax effects will make or break a project. Therefore, it is critical that taxes be dealt with correctly. Our tax laws are extremely complex, and they are subject to interpretation and to change. You can get assistance from your firm's accountants and tax lawyers, but even so, you should have a working knowledge of the current tax laws and their effects on cash flows.

An Overview of Depreciation

Suppose a firm buys a milling machine for $100,000 and uses it for five years, after which it is scrapped. The cost of the goods produced by the machine must include a charge for the machine, and this charge is called **depreciation.** In the following sections, we review some of the depreciation concepts covered in accounting courses.

Companies often calculate depreciation one way when figuring taxes and another way when reporting income to investors: many use the **straight-line** method for stockholder reporting (or "book" purposes), but they use the fastest rate permitted by law for tax purposes. Under the straight-line method used for stockholder reporting, one normally takes the cost of the asset, subtracts its estimated salvage value, and divides the net amount by the asset's useful economic life. For an asset with a five-year life, which costs $100,000 and has a $12,500 salvage value, the annual straight-line depreciation charge is ($100,000 − $12,500)/5 = $17,500. Note, however, as we discuss later, salvage value is *not* considered for tax depreciation purposes.

For tax purposes, Congress changes the permissible tax depreciation methods from time to time. Prior to 1954, the straight-line method was required for tax purposes, but in 1954 **accelerated** methods (double-declining balance and sum-of-years'-digits) were permitted. Then, in 1981, the old accelerated methods were replaced by a simpler procedure known as the Accelerated Cost Recovery System (ACRS). The ACRS system was changed again in 1986 as a part of the Tax Reform Act, and it is now known as the **Modified Accelerated Cost Recovery System (MACRS);** a 1993 tax law made further changes in this area.

Note that U.S. tax laws are very complicated, and in this text we can only provide an overview of MACRS designed to give you a basic understanding of the impact of depreciation on capital budgeting decisions. Further, the tax laws change so often that the numbers we present may be outdated before the book is even published. Thus, when dealing with tax depreciation in real-world situations, current Internal Revenue Service (IRS) publications or individuals with expertise in tax matters should be consulted.

Tax Depreciation Life

For tax purposes, the entire cost of an asset is expensed over its **depreciable life.** Historically, an asset's depreciable life was set equal to its estimated useful economic life; it was intended that an asset would be fully depreciated at approximately the same time that it reached the end of its useful economic life. However, MACRS totally abandoned that practice and set simple guidelines that created several classes of assets, each with a more-or-less arbitrarily prescribed life called a *recovery period* or *class life*. The MACRS class lives bear only a rough relationship to assets' expected useful economic lives.

A major effect of the MACRS system has been to shorten the depreciable lives of assets, thus giving businesses larger tax deductions early in the assets' lives, thereby increasing the present value of the cash flows. Table 11-2 describes the types of property that fit into the different class life groups, and Table 11-3 sets forth the MACRS recovery allowance percentages (depreciation rates) for selected classes of investment property.

Consider Table 11-2, which gives the MACRS class life and the types of assets that fall into each category. Property in the 27.5- and 39-year categories (real estate) must be depreciated by the straight-line method, but 3-, 5-, 7-, and 10-year property (personal property) can be depreciated either by the accelerated method set forth in Table 11-3 or by the straight-line method.[2]

As we saw earlier in the chapter, higher depreciation expenses result in lower taxes in the early years, hence a higher present value of cash flows. Therefore, since a firm has the choice of using straight-line rates or the accelerated rates shown in Table 11-3, most elect to use the accelerated rates.

The yearly recovery allowance, or depreciation expense, is determined by multiplying each asset's *depreciable basis* by the applicable recovery percentage shown in Table 11-3. Calculations are discussed in the following sections.

TABLE 11-2 | Major Classes and Asset Lives for MACRS

Class	Type of Property
3-year	Certain special manufacturing tools
5-year	Automobiles, light-duty trucks, computers, and certain special manufacturing equipment
7-year	Most industrial equipment, office furniture, and fixtures
10-year	Certain longer-lived types of equipment
27.5-year	Residential rental real property such as apartment buildings
39-year	All nonresidential real property, including commercial and industrial buildings

---

[2] As a benefit to very small companies, the Tax Code currently (2004) permits companies to *expense,* which is equivalent to depreciating over one year, up to $100,000 of equipment; see IRS Publication 946 for details. Thus, if a small company bought one asset worth up to $100,000, it could write the asset off in the year it was acquired. This is called "Section 179 expensing." We shall disregard this provision throughout the book. Also, Congress enacted the Job Creation and Worker Assistance Act of 2002 following the terrorist attacks on the World Trade Center and Pentagon. This act, among other things, temporarily changed how depreciation is charged for property acquired after September 10, 2001, and before September 11, 2004, and put in service before January 1, 2005. We shall disregard this provision throughout the book.

TABLE 11-3 | Recovery Allowance Percentage for Personal Property

Ownership Year	CLASS OF INVESTMENT			
	3-Year	5-Year	7-Year	10-Year
1	33%	20%	14%	10%
2	45	32	25	18
3	15	19	17	14
4	7	12	13	12
5		11	9	9
6		6	9	7
7			9	7
8			4	7
9				7
10				6
11				3
	100%	100%	100%	100%

Notes:

a. We developed these recovery allowance percentages based on the 200 percent declining balance method prescribed by MACRS, with a switch to straight-line depreciation at some point in the asset's life. For example, consider the 5-year recovery allowance percentages. The straight line percentage would be 20 percent per year, so the 200 percent declining balance multiplier is 2.0(20%) = 40% = 0.4. However, because the half-year convention applies, the MACRS percentage for Year 1 is 20 percent. For Year 2, there is 80 percent of the depreciable basis remaining to be depreciated, so the recovery allowance percentage is 0.40(80%) = 32%. In Year 3, 20% + 32% = 52% of the depreciation has been taken, leaving 48%, so the percentage is 0.4(48%) ≈ 19%. In Year 4, the percentage is 0.4(29%) ≈ 12%. After 4 years, straight-line depreciation exceeds the declining balance depreciation, so a switch is made to straight-line (this is permitted under the law). However, the half-year convention must also be applied at the end of the class life, and the remaining 17 percent of depreciation must be taken (amortized) over 1.5 years. Thus, the percentage in Year 5 is 17%/1.5 ≈ 11%, and in Year 6, 17% − 11% = 6%. Although the tax tables carry the allowance percentages out to two decimal places, we have rounded to the nearest whole number for ease of illustration.

b. Residential rental property (apartments) is depreciated over a 27.5-year life, whereas commercial and industrial structures are depreciated over 39 years. In both cases, straight-line depreciation must be used. The depreciation allowance for the first year is based, pro rata, on the month the asset was placed in service, with the remainder of the first year's depreciation being taken in the 28th or 40th year. A half-month convention is assumed; that is, an asset placed in service in February would receive 10.5 months of depreciation in the first year.

HALF-YEAR CONVENTION   Under MACRS, the assumption is generally made that property is placed in service in the middle of the first year. Thus, for 3-year class life property, the recovery period begins in the middle of the year the asset is placed in service and ends three years later. The effect of the *half-year convention* is to extend the recovery period out one more year, so 3-year class life property is depreciated over four calendar years, 5-year property is depreciated over six calendar years, and so on. This convention is incorporated into Table 11-3's recovery allowance percentages.[3]

DEPRECIABLE BASIS   The *depreciable basis* is a critical element of MACRS because each year's allowance (depreciation expense) depends jointly on the asset's depreciable

---

[3] The half-year convention also applies if the straight-line alternative is used, with half of one year's depreciation taken in the first year, a full year's depreciation taken in each of the remaining years of the asset's class life, and the remaining half-year's depreciation taken in the year following the end of the class life. You should recognize that virtually all companies have computerized depreciation systems. Each asset's depreciation pattern is programmed into the system at the time of its acquisition, and the computer aggregates the depreciation allowances for all assets when the accountants close the books and prepare financial statements and tax returns.

basis and its MACRS class life. The depreciable basis under MACRS is equal to the purchase price of the asset plus any shipping and installation costs. The basis is *not* adjusted for *salvage value* (which is the estimated market value of the asset at the end of its useful life) regardless of whether accelerated or straight-line depreciation is taken.

SALE OF A DEPRECIABLE ASSET   If a depreciable asset is sold, the sale price (actual salvage value) minus the then-existing undepreciated book value is added to operating income and taxed at the firm's marginal tax rate. For example, suppose a firm buys a 5-year class life asset for $100,000 and sells it at the end of the fourth year for $25,000. The asset's book value is equal to $100,000(0.11 + 0.06) = $100,000(0.17) = $17,000. Therefore, $25,000 − $17,000 = $8,000 is added to the firm's operating income and is taxed.

DEPRECIATION ILLUSTRATION   Assume that Stango Food Products buys a $150,000 machine that falls into the MACRS 5-year class life and places it into service on October 15, 2006. Stango must pay an additional $30,000 for delivery and installation. Salvage value is not considered, so the machine's depreciable basis is $180,000. (Delivery and installation charges are included in the depreciable basis rather than expensed in the year incurred.) Each year's recovery allowance (tax depreciation expense) is determined by multiplying the depreciable basis by the applicable recovery allowance percentage. Thus, the depreciation expense for 2006 is 0.20($180,000) = $36,000, and for 2007 it is 0.32($180,000) = $57,600. Similarly, the depreciation expense is $34,200 for 2008, $21,600 for 2009, $19,800 for 2010, and $10,800 for 2011. The total depreciation expense over the six-year recovery period is $180,000, which is equal to the depreciable basis of the machine.

As noted above, most firms use straight-line depreciation for stockholder reporting purposes but MACRS for tax purposes. *In this case, for capital budgeting purposes MACRS should be used.* In capital budgeting, we are concerned with cash flows, not reported income. Because MACRS depreciation is used for taxes, this type of depreciation must be used to determine the taxes that will be assessed against a particular project. Only if the depreciation method used for tax purposes is also used for capital budgeting analysis will we obtain an accurate cash flow estimate.

SELF-TEST QUESTIONS

What do the acronyms ACRS and MACRS stand for?
Briefly describe the tax depreciation system under MACRS.
How does the sale of a depreciable asset affect a firm's cash flows?

EVALUATING CAPITAL BUDGETING PROJECTS

e-resource

*For more discussion on replacement analysis decisions, refer to the Chapter 11 Web Extension on the textbook's Web site. Also, the file **CF2 Ch 11 Tool Kit.xls** provides an example of replacement analysis.*

Up to now, we have discussed several important aspects of cash flow analysis, but we have not seen how they affect capital budgeting decisions. Conceptually, capital budgeting is straightforward: A potential project creates value for the firm's shareholders if and only if the net present value of the incremental cash flows from the project is positive. In practice, however, estimating these cash flows can be difficult.

Incremental cash flows are affected by whether the project is an expansion project or replacement project. A **new expansion project** is defined as one where the firm invests in new assets to increase sales. Here the incremental cash flows are simply the project's cash inflows and outflows. In effect, the company is comparing what its value would be with and without the proposed project. By contrast, a **replacement project** occurs when the firm replaces an existing asset with a new one. In this case, the incremental cash flows are the firm's *additional* inflows and outflows that result from investing in the new project. In a replacement analysis, the company is comparing its value if it takes on the new project to its value if it continues to use the existing asset.

Despite these differences, the basic principles for evaluating expansion and replacement projects are the same. In each case, the cash flows typically include the following items:

1. *Initial investment outlay*. This includes the cost of the fixed assets associated with the project plus any initial investment in net operating working capital (NOWC), such as raw materials.
2. *Annual project cash flow*. The operating cash flow is the net operating profit after taxes (NOPAT) plus depreciation. Recall (a) that depreciation is added back because it is a noncash expense and (b) that financing costs (including interest expenses) are not subtracted because they are accounted for when the cash flow is discounted at the cost of capital. In addition, many projects have levels of NOWC that change during the project's life. For example, as sales increase, more NOWC is required, and as sales fall, less NOWC is needed. The cash flows associated with annual increases or reductions in NOWC must be included when calculating the project's annual cash flow.
3. *Terminal year cash flow*. At the end of the project's life, some extra cash flow is usually generated from the salvage value of the fixed assets, adjusted for taxes if the assets are not sold at their book value. Any return of net operating working capital not already accounted for in the annual cash flow must also be added to the terminal year cash flow.

The classification of cash flows isn't always as distinct as we have indicated. For example, in some projects the acquisition of fixed assets is phased in throughout the project's life, and for other projects some fixed assets are sold off at times other than the terminal year. The important thing to remember is to include all cash flows in your analysis, no matter how you classify them.

For each year of the project's life, the *net cash flow* is determined as the sum of the cash flows from each of the categories. These annual net cash flows are then plotted on a time line and used to calculate the project's NPV and IRR.

We will illustrate the principles of capital budgeting analysis by examining a new project being considered by Regency Integrated Chips (RIC), a large Nashville-based technology company. RIC's research and development department has been applying its expertise in microprocessor technology to develop a small computer designed to control home appliances. Once programmed, the computer will automatically control the heating and air-conditioning systems, security system, hot water heater, and even small appliances such as a coffee maker. By increasing a home's energy efficiency, the computer can cut costs enough to pay for itself within a few years. Development has now reached the stage where a decision must be made about whether or not to go forward with full-scale production.

RIC's marketing vice-president believes that annual sales would be 20,000 units if the units were priced at $3,000 each, so annual sales are estimated at $60 million. RIC expects no growth in unit sales, and it believes that the unit price will rise by 2 percent each year. The engineering department has reported that the project will require additional manufacturing space, and RIC currently has an option to purchase an existing building, at a cost of $12 million, which would meet this need. The building would be bought and paid for on December 31, 2006, and for depreciation purposes it would fall into the MACRS 39-year class.

The necessary equipment would be purchased and installed in late 2006, and it would also be paid for on December 31, 2006. The equipment would fall into the MACRS 5-year class, and it would cost $8 million, including transportation and installation.

The project's estimated economic life is four years. At the end of that time, the building is expected to have a market value of $7.5 million and a book value of $10.908 million, whereas the equipment would have a market value of $2 million and a book value of $1.36 million.

The production department has estimated that variable manufacturing costs would be $2,100 per unit, and that fixed overhead costs, excluding depreciation, would be $8 million a year. They expect variable costs to rise by 2 percent per year, and fixed costs to rise by 1 percent per year. Depreciation expenses would be determined in accordance with MACRS rates.

RIC's marginal federal-plus-state tax rate is 40 percent; its cost of capital is 12 percent; and, for capital budgeting purposes, the company's policy is to assume that operating cash flows occur at the end of each year. Because the plant would begin operations on January 1, 2007, the first operating cash flows would occur on December 31, 2007.

Several other points should be noted: (1) RIC is a relatively large corporation, with sales of more than $4 billion, and it takes on many investments each year. Thus, if the computer control project does not work out, it will not bankrupt the company—management can afford to take a chance on the computer control project. (2) If the project is accepted, the company will be contractually obligated to operate it for its full four-year life. Management must make this commitment to its component suppliers. (3) Returns on this project would be positively correlated with returns on RIC's other projects and also with the stock market—the project should do well if other parts of the firm and the general economy are strong.

Assume that you have been assigned to conduct the capital budgeting analysis. For now, assume that the project has the same risk as an average project, and use the corporate weighted average cost of capital, 12 percent.

Analysis of the Cash Flows

Capital projects can be analyzed using a calculator, paper and a pencil, or with a spreadsheet program such as *Excel*. Either way, you must set the analysis up as shown in Table 11-4 and go through the steps outlined in Parts 1 through 5 of the table. For exam purposes, you will probably have to work problems with a calculator. However, for reasons that will become obvious as you go through the chapter, in practice spreadsheets are virtually always used. Still, the steps involved in a capital budgeting analysis are the same whether you use a calculator or a computer.

Table 11-4, a printout from the file **CF2 Ch 11 Tool Kit.xls,** is divided into five parts: (1) Input Data, (2) Depreciation Schedule, (3) Net Salvage Values, (4) Projected Net Cash Flows, and (5) Key Output. There are also two extensions, Parts 6 and 7, that deal with risk analysis and which we will discuss later in the chapter when we cover sensitivity and scenario analyses. Note also that the table shows row and column indicators, so cells in the table have designations such as "Cell D77," which is the location of the cost of the building, found in Part 1, Input Data. The first row shown is Row 75; the previous rows contain information about the model that we omitted from the text. Finally, the numbers in the printed table are rounded from the actual numbers in the spreadsheet.

Part 1, the Input Data section, provides the basic data used in the analysis. The inputs are really "assumptions"—thus, in the analysis we *assume* that 20,000 units can be sold at a price of $3 per unit.[4] Some of the inputs are known with near certainty—for example, the 40 percent tax rate is not likely to change. Others are more speculative—units sold and the variable cost percentage are in this category. Obviously, if sales or costs are different from the assumed levels, then profits and cash flows, hence NPV and IRR, will differ from their projected levels. Later in the chapter, we discuss how changes in the inputs affect the results.

Part 2, which calculates depreciation over the project's four-year life, is divided into two sections, one for the building and one for the equipment. The first row in each section (Rows 88 and 92) gives the yearly depreciation rates as taken from Table 11-3. The

---

[4] Recall that the sales price is actually $3,000, but for convenience we show all dollars in thousands.

TABLE 11-4 | Analysis of a New (Expansion) Project: Parts 1 and 2

	A	B	C	D	E	F	G	H	I
75	Part 1. Input Data (in thousands of dollars)								
76							Key Output: NPV	=	$5,809
77	Building cost (= Depreciable basis)			$12,000					
78	Equipment cost (= Depreciable basis)			$8,000		Market value of building in 2010			$7,500
79	Net Operating WC/Sales			10%		Market value of equip. in 2010			$2,000
80	First year sales (in units)			20,000		Tax rate			40%
81	Growth rate in units sold			0.0%		WACC			12%
82	Sales price per unit			$3.00		Inflation: growth in sales price			2.0%
83	Variable cost per unit			$2.10		Inflation: growth in VC per unit			2.0%
84	Fixed costs			$8,000		Inflation: growth in fixed costs			1.0%
85									
86	Part 2. Depreciation Schedule[a]				Years				Cumulative Depr'n
87					1	2	3	4	
88	Building Depr'n Rate				1.3%	2.6%	2.6%	2.6%	
89	Building Depr'n				$156	$312	$312	$312	$1,092
90	Ending Book Val: Cost – Cum. Depr'n				11,844	11,532	11,220	$10,908	
91									
92	Equipment Depr'n Rate				20.0%	32.0%	19.0%	12.0%	
93	Equipment Depr'n				$1,600	$2,560	$1,520	$960	$6,640
94	Ending Book Val: Cost – Cum. Depr'n				6,400	3,840	2,320	$1,360	
95									
96	[a]The depreciation rates are multiplied by the depreciable basis ($12,000 for the building and $8,000 for the equipment) to determine the yearly depreciation expense. The correct depreciation percentages for the building depend upon the month that the building is put in service. Because this analysis assumes that all cash flows occur at the end of the year, and to prevent unnecessary complexity, we have rounded the depreciation percentages for the building. See the Tab named Depreciation for more details.								
97									

second row in each section (Rows 89 and 93) gives the dollars of depreciation, found as the rate times the asset's depreciable basis, which, in this example, is the initial cost. The third row (Rows 90 and 94) shows the book value at the end of Year 4, found by subtracting the accumulated depreciation from the depreciable basis.

Part 3 estimates the cash flows the firm will realize when it disposes of the assets. Row 101 shows the salvage value, which is the sales price the company expects to receive when it sells the assets four years hence. Row 102 shows the book values at the end of Year 4; these values were calculated in Part 2. Row 103 shows the expected gain or loss, defined as the difference between the sale price and the book value. As explained in notes c and d to Table 11-4, gains and losses are treated as ordinary income, not capital gains or losses.[5] Therefore, gains result in tax liabilities, and losses produce tax credits, that are equal to the gain or loss times the 40 percent tax rate. Taxes paid and tax credits are shown on

---

[5] Note again that if an asset is sold for exactly its book value, there will be no gain or loss, hence no tax liability or credit. However, if an asset is sold for other than its book value, a gain or loss will be created. For example, RIC's building will have a book value of $10,908, but the company expects to realize only $7,500 when it is sold. This would result in a loss of $3,408. This indicates that the building should have been depreciated at a faster rate—only if depreciation had been $3,408 larger would the book and market values have been equal. So, the Tax Code stipulates that losses on the sale of operating assets can be used to reduce ordinary income, just as depreciation reduces income. On the other hand, if an asset is sold for more than its book value, as is the case for the equipment, then this signifies that the depreciation rates were too high, so the gain is called "depreciation recapture" by the IRS and is taxed as ordinary income.

TABLE 11-4 | Analysis of a New (Expansion) Project: Part 3

	A	B	C	D	E	F	G	H	I
99	Part 3 of Table 11-4. Net Salvage Values in 2010								
100					Building	Equipment	Total		
101	Estimated Market Value in 2010				$7,500	$2,000			
102	Book Value in 2010[b]				10,908	1,360			
103	Expected Gain or Loss[c]				−3,408	640			
104	Taxes paid or tax credit				−1,363	256			
105	Net cash flow from salvage[d]				$8,863	$1,744	$10,607		
106									
107	[b]Book value equals depreciable basis (initial cost in this case) minus accumulated MACRS depreciation. For the building, accumulated								
108	depreciation equals $1,092, so book value equals $12,000 − $1,092 = $10,908. For the equipment, accumulated depreciation equals $6,640, so								
109	book value equals $8,000 − $6,640 = $1,360.								
110									
111	[c]Building: $7,500 market value − $10,908 book value = −$3,408, a loss. This represents a shortfall in depreciation taken versus true								
112	depreciation, and it is treated as an operating expense for 2010. Equipment: $2,000 market value − $1,360 book value = $640 profit. Here the								
113	depreciation charge exceeds the true depreciation, and the difference is called depreciation recapture. It is taxed as ordinary income in 2010.								
114	The actual book value at the time of disposition depends on the month of disposition. We have simplified the analysis and assumed that there will								
115	be a full year of depreciation in 2010.								
116	[d]Net cash flow from salvage equals salvage (market) value minus taxes. For the building, the loss results in a tax credit, so net salvage value =								
117	$7,500 − (−$1,363) = $8,863.								

Row 104. Row 105 shows the after-tax cash flow the company expects when it disposes of the asset, found as the expected sale price minus the tax liability or plus the credit. Thus, the firm expects to net $8,863 from the sale of the building and $1,744 from the equipment, for a total of $10,607.

Next, in Part 4, we use the information developed in Parts 1, 2, and 3 to find the projected cash flows over the project's life. Five periods are shown, from Year 0 (2006) to Year 4 (2010). The cash outlays required at Year 0 are the negative numbers in Column E for 2006, and their sum, −$26,000, is shown at the bottom in cell E149. Then, in the next four columns, we calculate the operating cash flows. We begin with sales revenues, found as the product of units sold and the sales price. Next, we subtract variable costs, which were assumed to be $2.10 per unit. We then deduct fixed operating costs and depreciation to obtain taxable operating income, or EBIT. When taxes (at a 40 percent rate) are subtracted, we are left with net operating profit after taxes, or NOPAT. Note, though, that we are seeking cash flows, not accounting income. Thus, depreciation must be added back.

RIC must purchase raw materials and replenish them each year as they are used. In Part 1 we assume that RIC must have an amount of NOWC on hand equal to 10 percent of the upcoming year's sales. For example, sales in Year 1 are $60,000, so RIC must have $6,000 in NOWC at Year 0, as shown in Cell E141. Because RIC had no NOWC prior to Year 0, it must make a $6,000 investment in NOWC at Year 0, as shown in Cell E142. Sales increase to $61,200 in Year 2, so RIC must have $6,120 of NOWC at Year 1. Because it already had $6,000 in NOWC on hand, its net investment at Year 1 is just $120, shown in Cell F142. Note that RIC will have no sales after Year 4, so it will require no NOWC at Year 4. Thus, it has a positive cash flow of $6,367 at Year 4 as working capital is sold but not replaced.

TABLE 11-4 | Analysis of a New (Expansion) Project: Part 4

	A	B	C	D	E	F	G	H	I
						Years			
119	Part 4 of Table 11-4. Projected Net Cash				**0**	**1**	**2**	**3**	**4**
120	Flows (Time line of annual cash flows)								
121					**2006**	**2007**	**2008**	**2009**	**2010**
122	*Investment Outlays: Long-Term Assets*								
123	Building				($12,000)				
124	Equipment				(8,000)				
125									
126	*Operating Cash Flows over the Project's Life*								
127	Units sold					20,000	20,000	20,000	20,000
128	Sales price					$3.00	$3.06	$3.12	$3.18
129	Sales revenue					$60,000	$61,200	$62,424	$63,672
130	Variable costs					42,000	42,840	43,697	44,571
131	Fixed operating costs					8,000	8,080	8,161	8,242
132	Depreciation (building)					156	312	312	312
133	Depreciation (equipment)					1,600	2,560	1,520	960
134	Oper. income before taxes (EBIT)					8,244	7,408	8,734	9,587
135	Taxes on operating income (40%)					3,298	2,963	3,494	3,835
136	Net Operating Profit After Taxes (NOPAT)					4,946	4,445	5,241	5,752
137	Add back depreciation					1,756	2,872	1,832	1,272
138	Operating cash flow					$6,702	$7,317	$7,073	$7,024
139									
140	*Cash Flows Due to Net Operating Working Capital*								
141	Net Operating Working Capital (based on sales)				$6,000	$6,120	$6,242	$6,367	$0
142	Cash flow due to investment in NOWC				($6,000)	($120)	($122)	($125)	$6,367
143									
144	*Salvage Cash Flows: Long-Term Assets*								
145	Net salvage cash flow: Building								$8,863
146	Net salvage cash flow: Equipment								1,744
147	Total salvage cash flows								$10,607
148									
149	Net Cash Flow (Time line of cash flows)				($26,000)	$6,582	$7,194	$6,948	$23,999
150									

When the project's life ends, the company will receive the "Salvage Cash Flows" as shown in the column for Year 4 in the lower part of the table. When the company disposes of the building and equipment at the end of Year 4, it will receive cash as estimated back in Part 3 of the table. Thus, the total salvage cash flow amounts to $10,607 as shown on Row 147. When we sum the subtotals in Part 4, we obtain the net cash flows shown on Row 149. Those cash flows constitute a *cash flow time line,* and they are then evaluated in Part 5 of Table 11-4.

Making the Decision

Part 5 of the table shows the standard evaluation criteria—NPV, IRR, MIRR, and payback—based on the cash flows shown on Row 149. The NPV is positive, the IRR and MIRR both exceed the 12 percent cost of capital, and the payback indicates that the project will return the invested funds in 3.22 years. Therefore, on the basis of the analysis thus

TABLE 11-4 | Analysis of a New (Expansion) Project: Part 5

	A	B	C	D	E	F	G	H	I
151	Part 5 of Table 11-4. Key Output and Appraisal of the Proposed Project								
152									
153	Net Present Value (at 12%)			$5,809					
154	IRR			20.12%					
155	MIRR			17.79%				Years	
156					0	1	2	3	4
157	Cumulative cash flow for payback				(26,000)	(19,418)	(12,223)	(5,275)	18,723
158	Cum. CF > 0, hence Payback Year:				FALSE	FALSE	FALSE	FALSE	3.22
159	Payback found with Excel function =			3.22	See note below for an explanation of the Excel calculation.				
160	Check: Payback = 3 + 5,275/23,999 =			3.22	Manual calculation for the base case.				
161									
162									
163	The Excel payback calculation is based on the logical IF function. Returns FALSE if the cumulative CF is negative or the actual payback if the cumulative CF is positive. Then, we use the MIN (minimum) function to find first year when payback is positive.								
164									
165									

far, it appears that the project should be accepted. Note, though, that we have been assuming that the project is about as risky as the company's average project. If the project were judged to be riskier than average, it would be necessary to increase the cost of capital, which might cause the NPV to become negative and leave the IRR and MIRR below the new WACC. Therefore, we cannot make a final decision until we evaluate the project's risk, the topic of a later section.

SELF-TEST QUESTION | What three types of cash flows must be considered when evaluating a proposed project?

ADJUSTING FOR INFLATION

Inflation is a fact of life in the United States and most other nations, so it must be considered in any sound capital budgeting analysis.

Inflation-Induced Bias

Note that *in the absence of inflation*, the real rate, r_r, would be equal to the nominal rate, r_n. Moreover, the real and nominal expected net cash flows—RCF_t and NCF_t—would also be equal. Remember that *real* interest rates and cash flows do not include inflation effects, while *nominal* rates and flows do reflect the effects of inflation. In particular, an inflation premium, IP, is built into all nominal market interest rates.

Suppose the expected rate of inflation is positive, and we expect *all* of the project's cash flows—including those related to depreciation—to rise at the rate i. Further, assume that this same inflation rate, i, is built into the market cost of capital as an inflation premium, IP = i. In this situation, the nominal net cash flow, NCF_t, will increase annually at the rate of i percent, producing this result:

$$NCF_t = RCF_t(1 + i)^t.$$

For example, if we expected a net cash flow of $100 in Year 5 in the absence of inflation, then with a 5 percent annual rate of inflation, $NCF_5 = \$100(1.05)^5 = \$127.63$.

In general, the cost of capital used as the discount rate in capital budgeting analysis is based on the market-determined costs of debt and equity, so it is a nominal rate. To convert a real interest rate, r_r, to a nominal rate, r_n, when the inflation rate is i, we use this formula:

$$(1 + r_n) = (1 + r_r)(1 + i).$$

For example, if the real cost of capital is 7 percent and the inflation rate is 5 percent, then $1 + r_n = (1.07)(1.05) = 1.1235$, so $r_n = 12.35\%$.[6]

Now if net cash flows increase at the rate of i percent per year, and if this same inflation premium is built into the firm's cost of capital, then the NPV would be calculated as follows:

$$\text{NPV (with inflation)} = \sum_{t=0}^{n} \frac{NCF_t}{(1 + r_n)^t} = \sum_{t=0}^{n} \frac{RCF_t(1 + i)^t}{(1 + r_r)^t(1 + i)^t}. \tag{11-1}$$

Since the $(1 + i)^t$ terms in the numerator and denominator cancel, we are left with

$$\text{NPV} = \sum_{t=0}^{n} \frac{RCF_t}{(1 + r_r)^t}.$$

Thus, if all costs and also the sales price, hence annual cash flows, are expected to rise at the same inflation rate that investors have built into the cost of capital, then the inflation-adjusted NPV as determined using Equation 11-1 is the same whether you discount nominal cash flows at a nominal rate or real cash flows at a real rate. For example, the PV of a real $100 at Year 5 at a real rate of 7 percent is $71.30 = \$100/(1.07)^5$. The PV of a nominal $127.63 at Year 5 at a nominal rate of 12.35 percent is also $71.30 = \$127.63/(1.1235)^5$.

However, some analysts mistakenly use base year, or constant (unadjusted), dollars throughout the analysis—say, 2006 dollars if the analysis is done in 2006—along with a cost of capital as determined in the marketplace as we described in Chapter 9. This is wrong: *If the cost of capital includes an inflation premium, as it typically does, but the cash flows are all stated in constant (unadjusted) dollars, then the calculated NPV will be lower than the true NPV.* The denominator will reflect inflation, but the numerator will not, and this will produce a downward-biased NPV.

Making the Inflation Adjustment

There are two ways to adjust for inflation. First, all project cash flows can be expressed as real (unadjusted) flows, with no consideration of inflation, and then the cost of capital can be adjusted to a real rate by removing the inflation premiums from the component costs. This approach is simple in theory, but to produce an unbiased NPV it requires (1) that all project cash flows, including depreciation, be affected identically by inflation, and (2) that this rate of increase equals the inflation rate built into investors' required returns. Because these assumptions do not necessarily hold in practice, this method is not commonly used.

The second method involves leaving the cost of capital in its nominal form, and then adjusting the individual cash flows to reflect expected inflation. This is what we did earlier in our RIC example as summarized in Table 11-4. There we assumed that sales prices and variable costs would increase at a rate of 2 percent per year, fixed costs would increase by 1 percent per year, and that depreciation charges would not be affected by inflation.

---

[6] To focus on inflation effects, we have simplified the situation somewhat. The actual project cost of capital is made up of debt and equity components, both of which are affected by inflation, but only the debt component is adjusted for tax effects. Thus, the relationship between nominal and real costs of capital is more complex than indicated in our discussion here.

One should always build inflation into the cash flow analysis, with the specific adjustment reflecting as accurately as possible the most likely set of circumstances. With a spreadsheet, it is easy to make the adjustments.

Our conclusions about inflation may be summarized as follows. First, inflation is critically important, for it can and does have major effects on businesses. Therefore, it must be recognized and dealt with. Second, the most effective way of dealing with inflation in capital budgeting analyses is to build inflation estimates into each cash flow element, using the best available information on how each element will be affected. Third, since we cannot estimate future inflation rates with precision, errors are bound to be made. Thus, inflation adds to the uncertainty, or riskiness, of capital budgeting as well as to its complexity.

SELF-TEST QUESTION What is the best way of handling inflation, and how does this procedure eliminate the potential bias?

PROJECT RISK ANALYSIS: TECHNIQUES FOR MEASURING STAND-ALONE RISK

Recall from Chapter 9 that there are three distinct types of risk: stand-alone risk, corporate risk, and market risk. Why should a project's stand-alone risk be important to anyone? In theory, this type of risk should be of little or no concern. However, it is actually of great importance for two reasons:

1. It is easier to estimate a project's stand-alone risk than its corporate risk, and it is far easier to measure stand-alone risk than market risk.
2. In the vast majority of cases, all three types of risk are highly correlated—if the general economy does well, so will the firm, and if the firm does well, so will most of its projects. Because of this high correlation, stand-alone risk is generally a good proxy for hard-to-measure corporate and market risk.

The starting point for analyzing a project's stand-alone risk involves determining the uncertainty inherent in its cash flows. To illustrate what is involved, consider again Regency Integrated Chips' appliance control computer project that we discussed above. Many of the key inputs shown in Part 1 of Table 11-4 are subject to uncertainty. For example, sales were projected at 20,000 units to be sold at a net price of $3,000 per unit. However, actual unit sales will almost certainly be somewhat higher or lower than 20,000, and the sales price will probably turn out to be different from the projected $3,000 per unit. *In effect, the sales quantity and price estimates are really expected values based on probability distributions, as are many of the other values that were shown in Part 1 of Table 11-4.* The distributions could be relatively "tight," reflecting small standard deviations and low risk, or they could be "wide," denoting a great deal of uncertainty about the actual value of the variable in question and thus a high degree of stand-alone risk.

The nature of the individual cash flow distributions, and their correlations with one another, determine the nature of the NPV probability distribution and, thus, the project's stand-alone risk. In the following sections, we discuss three techniques for assessing a project's stand-alone risk: (1) sensitivity analysis, (2) scenario analysis, and (3) Monte Carlo simulation.

Sensitivity Analysis

Intuitively, we know that many of the variables that determine a project's cash flows could turn out to be different from the values used in the analysis. We also know that a change in a key input variable, such as units sold, will cause the NPV to change. **Sensitivity analysis** is a technique that indicates how much NPV will change in response to a given change in an input variable, other things held constant.

Sensitivity analysis begins with a *base-case* situation, which is developed using the *expected* values for each input. To illustrate, consider the data given back in Table 11-4, where projected cash flows for RIC's computer project were shown. The values used to develop the table, including unit sales, sales price, fixed costs, and variable costs, are all most likely, or base-case, values, and the resulting $5.809 million NPV shown in Table 11-4 is called the **base-case NPV.** Now we ask a series of "what if" questions: "What if unit sales fall 15 percent below the most likely level?" "What if the sales price per unit falls?" "What if variable costs are $2.50 per unit rather than the expected $2.10?" Sensitivity analysis is designed to provide decision makers with answers to questions such as these.

In a sensitivity analysis, each variable is changed by several percentage points above and below the expected value, holding all other variables constant. Then a new NPV is calculated using each of these values. Finally, the set of NPVs is plotted to show how sensitive NPV is to changes in each variable. Figure 11-1 shows the computer project's sensitivity graphs for six of the input variables. The table below the graph gives the NPVs that were used to construct the graph. The slopes of the lines in the graph show how sensitive NPV is to changes in each of the inputs: *The steeper the slope, the more sensitive the NPV is to a change in the variable.* From the figure and the table, we see that the project's NPV is very sensitive to changes in the sales price and variable costs, fairly sensitive to changes in the growth rate and units sold, and not very sensitive to changes in either fixed costs or the cost of capital.

If we were comparing two projects, the one with the steeper sensitivity lines would be riskier, because for that project a relatively small error in estimating a variable such as unit sales would produce a large error in the project's expected NPV. Thus, sensitivity analysis can provide useful insights into the riskiness of a project.

CF

e-resource

Before we move on, we should note that spreadsheet computer programs such as *Excel* are ideally suited for sensitivity analysis. We used the Data Table feature in the file *CF2 Ch 11 Tool Kit.xls,* on the textbook's Web site, to generate the data for the graph in Figure 11-1. To conduct such an analysis by hand would be extremely time consuming.

Scenario Analysis

Although sensitivity analysis is probably the most widely used risk analysis technique, it does have limitations. For example, we saw earlier that the computer project's NPV is highly sensitive to changes in the sales price and the variable cost per unit. Those sensitivities suggest that the project is risky. Suppose, however, that Home Depot or Circuit City was anxious to get the new computer product and would sign a contract to purchase 20,000 units per year for four years at $3,000 per unit. Moreover, suppose Intel would agree to provide the principal component at a price that would ensure that the variable cost per unit would not exceed $2,100. Under these conditions, there would be a low probability of high or low sales prices and input costs, so the project would not be at all risky in spite of its sensitivity to those variables.

We see, then, that we need to extend sensitivity analysis to deal with the *probability distributions* of the inputs. In addition, it would be useful to vary more than one variable at a time so we could see the combined effects of changes in the variables. **Scenario analysis** provides these extensions—it brings in the probabilities of changes in the key variables, and it allows us to change more than one variable at a time. In a scenario analysis, the financial analyst begins with the **base case,** or most likely set of values for the input variables. Then, he or she asks marketing, engineering, and other operating managers to specify a **worst-case scenario** (low unit sales, low sales price, high variable costs, and so on) and a **best-case scenario.** Often, the best case and worst case are set so as to have a 25 percent

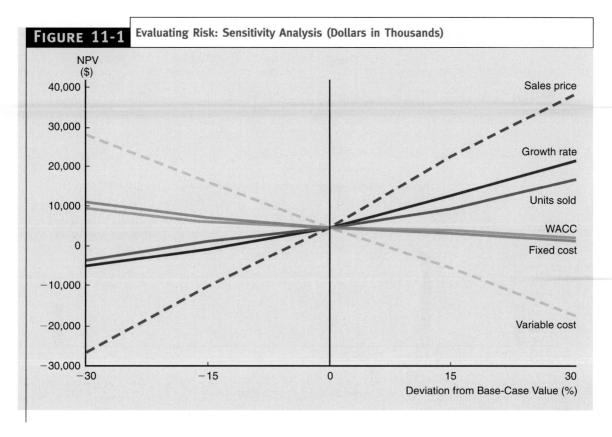

| **FIGURE 11-1** | Evaluating Risk: Sensitivity Analysis (Dollars in Thousands) |

NPV AT DIFFERENT DEVIATIONS FROM BASE

Deviation from Base Case	Sales Price	Variable Cost/Unit	Growth Rate	Year 1 Units Sold	Fixed Cost	WACC
−30%	($27,223)	$29,404	($ 4,923)	($ 3,628)	$10,243	$9,030
−15	(10,707)	17,607	(115)	1,091	8,026	7,362
0	5,809	5,809	5,809	5,809	5,809	5,809
15	22,326	(5,988)	12,987	10,528	3,593	4,363
30	38,842	(17,785)	21,556	15,247	1,376	3,014
Range	$66,064	$47,189	$26,479	$18,875	$ 8,867	$6,016

probability of conditions being that good or bad, and a 50 percent probability is assigned to the base-case conditions. Obviously, conditions could actually take on other values, but parameters such as these are useful to get people focused on the central issues in risk analysis.

The best-case, base-case, and worst-case values for RIC's computer project are shown in Table 11-5, along with a plot of the data. If the product is highly successful, then the combination of a high sales price, low production costs, high first year sales, and a strong growth rate in future sales will result in a very high NPV, $146 million. However, if things turn out badly, then the NPV would be −$37 million. The graphs show a very wide range of possibilities, indicating that this is indeed a very risky project. If the bad conditions materialize, this will not bankrupt the company—this is just one project for a large company. Still, losing $37 million would certainly not help the stock price or the career of the project's manager.

TABLE 11-5 Scenario Analysis (Dollars in Thousands)

Scenario	Probability	Sales Price	Unit Sales	Variable Costs	Growth Rate	NPV
Best case	25%	$3.90	26,000	$1.47	30%	$146,180
Base case	50	3.00	20,000	2.10	0	5,809
Worst case	25	2.10	14,000	2.73	−30	(37,257)
				Expected NPV =		$ 30,135
				Standard deviation =		$ 69,267
				Coefficient of variation = Standard deviation/Expected NPV =		2.30

Probability (%)

(37,257)   0   30,135   146,180   NPV ($)

5,809

Most likely

Mean of distribution = Expected value

Note: The scenario analysis calculations were performed in the *Excel* model, **CF2 Ch 11 Tool Kit.xls.**

The scenario probabilities and NPVs constitute a probability distribution of returns like those we dealt with in Chapter 5, except that the returns are measured in dollars instead of percentages (rates of return). The expected NPV (in thousands of dollars) is $30,135.[7]

CF

e-resource

See CF2 Ch 11 Tool Kit.xls for a scenario analysis using Excel Scenario Manager.

$$\text{Expected NPV} = \sum_{i=1}^{n} P_i(NPV_i)$$
$$= 0.25(\$146,180) + 0.50(\$5,809) + 0.25(-\$37,257)$$
$$= \$30,135.$$

The standard deviation of the NPV is $69,267 (in thousands of dollars):

$$\sigma_{NPV} = \sqrt{\sum_{i=1}^{n} P_i(NPV_i - \text{Expected NPV})^2}$$
$$= \sqrt{\begin{array}{l} 0.25(\$146,180 - \$30,135)^2 + 0.50(\$5,809 - \$30,135)^2 \\ + 0.25(-\$37,257 - \$30,135)^2 \end{array}}$$
$$= \$69,267.$$

Finally, the project's coefficient of variation is

$$CV_{NPV} = \frac{\sigma_{NPV}}{E(NPV)} = \frac{\$69,267}{\$30,135} = 2.30.$$

---

[7] Note that the expected NPV, $30,135, is *not* the same as the base-case NPV, $5,809 (in thousands). This is because the two uncertain variables, sales volume and sales price, are multiplied together to obtain dollar sales, and this process causes the NPV distribution to be skewed to the right. A big number times another big number produces a very big number, which, in turn, causes the average, or expected value, to increase.

Following are results from a survey of capital budgeting practices in Australia, Hong Kong, Indonesia, Malaysia, the Philippines, and Singapore.

Techniques for Evaluating Corporate Projects

Consistent with evidence on U.S. companies, most companies in this region evaluate projects using IRR, NPV, and payback. IRR use ranged from 86 percent (in Hong Kong) to 96 percent (in Australia). NPV use ranged from 81 percent (in the Philippines) to 96 percent (in Australia). Payback use ranged from 81 percent (in Indonesia) to 100 percent (in Hong Kong and the Philippines).

Techniques for Estimating the Cost of Equity Capital

Methods used to estimate the cost of equity varied considerably from country to country (see Table A).

We noted in Chapter 10 that the CAPM is used most often by U.S. firms. Except for Australia, this is not the case for Asian/Pacific firms, who instead more often use the other two approaches.

Techniques for Assessing Risk

Firms in these countries rely heavily on scenario and sensitivity analyses to assess project risk. They also use decision trees and Monte Carlo simulation, but less frequently than the other techniques (see Table B).

Source: From George W. Kester et al., "Capital Budgeting Practices in the Asia-Pacific Region: Australia, Hong Kong, Indonesia, Malaysia, Philippines, and Singapore," *Financial Practice and Education,* Vol. 9, no. 1, Spring/Summer 1999, 25–33. Reprinted by permission of Financial Management Association International, University of South Florida.

Table A

Method	Australia	Hong Kong	Indonesia	Malaysia	Philippines	Singapore
CAPM	72.7%	26.9%	0.0%	6.2%	24.1%	17.0%
Dividend yield plus growth rate	16.4	53.8	33.3	50.0	34.5	42.6
Cost of debt plus risk premium	10.9	23.1	53.4	37.5	58.6	42.6

Table B

Risk Assessment Technique	Australia	Hong Kong	Indonesia	Malaysia	Philippines	Singapore
Scenario analysis	96%	100%	94%	80%	97%	90%
Sensitivity analysis	100	100	88	83	94	79
Decision tree analysis	44	58	50	37	33	46
Monte Carlo simulation	38	35	25	9	24	35

The project's coefficient of variation can be compared with the coefficient of variation of RIC's "average" project to get an idea of the relative riskiness of the proposed project. RIC's existing projects, on average, have a coefficient of variation of about 1.0, so, on the basis of this stand-alone risk measure, we conclude that the project is much riskier than an "average" project.

Scenario analysis provides useful information about a project's stand-alone risk. However, it is limited in that it considers only a few discrete outcomes (NPVs), even though there are an infinite number of possibilities. We describe a more complete method of assessing a project's stand-alone risk in the next section.

Monte Carlo Simulation

Monte Carlo simulation ties together sensitivities and probability distributions. It grew out of work in the Manhattan Project to build the first atomic bomb, and was so named because it utilized the mathematics of casino gambling. While Monte Carlo simulation is considerably more complex than scenario analysis, simulation software packages make this process manageable. Many of these packages are included as add-ons to spreadsheet programs such as *Microsoft Excel*.

HIGH-TECH CFOs

Recent developments in technology have made it easier for corporations to utilize complex risk analysis techniques. New software and higher-powered computers enable financial managers to process large amounts of information, so technically astute finance people can consider a broad range of scenarios using computers to estimate the effects of changes in sales, operating costs, interest rates, the overall economy, and even the weather. Given such analysis, financial managers can make better decisions as to which course of action is most likely to maximize shareholder wealth.

Risk analysis can also take account of the correlation between various types of risk. For example, if interest rates and currencies tend to move together in a particular way, this tendency can be incorporated into the model. This can enable financial managers to make better estimates of the likelihood and effect of "worst-case" outcomes.

While this type of risk analysis is undeniably useful, it is only as good as the information and assumptions used in the models. Also, risk models frequently involve complex calculations, and they generate output that requires financial managers to have a fair amount of mathematical sophistication. However, technology is helping to solve these problems, and new programs have been developed to present risk analysis in an intuitive way. For example, Andrew Lo, an MIT finance professor, has developed a program that summarizes the risk, return, and liquidity profiles of various strategies using a new data visualization process that enables complicated relationships to be plotted along three-dimensional graphs that are easy to interpret. While some old-guard CFOs may bristle at these new approaches, younger and more computer-savvy CFOs are likely to embrace them. As Lo puts it: "The video-game generation just loves these 3-D tools."

Source: "The CFO Goes 3-D: Higher Math and Savvy Software Are Crucial," reprinted from October 28, 1996 issue of *Business Week* by special permission, copyright © 1996 by The McGraw-Hill Companies, Inc.

In a simulation analysis, the computer begins by picking at random a value for each variable—sales in units, the sales price, the variable cost per unit, and so on. Then those values are combined, and the project's NPV is calculated and stored in the computer's memory. Next, a second set of input values is selected at random, and a second NPV is calculated. This process is repeated perhaps 1,000 times, generating 1,000 NPVs. The mean and standard deviation of the set of NPVs is determined. The mean, or average value, is used as a measure of the project's expected NPV, and the standard deviation (or coefficient of variation) is used as a measure of risk.

Using this procedure, we conducted a simulation analysis of RIC's proposed project. As in our scenario analysis, we simplified the illustration by specifying the distributions for only four key variables: (1) sales price, (2) variable cost, (3) Year 1 units sold, and (4) growth rate.

We assumed that sales price can be represented by a continuous normal distribution with an expected value of $3.00 and a standard deviation of $0.35. Recall from Chapter 5 that there is about a 68 percent chance that the actual price will be within one standard deviation of the expected price, which results in a range of $2.65 to $3.35. Put another way, there is only a 32 percent chance that the price will fall outside the indicated range. Note too that there is less than a 1 percent chance that the actual price will be more than three standard deviations of the expected price, which gives us a range of $1.95 to $4.05. Therefore, the sales price is very unlikely to be less than $1.95 or more than $4.05.

RIC has existing labor contracts and strong relationships with some of its suppliers, which makes the variable cost less uncertain. In the simulation we assumed that the variable cost can be described by a triangular distribution, with a lower bound of $1.40, a most likely value of $2.10, and an upper bound of $2.50. Note that this is not a symmetric distribution. The lower bound is $0.70 less than the most likely value, but the upper bound is only $0.40 higher than the most likely value. This is because RIC has an active risk management program under which it hedges against increases in the prices of the commodities used in its production processes. The net effect is that RIC's hedging activities reduce its exposure to price increases but still allow it to take advantage of falling prices.

Based on preliminary purchase agreements with major customers, RIC is certain that sales in the first year will be at least 15,000 units. The marketing department believes the most likely demand will be 20,000 units, but it is possible that demand will be much higher. The plant can produce a maximum of 30,000 units in the first year, although production can be expanded in subsequent years if there is higher than expected demand. Therefore, we represented Year 1 unit sales with a triangular distribution with a lower bound of 15,000 units, a most likely value of 20,000 units, and an upper bound of 30,000 units.

The marketing department anticipates no growth in unit sales after the first year, but it recognizes that actual sales growth could be either positive or negative. Moreover, actual growth is likely to be positively correlated with units sold in the first year, which means that if demand is higher than expected in the first year, then growth will probably be higher than expected in subsequent years. We represented growth with a normal distribution having an expected value of 0 percent and a standard deviation of 15 percent. We also specified the correlation between Year 1 unit sales and growth in sales to be 0.65. Graphs of these probability distributions are in Figure 11-2.

We used these inputs and the model from *CF2 Ch 11 Tool Kit.xls* to conduct the simulation analysis. If you want to do the simulation yourself, you should first read the instructions in the file *Explanation of Simulation.doc*. This explains how to install an *Excel* add-in, *Simtools.xla*, which is necessary to run the simulation. After you have installed *Simtools.xla*, you can run the simulation analysis, which is in a separate spreadsheet,

CF
e-resource

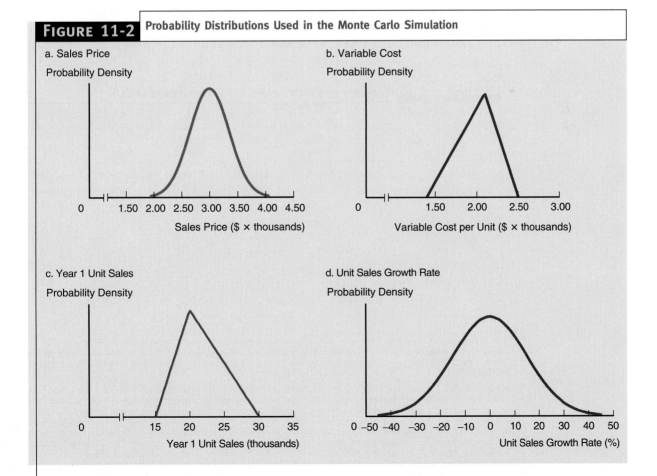

FIGURE 11-2 Probability Distributions Used in the Monte Carlo Simulation

a. Sales Price

Probability Density

1.50 2.00 2.50 3.00 3.50 4.00 4.50

Sales Price ($ × thousands)

b. Variable Cost

Probability Density

1.50 2.00 2.50 3.00

Variable Cost per Unit ($ × thousands)

c. Year 1 Unit Sales

Probability Density

15 20 25 30 35

Year 1 Unit Sales (thousands)

d. Unit Sales Growth Rate

Probability Density

−50 −40 −30 −20 −10 0 10 20 30 40 50

Unit Sales Growth Rate (%)

CF2 Ch 11 Tool Kit Simulation.xls.[8] All three files are included on the textbook's Web site. Using this model, we simulated 1,000 outcomes for the capital budgeting project. Table 11-6 presents selected results from the simulation.

After running the simulation, the first thing to do is to ensure that the results are consistent with our assumptions. The resulting mean and standard deviation of sales price are $3.01 and $0.35, respectively, which are virtually identical to our assumptions. Similarly, the resulting mean of −0.4 percent and standard deviation of 14.8 percent for growth are very close to our assumed distribution. The maximum for variable cost is $2.47, which is just under our specified maximum of $2.50, and the minimum is $1.40, which is equal to our specified minimum. Unit sales have a maximum of 29,741 and a minimum of 15,149, both of which are consistent with our assumptions. Finally, the resulting correlation between unit sales and growth is 0.664, which is very close to our assumed correlation of 0.65. Therefore, the results of the simulation are consistent with our assumptions.

Table 11-6 also reports summary statistics for the project's NPV. The mean is $13,867, which suggests that the project should be accepted. However, the range of outcomes is quite large, from a loss of $49,550 to a gain of $124,091, so the project is clearly risky. The standard deviation of $22,643 indicates that losses could easily occur, and this is consistent with this wide range of possible outcomes.[9] The coefficient of variation is 1.63, which is large compared with most of RIC's other projects. Table 11-6 also reports a median NPV of $10,607, which means that half the time the project will have an NPV greater than $10,607. The table also reports that 72.8 percent of the time we would expect the project to have a positive NPV.

A picture is worth a thousand words, and Figure 11-3 shows the probability distribution of the outcomes. Note that the distribution of outcomes is skewed to the right. As the figure shows, the potential downside losses are not as large as the potential upside gains. Our conclusion is that this is a very risky project, as indicated by the coefficient of variation, but it does have a positive expected NPV and the potential to be a home run.

TABLE 11-6 Summary of Simulation Results (Thousands of Dollars)

	RISKY INPUTS				OUTPUT
	Sales Price	Variable Cost	Unit Sales	Growth	NPV
Mean	$3.01	$2.00	21,662	−0.4%	$ 13,867
Standard deviation	0.35	0.23	3,201	14.8	22,643
Maximum	4.00	2.47	29,741	42.7	124,091
Minimum	1.92	1.40	15,149	−51.5	−49,550
Median					10,607
Probability of NPV > 0					72.8%
Coefficient of variation					1.63

[8] We are grateful to Professor Roger Myerson of Northwestern University for making *Simtools.xla* available to us.

Note too that there are a number of commercially available simulation programs that can be used with *Excel,* including *@Risk* and *Crystal Ball.* Many universities and companies have such a program installed on their networks, and they can also be installed on PCs.

[9] Note that the standard deviation of NPV in the simulation is much smaller than the standard deviation in the scenario analysis. In the scenario analysis, we assumed that all of the poor outcomes would occur together in the worst-case scenario, and all of the positive outcomes would occur together in the best-case scenario. In other words, we implicitly assumed that all of the risky variables were perfectly positively correlated. In the simulation, we assumed that the variables were independent, with the exception of the correlation between unit sales and growth. The independence of variables in the simulation reduces the range of outcomes. For example, in the simulation, sometimes the sales price is high, but the sales growth is low. In the scenario analysis, a high sales price is always coupled with high growth. Because the scenario analysis's assumption of perfect correlation is unlikely, simulation may provide a better estimate of project risk. However, if the standard deviations and correlations used as inputs in the simulation are not estimated accurately, then the simulation output will likewise be inaccurate.

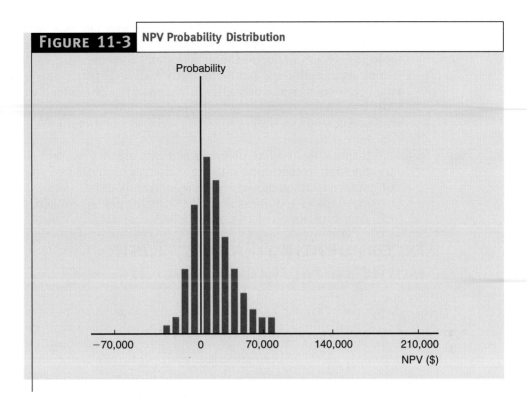

FIGURE 11-3 | NPV Probability Distribution

List two reasons why, in practice, a project's stand-alone risk is important.

Differentiate between sensitivity and scenario analyses. What advantage does scenario analysis have over sensitivity analysis?

What is Monte Carlo simulation?

PROJECT RISK CONCLUSIONS

We have discussed the three types of risk normally considered in capital budgeting analysis—stand-alone risk, within-firm (or corporate) risk, and market risk—and we have discussed ways of assessing each. However, two important questions remain: (1) Should firms be concerned with stand-alone or corporate risk in their capital budgeting decisions, and (2) what do we do when the stand-alone, within-firm, and market risk assessments lead to different conclusions?

These questions do not have easy answers. From a theoretical standpoint, well-diversified investors should be concerned only with market risk, managers should be concerned only with stock price maximization, and this should lead to the conclusion that market (beta) risk ought to be given virtually all the weight in capital budgeting decisions. However, if investors are not well diversified, if the CAPM does not operate exactly as theory says it should, or if measurement problems keep managers from having confidence in the CAPM approach in capital budgeting, it may be appropriate to give stand-alone and corporate risk more weight than financial theory suggests. Note also that the CAPM ignores bankruptcy costs, even though such costs can be substantial, and the probability of bankruptcy depends on a firm's corporate risk, not on its beta risk. Therefore, even well-diversified investors should want a firm's management to give at least some consideration to a project's corporate risk instead of concentrating entirely on market risk.

Although it would be nice to reconcile these problems and to measure project risk on some absolute scale, the best we can do in practice is to estimate project risk in a somewhat nebulous, relative sense. For example, we can generally say with a fair degree of confidence that a particular project has more or less stand-alone risk than the firm's average project. Then, assuming that stand-alone and corporate risk are highly correlated (which is typical), the project's stand-alone risk will be a good measure of its corporate risk. Finally, assuming that market risk and corporate risk are highly correlated (as is true for most companies), a project with more corporate risk than average will also have more market risk, and vice versa for projects with low corporate risk.

In theory, should a firm be concerned with stand-alone and corporate risk? Should the firm be concerned with these risks in practice?

If a project's stand-alone, corporate, and market risk are highly correlated, would this make the task of measuring risk easier or harder? Explain.

INCORPORATING PROJECT RISK INTO CAPITAL BUDGETING

As we described in Chapter 9, many firms calculate a cost of capital for each division, based on the division's market risk and capital structure. This is the first step toward incorporating risk analysis into capital budgeting decisions, but it is limited because it encompasses only market risk. Rather than directly estimating the corporate risk of a project, the risk management departments at many firms regularly assess the entire firm's likelihood of financial distress, based on current and proposed projects.[10] In other words, they assess a firm's corporate risk, given its portfolio of projects. This screening process will identify those projects that significantly increase corporate risk.

Suppose a proposed project doesn't significantly affect a firm's likelihood of financial distress, but it does have greater stand-alone risk than the typical project in a division. Two methods are used to incorporate this project risk into capital budgeting. One is called the *certainty equivalent* approach. Here every cash inflow that is not known with certainty is scaled down, and the riskier the flow, the lower its certainty equivalent value. The other method, and the one we focus on here, is the **risk-adjusted discount rate** approach, under which differential project risk is dealt with by changing the discount rate. Average-risk projects are discounted at the firm's average cost of capital, higher-risk projects are discounted at a higher cost of capital, and lower-risk projects are discounted at a rate below the firm's average cost of capital. Unfortunately, there is no good way of specifying exactly *how much* higher or lower these discount rates should be. Given the present state of the art, risk adjustments are necessarily judgmental and somewhat arbitrary.

How are risk-adjusted discount rates used to incorporate project risk into the capital budget decision process?

MANAGING RISK THROUGH PHASED DECISIONS: DECISION TREES

Up to this point we have focused primarily on techniques for estimating a project's stand-alone risk. Although this is an integral part of capital budgeting, managers are generally more interested in *reducing* risk than in *measuring* it. For example, sometimes projects can be structured so that expenditures do not have to be made all at one time, but, rather,

---

[10] These processes also measure the magnitude of the losses, which is often called *value at risk*.

can be made in stages over a period of years. This reduces risk by giving managers the opportunity to reevaluate decisions using new information and then either investing additional funds or terminating the project. Such projects can be evaluated using *decision trees*.

The Basic Decision Tree

Suppose United Robotics is considering the production of an industrial robot for the television manufacturing industry. The net investment for this project can be broken down into stages, as set forth in Figure 11-4:

STAGE 1. At t = 0, which in this case is sometime in the near future, conduct a $500,000 study of the market potential for robots in television assembly lines.

STAGE 2. If it appears that a sizable market does exist, then at t = 1 spend $1,000,000 to design and build a prototype robot. This robot would then be evaluated by television engineers, and their reactions would determine whether the firm should proceed with the project.

STAGE 3. If reaction to the prototype robot is good, then at t = 2 build a production plant at a net cost of $10,000,000. If this stage were reached, the project would generate either high, medium, or low net cash flows over the following four years.

STAGE 4. At t = 3 market acceptance will be known. If demand is low, the firm will terminate the project and avoid the negative cash flows in Years 4 and 5.

A **decision tree** such as the one in Figure 11-4 can be used to analyze such multistage, or sequential, decisions. Here we assume that one year goes by between decisions. Each circle represents a decision point, and it is called a **decision node**. The dollar value to the left of each decision node represents the net investment required at that decision point, and the cash flows shown under t = 3 to t = 5 represent the cash inflows if the project is pushed on to completion. Each diagonal line represents a **branch** of the decision tree, and each branch has an estimated probability. For example, if the firm decides to "go" with the project at Decision Point 1, it will spend $500,000 on a marketing study. Management estimates that there is a 0.8 probability that the study will produce favorable results, leading to the decision to move on to Stage 2, and a 0.2 probability that the marketing study will produce negative results, indicating that the project should be canceled after Stage 1. If the project is canceled, the cost to the company will be the $500,000 for the initial marketing study, and it will be a loss.

FIGURE 11-4	United Robotics: Decision Tree Analysis (Thousands of Dollars)

t = 0	t = 1	t = 2	t = 3	t = 4	t = 5	Joint Probability	NPV	Product: Prob. × NPV
			$18,000	$18,000	$18,000	0.144	$25,635	$ 3,691
	($10,000)		$8,000	$8,000	$8,000	0.192	$6,149	$ 1,181
	($1,000)		($2,000)	Stop		0.144	($10,883)	($ 1,567)
($500)		Stop				0.320	($1,397)	($ 447)
	Stop					0.200	($500)	($ 100)
						1.000	Expected NPV =	$ 2,758
							σ =	$10,584

If the marketing study yields positive results, then United Robotics will spend $1,000,000 on the prototype robot at Decision Point 2. Management estimates (before even making the initial $500,000 investment) that there is a 60 percent probability that the television engineers will find the robot useful and a 40 percent probability that they will not like it.

If the engineers like the robot, the firm will spend the final $10,000,000 to build the plant and go into production. If the engineers do not like the prototype, the project will be dropped. If the firm does go into production, the operating cash flows over the project's four-year life will depend on how well the market accepts the final product. There is a 30 percent chance that acceptance will be quite good and net cash flows will be $18 million per year, a 40 percent probability of $8 million each year, and a 30 percent chance of losing $2 million. These cash flows are shown under Years 3 through 5.

In summary, the decision tree in Figure 11-4 defines the decision nodes and the branches that leave the nodes. There are two types of nodes, decision nodes and outcome nodes. Decision nodes are the points at which management can respond to new information. The first decision node is at t = 1, after the company has completed the marketing study (Decision Point 1 in Figure 11-4). The second decision node is at t = 2, after the company has completed the prototype study (Decision Point 2 in Figure 11-4). The outcome nodes show the possible results if a particular decision is taken. There is one relevant outcome node (Decision Point 3 in Figure 11-4), the one occurring at t = 3, and its branches show the possible cash flows if the company goes ahead with the industrial robot project. There is one more decision node, Decision Point 4, at which United Robotics terminates the project if acceptance is low. Note that the decision tree also shows the probabilities of moving into each branch that leaves a node.

The column of joint probabilities in Figure 11-4 gives the probability of occurrence of each branch, hence of each NPV. Each joint probability is obtained by multiplying together all probabilities on a particular branch. For example, the probability that the company will, if Stage 1 is undertaken, move through Stages 2 and 3, and that a strong demand will produce $18,000,000 per year of inflows, is (0.8)(0.6)(0.3) = 0.144 = 14.4%.

The company has a cost of capital of 11.5 percent, and management assumes initially that the project is of average risk. The NPV of the top (most favorable) branch as shown in the next-to-last column is $25,635 (in thousands of dollars):

$$\text{NPV} = -\$500 - \frac{\$1,000}{(1.115)^1} - \frac{\$10,000}{(1.115)^2} + \frac{\$18,000}{(1.115)^3} + \frac{\$18,000}{(1.115)^4} + \frac{\$18,000}{(1.115)^5}$$

$$= \$25,635.$$

The NPVs for other branches were calculated similarly.

The last column in Figure 11-4 gives the product of the NPV for each branch times the joint probability of that branch, and the sum of these products is the project's expected NPV. Based on the expectations set forth in Figure 11-4 and a cost of capital of 11.5 percent, the project's expected NPV is $2.758 million.

As this example shows, decision tree analysis requires managers to explicitly articulate the types of risk a project faces and to develop responses to potential scenarios. Note also that our example could be extended to cover many other types of decisions, and could even be incorporated into a simulation analysis. All in all, decision tree analysis is a valuable tool for analyzing project risk.[11]

SELF-TEST QUESTION

What is a decision tree? A branch? A node?

---

[11] In the United Robotics example we glossed over an important issue, namely, the appropriate cost of capital for the project. Adding decision nodes to a project clearly changes its risk, so we would expect the cost of capital for a project with few decision nodes to have a different risk than one with many nodes. If this were so, we would expect the projects to have different costs of capital. In fact, we might expect the cost of capital to change over time as the project moves to different stages, since the stages themselves differ in risk.

INTRODUCTION TO REAL OPTIONS

According to traditional capital budgeting theory, a project's NPV is the present value of its expected future cash flows, discounted at a rate that reflects the riskiness of the expected future cash flows. Note, however, that this says nothing about actions that can be taken after the project has been accepted and placed in operation that might cause the cash flows to increase. In other words, traditional capital budgeting theory assumes that a project is like a roulette wheel. A gambler can choose whether or not to spin the wheel, but once the wheel has been spun, there is nothing he or she can do to influence the outcome. Once the game begins, the outcome depends purely on chance, with no skill involved.

Contrast roulette with other games, such as draw poker. Chance plays a role in poker, and it continues to play a role after the initial deal because players receive additional cards throughout the game. However, poker players are able to respond to their opponents' actions, so skillful players usually win.

Capital budgeting decisions have more in common with poker than roulette because (1) chance plays a continuing role throughout the life of the project but (2) managers can respond to changing market conditions and to competitors' actions. Opportunities to respond to changing circumstances are called **managerial options** because they give managers a chance to influence the outcome of a project. They are also called **strategic options** because they are often associated with large, strategic projects rather than routine maintenance projects. Finally, they are called **real options,** which are differentiated from financial options because they involve real, rather than financial, assets. The following sections describe several types of projects with **embedded options**.

Investment Timing Options

Conventional NPV analysis implicitly assumes that projects will either be accepted or rejected, which implies that they will be undertaken now or never. In practice, however, companies sometimes have a third choice—delay the decision until later, when more information is available. Such **investment timing options** can dramatically affect a project's estimated profitability and risk.

For example, suppose Sony plans to introduce an interactive DVD-TV system, and your software company has two alternatives: (1) immediately begin full-scale production of game software on DVDs for the new system or (2) delay investment in the project until you get a better idea of the size of the market for interactive DVDs. You might prefer delaying implementation. Keep in mind, though, that the *option to delay* is valuable only if it more than offsets any harm that might come from delaying. For example, if you delay, some other company might establish a loyal customer base that makes it difficult for your company to later enter the market. The option to delay is usually most valuable to firms with proprietary technology, patents, licenses, or other barriers to entry, because these factors lessen the threat of competition. The option to delay is valuable when market demand is uncertain, but it is also valuable during periods of volatile interest rates, since the ability to wait can allow firms to delay raising capital for projects until interest rates are lower.

Growth Options

A **growth option** allows a company to increase its capacity if market conditions are better than expected. There are several types of growth options. One lets a company *increase the capacity of an existing product line.* A "peaking unit" power plant illustrates this type of growth option. Such units have high variable costs and are used to produce additional power only if demand and therefore prices are high.

The second type of growth option allows a company to *expand into new geographic markets.* Many companies are investing in Eastern Europe, Russia, and China even though standard NPV analysis produces negative NPVs. However, if these developing markets really take off, the option to open more facilities could be quite valuable.

The third type of growth option is the opportunity to *add new products,* including complementary products and successive "generations" of the original product. Toshiba probably lost money on its first laptop computers, but the manufacturing skills and consumer recognition it gained helped turn subsequent generations of laptops into money makers. In addition, Toshiba used its experience and name recognition in laptops as a springboard into the desktop computer market.

Abandonment Options

Many projects contain an **abandonment option.** When evaluating a potential project, standard DCF analysis assumes that the assets will be used over a specified economic life. While some projects must be operated over their full economic life, even though market conditions might deteriorate and cause lower than expected cash flows, others can be abandoned. For example, some contracts between automobile manufacturers and their suppliers specify the quantity and price of the parts that must be delivered. If the supplier's labor costs increase, then the supplier might well lose money on each part it ships. Including the option to abandon in such a contract might be quite valuable.

Note too that some projects can be structured so that they provide the option to *reduce capacity or temporarily suspend operations.* Such options are common in the natural resource industry, including mining, oil, and timber, and they should be reflected in the analysis when NPVs are being estimated.

Flexibility Options

Many projects offer **flexibility options** that permit the firm to alter operations depending on how conditions change during the life of the project. Typically, either inputs or outputs (or both) can be changed. BMW's Spartanburg, South Carolina, auto assembly plant provides a good example of output flexibility. BMW needed the plant to produce sports coupes. If it built the plant configured to produce only these vehicles, the construction cost would be minimized. However, the company thought that later on it might want to switch production to some other vehicle type, and that would be difficult if the plant were designed just for coupes. Therefore, BMW decided to spend additional funds to construct a more flexible plant—one that could produce different types of vehicles should demand patterns shift. Sure enough, things did change. Demand for coupes dropped a bit and that for sports utility vehicles soared. But BMW was ready, and the Spartanburg plant is now spewing out hot-selling SUVs. The plant's cash flows are much higher than they would have been without the flexibility option that BMW "bought" by paying more to build a more flexible plant.

Electric power plants provide an example of input flexibility. Utilities can build plants that generate electricity by burning coal, oil, or natural gas. The prices of those fuels change over time, depending on events in the Middle East, changing environmental policies, and weather conditions. Some years ago, virtually all power plants were designed to burn just one type of fuel, because this resulted in the lowest construction cost. However, as fuel cost volatility increased, power companies began to build higher-cost but more flexible plants, especially ones that could switch from oil to gas and back again, depending on relative fuel prices.

Valuing Real Options

A full treatment of real option valuation is beyond the scope of this book, but there are some things we can say. First, if your project has an embedded real option, you should at least recognize and articulate its existence. Second, we know that a financial option is more valuable if it has a long time until maturity or if the underlying asset is very risky.

If either of these characteristics applies to your real option, then you know that its value is relatively high, qualitatively speaking. Third, you might be able to model the real option along the lines of a decision tree. This will give you an approximate value, but keep in mind that you may not have a good estimate of the appropriate discount rate, because the real option changes the risk, and hence the required return, of the project.[12]

SELF-TEST QUESTION   Name some different types of real options.

---

[12] For more on real option valuation, see Eugene F. Brigham and Michael C. Ehrhardt, *Financial Management: Theory and Practice*, 11th ed. (Mason, OH: South-Western Publishing, 2004), chap. 12; M. Amram and N. Kulatilaka, *Real Options: Managing Strategic Investment in an Uncertain World* (Boston, MA: Harvard Business School Press, 1999); and M. Brennan and L. Trigeorgis, *Project Flexibility, Agency, and Competition: New Developments in the Theory and Application of Real Options* (New York: Oxford Press, 2000).

SUMMARY

Throughout the book, we have indicated that the value of any asset depends on the amount, timing, and riskiness of the cash flows it produces. In this chapter, we developed a framework for analyzing a project's cash flows and risk. The key concepts covered are listed below.

- The most important (and most difficult) step in analyzing a capital budgeting project is **estimating the incremental after-tax cash flows** the project will produce.
- **Project cash flow** is different from accounting income. Project cash flow reflects (1) **cash outlays for fixed assets,** (2) the **tax shield provided by depreciation,** and (3) cash flows due to **changes in net operating working capital.** Project cash flow does not include **interest payments.**
- In determining incremental cash flows, **opportunity costs** (the cash flows forgone by using an asset) must be included, but **sunk costs** (cash outlays that have been made and that cannot be recouped) are not included. Any **externalities** (effects of a project on other parts of the firm) should also be reflected in the analysis.
- **Cannibalization** occurs when a new project leads to a reduction in sales of an existing product.
- **Tax laws** affect cash flow analysis in two ways: (1) They reduce operating cash flows, and (2) they determine the depreciation expense that can be taken in each year.
- Capital projects often require additional investments in **net operating working capital (NOWC).**
- The incremental cash flows from a typical project can be classified into three categories: (1) **initial investment outlay,** (2) **operating cash flows over the project's life,** and (3) **terminal year cash flows.**
- **Inflation effects** must be considered in project analysis. The best procedure is to build expected inflation into the cash flow estimates.
- Since stockholders are generally diversified, **market risk** is theoretically the most relevant measure of risk. Market, or beta, risk is important because beta affects the cost of capital, which, in turn, affects stock prices.
- **Corporate risk** is important because it influences the firm's ability to use low-cost debt, to maintain smooth operations over time, and to avoid crises that might consume management's energy and disrupt its employees, customers, suppliers, and community.
- **Sensitivity analysis** is a technique that shows how much a project's NPV will change in response to a given change in an input variable such as sales, other things held constant.

- **Scenario analysis** is a risk analysis technique in which the best- and worst-case NPVs are compared with the project's expected NPV.
- **Monte Carlo simulation** is a risk analysis technique that uses a computer to simulate future events and thus to estimate the profitability and riskiness of a project.
- The **risk-adjusted discount rate**, or **project cost of capital**, is the rate used to evaluate a particular project. It is based on the corporate WACC, which is increased for projects that are riskier than the firm's average project but decreased for less risky projects.
- **Decision tree analysis** shows how different decisions in a project's life affect its value.
- Opportunities to respond to changing circumstances are called **managerial options** because they give managers the option to influence the outcome of a project. They are also called **strategic options** because they are often associated with large, strategic projects rather than routine maintenance projects. Finally, they are also called **real options** because they involve "real," rather than "financial," assets. Many projects include a variety of **embedded options** that can dramatically affect the true NPV.
- An **investment timing option** involves not only the decision of *whether* to proceed with a project but also the decision of *when* to proceed with it. This opportunity to affect a project's timing can dramatically change its estimated value.
- A **growth option** occurs if an investment creates the opportunity to make other potentially profitable investments that would not otherwise be possible. These include (1) options to expand output, (2) options to enter a new geographical market, and (3) options to introduce complementary products or successive generations of products.
- The **abandonment option** is the ability to abandon a project if the operating cash flows and/or abandonment value turn out to be lower than expected. It reduces the risk of a project and increases its value. Instead of total abandonment, some options allow a company to reduce capacity or temporarily suspend operations.
- A **flexibility option** is the option to modify operations depending on how conditions develop during a project's life, especially the type of output produced or the inputs used.

QUESTIONS

(11-1) Define each of the following terms:
   a. Cash flow; accounting income
   b. Incremental cash flow; sunk cost; opportunity cost
   c. Net operating working capital changes; salvage value
   d. Real rate of return, r_r, versus nominal rate of return, r_n
   e. Sensitivity analysis; scenario analysis; Monte Carlo simulation analysis
   f. Risk-adjusted discount rate; project cost of capital
   g. Real options; managerial options; strategic options; embedded options
   h. Investment timing option; growth option; abandonment option; flexibility option

(11-2) Operating cash flows, rather than accounting profits, are listed in Table 11-4. What is the basis for this emphasis on cash flows as opposed to net income?

(11-3) Why is it true, in general, that a failure to adjust expected cash flows for expected inflation biases the calculated NPV downward?

(11-4) Explain why sunk costs should not be included in a capital budgeting analysis, but opportunity costs and externalities should be included.

(11-5) Explain how net operating working capital is recovered at the end of a project's life, and why it is included in a capital budgeting analysis.

(11-6) Define (a) simulation analysis, (b) scenario analysis, and (c) sensitivity analysis.

SELF-TEST PROBLEMS   Solutions Appear in Appendix A

(ST-1)

New Project Analysis

You have been asked by the president of the Farr Construction Company to evaluate the proposed acquisition of a new earth mover. The mover's basic price is $50,000, and it would cost another $10,000 to modify it for special use. Assume that the mover falls into the MACRS 3-year class, it would be sold after 3 years for $20,000, and it would require an increase in net working capital (spare parts inventory) of $2,000. The earth mover would have no effect on revenues, but it is expected to save the firm $20,000 per year in before-tax operating costs, mainly labor. The firm's marginal federal-plus-state tax rate is 40 percent.

a. What is the net cost of the earth mover? (That is, what are the Year 0 cash flows?)
b. What are the operating cash flows in Years 1, 2, and 3?
c. What are the additional (nonoperating) cash flows in Year 3?
d. If the project's cost of capital is 10 percent, should the earth mover be purchased?

(ST-2)

Corporate Risk Analysis

The staff of Porter Manufacturing has estimated the following net after-tax cash flows and probabilities for a new manufacturing process:

	NET AFTER-TAX CASH FLOWS		
Year	P = 0.2	P = 0.6	P = 0.2
0	($100,000)	($100,000)	($100,000)
1	20,000	30,000	40,000
2	20,000	30,000	40,000
3	20,000	30,000	40,000
4	20,000	30,000	40,000
5	20,000	30,000	40,000
5*	0	20,000	30,000

Line 0 gives the cost of the process, Lines 1 through 5 give operating cash flows, and Line 5* contains the estimated salvage values. Porter's cost of capital for an average-risk project is 10 percent.

a. Assume that the project has average risk. Find the project's expected NPV. (Hint: Use expected values for the net cash flow in each year.)
b. Find the best-case and worst-case NPVs. What is the probability of occurrence of the worst case if the cash flows are perfectly dependent (perfectly positively correlated) over time? If they are independent over time?
c. Assume that all the cash flows are perfectly positively correlated, that is, there are only three possible cash flow streams over time: (1) the worst case, (2) the most likely, or base, case, and (3) the best case, with probabilities of 0.2, 0.6, and 0.2, respectively. These cases are represented by each of the columns in the table. Find the expected NPV, its standard deviation, and its coefficient of variation.

PROBLEMS

(11-1)

Investment Outlay

Johnson Industries is considering an expansion project. The necessary equipment could be purchased for $9 million, and the project would also require an initial $3 million investment in net operating working capital. The company's tax rate is 40 percent. What is the project's initial investment outlay?

(11-2)

Operating Cash Flow

Nixon Communications is trying to estimate the first-year operating cash flow (at t = 1) for a proposed project. The financial staff has collected the following information:

Projected sales	$10 million
Operating costs (not including depreciation)	$7 million
Depreciation	$2 million
Interest expense	$2 million

The company faces a 40 percent tax rate. What is the project's operating cash flow for the first year (t = 1)?

(11-3)
Net Salvage Value
Carter Air Lines is now in the terminal year of a project. The equipment originally cost $20 million, of which 80 percent has been depreciated. Carter can sell the used equipment today to another airline for $5 million, and its tax rate is 40 percent. What is the equipment's after-tax net salvage value?

(11-4)
New Project Analysis
The Campbell Company is evaluating the proposed acquisition of a new milling machine. The machine's base price is $108,000, and it would cost another $12,500 to modify it for special use by your firm. The machine falls into the MACRS 3-year class, and it would be sold after 3 years for $65,000. The machine would require an increase in net working capital (inventory) of $5,500. The milling machine would have no effect on revenues, but it is expected to save the firm $44,000 per year in before-tax operating costs, mainly labor. Campbell's marginal tax rate is 35 percent.
a. What is the net cost of the machine for capital budgeting purposes? (That is, what is the Year 0 net cash flow?)
b. What are the net operating cash flows in Years 1, 2, and 3?
c. What is the additional Year 3 cash flow (that is, the after-tax salvage and the return of working capital)?
d. If the project's cost of capital is 12 percent, should the machine be purchased?

(11-5)
New Project Analysis
You have been asked by the president of your company to evaluate the proposed acquisition of a new spectrometer for the firm's R&D department. The equipment's basic price is $70,000, and it would cost another $15,000 to modify it for special use by your firm. The spectrometer, which falls into the MACRS 3-year class, would be sold after 3 years for $30,000. Use of the equipment would require an increase in net working capital (spare parts inventory) of $4,000. The spectrometer would have no effect on revenues, but it is expected to save the firm $25,000 per year in before-tax operating costs, mainly labor. The firm's marginal federal-plus-state tax rate is 40 percent.
a. What is the net cost of the spectrometer? (That is, what is the Year 0 net cash flow?)
b. What are the net operating cash flows in Years 1, 2, and 3?
c. What is the additional (nonoperating) cash flow in Year 3?
d. If the project's cost of capital is 10 percent, should the spectrometer be purchased?

(11-6)
Inflation Adjustments
The Rodriguez Company is considering an average-risk investment in a mineral water spring project that has a cost of $150,000. The project will produce 1,000 cases of mineral water per year indefinitely. The current sales price is $138 per case, and the current cost per case (all variable) is $105. The firm is taxed at a rate of 34 percent. Both prices and costs are expected to rise at a rate of 6 percent per year. The firm uses only equity, and it has a cost of capital of 15 percent. Assume that cash flows consist only of after-tax profits, since the spring has an indefinite life and will not be depreciated.
a. Should the firm accept the project? (Hint: The project is a perpetuity, so you must use the formula for a perpetuity to find its NPV.)
b. If total costs consisted of a fixed cost of $10,000 per year and variable costs of $95 per unit, and if only the variable costs were expected to increase with inflation, would this make the project better or worse? Continue with the assumption that the sales price will rise with inflation.

(11-7)
Scenario Analysis
Shao Industries is considering a proposed project for its capital budget. The company estimates that the project's NPV is $12 million. This estimate assumes that the economy and market conditions will be average over the next few years. The company's

CFO, however, forecasts that there is only a 50 percent chance that the economy will be average. Recognizing this uncertainty, she has also performed the following scenario analysis:

Economic Scenario	Probability of Outcome	NPV
Recession	0.05	($70 million)
Below average	0.20	(25 million)
Average	0.50	12 million
Above average	0.20	20 million
Boom	0.05	30 million

What is the project's expected NPV, its standard deviation, and its coefficient of variation?

(11-8)
Risky Cash Flows
The Bartram-Pulley Company (BPC) must decide between two mutually exclusive investment projects. Each project costs $6,750 and has an expected life of 3 years. Annual net cash flows from each project begin 1 year after the initial investment is made and have the following probability distributions:

PROJECT A		PROJECT B	
Probability	Net Cash Flows	Probability	Net Cash Flows
0.2	$6,000	0.2	$ 0
0.6	6,750	0.6	6,750
0.2	7,500	0.2	18,000

BPC has decided to evaluate the riskier project at a 12 percent rate and the less risky project at a 10 percent rate.
a. What is the expected value of the annual net cash flows from each project? What is the coefficient of variation (CV)? (Hint: $\sigma_B = \$5,798$ and $CV_B = 0.76$.)
b. What is the risk-adjusted NPV of each project?
c. If it were known that Project B was negatively correlated with other cash flows of the firm whereas Project A was positively correlated, how would this knowledge affect the decision? If Project B's cash flows were negatively correlated with gross domestic product (GDP), would that influence your assessment of its risk?

(11-9)
Simulation
Singleton Supplies Corporation (SSC) manufactures medical products for hospitals, clinics, and nursing homes. SSC may introduce a new type of X-ray scanner designed to identify certain types of cancers in their early stages. There are a number of uncertainties about the proposed project, but the following data are believed to be reasonably accurate.

	Probability	Value	Random Numbers
Developmental costs	0.3	$2,000,000	00–29
	0.4	4,000,000	30–69
	0.3	6,000,000	70–99
Project life	0.2	3 years	00–19
	0.6	8 years	20–79
	0.2	13 years	80–99
Sales in units	0.2	100	00–19
	0.6	200	20–79
	0.2	300	80–99
Sales price	0.1	$13,000	00–09
	0.8	13,500	10–89
	0.1	14,000	90–99
Cost per unit (excluding developmental costs)	0.3	$5,000	00–29
	0.4	6,000	30–69
	0.3	7,000	70–99

SSC uses a cost of capital of 15 percent to analyze average-risk projects, 12 percent for low-risk projects, and 18 percent for high-risk projects. These risk adjustments reflect primarily the uncertainty about each project's NPV and IRR as measured by the coefficients of variation of NPV and IRR. SSC is in the 40 percent federal-plus-state income tax bracket.

a. What is the expected IRR for the X-ray scanner project? Base your answer on the expected values of the variables. Also, assume the after-tax "profits" figure you develop is equal to annual cash flows. All facilities are leased, so depreciation may be disregarded. Can you determine the value of σ_{IRR} short of actual simulation or a fairly complex statistical analysis?

b. Assume that SSC uses a 15 percent cost of capital for this project. What is the project's NPV? Could you estimate σ_{NPV} without either simulation or a complex statistical analysis?

c. Show the process by which a computer would perform a simulation analysis for this project. Use the random numbers 44, 17, 16, 58, 1; 79, 83, 86; and 19, 62, 6 to illustrate the process with the first computer run. Actually calculate the first-run NPV and IRR. Assume that the cash flows for each year are independent of cash flows for other years. Also, assume that the computer operates as follows: (1) A developmental cost and a project life are estimated for the first run using the first two random numbers. (2) Next, sales volume, sales price, and cost per unit are estimated using the next three random numbers and used to derive a cash flow for the first year. (3) Then, the next three random numbers are used to estimate sales volume, sales price, and cost per unit for the second year, hence the cash flow for the second year. (4) Cash flows for other years are developed similarly, on out to the first run's estimated life. (5) With the developmental cost and the cash flow stream established, NPV and IRR for the first run are derived and stored in the computer's memory. (6) The process is repeated to generate perhaps 500 other NPVs and IRRs. (7) Frequency distributions for NPV and IRR are plotted by the computer, and the distributions' means and standard deviations are calculated.

(11-10)
Sequential Decisions   The Yoran Yacht Company (YYC), a prominent sailboat builder in Newport, may design a new 30-foot sailboat based on the "winged" keels first introduced on the 12-meter yachts that raced for the America's Cup.

First, YYC would have to invest $10,000 at t = 0 for the design and model tank testing of the new boat. YYC's managers believe that there is a 60 percent probability that this phase will be successful and the project will continue. If Stage 1 is not successful, the project will be abandoned with zero salvage value.

The next stage, if undertaken, would consist of making the molds and producing two prototype boats. This would cost $500,000 at t = 1. If the boats test well, YYC would go into production. If they do not, the molds and prototypes could be sold for $100,000. The managers estimate that the probability is 80 percent that the boats will pass testing, and that Stage 3 will be undertaken.

Stage 3 consists of converting an unused production line to produce the new design. This would cost $1,000,000 at t = 2. If the economy is strong at this point, the net value of sales would be $3,000,000, while if the economy is weak, the net value would be $1,500,000. Both net values occur at t = 3, and each state of the economy has a probability of 0.5. YYC's corporate cost of capital is 12 percent.

a. Assume that this project has average risk. Construct a decision tree and determine the project's expected NPV.

b. Find the project's standard deviation of NPV and coefficient of variation (CV) of NPV. If YYC's average project had a CV of between 1.0 and 2.0, would this project be of high, low, or average stand-alone risk?

SPREADSHEET PROBLEM

(11-11)
Build a Model: Issues in Capital Budgeting   Start with the partial model in the file *CF2 Ch 11 P11 Build a Model.xls* from the textbook's Web site. Webmasters.com has developed a powerful new server that would be used for corporations' Internet activities. It would cost $10 million to buy

the equipment necessary to manufacture the server, and it would require net operating working capital equal to 10 percent of sales. The servers would sell for $24,000 per unit, and Webmasters believes that variable costs would amount to $17,500 per unit. After the first year the sales price and variable costs will increase at the inflation rate of 3 percent. The company's fixed costs would be $1 million per year and would increase with inflation. It would take 1 year to buy the required equipment and set up operations, and the server project would have a life of 4 years. If the project is undertaken, it must be continued for the entire 4 years. Also, the project's returns are expected to be highly correlated with returns on the firm's other assets. The firm believes it could sell 1,000 units per year.

The equipment would be depreciated over a 5-year period, using MACRS rates. The estimated market value of the equipment at the end of the project's 4-year life is $500,000. Webmasters' federal-plus-state tax rate is 40 percent. Its cost of capital is 10 percent for average-risk projects, defined as projects with a coefficient of variation of NPV between 0.8 and 1.2. Low-risk projects are evaluated with a WACC of 8 percent, and high-risk projects at 13 percent.

a. Develop a spreadsheet model and use it to find the project's NPV, IRR, and payback.

b. Now conduct a sensitivity analysis to determine the sensitivity of NPV to changes in the sales price, variable costs per unit, and number of units sold. Set these variables' values at 10 percent and 20 percent above and below their base-case values. Include a graph in your analysis.

c. Now conduct a scenario analysis. Assume that there is a 25 percent probability that "best-case" conditions, with each of the variables discussed in part b being 20 percent better than its base-case value, will occur. There is a 25 percent probability of "worst-case" conditions, with the variables 20 percent worse than base, and a 50 percent probability of base-case conditions.

d. If the project appears to be more or less risky than an average project, find its risk-adjusted NPV, IRR, and payback.

e. On the basis of information in the problem, would you recommend that the project be accepted?

CYBERPROBLEM

Please go to our Web site, **http://ehrhardt.swlearning.com**, to access any Cyberproblems.

THOMSON ONE
Business School Edition

Please go to **http://ehrhardt.swlearning.com** to access any Thomson ONE—Business School Edition problems.

MINI CASE

Shrieves Casting Company is considering adding a new line to its product mix, and the capital budgeting analysis is being conducted by Sidney Johnson, a recently graduated MBA. The production line would be set up in unused space in Shrieves's main plant. The machinery's invoice price would be approximately $200,000, another $10,000 in shipping charges would be required, and it would cost an additional $30,000 to install the equipment. The machinery has an economic life of 4 years, and Shrieves has obtained a special tax ruling that places the equipment in the MACRS 3-year class. The machinery is expected to have a salvage value of $25,000 after 4 years of use.

The new line would generate incremental sales of 1,250 units per year for 4 years at an incremental cost of $100 per unit in the first year, excluding depreciation. Each unit can be sold for $200 in the first year. The sales price and cost are both expected to increase by 3 percent per year due to inflation. Further, to handle the new line, the firm's net operating working capital would have to increase by an amount equal to 12 percent of sales revenues. The firm's tax rate is 40 percent, and its overall weighted average cost of capital is 10 percent.

e-resource

the equipment necessary to manufacture the server, and it would require net operating working capital equal to 10 percent of sales. The servers would sell for $24,000 per unit, and Webmasters believes that variable costs would amount to $17,500 per unit. After the first year the sales price and variable costs will increase at the inflation rate of 3 percent. The company's fixed costs would be $1 million per year and would increase with inflation. It would take 1 year to buy the required equipment and set up operations, and the server project would have a life of 4 years. If the project is undertaken, it must be continued for the entire 4 years. Also, the project's returns are expected to be highly correlated with returns on the firm's other assets. The firm believes it could sell 1,000 units per year.

The equipment would be depreciated over a 5-year period, using MACRS rates. The estimated market value of the equipment at the end of the project's 4-year life is $500,000. Webmasters' federal-plus-state tax rate is 40 percent. Its cost of capital is 10 percent for average-risk projects, defined as projects with a coefficient of variation of NPV between 0.8 and 1.2. Low-risk projects are evaluated with a WACC of 8 percent, and high-risk projects at 13 percent.

a. Develop a spreadsheet model and use it to find the project's NPV, IRR, and payback.

b. Now conduct a sensitivity analysis to determine the sensitivity of NPV to changes in the sales price, variable costs per unit, and number of units sold. Set these variables' values at 10 percent and 20 percent above and below their base-case values. Include a graph in your analysis.

c. Now conduct a scenario analysis. Assume that there is a 25 percent probability that "best-case" conditions, with each of the variables discussed in part b being 20 percent better than its base-case value, will occur. There is a 25 percent probability of "worst-case" conditions, with the variables 20 percent worse than base, and a 50 percent probability of base-case conditions.

d. If the project appears to be more or less risky than an average project, find its risk-adjusted NPV, IRR, and payback.

e. On the basis of information in the problem, would you recommend that the project be accepted?

CYBERPROBLEM

Please go to our Web site, **http://ehrhardt.swlearning.com**, to access any Cyberproblems.

THOMSON ONE
Business School Edition

Please go to **http://ehrhardt.swlearning.com** to access any Thomson ONE—Business School Edition problems.

MINI CASE

Shrieves Casting Company is considering adding a new line to its product mix, and the capital budgeting analysis is being conducted by Sidney Johnson, a recently graduated MBA. The production line would be set up in unused space in Shrieves's main plant. The machinery's invoice price would be approximately $200,000, another $10,000 in shipping charges would be required, and it would cost an additional $30,000 to install the equipment. The machinery has an economic life of 4 years, and Shrieves has obtained a special tax ruling that places the equipment in the MACRS 3-year class. The machinery is expected to have a salvage value of $25,000 after 4 years of use.

The new line would generate incremental sales of 1,250 units per year for 4 years at an incremental cost of $100 per unit in the first year, excluding depreciation. Each unit can be sold for $200 in the first year. The sales price and cost are both expected to increase by 3 percent per year due to inflation. Further, to handle the new line, the firm's net operating working capital would have to increase by an amount equal to 12 percent of sales revenues. The firm's tax rate is 40 percent, and its overall weighted average cost of capital is 10 percent.

a. Define "incremental cash flow."

   (1) Should you subtract interest expense or dividends when calculating project cash flow?

   (2) Suppose the firm had spent $100,000 last year to rehabilitate the production line site. Should this be included in the analysis? Explain.

   (3) Now assume that the plant space could be leased out to another firm at $25,000 per year. Should this be included in the analysis? If so, how?

   (4) Finally, assume that the new product line is expected to decrease sales of the firm's other lines by $50,000 per year. Should this be considered in the analysis? If so, how?

b. Disregard the assumptions in part a. What is Shrieves's depreciable basis? What are the annual depreciation expenses?

c. Calculate the annual sales revenues and costs (other than depreciation). Why is it important to include inflation when estimating cash flows?

d. Construct annual incremental operating cash flow statements.

e. Estimate the required net operating working capital for each year and the cash flow due to investments in net operating working capital.

f. Calculate the after-tax salvage cash flow.

g. Calculate the net cash flows for each year. Based on these cash flows, what are the project's NPV, IRR, MIRR, and payback? Do these indicators suggest that the project should be undertaken?

h. What does the term "risk" mean in the context of capital budgeting; to what extent can risk be quantified; and when risk is quantified, is the quantification based primarily on statistical analysis of historical data or on subjective, judgmental estimates?

i. (1) What are the three types of risk that are relevant in capital budgeting?

   (2) How is each of these risk types measured, and how do they relate to one another?

   (3) How is each type of risk used in the capital budgeting process?

j. (1) What is sensitivity analysis?

   (2) Perform a sensitivity analysis on the unit sales, salvage value, and cost of capital for the project. Assume that each of these variables can vary from its base-case, or expected, value by ± 10, 20, and 30 percent. Include a sensitivity diagram, and discuss the results.

   (3) What is the primary weakness of sensitivity analysis? What is its primary usefulness?

k. Assume that Sidney Johnson is confident of her estimates of all the variables that affect the project's cash flows except unit sales and sales price. If product acceptance is poor, unit sales would be only 900 units a year and the unit price would only be $160; a strong consumer response would produce sales of 1,600 units and a unit price of $240. Johnson believes that there is a 25 percent chance of poor acceptance, a 25 percent chance of excellent acceptance, and a 50 percent chance of average acceptance (the base case).

   (1) What is scenario analysis?

   (2) What is the worst-case NPV? The best-case NPV?

   (3) Use the worst-, most likely, and best-case NPVs and probabilities of occurrence to find the project's expected NPV, standard deviation, and coefficient of variation.

l. Are there problems with scenario analysis? Define simulation analysis, and discuss its principal advantages and disadvantages.

m. (1) Assume that Shrieves's average project has a coefficient of variation in the range of 0.2 to 0.4. Would the new line be classified as high risk, average risk, or low risk? What type of risk is being measured here?

   (2) Shrieves typically adds or subtracts 3 percentage points to the overall cost of capital to adjust for risk. Should the new line be accepted?

   (3) Are there any subjective risk factors that should be considered before the final decision is made?

n. What is a real option? What are some types of real options?

SELECTED ADDITIONAL REFERENCES AND CASES

A paper on the effect of inflation on capital budgeting is

Mehta, Dileep R., Michael D. Curley, and Hung-Gay Fung, "Inflation, Cost of Capital, and Capital Budgeting Procedures," *Financial Management*, Winter 1984, 48–54.

The following articles pertain to other topics in this chapter:

Kroll, Yoram, "On the Differences between Accrual Accounting Figures and Cash Flows: The Case of Working Capital," *Financial Management*, Spring 1985, 75–82.

Mukherjee, Tarun K., "Reducing the Uncertainty-Induced Bias in Capital Budgeting Decisions—A Hurdle Rate Approach," *Journal of Business Finance & Accounting*, September 1991, 747–753.

The literature on risk analysis in capital budgeting is vast; here is a small but useful selection of additional references that bear directly on the topics covered in this chapter:

Butler, J. S., and Barry Schachter, "The Investment Decision: Estimation Risk and Risk Adjusted Discount Rates," *Financial Management*, Winter 1989, 13–22.

Weaver, Samuel C., Peter J. Clemmens III, Jack A. Gunn, and Bruce D. Danneburg, "Divisional Hurdle Rates and the Cost of Capital," *Financial Management*, Spring 1989, 18–25.

The following cases from the Finance Online Case Library *cover many of the concepts discussed in this chapter and are available at* **http://www.textchoice.com:**

Case 12, "Indian River Citrus Company (A)," Case 12A, "Cranfield, Inc. (A)," Case 14, "Robert Montoya, Inc." focus on cash flow estimation. Case 13, "Indian River Citrus (B)," Case 13A, "Cranfield, Inc. (B)," Case 13B, "Tasty Foods (B)," Case 13C, "Heavenly Foods," and Case 15, "Robert Montoya, Inc. (B)," illustrate project risk analysis. Case 58, "Universal Corporation," is a comprehensive case that illustrates Chapters 10 and 11, as do Cases 47 and 48, "The Western Company (A and B)."

Corporate Valuation

CHAPTER 12

Financial Planning and Forecasting Financial Statements

Many managers compare financial planning with having a root canal: time consuming and painful. Even worse, they are left with nagging doubts that the results might not be very reliable. According to a recent survey of finance professionals, only 45 percent are satisfied with their current planning process, and 90 percent believe it is too cumbersome. Nevertheless, 71 percent of the finance professionals believe long-term strategic planning is the single most critical activity for future success.

What's wrong with the current planning process? First, it's too slow. The process typically starts in July and ends in December. Second, it's too labor intensive, with the average company requiring 13 employees to spend the equivalent of 4.33 person-years.

The process begins with data acquisition, including sales revenues, costs, inventories, batch sizes, defect rates, the number of repeat customers, product mix by customer type, and hours of employee training. Unfortunately, only 24 percent of companies currently have a unified planning and reporting system—most have stand-alone software packages and spreadsheets that vary from division to division, making data acquisition time consuming and error filled.

Instead of basing growth and performance targets on analysis, they are often set through negotiation between staff managers who make the budgets and line managers who must execute them. Fully 66 percent of managers believe planning is influenced more by politics than by strategy.

It's not surprising that many companies are reengineering their processes. Using information technology that standardizes data, links data throughout the company, and pulls data directly into the planning process, many companies are dramatically shortening the planning cycle. For example, Sprint replaced annual budgets with quarterly reviews, and Nationwide Financial Services reduced its budget cycle from four months to a few weeks. Similar changes are occurring in forecasting, with analysis replacing politics. A recent survey reported that 81 percent of companies use trend-based projections, 41 percent use activity based management (that is, linking financial forecasts to nonfinancial data), and 22 percent use simulations.

As a result of better data, better forecasting techniques, and shorter planning cycles, many companies now have more accurate and useful financial plans.

Sources: Fritz McCormick, "Fewer and Fewer Beans," *CFO,* October 1999, 18; Susan Arterian, "Sprint Retools the Budget Process," *CFO,* September 1997, 88–91; Russ Banham, "The Revolution in Planning," *CFO,* August 1999, 46–56; and Cathy Lazere, "All Together Now," *CFO,* February 1998, 28–36.

e-resource

The textbook's Web site contains an Excel file that will guide you through the chapter's calculations. The file for this chapter is **CF2 Ch 12 Tool Kit.xls,** *and we encourage you to open the file and follow along as you read the chapter.*

Managers use **pro forma,** or **projected, financial statements** in four ways: (1) By looking at projected statements, they can assess whether the firm's anticipated performance is in line with the firm's own general targets and with investors' expectations. (2) Pro forma statements can be used to estimate the effect of proposed operating changes, enabling managers to conduct "what if" analyses. (3) Managers use pro forma statements to anticipate the firm's future financing needs. (4) Managers forecast free cash flows under different operating plans, forecast their capital requirements, and then choose the plan that maximizes shareholder value. Security analysts make the same types of projections, forecasting future earnings, cash flows, and stock prices.

OVERVIEW OF FINANCIAL PLANNING

Our primary objective in this book is to explain what managers can do to make their companies more valuable. However, value creation is impossible unless the company has a well-articulated plan. As Yogi Berra once said, "You've got to be careful if you don't know where you're going, because you might not get there."

Strategic Plans

Strategic plans usually begin with a statement of the overall *corporate purpose.* Many companies are very clear about their corporate purpose: "Our mission is to maximize shareowner value over time."

This corporate purpose is increasingly common for U.S. companies, but that has not always been the case. For example, Varian Associates, Inc., a New York Stock Exchange company with sales of almost $2 billion, was, in 1990, regarded as one of the most technologically advanced electronics companies. However, Varian's management was more concerned with developing new technology than with marketing it, and its stock price was lower than it had been ten years earlier. Some of the larger stockholders were intensely unhappy with the state of affairs, and management was faced with the threat of a proxy fight or forced merger. In 1991, management announced a change in policy and stated that it would, in the future, emphasize both technological excellence *and* profitability, rather than focusing primarily on technology. Earnings improved dramatically, and the stock price rose from $6.75 to more than $60 four years after the change in corporate purpose.

A corporate focus on creating wealth for the company's owners is not yet as common abroad as it is in the United States. For example, Veba AG, one of Germany's largest companies, created a stir in 1996 when it stated in its annual report that "Our commitment is to create value for you, our shareholders." This was quite different from the usual German model, in which companies have representatives from labor on their boards of directors and which explicitly state their commitments to a variety of stakeholders. As one might expect, Veba's stock has consistently outperformed the average German stock. As the trend in international investing continues, more and more non-U.S. companies are adopting a corporate purpose similar to that of Varian and Veba.

Corporate scope defines a firm's lines of business and geographic area of operations. For example, Coca-Cola limits its products to soft drinks, but on a global scale. Pepsi-Cola recently followed Coke's lead—it restricted its scope by spinning off its food service

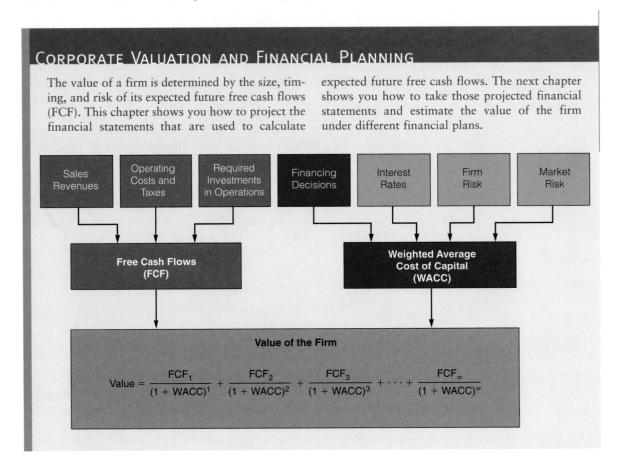

CORPORATE VALUATION AND FINANCIAL PLANNING

The value of a firm is determined by the size, timing, and risk of its expected future free cash flows (FCF). This chapter shows you how to project the financial statements that are used to calculate expected future free cash flows. The next chapter shows you how to take those projected financial statements and estimate the value of the firm under different financial plans.

businesses. In fact, several studies have found that the market tends to value focused firms more highly than diversified firms.[1]

The corporate purpose states the general philosophy of the business, but it does not provide managers with operational objectives. The *statement of corporate objectives* sets forth specific goals to guide management. Most organizations have both qualitative and quantitative objectives. A typical quantitative objective might be attaining a 50 percent market share, a 20 percent ROE, a 10 percent earnings growth rate, or a $100 million economic value added (EVA).

Once a firm has defined its purpose, scope, and objectives, it must develop a strategy for achieving its goals. *Corporate strategies* are broad approaches rather than detailed plans. For example, one airline may have a strategy of offering no-frills service between a limited number of cities, while another's strategy may be to offer "staterooms in the sky." Any such strategy should be compatible with the firm's purpose, scope, and objectives.

Operating Plans

Operating plans provide detailed implementation guidance to help meet the corporate objectives. These plans can be developed for any time horizon, but most companies use a five-year horizon. A five-year plan is detailed for the first year, with each succeeding year's plan becoming less specific. The plan explains who is responsible for each particular function, when specific tasks are to be accomplished, sales and profit targets, and the like.

[1] See, for example, Philip G. Berger and Eli Ofek, "Diversification's Effect on Firm Value," *Journal of Financial Economics,* Vol. 37, no. 1, 39–66 (1995); and Larry Lang and René Stulz, "Tobin's Q, Corporate Diversification, and Firm Performance," *Journal of Political Economy,* Vol. 102, Issue 6, 1248–1280 (1994).

Large, multidivisional companies such as General Electric break down their operating plans by divisions. Thus, each division has its own goals, mission, and plan for meeting its objectives, and these plans are then consolidated to form the corporate plan.

The Financial Plan

The financial planning process has five steps:

1. Project financial statements to analyze the effects of the operating plan on projected profits and financial ratios.
2. Determine the funds needed to support the five-year plan.
3. Forecast the funds to be generated internally and identify those to be obtained from external sources, subject to any constraints due to borrowing convenants, such as restrictions on the debt ratio, the current ratio, and the coverage ratios.
4. Establish a performance-based management compensation system that rewards employees for creating shareholder wealth.
5. Monitor operations after implementing the plan, identify the cause of any deviations, and take corrective actions.

In the remainder of this chapter, we explain how to create a financial plan, including its three key components: (1) the sales forecast, (2) pro forma financial statements, and (3) the external financing plan. We discuss compensation in Chapter 13.

SELF-TEST QUESTIONS
What are four ways that managers use pro forma statements?
Briefly explain the following terms: (1) corporate purpose, (2) corporate scope, (3) corporate objectives, and (4) corporate strategies.
Briefly describe the contents of an operating plan.
What are the steps of the financial planning process?

SALES FORECAST

e-resource

See *CF2 Ch 12 Tool Kit.xls* for details.

The **sales forecast** generally starts with a review of sales during the past five to ten years, expressed in a graph such as that in Figure 12-1. The first part of the graph shows five years of historical sales for MicroDrive. The graph could have contained 10 years of sales data, but MicroDrive typically focuses on sales figures for the latest five years because the firm's studies have shown that its future growth is more closely related to recent events than to the distant past.

Entire courses are devoted to forecasting sales, so we can only touch on the basic elements here. However, forecasting the future sales growth rate always begins with a look at past growth. For example, the average of MicroDrive's recent annual growth rates is 10.3 percent. However, the compound growth rate from 2001 to 2005 is the solution value for g in the equation

$$\$2,058 \ (1 + g)^4 = \$3,000,$$

and it can be found by solving the equation or with a financial calculator, entering $N = 4$, $PV = -2058$, $PMT = 0$, $FV = 3000$, and then pressing I to get $g = 9.9$ percent.

The preceding approaches are simple, but both can be poor representations of past growth. First, the arithmetic average procedure generally produces numbers that are too high. To illustrate why, suppose sales grew by 100 percent one year and then fell by -50 percent the next year. There would actually be zero growth over the two years, but the calculated average growth rate would be 25 percent. Similarly, the point-to-point procedure is not reliable because if either the beginning or ending year is an "outlier" in the sense of

e-resource

See *CF2 Ch 12 Tool Kit.xls* for details.

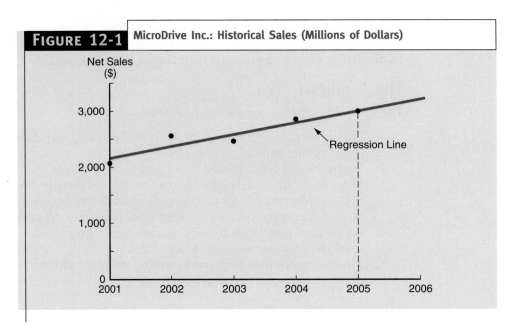

FIGURE 12-1 MicroDrive Inc.: Historical Sales (Millions of Dollars)

Year	Sales	Annual Growth Rate
2001	$2,058	
2002	2,534	23.1%
2003	2,472	−2.4
2004	2,850	15.3
2005	3,000	5.3
		Average = 10.3%

being above or below the trend line shown in Figure 12-1, then the calculated growth rate will not be representative of past growth. The solution to these problems is to use a regression approach, where a curve is fitted to the historic sales data and then the slope of that curve is used to measure historic growth. If we expect a constant growth rate (as opposed to a constant dollar amount, which would mean a declining growth rate), then the regression should be based on the natural log of sales, not sales itself. With a spreadsheet, this is not a difficult calculation, and by far the easiest way to calculate the growth rate is with *Excel*'s LOGEST function. Simply type the years and sales into a spreadsheet, click f_x on the menu bar, select Statistical functions, and then choose the LOGEST function. Highlight the sales range for the Y variable and the years range for X in the function dialog box, and then click OK. The result will be 1 + g, so you finish by subtracting 1 to get the growth rate. For MicroDrive, the growth rate is 9.1 percent.[2]

Although it is useful to calculate the past growth rate in sales, much more is involved in estimating future sales. Future sales will depend on the economy (both domestic and global), the industry's prospects, the company's current product line, proposed products that are in the pipeline, and marketing campaigns. When MicroDrive incorporated these issues into its analysis, it estimated 10 percent expected growth for the upcoming year.

If the sales forecast is off, the consequences can be serious. First, if the market expands by *more* than MicroDrive has anticipated, the company will not be able to meet demand.

e-resource

---

[2] These approaches are demonstrated in the *CF2 Ch 12 Tool Kit.xls*. Also, the Chapter 9 Web Extension illustrates these approaches when estimating dividend growth rates.

Its customers will end up buying competitors' products, and MicroDrive will lose market share. On the other hand, if its projections are overly optimistic, MicroDrive could end up with too much plant, equipment, and inventory, which hurts free cash flow and stock prices. If MicroDrive had financed an unnecessary expansion with debt, high interest charges would compound its problems. Thus, an accurate sales forecast is critical to the firm's well-being.

SELF-TEST QUESTIONS   List some factors that should be considered when developing a sales forecast. Explain why an accurate sales forecast is critical to profitability.

FINANCIAL STATEMENT FORECASTING: THE PERCENT OF SALES METHOD

Once sales have been forecasted, we must forecast future balance sheets and income statements. The most commonly used technique is the **percent of sales method,** which begins with the sales forecast, expressed as an annual growth rate in dollar sales revenues. Many items on the income statement and balance sheets are assumed to increase proportionally with sales, with their values for a particular year estimated as percentages of the forecasted sales for that year. The remaining items on the forecasted statements—items that are not tied directly to sales—depend on the company's dividend policy and its relative use of debt and equity financing.

In the following sections we explain the percent of sales method and use it to forecast MicroDrive's financial statements.[3]

Step 1. Analyze the Historical Ratios

The first step is to analyze the historical ratios. This differs somewhat from the ratio analysis of Chapter 4, since the objective here is to forecast the future, or pro forma, financial statements. The percent of sales method assumes that costs in a given year will be some specified percentage of that year's sales. Thus, we begin our analysis by calculating the ratio of costs to sales for several past years. We illustrate the method using only two years of data for MicroDrive, but a thorough analysis should have at least five years of historical data. Table 12-1 shows MicroDrive's ratio of costs to sales for the past two years. In 2004, MicroDrive had an 87.6 percent ratio of costs to sales, and the ratio dropped to 87.2

e-resource

See CF2 Ch 12 Tool Kit.xls for details.

TABLE 12-1 | Historical Ratios for MicroDrive Inc.

	Actual 2004	Actual 2005	Historical Average	Industry Average
Costs to sales	87.6%	87.2%	87.4%	87.1%
Depreciation to net plant and equipment	10.3	10.0	10.2	10.2
Cash to sales	0.5	0.3	0.4	1.0
Accounts receivable to sales	11.1	12.5	11.8	10.0
Inventory to sales	14.6	20.5	17.5	11.1
Net plant and equipment to sales	30.5	33.3	31.9	33.3
Accounts payable to sales	1.1	2.0	1.5	1.0
Accruals to sales	4.6	4.7	4.6	2.0

[3] For a much more detailed treatment of financial forecasting, see P. Daves, M. Ehrhardt, and R. Shrieves, *Corporate Valuation: A Guide for Managers and Investors* (Mason, OH: South-Western Publishing, 2004).

percent in 2005. The table also shows the historical average, which in this case is the average of the two prior years. The last column shows the ratio of costs to sales for the industry composite, which is the sum of the financial statements for all firms in the industry. Note that MicroDrive has improved its costs/sales ratio, but it still is higher than the industry average.

The table also shows the ratio of depreciation to net plant and equipment. Because depreciation depends on the asset base, it is more reasonable to forecast depreciation as a percent of net plant and equipment rather than of sales.

Many other items on MicroDrive's balance sheets will also increase with sales. The company writes and deposits checks every day. Because managers don't know exactly when all of the checks will clear, they can't predict exactly what the balance in their checking accounts will be on any given day. Therefore, they must maintain a balance of cash and cash equivalents (such as very short-term marketable securities) to avoid overdrawing their accounts. We discuss the issue of cash management in Chapter 16, but for now we simply assume that the cash required to support the company's operations is proportional to its sales. Table 12-1 shows the ratio of cash to sales for the past two years, as well as the historical average and the industry composite ratio. All of the remaining pro forma balance sheet ratios, which we discuss below, also are shown in Table 12-1.

Unless a company changes its credit policy or has a change in its customer base, accounts receivable should be proportional to sales. Furthermore, as sales increase, firms generally must carry more inventories. Chapter 16 discusses inventory management in detail, but for now we assume that inventory will also be proportional to sales.

It might be reasonable to assume that cash, accounts receivable, and inventories will be proportional to sales, but will the amount of net plant and equipment go up and down as sales go up and down? The correct answer could be either yes or no. When companies acquire plant and equipment, they often install more capacity than they currently need due to economies of scale in building capacity. Moreover, even if a plant is operating at its maximum rated capacity, most companies can produce additional units by reducing downtime for scheduled maintenance, by running machinery at a higher than optimal speed, or by adding a second or third shift. Therefore, at least in the short run, companies may not have a very close relationship between sales and net plant and equipment.

However, some companies do have a fixed relationship between sales and plant and equipment, even in the short term. For example, new stores in many retail chains achieve the same sales during their first year as the chain's existing stores. The only way such retailers can grow (beyond inflation) is by adding new stores. Such companies therefore have a strong proportional relationship between fixed assets and sales.

Finally, in the long term there is a strong relationship between sales and net plant and equipment for virtually all companies: Few companies can continue to increase sales unless they eventually add capacity. Therefore, as a first approximation it is reasonable to assume that the long-term ratio of net plant and equipment to sales will be constant.

For the first years in a forecast, managers generally build in the actual planned expenditures on plant and equipment. If those estimates are not available, it is generally best to assume a constant ratio of net plant and equipment to sales.

Some items on the liability side of the balance sheet can be expected to increase spontaneously with sales, producing what are called **spontaneously generated funds.** The two primary types of spontaneous funds are accounts payable and accruals. Regarding payables, as sales increase, so will purchases of raw materials, and those larger purchases will spontaneously lead to a higher level of accounts payable. Similarly, more sales will require more labor, while higher sales normally result in higher taxable income and thus taxes. Therefore, accrued wages and taxes both increase.

All of the historical ratios are shown in Table 12-1. Using these ratios, along with the industry composite ratios and a knowledge of MicroDrive's operating plans and industry trends, its managers are ready to begin forecasting the projected, or pro forma, financial statements.

Step 2. Forecast the Income Statement

In this section we explain how to forecast the income statement, and in the following section we forecast the balance sheet. Although we cover these topics in two separate sections, the forecasted financial statements are actually integrated with one another and with the previous year's statements. For example, the income statement item "depreciation" depends on net plant and equipment, which is a balance sheet item, and "retained earnings," which is a balance sheet item, depends on the previous year's retained earnings, the forecasted net income, and the firm's dividend policy. Keep this interrelatedness in mind as you go through the forecast.

FORECAST SALES   Table 12-2 shows the forecasted income statement. Management forecasts that sales will grow by 10 percent. Thus, forecasted sales, shown in Row 1, Column 3, is the product of $3,000 million prior year's sales and (1 + g), or $3,000(1.1) = $3,300 million.

e-resource

See CF2 Ch 12 Tool Kit.xls for details.

FORECAST EARNINGS BEFORE INTEREST AND TAXES (EBIT)   Table 12-1 shows that MicroDrive's ratio of costs to sales for the most recent year was 87.2 percent ($2,616/$3,000 = 0.872). Thus, to get a dollar of sales, MicroDrive had to incur 87.2 cents of costs. Initially, we assume that the cost structure will remain unchanged. Later on, we explore the impact of changes in the cost structure, but for now we assume that forecasted costs will equal 87.2 percent of forecasted sales. See Row 2 of Table 12-2.

The most recent ratio of depreciation to net plant and equipment, shown in Table 12-1, was 10 percent ($100/$1,000 = 0.10), and MicroDrive's managers believe this is a good estimate of future depreciation rates. As we show later in Table 12-3, the forecasted net plant and equipment is $1,100 million. Therefore, forecasted depreciation is 0.10($1,100) = $110 million. Notice how a balance sheet item, net plant and equipment, affects the charge for depreciation, which is an income statement item.

Total operating costs, shown on Row 4, are the sum of costs of goods sold plus depreciation, and EBIT is then found by subtraction.

TABLE 12-2 | MicroDrive Inc.: Actual and Projected Income Statements (Millions of Dollars Except for Per Share Data)

	Actual 2005 (1)	Forecast Basis (2)	Forecast for 2006 (3)
1. Sales	$3,000.0	110% × 2005 Sales =	$3,300.0
2. Costs except depreciation	2,616.2	87.2% × 2006 Sales =	2,877.6
3. Depreciation expense	100.0	10% × 2006 Net plant =	110.0
4. Total operating costs	$2,716.2		$2,987.6
5. EBIT	$ 283.8		$ 312.4
6. Less interest	88.0	(See text for explanation)	92.8
7. Earnings before taxes (EBT)	$ 195.8		$ 219.6
8. Taxes (40%)	78.3		87.8
9. NI before preferred dividends	$ 117.5		$ 131.8
10. Preferred dividends	4.0	Dividend rate × 2005 preferred =	4.0
11. NI available to common	$ 113.5		$ 127.8
12. Shares of common equity	50.0		50.0
13. Dividends per share	$ 1.15	108% × 2005 DPS =	$ 1.25
14. Dividends to common	$ 57.5	2006 DPS × Number of shares =	$ 62.5
15. Additions to retained earnings	$ 56.0		$ 65.3

FORECAST INTEREST EXPENSE   How should we forecast the interest charges? The actual net interest expense is the sum of the firm's daily interest charges less its daily interest income, if any, from short-term investments. Most companies have a variety of different debt obligations with different fixed interest rates and/or floating interest rates. For example, bonds issued in different years generally have different fixed rates, while most bank loans have rates that vary with interest rates in the economy. Given this situation, it is impossible to forecast the exact interest expense for the upcoming year, so we make two simplifying assumptions.

Assumption 1.   Specifying the Balance of Debt for Computing Interest Expense   As noted above, interest on bank loans is calculated daily, based on the amount of debt at the beginning of the day, while bond interest depends on the amount of bonds outstanding. If debt remained constant all during the year, the correct balance to use when forecasting the annual interest expense would be the amount of debt at the beginning of the year, which is the same as the debt shown on the balance sheets at the end of the previous year. But how should you forecast the annual interest expense if debt is expected to change during the year, which is typical for most companies? One option would be to base the interest expense on the debt balance shown at the end of the forecasted year, but this has two disadvantages. First, this would charge a full year's interest on the additional debt, which would imply that the debt was put in place on January 1. Because this is usually not true, that forecast would overstate the most likely interest expense. Second, this assumption causes circularity in the spreadsheet. We discuss this in detail in the Web Extension to this chapter, but the short explanation is that additional debt causes additional interest expense, which reduces the addition to retained earnings, which in turn requires a higher level of debt, which causes still more interest expense, and the cycle keeps repeating. This is called **financing feedback**. Spreadsheets can deal with this problem (see the Web Extension to this chapter), but it adds complexity to the model that might not be worth the benefits.

e-resource

A similar approach would be to base the interest expense on the average of the debt at the beginning and end of the year. This approach would produce the correct interest expense only if debt were added evenly throughout the year, which is a big assumption. In addition, it also results in a circular model with all its complexity.

A third approach, which we illustrate below, works well for most situations. We base the interest expense on the amount of debt at the beginning of the year as shown on the previous year's balance sheet. However, since this will underestimate the true interest expense if debt increases throughout the year, as it usually does for most companies, we use an interest rate that is about 0.5 percent higher than the rate we actually expect. This approach provides reasonably accurate forecasts without greatly increasing the model's complexity. Keep in mind, though, that this simple approach might not work well in all situations, so see the Web Extension to this chapter if you want to implement the more complex modeling technique.

Assumption 2.   Specifying Interest Rates   As noted earlier, different loans have different interest rates. Rather than trying to specify the rate on each separate debt issue, we usually specify only two rates, one for short-term notes payable and one for long-term bonds. The interest rate on short-term debt usually floats, and because the best estimate of future rates is generally the current rate, it is most reasonable to apply the current market rate to short-term loans. For MicroDrive, the appropriate short-term rate is about 8.5 percent, which we rounded up to 9 percent because we will apply it to the debt at the beginning of the year.

Most companies' long-term debt consists of several different bond issues with different interest rates. During the course of the year, some of this debt may be paid off, and some new long-term debt may be added. Rather than try to estimate the interest expense for each particular issue, we apply a single interest rate to the total amount of long-term debt. This rate is an average of the rates on the currently outstanding long-term bonds and the rate that is expected on any new long-term debt. The average rate on MicroDrive's existing long-term bonds is about 10 percent, and it would have to pay about 10.5 percent on new long-term bonds. The average rate on old and new bonds would be somewhere between 10 and 10.5 percent, which we round up to 11 percent because we are going to apply it to the debt at the beginning of the year, as explained above.

Calculating Interest Expense   The forecasted interest expense is the net interest paid on short-term financing plus the interest on long-term bonds. We estimate the net interest on short-term financing by first finding the interest expense on notes payable and then subtracting any interest income from short-term investments. We base interest charges on the amount of short-term debt at the beginning of the year (which is the debt at the end of the previous year), and we note that MicroDrive had no short-term investments. Therefore, MicroDrive's net short-term interest is 0.09($110) − 0.09($0) = $9.9 million. The interest on long-term bonds is 0.11($754.0) = $82.94, rounded to $82.9 million. Therefore, the total interest expense is $9.9 + $82.9 = $92.8 million.

COMPLETING THE INCOME STATEMENT   Earnings before taxes (EBT) is calculated by subtracting interest from EBIT, and then we deduct taxes calculated at a 40 percent rate. The resulting net income before preferred dividends for 2006, which is $131.8 million, is shown on Row 9 of Table 12-2. MicroDrive's preferred stock pays a dividend of 10 percent. Based on the amount of preferred stock at the beginning of the year, the preferred dividends are 0.10($40) = $4 million. Thus, MicroDrive's forecasted net income available to common stock is $127.8 million, shown in Row 11.

Row 12 shows the number of shares of common stock, and Row 13 shows the most recent dividend per share, $1.15. MicroDrive does not plan to issue any new shares, but it does plan to increase the dividend by 8 percent, resulting in a forecasted dividend of 1.08($1.15) = $1.242, rounded up to $1.25 per share. With 50 million shares, the total forecasted dividend is 50($1.25) = $62.5 million. The forecasted addition to retained earnings is equal to the net income available to common stockholders minus the total dividends: $127.8 − $62.5 = $65.3 million, as shown on Row 15.

Step 3. Forecast the Balance Sheet

Before going into the details of forecasting balance sheets, let's take a look at the big picture. First, a company must have assets to support the sales as forecasted on the income statement, and if sales are growing, then assets typically must also grow. Second, if assets are to grow, then the company must obtain funds to purchase the new assets. Third, the needed funds can come from internal sources, mainly as reinvested earnings, or externally, from the sale of short-term investments, from new loans (either notes payable or long-term bonds), from new stock issues, or by increasing operating current liabilities, mainly accounts payable or accruals. Here are the steps: (1) Determine the amount of new assets needed to support the forecasted sales, (2) determine the amount of internal funds that will be available, and (3) plan to raise any required additional financing. This sounds simple, but the devil is in the details.

Let's start with the assets required to support sales. Notice that these consist of operating current assets plus operating long-term assets. The percent of sales approach assumes initially that each class of assets is proportional to sales, so we can forecast all of the assets on MicroDrive's balance sheet except for short-term investments, which is a nonoperating asset. Many firms use short-term investments as a temporary repository for any extra cash, or as a "slush fund" for use in times when operating cash flows are lower than expected. We'll show how to forecast the final level of short-term investments shortly, but for now we assume that MicroDrive plans to maintain its current level of short-term investments.

The liability side of the balance sheet is a little trickier because it involves both operating effects driven by the sales and costs forecasts and financial effects that result from management's financial policy decisions. The percent of sales method is based on the assumption that accounts payable and accruals are both proportional to sales, so given the sales forecast we can forecast operating current liabilities. Forecasting the other liability and equity items is more complicated, because these are affected by the firm's financial policies, which can vary widely. We explain one fairly typical set of financial policies below, and we go through the calculations in detail in the chapter spreadsheet model, *CF2 Ch 12 Tool Kit.xls*. However, there are many other possible policies. The Web Extension to this chapter describes a procedure that can be used to develop a model to fit any set of financial policies.

First, note that most mature companies rarely issue new common stock, so the forecast for common stock is usually the previous year's common stock.

Second, most firms increase their dividends at a fairly steady rate, which allows us to forecast dividend payments; see Chapter 15 for a discussion of dividend policy. Subtracting forecasted dividends from forecasted net income gives the additions to retained earnings, which allows us to specify the forecasted amount of total common equity.

Third, most firms do not use preferred stock, and those that do issue it infrequently. Therefore, we assume that the forecasted preferred stock is equal to last year's preferred stock.

Fourth, issuing more long-term bonds is a major event for most firms, and it often requires approval from the board of directors. Chapter 15 discusses long-term debt financing in detail, but for now we simply assume that MicroDrive will not issue any new long-term debt, at least in the initial forecast.

Fifth, many firms use short-term bank loans, shown on the balance sheet as notes payable, as a financial "shock absorber." When extra funding is needed, they draw down their lines of credit, thus increasing notes payable, until their short-term debt has risen to an unacceptably high level, at which point they arrange long-term financing. When they secure the long-term financing, they pay off some of their short-term debt to bring it down to an acceptable level. We will explain how to forecast the final level of notes payable shortly, but initially we assume that MicroDrive will simply maintain its current level of notes payable.

At this point, all of the items on the liability and equity side of the balance sheet have been specified. If we were extraordinarily lucky, the sources of financing would exactly equal the required assets. In this case, we would have exactly enough financing to acquire the assets needed to support the forecasted level of sales. But in all our years of forecasting, we have never had this happen, and you probably won't be any luckier. Therefore, we define the term **additional funds needed (AFN)** as the required assets minus the specified sources of financing. If the required additional financing is positive, then we need to raise additional funds, and we "plug" this amount into the balance sheet as additional notes payable. For example, suppose the required assets equal $2,500 million and the specified sources of financing total $2,400 million. The required additional financing is $2,500 − $2,400 = $100 million. We assume that the firm would raise this $100 million as notes payable, thus increasing the old notes payable by $100 million.

If the AFN were negative, this would mean that we are forecasting having more capital than we need. Initially, we assume that any extra funds will be used to purchase additional short-term investments, so we would "plug" the amount (the absolute value of the AFN) into short-term investments on the asset side of the balance sheet. For example, suppose the required assets equal only $2,200 million and the specified sources of financing total $2,400 million. The required additional financing is $2,200 − $2,400 = −$200 million. Thus, the firm would have an extra $200 million that it could use to purchase short-term investments. Notice that total assets would now equal $2,200 + $200 = $2,400 million, which is exactly equal to the total sources of financing.

Before we apply this model to MicroDrive, a couple of points are worth noting. First, financial policies are not etched in stone. For example, if the forecast is for a very large need for financing, the firm might decide to issue more long-term debt or equity rather than finance the entire shortfall with notes payable. Similarly, a company with negative required additional financing might decide to use the funds to pay a special dividend, to pay off some of its debt, or even to buy back some of its stock. As we discuss, managers generally go over the initial forecast and then go back and make changes to the plan. Financial planning is truly an iterative process—managers formulate a plan, analyze the results, modify either the operating plan or their financial policies, observe the new results, and repeat the process until they are comfortable with the forecast.

Second, the plug approach that we outlined specifies the additional amount of *either* notes payable or short-term investments, but not both. If the AFN is positive, we assume that the firm will add to notes payable but leave short-term investments at their current level. If the AFN is negative, it will add to short-term investments but not to notes payable. Now let's apply these concepts to MicroDrive.

FORECAST OPERATING ASSETS As noted earlier, MicroDrive's assets must increase if sales are to increase. The company's most recent ratio of cash to sales was approximately 0.33 percent ($10/$3,000 = 0.003333), and management believes this ratio should remain constant. Therefore, the forecasted cash balance, shown in Row 1 of Table 12-3, is 0.003333($3,300) = $11 million.

TABLE 12-3 | MicroDrive Inc.: Actual and Projected Balance Sheets (Millions of Dollars)

	Actual 2005 (1)	Forecast Basis (2)	Forecast for 2006 (3)
Assets			
1. Cash	$ 10.0	0.33% × 2006 Sales =	$ 11.0
2. Short-term investments	0.0	Previous plus "plug" if needed	0.0
3. Accounts receivable	375.0	12.50% × 2006 Sales =	412.5
4. Inventories	615.0	20.50% × 2006 Sales =	676.5
5. Total current assets	$1,000.0		$1,100.0
6. Net plant and equipment	1,000.0	33.33% × 2006 Sales =	1,100.0
7. Total assets	$2,000.0		$2,200.0
Liabilities and Equity			
8. Accounts payable	$ 60.0	2.00% × 2006 Sales =	$ 66.0
9. Accruals	140.0	4.67% × 2006 Sales =	154.0
10. Notes payable	110.0	Previous plus "plug" if needed	224.7
11. Total current liabilities	$ 310.0		$ 444.7
12. Long-term bonds	754.0	Same: no new issue	754.0
13. Total liabilities	$1,064.0		$1,198.7
14. Preferred stock	40.0	Same: no new issue	40.0
15. Common stock	130.0	Same: no new issue	130.0
16. Retained earnings	766.0	2005 RE + 2006 Additions to RE =	831.3
17. Total common equity	896.0		961.3
18. Total liabilities and equity	$2,000.0		$2,200.0
19. Required assets[a]			$2,200.0
20. Specified sources of financing[b]			2,085.3
21. Additional funds needed (AFN)			$ 114.7
22. Required additional notes payable			$ 114.7
23. Additional short-term investments			0.0

[a]Required assets include all of the forecasted operating assets, plus short-term investments from the previous year.

[b]Specified sources of financing include forecasted operating current liabilities, forecasted long-term bonds, forecasted preferred stock, forecasted common equity, and the amount of notes payable from the previous year.

The ratio of accounts receivable to sales was $375/$3,000 = 0.125 = 12.5 percent. For now we assume that the credit policy and customers' paying patterns will remain constant, so the forecast for accounts receivable is 0.125($3,300) = $412.5 million, as shown in Row 3.

The most recent inventory to sales ratio was $615/$3,000 = 0.205 = 20.5 percent. Assuming no change in MicroDrive's inventory policy, the forecasted inventory is 0.205($3,300) = $676.5 million, as shown in Row 4.

The ratio of net plant and equipment to sales was $1,000/$3,000 = 0.3333 = 33.33 percent. MicroDrive's net plant and equipment have grown fairly steadily in the past, and its managers expect steady future growth. Therefore, they forecast that they will need net plant and equipment of 0.3333($3,300) = $1,100 million.

Next, we make the temporary assumption that short-term investments will remain at their current level. We will return to this point after we forecast the rest of the balance sheet.

FORECAST OPERATING CURRENT LIABILITIES   As noted earlier, operating current liabilities are called **spontaneously generated funds** because they increase automatically, as sales increase. MicroDrive's most recent ratio of accounts payable to sales was $60/$3,000 = 0.02 = 2 percent. Assuming that the payables policy will not change, the forecasted level of accounts payable is 0.02($3,300) = $66 million as shown in Row 8. The most recent ratio of accruals to sales was $140/$3,000 = 0.0467 = 4.67 percent. There is no reason to expect a change in this ratio, so the forecasted level of accruals is 0.0467($3,300) = $154 million.

FORECAST ITEMS DETERMINED BY FINANCIAL POLICY DECISIONS   In its initial financial plan, MicroDrive kept long-term debt at the 2005 level, as shown in Row 12. The company's policy is to not issue any additional shares of preferred or common stock barring extraordinary circumstances. Therefore, its forecasts for preferred and common stock, shown in Rows 14 and 15, are the 2005 levels. MicroDrive plans to increase its dividend per share by about 8 percent per year. As shown in Row 15 in Table 12-2, this policy, when combined with the forecasted level of net income, results in a $65.3 million addition to retained earnings. On the balance sheet, the forecasted level of retained earnings is equal to the 2005 retained earnings plus the forecasted addition to retained earnings, or $766.0 + $65.3 = $831.3 million. Again, note that we make the temporary assumption that notes payable remain at their 2005 level.

Step 4. Raising the Additional Funds Needed

Based on the forecasted balance sheet, MicroDrive will need $2,200 million of operating assets to support its forecasted $3,300 million of sales. We define required assets as the sum of its forecasted operating assets plus the previous amount of short-term investments. Since MicroDrive had no short-term investments in 2005, its required assets are simply $2,200 million, as shown in Row 19 of Table 12-3.

We define the specified sources of financing as the sum of forecasted levels of operating current liabilities, long-term debt, preferred stock, and common equity, plus notes payable carried over from the previous year:

Accounts payable	$ 66.0
Accruals	154.0
Notes payable (carryover)	110.0
Long-term bonds	754.0
Preferred stock	40.0
Common stock	130.0
Retained earnings	831.3
Total	$2,085.3

Based on its required assets and specified sources of financing, MicroDrive's AFN is $2,200 − $2,085.3 = $114.7 million, as shown in Rows 19, 20, and 21 of Table 12-3. Because the AFN is positive, MicroDrive needs $114.7 million of additional financing, and its initial financial policy is to obtain these funds as notes payable. Therefore, we add $114.7 million into notes payable (Row 10 of Table 12-3), bringing the forecasted total to $110 + $114.7 = $224.7 million. Because we added notes payable, we don't add any short-term investment, and so this completes the initial forecast. Now it is time to analyze the plan and consider potential changes.

Analysis of the Forecast

The 2006 forecast as developed above is only the first part of MicroDrive's total forecasting process. We must next examine the projected statements and determine whether the forecast meets the financial targets as set forth in the five-year financial plan. If the statements do not meet the targets, then elements of the forecast must be changed.

Table 12-4 shows MicroDrive's most recent actual ratios, its projected ratios, and the latest industry average ratios. (The table also shows a "Revised Forecast" in the third column, which we will discuss later. Disregard the revised data for now.) The firm's financial condition at the close of 2005 was weak, with many ratios being well below the industry averages. For example, MicroDrive's current ratio, based on Column 1 of Table 12-4, was only 3.2 versus 4.2 for an average competitor.

The "Inputs" section shown on the top three rows of the table provides data on three of the model's key drivers: (1) costs (excluding depreciation) as a percentage of sales, (2) accounts receivable as a percentage of sales, and (3) inventory as a percentage of sales. The preliminary forecast in Column 2 assumes these variables remain constant. While MicroDrive's cost-to-sales ratio is only slightly worse than the industry average, its ratios of accounts receivable to sales and inventory to sales are significantly higher than those of its competitors. Its investment in inventories and receivables is too high, causing its returns on assets, equity, and invested capital as shown in the lower part of the table to be too low. Therefore, MicroDrive should make operational changes designed to reduce its current assets.

The "Ratios" section of Table 12-4 provides more details regarding the firm's weaknesses. MicroDrive's asset management ratios are much worse than the industry averages. For example, its total assets turnover ratio is 1.5 versus an industry average of 1.8. Its poor asset management ratios drag down the return on invested capital (9.5 percent for MicroDrive versus 11.4 percent for the industry average). Furthermore, MicroDrive must carry more than the average amount of debt to support its excessive assets, and the extra interest expense reduces its profit margin to 3.9 percent versus 5.0 percent for the industry. Much of the debt is short term, and this results in a current ratio of 2.5 versus the 4.2 industry average. These problems will persist unless management takes action to improve things.

After reviewing its preliminary forecast, management decided to take three steps to improve its financial condition: (1) It decided to lay off some workers and close certain operations. It forecasted that these steps would lower operating costs (excluding depreciation) from the current 87.2 to 86 percent of sales as shown in Column 3 of Table 12-4. (2) By screening credit customers more closely and being more aggressive in collecting past-due accounts, the company believes it can reduce the ratio of accounts receivable to sales from 12.5 to 11.8 percent. (3) Finally, management thinks it can reduce the inventory-to-sales ratio from 20.5 to 16.7 percent through the use of tighter inventory controls.[4]

These projected operational changes were then used to create a revised set of forecasted statements for 2006. We do not show the new financial statements, but the revised ratios

---

[4] We will discuss receivables and inventory management in detail in Chapter 16.

TABLE 12-4 | Model Inputs, AFN, and Key Ratios (Millions of Dollars)

	Actual 2005 (1)	Preliminary Forecast for 2006 (2)	Revised Forecast for 2006 (3)	Industry Average 2005 (4)
Model Inputs				
Costs (excluding depreciation) as percentage of sales	87.2%	87.2%	86.0%	87.1%
Accounts receivable as percentage of sales	12.5	12.5	11.8	10.0
Inventory as percentage of sales	20.5	20.5	16.7	11.1
Model Outputs				
NOPAT (net operating profit after taxes)[a]	$170.3	$187.4	$211.2	
Net operating working capital[b]	$800.0	$880.0	$731.5	
Total operating capital[c]	$1,800.0	$1,980.0	$1,831.5	
Free cash flow (FCF)[d]	($174.7)	$7.4	$179.7	
AFN		$114.7	($57.5)	
Ratios				
Current ratio	3.2×	2.5×	3.1×	4.2×
Inventory turnover	4.9×	4.9×	6.0×	9.0×
Days sales outstanding	45.6×	45.6×	43.1×	36.0×
Total assets turnover	1.5×	1.5×	1.6×	1.8×
Debt ratio	53.2%	54.5%	51.4%	40.0%
Profit margin	3.8%	3.9%	4.6%	5.0%
Return on assets	5.7%	5.8%	7.2%	9.0%
Return on equity	12.7%	13.3%	15.4%	15.0%
Return on invested capital (NOPAT/Total operating capital)	9.5%	9.5%	11.5%	11.4%

[a]NOPAT = EBIT × (1 − T) from Table 12-2.
[b]Net operating working capital = Cash + Accounts receivable + Inventories − Accounts payable − Accruals from Table 12-3.
[c]Total operating capital = Net operating working capital + Net plant and equipment from Table 12-3.
[d]Free cash flow = NOPAT − Investment in total operating capital.

e-resource

See CF2 Ch 12 Tool Kit.xls for details.

are shown in the third column of Table 12-4. You can see the details in the chapter spreadsheet model, **CF2 Ch 12 Tool Kit.xls.** Here are the highlights of the revised forecast:

1. The reduction in operating costs improved the 2006 NOPAT, or net operating profit after taxes, by $23.8 million. Even more impressive, the improvements in the receivables policy and in inventory management reduced receivables and inventories by $148.5 million. The net result of the increase in NOPAT and the reduction of operating current assets was a very large increase in free cash flow for 2006, from a previously estimated $7.4 million to $179.7 million.

2. The profit margin improved to 4.6 percent. However, the firm's profit margin still lagged the industry average because its high debt ratio results in higher-than-average interest payments.

3. The increase in the profit margin resulted in an increase in projected retained earnings. More importantly, by tightening inventory controls and reducing the days sales outstanding, MicroDrive projected a reduction in inventories and receivables. Taken together, these actions resulted in a *negative* AFN of $57.5 million, which

means that MicroDrive would actually generate $57.5 million more from internal operations and its financing plan than it needs for new assets. Under its current financial policy, MicroDrive would have $110 million in notes payable (the amount it carried over from the previous year) and $57.5 million in short-term investments. (Note: MicroDrive's managers considered using the $57.5 million to pay down some of the debt but decided instead to keep it as a liquid asset, which gives them the flexibility to quickly fund any new projects created by their R&D department.) The net effect is a significant reduction in MicroDrive's debt ratio, although it is still above the industry average.

4. These actions would also raise the rate of return on assets from 5.8 to 7.2 percent, and they would boost the return on equity from 13.3 to 15.4 percent, which is even higher than the industry average.

Although MicroDrive's managers believed that the revised forecast is achievable, they were not sure of this. Accordingly, they wanted to know how variations in sales would affect the forecast. Therefore, they ran a spreadsheet model using several different sales growth rates, and analyzed the results to see how the ratios would change under different growth scenarios. To illustrate, if the sales growth rate increased from 10 to 20 percent, the AFN would change dramatically, from a $57.5 million *surplus* to an $89.8 million *shortfall* because more assets would be required to finance the additional sales.

The spreadsheet model was also used to evaluate dividend policy. If MicroDrive decided to reduce its dividend growth rate, then additional funds would be generated, and those funds could be invested in plant, equipment, and inventories; used to reduce debt; or used to repurchase stock.

We see, then, that forecasting is an iterative process. For planning purposes, the financial staff develops a preliminary forecast based on a continuation of past policies and trends. This provides a starting point, or "baseline" forecast. Next, the projections are modified to see what effects alternative operating plans would have on the firm's earnings and financial condition. This results in a revised forecast. Then alternative operating plans are examined under different sales growth scenarios, and the model is used to evaluate both dividend policy and capital structure decisions.

Finally, the projected statements can be used to estimate the effect of different plans on MicroDrive's stock price. This is called value-based management, and is covered in Chapter 13.

SELF-TEST QUESTIONS
What is the AFN, and how is the percent of sales method used to estimate it?
Why do accounts payable and accruals provide "spontaneous funds" to a growing firm?

THE AFN FORMULA

Most firms forecast their capital requirements by constructing pro forma income statements and balance sheets as described above. However, if the ratios are expected to remain constant, then the following formula can be used to forecast financial requirements. Here we apply the formula to MicroDrive based on the 2005 data, not the revised data, as the revised data do not assume constant ratios.

Additional funds needed	=	Required increase in assets	−	Spontaneous increase in liabilities	−	Increase in retained earnings	(12-1)
AFN	=	$(A^*/S_0)\Delta S$	−	$(L^*/S_0)\Delta S$	−	$MS_1(RR).$	

The symbols in Equation 12-1 are defined below:

AFN = additional funds needed.

A^* = assets that are tied directly to sales, hence must increase if sales are to increase. Note that A designates total assets and A^* designates those assets that must increase if sales are to increase. When the firm is operating at full capacity, as is the case here, $A^* = A$. Often, though, A^* and A are not equal, and either the equation must be modified or we must use the projected financial statement method.

S_0 = sales during the last year.

A^*/S_0 = percentage of required assets to sales, which also shows the required dollar increase in assets per \$1 increase in sales. $A^*/S_0 = \$2,000/\$3,000 = 0.6667$ for MicroDrive. Thus, for every \$1 increase in sales, assets must increase by about 67 cents.

L^* = liabilities that increase spontaneously. L^* is normally much less than total liabilities (L). Spontaneous liabilities include accounts payable and accruals, but not bank loans and bonds.

L^*/S_0 = liabilities that increase spontaneously as a percentage of sales, or spontaneously generated financing per \$1 increase in sales. $L^*/S_0 = (\$60 + \$140)/\$3,000 = 0.0667$ for MicroDrive. Thus, every \$1 increase in sales generates about 7 cents of spontaneous financing.

S_1 = total sales projected for next year. Note that S_0 designates last year's sales, and $S_1 = \$3,300$ million for MicroDrive.

ΔS = change in sales $= S_1 - S_0 = \$3,300$ million $- \$3,000$ million $= \$300$ million for MicroDrive.

M = profit margin, or profit per \$1 of sales. $M = \$114/\$3,000 = 0.0380$ for MicroDrive. So, MicroDrive earns 3.8 cents on each dollar of sales.

RR = retention ratio, which is the percentage of net income that is retained. For MicroDrive, $RR = \$56/\$114 = 0.491$. RR is also equal to $1 -$ payout ratio, since the retention ratio and the payout ratio must total to $1.0 = 100\%$.

Inserting values for MicroDrive into Equation 12-1, we find the additional funds needed to be \$118 million:

$$AFN = \begin{bmatrix} \text{Required} \\ \text{asset} \\ \text{increase} \end{bmatrix} - \begin{bmatrix} \text{Spontaneous} \\ \text{liability} \\ \text{increase} \end{bmatrix} - \begin{bmatrix} \text{Increase} \\ \text{in retained} \\ \text{earnings} \end{bmatrix}$$

$$= 0.667(\Delta S) - 0.067(\Delta S) - 0.038(S_1)(0.491)$$
$$= 0.667(\$300 \text{ million}) - 0.067(\$300 \text{ million})$$
$$\quad - 0.038(\$3,300 \text{ million})(0.491)$$
$$= \$200 \text{ million} - \$20 \text{ million} - \$62 \text{ million}$$
$$= \$118 \text{ million}.$$

To increase sales by \$300 million, the formula suggests that MicroDrive must increase assets by \$200 million. The \$200 million of new assets must be financed in some manner. Of the total, \$20 million will come from a spontaneous increase in liabilities, while another \$62 million will be obtained from retained earnings. The remaining \$118 million must be raised from external sources. This value is an approximation, but it is only slightly different from the AFN figure (\$114.7 million) we developed in Table 12-3.

The AFN equation shows that external financing requirements depend on five key factors:

- **Sales growth (ΔS).** Rapidly growing companies require large increases in assets, and more external financing, other things held constant.

- **Capital intensity (A^*/S_0).** The amount of assets required per dollar of sales, A^*/S_0 in Equation 12-1, is called the **capital intensity ratio.** This ratio has a major effect on capital requirements. Companies with higher assets-to-sales ratios require more assets for a given increase in sales, hence a greater need for external financing.
- **Spontaneous liabilities-to-sales ratio (L^*/S_0).** Companies that spontaneously generate a large amount of liabilities from accounts payable and accruals will have a relatively lower need for external financing.
- **Profit margin (M).** The higher the profit margin, the larger the net income available to support increases in assets, hence the lower the need for external financing.
- **Retention ratio (RR).** Companies that retain more of their earnings as opposed to paying them out as dividends will generate more retained earnings and thus have less need for external financing.

Note that Equation 12-1 provides an accurate forecast only for companies whose ratios are all expected to remain constant. It is useful to obtain a quick "back of the envelope" estimate of external financing requirements for nonconstant ratio companies, but in the planning process one should calculate the actual additional funds needed by the projected financial statement method.

SELF-TEST QUESTIONS If all ratios are expected to remain constant, a formula can be used to forecast AFN. Give the formula and briefly explain it.

How do the following factors affect external capital requirements: (1) retention ratio, (2) capital intensity, and (3) profit margin?

FORECASTING FINANCIAL REQUIREMENTS WHEN THE BALANCE SHEET RATIOS ARE SUBJECT TO CHANGE

Both the AFN formula and the projected financial statement method as we initially used it assume that the ratios of assets and liabilities to sales (A^*/S_0 and L^*/S_0) remain constant over time. This, in turn, requires the assumption that each "spontaneous" asset and liability item increases at the same rate as sales. In graph form, this implies the type of relationship shown in Panel a of Figure 12-2, a relationship that is (1) linear and (2) passes through the origin. Under those conditions, if the company's sales increase from $200 million to $400 million, or by 100 percent, inventory will also increase by 100 percent, from $100 million to $200 million.

The assumption of constant ratios and identical growth rates is appropriate at times, but there are times when it is incorrect. Three such conditions are described in the following sections.

Economies of Scale

There are economies of scale in the use of many kinds of assets, and when economies occur, the ratios are likely to change over time as the size of the firm increases. For example, retailers often need to maintain base stocks of different inventory items, even if current sales are quite low. As sales expand, inventories may then grow less rapidly than sales, so the ratio of inventory to sales (I/S) declines. This situation is depicted in Panel b of Figure 12-2. Here we see that the inventory/sales ratio is 1.5, or 150 percent, when sales are $200 million, but the ratio declines to 1.0 when sales climb to $400 million.

The relationship in Panel b is linear, but nonlinear relationships often exist. Indeed, if the firm uses one popular model for establishing inventory levels (the EOQ model), its inventories will rise with the square root of sales. This situation is shown in Panel c of Figure 12-2, which shows a curved line whose slope decreases at higher sales levels. In this situation, very large increases in sales would require very little additional inventory.

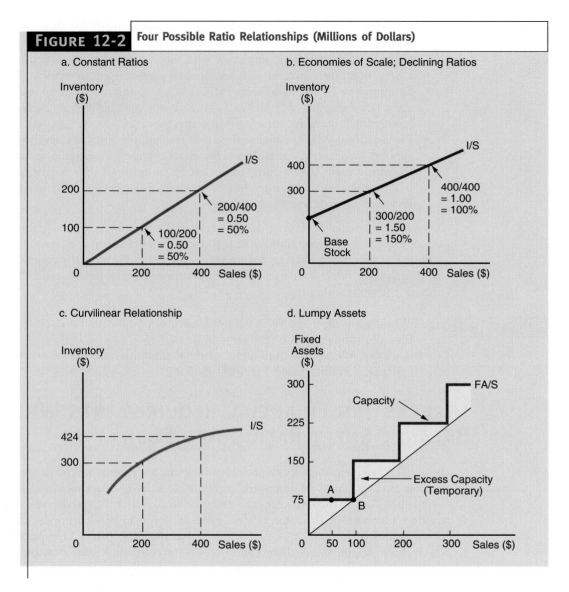

FIGURE 12-2 Four Possible Ratio Relationships (Millions of Dollars)

a. Constant Ratios

b. Economies of Scale; Declining Ratios

c. Curvilinear Relationship

d. Lumpy Assets

CF

e-resource

See the Web Extension to this chapter for more on forecasting when variables are not proportional to sales.

Lumpy Assets

In many industries, technological considerations dictate that if a firm is to be competitive, it must add fixed assets in large, discrete units; such assets are often referred to as **lumpy assets.** In the paper industry, for example, there are strong economies of scale in basic paper mill equipment, so when a paper company expands capacity, it must do so in large, lumpy increments. This type of situation is depicted in Panel d of Figure 12-2. Here we assume that the minimum economically efficient plant has a cost of $75 million, and that such a plant can produce enough output to reach a sales level of $100 million. If the firm is to be competitive, it simply must have at least $75 million of fixed assets.

Lumpy assets have a major effect on the fixed assets/sales (FA/S) ratio at different sales levels and, consequently, on financial requirements. At Point A in Panel d, which represents a sales level of $50 million, the fixed assets are $75 million, so the ratio FA/S = $75/$50 = 1.5. Sales can expand by $50 million, out to $100 million, with no additions to fixed assets. At that point, represented by Point B, the ratio FA/S = $75/$100 = 0.75.

However, since the firm is operating at capacity (sales of $100 million), even a small increase in sales would require a doubling of plant capacity, so a small projected sales increase would bring with it a very large financial requirement.[5]

Excess Capacity Adjustments

Consider again the MicroDrive example set forth in Tables 12-2 and 12-3, but now assume that excess capacity exists in fixed assets. Specifically, assume that fixed assets in 2005 were being utilized to only 96 percent of capacity. If fixed assets had been used to full capacity, 2005 sales could have been as high as $3,125 million versus the $3,000 million in actual sales:

$$\text{Full capacity sales} = \frac{\text{Actual sales}}{\text{Percentage of capacity at which fixed assets were operated}} \quad (12\text{-}2)$$

$$= \frac{\$3,000 \text{ million}}{0.96} = \$3,125 \text{ million}.$$

This suggests that MicroDrive's target fixed assets/sales ratio should be 32 percent rather than 33.3 percent:

$$\text{Target fixed assets/Sales} = \frac{\text{Actual fixed assets}}{\text{Full capacity sales}} \quad (12\text{-}3)$$

$$= \frac{\$1,000}{\$3,125} = 0.32 = 32\%.$$

Therefore, if sales are to increase to $3,300 million, then fixed assets would have to increase to $1,056 million:

$$\text{Required level of fixed assets} = (\text{Target fixed assets/Sales})(\text{Projected sales}) \quad (12\text{-}4)$$

$$= 0.32(\$3,300) = \$1,056 \text{ million}.$$

We previously forecasted that MicroDrive would need to increase fixed assets at the same rate as sales, or by 10 percent. That meant an increase from $1,000 million to $1,100 million, or by $100 million. Now we see that the actual required increase is only from $1,000 million to $1,056 million, or by $56 million. Thus, the capacity-adjusted forecast is $100 million − $56 million = $44 million less than the earlier forecast. With a smaller fixed asset requirement, the projected AFN would decline from an estimated $118 million to $118 million − $44 million = $74 million.

Note also that when excess capacity exists, sales can grow to the capacity sales as determined above with no increase in fixed assets, but sales beyond that level will require

---

[5] Several other points should be noted about Panel d of Figure 12-2. First, if the firm is operating at a sales level of $100 million or less, any expansion that calls for a sales increase above $100 million would require a *doubling* of the firm's fixed assets. A much smaller percentage increase would be involved if the firm were large enough to be operating a number of plants. Second, firms generally go to multiple shifts and take other actions to minimize the need for new fixed asset capacity as they approach Point B. However, these efforts can only go so far, and eventually a fixed asset expansion will be required. Third, firms often make arrangements to share excess capacity with other firms in their industry. For example, the situation in the electric utility industry is very much like that depicted in Panel d. However, electric companies often build jointly owned plants, or else they "take turns" building plants, and then they buy power from or sell power to other utilities to avoid building new plants that would be underutilized.

fixed asset additions as calculated in our example. The same situation could occur with respect to inventories, and the required additions would be determined in exactly the same manner as for fixed assets. Theoretically, the same situation could occur with other types of assets, but as a practical matter excess capacity normally exists only with respect to fixed assets and inventories.

SELF-TEST QUESTIONS | Explain how economies of scale and lumpy asset acquisition affect financial forecasting. If excess capacity exists, how will that affect the AFN?

SUMMARY

The key concepts covered are listed below:
- **Financial forecasting** generally begins with a forecast of the firm's sales, in terms of both units and dollars.
- Either the **projected,** or **pro forma, financial statement method** or the **AFN formula method** can be used to forecast financial requirements. The financial statement method is more reliable, and it also provides ratios that can be used to evaluate alternative business plans.
- A firm can determine its **additional funds needed (AFN)** by estimating the amount of new assets necessary to support the forecasted level of sales and then subtracting from that amount the spontaneous funds that will be generated from operations. The firm can then plan how to raise the AFN most efficiently.
- The **higher a firm's sales growth rate,** the **greater** will be its need for additional financing. Similarly, the **smaller its retention ratio,** the **greater** its need for additional funds.
- Adjustments must be made if **economies of scale** exist in the use of assets, if **excess capacity** exists, or if assets must be added in **lumpy increments.**
- **Linear regression** and **excess capacity adjustments** can be used to forecast asset requirements in situations where assets are not expected to grow at the same rate as sales.

QUESTIONS

(12-1) Define each of the following terms:
   a. Operating plan; financial plan; sales forecast
   b. Pro forma financial statement; percent of sales method
   c. Spontaneously generated funds
   d. Additional funds needed (AFN); AFN formula; capital intensity ratio
   e. Lumpy assets

(12-2) Certain liability and net worth items generally increase spontaneously with increases in sales. Put a check (√) by those items that typically increase spontaneously:

Accounts payable	_____	Mortgage bonds	_____
Notes payable to banks	_____	Common stock	_____
Accrued wages	_____	Retained earnings	_____
Accrued taxes	_____		

(12-3) The following equation can, under certain assumptions, be used to forecast financial requirements:

$$AFN = (A^*/S_0)(\Delta S) - (L^*/S_0)(\Delta S) - MS_1(RR).$$

Under what conditions does the equation give satisfactory predictions, and when should it *not* be used?

(12-4) Suppose a firm makes the following policy changes. If the change means that external, nonspontaneous financial requirements (AFN) will increase, indicate this by a (+); indicate a decrease by a (−); and indicate indeterminate or no effect by a (0). Think in terms of the immediate, short-run effect on funds requirements.

a. The dividend payout ratio is increased. _____

b. The firm decides to pay all suppliers on delivery, rather than after a 30-day delay, to take advantage of discounts for rapid payment. _____

c. The firm begins to sell on credit (previously all sales had been on a cash basis). _____

d. The firm's profit margin is eroded by increased competition; sales are steady. _____

SELF-TEST PROBLEMS   Solutions Appear in Appendix A

(ST-1)
Growth Rate

Weatherford Industries Inc. has the following ratios: $A^*/S_0 = 1.6$; $L^*/S_0 = 0.4$; profit margin = 0.10; and dividend payout ratio = 0.45, or 45 percent. Sales last year were $100 million. Assuming that these ratios will remain constant, use the AFN formula to determine the maximum growth rate Weatherford can achieve without having to employ nonspontaneous external funds.

(ST-2)
Additional Funds
Needed

Suppose Weatherford's financial consultants report (1) that the inventory turn-over ratio is sales/inventory = 3 times versus an industry average of 4 times and (2) that Weatherford could reduce inventories and thus raise its turnover to 4 without affecting sales, the profit margin, or the other asset turnover ratios. Under these conditions, use the AFN formula to determine the amount of additional funds Weatherford would require during each of the next 2 years if sales grew at a rate of 20 percent per year.

(ST-3)
Excess Capacity

Van Auken Lumber's 2005 financial statements are shown below.

Van Auken Lumber: Balance Sheet as of December 31, 2005 (Thousands of Dollars)

Cash	$ 1,800	Accounts payable	$ 7,200
Receivables	10,800	Notes payable	3,472
Inventories	12,600	Accruals	2,520
Total current assets	$25,200	Total current liabilities	$13,192
Net fixed assets	21,600	Mortgage bonds	5,000
		Common stock	2,000
		Retained earnings	26,608
Total assets	$46,800	Total liabilities and equity	$46,800

Van Auken Lumber: Income Statement for December 31, 2005 (Thousands of Dollars)

Sales	$36,000
Operating costs	30,783
Earnings before interest and taxes	$ 5,217
Interest	1,017
Earnings before taxes	$ 4,200
Taxes (40%)	1,680
Net income	$ 2,520
Dividends (60%)	$ 1,512
Addition to retained earnings	$ 1,008

a. Assume that the company was operating at full capacity in 2005 with regard to all items *except* fixed assets; fixed assets in 2005 were being utilized to only 75 percent of capacity. By what percentage could 2006 sales increase over 2005 sales without the need for an increase in fixed assets?

b. Now suppose 2006 sales increase by 25 percent over 2005 sales. How much additional external capital will be required? Assume that Van Auken cannot sell any fixed assets. (Hint: Use the percent of sales method to develop a pro forma balance sheet and income statement as in Tables 12-2 and 12-3.) Assume that any required financing is borrowed as notes payable. Use a 12 percent interest rate for all debt at the beginning of the year to forecast interest expense (cash does not earn interest), and use a pro forma income statement to determine the addition to retained earnings. (Another hint: Notes payable = $6,021.)

PROBLEMS

Carter Corporation's sales are expected to increase from $5 million in 2005 to $6 million in 2006, or by 20 percent. Its assets totaled $3 million at the end of 2005. Carter is at full capacity, so its assets must grow at the same rate as projected sales. At the end of 2005, current liabilities were $1 million, consisting of $250,000 of accounts payable, $500,000 of notes payable, and $250,000 of accruals. The after-tax profit margin is forecasted to be 5 percent, and the forecasted payout ratio is 70 percent. Use this information to answer Problems 12-1, 12-2, and 12-3.

(12-1)
AFN Formula
Use the AFN formula to forecast Carter's additional funds needed for the coming year.

(12-2)
AFN Formula
What would be the additional funds needed if the company's year-end 2005 assets had been $4 million? Assume that all other numbers are the same. Why is this AFN different from the one you found in Problem 12-1? Is the company's "capital intensity" the same or different?

(12-3)
AFN Formula
Return to the assumption that the company had $3 million in assets at the end of 2005, but now assume that the company pays no dividends. Under these assumptions, what would be the additional funds needed for the coming year? Why is this AFN different from the one you found in Problem 12-1?

(12-4)
Sales Increase
Pierce Furnishings generated $2.0 million in sales during 2005, and its year-end total assets were $1.5 million. Also, at year-end 2005, current liabilities were $500,000, consisting of $200,000 of notes payable, $200,000 of accounts payable, and $100,000 of accruals. Looking ahead to 2006, the company estimates that its assets must increase by 75 cents for every $1 increase in sales. Pierce's profit margin is 5 percent, and its payout ratio is 60 percent. How large a sales increase can the company achieve without having to raise funds externally?

(12-5)
Pro Forma Statements and Ratios
Upton Computers makes bulk purchases of small computers, stocks them in conveniently located warehouses, and ships them to its chain of retail stores. Upton's balance sheet as of December 31, 2005, is shown here (millions of dollars):

Cash	$ 3.5	Accounts payable	$ 9.0
Receivables	26.0	Notes payable	18.0
Inventories	58.0	Accruals	8.5
Total current assets	$ 87.5	Total current liabilities	$ 35.5
Net fixed assets	35.0	Mortgage loan	6.0
		Common stock	15.0
		Retained earnings	66.0
Total assets	$122.5	Total liabilities and equity	$122.5

Sales for 2005 were $350 million, while net income for the year was $10.5 million. Upton paid dividends of $4.2 million to common stockholders. The firm is operating at full capacity. Assume that all ratios remain constant.

a. If sales are projected to increase by $70 million, or 20 percent, during 2006, use the AFN equation to determine Upton's projected external capital requirements.

b. Construct Upton's pro forma balance sheet for December 31, 2006. Assume that all external capital requirements are met by bank loans and are reflected in notes payable. Assume Upton's profit margin and dividend payout ratio remain constant.

(12-6)
Additional Funds Needed

Stevens Textile's 2005 financial statements are shown below.

Stevens Textile: Balance Sheet as of December 31, 2005 (Thousands of Dollars)

Cash	$ 1,080	Accounts payable	$ 4,320
Receivables	6,480	Accruals	2,880
Inventories	9,000	Notes payable	2,100
Total current assets	$16,560	Total current liabilities	$ 9,300
Net fixed assets	12,600	Mortgage bonds	3,500
		Common stock	3,500
		Retained earnings	12,860
Total assets	$29,160	Total liabilities and equity	$29,160

Stevens Textile: Income Statement for December 31, 2005 (Thousands of Dollars)

Sales	$36,000
Operating costs	32,440
Earnings before interest and taxes	$ 3,560
Interest	460
Earnings before taxes	$ 3,100
Taxes (40%)	1,240
Net income	$ 1,860
Dividends (45%)	$ 837
Addition to retained earnings	$ 1,023

Suppose 2006 sales are projected to increase by 15 percent over 2005 sales. Determine the additional funds needed. Assume that the company was operating at full capacity in 2005, that it cannot sell off any of its fixed assets, and that any required financing will be borrowed as notes payable. Also, assume that assets, spontaneous liabilities, and operating costs are expected to increase by the same percentage as sales. Use the percent of sales method to develop a pro forma balance sheet and income statement for December 31, 2006. Use an interest rate of 10 percent on the balance of debt at the beginning of the year to compute interest (cash pays no interest). Use the pro forma income statement to determine the addition to retained earnings.

(12-7)
Additional Funds Needed

Garlington Technologies Inc.'s 2005 financial statements are shown below.

Garlington Technologies Inc.: Balance Sheet as of December 31, 2005

Cash	$ 180,000	Accounts payable	$ 360,000
Receivables	360,000	Notes payable	156,000
Inventories	720,000	Accruals	180,000
Total current assets	$1,260,000	Total current liabilities	$ 696,000
Fixed assets	1,440,000	Common stock	1,800,000
		Retained earnings	204,000
Total assets	$2,700,000	Total liabilities and equity	$2,700,000

Garlington Technologies Inc.: Income Statement for December 31, 2005

Sales	$3,600,000
Operating costs	3,279,720
EBIT	$ 320,280
Interest	18,280
EBT	$ 302,000
Taxes (40%)	120,800
Net income	$ 181,200
Dividends	$ 108,000

Suppose that in 2006 sales increase by 10 percent over 2005 sales and that 2006 dividends will increase to $112,000. Construct the pro forma financial statements using the percent of sales method. Assume the firm operated at full capacity in 2005. Use an interest rate of 13 percent on the debt balance at the beginning of the year. Assume that the AFN will be in the form of notes payable.

(12-8)   At year-end 2005, total assets for Bertin Inc. were $1.2 million and accounts payable
Long-Term Financing   were $375,000. Sales, which in 2005 were $2.5 million, are expected to increase by
Needed   25 percent in 2006. Total assets and accounts payable are proportional to sales and that relationship will be maintained. Bertin typically uses no current liabilities other than accounts payable. Common stock amounted to $425,000 in 2005, and retained earnings were $295,000. Bertin plans to sell new common stock in the amount of $75,000. The firm's profit margin on sales is 6 percent; 40 percent of earnings will be paid out as dividends.
    a. What was Bertin's total debt in 2005?
    b. How much new, long-term debt financing will be needed in 2006? (Hint: AFN − New stock = New long-term debt.) Do not consider any financing feedback effects.

(12-9)   The Booth Company's sales are forecasted to increase from $1,000 in 2005 to
Additional Funds Needed $2,000 in 2006. Here is the December 31, 2005, balance sheet:

Cash	$ 100	Accounts payable	$ 50
Accounts receivable	200	Notes payable	150
Inventories	200	Accruals	50
Net fixed assets	500	Long-term debt	400
		Common stock	100
		Retained earnings	250
Total assets	$1,000	Total liabilities and equity	$1,000

Booth's fixed assets were used to only 50 percent of capacity during 2005, but its current assets were at their proper levels. All assets except fixed assets increase at the same rate as sales, and fixed assets would also increase at the same rate if the current excess capacity did not exist. Booth's after-tax profit margin is forecasted to be 5 percent, and its payout ratio will be 60 percent. What is Booth's additional funds needed (AFN) for the coming year?

SPREADSHEET PROBLEM

(12-10)   Start with the partial model in the file *CF2 Ch 12 P10 Build a Model.xls* from the
Build a Model: Forecasting   textbook's Web site. Cumberland Industries' financial planners must forecast the
Financial Statements   company's financial results for the coming year. The forecast will be based on the percent of sales method, and any additional funds needed will be obtained by using a mix of notes payable, long-term debt, and common stock. No preferred stock will be

e-resource

issued. Data for the problem, including Cumberland Industries' balance sheet and income statement, can be found in the spreadsheet problem for Chapter 3. Use these data to answer the following questions.

a. Cumberland Industries has had the following sales since 2000. Assuming the historical trend continues, what will sales be in 2006?

Year	Sales
2000	$129,215,000
2001	180,901,000
2002	235,252,000
2003	294,065,000
2004	396,692,000
2005	455,150,000

Base your forecast on a spreadsheet regression analysis of the 2000–2005 sales. By what percentage are sales predicted to increase in 2006 over 2005? Is the sales growth rate increasing or decreasing?

b. Cumberland's management believes that the firm will actually experience a 20 percent increase in sales during 2006. Construct the 2006 pro forma financial statements. Cumberland will not issue any new stock or long-term bonds. Assume Cumberland will carry forward its current amounts of short-term investments and notes payable, prior to calculating AFN. Assume that any additional funds needed (AFN) will be raised as notes payable (if AFN is negative, Cumberland will purchase additional short-term investments). Use an interest rate of 9 percent for short-term debt (and for the interest income on short-term investments) and a rate of 11 percent for long-term debt. No interest is earned on cash. Use the beginning of year debt balances to calculate net interest expense. Assume dividends grow at an 8 percent rate.

c. Now create a graph that shows the sensitivity of AFN to the sales growth rate. To make this graph, compare the AFN at sales growth rates of 5, 10, 15, 20, 25, and 30 percent.

d. Calculate net operating working capital (NOWC), total operating capital, NOPAT, and operating cash flow (OCF) for 2005 and 2006. Also, calculate the free cash flow (FCF) for 2006.

e. Suppose Cumberland can reduce its inventory to sales ratio to 5 percent and its cost to sales ratio to 83 percent. What happens to AFN and FCF?

CYBERPROBLEM

Please go to our Web site, **http://ehrhardt.swlearning.com**, to access any Cyberproblems.

THOMSON ONE
Business School Edition

Please go to **http://ehrhardt.swlearning.com** to access any Thomson ONE—Business School Edition problems.

MINI CASE

Betty Simmons, the new financial manager of Southeast Chemicals (SEC), a Georgia producer of specialized chemicals for use in fruit orchards, must prepare a financial forecast for 2006. SEC's 2005 sales were $2 billion, and the marketing department is forecasting a 25 percent increase for 2006. Simmons thinks the company was operating at full capacity in 2005, but she is not sure about this. The 2005 financial statements, plus some other data, are shown below.

A. 2005 BALANCE SHEET (MILLIONS OF DOLLARS)

		Percent of Sales				Percent of Sales
Cash and securities	$ 20	1%	Accounts payable and accruals	$ 100	5%
Accounts receivable	240	12%	Notes payable	100	
Inventories	240	12%	Total current liabilities	$ 200	
Total current assets	$ 500		Long-term debt	100	
Net fixed assets	500	25%	Common stock	500	
			Retained earnings	200	
Total assets	$1,000		Total liabilities and equity	$1,000	

B. 2005 INCOME STATEMENT (MILLIONS OF DOLLARS)

		Percent of Sales
Sales	$2,000.00	
Cost of goods sold (COGS)	1,200.00	60%
Sales, general, and administrative costs (SGA)	700.00	35%
Earnings before interest and taxes	$ 100.00	
Interest	10.00	
Earnings before taxes	$ 90.00	
Taxes (40%)	36.00	
Net income	$ 54.00	
Dividends (40%)	21.60	
Addition to retained earnings	$ 32.40	

C. KEY RATIOS

	SEC	Industry
Profit margin	2.70%	4.00%
Return on equity	7.71	15.60
Days sales outstanding (365 days)	43.80 days	32.00 days
Inventory turnover	8.33×	11.00×
Fixed assets turnover	4.00	5.00
Debt/assets	30.00%	36.00%
Times interest earned	10×	9.40×
Current ratio	2.50	3.00
Return on invested capital (NOPAT/Operating capital)	6.67%	14.00%

   Assume that you were recently hired as Simmons's assistant, and your first major task is to help her develop the forecast. She asked you to begin by answering the following set of questions.

a. Describe three ways that pro forma statements are used in financial planning.

b. Explain the steps in financial forecasting.

c. Assume (1) that SEC was operating at full capacity in 2005 with respect to all assets, (2) that all assets must grow proportionally with sales, (3) that accounts payable and accruals will also grow in proportion to sales, and (4) that the 2005 profit margin and dividend payout will be maintained. Under these conditions, what will the company's financial requirements be for the coming year? Use the AFN equation to answer this question.

d. How would changes in these items affect the AFN: (1) sales increase? (2) the dividend payout ratio increases? (3) the profit margin increases? (4) the capital intensity ratio increases? and (5) SEC begins paying its suppliers sooner? (Consider each item separately and hold all other things constant.)

e. Briefly explain how to forecast financial statements using the percent of sales approach. Be sure to explain how to forecast interest expenses.

f. Now estimate the 2006 financial requirements using the percent of sales approach. Assume (1) that each type of asset, as well as payables, accruals, and fixed and variable costs, will be the same percent of sales in 2006 as in 2005; (2) that the payout ratio is held constant at 40 percent; (3) that external funds needed are financed 50 percent by notes payable and 50 percent by long-term debt (no new common stock will be issued); (4) that all debt carries an interest rate of 10 percent; and (5) interest expenses should be based on the balance of debt at the beginning of the year.

g. Why does the percent of sales approach produce a somewhat different AFN than the equation approach? Which method provides the more accurate forecast?

h. Calculate SEC's forecasted ratios, and compare them with the company's 2005 ratios and with the industry averages. Calculate SEC's forecasted free cash flow and return on invested capital (ROIC).

i. Based on comparisons between SEC's days sales outstanding (DSO) and inventory turnover ratios with the industry average figures, does it appear that SEC is operating efficiently with respect to its inventory and accounts receivable? Suppose SEC were able to bring these ratios into line with the industry averages and reduce its SGA/Sales ratio to 33 percent. What effect would this have on its AFN and its financial ratios? What effect would this have on free cash flow and ROIC?

j. Suppose you now learn that SEC's 2005 receivables and inventories were in line with required levels, given the firm's credit and inventory policies, but that excess capacity existed with regard to fixed assets. Specifically, fixed assets were operated at only 75 percent of capacity.

    (1) What level of sales could have existed in 2005 with the available fixed assets?

    (2) How would the existence of excess capacity in fixed assets affect the additional funds needed during 2006?

k. The relationship between sales and the various types of assets is important in financial forecasting. The percent of sales approach, under the assumption that each asset item grows at the same rate as sales, leads to an AFN forecast that is reasonably close to the forecast using the AFN equation. Explain how each of the following factors would affect the accuracy of financial forecasts based on the AFN equation: (1) economies of scale in the use of assets and (2) lumpy assets.

SELECTED ADDITIONAL REFERENCES AND CASES

For a more detailed explanation of financial forecasting and valuation, see

Daves, P., M. Ehrhardt, and R. Shrieves, *Corporate Valuation: A Guide for Managers and Investors* (Mason, OH: South-Western Publishing, 2004).

The heart of successful financial planning is the sales forecast. On this key subject, see

Hirschey, Mark, *Managerial Economics* (Mason, OH: South-Western Publishing, 2003).

Computer modeling is becoming increasingly important. For general references, see

Francis, Jack Clark, and Dexter R. Rowell, "A Simultaneous Equation Model of the Firm for Financial Analysis and Planning," *Financial Management,* Spring 1978, 29–44.

For an article on control, see

Bierman, Harold, "Beyond Cash Flow ROI," *Midland Corporate Finance Journal,* Winter 1988, 36–39.

The following cases from the Finance Online Case Library *cover many of the concepts discussed in this chapter and are available at* **http://www.textchoice.com:**

Case 37, "Space-Age Materials, Inc.," Case 38, "Automated Banking Management, Inc.," Case 38A, "Expert Systems," Case 38B, "Medical Management Systems, Inc.," and Case 63, "Dental Records, Inc.," which all focus on using the percent of sales forecasting method to forecast future financing requirements.

CHAPTER 13

Corporate Valuation, Value-Based Management, and Corporate Governance

For data on the NYSE Composite Index, go to *http:// www.nyse.com.* For data on Dell and Berkshire Hathaway, go to *http://finance .yahoo.com* and get quotes for DELL and BRKa.

If you had invested $1,000 in the NYSE Composite Index 10 years ago, your investment would have grown to $2,366, resulting in a 9.0 percent annual rate of return. Had you put the $1,000 in Berkshire Hathaway, you would now have $5,373, which is an 18.3 percent annual return. And if you had been really smart (or lucky) and invested in Dell, you would now have $100,912, which translates into a whopping 58.6 percent annual return! Berkshire Hathaway and Dell compete in very different industries and have very different strategies, yet both beat the market by sharing an operating philosophy: They created value for shareholders by focusing on the free cash flows of their underlying businesses. When this focus is applied systematically throughout a company, it is called value-based management, which is the central theme of this chapter.

Berkshire Hathaway's primary strategy has been to grow through acquisitions. Warren Buffett, Berkshire's CEO, wrote in a recent letter to shareholders that he seeks to own "businesses that generate cash and consistently earn above-average returns on their capital." When evaluating a potential acquisition, Buffett says he compares its purchase price with its "intrinsic value," which he defines as "the discounted value of the cash that can be taken out of a business during its remaining life." Thus, Buffett's growth strategy is governed by the principles of value-based management.

Instead of growing primarily through acquisitions, Dell has chosen to grow "organically" by expanding its existing businesses and developing new products and markets. For most companies, rapid growth in sales requires rapid growth in operating capital, which reduces free cash flow. But Dell is relentless in minimizing the amount of operating capital required to support sales. During the last five years, Dell's sales grew by 17.8 percent per year. However, Dell actually reduced its operating capital, largely because of reductions in inventory as a result of its build-to-order strategy and increases in its accounts payable. Even though its profit margin has fallen, it still exceeds the industry average. Thus, Dell has excelled at improving three primary drivers of value-based management: (1) Its sales growth rate was high. (2) Its profit margin exceeded the industry average. (3) Its capital requirements were held in check.

Sources: Various annual reports of Berkshire Hathaway Inc. and Dell Computers.

As we have emphasized throughout the book, maximizing shareholder value should be management's primary objective. However, to maximize value, managers need a tool for estimating the effects of alternative strategies. In this chapter, we develop and illustrate such a tool—the **corporate valuation model,** which is the present value of expected future free cash flows, discounted at the weighted average cost of capital. In a sense, the corporate valuation model is the culmination of all the material covered thus far, because it pulls together financial statements, cash flows, financial projections, time value of money, risk, and the cost of capital. Companies practice **value-based management** by systematically using the corporate valuation model to guide their decisions.

OVERVIEW OF CORPORATE VALUATION

e-resource

The textbook's Web site contains an Excel file that will guide you through the chapter's calculations. The file for this chapter is **CF2 Ch 13 Tool Kit.xls,** *and we encourage you to open the file and follow along as you read the chapter.*

As stated earlier, managers should evaluate the effects of alternative strategies on their firms' values. This really means forecasting financial statements under alternative strategies, finding the present value of each strategy's cash flow stream, and then choosing the strategy that provides the maximum value. The financial statements should be projected using the techniques and procedures discussed in Chapter 12, and the discount rate should be the risk-adjusted cost of capital as discussed in Chapter 9. But what model should managers use to discount the cash flows? One possibility is the dividend growth model from Chapter 7. However, that model is often unsuitable for managerial purposes. For example, suppose a startup company is formed to develop and market a new product. Its managers will focus on product development, marketing, and raising capital. They will probably be thinking about an eventual IPO, or perhaps the sale of the company to a larger firm—Cisco, Microsoft, Intel, IBM, or another of the industry leaders that buy hundreds of successful new companies each year. For the managers of such a startup, the decision to initiate dividend payments in the foreseeable future will be totally off the radar screen. Thus, the dividend growth model is not useful for valuing most startup companies.

Also, many established firms pay no dividends. Investors may expect them to pay dividends some time in the future, but when, and how much? As long as internal opportunities and acquisitions are so attractive, the initiation of dividends will be postponed, and this makes the dividend growth model of little use. Even Microsoft, one of the world's most successful companies, only started paying a tiny dividend in 2003.

Finally, the dividend growth model is generally of limited use for internal management purposes, even for a dividend-paying company. If the firm consisted of just one big asset, and that asset produced all of the cash flows used to pay dividends, then alternative strategies could be judged through the use of the dividend growth model. However, most firms have several different divisions with many assets, so the corporation's value depends on the cash flows from many different assets, and on the actions of many managers. These managers need a way to measure the effects of their decisions on corporate value, but the discounted dividend model isn't very useful because individual divisions don't pay dividends.

Fortunately, the corporate valuation model does not depend on dividends, and it can be applied to divisions and subunits as well as to the entire firm.

Another important aspect of value-based management is the concept of corporate governance. The corporate valuation model shows how corporate decisions affect *stockholders.* However, corporate decisions are made by managers, not stockholders, and maximizing shareholder wealth is not the same as individual managers maximizing their own

CORPORATE VALUATION: PUTTING THE PIECES TOGETHER

The value of a firm is determined by the size, timing, and risk of its expected future free cash flows (FCF). The last chapter showed how to project financial statements, and Chapter 3 showed how to calculate free cash flows. Chapter 9 explained how to estimate the weighted average cost of capital. This chapter puts the pieces together and shows how to calculate the value of a firm. It also shows how to use the valuation model as a guide for choosing among different corporate strategies and operating tactics.

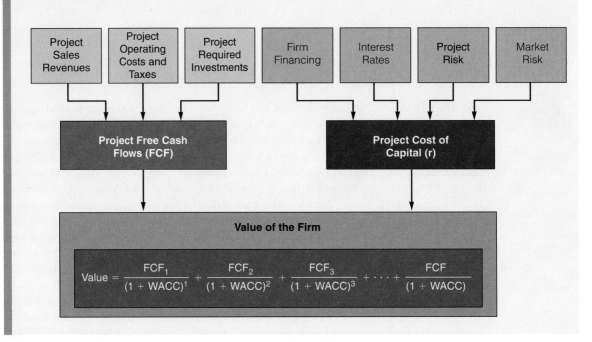

"satisfaction."[1] Thus, a key aspect of value-based management is making sure that managers focus on the goal of stockholder wealth maximization.

The set of rules and procedures used to motivate managers falls under the general heading of *corporate governance*. At the risk of oversimplification, it involves two primary mechanisms: "sticks" and "carrots." The sticks make it easier to replace a poorly performing CEO. They include (1) provisions in the corporate charter that affect the likelihood of a takeover and (2) the composition of the board of directors. The corporate charter may make it relatively easy for a takeover to occur, so that a poorly performing CEO can be replaced; or the charter may make a takeover more difficult, in which case poor managers can continue to perform poorly. The board of directors can consist of strong outsiders, who will likely monitor the CEO's performance closely and replace him or her if things are not going well, or of friends and colleagues of the CEO, who are willing to let things slide. The carrot involves the type of managerial compensation plan the company uses. If managerial compensation is linked to the firm's stock price or other value-based measures (such as EVA), then managers are more likely to focus on shareholder wealth maximization than if their compensation is just a fixed salary.

This chapter discusses the corporate valuation model, value-based management, and corporate governance, beginning with the corporate valuation model.

---

[1] A distinction is sometimes made between "executives" and "managers," with executives being corporate officers and other members of the top management team. We do not make that distinction in this book—all people with important decision-making powers are designated as "managers."

Why is the corporate valuation model applicable in more circumstances than the dividend growth model?

What is value-based management?

What is corporate governance?

THE CORPORATE VALUATION MODEL

Corporate assets are of two types: **operating** and **nonoperating.** Operating assets, in turn, take two forms: **assets-in-place** and **growth options.** Assets-in-place include such tangible assets as land, buildings, machines, and inventory, plus intangible assets such as patents, customer lists, reputation, and general know-how. Growth options are opportunities to expand that arise from the firm's current operating knowledge, experience, and other resources. The assets-in-place provide an expected stream of cash flows, and so do the growth options. To illustrate, Wal-Mart owns stores, inventory, and other tangible assets, it has a well-known name and reputation, and it has a lot of business know-how. These assets produce current sales and cash flows, and they also provide opportunities for new investments that will produce additional cash flows in the future. Similarly, Merck owns manufacturing plants, patents, and other real assets, and it has a knowledge base that facilitates the development of new drugs and thus new cash flow streams.

Most companies also own some nonoperating assets, which come in two forms. The first is a marketable securities portfolio over and above the cash needed to operate the business. For example, Ford Motor Company's automotive operation had about $17 billion in short-term investments as of June 2003, and this was in addition to $7 billion in cash. Second, Ford also had $2.5 billion of investments in other businesses, which were reported on the asset side of the balance sheet as "Equity in Net Assets of Affiliated Companies." In total Ford had $17 + $2.5 = $19.5 billion of nonoperating assets, compared with its $113 billion of automotive assets, or 15 percent of the total. For most companies, the percentage is much lower. For example, Wal-Mart's percentage of nonoperating assets was only 1 percent, which is more typical.

We see, then, that for most companies operating assets are far more important than nonoperating assets. Moreover, companies can influence the values of their operating assets, but the values of nonoperating assets are largely out of their direct control. Therefore, value-based management, hence this chapter, focuses on operating assets.

Estimating the Value of Operations

Tables 13-1 and 13-2 contain the actual 2005 and projected 2006 to 2009 financial statements for MagnaVision Inc., which produces optical systems for use in medical photography. (See Chapter 12 for more details on how to project financial statements.) Growth has been rapid in the past, but the market is becoming saturated, so the sales growth rate is expected to decline from 21 percent in 2006 to a sustainable rate of 5 percent in 2009 and beyond. Profit margins are expected to improve as the production process becomes more efficient and because MagnaVision will no longer be incurring marketing costs associated with the introduction of a major product. All items on the financial statements are projected to grow at a 5 percent rate after 2009. Note that the company does not pay a dividend, but it is expected to start paying out about 75 percent of its earnings beginning in 2008. (Chapter 15 explains in more detail how companies decide how much to pay out in dividends.)

Recall that free cash flow (FCF) is the cash from operations that is actually available for distribution to investors, including stockholders, bondholders, and preferred stockholders. The value of operations is the present value of the free cash flows the firm is expected to generate out into the future. Therefore, MagnaVision's value can be calculated as the

TABLE 13-1 | **MagnaVision Inc.: Income Statements**
| (Millions of Dollars Except for Per Share Data)

	ACTUAL		PROJECTED		
	2005	2006	2007[b]	2008	2009
Net sales	$700.0	$850.0	$1,000.0	$1,100.0	$1,155.0
Costs (except depreciation)	599.0	734.0	911.0	935.0	982.0
Depreciation	28.0	31.0	34.0	36.0	38.0
Total operating costs	$627.0	$765.0	$ 945.0	$ 971.0	$1,020.0
Earnings before interest and taxes (EBIT)	$ 73.0	$ 85.0	$ 55.0	$ 129.0	$ 135.0
Less: Net interest[a]	13.0	15.0	16.0	17.0	19.0
Earnings before taxes	$ 60.0	$ 70.0	$ 39.0	$ 112.0	$ 116.0
Taxes (40%)	24.0	28.0	15.6	44.8	46.4
Net income before preferred dividends	$ 36.0	$ 42.0	$ 23.4	$ 67.2	$ 69.6
Preferred dividends	6.0	7.0	7.4	8.0	8.3
Net income available for common dividends	$ 30.0	$ 35.0	$ 16.0	$ 59.2	$ 61.3
Common dividends	—	—	—	$ 44.2	$ 45.3
Addition to retained earnings	$ 30.0	$ 35.0	$ 16.0	$ 15.0	$ 16.0
Number of shares	100	100	100	100	100
Dividends per share	—	—	—	$ 0.442	$ 0.453

Notes:
[a]"Net interest" is interest paid on debt less interest earned on marketable securities. Both items could be shown separately on the income statements, but for this example we combine them and show net interest. MagnaVision pays more interest than it earns, hence its net interest is subtracted.
[b]Net income is projected to decline in 2007. This is due to the projected cost for a one-time marketing program in that year.

present value of its expected future free cash flows from operations, discounted at its weighted average cost of capital, WACC, plus the value of its nonoperating assets. Here is the equation for the value of operations, which is the firm's value as a going concern:

$$
\begin{aligned}
\text{Value of operations} = V_{op} &= \text{PV of expected future free cash flow} \\
&= \frac{FCF_1}{(1 + WACC)^1} + \frac{FCF_2}{(1 + WACC)^2} + \cdots + \frac{FCF_\infty}{(1 + WACC)^\infty} \\
&= \sum_{t=1}^{\infty} \frac{FCF_t}{(1 + WACC)^t}.
\end{aligned}
\tag{13-1}
$$

MagnaVision's cost of capital is 10.84 percent. To find its value of operations as a going concern, we use an approach similar to the nonconstant dividend growth model for stocks in Chapter 7, proceeding as follows:

1. Assume that the firm will experience nonconstant growth for N years, after which it will grow at some constant rate.
2. Calculate the expected free cash flow for each of the N nonconstant growth years.
3. Recognize that after Year N growth will be constant, so we can use the constant growth formula to find the firm's value at Year N. This is the sum of the PVs for year N + 1 and all subsequent years, discounted back to Year N.
4. Find the PV of the free cash flows for each of the N nonconstant growth years. Also, find the PV of the firm's value at Year N.

TABLE 13-2 | MagnaVision Inc.: Balance Sheets (Millions of Dollars)

	ACTUAL	PROJECTED			
	2005	2006	2007	2008	2009
Assets					
Cash	$ 17.0	$ 20.0	$ 22.0	$ 23.0	$ 24.0
Marketable securities[a]	63.0	70.0	80.0	84.0	88.0
Accounts receivable	85.0	100.0	110.0	116.0	121.0
Inventories	170.0	200.0	220.0	231.0	243.0
Total current assets	$ 335.0	$ 390.0	$ 432.0	$ 454.0	$ 476.0
Net plant and equipment	279.0	310.0	341.0	358.0	376.0
Total assets	$ 614.0	$ 700.0	$ 773.0	$ 812.0	$ 852.0
Liabilities and Equity					
Accounts payable	$ 17.0	$ 20.0	$ 22.0	$ 23.0	$ 24.0
Notes payable	123.0	140.0	160.0	168.0	176.0
Accruals	43.0	50.0	55.0	58.0	61.0
Total current liabilities	$ 183.0	$ 210.0	$ 237.0	$ 249.0	$ 261.0
Long-term bonds	124.0	140.0	160.0	168.0	176.0
Preferred stock	62.0	70.0	80.0	84.0	88.0
Common stock[b]	200.0	200.0	200.0	200.0	200.0
Retained earnings	45.0	80.0	96.0	111.0	127.0
Common equity	$ 245.0	$ 280.0	$ 296.0	$ 311.0	$ 327.0
Total liabilities and equity	$ 614.0	$ 700.0	$ 773.0	$ 812.0	$ 852.0

Notes:
[a]All assets except marketable securities are operating assets required to support sales. The marketable securities are financial assets not required in operations.
[b]Par plus paid-in capital.

5. Now sum all the PVs, those of the annual free cash flows during the nonconstant period plus the PV of the Year N value, to find the firm's value of operations.

Table 13-3 calculates free cash flow for each year, using procedures discussed in Chapter 3. Line 1, with data for 2005 from the balance sheets in Table 13-2, shows the required net operating working capital, or operating current assets minus operating current liabilities, for 2005:

$$\begin{pmatrix} \text{Required net} \\ \text{operating} \\ \text{working capital} \end{pmatrix} = \begin{pmatrix} \text{Cash +} \\ \text{Accounts receivable} \\ \text{+ Inventories} \end{pmatrix} - \begin{pmatrix} \text{Accounts} \\ \text{payable +} \\ \text{Accruals} \end{pmatrix}$$

$$= (\$17.00 + \$85.00 + \$170.00) - (\$17.00 + \$43.00)$$
$$= \$212.00.$$

Line 2 shows required net plant and equipment, and Line 3, which is the sum of Lines 1 and 2, shows the required net operating assets, also called total net operating capital, or just operating capital. For 2005, operating capital is $212 + $279 = $491 million.

Line 4 shows the required annual addition to operating capital, found as the change in operating capital from the previous year. For 2006, the required investment in operating capital is $560 − $491 = $69 million.

TABLE 13-3 | Calculating MagnaVision's Expected Free Cash Flow (Millions of Dollars)

	ACTUAL	PROJECTED			
	2005	2006	2007	2008	2009
Calculation of Free Cash Flow					
1. Required net operating working capital	$212.00	$250.00	$275.00	$289.00	$303.00
2. Required net plant and equipment	279.00	310.00	341.00	358.00	376.00
3. Required total net operating capital[a]	$491.00	$560.00	$616.00	$647.00	$679.00
4. Required net new investment in operating capital = change in total net operating capital from previous year		$ 69.00	$ 56.00	$ 31.00	$ 32.00
5. NOPAT [Net operating profit after taxes = EBIT × (1 − Tax rate)][b]		$ 51.00	$ 33.00	$ 77.40	$ 81.00
6. Less: Required investment in operating capital		69.00	56.00	31.00	32.00
7. Free cash flow		($ 18.00)	($ 23.00)	$ 46.40	$ 49.00

[a]The terms "total net operating capital," "operating capital," and "net operating assets" all mean the same thing.
[b]NOPAT declines in 2007 because of a marketing expenditure projected for that year. See Note b in Table 13-1.

Line 5 shows NOPAT, or net operating profit after taxes. Note that EBIT is operating earnings *before* taxes, while NOPAT is operating earnings *after* taxes. Therefore, NOPAT = EBIT(1 − T). With 2006 EBIT of $85 as shown in Table 13-1 and a tax rate of 40 percent, NOPAT as projected for 2006 is $51 million:

$$\text{NOPAT} = \text{EBIT}(1 - T) = \$85(1.0 - 0.4) = \$51 \text{ million.}$$

Although MagnaVision's operating capital is projected to produce $51 million of after-tax profits in 2006, the company must invest $69 million in new operating capital in 2006 to support its growth plan. Therefore, the free cash flow for 2006, shown on Line 7, is a negative $18 million:

$$\text{Free cash flow (FCF)} = \$51 - \$69 = -\$18 \text{ million.}$$

This negative free cash flow in the early years is typical for young, high-growth companies. Even though net operating profit after taxes (NOPAT) is positive in all years, free cash flow is negative because of the need to invest in operating assets. The negative free cash flow means the company will have to obtain new funds from investors, and the balance sheets in Table 13-2 show that notes payable, long-term bonds, and preferred stock all increase from 2005 to 2006. Stockholders will also help fund MagnaVision's growth—they will receive no dividends until 2008, so all of the net income from 2006 and 2007 will be reinvested. However, as growth slows, free cash flow will become positive, and MagnaVision plans to use some of its FCF to pay dividends beginning in 2008.[2]

A variant of the constant growth dividend model is shown below as Equation 13-2. This equation can be used to find the value of MagnaVision's operations at time N, when its free cash flows stabilize and begin to grow at a constant rate. This is the value of all FCFs beyond time N, discounted back to time N, which is 2009 for MagnaVision.

$$V_{\text{op(at time N)}} = \sum_{t=N+1}^{\infty} \frac{\text{FCF}_t}{(1 + \text{WACC})^{t-N}}$$

$$= \frac{\text{FCF}_N(1 + g)}{\text{WACC} - g} = \frac{\text{FCF}_{N+1}}{\text{WACC} - g}$$

(13-2)

[2] MagnaVision plans to increase its debt and preferred stock each year so as to maintain a constant capital structure. We discuss capital structure in detail in Chapter 14.

Based on a 10.84 percent cost of capital, $49 million of free cash flow in 2009, and a 5 percent growth rate, the value of MagnaVision's operations as of December 31, 2009, is forecasted to be $880.99 million:

$$V_{op(12/31/09)} = \frac{FCF_{12/31/09}(1 + g)}{WACC - g} = \frac{FCF_{12/31/10}}{WACC - g} \qquad \text{(13-2a)}$$

$$= \frac{\$49(1 + 0.05)}{0.1084 - 0.05} = \frac{\$51.45}{0.1084 - 0.05} = \$880.99.$$

This $880.99 million figure is called the company's **terminal, or horizon, value,** because it is the value at the end of the forecast period. It is also sometimes called a **continuing value.** In any case, it is the amount that MagnaVision could expect to receive if it sold its operating assets on December 31, 2009.

Figure 13-1 shows the free cash flow for each year during the nonconstant growth period, along with the horizon value of operations in 2009. To find the value of operations as of "today," December 31, 2005, we find the PV of each annual cash flow in Figure 13-1, discounting at the 10.84 percent cost of capital. The sum of the PVs is approximately $615 million, and it represents an estimate of the price MagnaVision could expect to receive if it sold its operating assets today, December 31, 2005.

Estimating the Price per Share

The total value of any company is the value of its operations plus the value of its nonoperating assets.[3] As the December 31, 2005, balance sheet in Table 13-2 shows, MagnaVision had $63 million of marketable securities on that date. Unlike operating assets, we do not have to calculate a present value for marketable securities because short-term financial assets as reported on the balance sheet are at, or close to, their market value. Therefore, MagnaVision's total value on December 31, 2005, is $615.27 + $63.00 = $678.27 million.

If the company's total value on December 31, 2005, is $678.27 million, what is the value of its common equity? First, the sum of notes payable and long-term debt is $123 + $124 = $247 million, and these securities have the first claim on assets and income. Accounts payable and accruals were netted out earlier when calculating free cash flow, so they have been accounted for. However, the preferred stock has a claim of $62 million, and it also ranks above the common. Therefore, the value left for common stockholders is $678.27 − $247 − $62 = $369.27 million.

FIGURE 13-1	Process for Finding the Value of Operations for a Nonconstant Growth Company

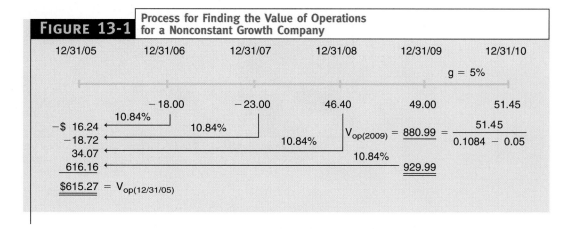

---

[3] The total value also includes the value of growth options not associated with assets-in-place, but MagnaVision has none.

Figure 13-2 is a bar chart that provides a breakdown of MagnaVision's value. The left bar shows the company's total value as the sum of its nonoperating assets plus its going concern value. Next, the middle bar shows the claim of each class of investors on that total value. Debtholders have the highest priority claim, and MagnaVision owes $123 million on notes payable and $124 million on long-term bonds, for a total of $247 million. The preferred stockholders have the next claim, $62 million. The remaining value belongs to the common equity, and it amounts to $678.27 − $247.00 − $62.00 = $369.27 million.[4] Finally, the bar on the right side divides the market value of the equity into the book value, which represents the actual investment stockholders have made, and the additional market value added by management (MVA).

Table 13-4 summarizes the calculations used to find MagnaVision's stock value. There are 100 million shares outstanding, and their total value is $369.27 million. Therefore, the value of a single share is $369.27/100 = $3.69.

The Dividend Growth Model Applied to MagnaVision

MagnaVision has not yet begun to pay dividends. However, as we saw in Table 13-1, a cash dividend of $0.442 per share is forecasted for 2008. The dividend is expected to grow by about 2.5 percent in 2009, and then at a constant 5 percent rate thereafter. MagnaVision's cost of equity is 14 percent. In this situation, we can apply the nonconstant dividend growth model as developed earlier in Chapter 7. Figure 13-3 shows that the value of MagnaVision's stock, based on this model, is $3.70 per share, which is the same as the value found using the corporate valuation model except for a rounding difference.

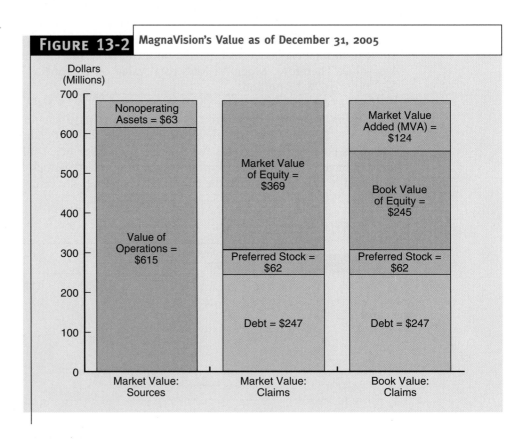

FIGURE 13-2 MagnaVision's Value as of December 31, 2005

---

[4] Rather than subtracting the book values of debt and preferred stock, it would be better to subtract their market values. In most cases, including this one, the book values of fixed income securities are close to their market values, and when this is true, one can simply work with their book values.

TABLE 13-4	Finding the Value of MagnaVision's Stock (Millions of Dollars Except for Per Share Data)	
1. Value of operations (present value of free cash flows)		$615.27
2. Plus value of nonoperating assets		63.00
3. Total market value of the firm		$678.27
4. Less: Value of debt		247.00
Value of preferred stock		62.00
5. Value of common equity		$369.27
6. Divide by number of shares		100.00
7. Value per share		$ 3.69

Comparing the Corporate Valuation and Dividend Growth Models

Because the corporate valuation and dividend growth models give the same answer, does it matter which model you choose? In general, it does. For example, if you were a financial analyst estimating the value of a mature company whose dividends are expected to grow steadily in the future, it would probably be more efficient to use the dividend growth model. Here you would only need to estimate the growth rate in dividends, not the entire set of pro forma financial statements.

However, if a company is paying a dividend but is still in the high-growth stage of its life cycle, you would need to project the future financial statements before you could make a reasonable estimate of future dividends. Then, because you would have already estimated future financial statements, it would be a toss-up as to whether the corporate valuation model or the dividend growth model would be easier to apply. Intel, which pays a dividend of about 16 cents versus earnings of about $0.97, is an example of a company to which you could apply either model.

Now suppose you were trying to estimate the value of a company that has never paid a dividend or a new firm that is about to go public, or a division that GE or some other large company is planning to sell. In all of these situations, you would have no choice: You would have to estimate future financial statements and use the corporate valuation model.

Actually, even if a company is paying steady dividends, much can be learned from the corporate valuation model, hence many analysts today use it for all types of valuations. The process of projecting the future financial statements can reveal quite a bit about the company's operations and financing needs. Also, such an analysis can provide insights into actions that might be taken to increase the company's value. This is value-based management, which we discuss in the next section.

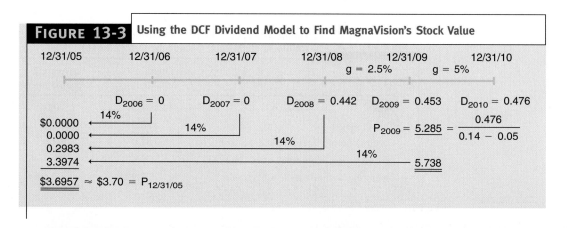

FIGURE 13-3 Using the DCF Dividend Model to Find MagnaVision's Stock Value

SELF-TEST QUESTIONS Give some examples of assets-in-place, growth options, and nonoperating assets.

Write out the equation for the value of operations.

What is the terminal, or horizon, value? Why is it also called the continuing value?

Explain how to estimate the price per share using the corporate valuation model.

VALUE-BASED MANAGEMENT

e-resource

See CF2 Ch 13 Tool Kit.xls for details.

Bell Electronics Inc. has two divisions, Memory and Instruments, with total sales of $1.5 billion and operating capital of $1.07 billion. Based on its current stock and bond prices, the company's total market value is about $1.215 billion, giving it an MVA of $145 million, found as $1.215 − $1.070 = $0.145 billion = $145 million. Because it has a positive MVA, Bell has created value for its investors. Even so, management is considering several new strategic plans in its efforts to increase the firm's value. All of Bell's assets are used in operations.

The Memory Division produces memory chips for such handheld electronic devices as cellular phones and PDAs (personal digital assistants), while the Instruments Division produces devices for measuring and controlling sewage and water treatment facilities. Table 13-5 shows the latest financial results for the two divisions and for the company as a whole.

As Table 13-5 shows, Bell Memory is the larger of the two divisions, with higher sales and more operating capital. Bell Memory is also more profitable, with a NOPAT/Sales ratio of 7.9 percent versus 7.2 percent for Bell Instruments. This year, as in other recent years, the focus of the initial strategic planning sessions was on the Memory division. Bell Memory has grown rapidly because of the phenomenal growth in consumer electronics, and this division rocketed past Instruments several years ago. Although Memory's growth had tapered off, senior management generally agreed that this division would receive the lion's share of corporate attention and resources because it is larger, more profitable, and, frankly, more exciting. After all, Bell Memory is associated with the glamorous market for telecommunications and personal electronic devices, whereas Bell Instruments is associated with sewage and sludge.

The financial assumptions and projections associated with the preliminary strategic plans for the two divisions are shown in Tables 13-6 and 13-7. Based on the initial strategic plans, each division is projected to have 5 percent annual growth for the next five years and thereafter. The strategic plans also assume that the cost structures of the two divisions will remain unchanged from the current year, 2005. Only partial financial projections are shown in Tables 13-6 and 13-7, but when Bell's management decides on a final strategic plan, it will develop complete financial statements for the company as a whole and use them to determine financing requirements, as described in Chapter 12.

TABLE 13-5	**Financial Results for Bell Electronics Inc.** (Millions of Dollars, Except for Percentages)		
	Division 1: Bell Memory	Division 2: Bell Instruments	Total Company
Sales	$1,000.0	$500.0	$1,500.0
Operating capital	870.0	200.0	1,070.0
Earnings before interest and taxes (EBIT)	131.0	60.0	191.0
Net operating profit after taxes (NOPAT)	78.6	36.0	114.6
Operating profitability (NOPAT/Sales)	7.9%	7.2%	7.6%

TABLE 13-6 | Initial Projections for the Bell Memory Division (Millions of Dollars, Except for Percentages)

	ACTUAL	PROJECTED[a]				
	2005	2006	2007	2008	2009	2010
PANEL A: INPUTS						
Sales growth rate		5%	5%	5%	5%	5%
Costs/sales	81%	81	81	81	81	81
Depreciation/net plant	10	10	10	10	10	10
Cash/sales	1	1	1	1	1	1
Accounts receivable/sales	8	8	8	8	8	8
Inventories/sales	30	30	30	30	30	30
Net plant/sales	59	59	59	59	59	59
Accounts payable/sales	5	5	5	5	5	5
Accruals/sales	6	6	6	6	6	6
Tax rate	40	40	40	40	40	40
PANEL B: PARTIAL INCOME STATEMENT						
Net sales	$1,000.0	$1,050.0	$1,102.5	$1,157.6	$1,215.5	$1,276.3
Costs (except depreciation)	810.0	850.5	893.0	937.7	984.6	1,033.8
Depreciation	59.0	62.0	65.0	68.3	71.7	75.3
Total operating costs	$ 869.0	$ 912.5	$ 958.1	$1,006.0	$1,056.3	$1,109.1
EBIT	$ 131.0	$ 137.6	$ 144.4	$ 151.6	$ 159.2	$ 167.2
PANEL C: PARTIAL BALANCE SHEETS						
Operating Assets						
Cash	$ 10.0	$ 10.5	$ 11.0	$ 11.6	$ 12.2	$ 12.8
Accounts receivable	80.0	84.0	88.2	92.6	97.2	102.1
Inventories	300.0	315.0	330.8	347.3	364.7	382.9
Operating current assets	$390.0	$409.5	$430.0	$451.5	$474.0	$497.7
Net plant and equipment	$590.0	$619.5	$650.5	$683.0	$717.1	$753.0
Operating Liabilities						
Accounts payable	$ 50.0	$ 52.5	$ 55.1	$ 57.9	$ 60.8	$ 63.8
Accruals	60.0	63.0	66.2	69.5	72.9	76.6
Operating current liabilities	$110.0	$115.5	$121.3	$127.3	$133.7	$140.4

[a]Projected figures may not total exactly due to rounding.

To evaluate the plans, Bell's management applied the corporate valuation model to each division, thus valuing them using the free cash flow valuation technique. Each division has a WACC of 10.5 percent, and Table 13-8 shows the results. The three key items are NOPAT, the required investment in operating capital, and the resulting free cash flows for each year. In addition, the table shows each division's horizon value of operations at 2010, which is the end of the five years of explicit forecasts, calculated with Equation 13-2. The value of operations at 2005 is the present value of the free cash flows and the horizon value, discounted at the weighted average cost of capital. As expected, Bell Memory has the greater value of operations, $709.6 million versus $505.5 million for Bell Instruments. However, the managers were surprised to see that Bell Memory's market value added (MVA) is *negative*: $709.6 value of operations − $870.0 operating capital = −$160.4 million. In contrast, Bell Instruments' MVA is positive: $505.5 value of operations − $200 operating capital = $305.5 million.

TABLE 13-7 | Initial Projections for the Bell Instruments Division
(Millions of Dollars, Except for Percentages)

	ACTUAL	PROJECTED[a]				
	2005	2006	2007	2008	2009	2010
PANEL A: INPUTS						
Sales growth rate		5%	5%	5%	5%	5%
Costs/sales	85%	85	85	85	85	85
Depreciation/net plant	10	10	10	10	10	10
Cash/sales	1	1	1	1	1	1
Accounts receivable/sales	5	5	5	5	5	5
Inventories/sales	15	15	15	15	15	15
Net plant/sales	30	30	30	30	30	30
Accounts payable/sales	5	5	5	5	5	5
Accruals/sales	6	6	6	6	6	6
Tax rate	40	40	40	40	40	40
PANEL B: PARTIAL INCOME STATEMENT						
Net sales	$500.0	$525.0	$551.3	$578.8	$607.8	$638.1
Costs (except depreciation)	$425.0	$446.3	$468.6	$492.0	$516.6	$542.4
Depreciation	15.0	15.8	16.5	17.4	18.2	19.1
Total operating costs	$440.0	$462.0	$485.1	$509.4	$534.8	$561.6
EBIT	$ 60.0	$ 63.0	$ 66.2	$ 69.5	$ 72.9	$ 76.6
PANEL C: PARTIAL BALANCE SHEETS						
Operating Assets						
Cash	$ 5.0	$ 5.3	$ 5.5	$ 5.8	$ 6.1	$ 6.4
Accounts receivable	25.0	26.3	27.6	28.9	30.4	31.9
Inventories	75.0	78.8	82.7	86.8	91.2	95.7
Operating current assets	$105.0	$110.3	$115.8	$121.6	$127.6	$134.0
Net plant and equipment	$150.0	$157.5	$165.4	$173.6	$182.3	$191.4
Operating Liabilities						
Accounts payable	$ 25.0	$ 26.3	$ 27.6	$ 28.9	$ 30.4	$ 31.9
Accruals	30.0	31.5	33.1	34.7	36.5	38.3
Operating current liabilities	$ 55.0	$ 57.8	$ 60.6	$ 63.7	$ 66.9	$ 70.2

[a]Projected figures may not total exactly due to rounding.

e-resource

A second strategic planning meeting was called to address this unexpected result. In it, Bell Memory's managers proposed a $20 million marketing campaign to boost their sales growth rate from 5 to 6 percent. They argued that because Bell Memory is so profitable, its value would be much higher if they could push up sales. Before accepting this proposal, though, the proposed changes were run through the valuation model. The managers changed the Bell Memory division's growth rate from 5 to 6 percent; see the file *CF2 Ch 13 Tool Kit.xls* on the textbook's Web site for details. To their surprise, the division's value of operations fell to $691.5 million, and its MVA also declined, from −$160.4 million to −$178.5 million. Although Bell Memory was profitable, increasing its sales growth actually reduced its value!

TABLE 13-8 | Initial FCF Valuation of Each Division
(Millions of Dollars, Except for Percentages)

	ACTUAL	PROJECTED				
	2005	2006	2007	2008	2009	2010
PANEL A: FCF VALUATION OF THE BELL MEMORY DIVISION						
Calculation of FCF						
Net operating working capital	$280.0	$294.0	$308.7	$ 324.1	$ 340.3	$ 357.4
Net plant	590.0	619.5	650.5	683.0	717.1	753.0
Net operating capital	$870.0	$913.5	$959.2	$1,007.1	$1,057.5	$1,110.4
Investment in operating capital		$ 43.5	$ 45.7	$ 48.0	$ 50.4	$ 52.9
NOPAT	$ 78.6	$ 82.5	$ 86.7	$ 91.0	$ 95.5	$ 100.3
Free cash flow		$ 39.0	$ 41.0	$ 43.0	$ 45.2	$ 47.4
Growth in FCF			5.0%	5.0%	5.0%	5.0%
Value of Operations						
Horizon value						$ 905.7
Value of operations	$709.6					
Divisional MVA (Value of operations − Capital)	($160.4)					
PANEL B: FCF VALUATION OF THE BELL INSTRUMENTS DIVISION						
Calculation of FCF						
Net operating working capital	$ 50.0	$ 52.5	$ 55.1	$ 57.9	$ 60.8	$ 63.8
Net plant	150.0	157.5	165.4	173.6	182.3	191.4
Net operating capital	$200.0	$210.0	$220.5	$231.5	$243.1	$255.3
Investment in operating capital		$ 10.0	$ 10.5	$ 11.0	$ 11.6	$ 12.2
NOPAT	$ 36.0	$ 37.8	$ 39.7	$ 41.7	$ 43.8	$ 45.9
Free cash flow		$ 27.8	$ 29.2	$ 30.6	$ 32.2	$ 33.8
Growth in FCF			5.0%	5.0%	5.0%	5.0%
Value of Operations						
Horizon value						$645.1
Value of operations	$505.5					
Divisional MVA (Value of operations − Capital)	$305.5					

Notes: The WACC is 10.5 percent for each division. The horizon value (HV) at 2010 is calculated using Equation 13-2, the constant growth formula for free cash flows $HV_{2010} = [FCF_{2010} \times (1 + g)](WACC - g)$. The value of operations is the present value of the horizon value and the free cash flows discounted at the WACC; calculated in a manner similar to Figure 13-1. Projected figures may not total exactly due to rounding. See the file *CF2 Ch 13 Tool Kit.xls* on the textbook's Web site for details.

To better understand these results, we can express the firm's value in terms of four fundamental wealth drivers:

g = growth in sales
OP = Operating profitability (OP) = NOPAT/Sales
CR = Capital requirements (CR) = Operating capital/Sales
$WACC$ = weighted average cost of capital

How do these drivers affect the value of a firm? First, the sales growth rate generally, but not always, has a positive effect on value, provided the company is profitable enough.

However, the effect can be negative if growth requires a great deal of capital, and the cost of that capital is high. Second, operating profitability, which measures the after-tax profit per dollar of sales, always has a positive effect—the higher the better. Third, the capital requirements ratio, which measures how much operating capital is needed to generate a dollar of sales, also has a consistent effect—the lower the CR the better, since a low CR means that the company can generate new sales with smaller amounts of new capital. Finally, the fourth factor, the WACC, also has a consistent effect—the lower it is, the higher the firm's value.

Another important metric in the corporate valuation model is the expected return on invested capital (EROIC), defined as the expected NOPAT for the coming year divided by the amount of operating capital at the beginning of the year (which is the end of the preceding year). Thus, EROIC represents the expected return on the capital that has already been invested. To illustrate, the EROIC of the Bell Memory division for 2010, the last year in the forecast period, is

$$\text{EROIC}_{2010} = \frac{\text{NOPAT}_{2011}}{\text{Capital}_{2010}} = \frac{\$100.3(1.05)}{\$1,110.4} = 9.5\%.$$

e-resource

See CF2 Ch 13 Tool Kit.xls for all calculations.

To see exactly how the four value drivers and expected ROIC determine value for a constant growth firm, we can start with Equation 13-2,

$$V_{\text{op(at time N)}} = \frac{\text{FCF}_{N+1}}{\text{WACC} - g}, \tag{13-2}$$

and rewrite it in terms of the value drivers:

$$V_{\text{op(at time N)}} = \text{Capital}_N + \left[\frac{\text{Sales}_N\,(1 + g)}{\text{WACC} - g}\right]\left[\text{OP} - \text{WACC}\left(\frac{\text{CR}}{1 + g}\right)\right]. \tag{13-3}$$

Equation 13-3 shows that the value of operations can be divided into two components: (1) the dollars of operating capital that investors have provided and (2) the additional value that management has added or subtracted, which is equivalent to MVA.

Note that the first bracket of Equation 13-3 shows the present value of growing sales, discounted at the WACC. This would be the MVA of a firm that has no costs and that never needs to invest additional capital. But firms do have costs and capital requirements, and their effect is shown in the second bracket. Here we see that, holding g constant, MVA will improve if operating profitability (OP) increases, capital requirements (CR) decrease, or WACC decreases.

Note that an increase in growth will not necessarily increase value. OP could be positive, but if CR is quite high, meaning that a lot of new capital is needed to support a given increase in sales, then the second bracket can be negative. In this situation, growth causes the term in the first bracket to increase, but it is being multiplied by a negative term in the second bracket, and the net result will be a decrease in MVA.

We can also rewrite Equation 13-2 in terms of EROIC:

$$V_{\text{op(at time N)}} = \text{Capital}_N + \frac{\text{Capital}_N(\text{EROIC}_N - \text{WACC})}{\text{WACC} - g}. \tag{13-4}$$

Equation 13-4 also breaks value into two components, the value of capital and the MVA, shown in the second term. This term for MVA shows that value depends on the spread between the expected return on invested capital, EROIC, and WACC. If EROIC is greater than WACC, then the return on capital is greater than the return investors expect, and management is adding value. In this case, an increase in the growth rate causes value to go up. If EROIC is exactly equal to WACC, then the firm is, in an economic sense, "breaking even." It has positive accounting profits and cash flow, but these cash flows are just sufficient to satisfy investors, causing value to exactly equal the amount of capital that has been provided. If EROIC is less than WACC, the term in brackets is negative, management is destroying value, and growth is harmful. Here the faster the growth rate is, the lower the firm's value.

We should also note that the insights from Equations 13-3 and 13-4 apply to all firms, but the equations themselves can only be applied to relatively stable firms whose growth has leveled out at a constant rate. For example, in 2001 Home Depot had been growing at around 20 percent per year, so we could not apply Equations 13-3 and 13-4 directly (although we could always apply Equation 13-1). Home Depot's NOPAT/sales ratio was 5.6 percent, which was excellent for its industry, but even though it was profitable, it had negative free cash flows. This is because Home Depot was still in its high-growth phase, which required enormous investments in operating capital. Home Depot's sales growth has slowed due to market saturation, and its free cash flows have become very large and positive. Note also that Home Depot currently has an expected ROIC of about 22 percent versus a WACC of only 10.5 percent. This large spread contributes to its $50 billion MVA.

Table 13-9 shows the value drivers for Bell's two divisions, measured at 2010, the end of the forecast period. We report these for the end of the forecast period because ratios can change during the forecast period due to input changes. By the end of the forecast period, however, all inputs and ratios should be stable.

Table 13-9 shows that both divisions have the same growth rate and the same WACC. Bell Memory is more profitable, but it also has much higher capital requirements. The result is that Bell Memory's expected ROIC is only 9.5 percent, well below its 10.5 percent WACC. Thus, growth doesn't help Bell Memory—indeed, it lowers the division's value.

Based on this analysis, Bell Memory's managers decided not to request funds for a marketing campaign. Instead, they developed a plan to reduce capital requirements. The new plan called for spending $50 million on an integrated supply chain information system that would allow them to cut their inventories/sales ratio from 30 percent to 20 percent and also reduce the net plant/sales ratio from 59 percent to 50 percent. Table 13-10 shows operating results based on this new plan. The value of operations increases from $709.6 million to $1.1574 billion, or by $447.8 million. Because this is well over the $50 million required to implement the plan, top management decided to approve the plan. Note also that MVA becomes positive at $287.4 million, and the divisional expected ROIC rises to 13.0 percent, well over the 10.5 percent WACC.

Bell Instruments' managers also used the valuation model to assess changes in plans for their division. Given their high expected ROIC, the Instruments division proposed (1) an

TABLE 13-9 | Bell Electronics' Forecasted Value Drivers for 2010

	Division 1: Bell Memory	Division 2: Bell Instruments
Growth, g	5.0%	5.0%
Profitability		
$(NOPAT_{2010}/Sales_{2010})$	7.9	7.2
Capital requirement		
$(Capital_{2010}/Sales_{2010})$	87.0	40.0
WACC	10.5	10.5
Expected return on invested capital, EROIC		
$[NOPAT_{2010}(1 + g)/Capital_{2010}]$	9.5	18.9

TABLE 13-10 | Comparison of the Preliminary and Final Plans
(Millions of Dollars, Except for Percentages)

	BELL MEMORY		BELL INSTRUMENTS	
	Preliminary	Final	Preliminary	Final
Inputs				
Sales growth rate, g	5%	5%	5%	6%
Inventories/sales	30	20	15	16
Net plant/sales	59	50	30	30
Results				
EROIC (2010)[a]	9.5%	13.0%	18.9%	18.6%
Invested (operating) capital (2010)[a]	$1,110.4	$867.9	$255.3	$274.3
Current value of operations (2005)[b]	$709.6	$1,157.4	$505.5	$570.1
Current MVA (2005)[b]	($160.4)	$287.4	$305.5	$370.1

Notes:
[a]We report EROIC and capital for the end of the forecast period because ratios can change during the forecast period if inputs change during the forecast period. By the end of the forecast period, however, all inputs and ratios should be stable.
[b]We report the value of operations and the MVA as of the current date, 2005, because we want to see the effect that the proposed plans have on the current value of the divisions.

aggressive marketing campaign and (2) an increase in inventories that would allow faster delivery and fewer stock-outs. Together, these changes would boost the growth rate from 5 to 6 percent. The direct cost to implement the plan was $20 million, but there was also an indirect cost in that significantly more inventories would have to be carried. Indeed, the ratio of inventories to sales was forecasted to increase from 15 to 16 percent.

Should Instruments' new plan be implemented? Table 13-10 shows the forecasted results. The capital requirements associated with the increased inventory caused the expected ROIC to fall from 18.9 to 18.6 percent, but (1) the 18.6 percent return greatly exceeds the 10.5 percent WACC, and (2) the spread between 18.6 percent and 10.5 percent would be earned on additional capital. This caused the forecasted value of operations to increase from $505.5 to $570.1 million, or by $64.6 million. An 18.6 percent return on $274.3 million of capital is more valuable than an 18.9 percent return on $255.3 million of capital.[5] You, or one of Bell's stockholders, would surely rather have an asset that provides a 50 percent return on an investment of $1,000 than one that provides a 100 percent return on an investment of $1. Therefore, the new plan should be accepted, even though it lowers the Instruments division's expected ROIC.

Sometimes companies focus on their profitability and growth, without giving adequate consideration to their capital requirements. This is a big mistake—all the wealth creation drivers must be taken into account, not just growth. Fortunately for Bell's investors, the revised plan was accepted. However, as this example illustrates, it is easy for a company to mistakenly focus only on profitability and growth. They are important, but so are the other value drivers—capital requirements and the weighted average cost of capital. Value-based management explicitly includes the effects of all the value drivers because it uses the corporate valuation model, and they are all embodied in the model.

SELF-TEST QUESTIONS | What are the four value drivers?
How is it possible that sales growth would decrease the value of a profitable firm?

---

[5] A potential fly in the ointment is the possibility that Bell has a compensation plan based on rates of return and not on changes in wealth. In such a plan, which is fairly typical, the managers might reject the new proposed strategic plan if it lowers ROIC and, hence, their bonuses, even though the plan is good for the company's stockholders. We discuss the effect of compensation plans in more detail later in the chapter.

The corporate valuation model, in which free cash flows are discounted at the weighted average cost of capital to determine the value of the company, lies at the heart of value-based management. Therefore, before adopting value-based management, managers would be wise to ask if the corporate valuation model produces results that are consistent with actual market values. The answer, according to a study by Copeland, Koller, and Murrin of the consulting firm McKinsey & Company, is a resounding yes. They applied the model to 35 companies and found a 0.94 correlation between the model's estimated values and the actual market values. Additional evidence of the model's usefulness was provided by McCafferty's recent survey, in which CFOs rated the corporate valuation model as the most important technique for estimating the value of a potential acquisition.

Finally, a recent *Fortune* article described how much corporations are paying consultants to help them implement the model. Marakon Associates, a leading advocate of value-based management, prides itself on having a single-minded view that a company should have one, and only one, goal—to increase shareholder wealth. It often takes Marakon several years to fully implement a value-based management system at a company. One reason for the lengthy implementation period is that

Marakon breaks the company into segments to determine where value is currently being created or destroyed. These segments might be divisions, product lines, customers, or even channels of distribution. "Deep drilling," as they call this process, is arduous and time consuming, and it requires a great deal of data and analysis. Also, and perhaps even more important, full implementation requires both a change in corporate culture and the creation of an "organization's collective ability to out-think its rivals." In other words, the skillset to use value-based management must permeate the entire company.

Although Marakon is a relatively small firm, with only 275 consultants versus almost 5,000 for McKinsey, it generates about $475,000 in revenue per consultant, which ties them with McKinsey as the most expensive consulting company. Note, though, that its rates seem to be justified. During the late 1990s, Marakon's client companies created an additional $68 billion of wealth versus what they would have created had they matched their industry peers' results.

Sources: Thomas A. Stewart, "Marakon Runners," *Fortune*, September 28, 1998, 153–158; Joseph McCafferty, "What Acquiring Minds Want to Know," *CFO*, February, 1999, 1; and Tom Copeland, Tim Koller, and Jack Murrin, *Valuation: Measuring and Managing the Value of Companies* (New York: John Wiley & Sons, 1994), 83.

CORPORATE GOVERNANCE AND SHAREHOLDER WEALTH

See the Web pages of CalPERS (the California Public Employees' Retirement System), http://www.calpers.org, and TIAA–CREF (Teachers Insurance and Annuity Association College Retirement Equity Fund), http://www.tiaa.org, for excellent discussions of shareholder-friendly corporate governance.

Shareholders want companies to hire managers who are able and willing to take whatever legal and ethical actions they can to maximize stock prices.[6] This obviously requires managers with technical competence, but it also requires managers who are willing to put forth the extra effort necessary to identify and implement value-adding activities. However, managers are people, and people have both personal and corporate goals. Logically, therefore, managers can be expected to act in their own self-interests, and if their self-interests are not aligned with those of stockholders, then corporate value will not be maximized. Managers may spend too much time golfing, lunching, surfing the net, and so forth, rather than focusing on corporate tasks, and they may also use corporate resources on activities that benefit themselves rather than shareholders. So, a key aspect of value-based management

[6] Notice that we said both legal and ethical actions. The accounting frauds perpetuated by Enron, WorldCom, and others that were uncovered in 2002 raised stock prices in the short run, but only because investors were misled about the companies' financial positions. Then, when the correct financial information was finally revealed, the stocks tanked. Investors who bought shares based on the fraudulent financial statements lost tens of billions of dollars. Releasing false financial statements is illegal. Aggressive earnings management and the use of misleading accounting tricks to pump up reported earnings is unethical, and executives should and will go to jail as a result of their shenanigans. When we speak of taking actions to maximize stock prices, we mean making operational or financial changes designed to maximize intrinsic stock value, not fooling investors with false or misleading financial reports.

is to motivate executives and other managers to actually take the actions required under value-based management.

This section deals with **corporate governance,** which is defined as the set of rules and procedures that ensure that managers do indeed employ the principles of value-based management. The essence of corporate governance is to make sure that the key share-holder objective—wealth maximization—is implemented. Most corporate governance provisions come in two forms, sticks and carrots. The primary stick is the *threat of removal,* either as a decision by the board of directors or as the result of a hostile takeover. If a firm's managers are maximizing the value of the resources entrusted to them, they need not fear the loss of their jobs. On the other hand, if managers are not maximizing value, they may well be removed, by their own boards of directors, by dissi-dent stockholders, or by other companies seeking to profit by installing a better manage-ment team. The main carrot is *compensation.* If compensation is strictly in the form of salary, then managers will have less incentive to focus on their firms' values than if com-pensation is somehow linked to their firms' performance, especially stock price perform-ance. We discuss different types of motivational devices in the following subsections.

Provisions to Prevent Managerial Entrenchment

Suppose a company has a weak board of directors and strong anti-takeover provisions in its corporate charter, causing senior managers to feel that there is little chance that they will be removed. In this case, management is said to be *entrenched.* Such a company faces a high risk of being poorly run, because entrenched managers are able to act in their own interests rather than in those of shareholders. For example, they can spend company money on such perquisites as lavish offices, memberships at country clubs, and corporate jets. Because these perks are not actually cash payments to the managers, they are called **nonpecuniary benefits.**

Also, entrenched managers are often reluctant to reduce fixed costs by closing or sell-ing off redundant plants, laying off employees whose services are no longer needed, and abandoning projects that show little promise of future profits. Managers often hate to admit mistakes, and they are also reluctant to lay off people, especially old friends and colleagues, even when these actions really should be taken. Entrenchment also enables managers to acquire other companies at too high a price, as well as to accept projects that make the company larger but that have negative MVAs. These actions occur be-cause managerial prestige and salary are associated with larger size, and they result in things that are bad for stockholders but good for the senior executives. Note, though, that if a firm has a strong board, dominated by shareholder-oriented people such as Warren Buffett, or if its charter does not make it too difficult for an outside group to seize control and oust a poorly performing management, then such value-destroying actions are minimized.

BARRIERS TO HOSTILE TAKEOVERS   Hostile takeovers usually occur when managers have not been willing or able to maximize the profit potential of the resources under their control. In such a situation, another company can acquire the poorly performing firm, replace its managers, increase free cash flow, and improve MVA. The following paragraphs describe some provisions that can be included in a corporate charter to make it harder for poorly performing managers to remain in control.[7]

A shareholder-friendly charter should ban **targeted share repurchases,** also known as **greenmail.** For example, suppose a company's stock is selling for $20 per share. Now a

---

[7] Some states have laws that go further than others to protect management. This is one reason that many companies are incor-porated in Delaware. Some companies have even shifted their state of incorporation to Delaware because their managers felt that a hostile takeover attempt was likely. Note that a "shareholder-friendly charter" could and would waive the company's rights to strong anti-takeover protection, even if the state allows it.

hostile bidder, who plans to replace management if the takeover is successful, buys 5 percent of the company's stock at the $20 price.[8] The raider then makes an offer to purchase the remainder of the stock for $30 per share. The company might offer to buy back the bidder's stock at a price of say $35 per share. This is called a targeted share repurchase, since the stock will be purchased only from the bidder and not from any other shareholders. Because the bidder paid only $20 per share for the stock, he or she would be making a quick profit of $15 per share, which could easily total several hundred million dollars. As a part of the deal, the raider would sign a document promising not to attempt to take over the company for a specified number of years, hence the buyback also is called greenmail. Greenmail hurts shareholders in two ways. First, they are left with $20 stock when they could have received $30 per share. Second, the company purchased stock from the bidder at $35 per share, which represents a direct loss by the remaining shareholders of $15 for each repurchased share.

Managers who buy back stock in targeted repurchases typically argue that their firms are worth more than the raiders offered, and that in time the "true value" will be revealed in the form of a much higher stock price. This situation might be true if a company were in the process of restructuring itself, or if new products with high potential were in the pipeline. But if the old management had been in power for a long time, and if it had a history of making empty promises, then one should question whether the true purpose of the buyback was to protect stockholders or management.

Another characteristic of a stockholder-friendly charter is that it does not contain a **shareholder rights provision,** better described as a **poison pill.** These provisions give the shareholders of target firms the right to buy a specified number of shares in the company at a very low price if an outside group or firm acquires a specified percentage of the firm's stock. Therefore, if a potential acquirer tries to take over a company, its other shareholders will be entitled to purchase additional shares of stock at a bargain price, thus seriously diluting the holdings of the raider. For this reason, these clauses are called poison pills, because if they are in the charter, the acquirer will end up swallowing a poison pill if the acquisition is successful. Obviously, the existence of a poison pill makes a takeover more difficult, and this helps to entrench management.

A third management entrenchment tool is a **restricted voting rights** provision, which automatically deprives a shareholder of voting rights if the shareholder owns more than a specified amount of stock. The board can grant voting rights to such a shareholder, but this is unlikely if the shareholder plans to take over the company.

EFFECTIVE MONITORING BY A STRONG BOARD OF DIRECTORS   High compensation and prestige go with a position on the board of a major company, so board seats are prized possessions. Board members typically want to retain their positions, and they are grateful to whoever helped get them on the board. This situation has important implications for corporate governance as it affects stockholders. First, note that 30 years ago a firm's CEO was in all likelihood also the chairman of its board. Moreover, many of the other board members were "insiders," that is, people who held managerial positions within the company, such as the CFO. The CEO, who could remove them from their inside position if they raised objections to his policies, generally nominated them to the board. Even outside board members usually had strong connections with the CEO through personal friendships, consulting or other fee-generating activities, or **interlocking boards of directors,** where Company A's CEO sits on Company B's board and B's CEO sits on A's board. In these situations, even the outside directors are not truly independent and impartial.

---

[8] Someone can, under the law, acquire up to 5 percent of a firm's stock without announcing the acquisition. Once the 5 percent limit has been hit, the acquirer must "announce" the acquisition by filing a report with the SEC, and the report must list not only the acquirer's position but also his or her intentions, such as a passive investment or a takeover. These reports are monitored closely, so as soon as one is filed, management is alerted to the imminent danger of a takeover.

Under an "old boy network" board as described above, the CEO had a much more protected position than is typical today. Now most boards are comprised primarily of outsiders who are not beholden to the CEO, which makes it much more likely that an ineffective CEO will be removed. Also, in earlier years board members were compensated in the form of salary, whereas today directors are generally given stock or options, so an ineffective management team costs the directors money. The changes in director compensation, together with directors' greater independence, have done much to improve the way boards monitor managerial performance and react to poor results.[9]

Why have these changes occurred? The primary reason has to do with a shift in the ownership of common stocks. Prior to the 1960s, most stock was owned by a large number of individual investors, each of whom owned a diversified portfolio of stocks. Because these individuals had just a small amount of any given company's stock, they could do little to influence its operations. Also, with just a small investment, it was not cost effective for them to monitor companies closely. Indeed, if a stockholder was dissatisfied, he or she would typically just "vote with his feet," that is, sell his or her stock. This situation began to change as institutional investors such as pension and mutual funds gained control of a larger and larger share of investment capital, and as they then acquired a larger and larger percentage of all outstanding stock. Given their large holdings, it makes sense for institutional investors to monitor management, and they have the clout to influence the board. In some cases, they have actually elected their own representatives to the board. For example, when TIAA–CREF, a huge private pension fund, became frustrated with the performance and leadership of Furr's/Bishop, a cafeteria chain, the fund led a fight that ousted the entire board and then elected a new board, which consisted only of outsiders.

In general, activist investors with large stakes in companies have been good for all shareholders. They have searched for firms with poor profitability, then replaced management with new teams that are well-versed in value-based management techniques, and thereby improved profitability. Not surprisingly, stock prices usually rise when the news comes out that a well-known activist investor has taken a major position in an underperforming company.

Note that activist investors can improve performance even if they don't go so far as to take over a firm. More often, they get a few people on the board, those people point out the firm's problems, and then the other board members change their attitudes and become less tolerant when they realize that the management team is not following the dictates of value-based management. Moreover, the firm's top managers recognize what will happen if they don't whip the company into shape, and they go about doing just that.

As power has shifted from CEOs to boards as a whole, there has been a tendency to replace insiders with strong, independent outsiders. Today, the typical board has about one-third insiders and two-thirds outsiders, and most outsiders are truly independent. Moreover, they are compensated primarily with stock rather than a straight salary. All of this has clearly decreased the patience of boards with poorly performing CEOs, and within the past several years the CEOs of Procter & Gamble, Coca-Cola, GM, IBM, Mattel, Campbell Soup, and Xerox, to name just a few, have been removed. This would have been unheard of 30 years ago.

---

[9] Note that boards can be elected by either cumulative or noncumulative voting. Under cumulative voting, each shareholder is given a number of votes equal to his or her shares times the number of board seats up for election. For example, the holder of 100 shares of stock will receive 1,000 votes if 10 seats are to be filled. Then, the shareholder can distribute his or her votes however he or she sees fit. One hundred votes could be cast for each of 10 candidates, or all 1,000 votes could be cast for one candidate. If noncumulative voting is used, our illustrative stockholder cannot concentrate his or her votes—no more than 100 votes can be cast for any one candidate.

With noncumulative voting, if management controls 51 percent of the shares, they can fill every seat on the board—dissident stockholders cannot put a representative on the board. With cumulative voting, however, if 10 seats are to be filled, dissidents can elect a representative, provided they have 10 percent plus one share of the stock.

Note also that bylaws specify whether the entire board is to be elected annually or if directors are to have staggered terms, with, say, one-third of the seats to be filled each year and directors to serve three-year terms. With staggered terms, fewer seats come up each year, making it harder for dissidents to gain representation on the board.

Using Compensation to Align Managerial and Shareholder Interests

In the preceding section we discussed the stick side of corporate governance. Now we turn to the carrot, managerial compensation. The typical CEO today receives a fixed salary plus a bonus that is zero if the firm's performance is poor but that rises as performance becomes better and better. Salary for an average executive amounts to about 21 percent of total compensation versus bonuses of about 79 percent. So, performance certainly matters![10]

Executive bonuses are based on a number of criteria, some reflecting short-term, or very recent, performance and others reflecting performance over a longer period. Bonuses also reflect internal operating statistics as well as stock prices, which reflect both internal operations and general stock market movements. On average, short-run operating factors such as this year's growth in earnings per share account for about 34 percent of the bonus, 20 percent is based on longer-term operating performance such as earnings growth over the last three years, and the remaining 46 percent is linked to the company's stock price. Bonuses can be paid in cash, in stock, or in options to buy stock. Moreover, they can be paid immediately after the relevant period (immediate vesting) or be awarded in stages over a number of years (deferred vesting). To illustrate deferred vesting, an executive might be awarded 10,000 shares of stock, but at the rate of 2,000 per year for each of the next five years, provided he or she is still with the company on each payment date.

STOCK OPTIONS   Stock-based compensation is often in the form of options. Chapter 8 explains option valuation in detail, but we discuss here how a standard stock option compensation plan works. Suppose IBM decides to grant an option to an employee, allowing him or her to purchase a specified number of IBM shares at a fixed price, called the **exercise price,** regardless of the actual price of the stock. The exercise price is usually set equal to the current stock price at the time the option is granted. Thus, if IBM's current price were $100, then the option would have an exercise price of $100. Options usually cannot be exercised until after some specified period (the **vesting period**), which is usually one to five years. Moreover, they have an **expiration date,** usually 10 years after issue. For our IBM example, assume that the vesting period is 3 years and the expiration date is 10 years. Thus, the employee can exercise the option 3 years after issue or wait as long as 10 years. Of course, the employee would not exercise unless IBM's stock is above the $100 exercise price, and if the price never rose above $100, the option would expire unexercised. However, if the stock price were above $100 on the expiration date, the option would surely be exercised.

Suppose the stock price had grown to $134 after five years, at which point the employee decided to exercise the option. He or she would buy stock from IBM for $100, so IBM would get only $100 for stock worth $134. The employee would (probably) sell the stock the same day he or she exercised the option, hence would receive in cash the $34 difference between the $134 stock price and the $100 exercise price. People often time the exercise of options to the purchase of a new home or some other large expenditure.

Let's suppose the employee is actually a senior executive and the grant was for options on 1 million shares. In this case, the executive would receive $34 for each option, or a total of $34 million. Keep in mind that this is in addition to an annual salary and other bonuses. The logic behind employee options is that they motivate people to work harder and smarter, thus making the company more valuable and benefiting shareholders. But take a closer look at this example. If the risk-free rate is 6.5 percent, the market risk premium is 6 percent, and IBM's beta is 1.09, then the expected return, based on the CAPM, is 13 percent [6.5% + 1.09(6%) = 13%]. IBM's dividend yield is only 0.4 percent, so the expected annual price appreciation must be around 12.6 percent (13% − 0.4% = 12.6%). Now note that if IBM's stock price grew from $100 to $134 over five years, that would translate to an annual growth rate of only 6 percent, not the 12.6 percent shareholders

[10] See Thomas A. Stewart, "CEO Pay: Mom Wouldn't Approve," *Fortune,* March 31, 1997, 119–120.

INTERNATIONAL CORPORATE GOVERNANCE

Corporate governance includes the following factors: (1) the likelihood that a poorly performing firm can be taken over; (2) whether the board of directors is dominated by insiders or outsiders; (3) the extent to which most of the stock is held by a few large "blockholders" versus many small shareholders; and (4) the size and form of executive compensation. A recent study compared Germany, Japan, and the United States.

First, note from the accompanying table that the threat of a takeover serves as a stick in the United States but not in Japan or Germany. This threat, which reduces management entrenchment, should benefit shareholders in the United States relative to the other two countries. Second, German and Japanese boards are larger than those in the United States, and Japanese boards consist primarily of insiders versus German and American boards, which have similar inside/outside mixes. It should be noted, though, that the boards of most large German corporations include representatives of labor, whereas U.S. boards represent just shareholders. Thus, it would appear that U.S. boards, with a higher percentage of outsiders, would have interests most closely aligned with those of shareholders.

German and Japanese firms are also more likely to be controlled by large blocks of stock than in the United States. Although pension and mutual funds, as well as other institutional investors, are increasingly important in the United States, block ownership is still less than in Germany and Japan. In both Germany and Japan, banks often own large blocks of stock, something that is not permitted by law in the United States, and corporations also own large blocks of stock in other corporations. In Japan, combinations of companies, called **keiretsus**, have cross-ownership of stock among the member companies, and these interlocking blocks distort the definition of an outside board member. For example, when the performance of a company in a keiretsu deteriorates, new directors are often appointed from the staffs of other members of the keiretsu. Such appointees might be classified officially as insiders, but they represent interests other than those of the troubled company's CEO.

In general, large blockholders are better able to monitor management than are small investors, so one might expect the blockholder factor to favor German and Japanese shareholders. However, these blockholders have other relationships with the company that might be detrimental to outside shareholders. For example, if one company buys from another, they might use transfer pricing to shift wealth to a favored company, or a company might be forced to buy from a sister company in spite of the availability of lower-cost resources from outside the group.

Executive compensation packages differ dramatically across the three countries, with U.S.

expected. Thus, the executive would receive $34 million for helping run a company that performed below shareholders' expectations. As this example illustrates, standard stock options do not necessarily link executives' wealth with that of shareholders.

Even worse, the events of the early 2000s showed that some executives are willing to illegally falsify financial statements in order to drive up stock prices just prior to exercising their stock options. In some notable cases, the subsequent stock price drop and loss of investor confidence has forced firms into bankruptcy. This behavior is certainly not in shareholders' best interest! As a result, companies today are experimenting with different types of compensation plans, with different vesting periods and different measures of performance.[11]

EMPLOYEE STOCK OWNERSHIP PLANS (ESOPs) Studies show that 90 percent of the employees who receive stock under **option** plans sell the stock as soon as they exercise their options, so the plans motivate employees only for a limited period.[12] Moreover,

---

[11] It should be noted that the empirical literature listed in the end-of-chapter references shows that the correlation between executive compensation and corporate performance is mixed. Some studies suggest that the type of compensation plan used affects company performance, while others suggest little if any effect. Note also that just as "all ships rise in a rising tide," so too do most stocks rise in a bull market such as the one during the 1990s. In a strong market, even the stocks of companies whose performance ranks in the bottom 10 percent of their peer group can rise and thus trigger handsome executive bonuses. This situation is leading to compensation plans that are based on *relative* as opposed to *absolute* stock price performance. For example, some compensation plans have indexed options, whose exercise prices depend on the performance of the market or of a subset of competitors.

[12] See Gary Laufman, "To Have and Have Not," *CFO*, March 1998, 58–66.

executives receiving by far the highest compensation. However, compensation plans are remarkably similar in terms of how sensitive total compensation is to corporate performance.

Which country's system of corporate governance is best from the standpoint of a shareholder whose goal is stock price maximization? There is no definitive answer. U.S. stocks have had the best performance in recent years. Moreover, German and Japanese companies are slowly moving toward the U.S. system with respect to size of compensation, and compensation plans in all three countries

are being linked ever stronger to performance. At the same time, though, U.S. companies are moving toward the others in the sense of having larger ownership blocks, and since those blocks are primarily held by pension and mutual funds rather than banks and related corporations, they better represent the interests of shareholders.

Source: Steven N. Kaplan, "Top Executive Incentives in Germany, Japan, and the USA: A Comparison," in *Executive Compensation and Shareholder Value,* Jennifer Carpenter and David Yermack, eds. (Boston: Kluwer Academic Publishers, 1999), 3–12.

International Characteristics of Corporate Governance

	Germany	Japan	United States
Threat of a takeover	Moderate	Low	High
Board of directors			
Size of board	26	21	14
Percent insiders	27%	91%	33%
Percent outsiders	73%	9%	67%
Are large blocks of stock typically owned by			
A controlling family?	Yes	No	No
Another corporation?	Yes	Yes	No
A bank?	Yes	Yes	No
Executive compensation			
Amount of compensation	Moderate	Low	High
Sensitivity to performance	Low to moderate	Low to moderate	Low to moderate

See *http://www .esopassociation .org for more on ESOPs.*

many companies limit their stock option plans to key managers and executives. To help provide long-term productivity gains, and also to help improve retirement incomes for all employees, Congress authorized the use of **Employee Stock Ownership Plans (ESOPs).** Today about 9,000 privately held companies and 1,000 publicly held firms have ESOPs, and more are being created every day. Typically, the ESOP's major asset is shares of the common stock of the company that created it, and of the 10,000 total ESOPs, about 2,500 of them actually own a majority of their company's stock.[13]

To illustrate how an ESOP works, consider Gallagher & Abbott Inc. (G&A), a Knoxville, Tennessee, construction company. G&A's simplified balance sheet is shown below:

G&A's Balance Sheet Prior to ESOP (millions of dollars)

Assets		Liabilities and Equity	
Cash	$ 10	Debt	$100
Other	190	Equity (1 million shares)	100
Total	$200	**Total**	$200

---

[13] See Eugene Pilotte, "Employee Stock Ownership Plans, Management Motives, and Shareholder Wealth: A Review of the Evidence," *Journal of Financial Education,* Spring 1997, 41–46; and Daniel Eisenberg, "No ESOP Fable," *Time,* May 10, 1999, 95.

Now G&A creates an ESOP, which is a new legal entity. The company issues 500,000 shares of new stock at $100 per share, or $50 million in total, which it sells to the ESOP. G&A's employees are the ESOP's stockholders, and each employee receives an ownership interest based on the size of his or her salary and years of service. The ESOP borrows the $50 million to buy the newly issued stock.[14] Financial institutions are willing to lend the ESOP the money because G&A signs a guarantee for the loan. Here is the company's new balance sheet:

G&A's Balance Sheet after the ESOP (millions of dollars)

Assets		Liabilities and Equity	
Cash	$ 60	Debt[a]	$100
Other	190	Equity (1.5 million shares)	150
Total	**$250**	**Total**	**$250**

[a]The company has guaranteed the ESOP's loan, and it has promised to make payments to the ESOP sufficient to retire the loan; but this does not show up on the balance sheet.

The company now has an additional $50 million of cash and $50 million more of book equity, but it has a de facto liability due to its guarantee of the ESOP's debt. It could use the cash to finance an expansion, but many companies use the cash to repurchase their own common stock, so we assume that G&A will do likewise. The company's new balance sheets, and that of the ESOP, are shown below:

G&A's Balance Sheet after the ESOP and Share Repurchase (millions of dollars)

Assets		Liabilities and Equity	
Cash	$ 10	Debt	$100
Other	190	Equity (1.5 million shares)	150
		Treasury stock	(50)
Total	**$200**	**Total**	**$200**

ESOP's Initial Balance Sheet (millions of dollars)

Assets		Liabilities and Equity	
G&A stock	$50	Debt	$50
		Equity	0
Total	**$50**	**Total**	**$50**

Note that while the company's balance sheet looks exactly as it did initially, there is really a huge difference—the footnote that discloses that the company has guaranteed the ESOP's debt, hence that it has an off-balance-sheet liability of $50 million. Moreover, because the ESOP has no equity, the guarantee is very real indeed. Finally, note that operating assets have not been increased at all, but the total debt outstanding and supported by those assets has increased by $50 million.[15]

If this were the whole story, there would be no reason to have an ESOP. However, G&A has promised to make payments to the ESOP in sufficient amounts to enable the ESOP to pay interest and principal charges on the debt so as to amortize the debt over 15 years. Thus, after 15 years the debt will be paid off, and the ESOP's equity holders, who

---

[14] Our description is somewhat simplified. Technically, the stock would be placed in a suspense account and then be allocated to employees as the debt is repaid.

[15] We assumed that the company used the $50 million paid to it by the ESOP to repurchase common stock and thus to increase its de facto debt. It could have used the $50 million to retire debt, in which case its true debt ratio would remain unchanged, or it could have used the money to support an expansion.

are the employees, will have equity with a book value of $50 million and a market value that could be much higher if G&A's stock increases, as it should over time. Then, as employees retire, the ESOP will distribute a pro rata amount of the G&A stock to each employee, who can then use it as a part of his or her retirement plan.

An ESOP is clearly beneficial for employees, but why would a company want to establish one? There are five primary reasons:

1. Congress passed the enabling legislation in hopes of enhancing employees' productivity and thus making the economy more efficient. In theory, if an employee has equity in the enterprise, he or she will work harder and smarter. Note too that if employees are more productive and creative, this will benefit outside shareholders, because productivity enhancements that benefit ESOP shareholders also benefit outside shareholders.

2. The ESOP represents additional compensation to employees, because in our example there is a $50 million (or more) transfer of wealth from existing shareholders to employees over the 15-year period. Presumably, if the ESOP were not created, then some other form of compensation would have been required, and that alternative compensation might not have the secondary benefit of enhancing productivity. Note too that the ESOP's payments to employees (as opposed to the payment by the company) come primarily at retirement, and Congress wanted to boost retirement incomes.

3. Depending on when an employee's rights to the ESOP are vested, the ESOP may help the firm retain employees.

4. There are also strong tax incentives to encourage a company to form an ESOP. First, Congress decreed that in cases where the ESOP owns 50 percent or more of the company's common stock, the financial institutions that lend money to ESOPs can exclude from taxable income 50 percent of the interest they receive on the loan. This improves the financial institutions' after-tax returns, making them willing to lend to ESOPs at below-market rates. Therefore, a company that establishes an ESOP can borrow through the ESOP at a lower rate than would otherwise be available—in our example, the $50 million of debt would be at a reduced rate.

   There is also a second tax advantage. If the company were to borrow directly, it could deduct interest but not principal payments from its taxable income. However, companies typically make the required payments to their ESOPs in the form of cash dividends. Dividends are not normally deductible from taxable income, *but cash dividends paid on ESOP stock are deductible if the dividends are paid to plan participants or are used to repay the loan.* Thus, companies whose ESOPs own 50 percent of their stock can in effect borrow on ESOP loans at subsidized rates and then deduct both the interest and principal payments made on the loans. American Airlines and Publix Supermarkets are two of the many firms that have used ESOPs to obtain this benefit, along with motivating employees by giving them an equity interest in the enterprise.

5. A less desirable use of ESOPs is to help companies avoid being acquired by another company. The company's CEO, or someone appointed by the CEO, typically acts as trustee for its ESOP, and the trustee is supposed to vote the ESOP's shares according to the will of the plan participants. Moreover, the participants, who are the company's employees, usually oppose takeovers because they frequently involve labor cutbacks. Therefore, if an ESOP owns a significant percentage of the company's shares, then management has a powerful tool for warding off takeovers. This is not good for outside stockholders.

Are ESOPs good for a company's shareholders? In theory, ESOPs motivate employees by providing them with an ownership interest. That should increase productivity and thereby enhance stock values. Moreover, tax incentives mitigate the costs associated with some ESOPs. However, an ESOP can be used to help entrench management, and that could hurt stockholders. How do the pros and cons balance out? The empirical evidence is not entirely clear, but certain findings are worth noting. First, if an ESOP is established to help defend against a takeover, then the firm's stock price typically falls when plans for the ESOP are announced. The market does not like the prospect of entrenching management and having to give up the premium normally associated with a takeover. However, if the ESOP is established for tax purposes and/or to motivate employees, the stock price generally goes up at the time of the announcement. In these cases, the company typically has a subsequent improvement in sales per employee and other long-term performance measures, which stimulates the stock price. Indeed, a recent study showed that companies with ESOPs enjoyed a 26 percent average annual stock return versus a return of only 19 percent for peer companies without ESOPs.[16] Therefore, it appears that ESOPs, if used appropriately, can be a powerful tool to help create shareholder value.

| SELF-TEST QUESTIONS |

What are two primary forms of corporate governance (that is, the carrot and the stick)?

What are three provisions in many corporate charters that deter takeovers?

Describe briefly how a typical stock option plan works.

What are ESOPs? What are some of their advantages and disadvantages?

---

[16] See Daniel Eisenberg, "No ESOP Fable," *Time*, May 10, 1999, 95.

SUMMARY

- **Corporate assets** consist of operating assets and financial, or nonoperating, assets.
- **Operating assets** take two forms: assets-in-place and growth options.
- **Assets-in-place** include the land, buildings, machines, and inventory that the firm uses in its operations to produce products and services.
- **Growth options** refer to opportunities the firm has to increase sales. They include opportunities arising from R&D expenditures, customer relationships, and the like.
- **Financial,** or **nonoperating, assets** are distinguished from operating assets and include items such as investments in marketable securities and noncontrolling interests in the stock of other companies.
- The **value of nonoperating assets** is usually close to the figure reported on the balance sheet.
- The **value of operations** is the present value of all the future free cash flows expected from operations when discounted at the weighted average cost of capital:

$$V_{op(at\ time\ 0)} = \sum_{t=1}^{\infty} \frac{FCF_t}{(1 + WACC)^t}.$$

- The **terminal,** or **horizon, value,** is the value of operations at the end of the explicit forecast period. It is also called the **continuing value,** and it is equal to the present value of all free cash flows beyond the forecast period, discounted back to the end of the forecast period at the weighted average cost of capital:

$$\text{Continuing value} = V_{op(at\ time\ N)} = \frac{FCF_{N+1}}{WACC - g} = \frac{FCF_N(1 + g)}{WACC - g}.$$

- The **corporate valuation model** can be used to calculate the total value of a company by finding the value of operations plus the value of nonoperating assets.

- The **value of equity** is the total value of the company minus the value of the debt and preferred stock. The **price per share** is the total value of the equity divided by the number of shares.
- **Value-based management** involves the systematic use of the corporate valuation model to evaluate a company's potential decisions.
- The four **value drivers** are (1) the growth rate in sales (g), (2) operating profitability (OP), which is measured by the ratio of NOPAT to sales, (3) capital requirements (CR) as measured by the ratio of operating capital to sales, and (4) the weighted average cost of capital (WACC).
- **Expected return on invested capital (EROIC)** is equal to expected NOPAT divided by the amount of capital that is available at the beginning of the year.
- A company creates value when the spread between expected ROIC and WACC is positive, that is, when EROIC − WACC > 0.
- **Corporate governance** involves the manner in which shareholders' objectives are implemented, and it is reflected in a company's policies and actions.
- The two primary mechanisms used in corporate governance are: (1) the threat of removal of a poorly performing CEO and (2) the type of plan used to compensate executives and managers.
- Poorly performing managers can be removed either by a takeover or by the company's own board of directors. Provisions in the corporate charter affect the difficulty of a successful takeover, and the composition of the board of directors affects the likelihood of a manager being removed by the board.
- **Managerial entrenchment** is most likely when a company has a weak board of directors coupled with strong anti-takeover provisions in its corporate charter. In this situation, the likelihood that badly performing senior managers will be fired is low.
- **Nonpecuniary benefits** are noncash perks such as lavish offices, memberships at country clubs, corporate jets, foreign junkets, and the like. Some of these expenditures may be cost effective, but others are wasteful and simply reduce profits. Such fat is almost always cut after a hostile takeover.
- **Targeted share repurchases,** also known as **greenmail,** occur when a company buys back stock from a potential acquiror at a higher-than-fair-market price. In return, the potential acquiror agrees not to attempt to take over the company.
- **Shareholder rights provisions,** also known as **poison pills,** allow existing shareholders to purchase additional shares of stock at a lower than market value if a potential acquiror purchases a controlling stake in the company.
- A **restricted voting rights** provision automatically deprives a shareholder of voting rights if the shareholder owns more than a specified amount of stock.
- **Interlocking boards of directors** occur when the CEO of Company A sits on the board of Company B, and B's CEO sits on A's board.
- A **stock option** provides for the purchase of a share of stock at a fixed price, called the **exercise price,** no matter what the actual price of the stock is. Stock options have an **expiration date,** after which they cannot be exercised.
- An **Employee Stock Ownership Plan,** or **ESOP,** is a plan that facilitates employees' ownership of stock in the company for which they work.

QUESTIONS

(13-1) Define each of the following terms:
   a. Assets-in-place; growth options; nonoperating assets
   b. Net operating working capital; operating capital; NOPAT; free cash flow
   c. Value of operations; horizon value; corporate valuation model
   d. Value-based management; value drivers; ROIC
   e. Managerial entrenchment; nonpecuniary benefits
   f. Greenmail; poison pills; restricted voting rights
   g. Stock option; ESOP

(13-2) Explain how to use the corporate valuation model to find the price per share of common equity.

(13-3) Explain how it is possible for sales growth to decrease the value of a profitable company.

(13-4) What are some actions an entrenched management might take that would harm shareholders?

(13-5) How is it possible for an employee stock option to be valuable even if the firm's stock price fails to meet shareholders' expectations?

SELF-TEST PROBLEM   Solution Appears in Appendix A

(ST-1)
Corporate Valuation

Watkins Inc. has never paid a dividend, and when it might begin paying dividends is unknown. Its current free cash flow is $100,000, and this FCF is expected to grow at a constant 7 percent rate. The weighted average cost of capital is WACC = 11%. Watkins currently holds $325,000 of nonoperating marketable securities. Its long-term debt is $1,000,000, but it has never issued preferred stock.
a.   Calculate Watkins' value of operations.
b.   Calculate the company's total value.
c.   Calculate the value of its common equity.

PROBLEMS

(13-1)
Free Cash Flow

Use the following income statements and balance sheets to calculate Garnet Inc.'s free cash flow for 2006.

Garnet Inc.

	2006	2005
INCOME STATEMENT		
Net sales	$530.0	$500.0
Costs (except depreciation)	400.0	380.0
Depreciation	30.0	25.0
Total operating costs	$430.0	$405.0
Earnings before interest and taxes (EBIT)	100.0	95.0
Less interest	23.0	21.0
Earnings before taxes	77.0	74.0
Taxes (40%)	30.8	29.6
Net income	$ 46.2	$ 44.4
BALANCE SHEET		
Assets		
Cash	$ 28.0	$ 27.0
Marketable securities	69.0	66.0
Accounts receivable	84.0	80.0
Inventories	112.0	106.0
Total current assets	$293.0	$279.0
Net plant and equipment	281.0	265.0
Total assets	$574.0	$544.0

	2006	2005
Liabilities and Equity		
Accounts payable	$ 56.0	$ 52.0
Notes payable	138.0	130.0
Accruals	28.0	28.0
Total current liabilities	$222.0	$210.0
Long-term bonds	173.0	164.0
Common stock	100.0	100.0
Retained earnings	79.0	70.0
Common equity	$179.0	$170.0
Total liabilities and equity	$574.0	$544.0

(13-2)
Value of Operations
EMC Corporation has never paid a dividend. Its current free cash flow is $400,000 and is expected to grow at a constant rate of 5 percent. The weighted average cost of capital is WACC = 12%. Calculate EMC's value of operations.

(13-3)
Value of Operations
Brooks Enterprises has never paid a dividend. Free cash flow is projected to be $80,000 and $100,000 for the next 2 years, respectively, and after the second year it is expected to grow at a constant rate of 8 percent. The company's weighted average cost of capital is WACC = 12%.
a. What is the terminal, or horizon, value of operations? (Hint: Find the value of all free cash flows beyond Year 2 discounted back to Year 2.)
b. Calculate the value of Brooks' operations.

(13-4)
Corporate Valuation
Dozier Corporation is a fast-growing supplier of office products. Analysts project the following free cash flows (FCFs) during the next 3 years, after which FCF is expected to grow at a constant 7 percent rate. Dozier's cost of capital is WACC = 13%.

Time	1	2	3
Free cash flow ($ millions)	−$20	$30	$40

a. What is Dozier's terminal, or horizon, value? (Hint: Find the value of all free cash flows beyond Year 3 discounted back to Year 3.)
b. What is the current value of operations for Dozier?
c. Suppose Dozier has $10 million in marketable securities, $100 million in debt, and 10 million shares of stock. What is the price per share?

(13-5)
Horizon Value
Current and projected free cash flows for Radell Global Operations are shown below. Growth is expected to be constant after 2007. The weighted average cost of capital is 11 percent. What is the horizon, or continuing, value at 2007?

	Actual 2005	PROJECTED 2006	2007	2008
Free cash flow (millions of dollars)	$606.82	$667.50	$707.55	$750.00

(13-6)
MVA
A company has capital of $200,000,000. It has an expected ROIC of 9 percent, forecasted constant growth of 5 percent, and a WACC of 10 percent. What is its value of operations? What is its MVA? (Hint: Use Equation 13-4.)

(13-7)
Horizon Value
You are given the following forecasted information for the year 2009: Sales = $300,000,000; Operating profitability (OP) = 6%; Capital requirements (CR) = 43%; Growth (g) = 5%; and the weighted average cost of capital (WACC) = 9.8%. If these values remain constant, what is the horizon value (that is, the 2009 value of operations)? (Hint: Use Equation 13-3.)

(13-8)
Value of Equity
The balance sheets of Hutter Amalgamated are shown below. If the 12/31/2005 value of operations is $756 million, what is the 12/31/2005 value of equity?

Balance Sheets, December 31, 2005 (Millions of Dollars)

Assets		Liabilities and Equity	
Cash	$ 20.0	Accounts payable	$ 19.0
Marketable securities	77.0	Notes payable	151.0
Accounts receivable	100.0	Accruals	51.0
Inventories	200.0	Total current liabilities	$221.0
Total current assets	$397.0	Long-term bonds	190.0
Net plant and equipment	279.0	Preferred stock	76.0
		Common stock (par plus PIC)	100.0
		Retained earnings	89.0
		Common equity	$189.0
Total assets	$676.0	Total liabilities and equity	$676.0

(13-9)
Price per Share

The balance sheets of Roop Industries are shown below. The 12/31/2005 value of operations is $651 million and there are 10 million shares of common equity. What is the price per share?

Balance Sheets, December 31, 2005 (Millions of Dollars)

Assets		Liabilities and Equity	
Cash	$ 20.0	Accounts payable	$ 19.0
Marketable securities	47.0	Notes payable	65.0
Accounts receivable	100.0	Accruals	51.0
Inventories	200.0	Total current liabilities	$135.0
Total current assets	$367.0	Long-term bonds	131.0
Net plant and equipment	279.0	Preferred stock	33.0
		Common stock (par plus PIC)	160.0
		Retained earnings	187.0
		Common equity	$347.0
Total assets	$646.0	Total liabilities and equity	$646.0

(13-10)
Corporate Valuation

The financial statements of Lioi Steel Fabricators are shown below, with the actual results for 2005 and the projections for 2006. Free cash flow is expected to grow at a 6 percent rate after 2006. The weighted average cost of capital is 11 percent.
a. If operating capital as of 12/31/2005 is $502.2 million, what is the free cash flow for 12/31/2006?
b. What is the horizon value as of 12/31/2006?
c. What is the value of operations as of 12/31/2005?
d. What is the total value of the company as of 12/31/2005?
e. What is the price per share for 12/31/2005?

Income Statement for the Year Ending December 31
(Millions of Dollars Except for Per Share Data)

	Actual 2005	Projected 2006
Net sales	$500.0	$530.0
Costs (except depreciation)	360.0	381.6
Depreciation	37.5	39.8
Total operating costs	$397.5	$421.4
Earnings before interest and tax	$102.5	108.6
Less interest	13.9	16.0
Earnings before taxes	$ 88.6	$ 92.6

	Actual 2005	Projected 2006
Taxes (40%)	35.4	37.0
Net income before preferred dividends	$ 53.2	$ 55.6
Preferred dividends	6.0	7.4
Net income avail. for common dividends	$ 47.2	$ 48.2
Common dividends	$ 40.8	$ 29.7
Addition to retained earnings	$ 6.4	$ 18.5
Number of shares	10	10
Dividends per share	$ 4.08	$ 2.97

Balance Sheets for December 31 (Millions of Dollars)

	Actual 2005	Projected 2006
Assets		
Cash	$ 5.3	$ 5.6
Marketable securities	49.9	51.9
Accounts receivable	53.0	56.2
Inventories	106.0	112.4
Total current assets	$214.2	$226.1
Net plant and equipment	375.0	397.5
Total assets	$589.2	$623.6
Liabilities and Equity		
Accounts payable	$ 9.6	$ 11.2
Notes payable	69.9	74.1
Accruals	27.5	28.1
Total current liabilities	$107.0	$113.4
Long-term bonds	140.8	148.2
Preferred stock	35.0	37.1
Common stock (par plus PIC)	160.0	160.0
Retained earnings	146.4	164.9
Common equity	$306.4	$324.9
Total liabilities and equity	$589.2	$623.6

SPREADSHEET PROBLEM

(13-11)
Build a Model:
Corporate Valuation

Start with the partial model in the file *CF2 Ch 13 P11 Build a Model.xls* from the textbook's Web site. The Henley Corporation is a privately held company specializing in lawn care products and services. The most recent financial statements are shown below.

Income Statement for the Year Ending December 31
(Millions of Dollars Except for Per Share Data)

	2005
Net sales	$800.0
Costs (except depreciation)	576.0
Depreciation	60.0
Total operating costs	$636.0
Earnings before interest and taxes	$164.0

	2005
Less interest	32.0
Earnings before taxes	$132.0
Taxes (40%)	52.8
Net income before preferred dividends	$ 79.2
Preferred dividends	1.4
Net income avail. for common dividends	$ 77.9
Common dividends	$ 31.1
Addition to retained earnings	$ 46.7
Number of shares (in millions)	10
Dividends per share	$ 3.11

Balance Sheets for December 31 (Millions of Dollars)

Assets	2005	Liabilities and Equity	2005
Cash	$ 8.0	Accounts payable	$ 16.0
Marketable securities	20.0	Notes payable	40.0
Accounts receivable	80.0	Accruals	40.0
Inventories	160.0	Total current liabilities	$ 96.0
Total current assets	$268.0	Long-term bonds	300.0
Net plant and equipment	600.0	Preferred stock	15.0
		Common stock (par plus PIC)	257.0
		Retained earnings	200.0
		Common equity	$457.0
Total assets	$868.0	Total liabilities and equity	$868.0

The ratios and selected information for the current and projected years are shown below.

	Actual 2005	PROJECTED			
		2006	2007	2008	2009
Sales growth rate		15%	10%	6%	6%
Costs/sales	72%	72	72	72	72
Depreciation/net PPE	10	10	10	10	10
Cash/sales	1	1	1	1	1
Accounts receivable/sales	10	10	10	10	10
Inventories/sales	20	20	20	20	20
Net PPE/sales	75	75	75	75	75
Accounts payable/sales	2	2	2	2	2
Accruals/sales	5	5	5	5	5
Tax rate	40	40	40	40	40
Weighted average cost of capital (WACC)	10.5	10.5	10.5	10.5	10.5

a. Forecast the parts of the income statement and balance sheets necessary to calculate free cash flow.

b. Calculate free cash flow for each projected year. Also calculate the growth rates of free cash flow each year to ensure that there is constant growth (that is, the same as the constant growth rate in sales) by the end of the forecast period.

c. Calculate operating profitability (OP = NOPAT/Sales), capital requirements (CR = Operating capital/Sales), and expected return on invested capital (EROIC = Expected NOPAT/Operating capital at beginning of year). Based on the spread between expected ROIC and WACC, do you think that the company will have a positive market value added (MVA = Market value of company − Book value of company = Value of operations − Operating capital)?

d. Calculate the value of operations and MVA. (Hint: First calculate the horizon value at the end of the forecast period, which is equal to the value of operations at the end of the forecast period. Assume that growth beyond the horizon is 6 percent.)

e. Calculate the price per share of common equity as of 12/31/2005.

CYBERPROBLEM

Please go to our Web site, **http://ehrhardt.swlearning.com**, to access any Cyberproblems.

THOMSON ONE
Business School Edition

Please go to **http://ehrhardt.swlearning.com** to access any Thomson ONE—Business School Edition problems.

MINI CASE

You have been hired as a consultant to Kulpa Fishing Supplies (KFS), a company that is seeking to increase its value. The company's CEO and founder, Mia Kulpa, has asked you to estimate the value of two privately held companies that KFS is considering acquiring. But first, the senior management of KFS would like for you to explain how to value companies that don't pay any dividends. You have structured your presentation around the following questions:

a. List the two types of assets that companies own.

b. What are assets-in-place? How can their value be estimated?

c. What are nonoperating assets? How can their value be estimated?

d. What is the total value of a corporation? Who has claims on this value?

e. The first acquisition target is a privately held company in a mature industry. The company currently has free cash flow of $20 million. Its WACC is 10 percent and it is expected to grow at a constant rate of 5 percent. The company has marketable securities of $100 million. It is financed with $200 million of debt, $50 million of preferred stock, and $210 million of book equity.

   (1) What is its value of operations?

   (2) What is its total corporate value? What is its value of equity?

   (3) What is its MVA (MVA = Total corporate value − Total book value)?

f. The second acquisition target is a privately held company in a growing industry. The target has recently borrowed $40 million to finance its expansion; it has no other debt or preferred stock. It pays no dividends and currently has no marketable securities. KFS expects the company to produce free cash flows of −$5 million in 1 year, $10 million in 2 years, and $20 million in 3 years. After 3 years, free cash flow will grow at a rate of 6 percent. Its WACC is 10 percent and it currently has 10 million shares of stock.

   (1) What is its horizon value (that is, its value of operations at Year 3)? What is its current value of operations (that is, at time zero)?

   (2) What is its value of equity on a price per share basis?

g. KFS is also interested in applying value-based management to its own divisions. Explain what value-based management is.

h. What are the four value drivers? How does each of them affect value?

i. What is expected return on invested capital (EROIC)? Why is the spread between expected ROIC and WACC so important?

j. KFS has two divisions. Both have current sales of $1,000, current expected growth of 5 percent, and a WACC of 10 percent. Division A has high profitability (OP = 6%) but high capital requirements (CR = 78%). Division B has low profitability (OP = 4%) but low capital requirements (CR = 27%). What is the MVA of each division, based on the current growth of 5 percent? What is the MVA of each division if growth is 6 percent?

k. What is the expected ROIC of each division for 5 percent growth and for 6 percent growth? How is this related to MVA?

l. The managers at KFS have heard that corporate governance can affect shareholder value. List for them the two primary mechanisms of corporate governance.

m. Why is entrenched management potentially harmful to shareholders?

n. List three provisions in the corporate charter that affect takeovers.

o. Explain the difference between insiders and outsiders on the board of directors. What are interlocking boards?

p. What is a stock option in a compensation plan?

SELECTED ADDITIONAL REFERENCES

For an explanation of corporate valuation, see

Daves, P., M. Ehrhardt, and R. Shrieves, *Corporate Valuation: A Guide for Managers and Investors* (Mason, OH: Thomson South-Western, 2004).

For explanations of corporate valuation and value-based management, see

Copeland, Tom, Tim Koller, and Jack Murrin, *Valuation: Measuring and Managing the Value of Companies,* 3rd ed. (New York: John Wiley & Sons, 2000).

Martin, John D., and J. William Petty, *Value Based Management: The Corporate Response to the Shareholder Revolution* (Boston: Harvard Business School Press, 2000).

McTaggart, James M., Peter W. Kontes, and Michael C. Mankins, *The Value Imperative* (New York: The Free Press, 1994).

Stewart, G. Bennett, *The Quest for Value* (New York: Harper Collins, 1991).

For additional discussions of corporate governance, see

Carpenter, Jennifer, and David Yermack, Editors, *Executive Compensation and Shareholder Value* (Boston: Kluwer Academic Publishers, 1999).

For more on EVA and performance, see

Peterson, Pamela P., and David R. Peterson, *Company Performance and Measures of Value Added* (The Research Foundation of the Institute of Chartered Financial Analysts, 1996).

Strategic Financing Decisions

CHAPTER 14

Capital Structure Decisions

A company can obtain long-term financing in the form of equity, debt, or some combination. The accompanying table shows the long-term debt ratios for different business sectors and selected individual companies within those industries. There are obvious differences between sectors' average debt ratios, with Technology having a very low average ratio (17 percent) and others, such as Utilities (62 percent), having much higher ratios. But notice that within each sector some companies have very low levels of debt, while others have very high levels. For example, the average debt ratio for Consumer/Noncyclical is 48 percent, but Starbucks has no long-term debt versus Kellogg's 73 percent. Why do we see such variation across companies and business sectors, and can a company make itself more valuable through its choice of debt ratio? Keep these questions in mind as you read the chapter.

For updates on a company's ratio, go to http://finance .yahoo.com, enter the ticker symbol for a stock quote, and select Profile after the quote comes up. Click on Ratio Comparisons (on the right side of the Profile sheet) for updates on the sector ratio. The long-term debt ratio in the table is the percent of long-term financing that comes from debt: (Long-term debt)/ (Long-term debt + Equity).

Sector and Company	Long-Term Debt Ratio	Sector and Company	Long-Term Debt Ratio
Technology	17%	**Consumer/Noncyclical**	48%
Agilent Technologies Inc. (A)	28	Starbucks Corporation (SBUX)	0
IKON Office Solutions (IKN)	48	Kellogg Company (K)	73
Energy	30	**Conglomerates**	57
ExxonMobil Corporation (XOM)	6	Minnesota Mining & Mfg. (MMM)	17
Chesapeake Energy Corp. (CHK)	46	Olin Corp. (OLN)	46
Health Care	24	**Utilities**	62
Patterson Dental Company (PDCO)	39	Reliant Energy Inc. (RRI)	56
HCA Inc. (HCA)	58	CMS Energy Corporation (CMS)	78
Transportation	35	**Services**	41
Roadway Corporation (ROAD)	44	Administaff Inc. (ASF)	25
Continental Airlines Inc. (CAL)	89	Allied Waste Industries (AW)	75
Basic Materials	48	**Consumer Cyclical**	72
Anglo American PLC (AAUK)	25	Callaway Golf Company (ELY)	0
Century Aluminum Company (CENX)	65	Black & Decker Corp. (BDK)	48
Capital Goods	48		
Winnebago Industries (WGO)	0		
Caterpillar Inc. (CAT)	70		

e-resource

*The textbook's Web site contains an Excel file that will guide you through the chapter's calculations. The file for this chapter is **CF2 Ch 14 Tool Kit.xls,** and we encourage you to open the file and follow along as you read the chapter.*

As we saw in Chapters 12 and 13, all firms need operating capital to support their sales. To acquire that operating capital, funds must be raised, usually as a combination of equity and debt. The firm's mixture of debt and equity is called its **capital structure.** Although actual levels of debt and equity may vary somewhat over time, most firms try to keep their financing mix close to a **target capital structure.** The **capital structure decisions** include a firm's choice of a target capital structure, the average maturity of its debt, and the specific sources of financing it chooses at any particular time. As with operating decisions, managers should make capital structure decisions designed to maximize the firm's value.

A PREVIEW OF CAPITAL STRUCTURE ISSUES

Recall from Chapter 13 that the value of a firm is the present value of its expected future free cash flows (FCFs), discounted at its weighted average cost of capital (WACC):[1]

$$V = \sum_{t=1}^{\infty} \frac{FCF_t}{(1 + WACC)^t}.$$

(14-1)

The WACC depends on the percentages of debt and equity (w_d and w_e), the cost of debt (r_d), the cost of stock (r_s), and the corporate tax rate (T):

$$WACC = w_d (1 - T)r_d + w_e r_s.$$

(14-2)

As these equations show, the only way any decision can change a firm's value is by affecting either free cash flows or the cost of capital. We discuss below some of the ways that a higher proportion of debt can affect WACC and/or FCF.

Debt Increases the Cost of Stock, r_s

Debtholders have a prior claim on the company's cash flows relative to shareholders, who are entitled only to any residual cash flow after debtholders have been paid. As we show later in a numerical example, the "fixed" claim of the debtholders causes the "residual" claim of the stockholders to become less certain, and this increases the cost of stock, r_s.

Debt Reduces the Taxes a Company Pays

Imagine that a company's cash flows are a pie, and three different groups get pieces of the pie. The first piece goes to the government in the form of taxes, the second goes to debtholders, and the third to shareholders. Companies can deduct interest expenses when calculating taxable income, which reduces the government's piece of the pie and leaves more pie available to debtholders and investors. This reduction in taxes reduces the after-tax cost of debt, as shown in Equation 14-2.

The Risk of Bankruptcy Increases the Cost of Debt, r_d

As debt increases, the probability of financial distress, or even bankruptcy, goes up. With higher bankruptcy risk, debtholders will insist on a higher promised return, which increases the pre-tax cost of debt, r_d.

---

[1] For simplicity, we assume that the firm has no nonoperating assets.

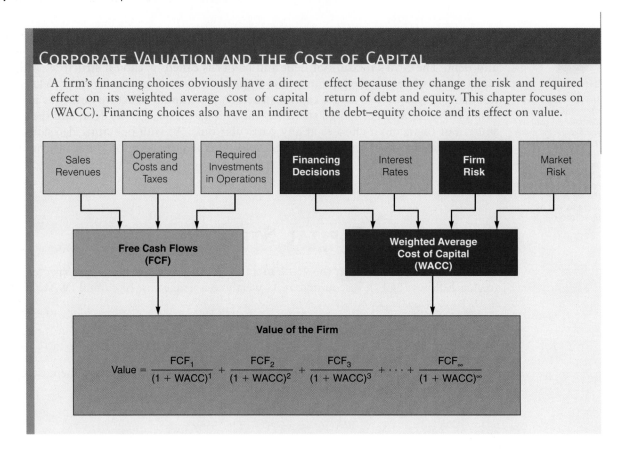

CORPORATE VALUATION AND THE COST OF CAPITAL

A firm's financing choices obviously have a direct effect on its weighted average cost of capital (WACC). Financing choices also have an indirect effect because they change the risk and required return of debt and equity. This chapter focuses on the debt–equity choice and its effect on value.

The Net Effect on the Weighted Average Cost of Capital

As Equation 14-2 shows, the WACC is a weighted average of relatively low-cost debt and high-cost equity. If we increase the proportion of debt, then the weight of low-cost debt (w_d) increases and the weight of high-cost equity (w_e) decreases. If all else remained the same, then the WACC would fall and the value of the firm in Equation 14-1 would increase. But the previous paragraphs show that all else doesn't remain the same: both r_d and r_s increase. While it should be clear that changing the capital structure affects all the variables in the WACC equation, it's not easy to say whether those changes increase the WACC, decrease it, or balance out exactly and leave the WACC unchanged. We'll return to this issue later, when we discuss capital structure theory.

Bankruptcy Risk Reduces Free Cash Flow

As the risk of bankruptcy increases, some customers may choose to buy from another company, which hurts sales. This, in turn, decreases net operating profit after taxes (NOPAT), thus reducing FCF. Financial distress also hurts the productivity of workers and managers, as they spend more time worrying about their next job rather than their current job. Again, this reduces NOPAT and FCF. Finally, suppliers tighten their credit standards, which reduces accounts payable and causes net operating working capital to increase, thus reducing FCF. Therefore, the risk of bankruptcy can decrease FCF and reduce the value of the firm.

Bankruptcy Risk Affects Agency Costs

Higher levels of debt may affect the behavior of managers in two opposing ways. First, when times are good, managers may waste cash flow on perquisites and nonnecessary expenditures. This is an agency cost, as described in Chapter 13. The good news is that the threat of bankruptcy reduces such wasteful spending, which increases FCF.

But the bad news is that a manager may become gun-shy and reject positive NPV projects if they are risky. From the stockholder's point of view it would be unfortunate if a risky project caused the company to go into bankruptcy, but note that other companies in the stockholder's portfolio may be taking on risky projects that turn out successfully. Since most stockholders are well diversified, they can afford for a manager to take on risky but positive NPV projects. But a manager's reputation and wealth are generally tied to a single company, so the project may be unacceptably risky from the manager's point of view. Thus, high debt can cause managers to forego positive NPV projects unless they are extremely safe. This is called the **underinvestment problem,** and it is another type of agency cost. Notice that debt can reduce one aspect of agency costs (wasteful spending) but may increase another (underinvestment), so the net effect on value isn't clear.

Issuing Equity Conveys a Signal to the Marketplace

Managers are in a better position to forecast a company's free cash flow than are investors, and academics call this **informational asymmetry.** Suppose a company's stock price is $50 per share. If managers are willing to issue new stock at $50 per share, investors reason that no one would sell anything for less than its true value. Therefore, the true value of the shares as seen by the managers with their superior information must be less than or equal to $50. Thus, investors perceive an equity issue as a negative signal, and this usually causes the stock price to fall.[2]

| SELF-TEST QUESTION | Briefly describe some ways in which the capital structure decision can affect the WACC and FCF. |

BUSINESS AND FINANCIAL RISK

In Chapter 5, when we examined risk from the viewpoint of a stock investor, we distinguished between *market risk,* which is measured by the firm's beta coefficient, and *stand-alone risk,* which includes both market risk and an element of risk that can be eliminated by diversification. Now we introduce two new dimensions of risk: (1) *business risk,* or the riskiness of the firm's stock if it uses no debt, and (2) *financial risk,* which is the additional risk placed on the common stockholders as a result of the firm's decision to use debt.[3]

Conceptually, each firm has a certain amount of risk inherent in its operations—this is its business risk. If it uses any debt, then in effect it is partitioning its investors into two groups and concentrating its business risk on one class—the common stockholders. The additional risk the stockholders of a leveraged firm face, over the risk they would face if the firm used no debt, is the firm's financial risk. For example, if half of a firm's capital is raised as debt and half as common equity, then each common stockholder would bear about twice as much risk as if only equity were used. Naturally, a leveraged firm's stockholders will demand more compensation for bearing the additional (financial) risk, so the required rate of return on common equity will increase with the use of debt. *In other words, the greater the use of debt, the greater the concentration of risk on the stockholders, and the higher the cost of common equity.* In the balance of this section, we examine business and financial risk within a stand-alone risk framework, which ignores the effects of diversification. Later, we analyze the effects of diversification.

---

[2] An exception to this rule is any situation with little informational asymmetry, such as a regulated utility. Also, some companies, such as startups or high-tech ventures, are unable to issue debt and so simply must issue equity; we discuss this later in the chapter.

[3] Preferred stock also adds to financial risk. To simplify matters, we concentrate on debt and common equity in this chapter.

Business Risk

As noted above, **business risk** is the risk a firm's common stockholders would face if the firm had no debt. Business risk arises from uncertainty in projections of the firm's cash flows, which in turn means uncertainty about its operating profit and its capital (investment) requirements. In other words, we do not know for sure how large operating profits will be, nor do we know how much we will have to invest to develop new products, build new plants, and so forth. The return on invested capital (ROIC) combines these two sources of uncertainty, and its variability can be used to measure business risk on a stand-alone basis:

$$\text{ROIC} = \frac{\text{NOPAT}}{\text{Capital}} = \frac{\text{EBIT} (1 - T)}{\text{Capital}}$$
$$= \frac{\text{Net income to common stockholders} + \text{After-tax interest payments}}{\text{Capital}}.$$

Here NOPAT is net operating profit after taxes, and capital is the required amount of operating capital, which is numerically equivalent to the sum of the firm's debt and common equity. Business risk can then be measured by the standard deviation of ROIC, σ_{ROIC}. If the firm's capital requirements are stable, then we can use the variability in EBIT, σ_{EBIT}, as an alternative measure of stand-alone business risk.

Business risk depends on a number of factors, as described below:

1. *Demand variability.* The more stable the demand for a firm's products, other things held constant, the lower its business risk.
2. *Sales price variability.* Firms whose products are sold in highly volatile markets are exposed to more business risk than similar firms whose output prices are more stable.
3. *Input cost variability.* Firms whose input costs are highly uncertain are exposed to a high degree of business risk.
4. *Ability to adjust output prices for changes in input costs.* Some firms are better able than others to raise their own output prices when input costs rise. The greater the ability to adjust output prices to reflect cost conditions, the lower the business risk.
5. *Ability to develop new products in a timely, cost-effective manner.* Firms in such high-tech industries as drugs and computers depend on a constant stream of new products. The faster its products become obsolete, the greater a firm's business risk.
6. *Foreign risk exposure.* Firms that generate a high percentage of their earnings overseas are subject to earnings declines due to exchange rate fluctuations. Also, if a firm operates in a politically unstable area, it may be subject to political risks. See Chapter 17 for a further discussion.
7. *The extent to which costs are fixed: operating leverage.* If a high percentage of its costs are fixed, hence do not decline when demand falls, then the firm is exposed to a relatively high degree of business risk. This factor is called *operating leverage,* and it is discussed at length in the next section.

Each of these factors is determined partly by the firm's industry characteristics, but each of them is also controllable to some extent by management. For example, most firms can, through their marketing policies, take actions to stabilize both unit sales and sales prices. However, this stabilization may require spending a great deal on advertising and/or price concessions to get commitments from customers to purchase fixed quantities at fixed prices in the future. Similarly, firms can reduce the volatility of future input costs by negotiating long-term labor and materials supply contracts, but they may have to pay prices above the current spot price to obtain these contracts. Many firms are also using hedging techniques to reduce business risk.

Operating Leverage

e-resource

See CF2 Ch14 Tool Kit.xls for detailed calculations.

In physics, leverage implies the use of a lever to raise a heavy object with a small force. In politics, if people have leverage, their smallest word or action can accomplish a lot. *In business terminology, a high degree of* **operating leverage**, *other factors held constant, implies that a relatively small change in sales results in a large change in EBIT.*

Other things held constant, the higher a firm's fixed costs, the greater its operating leverage. Higher fixed costs are generally associated with more highly automated, capital intensive firms and industries. However, businesses that employ highly skilled workers who must be retained and paid even during recessions also have relatively high fixed costs, as do firms with high product development costs, because the amortization of development costs is an element of fixed costs.

Consider Strasburg Electronics Company, a debt-free (unlevered) firm. Figure 14-1 illustrates the concept of operating leverage by comparing the results that Strasburg could expect if it used different degrees of operating leverage. Plan A calls for a relatively small amount of fixed costs, $20,000. Here the firm would not have much automated equipment, so its depreciation, maintenance, property taxes, and so on would be low. However, the total operating costs line has a relatively steep slope, indicating that variable costs per unit are higher than they would be if the firm used more operating leverage. Plan B calls for a higher level of fixed costs, $60,000. Here the firm uses automated equipment (with which one operator can turn out a few or many units at the same labor cost) to a much larger extent. The breakeven point is higher under Plan B—breakeven occurs at 60,000 units under Plan B versus only 40,000 units under Plan A.

We can calculate the breakeven quantity by recognizing that **operating breakeven** occurs when earnings before interest and taxes (EBIT) = 0:[4]

$$EBIT = PQ - VQ - F = 0. \tag{14-3}$$

Here P is average sales price per unit of output, Q is units of output, V is variable cost per unit, and F is fixed operating costs. If we solve for the breakeven quantity, Q_{BE}, we get this expression:

$$Q_{BE} = \frac{F}{P - V}. \tag{14-3a}$$

Thus for Plan A,

$$Q_{BE} = \frac{\$20,000}{\$2.00 - \$1.50} = 40,000 \text{ units,}$$

and for Plan B,

$$Q_{BE} = \frac{\$60,000}{\$2.00 - \$1.00} = 60,000 \text{ units.}$$

How does operating leverage affect business risk? *Other things held constant, the higher a firm's operating leverage, the higher its business risk.* The data in Figure 14-1 confirm this.

---

[4] This definition of breakeven does not include any fixed financial costs because Strasburg is an unlevered firm. If there were fixed financial costs, the firm would suffer an accounting loss at the operating breakeven point. We introduce financial costs shortly.

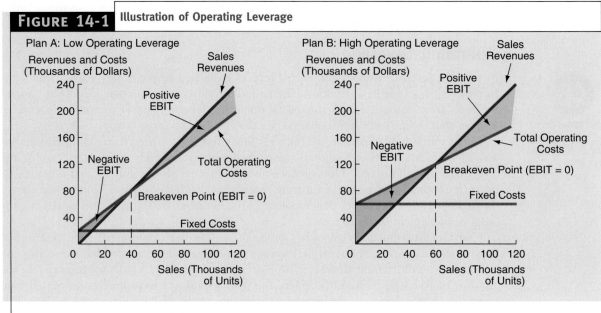

FIGURE 14-1 Illustration of Operating Leverage

	Plan A	Plan B
Price	$2.00	$2.00
Variable costs	$1.50	$1.00
Fixed costs	$20,000	$60,000
Capital	$200,000	$200,000
Tax rate	40%	40%

				PLAN A				PLAN B			
Demand	Probability	Units Sold	Dollar Sales	Operating Costs	Pre-Tax Operating Profit (EBIT)	Net Operating Profit after Taxes (NOPAT)	ROIC	Operating Costs	Pre-Tax Operating Profit (EBIT)	Net Operating Profit after Taxes (NOPAT)	ROIC
Terrible	0.05	0	$ 0	$ 20,000	($20,000)	($12,000)	−6.0%	$ 60,000	($ 60,000)	($36,000)	−18.0%
Poor	0.20	40,000	80,000	80,000	0	0	0.0	100,000	(20,000)	(12,000)	−6.0
Normal	0.50	100,000	200,000	170,000	30,000	18,000	9.0	160,000	40,000	24,000	12.0
Good	0.20	160,000	320,000	260,000	60,000	36,000	18.0	220,000	100,000	60,000	30.0
Wonderful	0.05	200,000	400,000	320,000	80,000	48,000	24.0%	260,000	140,000	84,000	42.0
Expected value:		100,000	$200,000	$170,000	$30,000	$18,000	9.0%	$160,000	$ 40,000	$24,000	12.0%
Standard deviation:					$24,698		7.4%		$ 49,396		14.8%
Coefficient of variation:					0.82		0.82		1.23		1.23

Notes:

a.   Operating costs = Variable costs + Fixed costs.

b.   The federal-plus-state tax rate is 40 percent, so NOPAT = EBIT (1 − Tax rate) = EBIT(0.6).

c.   ROIC = NOPAT/Capital.

d.   The breakeven sales level for Plan B is not shown in the table, but it is 60,000 units or $120,000.

e.   The expected values, standard deviations, and coefficients of variation were found using the procedures discussed in Chapter 5.

Plan A's lower operating leverage gives rise to a much lower range of possible EBITs, from −$20,000 if demand is terrible to $80,000 if demand is wonderful, with a standard deviation of $24,698. Plan B's EBIT range is much larger, from −$60,000 to $140,000, and it has a standard deviation of $49,396. Plan A's ROIC range is lower as well, from −6.0 percent to 24.0 percent, with a standard deviation of 7.4 percent, versus Plan B's ROIC range of from −18 percent to 42 percent, with a standard deviation of 14.8 percent, which is twice as high as A's.

Even though Plan B is riskier, note also that it has a higher expected EBIT and ROIC: $40,000 and 12 percent versus A's $30,000 and 9 percent. Therefore, Strasburg must make a choice between a project with a higher expected return but more risk and one with less risk but a lower return. For the rest of this analysis, we assume that Strasburg decided to go ahead with Plan B because management believes that the higher expected return is sufficient to compensate for the higher risk.

To a large extent, operating leverage is determined by technology. Electric utilities, telephone companies, airlines, steel mills, and chemical companies simply *must* have large investments in fixed assets; this results in high fixed costs and operating leverage. Similarly, drug, auto, computer, and other companies must spend heavily to develop new products, and product-development costs increase operating leverage. Grocery stores, on the other hand, generally have significantly lower fixed costs, hence lower operating leverage. Although industry factors do exert a major influence, all firms have some control over their operating leverage. For example, an electric utility can expand its generating capacity by building either a gas-fired or a coal-fired plant. The coal plant would require a larger investment and would have higher fixed costs, but its variable operating costs would be relatively low. The gas-fired plant, on the other hand, would require a smaller investment and would have lower fixed costs, but the variable costs (for gas) would be high. Thus, by its capital budgeting decisions, a utility (or any other company) can influence its operating leverage, hence its business risk.[5]

Financial Risk

Financial risk is the additional risk placed on the common stockholders as a result of the decision to finance with debt. Conceptually, stockholders face a certain amount of risk that is inherent in a firm's operations—this is its business risk, which is defined as the uncertainty inherent in projections of future ROIC. If a firm uses debt (financial leverage), this concentrates its business risk on its common stockholders. To illustrate, suppose ten people decide to form a corporation to manufacture disk drives. There is a certain amount of business risk in the operation. If the firm is capitalized only with common equity, and if each person buys 10 percent of the stock, then each investor shares equally in the business risk. However, suppose the firm is capitalized with 50 percent debt and 50 percent equity, with five of the investors putting up their capital as debt and the other five putting up their money as equity. In this case, the five investors who put up the equity will have to bear *virtually all* of the business risk, so the common stock will be much riskier than it would have been had the firm been financed only with equity. Thus, the use of debt, or **financial leverage**, concentrates the firm's business risk on its stockholders. This concentration of business risk occurs because debtholders, who receive fixed interest payments, bear none of the business risk.[6]

To illustrate the concentration of business risk, we can extend the Strasburg Electronics example. To date, the company has never used debt, but the treasurer is now considering a possible change in the capital structure. For now, assume that only two financing choices are being considered—remaining at zero debt, or shifting to $100,000 debt and $100,000 book equity.

First, focus on Section I of Table 14-1, which assumes that Strasburg uses no debt. Since debt is zero, interest is also zero, hence pre-tax income is equal to EBIT. Taxes at 40 percent are deducted to obtain net income, which is then divided by the $200,000 of book

CF

e-resource

See CF2 Ch14 Tool Kit.xls for detailed calculations.

CF

e-resource

---

[5] See the Web Extension to this chapter for additional discussion of the degree of operating leverage.

[6] Holders of corporate debt generally do bear some business risk, because they may lose some of their investment if the firm goes bankrupt. We discuss this in more depth later in the chapter.

TABLE 14-1	Effects of Financial Leverage: Strasburg Electronics Financed with Zero Debt or with $100,000 of Debt

SECTION I. ZERO DEBT

Debt   0

Book equity $200,000

Demand for Product (1)	Probability (2)	EBIT (3)	Interest (4)	Pre-Tax Income (5)	Taxes (40%) (6)	Net Income (7)	ROE (8)
Terrible	0.05	($ 60,000)	$0	($ 60,000)	($24,000)	($36,000)	−18.0%
Poor	0.20	(20,000)	0	(20,000)	(8,000)	(12,000)	−6.0
Normal	0.50	40,000	0	40,000	16,000	24,000	12.0
Good	0.20	100,000	0	100,000	40,000	60,000	30.0
Wonderful	0.05	140,000	0	140,000	56,000	84,000	42.0
Expected value:		$ 40,000	$0	$ 40,000	$16,000	$24,000	12.0%
Standard deviation:							14.8%
Coefficient of variation:							1.23

SECTION II. $100,000 OF DEBT

Debt $100,000

Book equity $100,000

Interest rate   10%

Demand for Product (1)	Probability (2)	EBIT (3)	Interest (4)	Pre-Tax Income (5)	Taxes (40%) (6)	Net Income (7)	ROE (8)
Terrible	0.05	($ 60,000)	$10,000	($ 70,000)	($28,000)	($42,000)	−42.0%
Poor	0.20	(20,000)	10,000	(30,000)	(12,000)	(18,000)	−18.0
Normal	0.50	40,000	10,000	30,000	12,000	18,000	18.0
Good	0.20	100,000	10,000	90,000	36,000	54,000	54.0
Wonderful	0.05	140,000	10,000	130,000	52,000	78,000	78.0
Expected value:		$ 40,000	$10,000	$ 30,000	$12,000	$18,000	18.0%
Standard deviation:							29.6%
Coefficient of variation:							1.65

Assumptions:
1. In terms of its operating leverage, Strasburg has chosen Plan B. The probability distribution and EBITs are obtained from Figure 14-1.
2. Sales and operating costs, hence EBIT, are not affected by the financing decision. Therefore, EBIT under both financing plans is identical, and it is taken from the EBIT column for Plan B in Figure 14-1.
3. All losses can be carried back to offset income in the prior year.

equity to calculate ROE. Note that Strasburg receives a tax credit if the demand is either terrible or poor (which are the two scenarios where net income is negative). Here we assume that Strasburg's losses can be carried back to offset income earned in the prior year. The ROE at each sales level is then multiplied by the probability of that sales level to calculate the 12 percent expected ROE. Note that this 12 percent is equal to the ROIC we found in Figure 14-1 for Plan B, since ROE is equal to ROIC if a firm has no debt.

Now let's look at the situation if Strasburg decides to use $100,000 of debt financing, shown in Section II of Table 14-1, with the debt costing 10 percent. Demand will not be affected, nor will operating costs, hence the EBIT columns are the same for the zero debt and $100,000 debt cases. However, the company will now have $100,000 of debt with a cost of 10 percent, hence its interest expense will be $10,000. This interest must be paid regardless of the state of the economy—if it is not paid, the company will be forced into bankruptcy, and stockholders will probably be wiped out. Therefore, we show a $10,000 cost in Column 4 as a fixed number for all demand conditions. Column 5 shows pre-tax income, Column 6 the applicable taxes, and Column 7 the resulting net income. When the net income figures are divided by the book equity—which will now be only $100,000 because $100,000 of the $200,000 total requirement was obtained as debt—we find the ROEs under each demand state. If demand is terrible and sales are zero, then a very large loss will be incurred, and the ROE will be −42.0 percent. However, if demand is wonderful, then ROE will be 78.0 percent. The probability-weighted average is the expected ROE, which is 18.0 percent if the company uses $100,000 of debt.

Typically, financing with debt increases the common stockholders' expected rate of return for an investment, but debt also increases the common stockholders' risk. This situation holds with our example—financial leverage raises the expected ROE from 12 percent to 18 percent, but it also increases the risk of the investment as seen by the increase in the standard deviation from 14.8 percent to 29.6 percent and the increase in the coefficient of variation from 1.23 to 1.65.[7]

We see, then, that using leverage has both good and bad effects: higher leverage increases expected ROE, but it also increases risk. The next section discusses how this trade-off between risk and return affects the value of the firm.

SELF-TEST QUESTIONS

What is business risk, and how can it be measured?

What are some determinants of business risk?

How does operating leverage affect business risk?

What is financial risk, and how does it arise?

Explain this statement: "Using leverage has both good and bad effects."

CAPITAL STRUCTURE THEORY

In the previous section, we showed how capital structure choices affect a firm's ROE and its risk. For a number of reasons, we would expect capital structures to vary considerably across industries. For example, pharmaceutical companies generally have very different capital structures than airline companies. Moreover, capital structures vary among firms within a given industry. What factors explain these differences? In an attempt to answer this question, academics and practitioners have developed a number of theories, and the theories have been subjected to many empirical tests. The following sections examine several of these theories.

Modigliani and Miller: No Taxes

Modern capital structure theory began in 1958, when Professors Franco Modigliani and Merton Miller (hereafter MM) published what has been called the most influential finance article ever written.[8] MM's study was based on some strong assumptions, including the following:

1. There are no brokerage costs.
2. There are no taxes.

---

[7] See Chapter 5 for a review of procedures for calculating the standard deviation and coefficient of variation. Recall that the advantage of the coefficient of variation is that it permits better comparisons when the expected values of ROEs vary, as they do here for the two capital structures.

[8] Franco Modigliani and Merton H. Miller, "The Cost of Capital, Corporation Finance, and the Theory of Investment," *American Economic Review,* June 1958. Modigliani and Miller both won Nobel Prizes for their work.

3. There are no bankruptcy costs.
4. Investors can borrow at the same rate as corporations.
5. All investors have the same information as management about the firm's future investment opportunities.
6. EBIT is not affected by the use of debt.

If these assumptions hold true, MM proved that a firm's value is unaffected by its capital structure, hence the following situation must exist:

$$V_L = V_U = S_L + D. \tag{14-4}$$

Here V_L is the value of a levered firm, which is equal to V_U, the value of an identical but unlevered firm. S_L is the value of the levered firm's stock, and D is the value of its debt.

Recall that the WACC is a combination of the cost of debt and the relatively higher cost of equity, r_s. As leverage increases, more weight is given to low-cost debt, but equity gets riskier, driving up r_s. Under MM's assumptions, r_s increases by exactly enough to keep the WACC constant. Put another way, if MM's assumptions are correct, it does not matter how a firm finances its operations, so capital structure decisions would be irrelevant.

Despite the fact that some of these assumptions are obviously unrealistic, MM's irrelevance result is extremely important. By indicating the conditions under which capital structure is irrelevant, MM also provided us with clues about what is required for capital structure to be relevant and hence to affect a firm's value. MM's work marked the beginning of modern capital structure research, and subsequent research has focused on relaxing the MM assumptions in order to develop a more realistic theory of capital structure.

Another extremely important aspect of MM's work was their thought process. To make a long story short, they imagined two portfolios. The first contained all the equity of the unlevered firm, and it generated cash flows in the form of dividends. The second portfolio contained all the levered firm's stock and debt, so its cash flows were the levered firm's dividends and interest payments. Under MM's assumptions, the cash flows of the two portfolios would be identical. They then concluded that if two portfolios produce the same cash flows, then they must have the same value.[9] As we showed in Chapter 8, this simple idea changed the entire financial world because it led to the development of options and derivatives. Thus, their paper's approach was just as important as its conclusions.

Modigliani and Miller: The Effect of Corporate Taxes

MM published a follow-up paper in 1963 in which they relaxed the assumption that there are no corporate taxes.[10] The Tax Code allows corporations to deduct interest payments as an expense, but dividend payments to stockholders are not deductible. This differential treatment encourages corporations to use debt in their capital structures. This means that interest payments reduce the taxes paid by a corporation, and if a corporation pays less to the government, more of its cash flow is available for its investors. In other words, the tax deductibility of the interest payments shields the firm's pre-tax income.

As in their earlier paper, MM introduced a second important way of looking at the effect of capital structure: The value of a levered firm is the value of an otherwise identi-

---

[9] They actually showed that if the values of the two portfolios differed, then an investor could engage in riskless arbitrage: The investor could create a trading strategy (buying one portfolio and selling the other) that had no risk, required none of the investor's own cash, and resulted in a positive cash flow for the investor. This would be such a desirable strategy that everyone would try to implement it. But if everyone tries to buy the same portfolio, its price will be driven up by market demand, and if everyone tries to sell a portfolio, its price will be driven down. The net result of the trading activity would be to change the portfolio's values until they were equal and no more arbitrage was possible.

[10] Franco Modigliani and Merton H. Miller, "Corporate Income Taxes and the Cost of Capital: A Correction," *American Economic Review* 53, June 1963, 433–443.

cal unlevered firm plus the value of any "side effects." While others expanded on this idea, the only side effect MM considered was the tax shield:

$$V_L = V_U + \text{Value of side effects} = V_U + \text{PV of tax shield.} \qquad (14\text{-}5)$$

Under their assumptions, they showed that the present value of the tax shield is equal to the corporate tax rate, T, multiplied by the amount of debt, D:

$$V_L = V_U + TD. \qquad (14\text{-}6)$$

With a tax rate of about 40 percent, this implies that every dollar of debt adds about 40 cents of value to the firm, and this leads to the conclusion that the optimal capital structure is virtually 100 percent debt. MM also showed that the cost of equity, r_s, increases as leverage increases, but that it doesn't increase quite as fast as it would if there were no taxes. As a result, under MM with corporate taxes the WACC falls as debt is added.

Miller: The Effect of Corporate and Personal Taxes

Merton Miller (this time without Modigliani) later brought in the effects of personal taxes.[11] He noted that all of the income from bonds is generally interest, which is taxed as personal income at rates (T_d) going up to 38.6 percent, while income from stocks generally comes partly from dividends and partly from capital gains. Further, long-term capital gains are taxed at a rate of 20 percent, and this tax is deferred until the stock is sold and the gain realized. If stock is held until the owner dies, no capital gains tax whatever must be paid. So, on average, returns on stocks are taxed at lower effective rates (T_s) than returns on debt.

Because of the tax situation, Miller argued that investors are willing to accept relatively low before-tax returns on stock relative to the before-tax returns on bonds. (The situation here is similar to that with tax-exempt municipal bonds as discussed in Chapter 6 and preferred stocks held by corporate investors as discussed in Chapter 7.) For example, an investor might require a return of 10 percent on Strasburg's bonds, and if stock income were taxed at the same rate as bond income, the required rate of return on Strasburg's

---

[11] Merton H. Miller, "Debt and Taxes," *Journal of Finance* 32, May 1977, 261–275. Miller was president of the American Finance Association, and he delivered the paper as his presidential address.

stock might be 16 percent because of the stock's greater risk. However, in view of the favorable treatment of income on the stock, investors might be willing to accept a before-tax return of only 14 percent on the stock.

Thus, as Miller pointed out, (1) the *deductibility of interest* favors the use of debt financing, but (2) the *more favorable tax treatment of income from stock* lowers the required rate of return on stock and thus favors the use of equity financing.

Miller showed that the net impact of corporate and personal taxes is given by this equation:

$$V_L = V_U + \left[1 - \frac{(1 - T_c)(1 - T_s)}{(1 - T_d)} \right] D. \tag{14-7}$$

Here T_c is the corporate tax rate, T_s is the personal tax rate on income from stocks, and T_d is the tax rate on income from debt. Miller argued that the marginal tax rates on stock and debt balance out in such a way that the bracketed term in Equation 14-7 is zero, so $V_L = V_U$, but most observers believe that there is still a tax advantage to debt. For example, with a 40 percent marginal corporate tax rate, a 30 percent marginal rate on debt, and a 12 percent marginal rate on stock, the advantage of debt financing is

$$V_L = V_U + \left[1 - \frac{(1 - 0.40)(1 - 0.12)}{(1 - 0.30)} \right] D \tag{14-7a}$$
$$= V_U + 0.25D.$$

Thus it appears as though the presence of personal taxes reduces but does not completely eliminate the advantage of debt financing.

Trade-Off Theory

MM's results also depend on the assumption that there are no **bankruptcy costs.** However, in practice bankruptcy can be quite costly. Firms in bankruptcy have very high legal and accounting expenses, and they also have a hard time retaining customers, suppliers, and employees. Moreover, bankruptcy often forces a firm to liquidate or sell assets for less than they would be worth if the firm were to continue operating. For example, if a steel manufacturer goes out of business, it might be hard to find buyers for the company's blast furnaces, even though they were quite expensive. Assets such as plant and equipment are often illiquid because they are configured to a company's individual needs and also because they are difficult to disassemble and move.

Note, too, that the *threat of bankruptcy,* not just bankruptcy per se, produces these problems. Key employees jump ship, suppliers refuse to grant credit, customers seek more stable suppliers, and lenders demand higher interest rates and impose more restrictive loan covenants if potential bankruptcy looms.

Bankruptcy-related problems are most likely to arise when a firm includes a great deal of debt in its capital structure. Therefore, bankruptcy costs discourage firms from pushing their use of debt to excessive levels.

Bankruptcy-related costs have two components: (1) the probability of financial distress and (2) the costs that would be incurred given that financial distress occurs. Firms whose earnings are more volatile, all else equal, face a greater chance of bankruptcy and, therefore, should use less debt than more stable firms. This is consistent with our earlier point that firms with high operating leverage, and thus greater business risk, should limit their use of financial leverage. Likewise, firms that would face high costs in the event of financial distress should rely less heavily on debt. For example, firms whose assets are illiquid and thus would have to be sold at "fire sale" prices should limit their use of debt financing.

The preceding arguments led to the development of what is called "the trade-off theory of leverage," in which firms trade off the benefits of debt financing (favorable corporate tax treatment) against the higher interest rates and bankruptcy costs. In essence, the trade-off theory says that the value of a levered firm is equal to the value of an unlevered firm plus the value of any side effects, which include the tax shield and the expected costs due to financial distress. A summary of the trade-off theory is expressed graphically in Figure 14-2. Here are some observations about the figure:

1. Under the assumptions of the Modigliani-Miller with-corporate-taxes paper, a firm's value will be maximized if it uses virtually 100 percent debt, and the line labeled "MM Result Incorporating the Effects of Corporate Taxation" in Figure 14-2 expresses the relationship between value and debt under their assumptions.

2. There is some threshold level of debt, labeled D_1 in Figure 14-2, below which the probability of bankruptcy is so low as to be immaterial. Beyond D_1, however, expected bankruptcy-related costs become increasingly important, and they reduce the tax benefits of debt at an increasing rate. In the range from D_1 to D_2, expected bankruptcy-related costs reduce but do not completely offset the tax benefits of debt, so the stock price rises (but at a decreasing rate) as the debt ratio increases. However, beyond D_2, expected bankruptcy-related costs exceed the tax benefits, so from this point on increasing the debt ratio lowers the value of the stock. Therefore, D_2 is the optimal capital structure. Of course, D_1 and D_2 vary from firm to firm, depending on their business risks and bankruptcy costs.

3. While theoretical and empirical work support the general shape of the curve in Figure 14-2, this graph must be taken as an approximation, not as a precisely defined function.

Signaling Theory

MM assumed that investors have the same information about a firm's prospects as its managers—this is called **symmetric information.** However, in fact managers often have better information than outside investors. This is called **asymmetric information,** and it

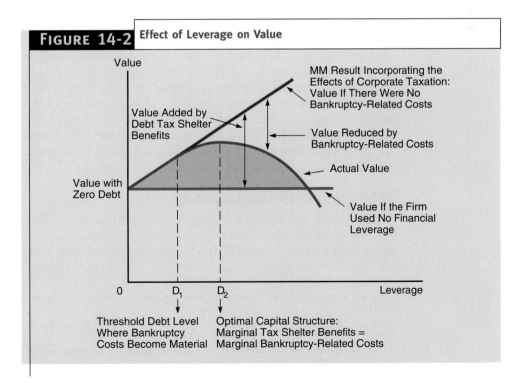

FIGURE 14-2   **Effect of Leverage on Value**

Value

MM Result Incorporating the Effects of Corporate Taxation: Value If There Were No Bankruptcy-Related Costs

Value Added by Debt Tax Shelter Benefits

Value Reduced by Bankruptcy-Related Costs

Actual Value

Value with Zero Debt

Value If the Firm Used No Financial Leverage

0   D_1 D_2 Leverage

Threshold Debt Level Where Bankruptcy Costs Become Material

Optimal Capital Structure: Marginal Tax Shelter Benefits = Marginal Bankruptcy-Related Costs

has an important effect on the optimal capital structure. To see why, consider two situations, one in which the company's managers know that its prospects are extremely positive (Firm P) and one in which the managers know that the future looks negative (Firm N).

Suppose, for example, that Firm P's R&D labs have just discovered a nonpatentable cure for the common cold. They want to keep the new product a secret as long as possible to delay competitors' entry into the market. New plants must be built to make the new product, so capital must be raised. How should Firm P's management raise the needed capital? If it sells stock, then, when profits from the new product start flowing in, the price of the stock would rise sharply, and the purchasers of the new stock would make a bonanza. The current stockholders (including the managers) would also do well, but not as well as they would have done if the company had not sold stock before the price increased, because then they would not have had to share the benefits of the new product with the new stockholders. *Therefore, one would expect a firm with very positive prospects to try to avoid selling stock and, rather, to raise any required new capital by other means, including using debt beyond the normal target capital structure.*[12]

Now let's consider Firm N. Suppose its managers have information that new orders are off sharply because a competitor has installed new technology that has improved its products' quality. Firm N must upgrade its own facilities, at a high cost, just to maintain its current sales. As a result, its return on investment will fall (but not by as much as if it took no action, which would lead to a 100 percent loss through bankruptcy). How should Firm N raise the needed capital? Here the situation is just the reverse of that facing Firm P, which did not want to sell stock so as to avoid having to share the benefits of future developments. *A firm with negative prospects would want to sell stock, which would mean bringing in new investors to share the losses!*[13] The conclusion from all this is that firms with extremely bright prospects prefer not to finance through new stock offerings, whereas firms with poor prospects like to finance with outside equity. How should you, as an investor, react to this conclusion? You ought to say, "If I see that a company plans to issue new stock, this should worry me because I know that management would not want to issue stock if future prospects looked good. However, management would want to issue stock if things looked bad. Therefore, I should lower my estimate of the firm's value, other things held constant, if it plans to issue new stock."

If you gave the above answer, your views would be consistent with those of sophisticated portfolio managers. *In a nutshell, the announcement of a stock offering is generally taken as a **signal** that the firm's prospects as seen by its management are not bright. Conversely, a debt offering is taken as a positive signal.* Notice that Firm N's managers cannot make a false signal to investors by mimicking Firm P and issuing debt. With its unfavorable future prospects, issuing debt could soon force Firm N into bankruptcy. Given the resulting damage to the personal wealth and reputations of N's managers, they cannot afford to mimic Firm P. All of this suggests that when a firm announces a new stock offering, more often than not the price of its stock will decline. Empirical studies have shown that this situation does indeed exist.[14]

Reserve Borrowing Capacity

Because issuing stock emits a negative signal and thus tends to depress the stock price, even if the company's prospects are bright, it should, in normal times, maintain a **reserve borrowing capacity** that can be used in the event that some especially good investment opportunity

---

[12] It would be illegal for Firm P's managers to personally purchase more shares on the basis of their inside knowledge of the new product.

[13] Of course, Firm N would have to make certain disclosures when it offered new shares to the public, but it might be able to meet the legal requirements without fully disclosing management's worst fears.

[14] Paul Asquith and David W. Mullins, Jr., "The Impact of Initiating Dividend Payments on Shareholders' Wealth," *Journal of Business,* January 1983, 77–96.

comes along. *This means that firms should, in normal times, use more equity and less debt than is suggested by the tax benefit/bankruptcy cost trade-off model expressed in Figure 14-2.*

The Pecking Order Hypothesis

The presence of flotation costs and asymmetric information may cause a firm to raise capital according to a **pecking order**. In this situation a firm first raises capital internally by reinvesting its net income and selling off its short-term marketable securities. When that supply of funds has been exhausted, the firm will issue debt and perhaps preferred stock. Only as a last resort will the firm issue common stock.

Using Debt Financing to Constrain Managers

Agency problems may arise if managers and shareholders have different objectives. Such conflicts are particularly likely when the firm's managers have too much cash at their disposal. Managers often use excess cash to finance pet projects or for perquisites such as nicer offices, corporate jets, and sky boxes at sports arenas, all of which may do little to maximize stock prices. Even worse, managers might be tempted to pay too much for an acquisition, something that could cost shareholders hundreds of millions. By contrast, managers with limited "excess cash flow" are less able to make wasteful expenditures.

Firms can reduce excess cash flow in a variety of ways. One way is to funnel some of it back to shareholders through higher dividends or stock repurchases. Another alternative is to shift the capital structure toward more debt in the hope that higher debt service requirements will force managers to be more disciplined. If debt is not serviced as required, the firm will be forced into bankruptcy, in which case its managers would likely lose their jobs. Therefore, a manager is less likely to buy an expensive new corporate jet if the firm has large debt service requirements that could cost the manager his or her job. In short, high levels of debt **bond the cash flow,** since much of it is precommitted to servicing the debt.

A leveraged buyout (LBO) is one way to bond cash flow. In an LBO debt is used to finance the purchase of a company's shares, after which the firm "goes private." Many leveraged buyouts, which were especially common during the late 1980s, were designed specifically to reduce corporate waste. As noted, high debt payments force managers to conserve cash by eliminating unnecessary expenditures.

Of course, increasing debt and reducing the available cash flow has its downside. It increases the risk of bankruptcy. One professor has argued that adding debt to a firm's capital structure is like putting a dagger into the steering wheel of a car.[15] The dagger—which points toward your stomach—motivates you to drive more carefully, but you may get stabbed if someone runs into you, even if you are being careful. The analogy applies to corporations in the following sense: Higher debt forces managers to be more careful with shareholders' money, but even well-run firms could face bankruptcy (get stabbed) if some event beyond their control such as a war, an earthquake, a strike, or a recession occurs. To complete the analogy, the capital structure decision comes down to deciding how big a dagger stockholders should use to keep managers in line.

Finally, too much debt may overconstrain managers. A large portion of a manager's personal wealth and reputation is tied to a single company, so managers are not well diversified. When faced with a positive NPV project that is risky, a manager may decide that it's not worth taking on the risk, even when well-diversified stockholders would find the risk acceptable. This is called the **underinvestment problem.** The more debt the firm has, the greater the likelihood of financial distress, and thus the greater the likelihood that managers will forego risky projects even if they have positive NPVs.

---

[15] Ben Bernake, "Is There Too Much Corporate Debt?" Federal Reserve Bank of Philadelphia *Business Review,* September/October 1989, 3–13.

The Investment Opportunity Set and Reserve Borrowing Capacity

Bankruptcy and financial distress are costly, and, as noted above, this can discourage highly leveraged firms from undertaking risky new investments. If potential new investments, although risky, have positive net present values, then high levels of debt can be doubly costly—the expected financial distress and bankruptcy costs are high, and the firm loses potential value by not making some potentially profitable investments. On the other hand, if a firm has very few profitable investment opportunities, then high levels of debt can keep managers from wasting money by investing in poor projects. For such companies, increases in the debt ratio can increase the value of the firm.

Thus, in addition to the tax, signaling, bankruptcy, and managerial constraint effects discussed earlier, the firm's optimal capital structure is related to its set of investment opportunities. Firms with many profitable opportunities should maintain their ability to invest by using low levels of debt, which is also consistent with maintaining reserve borrowing capacity. Firms with few profitable investment opportunities should use high levels of debt and thus have substantial interest payments, which means imposing managerial constraint through debt.[16]

Windows of Opportunity

If markets are efficient, then security prices should reflect all available information, so they are neither underpriced nor overpriced (except during the time it takes prices to move to a new equilibrium caused by the release of new information). The *windows of opportunity theory* states that managers don't believe this, but instead think that stock prices and interest rates are sometimes either too low or high relative to their true fundamental values. In particular, the theory suggests that managers issue equity when they believe stock market prices are abnormally high and issue debt when they believe interest rates are abnormally low. In other words, they try to time the market.[17] Notice that this differs from signaling theory because no asymmetric information is involved: These managers aren't basing their beliefs on insider information, just on a difference of opinion with the market consensus.

SELF-TEST QUESTIONS

Why does the MM theory with corporate taxes lead to 100 percent debt?
Explain how *asymmetric information* and *signals* affect capital structure decisions.
What is meant by *reserve borrowing capacity*, and why is it important to firms?
How can the use of debt serve to discipline managers?

CAPITAL STRUCTURE EVIDENCE AND IMPLICATIONS

There have been hundreds, perhaps even thousands, of papers testing the capital structure theories described in the previous section. We can only cover the highlights here; see the references at the end of the chapter if you would like more details.[18]

---

[16] Michael J. Barclay and Clifford W. Smith, Jr., "The Capital Structure Puzzle: Another Look at the Evidence," *Journal of Applied Corporate Finance*, Vol. 12, no. 1, Spring 1999, 8–20.

[17] See Malcolm Baker and Jeffrey Wurgler, "Market Timing and Capital Structure," *Journal of Finance*, Vol. 57, no. 1, (February 2002), 1–32.

[18] This section also draws heavily from: Barclay and Smith, "The Capital Structure Puzzle;" Jay Ritter, ed., *Recent Developments in Corporate Finance* (Northampton, MA: Edward Elgar Publishing Inc., 2005); and a presentation by Jay Ritter at the 2003 FMA meetings, "The Windows of Opportunity Theory of Capital Structure," available at **http://bear.cba.ufl.edu/ritter/ritterwp.htm.**

Empirical Evidence

Studies show that firms do benefit from the tax deductibility of interest payments, with a typical firm increasing in value by about $0.10 for every dollar of debt. This is much less than the corporate tax rate, so this supports the Miller model (with personal taxes) more than the MM model (with only corporate taxes). Recent evidence shows that the cost of bankruptcies can be as much as 10 to 20 percent of the firm's value.[19] Thus, the evidence shows the existence of tax benefits and financial distress costs, which provides support for the trade-off theory.

A particularly interesting study by Professors Mehotra, Mikkelson, and Partch examined the capital structure of firms that were spun off from their parents.[20] The financing choices of existing firms might be influenced by their past financing choices and by the costs of moving from one capital structure to another, but because spin-offs are newly created companies, managers can choose a capital structure without regard to these issues. The study finds that more profitable firms (which have a lower expected probability of bankruptcy) and more asset-intensive firms (which have better collateral and thus lower cost of bankruptcy should one occur) have higher levels of debt. These findings support the trade-off theory.

However, there is also evidence that is inconsistent with a static optimal target capital structure as implied by the trade-off theory. For example, stock prices are very volatile, which causes a firm's actual market-based debt ratio to deviate frequently from its target. However, such deviations don't cause firms to immediately issue or repurchase securities in an effort to return to the target. This inertia indicates that if there is an optimal capital structure as implied by the trade-off theory, firms don't try to maintain it very closely.

In fact, if stock prices have a big runup, which reduces the debt ratio, the trade-off theory suggests that firms should issue debt to return to their target. However, firms tend to do the opposite, and issue stock after big runups. This is much more consistent with the windows of opportunity theory, with managers trying to time the market by issuing stock when they perceive the market to be overvalued. Furthermore, firms tend to issue debt when stock prices and interest rates are low. The maturity of the issued debt seems to reflect an attempt to time interest rates: Firms tend to issue short-term debt if the term structure is upward sloping but long-term debt if the term structure is flat. Again, these facts suggest that managers try to time the market, which is consistent with the windows of opportunity theory.

Firms issue equity much less frequently than debt. On the surface, this seems to support both the pecking order hypothesis and the signaling hypothesis. The pecking order hypothesis predicts that firms with a high level of informational asymmetry, which causes equity issuances to be costly, should issue debt before issuing equity. However, we often see the opposite, with high-growth firms (which usually have greater informational asymmetry) issuing more equity than debt. Also, many highly profitable firms could afford to issue debt (which comes before equity in the pecking order) but instead choose to issue equity. With respect to the signaling hypothesis, consider the case of firms that have large increases in earnings that were unanticipated by the market. If managers have superior information, they would anticipate these upcoming performance improvements and issue debt before the increase. Such firms do, in fact, tend to issue debt slightly more frequently than other firms, but the difference isn't economically meaningful.

Many firms have less debt than might be expected, and many have large amounts of short-term investments. This is especially true for firms with high market/book ratios (which indicate many growth options and informational asymmetry problems). This

---

[19] The *expected cost* of financial distress is the product of bankruptcy costs and the probability of bankruptcy. At moderate levels of debt with low probabilities of bankruptcy, the expected cost of financial distress would be much less than actual bankruptcy costs if the firm failed.

[20] See V. Mehotra, W. Mikkelson, and M. Partch, "The Design of Financial Policies in Corporate Spin-offs," *Review of Financial Studies*, Winter 2003, 1359–1388.

behavior is consistent with the hypothesis that investment opportunities influence attempts to maintain reserve borrowing capacity. It is also consistent with tax considerations, since low-growth firms, which have more debt, are more likely to be able to use the tax shield. This behavior is not consistent with the pecking order hypothesis, where low-growth firms, which often have high free cash flow, would be able to avoid issuing debt by raising funds internally.

Summarizing these results, it appears that firms try to capture debt's tax benefits while avoiding financial distress costs. However, they also allow their debt ratios to deviate from the static optimal target ratio implied by the trade-off theory. There is a little evidence indicating that firms follow a pecking order and use security issuances as signals, but there is much more evidence in support of the windows of opportunity theory. Finally, it appears that firms often maintain reserve borrowing capacity, especially those with many growth opportunities or problems with informational asymmetry.

Implications for Managers

Managers should explicitly consider tax benefits when making capital structure decisions. Tax benefits obviously are more valuable for firms with high tax rates. Firms can utilize tax loss carry-forwards and carry-backs, but the time value of money means that tax benefits are more valuable for firms with stable, positive pre-tax income. Therefore, a firm whose sales are relatively stable can safely take on more debt and incur higher fixed charges than a company with volatile sales. Other things being equal, a firm with less operating leverage is better able to employ financial leverage because it will have less business risk and less volatile earnings.

Managers should also consider the expected cost of financial distress, which depends on the probability and cost of distress. Notice that stable sales and lower operating leverage provide tax benefits but also reduce the *probability* of financial distress. One *cost* of financial distress comes from lost investment opportunities. Firms with profitable investment opportunities need to be able to fund them, either by holding higher levels of marketable securities or by maintaining excess borrowing capacity. An astute corporate treasurer made this statement to the authors:

> Our company can earn a lot more money from good capital budgeting and operating decisions than from good financing decisions. Indeed, we are not sure exactly how financing decisions affect our stock price, but we know for sure that having to turn down a promising venture because funds are not available will reduce our long-run profitability.

Another cost of financial distress is the possibility of being forced to sell assets to meet liquidity needs. General-purpose assets that can be used by many businesses are relatively liquid and make good collateral in contrast to special-purpose assets. Thus, real estate companies are usually highly leveraged, whereas companies involved in technological research are not.

Asymmetric information also has a bearing on capital structure decisions. For example, suppose a firm has just successfully completed an R&D program, and it forecasts higher earnings in the immediate future. However, the new earnings are not yet anticipated by investors, hence are not reflected in the stock price. This company should not issue stock—it should finance with debt until the higher earnings materialize and are reflected in the stock price. Then it could issue common stock, retire the debt, and return to its target capital structure.

Managers should consider conditions in the stock and bond markets. For example, during a recent credit crunch, the junk bond market dried up, and there was simply no market at a "reasonable" interest rate for any new long-term bonds rated below BBB. Therefore, low-rated companies in need of capital were forced to go to the stock market or to the short-term debt market, regardless of their target capital structures. When conditions eased, however, these companies sold bonds to get their capital structures back on target.

Finally, managers should always consider lenders' and rating agencies' attitudes. For example, one large utility was recently told by Moody's and Standard & Poor's that its bonds would be downgraded if it issued more debt. This influenced its decision to finance its expansion with common equity. This doesn't mean that managers should never increase debt if it will cause their bond rating to fall, but managers should always factor this into their decision making.

SELF-TEST QUESTIONS

Which capital structure theories does the empirical evidence seem to support?
What issues should managers consider when making capital structure decisions?

ESTIMATING THE OPTIMAL CAPITAL STRUCTURE

Managers should choose the capital structure that maximizes shareholders' wealth. The basic approach is to consider a trial capital structure, based on the market values of the debt and equity, and then estimate the wealth of the shareholders under this capital structure. This approach is repeated until an optimal capital structure is identified. There are five steps for the analysis of each potential capital structure: (1) Estimate the interest rate the firm will pay. (2) Estimate the cost of equity. (3) Estimate the weighted average cost of capital. (4) Estimate the free cash flows and their present value, which is the value of the firm. (5) Deduct the value of the debt to find the shareholders' wealth, which we want to maximize. The following sections explain each of these steps, using the company we considered earlier, Strasburg Electronics.

1. Estimating the Cost of Debt

The CFO asked Strasburg's investment bankers to estimate the cost of debt at different capital structures. The investment bankers began by analyzing industry conditions and prospects. They appraised Strasburg's business risk, based on its past financial statements and its current technology and customer base. The bankers also projected pro forma statements under various capital structures and analyzed such key ratios as the current ratio and the times-interest-earned ratio. Finally, they factored in current conditions in the financial markets, including interest rates paid by firms in Strasburg's industry. Based on their analysis and judgment, they estimated interest rates at various capital structures as shown in Table 14-2, starting with an 8 percent cost of debt if 10 percent or less of its capital is obtained as debt. Notice that the cost of debt goes up as leverage and the threat of bankruptcy increase.

TABLE 14-2 | **The Cost of Debt for Strasburg Electronics with Different Capital Structures**

Percent Financed with Debt (w_d)	Cost of Debt (r_d)
0%	8.0%
10	8.0
20	8.1
30	8.5
40	9.0
50	11.0
60	14.0

Note: The capital structure weights are based on market values.

TAKING A LOOK AT GLOBAL CAPITAL STRUCTURES

To what extent does capital structure vary across different countries? The accompanying table, which is taken from a recent study by Raghuram Rajan and Luigi Zingales, both of the University of Chicago, shows the median debt ratios of firms in the largest industrial countries.

Rajan and Zingales also show that there is considerable variation in capital structure among firms within each of the seven countries. However, they also show that capital structures for the firms in each country are generally determined by a similar set of factors: firm size, profitability, market-to-book ratio, and the ratio of fixed assets to total assets. All in all, the Rajan-Zingales study suggests that the points developed in the chapter apply to firms all around the world.

Source: Raghuram G. Rajan and Luigi Zingales, "What Do We Know about Capital Structure? Some Evidence from International Data," *The Journal of Finance,* Vol. 50, no. 5, December 1995, 1421–1460.

Median Percentage of Debt to Total Assets in Different Countries

Country	Book Value Debt Ratio
Canada	32%
France	18
Germany	11
Italy	21
Japan	21
United Kingdom	10
United States	25

2. Estimating the Cost of Equity, r_s

An increase in the debt ratio also increases the risk faced by shareholders, and this has an effect on the cost of equity, r_s. Recall from Chapter 5 that a stock's beta is the relevant measure of risk for diversified investors. Moreover, it has been demonstrated, both theoretically and empirically, that beta increases with financial leverage. Indeed, Robert Hamada developed the following equation to specify the effect of financial leverage on beta:[21]

$$b = b_U[1 + (1 - T)(D/S)]. \tag{14-8}$$

Here D is the market value of the debt and S is the market value of the equity. The Hamada equation shows how increases in the market value debt/equity ratio increase beta. Here b_U is the firm's unlevered beta coefficient, that is, the beta it would have if it has no debt. In that case, beta would depend entirely upon business risk and thus be a measure of the firm's "basic business risk."

Note that beta is the only variable that can be influenced by management in the CAPM cost of equity equation, $r_s = r_{RF} + (RP_M)b$. The risk-free rate and market risk premium are determined by market forces that are beyond the firm's control. However, b is affected (1) by the firm's operating decisions as discussed earlier in the chapter, which affect b_U, and (2) by its capital structure decisions as reflected in its D/S ratio.

As a starting point, a firm can take its current beta, tax rate, and debt/equity ratio and calculate its **unlevered beta, b_U,** by simply transforming Equation 14-8 as follows:

$$b_U = b/[1 + (1 - T)(D/S)]. \tag{14-8a}$$

---

[21] See Robert S. Hamada, "Portfolio Analysis, Market Equilibrium, and Corporation Finance," *Journal of Finance,* March 1969, 13–31. Note that Thomas Conine and Maurry Tamarkin extended Hamada's work to include risky debt. See "Divisional Cost of Capital Estimation: Adjusting for Leverage," *Financial Management,* Spring 1985, 54–58.

Then, once b_U is determined, the Hamada equation can be used to estimate how changes in the debt/equity ratio would affect the leveraged beta, b, and thus the cost of equity, r_s.

We can apply the procedure to Strasburg Electronics. First, the risk-free rate of return, r_{RF}, is 6 percent, and the market risk premium, RP_M, is 6 percent. Next, we need the unlevered beta, b_U. Because Strasburg has no debt, D/S = 0. Therefore, its current beta of 1.0 is also its unlevered beta, hence b_U = 1.0. Therefore, Strasburg's current cost of equity is 12 percent:

$$r_s = r_{RF} + RP_M(b)$$
$$= 6\% + (6\%)(1.0)$$
$$= 6\% + 6\% = 12\%.$$

The first 6 percent is the risk-free rate, the second the risk premium. Because Strasburg currently uses no debt, it has no financial risk. Therefore, its 6 percent risk premium reflects only its business risk.

If Strasburg changes its capital structure by adding debt, this would increase the risk stockholders bear. That, in turn, would result in an additional risk premium. Conceptually, this situation would exist:

$$r_s = r_{RF} + \text{Premium for business risk} + \text{Premium for financial risk.}$$

Column 4 of Table 14-3 shows Strasburg's estimated beta for the capital structures under consideration. Figure 14-3 (using data calculated in Column 5 of Table 14-3) graphs Strasburg's required return on equity at different debt ratios. As the figure shows, r_s consists of the 6 percent risk-free rate, a constant 6 percent premium for business risk, and a premium for financial risk that starts at zero but rises at an increasing rate as the debt ratio increases.

TABLE 14-3 Strasburg's Optimal Capital Structure

Percent Financed with Debt, w_d (1)	Market Debt/Equity, D/S (2)[a]	After-Tax Cost of Debt, $(1 - T)r_d$ (3)[b]	Estimated Beta, b (4)[c]	Cost of Equity, r_s (5)[d]	WACC (6)[e]	Value of Firm, V (7)[f]
0%	0.00%	4.80%	1.00	12.0%	12.00%	$200,000
10	11.11	4.80	1.07	12.4	11.64	206,186
20	25.00	4.86	1.15	12.9	11.29	212,540
30	42.86	5.10	1.26	13.5	11.01	217,984
40	66.67	5.40	1.40	14.4	10.80	**222,222**
50	100.00	6.60	1.60	15.6	11.10	216,216
60	150.00	8.40	1.90	17.4	12.00	200,000

Notes:
[a] The D/S ratio is calculated as: $D/S = w_d/(1 - w_d)$.
[b] The interest rates are shown in Table 14-2, and the tax rate is 40 percent.
[c] The beta is estimated using Hamada's formula in Equation 14-8.
[d] The cost of equity is estimated using the CAPM formula: $r_s = r_{RF} + (RP_M)b$, where the risk free rate is 6 percent and the market risk premium is 6 percent.
[e] The weighted average cost of capital is calculated using Equation 14-2: $WACC = w_e r_s + w_d r_d (1 - T)$, where $w_e = (1 - w_d)$.
[f] The value of the firm is calculated using the free cash flow valuation formula in Equation 14-1, modified to reflect the fact that since Strasburg has zero growth, V = FCF/WACC. Strasburg has zero growth, so it requires no investment in capital and its FCF is equal to its NOPAT. Using the EBIT shown in Table 14-1:

$$FCF = NOPAT - \text{Investment in capital} = EBIT (1 - T) - 0$$
$$= \$40,000 (1 - 0.4) = \$24,000.$$

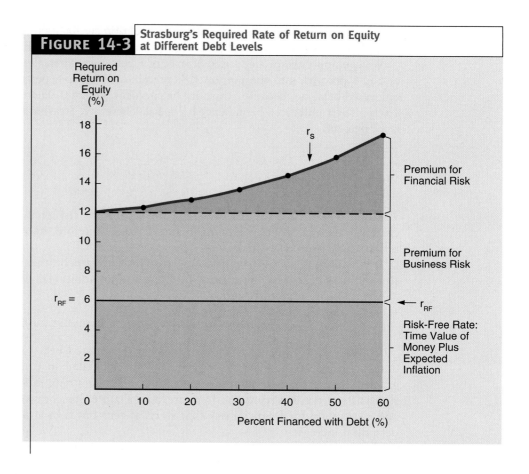

FIGURE 14-3   Strasburg's Required Rate of Return on Equity at Different Debt Levels

3. Estimating the Weighted Average Cost of Capital, WACC

Column 6 of Table 14-3 shows Strasburg's weighted average cost of capital, WACC, at different capital structures. Currently, it has no debt, so its capital structure is 100 percent equity, and at this point WACC = r_s = 12%. As Strasburg begins to use lower-cost debt, the WACC declines. However, as the debt ratio increases, the costs of both debt and equity rise, at first slowly but then at a faster and faster rate. Eventually, the increasing costs of the two components offset the fact that more low-cost debt is being used. At 40 percent debt, the WACC hits a minimum of 10.8 percent, and after that it rises with further increases in the debt ratio.

Note too that even though the component cost of equity is always higher than that of debt, using only lower-cost debt would not maximize value because of the feedback effects on the costs of debt and equity. If Strasburg were to issue more than 40 percent debt, it would then be relying more on the cheaper source of capital, but this lower cost would be more than offset by the fact that using more debt would raise the costs of both debt and equity.

4. Estimating the Firm's Value

We can estimate Strasburg's value using Equation 14-1. Because Strasburg has zero growth, we can use the constant growth version of Equation 14-1:

$$V = \frac{FCF}{WACC}. \qquad \textbf{(14-1a)}$$

Recall that FCF is net operating profit after taxes (NOPAT) minus the required net investment in capital. Table 14-1 shows that Strasburg has an expected EBIT of $40,000.

With a tax rate of 40 percent, its expected NOPAT is $24,000 = $40,000 (1 − 0.40). Since Strasburg has zero growth, its future net investments in operating assets will be zero, so its expected FCF is equal to NOPAT.

With zero debt, Strasburg has a WACC of 12 percent (shown in Column 6 of Table 14-3) and a value of

$$V = \frac{FCF}{WACC} = \frac{\$24,000}{0.12} = \$200,000.$$

Column 7 of Table 14-3 shows Strasburg's value at different capital structures.[22] Notice that the maximum value of $222,222 occurs at a capital structure with 40 percent debt, which is also the capital structure that minimizes the WACC.

5. Estimating Shareholder Wealth and Stock Price

Strasburg should now **recapitalize,** meaning that it should issue debt and use the proceeds to repurchase stock. The shareholders' wealth after the **recap,** as it is commonly called, would be equal to the payment they receive from the share repurchase plus the remaining value of their equity. To find the remaining value of equity, we need to specify how much debt is issued in the new capital structure. Since we know the percent of debt in the capital structure and the resulting value of the firm, we can find the dollar value of debt as follows:

$$D = w_d V.$$

For example, at the optimal capital structure of 40 percent debt, the dollar value of debt is about $88,889 = 0.40($222,222).

The market value of the remaining equity, S, is equal to the total value minus the value of the debt. At the optimal capital structure, the market value of equity is $133,333 = $222,222 − $88,889. Column 4 in Table 14-4 shows the market value of equity under the various capital structures. Notice that the value of equity declines as the percent financed with debt increases. At first glance, it looks like increasing leverage hurts shareholders. But keep in mind that the shareholders also receive cash equal to the amount of new debt when the company repurchases the stock:

Cash raised by issuing debt = $D - D_0$.

Here D_0 is the amount of debt the company had before the recap, which for Strasburg was zero.

For example, at the optimal capital structure, Strasburg will issue $88,889 in debt and use the proceeds to repurchase stock. Thus, the total wealth of the shareholders after the repurchase will be the cash they receive in the repurchase ($88,889) plus the value of their remaining equity ($133,333), for a total wealth of $222,222. Notice that their total wealth increases from its original level of $200,000 to the new level of $222,222, a gain of $22,222. This is exactly equal to the increase in total value experienced by Strasburg, so the shareholders reap the full rewards of the recapitalization.

Prior to the announced recap, Strasburg had a $200,000 market value of equity and 10,000 shares of stock outstanding (n_0). Therefore, its stock price prior to the recap was $20 per share ($200,000/10,000 = $20).

To find the price per share after the recap, consider the sequence of events. (1) The company announces the recap and issues new debt. (2) The company uses the proceeds from the debt issue to repurchase shares of stock. These events don't occur exactly simultaneously, so let's examine each event separately.

---

[22] In this analysis we assume that Strasburg's expected EBIT and FCF are constant for the various capital structures. In a more refined analysis we might try to estimate any possible declines in FCF at high levels of debt as the threat of bankruptcy becomes imminent.

TABLE 14-4 Strasburg's Stock Price and Earnings per Share

Percent Financed with Debt, w_d (1)	Value of Firm, V (2)[a]	Market Value of Debt, D (3)[b]	Market Value of Equity, S (4)[c]	Stock Price, P (5)[d]	Number of Shares after Repurchase, n (6)[e]	Net Income, NI (7)[f]	Earnings per Share, EPS (8)[g]
0%	$200,000	$ 0	$200,000	$20.00	10,000	$24,000	$2.40
10	206,186	20,619	185,567	20.62	9,000	23,010	2.56
20	212,540	42,508	170,032	21.25	8,000	21,934	2.74
30	217,984	65,395	152,589	21.80	7,000	20,665	2.95
40	**222,222**	**88,889**	**133,333**	**22.22**	**6,000**	**19,200**	**3.20**
50	216,216	108,108	108,108	21.62	5,000	16,865	3.37
60	200,000	120,000	80,000	20.00	4,000	13,920	3.48

Notes:
[a]The value of the firm is taken from Table 14-3.
[b]The value of debt is found by multiplying the percent of the firm financed with debt in Column 1 by the value of the firm in Column 2.
[c]The value of equity is found by subtracting the value of debt in Column 3 from the total value of the firm in Column 2.
[d]The number of outstanding shares prior to the recap is $n_0 = 10,000$. The stock price is $P = [S + (D - D_0)]/n_0 = [S + D]/10,000$.
[e]The number of shares after the recapitalizations is $n = S/P$.
[f]Net income is $NI = (EBIT - r_dD)(1 - T)$, where $EBIT = \$40,000$ (taken from Table 14-1), r_d comes from Table 14-2, and $T = 40\%$.
[g]$EPS = NI/n$.

STRASBURG ISSUES NEW DEBT   Strasburg announces its plans to recapitalize, and borrows $88,889. It has not yet repurchased the stock, and so the $88,889 of debt proceeds are temporarily used to purchase short-term investments such as T-bills or other marketable securities. Using the corporate valuation model from Chapter 13, the total corporate value is now equal to the value of operations, calculated by discounting the expected free cash flows by the new WACC, plus the value of any nonoperating assets such as short-term investments. Therefore, Strasburg's total value after issuing debt but before repurchasing stock is

Total corporate value = Value of operations + Value of short-term investments

$$= \$222,222 + \$88,889 = \$311,111.$$

Recall from Chapter 13 that the value of equity is the total corporate value minus the value of all debt. Therefore, the value of equity after the debt issue but prior to the repurchase, S_p, is

S_p = Value of equity after the debt issue but prior to the repurchase
= Total corporate value − Value of all debt

$$= \$311,111 - \$88,889 = \$222,222.$$

Although the corporate valuation model will always provide the correct value, there is a quicker and more intuitive way to determine S_p in a recapitalization. S_p reflects the wealth of the shareholders under the new capital structure, and, as we noted earlier, this is equal to the value of their equity after completion of the recapitalization plus the cash they receive in the repurchase. If all newly issued debt is used to repurchase stock, then that amount is $D - D_0$. Therefore, S_p is

$$S_p = S + (D - D_0)$$

$$= \$133,333 + (\$88,889 - \$0) = \$222,222.$$

This is exactly the same value as calculated above, but it can be computed with fewer steps and is perhaps a little more intuitive.

The price per share after issuing debt but prior to repurchasing stock, P_p, is

$$P_p = \text{Price per share after debt issue but prior to repurchase}$$
$$= \frac{\text{Value of equity after debt issue but prior to repurchase}}{\text{Number of shares outstanding prior to repurchase}}$$
$$= S_p/n_0$$

$$= \$222{,}222/10{,}000 = \$22.22.$$

STRASBURG REPURCHASES STOCK   What happens to the stock price during the repurchase? The short answer is "nothing." It is true that the additional debt will change the WACC and the stock price prior to the repurchase, but the subsequent repurchase itself will not affect the stock price.[23] To see why this is true, suppose the stock price was lower right before the repurchase than after the repurchase. If this were true, it would be possible for an investor to buy the stock the day before the repurchase and then reap a reward the very next day. Current stockholders would realize this and would refuse to sell the stock unless they were paid the price that is expected immediately after the repurchase.

Therefore, the post-repurchase price, P, is equal to the stock price after the debt issue but prior to the repurchase. Using the relationships in the previous section, we can write this as:[24]

$$P = S_p/n_0$$
$$= [S + (D - D_0)]/n_0.$$

(14-9)

Column 5 in Table 14-4 shows the price per share for the various capital structures. Notice that it, too, is maximized at the same capital structure that minimizes the WACC and maximizes the value of the firm.

Strasburg used the entire debt proceeds to repurchase stock, which means the number of repurchased shares is equal to the debt, D, divided by the repurchase price, P. Given 10,000 shares outstanding prior to the repurchase, the number of remaining shares after the repurchase, n, is

$$n = \text{Number of outstanding shares remaining after the repurchase}$$
$$= n_0 - (D/P).$$

At the optimal capital structure, Strasburg will repurchase $\$88{,}889/\$22.22 = 4{,}000$ shares of stock, leaving 6,000 shares outstanding (see Column 6 of Table 14-4).

The expected EBIT is $40,000, from Table 14-1. Using the appropriate interest rate, amount of debt, and tax rate we can calculate the net income (Column 7 in Table 14-4) and the earnings per share (Column 8).

---

[23] As we discuss in Chapter 15, a stock repurchase may be a signal of a company's future prospects, or it may be the way a company "announces" a change in capital structure, and either of those situations could have an impact on estimated free cash flows or WACC. However, neither situation applies to Strasburg.

[24] There are other ways to get to Equation 14-9. By definition, P = S/n. Since P is also the stock price immediately prior to the repurchase and all debt proceeds are used to repurchase stock, the dollar value of repurchased shares is $P(n_0 - n) = D - D_0$. We have two equations (one defining the price per share after the repurchase) and one defining the dollar value of repurchased stock. We have two unknowns, n and P. We can solve for the repurchase price: $P = (S + D - D_0)/n_0$.

Analyzing the Results

We summarize the results graphically in Figure 14-4. Notice that the cost of equity and the cost of debt both increase as debt increases. The WACC initially falls, but the rapidly increasing costs of equity and debt cause WACC to increase when the debt ratio goes

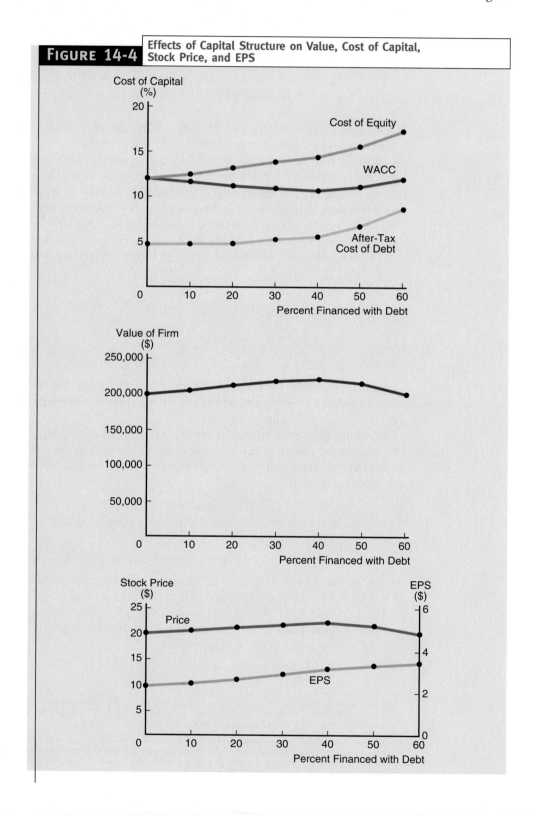

FIGURE 14-4 Effects of Capital Structure on Value, Cost of Capital, Stock Price, and EPS

above 40 percent. As indicated earlier, the minimum WACC and maximum corporate value occur at the same capital structure.

Now look closely at the curve for the value of the firm, and notice how flat it is around the optimal level of debt. Thus, it doesn't make a great deal of difference whether Strasburg's capital structure has 30 percent debt or 50 percent. Also, notice that the maximum value is about 11 percent greater than the value with no debt. Although this example is for a single company, the results are typical: The optimal capital structure can add 10 to 20 percent more value relative to zero debt, and there is a fairly wide region (from about 20 percent debt to 55 percent) over which value changes very little.

In Chapter 13 we looked at value-based management and saw how companies can increase their value by improving their operations. There is good news and bad news regarding this. The good news is that small improvements in operations can lead to huge increases in value. But the bad news is that it's often very hard to improve operations, especially if the company is already well managed.

If instead you seek to increase a firm's value by changing its capital structure, we again have good news and bad news. The good news is that changing capital structure is very easy—just call an investment banker and issue debt (or the reverse if the firm has too much debt). The bad news is that this will add only a relatively small amount of value. Of course, any additional value is better than none, so it's hard to understand why there are some mature firms with zero debt.

Finally, Figure 14-4 shows that Strasburg's EPS steadily increases with leverage, while its stock price reaches a maximum and then begins to decline. For some companies there is a capital structure that maximizes EPS, but this is generally not the same capital structure that maximizes stock price. This is one additional reason we focus on cash flows and value rather than earnings.

SELF-TEST QUESTIONS

What happens to the costs of debt and equity when the leverage increases? Explain.

Using the Hamada equation, show the effect of financial leverage on beta.

Using a graph and illustrative data, identify the premiums for financial risk and business risk at different debt levels. Do these premiums vary depending on the debt level? Explain.

Is expected EPS maximized at the optimal capital structure?

SUMMARY

This chapter examined the effects of financial leverage on stock prices, earnings per share, and the cost of capital. The key concepts covered are listed below:

- A firm's **optimal capital structure** is that mix of debt and equity that maximizes the stock price. At any point in time, management has a specific **target capital structure** in mind, presumably the optimal one, although this target may change over time.
- Several factors influence a firm's capital structure. These include its (1) **business risk**, (2) **tax position**, (3) need for **financial flexibility**, (4) **managerial conservatism or aggressiveness**, and (5) **growth opportunities.**
- **Business risk** is the riskiness inherent in the firm's operations if it uses no debt. A firm will have little business risk if the demand for its products is stable, if the prices of its inputs and products remain relatively constant, if it can adjust its prices freely if costs increase, and if a high percentage of its costs are variable and hence will decrease if sales decrease. Other things the same, the lower a firm's business risk, the higher its optimal debt ratio.

- **Financial leverage** is the extent to which fixed-income securities (debt and preferred stock) are used in a firm's capital structure. **Financial risk** is the added risk borne by stockholders as a result of financial leverage.
- **Operating leverage** is the extent to which fixed costs are used in a firm's operations. In business terminology, a high degree of operating leverage, other factors held constant, implies that a relatively small change in sales results in a large change in ROIC.
- Robert Hamada used the underlying assumptions of the CAPM, along with the Modigliani and Miller model, to develop the **Hamada equation,** which shows the effect of financial leverage on beta as follows:

$$b = b_U[1 + (1 - T)(D/S)].$$

Firms can take their current beta, tax rate, and debt/equity ratio to arrive at their **unlevered beta, b_U,** as follows:

$$b_U = b/[1 + (1 - T)(D/S)].$$

- **Modigliani and Miller** and their followers developed a **trade-off theory of capital structure.** They showed that debt is useful because interest is **tax deductible,** but also that debt brings with it costs associated with actual or potential bankruptcy. The optimal capital structure strikes a balance between the tax benefits of debt and the costs associated with bankruptcy.
- An alternative (or, really, complementary) theory of capital structure relates to the **signals** given to investors by a firm's decision to use debt versus stock to raise new capital. A stock issue sets off a negative signal, while using debt is a positive, or at least a neutral, signal. As a result, companies try to avoid having to issue stock by maintaining a **reserve borrowing capacity,** and this means using less debt in "normal" times than the MM trade-off theory would suggest.
- A firm's owners may decide to use a relatively large amount of debt to constrain the managers. A **high debt ratio raises the threat of bankruptcy,** which carries a cost but which also forces managers to be more careful and less wasteful with shareholders' money. Many of the corporate takeovers and leveraged buyouts in recent years were designed to improve efficiency by reducing the cash flow available to managers.

Although each firm has a theoretically optimal capital structure, as a practical matter we cannot estimate it with precision. Accordingly, financial executives generally treat the optimal capital structure as a range—for example, 40 to 50 percent debt—rather than as a precise point, such as 45 percent. The concepts discussed in this chapter help managers understand the factors they should consider when they set the target capital structure ranges for their firms.

QUESTIONS

(14-1) Define each of the following terms:
  a. Capital structure; business risk; financial risk
  b. Operating leverage; financial leverage, breakeven point
  c. Reserve borrowing capacity

(14-2) What term refers to the uncertainty inherent in projections of future ROIC?

(14-3) Firms with relatively high nonfinancial fixed costs are said to have a high degree of what?

(14-4) "One type of leverage affects both EBIT and EPS. The other type affects only EPS." Explain this statement.

(14-5) Why is the following statement true? "Other things being the same, firms with relatively stable sales are able to carry relatively high debt ratios."

(14-6) Why do public utility companies usually have capital structures that are different from those of retail firms?

(14-7) Why is EBIT generally considered to be independent of financial leverage? Why might EBIT actually be influenced by financial leverage at high debt levels?

(14-8) If a firm went from zero debt to successively higher levels of debt, why would you expect its stock price to first rise, then hit a peak, and then begin to decline?

SELF-TEST PROBLEMS   Solutions Appear in Appendix A

(ST-1)
Optimal Capital Structure

The Rogers Company is currently in this situation: (1) EBIT = $4.7 million; (2) tax rate, T = 40%; (3) value of debt, D = $2 million; (4) r_d = 10%; (5) r_s = 15%; (6) shares of stock outstanding, n_0 = 600,000; and stock price, P_0 = $30. The firm's market is stable, and it expects no growth, so all earnings are paid out as dividends. The debt consists of perpetual bonds.

a. What is the total market value of the firm's stock, S, and the firm's total market value, V?

b. What is the firm's weighted average cost of capital?

c. Suppose the firm can increase its debt so that its capital structure has 50 percent debt, based on market values (it will issue debt and buy back stock). At this level of debt, its cost of equity rises to 18.5 percent. Its interest rate on all debt will rise to 12 percent (it will have to call and refund the old debt). What is the WACC under this capital structure? What is the total value? How much debt will it issue, and what is the stock price after the repurchase? How many shares will remain outstanding after the repurchase?

(ST-2)
Hamada Equation

Lighter Industrial Corporation (LIC) is considering a large-scale recapitalization. Currently, LIC is financed with 25 percent debt and 75 percent equity. LIC is considering increasing its level of debt until it is financed with 60 percent debt and 40 percent equity. The beta on its common stock at the current level of debt is 1.5, the risk free rate is 6 percent, the market risk premium is 4 percent, and LIC faces a 40 percent federal-plus-state tax rate.

a. What is LIC's current cost of equity?

b. What is LIC's unlevered beta?

c. What will be the new beta and new cost of equity if LIC recapitalizes?

PROBLEMS

(14-1)
Operating Leverage and Breakeven

Schweser Satellites Inc. produces satellite earth stations that sell for $100,000 each. The firm's fixed costs, F, are $2 million; 50 earth stations are produced and sold each year; profits total $500,000; and the firm's assets (all equity financed) are $5 million. The firm estimates that it can change its production process, adding $4 million to investment and $500,000 to fixed operating costs. This change will (1) reduce variable costs per unit by $10,000 and (2) increase output by 20 units, but (3) the sales price on all units will have to be lowered to $95,000 to permit sales of the additional output. The firm has tax loss carry-forwards that cause its tax rate to be zero, its cost of equity is 15 percent, and it uses no debt.

a. Should the firm make the change?

b. Would the firm's operating leverage increase or decrease if it made the change? What about its breakeven point?

c. Would the new situation expose the firm to more or less business risk than the old one?

(14-2) Here are the estimated ROE distributions for Firms A, B, and C:

Business and
Financial Risk

	PROBABILITY				
	0.1	0.2	0.4	0.2	0.1
Firm A: ROE_A	0.0%	5.0%	10.0%	15.0%	20.0%
Firm B: ROE_B	(2.0)	5.0	12.0	19.0	26.0
Firm C: ROE_C	(5.0)	5.0	15.0	25.0	35.0

a. Calculate the expected value and standard deviation for Firm C's ROE. $ROE_A = 10.0\%$, $\sigma_A = 5.5\%$; $ROE_B = 12.0\%$, $\sigma_B = 7.7\%$.
b. Discuss the relative riskiness of the three firms' returns. (Assume that these distributions are expected to remain constant over time.)
c. Now suppose all three firms have the same standard deviation of basic earning power (EBIT/Total assets), $\sigma_A = \sigma_B = \sigma_C = 5.5\%$. What can we tell about the financial risk of each firm?

(14-3) The Rivoli Company has no debt outstanding, and its financial position is given by the following data:

Capital Structure
Analysis

Assets (book = market)	$3,000,000
EBIT	$500,000
Cost of equity, r_s	10%
Stock price, P_0	$15
Shares outstanding, n_0	200,000
Tax rate, T (federal-plus-state)	40%

The firm is considering selling bonds and simultaneously repurchasing some of its stock. If it moves to capital structure with 30 percent debt based on market values, its cost of equity, r_s, will increase to 11 percent to reflect the increased risk. Bonds can be sold at a cost, r_d, of 7 percent. Rivoli is a no-growth firm. Hence, all its earnings are paid out as dividends, and earnings are expectationally constant over time.
a. What effect would this use of leverage have on the value of the firm?
b. What would be the price of Rivoli's stock?
c. What happens to the firm's earnings per share after the recapitalization?
d. The $500,000 EBIT given previously is actually the expected value from the following probability distribution:

Probability	EBIT
0.10	($ 100,000)
0.20	200,000
0.40	500,000
0.20	800,000
0.10	1,100,000

Determine the times-interest-earned ratio for each probability. What is the probability of not covering the interest payment at the 30 percent debt level?

(14-4) Pettit Printing Company has a total market value of $100 million, consisting of 1 million shares selling for $50 per share and $50 million of 10 percent perpetual bonds now selling at par. The company's EBIT is $13.24 million, and its tax rate is 15 percent. Pettit can change its capital structure by either increasing its debt to 70 percent (based on market values) or decreasing it to 30 percent. If it decides to *increase* its use of leverage, it must call its old bonds and issue new ones with a 12 percent

Capital Structure
Analysis

coupon. If it decides to *decrease* its leverage, it will call in its old bonds and replace them with new 8 percent coupon bonds. The company will sell or repurchase stock at the new equilibrium price to complete the capital structure change.

The firm pays out all earnings as dividends; hence, its stock is a zero growth stock. Its current cost of equity, r_s, is 14 percent. If it increases leverage, r_s will be 16 percent. If it decreases leverage, r_s will be 13 percent. What is the firm's WACC and total corporate value under each capital structure?

(14-5)
Optimal Capital Structure with Hamada

Beckman Engineering and Associates (BEA) is considering a change in its capital structure. BEA currently has $20 million in debt carrying a rate of 8 percent, and its stock price is $40 per share with 2 million shares outstanding. BEA is a zero growth firm and pays out all of its earnings as dividends. EBIT is $14.933 million, and BEA faces a 40 percent federal-plus-state tax rate. The market risk premium is 4 percent, and the risk free rate is 6 percent. BEA is considering increasing its debt level to a capital structure with 40 percent debt, based on market values, and repurchasing shares with the extra money that it borrows. BEA will have to retire the old debt in order to issue new debt, and the rate on the new debt will be 9 percent. BEA has a beta of 1.0.

a. What is BEA's unlevered beta? Use market value D/S when unlevering.
b. What are BEA's new beta and cost of equity if it has 40 percent debt?
c. What are BEA's WACC and total value of the firm with 40 percent debt?

(14-6)
WACC and Optimal Capital Structure

Elliott Athletics is trying to determine its optimal capital structure, which now consists of only debt and common equity. The firm does not currently use preferred stock in its capital structure, and it does not plan to do so in the future. To estimate how much its debt would cost at different debt levels, the company's treasury staff has consulted with investment bankers and, on the basis of those discussions, has created the following table:

Market Debt-to-Value Ratio (w_d)	Market Equity-to-Value Ratio (w_e)	Market Debt-to-Equity Ratio (D/S)	Bond Rating	Before-Tax Cost of Debt (r_d)
0.0	1.0	0.00	A	7.0%
0.2	0.8	0.25	BBB	8.0
0.4	0.6	0.67	BB	10.0
0.6	0.4	1.50	C	12.0
0.8	0.2	4.00	D	15.0

Elliott uses the CAPM to estimate its cost of common equity, r_s. The company estimates that the risk-free rate is 5 percent, the market risk premium is 6 percent, and its tax rate is 40 percent. Elliott estimates that if it had no debt, its "unlevered" beta, b_U, would be 1.2. Based on this information, what is the firm's optimal capital structure, and what would the weighted average cost of capital be at the optimal capital structure?

SPREADSHEET PROBLEM

(14-7)
Build a Model: WACC and Optimal Capital Structure

e-resource

Start with the partial model in the file *CF2 Ch14 P07 Build a Model.xls* from the textbook's Web site. Rework Problem 14-6 using a spreadsheet model. After completing the problem as it appears, answer the following related questions.

a. Plot a graph of the after-tax cost of debt, the cost of equity, and the WACC versus the debt/value ratio.
b. Would the optimal capital structure change if the unlevered beta changed? To answer this question, do a sensitivity analysis of WACC on b_U for different levels of b_U.

CYBERPROBLEM

Please go to our Web site, **http://ehrhardt.swlearning.com**, to access any Cyberproblems.

THOMSON ONE
Business School Edition

Please go to **http://ehrhardt.swlearning.com** to access any Thomson ONE—Business School Edition problems.

MINI CASE

Assume you have just been hired as business manager of PizzaPalace, a pizza restaurant located adjacent to campus. The company's EBIT was $500,000 last year, and since the university's enrollment is capped, EBIT is expected to remain constant (in real terms) over time. Since no expansion capital will be required, PizzaPalace plans to pay out all earnings as dividends. The management group owns about 50 percent of the stock, and the stock is traded in the over-the-counter market.

The firm is currently financed with all equity; it has 100,000 shares outstanding; and $P_0 = \$25$ per share. When you took your corporate finance course, your instructor stated that most firms' owners would be financially better off if the firms used some debt. When you suggested this to your new boss, he encouraged you to pursue the idea. As a first step, assume that you obtained from the firm's investment banker the following estimated costs of debt for the firm at different capital structures:

Percent Financed with Debt, w_d	r_d
0%	—
20	8.0%
30	8.5
40	10.0
50	12.0

If the company were to recapitalize, debt would be issued, and the funds received would be used to repurchase stock. PizzaPalace is in the 40 percent state-plus-federal corporate tax bracket, its beta is 1.0, the risk-free rate is 6 percent, and the market risk premium is 6 percent.

a. Provide a brief overview of capital structure effects. Be sure to identify the ways in which capital structure can affect the weighted average cost of capital and free cash flows.

b. (1) What is business risk? What factors influence a firm's business risk?

   (2) What is operating leverage, and how does it affect a firm's business risk? Show the operating breakeven point if a company has fixed costs of $200, a sales price of $15, and variable costs of $10.

c. Now, to develop an example that can be presented to PizzaPalace's management to illustrate the effects of financial leverage, consider two hypothetical firms: Firm U, which uses no debt financing, and Firm L, which uses $10,000 of 12 percent debt. Both firms have $20,000 in assets, a 40 percent tax rate, and an expected EBIT of $3,000.

   (1) Construct partial income statements, which start with EBIT, for the two firms.

   (2) Now calculate ROE for both firms.

   (3) What does this example illustrate about the impact of financial leverage on ROE?

d. Explain the difference between financial risk and business risk.

e. Now consider the fact that EBIT is not known with certainty, but rather has the following probability distribution:

Economic State	Probability	EBIT
Bad	0.25	$2,000
Average	0.50	3,000
Good	0.25	4,000

Redo the part a analysis for Firms U and L, but add basic earnings power (BEP), return on invested capital (ROIC, defined as NOPAT/Capital = EBIT $(1 - T)$/TA for this company), and the times-interest-earned (TIE) ratio to the outcome measures. Find the values for each firm in each state of the economy, and then calculate the expected values. Finally, calculate the standard deviations. What does this example illustrate about the impact of debt financing on risk and return?

f. What does capital structure theory attempt to do? What lessons can be learned from capital structure theory? Be sure to address the MM models.

g. What does the empirical evidence say about capital structure theory? What are the implications for managers?

h. With the above points in mind, now consider the optimal capital structure for PizzaPalace.

   (1) For each capital structure under consideration, calculate the levered beta, the cost of equity, and the WACC.

   (2) Now calculate the corporate value, the value of the debt that will be issued, and the resulting market value of equity.

   (3) Calculate the resulting price per share, the number of shares repurchased, and the remaining shares.

i. Considering only the capital structures under analysis, what is PizzaPalace's optimal capital structure?

SELECTED ADDITIONAL REFERENCES AND CASES

The Journal of Applied Corporate Finance *periodically has roundtable discussions on capital structure. See the Spring 2001 issue (pages 9–41) and the Spring 1998 issue (pages 8–24) for some recent discussions.*

For an article on signaling, see

Baskin, Jonathon, "An Empirical Investigation of the Pecking Order Hypothesis," *Financial Management*, Spring 1989, 26–35.

For some insights into how practicing financial managers view the capital structure decision, see

Kamath, Ravindra R., "Long-Term Financing Decisions: Views and Practices of Financial Managers of NYSE Firms," *Financial Review*, May 1997, 331–356.

Norton, Edgar, "Factors Affecting Capital Structure Decisions," *Financial Review*, August 1991, 431–446.

Pinegar, J. Michael, and Lisa Wilbricht, "What Managers Think of Capital Structure Theory: A Survey," *Financial Management*, Winter 1989, 82–91.

To learn more about the link between market risk and operating and financial leverage, see

Callahan, Carolyn M., and Rosanne M. Mohr, "The Determinants of Systematic Risk: A Synthesis," *The Financial Review*, May 1989, 157–181.

Prezas, Alexandros P., "Effects of Debt on the Degrees of Operating and Financial Leverage," *Financial Management*, Summer 1987, 39–44.

Here are some additional articles that relate to this chapter:

Easterwood, John C., and Palani-Rajan Kadapakkam, "The Role of Private and Public Debt in Corporate Capital Structures," *Financial Management*, Autumn 1991, 49–57.

Garvey, Gerald T., "Leveraging the Underinvestment Problem: How High Debt and Management Shareholdings Solve the Agency Costs of Free Cash Flow," *Journal of Financial Research*, Summer 1992, 149–166.

Harris, Milton, and Artur Raviv, "Capital Structure and the Informational Role of Debt," *Journal of Finance*, June 1990, 321–349.

Israel, Ronen, "Capital Structure and the Market for Corporate Control: The Defensive Role of Debt Financing," *Journal of Finance*, September 1991, 1391–1409.

See the following two articles for additional insights into the relationship between industry characteristics and financial leverage:

Long, Michael, and Ileen Malitz, "The Investment-Financing Nexus: Some Empirical Evidence," *Midland Corporate Finance Journal*, Fall 1985, 53–59.

For a discussion of the international implications of capital structure, see

Rutterford, Janette, "An International Perspective on the Capital Structure Puzzle," *Midland Corporate Finance Journal*, Fall 1985, 60–72.

The following sources describe some empirical results from tests of capital structure theory:

Andrade, Gregor, and Steven Kaplan, "How Costly Is Financial (Not Economic) Distress? Evidence from Highly Leveraged Transactions That Became Distressed," *Journal of Finance*, Vol. 53, 1998, 1443–1493.

Baker, Malcolm, Robin Greenwood and Jeffrey Wurgler, "The Maturity of Debt Issues and Predictable Variation in Bond Returns," *Journal of Financial Economics*, Vol. 70, no. 2, November 2003, 261–291.

Frank, Murray Z., and Vidhan K. Goyal, "Testing the Pecking Order Theory of Capital Structure," *Journal of Financial Economics*, Vol. 67, no. 2, February 2003, 217–248.

Graham, John, and Campbell Harvey, "The Theory and Practice of Corporate Finance: Evidence from the Field," *Journal of Financial Economics*, Vol. 60, 2001, 187–243.

The following cases from the Finance Online Case Library *cover many of the concepts discussed in this chapter and are available at **http://www.textchoice.com**:*

Case 9, "Home Security Systems, Inc.," Case 10, "Kleen Kar, Inc.," Case 10A, "Mountain Springs, Inc." and Case 10B, "Greta Cosmetics, Inc.," which present a situation similar to the Strasburg example in the text.

CHAPTER 15

Distributions to Shareholders:
Dividends and Repurchases

A profitable company regularly faces three important questions: (1) How much of its free cash flow should it pass on to shareholders? (2) Should it provide this cash to stockholders by raising the dividend or by repurchasing stock? (3) Should it maintain a stable, consistent payment policy, or should it let the payments vary as conditions change?

In this chapter we discuss the issues that affect the answers to these questions. Most firms establish a policy that reflects their forecasted cash flows and capital expenditures, and then they try to stick to it. The policy can be changed, but this can cause problems because such changes inconvenience stockholders and may send unintended signals, which can harm stock prices. Still, economic circumstances do change, and occasionally such changes require firms to change their dividend policies.

One of the most striking examples of a dividend policy change occurred in May 1994, when FPL Group, a utility holding company whose primary subsidiary is Florida Power & Light, announced a cut in its quarterly dividend from $0.62 per share to $0.42. At the same time, FPL stated that it would buy back 10 million of its common shares over the next three years to bolster its stock price.[1]

Security analysts called the FPL decision a watershed event for the electric utility industry. FPL saw that its circumstances were changing—its core electric business was moving from a regulated monopoly environment to one of increasing competition, and the new environment required a stronger balance sheet and more financial flexibility than was consistent with its 90 percent payout policy.

What did the market think about FPL's dividend policy change? The company's stock price fell by 14 percent the day the announcement was made. In the past, hundreds of dividend cuts had been followed by sharply lower earnings, and that pattern had conditioned investors to expect the worst when companies reduced their dividends—this is the signaling effect, which is discussed later in the chapter. However, over the next few months, as they understood FPL's actions better, analysts began to praise the decision and to recommend the stock. As a result, FPL's stock outperformed the average utility and soon exceeded the preannouncement price.

---

[1] For a complete discussion of the FPL decision, see Dennis Soter, Eugene Brigham, and Paul Evanson, "The Dividend Cut Heard 'Round the World: The Case of FPL," *Journal of Applied Corporate Finance*, Spring 1996, 4–15.

CF

e-resource

*The textbook's Web site contains an Excel file that will guide you through the chapter's calculations. The file for this chapter is **CF2 Ch 15 Tool Kit.xls,** and we encourage you to open the file and follow along as you read the chapter.*

Successful companies generate net operating profit after taxes (NOPAT). A company's growth opportunities and replacement requirements, identified through capital budgeting and financial planning, determine the amount that should be invested in operating capital. Subtracting the investment in operating capital from NOPAT results in free cash flow (FCF), which is the amount of cash flow available for distribution to investors after paying expenses and taxes and making the necessary investments in operating capital. There are only five good uses of free cash flow: (1) pay interest expenses, (2) pay debt principal, (3) pay dividends, (4) repurchase stock, or (5) buy nonoperating assets such as Treasury bills or other marketable securities.[2] The capital structure choice determines the payments for interest expenses and debt principal, and a company's working capital policies (discussed in Chapter 16) determine its level of marketable securities. The remaining FCF should be distributed to shareholders, with the only choice being how much to distribute in the form of dividends versus stock repurchases.

Obviously, this is a simplification since companies (1) sometimes scale back their operating plans for sales and asset growth if such reductions are needed to maintain an existing dividend, (2) temporarily adjust their current financing mix in response to market conditions, and (3) often use marketable securities as shock absorbers for fluctuations in short-term cash flows. Still, there is interdependence among shareholder distributions, operating plans (which have the biggest impact on free cash flow), financing plans (which have the biggest impact on the cost of capital), and working capital policies (which determine the target level of marketable securities).

THE LEVEL OF DISTRIBUTIONS AND FIRM VALUE

An excellent source of recent dividend news for major corporations is available at the Web site of Corporate Financials Online at **http://www.cfonews .com/scs.** *By clicking the down arrow of the "News Category" box to the left of the screen, students may select "Dividends" to receive a list of companies with dividend news. Click on any company, and you will see its latest dividend news.*

Shareholder distributions for a wealth-maximizing firm affect the value of operations only to the extent that they change the cost of capital or investors' perceptions regarding expected free cash flow.[3] Here are the central questions addressed in this chapter: Can a company increase its value through its choice of **distribution policy**, defined as the *level* of distributions, the *form* of distributions (cash dividends versus stock repurchases), and the *stability* of distributions?

The answer depends in part on investors' preferences for returns as dividend yields versus capital gains. The mix of yield return versus gains return is determined by the **target distribution ratio**, which is the percentage of net income distributed to shareholders through cash dividends or stock repurchases, and the **target payout ratio**, which is the percentage of net income paid as a cash dividend. Notice that the payout ratio must be less than the distribution ratio since the distribution ratio includes stock repurchases as well as cash dividends.

A high distribution ratio and a high payout ratio mean that a company pays large dividends and has small, or zero, stock repurchases. In this situation, the dividend yield is relatively high and the expected capital gain is low. If a company has a large distribution ratio but a small payout ratio, then it pays low dividends but regularly repurchases stock, resulting in a low dividend yield but a relatively high expected capital gain yield. If a company has a low distribution ratio, then it must also have a relatively low payout ratio, again resulting in a low dividend yield and hopefully a relatively high capital gain. Therefore, a firm's **optimal distribution policy** must strike a balance between cash dividends and capital gains so as to maximize the stock price.

---

[2] Recall from Chapter 3 that the interest expense is after taxes and that a company doesn't need to spend FCF on operating assets since those expenditures were already deducted when calculating FCF. Also, most growing companies actually issue new debt each year rather than repay debt. This "negative use" of FCF provides more FCF for the other uses.

[3] Shareholder distributions also affect the level of marketable securities, a nonoperating asset, which in turn affects the stock price. This can also affect the stability of dividends, but this is normally a secondary effect.

CORPORATE VALUATION AND DISTRIBUTIONS TO SHAREHOLDERS

Free cash flow is the amount of cash available for distribution to all investors (shareholders and debtholders) after paying expenses and taxes, and making investments in the operating capital required to support the company's growth. Most of this book has focused on FCF generation, including its risk and expected level. In contrast, this chapter focuses on a use of FCF: How much FCF should be distributed to shareholders, and should it be distributed as dividends or stock repurchases? In addition, we show how distributions to shareholders are related to financing choices. Finally, we discuss ways that shareholders perceive distributions as signals regarding a firm's risk and expected future free cash flows.

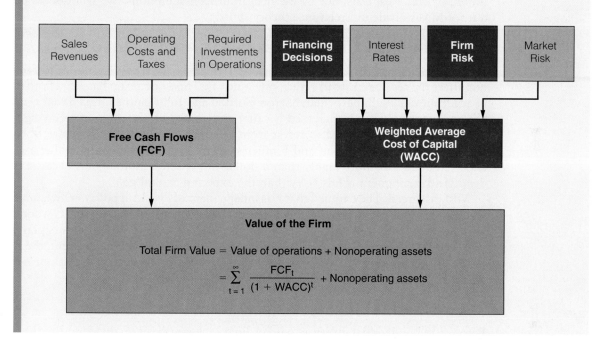

In this section we examine three theories of investor preferences for dividend yield versus capital gains: (1) the dividend irrelevance theory, (2) the "bird-in-the-hand" theory, and (3) the tax preference theory.

Dividend Irrelevance Theory

It has been argued that dividend policy has no effect on either the price of a firm's stock or its cost of capital. If dividend policy has no significant effects, then it would be *irrelevant*. The principal proponents of the **dividend irrelevance theory** are Merton Miller and Franco Modigliani (MM).[4] They argued that the firm's value is determined only by its basic earning power and its business risk. In other words, MM argued that the value of the firm depends only on the income produced by its assets, not on how this income is split between dividends and retained earnings.

To understand MM's argument, recognize that any shareholder can in theory construct his or her own dividend policy. For example, if a firm does not pay dividends, a shareholder who wants a 5 percent dividend can "create" it by selling 5 percent of his or her stock. Conversely, if a company pays a higher dividend than an investor desires, the investor can use

---

[4] Merton H. Miller and Franco Modigliani, "Dividend Policy, Growth, and the Valuation of Shares," *Journal of Business*, October 1961, 411–433.

the unwanted dividends to buy additional shares of the company's stock. If investors could buy and sell shares and thus create their own dividend policy without incurring costs, then the firm's dividend policy would truly be irrelevant. Note, though, that investors who want additional dividends must incur brokerage costs to sell shares and pay taxes on any capital gains. Investors who do not want dividends incur brokerage costs to purchase shares with their dividends. Because taxes and brokerage costs certainly exist, dividend policy may well be relevant.

In developing their dividend theory, MM made a number of assumptions, especially the absence of taxes and brokerage costs. Obviously, taxes and brokerage costs do exist, so the MM irrelevance theory may not be true. However, MM argued (correctly) that all economic theories are based on simplifying assumptions, and that the validity of a theory must be judged by empirical tests, not by the realism of its assumptions. We will discuss empirical tests of MM's dividend irrelevance theory shortly.

Bird-in-the-Hand Theory: Dividends Are Preferred

The principal conclusion of MM's dividend irrelevance theory is that dividend policy does not affect the required rate of return on equity, r_s. This conclusion has been hotly debated in academic circles. In particular, Myron Gordon and John Lintner argued that r_s *decreases* as the dividend payout is increased because investors are less certain of receiving the capital gains that are supposed to result from retaining earnings than they are of receiving dividend payments.[5] Gordon and Lintner said, in effect, that investors value a dollar of expected dividends more highly than a dollar of expected capital gains because the dividend yield component is less risky than the expected capital gain.

MM disagreed. They argued that r_s is independent of dividend policy, which implies that investors are indifferent between dividends and capital gains. MM called the Gordon-Lintner argument the **bird-in-the-hand** fallacy because, in MM's view, most investors plan to reinvest their dividends in the stock of the same or similar firms, and, in any event, the riskiness of the firm's cash flows to investors in the long run is determined by the riskiness of operating cash flows, not by dividend payout policy.

Tax Preference Theory: Capital Gains Are Preferred

Before 2003, individual investors paid ordinary income taxes on dividends but lower rates on long-term capital gains. The Jobs and Growth Act of 2003 changed this and reduced the tax rate on dividend income to the same as on long-term capital gains.[6] However, there are two reasons stock price appreciation is taxed more favorably than dividend income. First, due to time value effects, a dollar of taxes paid in the future has a lower effective cost than a dollar paid today. So even if dividends and gains are taxed equally, capital gains are never taxed sooner than dividends. Second, if a stock is held by someone until he or she dies, no capital gains tax is due at all—the beneficiaries who receive the stock can use the stock's value on the death day as their cost basis and thus completely escape the capital gains tax.

Because of these tax advantages, investors may prefer to have companies minimize dividends. If so, investors would be willing to pay more for low-payout companies than for otherwise similar high-payout companies.

---

[5] Myron J. Gordon, "Optimal Investment and Financing Policy," *Journal of Finance,* May 1963, 264–272; and John Lintner, "Dividends, Earnings, Leverage, Stock Prices, and the Supply of Capital to Corporations," *Review of Economics and Statistics,* August 1962, 243–269.

[6] Of course, nothing involving taxes is quite this simple. First, the dividend must be from a domestic company, and the investor must own the stock for more than 60 days during the 120-day period beginning 60 days before the ex-dividend date. There are other restrictions for dividends other than regular cash dividends. Under the new law, long-term capital gains are taxed at 5 percent for low-income investors (that is, those whose marginal tax rate is 15 percent or less) and at 15 percent for those with more income. Dividend income is taxed at those same rates through 2007. In 2008, the 5 percent capital gains (and dividend rate) drops to zero for low-income investors; there is no scheduled change for high-income investors in 2008. After 2008, the capital gains rates will revert to 10 percent and 20 percent, which were the capital gains rates in effect prior to the 2003 tax act.

Empirical Evidence and the Level of Shareholder Distributions

As Figure 15-1 shows, these three theories offer contradictory advice to corporate managers, so which, if any, should we believe? The most logical way to proceed is to test the theories empirically. Many such tests have been conducted, but their results have been unclear. There are two reasons for this: (1) For a valid statistical test, things other than distribution level must be held constant; that is, the sample companies must differ only in their distribution levels, and (2) we must be able to measure with a high degree of accuracy each firm's cost of equity. Neither of these two conditions holds: We cannot find a set of publicly owned firms that differ only in their distribution levels, nor can we obtain precise estimates of the cost of equity. Therefore, no one has yet identified a clear relationship between distribution level and the cost of equity or firm value.

Here is what the empirical evidence does tell us. First, the level of dividend payouts has been decreasing in the last 30 years.[7] In 1978, about 66.5 percent of NYSE, AMEX, and Nasdaq firms paid a dividend. In 1999, only 20.8 percent paid a dividend. As a percent of net income, the average dividend payout ratio fell from 22.3 percent in 1974 to 13.8

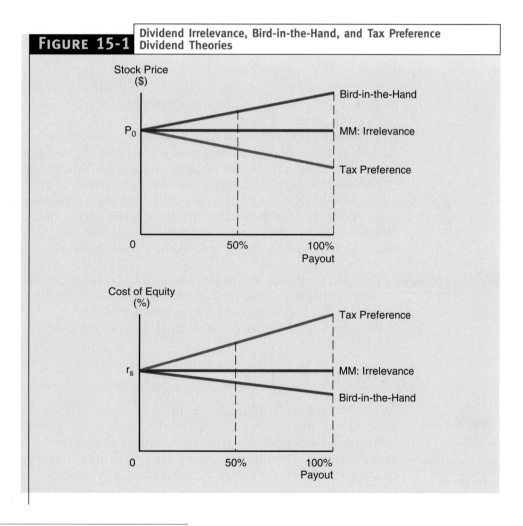

FIGURE 15-1 Dividend Irrelevance, Bird-in-the-Hand, and Tax Preference Dividend Theories

[7] See Gustavo Grullon and Roni Michaely, "Dividends, Share Repurchases, and the Substitution Hypothesis," *Journal of Finance*, Vol. 57, no. 4, August 2002, 1649–1684; or see Eugene Fama and Kenneth French, "Disappearing Dividends: Changing Firm Characteristics or Lower Propensity to Pay?" *Journal of Applied Corporate Finance*, Vol. 14, no. 1, Spring 2001, 67–79.

DIVIDEND YIELDS AROUND THE WORLD

Dividend yields vary considerably in different stock markets throughout the world. In 1999 in the United States, dividend yields averaged 1.6 percent for the large blue chip stocks in the Dow Jones Industrials, 1.2 percent for a broader sample of stocks in the S&P 500, and 0.3 percent for stocks in the high-tech-dominated Nasdaq. Outside the United States, average dividend yields ranged from 5.7 percent in New Zealand to 0.7 percent in Taiwan. The accompanying table summarizes the dividend picture in 1999.

World Stock Market (Index)	Dividend Yield	World Stock Market (Index)	Dividend Yield
New Zealand	5.7%	United States (Dow Jones Industrials)	1.6
Australia	3.1	Canada (TSE 300)	1.5
Britain FTSE 100	2.4	United States (S&P 500)	1.2
Hong Kong	2.4	Mexico	1.1
France	2.1	Japan Nikkei	0.7
Germany	2.1	Taiwan	0.7
Belgium	2.0	United States (Nasdaq)	0.3
Singapore	1.7		

Source: From Alexandra Eadie, "On the Grid Looking for Dividend Yield Around the World," *The Globe and Mail*, June 23, 1999, B16. Eadie's source was Bloomberg Financial Services. Reprinted with permission from *The Globe and Mail*.

percent in 1998. Second, the average repurchase payout rose from 3.7 to 13.6 percent, causing the percent of total distributions to remain fairly stable at around 26 to 28 percent. While total distributions have been fairly steady, there is considerable variation in the level and form of payout among individual firms. We take a closer look at stock repurchases later in the chapter, but for now we focus on dividend payments.

Although investors in the aggregate cannot be shown to prefer either higher or lower distribution levels, the evidence does show that individual investors have strong preferences. Evidence also shows that investors prefer stable, predictable dividend payouts (regardless of the payout level), and that they interpret dividend changes as signals about the firm's future prospects. We discuss these issues in the next several sections.

SELF-TEST QUESTIONS
What did Modigliani and Miller assume about taxes and brokerage costs when they developed their dividend irrelevance theory?

How did the bird-in-the-hand theory get its name?

What have been the results of empirical tests of the dividend theories?

CLIENTELE EFFECT

For updates of industry payout ratios, go to **http://yahoo .investor.reuters.com.** *After picking a company, select Ratios, then select Dividend.*

As we indicated earlier, different groups, or *clienteles,* of stockholders prefer different dividend payout policies. For example, retired individuals, pension funds, and university endowment funds generally prefer cash income, so they may want the firm to pay out a high percentage of its earnings. Such investors are often in low or even zero tax brackets, so taxes are of no concern. On the other hand, stockholders in their peak earning years might prefer reinvestment, because they have less need for current investment income and would simply reinvest dividends received, after first paying income taxes on those dividends.

If a firm retains and reinvests income rather than paying dividends, those stockholders who need current income would be disadvantaged. The value of their stock might increase, but they would be forced to go to the trouble and expense of selling off some of their shares to obtain cash. Also, some institutional investors (or trustees for individuals) would be legally precluded from selling stock and then "spending capital." On the other hand, stockholders who are saving rather than spending dividends might favor the low dividend policy, for the less the firm pays out in dividends, the less these stockholders will have to pay in current taxes, and the less trouble and expense they will have to go through to reinvest their after-tax dividends. Therefore, investors who want current investment income should own shares in high dividend payout firms, while investors with no need for current investment income should own shares in low dividend payout firms. For example, investors seeking high cash income might invest in electric utilities, which averaged a 55 percent payout in 2004, while those favoring growth could invest in the software industry, which paid out only 12 percent during the same time period.

To the extent that stockholders can switch firms, a firm can change from one dividend payout policy to another and then let stockholders who do not like the new policy sell to other investors who do. However, frequent switching would be inefficient because of (1) brokerage costs, (2) the likelihood that stockholders who are selling will have to pay capital gains taxes, and (3) a possible shortage of investors who like the firm's newly adopted dividend policy. Thus, management should be hesitant to change its dividend policy, because a change might cause current shareholders to sell their stock, forcing the stock price down. Such a price decline might be temporary, but it might also be permanent—if few new investors are attracted by the new dividend policy, then the stock price would remain depressed. Of course, the new policy might attract an even larger clientele than the firm had before, in which case the stock price would rise.

Evidence from several studies suggests that there is in fact a **clientele effect**.[8] MM and others have argued that one clientele is as good as another, so the existence of a clientele effect does not necessarily imply that one dividend policy is better than any other. MM may be wrong, though, and neither they nor anyone else can prove that the aggregate makeup of investors permits firms to disregard clientele effects. This issue, like most others in the dividend arena, is still up in the air.

SELF-TEST QUESTION Define the clientele effect and explain how it affects dividend policy.

INFORMATION CONTENT, OR SIGNALING, HYPOTHESIS

When MM set forth their dividend irrelevance theory, they assumed that everyone—investors and managers alike—has identical information regarding the firm's future earnings and dividends. In reality, however, different investors have different views on both the level of future dividend payments and the uncertainty inherent in those payments, and managers have better information about future prospects than public stockholders.

It has been observed that an increase in the dividend is often accompanied by an increase in the price of a stock, while a dividend cut generally leads to a stock price decline. Some have argued that this indicates that investors prefer dividends to capital gains. However, MM argued differently. They noted the well-established fact that corporations are reluctant to cut dividends, hence do not raise dividends unless they anticipate higher earnings in the future. Thus, MM argued that a higher-than-expected dividend increase is a "signal" to investors that the firm's management forecasts good future earnings. Conversely, a dividend reduction, or a smaller-than-expected increase, is a signal that management is forecasting poor earnings in the future. Thus, MM argued that investors' reactions to changes in dividend policy do not necessarily show that investors prefer dividends to

---

[8] For example, see R. Richardson Pettit, "Taxes, Transactions Costs and the Clientele Effect of Dividends," *The Journal of Financial Economics*, December 1977, 419–436.

retained earnings. Rather, they argue that price changes following dividend actions simply indicate that there is an important **information, or signaling, content** in dividend announcements.

The initiation of a dividend by a firm that formerly paid no dividend is certainly a significant change in distribution policy. It appears that initiating firms' future earnings and cash flows are less risky than before the initiation. However, the evidence is mixed regarding the future profitability of initiating firms: Some studies find slightly higher earnings after the initiation, while others find no significant change in earnings.[9] What happens when firms with existing dividends unexpectedly increase or decrease the dividend? Early studies, using small data samples, concluded that unexpected dividend changes did not provide a signal about future earnings.[10] However, more recent data with larger samples provide mixed evidence.[11] On average, firms that cut dividends have had poor earnings in recent years but have actually improved earnings in subsequent years. Firms that increase dividends have had earnings increases in recent years but don't appear to have had subsequent earnings increases. However, they don't have subsequent declines in earnings either, so it appears that the increase in dividends signals that past earnings increases were not temporary. Also, a relatively large number of firms that expect a large permanent increase in cash flow (as opposed to earnings) do in fact increase their dividend payouts in the year prior to the cash flow increase.

All in all, there is clearly some information content in dividend announcements: Stock prices tend to fall when dividends are cut, even if they don't always rise when dividends are increased. However, this doesn't necessarily validate the signaling hypothesis since it is difficult to tell whether any stock price changes that follow changes in dividends reflect only signaling effects or both signaling and dividend preferences.

SELF-TEST QUESTION | Define information content, and explain how it affects dividend policy.

IMPLICATIONS FOR DIVIDEND STABILITY

The clientele effect and the information content in dividend announcements definitely have implications regarding the desirability of stable versus volatile dividends. For example, many stockholders rely on dividends to meet expenses, and they would be seriously inconvenienced if the dividend stream were unstable. Further, reducing dividends to make funds available for capital investment could send incorrect signals to investors, who might push down the stock price because they interpreted the dividend cut to mean that the company's future earnings prospects have been diminished. Thus, maximizing its stock price probably requires a firm to maintain a steady dividend policy. Because sales and earnings are expected to grow for most firms, a stable dividend policy means that a company's regular cash dividends should also grow at a steady, predictable rate.

SELF-TEST QUESTION | Why do the clientele effect and the information content hypotheses imply that investors prefer stable dividends?

[9] See Edward Dyl and Robert Weigand, "The Information Content of Dividend Initiations: Additional Evidence," *Financial Management*, Vol. 27, no. 3, Autumn 1998, 27–35; P. Asquith and D. Mullins, "The Impact of Initiating Dividend Payments on Shareholders' Wealth," *Journal of Business*, January 1983, 77–96; and P. Healy and K. Palepu, "Earnings Information Conveyed by Dividend Initiations and Omissions," *Journal of Financial Economics*, September 1988, 149–175.

[10] For example, see N. Gonedes, "Corporate Signaling, External Accounting, and Capital Market Equilibrium: Evidence of Dividends, Income, and Extraordinary Items," *Journal of Accounting Research*, Spring 1978, 26–79; and R. Watts, "The Information Content of Dividends," *Journal of Business*, April 1973, 191–211.

[11] See Shlomo Benartzi, Roni Michaely, and Richard Thaler, "Do Changes in Dividends Signal the Future or the Past?" *Journal of Finance*, Vol. 52, no. 3, July 1997, 1007–1034; and Yaron Brook, William Charlton, Jr., and Robert J. Hendershott, "Do Firms Use Dividends to Signal Large Future Cash Flow Increases?" *Financial Management*, Vol. 27, no. 3, Autumn, 1998, 46–57.

SETTING THE TARGET DISTRIBUTION LEVEL: THE RESIDUAL DISTRIBUTION MODEL

When deciding how much cash to distribute to stockholders, two points should be kept in mind: (1) The overriding objective is to maximize shareholder value, and (2) the firm's cash flows really belong to its shareholders, so management should refrain from retaining income unless they can reinvest it to produce returns higher than shareholders could themselves earn by investing the cash in investments of equal risk. On the other hand, recall from Chapter 9 that internal equity (reinvested earnings) is cheaper than external equity (new common stock issues) because it avoids flotation costs. This encourages firms to retain earnings so as to avoid having to issue new stock.

When establishing a distribution policy, one size does not fit all. Some firms produce a lot of cash but have limited investment opportunities—this is true for firms in profitable but mature industries where few opportunities for growth exist. Such firms typically distribute a large percentage of their cash to shareholders, thereby attracting investment clienteles that prefer high dividends. Other firms generate little or no excess cash since they have many good investment opportunities. Such firms generally distribute little or no cash but enjoy rising earnings and stock prices, thereby attracting investors who prefer capital gains.

As Table 15-1 suggests, dividend payouts and dividend yields for large corporations vary considerably. Generally, firms in stable, cash-producing industries such as utilities, financial services, and tobacco pay relatively high dividends, whereas companies in rapidly growing industries such as computer software tend to pay lower dividends.

For a given firm, the optimal distribution ratio is a function of four factors: (1) investors' preferences for dividends versus capital gains, (2) the firm's investment opportunities,

TABLE 15-1 | Dividend Payouts (May 2004)

Company	Industry	Dividend Payout	Dividend Yield
I. Companies That Pay High Dividends			
WD-40 Company (WDFC)	Household products	50%	2.6%
Empire District Electric (EDE)	Electric utility	117	6.4
Rayonier Inc. (RYN)	Forest products	52	5.6
R. J. Reynolds Tobacco (RJR)	Tobacco products	NM[a]	6.6
Union Planters Corp. (UPC)	Regional banks	59	4.6
Ingles Markets Inc. (IMKTA)	Retail (grocery)	73	6.1
II. Companies That Pay Little or No Dividends			
Tiffany and Company (TIF)	Specialty retail	13%	0.7%
Harley-Davidson Inc. (HDI)	Recreational products	9	0.7
Aaron Rents Inc. (RNT)	Rental and leasing	2	0.1
Delta Air Lines Inc. (DAL)	Airline	0.0	0.0
Papa John's Intl. Inc. (PZZA)	Restaurants	0.0	0.0
Microsoft Corp. (MSFT)	Software and programming	23	0.6

[a]Reported a loss, so its dividend payout ratio is not meaningful (NM).

Source: **http://yahoo.investor.reuters.com**, May 2004.

(3) its target capital structure, and (4) the availability and cost of external capital. The last three elements are combined in what we call the **residual distribution model.** Under this model a firm follows these four steps when establishing its target distribution ratio: (1) It determines the optimal capital budget; (2) it determines the amount of equity needed to finance that budget, given its target capital structure; (3) it uses reinvested earnings to meet equity requirements to the extent possible; and (4) it pays dividends or repurchases stock only if more earnings are available than are needed to support the optimal capital budget. The word *residual* implies "leftover," and the residual policy implies that distributions are paid out of "leftover" earnings.

If a firm rigidly follows the residual distribution policy, then distributions paid in any given year can be expressed as follows:

$$
\begin{aligned}
\text{Distributions} &= \text{Net income} - \begin{array}{l} \text{Retained earnings needed to} \\ \text{finance new investments} \end{array} \\
&= \text{Net income} - \begin{array}{l} [(\text{Target equity ratio}) \\ \times (\text{Total capital budget})]. \end{array}
\end{aligned}
\tag{15-1}
$$

For example, suppose the target equity ratio is 60 percent and the firm plans to spend $50 million on capital projects. In that case, it would need $50(0.6) = $30 million of common equity. Then, if its net income were $100 million, its distributions would be $100 − $30 = $70 million. So, if the company had $100 million of earnings and a capital budget of $50 million, it would use $30 million of the retained earnings plus $50 − $30 = $20 million of new debt to finance the capital budget, and this would keep its capital structure on target. Note that the amount of equity needed to finance new investments might exceed the net income; in our example, this would happen if the capital budget were $200 million. In that case, no distributions would be paid, and the company would have to issue new common stock in order to maintain its target capital structure.

Most firms have a target capital structure that calls for at least some debt, so new financing is done partly with debt and partly with equity. As long as the firm finances with the optimal mix of debt and equity, and provided it uses only internally generated equity (retained earnings), then the marginal cost of each new dollar of capital will be minimized. Internally generated equity is available for financing a certain amount of new investment, but beyond that amount, the firm must turn to more expensive new common stock. At the point where new stock must be sold, the cost of equity, and consequently the marginal cost of capital, rises.

To illustrate these points, consider the case of Texas and Western (T&W) Transport Company. T&W's overall composite cost of capital is 10 percent. However, this cost assumes that all new equity comes from retained earnings. If the company must issue new stock, its cost of capital will be higher. T&W has $60 million in net income and a target capital structure of 60 percent equity and 40 percent debt. Provided that it does not make any cash distributions, T&W could make net investments (investments in addition to asset replacements from depreciation) of $100 million, consisting of $60 million from reinvested earnings plus $40 million of new debt supported by the retained earnings, at a 10 percent marginal cost of capital. If the capital budget exceeded $100 million, the required equity component would exceed net income, which is of course the maximum amount of reinvested earnings. In this case, T&W would have to issue new common stock, thereby pushing its cost of capital above 10 percent.

At the beginning of its planning period, T&W's financial staff considers all proposed projects for the upcoming period. Independent projects are accepted if their estimated returns exceed the risk-adjusted cost of capital. In choosing among mutually exclusive projects, T&W chooses the project with the highest positive NPV. The capital budget represents the amount of capital that is required to finance all accepted projects. If T&W

TABLE 15-2 | T&W's Distribution Ratio with $60 Million of Net Income When Faced with Different Investment Opportunities (Millions of Dollars)

	INVESTMENT OPPORTUNITIES		
	Poor	Average	Good
Capital budget	$40	$70	$150
Net income	60	60	60
Required equity (0.6 × Capital budget)	24	42	90
Distributions paid (NI − Required equity)	$36	$18	−$ 30a
Distribution ratio (Dividend/NI)	60%	30%	0%

aWith a $150 million capital budget, T&W would retain all of its earnings and also issue $30 million of new stock.

follows a strict residual distribution policy, we can see from Table 15-2 that there may be changes in the distribution ratio.

If T&W forecasts poor investment opportunities, its estimated capital budget will be only $40 million. To maintain the target capital structure, 40 percent of this capital ($16 million) must be raised as debt, and 60 percent ($24 million) must be equity. If it followed a strict residual policy, T&W would retain $24 million of its $60 million earnings to help finance new investments, then distribute the remaining $36 million to shareholders. Under this scenario, the company's distribution ratio would be $36 million/$60 million = 0.6 = 60%.

By contrast, if the company's investment opportunities are average, its optimal capital budget would rise to $70 million. Here it would require $42 million of retained earnings, so distributions would be $60 – $42 = $18 million, for a ratio of $18/$60 = 30%. Finally, if investment opportunities are good, the capital budget would be $150 million, which would require 0.6($150) = $90 million of equity. T&W would retain all of its net income ($60 million), thus make no distributions. Moreover, since the required equity exceeds the retained earnings, the company would have to issue some new common stock to maintain the target capital structure.

Since both investment opportunities and earnings will surely vary from year to year, strict adherence to the residual distribution policy would result in unstable distributions. One year the firm might make no distributions because it needed the money to finance good investment opportunities, but the next year it might make a large distribution because investment opportunities were poor and it therefore did not need to retain much. Similarly, fluctuating earnings could also lead to variable distributions, even if investment opportunities were stable. To this point, we have not said whether distributions should be in the form of dividends, stock repurchases, or some combination. The next sections discuss some specific issues associated with dividend payments and stock repurchases, followed by a comparison of their relative advantages and disadvantages.

SELF-TEST QUESTION Explain the logic of the residual dividend model and the steps a firm would take to implement it.

DISTRIBUTIONS IN THE FORM OF DIVIDENDS

This section explains how the volatile distributions implied by the residual model affect the use of dividends as a form of distribution. It also describes some of the institutional features associated with dividend payments.

Dividends and the Residual Model

If distributions were in the form of dividends, then rigidly following the residual policy would lead to fluctuating, unstable dividends. Since investors dislike volatile dividends, r_s would be high, and the stock price low. Therefore, firms should

1. Estimate earnings and investment opportunities, on average, over the next five or so years.
2. Use this forecasted information and the target capital structure to find the average residual model distributions and dollars of dividends during the planning period.
3. Then set a *target payout ratio* based on the average projected data.

Thus, firms should use the residual policy to help set their long-run target distribution ratios, but not as a guide to the distribution in any one year.

Companies use the residual distribution model as discussed above to help understand the determinants of an optimal dividend policy, along with computerized financial forecasting models. Most larger corporations forecast their financial statements over the next five to ten years. Information on projected capital expenditures and working capital requirements is entered into the model, along with sales forecasts, profit margins, depreciation, and the other elements required to forecast cash flows. The target capital structure is also specified, and the model shows the amount of debt and equity that will be required to meet the capital budgeting requirements while maintaining the target capital structure. Then, dividend payments are introduced. Naturally, the higher the payout ratio, the greater the required external equity. Most companies use the model to find a dividend pattern over the forecast period (generally five years) that will provide sufficient equity to support the capital budget without forcing it to sell new common stock or move the capital structure ratios outside the optimal range.

Some companies set a very low "regular" dividend and then supplement it with an "extra" dividend when times are good. General Motors, Ford, and other auto companies have followed the **low-regular-dividend-plus-extras** policy in the past. Each company announced a low regular dividend that it was sure could be maintained "through hell or high water," and stockholders could count on receiving that dividend under all conditions. Then, when times were good and profits and cash flows were high, the companies either paid a specially designated extra dividend or repurchased shares of stock. Investors recognized that the extras might not be maintained in the future, so they did not interpret them as a signal that the companies' earnings were going up permanently, nor did they take the elimination of the extra as a negative signal.

At times, however, companies must make substantial cuts in dividends in order to conserve cash. In October 2000, facing increasing competition, technology changes, a decline in its bond rating, and a cutoff from the commercial paper market, Xerox Corporation rolled back its quarterly dividend from $0.20 per share to $0.05 per share. This was a dividend rate not seen by Xerox shareholders since 1966. In the week prior to the dividend cut, the share price had declined significantly in response to an announcement that there would be a loss for the quarter rather than a modest profit, and a warning that a dividend cut was being considered. Xerox took a substantial stock price hit when it conceded that cash flows would not be sufficient to cover the old dividend—the price declined from about $15 to about $8. However, some analysts viewed the cut as a positive action that would preserve cash and maintain Xerox's ability to service its debt.

Dividend Payment Procedures

Dividends are normally paid quarterly, and, if conditions permit, the dividend is increased once each year. For example, Katz Corporation paid $0.50 per quarter in 2005, or at an annual rate of $2.00. In common financial parlance, we say that in 2005 Katz's *regular quarterly dividend* was $0.50, and its *annual dividend* was $2.00. In late 2005, Katz's board of directors met, reviewed projections for 2006, and decided to keep the 2006 dividend at $2.00. The directors announced the $2 rate, so stockholders could count on receiving it unless the company experienced unanticipated operating problems.

The actual payment procedure is as follows:

1. *Declaration date.* On the **declaration date**—say, on November 8—the directors meet and declare the regular dividend, issuing a statement similar to the following: "On November 8, 2005, the directors of Katz Corporation met and declared the regular quarterly dividend of 50 cents per share, payable to holders of record on December 9, payment to be made on January 3, 2006." For accounting purposes, the declared dividend becomes an actual liability on the declaration date. If a balance sheet were constructed, the amount ($0.50) × (Number of shares outstanding) would appear as a current liability, and retained earnings would be reduced by a like amount.

2. *Holder-of-record date.* At the close of business on the **holder-of-record date,** December 9, the company closes its stock transfer books and makes up a list of shareholders as of that date. If Katz Corporation is notified of the sale before 5 P.M. on December 9, then the new owner receives the dividend. However, if notification is received on or after December 10, the previous owner gets the dividend check.

3. *Ex-dividend date.* Suppose Jean Buyer buys 100 shares of stock from John Seller on December 6. Will the company be notified of the transfer in time to list Buyer as the new owner and thus pay the dividend to her? To avoid conflict, the securities industry has set up a convention under which the right to the dividend remains with the stock until two business days prior to the holder-of-record date; on the second day before that date, the right to the dividend no longer goes with the shares. The date when the right to the dividend leaves the stock is called the **ex-dividend date.** In this case, the ex-dividend date is two days prior to December 9, or December 7:

Dividend goes with stock:	December 6
Ex-dividend date:	December 7
	December 8
Holder-of-record date:	December 9

Therefore, if Buyer is to receive the dividend, she must buy the stock on or before December 6. If she buys it on December 7 or later, Seller will receive the dividend because he will be the official holder of record.

Katz's dividend amounts to $0.50, so the ex-dividend date is important. Barring fluctuations in the stock market, we would normally expect the price of a stock to drop by approximately the amount of the dividend on the ex-dividend date. Thus, if Katz closed at $30.50 on December 6, it would probably open at about $30 on December 7.

4. *Payment date.* The company actually mails the checks to the holders of record on January 3, the **payment date.**

SELF-TEST QUESTIONS

Why is the residual model more likely to be used to establish a long-run payout target than to set the actual year-by-year dividend payout ratio?

How do firms use planning models to help set dividend policy?

Explain the procedures used to actually pay the dividend.

Why is the ex-dividend date important to investors?

DISTRIBUTIONS THROUGH STOCK REPURCHASES

Stock repurchases, which occur when a company buys back some of its own outstanding stock, have become an important part of the financial landscape.[12] In fact, large companies have repurchased more shares than they have issued since 1985. Repurchases have also become the preferred method of initiating cash distributions to shareholders. In 1998, 81 percent of those firms initiating a distribution did so with a stock repurchase instead of a cash dividend, substantially higher than the 27 percent doing so in 1973.[13] Stock repurchases have also steadily replaced dividends as a form of distribution, with more cash returned to shareholders in repurchases than as dividend payments since 1998. This section discusses stock repurchases and their effect on value.

Three principal situations lead to stock repurchases. First, a company may decide to increase its leverage by issuing debt and using the proceeds to repurchase stock, as we described in Chapter 14. Second, many firms have given their employees stock options, and they repurchase stock for use when employees exercise the options. In this case, the number of outstanding shares reverts to its pre-repurchase level after the options are exercised. Third, a company may have excess cash. This may be due to a one-time cash inflow, such as the sale of a division, or it may simply be that the company is generating more free cash flow than it needs to service its debt.[14]

Stock repurchases are usually made in one of three ways: (1) A publicly owned firm can buy back its own stock through a broker on the open market.[15] (2) The firm can make a tender offer, under which it permits stockholders to send in (that is, "tender") shares in exchange for a specified price per share. In this case, the firm generally indicates that it will buy up to a specified number of shares within a stated time period (usually about two weeks). If more shares are tendered than the company wants to buy, purchases are made on a pro rata basis. (3) The firm can purchase a block of shares from one large holder on a negotiated basis. This is a targeted stock repurchase as discussed in Chapter 13.

The Effects of Stock Repurchases

Suppose a company has some extra cash, perhaps due to the sale of a division, and it plans to use that cash to repurchase stock.[16] To keep the example simple, we assume the company has no debt. The current stock price, P_0, is $20 and the company has 2 million outstanding shares, n_0, for a total market capitalization of $40 million. The company has $5 million in marketable securities (that is, extra cash) from the recent sale of a division.

As described in the corporate valuation model of Chapter 13, the company's value of operations, V_{op}, is the present value of its expected future free cash flows, discounted at the WACC.[17] Notice that the repurchase will not affect the FCFs or the WACC, so the

---

[12] The repurchased stock is called "treasury stock" and is shown as a negative value on the company's detailed balance sheet. On the consolidated balance sheet, treasury shares are deducted to find shares outstanding, and the price paid for the repurchased shares is deducted when determining common equity.

[13] See Gustavo Grullon and David Ikenberry, "What Do We Know about Stock Repurchases?" *Journal of Applied Corporate Finance,* Spring 2000, 31–51.

[14] See Benton Gup and Doowoo Nam, "Stock Buybacks, Corporate Performance, and EVA," *Journal of Applied Corporate Finance*, Vol. 14, no. 1, Spring 2001, 99–110, which shows that firms that repurchase stock have superior operating performance than those that do not buy back stock, consistent with the notion that firms buy back stock when they generate additional free cash flow. Gup and Nam also show that the operating performance increases in the year after the buyback, indicating that the superior performance is sustainable.

[15] Many firms announce their plans to repurchase stock on the open market. For example, a company might announce that it plans to repurchase four million shares of stock. Interestingly, companies usually don't buy back all the shares they announce but instead repurchase only around 80 percent of the announced number. See Clifford Stephens and Michael Weisbach, "Actual Share Reacquisitions in Open-Market Repurchase Programs," *Journal of Finance*, Vol. 53, no. 1, February 1998, 313–333.

[16] See Chapter 14 for a description of a stock repurchase as part of a recapitalization.

[17] The WACC is based on the company's capital used in operations and does not include any effects due to the extra cash.

repurchase doesn't affect the value of operations. The total value of the company is the value of operations plus the value of the extra cash. We can find the price per share, P_0, by dividing the total value by the number of shares outstanding, n_0:

$$P_0 = \frac{V_{op} + \text{Extra cash}}{n_0}. \tag{15-2}$$

We can easily solve this for the value of operations: $V_{op} = P_0(n_0) - \text{Extra cash} = \$40 - \$5 = \$35$ million.

Now consider the repurchase. P is the repurchase price and n is the number of shares that will be outstanding after the repurchase. We can multiply the unknown repurchase price by the number of shares that are repurchased, and this must equal the extra cash that is being used in the repurchase:

$$P(n_0 - n) = \text{Extra cash}. \tag{15-3}$$

Since the company will have no extra cash after the repurchase, the stock price will be the value of operations divided by the remaining shares of stock:

$$P = \frac{V_{op}}{n}. \tag{15-4}$$

We know the current price (P_0), the current number of shares (n_0), and the amount of extra cash. This leaves three remaining unknown variables (P, n, and V_{op}) and three equations, so we can solve for the unknown variables.[18] The solution shows that $P = P_0 = \$20$. In other words, the repurchase itself does not change the stock price. However, the repurchase does change the number of outstanding shares. Rewriting Equation 15-4,

$$n = \frac{V_{op}}{P} = \frac{\$35 \text{ million}}{\$20} = 1.75 \text{ million.} \tag{15-5}$$

As a check, we can see that the total market capitalization before the repurchase was $40 million, $5 million was used to repurchase shares, and the total market capitalization after the repurchase is $35 million = P(n) = \$20(1.75 million). This should make sense, since the repurchase itself transferred $5 million of corporate assets to the individual shareholders. Notice that the aggregate wealth of the shareholders didn't change. It was $40 million prior to the repurchase, and it is $40 million afterward ($35 million in stock and $5 million in cash). Notice also that a repurchase of 250,000 shares of stock at a price of $20 equals the $5 million in cash used to repurchase the shares.

To summarize, the events leading up to a repurchase (the sale of a division, a recapitalization, or the generation of higher than normal free cash flows) can certainly change the stock price, but the repurchase itself doesn't change the stock price.

A Tale of Two Cash Distributions: Dividends versus Stock Repurchases

Suppose a company's current earnings are $400 million, it has 40 million shares of stock, and it pays out 50 percent of its earnings as dividends. Earnings are expected to grow at

---

[18] We can rewrite Equation 15-3 as Extra cash = $Pn_0 - Pn$ and Equation 15-4 as $V_{op} = Pn$. We then substitute these expressions for extra cash and V_{op} into Equation 15-2 and solve for P, which results in $P = P_0$.

a constant rate of 5 percent, and the cost of equity is 10 percent. Its current dividend per share is 0.50($400/40) = $5. Using the dividend growth model, the current stock price is

$$P_0 = \frac{D_1}{r_s - g} = \frac{D_0(1+g)}{r_s - g} = \frac{\$5(1+0.05)}{0.10 - 0.05} = \frac{\$5.25}{0.05} = \$105.$$

As the year progresses, the stock should climb in price by 10 percent to $115.5, but then fall by the amount of the dividend ($5.25) to $110.25 when the dividend is paid at Year 1.[19] This process will be repeated each year, as shown in Figure 15-2. Notice that the shareholders experience a 10 percent total return each year, with 5 percent as a dividend yield and 5 percent as a capital gain. Also, the total expected market value of equity after paying the dividend at the end of Year 1 is the price per share multiplied by the number of shares:

$$S_1 = \$110.25 \text{ (40 million)} = \$4,410 \text{ million}.$$

Suppose the company decides to use 50 percent of its earnings to repurchase stock each year instead of paying dividends. To find the current price per share, we discount the total payments to shareholders and divide that by the current number of shares. These payments are exactly equal to the total dividend payments in the original scenario, so the current price is the same for both dividend policies, ignoring any taxes or signaling effects. But what happens when the end of the year arrives? The stock price has grown to $115.50, just as for the cash dividend policy. But unlike the case of cash dividends in which the stock price falls by the amount of the dividend, the price per share doesn't change when a company repurchases stock, as shown earlier in this section (see Figure 15-2). This means that the total rate of return for a shareholder under the repurchase policy is 10 percent, with a zero dividend yield and a 10 percent capital gain.

Year 1 earnings will be $400(1.05) = $420 million, and the total amount of cash used to repurchase stock is 0.50($420 million) = $210 million. Using Equation 15-3, we can solve for the number of shares remaining, n, after the repurchase at Year 1:

$$P(n_0 - n) = \text{Cash purchase}$$
$$\$115.5(40 - n) = \$210 \text{ million}$$
$$n = [\$115.5(40) - \$210]/\$115.5 = 38.182 \text{ million}.$$

CF

e-resource

See **CF2 Ch 15 Tool Kit.xls** for all calculations.

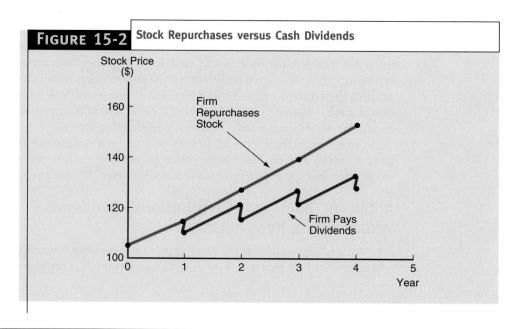

FIGURE 15-2 Stock Repurchases versus Cash Dividends

---

[19] This assumes no tax effects.

The total market value of equity at Year 1, S_1, is the price per share multiplied by the number of shares,

$$S_1 = \$115.5 \,(38.182 \text{ million}) = \$4{,}410 \text{ million},$$

which is identical to the market value of equity if the firm pays dividends instead of repurchasing stock.

This example illustrates three key results: (1) Ignoring possible tax effects and signals, the total market value of equity will be the same whether a firm pays dividends or repurchases stock. (2) The repurchase itself does not change the stock price (compared with using the cash to buy marketable securities), although it does reduce the number of outstanding shares. (3) The stock price for a company that repurchases its stock will climb faster than if it pays a dividend, but the total return to the shareholders will be the same.

SELF-TEST QUESTION   Explain how a repurchase changes the number of shares but not the stock price.

COMPARISON OF DIVIDENDS AND REPURCHASES

The advantages of repurchases are as follows:

1. Repurchase announcements are viewed as positive signals by investors because the repurchase is often motivated by management's belief that the firm's shares are undervalued.

2. The stockholders have a choice when the firm distributes cash by repurchasing stock—they can sell or not sell. Thus, those stockholders who need cash can sell back some of their shares, while those who do not want additional cash can simply retain their stock. With a cash dividend, on the other hand, stockholders must accept a dividend payment.

3. Dividends are "sticky" in the short run because managements are reluctant to raise the dividend if the increase cannot be maintained in the future—managements dislike cutting cash dividends because of the negative signal a cut gives. Hence, if the excess cash flow is thought to be only temporary, management may prefer to make the distribution in the form of a share repurchase rather than to declare an increased cash dividend that cannot be maintained.

4. Companies can use the residual model to set a *target cash distribution* level, then divide the distribution into a *dividend component* and a *repurchase component*. The dividend payout ratio will be relatively low, but the dividend itself will be relatively secure, and it will grow as a result of the declining number of shares outstanding. The company has more flexibility in adjusting the total distribution than it would if the entire distribution were in the form of cash dividends, because repurchases can be varied from year to year without giving off adverse signals. This procedure, which is what Florida Power & Light employed, has much to recommend it, and it is one reason for the dramatic increase in the volume of share repurchases.

5. Repurchases can be used to produce large-scale changes in capital structures. For example, several years ago Consolidated Edison decided to borrow $400 million and use the funds to repurchase some of its common stock. Thus, Con Ed was able to quickly change its capital structure.

6. Companies that use stock options as an important component of employee compensation can repurchase shares and then use those shares when employees exercise their options. This avoids having to issue new shares and thus diluting earnings. Microsoft and other high-tech companies have used this procedure in recent years.

Disadvantages of repurchases include the following:

1. Stockholders may not be indifferent between dividends and capital gains, and the price of the stock might benefit more from cash dividends than from repurchases.

Cash dividends are generally dependable, but repurchases are not.

2. The *selling* stockholders may not be fully aware of all the implications of a repurchase, or they may not have all the pertinent information about the corporation's present and future activities. However, firms generally announce repurchase programs before embarking on them to avoid potential stockholder suits.

3. The corporation may pay too much for the repurchased stock, to the disadvantage of remaining stockholders. If the firm seeks to acquire a relatively large amount of its stock, then the price may be bid above its equilibrium level and then fall after the firm ceases its repurchase operations.

When all the pros and cons on stock repurchases versus dividends have been totaled, where do we stand? Our conclusions may be summarized as follows:

1. Because of the deferred tax on capital gains, repurchases have a tax advantage over dividends as a way to distribute income to stockholders. This advantage is reinforced by the fact that repurchases provide cash to stockholders who want cash while allowing those who do not need current cash to delay its receipt. On the other hand, dividends are more dependable and are thus better suited for those who need a steady source of income.

2. Because of signaling effects, companies should not vary their dividends—that would lower investors' confidence in the company and adversely affect its cost of equity and its stock price. However, cash flows vary over time, as do investment opportunities, so the "proper" dividend in the residual model sense varies. To get around this problem, a company can set its dividend low enough to keep dividend payments from constraining operations and then use repurchases on a more or less regular basis to distribute excess cash. Such a procedure would provide regular, dependable dividends plus additional cash flow to those stockholders who want it.

3. Repurchases are also useful when a firm wants to make a large shift in its capital structure, wants to distribute cash from a one-time event such as the sale of a division, or wants to obtain shares for use in an employee stock option plan.

SELF-TEST QUESTIONS   What are some advantages and disadvantages of stock repurchases?
How can stock repurchases help a company operate in accordance with the residual distribution model?

OTHER FACTORS INFLUENCING DISTRIBUTIONS

In this section, we discuss several other factors that affect the dividend decision. These factors may be grouped into two broad categories: (1) constraints on dividend payments and (2) availability and cost of alternative sources of capital.

Constraints

1. *Bond indentures.* Debt contracts often limit dividend payments to earnings generated after the loan was granted. Also, debt contracts often stipulate that no dividends can be paid unless the current ratio, times-interest-earned ratio, and other safety ratios exceed stated minimums.

2. *Preferred stock restrictions.* Typically, common dividends cannot be paid if the company has omitted its preferred dividend. The preferred arrearages must be satisfied before common dividends can be resumed.

3. *Impairment of capital rule.* Dividend payments cannot exceed the balance sheet item "retained earnings." This legal restriction, known as the "impairment of capital rule," is designed to protect creditors. Without the rule, a company that is in trouble might distribute most of its assets to stockholders and leave its debthold-

ers out in the cold. (*Liquidating dividends* can be paid out of capital, but they must be indicated as such, and they must not reduce capital below the limits stated in debt contracts.)

4. *Availability of cash.* Cash dividends can be paid only with cash, so a shortage of cash in the bank can restrict dividend payments. However, the ability to borrow can offset this factor.

5. *Penalty tax on improperly accumulated earnings.* To prevent wealthy individuals from using corporations to avoid personal taxes, the Tax Code provides for a special surtax on improperly accumulated income. Thus, if the IRS can demonstrate that a firm's dividend payout ratio is being deliberately held down to help its stockholders avoid personal taxes, the firm is subject to heavy penalties. This factor is generally relevant only to privately owned firms.

Alternative Sources of Capital

1. *Cost of selling new stock.* If a firm needs to finance a given level of investment, it can obtain equity by retaining earnings or by issuing new common stock. If flotation costs (including any negative signaling effects of a stock offering) are high, r_e will be well above r_s, making it better to set a low payout ratio and to finance through retention rather than through the sale of new common stock. On the other hand, a high dividend payout ratio is more feasible for a firm whose flotation costs are low. Flotation costs differ among firms—for example, the flotation percentage is generally higher for small firms, so they tend to set low payout ratios.

2. *Ability to substitute debt for equity.* A firm can finance a given level of investment with either debt or equity. As noted above, low stock flotation costs permit a more flexible dividend policy because equity can be raised either by retaining earnings or by selling new stock. A similar situation holds for debt policy: If the firm can adjust its debt ratio without raising costs sharply, it can pay the expected dividend, even if earnings fluctuate, by increasing its debt ratio.

3. *Control.* If management is concerned about maintaining control, it may be reluctant to sell new stock, hence the company may retain more earnings than it otherwise would. However, if stockholders want higher dividends and a proxy fight looms, then the dividend will be increased.

SELF-TEST QUESTIONS What constraints affect dividend policy?
How does the availability and cost of outside capital affect dividend policy?

OVERVIEW OF THE DISTRIBUTION POLICY DECISION

In many ways, our discussion of distribution policy parallels our discussion of capital structure: We presented the relevant theories and issues, and we listed some additional factors that influence distribution policy, but we did not come up with any hard-and-fast guidelines that managers can follow. You should recognize that distribution decisions are exercises in informed judgment, not decisions that can be based on a precise mathematical model.

In practice, the distribution decision is made jointly with capital structure and capital budgeting decisions. The underlying reason for joining these decisions is asymmetric information, which influences managerial actions in two ways:

1. In general, managers do not want to issue new common stock. First, new common stock involves issuance costs—commissions, fees, and so on—and those costs can be avoided by using retained earnings to finance equity needs. Second, as we discussed in Chapter 14, asymmetric information causes investors to view new common stock issues as negative signals and thus lowers expectations regarding the

firm's future prospects. The end result is that the announcement of a new stock issue usually leads to a decrease in the stock price. Considering the total costs involved, including both issuance and asymmetric information costs, managers prefer to use retained earnings as the primary source of new equity.

2. Dividend changes provide signals about managers' beliefs as to their firms' future prospects. Thus, dividend reductions generally have a significant negative effect on a firm's stock price. Since managers recognize this, they try to set dollar dividends low enough so that there is only a remote chance that the dividend will have to be reduced in the future.

The effects of asymmetric information suggest that, to the extent possible, managers should avoid both new common stock sales and dividend cuts, because both actions tend to lower stock prices. Thus, in setting distribution policy, managers should begin by considering the firm's future investment opportunities relative to its projected internal sources of funds. The target capital structure also plays a part, but because the optimal capital structure is a *range,* firms can vary their actual capital structures somewhat from year to year. Since it is best to avoid issuing new common stock, the target long-term payout ratio should be designed to permit the firm to meet all of its equity capital requirements with retained earnings. *In effect, managers should use the residual model to set dividends, but in a long-term framework.* Finally, the current dollar dividend should be set so that there is an extremely low probability that the dividend, once set, will ever have to be lowered or omitted.

Of course, the dividend decision is made during the planning process, so there is uncertainty about future investment opportunities and operating cash flows. Thus, the actual payout ratio in any year will probably be above or below the firm's long-range target. However, the dollar dividend should be maintained, or increased as planned, unless the firm's financial condition deteriorates to the point where the planned policy simply cannot be maintained. A steady or increasing stream of dividends over the long run signals that the firm's financial condition is under control. Further, investor uncertainty is decreased by stable dividends, so a steady dividend stream reduces the negative effect of a new stock issue, should one become absolutely necessary.

In general, firms with superior investment opportunities should set lower payouts, hence retain more earnings, than firms with poor investment opportunities. The degree of uncertainty also influences the decision. If there is a great deal of uncertainty regarding the forecasts of free cash flows, which are defined here as the firm's operating cash flows minus mandatory equity investments, then it is best to be conservative and to set a lower current dollar dividend. Also, firms with postponable investment opportunities can afford to set a higher dollar dividend, because in times of stress investments can be postponed for a year or two, thus increasing the cash available for dividends. Finally, firms whose cost of capital is largely unaffected by changes in the debt ratio can also afford to set a higher payout ratio, because they can, in times of stress, more easily issue additional debt to maintain the capital budgeting program without having to cut dividends or issue stock.

Firms have only one opportunity to set the dividend payment from scratch. Therefore, today's dividend decisions are constrained by policies that were set in the past, hence setting a policy for the next five years necessarily begins with a review of the current situation.

Although we have outlined a rational process for managers to use when considering their firm's distribution policies, distribution policy still remains one of the most judgmental decisions managers must make. For this reason, distribution policy is always set by the board of directors—the financial staff analyzes the situation and makes a recommendation, but the board makes the final decision.

SELF-TEST QUESTION   Describe the decision process for distribution policy and dividend payout. Be sure to discuss all the factors that influence the decision.

STOCK SPLITS AND STOCK DIVIDENDS

Stock splits and stock dividends are related to the firm's cash dividend policy. The rationale for stock splits and dividends can best be explained through an example. We will use Porter Electronic Controls Inc., a $700 million electronic components manufacturer, for this purpose. Since its inception, Porter's markets have been expanding, and the company has enjoyed growth in sales and earnings. Some of its earnings have been paid out in dividends, but some are also retained each year, causing its earnings per share and stock price to grow. The company began its life with only a few thousand shares outstanding, and, after some years of growth, the stock price was so high that few people could afford to buy a "round lot" of 100 shares. Porter's CFO thought this limited the demand for the stock and thus kept the total market value of the firm below what it would have been if more shares, at a lower price, had been outstanding. To correct this situation, Porter "split its stock," as described in the next section.

Stock Splits

Although there is little empirical evidence to support the contention, there is nevertheless a widespread belief in financial circles that an *optimal price range* exists for stocks. "Optimal" means that if the price is within this range, the firm's value will be maximized. Many observers, including Porter's management, believe that the best range for most stocks is from $20 to $80 per share. Accordingly, if the price of Porter's stock rose to $80, management would probably declare a two-for-one **stock split,** thus doubling the number of shares outstanding, halving the earnings and dividends per share, and thereby lowering the stock price. Each stockholder would have more shares, but each share would be worth less. If the post-split price were $40, Porter's stockholders would be exactly as well off as before the split. However, if the stock price were to stabilize above $40, stockholders would be better off. Stock splits can be of any size—for example, the stock could be split two-for-one, three-for-one, one-and-a-half-for-one, or in any other way.

Sometimes a company will have a **reverse split.** For example, International Pictures Corp. (IPIX) developed the iPIX computer imaging technology, which allows a user to "walk through" a 360-degree view. Its stock price was in the $30 range prior to the dot-com crash of April 2000, but by August 2001 its price had fallen to $0.20 per share. One of Nasdaq's listing requirements is that the stock price must be above $1 per share, and Nasdaq was threatening to delist IPIX. To drive its price up, IPIX had a 1:10 reverse stock split before trading began on August 23, 2001, with its shareholders exchanging 10 shares of stock for a single new share. In theory, the stock price should have increased by a factor of 10, to around $2, but IPIX closed that day at a price of $1.46. Evidently, investors saw the reverse split as a negative signal.

Stock Dividends

Stock dividends are similar to stock splits in that they "divide the pie into smaller slices" without affecting the fundamental position of the current stockholders. On a 5 percent stock dividend, the holder of 100 shares would receive an additional 5 shares (without cost); on a 20 percent stock dividend, the same holder would receive 20 new shares; and so on. Again, the total number of shares is increased, so earnings, dividends, and price per share all decline.

If a firm wants to reduce the price of its stock, should it use a stock split or a stock dividend? Stock splits are generally used after a sharp price run-up to produce a large price reduction. Stock dividends used on a regular annual basis will keep the stock price more or less constrained. For example, if a firm's earnings and dividends were growing at about 10 percent per year, its stock price would tend to go up at about that same rate, and it would soon be outside the desired trading range. A 10 percent annual stock dividend would maintain the stock price within the optimal trading range. Note, though, that small stock dividends create bookkeeping problems and unnecessary expenses, so firms today use stock splits far more often than stock dividends.[20]

Effect on Stock Prices

If a company splits its stock or declares a stock dividend, will this increase the market value of its stock? Many empirical studies have sought to answer this question. Here is a summary of their findings.

1. On average, the price of a company's stock rises shortly after it announces a stock split or dividend.
2. However, these price increases are more the result of the fact that investors take stock splits/dividends as signals of higher future earnings and dividends than of a desire for stock dividends/splits per se. Because only companies whose managements think things look good tend to split their stocks, the announcement of a stock split is taken as a signal that earnings and cash dividends are likely to rise. Thus, the price increases associated with stock splits/dividends are probably the result of signals of favorable prospects for earnings and dividends, not a desire for stock splits/dividends per se.
3. If a company announces a stock split or stock dividend, its price will tend to rise. However, if during the next few months it does not announce an increase in earnings and dividends, then its stock price will drop back to the earlier level.
4. As we noted earlier, brokerage commissions are generally higher in percentage terms on lower-priced stocks. This means that it is more expensive to trade low-priced than high-priced stocks, and this, in turn, means that stock splits may reduce the liquidity of a company's shares. This particular piece of evidence suggests that stock splits/dividends might actually be harmful, although a lower price does mean that more investors can afford to trade in round lots (100 shares), which carry lower commissions than do odd lots (less than 100 shares).

What do we conclude from all this? From a purely economic standpoint, stock dividends and splits are just additional pieces of paper. However, they provide management with a relatively low-cost way of signaling that the firm's prospects look good. Further, we should note that since few large, publicly owned stocks sell at prices above several hundred dollars, we simply do not know what the effect would be if Microsoft, Wal-Mart, Hewlett-Packard, and other highly successful firms had never split their stocks, and consequently sold at prices in the thousands or even tens of thousands of dollars. All in all, it probably makes sense to employ stock dividends/splits when a firm's prospects are favorable, especially if the price of its stock has gone beyond the normal trading range.[21]

SELF-TEST QUESTIONS

What are stock splits and stock dividends?

How do stock splits and dividends affect stock prices?

In what situations should managers consider the use of stock splits?

In what situations should they consider the use of stock dividends?

---

[20] Accountants treat stock splits and stock dividends somewhat differently. For example, in a two-for-one stock split, the number of shares outstanding is doubled and the par value is halved, and that is about all there is to it. With a stock dividend, a bookkeeping entry is made transferring "retained earnings" to "common stock."

[21] It is interesting to note that Berkshire Hathaway, which is controlled by billionaire Warren Buffett, one of the most successful financiers of the twentieth century, has never had a stock split, and its stock (BRKa) sold on the NYSE for $89,000 per share in May 2004. But, in response to investment trusts that were being formed to sell fractional units of the stock, and thus, in effect, split it, Buffett himself created a new class of Berkshire Hathaway stock (Class B) worth about 1/30 of a Class A (regular) share.

DIVIDEND REINVESTMENT PLANS

During the 1970s, most large companies instituted **dividend reinvestment plans (DRIPs)**, under which stockholders can choose to automatically reinvest their dividends in the stock of the paying corporation.[22] Today most larger companies offer DRIPs, and although participation rates vary considerably, about 25 percent of the average firm's shareholders are enrolled. There are two types of DRIPs: (1) plans that involve only "old stock" that is already outstanding and (2) plans that involve newly issued stock. In either case, the stockholder must pay taxes on the amount of the dividends, even though stock rather than cash is received.

Under both types of DRIPs, stockholders choose between continuing to receive dividend checks or having the company use the dividends to buy more stock in the corporation. Under the "old stock" type of plan, if a stockholder elects reinvestment, a bank, acting as trustee, takes the total funds available for reinvestment, purchases the corporation's stock on the open market, and allocates the shares purchased to the participating stockholders' accounts on a pro rata basis. The transactions costs of buying shares (brokerage costs) are low because of volume purchases, so these plans benefit small stockholders who do not need cash dividends for current consumption.

The "new stock" type of DRIP uses the reinvested funds to buy newly issued stock, hence these plans raise new capital for the firm. AT&T, Union Carbide, and many other companies have had new stock plans in effect in recent years, using them to raise substantial amounts of new equity capital. No fees are charged to stockholders, and many companies offer stock at a discount of 3 percent to 5 percent below the actual market price. The companies offer discounts as a trade-off against flotation costs that would have been incurred if new stock had been issued through investment bankers rather than through the dividend reinvestment plans.

One interesting aspect of DRIPs is that they are forcing corporations to reexamine their basic dividend policies. A high participation rate in a DRIP suggests that stockholders might be better off if the firm simply reduced cash dividends, which would save stockholders some personal income taxes. Quite a few firms are surveying their stockholders to learn more about their preferences and to find out how they would react to a change in dividend policy. A more rational approach to basic dividend policy decisions may emerge from this research.

Note that companies start or stop using new stock DRIPs depending on their need for equity capital. Thus, both Union Carbide and AT&T recently stopped offering new stock DRIPs with a 5 percent discount because their needs for equity capital declined.

Some companies have expanded their DRIPs by moving to "open enrollment," whereby anyone can purchase the firm's stock directly and thus bypass brokers' commissions. ExxonMobil not only allows investors to buy their initial shares at no fee but also lets them pick up additional shares through automatic bank account withdrawals. Several plans, including ExxonMobil's, offer dividend reinvestment for individual retirement accounts, and some, such as U.S. West, allow participants to invest weekly or monthly rather than on the quarterly dividend schedule. In all of these plans, and many others, stockholders can invest more than the dividends they are foregoing—they simply send a check to the company and buy shares without a brokerage commission. According to First Chicago Trust, which handles the paperwork for 13 million shareholder DRIP accounts, at least half of all DRIPs will offer open enrollment, extra purchases, and other expanded services within the next few years.

---

[22] See Richard H. Pettway and R. Phil Malone, "Automatic Dividend Reinvestment Plans," *Financial Management*, Winter 1973, 11–18, for an old but still excellent discussion of the subject.

What are dividend reinvestment plans?

What are their advantages and disadvantages from both the stockholders' and the firm's perspectives?

SUMMARY

The key concepts covered in this chapter are listed below:

- **Distribution policy** involves three issues: (1) What fraction of earnings should be distributed? (2) Should the distribution be in the form of cash dividends or stock repurchases? (3) Should the firm maintain a steady, stable dividend growth rate?
- The **optimal distribution policy** strikes a balance between current dividends and future growth so as to maximize the firm's stock price.
- Miller and Modigliani developed the **dividend irrelevance theory,** which holds that a firm's dividend policy has no effect on either the value of its stock or its cost of capital.
- The **bird-in-the-hand theory** holds that the firm's value will be maximized by a high dividend payout ratio, because investors regard cash dividends as being less risky than potential capital gains.
- The **tax preference theory** states that because long-term capital gains are subject to somewhat less onerous taxes than dividends, investors prefer to have companies retain earnings rather than pay them out as dividends.
- **Empirical tests** of the three theories **have been inconclusive.** Therefore, academicians cannot tell corporate managers how a given change in dividend policy will affect stock prices and capital costs.
- Dividend policy should take account of the **information content of dividends (signaling)** and the **clientele effect.** The information content, or signaling, effect relates to the fact that investors regard an unexpected dividend change as a signal of management's forecast of future earnings. The clientele effect suggests that a firm will attract investors who like the firm's dividend payout policy. Both factors should be considered by firms that are considering a change in dividend policy.
- In practice, dividend paying firms follow a policy of paying a **steadily increasing dividend.** This policy provides investors with stable, dependable income, and departures from it give investors signals about management's expectations for future earnings.
- Most firms use the **residual distribution model** to set the long-run target distribution ratio at a level that will permit the firm to meet its equity requirements with retained earnings.
- Under a **stock repurchase plan,** a firm buys back some of its outstanding stock, thereby decreasing the number of shares, but leaving the stock price unchanged.
- **Legal constraints, investment opportunities, availability and cost of funds from other sources,** and **taxes** are also considered when firms establish dividend policies.
- A **stock split** increases the number of shares outstanding. Normally, splits reduce the price per share in proportion to the increase in shares because splits merely "divide the pie into smaller slices." However, firms generally split their stocks only if (1) the price is quite high and (2) management thinks the future is bright. Therefore, stock splits are often taken as positive signals and thus boost stock prices.
- A **stock dividend** is a dividend paid in additional shares rather than in cash. Both stock dividends and splits are used to keep stock prices within an "optimal" trading range.

- A **dividend reinvestment plan (DRIP)** allows stockholders to have the company automatically use dividends to purchase additional shares. DRIPs are popular because they allow stockholders to acquire additional shares without brokerage fees.

QUESTIONS

(15-1) Define each of the following terms:
- a. Optimal distribution policy
- b. Dividend irrelevance theory; bird-in-the-hand theory; tax preference theory
- c. Information content, or signaling, hypothesis; clientele effect
- d. Residual distribution model; extra dividend
- e. Declaration date; holder-of-record date; ex-dividend date; payment date
- f. Dividend reinvestment plan (DRIP)
- g. Stock split; stock dividend; stock repurchase

(15-2) How would each of the following changes tend to affect aggregate (that is, the average for all corporations) payout ratios, other things held constant? Explain your answers.
- a. An increase in the personal income tax rate.
- b. A liberalization of depreciation for federal income tax purposes—that is, faster tax write-offs.
- c. A rise in interest rates.
- d. An increase in corporate profits.
- e. A decline in investment opportunities.
- f. Permission for corporations to deduct dividends for tax purposes as they now do interest charges.
- g. A change in the Tax Code so that both realized and unrealized capital gains in any year were taxed at the same rate as dividends.

(15-3) What is the difference between a stock dividend and a stock split? As a stockholder, would you prefer to see your company declare a 100 percent stock dividend or a 2-for-1 split? Assume that either action is feasible.

(15-4) One position expressed in the financial literature is that firms set their dividends as a residual after using income to support new investment.
- a. Explain what a residual policy implies (assuming all distributions as dividends), illustrating your answer with a table showing how different investment opportunities could lead to different dividend payout ratios.
- b. Think back to Chapter 14, in which we considered the relationship between capital structure and the cost of capital. If the WACC-versus-debt-ratio plot was shaped like a sharp V, would this have a different implication for the importance of setting dividends according to the residual policy than if the plot was shaped like a shallow bowl (or a flattened U)?

(15-5) Indicate whether the following statements are true or false. If the statement is false, explain why.
- a. If a firm repurchases its stock in the open market, the shareholders who tender the stock are subject to capital gains taxes.
- b. If you own 100 shares in a company's stock and the company's stock splits 2-for-1, you will own 200 shares in the company following the split.
- c. Some dividend reinvestment plans increase the amount of equity capital available to the firm.
- d. The Tax Code encourages companies to pay a large percentage of their net income in the form of dividends.
- e. If your company has established a clientele of investors who prefer large dividends, the company is unlikely to adopt a residual dividend policy.
- f. If a firm follows a residual dividend policy, holding all else constant, its dividend payout will tend to rise whenever the firm's investment opportunities improve.

SELF-TEST PROBLEM   Solution Appears in Appendix A

(ST-1)
Alternative Dividend Payouts

Components Manufacturing Corporation (CMC) has an all-common-equity capital structure. It has 200,000 shares of $2 par value common stock outstanding. When CMC's founder, who was also its research director and most successful inventor, retired unexpectedly to the South Pacific in late 2005, CMC was left suddenly and permanently with materially lower growth expectations and relatively few attractive new investment opportunities. Unfortunately, there was no way to replace the founder's contributions to the firm. Previously, CMC found it necessary to plow back most of its earnings to finance growth, which averaged 12 percent per year. Future growth at a 5 percent rate is considered realistic, but that level would call for an increase in the dividend payout. Further, it now appears that new investment projects with at least the 14 percent rate of return required by CMC's stockholders ($r_s = 14\%$) would amount to only $800,000 for 2006 in comparison to a projected $2,000,000 of net income. If the existing 20 percent dividend payout were continued, retained earnings would be $1.6 million in 2006, but, as noted, investments that yield the 14 percent cost of capital would amount to only $800,000.

The one encouraging thing is that the high earnings from existing assets are expected to continue, and net income of $2 million is still expected for 2006. Given the dramatically changed circumstances, CMC's management is reviewing the firm's dividend policy.

a. Assuming that the acceptable 2006 investment projects would be financed entirely by earnings retained during the year, calculate DPS in 2006, assuming that CMC uses the residual distribution model and pays all distributions in the form of dividends.

b. What payout ratio does your answer to part a imply for 2006?

c. If a 60 percent payout ratio is maintained for the foreseeable future, what is your estimate of the present market price of the common stock? How does this compare with the market price that should have prevailed under the assumptions existing just before the news about the founder's retirement? If the two values of P_0 are different, comment on why.

PROBLEMS

(15-1)
Residual Distribution Model

Axel Telecommunications has a target capital structure that consists of 70 percent debt and 30 percent equity. The company anticipates that its capital budget for the upcoming year will be $3,000,000. If Axel reports net income of $2,000,000 and it follows a residual distribution model with all distributions as dividends, what will be its dividend payout ratio?

(15-2)
Stock Split

Gamma Medical's stock trades at $90 a share. The company is contemplating a 3-for-2 stock split. Assuming that the stock split will have no effect on the total market value of its equity, what will be the company's stock price following the stock split?

(15-3)
External Equity Financing

Northern Pacific Heating and Cooling Inc. has a 6-month backlog of orders for its patented solar heating system. To meet this demand, management plans to expand production capacity by 40 percent with a $10 million investment in plant and machinery. The firm wants to maintain a 40 percent debt-to-total-assets ratio in its capital structure; it also wants to maintain its past dividend policy of distributing 45 percent of last year's net income. In 2005, net income was $5 million. How much external equity must Northern Pacific seek at the beginning of 2006 to expand capacity as desired?

(15-4)
Residual Distribution Policy

Petersen Company has a capital budget of $1.2 million. The company wants to maintain a target capital structure which is 60 percent debt and 40 percent equity. The company forecasts that its net income this year will be $600,000. If the company follows a residual distribution model and pays all distributions as dividends, what will be its payout ratio?

(15-5)
Dividend Payout
The Wei Corporation expects next year's net income to be $15 million. The firm's debt ratio is currently 40 percent. Wei has $12 million of profitable investment opportunities, and it wishes to maintain its existing debt ratio. According to the residual distribution model (assuming all payments are in the form of dividends), how large should Wei's dividend payout ratio be next year?

(15-6)
Stock Split
After a 5-for-1 stock split, the Strasburg Company paid a dividend of $0.75 per new share, which represents a 9 percent increase over last year's pre-split dividend. What was last year's dividend per share?

(15-7)
Residual Distribution Policy
The Welch Company is considering three independent projects, each of which requires a $5 million investment. The estimated internal rate of return (IRR) and cost of capital for these projects are presented below:

Project H (high risk):	Cost of capital = 16%; IRR = 20%
Project M (medium risk):	Cost of capital = 12%; IRR = 10%
Project L (low risk):	Cost of capital = 8%; IRR = 9%

Note that the projects' cost of capital varies because the projects have different levels of risk. The company's optimal capital structure calls for 50 percent debt and 50 percent common equity. Welch expects to have net income of $7,287,500. If Welch bases its dividends on the residual model (all distributions are in the form of dividends), what will its payout ratio be?

(15-8)
Alternative Dividend Policies
In 2005 the Keenan Company paid dividends totaling $3,600,000 on net income of $10.8 million. 2005 was a normal year, and for the past 10 years, earnings have grown at a constant rate of 10 percent. However, in 2006, earnings are expected to jump to $14.4 million, and the firm expects to have profitable investment opportunities of $8.4 million. It is predicted that Keenan will not be able to maintain the 2006 level of earnings growth—the high 2006 earnings level is attributable to an exceptionally profitable new product line introduced that year—and the company will return to its previous 10 percent growth rate. Keenan's target debt ratio is 40 percent.
a. Calculate Keenan's total dividends for 2006 if it follows each of the following policies:
   (1) Its 2006 dividend payment is set to force dividends to grow at the long-run growth rate in earnings.
   (2) It continues the 2005 dividend payout ratio.
   (3) It uses a pure residual policy with all distributions in the form of dividends (40 percent of the $8.4 million investment is financed with debt).
   (4) It employs a regular-dividend-plus-extras policy, with the regular dividend being based on the long-run growth rate and the extra dividend being set according to the residual policy.
b. Which of the preceding policies would you recommend? Restrict your choices to the ones listed, but justify your answer.
c. Does a 2006 dividend of $9,000,000 seem reasonable in view of your answers to parts a and b? If not, should the dividend be higher or lower?

(15-9)
Alternative Dividend Policies
Buena Terra Corporation is reviewing its capital budget for the upcoming year. It has paid a $3.00 dividend per share (DPS) for the past several years, and its shareholders expect the dividend to remain constant for the next several years. The company's target capital structure is 60 percent equity and 40 percent debt; it has 1,000,000 shares of common equity outstanding; and its net income is $8 million. The company forecasts that it would require $10 million to fund all of its profitable (that is, positive NPV) projects for the upcoming year.
a. If Buena Terra follows the residual model and makes all distributions as dividends, how much retained earnings will it need to fund its capital budget?
b. If Buena Terra follows the residual model with all distributions in the form of dividends, what will be the company's dividend per share and payout ratio for the upcoming year?

c. If Buena Terra maintains its current $3.00 DPS for next year, how much retained earnings will be available for the firm's capital budget?

d. Can the company maintain its current capital structure, maintain the $3.00 DPS, and maintain a $10 million capital budget without having to raise new common stock?

e. Suppose that Buena Terra's management is firmly opposed to cutting the dividend; that is, it wishes to maintain the $3.00 dividend for the next year. Also assume that the company was committed to funding all profitable projects, and was willing to issue more debt (along with the available retained earnings) to help finance the company's capital budget. Assume that the resulting change in capital structure has a minimal impact on the company's composite cost of capital, so that the capital budget remains at $10 million. What portion of this year's capital budget would have to be financed with debt?

f. Suppose once again that Buena Terra's management wants to maintain the $3.00 DPS. In addition, the company wants to maintain its target capital structure (60 percent equity, 40 percent debt), and maintain its $10 million capital budget. What is the minimum dollar amount of new common stock that the company would have to issue in order to meet each of its objectives?

g. Now consider the case where Buena Terra's management wants to maintain the $3.00 DPS and its target capital structure, but it wants to avoid issuing new common stock. The company is willing to cut its capital budget in order to meet its other objectives. Assuming that the company's projects are divisible, what will be the company's capital budget for the next year?

h. What actions can a firm that follows the residual distribution policy take when its forecasted retained earnings are less than the retained earnings required to fund its capital budget?

e-resource

SPREADSHEET PROBLEM

(15-10)

Build a Model: Residual
Distribution Model

Start with the partial model in the file *CF2 Ch 15 P10 Build a Model.xls* from the textbook's Web site. Rework Problem 15-9, parts a through g, using a spreadsheet model.

CYBERPROBLEM

Please go to our Web site, **http://ehrhardt.swlearning.com**, to access any Cyberproblems.

THOMSON ONE
Business School Edition

Please go to **http://ehrhardt.swlearning.com** to access any Thomson ONE—Business School Edition problems.

MINI CASE

Southeastern Steel Company (SSC) was formed 5 years ago to exploit a new continuous-casting process. SSC's founders, Donald Brown and Margo Valencia, had been employed in the research department of a major integrated-steel company, but when that company decided against using the new process (which Brown and Valencia had developed), they decided to strike out on their own. One advantage of the new process was that it required relatively little capital in comparison with the typical steel company, so Brown and Valencia have been able to avoid issuing new stock, and thus they own all of the shares. However, SSC has now reached the stage where outside equity capital is necessary if the firm is to achieve its growth targets yet still maintain its target capital structure of 60 percent equity and 40 percent debt. Therefore, Brown and Valencia have decided to take the company public. Until now, Brown and Valencia have paid themselves reasonable salaries but routinely reinvested all after-tax earnings in the firm, so dividend policy has not been an issue. However, before talking with potential outside investors, they must decide on a dividend policy.

Assume that you were recently hired by Pierce Westerfield Carney (PWC), a national consulting firm, which has been asked to help SSC prepare for its public offering. Martha Millon, the senior PWC consultant in your group, has asked you to make a presentation to Brown and Valencia in which you review the theory of dividend policy and discuss the following questions.

a. (1) What is meant by the term "distribution policy"?

(2) The terms "irrelevance," "bird-in-the-hand," and "tax preference" have been used to describe three major theories regarding the way dividend payouts affect a firm's value. Explain what these terms mean, and briefly describe each theory.

(3) What do the three theories indicate regarding the actions management should take with respect to dividend payouts?

(4) What results have empirical studies of the dividend theories produced? How does all this affect what we can tell managers about dividend payouts?

b. Discuss (1) the information content, or signaling, hypothesis, (2) the clientele effect, and (3) their effects on distribution policy.

c. (1) Assume that SSC has an $800,000 capital budget planned for the coming year. You have determined that its present capital structure (60 percent equity and 40 percent debt) is optimal, and its net income is forecasted at $600,000. Use the residual distribution model approach to determine SSC's total dollar distribution. Assume for now that the distribution is in the form of a dividend. Then, explain what would happen if net income were forecasted at $400,000, or at $800,000.

(2) In general terms, how would a change in investment opportunities affect the payout ratio under the residual distribution policy?

(3) What are the advantages and disadvantages of the residual policy? (Hint: Don't neglect signaling and clientele effects.)

d. What are stock repurchases? Discuss the advantages and disadvantages of a firm's repurchasing its own shares.

e. Describe the series of steps that most firms take in setting dividend policy in practice.

f. What are stock splits and stock dividends? What are the advantages and disadvantages of stock splits and stock dividends?

g. What is a dividend reinvestment plan (DRIP), and how does it work?

SELECTED ADDITIONAL REFERENCES AND CASES

On stock dividends and stock splits, see

Baker, H. Kent, Aaron L. Phillips, and Gary E. Powell, "The Stock Distribution Puzzle: A Synthesis of the Literature on Stock Splits and Stock Dividends," *Financial Practice and Education,* Spring/Summer 1995, 24–37.

McNichols, Maureen, and Ajay Dravid, "Stock Dividends, Stock Splits, and Signaling," *Journal of Finance,* July 1990, 857–879.

On repurchases, see

Denis, David J., "Defensive Changes in Corporate Payout Policy: Share Repurchases and Special Dividends," *Journal of Finance,* December 1990, 1433–1456.

Gay, Gerald D., Jayant R. Kale, and Thomas H. Noe, "Share Repurchase Mechanisms: A Comparative Analysis of Efficacy, Shareholder Wealth and Corporate Control Effects," *Financial Management,* Spring 1991, 44–59.

Klein, April, and James Rosenfeld, "The Impact of Targeted Share Repurchases on the Wealth of Non-Participating Shareholders," *Journal of Financial Research,* Summer 1988, 89–97.

Netter, Jeffry M., and Mark L. Mitchell, "Stock-Repurchase Announcements and Insider Transactions after the October 1987 Stock Market Crash," *Financial Management,* Autumn 1989, 84–96.

Pugh, William, and John S. Jahera, Jr., "Stock Repurchases and Excess Returns: An Empirical Examination," *The Financial Review,* February 1990, 127–142.

Wansley, James W., William R. Lane, and Salil Sarkar, "Managements' View on Share Repurchase and Tender Offer Premiums," *Financial Management,* Autumn 1989, 97–110.

Woolridge, J. Randall, and Donald R. Chambers, "Reverse Splits and Shareholder Wealth," *Financial Management,* Autumn 1983, 5–15.

For surveys of managers' views on dividend policy, see

Baker, H. Kent, Gail E. Farrelly, and Richard B. Edelman, "A Survey of Management Views on Dividend Policy," *Financial Management,* Autumn 1985, 78–84.

Pruitt, Stephen W., and Lawrence J. Gitman, "The Interactions between the Investment, Financing, and Dividend Decisions of Major U.S. Firms," *Financial Review,* August 1991, 409–430.

Other pertinent articles include

Asquith, Paul, and David W. Mullins, Jr., "Signalling with Dividends, Stock Repurchases, and Equity Issues," *Financial Management,* Autumn 1986, 27–44.

Born, Jeffrey A., "Insider Ownership and Signals—Evidence from Dividend Initiation Announcement Effects," *Financial Management,* Spring 1988, 38–45.

Brennan, Michael J., and Anjan V. Thakor, "Shareholder Preferences and Dividend Policy," *Journal of Finance,* September 1990, 993–1018.

Chang, Rosita P., and S. Ghon Rhee, "The Impact of Personal Taxes on Corporate Dividend Policy and Capital Structure Decisions," *Financial Management,* Summer 1990, 21–31.

DeAngelo, Harry, and Linda DeAngelo, "Dividend Policy and Financial Distress: An Empirical Investigation of Troubled NYSE Firms," *Journal of Finance,* December 1990, 1415–1432.

DeAngelo, Harry, Linda DeAngelo, and Douglas J. Skinner, "Dividends and Losses," *Journal of Finance,* December 1992, 1837–1863.

Ghosh, Chinmoy, and J. Randall Woolridge, "An Analysis of Shareholder Reaction to Dividend Cuts and Omissions," *Journal of Financial Research,* Winter 1988, 281–294.

Healy, Paul M., and Krishna G. Palepu, "How Investors Interpret Changes in Corporate Financial Policy," *Journal of Applied Corporate Finance,* Fall 1989, 59–64.

Impson, C. Michael, and Imre Karafiath, "A Note on the Stock Market Reaction to Dividend Announcements," *The Financial Review,* May 1992, 259–271.

Kale, Jayant R., and Thomas H. Noe, "Dividends, Uncertainty, and Underwriting Costs Under Asymmetric Information," *Journal of Financial Research,* Winter 1990, 265–277.

Manakyan, Herman, and Carolyn Carroll, "An Empirical Examination of the Existence of a Signaling Value Function for Dividends," *Journal of Financial Research,* Fall 1990, 201–210.

Peterson, David R., and Pamela P. Peterson, "A Further Understanding of Stock Distributions: The Case of Reverse Stock Splits," *Journal of Financial Research,* Fall 1992, 189–205.

Peterson, Pamela P., David R. Peterson, and Norman H. Moore, "The Adoption of New-Issue Dividend Reinvestment Plans and Shareholder Wealth," *Financial Review,* May 1987, 221–232.

Talmor, Eli, and Sheridan Titman, "Taxes and Dividend Policy," *Financial Management,* Summer 1990, 32–35.

Wansley, James W., C. F. Sirmans, James D. Shilling, and Young-jin Lee, "Dividend Change Announcement Effects and Earnings Volatility and Timing," *Journal of Financial Research,* Spring 1991, 37–49.

Woolridge, J. Randall, and Chinmoy Ghosh, "Dividend Cuts: Do They Always Signal Bad News?" *Midland Corporate Finance Journal,* Summer 1985, 20–32.

The following cases from the Finance Online Case Library *cover many of the concepts discussed in this chapter and are available at* **http://www.textchoice.com:**

Case 19, "Georgia Atlantic Company," Case 19A, "Floral Fragrance, Inc.," Case 19B, "Cook Transportation, Inc.," and Case 20, "Bessemer Steel Products, Inc.," which illustrate the dividend policy decision. Case 60, "Consolidated Electric," is a longer and more comprehensive case on dividend policy.

Special Topics

CHAPTER 16

Working Capital Management

Dramatic improvements in microprocessor technology, along with equally dramatic growth in the Internet, have transformed the computer industry. Some companies have succeeded while others have failed. Despite some recent setbacks, Dell Computer has clearly been one of the most successful, as its sales have grown from roughly $5 billion in 1995 to more than $41 billion in 2004. There were many reasons for Dell's remarkable success, perhaps the most important being the company's impressive success in managing its working capital, which is the focus of this chapter.

Dell is able to build and deliver customized computers more rapidly and at a lower cost than its competitors, so it can underprice them. Traditionally, manufacturers of custom-designed products have had two choices. They could keep a large supply of inventory on hand to meet customer needs, or they could make their customers wait for weeks while the customized product was being built. Dell has used information technology to revolutionize its working capital management. First, it uses information technology to better coordinate with its suppliers. If a supplier wants to do business with Dell, it must link its information system with Dell's and provide the necessary components quickly and cheaply. Suppliers that adapt and meet Dell's demands are rewarded with increased business. Second, Dell uses information technology to collect data that enable it to better customize products for its customers. For example, Dell has been able to capture most of the Ford Motor Company's PC business by anticipating and quickly filling its orders.

Sound working capital management is necessary if a company wants to compete in the information age, and the lessons taught by Dell extend to other industries. Indeed, in an interview with *The Wall Street Journal*, Michael Dell, founder and CEO of Dell Computer, discussed how traditional manufacturers, such as the automobile companies, could use Dell's experience to improve their operations. The article included his five points on how to build a better car:

1. Use the Internet to lower the costs of linking manufacturers, suppliers, and dealers.
2. Turn over to an outside specialist any operation that is not central to the business.
3. Accelerate the pace of change, and get employees conditioned to accept change.
4. Experiment with Internet businesses. Set up trials to see what happens when customers can access information more easily, and in ways never before possible.
5. Think about what could be done with the capital freed up by shedding excessive inventory and other redundant assets.

Sources: J. William Gurley and Jane Hodges, "A Dell for Every Industry," *Fortune,* October 12, 1998, 167–172; and Gary McWilliams and Joseph B. White, "Dell to Detroit: Get into Gear Online!" *The Wall Street Journal,* December 1, 1999, B1.

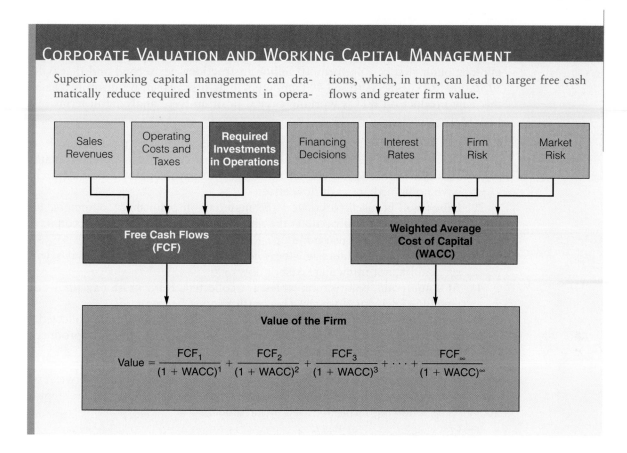

CORPORATE VALUATION AND WORKING CAPITAL MANAGEMENT

Superior working capital management can dramatically reduce required investments in operations, which, in turn, can lead to larger free cash flows and greater firm value.

| Sales Revenues | Operating Costs and Taxes | **Required Investments in Operations** | Financing Decisions | Interest Rates | Firm Risk | Market Risk |

Free Cash Flows (FCF)

Weighted Average Cost of Capital (WACC)

Value of the Firm

$$\text{Value} = \frac{FCF_1}{(1 + WACC)^1} + \frac{FCF_2}{(1 + WACC)^2} + \frac{FCF_3}{(1 + WACC)^3} + \cdots + \frac{FCF_\infty}{(1 + WACC)^\infty}$$

e-resource

*The textbook's Web site contains an Excel file that will guide you through the chapter's calculations. The file for this chapter is **CF2 Ch 16 Tool Kit.xls,** and we encourage you to open the file and follow along as you read the chapter.*

Working capital management involves two basic questions: (1) What is the appropriate amount of working capital, both in total and for each specific account, and (2) how should working capital be financed? Note that sound working capital management goes beyond finance. Indeed, the ideas for improving working capital management often stem from other disciplines. For example, experts in logistics, operations management, and information technology often work with the marketing group to develop a better way to deliver the firm's products. Where finance comes into play is in evaluating the profitability of alternative proposals. In addition, financial managers determine how much cash a company must keep on hand, and how much short-term financing it should use.

We begin our discussion of working capital policy by reviewing some basic definitions and concepts:

1. **Working capital,** sometimes called *gross working capital,* simply refers to current assets used in operations.
2. **Net working capital** is defined as current assets minus current liabilities.
3. **Net operating working capital (NOWC)** is defined as operating current assets minus operating current liabilities. Generally, NOWC is equal to cash, accounts receivable, and inventories, less accounts payable and accruals.

The next section shows how working capital affects cash flows.

THE CASH CONVERSION CYCLE

Firms typically follow a cycle in which they purchase inventory, sell goods on credit, and then collect accounts receivable. This cycle is referred to as the *cash conversion cycle.*

An Illustration

Consider Real Time Computer Corporation (RTC), which in early 2005 introduced a new minicomputer that can perform 10 billion instructions per second and that will sell for $250,000. RTC expects to sell 40 computers in its first year of production. The effects of this new product on RTC's working capital position were analyzed in terms of the following five steps:

1. RTC will order and then receive the materials it needs to produce the 40 computers it expects to sell. Because RTC and most other firms purchase materials on credit, this transaction will create an account payable. However, the purchase will have no immediate cash flow effect.
2. Labor will be used to convert the materials into finished computers. However, wages will not be fully paid at the time the work is done, so, like accounts payable, accrued wages will also build up.
3. The finished computers will be sold, but on credit. Therefore, sales will create receivables, not immediate cash inflows.
4. At some point before receivables are collected, RTC must pay off its accounts payable and accrued wages. This outflow must be financed.
5. The cycle will be completed when RTC's receivables have been collected. At that time, the company can pay off the credit that was used to finance production, and it can then repeat the cycle.

The **cash conversion cycle model,** which focuses on the length of time between when the company makes payments and when it receives cash inflows, formalizes the steps outlined above.[1] The following terms are used in the model:

1. **Inventory conversion period,** which is the average time required to convert materials into finished goods and then to sell those goods. Note that the inventory conversion period is calculated by dividing inventory by sales per day. For example, if average inventories are $2 million and sales are $10 million, then the inventory conversion period is 73 days:

$$\text{Inventory conversion period} = \frac{\text{Inventory}}{\text{Sales per day}} \qquad \text{(16-1)}$$

$$= \frac{\$2,000,000}{\$10,000,000/365}$$

$$= 73 \text{ days.}$$

   Thus, it takes an average of 73 days to convert materials into finished goods and then to sell those goods.[2]

2. **Receivables collection period,** which is the average length of time required to convert the firm's receivables into cash, that is, to collect cash following a sale. The receivables collection period is also called the *days sales outstanding (DSO),* and it is calculated by dividing accounts receivable by the average credit sales per day.

---

[1] See Verlyn D. Richards and Eugene J. Laughlin, "A Cash Conversion Cycle Approach to Liquidity Analysis," *Financial Management,* Spring 1980, 32–38.

[2] Some analysts define the inventory conversion period as inventory divided by daily cost of goods sold. However, most published sources use the formula we show in Equation 16-1. In addition, some analysts use a 360-day year; however, unless stated otherwise, we will base all our calculations on a 365-day year.

If receivables are \$657,534 and sales are \$10 million, the receivables collection period is

$$\text{Receivables collection period} = \text{DSO} = \frac{\text{Receivables}}{\text{Sales}/365} \qquad \text{(16-2)}$$

$$= \frac{\$657,534}{\$10,000,000/365} = 24 \text{ days.}$$

Thus, it takes 24 days after a sale to convert the receivables into cash.

3. **Payables deferral period,** which is the average length of time between the purchase of materials and labor and the payment of cash for them. For example, if the firm on average has 30 days to pay for labor and materials, if its cost of goods sold is \$8 million per year, and if its accounts payable average \$657,534, then its payables deferral period can be calculated as follows:

$$\text{Payables deferral period} = \frac{\text{Payables}}{\text{Purchases per day}}$$
$$= \frac{\text{Payables}}{\text{Cost of goods sold}/365} \qquad \text{(16-3)}$$

$$= \frac{\$657,534}{\$8,000,000/365}$$
$$= 30 \text{ days.}$$

The calculated figure is consistent with the stated 30-day payment period.[3]

4. **Cash conversion cycle,** which nets out the three periods just defined and which therefore equals the length of time between the firm's actual cash expenditures to pay for productive resources (materials and labor) and its own cash receipts from the sale of products (that is, the length of time between paying for labor and materials and collecting on receivables). The cash conversion cycle thus equals the average length of time a dollar is tied up in current assets.

We can now use these definitions to analyze the cash conversion cycle. First, the concept is diagrammed in Figure 16-1. Each component is given a number, and the cash conversion cycle can be expressed by this equation:

(1) Inventory conversion period	+	(2) Receivables collection period	−	(3) Payables deferral period	=	(4) Cash conversion . cycle	(16-4)

To illustrate, suppose it takes Real Time an average of 73 days to convert raw materials to computers and then to sell them, and another 24 days to collect on receivables. However,

---

[3] Some sources define the payables deferral period as payables divided by daily sales.

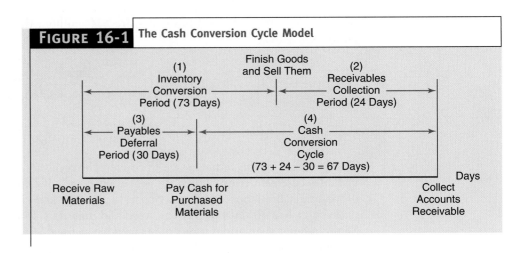

FIGURE 16-1 The Cash Conversion Cycle Model

30 days normally elapse between receipt of raw materials and payment for them. Therefore, the cash conversion cycle would be 67 days:

Days in cash conversion cycle = 73 days + 24 days − 30 days = 67 days.

To look at it another way,

Cash inflow delay − Payment delay = Net delay
(73 days + 24 days) − 30 days = 67 days.

Shortening the Cash Conversion Cycle

Given these data, RTC knows when it starts producing a computer that it will have to finance the manufacturing costs for a 67-day period. The firm's goal should be to shorten its cash conversion cycle as much as possible without hurting operations. This would increase RTC's value, because the shorter the cash conversion cycle, the lower the required net operating working capital, and the higher the resulting free cash flow.

The cash conversion cycle can be shortened (1) by reducing the inventory conversion period by processing and selling goods more quickly, (2) by reducing the receivables collection period by speeding up collections, or (3) by lengthening the payables deferral period by slowing down the firm's own payments. To the extent that these actions can be taken *without increasing costs or depressing sales,* they should be carried out.

Benefits

We can illustrate the benefits of shortening the cash conversion cycle by looking again at Real Time Computer Corporation. As shown in Table 16-1, RTC currently has $2 million tied up in net operating working capital. Suppose RTC can improve its logistics and production processes so that its inventory conversion period drops to 65 days. The firm can also cut its receivable collection period to 23 days by billing customers daily rather than batching bills every other day as it now does. Finally, it can increase its payables deferral period by using remote disbursements, as discussed later in this chapter. Table 16-1 shows that the net effects of these improvements are a 10-day reduction in the cash conversion cycle and a $268,493 reduction in net operating capital.

Recall that free cash flow (FCF) is equal to NOPAT minus the net investments in operating capital. Therefore, if working capital decreases, FCF increases by that same amount. RTC's reduction in its cash conversion cycle would lead to a $268,493 increase in FCF. If sales stay at the same level, then the reduction in working capital would simply be a one-time cash inflow. However, suppose sales grow. When a company improves its working

TABLE 16-1 | Benefits from Improving the Cash Conversion Cycle

	Original	Improved
Annual sales	$10,000,000	$10,000,000
Cost of goods sold (COGS)	8,000,000	8,000,000
Inventory conversion period (days)	73	65
Receivables collection period (days)	24	23
Payable deferral period (days)	(30)	(31)
Cash conversion cycle (days)	67	57
Inventory[a]	$ 2,000,000	$ 1,780,822
Receivables[b]	657,534	630,137
Payables[c]	(657,534)	(679,452)
Net operating working capital (NOWC)	$ 2,000,000	$ 1,731,507
Improvement in free cash flow = Original NOWC − Improved NOWC		$ 268,493

Notes:
[a]Inventory = (Inventory conversion period)(Sales/365)
[b]Receivables = (Receivables collection period)(Sales/365)
[c]Payables = (Payables deferral period)(COGS/365)

capital processes, they usually remain at their improved level. If the NOWC/Sales ratio remains at its new level, proportionately less working capital will be required to support the additional future sales, leading to an increase in projected FCF for each future year.

For example, if RTC's sales and costs increase next year by 10 percent, then its NOWC would also increase by 10 percent. Under the original working capital situation, the projected NOWC would be 1.10($2,000,000) = $2,200,000, which means RTC would have to make an investment of $2,200,000 − $2,000,000 = $200,000 in new working capital. Under the improved scenario, the projected NOWC would be 1.10($1,731,507) = $1,904,658. Its new projected investment is only $1,904,658 − $1,731,507 = $173,151, which is $26,849 less than was required under the original scenario ($2,000,000 − $1,731,507 = $268,493). As this example shows, not only does the improvement in working capital process produce a one-time free cash flow of $268,493 at the time of the improvement, but it also leads to an improved FCF of $26,849 in the next year, with additional improvements in future years. Therefore, an improvement in working capital management is a gift that keeps on giving.

The combination of the one-time cash inflow and the long-term improvement in free cash flow can add substantial value to a company. Two professors, Hyun-Han Shin and Luc Soenen, studied more than 2,900 companies during a recent 20-year period and found a strong relationship between a company's cash conversion cycle and its performance.[4] In particular, their results show that for the average company a 10-day improvement in the cash conversion cycle was associated with an increase in pre-tax operating profit margin from 12.76 to 13.02 percent. They also demonstrated that companies with a cash conversion cycle 10 days shorter than average also had an annual stock return that was 1.7 percentage points higher than that of an average company, even after adjusting for differences in risk. Given results like these, it's no wonder firms now place so much emphasis on working capital management!

---

[4] See Hyun-Han Shin and Luc Soenen, "Efficiency of Working Capital Management and Corporate Profitability," *Financial Practice and Education,* Fall/Winter 1998, 37–45.

SELF-TEST QUESTIONS
Define the following terms: inventory conversion period, receivables collection period, and payables deferral period. Give the equation for each term.

What is the cash conversion cycle? What is its equation?

What should the firm's goal be regarding the cash conversion cycle? Explain your answer.

What are some actions the firm can take to shorten its cash conversion cycle?

ALTERNATIVE NET OPERATING WORKING CAPITAL POLICIES

A **relaxed working capital policy** is one in which relatively large amounts of cash and inventories are carried, where sales are stimulated by the use of a credit policy that provides liberal financing to customers and a corresponding high level of receivables, and where a company doesn't take advantage of credit provided by accruals and accounts payable. Conversely, with a **restricted working capital policy,** the holdings of cash, inventories, and receivables are minimized, and accruals and payables are maximized. Under the restricted policy, NOWC is turned over more frequently, so each dollar of NOWC is forced to "work harder." A **moderate working capital policy** is between the two extremes.

Under conditions of certainty—when sales, costs, lead times, payment periods, and so on, are known for sure—all firms would hold only minimal levels of working capital. Any larger amounts would increase the need for external funding without a corresponding increase in profits, while any smaller holdings would involve late payments to suppliers along with lost sales due to inventory shortages and an overly restrictive credit policy.

However, the picture changes when uncertainty is introduced. Here the firm requires some minimum amount of cash and inventories based on expected payments, expected sales, expected order lead times, and so on, plus additional holdings, or *safety stocks,* which enable it to deal with departures from the expected values. Similarly, accounts receivable levels are determined by credit terms, and the tougher the credit terms, the lower the receivables for any given level of sales. With a restricted policy, the firm would hold minimal safety stocks of cash and inventories, and it would have a tight credit policy even though this meant running the risk of losing sales. A restricted, lean-and-mean working capital policy generally provides the highest expected return on this investment, but it entails the greatest risk, while the reverse is true under a relaxed policy. The moderate policy falls in between the two extremes in terms of expected risk and return.

Recall that NOWC consists of cash, inventory, and accounts receivable, less accruals and accounts payable. Firms face a fundamental trade-off: Working capital is necessary to conduct business, and the greater the working capital, the smaller the danger of running short, hence the lower the firm's operating risk. However, holding working capital is costly—it reduces a firm's return on invested capital (ROIC), free cash flow, and value. The following sections discuss the individual components of NOWC.

SELF-TEST QUESTIONS
Identify and explain three alternative working capital policies.

What are the principal components of net operating working capital?

What are the reasons for not wanting to hold too little working capital? For not wanting to hold too much?

CASH MANAGEMENT

Approximately 1.5 percent of the average industrial firm's assets are held in the form of cash, which is defined as demand deposits plus currency. Cash is often called a "nonearning asset." It is needed to pay for labor and raw materials, to buy fixed assets, to pay taxes, to service debt, to pay dividends, and so on. However, cash itself (and also most commercial checking

THE BEST AT MANAGING WORKING CAPITAL

What do General Dynamics, Delta Air Lines, Pepsico, Costco Wholesale, Texas Instruments, and Burlington Northern Santa Fe have in common? Each of these companies leads its industry in CFO magazine's annual survey of working capital management, which covers 1,000 firms with sales greater than $500 million. Each company is rated on the number of days tied up in working capital (DWC), defined as (Receivables + Inventory − Payables)/Daily sales.

The typical DWC is about 56. Burlington Northern Santa Fe (BNSF) has an outstanding DWC of −39 days versus an industry average of 43! BNSF achieved this by reengineering its accounts receivable process, starting with the number of days it takes to submit a bill to customers. In 1997 it had about 50,000 bills on hand each day that had not yet been priced and rendered to customers. By working on its information systems, BNSF was

able to automate much of the process, and it reduced unprocessed bills to about 15,000. BNSF then turned its attention to the number of days it takes a customer to pay. They found that their large customers would receive a batch of bills, but not pay any of them if the customer disputed any single bill in the batch. Working closely with marketing and sales, BNSF was able to greatly reduce the number of disputed bills. The net result of these efforts was a decrease in the days sales outstanding from 50 to 7. When coupled with very little inventory and its own ability to delay payments to its suppliers, BNSF's cash conversion cycle became negative. This increased its free cash flow to such an extent that BNSF was able to implement a large stock repurchase program.

Source: Various issues of *CFO*. For an update, see http://www.cfo.com and search for "working capital annual survey."

accounts) earns no interest. Thus, the goal of the cash manager is to minimize the amount of cash the firm must hold for use in conducting its normal business activities, yet, at the same time, to have sufficient cash (1) to take trade discounts, (2) to maintain its credit rating, and (3) to meet unexpected cash needs. We begin our analysis with a discussion of the reasons for holding cash.

Reasons for Holding Cash

Firms hold cash for two primary reasons:

1. *Transactions.* Cash balances are necessary in business operations. Payments must be made in cash, and receipts are deposited in the cash account. Cash balances associated with routine payments and collections are known as **transactions balances.** Cash inflows and outflows are unpredictable, with the degree of predictability varying among firms and industries. Therefore, firms need to hold some cash in reserve for random, unforeseen fluctuations in inflows and outflows. These "safety stocks" are called **precautionary balances,** and the less predictable the firm's cash flows, the larger such balances should be.

2. *Compensation to banks for providing loans and services.* A bank makes money by lending out funds that have been deposited with it, so the larger its deposits, the better the bank's profit position. If a bank is providing services to a customer, it may require the customer to leave a minimum balance on deposit to help offset the costs of providing the services. Also, banks may require borrowers to hold deposits at the bank. Both types of deposits are called **compensating balances.** In a 1979 survey, 84.7 percent of responding companies reported that they were required to maintain compensating balances to help pay for bank services.[5] Only 13.3 percent reported paying direct fees for banking services. By 1996 those findings were

---

[5] See Lawrence J. Gitman, E. A. Moses, and I. T. White, "An Assessment of Corporate Cash Management Practices," *Financial Management*, Vol. 14, no. 1, Spring 1979, 32–41.

reversed: only 28 percent paid for bank services with compensating balances, while 83 percent paid direct fees.[6] So, while the use of compensating balances to pay for services has declined, it is still a reason some companies hold so much cash.

In addition to holding cash for transactions, precautionary, and compensating balances, it is essential that the firm have sufficient cash to take **trade discounts.** Suppliers frequently offer customers discounts for early payment of bills. As we will see later in this chapter, the cost of not taking discounts is very high, so firms should have enough cash to permit payment of bills in time to take discounts.

Finally, firms often hold short-term investments in excess of the cash needed to support operations. We discuss short-term investments later in the chapter.

SELF-TEST QUESTIONS Why is cash management important?
What are the two primary motives for holding cash?

THE CASH BUDGET

The **cash budget** shows the firm's projected cash inflows and outflows over some specified period. Generally, firms use a monthly cash budget forecasted over the next year, plus a more detailed daily or weekly cash budget for the coming month. The monthly cash budgets are used for planning purposes, and the daily or weekly budgets for actual cash control.

In Chapter 12, we saw that MicroDrive's projected sales were $3,300 million, resulting in a net cash flow from operations of $163 million. When all expenditures and financing flows are considered, its cash account was projected to increase by $1 million. Does this mean that it will not have to worry about cash shortages during the year? To answer this question, we must construct the cash budget.

To simplify the example, we will only consider the cash budget for the last half of the year. Further, we will not list every cash flow but rather focus on the operating cash flows. Sales peak in September, and all sales are made on terms of 2/10, net 40, meaning that a 2 percent discount is allowed if payment is made within 10 days, and, if the discount is not taken, the full amount is due in 40 days. However, like most companies, MicroDrive finds that some of its customers delay payment up to 90 days. Experience has shown that payment on 20 percent of dollar sales is made during the month in which the sale is made—these are the discount sales. On 70 percent of sales, payment is made during the month immediately following the month of sale, and on 10 percent of sales, payment is made in the second month following the month of sale.

Costs average 70 percent of the sales prices of the finished products. These purchases are generally made one month before the firm expects to sell the finished products, but MicroDrive's terms with its suppliers allow it to delay payments for 30 days. Accordingly, if July sales are forecasted at $300 million, then purchases during June will amount to $210 million, and this amount will actually be paid in July.

Such other cash expenditures as wages and lease payments are also built into the cash budget, and MicroDrive must make estimated tax payments of $30 million on September 15 and $20 million on December 15. Also, a $100 million payment for a new plant must be made in October. Assuming that the **target cash balance** is $10 million, and that it projects $15 million to be on hand on July 1, 2006, what will its monthly cash surpluses or shortfalls be for the period from July to December?

The monthly cash flows are shown in Table 16-2. Section I of the table provides a worksheet for calculating both collections on sales and payments on purchases. Line 1 gives the

[6] See Charles E. Maxwell, Lawrence J. Gitman, and Stephanie A. M. Smith, "Working Capital Management and Financial-Service Consumption Preferences of US and Foreign Firms: A Comparison of 1979 and 1996 Preferences," *Financial Practice and Education,* Fall/Winter 1998, 46–52.

TABLE 16-2 | MicroDrive Inc.: Cash Budget (Millions of Dollars)

	May	Jun	Jul	Aug	Sep	Oct	Nov	Dec
I. COLLECTIONS AND PURCHASES WORKSHEET								
(1) Sales (gross)[a]	$200	$250	$300	$400	$500	$350	$250	$200
Collections								
(2) During month of sale: (0.2)(0.98)(month's sales)			59	78	98	69	49	39
(3) During first month after sale: 0.7(previous month's sales)			175	210	280	350	245	175
(4) During second month after sale: 0.1(sales 2 months ago)			20	25	30	40	50	35
(5) Total collections (2 + 3 + 4)			$254	$313	$408	$459	$344	$249
Purchases								
(6) 0.7(next month's sales)		$210	$280	$350	$245	$175	$140	
(7) Payments (prior month's purchases)			$210	$280	$350	$245	$175	$140
II. CASH GAIN OR LOSS FOR MONTH								
(8) Collections (from Section I)			$254	$313	$408	$ 459	$344	$249
(9) Payments for purchases (from Section I)			$210	$280	$350	$ 245	$175	$140
(10) Wages and salaries			30	40	50	40	30	30
(11) Lease payments			15	15	15	15	15	15
(12) Other expenses			10	15	20	15	10	10
(13) Taxes					30			20
(14) Payment for plant construction						100		
(15) Total payments			$265	$350	$465	$ 415	$230	$215
(16) Net cash gain (loss) during month (Line 8 − Line 15)			($ 11)	($ 37)	($ 57)	$ 44	$114	$ 34
III. LOAN REQUIREMENT OR CASH SURPLUS								
(17) Cash at start of month if no borrowing is done[b]			$ 15	$ 4	($ 33)	($ 90)	($ 46)	$ 68
(18) Cumulative cash: cash at start if no borrowing + gain or − loss (Line 16 + Line 17)			$ 4	($ 33)	($ 90)	($ 46)	$ 68	$102
(19) Target cash balance			10	10	10	10	10	10
(20) Cumulative surplus cash or loans outstanding to maintain $10 target cash balance (Line 18 − Line 19)[c]			($ 6)	($ 43)	($100)	($ 56)	$ 58	$ 92

Notes:

[a]Although the budget period is July through December, sales and purchases data for May and June are needed to determine collections and payments during July and August.

[b]The amount shown on Line 17 for July, the $15 balance (in millions), is on hand initially. The values shown for each of the following months on Line 17 are equal to the cumulative cash as shown on Line 18 for the preceding month; for example, the $4 shown on Line 17 for August is taken from Line 18 in the July column.

[c]When the target cash balance of $10 (Line 19) is deducted from the cumulative cash balance (Line 18), a resulting negative figure on Line 20 (shown in parentheses) represents a required loan, whereas a positive figure represents surplus cash. Loans are required from July through October, and surpluses are expected during November and December. Note also that firms can borrow or pay off loans on a daily basis, so the $6 borrowed during July would be done on a daily basis, as needed, and during October the $100 loan that existed at the beginning of the month would be reduced daily to the $56 ending balance, which, in turn, would be completely paid off during November.

sales forecast for the period from May through December. (May and June sales are necessary to determine collections for July and August.) Next, Lines 2 through 5 show cash collections. Line 2 shows that 20 percent of the sales during any given month are collected

THE GREAT DEBATE: HOW MUCH CASH IS ENOUGH?

"I hate cash on hand," says Fred Salerno, Bell Atlantic's CFO. According to a recent survey, Salerno has backed up his talk with actions. When rated on the number of days of operating expenses held in cash (DOEHIC), Bell Atlantic leads its industry with a DOEHIC of 6 days versus an industry average of 27. Put another way, Bell Atlantic has cash holdings equal to only 0.90 percent of sales as compared with an industry median cash/sales ratio of 5.20 percent.

A great relationship with its banks is a key to keeping low cash levels. Jim Hopwood, treasurer of Wickes, says, "We have a credit revolver if we ever need it." The same is true at Haverty Furniture, where CFO Dennis Fink says, "You don't have to worry about predicting short-term fluctuations in cash flow," if you have solid bank commitments.

Treasurer Wayne Smith of Avery Dennison says that their low cash holdings have reduced their net operating working capital to such an extent that their return on invested capital (ROIC) is 3 percentage points higher than it would be if their cash holdings were at the industry average. He goes on to say that this adds a lot of economic value to their company.

Despite these and other comments about the advantages of low cash holdings, many companies still hold extremely large amounts of cash and marketable securities, including Procter & Gamble ($2.6 billion, 32 days DOEHIC, 7.1 percent cash/sales) and Ford Motor Company ($24 billion, 76 DOEHIC). When asked about the appropriate level of cash holdings, Ford CFO Henry Wallace refused to be pinned down, saying, "There is no answer for a company this size." However, it is interesting to note that Ford recently completed a huge stock repurchase, reducing its cash by about $10 billion.

Source: S. L. Mintz, "Lean Green Machine," *CFO*, July 2000, 76–94.

---

during that month. Customers who pay in the first month, however, take the discount, so the cash collected in the month of sale is reduced by 2 percent; for example, collections during July for the $300 million of sales in that month will be 20 percent times sales times 1.0 minus the 2 percent discount = (0.20)($300)(0.98) ≈ $59 million. Line 3 shows the collections on the previous month's sales, or 70 percent of sales in the preceding month; for example, in July, 70 percent of the $250 million June sales, or $175 million, will be collected. Line 4 gives collections from sales two months earlier, or 10 percent of sales in that month; for example, the July collections for May sales are (0.10)($200) = $20 million. The collections during each month are summed and shown on Line 5; thus, the July collections represent 20 percent of July sales (minus the discount) plus 70 percent of June sales plus 10 percent of May sales, or $254 million in total.

Next, payments for purchases of raw materials are shown. July sales are forecasted at $300 million, so MicroDrive will purchase $210 million of materials in June (Line 6) and pay for these purchases in July (Line 7). Similarly, MicroDrive will purchase $280 million of materials in July to meet August's forecasted sales of $400 million.

With Section I completed, Section II can be constructed. Cash from collections is shown on Line 8. Lines 9 through 14 list payments made during each month, and these payments are summed on Line 15. The difference between cash receipts and cash payments (Line 8 minus Line 15) is the net cash gain or loss during the month. For July there is a net cash loss of $11 million, as shown on Line 16.

In Section III, we first determine the cash balance MicroDrive would have at the start of each month, assuming no borrowing is done. This is shown on Line 17. MicroDrive will have $15 million on hand on July 1. The beginning cash balance (Line 17) is then added to the net cash gain or loss during the month (Line 16) to obtain the cumulative cash that would be on hand if no financing were done (Line 18). At the end of July, MicroDrive forecasts a cumulative cash balance of $4 million in the absence of borrowing.

The target cash balance, $10 million, is then subtracted from the cumulative cash balance to determine the firm's borrowing requirements, shown in parentheses, or its surplus cash. Because MicroDrive expects to have cumulative cash, as shown on Line 18, of only $4 million in July, it will have to borrow $6 million to bring the cash account up to the target balance of $10 million. Assuming that this amount is indeed borrowed, loans outstanding will total $6 million at the end of July. (MicroDrive did not have any loans outstanding on July 1.) The cash surplus or required loan balance is given on Line 20; a positive value indicates a cash surplus, whereas a negative value indicates a loan requirement. Note that the surplus cash or loan requirement shown on Line 20 is a *cumulative amount*. MicroDrive must borrow $6 million in July. Then, it has an additional cash shortfall during August of $37 million as reported on Line 16, so its total loan requirement at the end of August is $6 + $37 = $43 million, as reported on Line 20. MicroDrive's arrangement with the bank permits it to increase its outstanding loans on a daily basis, up to a prearranged maximum, just as you could increase the amount you owe on a credit card. MicroDrive will use any surplus funds it generates to pay off its loans, and because the loan can be paid down at any time, on a daily basis, the firm will never have both a cash surplus and an outstanding loan balance.

This same procedure is used in the following months. Sales will peak in September, accompanied by increased payments for purchases, wages, and other items. Receipts from sales will also go up, but the firm will still be left with a $57 million net cash outflow during the month. The total loan requirement at the end of September will hit a peak of $100 million, the cumulative cash plus the target cash balance. The $100 million can also be found as the $43 million needed at the end of August plus the $57 million cash deficit for September.

Sales, purchases, and payments for past purchases will fall sharply in October, but collections will be the highest of any month because they will reflect the high September sales. As a result, MicroDrive will enjoy a healthy $44 million net cash gain during October. This net gain can be used to pay off borrowings, so loans outstanding will decline by $44 million, to $56 million.

MicroDrive will have an even larger cash surplus in November, which will permit it to pay off all of its loans. In fact, the company is expected to have $58 million in surplus cash by the month's end, and another cash surplus in December will swell the excess cash to $92 million. With such a large amount of unneeded funds, MicroDrive's treasurer will certainly want to invest in interest-bearing securities or to put the funds to use in some other way.

We intentionally kept this cash budget simple for illustrative purposes, but here are some potential refinements that you could easily incorporate: (1) Add dividend payments, stock issues, bond sales, interest income, and interest expenses. (2) Create a cash budget to determine weekly, or even daily, cash requirements. (3) Use simulation to estimate the probability distribution for the cash requirements. (4) Allow the target cash balance to vary over time, reflecting the seasonal nature of sales and operating activity.

| SELF-TEST QUESTIONS | What is the purpose of the cash budget? |
| What are the three major sections of a cash budget? |

CASH MANAGEMENT TECHNIQUES

Most business is conducted by large firms, many of which operate regionally, nationally, or even globally. They collect cash from many sources and make payments from a number of different cities or even countries. For example, companies such as IBM, General Motors, and Hewlett-Packard have manufacturing plants all around the world, even more sales offices, and bank accounts in virtually every city where they do business. Their collection points follow sales patterns. Some disbursements are made from local offices, but most are made in the cities where manufacturing occurs, or else from the home office. Thus, a major corporation might have hundreds or even thousands of bank accounts, and since there is no reason to think that inflows and outflows will balance in each account, a system must be in place to transfer funds from where they come in to where they are needed, to arrange loans to cover net corporate shortfalls, and to invest net corporate surpluses without delay. We discuss the most commonly used techniques for accomplishing these tasks in the following sections.

Cash Flow Synchronization

If you as an individual were to receive income once a year, you would probably put it in the bank, draw down your account periodically, and have an average balance for the year equal to about half your annual income. If instead you could arrange to receive income weekly and to pay rent, tuition, and other charges on a weekly basis, and if you were confident of your forecasted inflows and outflows, then you could hold a tiny average cash balance.

Exactly the same situation holds for businesses—by improving their forecasts and by timing cash receipts to coincide with cash requirements, firms can hold their transactions balances to a minimum. Recognizing this, utility companies, oil companies, credit card companies, and so on, arrange to bill customers, and to pay their own bills, on regular "billing cycles" throughout the month. This **synchronization of cash flows** provides cash when it is needed and thus enables firms to reduce the cash balances needed to support operations.

Speed Up the Check-Clearing Process

When a customer writes and mails a check, the funds are not available to the receiving firm until the **check-clearing** process has been completed. The bank must first make sure that the deposited check is good and the funds are available before it will give cash to the company.

In practice, it may take a long time for a firm to process incoming checks and obtain the use of the money. A check must first be delivered through the mail and then be cleared through the banking system before the money can be put to use. Checks received from the customers in distant cities are especially subject to delays because of mail delays and also because more banks are involved. For example, assume that we receive a check and deposit it in our bank. Our bank must send the check to the bank on which it was drawn. Only when this latter bank transfers funds to our bank are the funds available for us to use. Checks are generally cleared through the Federal Reserve System or through a clearinghouse set up by the banks in a particular city. Of course, if the check is deposited in the same bank on which it was drawn, that bank merely transfers funds by bookkeeping entries from one depositor to another. The length of time required for checks to clear is thus a function of the distance between the payer's and the payee's bank. In the case of private clearinghouses, clearing can range from one to three days. Checks are generally cleared through the Federal Reserve System in about two days, but mail delays can slow down things on each end of the Fed's involvement in the process.

Using Float

Float is defined as the difference between the balance shown in a firm's (or individual's) checkbook and the balance on the bank's records. Suppose a firm writes, on average, checks in the amount of $5,000 each day, and it takes six days for these checks to clear and be deducted from the firm's bank account. This will cause the firm's own checkbook to show a balance $30,000 smaller than the balance on the bank's records; this difference is called **disbursement float**. Now suppose the firm also receives checks in the amount of $5,000 daily, but it loses four days while they are being deposited and cleared. This will result in $20,000 of **collections float**. In total, the firm's **net float**—the difference between the $30,000 positive disbursement float and the $20,000 negative collections float—will be $10,000.

Delays that cause float arise because it takes time for checks (1) to travel through the mail (mail float), (2) to be processed by the receiving firm (processing float), and (3) to clear through the banking system (clearing, or availability, float). Basically, the size of a firm's net float is a function of its ability to speed up collections on checks it receives and to slow down collections on checks it writes. Efficient firms go to great lengths to speed up the processing of incoming checks, thus putting the funds to work faster, and they try to stretch their own payments out as long as possible, sometimes by disbursing checks from banks in remote locations.

Speeding Up Receipts

Two major techniques are now used both to speed collections and to get funds where they are needed: (1) lockbox plans and (2) payment by wire or automatic debit.

LOCKBOXES   A **lockbox plan** is one of the oldest cash management tools. In a lockbox system, incoming checks are sent to post office boxes rather than to corporate headquarters. For example, a firm headquartered in New York City might have its West Coast customers send their payments to a box in San Francisco, its customers in the Southwest send their checks to Dallas, and so on, rather than having all checks sent to New York City. Several times a day a local bank will collect the contents of the lockbox and deposit the checks into the company's local account. In fact, some banks even have their lockbox operation located in the same facility as the post office. The bank then provides the firm with a daily record of the receipts collected, usually via an electronic data transmission system in a format that permits online updating of the firm's accounts receivable records.

A lockbox system reduces the time required for a firm to receive incoming checks, to deposit them, and to get them cleared through the banking system so the funds are available for use. Lockbox services can accelerate the availability of funds by two to five days over the "regular" system.

PAYMENT BY WIRE OR AUTOMATIC DEBIT   Firms are increasingly demanding payments of larger bills by wire, or even by automatic electronic debits. Under an electronic debit system, funds are automatically deducted from one account and added to another. This is, of course, the ultimate in a speeded-up collection process, and computer technology is making such a process increasingly feasible and efficient, even for retail transactions.

| SELF-TEST QUESTIONS | What is float? How do firms use float to increase cash management efficiency? What are some methods firms can use to accelerate receipts? |

INVENTORY

Inventory management techniques are covered in depth in production management courses. Still, since financial managers have a responsibility both for raising the capital needed to carry inventory and for the firm's overall profitability, we need to cover the financial aspects of inventory management here.

The twin goals of inventory management are (1) to ensure that the inventories needed to sustain operations are available, but (2) to hold the costs of ordering and carrying inventories to the lowest possible level. While analyzing improvements in the cash conversion cycle, we identified some of the cash flows associated with a reduction in inventory. In addition to the points made earlier, lower inventory levels reduce costs due to storage and handling, insurance, property taxes, and spoilage or obsolescence.

Consider Trane Corporation, which makes air conditioners, and recently adopted just-in-time inventory procedures. In the past, Trane produced parts on a steady basis, stored them as inventory, and had them ready whenever the company received an order for a batch of air conditioners. However, the company reached the point where its inventory covered an area equal to three football fields, and it still sometimes took as long as 15 days to fill an order. To make matters worse, occasionally some of the necessary components simply could not be located, while in other instances the components were located but found to have been damaged from long storage.

Then Trane adopted a new inventory policy—it began producing components only after an order is received, and then sending the parts directly from the machines that make them to the final assembly line. The net effect: Inventories fell nearly 40 percent even as sales increased by 30 percent.

However, there are costs associated with holding too little inventory, and these costs can be severe. Generally, if a business carries small inventories, it must reorder frequently. This increases ordering costs. Even more important, firms can miss out on profitable sales, and also suffer a loss of goodwill that can lead to lower future sales if they experience stockouts. So, it is important to have enough inventory on hand to meet customer demands.

SELF-TEST QUESTION   What are some costs associated with high inventories? With low inventories?

RECEIVABLES MANAGEMENT

Firms would, in general, rather sell for cash than on credit, but competitive pressures force most firms to offer credit. Thus, goods are shipped, inventories are reduced, and an **account receivable** is created.[7] Eventually, the customer will pay the account, at which time (1) the firm will receive cash and (2) its receivables will decline. Carrying receivables has both direct and indirect costs, but it also has an important benefit—increased sales.

Receivables management begins with the credit policy, but a monitoring system is also important. Corrective action is often needed, and the only way to know whether the situation is getting out of hand is with a good receivables control system.

Credit Policy

The success or failure of a business depends primarily on the demand for its products—as a rule, the higher its sales, the larger its profits and the higher its stock price. Sales, in turn, depend on a number of factors, some exogenous but others under the firm's control. The major controllable determinants of demand are sales prices, product quality, advertising, and the firm's **credit policy**. Credit policy, in turn, consists of these four variables:

1. *Credit period,* which is the length of time buyers are given to pay for their purchases. For example, credit terms of "2/10, net 30" indicate that buyers may take up to 30 days to pay.
2. *Discounts* given for early payment, including the discount percentage and how rapidly payment must be made to qualify for the discount. The credit terms "2/10, net 30" allow buyers to take a 2 percent discount if they pay within 10 days. Otherwise, they must pay the full amount within 30 days.
3. *Credit standards,* which refer to the required financial strength of acceptable credit customers. Lower credit standards boost sales, but also increase bad debts.
4. *Collection policy,* which is measured by its toughness or laxity in attempting to collect on slow-paying accounts. A tough policy may speed up collections, but it might also anger customers, causing them to take their business elsewhere.

The credit manager is responsible for administering the firm's credit policy. However, because of the pervasive importance of credit, the credit policy itself is normally established by the executive committee, which usually consists of the president plus the vice-presidents of finance, marketing, and production.

---

[7] Whenever goods are sold on credit, two accounts are created—an asset item entitled *accounts receivable* appears on the books of the selling firm, and a liability item called *accounts payable* appears on the books of the purchaser. At this point, we are analyzing the transaction from the viewpoint of the seller, so we are concentrating on the variables under its control, in this case, the receivables. We examine the transaction from the viewpoint of the purchaser later in this chapter, where we discuss accounts payable as a source of funds and consider their cost.

SUPPLY CHAIN MANAGEMENT

Herman Miller Inc. manufactures a wide variety of office furniture and a typical order from a single customer might require work at five different plants. Each plant uses components from different suppliers, and each plant works on orders for many customers. Imagine all the coordination that is required. The sales force generates the order, the purchasing department orders components from suppliers, and the suppliers must order materials from their own suppliers. Then, the suppliers ship the components to Herman Miller, the factory builds the product, the different products are gathered together to complete the order, and then the order is shipped to the customer. If one part of that process malfunctions, then the order will be delayed, inventory will pile up, extra costs to expedite the order will be incurred, and the customer's goodwill will be damaged, which will hurt future sales growth.

To prevent such consequences, many companies are turning to a process called supply chain management (SCM). The key element in SCM is sharing information all the way from the point-of-sale at the product's retailer to the suppliers, and even back to the suppliers' suppliers. SCM requires special software, but even more important, it requires cooperation between the different companies and departments in the supply chain. This new culture of open communication is often difficult for many companies—they are reluctant to divulge operating information. For example, EMC Corp., a manufacturer of data storage systems, has become deeply involved in the design processes and financial controls of its key suppliers. Many of EMC's suppliers were initially wary of these new relationships. However, SCM has been a win-win situation, with increases in value for EMC and its suppliers.

The same is true at many other companies. After implementing SCM, Herman Miller was able to reduce its days of inventory on hand by a week, and to cut two weeks off of delivery times to customers. Herman Miller was also able to operate its plants at a 20 percent higher volume without additional capital expenditures. As another example, Heineken USA can now get beer from its breweries to its customers' shelves in less than six weeks, compared with 10 to 12 weeks before implementing SCM. As these and other companies have found, SCM increases free cash flows, and that leads to higher stock prices.

Sources: Elaine L. Appleton, "Supply Chain Brain," *CFO*, July 1997, 51–54; and Kris Frieswick, "Up Close and Virtual," *CFO*, April 1998, 87–91.

The Accumulation of Receivables

The total amount of accounts receivable outstanding at any given time is determined by two factors: (1) the volume of credit sales and (2) the average length of time between sales and collections. For example, suppose Boston Lumber Company (BLC), a wholesale distributor of lumber products, opens a warehouse on January 1 and, starting the first day, makes sales of $1,000 each day. For simplicity, we assume that all sales are on credit, and customers are given 10 days to pay. At the end of the first day, accounts receivable will be $1,000; they will rise to $2,000 by the end of the second day; and by January 10, they will have risen to 10($1,000) = $10,000. On January 11, another $1,000 will be added to receivables, but payments for sales made on January 1 will reduce receivables by $1,000, so total accounts receivable will remain constant at $10,000. In general, once the firm's operations have stabilized, this situation will exist:

$$\begin{array}{ccc} \text{Accounts} & = & \text{Credit sales} \times \text{Length of} \\ \text{receivable} & & \text{per day} \quad \text{collection period} \end{array} \qquad \text{(16-5)}$$

$$= \quad \$1,000 \quad \times \quad 10 \text{ days} \quad = \$10,000.$$

If either credit sales or the collection period changes, such changes will be reflected in accounts receivable.

Monitoring the Receivables Position

Investors—both stockholders and bank loan officers—should pay close attention to accounts receivable management, for, as we shall see, one can be misled by reported financial statements and later suffer serious losses on an investment.

When a credit sale is made, the following events occur: (1) Inventories are reduced by the cost of goods sold, (2) accounts receivable are increased by the sales price, and (3) the difference is profit, which is added to retained earnings. If the sale is for cash, then the cash from the sale has actually been received by the firm, but if the sale is on credit, the firm will not receive the cash from the sale unless and until the account is collected. Firms have been known to encourage "sales" to very weak customers in order to report high profits. This could boost the firm's stock price, at least until credit losses begin to lower earnings, at which time the stock price will fall. Analyses along the lines suggested in the following sections will detect any such questionable practice, as well as any unconscious deterioration in the quality of accounts receivable. Such early detection could help both investors and bankers avoid losses.

DAYS SALES OUTSTANDING (DSO)   Suppose Super Sets Inc., a television manufacturer, sells 200,000 television sets a year at a price of $198 each. Further, assume that all sales are on credit with the following terms: if payment is made within 10 days, customers will receive a 2 percent discount; otherwise the full amount is due within 30 days. Finally, assume that 70 percent of the customers take discounts and pay on Day 10, while the other 30 percent pay on Day 30.

Super Sets's **days sales outstanding (DSO),** sometimes called the *average collection period (ACP),* is 16 days:

$$DSO = ACP = 0.7(10 \text{ days}) + 0.3(30 \text{ days}) = 16 \text{ days.}$$

Super Sets's *average daily sales (ADS)* is $108,493:

$$ADS = \frac{\text{Annual sales}}{365} = \frac{(\text{Units sold})(\text{Sales price})}{365} \qquad \text{(16-6)}$$

$$= \frac{200,000(\$198)}{365} = \frac{\$39,600,000}{365} = \$108,493.$$

Super Sets's accounts receivable, assuming a constant, uniform rate of sales throughout the year, will at any point in time be $1,735,888:

$$\text{Receivables} = (ADS)(DSO) \qquad \text{(16-7)}$$

$$= (\$108,493)(16) = \$1,735,888.$$

Note also that its DSO, or average collection period, is a measure of the average length of time it takes Super Sets's customers to pay off their credit purchases, and the DSO is often compared with an industry average DSO. For example, if all television manufacturers sell on the same credit terms, and if the industry average DSO is 25 days versus Super Sets's 16 days, then Super Sets either has a higher percentage of discount customers or else its credit department is exceptionally good at ensuring prompt payment.

Finally, note that if you know both the annual sales and the receivables balance, you can calculate DSO as follows:

$$DSO = \frac{\text{Receivables}}{\text{Sales per day}} = \frac{\$1,735,888}{\$108,493} = 16 \text{ days.}$$

The DSO can also be compared with the firm's own credit terms. For example, suppose Super Sets's DSO had been averaging 35 days. With a 35-day DSO, some customers would obviously be taking more than 30 days to pay their bills. In fact, if many customers were paying within 10 days to take advantage of the discount, the others must, on average, be taking much longer than 35 days. One way to check this possibility is to use an aging schedule as described in the next section.

AGING SCHEDULES   An **aging schedule** breaks down a firm's receivables by age of account. Table 16-3 contains the December 31, 2005, aging schedules of two television manufacturers, Super Sets and Wonder Vision. Both firms offer the same credit terms, and both show the same total receivables. However, Super Sets's aging schedule indicates that all of its customers pay on time—70 percent pay on Day 10 while 30 percent pay on Day 30. Wonder Vision's schedule, which is more typical, shows that many of its customers are not abiding by its credit terms—some 27 percent of its receivables are more than 30 days past due, even though Wonder Vision's credit terms call for full payment by Day 30.

Aging schedules cannot be constructed from the type of summary data reported in financial statements; they must be developed from the firm's accounts receivable ledger. However, well-run firms have computerized their accounts receivable records, so it is easy to determine the age of each invoice, to sort electronically by age categories, and thus to generate an aging schedule.

Management should constantly monitor both the DSO and the aging schedule to detect trends, to see how the firm's collection experience compares with its credit terms, and to see how effectively the credit department is operating in comparison with other firms in the industry. If the DSO starts to lengthen, or if the aging schedule begins to show an increasing percentage of past-due accounts, then the firm's credit policy may need to be tightened.

Although a change in the DSO or the aging schedule should signal the firm to investigate its credit policy, a deterioration in either of these measures does not necessarily indicate that the firm's credit policy has weakened. In fact, if a firm experiences sharp seasonal variations, or if it is growing rapidly, then both the aging schedule and the DSO may be distorted. To see this point, note that the DSO is calculated as follows:

$$DSO = \frac{Accounts\ receivable}{Sales/365}.$$

Since receivables at a given point in time reflect sales in the last month or so, but sales as shown in the denominator of the equation are for the last 12 months, a seasonal increase in sales will increase the numerator more than the denominator, hence will raise the DSO. This will occur even if customers are still paying exactly as before. Similar problems arise

TABLE 16-3 | Aging Schedules

Age of Account (Days)	SUPER SETS Value of Account	Percentage of Total Value	WONDER VISION Value of Account	Percentage of Total Value
0–10	$1,215,122	70%	$ 815,867	47%
11–30	520,766	30	451,331	26
31–45	0	0	260,383	15
46–60	0	0	173,589	10
Over 60	0	0	34,718	2
Total receivables	$1,735,888	100%	$1,735,888	100%

with the aging schedule if sales fluctuate widely. Therefore, a change in either the DSO or the aging schedule should be taken as a signal to investigate further, but not necessarily as a sign that the firm's credit policy has weakened.

SELF-TEST QUESTIONS

Explain how a new firm's receivables balance is built up over time.

Define days sales outstanding (DSO). What can be learned from it? How is it affected by sales fluctuations?

What is an aging schedule? What can be learned from it? How is it affected by sales fluctuations?

ACCRUALS AND ACCOUNTS PAYABLE (TRADE CREDIT)

Recall that net operating working capital is equal to operating current assets minus operating current liabilities. The previous sections discussed the management of operating current assets (cash, inventory, and accounts receivable), and the following sections discuss the two major types of operating current liabilities, accruals and accounts payable.

Accruals

Firms generally pay employees on a weekly, biweekly, or monthly basis, so the balance sheet will typically show some accrued wages. Similarly, the firm's own estimated income taxes, Social Security and income taxes withheld from employee payrolls, and sales taxes collected are generally paid on a weekly, monthly, or quarterly basis, hence the balance sheet will typically show some accrued taxes along with accrued wages.

These **accruals** increase automatically, or spontaneously, as a firm's operations expand. However, a firm cannot ordinarily control its accruals: The timing of wage payments is set by economic forces and industry custom, while tax payment dates are established by law. Thus, firms use all the accruals they can, but they have little control over the levels of these accounts.

Accounts Payable (Trade Credit)

Firms generally make purchases from other firms on credit, recording the debt as an *account payable*. Accounts payable, or **trade credit,** is the largest single category of operating current liabilities, representing about 40 percent of the current liabilities of the average nonfinancial corporation. The percentage is somewhat larger for smaller firms: Because small companies often do not qualify for financing from other sources, they rely especially heavily on trade credit.

Trade credit is a "spontaneous" source of financing in the sense that it arises from ordinary business transactions. For example, suppose a firm makes average purchases of $2,000 a day on terms of net 30, meaning that it must pay for goods 30 days after the invoice date. On average, it will owe 30 times $2,000, or $60,000, to its suppliers. If its sales, and consequently its purchases, were to double, then its accounts payable would also double, to $120,000. So, simply by growing, the firm would spontaneously generate an additional $60,000 of financing. Similarly, if the terms under which it bought were extended from 30 to 40 days, its accounts payable would expand from $60,000 to $80,000. Thus, lengthening the credit period, as well as expanding sales and purchases, generates additional financing.

The Cost of Trade Credit

Firms that sell on credit have a *credit policy* that includes certain *terms of credit*. For example, Microchip Electronics sells on terms of 2/10, net 30, meaning that it gives its customers a 2 percent discount if they pay within 10 days of the invoice date, but the full invoice amount is due and payable within 30 days if the discount is not taken.

Note that the true price of Microchip's products is the net price, or 0.98 times the list price, because any customer can purchase an item at that price as long as the customer pays within 10 days. Now consider Personal Computer Company (PCC), which buys its memory chips from Microchip. One commonly used memory chip is listed at $100, so the "true" price to PCC is $98. Now if PCC wants an additional 20 days of credit beyond the 10-day discount period, it must incur a finance charge of $2 per chip for that credit. Thus, the $100 list price consists of two components:

$$\text{List price} = \$98 \text{ true price} + \$2 \text{ finance charge.}$$

The question PCC must ask before it turns down the discount to obtain the additional 20 days of credit from Microchip is this: Could we obtain credit under better terms from some other lender, say, a bank? In other words, could 20 days of credit be obtained for less than $2 per chip?

PCC buys an average of $11,923,333 of memory chips from Microchip each year at the net, or true, price. This amounts to $11,923,333/365 = $32,666.67 per day. For simplicity, assume that Microchip is PCC's only supplier. If PCC decides not to take the additional trade credit—that is, if it pays on the 10th day and takes the discount—its payables will average 10($32,666.67) = $326,667. Thus, PCC will be receiving $326,667 of credit from Microchip.

Now suppose PCC decides to take the additional 20 days credit and thus must pay the finance charge. Since PCC will now pay on the 30th day, its accounts payable will increase to 30($32,666.67) = $980,000.[8] Microchip will now be supplying PCC with an additional $980,000 − $326,667 = $653,333 of credit, which PCC could use to build up its cash account, to pay off debt, to expand inventories, or even to extend credit to its own customers, hence increasing its own accounts receivable.

The additional trade credit offered by Microchip has a cost—PCC must pay a finance charge equal to the 2 percent discount it is forgoing. PCC buys $11,923,333 of chips at the true price, and the added finance charges increase the total cost to $11,923,333/0.98 = $12,166,666. Therefore, the annual financing cost is $12,166,666 − $11,923,333 = $243,333. Dividing the $243,333 financing cost by the $653,333 of additional credit, we find the nominal annual cost rate of the additional trade credit to be 37.2 percent:

$$\text{Nominal annual cost} = \frac{\$243,333}{\$653,333} = 37.2\%.$$

If PCC can borrow from its bank (or from other sources) at an interest rate less than 37.2 percent, it should take discounts and forgo the additional trade credit.

The following equation can be used to calculate the nominal cost, on an annual basis, of not taking discounts, illustrated with terms of 2/10, net 30:

$$\begin{array}{c}\text{Nominal}\\\text{annual}\\\text{cost}\end{array} = \frac{\text{Discount percent}}{100 - \begin{array}{c}\text{Discount}\\\text{percent}\end{array}} \times \frac{365 \text{ days}}{\begin{array}{c}\text{Days credit is}\\\text{outstanding}\end{array} - \begin{array}{c}\text{Discount}\\\text{period}\end{array}} \qquad (16\text{-}8)$$

$$= \frac{2}{98} \times \frac{365}{20} = 2.04\% \times 18.25 = 37.2\%.$$

The numerator of the first term, Discount percent, is the cost per dollar of credit, while the denominator in this term, 100 − Discount percent, represents the funds made available

[8] A question arises here: Should accounts payable reflect gross purchases or purchases net of discounts? Generally accepted accounting principles permit either treatment if the difference is not material, but if the discount is material, then the transaction must be recorded net of discounts, or at "true" prices. Then, the higher payment that results from not taking discounts is reported as an additional expense called "discounts lost." Thus, *we show accounts payable net of discounts even if the company does not expect to take discounts.*

by not taking the discount. Thus, the first term, 2.04%, is the cost per period for the trade credit. The denominator of the second term is the number of days of extra credit obtained by not taking the discount, so the entire second term shows how many times each year the cost is incurred, 18.25 times in this example.

The nominal annual cost formula does not take account of compounding, and in effective annual interest terms, the cost of trade credit is even higher. The discount amounts to interest, and with terms of 2/10, net 30, the firm gains use of the funds for $30 - 10 = 20$ days, so there are $365/20 = 18.25$ "interest periods" per year. Remember that the first term in Equation 16-8, (Discount percent)/(100 − Discount percent) = 0.02/0.98 = 0.0204, is the periodic interest rate. This rate is paid 18.25 times each year, so the effective annual cost of trade credit is

$$\text{Effective annual rate} = (1.0204)^{18.25} - 1.0 = 1.4459 - 1.0 = 44.6\%.$$

Thus, the 37.2 percent nominal cost calculated with Equation 16-8 understates the true cost.

Note, however, that the cost of trade credit can be reduced by paying late. Thus, if PCC could get away with paying in 60 days rather than in the specified 30 days, then the effective credit period would become $60 - 10 = 50$ days, the number of times the discount would be lost would fall to $365/50 = 7.3$, and the nominal cost would drop from 37.2 percent to $2.04\% \times 7.3 = 14.9\%$. The effective annual rate would drop from 44.6 to 15.9 percent:

$$\text{Effective annual rate} = (1.0204)^{7.3} - 1.0 = 1.1589 - 1.0 = 15.9\%.$$

In periods of excess capacity, firms may be able to get away with deliberately paying late, or **stretching accounts payable.** However, they will also suffer a variety of problems associated with being branded a "slow payer." These problems are discussed later in the chapter.

The costs of the additional trade credit from forgoing discounts under some other purchase terms are shown below:

Credit Terms	COST OF ADDITIONAL CREDIT IF THE CASH DISCOUNT IS NOT TAKEN	
	Nominal Cost	Effective Cost
1/10, net 20	36.9%	44.3%
1/10, net 30	18.4	20.1
2/10, net 20	74.5	109.0
3/15, net 45	37.6	44.9

As these figures show, the cost of not taking discounts can be substantial. Incidentally, throughout the chapter, we assume that payments are made either on the *last day* for taking discounts or on the *last day* of the credit period, unless otherwise noted. It would be foolish to pay, say, on the 5th day or on the 20th day if the credit terms were 2/10, net 30.[9]

On the basis of the preceding discussion, trade credit can be divided into two components: (1) **free trade credit,** which involves credit received during the discount period, and

---

[9] A financial calculator can also be used to determine the cost of trade credit. If the terms of credit are 2/10, net 30, this implies that for every $100 of goods purchased at the full list price, the customer has the choice of paying the full amount in 30 days or else paying $98 in 10 days. If a customer decides not to take the discount, then it is in effect borrowing $98, the amount it would otherwise have to pay, from Day 11 to Day 30, or for 20 days. It will then have to pay $100, which is the $98 loan plus a $2 financing charge, at the end of the 20-day loan period. To calculate the interest rate, enter N = 1, PV = 98, PMT = 0, FV = −100, and then press I to obtain 2.04 percent. This is the rate for 20 days. To calculate the effective annual interest rate on a 365-day basis, enter N = 20/365 = 0.05479, PV = 98, PMT = 0, FV = −100, and then press I to obtain 44.6 percent. The 20/365 = 0.05479 is the fraction of a year the "loan" is outstanding, and the 44.6 percent is the annualized cost of not taking discounts.

(2) **costly trade credit,** which involves credit in excess of the free trade credit and whose cost is an implicit one based on the forgone discounts. *Firms should always use the free component, but they should use the costly component only after analyzing the cost of this capital to make sure that it is less than the cost of funds that could be obtained from other sources.* Under the terms of trade found in most industries, the costly component is relatively expensive, so stronger firms will avoid using it.

SELF-TEST QUESTIONS   What are accruals? How much control do managers have over accruals?

What is trade credit?

What is the difference between free trade credit and costly trade credit?

How does the cost of costly trade credit generally compare with the cost of short-term bank loans?

ALTERNATIVE SHORT-TERM FINANCING POLICIES

Up until this point we have focused on the management of net operating working capital. We now turn our attention to decisions involving short-term investments and short-term financing.

Most businesses experience seasonal and/or cyclical fluctuations. For example, construction firms have peaks in the spring and summer, retailers peak around Christmas, and the manufacturers who supply both construction companies and retailers follow similar patterns. Similarly, virtually all businesses must build up net operating working capital (NOWC) when the economy is strong, but they then sell off inventories and reduce receivables when the economy slacks off. Still, NOWC rarely drops to zero—companies have some **permanent NOWC,** which is the NOWC on hand at the low point of the cycle. Then, as sales increase during the upswing, NOWC must be increased, and the additional NOWC is defined as **temporary NOWC.** The manner in which the permanent and temporary NOWC are financed is called the firm's *short-term financing policy.*

Maturity Matching, or "Self-Liquidating," Approach

The **maturity matching,** or **"self-liquidating," approach** calls for matching asset and liability maturities as shown in Panel a of Figure 16-2. This strategy minimizes the risk that the firm will be unable to pay off its maturing obligations. To illustrate, suppose a company borrows on a one-year basis and uses the funds obtained to build and equip a plant. Cash flows from the plant (profits plus depreciation) would not be sufficient to pay off the loan at the end of only one year, so the loan would have to be renewed. If for some reason the lender refused to renew the loan, then the company would have problems. Had the plant been financed with long-term debt, however, the required loan payments would have been better matched with cash flows from profits and depreciation, and the problem of renewal would not have arisen.

At the limit, a firm could attempt to match exactly the maturity structure of its assets and liabilities. Inventory expected to be sold in 30 days could be financed with a 30-day bank loan; a machine expected to last for 5 years could be financed with a 5-year loan; a 20-year building could be financed with a 20-year mortgage bond; and so forth. In practice, firms don't actually finance each specific asset with a type of capital that has a maturity equal to the asset's life. However, academic studies do show that most firms tend to finance short-term assets from short-term sources and long-term assets from long-term sources.[10]

---

[10] For example, see William Beranek, Christopher Cornwell, and Sunho Choi, "External Financing, Liquidity, and Capital Expenditures," *Journal of Financial Research,* Summer 1995, 207–222.

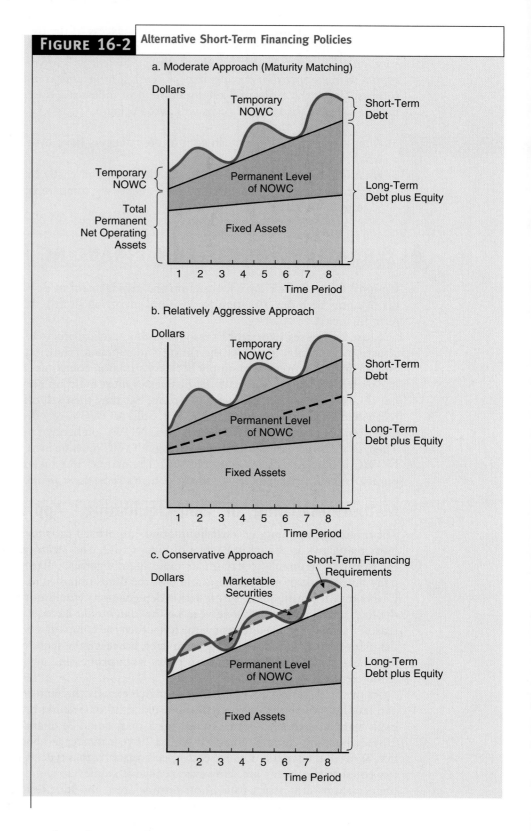

FIGURE 16-2 Alternative Short-Term Financing Policies

a. Moderate Approach (Maturity Matching)

b. Relatively Aggressive Approach

c. Conservative Approach

Aggressive Approach

Panel b of Figure 16-2 illustrates the situation for a relatively aggressive firm that finances all of its fixed assets with long-term capital and part of its permanent NOWC with short-term debt. Note that we used the term "relatively" in the title for Panel b because there can be different *degrees* of aggressiveness. For example, the dashed line in Panel b could have been drawn *below* the line designating fixed assets, indicating that all of the permanent NOWC and part of the fixed assets were financed with short-term credit; this would be a highly aggressive, extremely nonconservative position, and the firm would be very much subject to dangers from rising interest rates as well as to loan renewal problems. However, short-term debt is often cheaper than long-term debt, and some firms are willing to sacrifice safety for the chance of higher profits.

Conservative Approach

Panel c of Figure 16-2 has the dashed line *above* the line designating permanent NOWC, indicating that long-term sources are being used to finance all permanent operating asset requirements and also to meet some of the seasonal needs. In this situation, the firm uses a small amount of short-term debt to meet its peak requirements, but it also meets a part of its seasonal needs by "storing liquidity" in the form of marketable securities. The humps above the dashed line represent short-term financing, while the troughs below the dashed line represent short-term investing. Panel c represents a very safe, conservative current asset financing policy.

What is meant by the term "permanent NOWC"?
What is meant by the term "temporary NOWC"?
What are three alternative short-term financing policies? Is one best?

SHORT-TERM INVESTMENTS: MARKETABLE SECURITIES

Realistically, the management of cash and marketable securities cannot be separated—management of one implies management of the other. In the first part of the chapter, we focused on cash management. Now, we turn to **marketable securities.**

Marketable securities typically provide much lower yields than operating assets. For example, recently DaimlerChrysler held approximately a $7 billion portfolio of short-term marketable securities that provided a much lower yield than its operating assets. Why would a company such as DaimlerChrysler have such large holdings of low-yielding assets?

In many cases, companies hold marketable securities for the same reasons they hold cash. Although these securities are not the same as cash, in most cases they can be converted to cash on very short notice (often just a few minutes) with a single telephone call. Moreover, while cash and most commercial checking accounts yield nothing, marketable securities provide at least a modest return. For this reason, many firms hold at least some marketable securities in lieu of larger cash balances, liquidating part of the portfolio to increase the cash account when cash outflows exceed inflows. In such situations, the marketable securities could be used as a substitute for transactions balances or for precautionary balances. In most cases, the securities are held primarily for precautionary purposes—most firms prefer to rely on bank credit to make temporary transactions, but they may still hold some liquid assets to guard against a possible shortage of bank credit during difficult times.

There are both benefits and costs associated with holding marketable securities. The benefits are twofold: (1) the firm reduces risk and transactions costs because it won't have to issue securities or borrow as frequently to raise cash; and (2) it will have ready cash to take advantage of bargain purchases or growth opportunities. Funds held for the second reason are called **speculative balances.** The primary disadvantage is that the after-tax return on short-term securities is very low. Thus, firms face a trade-off between benefits and costs.

Recent research supports this trade-off hypothesis as an explanation for firms' cash holdings.[11] Firms with high growth opportunities suffer the most if they don't have ready cash to quickly take advantage of an opportunity, and the data show that these firms do hold relatively high levels of marketable securities. Firms with volatile cash flows are the ones most likely to run low on cash, so they tend to hold high levels of cash. In contrast, cash holdings are less important to large firms with high credit ratings, because they have quick and inexpensive access to capital markets. As expected, such firms hold relatively low levels of cash. Of course, there will always be outliers such as Ford, which is large, strong, and cash-rich, but volatile firms with good growth opportunities are still the ones with the most marketable securities, on average.

SELF-TEST QUESTION	Why might a company hold low-yielding marketable securities when it could earn a much higher return on operating assets?

SHORT-TERM FINANCING

The three possible short-term financing policies described earlier were distinguished by the relative amounts of short-term debt used under each policy. The aggressive policy called for the greatest use of short-term debt, while the conservative policy called for the least. Maturity matching fell in between. Although short-term credit is generally riskier than long-term credit, using short-term funds does have some significant advantages. The pros and cons of short-term financing are considered in this section.

Advantages of Short-Term Financing

First, a short-term loan can be obtained much faster than long-term credit. Lenders will insist on a more thorough financial examination before extending long-term credit, and the loan agreement will have to be spelled out in considerable detail because a lot can happen during the life of a 10- to 20-year loan. Therefore, if funds are needed in a hurry, the firm should look to the short-term markets.

Second, if its needs for funds are seasonal or cyclical, a firm may not want to commit itself to long-term debt: (1) Flotation costs are higher for long-term debt than for short-term credit. (2) Although long-term debt can be repaid early, provided the loan agreement includes a prepayment provision, prepayment penalties can be expensive. Accordingly, if a firm thinks its need for funds will diminish in the near future, it should choose short-term debt. (3) Long-term loan agreements always contain provisions, or covenants, which constrain the firm's future actions. Short-term credit agreements are generally less restrictive.

Third, the yield curve is normally upward sloping, indicating that interest rates are generally lower on short-term debt. Thus, under normal conditions, interest costs at the time the funds are obtained will be lower if the firm borrows on a short-term rather than a long-term basis.

Disadvantages of Short-Term Debt

Even though short-term rates are often lower than long-term rates, short-term credit is riskier for two reasons: (1) If a firm borrows on a long-term basis, its interest costs will be relatively stable over time, but if it uses short-term credit, its interest expense will fluctuate widely, at times going quite high. For example, the rate banks charge large corporations for short-term debt more than tripled over a two-year period in the 1980s, rising from 6.25 to 21 percent. Many firms that had borrowed heavily on a short-term

---

[11] See Tim Opler, Lee Pinkowitz, René Stulz, and Rohan Williamson, "The Determinants and Implications of Corporate Cash Holdings," *Journal of Financial Economics,* Vol. 52, 1999, 3–46.

basis simply could not meet their rising interest costs, and as a result, bankruptcies hit record levels during that period. (2) If a firm borrows heavily on a short-term basis, a temporary recession may render it unable to repay this debt. If the borrower is in a weak financial position, the lender may not extend the loan, which could force the firm into bankruptcy.

SELF-TEST QUESTION   What are the advantages and disadvantages of short-term debt over long-term debt?

SHORT-TERM BANK LOANS

Loans from commercial banks generally appear on balance sheets as notes payable. A bank's influence is actually greater than it appears from the dollar amounts because banks provide *nonspontaneous* funds. As a firm's financing needs increase, it requests additional funds from its bank. If the request is denied, the firm may be forced to abandon attractive growth opportunities. The key features of bank loans are discussed in the following paragraphs.

Maturity

Although banks do make longer-term loans, *the bulk of their lending is on a short-term basis*—about two-thirds of all bank loans mature in a year or less. Bank loans to businesses are frequently written as 90-day notes, so the loan must be repaid or renewed at the end of 90 days. Of course, if a borrower's financial position has deteriorated, the bank may refuse to renew the loan. This can mean serious trouble for the borrower.

Promissory Note

When a bank loan is approved, the agreement is executed by signing a **promissory note.** The note specifies (1) the amount borrowed; (2) the interest rate; (3) the repayment schedule, which can call for either a lump sum or a series of installments; (4) any collateral that might have to be put up as security for the loan; and (5) any other terms and conditions to which the bank and the borrower have agreed. When the note is signed, the bank credits the borrower's checking account with the funds, so on the borrower's balance sheet both cash and notes payable increase.

Compensating Balances

Banks sometimes require borrowers to maintain an average demand deposit (checking account) balance equal to from 10 to 20 percent of the face amount of the loan. This is called a **compensating balance,** and such balances raise the effective interest rate on the loans. For example, if a firm needs $80,000 to pay off outstanding obligations, but if it must maintain a 20 percent compensating balance, then it must borrow $100,000 to obtain a usable $80,000. If the stated annual interest rate is 8 percent, the effective cost is actually 10 percent: $8,000 interest divided by $80,000 of usable funds equals 10 percent.[12]

As we noted earlier in the chapter, recent surveys indicate that compensating balances are much less common now than 20 years ago. In fact, compensating balances are now illegal in many states. Despite this trend, some small banks in states where compensating balances are legal still require their customers to maintain compensating balances.

---

[12] Note, however, that the compensating balance may be set as a minimum monthly *average,* and if the firm would maintain this average anyway, the compensating balance requirement would not raise the effective interest rate. Also, note that these *loan* compensating balances are added to any compensating balances that the firm's bank may require for *services performed,* such as clearing checks.

Informal Line of Credit

A **line of credit** is an informal agreement between a bank and a borrower indicating the maximum credit the bank will extend to the borrower. For example, on December 31, a bank loan officer might indicate to a financial manager that the bank regards the firm as being "good" for up to $80,000 during the forthcoming year, provided the borrower's financial condition does not deteriorate. If on January 10 the financial manager signs a promissory note for $15,000 for 90 days, this would be called "taking down" $15,000 of the total line of credit. This amount would be credited to the firm's checking account at the bank, and before repayment of the $15,000, the firm could borrow additional amounts up to a total of $80,000 outstanding at any one time.

Revolving Credit Agreement

A **revolving credit agreement** is a formal line of credit often used by large firms. To illustrate, in 2004 Texas Petroleum Company negotiated a revolving credit agreement for $100 million with a group of banks. The banks were formally committed for four years to lend the firm up to $100 million if the funds were needed. Texas Petroleum, in turn, paid an annual commitment fee of ¼ of 1 percent on the unused balance of the commitment to compensate the banks for making the commitment. Thus, if Texas Petroleum did not take down any of the $100 million commitment during a year, it would still be required to pay a $250,000 annual fee, normally in monthly installments of $20,833.33. If it borrowed $50 million on the first day of the agreement, the unused portion of the line of credit would fall to $50 million, and the annual fee would fall to $125,000. Of course, interest would also have to be paid on the money Texas Petroleum actually borrowed. As a general rule, the interest rate on "revolvers" is pegged to the prime rate, the T-bill rate, or some other market rate, so the cost of the loan varies over time as interest rates change. Texas Petroleum's rate was set at prime plus 0.5 percentage point.

Note that a revolving credit agreement is very similar to an informal line of credit, but with an important difference: The bank has a *legal obligation* to honor a revolving credit agreement, and it receives a commitment fee. Neither the legal obligation nor the fee exists under the informal line of credit.

Often a line of credit will have a **cleanup clause** that requires the borrower to reduce the loan balance to zero at least once a year. Keep in mind that a line of credit typically is designed to help finance negative operating cash flows that are incurred as a natural part of a company's business cycle, not as a source of permanent capital. For example, the total annual operating cash flow of Toys "Я" Us is normally positive, even though its operating cash flow is negative during the fall as it builds up inventory for the Christmas season. However, Toys "Я" Us has large positive cash flows in December through February, as it collects on Christmas sales. Their bankers would expect Toys "Я" Us to use those positive cash flows to pay off balances that had been drawn against their credit lines. Otherwise, Toys "Я" Us would be using its credit lines as a permanent source of financing.

SELF-TEST QUESTION | Explain how a firm that expects to need funds during the coming year might make sure the needed funds will be available.

COMMERCIAL PAPER

Commercial paper is a type of unsecured promissory note issued by large, strong firms and sold primarily to other business firms, to insurance companies, to pension funds, to money market mutual funds, and to banks. In mid-2004, there was approximately $1,346 billion of commercial paper outstanding, versus about $876 billion of commercial and industrial bank loans. Much of this commercial paper outstanding is issued by financial institutions.

Maturity and Cost

Maturities of commercial paper generally vary from one day to nine months, with an average of about five months.[13] The interest rate on commercial paper fluctuates with supply and demand conditions—it is determined in the marketplace, varying daily as conditions change. Recently, commercial paper rates have ranged from 1½ to 3½ percentage points below the stated prime rate, and up to ½ of a percentage point above the T-bill rate. For example, in May 2004, the average rate on three-month commercial paper was 1.22 percent, the stated prime rate was 4.00 percent, and the three-month T-bill rate was 1.06 percent.

Use of Commercial Paper

The use of commercial paper is restricted to a comparatively small number of very large concerns that are exceptionally good credit risks. Dealers prefer to handle the paper of firms whose net worth is $100 million or more and whose annual borrowing exceeds $10 million. One potential problem with commercial paper is that a debtor who is in temporary financial difficulty may receive little help because commercial paper dealings are generally less personal than are bank relationships. Thus, banks are generally more able and willing to help a good customer weather a temporary storm than is a commercial paper dealer. On the other hand, using commercial paper permits a corporation to tap a wide range of credit sources, including financial institutions outside its own area and industrial corporations across the country, and this can reduce interest costs.

SELF-TEST QUESTIONS

What is commercial paper?

What types of companies can use commercial paper to meet their short-term financing needs?

How does the cost of commercial paper compare with the cost of short-term bank loans? With the cost of Treasury bills?

USE OF SECURITY IN SHORT-TERM FINANCING

Thus far, we have not addressed the question of whether or not short-term loans should be secured. Commercial paper is never secured, but other types of loans can be secured if this is deemed necessary or desirable. Other things held constant, it is better to borrow on an unsecured basis, since the bookkeeping costs of **secured loans** are often high. However, firms often find that they can borrow only if they put up some type of collateral to protect the lender, or that by using security they can borrow at a much lower rate.

Several different kinds of collateral can be employed, including marketable stocks or bonds, land or buildings, equipment, inventory, and accounts receivable. Marketable securities make excellent collateral, but few firms that need loans also hold portfolios of stocks and bonds. Similarly, real property (land and buildings) and equipment are good forms of collateral, but they are generally used as security for long-term loans rather than for working capital loans. Therefore, most secured short-term business borrowing involves the use of accounts receivable and inventories as collateral.

To understand the use of security, consider the case of a Chicago hardware dealer who wanted to modernize and expand his store. He requested a $200,000 bank loan. After examining his business's financial statements, the bank indicated that it would lend him a maximum of $100,000 and that the effective interest rate would be 12.1 percent. The

---

[13] The maximum maturity without SEC registration is 270 days. Also, commercial paper can only be sold to "sophisticated" investors; otherwise, SEC registration would be required even for maturities of 270 days or less.

owner had a substantial personal portfolio of stocks, and he offered to put up $300,000 of high-quality stocks to support the $200,000 loan. The bank then granted the full $200,000 loan, and at the prime rate of 9.5 percent. The store owner might also have used his inventories or receivables as security for the loan, but processing costs would have been high.[14]

For a more detailed discussion of secured financing, see the Web Extension to this chapter on the textbook's Web site.

What is a secured loan?

What are some types of current assets that are pledged as security for short-term loans?

---

[14] The term "asset-based financing" is often used as a synonym for "secured financing." In recent years, accounts receivable have been used as security for long-term bonds, and this permits corporations to borrow from lenders such as pension funds rather than being restricted to banks and other traditional short-term lenders.

SUMMARY

This chapter discussed working capital management and short-term financing. The key concepts covered are listed below.

- **Working capital** refers to current assets, and **net working capital** is defined as current assets minus current liabilities. **Net operating working capital** is defined as operating current assets minus operating current liabilities.
- The **cash conversion cycle model** focuses on the length of time between when the company makes payments and when it receives cash inflows.
- The **inventory conversion period** is the average time required to convert materials into finished goods and then to sell those goods.

$$\text{Inventory conversion period} = \text{Inventory/Sales per day.}$$

- The **receivables collection period** is the average length of time required to convert the firm's receivables into cash, that is, to collect cash following a sale.

$$\text{Receivables collection period} = \text{DSO} = \text{Receivables/(Sales/365).}$$

- The **payables deferral period** is the average length of time between the purchase of materials and labor and the payment of cash for them.

$$\text{Payables deferral period} = \text{Payables/Purchases per day.}$$

- The **cash conversion cycle** equals the length of time between the firm's actual cash expenditures to pay for productive resources (materials and labor) and its own cash receipts from the sale of products (that is, the length of time between paying for labor and materials and collecting on receivables).

$$
\begin{array}{ccccc}
\text{Cash} & & \text{Inventory} & \text{Receivables} & \text{Payables} \\
\text{conversion} & = & \text{conversion} + & \text{collection} - & \text{deferral} \; . \\
\text{cycle} & & \text{period} & \text{period} & \text{period}
\end{array}
$$

- Under a **relaxed working capital policy,** a firm would hold relatively large amounts of each type of current asset. Under a **restricted working capital policy,** the firm would hold minimal amounts of these items.
- The **primary goal of cash management** is to reduce the amount of cash to the minimum necessary to conduct business.

- The **transactions balance** is the cash necessary to conduct day-to-day business, whereas the **precautionary balance** is a cash reserve held to meet random, unforeseen needs. A **compensating balance** is a minimum checking account balance that a bank requires as compensation either for services provided or as part of a loan agreement.
- A **cash budget** is a schedule showing projected cash inflows and outflows over some period. The cash budget is used to predict cash surpluses and deficits, and it is the primary cash management planning tool.
- The twin goals of **inventory management** are (1) to ensure that the inventories needed to sustain operations are available, but (2) to hold the costs of ordering and carrying inventories to the lowest possible level.
- **Inventory costs** can be divided into three types: carrying costs, ordering costs, and stock-out costs. In general, carrying costs increase as the level of inventory rises, but ordering costs and stock-out costs decline with larger inventory holdings.
- When a firm sells goods to a customer on credit, an **account receivable** is created.
- A firm can use an **aging schedule** and the **days sales outstanding (DSO)** to help keep track of its receivables position and to help avoid an increase in bad debts.
- A firm's **credit policy** consists of four elements: (1) credit period, (2) discounts given for early payment, (3) credit standards, and (4) collection policy.
- **Permanent net operating working capital** is the NOWC that the firm holds even during slack times, whereas **temporary NOWC** is the additional NOWC needed during seasonal or cyclical peaks. The methods used to finance permanent and temporary NOWC define the firm's **short-term financing policy.**
- A **moderate** approach to short-term financing involves matching, to the extent possible, the maturities of assets and liabilities, so that temporary NOWC is financed with short-term debt, and permanent NOWC and fixed assets are financed with long-term debt or equity. Under an **aggressive** approach, some permanent NOWC, and perhaps even some fixed assets, are financed with short-term debt. A **conservative** approach would be to use long-term sources to finance all permanent operating capital and some of the temporary NOWC.
- The advantages of short-term credit are (1) the **speed** with which short-term loans can be arranged, (2) increased **flexibility,** and (3) the fact that short-term **interest rates** are generally **lower** than long-term rates. The principal disadvantage of short-term credit is the **extra risk** the borrower must bear because (1) the lender can demand payment on short notice and (2) the cost of the loan will increase if interest rates rise.
- **Accounts payable,** or trade credit, arises spontaneously as a result of credit purchases. Firms should use all the **free trade credit** they can obtain, but they should use **costly trade credit** only if it is less expensive than other forms of short-term debt. Suppliers often offer discounts to customers who pay within a stated discount period. The following equation may be used to calculate the nominal cost, on an annual basis, of not taking discounts:

$$\frac{\text{Nominal}}{\text{cost}} = \frac{\text{Discount percent}}{100 - \frac{\text{Discount}}{\text{percent}}} \times \frac{365 \text{ days}}{\frac{\text{Days credit is}}{\text{outstanding}} - \frac{\text{Discount}}{\text{period}}}.$$

- **Bank loans** are an important source of short-term credit. When a bank loan is approved, a **promissory note** is signed. It specifies: (1) the amount borrowed, (2) the percentage interest rate, (3) the repayment schedule, (4) the collateral, and (5) any other conditions to which the parties have agreed.
- Banks sometimes require borrowers to maintain **compensating balances,** which are deposit requirements set at between 10 and 20 percent of the loan amount. Compensating balances raise the effective interest rate on bank loans.
- A **line of credit** is an informal agreement between the bank and the borrower indicating the maximum amount of credit the bank will extend to the borrower.
- A **revolving credit agreement** is a formal line of credit often used by large firms; it involves a **commitment fee.**

- **Commercial paper** is unsecured short-term debt issued by large, financially strong corporations. Although the cost of commercial paper is lower than the cost of bank loans, it can be used only by large firms with exceptionally strong credit ratings.
- Sometimes a borrower will find that it is necessary to borrow on a **secured basis,** in which case the borrower pledges assets such as real estate, securities, equipment, inventories, or accounts receivable as collateral for the loan.

QUESTIONS

(16-1) Define each of the following terms:
  a. Working capital; net working capital; net operating working capital
  b. Inventory conversion period; receivables collection period; payables deferral period; cash conversion cycle
  c. Relaxed NOWC policy; restricted NOWC policy; moderate NOWC policy
  d. Transactions balance; compensating balance; precautionary balance
  e. Cash budget; target cash balance
  f. Trade discounts
  g. Account receivable; days sales outstanding; aging schedule
  h. Credit policy; credit period; credit standards; collection policy; cash discounts
  i. Permanent NOWC; temporary NOWC
  j. Moderate short-term financing policy; aggressive short-term financing policy; conservative short-term financing policy
  k. Maturity matching, or "self-liquidating," approach
  l. Accruals
  m. Trade credit; stretching accounts payable; free trade credit; costly trade credit
  n. Promissory note; line of credit; revolving credit agreement
  o. Commercial paper; secured loan

(16-2) What are the two principal reasons for holding cash? Can a firm estimate its target cash balance by summing the cash held to satisfy each of the two reasons?

(16-3) Is it true that when one firm sells to another on credit, the seller records the transaction as an account receivable while the buyer records it as an account payable and that, disregarding discounts, the receivable typically exceeds the payable by the amount of profit on the sale?

(16-4) What are the four elements of a firm's credit policy? To what extent can firms set their own credit policies as opposed to having to accept policies that are dictated by "the competition"?

(16-5) What are the advantages of matching the maturities of assets and liabilities? What are the disadvantages?

(16-6) From the standpoint of the borrower, is long-term or short-term credit riskier? Explain. Would it ever make sense to borrow on a short-term basis if short-term rates were above long-term rates?

(16-7) "Firms can control their accruals within fairly wide limits." Discuss.

(16-8) Is it true that most firms are able to obtain some free trade credit and that additional trade credit is often available, but at a cost? Explain.

(16-9) What kinds of firms use commercial paper?

SELF-TEST PROBLEMS   Solutions Appear in Appendix A

(ST-1) The Calgary Company is attempting to establish a current assets policy. Fixed assets
Working Capital Policy   are $600,000, and the firm plans to maintain a 50 percent debt-to-assets ratio. Calgary

has no operating current liabilities. The interest rate is 10 percent on all debt. Three alternative current asset policies are under consideration: 40, 50, and 60 percent of projected sales. The company expects to earn 15 percent before interest and taxes on sales of $3 million. Calgary's effective federal-plus-state tax rate is 40 percent. What is the expected return on equity under each alternative?

(ST-2)
Current Asset Financing

Vanderheiden Press Inc. and the Herrenhouse Publishing Company had the following balance sheets as of December 31, 2005 (thousands of dollars):

	Vanderheiden Press	Herrenhouse Publishing
Current assets	$100,000	$ 80,000
Fixed assets (net)	100,000	120,000
Total assets	$200,000	$200,000
Current liabilities	$ 20,000	$ 80,000
Long-term debt	80,000	20,000
Common stock	50,000	50,000
Retained earnings	50,000	50,000
Total liabilities and equity	$200,000	$200,000

Earnings before interest and taxes for both firms are $30 million, and the effective federal-plus-state tax rate is 40 percent.
a. What is the return on equity for each firm if the interest rate on current liabilities is 10 percent and the rate on long-term debt is 13 percent?
b. Assume that the short-term rate rises to 20 percent. While the rate on new long-term debt rises to 16 percent, the rate on existing long-term debt remains unchanged. What would be the return on equity for Vanderheiden Press and Herrenhouse Publishing under these conditions?
c. Which company is in a riskier position? Why?

PROBLEMS

(16-1)
Cash Management

Williams & Sons last year reported sales of $10 million and an inventory turnover ratio of 2. The company is now adopting a new inventory system. If the new system is able to reduce the firm's inventory level and increase the firm's inventory turnover ratio to 5, while maintaining the same level of sales, how much cash will be freed up?

(16-2)
Receivables Investment

Medwig Corporation has a DSO of 17 days. The company averages $3,500 in credit sales each day. What is the company's average accounts receivable?

(16-3)
Cost of Trade Credit

What is the nominal and effective cost of trade credit under the credit terms of 3/15, net 30?

(16-4)
Cost of Trade Credit

A large retailer obtains merchandise under the credit terms of 1/15, net 45, but routinely takes 60 days to pay its bills. Given that the retailer is an important customer, suppliers allow the firm to stretch its credit terms. What is the retailer's effective cost of trade credit?

(16-5)
Accounts Payable

A chain of appliance stores, APP Corporation, purchases inventory with a net price of $500,000 each day. The company purchases the inventory under the credit terms of 2/15, net 40. APP always takes the discount, but takes the full 15 days to pay its bills. What is the average accounts payable for APP?

(16-6)
Receivables Investment

McDowell Industries sells on terms of 3/10, net 30. Total sales for the year are $912,500. Forty percent of the customers pay on the 10th day and take discounts; the other 60 percent pay, on average, 40 days after their purchases.
a. What is the days sales outstanding?

b.   What is the average amount of receivables?

c.   What would happen to average receivables if McDowell toughened up on its collection policy with the result that all nondiscount customers paid on the 30th day?

(16-7)
Cost of Trade Credit
Calculate the nominal annual cost of nonfree trade credit under each of the following terms. Assume payment is made either on the due date or on the discount date.
a.   1/15, net 20.
b.   2/10, net 60.
c.   3/10, net 45.
d.   2/10, net 45.
e.   2/15, net 40.

(16-8)
Cost of Trade Credit
a.   If a firm buys under terms of 3/15, net 45, but actually pays on the 20th day and *still takes the discount,* what is the nominal cost of its nonfree trade credit?
b.   Does it receive more or less credit than it would if it paid within 15 days?

(16-9)
Cost of Trade Credit
Grunewald Industries sells on terms of 2/10, net 40. Gross sales last year were $4,562,500, and accounts receivable averaged $437,500. Half of Grunewald's customers paid on the 10th day and took discounts. What are the nominal and effective costs of trade credit to Grunewald's nondiscount customers? (Hint: Calculate sales/day based on a 365-day year; then get average receivables of discount customers; then find the DSO for the nondiscount customers.)

(16-10)
Effective Cost of Trade Credit
The D.J. Masson Corporation needs to raise $500,000 for 1 year to supply working capital to a new store. Masson buys from its suppliers on terms of 3/10, net 90, and it currently pays on the 10th day and takes discounts, but it could forgo discounts, pay on the 90th day, and get the needed $500,000 in the form of costly trade credit. What is the effective annual interest rate of the costly trade credit?

(16-11)
Cash Conversion Cycle
The Zocco Corporation has an inventory conversion period of 75 days, a receivables collection period of 38 days, and a payables deferral period of 30 days.
a.   What is the length of the firm's cash conversion cycle?
b.   If Zocco's annual sales are $3,421,875 and all sales are on credit, what is the firm's investment in accounts receivable?
c.   How many times per year does Zocco turn over its inventory?

(16-12)
Working Capital Cash Flow Cycle
The Christie Corporation is trying to determine the effect of its inventory turnover ratio and days sales outstanding (DSO) on its cash flow cycle. Christie's sales last year (all on credit) were $150,000, and it earned a net profit of 6 percent, or $9,000. It turned over its inventory 5 times during the year, and its DSO was 36.5 days. The firm had fixed assets totaling $35,000. Christie's payables deferral period is 40 days.
a.   Calculate Christie's cash conversion cycle.
b.   Assuming Christie holds negligible amounts of cash and marketable securities, calculate its total assets turnover and ROA.
c.   Suppose Christie's managers believe that the inventory turnover can be raised to 7.3 times. What would Christie's cash conversion cycle, total assets turnover, and ROA have been if the inventory turnover had been 7.3 for the year?

(16-13)
Working Capital Policy
The Rentz Corporation is attempting to determine the optimal level of current assets for the coming year. Management expects sales to increase to approximately $2 million as a result of an asset expansion presently being undertaken. Fixed assets total $1 million, and the firm wishes to maintain a 60 percent debt ratio. Rentz's interest cost is currently 8 percent on both short-term and longer-term debt (which the firm uses in its permanent structure). Three alternatives regarding the projected current asset level are available to the firm: (1) a tight policy requiring current assets of only 45 percent of projected sales, (2) a moderate policy of 50 percent of sales in current assets, and (3) a relaxed policy requiring current assets of 60 percent of sales. The firm expects to generate earnings before interest and taxes at a rate of 12 percent on total sales.
a.   What is the expected return on equity under each current asset level? (Assume a 40 percent effective federal-plus-state tax rate.)

b. In this problem, we have assumed that the level of expected sales is independent of current asset policy. Is this a valid assumption?

c. How would the overall riskiness of the firm vary under each policy?

(16-14)
Cash Budgeting

Dorothy Koehl recently leased space in the Southside Mall and opened a new business, Koehl's Doll Shop. Business has been good, but Koehl has frequently run out of cash. This has necessitated late payment on certain orders, which, in turn, is beginning to cause a problem with suppliers. Koehl plans to borrow from the bank to have cash ready as needed, but first she needs a forecast of just how much she must borrow. Accordingly, she has asked you to prepare a cash budget for the critical period around Christmas, when needs will be especially high.

Sales are made on a cash basis only. Koehl's purchases must be paid for during the following month. Koehl pays herself a salary of $4,800 per month, and the rent is $2,000 per month. In addition, she must make a tax payment of $12,000 in December. The current cash on hand (on December 1) is $400, but Koehl has agreed to maintain an average bank balance of $6,000—this is her target cash balance. (Disregard till cash, which is insignificant because Koehl keeps only a small amount on hand in order to lessen the chances of robbery.)

The estimated sales and purchases for December, January, and February are shown below. Purchases during November amounted to $140,000.

	Sales	Purchases
December	$160,000	$40,000
January	40,000	40,000
February	60,000	40,000

a. Prepare a cash budget for December, January, and February.

b. Now, suppose Koehl were to start selling on a credit basis on December 1, giving customers 30 days to pay. All customers accept these terms, and all other facts in the problem are unchanged. What would the company's loan requirements be at the end of December in this case? (Hint: The calculations required to answer this question are minimal.)

(16-15)
Cash Discounts

Suppose a firm makes purchases of $3.65 million per year under terms of 2/10, net 30, and takes discounts.

a. What is the average amount of accounts payable net of discounts? (Assume that the $3.65 million of purchases is net of discounts—that is, gross purchases are $3,724,490, discounts are $74,490, and net purchases are $3.65 million.)

b. Is there a cost of the trade credit the firm uses?

c. If the firm did not take discounts but it did pay on the due date, what would be its average payables and the cost of this nonfree trade credit?

d. What would its cost of not taking discounts be if it could stretch its payments to 40 days?

(16-16)
Trade Credit

The Thompson Corporation projects an increase in sales from $1.5 million to $2 million, but it needs an additional $300,000 of current assets to support this expansion. Thompson can finance the expansion by no longer taking discounts, thus increasing accounts payable. Thompson purchases under terms of 2/10, net 30, but it can delay payment for an additional 35 days—paying in 65 days and thus becoming 35 days past due—without a penalty because of its suppliers' current excess capacity problems. What is the effective, or equivalent, annual cost of the trade credit?

(16-17)
Bank Financing

The Raattama Corporation had sales of $3.5 million last year, and it earned a 5 percent return, after taxes, on sales. Recently, the company has fallen behind in its accounts payable. Although its terms of purchase are net 30 days, its accounts payable represent 60 days' purchases. The company's treasurer is seeking to increase bank borrowings in order to become current in meeting its trade obligations (that is, to have 30 days' payables outstanding). The company's balance sheet is as follows (thousands of dollars):

Cash	$ 100	Accounts payable	$ 600
Accounts receivable	300	Bank loans	700
Inventory	1,400	Accruals	200
Current assets	$1,800	Current liabilities	$1,500
Land and buildings	600	Mortgage on real estate	700
Equipment	600	Common stock, $0.10 par	300
		Retained earnings	500
Total assets	$3,000	Total liabilities and equity	$3,000

a. How much bank financing is needed to eliminate the past-due accounts payable?
b. Would you as a bank loan officer make the loan? Why or why not?

SPREADSHEET PROBLEM

(16-18)

Build a Model: Cash Budgeting

CF

e-resource

Start with the partial model in the file *CF2 Ch 16 P18 Build a Model.xls* from the textbook's Web site.

Helen Bowers, owner of Helen's Fashion Designs, is planning to request a line of credit from her bank. She has estimated the following sales forecasts for the firm for parts of 2006 and 2007:

	Sales	Labor and Raw Materials
May 2006	$180,000	$ 90,000
June	180,000	90,000
July	360,000	126,000
August	540,000	882,000
September	720,000	306,000
October	360,000	234,000
November	360,000	162,000
December	90,000	90,000
January 2007	180,000	NA

Collection estimates obtained from the credit and collection department are as follows: collections within the month of sale, 10 percent; collections the month following the sale, 75 percent; collections the second month following the sale, 15 percent. Payments for labor and raw materials are typically made during the month following the one in which these costs have been incurred. Total labor and raw materials costs are estimated for each month as shown above.

General and administrative salaries will amount to approximately $27,000 a month; lease payments under long-term lease contracts will be $9,000 a month; depreciation charges will be $36,000 a month; miscellaneous expenses will be $2,700 a month; income tax payments of $63,000 will be due in both September and December; and a progress payment of $180,000 on a new design studio must be paid in October. Cash on hand on July 1 will amount to $132,000, and a minimum cash balance of $90,000 will be maintained throughout the cash budget period.

a. Prepare a monthly cash budget for the last 6 months of 2006.
b. Prepare an estimate of the required financing (or excess funds)—that is, the amount of money Bowers will need to borrow (or will have available to invest)—for each month during that period.
c. Assume that receipts from sales come in uniformly during the month (that is, cash receipts come in at the rate of 1/30 each day), but all outflows are paid on the 5th of the month. Will this have an effect on the cash budget—in other words,

would the cash budget you have prepared be valid under these assumptions? If not, what can be done to make a valid estimate of peak financing requirements? No calculations are required, although calculations can be used to illustrate the effects.

d. Bowers produces on a seasonal basis, just ahead of sales. Without making any calculations, discuss how the company's current ratio and debt ratio would vary during the year assuming all financial requirements were met by short-term bank loans. Could changes in these ratios affect the firm's ability to obtain bank credit?

e. If its customers began to pay late, this would slow down collections and thus increase the required loan amount. Also, if sales dropped off, this would have an effect on the required loan. Do a sensitivity analysis that shows the effects of these two factors on the maximum loan requirement.

CYBERPROBLEM

Please go to our Web site, **http://ehrhardt.swlearning.com**, to access any Cyberproblems.

THOMSON ONE
Business School Edition

Please go to **http://ehrhardt.swlearning.com** to access any Thomson ONE—Business School Edition problems.

MINI CASE

Dan Barnes, financial manager of Ski Equipment Inc. (SKI), is excited, but apprehensive. The company's founder recently sold his 51 percent controlling block of stock to Kent Koren, who is a big fan of EVA (Economic Value Added). EVA is found by taking the after-tax operating profit and then subtracting the dollar cost of all the capital the firm uses:

$$EVA = NOPAT - \text{Capital costs}$$
$$= EBIT(1 - T) - WACC(\text{Capital employed}).$$

If EVA is positive, then the firm is creating value. On the other hand, if EVA is negative, the firm is not covering its cost of capital, and stockholders' value is being eroded. Koren rewards managers handsomely if they create value, but those whose operations produce negative EVAs are soon looking for work. Koren frequently points out that if a company can generate its current level of sales with fewer assets, it would need less capital. That would, other things held constant, lower capital costs and increase its EVA.

Shortly after he took control of SKI, Kent Koren met with SKI's senior executives to tell them of his plans for the company. First, he presented some EVA data that convinced everyone that SKI had not been creating value in recent years. He then stated, in no uncertain terms, that this situation must change. He noted that SKI's designs of skis, boots, and clothing are acclaimed throughout the industry, but something is seriously amiss elsewhere in the company. Costs are too high, prices are too low, or the company employs too much capital, and he wants SKI's managers to correct the problem or else.

Barnes has long felt that SKI's working capital situation should be studied—the company may have the optimal amounts of cash, securities, receivables, and inventories, but it may also have too much or too little of these items. In the past, the production manager resisted Barnes's efforts to question his holdings of raw materials inventories, the marketing manager resisted questions about finished goods, the sales staff resisted questions about credit policy (which affects accounts receivable), and the treasurer did not want to talk about her cash and securities balances. Koren's speech made it clear that such resistance would no longer be tolerated.

Barnes also knows that decisions about working capital cannot be made in a vacuum. For example, if inventories could be lowered without adversely affecting operations, then less capital would be required, the dollar cost of capital would decline, and EVA would increase. However, lower raw materials inventories might lead to production slowdowns and higher costs, while lower finished goods inventories might lead to the loss of profitable sales. So, before inventories are changed, it will be necessary to study operating as well as financial effects. The situation is the same with regard to cash and receivables. Barnes began collecting the ratios shown below.

	SKI	Industry
Current	1.75	2.25
Quick	0.83	1.20
Debt/assets	58.76%	50.00%
Turnover of cash and securities	16.67	22.22
Days sales outstanding (365-day basis)	45.63	32.00
Inventory turnover	4.82	7.00
Fixed assets turnover	11.35	12.00
Total assets turnover	2.08	3.00
Profit margin on sales	2.07%	3.50%
Return on equity (ROE)	10.45%	21.00%
Payables deferral period	30.00	33.00

	Nov	Dec	Jan	Feb	Mar	Apr
I. COLLECTIONS AND PURCHASES WORKSHEET						
(1) Sales (gross)	$71,218	$ 68,212	$ 65,213	$ 52,475	$42,909	$30,524
Collections						
(2) During month of sale (0.2)(0.98)(month's sales)			12,781.75	10,285.10		
(3) During first month after sale (0.7)(previous month's sales)			47,748.40	45,649.10		
(4) During second month after sale (0.1)(sales 2 months ago)			7,121.80	6,821.20		
(5) Total collections (Lines 2 + 3 + 4)			$67,651.95	$62,755.40		
Purchases						
(6) (0.85)(forecasted sales 2 months from now)		$44,603.75	$36,472.65	$25,945.40		
(7) Payments (1-month lag)			44,603.75	36,472.65		
II. CASH GAIN OR LOSS FOR MONTH						
(8) Collections (from Section I)			$67,651.95	$62,755.40		
(9) Payments for purchases (from Section I)			44,603.75	36,472.65		
(10) Wages and salaries			6,690.56	5,470.90		
(11) Rent			2,500.00	2,500.00		
(12) Taxes						
(13) Total payments			$53,794.31	$44,443.55		
(14) Net cash gain (loss) during month (Line 8 – Line 13)			$13,857.64	$18,311.85		
III. CASH SURPLUS OR LOAN REQUIREMENT						
(15) Cash at beginning of month if no borrowing is done			$ 3,000.00	$16,857.64		
(16) Cumulative cash (cash at start + gain or − loss = Line 14 + Line 15)			16,857.64	35,169.49		
(17) Target cash balance			1,500.00	1,500.00		
(18) Cumulative surplus cash or loans outstanding to maintain $1,500 target cash balance (Line 16 − Line 17)			$15,357.64	$33,669.49		

a. Barnes plans to use the preceding ratios as the starting point for discussions with SKI's operating executives. He wants everyone to think about the pros and cons of changing each type of current asset and how changes would interact to affect profits and EVA. Based on the data, does SKI seem to be following a relaxed, moderate, or restricted working capital policy?

b. How can one distinguish between a relaxed but rational working capital policy and a situation in which a firm simply has a lot of current assets because it is inefficient? Does SKI's working capital policy seem appropriate?

c. Calculate the firm's cash conversion cycle. Assume a 365-day year.

d. What might SKI do to reduce its cash without harming operations?

In an attempt to better understand SKI's cash position, Barnes developed a cash budget. Data for the first 2 months of the year are shown above. (Note that Barnes's preliminary cash budget does not account for interest income or interest expense.) He has the figures for the other months, but they are not shown.

e. Should depreciation expense be explicitly included in the cash budget? Why or why not?

f. In his preliminary cash budget, Barnes has assumed that all sales are collected and, thus, that SKI has no bad debts. Is this realistic? If not, how would bad debts be dealt with in a cash budgeting sense? (Hint: Bad debts will affect collections but not purchases.)

g. Barnes's cash budget for the entire year, although not given here, is based heavily on his forecast for monthly sales. Sales are expected to be extremely low between May and September but then increase dramatically in the fall and winter. November is typically the firm's best month, when SKI ships equipment to retailers for the holiday season. Interestingly, Barnes's forecasted cash budget indicates that the company's cash holdings will exceed the targeted cash balance every month except for October and November, when shipments will be high but collections will not be coming in until later. Based on the ratios shown earlier, does it appear that SKI's target cash balance is appropriate? In addition to possibly lowering the target cash balance, what actions might SKI take to better improve its cash management policies, and how might that affect its EVA?

h. What reasons might SKI have for maintaining a relatively high amount of cash?

i. What are the three categories of inventory costs? If the company takes steps to reduce its inventory, what effect would this have on the various costs of holding inventory?

j. Is there any reason to think that SKI may be holding too much inventory? If so, how would that affect EVA and ROE?

k. If the company reduces its inventory without adversely affecting sales, what effect should this have on the company's cash position (1) in the short run and (2) in the long run? Explain in terms of the cash budget and the balance sheet.

l. Barnes knows that SKI sells on the same credit terms as other firms in its industry. Use the ratios presented earlier to explain whether SKI's customers pay more or less promptly than those of its competitors. If there are differences, does that suggest that SKI should tighten or loosen its credit policy? What four variables make up a firm's credit policy, and in what direction should each be changed by SKI?

m. Does SKI face any risks if it tightens its credit policy?

n. If the company reduces its DSO without seriously affecting sales, what effect would this have on its cash position (1) in the short run and (2) in the long run? Answer in terms of the cash budget and the balance sheet. What effect should this have on EVA in the long run?

In addition to improving the management of its current assets, SKI is also reviewing the ways in which it finances its current assets. With this concern in mind, Dan is also trying to answer the following questions.

o. Is it likely that SKI could make significantly greater use of accruals?

p. Assume that SKI buys on terms of 1/10, net 30, but that it can get away with paying on the 40th day if it chooses not to take discounts. Also, assume that it purchases $506,985 of equipment per year, net of discounts. How much free trade credit can the company get, how much costly trade credit can it get, and what is the percentage cost of the costly credit? Should SKI take discounts?

q. SKI tries to match the maturity of its assets and liabilities. Describe how SKI could adopt either a more aggressive or more conservative financing policy.

r. What are the advantages and disadvantages of using short-term debt as a source of financing?

s. Would it be feasible for SKI to finance with commercial paper?

SELECTED ADDITIONAL REFERENCES AND CASES

Gallinger, George W., and P. Basil Healy, *Liquidity Analysis and Management* (Reading, MA: Addison-Wesley, 1991).

Hill, Ned C., and William L. Sartoris, *Short-Term Financial Management* (New York: Prentice-Hall, 1995).

Maness, Terry S., and John T. Zietlow, *Short-Term Financial Management* (Mason, OH: Thomson South-Western, 2004).

The following articles provide more information on short-term financial management:

Gentry, James A., "State of the Art of Short-Run Financial Management," *Financial Management,* Summer 1998, 41–57.

Gentry, James A., and Jesus M. De La Garza, "Monitoring Accounts Payables," *Financial Review,* November 1990, 559–576.

Gentry, James A., R. Vaidyanathan, and Hei Wai Lee, "A Weighted Cash Conversion Cycle," *Financial Management,* Spring 1990, 90–99.

Mitchell, Karlyn, "The Debt Maturity Choice: An Empirical Investigation," *Journal of Financial Research,* Winter 1993, 309–320.

For more information on cash management, see

Summers, Bruce J., "Clearing and Payment Systems: The Role of the Central Bank," *Federal Reserve Bulletin,* February 1991, 81–91.

Wood, John C., and Dolores D. Smith, "Electronic Transfer of Government Benefits," *Federal Reserve Bulletin,* April 1991, 204–207.

Stone, Bernell K., and Tom W. Miller, "Daily Cash Forecasting with Multiplicative Models of Cash Flow Patterns," *Financial Management,* Winter 1987, 45–54.

For more information on marketable securities, see

Brown, Keith C., and Scott L. Lummer, "A Reexamination of the Covered Call Option Strategy for Corporate Cash Management," *Financial Management,* Summer 1986, 13–17.

Kamath, Ravindra R., et al., "Management of Excess Cash: Practices and Developments," *Financial Management,* Autumn 1985, 70–77.

Zivney, Terry L., and Michael J. Alderson, "Hedged Dividend Capture with Stock Index Options," *Financial Management,* Summer 1986, 5–12.

For additional insights into the problems of inventory management, see

Followill, Richard A., Michael Schellenger, and Patrick H. Marchard, "Economic Order Quantities, Volume Discounts, and Wealth Maximization," *The Financial Review,* February 1990, 143–152.

Articles that address credit policy and receivables management include the following:

Gallinger, George W., and A. James Ifflander, "Monitoring Accounts Receivable Using Variance Analysis," *Financial Management,* Winter 1986, 69–76.

Mian, Shehzad L., and Clifford W. Smith, "Extending Trade Credit and Financing Receivables," *Journal of Applied Corporate Finance,* Spring 1994, 75–84.

For more on trade credit, see

Adams, Paul D., Steve B. Wyatt, and Yong H. Kim, "A Contingent Claims Analysis of Trade Credit," *Financial Management,* Autumn 1992, 104–112.

The following cases from the Finance Online Case Library *cover many of the concepts discussed in this chapter and are available at http://www.textchoice.com:*

Case 29, "Office Mates, Inc.," which illustrates how changes in current asset policy affect expected profitability and risk.

Case 32, "Alpine Wear, Inc.," which illustrates the mechanics of the cash budget and the rationale behind its use.

Case 32A, "Toy World, Inc.," and Case 32B, "Sorenson Stove Company," which deal with cash budgeting.

Case 33, "Upscale Toddlers, Inc.," which deals with credit policy changes.

Case 34, "Texas Rose Company," which focuses on receivables management.

Case 62, "Western Supply Company," which illustrates the effects of a change in credit policy on corporate profitability and cash flow.

CHAPTER 17

Multinational Corporate Finance*

From the end of World War II until the 1970s, the United States dominated the world economy. However, that situation no longer exists. Raw materials, finished goods, services, and money flow freely across most national boundaries, as do innovative ideas and new technologies. World-class U.S. companies are making breakthroughs in foreign labs, obtaining capital from foreign investors, and putting foreign employees on the fast track to the top. Dozens of top U.S. manufacturers, including Dow Chemical, Colgate-Palmolive, Gillette, Hewlett-Packard, and Xerox, sell more of their products outside the United States than they do at home. Service firms are not far behind, as Citigroup, Disney, McDonald's, and Time Warner all receive more than 20 percent of their revenues from foreign sales.

Successful global companies must conduct business in different economies, and they must be sensitive to the many subtleties of different cultures and political systems. Accordingly, they find it useful to blend into the foreign landscape to win product acceptance and avoid political problems.

At the same time, foreign-based multinationals are arriving on American shores in ever greater numbers. Sweden's ABB, the Netherlands' Philips, France's Thomson, and Japan's Fujitsu and Honda are all waging campaigns to be identified as American companies that employ Americans, transfer technology to America, and help the U.S. trade balance. Few Americans know or care that Thomson owns the RCA and General Electric names in consumer electronics, or that Philips owns Magnavox.

The emergence of "world companies" raises a host of questions for governments. For example, should domestic firms be favored, or does it make no difference what a company's nationality is as long as it provides domestic jobs? Should a company make an effort to keep jobs in its home country, or should it produce or provide services where costs are lowest? What nation controls the technology developed by a multinational corporation, particularly if the technology can be used in military applications? Must a multinational company adhere to rules imposed in its home country with respect to its operations outside the home country? Keep these questions in mind as you read this chapter. When you finish it, you should have a better appreciation of both the problems facing governments and the difficult but profitable opportunities facing managers of multinational companies.

---

*This chapter was coauthored with Professor Roy Crum of the University of Florida and Subu Venkataraman with Morgan Stanley.

Managers of multinational companies must deal with a wide range of issues that are not present when a company operates in a single country. In this chapter, we highlight the key differences between multinational and domestic corporations, and we discuss the effect these differences have on the financial management of multinational businesses.

MULTINATIONAL, OR GLOBAL, CORPORATIONS

e-resource

The textbook's Web site contains an Excel file that will guide you through the chapter's calculations. The file for this chapter is **CF2 Ch 17 Tool Kit.xls,** *and we encourage you to open the file and follow along as you read the chapter.*

The term **multinational,** or **global, corporation** is used to describe a firm that operates in an integrated fashion in a number of countries. During the past 20 years, a new and fundamentally different form of international commercial activity has developed, and this has greatly increased worldwide economic and political interdependence. Rather than merely buying resources from and selling goods to foreign nations, multinational firms now make direct investments in fully integrated operations, from extraction of raw materials, through the manufacturing process, to distribution to consumers throughout the world. Today, multinational corporate networks control a large and growing share of the world's technological, marketing, and productive resources.

Companies, both U.S. and foreign, "go global" for six primary reasons:

1. *To broaden their markets.* After a company has saturated its home market, growth opportunities are often better in foreign markets. Thus, such homegrown firms as Coca-Cola and McDonald's are aggressively expanding into overseas markets, and foreign firms such as Sony and Toshiba now dominate the U.S. consumer electronics market. Also, as products become more complex, and development becomes more expensive, it is necessary to sell more units to cover overhead costs, so larger markets are critical. Thus, movie companies have "gone global" to get the volume necessary to support pictures such as *Lord of the Rings.*

2. *To seek raw materials.* Many U.S. oil companies, such as ExxonMobil, have major subsidiaries around the world to ensure access to the basic resources needed to sustain the companies' primary business line.

3. *To seek new technology.* No single nation holds a commanding advantage in all technologies, so companies are scouring the globe for leading scientific and design ideas. For example, Xerox has introduced more than 80 different office copiers in the United States that were engineered and built by its Japanese joint venture, Fuji Xerox. Similarly, versions of the superconcentrated detergent that Procter & Gamble first formulated in Japan in response to a rival's product are now being marketed in Europe and the United States.

4. *To seek production efficiency.* Companies in high-cost countries are shifting production to low-cost regions. For example, GE has production and assembly plants in Mexico, South Korea, and Singapore, and Japanese manufacturers are shifting some of their production to lower-cost countries in the Pacific Rim. BMW, in response to high production costs in Germany, has built assembly plants in the United States. The ability to shift production from country to country has important implications for labor costs in all countries. For example, when Xerox threatened to move its copier rebuilding work to Mexico, its union in Rochester agreed to work rule changes and productivity improvements that kept the operation in the United States. Some multinational companies make decisions almost daily on where to shift production. When Dow Chemical saw European demand for a certain solvent declining, the company scaled back production at a German plant and shifted its production to another chemical that had previously been imported from the United States. Relying on complex computer models for making such decisions, Dow runs its plants at peak capacity and thus keeps capital costs down.

5. *To avoid political and regulatory hurdles.* The primary reason Japanese auto companies moved production to the United States was to get around U.S. import quo-

tas. Now Honda, Nissan, Toyota, Mazda, and Mitsubishi are all assembling vehicles in the United States. One of the factors that prompted U.S. pharmaceutical maker SmithKline and Britain's Beecham to merge was that they wanted to avoid licensing and regulatory delays in their largest markets, Western Europe and the United States. Now SmithKline Beecham can identify itself as an inside player in both Europe and the United States. Similarly, when Germany's BASF launched biotechnology research at home, it confronted legal and political challenges from the environmentally conscious Green movement. In response, BASF shifted its cancer and immune system research to two laboratories in the Boston suburbs. This location is attractive not only because of its large number of engineers and scientists but also because the Boston area has resolved controversies involving safety, animal rights, and the environment. "We decided it would be better to have the laboratories located where we have fewer insecurities about what will happen in the future," said Rolf-Dieter Acker, BASF's director of biotechnology research.

6. *To diversify*. By establishing worldwide production facilities and markets, firms can cushion the impact of adverse economic trends in any single country. For example, General Motors softened the blow of poor sales in the United States during a recent recession with strong sales by its European subsidiaries. In general, geographic diversification works because the economic ups and downs of different countries are not perfectly correlated. Therefore, companies investing overseas benefit from diversification in the same way that individuals benefit from investing in a broad portfolio of stocks.

Interesting reports about the effect of trade on the U.S. economy can be found on the United States Trade Representative's home page at http://www .ustr.gov.

Over the past 10 to 15 years, there has been an increasing amount of investment in the United States by foreign corporations, and in foreign nations by U.S. corporations. This trend is important because of its implications for eroding the traditional doctrine of independence and self-reliance that has been a hallmark of U.S. policy. Just as U.S. corporations with extensive overseas operations are said to use their economic power to exert substantial economic and political influence over host governments in many parts of the world, it is feared that foreign corporations are gaining similar sway over U.S. policy. These developments suggest an increasing degree of mutual influence and interdependence among business enterprises and nations, to which the United States is not immune.

SELF-TEST QUESTIONS	What is a multinational corporation?
	Why do companies "go global"?

MULTINATIONAL VERSUS DOMESTIC FINANCIAL MANAGEMENT

In theory, the concepts and procedures discussed in earlier chapters are valid for both domestic and multinational operations. However, six major factors distinguish financial management in firms operating entirely within a single country from firms that operate globally:

1. *Different currency denominations*. Cash flows in various parts of a multinational corporate system will be denominated in different currencies. Hence, an analysis of exchange rates must be included in all financial analyses.

2. *Economic and legal ramifications*. Each country has its own unique economic and legal systems, and these differences can cause significant problems when a corporation tries to coordinate and control its worldwide operations. For example, differences in tax laws among countries can cause a given economic transaction to have strikingly different after-tax consequences, depending on where the transaction

THE EURO: WHAT YOU NEED TO KNOW

Twelve countries have adopted the euro: Greece, Belgium, Austria, Finland, France, Luxembourg, Italy, the Netherlands, Germany, Spain, Ireland, and Portugal. Britain, Switzerland, and the Scandinavian countries chose not to join the economic and monetary union (EMU) because they did not want to give up control of their currencies.

Euro bills and coins began circulating January 1, 2002. After euro bills and coins began circulating, there was a six-month phase-in period, but now all transactions must be made in euros. (People with the previous currencies still have 10 more years to convert them at a bank at a fixed exchange rate.)

The value of the euro fluctuates relative to other currencies, such as the U.S. dollar. Finally, instead of each country having a central bank to manage its currency, the European Central Bank, located in Frankfurt, Germany, sets interest rates and manages monetary policy for the entire region.

Source: From Helene Cooper, "Europe Unites: The Launch of the Euro; The Euro: What You Need to Know," *The Wall Street Journal,* January 4, 1999, A5.

For more on the euro, see http:// www.europa.eu.int/ euro/entry.html.

occurs. Similarly, differences in legal systems of host nations, such as the Common Law of Great Britain versus the French Civil Law, complicate matters ranging from the simple recording of business transactions to the role played by the judiciary in resolving conflicts. Such differences can restrict multinational corporations' flexibility in deploying resources, and can even make procedures that are required in one part of the company illegal in another part. These differences also make it difficult for executives trained in one country to move easily to another.

3. *Language differences.* The ability to communicate is critical in all business transactions, and here U.S. citizens are often at a disadvantage because we are generally fluent only in English, while European and Japanese businesspeople are usually fluent in several languages, including English. Thus, they can penetrate our markets more easily than we can penetrate theirs.

4. *Cultural differences.* Even within geographic regions that are considered relatively homogeneous, different countries have unique cultural heritages that shape values and influence the conduct of business. Multinational corporations find that matters such as defining the appropriate goals of the firm, attitudes toward risk, dealings with employees, and the ability to curtail unprofitable operations vary dramatically from one country to the next.

5. *Role of governments.* Most financial models assume the existence of a competitive marketplace in which the terms of trade are determined by the participants. The government, through its power to establish basic ground rules, is involved in the process, but its role is minimal. Thus, the market provides the primary barometer of success, and it gives the best clues about what must be done to remain competitive. This view of the process is reasonably correct for the United States and Western Europe, but it does not accurately describe the situation in most of the world. Frequently, the terms under which companies compete, the actions that must be taken or avoided, and the terms of trade on various transactions are determined not in the marketplace but by direct negotiation between host governments and multinational corporations. This is essentially a political process, and it must be treated as such. Thus, our traditional financial models have to be recast to include political and other noneconomic aspects of the decision process.

6. *Political risk.* A nation is free to place constraints on the transfer of corporate resources and even to expropriate without compensation assets within its boundaries. This is *political risk,* and it tends to be largely a given rather than a variable that can be changed by negotiation. Political risk varies from country to country, and it must be addressed explicitly in any financial analysis. Another aspect of

political risk is terrorism against U.S. firms or executives. For example, U.S. and Japanese executives have been kidnapped and held for ransom—with some killed to prove that the kidnappers were serious—in several South American countries.

These six factors complicate financial management, and they increase the risks faced by multinational firms. However, the prospects for high returns, diversification benefits, and other factors make it worthwhile for firms to accept these risks and learn how to manage them.

SELF-TEST QUESTION   Identify and briefly discuss six major factors that complicate financial management in multinational firms.

EXCHANGE RATES

The Bloomberg World Currency Values site provides up-to-the-minute foreign currency values versus the U.S. dollar, as well as a cross-currency table similar to that found in The Wall Street Journal *for the world's major currencies. The site can be accessed at http://www .bloomberg.com/ markets/currencies/ fxc.html.*

An **exchange rate** specifies the number of units of a given currency that can be purchased with one unit of another currency. Exchange rates appear daily in the financial sections of newspapers, such as *The Wall Street Journal,* and at financial Web sites, such as **http://www.bloomberg.com**. The values shown in Column 1 of Table 17-1 are the number of U.S. dollars required to purchase one unit of a foreign currency; this is called a **direct quotation.** Direct quotations have a dollar sign in their quotation and state the number of dollars per foreign currency unit, such as dollars per euro. Thus, the direct U.S. dollar quotation for the euro is $1.2290, because one euro could be bought for 1.2290 dollars.

The exchange rates given in Column 2 represent the number of units of a foreign currency that can be purchased for one U.S. dollar; these are called **indirect quotations.** Indirect quotations often begin with the foreign currency's equivalent to the dollar sign and express the foreign currency per dollar, such as euros per dollar. Thus, the indirect quotation for the euro is €0.8137. (The "€" stands for *euro,* and it is analogous to the symbol "$.")

Normal practice in currency trading centers is to use the indirect quotations (Column 2) for all currencies other than British pounds and euros, for which the direct quotations are given. Thus we speak of the pound as "selling at 1.8401 dollars, or at $1.8401," and the euro as "selling at $1.2290." For all other currencies, say, the Japanese yen, we would quote the dollars as "being at ¥111.0371," where the "¥" stands for *yen* and is analogous

TABLE 17-1 | Selected Exchange Rates

	Direct Quotation: U.S. Dollars Required to Buy One Unit of Foreign Currency (1)	Indirect Quotation: Number of Units of Foreign Currency per U.S. Dollar (2)
Canadian dollar	$0.7401	1.3512
Japanese yen	0.0090	111.0371
Mexican peso	0.0876	11.4181
Swiss franc	0.8070	1.2392
U.K. (British) pound	1.8401	0.5434
Euro	1.2290	0.8137

Note: British pounds and euros are quoted as direct quotations, so Column 2 equals 1.0 divided by Column 1 for these currencies. All other currencies are quoted as indirect quotations, so Column 1 equals 1.0 divided by Column 2 for these currencies.

Source: The Wall Street Journal, **http://online.wsj.com**; quotes for June 4, 2004.

to the symbol "$." This convention eliminates confusion when comparing quotations from one trading center—say, New York—with those from another—say, London or Zurich.

We can use the data in Table 17-1 to show how to work with exchange rates. Suppose a tourist flies from New York to London, then to Paris, and then on to Geneva. She then flies to Montreal, and finally back to New York. Her tour includes lodging, food, and transportation, but she must pay for any other expenses. When she arrives at London's Heathrow Airport, she goes to the bank to check the foreign exchange listings. The rate she observes for U.S. dollars is $1.8401; this means that £1 will cost $1.8401. Assume that she exchanges $3,000:

$$\$3,000 = \frac{\$3,000}{\$1.8401 \text{ per pound}} = £1630.35$$

and enjoys a week's vacation in London, ending with £1,000.

After taking a train under the Channel to France, she realizes that she needs to exchange her 1,000 remaining pounds for euros. However, what she sees on the board is the direct quotation for dollars per pound and the direct quotation for dollars per euro. The exchange rate between any two currencies other than dollars is called a **cross rate.** Cross rates are actually calculated on the basis of various currencies relative to the U.S. dollar. For example, the cross rate between British pounds and euros is computed as follows:

$$\text{Cross rate of euros per pound} = \frac{\$1.8401 \text{ per pound}}{\$1.2290 \text{ per euro}} = 1.4972 \text{ euros per pound.}$$

Therefore, for every British pound she would receive 1.4972 euros, so she would receive 1.4972 (1,000) = 1,497.20 euros.

She has 800 euros remaining when she finishes touring in France and arrives in Geneva. She again needs to determine a cross rate, this time between euros and Swiss francs. The quotes she sees, as shown in Table 17-1, are a direct quote for euros ($1.2290 per euro) and an indirect quote for Swiss francs (SFr 1.2392 per dollar). To find the cross rate for Swiss francs per euro, she makes the following calculation:

$$\begin{aligned}
\text{Cross rate of Swiss francs per euro} &= \left(\frac{\text{Swiss francs}}{\text{Dollar}}\right)\left(\frac{\text{Dollars}}{\text{euro}}\right)\\
&= (\text{SFr } 1.2392 \text{ per dollar})(\$1.2290 \text{ per euro})\\
&= 1.5230 \text{ Swiss francs per euro.}
\end{aligned}$$

Therefore, for every euro she would receive 1.5230 Swiss francs, so she would receive 1.5230(800) = 1,218.40 Swiss francs.

She has 500 Swiss francs remaining when she leaves Geneva and arrives in Montreal. She again needs to determine a cross rate, this time between Swiss francs and Canadian dollars. The quotes she sees, as shown in Table 17-1, are an indirect quote for Swiss francs (SFr 1.2392 per dollar) and an indirect quote for Canadian dollars (1.3512 Canadian dollars per U.S. dollar). To find the cross rate for Canadian dollars per Swiss franc, she makes the following calculation:

$$\begin{aligned}
\text{Cross rate of Canadian dollars per Swiss franc} &= \frac{\left(\dfrac{\text{Canadian dollars}}{\text{U.S. dollar}}\right)}{\left(\dfrac{\text{Swiss francs}}{\text{U.S. dollar}}\right)}\\[2ex]
&= \frac{(1.3512 \text{ Canadian dollars per U.S. dollar})}{(\text{SFr } 1.2392 \text{ per U.S. dollar})}\\[2ex]
&= 1.0904 \text{ Canadian dollar per Swiss franc.}
\end{aligned}$$

For a nice currency calculator to determine the exchange rate between any two currencies, see http://www.finance .yahoo.com/currency.

Therefore, she would receive 1.0904(500) = 545.20 Canadian dollars.

After leaving Montreal and arriving at New York, she has 100 Canadian dollars remaining. She sees the indirect quote for Canadian dollars and converts the 100 Canadian dollars to U.S. dollars as follows:

$$100 \text{ Canadian dollars} = \frac{100 \text{ Canadian dollars}}{1.3512 \text{ Canadian dollars per U.S. dollar}} = \$74.01$$

In this example, we made three assumptions. First, we assumed that our traveler had to calculate all the cross rates. For retail transactions, it is customary to display the cross rates directly instead of a series of dollar rates. Second, we assumed that exchange rates remain constant over time. Actually, exchange rates vary every day, often dramatically. We will have more to say about exchange rate fluctuations in the next section. Finally, we assumed that there were no transactions costs involved in exchanging currencies. In reality, small retail exchange transactions such as those in our example usually involve fixed and/or sliding scale fees that can easily consume 5 or more percent of the transaction amount. However, credit card purchases minimize these fees.

Major business publications, such as *The Wall Street Journal*, and Web sites, such as **http://www.bloomberg.com**, regularly report cross rates among key currencies. A set of cross rates is given in Table 17-2. When examining the table, note the following points:

1. Column 1 gives indirect quotes for dollars, that is, units of a foreign currency that can be bought with one U.S. dollar. Examples: $1 will buy 0.8137 euro or 1.2392 Swiss francs. Note the consistency with Table 17-1, Column 2.
2. Other columns show number of units of other currencies that can be bought with one pound, one Swiss franc, etc. For example, the euro column shows that 1 euro will buy 1.6606 Canadian dollars, 136.4646 Japanese yen, or 1.2290 U.S. dollars.
3. The rows show direct quotes, that is, number of units of the currency of the country listed in the left column required to buy one unit of the currency listed in the top row. The bottom row is particularly important for U.S. companies, as it shows the direct quotes for the U.S. dollar. This row is consistent with Column 1 of Table 17-1.
4. Note that the values on the bottom row of Table 17-2 are reciprocals of the corresponding values in the first column. For example, the U.K. row in the first column shows 0.5434 pound per dollar, and the pound column in the bottom row shows 1/0.5434 = 1.8401 dollars per pound.
5. Now notice, by reading down the euro column, that one euro was worth 1.5230 Swiss francs. This is the same cross rate that we calculated for the U.S. tourist in our example.

TABLE 17-2 | Key Currency Cross Rates

	Dollar	Euro	Pound	SFranc	Peso	Yen	CdnDlr
Canada	1.3512	1.6606	2.4863	1.0904	0.1183	0.0122	—
Japan	111.0371	136.4646	204.3194	89.6039	9.7247	—	82.1767
Mexico	11.4181	14.0328	21.0104	9.2141	—	0.1028	8.4503
Switzerland	1.2392	1.5230	2.2803	—	0.1085	0.0112	0.9171
United Kingdom	0.5434	0.6679	—	0.4385	0.0476	0.0049	0.4022
Euro	0.8137	—	1.4972	0.6566	0.0713	0.0073	0.6022
United States	—	1.2290	1.8401	0.8070	0.0876	0.0090	0.7401

Source: Derived from Table 17-1; quotes for June 4, 2004.

The tie-in with the dollar ensures that all currencies are related to one another in a consistent manner. If this consistency did not exist, currency traders could profit by buying undervalued and selling overvalued currencies. This process, known as *arbitrage,* works to bring about an equilibrium wherein the same relationship described earlier would exist. Currency traders are constantly operating in the market, seeking small inconsistencies from which they can profit. The traders' existence enables the rest of us to assume that currency markets are in equilibrium and that, at any point in time, cross rates are all internally consistent.

SELF-TEST QUESTIONS

What is an exchange rate?

Explain the difference between direct and indirect quotations.

What is a cross rate?

THE INTERNATIONAL MONETARY SYSTEM

Just as the demand for consumer goods, such as for Tommy Hilfiger jeans and Nike shoes, changes over time, so does the demand for currency. One factor affecting currency demand is the balance of trade between two countries. For example, U.S. importers must buy yen to pay for Japanese goods, whereas Japanese importers must buy U.S. dollars to pay for U.S. goods. If U.S. imports from Japan were to exceed U.S. exports to Japan, then the U.S. would have a **trade deficit** with Japan, and there would be a greater demand for yen than for dollars. Capital movements also affect currency demand. For example, suppose interest rates in the United States were higher than those in Japan. To take advantage of high U.S. interest rates, Japanese banks, corporations, and sophisticated individuals would buy dollars with yen and then use those dollars to purchase high-yielding U.S. securities. This would create greater demand for dollars than for yen.

Without any government intervention, the relative prices of yen and dollars would fluctuate in response to changes in supply and demand in much the same way that prices of consumer goods fluctuate. For example, if U.S. consumers were to increase their demand for Japanese electronic products, then the accompanying increase in demand for yen would cause its value to increase relative to the dollar. In this situation, the strong yen would be due to fundamental economic forces.

However, governments can and do intervene. A country's central bank can artificially prop up its currency by using its reserves of gold or foreign currencies to purchase its own currency in the open market. This creates artificial demand for its own currency, causing its value to be artificially high. A central bank can also keep its currency at an artificially low value by selling its own currency in the open markets. This increases the currency's supply, which reduces its price.

Why might an artificially low currency be a problem? After all, a cheap currency makes it less expensive for other nations to purchase the country's goods, which creates jobs in the exporting country. However, an artificially low currency value raises the cost of imports, which increases inflation. In addition, high import prices allow competing domestic manufacturers to raise their prices as well, further boosting inflation. The government intervention that causes the artificially low value also contributes to inflation: When a government creates currency to sell in the open markets, this increases the money supply, and, all else held constant, an increasing money supply leads to still more inflation. Thus, artificially holding down the value of a currency stimulates exports but at the expense of potentially overheating and inflating the economy. Also, other countries— whose economies are being weakened because their manufacturers cannot compete against the artificially low prices—may retaliate and impose tariffs or other restrictions on the country that is holding its currency value down.

For example, China has for several years artificially held down the value of the yuan (also called the rinminbi). This has helped make it number 1 in exports and greatly stimulated its economy. However, in 2004 the Chinese economy was growing at an unsustainably high rate, and inflation was rising rapidly. The United States and other nations were putting pressure on the Chinese government to allow the yuan to rise, which would help their economies by slowing Chinese exports and stimulating their own exports to China.

A currency that is artificially high has the opposite effects: Inflation will be held down, and citizens can purchase imported goods at low domestic prices, but exporting industries are hurt, as are domestic industries that compete with the cheap imports. Because there is relatively little external demand for the currency, the government will have to create demand by purchasing its own currency, paying with either gold or foreign currencies held by its central bank. Over time, supporting an inflated currency can deplete the gold and foreign currency reserves, making it impossible to continue propping up the currency.

The following sections describe ways that governments handle changes in currency demands.

The Bretton Woods Fixed Exchange Rate System

From the end of World War II until August 1971, most of the industrialized world operated under the Bretton Woods **fixed exchange rate system** administered by the International Monetary Fund (IMF). Under this system, the U.S. dollar was linked to gold (at $35 per ounce), and other currencies were then tied to the dollar. The United States took actions to keep the price of gold at $35 per ounce, and central banks acted to keep exchange rates between other currencies and the dollar within narrow limits. For example, when the demand for pounds was falling, the Bank of England would step in and buy pounds to push up their price, offering gold or foreign currencies in exchange for pounds. Conversely, when the demand for pounds was too high, the Bank of England would sell pounds for dollars or gold. The Federal Reserve in the United States performed the same functions, and central banks of other countries operated similarly. These actions artificially matched supply and demand, keeping exchange rates stable, but they didn't address the underlying imbalance. For example, if the high demand for pounds occurred because British productivity was rising and British goods were improving in quality, then the underlying demand for pounds would continue in spite of central bank intervention. In such a situation the Bank of England would find it necessary to continually sell pounds indefinitely. If the central bank stopped selling pounds, their value would rise; that is, the pound would strengthen and exceed the agreed upon limits.

Modern Exchange Rate Systems

Many countries found it difficult and economically painful to maintain the fixed exchange rates required by Bretton Woods. This system began to crumble in August 1971, and it was abandoned completely by the end of 1973. The following sections describe several modern exchange rate systems.

FLOATING RATES   In the early 1970s, the U.S. dollar was cut loose from the gold standard and, in effect, allowed to "float." The United States and most other major industrial nations currently operate under a system of **floating exchange rates**, whereby currency prices are allowed to seek their own levels, with only modest central bank intervention to smooth out extreme exchange rate fluctuations. For example, suppose the dollar cost of a pound were $1.8401 as shown in Table 17-1. If there were excessive demand for pounds caused by a U.S. trade deficit with Great Britain, then the price of pounds might increase to $2. In this situation, the pound is said to be *appreciating*, because a pound would now buy more dollars. In other words, a pound is now worth more than it was. This is called **currency appreciation**. Conversely, the dollar would be *depreciating*, because the dollar now buys fewer pounds (a dollar would previously buy 1/1.8401 = 0.5434 pound, but afterward it would buy only 1/2 = 0.5 pound). This is called **currency depreciation**. Notice that the more costly pound would make British imports more expensive to U.S. consumers, which would reduce imports—and, consequently, the demand for pounds—until the exchange rate reached equilibrium.

Exchange rate fluctuations can have a profound effect on profits. For example, in 1985 it cost Honda Motors 2,380,000 yen to build a particular model in Japan and ship it to the United States. The model carried a U.S. sticker price of $12,000. Because the $12,000 sales price was the equivalent of (238 yen per dollar)($12,000) = 2,856,000 yen, which was 20 percent above the 2,380,000 yen cost, the automaker had built a 20 percent markup into the U.S. sales price. However, three years later the dollar had depreciated to 128 yen. Now if the car still sold for $12,000, the yen return to Honda would be only (128 yen per dollar)($12,000) = 1,536,000 yen, and the automaker would be losing about 35 percent on each auto sold. Therefore, the depreciation of the dollar against the yen turned a healthy profit into a huge loss. In fact, for Honda to maintain its 20 percent markup, the model would have to sell in the United States for 2,856,000 yen/(128 yen per dollar) = $22,312.50. This situation, which grew even worse, led Honda to build its most popular model, the Accord, in Marysville, Ohio.

The inherent volatility of exchange rates under a floating system increases the uncertainty of the cash flows for a multinational corporation. Because its cash flows are generated in many parts of the world, they are denominated in many different currencies. When exchange rates change, the dollar-equivalent value of the company's consolidated cash flows also fluctuates. For example, Toyota estimates that each 1 yen drop in the dollar reduces the company's annual net income by about 10 billion yen. This is known as **exchange rate risk**, and it is a major factor differentiating a global company from a purely domestic one.

According to the International Monetary Fund, about 36 currencies have floating exchange rates, including the dollar, euro, pound, and yen. The following sections describe other exchange-rate regimes.

OTHER EXCHANGE-RATE REGIMES

The International Monetary Fund reports a full listing of exchange rate arrangements. See http://www.imf.org/ external/np/mfd/er/ index.asp. The IMF also publishes a more detailed listing in its Annual Report on Exchange Arrangements and Exchange Restrictions. *For another listing of world currencies, see http://fx.sauder .ubc.ca/currency_ table.html.*

A few countries don't have their own separate legal tender, but instead use the currency of another nation. For example, Ecuador has used the U.S. dollar since September 2000. Other countries belong to a monetary union, such as the 12 European Monetary Union nations whose currency is the euro. Member nations of the Eastern Caribbean Currency Union, the West African Economic and Monetary Union (WAEMU), and the Central African Economic and Monetary Community (CAEMC) use their respective union's currency. The euro is allowed to float, but the currencies of the other unions are pegged to some other currency. For example, the Eastern Caribbean dollar is pegged to the U.S. dollar, and the CFA franc (used by both the WAEMU and CAEMC) is pegged to the euro.

As indicated earlier, countries with **pegged exchange rates** establish a fixed exchange rate with some other major currency or basket of currencies. When a government lowers the target fixed exchange rate, this is called **devaluation**, and when it increases the rate it is called **revaluation**. For example, from 1991 through early 2002, Argentina had a fixed exchange rate of 1 peso per U.S. dollar. Imports were high, exports were low, and the Argentinean government had to purchase huge amounts of pesos to maintain that artificially high exchange rate. The government borrowed heavily to finance these purchases, and eventually it was unable to continue supporting the peso. (Indeed, the government defaulted on some of its obligations). As a result, the government had to devalue the peso to 1.4 pesos per dollar in early 2002. Notice that this made the peso weaker: Before the devaluation, 1 peso would buy 1 dollar, but afterward 1 peso would buy only 71 cents (1.4 pesos per dollar = 1/1.4 = 0.71 dollar per peso). The devaluation lowered the prices of Argentine goods on the world market, which helped its exporters, but prices rose for imported goods, including oil. The initial shock to the Argentine economy was severe, as employment fell in those industries that were not exporters. The problem was exacerbated because many Argentine companies and individuals had borrowed using debt denominated in dollars, which instantly cost much more to service. However, by mid-2004 the economy was improving, with exports up, tourism up, and employment higher. Still, the initial pain caused by devaluation helps explain why many countries with fixed exchange rates tend to postpone needed measures until economic pressures build to explosive proportions.

Many countries have abandoned pegged exchange rates and now allow their currencies to float. For example, Mexico had a pegged exchange rate prior to 1994, but it depleted its foreign reserves trying to support the peso and was forced to devalue the peso in 1994. Mexico's currency now floats, as does that of Argentina.

A pegged exchange rate per se isn't necessarily a deterrent to direct investment in the country by foreign corporations, as long as the local government's central bank supports the currency and devaluations are unlikely. This was generally the case in the Bretton Woods era, and so those currencies were considered to be **convertible** because the nation that issued it allowed it to be traded in the currency markets and was willing to redeem it at market rates. This is true today for all floating-rate currencies, which are also called **hard currencies** because of their convertibility. Some pegged currencies are also at least partially convertible, because their central banks will redeem them at market rates under specified conditions.

However, some countries peg the exchange rate but do not allow their currencies to be traded on world markets. For example, the Chinese yuan is pegged at about 8.3 yuan per dollar. However, the yuan can be legally used and exchanged only within China. Furthermore, the Chinese government imposes restrictions on both residents and nonresidents from freely converting their holdings of yuans into another currency. Thus, the yuan is a **nonconvertible currency**, also called a **soft currency**. When official exchange rates differ from "market rates" or when there are restrictions on convertibility, a black market will often arise. For example, in mid-2004 Venezuela's official exchange rate was about 1,900 bolivars per dollar, but black market prices were estimated to be over 3,200.

A nonconvertible currency creates problems for foreign companies looking to make direct investments. For example, consider the situation faced by Pizza Hut when it wanted to open a chain of restaurants in the former Soviet Union. The Russian ruble was not convertible, so Pizza Hut could not take the profits from its restaurants out of the Soviet Union in the form of dollars. There was no mechanism to exchange the rubles it earned in Russia for dollars, so the investment in the Soviet Union was essentially worthless to a U.S. company. However, Pizza Hut arranged to use the ruble profit from the restaurants to buy Russian vodka, which it then shipped to the United States and sold for dollars. Pizza Hut managed to work things out, but lack of convertibility significantly inhibits the ability of a country to attract foreign investment.

SELF-TEST QUESTIONS	What is the difference between a fixed exchange rate system and a floating rate system?

What are pegged exchange rates?

What does it mean to say that the dollar is depreciating with respect to the euro? For a U.S. consumer of European goods, would this be good or bad? How could changes in consumption arrest the decline of the dollar?

What is a convertible currency?

TRADING IN FOREIGN EXCHANGE

Importers, exporters, tourists, and governments buy and sell currencies in the foreign exchange market. For example, when a U.S. trader imports automobiles from Japan, payment will probably be made in Japanese yen. The importer buys yen (through its bank) in the foreign exchange market, much as one buys common stocks on the New York Stock

Exchange or pork bellies on the Chicago Mercantile Exchange. However, whereas stock and commodity exchanges have organized trading floors, the foreign exchange market consists of a network of brokers and banks based in New York, London, Tokyo, and other financial centers. Most buy and sell orders are conducted by computer and telephone.[1]

Spot Rates and Forward Rates

Currency futures prices are available from the Chicago Mercantile Exchange (CME) on their Web site at http://www.cme.com. Currency spot and forward rates are available from the Bank of Montreal Financial Group at http://www4.bmo.com and the New York Federal Reserve Bank at http://www.federalreserve.gov.

The exchange rates shown earlier in Tables 17-1 and 17-2 are known as **spot rates,** which means the rate paid for delivery of the currency "on the spot" or, in reality, no more than two days after the day of the trade. For most of the world's major currencies, it is also possible to buy (or sell) currencies for delivery at some agreed-upon future date, usually 30, 90, or 180 days from the day the transaction is negotiated. This rate is known as the **forward exchange rate.**

For example, suppose a U.S. firm must pay 500 million yen to a Japanese firm in 30 days, and the current spot rate is 111.0371 yen per dollar. Unless spot rates change, the U.S. firm will pay the Japanese firm the equivalent of $4.503 million (500 million yen divided by 111.0371 yen per dollar) in 30 days. But if the spot rate falls to 100 yen per dollar, for example, the U.S. firm will have to pay the equivalent of $5 million. The treasurer of the U.S. firm can avoid this risk by entering into a 30-day forward exchange contract. This contract promises delivery of yen to the U.S. firm in 30 days at a guaranteed price of 110.9262 yen per dollar. No cash changes hands at the time the treasurer signs the forward contract, although the U.S. firm might have to put some collateral down as a guarantee against default. Because the firm can use an interest-bearing instrument for the collateral, though, this requirement is not costly. The counterparty to the forward contract must deliver the yen to the U.S. firm in 30 days, and the U.S. firm is obligated to purchase the 500 million yen at the previously agreed-upon rate of 110.9262 yen per dollar. Therefore, the treasurer of the U.S. firm is able to lock in a payment equivalent to $4.508 million, no matter what happens to spot rates. This technique is called "hedging."

Forward rates for 30-, 90-, and 180-day delivery, along with the current spot rates for some commonly traded currencies, are given in Table 17-3. If you can obtain *more* of the

TABLE 17-3 | Selected Spot and Forward Exchange Rates; Indirect Quotation: Number of Units of Foreign Currency per U.S. Dollar

		FORWARD RATES[a]			
	Spot Rate	30 Days	90 Days	180 Days	Forward Rate at a Premium or Discount[b]
Britain (pound)	0.5434	0.5449	0.5479	0.5521	Discount
Canada (dollar)	1.3512	1.3523	1.3537	1.3554	Discount
Japan (yen)	111.0371	110.9262	110.6317	110.0837	Premium
Switzerland (franc)	1.2392	1.2382	1.2359	1.2318	Premium

Notes:

[a]These are representative quotes as provided by a sample of New York banks. Forward rates for other currencies and for other lengths of time can often be negotiated.

[b]When it takes more units of a foreign currency to buy one dollar in the future, the value of the foreign currency is less in the forward market than in the spot market, hence the forward rate is at a *discount* to the spot rate.

Source: The Wall Street Journal, http://online.wsj.com; quotes for June 4, 2004.

---

[1] For a more detailed explanation of exchange rate determination and operations of the foreign exchange market, see Mark Eaker, Frank Fabozzi, and Dwight Grant, *International Corporate Finance* (Fort Worth, TX: The Dryden Press, 1996).

foreign currency for a dollar in the forward than in the spot market, the forward currency is less valuable than the spot currency, and the forward currency is said to be selling at a **discount**. In other words, if the foreign currency is expected to depreciate (based on the forward rates), then the spot rate is at a discount. Conversely, since a dollar would buy *fewer* yen and francs in the forward than in the spot market, the forward yen and francs are selling at a **premium**.

SELF-TEST QUESTIONS Differentiate between spot and forward exchange rates.
Explain what it means for a forward currency to sell at a discount and at a premium.

INTEREST RATE PARITY

Market forces determine whether a currency sells at a forward premium or discount, and the general relationship between spot and forward exchange rates is specified by a concept called "interest rate parity."

Interest rate parity holds that investors should expect to earn the same return on security investments in all countries after adjusting for risk. It recognizes that when you invest in a country other than your home country, you are affected by two forces—returns on the investment itself and changes in the exchange rate. It follows that your overall return will be higher than the investment's stated return if the currency in which your investment is denominated appreciates relative to your home currency. Likewise, your overall return will be lower if the foreign currency you receive declines in value.

To illustrate interest rate parity, consider the case of a U.S. investor who can buy default-free 180-day Swiss bonds that promise a 4 percent nominal annual return. The 180-day Swiss interest rate, r_f, is 4%/2 = 2% because 180 days is one-half of a 360-day year. Assume also that the indirect quotation for the spot exchange rate is 1.2392 Swiss francs per dollar, as shown in Table 17-3. Finally, assume that the 180-day forward exchange rate is 1.2318 Swiss francs per dollar, which means that in 180 days the investor can exchange one dollar for 1.2318 Swiss francs.

The U.S. investor could receive a 4 percent annualized return denominated in Swiss francs, but if he or she ultimately wants to consume goods in the United States, those Swiss francs must be converted to dollars. The dollar return on the investment depends, therefore, on what happens to exchange rates over the next six months. However, the investor can lock in the dollar return by selling the foreign currency in the forward market. For example, the investor could simultaneously:

1. Convert $1,000 to 1,239.20 Swiss francs in the spot market: $1,000(1.2392 Swiss francs per dollar) = 1,239.20 Swiss francs.
2. Invest the Swiss francs in a 180-day Swiss bond that has a 4 percent annual return, or a 2 percent semiannual return. This investment will pay 1,239.20(1.02) = 1,263.98 Swiss francs in 180 days.
3. Agree today to exchange the Swiss francs in 180 days at the rate of 1.2318 Swiss francs per dollar, for a total of (1,263.98 Swiss francs)/(1.2318 Swiss francs per dollar) = $1,026.12.

This investment, therefore, has an expected 180-day return of $26.12/$1,000 = 2.612%, which translates into a nominal annual return of 2(2.612%) = 5.22%. In this case, 4 percent of the expected 5.22 percent is coming from the bond itself, and 1.22 percent arises because the market believes the Swiss franc will strengthen relative to the dollar. Note that by locking in the forward rate today, the investor has eliminated all exchange rate risk.

HUNGRY FOR A BIG MAC? GO TO THE PHILIPPINES!

Purchasing power parity (PPP) implies that the same product will sell for the same price in every country after adjusting for current exchange rates. One problem when testing to see if PPP holds is that it assumes that goods consumed in different countries are of the same quality. For example, if you find that a product is more expensive in Switzerland than it is in Canada, one explanation is that PPP fails to hold, but another explanation is that the product sold in Switzerland is of a higher quality and therefore deserves a higher price.

One way to test for PPP is to find goods that have the same quality worldwide. With this in mind, *The Economist* magazine occasionally compares the prices of a well-known good whose quality is the same in nearly 120 different countries: the McDonald's Big Mac hamburger.

The table on the next page provides information collected during 2004. The first column shows the price of a Big Mac in the local currency. Column 2 calculates the price of the Big Mac in terms of the U.S. dollar—this is obtained by dividing the local price by the actual exchange rate at that time.[a] For example, a Big Mac costs 2.73 euros in the EMU area. Given an exchange rate of 1.20 dollar per euro, this implies that the dollar price of a Big Mac is (2.73 euros)(1.20 dollar per euro) = $3.28.

The third column backs out the implied exchange rate that would hold under PPP. This is obtained

by dividing the price of the Big Mac in each local currency by its U.S. price. For example, a Big Mac costs 42.05 rubles in Russia, and $2.90 in the United States. If PPP holds, the exchange rate should be 14.50 rubles per dollar (42.05 rubles/$2.90).

Comparing the implied exchange rate to the actual exchange rate in Column 4, we see the extent to which the local currency is under- or overvalued relative to the dollar. Given that the actual exchange rate at the time was 29.00 rubles per dollar, this implies that the ruble was 50 percent undervalued.

The evidence suggests that strict PPP does not hold, but the Big Mac test may shed some insights about where exchange rates are headed. Other than a few European countries, most of the other currencies are undervalued against the dollar. The Big Mac 2004 test suggests that European currencies will fall over the next year or so, but that most others will rise.

One last benefit of the Big Mac test is that it tells us the cheapest places to find a Big Mac. According to the data, if you are looking for a Big Mac, head to the Philippines, and avoid Switzerland.

[a]Except when the quote is a direct quote, like it is for euros and pounds. Then the local price is multiplied by the exchange rate.

Source: Based on information contained within "Food for Thought," *The Economist*, May 27, 2004, and **http://www.economist.com/ markets/Bigmac/Index.cfm.**

And since the Swiss bond is assumed to be default-free, the investor is certain to earn a 5.22 percent annual dollar return.

Interest rate parity implies that an investment in the United States with the same risk as the Swiss bond should also have a return of 5.22 percent. We can express interest rate parity by the following equation:

$$\frac{\text{Forward exchange rate}}{\text{Spot exchange rate}} = \frac{(1 + r_h)}{(1 + r_f)}. \tag{17-1}$$

Here r_h is the periodic interest rate in the home country, r_f is the periodic interest rate in the foreign country, and the forward and exchange rates are expressed as direct quotations (that is, dollars per foreign currency).

Using Table 17-3, the direct spot quotation is 0.80697 dollar per Swiss franc = (1/1.2392 Swiss francs per dollar), and the direct 180-day forward quotation is 0.81182 = (1/1.2318). Using Equation 17-1, we can solve for the equivalent home rate, r_h:

$$\frac{\text{Forward exchange rate}}{\text{Spot exchange rate}} = \frac{(1 + r_h)}{(1 + f_f)} = \frac{(1 + r_h)}{(1 + 0.02)} = \frac{0.81182}{0.80697} \tag{17-1a}$$

$$(1 + r_h) = \left(\frac{0.81182}{0.80697}\right)(1 + 0.02) = 1.026130.$$

	BIG MAC PRICES		Implied Exchange Rate Based on PPP[a] (3)	Actual $ Exchange Rate (4)	Local Currency Under(−)/Over(+) Valuation[b](%) (5)
	In Local Currency (1)	In Dollars (2)			
United States[c]	$2.90	2.90			
Argentina	Peso4.35	1.48	1.50	2.94	−49
Australia	A$3.27	2.27	1.12	1.44	−22
Britain	£1.88	3.37	1.54[d]	1.79	16
Canada	C$3.22	2.33	1.10	1.38	−20
China	Yuan10.52	1.26	3.59	8.35	−57
Denmark	DKr27.70	4.46	9.57	6.21	54
Euro area	€2.73	3.28	1.06[e]	1.20	13
Hong Kong	HK$12.03	1.54	4.14	7.81	−47
Japan	¥263.01	2.33	90.30	112.88	−20
Malaysia	M$5.03	1.33	1.74	3.78	−54
Mexico	Peso23.92	2.08	8.28	11.50	−28
Philippines	Peso68.08	1.23	23.80	55.35	−57
Russia	Ruble42.05	1.45	14.50	29.00	−50
Switzerland	SFr6.27	4.90	2.17	1.28	69

Notes:
[a]Purchasing power parity local price divided by price in the United States.
[b]Against dollar.
[c]Average of New York, Chicago, San Francisco, and Atlanta.
[d]Dollars per pound.
[e]Dollars per euro.
Source: "Food for Thought" *The Economist*, May 27, 2004; and **http://www.economist.com/markets/Bigmac/Index.cfm.**

The periodic home interest rate is 2.612 percent, and the annualized home interest rate is $(2.612\%)(2) = 5.22\%$, the same value we found above.

After accounting for exchange rates, interest rate parity states that bonds in the home country and the foreign country must have the same effective rate of return. In this example, the U.S. bond must yield 5.22 percent to provide the same return as the 4 percent Swiss bond. If one bond provides a higher return, investors will sell their low-return bond and flock to the high-return bond. This activity will cause the price of the low-return bond to fall (which pushes up its yield) and the price of the high-return bond to increase (driving down its yield). This will continue until the two bonds again have the same returns after accounting for exchange rates.

In other words, interest rate parity implies that an investment in the United States with the same risk as a Swiss bond should have a dollar value return of 5.22 percent. Solving for r_h in Equation 17-1, we indeed find that the predicted interest rate in the United States is 5.22 percent.

Interest rate parity shows why a particular currency might be at a forward premium or discount. Note that a currency is at a forward premium whenever domestic interest rates are higher than foreign interest rates. Discounts prevail if domestic interest rates are lower than foreign interest rates. If these conditions do not hold, then arbitrage will soon force interest rates and exchange rates back to parity.

SELF-TEST QUESTION | Briefly explain interest rate parity, illustrating it with an example.

PURCHASING POWER PARITY

We have discussed exchange rates in some detail, and we have considered the relationship between spot and forward exchange rates. However, we have not yet addressed the fundamental question: What determines the spot level of exchange rates in each country? While exchange rates are influenced by a multitude of factors that are difficult to predict, particularly on a day-to-day basis, over the long run market forces work to ensure that similar goods sell for similar prices in different countries after taking exchange rates into account. This relationship is known as "purchasing power parity."

Purchasing power parity (PPP), sometimes referred to as the *law of one price*, implies that the levels of exchange rates and prices adjust so as to cause identical goods to cost the same amount in different countries. For example, if a pair of tennis shoes costs $150 in the United States and 100 pounds in Britain, PPP implies that the exchange rate be $1.50 per pound. Consumers could purchase the shoes in Britain for 100 pounds, or they could exchange their 100 pounds for $150 and then purchase the same shoes in the United States at the same effective cost, assuming no transaction or transportation costs. Here is the equation for purchasing power parity:

$$P_h = (P_f)(\text{Spot rate}), \qquad (17\text{-}2)$$

or

$$\text{Spot rate} = \frac{P_h}{P_f}. \qquad (17\text{-}2a)$$

Here

P_h= the price of the good in the home country ($150, assuming the United States is the home country).
P_f= the price of the good in the foreign country (100 pounds).

Note that the spot market exchange rate is expressed as the number of units of home currency that can be exchanged for one unit of foreign currency ($1.50 per pound).

PPP assumes that market forces will eliminate situations in which the same product sells at a different price overseas. For example, if the shoes cost $140 in the United States, importers/exporters could purchase them in the United States for $140, sell them for 100 pounds in Britain, exchange the 100 pounds for $150 in the foreign exchange market, and earn a profit of $10 on every pair of shoes. Ultimately, this trading activity would increase the demand for shoes in the United States and thus raise P_h, increase the supply of shoes in Britain and thus reduce P_f, and increase the demand for dollars in the foreign exchange market and thus reduce the spot rate. Each of these actions works to restore PPP.

Note that PPP assumes that there are no transportation or transaction costs, or import restrictions, all of which limit the ability to ship goods between countries. In many cases, these assumptions are incorrect, which explains why PPP is often violated. An additional problem for empirical tests of the PPP theorem is that products in different countries are rarely identical. Frequently, there are real or perceived differences in quality, which can lead to price differences in different countries.

Still, the concepts of interest rate and purchasing power parity are critically important to those engaged in international activities. Companies and investors must anticipate changes in interest rates, inflation, and exchange rates, and they often try to hedge the risks of adverse movements in these factors. The parity relationships are extremely useful when anticipating future conditions.

SELF-TEST QUESTION   What is meant by purchasing power parity? Illustrate it.

INFLATION, INTEREST RATES, AND EXCHANGE RATES

Relative inflation rates, or the rates of inflation in foreign countries compared with that in the home country, have many implications for multinational financial decisions. Obviously, relative inflation rates will greatly influence future production costs at home and abroad. Equally important, inflation has a dominant influence on relative interest rates and exchange rates. Both of these factors influence decisions by multinational corporations for financing their foreign investments, and both have an important effect on the profitability of foreign investments.

For current international interest rates, go to http://www .bloomberg.com and select Market Data. Then select Rates and Bonds.

The currencies of countries with higher inflation rates than that of the United States by definition *depreciate* over time against the dollar. Countries where this has occurred include Mexico and all the South American nations. On the other hand, the currencies of Switzerland and Japan, which have had less inflation than the United States, have generally *appreciated* against the dollar. *In fact, a foreign currency will, on average, depreciate or appreciate at a percentage rate approximately equal to the amount by which its inflation rate exceeds or is less than the U.S. rate.*

Relative inflation rates also affect interest rates. The interest rate in any country is largely determined by its inflation rate. Therefore, countries currently experiencing higher rates of inflation than the United States also tend to have higher interest rates. The reverse is true for countries with lower inflation rates.

It is tempting for a multinational corporation to borrow in countries with the lowest interest rates. However, this is not always a good strategy. Suppose, for example, that interest rates in Switzerland are lower than those in the United States because of Switzerland's lower inflation rate. A U.S. multinational firm could therefore save interest by borrowing in Switzerland. However, because of relative inflation rates, the Swiss franc will probably appreciate in the future, causing the dollar cost of annual interest and principal payments on Swiss debt to rise over time. Thus, *the lower interest rate could be more than offset by losses from currency appreciation.* Similarly, multinational corporations should not necessarily avoid borrowing in a country such as Brazil, where interest rates have been very high, because future depreciation of the Brazilian real could make such borrowing end up being relatively inexpensive.

SELF-TEST QUESTIONS

What effects do relative inflation rates have on relative interest rates?
What happens over time to the currencies of countries with higher inflation rates than that of the United States? To those with lower inflation rates?
Why might a multinational corporation decide to borrow in a country such as Brazil, where interest rates are high, rather than in a country like Switzerland, where interest rates are low?

INTERNATIONAL MONEY AND CAPITAL MARKETS

One way for U.S. citizens to invest in world markets is to buy the stocks of U.S. multinational corporations that invest directly in foreign countries. Another way is to purchase foreign securities—stocks, bonds, or money market instruments issued by foreign companies. Security investments are known as *portfolio investments,* and they are distinguished from *direct investments* in physical assets by U.S. corporations.

From World War II through the 1960s, the U.S. capital markets dominated world markets. Today, however, the value of U.S. securities represents less than one-fourth the value of all securities. Given this situation, it is important for both corporate managers and investors to have an understanding of international markets. Moreover, these markets often offer better opportunities for raising or investing capital than are available domestically.

Eurodollar Market

A **Eurodollar** is a U.S. dollar deposited in a bank outside the United States. (Although they are called Eurodollars because they originated in Europe, Eurodollars are really any dollars deposited in any part of the world other than the United States.) The bank in which the deposit is made may be a non-U.S. bank, such as Barclay's Bank in London; the foreign branch of a U.S. bank, such as Citibank's Paris branch; or even a foreign branch of a third-country bank, such as Barclay's Munich branch. Most Eurodollar deposits are for $500,000 or more, and they have maturities ranging from overnight to about one year.

The major difference between Eurodollar deposits and regular U.S. time deposits is their geographic locations. The two types of deposits do not involve different currencies—in both cases, dollars are on deposit. However, Eurodollars are outside the direct control of the U.S. monetary authorities, so U.S. banking regulations, including reserve requirements and FDIC insurance premiums, do not apply. The absence of these costs means that the interest rate paid on Eurodollar deposits can be higher than domestic U.S. rates on equivalent instruments.

Although the dollar is the leading international currency, British pounds, euros, Swiss francs, Japanese yen, and other currencies are also deposited outside their home countries; these *Eurocurrencies* are handled in exactly the same way as Eurodollars.

Eurodollars are borrowed by U.S. and foreign corporations for various purposes, but especially to pay for goods imported from the United States and to invest in U.S. security markets. Also, U.S. dollars are used as an international currency, or international medium of exchange, and many Eurodollars are used for this purpose. It is interesting to note that Eurodollars were actually "invented" by the Soviets in 1946. International merchants did not trust the Soviets or their rubles, so the Soviets bought some dollars (for gold), deposited them in a Paris bank, and then used these dollars to buy goods in the world markets. Others found it convenient to use dollars this same way, and soon the Eurodollar market was in full swing.

Eurodollars are usually held in interest-bearing accounts. The interest rate paid on these deposits depends (1) on the bank's lending rate, as the interest a bank earns on loans determines its willingness and ability to pay interest on deposits, and (2) on rates of return available on U.S. money market instruments. If money market rates in the United States were above Eurodollar deposit rates, these dollars would be sent back and invested in the United States, whereas if Eurodollar deposit rates were significantly above U.S. rates, which is more often the case, more dollars would be sent out of the United States to become Eurodollars. Given the existence of the Eurodollar market and the electronic flow of dollars to and from the United States, it is easy to see why interest rates in the United States cannot be insulated from those in other parts of the world.

Interest rates on Eurodollar deposits (and loans) are tied to a standard rate known by the acronym *LIBOR*, which stands for *London Interbank Offer Rate*. LIBOR is the rate of interest offered by the largest and strongest London banks on dollar deposits of significant size. In June 2004, LIBOR rates were just a little below domestic U.S. bank rates on time deposits of the same maturity—1.36 percent for three-month CDs versus 1.33 percent for LIBOR CDs. The Eurodollar market is essentially a short-term market; most loans and deposits are for less than one year.

International Bond Markets

Any bond sold outside the country of the borrower is called an *international bond*. However, there are two important types of international bonds: foreign bonds and Eurobonds. **Foreign bonds** are bonds sold by a foreign borrower but denominated in the currency of the country in which the issue is sold. For instance, Nortel Networks (a Canadian company) may need U.S. dollars to finance the operations of its subsidiaries in the United States. If it decides to raise the needed capital in the United States, the bond will be underwritten by a syndicate of U.S. investment bankers, denominated in U.S. dollars, and sold to U.S. investors in accordance with SEC and applicable state regulations. Except for the foreign origin of the borrower, this bond will be indistinguishable from those issued by equivalent U.S. corporations. Since Nortel is a foreign corporation, however, the bond would be a foreign bond. Furthermore, because it is denominated in dollars and sold in the United States under SEC regulations, it is also called a **Yankee bond**. In contrast, if Nortel issued bonds in Mexico denominated in pesos, it would be a foreign bond, but not a Yankee bond.

The term **Eurobond** is used to designate any bond issued in one country but denominated in the currency of some other country. Examples include a Ford Motor Company issue denominated in dollars and sold in Germany, or a British firm's sale of euro-denominated bonds in Switzerland. The institutional arrangements by which Eurobonds are marketed are different than those for most other bond issues, with the most important distinction being a far lower level of required disclosure than is usually found for bonds issued in domestic markets, particularly in the United States. Governments tend to be less strict when regulating securities denominated in foreign currencies, because the bonds' purchasers are generally more "sophisticated." The lower disclosure requirements result in lower total transaction costs for Eurobonds.

Eurobonds appeal to investors for several reasons. Generally, they are issued in bearer form rather than as registered bonds, so the names and nationalities of investors are not recorded. Individuals who desire anonymity, whether for privacy reasons or for tax avoidance, like Eurobonds. Similarly, most governments do not withhold taxes on interest payments associated with Eurobonds. If the investor requires an effective yield of 10 percent, a Eurobond that is exempt from tax withholding would need a coupon rate of 10 percent. Another type of bond—for instance, a domestic issue subject to a 30 percent withholding tax on interest paid to foreigners—would need a coupon rate of 14.3 percent to yield an after-withholding rate of 10 percent. Investors who desire secrecy would not want to file for a refund of the tax, so they would prefer to hold the Eurobond.

More than half of all Eurobonds are denominated in dollars. Bonds in Japanese yen, German marks, and Dutch guilders account for most of the rest. Although centered in Europe, Eurobonds are truly international. Their underwriting syndicates include investment bankers from all parts of the world, and the bonds are sold to investors not only in Europe but also in such faraway places as Bahrain and Singapore. Up to a few years ago, Eurobonds were issued solely by multinational firms, by international financial institutions, or by national governments. Today, however, the Eurobond market is also being tapped by purely domestic U.S. firms, because they often find that by borrowing overseas they can lower their debt costs.

International Stock Markets

New issues of stock are sold in international markets for a variety of reasons. For example, a non-U.S. firm might sell an equity issue in the United States because it can tap a much larger source of capital than in its home country. Also, a U.S. firm might tap a foreign market because it wants to create an equity market presence to accompany its operations in that country. Large multinational companies also occasionally issue new stock simultaneously in multiple countries. For example, Alcan Aluminum, a Canadian company, recently issued new stock in Canada, Europe, and the United States simultaneously, using different underwriting syndicates in each market.

In addition to new issues, outstanding stocks of large multinational companies are increasingly being listed on multiple international exchanges. For example, Coca-Cola's stock is traded on six stock exchanges in the United States, four stock exchanges in Switzerland, and the Frankfurt stock exchange in Germany. Some 500 foreign stocks are listed in the United States—an example here is Royal Dutch Petroleum, which is listed on the NYSE.

U.S. investors can also invest in foreign companies through American Depository Receipts (ADRs), which are certificates representing ownership of foreign stock held in trust. About 1,700 ADRs are now available in the United States, with most of them traded on the over-the-counter (OTC) market. However, more and more ADRs are being listed on the New York Stock Exchange, including England's British Airways, Japan's Honda Motors, and Italy's Fiat Group.

SELF-TEST QUESTIONS Differentiate between foreign portfolio investments and direct foreign investments.

What are Eurodollars?

Has the development of the Eurodollar market made it easier or more difficult for the Federal Reserve to control U.S. interest rates?

Differentiate between foreign bonds and Eurobonds.

Why do Eurobonds appeal to investors?

MULTINATIONAL CAPITAL BUDGETING

Up to now, we have discussed the general environment in which multinational firms operate. In the remainder of the chapter, we see how international factors affect key corporate decisions, beginning with capital budgeting. Although the same basic principles apply to capital budgeting for both foreign and domestic operations, there are some key differences, including types of risks the firm faces, cash flow estimation, and project analysis.

Risk Exposure

Foreign projects may be more or less risky than equivalent domestic projects, and that can lead to differences in the cost of capital. Higher risk for foreign projects tends to result from two primary sources: (1) exchange rate risk and (2) political risk. However, international diversification might result in a lower risk.

Exchange rate risk relates to the value of the basic cash flows in the parent company's home currency. Foreign currency cash flows turned over to the parent must be converted into U.S. dollars, so projected cash flows must be translated to dollars at the expected future exchange rates. An analysis should be conducted to ascertain the effects of exchange rate variations on dollar cash flows, and, on the basis of this analysis, an exchange rate risk premium should be added to the domestic cost of capital. It is sometimes possible to hedge against exchange rate risk, but it may not be possible to hedge completely, especially on long-term projects. If hedging is used, the costs of doing so must be subtracted from the project's operating cash flows.

Political risk refers to potential actions by a host government that would reduce the value of a company's investment. It includes at one extreme expropriation of the subsidiary's assets without compensation, but it also includes less drastic actions that reduce the value of the parent firm's investment in the foreign subsidiary. Included here are higher taxes, tighter repatriation or currency controls, and restrictions on prices charged. The risk of expropriation is small in traditionally friendly and stable countries such as Great Britain or Switzerland. However, in Latin America, Africa, the Far East, and Eastern Europe, the risk may be substantial. Past expropriations include those of ITT and Anaconda Copper in Chile, Gulf Oil in Bolivia, Occidental Petroleum in Libya, Enron Corporation in Peru, and the assets of many companies in Iraq, Iran, and Cuba.

Note that companies can take steps to reduce the potential loss from expropriation, including one or more of the following:

1. Finance the subsidiary with local capital.
2. Structure operations so that the subsidiary has value only as a part of the integrated corporate system.

3. Obtain insurance against economic losses from expropriation from a source such as the Overseas Private Investment Corporation (OPIC).

If OPIC insurance is purchased, the premiums paid must be added to the project's cost.

Several organizations rate countries according to different aspects of risk. For example, Transparency International (TI) ranks countries based on perceived corruption, which is an important part of political risk. Table 17-4 shows selected countries. TI rates Finland as the most honest country, while Nigeria and Bangladesh are the lowest two. The United States is tied for eighteenth.

Cash Flow Estimation

Cash flow estimation is more complex for foreign than domestic investments. Most multinational firms set up separate subsidiaries in each foreign country in which they operate, and the relevant cash flows for the parent company are the dividends and royalties paid by the subsidiaries to the parent, translated into dollars. Dividends and royalties are normally taxed by both foreign and home country governments, although the home country may allow credits for some or all of the foreign taxes paid. Furthermore, a foreign government may restrict the amount of the cash that may be **repatriated** to the parent company. For example, some governments place a ceiling, stated as a percentage of the company's net worth, on the amount of cash dividends that a subsidiary can pay to its parent. Such restrictions are normally intended to force multinational firms to reinvest earnings in the foreign country, although restrictions are sometimes imposed to prevent large currency outflows, which might disrupt the exchange rate.

Whatever the host country's motivation for blocking repatriation of profits, the result is that the parent corporation cannot use cash flows blocked in the foreign country to pay dividends to its shareholders or to invest elsewhere in the business. Hence, from the perspective of the parent organization, the cash flows relevant for foreign investment analysis are the cash flows that the subsidiary is actually expected to send back to the parent. Note, though, that if returns on investments in the foreign country are attractive, and if blockages are expected to be lifted in the future, then current blockages may not be bad, but dealing with this situation does complicate the cash flow estimation process.

TABLE 17-4 | The Transparency International Corruption Perceptions Index (CPI)

TOP-RANKED COUNTRIES			BOTTOM-RANKED COUNTRIES		
Rank	Country	2003 CPI Score	Rank	Country	2003 CPI Score
1	Finland	9.7	118 (tie)	Cote d'Ivoire	2.1
2	Iceland	9.6		Kyrgyzstan	2.1
3 (tie)	Denmark	9.5		Libya	2.1
	New Zealand	9.5		Papua New	
5	Singapore	9.4		Guinea	2.1
6	Sweden	9.3	124 (tie)	Angola	1.8
7	Netherlands	8.9		Azerbaijan	1.8
8 (tie)	Australia	8.8		Cameroon	1.8
	Norway	8.8		Georgia	1.8
	Switzerland	8.8		Tajikistan	1.8
11 (tie)	Canada	8.7	129 (tie)	Myanmar	1.6
	Luxembourg	8.7		Paraguay	1.6
	United Kingdom	8.7	131	Haiti	1.5
			132	Nigeria	1.4
			133	Bangladesh	1.3

Source: **http://www.transparency.org/**.

Some companies attempt to circumvent repatriation restrictions (and also lower taxes paid) through the use of transfer pricing. For example, a foreign subsidiary might obtain raw materials or other input components from the parent. The price the subsidiary pays the parent is called a **transfer price**. If the transfer price is very high, then the foreign subsidiary's costs will be very high, leaving little or no profit to repatriate. However, the parent's profit will be higher because it sold to the subsidiary at an inflated transfer price. The net result is that the parent receives cash flows from the subsidiary via transfer pricing rather than as repatriated dividends. Transfer pricing can also be used to shift profits from high-tax to low-tax jurisdictions. Of course, governments are well aware of these possibilities, so governmental auditors are on guard to prevent abusive transfer pricing.

Project Analysis

First, consider a domestic project that requires foreign raw materials, or one where the finished product will be sold in a foreign market. Because the operation is based in the United States, any projected nondollar cash flows—costs in the first example and revenues in the second—should be converted into dollars. This conversion does not present much of a problem for cash flows to be paid or received in the short run, but there is a significant problem in estimating exchange rates for converting long-term foreign cash flows into dollars because forward exchange rates are usually not available for more than 180 days into the future. However, long-term expected forward exchange rates can be estimated using the interest rate parity relationship set forth in Equation 17-1. For example, if a foreign cash flow is expected to occur in one year, then the one-year forward exchange rate can be estimated using domestic and foreign government bonds maturing in one year. Similarly, the two-year exchange rate can be estimated using two-year bonds. Thus, foreign cash flows can be converted into dollars and added to the project's other projected cash flows, and then the project's NPV can be calculated based on the project's cost of capital.

Now consider a project that will be based overseas, where most expected future cash flows will be denominated in a foreign currency. Two approaches can be used to estimate such a project's NPV. Both begin by forecasting the future cash flows denominated in the foreign currency and then determining the annual repatriations to the United States, denominated in the foreign currency. Under the first approach, we convert the expected future repatriations to dollars (as described earlier), and then find the NPV using the project's cost of capital. Under the second approach, we take the projected repatriations, denominated in the foreign currency, and discount them at the foreign cost of capital, which reflects foreign interest rates and relevant risk premiums. This produces an NPV denominated in the foreign currency, which can be converted into a dollar-denominated NPV using the spot exchange rate.

The following example illustrates the first approach. A U.S. company has the opportunity to lease a manufacturing facility in Great Britain for three years. The company must spend £20 million initially to refurbish the plant. The expected net cash flows from the plant for the next three years, in millions, are $CF_1 = £7$, $CF_2 = £9$, and $CF_3 = £11$. A similar project in the United States would have a risk adjusted cost of capital of 10 percent. The first step is to estimate the expected exchange rates at the end of one, two, and three years using the interest rate parity equation:

$$\text{Expected forward exchange rate} = \text{Spot exchange rate} \left(\frac{1 + r_h}{1 + r_f} \right) \qquad \text{(17-1b)}$$

where the exchange rates are expressed in direct quotations. We are using the interest rate parity equation to calculate forward rates because market-based forward rates for maturities longer than a year are not generally available.

STOCK MARKET INDICES AROUND THE WORLD

In the United States the Dow Jones Industrial Average (^DJI) is the most well-known stock market index. Similar indices also exist for each major world financial center.

Hong Kong (^HSI)

In Hong Kong, the primary stock index is the Hang Seng. Created by HSI Services Limited, the Hang Seng index is composed of 33 large stocks.

Great Britain (^FTSE)

The FT-SE 100 Index (pronounced "footsie") is the most widely followed indicator of equity investments in Great Britain. It is a value-weighted index composed of the 100 largest companies on the London Stock Exchange.

Japan (^N225)

In Japan, the principal barometer of stock performance is the Nikkei 225 Index. The index consists of highly liquid equity issues thought to be representative of the Japanese economy.

Germany (^GDAXI)

The Deutscher Aktienindex, commonly called the DAX, is an index comprised of the 30 largest companies trading on the Frankfurt Stock Exchange.

India (^BSESN)

Of the 22 stock exchanges in India, the Bombay Stock Exchange (BSE) is the largest, with more than 6,000 listed stocks and approximately two-thirds of the country's total trading volume. Established in 1875, the exchange is also the oldest in Asia. Its yardstick is the BSE Sensex, an index of 30 publicly traded Indian stocks that account for one-fifth of the BSE's market capitalization.

Note: For easy access to world indices, see **http://finance.yahoo.com/m2** and use the "ticker" symbols shown in parentheses.

Relative Ten-Year Performance (Starting Values = 100)

	United States	Germany	Great Britain	Hong Kong	India	Japan
May 1994	100	100	100	100	100	100
May 2004	271	184	149	128	124	54

Suppose the spot exchange rate is 1.8000 dollars per pound. Interest rates on U.S. and U.K. government bonds are shown below, along with the expected forward rate implied by the interest rate parity relationship in Equation 17-1b:

Maturity (in years)	r_h	r_f	Spot Rate ($/£)	Expected Forward Rate Based on Equation 17-1b ($/£)
1	2.0%	4.6%	1.8000	1.7553
2	2.8	5.0	1.8000	1.7623
3	3.5	5.2	1.8000	1.7709

The current dollar cost of the project is £20(1.8000 $/£) = $36 million. The Year 1 cash flow in dollars is £7(1.7553 $/£) = $12.29 million. Table 17-5 shows the complete time line and the net present value of $2.92 million.

SELF-TEST QUESTIONS List some key differences in capital budgeting as applied to foreign versus domestic operations.

What are the relevant cash flows for an international investment—the cash flow produced by the subsidiary in the country where it operates or the cash flows in dollars that it sends to its parent company?

Why might the cost of capital for a foreign project differ from that of an equivalent domestic project? Could it be lower?

What adjustments might be made to the domestic cost of capital for a foreign investment due to exchange rate risk and political risk?

TABLE 17-5 | Net Present Value of International Investment
(cash flows in millions)

	Year			
	0	1	2	3
Cash flows in pounds	−£20	£7	£9	£11
Expected exchange rates	1.8000	1.7553	1.7623	1.7709
Cash flows in dollars	−$36.00	$12.29	$15.86	$19.48
Project cost of capital =	10%			
NPV =	$2.92			

INTERNATIONAL CAPITAL STRUCTURES

Companies' capital structures vary among countries. For example, the Organization for Economic Cooperation and Development (OECD) recently reported that, on average, Japanese firms use 85 percent debt to total assets (in book value terms), German firms use 64 percent, and U.S. firms use 55 percent. One problem, however, when interpreting these numbers is that different countries often use very different accounting conventions with regard to (1) reporting assets on a historical- versus a replacement-cost basis, (2) the treatment of leased assets, (3) pension plan funding, and (4) capitalizing versus expensing R&D costs. These differences make it difficult to compare capital structures.

A study by Raghuram Rajan and Luigi Zingales of the University of Chicago attempted to control for differences in accounting practices. In their study, Rajan and Zingales used a database that covered fewer firms than the OECD but that provided a more complete breakdown of balance sheet data. They concluded that differences in accounting practices can explain much of the cross-country variation in capital structures.

Rajan and Zingales's results are summarized in Table 17-6. There are a number of different ways to measure capital structure. One measure is the average ratio of total liabilities to total assets—this is similar to the measure used by the OECD, and it is reported in Column 1. Based on this measure, German and Japanese firms appear to be more highly levered than U.S. firms. However, if you look at Column 2, where capital structure is measured by interest-bearing debt to total assets, it appears that German firms use less leverage than U.S. and Japanese firms. What explains this difference? Rajan and Zingales argue that much of this difference is explained by the way German firms account for pension liabilities. German firms generally include all pension liabilities (and their offsetting assets) on the balance sheet, whereas firms in other countries (including the United States) generally "net out" pension assets and liabilities on their balance sheets. To see the importance of this difference, consider a firm with $10 million in liabilities (not including pension liabilities) and $20 million in assets (not including pension assets). Assume that the firm has $10 million in pension liabilities that are fully funded by $10 million in pension assets. Therefore, net pension liabilities are zero. If this firm were in the United States, it would report a ratio of total liabilities to total assets equal to 50 percent ($10 million/$20 million). By contrast, if this firm operated in Germany, both its pension assets and liabilities would be reported on the balance sheet. The firm would have $20 million in liabilities and $30 million in assets—or a 67 percent ($20 million/$30 million) ratio of total liabilities to total assets. Total debt is the sum of short-term debt and long-term debt and excludes other liabilities including pension liabilities. Therefore, the measure of total debt to total assets provides a more comparable measure of leverage across different countries.

Rajan and Zingales also make a variety of adjustments that attempt to control for other differences in accounting practices. The effects of these adjustments are reported in Columns 3 and 4. Overall, the evidence suggests that companies in Germany and the

TABLE 17-6 | Median Capital Structures among Large Industrialized Countries (Measured in Terms of Book Value)

Country	Total Liabilities to Total Assets (Unadjusted for Accounting Differences) (1)	Interest-Bearing Debt to Total Assets (Unadjusted for Accounting Differences) (2)	Total Liabilities to Total Assets (Adjusted for Accounting Differences) (3)	Debt to Total Assets (Adjusted for Accounting Differences) (4)	Times-Interest-Earned (TIE) Ratio (5)
Canada	56%	32%	48%	32%	1.55×
France	71	25	69	18	2.64
Germany	73	16	50	11	3.20
Italy	70	27	68	21	1.81
Japan	69	35	62	21	2.46
United Kingdom	54	18	47	10	4.79
United States	58	27	52	25	2.41
Mean	64%	26%	57%	20%	2.69×
Standard deviation	8%	7%	10%	8%	1.07×

Source: Raghuram Rajan and Luigi Zingales, "What Do We Know about Capital Structure? Some Evidence from International Data," *The Journal of Finance*, Vol. 50, no. 5, December 1995, 1421–1460. Published by Blackwell Publishing.

United Kingdom tend to have less leverage, whereas firms in Canada appear to have more leverage, relative to firms in the United States, France, Italy, and Japan. This conclusion is supported by data in the final column, which shows the average times-interest-earned ratio for firms in a number of different countries. Recall from Chapter 4 that the times-interest-earned ratio is the ratio of operating income (EBIT) to interest expense. This measure indicates how much cash the firm has available to service its interest expense. In general, firms with more leverage have a lower times-interest-earned ratio. The data indicate that this ratio is highest in the United Kingdom and Germany and lowest in Canada.

> SELF-TEST QUESTION   Do international differences in financial leverage exist? Explain.

MULTINATIONAL WORKING CAPITAL MANAGEMENT

Cash Management

The goals of cash management in a multinational corporation are similar to those in a purely domestic corporation: (1) to speed up collections, slow down disbursements, and thus maximize net float; (2) to shift cash as rapidly as possible from those parts of the business where it is not needed to those parts where it is needed; and (3) to maximize the risk-adjusted, after-tax rate of return on temporary cash balances. Multinational companies use the same general procedures for achieving these goals as domestic firms, but because of longer distances and more serious mail delays, such devices as lockbox systems and electronic funds transfers are especially important.

Although multinational and domestic corporations have the same objectives and use similar procedures, multinational corporations face a far more complex task. As noted earlier in our discussion of political risk, foreign governments often place restrictions on transfers of funds out of the country, so although IBM can transfer money from its Salt Lake City office to its New York concentration bank just by pressing a few buttons, a similar transfer from its Buenos Aires office is far more complex. Buenos Aires funds must be converted to dollars before the transfer. If there is a shortage of dollars in Argentina, or if the Argentinean government wants to conserve dollars so they will be available for the purchase of strategic materials, then conversion, hence the transfer, may be blocked. Even if no dollar shortage exists in Argentina, the government may still restrict funds outflows if those funds represent profits or depreciation rather than payments for purchased materials or equipment, because many countries, especially those that are less developed, want profits reinvested in the country in order to stimulate economic growth.

Once it has been determined what funds can be transferred, the next task is to get those funds to locations where they will earn the highest returns. Whereas domestic corporations tend to think in terms of domestic securities, multinationals are more likely to be aware of investment opportunities all around the world. Most multinational corporations use one or more global concentration banks, located in money centers such as London, New York, Tokyo, Zurich, or Singapore, and their staffs in those cities, working with international bankers, are able to take advantage of the best rates available anywhere in the world.

Credit Management

Consider the international cash conversion cycle for a foreign company importing from the United States: The order is placed, the goods are shipped, an account payable is created for the importer and an account receivable is created for the exporter, the goods arrive in the foreign country, the importer sells them, and the importer collects on the sales. At some point in this process the importer pays off the account payable, which is usually before the importer collects on its own sales. Notice that the importer must finance the transaction from the time it pays the account payable until it collects on its sales. In many poorer, less-developed nations, the capital markets are not adequate to enable the importer to finance the cash conversion cycle. Even when foreign capital markets are available, the additional shipping time might lengthen the cash conversion cycle to such an extent that the importer can't afford the financing costs. Thus, there is enormous pressure on the exporter to grant credit, often with very lengthy payment periods.

But now consider the situation from the exporter's point of view. First, it is much more difficult for the exporter to perform a credit analysis on a foreign customer. Second, the exporter must also worry about exchange-rate fluctuations between the time of the sale and the time the receivable is collected. For example, if IBM sold a computer to a Japanese customer for 90 million yen when the exchange rate was 90 yen to the dollar, IBM would obtain 90,000,000/90 = $1,000,000 for the computer. However, if it sold the computer on terms of net/6 months, and if the yen fell against the dollar so that 1 dollar would now buy 112.5 yen, IBM would end up realizing only 90,000,000/112.5 = $800,000 when it collected the receivable. Hedging with forward contracts can reduce this exchange rate risk, but what about the credit risk?

One possibility is for the importer to obtain a letter of credit from its bank, whereby the bank certifies that the importer will meet the terms of the account payable or else the bank will pay. However, the importer often must pay the bank a relatively large fee for the letter of credit, and letters of credit might not be available to companies in developing countries.

A second option is for the importer to essentially write a check to the exporter at the time of the purchase, but one that is postdated so that it cannot be cashed until the account payable's due date. If the importer's bank promises that it will "accept" the check even if there are insufficient funds in the importer's account, then the check becomes a financial instrument that is called a **banker's acceptance**. If the bank is strong, then this virtually eliminates the credit risk. In addition, the exporter can then sell this banker's acceptance in the secondary market if it needs funds immediately. Of course, it must sell the banker's acceptance at a discount to reflect the time value of money, because the banker's acceptance is essentially a short-term financial security that pays no interest, similar to a T-bill.

Financing an international transaction via a banker's acceptance has many benefits for the exporter, but the importer often must pay the bank a relatively large fee, and this service might not be available to companies in developing countries.

A third alternative is for the exporter to purchase export credit insurance, in which an insurer makes a commitment to pay the exporter even if the importer defaults. Sometimes the "insurer" is a government agency, such as the Japanese Ministry of International Trade and Industry (MITI) or the United States Export-Import Bank. But the last decade has seen a dramatic increase in the availability of export credit insurance from private insurance companies. These large insurance companies have developed expertise in international credit analysis and they can spread the risk over a large number of customers. These advantages allow them to offer credit insurance at rates that often make it less costly than either letters of credit or banker's acceptances. In fact, export credit insurance has been so successful that it has virtually killed the market for bankers' acceptances and has become the primary method companies use to manage the credit risk of international sales.

Inventory Management

As with most other aspects of finance, inventory management for a firm in a multinational setting is similar to but more complex than for a purely domestic firm. First, there is the matter of the physical location of inventories. For example, where should ExxonMobil keep its stockpiles of crude oil and refined products? It has refineries and marketing centers located worldwide, and one alternative is to keep items concentrated in a few strategic spots from which they can then be shipped as needs arise. Such a strategy might minimize the total amount of inventories needed and thus might minimize the investment in inventories. Note, though, that consideration will have to be given to potential delays in getting goods from central storage locations to user locations all around the world. Both working stocks and safety stocks would have to be maintained at each user location, as well as at the strategic storage centers. Problems like the Iraqi occupation of Kuwait in 1990 and the subsequent trade embargo, which brought with it the potential for a shutdown of production of about 25 percent of the world's oil supply, complicate matters further.

Exchange rates also influence inventory policy. If a local currency, say, the Danish krone, were expected to rise in value against the dollar, a U.S. company operating in Denmark would want to increase stocks of local products before the rise in the krone, and vice versa if the krone were expected to fall.

Another factor that must be considered is the possibility of import or export quotas or tariffs. For example, Apple Computer Company was buying certain memory chips from Japanese suppliers at a bargain price. Then U.S. chipmakers accused the Japanese of dumping chips in the U.S. market at prices below cost, so they sought to force the Japanese to raise prices.[2] That led Apple to increase its chip inventory. Then computer sales slacked off, and Apple ended up with an oversupply of obsolete computer chips. As a result, Apple's profits were hurt and its stock price fell, demonstrating once more the importance of careful inventory management.

As mentioned earlier, another danger in certain countries is the threat of expropriation. If that threat is large, inventory holdings will be minimized, and goods will be brought in only as needed. Similarly, if the operation involves extraction of raw materials such as oil

---

[2] The term "dumping" warrants explanation, because the practice is so potentially important in international markets. Suppose Japanese chipmakers have excess capacity. A particular chip has a variable cost of $25, and its "fully allocated cost," which is the $25 plus total fixed cost per unit of output, is $40. Now suppose the Japanese firm can sell chips in the United States at $35 per unit, but if it charges $40, it will not make any sales because U.S. chipmakers sell for $35.50. If the Japanese firm sells at $35, it will cover variable cost plus make a contribution to fixed overhead, so selling at $35 makes sense. Continuing, if the Japanese firm can sell in Japan at $40, but U.S. firms are excluded from Japanese markets by import duties or other barriers, the Japanese will have a huge advantage over U.S. manufacturers. This practice of selling goods at lower prices in foreign markets than at home is called "dumping." U.S. firms are required by antitrust laws to offer the same price to all customers and, therefore, cannot engage in dumping.

or bauxite, processing plants may be moved offshore rather than located close to the production site.

Taxes have two effects on multinational inventory management. First, countries often impose property taxes on assets, including inventories, and when this is done, the tax is based on holdings as of a specific date, say, January 1 or March 1. Such rules make it advantageous for a multinational firm (1) to schedule production so that inventories are low on the assessment date, and (2) if assessment dates vary among countries in a region, to hold safety stocks in different countries at different times during the year.

Finally, multinational firms may consider the possibility of at-sea storage. Oil, chemical, grain, and other companies that deal in a bulk commodity that must be stored in some type of tank can often buy tankers at a cost not much greater—or perhaps even less, considering land cost—than land-based facilities. Loaded tankers can then be kept at sea or at anchor in some strategic location. This eliminates the danger of expropriation, minimizes the property tax problem, and maximizes flexibility with regard to shipping to areas where needs are greatest or prices highest.

This discussion has only scratched the surface of inventory management in the multinational corporation—the task is much more complex than for a purely domestic firm. However, the greater the degree of complexity, the greater the rewards from superior performance, so if you want challenge along with potentially high rewards, look to the international arena.

| SELF-TEST QUESTIONS |

What are some factors that make cash management especially complicated in a multinational corporation?

Why is granting credit especially risky in an international context?

Why is inventory management especially important for a multinational firm?

SUMMARY

Multinational companies have more opportunities but also face different risks than do companies that operate only in their home market. The chapter discussed many of the key trends affecting the global markets today, and it described the most important differences between multinational and domestic financial management. The key concepts are listed below:

- **International operations** are becoming increasingly important to individual firms and to the national economy. A **multinational, or global, corporation** is a firm that operates in an integrated fashion in a number of countries.
- Companies "go global" for six primary reasons: (1) **to expand their markets,** (2) **to obtain raw materials,** (3) **to seek new technology,** (4) **to lower production costs,** (5) **to avoid trade barriers,** and (6) **to diversify.**
- Six major factors distinguish financial management as practiced by domestic firms from that practiced by multinational corporations: (1) **different currency denominations,** (2) **different economic and legal structures,** (3) **languages,** (4) **cultural differences,** (5) **role of governments,** and (6) **political risk.**
- When discussing **exchange rates,** the number of U.S. dollars required to purchase one unit of a foreign currency is called a **direct quotation,** while the number of units of foreign currency that can be purchased for one U.S. dollar is an **indirect quotation.**
- **Exchange rate fluctuations** make it difficult to estimate the dollars that overseas operations will produce.

- Prior to August 1971, the world was on a **fixed exchange rate system** whereby the U.S. dollar was linked to gold, and other currencies were then tied to the dollar. After August 1971, the world monetary system changed to a **floating system** under which major world currency rates float with market forces, largely unrestricted by governmental intervention. The central bank of each country does operate in the foreign exchange market, buying and selling currencies to smooth out exchange rate fluctuations, but only to a limited extent.
- The consolidation of the European market has had a profound impact on European exchange rates. The exchange rates for the currencies of each of the participating countries were fixed relative to the **euro.** Consequently, the cross rates between the various participating currencies were also fixed. However, the value of the euro continues to fluctuate.
- **Pegged exchange rates** occur when a country establishes a fixed exchange rate with a major currency. Consequently, the values of pegged currencies move together over time.
- A **convertible currency** is one that may be readily exchanged for other currencies.
- **Spot rates** are the rates paid for delivery of currency "on the spot," while the **forward exchange rate** is the rate paid for delivery at some agreed-upon future date, usually 30, 90, or 180 days from the day the transaction is negotiated. The forward rate can be at either a **premium** or a **discount** to the spot rate.
- **Interest rate parity** holds that investors should expect to earn the same risk-free return in all countries after adjusting for exchange rates.
- **Purchasing power parity,** sometimes referred to as the *law of one price,* implies that the level of exchange rates adjusts so that identical goods cost the same in different countries.
- Granting credit is more risky in an international context because, in addition to the normal risks of default, the multinational firm must worry about **exchange rate changes** between the time a sale is made and the time a receivable is collected.
- Credit policy is important for a multinational firm for two reasons: (1) Much trade is with less-developed nations, and in such situations granting credit is a necessary condition for doing business. (2) The governments of nations such as Japan whose economic health depends upon exports often help their firms compete by granting credit to foreign customers.
- Foreign investments are similar to domestic investments, but political risk and exchange rate risk must be considered. **Political risk** is the risk that the foreign government will take some action that will decrease the value of the investment, while **exchange rate risk** is the risk of losses due to fluctuations in the value of the dollar relative to the values of foreign currencies.
- Investments in **international capital projects** expose firms to exchange rate risk and political risk. The relevant cash flows in international capital budgeting are the dollars that can be **repatriated** to the parent company.
- **Eurodollars** are U.S. dollars deposited in banks outside the United States. Interest rates on Eurodollars are tied to **LIBOR,** the London Interbank Offer Rate.
- U.S. firms often find that they can raise long-term capital at a lower cost outside the United States by selling bonds in the **international capital markets.** International bonds may be either **foreign bonds,** which are exactly like regular domestic bonds except that the issuer is a foreign company, or **Eurobonds,** which are bonds sold in a foreign country but denominated in the currency of the issuing company's home country.

QUESTIONS

(17-1) Define each of the following terms:
    a. Multinational corporation
    b. Exchange rate; fixed exchange rate system; floating exchange rates
    c. Trade deficit; devaluation; revaluation

d. Exchange rate risk; convertible currency; pegged exchange rates
e. Interest rate parity; purchasing power parity
f. Spot rate; forward exchange rate; discount on forward rate; premium on forward rate
g. Repatriation of earnings; political risk
h. Eurodollar; Eurobond; international bond; foreign bond
i. The euro

(17-2) Under the fixed exchange rate system, what was the currency against which all other currency values were defined? Why?

(17-3) Exchange rates fluctuate under both the fixed exchange rate and floating exchange rate systems. What, then, is the difference between the two systems?

(17-4) If the Swiss franc depreciates against the U.S. dollar, can a dollar buy more or fewer Swiss francs as a result?

(17-5) If the United States imports more goods from abroad than it exports, foreigners will tend to have a surplus of U.S. dollars. What will this do to the value of the dollar with respect to foreign currencies? What is the corresponding effect on foreign investments in the United States?

(17-6) Why do U.S. corporations build manufacturing plants abroad when they could build them at home?

(17-7) Should firms require higher rates of return on foreign projects than on identical projects located at home? Explain.

(17-8) What is a Eurodollar? If a French citizen deposits $10,000 in Chase Manhattan Bank in New York, have Eurodollars been created? What if the deposit is made in Barclay's Bank in London? Chase Manhattan's Paris branch? Does the existence of the Eurodollar market make the Federal Reserve's job of controlling U.S. interest rates easier or more difficult? Explain.

(17-9) Does interest rate parity imply that interest rates are the same in all countries?

(17-10) Why might purchasing power parity fail to hold?

SELF-TEST PROBLEM   Solution Appears in Appendix A

(ST-1) Suppose the exchange rate between U.S. dollars and EMU euros is €0.98 = $1.00,
Cross Rates and the exchange rate between the U.S. dollar and the Canadian dollar is $1.00 = C$1.50. What is the cross rate of euros to Candian dollars?

PROBLEMS

(17-1) A currency trader observes that in the spot exchange market, 1 U.S. dollar can be
Cross Rates exchanged for 9 Mexican pesos or for 111.23 Japanese yen. What is the cross-exchange rate between the yen and the peso; that is, how many yen would you receive for every peso exchanged?

(17-2) Six-month T-bills have a nominal rate of 7 percent, while default-free Japanese
Interest Rate Parity bonds that mature in 6 months have a nominal rate of 5.5 percent. In the spot exchange market, 1 yen equals $0.009. If interest rate parity holds, what is the 6-month forward exchange rate?

(17-3) A television set costs $500 in the United States. The same set costs 550 euros in
Purchasing Power Parity France. If purchasing power parity holds, what is the spot exchange rate between the euro and the dollar?

(17-4)
Exchange Rate
If British pounds sell for $1.50 (U.S.) per pound, what should dollars sell for in pounds per dollar?

(17-5)
Currency Appreciation
Suppose that 1 Swiss franc could be purchased in the foreign exchange market for 60 U.S. cents today. If the franc appreciated 10 percent tomorrow against the dollar, how many francs would a dollar buy tomorrow?

(17-6)
Cross Exchange Rates
Suppose the exchange rate between U.S. dollars and the Swiss franc was SFr1.6 = $1, and the exchange rate between the dollar and the British pound was £1 = $1.50. What was the exchange rate between francs and pounds?

(17-7)
Exchange Gains and Losses
You are the vice president of International InfoXchange, headquartered in Chicago, Illinois. All shareholders of the firm live in the United States. Earlier this month, you obtained a loan of 5 million Canadian dollars from a bank in Toronto to finance the construction of a new plant in Montreal. At the time the loan was received, the exchange rate was 75 U.S. cents to the Canadian dollar. By the end of the month, it has unexpectedly dropped to 70 cents. Has your company made a gain or loss as a result, and by how much?

(17-8)
Results of Exchange Rate Changes
Early in September 1983, it took 245 Japanese yen to equal $1. More than 20 years later that exchange rate had fallen to 108 yen to $1. Assume the price of a Japanese-manufactured automobile was $8,000 in September 1983 and that its price changes were in direct relation to exchange rates.
a. Has the price, in dollars, of the automobile increased or decreased during the 20-year period because of changes in the exchange rate?
b. What would the dollar price of the car be, assuming the car's price changes only with exchange rates?

(17-9)
Spot and Forward Rates
Boisjoly Watch Imports has agreed to purchase 15,000 Swiss watches for 1 million francs at today's spot rate. The firm's financial manager, James Desreumaux, has noted the following current spot and forward rates:

	U.S. Dollar/Franc	Franc/U.S. Dollar
Spot	1.6590	0.6028
30-day forward	1.6540	0.6046
90-day forward	1.6460	0.6075
180-day forward	1.6400	0.6098

On the same day, Desreumaux agrees to purchase 15,000 more watches in 3 months at the same price of 1 million francs.
a. What is the price of the watches, in U.S. dollars, if purchased at today's spot rate?
b. What is the cost, in dollars, of the second 15,000 batch if payment is made in 90 days and the spot rate at that time equals today's 90-day forward rate?
c. If the exchange rate for the Swiss franc is 0.50 to $1 in 90 days, how much will he have to pay for the watches (in dollars)?

(17-10)
Interest Rate Parity
Assume that interest rate parity holds and that 90-day risk-free securities yield 5 percent in the United States and 5.3 percent in Germany. In the spot market, 1 euro equals $0.80 dollar.
a. Is the 90-day forward rate trading at a premium or discount relative to the spot rate?
b. What is the 90-day forward rate?

(17-11)
Interest Rate Parity
Assume that interest rate parity holds. In both the spot market and the 90-day forward market 1 Japanese yen equals 0.0086 dollar. The 90-day risk-free securities yield 4.6 percent in Japan. What is the yield on 90-day risk-free securities in the United States?

(17-12)
Purchasing Power Parity
In the spot market 7.8 pesos can be exchanged for 1 U.S. dollar. A compact disk costs $15 in the United States. If purchasing power parity holds, what should be the price of the same disk in Mexico?

SPREADSHEET PROBLEM

(17-13)
Build a Model:
Multinational Financial
Management

e-resource

Start with the partial model in the file *CF2 Ch 17 P13 Build a Model.xls* from the textbook's Web site. Yohe Telecommunications is a multinational corporation that produces and distributes telecommunications technology. Although its corporate headquarters are located in Maitland, Florida, Yohe usually must buy its raw materials in several different foreign countries using several different foreign currencies. The matter is further complicated because Yohe usually sells its products in other foreign countries. One product in particular, the SY-20 radio transmitter, draws its principal components, Component X, Component Y, and Component Z, from Germany, Mexico, and England, respectively. Specifically, Component X costs 84 euros, Component Y costs 650 Mexican pesos, and Component Z costs 105 British pounds. The largest market for the SY-20 is in Japan, where it sells for 38,000 Japanese yen. Naturally, Yohe is intimately concerned with economic conditions that could adversely affect dollar exchange rates. You will find Tables 17-1, 17-2, and 17-3 useful for this problem.

a.   How much, in dollars, does it cost for Yohe to produce the SY-20? What is the dollar sale price of the SY-20?

b.   What is the dollar profit that Yohe makes on the sale of the SY-20? What is the percentage profit?

c.   If the U.S. dollar were to weaken by 10 percent against all foreign currencies, what would be the dollar profit for the SY-20?

d.   If the U.S. dollar were to weaken by 10 percent only against the Japanese yen and remained constant relative to all other foreign currencies, what would be the dollar and percentage profits for the SY-20?

e.   Using the forward exchange information from Table 17-3, calculate the return on 1-year securities in England, if the rate of return on 1-year securities in the United States is 4.9 percent.

f.   Assuming that purchasing power parity (PPP) holds, what would be the sale price of the SY-20 if it were sold in England rather than Japan?

CYBERPROBLEM

Please go to our Web site, **http://ehrhardt.swlearning.com**, to access any Cyberproblems.

THOMSON ONE
Business School Edition

Please go to **http://ehrhardt.swlearning.com** to access any Thomson ONE—Business School Edition problems.

MINI CASE

Citrus Products Inc. is a medium-sized producer of citrus juice drinks with groves in Indian River County, Florida. Until now, the company has confined its operations and sales to the United States, but its CEO, George Gaynor, wants to expand into Europe. The first step would be to set up sales subsidiaries in Spain and Sweden, then to set up a production plant in Spain, and, finally, to distribute the product throughout the European common market. The firm's financial manager, Ruth Schmidt, is enthusiastic about the plan, but she is worried about the implications of the foreign expansion on the firm's financial management process. She has asked you, the firm's most recently hired financial analyst, to develop a 1-hour tutorial package that explains the basics of multinational financial management. The tutorial will be presented at the next board of directors' meeting. To get you started, Schmidt has supplied you with the following list of questions.

a.   What is a multinational corporation? Why do firms expand into other countries?

b.   What are the six major factors that distinguish multinational financial management from financial management as practiced by a purely domestic firm?

c. Consider the following illustrative exchange rates.

	U.S. Dollars Required to Buy One Unit of Foreign Currency
Euro	0.8000
Swedish krona	0.1000

(1) Are these currency prices direct quotations or indirect quotations?

(2) Calculate the indirect quotations for euros and kronas.

(3) What is a cross rate? Calculate the two cross rates between euros and kronas.

(4) Assume Citrus Products can produce a liter of orange juice and ship it to Spain for $1.75. If the firm wants a 50 percent markup on the product, what should the orange juice sell for in Spain?

(5) Now, assume Citrus Products begins producing the same liter of orange juice in Spain. The product costs 2.0 euros to produce and ship to Sweden, where it can be sold for 20 kronas. What is the dollar profit on the sale?

(6) What is exchange rate risk?

d. Briefly describe the current international monetary system. How does the current system differ from the system that was in place prior to August 1971?

e. What is a convertible currency? What problems arise when a multinational company operates in a country whose currency is not convertible?

f. What is the difference between spot rates and forward rates? When is the forward rate at a premium to the spot rate? At a discount?

g. What is interest rate parity? Currently, you can exchange 1 euro for 0.8100 dollar in the 180-day forward market, and the risk-free rate on 180-day securities is 6 percent in the United States and 4 percent in Spain. Does interest rate parity hold? If not, which securities offer the highest expected return?

h. What is purchasing power parity? If grapefruit juice costs $2.00 a liter in the United States and purchasing power parity holds, what should be the price of grapefruit juice in Spain?

i. What effect does relative inflation have on interest rates and exchange rates?

j. Briefly discuss the international capital markets.

k. To what extent do average capital structures vary across different countries?

l. Briefly describe special problems that occur in multinational capital budgeting and describe the process for evaluating a foreign project. Now consider the following project: A U.S. company has the opportunity to lease a manufacturing facility in Japan for 2 years. The company must spend ¥1 billion initially to refurbish the plant. The expected net cash flows from the plant for the next two years, in millions, are $CF_1 = ¥500$ and $CF_2 = ¥800$. A similar project in the United States would have a risk adjusted cost of capital of 10 percent. In the United States, a 1-year government bond pays 2 percent interest and a 2-year bond pays 2.8 percent. In Japan, a 1-year bond pays 0.05 percent and a 2-year bond pays 0.26 percent. What is the project's NPV?

m. Briefly discuss special factors associated with the following areas of multinational working capital management:

(1) Cash management.

(2) Credit management.

(3) Inventory management.

SELECTED ADDITIONAL REFERENCES AND CASES

Perhaps the best way to obtain more information on multinational financial management is to consult one of the many excellent textbooks on the subject. For example, see

Eaker, Mark R., Frank J. Fabozzi, and Dwight Grant, *International Corporate Finance* (Fort Worth, TX: The Dryden Press, 1996).

Levi, Maurice, *International Finance* (New York: McGraw-Hill, 1996).

Madura, Jeff, *International Financial Management* (Mason, OH: Thomson/South-Western, 2003).

For some articles on multinational financial management, see

Carre, Herve, and Karen H. Johnson, "Progress Toward a European Monetary Union," *Federal Reserve Bulletin*, October 1991, 769–783.

Choi, Jongmoo Jay, and Anita Mehra Prasad, "Exchange Risk Sensitivity and Its Determinants: A Firm and Industry Analysis of U.S. Multinationals," *Financial Management*, Autumn 1995, 77–88.

Frankel, Jeffrey A., "The Japanese Cost of Finance," *Financial Management*, Spring 1991, 95–127.

Hammer, Jerry A., "Hedging Performance and Hedging Objectives: Tests of New Performance Measures in the Foreign Currency Market," *Journal of Financial Research*, Winter 1990, 307–323.

Hunter, William C., and Stephen G. Timme, "A Stochastic Dominance Approach to Evaluating Foreign Exchange Hedging Strategies," *Financial Management*, Autumn 1992, 104–112.

Kester, George W., Rosita P. Chang, and Kai-Chong Tsui, "Corporate Financial Policy in the Pacific Basin: Hong Kong and Singapore," *Financial Practice and Education*, Spring/Summer 1994, 117–127.

Lee, Insup, and Steve B. Wyatt, "The Effects of International Joint Ventures on Shareholder Wealth," *Financial Review*, November 1990.

Mahajan, Arvind, "Pricing Expropriation Risk," *Financial Management*, Winter 1990, 77–86.

Pauls, B. Dianne, "U.S. Exchange Rate Policy: Bretton Woods to Present," *Federal Reserve Bulletin*, November 1990, 891–908.

The following case from the Finance Online Case Library *covers many of the concepts discussed in this chapter and is available at* **http://www.textchoice.com:**

Case 18, "Alaska Oil Corporation."

Solutions to Self-Test Problems

Chapter 1

ST-1 a. Average = (4% + 5% + 6% + 7%)/4 = 22%/4 = 5.5%.

b. $r_{\text{T-bond}} = r^* + IP = 2\% + 5.5\% = 7.5\%$.

c. If the 5-year T-bond rate is 8 percent, the inflation rate is expected to average approximately 8% − 2% = 6% during the next 5 years. Thus, the implied Year 5 inflation rate is 8 percent:

$$6\% = (4\% + 5\% + 6\% + 7\% + I_5)/5$$
$$30\% = 22\% + I_5$$
$$I_5 = 8\%.$$

Chapter 2

ST-1 a.

0	8%	1	2	3	4
		−1,000			FV = ?

$1,000 is being compounded for 3 years, so your balance at Year 4 is $1,259.71:

$$FV_n = PV(1 + i)^n = \$1{,}000(1 + 0.08)^3 = \$1{,}259.71.$$

Alternatively, using a financial calculator, input N = 3, I = 8, PV = −1000, PMT = 0, and FV = ? FV = $1,259.71.

b.

0		4	8	12	16
2%					
	−1,000				FV = ?

Use FVIF for 2%, 3 × 4 = 12 periods:

$$FV_{12} = \$1{,}000(FVIF_{2\%,12}) = \$1{,}000(1 + 0.02)^{12} = \$1{,}000(1.2682) = \$1{,}268.20.$$

Alternatively, using a financial calculator, input N = 12, I = 2, PV = −1000, PMT = 0, and FV = ? FV = $1,268.24. (Note that a rounding difference occurs.)

c.

0	8%	1	2	3	4
		250	250	250	250
					FV = ?

As you work this problem, keep in mind that the payments are made at the end of each period. Therefore, you may solve this problem by finding the future value of an annuity of $250 for 4 years at 8 percent:

$$FVA_4 = PMT(FVIFA_{i,n}) = \$250\left(\frac{(1 + 0.08)^4 - 1}{0.08}\right) = \$250(4.5061) = \$1{,}126.53.$$

Alternatively, using a financial calculator, input N = 4, I = 8, PV = 0, PMT = −250, and FV = ? FV = $1,126.53.

d.

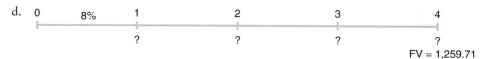

N = 4; I = 8; PV = 0; FV = 1259.71; PMT = ?; PMT = $279.56.

Alternatively,

$$PMT(FVIFA_{8\%,4}) = FVA_4$$

$$PMT\left(\frac{(1 + 0.08)^4 - 1}{0.08}\right) = \$1,259.71$$

$$PMT(4.5061) = \$1,259.71$$

$$PMT = \$1,259.71/4.5061 = \$279.56.$$

Therefore, you would have to make 4 payments of $279.56 each to have a balance of $1,259.71 in 4 years.

ST-2 a. Set up a time line like the one in the preceding problem:

Note that your deposit will grow for 3 years at 8 percent. The deposit at Year 1 is the PV, and the FV is $1,000. Here is the solution:

N = 3; I = 8; PMT = 0; FV = 1000; PV = ?; PV = $793.83.

Alternatively,

$$FV_3(PVIF_{8\%,3}) = PV$$

$$\$1,000\left(\frac{1}{(1 + 0.08)^3}\right) = PV$$

$$PV = \$1,000(0.7938) = \$793.80 = \text{Initial deposit to accumulate } \$1,000.$$

(Difference due to rounding.)

b.

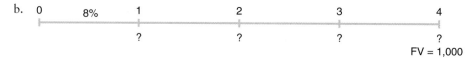

Here we are dealing with a 4-year annuity whose first payment occurs 1 year from today, and whose future value must equal $1,000. You should modify the time line to help visualize the situation. Here is the solution:

N = 4; I = 8; PV = 0; FV = 1000; PMT = ?; PMT = $221.92.

Alternatively,

$$PMT(FVIFA_{8\%,4}) = FVA_4$$

$$PMT\left(\frac{(1 + 0.08)^4 - 1}{0.08}\right) = \$1,000$$

$$PMT = \frac{\$1,000}{4.5061} = \$221.92 = \begin{array}{l}\text{Payment necessary}\\ \text{to accumulate } \$1,000\end{array}$$

c. This problem can be approached in several ways. Perhaps the simpliest is to ask this question: "If I received $750 1 year from now and deposited it to earn 8 percent, would I have the required $1,000 4 years from now?" The answer is no:

$$FV_3 = \$750(1.08)(1.08)(1.08) = \$944.78.$$

This indicates that you should let your father make the payments rather than accept the lump sum of $750.

You could also compare the $750 with the PV of the payments:

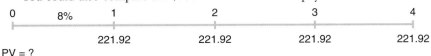

$N = 4; I = 8; PMT = -221.92; FV = 0; PV = ?; PV = \$735.03.$

Alternatively,

$$PMT(PVIFA_{8\%,4}) = PVA_4$$

$$\$221.92\left(\frac{1 - \dfrac{1}{(1 + 0.08)^4}}{0.08}\right) = PVA_4$$

$$\$221.92(3.3121) = \$735.02 = \begin{matrix}\text{Present value} \\ \text{of the required payments}\end{matrix}$$

(Difference due to rounding.)

This is less than the $750 lump sum offer, so your initial reaction might be to accept the lump sum of $750. However, this would be a mistake. The problem is that when you found the $735.02 PV of the annuity, you were finding the value of the annuity *today*. You were comparing $735.02 today with the lump sum of $750 1 year from now. This is, of course, invalid. What you should have done was take the $735.02, recognize that this is the PV of an annuity as of today, multiply $735.02 by 1.08 to get $793.82, and compare $793.82 with the lump sum of $750. You would then take your father's offer to make the payments rather than take the lump sum 1 year from now.

d.

$N = 3; PV = -750; PMT = 0; FV = 1000; I = ?; I = 10.0642\%.$

e.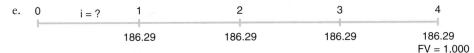

$N = 4; PV = 0; PMT = -186.29; FV = 1000; I = ?; I = 19.9997\%.$

You might be able to find a borrower willing to offer you a 20 percent interest rate, but there would be some risk involved—he or she might not actually pay you your $1,000!

f.

Find the future value of the original $400 deposit:

$$FV_6 = PV(FVIF_{4\%,6}) = \$400(1 + 0.04)^6 = \$400(1.2653) = \$506.12.$$

This means that at Year 4, you need an additional sum of \$493.88:

$$\$1,000.00 = \$506.12 = \$493.88.$$

This will be accumulated by making 6 equal payments which earn 8 percent compounded semiannually, or 4 percent each 6 months:

N = 6; I = 4; PV = 0; FV = 493.88; PMT = ?; PMT = \$74.46.

Alternatively,

$$PMT(FVIFA_{4\%,6}) = FVA_6$$

$$PMT\left(\frac{(1 + 0.04)^6 - 1}{0.04}\right) = \$493.88$$

$$PMT = \frac{\$493.88}{6.6330} = \$74.46.$$

Alternatively, using a financial calculator, input N = 6, I = 4, PV = −400, FV = 1000, and PMT = ?; PMT = \$74.46.

g.

$$\text{Effective annual rate} = \left(1 + \frac{i_{Nom}}{m}\right)^m - 1.0$$

$$= \left(1 + \frac{0.08}{2}\right)^2 - 1 = (1.04)^2 - 1$$

$$= 1.0816 - 1 = 0.0816 = 8.16\%.$$

ST-3 Bank A's effective annual rate is 8.24 percent:

$$\text{Effective annual rate} = \left(1 + \frac{0.08}{4}\right)^4 - 1.0$$

$$= (1.02)^4 - 1 = 1.0824 - 1$$

$$= 0.0824 = 8.24\%.$$

Now Bank B must have the same effective annual rate:

$$\left(1 + \frac{i}{12}\right)^{12} - 1.0 = 0.0824$$

$$\left(1 + \frac{i}{12}\right)^{12} = 1.0824$$

$$1 + \frac{i}{12} = (1.0824)^{1/12}$$

$$1 + \frac{i}{12} = 1.00662$$

$$\frac{i}{12} = 0.00662$$

$$i = 0.07944 = 7.94\%.$$

Thus, the two banks have different quoted rates—Bank A's quoted rate is 8 percent, while Bank B's quoted rate is 7.94 percent; however, both banks have the same effective annual rate of 8.24 percent. The difference in their quoted rates is due to the difference in compounding frequency.

Chapter 3

ST-1 a.

EBIT	\$5,000,000
Interest	1,000,000
EBT	\$4,000,000
Taxes (40%)	1,600,000
Net income	\$2,400,000

b.
$$NCF = NI + DEP$$
$$= \$2,400,000 + \$1,000,000 = \$3,400,000.$$

c.
$$NOPAT = EBIT(1 - T)$$
$$= \$5,000,000(0.6)$$
$$= \$3,000,000.$$

d.
$$FCF = NOPAT - \text{Net investment in operating capital}$$
$$= \$3,000,000 - (\$25,000,000 - \$24,000,000)$$
$$= \$2,000,0000.$$

e.
$$EVA = EBIT(1 - T) - (\text{Total capital})(\text{After-tax cost of capital})$$
$$= \$5,000,000(0.6) - (\$25,000,000)(0.10)$$
$$= \$3,000,000 - \$2,500,000 = \$500,000.$$

Chapter 4

ST-1 Billingsworth paid $2 in dividends and retained $2 per share. Since total retained earnings rose by $12 million, there must be 6 million shares outstanding. With a book value of $40 per share, total common equity must be $40(6 million) = $240 million. Since Billingsworth has $120 million of debt, its debt ratio must be 33.3 percent:

$$\frac{\text{Debt}}{\text{Assets}} = \frac{\text{Debt}}{\text{Debt} + \text{Equity}} = \frac{\$120 \text{ million}}{\$120 \text{ million} + \$240 \text{ million}}$$
$$= 0.333 = 33.3\%.$$

ST-2 a. In answering questions such as this, always begin by writing down the relevant definitional equations, then start filling in numbers. Note that the extra zeros indicating millions have been deleted in the calculations below.

(1)
$$DSO = \frac{\text{Accounts receivable}}{\text{Sales}/365}$$
$$40.55 = \frac{\text{A/R}}{\$1,000/365}$$
$$\text{A/R} = 40.55(\$2.7397) = \$111.1 \text{ million.}$$

(2)
$$\text{Quick ratio} = \frac{\text{Current assets} - \text{Inventories}}{\text{Current liabilities}} = 2.0$$
$$= \frac{\text{Cash and marketable securities} + \text{A/R}}{\text{Current liabilities}} = 2.0$$
$$2.0 = \frac{\$100 + \$111.1}{\text{Current liabilities}}$$
$$\text{Current liabilities} = (\$100 + \$111.1)/2 = \$105.5 \text{ million.}$$

(3)
$$\text{Current ratio} = \frac{\text{Current assets}}{\text{Current liabilities}} = 3.0$$
$$= \frac{\text{Current assets}}{\$105.5} = 3.0$$
$$\text{Current assets} = 3.0(\$105.5) = \$316.50 \text{ million.}$$

(4)
$$\text{Total assets} = \text{Current assets} + \text{Fixed assets}$$
$$= \$316.5 + \$283.5 = \$600 \text{ million.}$$

(5)
$$\text{ROA} = \text{Profit margin} \times \text{Total assets turnover}$$
$$= \frac{\text{Net income}}{\text{Sales}} \times \frac{\text{Sales}}{\text{Total assets}}$$
$$= \frac{\$50}{\$1,000} \times \frac{\$1,000}{\$600}$$
$$= 0.05 \times 1.667 = 0.0833 = 8.33\%.$$

(6)
$$\text{ROE} = \text{ROA} \times \frac{\text{Assets}}{\text{Equity}}$$
$$12.0\% = 8.33\% \times \frac{\$600}{\text{Equity}}$$
$$\text{Equity} = \frac{(8.33\%)(\$600)}{12.0\%}$$
$$= \$416.50 \text{ million.}$$

(7)
$$\text{Total assets} = \text{Total claims} = \$600 \text{ million}$$
$$\text{Current liabilities} + \text{Long-term debt} + \text{Equity} = \$600 \text{ million}$$
$$\$105.5 + \text{Long-term debt} + \$416.5 = \$600 \text{ million}$$
$$\text{Long-term debt} = \$600 - \$105.5 - \$416.5 = \$78 \text{ million.}$$

Note: We could have found equity as follows:
$$\text{ROE} = \frac{\text{Net income}}{\text{Equity}}$$
$$12.0\% = \frac{\$50}{\text{Equity}}$$
$$\text{Equity} = \$50/0.12$$
$$= \$416.67 \text{ million (rounding difference).}$$

Then we could have gone on to find current liabilities and long-term debt.

b. Kaiser's average sales per day were $\$1,000/365 = \$2.7397$ million. Its DSO was 40.55, so A/R = 40.55($\$2.7397$) = $\$111.1$ million. Its new DSO of 30.4 would cause A/R = 30.4($\$2.7397$) = $\$83.3$ million. The reduction in receivables would be $\$111.1 - \$83.3 = \$27.8$ million, which would equal the amount of cash generated.

(1)
$$\text{New equity} = \text{Old equity} - \text{Stock bought back}$$
$$= \$416.5 - \$27.8$$
$$= \$388.7 \text{ million.}$$

Thus,
$$\text{New ROE} = \frac{\text{Net income}}{\text{New equity}}$$
$$= \frac{\$50}{\$388.7}$$
$$= 12.86\% \text{ (versus old ROE of 12.0\%).}$$

(2)
$$\text{New ROA} = \frac{\text{Net income}}{\text{Total assets} - \text{Reduction in A/R}}$$
$$= \frac{\$50}{\$600 - \$27.8}$$
$$= 8.74\% \text{ (versus old ROA of 8.33\%).}$$

(3) The old debt is the same as the new debt:
$$\text{Debt} = \text{Total claims} - \text{Equity}$$
$$= \$600 - \$416.5 = \$183.5 \text{ million.}$$

Old total assets = $600 million.

New total assets = Old total assets − Reduction in A/R

= $600 − $27.8

= $572.2 million.

Therefore,

$$\frac{\text{Debt}}{\text{Old total assets}} = \frac{\$183.5}{\$600} = 30.6\%,$$

while

$$\frac{\text{New debt}}{\text{New total assets}} = \frac{\$183.5}{\$572.2} = 32.1\%.$$

Chapter 5

ST-1 a. The average rate of return for each stock is calculated simply by averaging the returns over the 5-year period. The average return for each stock is 12 percent, calculated for Stock A as follows:

$$r_{Avg} = (-18\% + 44\% - 22\% + 22\% + 34\%)/5$$

$$= 12\%.$$

The realized rate of return on a portfolio made up of Stock A and Stock B would be calculated by finding the average return in each year as r_A(% of Stock A) + r_B(% of Stock B) and then averaging these yearly returns:

Year	Portfolio AB's Return, r_{AB}
2001	(21%)
2002	34
2003	(13)
2004	15
2005	45
	r_{Avg} = 12%

b. The standard deviation of returns is estimated, using Equation 5-3a, as follows:

$$\text{Estimated } \sigma = S = \sqrt{\frac{\sum_{t=1}^{n} (\bar{r}_t - \bar{r}_{Avg})^2}{n - 1}}. \tag{5-3a}$$

For Stock A, the estimated σ is 30 percent:

$$\sigma_A = \sqrt{\frac{(-18 - 12)^2 + (44 - 12)^2 + (-22 - 12)^2 + (22 - 12)^2 + (34 - 12)^2}{5 - 1}}$$

$$= \sqrt{\frac{3,664}{4}} = 30.265\% \approx 30\%.$$

The standard deviation of returns for Stock B and for the portfolio are similarly determined and they are as follows:

	Stock A	Stock B	Portfolio AB
Standard deviation	30	30	29

c. Because the risk reduction from diversification is small (σ_{AB} falls only from 30 to 29 percent), the most likely value of the correlation coefficient is 0.8. If the correlation coefficient were −0.8, the risk reduction would be much larger. In fact, the correlation coefficient between Stocks A and B is 0.8.

d. If more randomly selected stocks were added to a portfolio, σ_p would decline to somewhere in the vicinity of 20 percent; see Figure 5-7. σ_p would remain constant only if the correlation coefficient were +1.0, which is most unlikely. σ_p would decline to zero only if the correlation coefficient, ρ, were equal to zero and a large number of stocks were added to the portfolio, or if the proper proportions were held in a two-stock portfolio with $\rho = -1.0$.

ST-2 a.
$$b = (0.6)(0.70) + (0.25)(0.90) + (0.1)(1.30) + (0.05)(1.50)$$
$$= 0.42 + 0.225 + 0.13 + 0.075 = 0.85.$$

b.
$$r_{RF} = 6\%; RP_M = 5\%; b = 0.85.$$
$$r = 6\% + (5\%)(0.85)$$
$$= 10.25\%.$$

c.
$$b_N = (0.5)(0.70) + (0.25)(0.09) + (0.1)(1.30) + (0.15)(1.50)$$
$$= 0.35 + 0.225 + 0.13 + 0.225$$
$$= 0.93.$$
$$r = 6\% + (5\%)(0.93)$$
$$= 10.65\%.$$

Chapter 6

ST-1 a. Pennington's bonds were sold at par; therefore, the original YTM equaled the coupon rate of 12%.

b.
$$V_B = \sum_{t=1}^{50} \frac{\$120/2}{\left(1 + \dfrac{0.10}{2}\right)^t} + \frac{\$1,000}{\left(1 + \dfrac{0.10}{2}\right)^{50}}$$

$$= \$60\left(\frac{1 - \dfrac{1}{(1 + 0.05)^{50}}}{0.05}\right) + \$1,000\left(\frac{1}{(1 + 0.05)^{50}}\right)$$

$$= \$60(18.2559) + \$1,000(0.0872)$$

$$= \$1,095.35 + \$87.20 = \$1,182.55.$$

Alternatively, with a financial calculator, input the following: N = 50, I = 5, PMT = 60, FV = 1000, and PV = ? PV = −$1,182.56.

c.
$$\text{Current yield} = \text{Annual coupon payment/Price}$$
$$= \$120/\$1,182.55$$
$$= 0.1015 = 10.15\%.$$
$$\text{Capital gains yield} = \text{Total yield} - \text{Current yield}$$
$$= 10\% - 10.15\% = -0.15\%.$$

d.
$$\$916.42 = \sum_{t=1}^{13} \frac{\$60}{(1 + r_d/2)^t} + \frac{\$1,000}{(1 + r_d/2)^{13}}.$$

With a financial calculator, input the following: N = 13, PV = −916.42, PMT = 60, FV = 1000, and $r_d/2$ = I = ? Calculator solution = $r_d/2$ = 7.00%; therefore, r_d = 14.00%.

e.
$$\text{Current yield} = \$120/\$916.42 = 13.09\%.$$
$$\text{Capital gains yield} = 14\% - 13.09\% = 0.91\%.$$

f. The following time line illustrates the years to maturity of the bond:

| 1/1/05 | 7/01/05 | 12/31/05 | 7/1/06 | 12/31/06 | 12/31/11 |

3/1/05

Thus, on March 1, 2005, there were $13\frac{2}{3}$ periods left before the bond matured. Bond traders actually use the following procedure to determine the price of the bond:

(1) Find the price of the bond on the next coupon date, July 1, 2005.

$$V_{B\ 7/1/05} = \$60\left(\frac{1 - \dfrac{1}{(1 + 0.0775)^{13}}}{0.0775}\right) + \$1,000\left(\frac{1}{(1 + 0.0775)^{13}}\right)$$

$$= \$60(8.0136) + \$1,000(0.3789)$$

$$= \$859.72.$$

With a financial calculator, N = 13, I = 7.75, PV = ?, PMT = 60, FV = 1000, and we get PV = −859.76.

(2) Add the coupon, $60, to the bond price to get the total value, TV, of the bond on the next interest payment date: TV = $859.72 + $60.00 = $919.72.

(3) Discount this total value back to the purchase date:

$$\text{Value at purchase date (March 1, 2005)} = \$919.72\left(\frac{1}{(1 + 0.0775)^{(4/6)}}\right)$$

$$= \$919.72(0.9515)$$

$$= \$875.11.$$

(4) Therefore, you would have written a check for $875.11 to complete the transaction. Of this amount, $20 = (1/3)($60) would represent accrued interest and $855.11 would represent the bond's basic value. This breakdown would affect both your taxes and those of the seller.

(5) This problem could be solved *very* easily using a spreadsheet or a financial calculator with a bond valuation function.

Chapter 7

ST-1 The first step is to solve for g, the unknown variable, in the constant growth equation. Since D_1 is unknown but D_0 is known, substitute $D_0(1 + g)$ as follows:

$$\hat{P}_0 = P_0 = \frac{D_1}{r_s - g} = \frac{D_0(1 + g)}{r_s - g}$$

$$\$36 = \frac{\$2.40(1 + g)}{0.12 - g}.$$

Solving for g, we find the growth rate to be 5 percent:

$$\$4.32 - \$36g = \$2.40 + \$2.40g$$

$$\$38.4g = \$1.92$$

$$g = 0.05 = 5\%.$$

The next step is to use the growth rate to project the stock price 5 years hence:

$$\hat{P}_5 = \frac{D_0(1 + g)^6}{r_s - g}$$

$$= \frac{\$2.40(1.05)^6}{0.12 - 0.05}$$

$$= \$45.95.$$

[Alternatively, $\hat{P}_5 = \$36(1.05)^5 = \$45.95$.]

Therefore, Ewald Company's expected stock price 5 years from now, $\hat{P}_5$ is $45.95.

ST-2 a. (1) Calculate the PV of the dividends paid during the supernormal growth period:

$$D_1 = \$1.1500(1.15) = \$1.3225.$$
$$D_2 = \$1.3225(1.15) = \$1.5209.$$
$$D_3 = \$1.5209(1.13) = \$1.7186.$$
$$PVD = \$1.3225(0.8929) + \$1.5209(0.7972) + \$1.7186(0.7118)$$
$$= \$1.1809 + \$1.2125 + \$1.2233$$
$$= \$3.6167 \approx \$3.62.$$

(2) Find the PV of Snyder's stock price at the end of Year 3:

$$\hat{P}_3 = \frac{D_4}{r_s - g} = \frac{D_3(1 + g)}{r_s - g}$$
$$= \frac{\$1.7186(1.06)}{0.12 - 0.06}$$
$$= \$30.36.$$
$$PV\ \hat{P}_3 = \$30.36(0.7118) = \$21.61.$$

(3) Sum the two components to find the value of the stock today:

$$\hat{P}_0 = \$3.62 + \$21.61 = \$25.23.$$

Alternatively, the cash flows can be placed on a time line as follows:

Enter the cash flows into the cash flow register, I = 12, and press the NPV key to obtain $P_0 = \$25.23$.

b.

$$\hat{P}_1 = \$1.5209(0.8929) + \$1.7186(0.7972) + \$30.36(0.7972)$$
$$= \$1.3580 + \$1.3701 + \$24.2030$$
$$= \$26.9311 \approx \$26.93.$$
(Calculator solution: $26.93.)
$$\hat{P}_2 = \$1.7186(0.8929) + \$30.36(0.8929)$$
$$= \$1.5345 + \$27.1084$$
$$= \$28.6429 \approx \$28.64.$$
(Calculator solution: $28.64.)

c.

Year	Dividend Yield	+	Capital Gains Yield	=	Total Return
1	$\frac{\$1.3225}{\$25.23} \approx 5.24\%$ +		$\frac{\$26.93 - \$25.23}{\$25.23} \approx 6.74\%$		$\approx 12\%$
2	$\frac{\$1.5209}{\$26.93} \approx 5.65\%$ +		$\frac{\$28.64 - \$26.93}{\$26.93} \approx 6.35\%$		$\approx 12\%$
3	$\frac{\$1.7186}{\$28.64} \approx 6.00\%$ +		$\frac{\$30.36 - \$28.64}{\$28.64} \approx 6.00\%$		$\approx 12\%$

Chapter 8

ST-1 a.
$$\text{Exercise value} = \text{Current stock price} - \text{Strike price}$$
$$= \$30 - \$25 = \$5.$$

b.
$$\text{Premium} = \text{Option price} - \text{Exercise value}$$
$$= \$7 - \$5 = \$2.$$

ST-2 a. An increase in stock price increases the value of a call option because it increases the size of the profit should the option be exercised.

b. An increase in volatility means that the stock price might become much higher or much lower than the strike price. Stock prices higher than the strike price lead to high exercise values, but the exercise value will never be less than zero, no matter how low the stock price. So volatility increases the upside potential without increasing the downside risk. Therefore, volatility increases the value of a call option.

c. As the risk-free rate increases, the present value of the cost of exercising the option in the future decreases, which causes the value of the call option to increase.

d. A decrease in the time remaining until expiration reduces the chance that the stock price will go up very much. Therefore, a decrease in time reduces the value of a call option.

Chapter 9

ST-1 a. Component costs are as follows:

Debt at $r_d = 9\%$:

$$r_d(1 - T) = 9\%(0.6) = 5.4\%.$$

Preferred with F = 5%:

$$r_{ps} = \frac{\text{Preferred dividend}}{P_n} = \frac{\$9}{\$100(.95)} = 9.5\%.$$

Common with DCF:

$$r_s = \frac{D_1}{P_0} + g = \frac{\$3.922}{\$60} + 6\% = 12.5\%.$$

Common with CAPM:

$$r_s = 6\% + 1.3(5\%) = 12.5\%.$$

b.
$$WACC = w_d r_d(1 - T) + w_{ps}r_{ps} + w_{ce}r_s$$
$$= 0.25(9\%)(1 - 0.4) + 0.15(9.5\%) + 0.60(12.5\%)$$
$$= 10.275\%.$$

Chapter 10

ST-1 a. **Payback:**

To determine the payback, construct the cumulative cash flows for each project:

	Cumulative Cash Flows	
Year	Project X	Project Y
0	($10,000)	($10,000)
1	(3,500)	(6,500)
2	(500)	(3,000)
3	2,500	500
4	3,500	4,000

$$\text{Payback}_X = 2 + \frac{\$500}{\$3,000} = 2.17 \text{ years.}$$

$$\text{Payback}_Y = 2 + \frac{\$3,000}{\$3,500} = 2.86 \text{ years.}$$

Net Present Value (NPV):

$$NPV_X = -\$10,000 + \frac{\$6,500}{(1.12)^1} + \frac{\$3,000}{(1.12)^2} + \frac{\$3,000}{(1.12)^3} + \frac{\$1,000}{(1.12)^4}$$

$$= \$966.01.$$

$$NPV_Y = -\$10,000 + \frac{\$3,500}{(1.12)^1} + \frac{\$3,500}{(1.12)^2} + \frac{\$3,500}{(1.12)^3} + \frac{\$3,500}{(1.12)^4}$$

$$= \$630.72.$$

Alternatively, using a financial calculator, input the cash flows into the cash flow register, enter I = 12, and then press the NPV key to obtain $NPV_X = \$966.01$ and $NPV_Y = \$630.72$.

Internal Rate of Return (IRR):

To solve for each project's IRR, find the discount rates which equate each NPV to zero:

$$IRR_X = 18.0\%.$$
$$IRR_Y = 15.0\%.$$

Modified Internal Rate of Return (MIRR):

To obtain each project's MIRR, begin by finding each project's terminal value (TV) of cash inflows:

$$TV_X = \$6,500(1.12)^3 + \$3,000(1.12)^2$$
$$+ 3,000(1.12)^1 + \$1,000 = \$17,255.23.$$

$$TV_Y = \$3,500(1.12)^3 + \$3,500(1.12)^2$$
$$+ \$3,500(1.12)^1 + \$3,500 = \$16,727.65.$$

Now, each project's MIRR is that discount rate which equates the PV of the TV to each project's cost, $10,000:

$$MIRR_X = 14.61\%.$$

$$MIRR_Y = 13.73\%.$$

b. The following table summarizes the project rankings by each method:

	Project That Ranks Higher
Payback	X
NPV	X
IRR	X
MIRR	X

Note that all methods rank Project X over Project Y. In addition, both projects are acceptable under the NPV, IRR, and MIRR criteria. Thus, both projects should be accepted if they are independent.

c. In this case, we would choose the project with the higher NPV at r = 12%, or Project X.

d. To determine the effects of changing the cost of capital, plot the NPV profiles of each project. The crossover rate occurs at about 6 to 7 percent (6.2%). See the graph below.

   If the firm's cost of capital is less than 6 percent, a conflict exists because $NPV_Y > NPV_X$, but $IRR_X > IRR_Y$. Therefore, if r were 5 percent, a conflict would exist. Note, however, that when r = 5.0%, $MIRR_X = 10.64\%$ and $MIRR_Y = 10.83\%$; hence, the modified IRR ranks the projects correctly, even if r is to the left of the crossover point.

e. The basic cause of the conflict is differing reinvestment rate assumptions between NPV and IRR. NPV assumes that cash flows can be reinvested at the cost of capital, while IRR assumes reinvestment at the (generally) higher IRR. The high reinvestment rate assumption under IRR makes early cash flows especially valuable, and hence short-term projects look better under IRR.

NPV Profiles for Projects X and Y

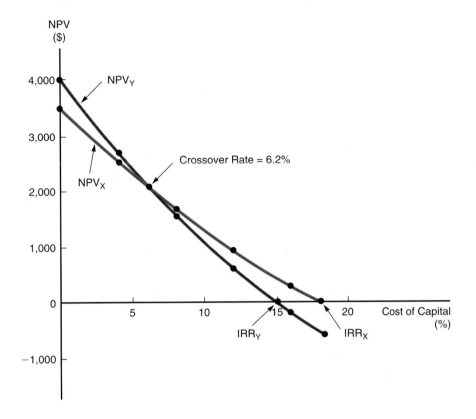

Cost of Capital	NPV_X	NPV_Y
0%	$3,500	$4,000
4	2,545	2,705
8	1,707	1,592
12	966	631
16	307	(206)
18	5	(585)

Chapter 11

ST-1 a. **Estimated Investment Requirements:**

Price	($50,000)
Modification	(10,000)
Change in net working capital	(2,000)
Total investment	($62,000)

b. **Operating Cash Flows:**

	Year 1	Year 2	Year 3
1. After-tax cost savings[a]	$12,000	$12,000	$12,000
2. Depreciation[b]	19,800	27,000	9,000
3. Depreciation tax savings[c]	7,920	10,800	3,600
Operating cash flow (1 + 3)	$19,920	$22,800	$15,600

[a]$20,000(1 − T).
[b]Depreciable basis = $60,000; the MACRS percentage allowances are 0.33, 0.45, and 0.15 in Years 1, 2, and 3, respectively; hence, depreciation in Year 1 = 0.33($60,000) = $19,800, and so on. There will remain $4,200, or 7 percent, undepreciated after Year 3; it would normally be taken in Year 4.
[c]Depreciation tax savings = T(Depreciation) = 0.4($19,800) = $7,920 in Year 1, and so on.

c. **Termination Cash Flow:**

Salvage value	$20,000
Tax on salvage value[a]	(6,320)
Net working capital recovery	2,000
Termination cash flow	$15,680

[a]Sales price	$20,000
Less book value	4,200
Taxable income	$15,800
Tax at 40%	$ 6,320

$$\text{Book value} = \text{Depreciation basis} - \text{Accumulated depreciation}$$
$$= \$60,000 - \$55,800 = \$4,200.$$

d. **Project NPV:**

0	10%	1	2	3
−62,000		19,920	22,800	31,280

$$NPV = -\$62,000 + \frac{\$19,920}{(1.10)^1} + \frac{\$22,800}{(1.10)^2} + \frac{\$31,280}{(1.10)^3}$$
$$= -\$1,547.$$

Alternatively, using a financial calculator, input the cash flows into the cash flow register, enter I = 10, and then press the NPV key to obtain NPV = −$1,547. Because the earthmover has a negative NPV, it should not be purchased.

ST-2 a. First, find the expected cash flows:

Year		Expected Cash Flows		
0	0.2(−$100,000)	+0.6(−$100,000)	+0.2(−$100,000)	= ($100,000)
1	0.2($20,000)	+0.6($30,000)	+0.2($40,000)	= $30,000
2				$30,000
3				$30,000
4				$30,000
5				$30,000
5*	0.2($0)	+0.6($20,000)	+0.2($30,000)	= $18,000

0	10%	1	2	3	4	5
−100,000		30,000	30,000	30,000	30,000	48,000

Next, determine the NPV based on the expected cash flows:

$$NPV = -\$100,000 + \frac{\$30,000}{(1.10)^1} + \frac{\$30,000}{(1.10)^2} + \frac{\$30,000}{(1.10)^3}$$

$$+ \frac{\$30,000}{(1.10)^4} + \frac{\$48,000}{(1.10)^5} = \$24,900.$$

Alternatively, using a financial calculator, input the cash flows in the cash flow register, enter I = 10, and then press the NPV key to obtain NPV = $24,900.

b. For the worst case, the cash flow values from the cash flow column farthest on the left are used to calculate NPV:

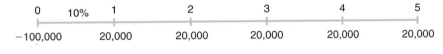

$$NPV = -\$100,000 + \frac{\$20,000}{(1.10)^1} + \frac{\$20,000}{(1.10)^2} + \frac{\$20,000}{(1.10)^3}$$

$$+ \frac{\$20,000}{(1.10)^4} + \frac{\$20,000}{(1.10)^5} = -\$24,184.$$

Similarly, for the best case, use the values from the column farthest on the right. Here the NPV is $70,259.

If the cash flows are perfectly dependent, then the low cash flow in the first year will mean a low cash flow in every year. Thus, the probability of the worst case occurring is the probability of getting the $20,000 net cash flow in Year 1, or 20 percent. If the cash flows are independent, the cash flow in each year can be low, high, or average, and the probability of getting all low cash flows will be

$$0.2(0.2)(0.2)(0.2)(0.2) = 0.2^5 = 0.00032 = 0.032\%.$$

c. The base-case NPV is found using the most likely cash flows and is equal to $26,142. This value differs from the expected NPV of $24,900 because the Year 5 cash flows are not symmetric. Under these conditions, the NPV distribution is as follows:

P	NPV
0.2	($24,184)
0.6	26,142
0.2	70,259

Thus, the expected NPV is 0.2(−$24,184) + 0.6($26,142) + 0.2($70,259) = $24,900. As is generally the case, the expected NPV is the same as the NPV of the expected cash flows found in part a. The standard deviation is $29,904:

$$\sigma^2_{NPV} = 0.2(-\$24,184 - \$24,900)^2 + 0.6(\$26,142 - \$24,900)^2$$

$$+ 0.2(\$70,259 - \$24,900)^2$$

$$= \$894,261,126.$$

$$\sigma_{NPV} = \sqrt{\$894,261,126} = \$29,904.$$

The coefficient of variation, CV, is $29,904/$24,900 = 1.20.

Chapter 12

ST-1   To solve this problem, we will define ΔS as the change in sales and g as the growth rate in sales, and then we use the three following equations:

$$\Delta S = S_0 g.$$

$$S_1 = S_0(1 + g).$$

$$AFN = (A^*/S_0)(DS) - (L^*/S_0)(DS) - MS_1(1 - d).$$

Set AFN = 0, substitute in known values for A^*/S_0, L^*/S_0, M, d, and S_0, and then solve for g:

$$0 = 1.6(\$100g) - 0.4(\$100g) - 0.10[\$100(1 + g)](0.55)$$
$$= \$160g - \$40g - 0.055(\$100 + \$100g)$$
$$= \$160g - \$40g - \$5.5 - \$5.5g$$
$$\$114.5g = \$5.5$$
$$g = \$5.5/\$114.5 = 0.048 = 4.8\%$$
$$= \text{Maximum growth rate without external financing.}$$

ST-2　Assets consist of cash, marketable securities, receivables, inventories, and fixed assets. Therefore, we can break the A^*/S_0 ratio into its components—cash/sales, inventories/sales, and so forth. Then,

$$\frac{A^*}{S_0} = \frac{A^* - \text{Inventories}}{S_0} + \frac{\text{Inventories}}{S_0} = 1.6.$$

We know that the inventory turnover ratio is sales/inventories = 3 times, so inventories/sales = 1/3 = 0.3333. Further, if the inventory turnover ratio can be increased to 4 times, then the inventory/sales ratio will fall to 1/4 = 0.25, a difference of 0.3333 − 0.2500 = 0.0833. This, in turn, causes the A^*/S_0 ratio to fall from A^*/S_0 = 1.6 to A^*/S_0 = 1.6 − 0.0833 = 1.5167. This change has two effects: First, it changes the AFN equation, and second, it means that Weatherford currently has excessive inventories. Because it is costly to hold excess inventories, Weatherford will want to reduce its inventory holdings by not replacing inventories until the excess amounts have been used. We can account for this by setting up the revised AFN equation (using the new A^*/S_0 ratio), estimating the funds that will be needed next year if no excess inventories are currently on hand, and then subtracting out the excess inventories which are currently on hand:

Present Conditions:

$$\frac{\text{Sales}}{\text{Inventories}} = \frac{\$100}{\text{Inventories}} = 3,$$

so

$$\text{Inventories} = \$100/3 = \$33.3 \text{ million at present.}$$

New Conditions:

$$\frac{\text{Sales}}{\text{Inventories}} = \frac{\$100}{\text{Inventories}} = 4,$$

so

$$\text{New level of inventories} = \$100/4 = \$25 \text{ million.}$$

Therefore,

$$\text{Excess inventories} = \$33.3 - \$25 = \$8.3 \text{ million.}$$

Forecast of Funds Needed, First Year:

$$\text{DS in first year} = 0.2(\$100 \text{ million}) = \$20 \text{ million.}$$
$$\text{AFN} = 1.5167(\$20) - 0.4(\$20) - 0.1(0.55)(\$120) - \$8.3$$
$$= \$30.3 - \$8 - \$6.6 - \$8.3$$
$$= \$7.4 \text{ million.}$$

Forecast of Funds Needed, Second Year:

$$\Delta S \text{ in second year} = gS_1 = 0.2(\$120 \text{ million}) = \$24 \text{ million.}$$
$$\text{AFN} = 1.5167(\$24) - 0.4(\$24) - 0.1(0.55)(\$144)$$
$$= \$36.4 - \$9.6 - \$7.9$$
$$= \$18.9 \text{ million.}$$

ST-3 a.

$$\text{Full capacity sales} = \frac{\text{Current sales}}{\text{Percentage of capacity at which}} = \frac{\$36,000}{0.75} = \$48,000.$$

FA were operated

$$\text{Percentage increase} = \frac{\text{New sales} - \text{Old sales}}{\text{Old sales}} = \frac{\$48,000 - \$36,000}{\$36,000} = 0.33$$

$$= 33\%.$$

Therefore, sales could expand by 33 percent before Van Auken Lumber would need to add fixed assets.

b. Because none of the operating ratios are assumed to change, it is easier to let the appropriate items increase at the sales growth rate.

Van Auken Lumber: Pro Forma Income Statement for December 31, 2006 (Thousands of Dollars)

	2005	Forecast Basis	Pro Forma 2006
Sales	$36,000	1.25 (Sales$_{05}$)	$45,000
Operating costs	30,783	85.508% (Sales$_{06}$)	38,479
EBIT	$ 5,217		$ 6,521
Interest	717	12% 2005 Debt	1,017
EBT	$ 4,500		$ 5,504
Taxes (40%)	1,800		2,202
Net income	$ 2,700		$ 3,302
Dividends (60%)	$ 1,620		$ 1,981
Addition to RE	$ 1,080		$ 1,321

Van Auken Lumber: Pro Forma Balance Sheet for December 31, 2006 (Thousands of Dollars)

	2005	Percent of 2006 Sales	Additions	2006	AFN	2006 After AFN
Cash	$ 1,800	5.000%		$ 2,250		$ 2,250
Receivables	10,800	30.000		13,500		13,500
Inventories	12,600	35.000		15,750		15,750
Total current assets	$25,200			$31,500		$31,500
Net fixed assets	21,600	—		21,600[a]		21,600
Total assets	$46,800	—		$53,100		$53,100
Accounts payable	$ 7,200	20.000		$ 9,000		$ 9,000
Notes payable	3,472			3,472	+2,549	6,021
Accruals	2,520	7.000		3,150		3,150
Total current liabilities	$13,192			$15,622		$18,171
Mortgage bonds	5,000			5,000		5,000
Common stock	2,000			2,000		2,000
Retained earnings	26,608		1,321[b]	27,929		27,929
Total liabilities and equity	$46,800			$50,551		$53,100
AFN =				$ 2,549		

[a]From part a we know that sales can increase by 33% before additions to fixed assets are needed.
[b]See income statement.

Chapter 13

ST-1   a.
$$V_{op} = \frac{FCF(1 + g)}{WACC - g} = \frac{\$100{,}000(1 + 0.07)}{0.11 - 0.07} = \$2{,}675{,}000.$$

b.
Total value = Value of operations + Value of nonoperating assets
$$= \$2{,}675{,}000 + \$325{,}000 = \$3{,}000{,}000.$$

c.
Value of equity = Total value − Value of debt
$$= \$3{,}000{,}000 - \$1{,}000{,}000 = \$2{,}000{,}000.$$

Chapter 14

ST-1   a.
$$S = P_0 n = \$30(600{,}000) = \$18{,}000{,}000$$
$$V = D + S = \$2{,}000{,}000 + \$18{,}000{,}000 = \$20{,}000{,}000$$

b.
$$D/V = \$2{,}000{,}000/\$20{,}000{,}000 = 0.10.$$
$$S/V = \$18{,}000{,}000/\$20{,}000{,}000 = 0.90.$$
$$WACC = (D/V)r_d(1 - T) + (S/V)r_s$$
$$= (0.10)(10\%)(0.60) + (0.90)(15\%) = 14.1\%.$$

c.
$$WACC = (0.50)(12\%)(0.60) + (0.50)(18.5\%) = 12.85\%.$$
Since g = 0, FCF = NOPAT.

$$V = FCF/WACC = NOPAT(1 - T)/0.1285 = \$4{,}700{,}000(0.60)/0.1285.$$
$$= \$21{,}945{,}525.292.$$
$$D = w_d(V) = 0.50(\$21{,}945{,}525.292) = \$10{,}972{,}762.646.$$

Since it started with $2 million debt, it will issue:
$$\$8{,}972{,}762.646 = \$10{,}972{,}762.646 - \$2{,}000{,}000.$$
$$S = V - D = \$21{,}945{,}525.292 - \$10{,}972{,}762.646 = \$10{,}972{,}762.646$$
$$New\ P = (S + D - D_0)/n_0$$
$$= (\$10{,}972{,}762.646 + \$10{,}972{,}762.646 - \$2{,}000{,}000)/600{,}000$$
$$= \$33.243$$

It used the proceeds of the new debt, $8,972,762.646, to repurchase X shares of stock at a price of $33.243 per share. The number of shares it will repurchase is X = $8,972,762.646/$33.243 = 269,914.347 ≈ 269,914. Therefore, there are 600,000 − 269,914 = 330,086. As a check the stock price should equal the market value of equity, S, divided by the number of shares: P_0 = $10,972,762.646/330,086 = $33.242.

ST-2   a. LIC's current cost of equity is 6% + 1.5(4%) = 12%.
      b. LIC's unlevered beta is 1.5/[1 + (1 − 0.40)(25/75)] = 1.5/1.2 = 1.25.
      c. LIC's levered beta at D/S = 60/40 = 1.5 is 1.25[1 + (1 − 0.40)(1.5)] = 2.375. LIC's new cost of capital will be 6% + (2.375)(4%) = 15.5%.

Chapter 15

ST-1   a.

Projected net income	$2,000,000
Less projected capital investments	800,000
Available residual	$1,200,000
Shares outstanding	200,000

$$DPS = \$1{,}200{,}000/200{,}000\ shares = \$6 = D_1.$$

b.

$$EPS = \$2,000,000/200,000 \text{ shares} = \$10.$$

Payout ratio = DPS/EPS = \$6/\$10 = 60%, or

Total dividends/NI = \$1,200,000/\$2,000,000 = 60%.

c.

$$\text{Currently, } P_0 = \frac{D_1}{r_s - g} = \frac{\$6}{0.14 - 0.05} = \frac{\$6}{0.09} = \$66.67.$$

Under the former circumstances, D_1 would be based on a 20 percent payout on \$10 EPS, or \$2. With $r_s = 14\%$ and $g = 12\%$, we solve for P_0:

$$P_0 = \frac{D_1}{r_s - g} = \frac{\$2}{0.14 - 0.12} = \frac{\$2}{0.02} = \$100.$$

Although CMC has suffered a severe setback, its existing assets will continue to provide a good income stream. More of these earnings should now be passed on to the shareholders, as the slowed internal growth has reduced the need for funds. However, the net result is a 33 percent decrease in the value of the shares.

Chapter 16

ST-1   **The Calgary Company: Alternative Balance Sheets**

	Restricted (40%)	Moderate (50%)	Relaxed (60%)
Current assets (% of sales)	$1,200,000	$1,500,000	$1,800,000
Fixed assets	600,000	600,000	600,000
Total assets	$1,800,000	$2,100,000	$2,400,000
Debt	$ 900,000	$1,050,000	$1,200,000
Equity	900,000	1,050,000	1,200,000
Total liabilities and equity	$1,800,000	$2,100,000	$2,400,000

The Calgary Company: Alternative Income Statements

	Restricted	Moderate	Relaxed
Sales	$3,000,000	$3,000,000	$3,000,000
EBIT	450,000	450,000	450,000
Interest (10%)	90,000	105,000	120,000
Earnings before taxes	$ 360,000	$ 345,000	$ 330,000
Taxes (40%)	144,000	138,000	132,000
Net income	$ 216,000	$ 207,000	$ 198,000
ROE	24.0%	19.7%	16.5%

ST-2   a. and b.

Income Statements for Year Ended December 31, 2005 (Thousands of Dollars)

	Vanderheiden Press		Herrenhouse Publishing	
	a	b	a	b
EBIT	$ 30,000	$ 30,000	$ 30,000	$ 30,000
Interest	12,400	14,400	10,600	18,600
Taxable income	$ 17,600	$ 15,600	$ 19,400	$ 11,400
Taxes (40%)	7,040	6,240	7,760	4,560
Net income	$ 10,560	$ 9,360	$ 11,640	$ 6,840
Equity	$100,000	$100,000	$100,000	$100,000
Return on equity	10.56%	9.36%	11.64%	6.84%

The Vanderheiden Press has a higher ROE when short-term interest rates are high, whereas Herrenhouse Publishing does better when rates are lower.

c. Herrenhouse's position is riskier. First, its profits and return on equity are much more volatile than Vanderheiden's. Second, Herrenhouse must renew its large short-term loan every year, and if the renewal comes up at a time when money is very tight, when its business is depressed, or both, then Herrenhouse could be denied credit, which could put it out of business.

Chapter 17

ST-1

$$\frac{\text{Euros}}{\text{C\$}} = \frac{\text{Euros}}{\text{US\$}} \times \frac{\text{US\$}}{\text{C\$}}$$

$$= \frac{0.98}{\$1} \times \frac{\$1}{1.5} = \frac{0.98}{1.5} = 0.6533 \text{ euro per Canadian dollar.}$$

Answers to End-of-Chapter Problems

We present here some intermediate steps and final answers to selected end-of-chapter problems. Please note that your answer may differ slightly from ours due to rounding differences. Also, although we hope not, some of the problems may have more than one correct solution, depending upon what assumptions are made in working the problem. Finally, many of the problems involve some verbal discussion as well as numerical calculations; this verbal material is not presented here.

1-1 6%; 6.33%.

1-2 1.5%.

1-3 0.2%.

1-4 6.8%.

1-5 1.5%.

1-6 6.0%.

1-7 a. $r_1 = 9.20\%$; $r_5 = 7.20\%$.

2-1 a. $530.
    b. $561.80.
    c. $471.70.
    d. $445.00.

2-2 a. $895.40.
    b. $1,552.90.
    c. $279.20.
    d. $i = 12\%$; $500.03.
      $i = 6\%$; $867.14.

2-3 a. $n \approx 10$ years.
    b. $n \approx 7$ years.
    c. $n \approx 4$ years.
    d. $n \approx 1$ year.

2-4 a. $6,374.96.
    b. $1,105.12.
    c. $2,000.00.
    d. (1) $7,012.46.
       (2) $1,160.38.
       (3) $2,000.00.

2-5 a. $2,457.83.
    b. $865.90.
    c. $2,000.00.
    d. (1) $2,703.62.
       (2) $909.20.
       (3) $2,000.00.

2-6 a. $PV_A = \$1,251.25$.
      $PV_B = \$1,300.32$.
    b. $PV_A = \$1,600$.
      $PV_B = \$1,600$.

2-7 a. 7%.
    b. 7%.
    c. 9%.
    d. 15%.

2-8 a. $881.17.
    b. $895.42.
    c. $903.06.
    d. $908.35.

2-9 a. $279.20.
    b. $276.84.
    c. $443.72.

2-10 a. $5,272.32.
     b. $5,374.07.

2-11 a. Universal, EAR = 7%.
       Regional, EAR = 6.14%.

2-12 a. PMT = $6,594.94.
       $\text{Interest}_1 = \$2,500$.
       $\text{Interest}_2 = \$2,090.51$.
     b. $13,189.87.
     c. $8,137.27.

2-13 a. $i \approx 15\%$.

2-14 $i = 7.18\%$.

2-15 $i = 9\%$.

2-16 a. $33,872.11.
     b. (1). $26,243.04.
       (2). $0.

2-17 15 years.

2-18 6 years; $1,106.01.

2-19 (1). $1,428.57.
     (2). $714.29.

2-20 $893.26.

2-21 $984.88.

2-22 57.18%.

2-23 a. $1,432.02.
     b. $93.07.

2-24 $i_{Nom} = 15.19\%$.

2-25 PMT = $36,949.61.

3-1 5.8%.

3-2 25%.

3-3 Tax = $107,855; NI = $222,145; Marginal tax rate = 39%; Average tax rate = 33.8%.

3-4 a. Tax = $3,575,000.
b. Tax = $350,000.
c. Tax = $105,000.

3-5 AT&T preferred stock = 5.37%; Florida bond = 5%.

3-6 NI = $450,000; NCF = $650,000.

3-7 a. $2,400,000.
b. NI = $0; NCF = $3,000,000.
c. NI = $1,350,000; NCF = $2,100,000.

3-8 a. NOPAT = $90,000,000.
b. $NOWC_{04}$ = $210,000,000; $NOWC_{05}$ = $192,000,000.
c. Operating capital$_{04}$ = $460,000,000; Operating capital$_{05}$ = $492,000,000.
d. FCF = $58,000,000.

3-9 Refund = $120,000.
Future taxes = $0; $0; $40,000; $60,000; $60,000.

4-1 CL = $2,000,000; Inv = $1,000,000.

4-2 AR = $800,000.

4-3 D/A = 58.33%.

4-4 S/TA = 5; TA/E = 1.5.

4-5 Net profit margin = 2%; D/A = 40%.

4-6 $262,500; 1.19×.

4-7 Sales = $2,592,000; DSO = 36.33 days.

4-8 TIE = 3.86×.

4-9 a. Current ratio = 1.98×; DSO = 76 days; Total assets turnover = 1.7×; Debt ratio = 61.9%.

4-10 A/P = $90,000; Inv = $90,000; FA = $138,000.

4-11 a. Quick ratio = 0.8×; DSO = 37 days; ROE = 13.1%; Debt ratio = 54.8%.

5-1 $\hat{r}$ = 11.40%; σ = 26.69%; CV = 2.34.

5-2 b = 1.12.

5-3 r_M = 11%; r_s = 12.2%.

5-4 r_s = 10.90%.

5-5 a. $\hat{r}_M$ = 13.5%; $\hat{r}_j$ = 11.6%.
b. $σ_M$ = 3.85%; $σ_j$ = 6.22%.
c. CV_M = 0.29; CV_j = 0.54.

5-6 a. b_A = 1.40.
b. r_A = 15%.

5-7 a. r_i = 15.5%.
b. (1). r_M = 15%; r_i = 16.5%.
(2). r_M = 13%; r_i = 14.5%.
c. (1). r_i = 18.1%.

(2). r_i = 14.2%.

5-8 b_N = 1.16.

5-9 b_p = 0.7625; r_p = 12.1%.

5-10 b_N = 1.1250.

5-11 4.5%.

5-12 a. $\bar{r}_A$ = 11.30%; $\bar{r}_B$ = 11.3%.
b. $\bar{r}_p$ = 11.3%.
c. $σ_A$ = 20.8%; $σ_B$ = 20.8%; $σ_p$ = 20.1%.
d. CV_A = 1.84; CV_B = 1.84; CV_p = 1.78.

5-13 a. b_X = 1.3471; b_Y = 0.6508.
b. r_X = 12.7355%; r_Y = 9.254%.
c. r_p = 12.04%.

6-1 $935.82.

6-2 12.48%.

6-3 YTM = 6.62%; YTC = 6.49%.

6-4 8.55%.

6-5 $1,028.60.

6-6 a. 5%: V_L = $1,518.98; V_S = $1,047.62.
8%: V_L = $1,171.19; V_S = $1,018.52.
12%: V_L = $863.78; V_S = $982.14.

6-7 a. YTM at $829 ≈ 15%; YTM at $1,104 = 6%.

6-8 15.03%.

6-9 a. 10.37%.
b. 10.91%.
c. −0.54%.
d. 10.15%.

6-10 8.65%.

6-11 10.78%.

6-12 YTC = 6.47%.

6-13 a. $1,251.22.
b. $898.94.

6-14 10-year, 10% coupon: $1,134.20, $1,210.71, 6.75%;
10-year zero: $463.19, $508.35, 9.75%;
5-year zero: $680.58, $712.99, 4.76%;
30-year zero: $99.38, $131.37, 32.19%;
$100 perpetuity: $1,250, $1,428.57, 14.29%.

6-15 a. C_0 = $1,012.79; Z_0 = $693.04;
C_1 = $1,010.02; Z_1 = $759.57;
C_2 = $1,006.98; Z_2 = $832.49;
C_3 = $1,003.65; Z_3 = $912.41;
C_4 = $1,000.00; Z_4 = $1,000.00.

7-1 D_1 = $1.5750; D_3 = $1.7364; D_5 = $2.1011.

7-2 $\hat{P}_0$ = $6.25.

7-3 $\hat{P}_1$ = $22.00; $\hat{r}_s$ = 15.50%.

7-4 r_{ps} = 8.33%.

7-5 $50.50.

7-6 $g = 9\%$.

7-7 $\hat{P}_3 = \$27.32$.

7-8 a. 13.3%.
b. 10%.
c. 8%.
d. 5.7%.

7-9 $23.75.

7-10 a. $r_C = 10.6\%$; $r_D = 7\%$.

7-11 $25.03.

7-12 $\hat{P}_0 = \$19.89$.

7-13 a. $125.
b. $83.33.

7-14 a. $D_1 = \$2.10$; $D_2 = \$2.21$; $D_3 = \$2.32$.
b. PV = $5.29.
c. $24.72.
d. $30.01.
e. $30.00.

7-15 a. 7%.
b. 5%.
c. 12%.

7-16 a. (1). $9.50.
(2). $13.33.
(3). $21.00.
(4). $44.00.

7-17 a. $D_1 = \$2.01$; $D_3 = \$2.66$; $D_5 = \$3.52$.
b. $\hat{P}_0 = \$39.42$.
c. Dividend yield t = 0, 5.10%; t = 5, 7.00%.
Capital gains yield t = 0, 6.9%; t = 5, 5%.

7-18 a. $\hat{P}_0 = \$54.11$.
Dividend yield = 3.55%.
Capital gains yield = 6.45%.
c. Dividend yield = 4%.
Capital gains yield = 6%.

7-19 a. $\hat{P}_0 = \$21.43$.
b. $\hat{P}_0 = \$26.47$.
c. $\hat{P}_0 = \$32.14$.
d. $\hat{P}_0 = \$40.54$.

8-1 $1.67.

8-2 $27.00; $37.00.

8-3 $1.90.

8-4 $2.39.

8-5 $1.91.

8-6 $3.70.

9-1 $r_s = 13\%$.

9-2 $r_{ps} = 8\%$.

9-3 $r_s = 15\%$.

9-4 a. 13%.
b. 10.4%.
c. 8.45%.

9-5 7.80%.

9-6 11.94%.

9-7 7.2%.

9-8 a. 16.3%.
b. 15.4%.
c. 16%.

9-9 a. 8%.
b. $2.81.
c. 15.81%.

9-10 a. $g = 3\%$.
b. $EPS_1 = \$5.562$.

9-11 a. $15,000,000.
b. 8.4%.

9-12 Short-term debt = 11.14%.
Long-term debt = 22.03%.
Common equity = 66.83%.

9-13 $w_{d(Short)} = 0\%$; $w_{d(Long)} = 20\%$; $w_{ps} = 4\%$; $w_{ce} = 76\%$. r_d (After-tax) = 7.2%; $r_{ps} = 11.6\%$; $r_s \approx 17.5\%$.

9-14 $r_s = 16.1\%$.

9-15 $(1-T)r_d = 5.57\%$.

10-1 a. 4.34 years.
b. DPP = 6.51 years.
c. NPV = $7,486.20.
d. IRR = 16%.
e. MIRR = 13.89%.

10-2 5%: $NPV_A = \$16,108,952$; $NPV_B = \$18,300,939$.
10%: $NPV_A = \$12,836,213$; $NPV_B = \$15,954,170$.
15%: $NPV_A = \$10,059,587$; $NPV_B = \$13,897,838$.

10-3 $NPV_T = \$409$; $IRR_T = 15\%$; $MIRR_T = 14.54\%$;
Accept: $NPV_P = \$3,318$; $IRR_P = 20\%$; $MIRR_P = 17.19\%$; Accept.

10-4 $NPV_E = \$3,861$; $IRR_E = 18\%$; $NPV_G = \$3,057$; $IRR_G = 18\%$; Purchase electric-powered forklift; it has a higher NPV.

10-5 $NPV_S = \$814.33$; $NPV_L = \$1,675.34$; $IRR_S = 15.24\%$; $IRR_L = 14.67\%$; $MIRR_S = 13.77\%$; $MIRR_L = 13.46\%$; $PI_S = 1.081$; $PI_L = 1.067$.

10-6 $MIRR_X = 13.59\%$; $MIRR_Y = 13.10\%$.

10-7 a. NPV = $136,578; IRR = 19.22%.

10-8 b. $IRR_A = 18.1\%$; $IRR_B = 24.0\%$.
c. 10%: $NPV_A = \$283.34$; $NPV_B = \$178.60$.
17%: $NPV_A = \$31.05$; $NPV_B = \$75.95$.
d. (1). $MIRR_A = 14.07\%$; $MIRR_B = 15.89\%$.
(2). $MIRR_A = 17.57\%$; $MIRR_B = 19.91\%$.
e. 14.53%.

10-9 a. $0; −$10,250,000; $1,750,000.
b. 16.07%.

10-10 a. $NPV_A = \$18,108,510$; $NPV_B = \$13,946,117$;
$IRR_A = 15.03\%$; $IRR_B = 22.26\%$.
b. $NPV_\Delta = \$4,162,393$; $IRR_\Delta = 11.71\%$.

10-11 b. 8%: NPV < 0; 14%: NPV > 0.
d. 7.61%; 15.58%.

10-12 a. Undefined.
b. $NPV_C = -\$911,067$; $NPV_F = -\$838,834$.

10-13 a. A = 2.67 years; B = 1.5 years.
b. A = 3.07 years; B = 1.825 years.
c. $NPV_A = \$12,739,908$; choose both.
d. $NPV_A = \$18,243,813$; choose A.
e. $NPV_B = \$8,643,390$; choose B.
f. 13.53%.
g. $MIRR_A = 21.93\%$; $MIRR_B = 20.96\%$.

10-14 Extended $NPV_A = \$12.76$ million; $NPV_B = \$9.26$ million.

10-15 Machine A; Extended $NPV_A = \$4.51$ million; $NPV_B = \$3.67$ million.

10-16 NPV of 360-6 = $22,256.
Extended NPV of 190-3 = $20,070.

10-17 a. 3 years.
b. No.

11-1 $12,000,000.

11-2 $2,600,000.

11-3 $4,600,000.

11-4 a. −$126,000.
b. $42,518; $47,579; $34,926.
c. $50,702.
d. NPV = $10,841; Purchase.

11-5 a. ($89,000).
b. $26,220; $30,300; $20,100.
c. $24,380.
d. NPV = −$6,704; Don't purchase.

11-6 a. NPV = $106,537.

11-7 E(NPV) = $3 million; $\sigma_{NPV} = \$23.622$ million; $CV_{NPV} = 7.874$.

11-8 a. Expected $CF_A = \$6,750$;
Expected $CF_B = \$7,650$;
$CV_A = 0.0703$.
b. $NPV_A = \$10,036$; $NPV_B = \$11,624$.

11-9 a. E(IRR) ≈ 15.3%.
b. $38,589.

11-10 a. $117,779.
b. $\sigma_{NPV} = \$445,060$;
$CV_{NPV} = 3.78$.

12-1 AFN = $410,000.

12-2 AFN = $610,000.

12-3 AFN = $200,000.

12-4 ΔS = $68,965.52.

12-5 a. $13.44 million.
b. Notes payable = $31.44 million.

12-6 a. Total assets = $33,534;
AFN = $2,128.
b. Notes payable = $4,228.

12-7 a. AFN = $128,783.
b. Notes payable = $284,783.

12-8 a. $480,000.
b. $18,750.

12-9 AFN = $360.

13-1 FCF = $37.0.

13-2 $V_{op} = \$6,000,000$.

13-3 a. $V_{op2} = \$2,700,000$.
b. $2,303,571.43.

13-4 a. $713.33.
b. $527.89.
c. $43.79.

13-5 V_{op} at 2007 = $15,000.

13-6 $V_{op} = \$160,000,000$.
MVA = −$40,000,000.

13-7 $259,375,000.

13-8 $416 million.

13-9 $46.90.

13-10 a. $34.96 million.
b. $741.152 million.
c. $699.20 million.
d. $749.10 million.
e. $50.34.

14-1 a. ROI = 21.25% > WACC = 15%.
b. (1). $OL_{Old} = 44.44\%$; $OL_{New} = 47.17\%$.
(2). $Q_{BEOld} = 40$; $Q_{BENew} = 45.45$.

14-2 a. $ROE_C = 15\%$; $\sigma_C = 11\%$.

14-3 a. V = $3,348,214.
b. $16.74.
c. $1.84.
d. 10%.

14-4 30% debt: WACC = 11.14%; = $101.023 million.
50% debt: WACC = 11.25%; = $100 million.
70% debt: WACC = 11.94%; = $94.255 million.

14-5 a. 0.870.
b. $b_L = 1.218$; $r_s = 10.872\%$.
c. WACC = 8.683%; V = $103.188 million.

14-6 11.45%.

15-1 Payout = 55%.

15-2 $P_0 = \$60$.

15-3 $3,250,000.

15-4 Payout = 20%.

15-5 Payout = 52%.

15-6 D_0 = $3.44.

15-7 Payout = 31.39%.

15-8 a. (1) $3,960,000.
    (2) $4,800,000.
    (3) $9,360,000.
    (4) Regular = $3,960,000;
        Extra = $5,400,000.

15-9 a. $6,000,000.
   b. DPS = $2.00; Payout = 25%.
   c. $5,000,000.
   d. No.
   e. 50%.
   f. $1,000,000.
   g. $8,333,333.

16-1 $3,000,000.

16-2 A/R = $59,500.

16-3 r_{Nom} = 75.26%; EAR = 109.84%.

16-4 EAR = 8.49%.

16-5 $7,500,000.

16-6 a. DSO = 28 days.
   b. A/R = $70,000.
   c. A/R = $55,000.

16-7 a. 73.74%.
   b. 14.9%.
   c. 32.25%.
   d. 21.28%.
   e. 29.80%.

16-8 a. 45.15%.
   b. More.

16-9 Nominal cost = 14.90%; Effective cost = 15.89%.

16-10 14.91%.

16-11 a. 83 days.
   b. $356,250.
   c. 4.87×.

16-12 a. 69.5 days.
   b. (1) 1.875×.
      (2) 11.25%.
   c. (1) 46.5 days.
      (2) 2.1262×.
      (3) 12.76%.

16-13 a. ROE_T = 11.75%; ROE_M = 10.80%; ROE_R = 9.16%.

16-14 a. Dec. deficit = $4,400;
      Jan. deficit = $11,200; Feb.
      surplus = $2,000.
   b. $164,400.

16-15 a. $100,000.
   c. (1) $300,000.
      (2) Nominal cost = 37.24%;
          Effective cost = 44.59%.
   d. Nominal cost = 24.83%;
      Effective cost = 27.86%.

16-16 14.35%.

16-17 a. $300,000.

17-1 12.358 yen per peso.

17-2 f_t = $0.00907.

17-3 1 euro = $0.9091 or $1 = 1.1 euro.

17-4 0.6667 pound per dollar.

17-5 1.5152 SFr.

17-6 14.16 Swiss francs per pound.

17-7 +$250,000.

17-8 b. $18,148.00.

17-9 a. $1,659,000.
   b. $1,646,000.
   c. $2,000,000.

17-10 b. f_t = $0.7994.

17-11 $r_{Nom-U.S.}$ = 4.6%.

17-12 117 pesos.

Selected Equations and Data

Chapter 1

$$\text{Value} = \frac{FCF_1}{(1 + WACC)} + \frac{FCF_2}{(1 + WACC)^2} + \cdots + \frac{FCF_\infty}{(1 + WACC)^\infty}$$

Quoted interest rate $= r = r^* + IP + DRP + LP + MRP$.

$r_{T\text{-bill}} = r_{RF} = r^* + IP$.

$$IP_n = \frac{I_1 + I_2 + \cdots + I_n}{n}.$$

Chapter 2

$FV_n = PV(1 + i)^n = PV(FVIF_{i,n})$.

$$PV = FV_n\left(\frac{1}{1 + i}\right)^n = FV_n(1 + i)^{-n} = FV_n(PVIF_{i,n}).$$

$$PVIF_{i,n} = \frac{1}{FVIF_{i,n}}.$$

$$FVIFA_{i,n} = \sum_{t=1}^{n} (1 + i)^{n-t} = \frac{(1 + i)^n - 1}{i}.$$

$$PVIFA_{i,n} = \sum_{t=1}^{n} \frac{1}{(1 + i)^t} = \frac{1 - \dfrac{1}{(1 + i)^n}}{i} = \frac{1}{i} - \frac{1}{i(1 + i)^n}.$$

$FVA_n = PMT(FVIFA_{i,n})$.

$FVA_n(\text{Annuity due}) = PMT(FVIFA_{i,n})(1 + i)$.

$PVA_n = PMT(PVIFA_{i,n})$.

$PVA_n(\text{Annuity due}) = PMT(PVIFA_{i,n})(1 + i)$.

$$PV(\text{Perpetuity}) = \frac{\text{Payment}}{\text{Interest rate}} = \frac{PMT}{i}.$$

$$PV_{\text{Uneven stream}} = \sum_{t=1}^{n} CF_t\left(\frac{1}{1 + i}\right)^t = \sum_{t=1}^{n} CF_t(PVIF_{i,t}).$$

$$FV_{\text{Uneven stream}} = \sum_{t=1}^{n} CF_t(1 + i)^{n-t} = \sum_{t=1}^{n} CF_t(FVIF_{i,n-t}).$$

$$FV_n = PV\left(1 + \frac{i_{\text{Nom}}}{m}\right)^{mn}.$$

$$\text{Effective annual rate} = \left(1 + \frac{i_{\text{Nom}}}{m}\right)^m - 1.0.$$

Periodic rate $= i_{Nom}/m$.

$i_{Nom} = $ APR $= $ (Periodic rate)(m).

Chapter 3

NOWC $= $ Net operating working capital

$\qquad = $ Operating current assets $-$ operating current liabilities.

Total net operating capital $= $ (Net operating working capital) $+$ (Operating long-term assets).

NOPAT $= $ Net operating profit after taxes $= $ EBIT(1 $-$ Tax rate).

Free cash flow (FCF) $= $ NOPAT $-$ Net investment in operating capital.

WACC $= $ Weighted average cost of capital.

Return on invested capital (ROIC) $= \dfrac{\text{NOPAT}}{\text{Operating capital}}$.

MVA $= $ (Market value of equity $+$ Market value of debt) $-$ Capital supplied by investors

$\qquad = $ Market value of equity $-$ Equity capital supplied by shareholders

$\qquad = $ (Shares outstanding)(Stock price) $-$ Total common equity.

EVA $= $ NOPAT $-$ (WACC)(Operating capital).

$\qquad = $ Operating capital (ROIC $-$ WACC).

Chapter 4

Current ratio $= \dfrac{\text{Current assets}}{\text{Current liabilities}}$.

Quick, or acid test, ratio $= \dfrac{\text{Current assets} - \text{Inventories}}{\text{Current liabilities}}$.

Inventory turnover ratio $= \dfrac{\text{Sales}}{\text{Inventories}}$.

DSO $= $ Days sales outstanding $= \dfrac{\text{Receivables}}{\text{Average sales per day}} = \dfrac{\text{Receivables}}{\text{Annual sales}/365}$.

Fixed assets turnover ratio $= \dfrac{\text{Sales}}{\text{Net fixed assets}}$.

Total assets turnover ratio $= \dfrac{\text{Sales}}{\text{Total assets}}$.

Debt ratio $= \dfrac{\text{Total debt}}{\text{Total assets}}$.

$D/E = \dfrac{D/A}{1 - D/A}$, and $D/A = \dfrac{D/E}{1 + D/E}$.

Equity multiplier $= \dfrac{\text{Total assets}}{\text{Equity}} = \dfrac{A}{E}$.

Debt ratio $= 1 - \dfrac{1}{\text{Equity multiplier}}$.

Times-interest-earned (TIE) ratio $= \dfrac{\text{EBIT}}{\text{Interest charges}}$.

EBITDA coverage ratio $= \dfrac{\text{EBITDA} + \text{Lease payments}}{\text{Interest charges} + \text{Principal payments} + \text{Lease payments}}$.

Profit margin on sales $= \dfrac{\text{Net income available to common stockholders}}{\text{Sales}}$.

$$\text{Basic earning power ratio} = \frac{\text{EBIT}}{\text{Total assets}}.$$

$$\text{Return on total assets (ROA)} = \frac{\text{Net income available to common stockholders}}{\text{Total assets}}.$$

$$\text{Return on common equity (ROE)} = \frac{\text{Net income available to common stockholders}}{\text{Common equity}}.$$

$$\text{Price/earnings (P/E) ratio} = \frac{\text{Price per share}}{\text{Earnings per share}}.$$

$$\text{Book value per share} = \frac{\text{Common equity}}{\text{Shares outstanding}}.$$

$$\text{Market/book (M/B) ratio} = \frac{\text{Market price per share}}{\text{Book value per share}}.$$

$$\text{Price/cash flow ratio} = \frac{\text{Price per share}}{\text{Cash flow per share}}.$$

$$\text{ROE} = \text{ROA} \times \text{Equity multiplier}$$

$$= (\text{Profit margin})\,(\text{Total assets turnover})\,(\text{Equity multiplier})$$

$$= \left(\frac{\text{Net income}}{\text{Sales}}\right)\left(\frac{\text{Sales}}{\text{Total assets}}\right)\left(\frac{\text{Total assets}}{\text{Common equity}}\right)$$

$$= \frac{\text{Net income}}{\text{Common equity}}.$$

Chapter 5

$$\text{Expected rate of return} = \hat{r} = \sum_{i=1}^{n} P_i r_i.$$

$$\text{Historical average, } \bar{r}_{\text{Avg}} = \frac{\sum_{t=1}^{n} \bar{r}_t}{n}$$

$$\text{Variance} = \sigma^2 = \sum_{i=1}^{n} (r_i - \hat{r})^2 P_i.$$

$$\text{Standard deviation} = \sigma = \sqrt{\sum_{i=1}^{n} (r_i - \hat{r})^2 P_i}.$$

$$\sigma \text{ historical} = \sqrt{\frac{\sum_{t=1}^{n} (\bar{r}_t - \bar{r}_{\text{Avg}})^2}{n - 1}}$$

$$CV = \frac{\sigma}{\hat{r}}.$$

$$\hat{r}_p = \sum_{i=1}^{n} w_i \hat{r}_i.$$

$$\sigma_p = \sqrt{\sum_{i=1}^{n} (r_{pi} - \hat{r}_p)^2 P_i}.$$

$$b_i = \left(\frac{\sigma_i}{\sigma_M}\right)\rho_{iM}.$$

$$b_p = \sum_{i=1}^{n} w_i b_i.$$

Required return on stock market $= r_M$.

Market risk premium $(RP_M) = r_M - r_{RF}$.

$RP_i = (r_M - r_{RF})b_i = (RP_M)b_i$.

SML: $r_i = r_{RF} + (r_M - r_{RF})b_i = r_{RF} + (RP_M)b_i$.

Chapter 6

$$V_B = \sum_{t=1}^{N} \frac{INT}{(1 + r_d)^t} + \frac{M}{(1 + r_d)^N}$$

$$V_B = \sum_{t=1}^{2N} \frac{INT/2}{(1 + r_d/2)^t} + \frac{M}{(1 + r_d/2)^{2N}} = \frac{INT}{2}(PVIFA_{r_d/2,2N}) + M(PVIF_{r_d/2,2N}).$$

$$\text{Price of callable bond} = \sum_{t=1}^{N} \frac{INT}{(1 + r_d)^t} + \frac{\text{Call price}}{(1 + r_d)^N}.$$

Chapter 7

$$\hat{P}_0 = \text{PV of expected future dividends} = \sum_{t=1}^{\infty} \frac{D_t}{(1 + r_s)^t}.$$

$$\hat{P}_0 = \frac{D_0(1 + g)}{r_s - g} = \frac{D_1}{r_s - g}.$$

$$\hat{r}_s = \frac{D_1}{P_0} + g.$$

$$\bar{r}_s = \text{Actual dividend yield} + \text{Actual capital gains yield}.$$

$$V_{ps} = \frac{D_{ps}}{r_{ps}}.$$

$$r_{ps} = \frac{D_{ps}}{V_{ps}}.$$

Chapter 8

Exercise value $=$ Current price of stock $-$ Strike price.

$V = P[N(d_1)] - Xe^{-r_{RF}t}[N(d_2)]$.

$$d_1 = \frac{\ln(P/X) + [r_{RF} + (\sigma^2/2)]t}{\sigma\sqrt{t}}.$$

$d_2 = d_1 - \sigma\sqrt{t}$.

Chapter 9

After-tax component cost of debt $= r_d(1 - T)$.

Component cost of preferred stock $= r_{ps} = \dfrac{D_{ps}}{P_n}$.

$r_s = \hat{r}_s = r_{RF} + RP_M = D_1/P_0 + \text{expected g}$.

$r_s = r_{RF} + (r_M - r_{RF})b_i = r_{RF} + b_i\, RP_M$

$r_s = \text{Bond yield} + \text{Risk premium}$.

$g = (\text{Retention rate})(\text{ROE}) = (1.0 - \text{Payout rate})(\text{ROE})$.

$WACC = w_d r_d(1 - T) + w_{ps}r_{ps} + w_{ce}r_s$.

Chapter 10

$$\text{Payback period} = \text{Year before full recovery} + \frac{\text{Unrecovered cost at start of year}}{\text{Cash flow during year}}.$$

$$\text{NPV} = CF_0 + \frac{CF_1}{(1 + r)^1} + \frac{CF_2}{(1 + r)^2} + \cdots + \frac{CF_n}{(1 + r)^n}$$

$$= \sum_{t=0}^{n} \frac{CF}{(1 + r)^t}.$$

$$\text{IRR: } CF_0 + \frac{CF_1}{(1 + IRR)^1} + \frac{CF_2}{(1 + IRR)^2} + \cdots + \frac{CF_n}{(1 + IRR)^n} = 0.$$

$$\sum_{t=0}^{n} \frac{CF_t}{(1 + IRR)^t} = 0.$$

MIRR: PV costs = PV terminal value

$$\sum_{t=0}^{n} \frac{COF_t}{(1 + r)^t} = \frac{\sum_{t=0}^{n} CIF_t(1 + r)^{n-t}}{(1 + MIRR)^n}$$

$$\text{PV costs} = \frac{TV}{(1 + MIRR)^n}.$$

$$\text{PI} = \frac{\text{PV of future cash flows}}{\text{Initial cost}} = \frac{\sum_{t=1}^{n} \frac{CF_t}{(1 + r)^t}}{CF_0}.$$

Chapter 11

$$\text{NPV} = \sum_{t=0}^{n} \frac{NCF_t}{(1 + r_n)^t} = \sum_{t=0}^{n} \frac{RCF_t(1 + i)^t}{(1 + r_r)^t(1 + i)^t} = \sum_{t=0}^{n} \frac{RCF_t}{(1 + r_r)^t}$$

$$\sigma_{NPV} = \sqrt{\sum_{i=1}^{n} P_i[NPV_i - E(NPV)]^2}.$$

$$CV_{NPV} = \frac{\sigma_{NPV}}{E(NPV)}.$$

Chapter 12

$$\text{AFN} = (A^*/S_0)\Delta S - (L^*/S_0)\Delta S - MS_1(1 - d).$$

Chapter 13

V_{op} = Value of operations

= PV of expected future free cash flows

$$= \sum_{t=1}^{\infty} \frac{FCF_t}{(1 + WACC)^t}.$$

$$\text{Horizon value (HV): } HV_T = \frac{FCF_T(1 + g)}{WACC - g} = \frac{FCF_{T+1}}{WACC - g}.$$

Total value = V_{op} + Value of nonoperating assets.

Value of equity = Total value − Preferred stock − Debt.

$$\text{Operating profitability (OP): } OP = \frac{NOPAT}{Sales}.$$

Capital requirements (CR): $CR = \dfrac{\text{Operating capital}}{\text{Sales}}$.

For constant growth:

V_{op} at time $N = Capital_N$

$$+ \left[\frac{Sales_N(1 + g)}{WACC - g}\right]\left[OP - WACC\left(\frac{CR}{1 + g}\right)\right].$$

Expected return on invested capital (EROIC): $EROIC_T = \dfrac{NOPAT_{T+1}}{Capital}$.

For constant growth: V_{op} at time $N = Capital_N + \dfrac{Capital_N(EROIC_N - WACC)}{WACC - g}$.

Chapter 14

Return on invested capital (ROIC) $= \dfrac{NOPAT}{Capital}$.

$EBIT = PQ - VQ - F$.

$Q_{BE} = \dfrac{F}{P - V}$.

$b = b_U[1 + (1 - T)(D/S)]$.

$b_U = b/[1 + (1 - T)(D/S)]$.

$D/S = \dfrac{D/A}{1 - D/A}$.

$r_s = r_{RF} + \text{Premium for business risk} + \text{Premium for financial risk}$.

MM, no taxes: $V_L = V_U$.

MM, corporate taxes: $V_L = V_U + TD$.

Miller, personal taxes: $V_L = V_U + \left[1 - \dfrac{(1 - T_c)(1 - T_s)}{(1 - T_d)}\right]D$.

$WACC = r_s w_e + r_d(1 - T)w_d$

$V_L = D + S$

If growth is zero, then the value of a levered firm is $V_L = \dfrac{FCF}{WACC} = \dfrac{(EBIT)(1 - T)}{WACC}$

$D = w_d V$

$S = w_e V$

$P = [S + (D - D_0)]/n_0$

$S_p = S + (D - D_0)$

$P_p = S_p/n_0$

$n = n_0 - (D/P)$

$EPS = \dfrac{NI}{n} = \dfrac{(EBIT - r_d D)(1 - T)}{n}$

$n - n_0 = (D - D_0)/P$

Chapter 15

Distributions = Net income $-$ [(Target equity ratio)(Total capital budget)].

Chapter 16

$$\text{Inventory conversion period} = \frac{\text{Inventory}}{\text{Sales/365}}.$$

$$\text{Receivables collection period} = \text{DSO} = \frac{\text{Receivables}}{\text{Sales/365}}.$$

$$\text{Payables deferral period} = \text{Payables/Credit purchases per day}$$
$$= \text{Payables/(Cost of goods sold/365)}.$$

$$\begin{matrix} \text{Inventory} \\ \text{conversion} \\ \text{period} \end{matrix} + \begin{matrix} \text{Receivables} \\ \text{collection} \\ \text{period} \end{matrix} - \begin{matrix} \text{Payables} \\ \text{deferral} \\ \text{period} \end{matrix} = \begin{matrix} \text{Cash} \\ \text{conversion} \\ \text{cycle} \end{matrix}.$$

$$\text{A/R} = \text{Credit sales per day} \times \text{Length of collection period}.$$

$$\text{Receivables} = (\text{Annual daily sales})(\text{DSO}).$$

$$\text{Nominal cost of payables} = \frac{\text{Discount percent}}{100 - \text{Discount percent}} \times \frac{365}{\text{Days credit is outstanding} - \text{Discount period}}.$$

Chapter 17

$$\frac{\text{Forward exchange rate}}{\text{Spot exchange rate}} = \frac{(1 + r_h)}{(1 + r_f)}.$$

$$P_h = (P_f)(\text{Spot rate}).$$

$$\text{Spot rate} = \frac{P_h}{P_f}.$$

Mathematical Table

TABLE D-1 — Values of the Areas under the Standard Normal Distribution Function

Z	0.00	0.01	0.02	0.03	0.04	0.05	0.06	0.07	0.08	0.09
0.0	.0000	.0040	.0080	.0120	.0160	.0199	.0239	.0279	.0319	.0359
0.1	.0398	.0438	.0478	.0517	.0557	.0596	.0636	.0675	.0714	.0753
0.2	.0793	.0832	.0871	.0910	.0948	.0987	.1026	.1064	.1103	.1141
0.3	.1179	.1217	.1255	.1293	.1331	.1368	.1406	.1443	.1480	.1517
0.4	.1554	.1591	.1628	.1664	.1700	.1736	.1772	.1808	.1844	.1879
0.5	.1915	.1950	.1985	.2019	.2054	.2088	.2123	.2157	.2190	.2224
0.6	.2257	.2291	.2324	.2357	.2389	.2422	.2454	.2486	.2517	.2549
0.7	.2580	.2611	.2642	.2673	.2704	.2734	.2764	.2794	.2823	.2852
0.8	.2881	.2910	.2939	.2967	.2995	.3023	.3051	.3078	.3106	.3133
0.9	.3159	.3186	.3212	.3238	.3264	.3289	.3315	.3340	.3365	.3389
1.0	.3413	.3438	.3461	.3485	.3508	.3531	.3554	.3577	.3599	.3621
1.1	.3643	.3665	.3686	.3708	.3729	.3749	.3770	.3790	.3810	.3830
1.2	.3849	.3869	.3888	.3907	.3925	.3944	.3962	.3980	.3997	.4015
1.3	.4032	.4049	.4066	.4082	.4099	.4115	.4131	.4147	.4162	.4177
1.4	.4192	.4207	.4222	.4236	.4251	.4265	.4279	.4292	.4306	.4319
1.5	.4332	.4345	.4357	.4370	.4382	.4394	.4406	.4418	.4429	.4441
1.6	.4452	.4463	.4474	.4484	.4495	.4505	.4515	.4525	.4535	.4545
1.7	.4554	.4564	.4573	.4582	.4591	.4599	.4608	.4616	.4625	.4633
1.8	.4641	.4649	.4656	.4664	.4671	.4678	.4686	.4693	.4699	.4706
1.9	.4713	.4719	.4726	.4732	.4738	.4744	.4750	.4756	.4761	.4767
2.0	.4773	.4778	.4783	.4788	.4793	.4798	.4803	.4808	.4812	.4817
2.1	.4821	.4826	.4830	.4834	.4838	.4842	.4846	.4850	.4854	.4857
2.2	.4861	.4864	.4868	.4871	.4875	.4878	.4881	.4884	.4887	.4890
2.3	.4893	.4896	.4898	.4901	.4904	.4906	.4909	.4911	.4913	.4916
2.4	.4918	.4920	.4922	.4925	.4927	.4929	.4931	.4932	.4934	.4936
2.5	.4938	.4940	.4941	.4943	.4945	.4946	.4948	.4949	.4951	.4952
2.6	.4953	.4955	.4956	.4957	.4959	.4960	.4961	.4962	.4963	.4964
2.7	.4965	.4966	.4967	.4968	.4969	.4970	.4971	.4972	.4973	.4974
2.8	.4974	.4975	.4976	.4977	.4977	.4978	.4979	.4979	.4980	.4981
2.9	.4981	.4982	.4982	.4982	.4984	.4984	.4985	.4985	.4986	.4986
3.0	.4987	.4987	.4987	.4988	.4988	.4989	.4989	.4989	.4990	.4990

account receivable Created when a good is shipped or a service is performed, but payment for that good is not made on a cash basis but on a credit basis.

accounting income Income as defined by Generally Accepted Accounting Principles (GAAP).

accounting profit A firm's net income as reported on its income statement.

actual, or realized, rate of return, $\bar{r}_s$ The rate of return that was actually realized at the end of some holding period.

additional funds needed (AFN) Those funds required from external sources to increase the firm's assets to support a sales increase. A sales increase will normally require an increase in assets. However, some of this increase is usually offset by a spontaneous increase in liabilities as well as by earnings retained in the firm. Those funds that are required but not generated internally must be obtained from external sources.

aggressive short-term financing policy Refers to a policy in which a firm finances all of its fixed assets with long-term capital but part of its permanent current assets with short-term, nonspontaneous credit.

aging schedule Breaks down accounts receivable according to how long they have been outstanding. This gives the firm a more complete picture of the structure of accounts receivable than that provided by days sales outstanding.

amortization A noncash charge against intangible assets, such as goodwill.

amortization schedule A table that breaks down the periodic fixed payment of an installment loan into its principal and interest components.

amortized loan A loan repaid in equal periodic amounts (or "killed off" over time).

annual report A report issued annually by a corporation to its stockholders. It contains basic financial statements, as well as management's opinion of the past year's operations and the firm's future prospects.

annuity A series of payments of a fixed amount for a specified number of periods.

annuity due An annuity with payments occurring at the beginning of each period.

APR The nominal annual interest rate, also called the annual percentage rate.

asset management ratios A set of ratios that measure how effectively a firm is managing its assets.

assets-in-place Refers to the land, buildings, machines, and inventory that the firm uses in its operations to produce its products and services. Also known as operating assets.

average tax rate Calculated by taking the total amount of tax paid divided by taxable income.

balance sheet A statement of the firm's financial position at a specific point in time. It specifically lists the firm's assets on the left side of the balance sheet, while the right side shows its liabilities and equity, or the claims against these assets.

basic earning power (BEP) ratio Calculated by dividing earnings before interest and taxes by total assets. This ratio shows the raw earning power of the firm's assets, before the influence of taxes and leverage.

benchmarking When a firm compares its ratios to other leading companies in the same industry.

beta coefficient, b A measure of a stock's market risk, or the extent to which the returns on a given stock move with the stock market.

bird-in-the-hand theory Assumes that investors value a dollar of dividends more highly than a dollar of expected capital gains because the dividend yield component, D_1/P_0, is less risky than the g component in the total expected return equation $\hat{r}_s = D_1/P_0 + g$.

Black-Scholes Option Pricing Model Widely used by option traders to value options.

bond A promissory note issued by a business or a governmental unit.

book value per share Common equity divided by the number of shares outstanding.

breakeven point The level of unit sales at which costs equal revenues. Breakeven analysis may be performed with or without the inclusion of financial costs. If financial costs are not included, breakeven occurs when earnings before interest and taxes equals zero. If financial costs are included, breakeven occurs when earnings before taxes equals zero.

business risk The risk inherent in the operations of the firm, prior to the financing decision. Thus, business risk is the uncertainty inherent in a total risk sense, future operating income, or earnings before interest and taxes. Business risk is caused by many factors. Two of the most important are sales variability and operating leverage.

call option An option that allows the holder to buy the asset at some predetermined price within a specified period of time.

call provision Gives the issuing corporation the right to call the bonds for redemption. The call provision generally states that if the bonds are called, the company must pay the bondholders an amount greater than the par value, a call premium. Most bonds contain a call provision.

capacity option Allows a company to change the capacity of its output in response to changing market conditions. This includes the option to contract or expand production. It also includes the option to abandon a project if market conditions deteriorate too much.

Capital Asset Pricing Model (CAPM) A model based on the proposition that any stock's required rate of return is equal to the risk-free rate of return plus a risk premium reflecting only the risk remaining after diversification. The CAPM equation is $r_i = r_{RF} + b_i(r_M - r_{RF})$.

capital budget Outlines the planned expenditures on fixed assets.

capital budgeting The whole process of analyzing projects and deciding whether they should be included in the capital budget.

capital gain (loss) The profit (loss) from the sale of a capital asset for more (less) than its purchase price.

capital gains yield Results from changing prices and is calculated as $(P_1 - P_0)/P_0$, where P_0 is the beginning-of-period price and P_1 is the end-of-period price.

capital intensity ratio The dollar amount of assets required to produce a dollar of sales. The capital intensity ratio is the reciprocal of the total assets turnover ratio.

capital market Capital markets are the financial markets for long-term debt and corporate stocks. The New York Stock Exchange is an example of a capital market.

capital rationing Occurs when management places a constraint on the size of the firm's capital budget during a particular period.

capital structure The manner in which a firm's assets are financed; that is, the right side of the balance sheet. Capital structure is normally expressed as the percentage of each type of capital used by the firm such as debt, preferred stock, and common equity.

cash budget A schedule showing cash flows (receipts, disbursements, and cash balances) for a firm over a specified period.

cash conversion cycle The length of time between the firm's actual cash expenditures on productive resources (materials and labor) and its own cash receipts from the sale of products (that is, the length of time between paying for labor and materials and collecting on receivables). Thus, the cash conversion cycle equals the length of time the firm has funds tied up in current assets.

cash discounts The amount by which a seller is willing to reduce the invoice price in order to be paid immediately, rather than in the future. A cash discount might be 2/10, net 30, which means a 2 percent discount if the bill is paid within 10 days, otherwise the entire amount is due within 30 days.

classified stock Sometimes created by a firm to meet special needs and circumstances. Generally, when special classifications of stock are used, one type is designated "Class A," another as "Class B," and so on. For example, Class A might be entitled to receive dividends before dividends can be paid on Class B stock. Class B might have the exclusive right to vote.

clientele effect The attraction of companies with specific dividend policies to those investors whose needs are best served by those policies. Thus, companies with high dividends will have a clientele of investors with low marginal tax rates and strong desires for current income. Similarly, companies with low dividends will attract a clientele with little need for current income and who often have high marginal tax rates.

closely held corporation Refers to companies that are so small that their common stocks are not actively traded; they are owned by only a few people, usually the companies' managers.

coefficient of variation (CV) Equal to the standard deviation divided by the expected return; it is a standardized risk measure that allows comparisons between investments having different expected returns and standard deviations.

collection policy The procedure for collecting accounts receivable. A change in collection policy will affect sales, days sales outstanding, bad debt losses, and the percentage of customers taking discounts.

commercial paper Unsecured, short-term promissory notes of large firms, usually issued in denominations of $100,000 or more and having an interest rate of somewhat below the prime rate.

common stockholders' equity (net worth) The capital supplied by common stockholders—capital stock, paid-in capital, retained earnings, and, occasionally, certain reserves. Paid-in capital is the difference between the stock's par value and what stockholders paid when they bought newly issued shares.

comparative ratio analysis Compares a firm's own ratios to other leading companies in the same industry. This technique is also known as benchmarking.

compensating balance (CB) A minimum checking account balance that a firm must maintain with a bank to compensate the bank for services rendered or for making the loan; generally equal to 10 to 20 percent of the loans outstanding.

compounding Compounding is the process of finding the future value of a single payment or series of payments.

computer/telephone network Consists of all the facilities that provide for security transactions not conducted at a physical location exchange. These facilities are, basically, the communications networks that link buyers and sellers. An example is Nasdaq.

conservative short-term financing policy Refers to using permanent capital to finance all permanent asset requirements as well as to meet some or all of the seasonal demands.

consol Another term for perpetuity. Consols were originally bonds issued by England in 1815 to consolidate past debt.

continuous probability distribution Contains an infinite number of outcomes and is graphed from $-\infty$ and $+\infty$.

convertible bond Security that is convertible into shares of common stock, at a fixed price, at the option of the bondholder.

convertible currency A currency that can be traded in the currency markets and can be redeemed at current market rates.

corporate bond Debt issued by corporations and exposed to default risk. Different corporate bonds have different levels of default risk, depending on the issuing company's characteristics and on the terms of the specific bond.

corporate valuation model Defines the total value of a company as the value of operations plus the value of nonoperating assets plus the value of growth options.

corporation A legal entity created by a state; it is separate and distinct from its owners and managers.

correlation The tendency of two variables to move together.

correlation coefficient, ρ (rho) A standardized measure of how two random variables covary. A correlation coefficient (ρ) of $+1.0$ means that the two variables move up and down in perfect synchronization, while a coefficient of -1.0 means the variables always move in opposite directions. A correlation coefficient of zero suggests that the two variables are not related to one another; that is, they are independent.

cost of common stock, r_s The return required by the firm's common stockholders. It is usually calculated using the Capital Asset Pricing Model or the dividend growth model.

cost of new external common equity, r_e Projects financed with external equity must earn a higher rate of return because the project must cover the flotation costs. Thus, the cost of new common equity is higher than that of common equity raised internally by reinvesting earnings.

cost of preferred stock, r_{ps} The return required by the firm's preferred stockholders. The cost of preferred stock, r_{ps}, is the cost to the firm of issuing new preferred stock. For perpetual preferred, it is the preferred dividend, D_{ps}, divided by the net issuing price, P_n.

costly trade credit Credit taken in excess of free trade credit whose cost is equal to the discount lost.

coupon interest rate Stated rate of interest on a bond, defined as the coupon payment divided by the par value.

coupon payment Dollar amount of interest paid to each bondholder on the interest payment dates.

coverage ratio Similar to the times-interest-earned ratio, but it recognizes that many firms lease assets and also must make sinking fund payments. It is found by adding earnings before interest, taxes, depreciation, and amortization to lease payments, then dividing this total by interest charges, lease payments, and sinking fund payments over 1 minus the tax rate.

credit period The length of time for which credit is extended. If the credit period is lengthened, sales will generally increase, as will accounts receivable. This will increase the financing needs and possibly increase bad debt losses. A shortening of the credit period will have the opposite effect.

credit policy The firm's policy on granting and collecting credit. There are four elements of credit policy, or credit policy variables: credit period, credit standards, collection policy, and discounts.

credit standards The financial strength and creditworthiness that qualifies a customer for a firm's regular credit terms.

credit terms Statements of the credit period and any discounts offered, for example, 2/10, net 30.

crossover rate The cost of capital at which the NPV profiles for two projects intersect.

current ratio Indicates the extent to which current liabilities are covered by those assets expected to be converted to cash in the near future; it is found by dividing current assets by current liabilities.

current yield (on a bond) The annual coupon payment divided by the current market price.

days sales outstanding (DSO) Used to appraise accounts receivable and indicates the length of time the firm must wait after making a sale before receiving cash. It is found by dividing receivables by average sales per day.

DCF (discounted cash flow) techniques The net present value (NPV) and internal rate of return (IRR) techniques are discounted cash flow (DCF) evaluation techniques. These are called DCF methods because they explicitly recognize the time value of money.

dealer market Refers to when a dealer holds an inventory of the security and makes a market by offering to buy or sell. Others who wish to buy or sell can see the offers made by the dealers and can contact the dealer of their choice to arrange a transaction.

debenture This is an unsecured bond, and, as such, it provides no lien against specific property as security for the obligation. Debenture holders are, therefore, general creditors whose claims are protected by property not otherwise pledged.

debt ratio The ratio of total liabilities to total assets, it measures the percentage of funds provided by creditors.

decision trees A form of scenario analysis in which different actions are taken in different scenarios.

declaration date The date on which a firm's directors issue a statement declaring a dividend.

default risk The risk that a borrower will not pay the interest and/or principal on a loan as it becomes due. If the issuer defaults, investors receive less than the promised return on the bond. Default risk is influenced by both the financial strength of the issuer and the terms of the bond contract, especially whether collateral has been pledged to secure the bond. The greater the default risk, the higher the bond's yield to maturity.

default risk premium (DRP) Default risk is the risk that a borrower will not pay the interest and/or principal on a loan as they become due. Thus, a default risk premium (DRP) is added to the real risk-free rate to compensate investors for bearing default risk.

depreciation A noncash charge against tangible assets, such as buildings or machines. It is taken for the purpose of showing an asset's estimated dollar cost of the capital equipment used up in the production process.

derivative Claims whose value depends on what happens to the value of some other asset. Futures and options are two important types of derivatives, and their values depend on what happens to the

prices of other assets. Therefore, the value of a derivative security is derived from the value of an underlying real asset or other security.

devaluation The lowering, by governmental action, of the price of its currency relative to another currency. For example, in 1967 the British pound was devalued from $2.80 per pound to $2.50 per pound.

development bond A tax-exempt bond sold by state and local governments whose proceeds are made available to corporations for specific uses deemed (by Congress) to be in the public interest.

discount bond Bond prices and interest rates are inversely related; that is, they tend to move in the opposite direction from one another. A fixed-rate bond will sell at par when its coupon interest rate is equal to the going rate of interest, r_d. When the going rate of interest is above the coupon rate, a fixed-rate bond will sell at a "discount" below its par value. If current interest rates are below the coupon rate, a fixed-rate bond will sell at a "premium" above its par value.

discount on forward rate Occurs when the forward exchange rate differs from the spot rate. When the forward rate is below the spot rate, the forward rate is said to be at a discount.

discounted payback period The number of years it takes a firm to recover its project investment based on discounted cash flows.

discounting The process of finding the present value of a single payment or series of payments.

distribution policy The policy that sets the level of distributions and the form of the distributions (dividends and stock repurchases).

diversifiable risk Refers to that part of a security's total risk associated with random events not affecting the market as a whole. This risk can be eliminated by proper diversification. Also known as company-specific risk.

dividend irrelevance theory Holds that dividend policy has no effect on either the price of a firm's stock or its cost of capital.

dividend reinvestment plan (DRIP) Allows stockholders to automatically purchase shares of common stock of the paying corporation in lieu of receiving cash dividends. There are two types of plans—one involves only stock that is already outstanding, while the other involves newly issued stock. In the first type, the dividends of all participants are pooled and the stock is purchased on the open market. Participants benefit from lower transaction costs. In the second type, the company issues new shares to the participants. Thus, the company issues stock in lieu of the cash dividend.

dividend yield Defined as either the end-of-period dividend divided by the beginning-of-period price or the ratio of the current dividend to the current price. Valuation formulas use the former definition.

Du Pont chart A chart designed to show the relationships among return on investment, asset turnover, profit margin, and leverage.

Du Pont equation A formula that shows that the rate of return on equity can be found as the product of the profit margin times the total assets turnover times the equity multiplier.

EBITDA Earnings before interest, taxes, depreciation, and amortization.

ECN (electronic communications network) Orders from potential buyers and sellers are automatically matched, and the transaction is automatically completed.

economic life The number of years a project should be operated to maximize its net present value; often less than the maximum potential life.

economic value added (EVA) A method used to measure a firm's true profitability. EVA is found by taking the firm's after-tax operating profit and subtracting the annual cost of all the capital a firm uses. If the firm generates a positive EVA, its management has created value for its shareholders. If the EVA is negative, management has destroyed shareholder value.

effective annual rate (EAR) The rate that, under annual compounding, would have produced the same future value at the end of one year as was produced by more frequent compounding, say, quarterly. If the compounding occurs annually, the effective annual rate and the nominal rate are the same. If compounding occurs more frequently, the effective annual rate is greater than the nominal rate.

efficient markets hypothesis (EMH) States (1) that stocks are always in equilibrium and (2) that it is impossible for an investor to consistently "beat the market." The EMH assumes that all important information regarding a stock is reflected in the price of that stock.

embedded options Options that are a part of another project. Also called real options, managerial options, and strategic options.

entrenchment Occurs when a company has such a weak board of directors and has such strong anti-takeover provisions in its corporate charter that senior managers feel there is very little chance that they will be removed.

equilibrium The condition under which intrinsic value of a security is equal to its price; also, its expected return is equal to its required return.

ESOP (employee stock ownership plan) A type of retirement plan in which employees own stock in the company.

euro A currency used by the nations in the European Monetary Union who signed the Treaty of Maastricht.

eurobond Any bond sold in some country other than the one in whose currency the bond is denom- inated. Thus, a U.S. firm selling dollar bonds in Switzerland is selling eurobonds.

eurodollar A U.S. dollar on deposit in a foreign bank or a foreign branch of a U.S. bank. Eurodollars are used to conduct transactions throughout Europe and the rest of the world.

exchange rate Specifies the number of units of a given currency that can be purchased for one unit of another currency.

exchange rate risk Refers to the fluctuation in exchange rates between currencies over time.

ex-dividend date The date when the right to the dividend leaves the stock. This date was established by stockbrokers to avoid confusion and is four business days prior to the holder-of-record-date. If the stock sale is made prior to the ex-dividend date, the dividend is paid to the buyer. If the stock is bought on or after the ex-dividend date, the dividend is paid to the seller.

exercise value Equal to the current price of the stock (underlying the option) less the striking price of the option.

expectations theory States that the slope of the yield curve depends on expectations about future inflation rates and interest rates. Thus, if the annual rate of inflation and future interest rates are expected to increase, the yield curve will be upward sloping, whereas the curve will be downward sloping if the annual rates are expected to decrease.

expected rate of return, $\hat{r}_s$ The rate of return expected on a stock given its current price and expected future cash flows. If the stock is in equilibrium, the required rate of return will equal the expected rate of return.

extra dividend A dividend paid, in addition to the regular dividend, when earnings permit. Firms with volatile earnings may have a low regular dividend that can be maintained even in low-profit (or high-capital-investment) years and then supplement it with an extra dividend when excess funds are available.

financial intermediary A financial intermediary buys securities with funds that it obtains by issuing its own securities. An example is a common stock mutual fund that buys common stocks with funds obtained by issuing shares in the mutual fund.

financial leverage The extent to which fixed-income securities (debt and preferred stock) are used in a firm's capital structure. If a high percentage of a firm's capital structure is in the form of debt and preferred stock, then the firm is said to have a high degree of financial leverage.

financial risk The risk added by the use of debt financing. Debt financing increases the variability of earnings before taxes (but after interest); thus, along with business risk, it contributes to the uncertainty of net income and earnings per share.

Business risk plus financial risk equals total corporate risk.

financial service corporation   Offers a wide range of financial services such as brokerage operations, insurance, and commercial banking.

fixed assets turnover ratio   Measures how effectively the firm uses its plant and equipment. It is the ratio of sales to net fixed assets.

fixed exchange rate system   System in effect from the end of World War II until August 1971. Under the system, the U.S. dollar was linked to gold at the rate of $35 per ounce, and other currencies were then tied to the dollar.

floating exchange rates   System currently in effect where the forces of supply and demand are allowed to determine currency prices with little government intervention.

floating-rate bond   Bond whose coupon payment may vary over time. The coupon rate is usually linked to the rate on some other security, such as a Treasury security, or to some other rate, such as the prime rate or LIBOR.

flotation cost, F   Those costs occurring when a company issues a new security, including fees to an investment banker and legal fees.

foreign bond   A bond sold by a foreign borrower but denominated in the currency of the country in which the issue is sold. Thus, a U.S. firm selling bonds denominated in Swiss francs in Switzerland is selling foreign bonds.

foreign trade deficit   Occurs when businesses and individuals in the United States import more goods from foreign countries than are exported.

forward exchange rate   The prevailing exchange rate for exchange (delivery) at some agreed-upon future date, usually 30, 90, or 180 days from the day the transaction is negotiated.

founders' shares   Stock owned by the firm's founders that has sole voting rights but restricted dividends for a specified number of years.

free cash flow (FCF)   The cash flow actually available for distribution to all investors after the company has made all investments in fixed assets and working capital necessary to sustain ongoing operations.

free trade credit   Credit received during the discount period.

FV_n   The ending amount in an account, where n is the number of periods the money is left in the account.

FVA_n   The ending value of a stream of equal payments, where n is the number of payments of the annuity.

$FVIF_{i,n}$ The future value interest factor for a lump sum left in an account for n periods paying i percent interest per period.

$FVIFA_{i,n}$ The future value interest factor for an ordinary annuity of n periodic payments paying i percent interest per period.

going public   The act of selling stock to the public at large by a closely held corporation or its principal stockholders.

greenmail   Targeted share repurchases that occur when a company buys back stock from a potential acquirer at a higher-than-fair-market price. In return, the potential acquirer agrees not to attempt to take over the company.

growth option   Occurs if an investment creates the opportunity to make other potentially profitable investments that would not otherwise be possible, including options to expand output, options to enter a new geographical market, and options to introduce complementary products or successive generations of products.

holder-of-record date   If a company lists the stockholder as an owner on the holder-of-record date, then the stockholder receives the dividend.

horizon value   The value of operations at the end of the explicit forecast period. It is equal to the present value of all free cash flows beyond the forecast period, discounted back to the end of the forecast period at the weighted average cost of capital.

hurdle rate   The project cost of capital, or discount rate. It is the rate used in discounting future cash flows in the net present value method, and it is the rate that is compared with the internal rate of return.

improper accumulation   The retention of earnings by a business for the purpose of enabling stockholders to avoid personal income taxes on dividends.

income bond   Pays interest only if the interest is earned. These securities cannot bankrupt a company, but from an investor's standpoint, they are riskier than "regular" bonds.

income statement   Summarizes the firm's revenues and expenses over an accounting period. Net sales are shown at the top of each statement, after which various costs, including income taxes, are subtracted to obtain the net income available to common stockholders. The bottom of the statement reports earnings and dividends per share.

incremental cash flow   Those cash flows that arise solely from the asset that is being evaluated.

indentures   A legal document that spells out the rights of both bondholders and the issuing corporation.

independent projects   Projects that can be accepted or rejected individually.

indexed, or purchasing power, bond   The interest rate of such a bond is based on an inflation index such as the consumer price index (CPI), so the interest paid rises automatically when the inflation rate rises, thus protecting the bondholders against inflation.

inflation premium (IP)   The inflation premium is the premium added to the real risk-free rate of interest to compensate for the expected loss of purchasing power. The inflation premium is the average rate of inflation expected over the life of the security.

information content, or signaling, hypothesis A theory that holds that investors regard dividend changes as "signals" of management forecasts. Thus, when dividends are raised, this is viewed by investors as recognition by management of future earnings increases. Therefore, if a firm's stock price increases with a dividend increase, the reason may not be investor preference for dividends but expectations of higher future earnings. Conversely, a dividend reduction may signal that management is forecasting poor earnings in the future.

initial public offering (IPO) Occurs when a closely held corporation or its principal stockholders sell stock to the public at large.

initial public offering (IPO) market Going public is the act of selling stock to the public at large by a closely held corporation or its principal stockholders, and this market is often termed the initial public offering market.

i_{Nom} The nominal, or quoted, interest rate.

interest rate parity Holds that investors should expect to earn the same return in all countries after adjusting for risk.

interest rate risk Risk from changing interest rates. The longer the maturity of the bond, the greater the exposure to interest rate risk.

internal rate of return (IRR) method The discount rate that equates the present value of the expected future cash inflows and outflows. IRR measures the rate of return on a project, but it assumes that all cash flows can be reinvested at the IRR rate.

international bond Any bond sold outside of the country of the borrower. There are two types of international bonds: eurobonds and foreign bonds.

intrinsic value, $\hat{P}_0$ The present value of the expected future cash flows.

inventory conversion period The average length of time to convert materials into finished goods and then to sell them; calculated by dividing total inventory by sales per day.

inventory turnover ratio Sales divided by inventories.

inverted ("abnormal") yield curve A downward-sloping yield curve is termed "abnormal" or "inverted."

investment banker A middleman between businesses and investors. Investment banking houses assist in the design of corporate securities and then sell them to investors in the primary markets.

investment-grade bond Securities with ratings of Baa/BBB or above.

investment timing option Gives companies the option to delay a project rather than implement it immediately. This option to wait allows a company to reduce the uncertainty of market conditions before it decides to implement the project.

junk bond High-risk, high-yield bond issued to finance leveraged buyouts, mergers, or troubled companies.

limited liability partnership Combines the limited liability advantage of a corporation with the tax advantages of a partnership. Sometimes called a limited liability company (LLC).

limited partnership Liabilities, investment returns, and control are limited for the limited partners, while general partners have unlimited liability and control.

line of credit An arrangement in which a bank agrees to lend up to a specified maximum amount of funds during a designated period.

liquidity Liquidity refers to a firm's cash and marketable securities position and to its ability to meet maturing obligations. A liquid asset is any asset that can be quickly sold and converted to cash at its "fair" value. Active markets provide liquidity.

liquidity premium (LP) Added to the real risk-free rate of interest, in addition to other premiums, if a security is not liquid.

liquidity ratio A ratio that shows the relationship of a firm's cash and other current assets to its current liabilities.

lumpy assets Those assets that cannot be acquired smoothly but that require large, discrete additions. For example, an electric utility that is operating at full capacity cannot add a small amount of generating capacity, at least not economically.

managerial options Options that give opportunities to managers to respond to changing market conditions. Also called real options.

marginal tax rate Defined as the tax rate on the last unit of income.

market portfolio A portfolio consisting of all stocks.

market risk That part of a security's total risk that cannot be eliminated by diversification. It is measured by the beta coefficient.

market risk premium (RP_M) The difference between the expected return on the market and the risk-free rate.

market value added (MVA) The difference between the market value of the firm (that is, the sum of the market value of common equity, the market value of debt, and the market value of preferred stock) and the book value of the firm's common equity, debt, and preferred stock. If the book values of debt and preferred stock are equal to their market values, then MVA is also equal to the difference between the market value of equity and the amount of equity capital that investors supplied.

market value ratios Relate the firm's stock price to its earnings and book value per share.

market/book (M/B) ratio The market price per share divided by the book value per share.

maturity date   The date when the bond's par value is repaid to the bondholder. Maturity dates generally range from 10 to 40 years from the time of issue.

maturity risk premium (MRP)   A premium that must be added to the real risk-free rate of interest to compensate for interest rate risk that depends on a bond's maturity. Interest rate risk arises from the fact that bond prices decline when interest rates rise. Under these circumstances, selling a bond prior to maturity will result in a capital loss, and the longer the term to maturity, the larger the loss.

moderate net operating working capital policy   A policy that matches asset and liability maturities. It is also referred to as the maturity matching, or "self-liquidating" approach.

modified internal rate of return (MIRR) method   Assumes that cash flows from all projects are reinvested at the cost of capital as opposed to the project's own IRR. This makes the modified internal rate of return a better indicator of a project's true profitability.

money market   A financial market for debt securities with maturities of less than one year (short term). The New York money market is the world's largest.

money market fund   Mutual funds that invest in short-term debt instruments and offer their investors check-writing privileges; thus, they are essentially interest-bearing checking accounts.

Monte Carlo simulation analysis   A risk analysis technique in which a computer is used to simulate probable future events and thus to estimate the profitability and risk of a project.

mortgage bond   The corporation pledges certain assets as security for the bond. All such bonds are written subject to an indenture.

multinational corporation   A corporation that operates in two or more countries.

municipal bond   Issued by state and local governments. The interest earned on most municipal bonds is exempt from federal taxes and also from state taxes if the holder is a resident of the issuing state.

municipal bond insurance   An insurance company guarantees to pay the coupon and principal payments should the issuer of the bond (the municipality) default. This reduces the risk to investors who are willing to accept a lower coupon rate for an insured bond issue compared with an uninsured issue.

mutual fund   A corporation that sells shares in the fund and uses the proceeds to buy stocks, long-term bonds, or short-term debt instruments. The resulting dividends, interest, and capital gains are distributed to the fund's shareholders after the deduction of operating expenses. Some funds specialize in certain types of securities, such as growth stocks, international stocks, or municipal bonds.

mutually exclusive projects   Projects that cannot be performed at the same time. A company could choose either Project 1 or Project 2, or it can reject both, but it cannot accept both projects.

net cash flow   The sum of net income plus non-cash adjustments.

net operating working capital (NOWC)   Operating current assets minus operating current liabilities. Operating current assets are the current assets used to support operations, such as cash, accounts receivable, and inventory. They do not include short-term investments. Operating current liabilities are the current liabilities that are a natural consequence of the firm's operations, such as accounts payable and accruals. They do not include notes payable or any other short-term debt that charges interest.

net present value (NPV) method   The present value of the project's expected future cash flows, discounted at the appropriate cost of capital. NPV is a direct measure of the value of the project to shareholders.

net working capital   Current assets minus current liabilities.

nominal (quoted) interest rate, i_{Nom}   The rate of interest stated in a contract. If the compounding occurs annually, the effective annual rate and the nominal rate are the same. If compounding occurs more frequently, the effective annual rate is greater than the nominal rate. The nominal annual interest rate is also called the annual percentage rate, or APR.

nominal rate of return, r_n   Includes an inflation adjustment (premium). Thus, if nominal rates of return are used in the capital budgeting process, the net cash flows must also be nominal.

nominal risk-free rate of interest, r_{RF}   The real risk-free rate plus a premium for expected inflation. The short-term nominal risk-free rate is usually approximated by the U.S. Treasury bill rate, while the long-term nominal risk-free rate is approximated by the rate on U.S. Treasury bonds.

nonnormal cash flow projects   Projects with a large cash outflow either sometime during or at the end of their lives. A common problem encountered when evaluating projects with nonnormal cash flows is multiple internal rates of return.

nonoperating assets   Include investments in marketable securities and noncontrolling interests in the stock of other companies.

nonpecuniary benefits   Perks that are not actual cash payments, such as lavish offices, memberships at country clubs, corporate jets, and excessively large staffs.

NOPAT (net operating profit after taxes)   The amount of profit a company would generate if it had no debt and no financial assets.

normal cash flow projects A project in which one or more cash outflows (costs) are followed by a series of cash inflows.

normal yield curve When the yield curve slopes upward, it is said to be "normal," because it is like this most of the time.

open outcry auction A method of matching buyers and sellers. The buyers and sellers are face-to-face, with each stating the prices at which they will buy or sell.

operating capital The sum of net operating working capital and operating long-term assets, such as net plant and equipment. Operating capital also is equal to the net amount of capital raised from investors. This is the amount of interest-bearing debt plus preferred stock plus common equity minus short-term investments. Also called total net operating capital, net operating capital, or net operating assets.

operating current assets The current assets used to support operations, such as cash, accounts receivable, and inventory. It does not include short-term investments.

operating current liabilities The current liabilities that are a natural consequence of the firm's operations, such as accounts payable and accruals. It does not include notes payable or any other short-term debt that charges interest.

operating leverage The extent to which fixed costs are used in a firm's operations. If a high percentage of a firm's total costs are fixed costs, then the firm is said to have a high degree of operating leverage. Operating leverage is a measure of one element of business risk but does not include the second major element, sales variability.

opportunity cost A cash flow that a firm must forgo to accept a project. For example, if the project requires the use of a building that could otherwise be sold, the market value of the building is an opportunity cost of the project.

opportunity cost rate The rate of return available on the best alternative investment of similar risk.

optimal distribution policy The distribution policy that maximizes the value of the firm by choosing the optimal level and form of distributions (dividends and stock repurchases).

optimal dividend policy The dividend policy that strikes a balance between current dividends and future growth and maximizes the firm's stock price.

option A contract that gives its holder the right to buy or sell an asset at some predetermined price within a specified period of time.

ordinary (deferred) annuity An annuity with a fixed number of equal payments occurring at the end of each period.

original issue discount (OID) bond In general, any bond originally offered at a price significantly below its par value.

par value The nominal or face value of a stock or bond. The par value of a bond generally represents the amount of money that the firm borrows and promises to repay at some future date. The par value of a bond is often $1,000, but can be $5,000 or more.

partnership Exists when two or more persons associate to conduct a business.

payable deferral period The average length of time between a firm's purchase of materials and labor and the payment of cash for them. It is calculated by dividing accounts payable by credit purchases per day (Cost of goods sold/365).

payback period The number of years it takes a firm to recover its project investment. Payback does not capture a project's entire cash flow stream and is thus not the preferred evaluation method. Note, however, that the payback does measure a project's liquidity, and hence many firms use it as a risk measure.

payment date The date on which a firm actually mails dividend checks.

pegged exchange rates Refers to the rate fixed against a major currency such as the U.S. dollar. Consequently, the values of the pegged currencies move together over time.

percent of sales method Many items on the income statement and balance sheets are assumed to increase proportionally with sales. As sales increase, these items that are tied to sales also increase, and the values of these items for a particular year are estimated as percentages of the forecasted sales for that year.

periodic rate, i_{PER} The rate charged by a lender or paid by a borrower each period. It can be a rate per year, per six-month period, per quarter, per month, per day, or per any other time interval (usually one year or less).

permanent net operating working capital The NOWC required when the economy is weak and seasonal sales are at their low point. Thus, this level of NOWC always requires financing and can be regarded as permanent.

perpetuity A series of payments of a fixed amount that last indefinitely.

physical location exchanges Exchanges, such as the New York Stock Exchange, that facilitate trading of securities at a particular location.

PMT Equal to the dollar amount of an equal, or constant cash flow (an annuity).

poison pill Shareholder rights provisions that allow existing shareholders in a company to purchase additional shares of stock at a lower than market value if a potential acquirer purchases a controlling stake in the company.

political risk Refers to the possibility of expropriation and the unanticipated restriction of cash flows to the parent by a foreign government.

post-audit The final aspect of the capital budgeting process. It is a feedback process in which the actual results are compared with those predicted in the original capital budgeting analysis. The post-audit has several purposes, the most important being to improve forecasts and improve operations.

precautionary balance A cash balance held in reserve for random, unforeseen fluctuations in cash inflows and outflows.

preemptive right Gives the current shareholders the right to purchase any new shares issued in proportion to their current holdings. The preemptive right enables current owners to maintain their proportionate share of ownership and control of the business.

preferred stock A hybrid—it is similar to bonds in some respects and to common stock in other respects. Preferred dividends are similar to interest payments on bonds in that they are fixed in amount and generally must be paid before common stock dividends can be paid. If the preferred dividend is not earned, the directors can omit it without throwing the company into bankruptcy.

premium bond Bond prices and interest rates are inversely related; that is, they tend to move in the opposite direction from one another. A fixed-rate bond will sell at par when its coupon interest rate is equal to the going rate of interest, r_d. When the going rate of interest is above the coupon rate, a fixed-rate bond will sell at a "discount" below its par value. If current interest rates are below the coupon rate, a fixed-rate bond will sell at a "premium" above its par value.

premium on forward rate Occurs when the forward exchange rate differs from the spot rate. When the forward rate is above the spot rate, it is said to be at a premium.

price/cash flow ratio Calculated by dividing price per share by cash flow per share. This shows how much investors are willing to pay per dollar of cash flow.

price/earnings (P/E) ratio Calculated by dividing price per share by earnings per share. This shows how much investors are willing to pay per dollar of reported profits.

primary markets The markets in which newly issued securities are sold for the first time.

private markets Transactions are worked out directly between two parties and structured in any manner that appeals to them. Bank loans and private placements of debt with insurance companies are examples of private market transactions.

pro forma financial statement Shows how an actual statement would look if certain assumptions are realized.

probability distribution A listing, chart, or graph of all possible outcomes, such as expected rates of return, with a probability assigned to each outcome.

professional corporation (PC) Enjoys most of the benefits of incorporation, but the participants are not relieved of professional (malpractice) liability. Known in some states as a professional association (PA).

profit margin on sales Calculated by dividing net income by sales; gives the profit per dollar of sales.

profitability index Found by dividing the project's present value of future cash flows by its initial cost. A profitability index greater than 1 is equivalent to a positive net present value project.

profitability ratios A group of ratios that show the combined effects of liquidity, asset management, and debt on operations.

progressive tax The higher one's income, the larger the percentage paid in taxes.

project cost of capital The risk-adjusted discount rate for that project.

promissory note A document specifying the terms and conditions of a loan, including the amount, interest rate, and repayment schedule.

proxy A document giving one person the authority to act for another, typically the power to vote shares of common stock.

proxy fight An attempt to take over a company in which an outside group solicits existing shareholders' proxies, which are authorizations to vote shares in a shareholders' meeting, in an effort to overthrow management and take control of the business.

public markets In public markets, standardized contracts are traded on organized exchanges. Securities that are issued in public markets, such as common stock and corporate bonds, are ultimately held by a large number of individuals.

publicly owned corporation In most larger companies, the stock is owned by a large number of investors, most of whom are not active in management.

purchasing power parity Implies that the level of exchange rates adjusts so that identical goods cost the same in different countries. Sometimes referred to as the "law of one price."

put option Allows the holder to sell the asset at some predetermined price within a specified period of time.

PV (present value) The value today of a future payment, or stream of payments, discounted at the appropriate rate of interest. PV is also the beginning amount that will grow to some future value.

PVA_n The value today of a future stream of equal payments (an annuity).

$PVIF_{i,n}$ The present value interest factor for a lump sum received n periods in the future discounted at i percent per period.

$PVIFA_{i,n}$ The present value interest factor for an ordinary annuity of n periodic payments discounted at i percent interest per period.

quick, or acid test, ratio Found by taking current assets less inventories and then dividing by current liabilities.

real options Occur when managers can influence the size and risk of a project's cash flows by taking different actions during the project's life. They are referred to as real options because they deal with real as opposed to financial assets. They are also called managerial options because they give opportunities to managers to respond to changing market conditions. Sometimes they are called strategic options because they often deal with strategic issues. Finally, they are also called embedded options because they are a part of another project.

real rate of return, r_r Contains no adjustment for expected inflation. If net cash flows from a project do not include inflation adjustments, then the cash flows should be discounted at the real cost of capital. In a similar manner, the internal rate of return resulting from real net cash flows should be compared with the real cost of capital.

real risk-free rate of interest, r^* The interest rate that equalizes the aggregate supply of, and demand for, riskless securities in an economy with zero inflation. The real risk-free rate could also be called the pure rate of interest since it is the rate of interest that would exist on very short-term, default-free U.S. Treasury securities if the expected rate of inflation were zero.

realized rate of return, r The actual return an investor receives on his or her investment. It can be quite different than the expected return.

receivables collection period The average length of time required to convert a firm's receivables into cash. It is calculated by dividing accounts receivable by sales per day.

redeemable bond Gives investors the right to sell the bonds back to the corporation at a price that is usually close to the par value. If interest rates rise, investors can redeem the bonds and reinvest at the higher rates.

reinvestment rate risk Occurs when a short-term debt security must be "rolled over." If interest rates have fallen, the reinvestment of principal will be at a lower rate, with correspondingly lower interest payments and ending value.

relaxed net operating working capital policy A policy under which relatively large amounts of cash, marketable securities, and inventories are carried and under which sales are stimulated by a liberal credit policy, resulting in a high level of receivables.

repatriation of earnings The cash flow, usually in the form of dividends or royalties, from the foreign branch or subsidiary to the parent company. These cash flows must be converted to the currency of the parent, and thus are subject to future exchange rate changes. A foreign government may restrict the amount of cash that may be repatriated.

replacement chain A method of comparing mutually exclusive projects that have unequal lives. Each project is replicated such that they will both terminate in a common year. If projects with lives of 3 years and 5 years are being evaluated, the 3-year project would be replicated five times and the 5-year project replicated three times; thus, both projects would terminate in 15 years.

required rate of return, r_s The minimum acceptable rate of return considering both its risk and the returns available on other investments.

reserve borrowing capacity Exists when a firm uses less debt under "normal" conditions than called for by the trade-off theory. This allows the firm some flexibility to use debt in the future when additional capital is needed.

residual distribution model States that firms should pay dividends only when more earnings are available than needed to support the optimal capital budget.

restricted net operating working capital policy A policy under which holdings of cash, securities, inventories, and receivables are minimized.

restricted voting rights A provision that automatically deprives a shareholder of voting rights if the shareholder owns more than a specified amount of stock.

retained earnings The portion of the firm's earnings that have been saved rather than paid out as dividends.

return on common equity (ROE) Found by dividing net income into common equity.

return on invested capital (ROIC) Net operating profit after taxes divided by the operating capital.

return on total assets (ROA) The ratio of net income to total assets.

revaluation Occurs when the relative price of a currency is increased. It is the opposite of devaluation.

revolving credit agreement A formal, committed line of credit extended by a bank or other lending institution.

risk aversion An investor's dislike of risk and need for a higher rate of return as an inducement to buy riskier securities.

risk premium for stock i, RP_i The extra return that an investor requires to hold risky stock i instead of a risk-free asset.

risk-adjusted discount rate Incorporates the riskiness of the project's cash flows. The cost of capital to the firm reflects the average risk of the firm's existing projects. Thus, new projects that are riskier than existing projects should have a higher risk-adjusted discount rate. Conversely, projects with less risk should have a lower risk-adjusted discount rate.

S corporation A small corporation that, under Subchapter S of the Internal Revenue Code, elects to be taxed as a proprietorship or a partnership yet retains limited liability and other benefits of the corporate form of organization.

salvage value The market value of an asset after its useful life.

scenario analysis A shorter version of simulation analysis that uses only a few outcomes. Often the outcomes are for three scenarios: optimistic, pessimistic, and most likely.

seasonal effects on ratios Seasonal factors can distort ratio analysis. At certain times of the year a firm may have excessive inventories in preparation for a "season" of high demand. Therefore, an inventory turnover ratio taken at this time, as opposed to after the season, will be radically distorted.

secondary markets Markets in which securities are resold after initial issue in the primary market. The New York Stock Exchange is an example.

secured loan A loan backed by collateral, often for inventories or receivables.

security-market-line (SML) Represents, in a graphical form, the relationship between the risk of an asset as measured by its beta and the required rates of return for individual securities. The SML equation is essentially the Capital Asset Pricing Model: $r_i = r_{RF} + b_i(r_M - r_{RF})$.

semistrong-form market efficiency States that current market prices reflect all publicly available information. Therefore, the only way to gain abnormal returns on a stock is to possess inside information about the company's stock.

sensitivity analysis Indicates exactly how much net present value will change in response to a given change in an input variable, other things held constant. Sensitivity analysis is sometimes called "what if" analysis because it answers this type of question.

sinking fund Facilitates the orderly retirement of a bond issue. This can be achieved in one of two ways: (1) The company can call in for redemption (at par value) a certain percentage of bonds each year, or (2) the company may buy the required amount of bonds on the open market.

sole proprietorship A proprietorship, or sole proprietorship, is a business owned by one individual.

spontaneously generated funds Funds generated if a liability account increases spontaneously (automatically) as sales increase. An increase in a liability account is a source of funds; thus funds have been generated. Two examples of spontaneous liability accounts are accounts payable and accrued wages. Note that notes payable, although a current liability account, is not a spontaneous source of funds since an increase in notes payable requires a specific action between the firm and a creditor.

spot rate The exchange rate that applies to "on the spot" trades, or, more precisely, exchanges that occur two days following the day of trade (in other words, current exchanges).

stand-alone risk The risk an investor takes by holding only one asset.

standard deviation, σ A statistical measure of the variability of a set of observations. It is the square root of the variance.

statement of cash flows Reports the effect of a firm's operating, investing, and financing activities on cash flows over an accounting period.

statement of retained earnings Shows how much of the firm's earnings were retained in the business rather than paid out in dividends. Note that retained earnings represent a claim against assets, not assets per se. Firms retain earnings primarily to expand the business, not to accumulate cash in a bank account.

stock dividend Increases the number of shares outstanding, but at a slower rate than splits. Current shareholders receive additional shares on some proportional basis. Thus, a holder of 100 shares would receive 5 additional shares at no cost if a 5 percent stock dividend were declared.

stock option Allows its owner to purchase a share of stock at a fixed price, called the exercise price, no matter what the actual price of the stock is. Stock options always have an expiration date, after which they cannot be exercised.

stock repurchase Occurs when a firm repurchases its own stock. These shares of stock are then referred to as treasury stock.

stock split Current shareholders are given some number (or fraction) of shares for each stock share owned. Thus, in a three-for-one split, each shareholder would receive three new shares in exchange for each old share, thereby tripling the number of shares outstanding. Stock splits usually occur when the stock price is outside of the optimal trading range.

strategic options Options that often deal with strategic issues. Also called real options and managerial options.

stretching accounts payable The practice of deliberately paying accounts late.

strike price The price stated in the option contract at which the security can be bought (or sold). For example, if the underlying stock sells for $50 and the strike price is $20, the exercise value of the option would be $30. Also called the exercise price.

strong-form market efficiency Assumes that all information pertaining to a stock, whether public or inside information, is reflected in current market prices. Thus, no investors would be able to earn abnormal returns in the stock market.

subordinated debenture Debentures that have claims on assets, in the event of bankruptcy, only after senior debt as named in the subordinated debt's indenture has been paid off. Subordinated debentures may be subordinated to designated notes payable or to all other debt.

sunk cost A cost that has already occurred and is not affected by the capital project decision. Sunk costs are not relevant to capital budgeting decisions.

takeover An action whereby a person or group succeeds in ousting a firm's management and taking control of the company.

target capital structure The relative amount of debt, preferred stock, and common equity that the firm desires. The weighted average cost of capital should be based on these target weights.

target cash balance The desired cash balance that a firm plans to maintain in order to conduct business.

tax loss carry-back and carry-forward Ordinary corporate operating losses can be carried backward for 2 years or forward for 20 years to offset taxable income in a given year.

tax preference theory Proposes that investors prefer capital gains over dividends, because capital gains taxes can be deferred into the future, but taxes on dividends must be paid as the dividends are received.

taxable income Gross income less a set of exemptions and deductions that are spelled out in the instructions to the tax forms individuals must file.

temporary net operating working capital The NOWC required above the permanent level when the economy is strong and/or seasonal sales are high.

term structure of interest rates The relationship between yield to maturity and term to maturity for bonds of a single risk class.

time line A graphical representation used to show the timing of cash flows.

times-interest-earned (TIE) ratio Determined by dividing earnings before interest and taxes by the interest charges. This ratio measures the extent to which operating income can decline before the firm is unable to meet its annual interest costs.

total assets turnover ratio Measures the turnover of all the firm's assets; it is calculated by dividing sales by total assets.

trade credit Debt arising from credit sales and recorded as an account receivable by the seller and as an account payable by the buyer.

trade deficit Occurs when a country imports more goods from abroad than it exports.

trade discounts Price reductions that suppliers offer customers for early payment of bills.

transactions balance The cash balance associated with payments and collections; the balance necessary for day-to-day operations.

Treasury bonds Bonds issued by the federal government and not exposed to default risk. Sometimes referred to as government bonds.

trend analysis An analysis of a firm's financial ratios over time. It is used to estimate the likelihood of improvement or deterioration in its financial situation.

value-based management Managing a firm with shareholder value in mind. It typically involves use of a model of shareholder value, like the corporate valuation model.

value drivers Growth rate in sales (g), operating profitability (OP = NOPAT/Sales), capital requirements (CR = Capital/Sales), and the weighted average cost of capital (WACC).

value of operations The present value of all the future free cash flows that are expected from current assets-in-place and the expected growth of assets-in-place when discounted at the weighted average cost of capital.

variance, σ^2 A measure of the distribution's variability. It is the sum of the squared deviations about the expected value.

warrant A call option issued by a company allowing the holder to buy a stated number of shares of stock from a company at a specified price. Warrants are generally distributed with debt, or preferred stock, to induce investors to buy those securities at lower cost.

weak-form market efficiency Assumes that all information contained in past price movements is fully reflected in current market prices. Thus, information about recent trends in a stock's price is of no use in selecting a stock.

weighted average cost of capital (WACC) The weighted average of the after-tax component costs of capital—debt, preferred stock, and common equity. Each weighting factor is the proportion of that type of capital in the optimal, or target, capital structure.

window dressing A technique employed by firms to make their financial statements look better than they really are.

working capital A firm's investment in short-term assets—cash, marketable securities, inventory, and accounts receivable.

yield curve The curve that results when yield to maturity is plotted on the Y axis with term to maturity on the X axis.

yield to call (YTC) The rate of interest earned on a bond if it is called. If current interest rates are well below an outstanding callable bond's coupon rate, the YTC may be a more relevant estimate of expected return than the YTM, since the bond is likely to be called.

yield to maturity (YTM) The rate of interest earned on a bond if it is held to maturity.

zero coupon bond Pays no coupons at all, but is offered at a substantial discount below its par value and hence provides capital appreciation rather than interest income.